"You're probably thinking that if someone has the gall to call his book a Bible, it had better be pretty good. If you're not thinking that, it's probably because you've already experienced the *Photoshop Bible* and you know it's good."
— Krissy Harris, *Los Angeles Times*

"Definitely the top book out on the market today. You won't find a better source of information on Photoshop."
— Jacquelin Vanderwood, *The Internet Eye Magazine*

"The *Photoshop Bible* is a must-have encyclopedia of Photoshop info. It's a tribute to Deke's knowledge that even the most veteran Photoshop users find the *Bible* required reading."
— Jeff Schewe, leading photographer and digital artist

"If I were stuck on a desert island and I could only have just one book on Photoshop, hands down, this would be the one!"
— Scott Kelby, President, National Association of Photoshop Professionals

"When I have a question, I know Deke can tell me the answer, clearly and thoroughly. If you're seriously interested in the world's premiere image-editing program and can only buy one book, this should be it."
— Howard Millard, *eDigitalPhoto.com*

"Photoshop has become a heavy, industrial program. For that. you need an industrial encyclopedia of information. You need the *Bible*!"
— Fred Showker, Publisher, *DT&G Magazine*

"Deke is the best Photoshop writer on the planet. When I consider the years of experience and preparation that have gone into *Photoshop Bible*, I'm stunned. The value of this book far exceeds the purchase price."
— John Nemerovski, "Book Bytes" columnist, *My Mac Magazine*

Photoshop® 7 Bible

Photoshop® 7 Bible

Deke McClelland

Wiley Publishing, Inc.

Photoshop® 7 Bible

Published by
Wiley Publishing, Inc.
909 Third Avenue
New York, NY 10022
www.wiley.com

Copyright © 2002 by Wiley Publishing, Inc.,
Indianapolis, Indiana

Library of Congress Control Number: 2002107895

ISBN: 0-7645-3694-X

Manufactured in the United States of America

10 9 8 7 6 5 4 3

1O/SR/QY/QS/IN

Published by Wiley Publishing, Inc., Indianapolis,
Indiana

Published simultaneously in Canada

For general information on our other products and services or to obtain technical support, please contact our Customer Care Department within the U.S. at 800-762-2974, outside the U.S. at 317-572-3993 or fax 317-572-4002.

Wiley also publishes its books in a variety of electronic formats. Some content that appears in print may not be available in electronic books.

Trademarks: Wiley, the Wiley Publishing logo, and related trade dress are trademarks or registered trademarks of Wiley Publishing, Inc., in the United States and other countries, and may not be used without written permission. Photoshop is a trademark or registered trademark of Adobe Systems, Inc. All other trademarks are the property of their respective owners. Wiley Publishing, Inc., is not associated with any product or vendor mentioned in this book.

About the Author

In 1985, **Deke McClelland** oversaw the implementation of the first personal computer-based production department in Boulder, Colorado. He later graduated to be artistic director for Publishing Resources, one of the earliest all-PostScript service bureaus in the United States.

These days, Deke is a well-known expert and lecturer on Adobe Photoshop and the larger realm of computer graphics and design. He serves as host to the interactive "Best of Photoshop 7.0" that ships with Photoshop as well as the exhaustive and entertaining *Total Training for Adobe Photoshop 7* (*www.totaltraining.com*). His other DVD- and CD-based video series include *Digital Photography with Photoshop Elements*, *Total Training for Adobe Illustrator 10*, *Total Training for Adobe InDesign 2*, and *Total Training for PageMaker 7* (all Total Training).

In addition to his videos, Deke is author of the award-winning titles *Photoshop 7 Bible* and *Photoshop 7 Bible, Professional Edition* (both Wiley Publishing, Inc.), now in their tenth year with more copies in print than any other guides on computer graphics. Other best-selling titles include *Photoshop 7 For Dummies, Photoshop Elements 2 For Dummies, Look & Learn Photoshop*, and *Web Design Studio Secrets* (all Wiley Publishing, Inc.), as well as *Real World Illustrator 10*, *Real World Digital Photography*, and *Adobe Master Class: Design Invitational* (all Peachpit Press).

In 1989, Deke won the Benjamin Franklin Award for Best Computer Book. Since then, he has received honors from the Society for Technical Communication (once in 1994 and twice in 1999), the American Society of Business Press Editors (1995 and 2000), the Western Publications Association (1999), and the Computer Press Association (1990, 1992, 1994, 1995, 1997, and twice in 2000). In 1999, Book Bytes named Deke its Author of the Year.

In addition to his other credits, Deke is an Adobe Certified Expert, a member of the PhotoshopWorld Instructor Dream Team, a featured speaker on the 2002 MacMania cruise of Alaska's Inside Passage, and a contributing editor for *Macworld* and *Photoshop User* magazines.

Credits

Revisions by
Galen Fott

Acquisitions Editor
Tom Heine

Project Editor
Amy Thomas Buscaglia

Technical Editor
Rod Wynne-Powell

Copy Editor
Jerelind Charles

Editorial Manager
Rev Mengle

**Vice President and
Executive Group Publisher**
Richard Swadley

**Vice President and
Executive Publisher**
Bob Ipsen

Executive Editorial Director
Mary Bednarek

Project Coordinator
Regina Snyder

Graphics and Production Specialists
Beth Brooks, Sean Decker,
Melanie DesJardins, Clint Lahnen,
Laurie Petrone, Brent Savage

Quality Control Technicians
John Bitter, Andy Hollandbeck,
Angel Perez, Carl Pierce, Linda Quigley

Proofreading
TECHBOOKS Production Services

Indexing
Sharon Hilgenberg

To my darling Elizabeth
without whom life as I now
know it would not be possible.

— D

Foreword

A Tour of the Pixel Mines

If you are reading this foreword, it probably means that you've purchased a copy of Adobe Photoshop 7.0, and for that I and the rest of the Photoshop team at Adobe thank you.

Adobe Photoshop is a deep product. While some of its riches are, we hope, relatively evident on the surface, many of them take digging to get to. That's essentially the way things have to be given a limited amount of space at the surface and a desire not to entirely overwhelm users on first launch. If you want to get a feel for this, take a moment and bring up the Layer Style dialog or the Brushes palette and imagine all of the controls in all of the panels being visible when Photoshop first launched. Not a pretty thought. One approach—the approach taken in Photoshop Elements—would simply be to not make those controls available anywhere. Photoshop, however, is a tool for professionals and people who like to fancy themselves professionals, and not including options simply because it would be too overwhelming would be underestimating our users.

But let's say you're just starting out. You wander around and pick up a few pretty rocks, find some interesting things to do with your image without working too hard, and then you wonder whether there's more. That's when it's time to start digging.

Now digging a hole can be a chore. Or it can be a grand adventure like my three-year-old digging for buried treasure. Deke is in some sense the world's oldest three-year-old. He dives into Photoshop and drags you along not just with enthusiasm but with giddy enthusiasm. Some might say "demented enthusiasm."

On the other hand, Deke is also a wizened old pixel miner who has been down this way many times before. He already knows where the veins of riches are and he knows where the pitfalls are. He isn't shy about sharing his opinions, and he is only too happy to let you know when he disagrees with our choices.

What you'll get from letting Deke be your guide through the pixel mines is a rich, colorful, and exciting ride. Deke will grab you and drag you along at breakneck speed through a long and varied course as he gushes with excitement about all that he has to show you. But don't worry. He knows where he's going, and once you've completed the journey with him, you'll be well prepared to dig for treasure on your own.

Have fun!

Mark Hamburg
Principal Scientist, Adobe Systems Incorporated
June 2002

Preface

It's hard to know how to introduce a book. Especially one as gargantuan as this. I feel like I should lead with something momentous, something that you'll remember. Something that'll make you want to buy this book, take it home, and love it forever. But all I can think of is the following:

Hello and welcome to the *Photoshop Bible*, the bestselling big fat book on Photoshop in publishing history. I've done my best to cover everything and make my prose at least occasionally entertaining. Naturally, I hope you learn a lot, but I also hope you have a really swell time while you're at it. Because if you're not having fun, then your enemies are surely gloating. Unless you don't have any enemies, in which case you must be having fun because you're such a pleasure to be around. Kudos to you, friend.

As you prepare yourself for the sheer joy you're about to experience, let me tell you a little something about this book. Now in its ninth year, the *Photoshop Bible* is the longest continuously published title on Adobe Photoshop. Not coincidentally, it also happens to be the bestselling reference guide on the topic, with a total of 12 U.S. editions, dozens of localized translations in foreign lands, and more than a million copies in print worldwide. This makes it not only the most successful book of its kind, but one of the most successful books on any electronic publishing topic ever printed.

Of course, "bestseller" doesn't necessarily translate to "best" — once upon a time, Furbies were all the rage. But the *Photoshop Bible* seems to have withstood the test of time, and while I may have inertia to thank, I hope the book's enduring appeal is at least in part the result of the time and effort I put into it.

The driving philosophy behind the *Photoshop Bible* is a simple one: Even the most intimidating topic can be made easy if it's explained properly. This goes double when the subject of the discussion is something as modest as a piece of software. Photoshop isn't some remarkable work of nature that defies our comprehension. It's nothing more that a commercial product designed by a bunch of regular people like you for the express purpose of being understood and put to use by a bunch of regular people like you. If I can't explain something that inherently straightforward, then shame on me.

I've made it my mission to address every topic head on — no cop-outs, no apologies. Everything's here, from the practical benefits of creating accurate masks to the theoretical wonders of designing your own custom layer styles. I wasn't born with this knowledge, and there are plenty of times when I'm learning with you. But when I don't know how something works, I do the research and figure it out, sometimes discussing features directly with the programmers, sometimes taking advantage of other sources. My job is to find out the answers, make sure those answers make sense, and pass them along to you as clearly as I can.

I also provide background, opinions, and occasional attempts at chummy, even crummy humor. A dry listing of features followed by ponderous discussions of how they work doesn't mean squat unless I explain why the feature is there, where it fits into your workflow, and — on occasion — whether or not it's the best solution. I am alternatively cranky, excited, and just plain giddy as I explain Photoshop, and I make no effort to contain my criticisms or enthusiasm. This book is me walking you through the program as subjectively as I would explain it to a friend.

About This Edition of the Book

I try to make every update to the *Photoshop Bible* special, particularly for those of you who purchase the book on a regular basis. But this time, I really went overboard, and I hope it shows. In addition to making the usual detailed changes to every single page of the book — as well as documenting all the new features including the file browser, customizable Brushes palette, the healing brush, the Pattern Maker, workspaces and tool presets, Auto Color, the new blend modes, the spell checker, and so on — I overhauled existing discussions of layer styles, blending options, the Liquify command, masking, and many of the core filters and color adjustment options. More than half the chapters received heavy alterations or complete rewrites.

But frankly, that happens every edition. What's special about the *Photoshop 7 Bible* is the graphics. For the first time since the inception of this book, I replaced virtually every image in the book. Out of roughly 600 figures, about 30 are pickups from previous editions, meaning that fully 95 percent are either reworked or, much more likely, entirely new to this edition. In replacing the images, I also dramatically improved their clarity, quality, and resolution, with some images soaring as high as 600 pixels per inch. Most graphics include labels, so you can tell what's going on at a glance. And perhaps most exciting, I redesigned the color plates, so that each plate fills an entire page and each image makes sense on its own.

Not including the considerable efforts of my extremely capable collaborators, *InDesign For Dummies* coauthor Amy Thomas Buscaglia and *Photoshop Elements For Dummies* coauthor and *Total Photoshop* writer Galen Fott, I spent more time on the *Photoshop 7 Bible* than I have on any other since I wrote the very first edition in 1993. Amy, Galen, and I hope you agree, it was time well spent.

Like all versions of the *Photoshop Bible*, this is a reference guide, not a tutorial. I do not make the images in this book available for download for two reasons. First, many are commercial stock images; understandably, their photographers would frown on me giving away their artwork for free. Second, the techniques discussed in this book are designed to work on *your* images. There's no need to slog through a tutorial before you can apply what you've learned to your own work; you can set right in making practical use of these techniques immediately.

However, you should note that some streamlining has occurred to keep down the size of the book and reduce its price. First, there is no CD, to which I for one say good riddance. This is a book, not a piece of software, and I have long considered the CD to be extraneous. Second, the *Photoshop 7 Bible* covers all things Photoshop, but limits itself to Photoshop only. I do not discuss Photoshop's companion product, ImageReady. If learning ImageReady is important to you, put this book down and get the hardbound *Photoshop 7 Bible, Professional Edition* instead, which includes more color pages and advanced information.

And lest I forget, two more special bonuses to this edition. First, we have a new technical editor, Rod Wynne-Powell, whose job it is to maintain the technical accuracy of this title. An active beta user and author of *Photoshop Made Simple*, Rod has proven to be one of the most meticulous and insightful technical editors it's ever been my pleasure to work with. Second, we are fortunate to have back one of the original contributors to the *Photoshop Bible*, indexer Sharon Hilgenberg. Once upon a time, the index for the *Bible* could not be beat; now it is great again.

Conventions

Every computer book conforms to its own special brand of logic, and this one is no exception. Although I try to avoid pig Latin — ellway, orfay hetay ostmay artpay — I do subscribe to a handful of conventions that you may not immediately recognize.

Vocabulary

Call it computerese, call it technobabble, call it the indecipherable gibberish of incorrigible propeller heads. The fact is, I can't explain Photoshop in graphic and gruesome detail without occasionally reverting to the specialized language of the trade. However, to help you keep up, I can and have italicized vocabulary words (as in *random-access memory*) with which you may not be familiar, or which I use in an unusual context. An italicized term is followed by a definition.

If you come across a strange word that is *not* italicized (that bit of italics was for emphasis), look it up in the index to find the first reference to the word in the book.

Commands and options

To distinguish the literal names of commands, dialog boxes, buttons, and so on, I capitalize the first letter in each word (for example, *click the Cancel button*). The only exceptions are option names, which can be six or seven words long and filled with prepositions such as *to* and *of*. Traditionally, prepositions and articles (*a, an, the*) don't appear in initial caps, and this book follows that time-honored rule, too.

When discussing menus and commands, I use an arrow symbol to indicate hierarchy. For example, *Choose File ⇨ Open* means to choose the Open command from the File menu. If you have to display a submenu to reach a command, I list the command used to display the submenu between the menu name and the final command. *Choose Image ⇨ Adjustments ⇨ Invert* means to choose the Adjustments command from the Image menu and then choose the Invert command from the Adjustments submenu.

The whole platform thing

This is a cross-platform book, meaning that it's written for both Windows and Macintosh users. Photoshop is virtually identical on the two platforms, so it makes little difference. However, the PC and Mac keyboards are different. The Ctrl key on the PC translates to the Command key (⌘) on the Mac. Alt translates to Option. And because Apple's mice do not include right mouse buttons, right-clicking on the PC becomes Control-clicking on the Mac. Throughout the course of this book, I try to make things as unambiguous as possible by mentioning the Windows keystroke first with the Macintosh equivalent in parentheses.

Version numbers

A new piece of software comes out every 15 minutes. That's not a real statistic, mind you, but I bet I'm not far off. As I write this, Photoshop has advanced to Version 7.0. But by the time you read this, the version number may be seven hundredths of a percentage point higher. So know that when I write *Photoshop 7*, I mean any version of Photoshop short of 8.

Similarly, when I write *Photoshop 6*, I mean Versions 6.0 and 6.0.1; *Photoshop 5* means Versions 5.0, 5.0.2, and 5.5; *Photoshop 4* means Versions 4.0 and 4.0.1; *Photoshop 3,* means Versions 3.0, 3.0.1, 3.0.3, 3.0.4, and 3.0.5 — well, you get the idea.

Icons

Like just about every computer book currently available on your greengrocer's shelves, this one includes alluring icons that focus your eyeballs smack dab on important information. The icons make it easy for folks who just like to skim books to figure out what the heck's going on. Icons serve as little insurance policies against short attention spans. On the whole, the icons are self-explanatory, but I'll explain them anyway.

The Caution icon warns you that a step you're about to take may produce disastrous results. Well, perhaps "disastrous" is an exaggeration. Inconvenient, then. Uncomfortable. For heaven's sake, use caution.

The Note icon highlights some little tidbit of information I've decided to share with you that seemed at the time to be remotely related to the topic at hand. I might tell you how an option came into existence, why a feature is implemented the way it is, or how things used to be better back in the old days.

The Photoshop 7 icon explains an option, command, or other feature that is brand-spanking new to this latest revision. If you're already familiar with previous versions of Photoshop, you might just want to plow through the book looking for Photoshop 7 icons and see what new stuff is out there.

This book is bursting with tips and techniques. If I were to highlight every one of them, whole pages would be gray with triangles popping out all over the place. The Tip icon calls attention to shortcuts that are specifically applicable to the Photoshop application. For the bigger, more useful power tips, I'm afraid you'll have to actually read the text.

The Cross-Reference icon tells you where to go for information related to the current topic. I included one a few pages back and you probably read it without thinking twice. That means you're either sharp as a tack or an experienced computer-book user. Either way, you won't have any trouble with this icon.

I thought of including one more icon that alerted you to every new bit of information — whether Photoshop 7-dependent or not — that's included in this book. But I found myself using it every other paragraph. Besides, that would have robbed you of the fun of discovering the new stuff.

How to Bug Me

Even in its millionth edition, scanned by the eyes of hundreds of thousands of readers and scrutinized intensely for months at a time by myself and my editors, I'll bet someone, somewhere will still manage to locate errors and oversights. If you notice those kinds of things and you have a few spare moments, please let me know what you think. I always appreciate readers' comments.

If you want to share your insights, comments, or corrections, please e-mail me at *p7bible@dekemc.com*. Don't fret if you don't hear from me for a few days, or months, or ever. I read every letter and try to implement nearly every constructive idea anyone bothers to send me. But because I receive hundreds of reader letters a week, I can respond to only a small percentage of them.

Please, do not write to ask me why your copy of Photoshop is misbehaving on your specific computer. I was not involved in developing Photoshop, I am not employed by Adobe, and I am not trained in product support. Adobe can answer your technical support questions way better than I can, so I leave it to the experts.

Now, without further ado, I urge you to turn the page and advance forward into the great untamed frontier of image editing. Soon, you will know things you never knew before, you will see things you never saw before, you will gain insights and shed pounds from the expenditure of pure thinking energy. (Such results are not typical.) But whatever you do, don't take this book to bed, fall asleep, and let it topple onto your face. It will crush you like a squishy-squashy ooshy-bug, only more messily.

Contents at a Glance

Contents

Part III: Selections, Masks, and Filters   369

Part IV: Layers, Objects, and Text   633

Chapter 12: Working with Layers 635

Welcome to Photoshop

Introducing Photoshop 7

What Is Photoshop?

Many of you already know the answer to this question. You know what Photoshop does, the various purposes it serves, where it fits into the computer design scheme, how much it costs at 15 different mail order sites, its complete history (from its inception as a bit of image conversion code called Display to its first shipping version Barneyscan XP to the present day), and the names of everyone on the development team. You're the folks who keep me awake at night, because it's the job of this book to share information on Photoshop that even *you* didn't know.

But just as likely, you're part of the larger group of people who have a vague sense of what Photoshop does but are a little shaky on some of the details. You know the program lets you modify photographs, for example, but how exactly it does this is far from crystal clear. Or perhaps you have no idea what Photoshop is. Someone installed the program on your computer, threw this book in your lap, and said, "Go!" If one of these latter scenarios describes you, don't worry—we were all beginners at Photoshop once and we'll all have ample opportunity to be beginners at something else in the future. So before we go any further, let's get one thing settled for once and for all: just what exactly is Photoshop?

Adobe Photoshop—Photoshop is the name of the software, Adobe Systems is the name of the company that develops and sells it—is a professional-level image-editing application. It allows you to create images from whole cloth or, more likely, modify scanned artwork and digital photographs. Photoshop is available for use on computers equipped with either Microsoft Windows or Apple's Macintosh operating system.

Mind you, Photoshop isn't just any image-editing application, it's the most powerful, most ubiquitous image-editing application in the world. Despite hefty competition over the years from more than a hundred programs ranging in price from virtually free to a few thousand dollars a pop, Photoshop remains the most popular design software in use today. Where professional image editing is concerned, Photoshop's not just the market leader, it's the only game in town.

Such a lack of competition is rarely a good thing. But in Photoshop's case, it has played out remarkably well. The program's historically lopsided sales advantage has provided Adobe with a clear incentive to reinvest in Photoshop and regularly enhance, even overhaul, its capabilities. It's as if each new version of Photoshop is competing with its predecessors for the hearts and minds of the digital art community. Meanwhile, other vendors have had to devote smaller resources to playing catch-up. Some, such as Jasc Software, with its Windows-only Paint Shop Pro, have hung in there and remained commercially viable. But such success stories are few and far between. Although competitors have provided some interesting and sometimes amazing capabilities, the sums of their parts have more often than not fallen well short of Photoshop's.

As a result, Photoshop rides a self-perpetuating wave of market leadership. It wasn't always the best image editor, nor was it the first. But its deceptively straightforward interface combined with a few terrific core functions made it a hit from the moment of its first release. More than a dozen years later — thanks to substantial capital injections from Adobe and highly creative programming on the parts of Photoshop's engineering staff and its originator Thomas Knoll — Photoshop has evolved into the most popular program of its kind.

Image-Editing Theory

Like any *image editor*, Photoshop enables you to alter photographs and other scanned artwork. You can retouch an image, apply special effects, swap details between photos, introduce text and logos, adjust color balance, and even sharpen the focus of a photograph. Photoshop also provides everything you need to create artwork from scratch, including a suite of vector drawing tools and a highly specialized painting palette. These tools are fully compatible with pressure-sensitive tablets, so you can create naturalistic images that closely mimic watercolors and oils.

Bitmaps versus vectors

Image editors fall into the larger software category of *painting programs*. In a painting program, you draw a line, and the application converts it to tiny square dots called *pixels*. The painting itself is called a *bitmapped image*, but *bitmap* and *image* are equally acceptable terms.

Photoshop uses the term *bitmap* exclusively to mean a black-and-white image, the logic being that each pixel conforms to one *bit* of data, 0 or 1 (off or on). In order to avoid awkward syllabic mergers such as *pix-map*—and because forcing a distinction between working with exactly two colors or anywhere from four to 16 million colors is entirely arbitrary—I use the term bitmap more broadly to mean any image composed of a fixed number of pixels, regardless of the number of colors involved.

What about other graphics applications, such as Adobe's own Illustrator? Applications such as Illustrator, Macromedia FreeHand, and CorelDraw fall into a different category of software called *drawing programs*. Drawings comprise *vector objects*, which are independent, mathematically defined lines and shapes. For this reason, drawing programs are sometimes said to be *vector-based* or *object-oriented*.

As luck would have it, Photoshop spans the chasm between conventional painting and drawing programs by providing many of the best features of both. In addition to its wealth of image editing and organic painting capabilities, Photoshop permits you to add vector-based text and shapes to your photographic images. These features don't altogether take the place of a drawing program but they help to make Photoshop an increasingly flexible and dynamic image-creation environment.

The ups and downs of painting

As you might expect, painting programs and drawing programs each have their strengths and weaknesses. The strength of a painting program is that it offers an extremely straightforward approach to creating images. For example, although many of Photoshop's features are complex—*exceedingly* complex on occasion—its core painting tools are as easy to use as a pencil. You alternately draw and erase until you reach a desired effect, just as you've been doing since grade school.

In addition to being simple to use, each of Photoshop's core painting tools is fully customizable. It's as if you have access to an infinite variety of crayons, colored pencils, pastels, airbrushes, watercolors, and so on, all of which are entirely erasable. Doodling on the phone book was never so much fun.

Because painting programs rely on pixels, they are ideally suited to electronic photography. Whether captured with a scanner or digital camera, an electronic photograph is composed of thousands or even tens of millions of colored pixels. A drawing program like Illustrator may let you import such a photograph and apply very simple edits, but Photoshop gives you complete control over every pixel, entire collections of pixels, or independent elements of pixels. As witnessed by a quick examination of the pictures in this book, a photograph can become anything.

The downside of paintings and electronic photos is that they are ultimately finite in scale. Because a bitmap contains a fixed number of pixels, the *resolution* of an image—the number of pixels in an inch, centimeter, or other allotted space—changes with respect to the size at which the image is printed. Print the image small, and the pixels become tiny, which increases the resolution of the image. Like the millions of cells in your body, tiny pixels become too small to see and thus blend together to form a cohesive whole, as in the first image in Figure 1-1. Print the image large and the pixels grow, which decreases the resolution. Large pixels are like cells viewed through a microscope; once you can distinguish them independently, the image falls apart, as in the second example in the figure. The results are jagged edges and blocky transitions. The only way to remedy this problem is to increase the number of pixels in the image, which increases the size of the file on disk.

Continuous-tone image   same, pixels enlarged to 500%

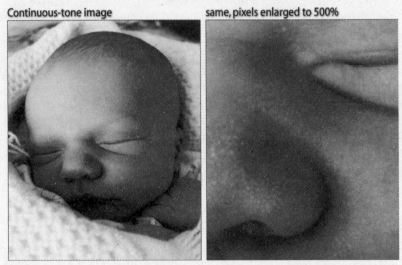

Figure 1-1: When printed small, an image appears smooth and sharp (left). But when enlarged, the image breaks down into jagged transitions and grain (right).

Bear in mind that this is a very simplified explanation of how images work. For a more complete description that includes techniques for maximizing image resolution and quality, read "How Images Work," at the outset of Chapter 3.

The downs and ups of drawing

The process of creating a vector-based drawing might more aptly be termed "constructing," because you actually build lines and shapes point by point and stack them on top of each other to create a finished image. Each object is independently editable — one of the key structural advantages of an object-oriented approach — but you're still faced with the task of building your artwork one chunk at a time.

Nevertheless, because a drawing program defines lines, shapes, and text as mathematical equations, these objects automatically conform to the full resolution of the output device, whether it's a laser printer, imagesetter, or film recorder. The drawing program sends the math to the printer and the printer *renders* the math to paper or film. In other words, the printer converts the drawing program's equations to printer pixels. Your printer offers far more pixels than your screen — a 600-dot-per-inch (dpi) laser printer, for example, offers 600 pixels per inch (dots equal pixels), whereas most screens are limited to 150 pixels per inch or fewer. So the printed drawing appears smooth and sharply focused regardless of the size at which you print it, as shown in Figure 1-2.

Vector-based illustration   same, lines & shapes enlarged to 500%

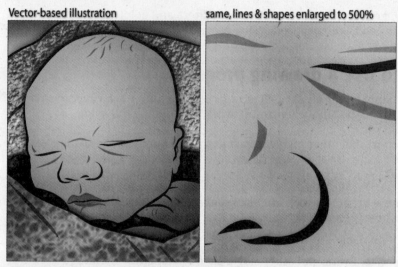

Figure 1-2: Small or large, a drawing prints super sharp. But it's also more work to create. Despite its simplicity, I ended up pouring several hours of labor into this piece.

Another advantage of drawings is that they take up relatively little room on disk. The file size of a drawing depends on the quantity and complexity of the objects the drawing contains. Thus, the file size has almost nothing to do with the size of the printed image, which is just the opposite of the way bitmapped images work. A thumbnail drawing of a garden that contains hundreds of leaves and petals consumes several times more disk space than a poster-sized drawing that comprises three rectangles.

When to use Photoshop

Thanks to their specialized methods, painting programs and drawing programs fulfill distinct and divergent purposes. Photoshop and other painting programs are best suited to creating and editing the following kinds of artwork:

✦ Scanned photos, including photographic collages and embellishments that originate from scans

✦ Images captured with any type of digital camera

✦ Still frames scanned from videotape or film

✦ Realistic artwork that relies on the play between naturalistic highlights, midranges, and shadows

✦ Impressionistic-type artwork and other images created for purely personal or aesthetic purposes

✦ Logos and other display type featuring soft edges, reflections, or tapering shadows

✦ Special effects that require the use of filters and color enhancements you simply can't achieve in a drawing program

When to use a drawing program

You're probably better off using Illustrator or some other drawing program if you're interested in creating more stylized artwork, such as the following:

✦ Poster art and other high-contrast graphics that heighten the appearance of reality

✦ Architectural plans, product designs, or other precise line drawings

✦ Business graphics, such as charts and other "infographics" that reflect data or show how things work

✦ Traditional logos and text effects that require crisp, ultrasmooth edges

✦ Brochures, flyers, and other single-page documents that mingle artwork, logos, and body-copy text (such as the text you're reading now)

If you're serious about computer graphics, you should own at least one painting program and one drawing program. If I had to rely exclusively on two graphics applications for producing still, two-dimensional images, I would choose Photoshop and Illustrator. Adobe has done a fine job of establishing symmetry between the two programs so that they share common interface elements and keyboard short-cuts. Learn one and the other makes a lot more sense.

For those who are interested, I write a cradle-to-grave guide to Illustrator called *Real World Illustrator*, published by Peachpit Press. I'm also the host of a handful of video training series, including not only *Total Training for Adobe Illustrator*, but also *Total Training for Adobe Photoshop* and *Total Training for Adobe InDesign*, all from Total Training (*www.totaltraining.com*).

Fast Track to Photoshop 7

Now that we've reviewed the fundamentals, let's turn our attention from the wider world of image editing to the comparatively narrow realm of Photoshop 7. Namely, what hot new features does this upgrade have to offer? Particularly given that these days, Photoshop's only competition is its glorious past, what is it about Version 7 that distinguishes it from previous versions of the program?

In short, Photoshop 7 is the back-to-basics upgrade. It lets you organize your images more efficiently, paint more creatively, retouch imperfections with greater skill, and save tool and palette settings for later use. But like any upgrade to Photoshop, there's a lot more going on than may at first meet the eye. Which is why the following list tells all. Here I've compiled a few of the most prominent features that are new to Photoshop 7, in rough order of importance. I also point you to the chapter where you can sniff around for more information:

✦ **The file browser (Chapter 3):** For years, less expensive image editors, including Paint Shop Pro and Adobe's own Photoshop Elements, have offered browsers that let you preview entire folders full of images at a time. Thankfully for digital photographers and others wading through squillions of images, Photoshop 7 now offers a browser as well. Available either as a palette or an independent window, the file browser lets you rename and move files, rotate and rank images, and view the Exchangeable Image File (EXIF) data captured by modern digital cameras. Robust and well implemented, the file browser is likely to rank as many designers' favorite new feature.

✦ **The Brushes palette (Chapter 5):** Photoshop has never been known for its painting abilities, but that's about to change. Adobe assigned programmer Jerry Harris, codeveloper of the Macintosh computer's first color painting program, PixelPaint, to the task of revamping the painting engine. The result is Photoshop 7's most impressive new feature, not just for artists but for anyone who touches a brush, whether to retouch, mask, dodge, or smear. The restored Brushes palette sports multiple panels and more than 50 new settings and variables. Most parameters respond to input from pressure-sensitive tablets. Photoshop 7 even introduces support for more sophisticated stylus input such as tilt and stylus wheel, bringing the program up to speed with the latest hardware innovations.

✦ **The healing tools (Chapter 7):** With the advent of digital photography, more and more designers are finding themselves in need of retouching solutions. Yet as far back as Version 1, Photoshop's only answer has been the labor-intensive stamp tool, which copies colors from one portion of an image and applies them to another. Photoshop 7 steps to the plate with two new cloning tools, the healing brush and the patch tool. The healing brush clones the texture from one portion of the image and draws the color from the area around the brushstroke. Meanwhile, the patch tool applies this same principle to the task of healing entire selections. By sampling color and texture independently, Photoshop is able to create patches that appear consistent with their surroundings.

✦ **Workspace and tool presets (Chapter 2):** If some days, Photoshop feels more like your home than, well, your home, then you probably spend a lot of time moving palettes, adjusting tool settings, and generally tweaking your environment. This is especially true if you occasionally change monitor resolutions, as when gauging artwork for the Web. To expedite your housekeeping,

Photoshop 7 offers the ability to save workspaces and tool presets. A workspace records all palette and toolbox locations to better facilitate, say, file browsing, retouching, layer management, or Web design. They're also particularly useful in multiuser environments, where one person wants the screen one way and another wants it another way. Tool presets let you configure personalized tools loaded with custom brushes, clone settings, selection modifiers, and more. Not only do presets save you time, but they also permit you to keep a record of how you create an effect so you can replicate it without a lot of fuss.

✦ **Spell check and replace (Chapter 15):** If you create a lot of text in Photoshop — as when comping page layouts or Web designs — you'll appreciate the spell checker, identical to those found inside other Adobe applications. You can also search and replace passages of text.

✦ **Liquify (Chapter 11):** Introduced in Photoshop 6, the Liquify filter lets you distort an image by painting inside it with a collection of tools. Though widely popular, there was general agreement it needed work. And work it has received. You can now zoom and scroll inside the Liquify dialog box, as well as take advantage of unlimited undos. You can also preview multiple layers for reference and save a distortion grid for use on another image.

✦ **Pattern Maker (Chapter 7):** Photoshop 7's custom brushes and healing tools give the option to use repeating patterns as textures. The program ships with a slew of predefined patterns, but you can also create your own using the Pattern Maker filter. While it saves time by automatically generating complex patterns from a selected portion of an image, you have no way to paint or edit inside the filter. So be prepared for a little bit of trial and error.

✦ **Auto Color (Chapter 17):** The quick-fix commands Auto Levels and Auto Contrast correct the lightest and darkest colors in an image, but they scrupulously avoid the midtones. The new Auto Color command corrects gamma values with the hope of removing color casts. Better still, you can customize the command to better suit your exacting needs.

✦ **Blending options (Chapter 13):** Photoshop 7 introduces five new blend modes, which permit you to mix the colors in brushstrokes and layers to create custom dissolves and other effects. To help minimize confusion, blend modes are organized more logically, with all modes that lighten an image in one group and all that darken in another. Photoshop 7 also makes it more convenient to mask layer effects and adjust the opacity of pixels independently of effects.

✦ **Renaming layers (Chapter 12):** Every update to Photoshop, I like to take credit for a new feature, and this one is it. Photoshop 6 required you to Option-double-click on a layer to rename it. Everybody hated that technique, but I was the guy who suggested that Photoshop 7 let you rename a layer directly inside the Layers palette. The same now goes for channels, paths, actions, tool presets, swatches, and styles. Who's got the vision? I do, baby. I can see for miles and miles.

✦ **Airbrush almighty (Chapter 5):** Some longtime users will be surprised by the disappearance of the venerable airbrush. But like Obi-Won Kenobi cut down by Darth Vader, freeing the airbrush from the mortal coil of the toolbox has made it omnipresent. By making the airbrush a toggle available to a wide range of painting and editing tools — including the history brush and clone stamp tool — Photoshop 7 permits you to use any brush to lay down a continuous stream of color, even when you hold the cursor still. You can also control the rate at which an effect flows, analogous to the airbrush's old Pressure setting.

✦ **Better eyedropper (Chapter 4):** My favorite hidden feature is a minor but momentous change to the eyedropper. You can now sample any color you can see on screen by dragging from the image window into the background. No more need to copy and paste a color from, say, Illustrator, QuarkXPress, or InDesign; you can sample it directly without ever leaving Photoshop.

✦ **Tapered path stroking (Chapter 8):** When stroking vector-based paths with brushstrokes, you can instruct Photoshop to simulate pressure sensitivity. This permits you to create smoothly tapering lines and edits, even if you don't own a pressure-sensitive tablet.

✦ **Improved Picture Package (Chapter 18):** Previously, the Picture Package command let you print multiple copies of a single photo, great for creating pages of proofs. Now you have the option of previewing how your photographs will print, as well as mixing two or more images on a page or printing multiple sets of images at a time. You can also label the pictures to add copyright notices or protect proofs from reproduction.

✦ **PDF passwords (Chapter 3):** When saving annotated PDF images for viewing in Acrobat or the like, you can now assign passwords and disable printing or copying.

For you Macintosh users, Photoshop 7 is Carbonized, meaning that it runs directly under OS X, sports the candy-coated aqua interface, and exploits protected memory, preemptive multitasking, and persistent image display. (Note, however, Adobe engineers report that Photoshop runs about five percent slower under OS X than it does under OS 9.2.) Photoshop 7 is also up to speed with recent developments on the Windows side, including Windows XP and later. The upshot is, regardless of your operating system, you're good to go.

Photoshop's companion program, ImageReady 7, also introduces its own share of upgrades. You can optimize the area inside a vector shape independently of other portions of an image. The revamped Rollovers palette tracks slices and lets you manage animations, image maps, and JavaScript rollovers more easily than before. In both Photoshop and ImageReady, you can dither transparent areas inside GIF images and export graphics to the black-and-white WBMP format, used by Web-surfing cell phones and the like. As I mentioned in the preface, for complete information on creating Web graphics with Photoshop and ImageReady, please refer to the hardbound edition of this title, *Photoshop 7 Bible, Professional Edition*.

The result is yet another very strong upgrade to Photoshop. I've heard some folks go so far as to call this the best upgrade to Photoshop ever. Personally, I don't share that opinion—Versions 3, 5, and 6 were more substantial, each in its own way—but Photoshop 7 is no slouch. I would rank it above Versions 2, 2.5, 4, and 5.5, so I guess that makes Version 7 the most representative upgrade to date and a baseline by which all future upgrades will be measured. And if I wish Photoshop 7 had perhaps offered a few more features—such as the ability to edit keyboard shortcuts, pile on editable filter layers, and apply envelope distortions—I am pleasantly surprised by what it does offer and find little fault with its implementation.

Besides, who cares if this is the best upgrade to Photoshop when you hold in your hands the best upgrade to the *Photoshop Bible*? With new imagery and examples throughout, huge rewrites and expanded discussions, and documentation of all new features in their proper context, what more could you need? Just remember to keep an eye peeled for the Photoshop 7 icon and you'll be over the hump and into the image-editing groove in no time.

✦　　✦　　✦

Inside Photoshop

A First Look at Photoshop 7

These days, most computer applications speak a common graphical language, and Photoshop is no exception. It subscribes to the basic language of on-screen nouns and verbs that is spoken by the operating system. As a result, Photoshop may seem tolerably comprehensible the first time you meet it. Without any prior knowledge of its origins or behavior, you should be able to pick up a brush and specify a color in a matter of a few seconds, simply based on the rudimentary vocabulary that you've picked up from other programs. After years of staring into cathode ray tubes, you can't help but get the picture.

But Photoshop has its own special dialect, one that differs from every other program out there. The dialect is so distinct that it's only peripherally understood by other applications, including those from Adobe, the very siblings that Photoshop grew up with. Photoshop has its own way of turning a phrase, it speaks its words in a different order than you might expect, and yes, it uses a lot of strange and sometimes unsettling jargon that it has picked up on the street. Photoshop is always and will forever be a foreigner unnaturally introduced to your hard drive. For all you may think you share in common, it doesn't know you and you don't know it.

Even you experienced users — you hearty few who have carried on more conversations with Photoshop than you have with most of your friends and family — may find yourselves perplexed at times when negotiating with Version 7. The program speaks differently every time it upgrades. In fact, it's wrong to think of Photoshop 7 as an older, wiser version of its original self. This is a completely new beast, bearing about as much resemblance to Photoshop 1.0 as you bear to a rhesus monkey.

So in this chapter, I introduce to you the Seventh Beast, insubordinate child of its ancestors, spoiler of photographic traditions, and speaker of the new language that you now have to learn. These pages represent a low-level primer you need to ingest before you can utter so much as a coherent "gack!" Granted, it comes to you second hand—I am a non-native myself, with my own peculiar dialect as you'll discover—but given that Photoshop 7 itself is the only native speaker on the planet, this foreigner's perspective will have to do.

The splash screen

Shortly after you launch Photoshop, the splash screen appears. The splash screen explains the launching process by flashing the names of plug-in modules as they load and listing the various initialization procedures.

On the PC, you can access the splash screen at any time by choosing Help ➪ About Photoshop. In Macintosh OS X, choose About Photoshop from the Photoshop menu. In Mac OS 9, choose About Photoshop from the Apple menu. After a few seconds, the list of programmers and copyright statements at the bottom of the screen starts to scroll. Press Alt (Win) or Option (Mac) to make the list scroll more quickly. To make the splash screen go away, just click it.

If you've ever tried to launch Photoshop on a networked computer while another computer on the network is already running a copy of Photoshop using the same serial number, you're familiar with the message "Could not initialize Photoshop because So And So is already running a copy of Adobe Photoshop with this serial number." There are two important things to note here: One is that you can work around this by simply detaching the second computer from the network before you launch Photoshop. Once the application is open, re-network the computer, and you'll be up and running. And the other important thing to note is that with Mac OS X, the previously-described same-serial-number network problem doesn't occur at all.

Online resources

Click the icon at the top of the toolbox or choose Help ➪ Adobe Online to open another splash screen titled Adobe Online. Pictured in Figure 2-1, this screen provides access to Adobe's Internet-based resources, which include technical support, tips and tricks, and information about upgrades and related products. You also can choose one of the other commands on the Help menu to link directly to a few specific areas of the online resources.

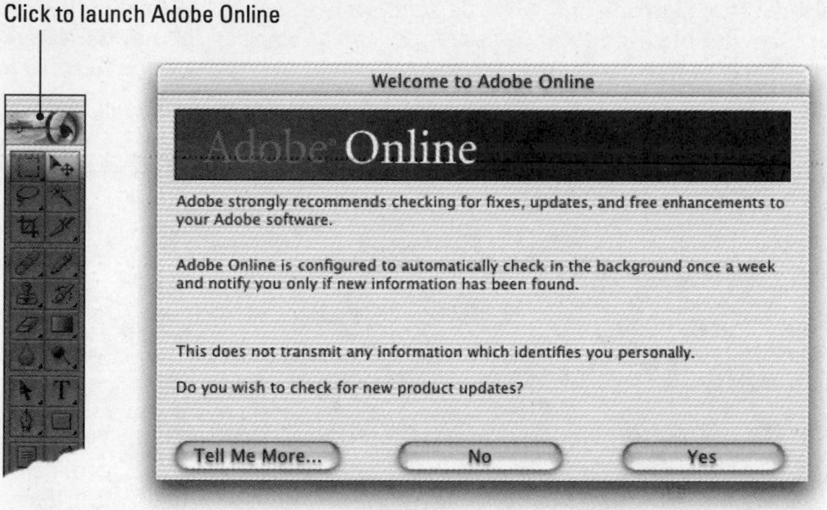

Click to launch Adobe Online

Figure 2-1: Adobe offers a series of online support options for Photoshop 7.

If you want to know more about Adobe Online, click the Tell Me More button and your Web browser will fire up and take you to an informational Web page. After reading this, you'll probably come to the conclusion that checking for updates is a good thing (and it is), so go ahead and click the Yes button on the Adobe Online splash screen. To tell Photoshop how you want your online help delivered — including whether you want Adobe to automatically check for product updates — click the Preferences button to display the Preferences dialog box. After setting your preferences, click OK and check for any updates by clicking the Updates button. Unless you uncheck the "Do not display this dialog again" check box, from this time forward choosing Help ⇨ Adobe Online in Photoshop will automatically launch your Web browser and take you to the Adobe home page. You can also click the Go Online button to visit the home page immediately. (If you have problems, connect to the Internet, start your browser as you normally do, and then return to Photoshop and choose Adobe Online again.) You can return to the Adobe Online preferences at any time by choosing Adobe Online from the Preferences submenu.

The Photoshop Desktop

After the launch process is complete, the Photoshop desktop consumes the foreground. Figure 2-2 shows the Photoshop 7 desktop as it appears on a PC when an image is open and all palettes are visible. Figure 2-3 shows the same scenario as it appears on a Mac running Mac OS X.

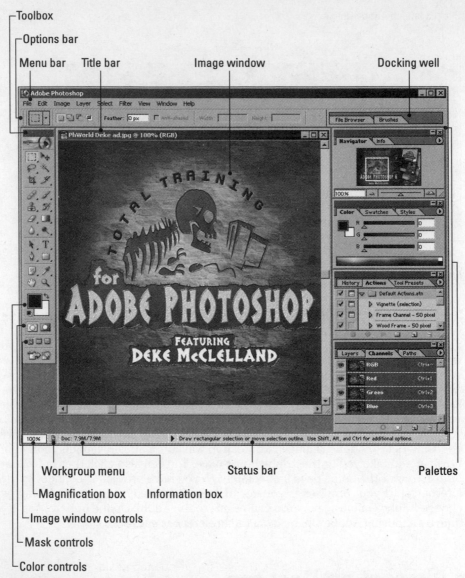

Toolbox

Options bar

Menu bar   Title bar   Image window   Docking well

Workgroup menu   Status bar   Palettes

Magnification box   Information box

Image window controls

Mask controls

Color controls

Figure 2-2: The Photoshop 7 desktop as it looks on a PC with a 17-inch screen.

Many of the elements that make up the Photoshop desktop are well known to folks familiar with the Windows or Macintosh environments. For example, the menu bar provides access to menus and commands. You can drag the title bar to move the image window. And the scroll bars let you look at hidden portions of the image.

Toolbox

Options bar

Menu bar   Title bar   Image window   Docking well

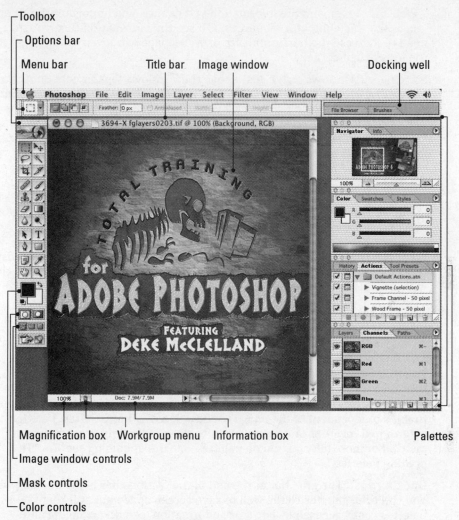

Magnification box   Workgroup menu   Information box   Palettes

Image window controls

Mask controls

Color controls

Figure 2-3: The Photoshop 7 desktop as it looks on a Mac running Mac OS X.

Other potentially less-familiar elements of the Photoshop desktop work as follows:

✦ **Image window:** Like any halfway decent product, Photoshop lets you open multiple documents at a time. Each open image resides inside its own window. In Mac OS X, click the green zoom button in the upper-left corner of the title bar to resize the window to fit the image. In Mac OS 9, click the zoom box in the upper-right corner of the image window. Also worth noting on the Mac are the special boxes in the lower-left corner of the image window (see Figure 2-3). The magnification box tells you the current view size, the Workgroup pop-up menu gives you easy access to useful commands for sharing files over a WebDAV server, and the information box can tell you important things about image size and computer resources. (To see the information box, you may need to increase the horizontal size of your image window by dragging it from the lower-right corner.)

✦ **Status bar (Windows only):** Just above the Windows taskbar sits Photoshop's status bar, which provides running commentary on the active tool and image. (If the status bar doesn't appear on your screen, choose Window ➪ Status Bar.) The left end of the status bar features the magnification box, the Workgroup pop-up menu, and the information box, all of which are described in the previous paragraph.

For complete information on the magnification box, read the "Navigating in Photoshop" section later in this chapter. For more on the Workgroup pop-up menu, see the "File Handling" section, later in this chapter. The very next section explains the information box.

✦ **Toolbox:** The toolbox icons provide one-click access to the various Photoshop tools. To select a tool, click its icon. Then use the tool by clicking or dragging with it inside the image window.

The bottom four rows of the toolbox contain controls for changing your paint colors, entering and exiting the quick mask mode, changing the screen area available for image display, and switching to Adobe ImageReady (which ships with Photoshop).

✦ **Floating palettes:** Photoshop 7 offers a total of 15 palettes, three more than Version 6. (This number excludes the toolbox and the Options bar, which are technically palettes as well.) Each palette is said to be "floating," which means that it's independent of the image window and of other palettes. Palettes can be grouped together or dragged apart to float separately according to your tastes. For more information on palettes, see the upcoming section "The floating palettes."

✦ **Docking well:** The gray bar at the end of the Options bar is the docking well. You can drag palettes to the well to save screen space but still keep the palettes easily accessible. For more information, see "Rearranging and docking palettes," later in this chapter.

Unfortunately, the docking well is only visible if you use a screen resolution with a horizontal pixel display of more than 800 pixels.

The information box

The information box is Photoshop's way of passing you a memo marked FYI. No biggie, nothing to fret about, just a little bit of info you might want to know. As an unusually obliging piece of software, Photoshop likes to keep its human masters informed on the latest developments.

Document size

By default, the information box contains two numbers divided by a slash. The first number is the size of the base image in memory. The second number takes into account any additional layers in your image.

Photoshop calculates the first value by multiplying the height and width of the image (both in pixels) by the *bit depth* of the image, which is the size of each pixel in memory. Consider a typical full-color, 640 × 480-pixel image. A full-color image takes up 24 bits of memory per pixel (which is why it's called a 24-bit image). There are 8 bits in a byte, so 24 bits translates to 3 bytes. Multiply that by the number of pixels and you get 640 × 480 × 3 = 921,600 bytes. Because there are 1,024 bytes in a kilobyte, 921,600 bytes is exactly 900K. Try it yourself — open a 640 × 480-pixel RGB image and you'll see that the first number in the information box reads 900K. Now you know why.

But it's the second value, the one that factors in the layers, that represents the real amount of memory that Photoshop needs. If the image contains one layer only, the numbers before and after the slash are the same. Otherwise, Photoshop measures the opaque pixels in each layer and adds approximately 1 byte of overhead per pixel to calculate the transparency. The second number also grows to accommodate paths, masks, spot-color channels, undoable operations, and miscellaneous data required by the image cache.

Now obviously, it's not necessary that you be able to predict these values (which is lucky, because predicting the second value is virtually impossible). Photoshop asks no help when calculating the values in the information box and will summarily ignore any help you might care to offer. But it's a good idea to know what's going on as you start piling layers on top of an image. The larger the preview numbers grow, the more work Photoshop has to do and the slower it's likely to perform.

Image position

The Print Options feature introduced in Photoshop 6 has now been rechristened Print with Preview. This welcome feature enables you to position a picture precisely on a page before printing. You can find Print with Preview in the File menu, near the other printing commands; skip to Chapter 18 for details on using this tool.

To get a rough idea of the current image position, however, click and hold on the information box. Photoshop displays a pop-up window showing the size and placement of the image in relation to the paper. The preview also shows the approximate placement of crop marks and other elements requested in the Show More Options section of the Print with Preview dialog box.

Press Alt (Win) or Option (Mac) and mouse down on the information box to view the size, channels, and resolution of the image.

You can also Ctrl-click (⌘-click on the Mac) the information box to see the tile sizes. Photoshop uses *tiles* to calculate pixel manipulations. If you confine your work to a single tile, it will probably go faster than if you slop a little over into a second tile. But who cares? Unless you're some kind of tile-reading robot, this technical information is rarely of any practical use.

Click the right-pointing arrowhead next to the information box to display a pop-up menu of seven options. The first option — Document Sizes — is selected by default. This option displays the image-size values described in the previous section. You can find out what information the other choices provide in the next few sections.

The prefix displayed before the values in the information box indicates which of the options is active: Doc shows that Document Sizes is selected; Scr, Scratch Sizes; and Eff, Efficiency. When the Timing option is active, an *s* appears after the numerical value. If a tool name appears in the information box, you know the final option, Current Tool, is active. Similarly, if you see a color profile statement such as "Untagged RGB" or a couple of measurements, such as "640 pixels x 480 pixels", you're looking at the Document Profile or Document Dimensions setting, respectively.

Image color profile

If you work regularly with many different color profiles, you may find the Document Profile option handy. When you select this option, the name of the current color profile appears in the information box. Chapter 16 tells you everything you need to know about color profiles.

Document measurements

Similar to Alt- or Option-clicking on the information box, selecting Document Dimensions gives you a quick readout of the width-by-height measurements of your document. The unit of measurement is set in the Units & Rulers panel of Photoshop's Preferences dialog box.

Memory consumption and availability

When you select Scratch Sizes, Photoshop changes the values in the information box to represent memory consumption and availability. The first value is the amount of room required to hold the currently open images in RAM. The second value indicates the total amount of RAM that Photoshop has to work with. For the program to run at top efficiency, the first number must be smaller than the second.

In the old days, the number before the slash was generally equal to between three and five times the size of all open images, including layers. But thanks to the advent of multiple undos, this value can grow to more than one hundred times as big as any one image. This is because Photoshop has to store each operation in memory on the off chance that you may want to undo to a previous point in time. For each and every action, Photoshop nudges the first value upward until you reach the ceiling of undoable operations.

The second value is simply equal to the amount of memory available to your images after the Photoshop application itself has loaded. For example, suppose Photoshop has 100MB of RAM at its disposal. The code that makes up the Photoshop application consumes about 15MB, so that leaves 85MB to hold and edit images.

If the second value is bigger than the first, then all is happiness and Photoshop is running as fast as your particular brand of computer permits. But if the first value is larger, Photoshop has to dig into its supply of *virtual memory*, a disk-bound adjunct to RAM. Virtual memory makes Photoshop run more slowly because the program must swap portions of the image on and off your hard disk. The simple fact is, disks have moving parts and RAM does not. That means disk-bound "virtual" memory is slower than real memory.

To increase the size of the value after the slash, you have to get more RAM to your images in one of the following ways:

✦ Purchase more RAM. Installing an adequate supply of memory is the single best way to make Photoshop run more quickly.

✦ Quit other applications so that only Photoshop is running.

✦ Quit Photoshop and remove any filters that you don't need from the Plug-Ins folder (which resides in the same folder as the Photoshop 7 application). Don't throw the filters away, just move them to a location outside the Plug-Ins folder so they won't load into RAM when you launch Photoshop.

✦ On the PC and in Mac OS X, choose Memory & Image Cache in the Preferences submenu and increase the Memory Usage value as explained later in this chapter.

✦ In Mac OS 9, press ⌘-Q to quit Photoshop. Then select the Photoshop application icon at the Finder desktop level, press ⌘-I, find the Memory Requirements option in the resulting dialog box, and raise the Preferred Size value.

Operating efficiency

When you select the Efficiency option, Photoshop lists the amount of time it spends running operations in RAM compared with swapping data back and forth between the hard disk. A value of 100 percent is the best-case scenario. It means Photoshop never has to rely on scratch files. Low values indicate higher reliance on the hard disk and, as a result, slower operations. Adobe recommends that if the value falls below 75 percent, you should either assign more memory to Photoshop or purchase more RAM for your computer.

The Efficiency option is a reality check. If it seems Photoshop is dragging its feet, and you hear it writing to your hard disk a little too often, you can refer to the Efficiency rating to see if performance is as bad as you suspect. Keep in mind, hearing Photoshop occasionally write to disk is not, in and of itself, cause for concern. All versions of Photoshop since 3.0 automatically copy open images to a disk buffer in case virtual memory is later warranted. In fact, this is the reason Adobe added the Efficiency option to Version 3.0.1 — to quash fears that a few sparks from your hard drive indicated anything less than peak performance.

Photoshop operations timing

If you select Timing, the information box tells how long Photoshop took to perform the last operation (including background tasks, such as transferring an image to the system Clipboard). Adobe may have added this option to help testing facilities run their Photoshop tests. But built-in timing helps you as well.

For example, suppose you're trying to decide whether to purchase a new computer. You read a magazine article comparing the newest super-fast system. You can run the same filters with the same settings on your computer and see how much slower your results are, all without picking up a stopwatch.

At the risk of starting interoffice feuding, the Timing option also provides you with a mechanism for testing your computer against those of coworkers and friends. The Timing option serves as a neutral arbitrator, enabling you and an associate to test identical operations over the phone. Like Efficiency, Timing is a reality check. If you and your associate own similarly configured computers and your Timing values are vastly different, something's wrong.

The active tool

Choose Current Tool, and Photoshop displays the name of the active tool. Why do you need such a condescending option? Surely you're not so far gone that you need Photoshop telling you what you already know. Adobe's intention is not to drum you over the head with redundant information, but to offer a helping hand if you find the tool configuration confusing. Also, on the PC, the tool name serves as a companion to the tool description to the right of it in the status bar. Now you see not just what the tool does, but what the tool is.

Still, my guess is that this option will prove as rarely useful to everyday image editing as Timing. Use it if you're having problems when first using Photoshop 7 and then set it back to Document Sizes, Scratch Sizes, or Efficiency. The original three options continue to be the best.

The tools

After the seismic changes that Photoshop's toolbox endured in the move from Version 5 to Version 6, Photoshop 7's changes are exceedingly minor. Here's a quick summary:

✦ The powers of the airbrush tool have been subsumed by the newly-renamed brush tool.

✦ The dearly departed airbrush willed its dwelling to the new kids on the block, the healing brush and patch tools.

✦ The Tool Formerly Known as Paintbrush wasn't the only tool to undergo a name change; the path component selection tool has dropped its middle name, and is now known simply as the path selection tool.

✦ Meanwhile, the type tool is now known as the horizontal type tool. This signifies a happy turn of events in the never-ending soap opera that is the Photoshop toolbox. In Version 5 there were four different type tools, but Version 6 broke up this happy family, demoting three of the tools to mere options in the Options bar. Now in Version 7, things are once again as they were in Version 5, and the horizontal type tool now shares accommodations with the vertical type tool, the horizontal type mask tool, and the vertical type mask tool.

✦ The icons in the toolbox now have a lovely shaded dimensional look to them, and they light up colorfully when your cursor passes over them. Some icons have been completely redesigned; frequent users of the custom shape tool will be happy to note that its icon no longer resembles a squashed bug.

When multiple tools share a single toolbox slot, you select the tool you want from a menu-style list, as shown in Figure 2-4. A tiny triangle in the lower-right corner of an icon indicates that more tools lurk beneath the surface. You can click the triangle and then click the name of the tool you want to use. Or, to get the job done with one less click, just drag from the icon onto the name of the tool and then release the mouse button.

Tip

You can cycle between the tools in the pop-up menu by Alt-clicking (Win) or Option-clicking (Mac) a tool icon. Pressing the key that appears to the right of the tool names also does the trick — however, depending on a tool setting that you establish in the Preferences dialog box, you may need to press Shift with the key. (See the upcoming section, "General preferences.")

Also, when you hover your cursor over a tool, Photoshop tells you the name of the tool and how to select it from the keyboard. If you find the tool tips irritating, turn to "General preferences" to find out how to turn them off.

Note

I've catalogued each tool in the following lengthy list, with tool icons, pithy summaries, and the chapter (if any) to which you can refer for more information. No need to read the list word for word; just use it as a reference to get acquainted with the new program. The list presents the tools in the order that they appear in the toolbox. Incidentally, unless otherwise noted, each of the following descriptions tells how to use the tool inside the image window. For example, if an item says drag, you click the tool's icon to select the tool and then drag in the image window; you don't drag on the tool icon itself.

Drag from tool

... to display pop-up menu

Figure 2-4: Drag from any tool icon with a triangle to display a pop-up menu of alternate tools.

Rectangular marquee (Chapter 8): Drag with this tool to enclose a portion of the image in a rectangular marquee, which is a pattern of moving dash marks indicating the boundary of a selection.

Shift-drag to add to a selection; Alt-drag (Win) or Option-drag (Mac) to delete from a selection. The same goes for the other marquee tools, as well as the lassos and magic wand. As an alternative to using these time-honored shortcuts, you can click mode icons in the Options bar to change the behavior of the selection tools.

Elliptical marquee (Chapter 8): Drag with the elliptical marquee tool to enclose a portion of the window in an oval marquee.

Single-row marquee (Chapter 8): Click with the single-row marquee to select an entire horizontal row of pixels that stretches all the way across the image. You can also drag with the tool to position the selection. You rarely need it, but when you do, here it is.

Single-column marquee (Chapter 8): Same as the single-row marquee, except the single-column marquee selects an entire vertical column of pixels. Again, not a particularly useful tool.

Move (Chapter 8): Drag to move a selection or layer. In fact, the move tool is the exclusive means for moving and cloning portions of an image. You can also Ctrl-drag (Win) or ⌘-drag (Mac) selections with any tools except the shape, path, and slicing tools, but only because Ctrl (⌘ on the Mac) temporarily accesses the move tool.

 Lasso (Chapter 8): Drag with the lasso tool to select a free-form portion of the image. You can also Alt-click (Win) or Option-click (Mac) with the lasso to create a straight-sided selection outline.

 Polygonal lasso (Chapter 8): Click hither and yon with this tool to draw a straight-sided selection outline (just like Alt-clicking or Option-clicking with the standard lasso). Each click sets a corner point in the selection.

Magnetic lasso (Chapter 8): As you drag with the magnetic lasso tool, the selection outline automatically sticks to the edge of the foreground image. Bear in mind, however, that Photoshop's idea of an edge may not jibe with yours. Like any automated tool, the magnetic lasso sometimes works wonders, other times it's more trouble than it's worth.

 The magnetic lasso automatically lays down points as you drag. If you don't like a point and you want to get rid of it, press the Backspace (Win) or Delete (Mac) key.

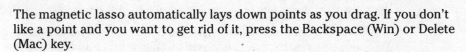 **Magic wand (Chapter 8):** Click with the magic wand tool to select a contiguous area of similarly colored pixels. To select discontiguous areas, click in one area and then Shift-click in another. Deselect the Contiguous tool option and click once to select similar colors throughout the image.

Crop (Chapter 3): Drag with the crop tool to enclose the portion of the image you want to retain in a rectangular boundary. Photoshop tints areas outside the boundary to help you better see which image areas will go and which will stay when you apply the crop. The crop boundary sports several square handles you can drag to resize the cropped area. Drag outside the boundary to rotate it; drag inside to move it. Press Enter or Return to apply the crop or Escape to cancel.

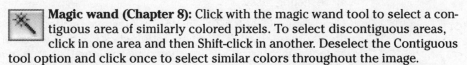 **Slice:** The slice tool and its companion, the slice select tool, come into play when you're creating Web graphics. You can cut images into rectangular sections — known as slices — so that you can apply Web effects, such as links, rollovers, and animations, to different areas of the same image. Drag with the slice tool to define the area that you want to turn into a slice.

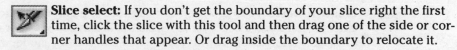 **Slice select:** If you don't get the boundary of your slice right the first time, click the slice with this tool and then drag one of the side or corner handles that appear. Or drag inside the boundary to relocate it.

Press Ctrl (Win) or ⌘ (Mac) when the slice tool is active to temporarily access the slice select tool, and vice versa.

Healing brush (Chapter 7): The clone stamp tool (also known to long-time Photoshop users as the rubber stamp tool) has always seemed like a miracle worker when removing unwanted elements from images. While excellent results were possible, one still had to be very careful so that the texture and shading of the cloned area matched the area you were replacing. While the new healing brush tool seems at first use just like the clone stamp tool, the special "healing" process lets you clone details from one area without obscuring the texture and shading of the other.

Patch (Chapter 7): Similar to the healing brush, the patch tool lets you use the same new "healing" technology by making selections and dragging them to new locations. It's generally useful for healing larger areas of the image.

Brush (Chapter 5): Don't think that the departure of the airbrush tool makes Photoshop a less interesting application for painting. In fact, Airbrush is now just one of many settings to be found in the new Brushes palette. Painting has received a major boost in Version 7, and while the Brushes palette is customization central for the brush tool, don't neglect to check out the interesting new presets available in the brush tool's Options bar.

Pencil (Chapter 5): Drag with the pencil tool to paint jagged, hard-edged lines. Its main purpose is to clean up individual pixels when you're feeling fussy.

Clone stamp (Chapter 7): This tool copies one portion of the image onto another. Alt-click (Win) or Option-click (Mac) the part of your image you want to clone, and then drag to clone that area to another portion of the image.

Pattern stamp (Chapter 7): The pattern stamp tool lets you paint with a pattern. Either choose a preset or define your own pattern using Edit ➪ Define Pattern and then paint away.

History brush (Chapter 7): The history brush reverts portions of the image to any of a handful of previous states throughout the recent history of the image. To specify the state that you want to revert to, click in the first column of the History palette. It's like an undo brush, except way, way better.

Art history brush (Chapter 7): Like the history brush, the art history brush paints with pixels from a previous image state. But with this brush, you get a variety of brush options that create different artistic effects.

Eraser (Chapter 7): Drag with the eraser tool to paint in the background color or erase areas in a layer to reveal the layers below. Alt-drag (Win) or Option-drag (Mac) to switch to the Erase to History mode, which reverts the image to a previous state just as if you were using the history brush.

Background eraser (Chapter 9): The background eraser rubs away the background from an image as you drag along the border between the background and foreground. If you don't wield this tool carefully, though, you wind up erasing both background and foreground.

Magic eraser (Chapter 9): The magic eraser came from the same gene pool that produced the magic wand. When you click with the magic wand, Photoshop selects a range of similarly colored pixels; click with the magic eraser, and you erase instead of select.

Gradient (Chapter 6): Drag with this tool to fill a selection with a gradual transition of colors, commonly called a *gradient*. You can click the gradient icon in the toolbox and select a gradient style from the Options bar.

Paint bucket (Chapter 6): Click with the paint bucket tool to fill a contiguous area of similarly colored pixels with the foreground color or a predefined pattern.

Blur (Chapter 5): Drag with the blur tool to diffuse the contrast between neighboring pixels, which blurs the focus of the image. You can also Alt-drag (Win) or Option-drag (Mac) to sharpen the image.

Sharpen (Chapter 5): Drag with this tool to increase the contrast between pixels, which sharpens the focus. Alt-drag (Win) or Option-drag (Mac) when this tool is active to blur the image.

Smudge (Chapter 5): The smudge tool works just as its name implies; drag with the tool to smear colors inside the image.

Dodge (Chapter 5): Drag with the dodge tool to lighten pixels in the image. Alt-drag (Win) or Option-drag (Mac) to darken the image.

Burn (Chapter 5): Drag with the burn tool to darken pixels. Press Alt (Win) or Option (Mac) to temporarily access the dodge tool and lighten pixels.

Sponge (Chapter 5): Drag with the sponge tool to decrease the amount of saturation in an image so the colors appear more drab, and eventually gray. You can also increase color saturation by changing the Mode setting in the Options bar from Desaturate to Saturate.

Path selection (Chapter 8): Click anywhere inside a path to select the entire path. If you click inside a path that contains multiple subpaths, Photoshop selects the subpath under the tool cursor. Shift-click to select additional paths or subpaths. You also use this tool and the direct selection tool, described next, to select and manipulate lines and shapes drawn with the shape tools.

Direct selection (Chapter 8): To select and edit a segment in a selected path or shape, click it or drag over it with this tool. Press Shift while using the tool to select additional segments. Or Alt-click (Option-click on the Mac) inside a path or shape to select and edit the whole object.

Horizontal type (Chapter 15): Also known simply as the type tool, click with this tool to add text to your image. As of Photoshop 6, you can enter and edit text directly in the image window—those days of fooling around with the Type Tool dialog box are happily long gone.

  Vertical type (Chapter 15): The vertical type tool behaves just as the horizontal type tool does, except that your text is oriented vertically in the image.

 Horizontal type mask (Chapter 15): As you might expect, this tool creates horizontal type. The twist is that the type doesn't appear directly in the image, but rather as a mask, with an active selection around the shapes of the letters.

 Vertical type mask (Chapter 15): Combine the verticality of the vertical type tool with the mask-iness of the horizontal type mask tool, and you've got—what else?—the vertical type mask tool. Use it to create an active selection of vertically oriented text.

 Pen (Chapter 8): Click and drag with the pen tool to set points in the image window. Photoshop draws an editable path outline—much like a path in Illustrator—that you can convert to a selection outline or stroke with color.

 Freeform pen (Chapter 8): Drag with this tool to draw freehand paths or vector masks. Photoshop automatically adds points along the path as it sees fit. If you select the Magnetic check box in the Options bar, the freeform pen morphs into the magnetic pen introduced in Version 5.5. Deselect the check box to return to the freeform pen.

 Add anchor point (Chapter 8): To insert a point in a path, click a path segment with this tool.

 Delete anchor point (Chapter 8): Click a point to remove the point without interrupting the outline of the path. Photoshop automatically draws a new segment between the neighboring points.

 Convert point (Chapter 8): Points in a path come in different varieties, some indicating corners and others indicating smooth arcs. The convert point tool enables you to change one kind of point to another. Drag a point to convert it from a corner to an arc. Click a point to convert it from an arc to a sharp corner.

 Rectangle (Chapter 14): One of the five vector drawing tools provided by Photoshop 7, this tool draws rectangles filled with the foreground color. Just drag to create a rectangle; Shift-drag to draw a square.

Rounded rectangle (Chapter 14): Prefer your boxes with nice, curved corners instead of sharp, 90-degree angles? Drag or Shift-drag with the rounded rectangle tool.

 You can opt to create rasterized shapes and lines with the rectangle, rounded rectangle, ellipse, polygon, line, and custom shape tools. See Chapter 14 for details.

Ellipse (Chapter 14): You look pretty smart to me, so you probably already figured out that you drag with this tool to draw an ellipse and Shift-drag to draw a circle.

 Polygon (Chapter 14): By default, dragging with this tool creates a 5-sided polygon. Controls available in the Options bar enable you to change the number of sides or set the tool to create star shapes.

 Line (Chapter 14): Drag with the line tool to create a straight line. But before you do, travel to the Options bar to set the line thickness and specify whether you want arrowheads at the ends of the line.

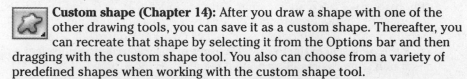 **Custom shape (Chapter 14):** After you draw a shape with one of the other drawing tools, you can save it as a custom shape. Thereafter, you can recreate that shape by selecting it from the Options bar and then dragging with the custom shape tool. You also can choose from a variety of predefined shapes when working with the custom shape tool.

 Notes (Chapter 3): Use this tool to create a little sticky note on which you can jot down thoughts, ideas, and other pertinent info that you want to share with other people who work with the image — or that you simply want to remember the next time you open the image. After you create the note, Photoshop displays a note icon in the image window; double-click the icon to see what you had to say.

 Audio annotation (Chapter 3): If you prefer the spoken word to the written one, you can annotate your images with an audio clip, assuming that you have a microphone and sound card for your computer. As with the notes tool, an audio icon appears in the image window after you record your message. Clicking the icon plays the audio clip.

 Eyedropper (Chapter 4): Click with the eyedropper tool on a color in the image window to make that color the foreground color. Alt-click (Win) or Option-click (Mac) a color to make that color the background color.

Color sampler (Chapter 4): Click as many as four locations in an image to evaluate the colors of those pixels in the Info palette. After you set a point, you can move it by dragging it to a different pixel.

Measure (Chapter 12): The measure tool lets you measure distances and directions inside the image window. Just drag from one point to another and note the measurement data in the Info palette or the Options bar. You can also drag the endpoints of your line to take new measurements. And by Alt-dragging (Win) or Option-dragging (Mac) an endpoint, you can create a sort of virtual protractor that measures angles.

Hand (Chapter 2): Drag inside the image window with the hand tool to scroll the window so you can see a different portion of the image. Double-click the hand tool icon to magnify or reduce the image so it fits on the screen in its entirety. When the hand tool is active, you can click buttons in the Options bar to display the image at the actual-pixels, fit-on-screen, or print-size view sizes.

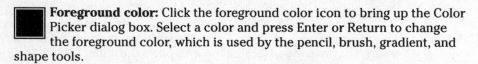

Zoom (Chapter 2): Click with the zoom tool to magnify the image so you can see individual pixels more clearly. Alt-click (Win) or Option-click (Mac) to step back from the image and take in a broader view. Drag to enclose the specific portion of the image you want to magnify. And, finally, double-click the zoom tool icon inside the toolbox to restore the image to 100-percent view size.

You can modify the performance of any tool but the measure tool by adjusting the settings in the Options bar. To change the unit of measurement used by the measure tool, double-click the ruler or choose Edit ⇨ Preferences ⇨ Units & Rulers (Photoshop ⇨ Preferences ⇨ Units & Rulers in Mac OS X) to display the Units & Rulers panel of the Preferences dialog box. Then select the unit from the Rulers pop-up menu. Or, even quicker, right-click (Win) or Control-click (Mac) the ruler or click the plus sign in the lower-left corner of the Info palette and select a measurement unit from the resulting pop-up menu.

The toolbox controls

Well, that pretty much wraps it up for the Photoshop 7 tools. It was a breathtakingly dull tale, but one that had to be told. But the excitement isn't over yet. Gather the kittens and hold onto your mittens as we explore the ten controls that grace the lower portion of the toolbox:

Foreground color: Click the foreground color icon to bring up the Color Picker dialog box. Select a color and press Enter or Return to change the foreground color, which is used by the pencil, brush, gradient, and shape tools.

I'm not sure why, but many users make the mistake of double-clicking the foreground or background color icons when they first start using Photoshop. A single click is all that's needed. Experienced users don't even bother with the Color Picker — they stick to the more convenient Color palette.

Background color: Click the background color icon to display the Color Picker and change the background color, which is used by the eraser and gradient tools. Photoshop also uses the background color to fill a selected area on the background layer when you press the Backspace or Delete key.

 Switch colors: Click the switch colors icon to exchange the foreground and background colors.

 Default colors: Click this icon to return to the default foreground and background colors — black and white, respectively.

At any time, you can quickly make the foreground color white by clicking the default colors icon and then clicking the switch colors icon. Or just press D (for default colors) and then X (for switch colors).

Marching ants: Click this icon to exit Photoshop's quick mask mode and view selection outlines as animated dotted lines that look like marching ants, hence the name. (Adobe calls this the "standard" mode, but I think marching ants mode better describes how it works.)

Quick mask: Click here to enter the quick mask mode, which enables you to edit selection boundaries using painting tools. The marching ants vanish and the image appears half covered by a translucent layer of red, like a rubylith in traditional paste-up. The red layer covers the deselected—or masked—portions of the image. Paint with black to extend the masked areas, thereby subtracting from the selection. Paint with white to erase the mask, thereby adding to the selection.

The quick mask mode is too complex a topic to sum up in a few sentences. If you can't wait to find out what it's all about, check out Chapter 9.

Standard window: Click this icon to display the foreground image in a standard window, as shown earlier in Figures 2-2 and 2-3. Every image appears in the standard window mode when you first open it.

Full screen with menu bar: If you can't see enough of your image inside a standard window, click this icon. The title bar and scroll bars disappear, as do all background windows and the Windows taskbar, but the menu bar and palettes remain visible, as shown in Figure 2-5. (You can still access other open images by choosing their names from the Window menu.) A light gray background fills any empty area around the image.

This is similar to the effect that you get when you click the maximize button in the upper-right corner of the image window on a PC. However, you probably want to avoid maximizing images; use the toolbox controls instead. Photoshop has a habit of resizing a maximized window whenever you zoom with the commands under the View menu. If you use the toolbox controls, you don't have that problem.

When the image doesn't consume the entire image window, the empty portion of the window appears gray when you're working in the standard window or full screen with menu bar modes. To change it to a different color—such as black—select a color and Shift-click in the gray area with the paint bucket tool.

Absolute full screen: If you still can't see enough of your image, click the rightmost of the image window controls to see the photo set against a neutral black background. (You can't change the color of this backdrop—it's always black.) The menu bar disappears, limiting your access to commands, but you can still access many commands using keyboard shortcuts. Only the toolbox and palettes remain visible.

As noted in the tool tips, pressing the F key lets you cycle through these three options. If you need access to a menu command when working in the absolute full screen mode, press Shift+F to display the menu bar. Press Shift+F again to hide it.

Figure 2-5: Click the middle icon at the bottom of the toolbox to hide the title bar and scroll bars.

If Photoshop's screen elements interfere with your view of an image, you can hide all palettes — including the toolbox and Options bar — by pressing the Tab key. To bring the hidden palettes back into view, press Tab again.

You can hide the palettes but leave the toolbox and Options bar on screen by pressing Shift+Tab. Press Shift+Tab again to bring the palettes back. (Pressing Tab while the standard palettes are gone hides the toolbox and Options bar.) If the rulers are turned on, they remain visible at all times. Press Ctrl+R (⌘-R on the Mac) to toggle the ruler display off and on.

Here's one more tip for good measure: Shift-click the icon for absolute full screen to switch the display mode for all open images. Then press Ctrl+Tab (Control-Tab on the Mac) to cycle through the open images. This same trick works for the standard and full screen with menu bar modes.

 Go to ImageReady: Click this icon to switch to ImageReady, Photoshop's companion Web graphics program.

The Options bar

Spanning the width of the Photoshop window, the Options bar (labeled back in
Figures 2-2 and 2-3) contains the major controls for the tools in the toolbox. You
establish tool settings by selecting check boxes, clicking icons, and choosing
options from pop-up menus in the bar. In other words, think of the Options bar as
just another floating palette, albeit a long, skinny one. (Longtime Photoshop users
will remember that the Options bar actually used to be a floating Options palette.)
However, you use different tactics to hide, display, and relocate the Options bar
than you do a regular palette:

✦ Choose Window ➪ Options or double-click any tool icon in the toolbox to
toggle on the display of the Options bar. (You should see a checkmark to the
left of the command when the Options bar is visible.) Choose Window ➪
Options again to toggle off the Options bar. You also can press Tab to toggle
the display of the Options bar and all other palettes on and off.

✦ By default, the Options bar is docked at the top of the program window. Drag
the vertical handle at the left end of the bar to relocate it. If you drag the bar
to the top or bottom of the window, it becomes docked again.

✦ Unfortunately, you can't change the size or shape of the Options bar.

You can attach regular palettes to the Options bar by dragging them onto the
docking well at the right end of the bar. The upcoming section, "Rearranging
and docking palettes," tells all.

Tool presets

In Photoshop 6, the current tool icon that appeared at the far left end of the
Options bar was little more than just an icon. True, you could give it a click and
access a tiny pop-up menu, which allowed you to either reset that single tool to its
default settings or reset all tools to their defaults. But in Version 7, this icon has
become one of the main hubs of activity for a brand new concept: tool presets.

Let's say you frequently make 3¼ by 4 inch prints from your printer. This probably
also means that you frequently set the crop tool for those specific dimensions. If
you use the crop tool for some other purpose, however, the next time you want to
make a 3¼ by 4 inch print, you'll have to reenter those measurements again. Tool
presets let you save specific tool settings so that you can quickly access them
without having to do a lot of typing and tweaking.

Adobe was apparently so excited by this concept that it also gave tool presets a
floating palette of their own. You may think the Options bar icon is more convenient
because it's on the same side of the screen as the toolbox; then again, if the floating
Tool Presets palette is visible, you may be able to access the desired preset with a
single click. Either way, the palette gives you access to the same settings and
choices as the Options bar icon does.

Start by selecting a tool and adjusting the settings until they're perfect. Set up the ideal gradient and direction settings for the gradient tool, a frequently-used tolerance for the magic wand, or a combination of font, size, and alignment options for the type tool. Here are ways you can save those settings as a tool preset:

✦ Choose Window ➪ Tool Presets to display the Tool Presets palette. Then click the new tool preset icon at the bottom of the palette (labeled in Figure 2-6).

✦ Click the current tool icon in the Options bar; then click the new tool preset icon below the flyout menu arrow in the upper-right corner of the drop-down palette.

✦ Choose New Tool Preset from either the Tool Presets floating palette menu or the palette menu accessible from the drop-down palette in the Options bar (shown in Figure 2-6).

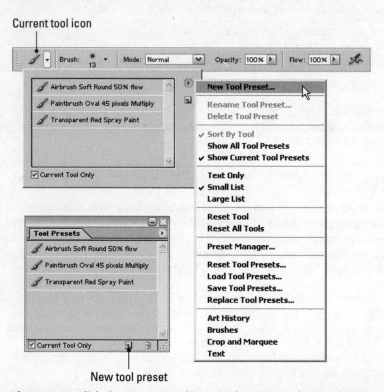

Figure 2-6: Click the current tool icon in the Options bar or choose Window ➪ Tool Presets to display options for creating new tool presets.

Any of these methods will take you to a small dialog box where you can enter a descriptive name for your tool settings. Some tools also have a check box where you can choose to include or exclude a particular setting from the preset, such as the color for the brush tool or the pattern for the pattern stamp tool. Click OK, and your newly-named group of tool settings will appear in the list. From here on out, clicking on this preset will load that group of settings into the Options bar. If you're having a hard time finding a preset, make sure the Current Tool Only option is checked; this will make only presets for the current tool appear in the list.

Whether you access the Tool Presets menu from the Options bar or from the Tool Presets palette, you can choose from the following additional options:

✦ Rename Tool Preset and Delete Tool Preset let you perform those functions on the currently selected tool preset.

✦ Sort By Tool is only active if the Current Tool Only option is unchecked; it groups the presets in the list by tool.

✦ Show All Tool Presets and Show Current Tool Presets toggle off and on the Current Tool Only check box.

✦ There are three options for viewing the list: Text Only, which lets you see the most options on-screen at one time; Small List, which adds a small icon; and Large List, which gives you the icon along with larger text.

✦ Reset Tool and Reset All Tools are carryovers from Photoshop 6, letting you restore either the current tool or all tools to their default settings. This has no effect on your collection of tool presets.

✦ Reset Tool Presets, Load Tool Presets, Save Tool Presets, and Replace Tool Presets all let you deal with groups of presets. Reset takes you back to the default set of tool presets, giving you the option to append the default set to the current set or to replace it entirely with the default set; Load gives you access to a previously saved groups of presets; Save lets you save the group of presets to disk for future use, and Replace wipes out the current group of presets in favor of the presaved group of your choice.

✦ Preset Manager takes you to Adobe's gift to the obsessively organized: the Preset Manager dialog box. Here you can store and manage all of your preset collections, as I explain in the very next section.

The Preset Manager

Tool presets are actually only the latest addition to the Preset Manager, a nifty innovation introduced in Photoshop 6. This handy tool lets you organize and store presets in eight different categories: Brushes, Swatches, Gradients, Styles, Patterns, Contours, Custom Shapes, and Tools. In addition to choosing Preset Manager from the palette menus of the Tool Presets, Brushes, Swatches, and Styles palettes, you can always access the Preset Manager dialog box (shown in Figure 2-7) by choosing Edit ⇨ Preset Manager. Then choose a category from the Preset Type pop-up menu.

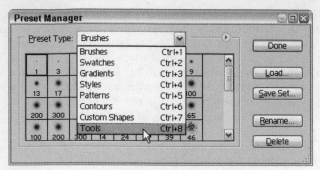

Figure 2-7: The Preset Manager dialog box lets you store and organize presets for eight different categories.

If you click the right-pointing arrowhead to the left of the Done button, you display a pop-up menu with some of the same options found in the Tool Presets palette menu. For example, you can choose to replace the current preset collection with another or return to the default collection. To append a collection, click the Load button. Alternatively, click a collection name in the pop-up menu, in which case you have the choice of appending or replacing the current collection with the new one. In addition, you can click a preset and then click Delete to remove the preset or Rename to change the preset's name. If you want to dump or rename a bunch of presets, Shift-click them and then click Delete or Rename. To select all presets, press Ctrl+A (⌘-A on the Mac). If you press the Alt or Option key, you get a scissors cursor with which you can click a preset to delete it.

Aside from being able to delete or rename a batch of presets at one time, the best reason for bothering with the Preset Manager is to create a new preset collection out of presets from an existing set or sets. Load the collection that you want to use as a basis for the new set. Then Shift-click to select presets for the new set — or press Ctrl+A (⌘-A on the Mac) to select all presets — and click Save Set. Give the collection a name and store it in the suggested folder.

Note that you can't overwrite any existing preset files. Also, after you add a new preset, you must save it as part of a collection, either via the palette menu or the Preset Manager. Otherwise Photoshop deletes the preset if you replace the current preset collection with another.

The floating palettes

When you first launch Photoshop, all the palettes appear either on screen or in the docking well except for two: the Character and Paragraph palettes. These two palettes don't display automatically; you must choose Show Character or Show Paragraph from the Window menu or click the Palettes button in the Options bar while a type tool is active. Other than that, these palettes look and behave just like the other palettes, which look and behave much like they have since Version 3.

Each palette contains most or all of the elements labeled in Figure 2-8. (Note that on the Mac, the close button is positioned on the far left side of the title bar.) Some palettes lack scroll bars, others lack size boxes, but that's just to keep things from getting too predictable.

There's one palette that plays by its own rules and pays no attention to the underlying palette logic built into Photoshop: The new File Browser palette. In fact, as you work with the File Browser, you may begin to feel that it's not really a palette at all, but more like a dialog box in palette's clothing. I'll take a full look at this powerful new feature in Chapter 3; for now, if you want to experiment with the File Browser, you'll find it hiding out in the Options bar's palette well by default.

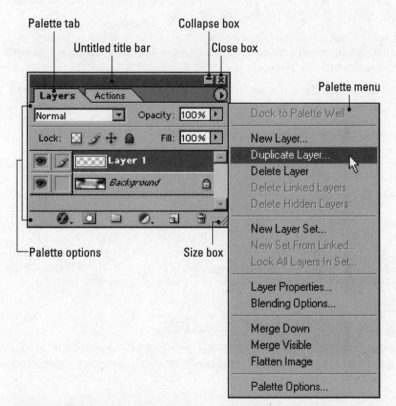

Figure 2-8: Most palettes include the same basic elements as the Layers palette, shown here.

Many palette elements are miniature versions of the elements that accompany any window. For example, the close box and title bar work identically to their image-window counterparts. The title bar lacks a title—I have a lobbyist in Washington working on getting the name changed to "untitled bar" as we speak—but you can still drag it to move the palette to a different location on screen.

Photoshop automatically snaps palettes into alignment with other palettes. To snap a palette to the edge of the screen, Shift-click its title bar. You can also Shift-drag the title bar to move the palette around the perimeter of the screen or to snap the palette from one edge of the screen to the other. (This tip also works with the toolbox.)

Four elements are unique to floating palettes:

✦ **Palette options:** Each floating palette offers its own collection of options. These options may include icons, pop-up menus, slider bars, you name it.

✦ **Palette menu:** Click the right-pointing arrowhead to display a menu of commands specific to the palette. These commands enable you to manipulate the palette options and adjust preference settings.

✦ **Palette tabs:** Click a palette tab to move it to the front of the palette group. (You can also select the palette commands from the Window menu, but it's more convenient to click a tab.)

✦ **Collapse box:** Click the collapse box to decrease the amount of space consumed by the palette. If you previously enlarged the palette by dragging the size box, your first click reduces the palette back to its default size. After that, clicking the collapse box hides all but the most essential palette options.

In most cases, collapsing a palette hides all options and leaves only the tabs visible. But in the case of the Color and Layers palettes, clicking the collapse box leaves a sliver of palette options intact, as demonstrated in the middle example of Figure 2-9. To eliminate all options — as in the last example — Alt-click (Win) or Option-click (Mac) the collapse box. You can also double-click one of the tabs or in the empty area to the right of the tabs. And if your palette is located at the bottom edge of the screen, collapsing the palette will make it collapse downward, leaving the visible part of the collapsed palette hugging the bottom of the screen. These tricks work even if you've enlarged the palette by dragging the size box.

Rearranging and docking palettes

Photoshop makes it easy to regroup palettes to suit the way you work. You can dock palettes to each other or to the Options bar. You're king of the palette hill, as it were.

To attach a floating palette to the Options bar, as shown in Figure 2-10, drag the palette tab to the docking well. After you dock the palette, you see just the palette tab in the Options bar. Click the tab to display the palette, as shown in the figure. When you click outside the palette, the palette closes automatically.

If you don't see the docking well, you need to raise your monitor resolution. The docking well isn't accessible at monitor resolutions of 800 pixels wide or less.

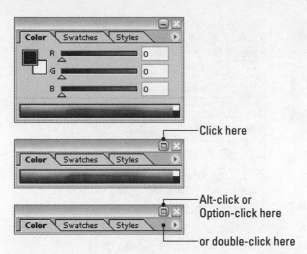

Click here

Alt-click or
Option-click here

or double-click here

Figure 2-9: The Color palette shown at full size (top), partially collapsed (middle), and fully collapsed (bottom).

Docking well

Figure 2-10: Attach palettes to the Options bar by dragging them to the docking well.

In addition to docking palettes in the Options bar, you can dock palettes to each other. Drag a palette tab to the bottom of another palette and release the mouse button when just the bottom of the other palette appears highlighted, as shown in the left side of Figure 2-11. The dragged palette grabs hold of the other palette's tail and doesn't let go. Now you can keep both palettes visible but move, close, collapse, and resize the two as a single entity, as shown in the right half of the figure.

Tip

When you dock a resizable palette to another resizable palette, you can resize the palettes like so:

✦ Place your cursor over the border between two stacked palettes until you see the double-headed arrow cursor. Then drag down to enlarge the upper palette and shrink the lower one. Drag up to enlarge the lower palette and shrink the upper one. The overall size of the docked palettes doesn't change.

✦ Alt-drag (Win) or Option-drag (Mac) the border to resize the upper palette only.

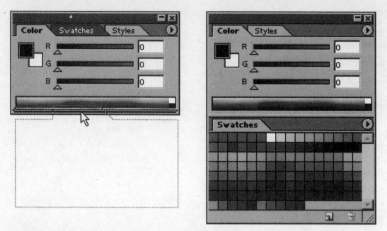

Figure 2-11: Drag a palette tab to the bottom of another palette (left) to dock the two palettes together (right).

Still not happy with your palette layout? You can shuffle palettes at will, moving a single palette from one group to another or giving it complete independence from any group. To separate a palette from the herd, drag its tab away from the palette group, as demonstrated in the left column in Figure 2-12. To add the palette to a palette group, drag its tab onto the palette group, as shown in the middle column. The right column shows the results of the two maneuvers I made in the first two columns.

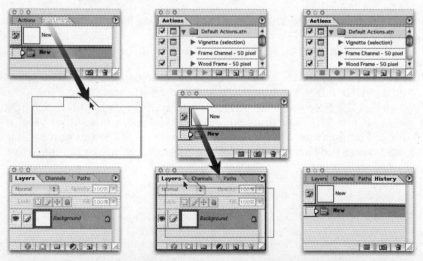

Figure 2-12: Dragging a palette tab out of a palette group (left) separates the palette from its original family (middle). Dragging a palette tab onto another palette group (middle) adds that palette to the group (right).

The Reset Palette Locations command (Window ⇨ Workspace ⇨ Reset Palette Locations), introduced in Photoshop 6, makes it easy to restore your palette setup to the neat and tidy defaults. But Version 7 takes this concept one step further, allowing you to save and recall your own palette arrangements. This makes it easy for individual users to share the same Photoshop application; if your wacky co-worker can't function in the application unless the toolbox is moved to the *right* side of the screen, you can choose Window ⇨ Workspace ⇨ Save Workspace, name the workspace Wacky's Workspace (or whatever you desire), and click Save. From now on, you can access this saved workspace in the Window ⇨ Workspace menu. And when Mr. or Ms. Wacky gets promoted above you and finally has his or her own computer, you can choose Window ⇨ Workspace ⇨ Delete Workspace and choose from a pop-up list of all saved workspaces.

Tabbing through the options

I mentioned earlier that you can hide the palettes by pressing Shift+Tab and that you can hide the palettes, toolbox, and Options bar by pressing Tab. But this keyboard trick doesn't work if an option box is active.

For example, suppose you click inside the R option box in the Color palette. This activates the option. Now press Tab. Rather than hiding the palettes, Photoshop advances you to the next option box in the palette, G. To move backward through the options, press Shift+Tab. This trick applies to the Options bar as well as to the standard palettes.

To apply an option box value and return focus to the image window, press Enter or Return. This deactivates the palette options. If an option box remains active, certain keyboard tricks — such as pressing a key to select a tool — won't work properly. Photoshop either ignores the shortcut or beeps at you for pressing a key the option box doesn't like.

While you're working in the image window, you can return focus to the Options bar from the keyboard. When you press Enter or Return, Photoshop displays the Options bar, if it's not already visible. If the Options bar offers an option box for the active tool, Photoshop highlights the contents of the option box. You can then tab around to reach the option you want to change, enter a new value, and press Enter or Return to get out.

Navigating in Photoshop

All graphics and desktop publishing programs provide a variety of navigational tools and functions that enable you to scoot around the screen, visit the heartlands and nether regions, examine the fine details, and take in the big picture. And Photoshop is no exception. In fact, Photoshop's navigation tools would make Magellan drool (were he inclined to edit an image or two).

The view size

You can change the view size—the size at which an image appears on screen—so you can either see more of an image or concentrate on individual pixels. Each change in view size is expressed as a zoom ratio, which is the ratio between screen pixels and image pixels. Photoshop displays the zoom ratio as a percentage value in the title bar as well as in the magnification box. The 100-percent zoom ratio shows one image pixel for each screen pixel (and is therefore equivalent to the old 1:1 zoom ratio in Photoshop 3 and earlier). A 200 percent zoom ratio doubles the size of the image pixels on screen, and so on.

Actual pixels

Photoshop calls the 100-percent zoom ratio the *actual-pixels* view. This is the most accurate view size because you can see the image as it really is. Reduced view sizes drop pixels; magnified view sizes stretch pixels. Only the actual-pixels view displays each pixel without a trace of screen distortion.

You can switch to this most accurate of view sizes at any time using one of the following techniques:

✦ Choose View ➪ Actual Pixels.

✦ Press Ctrl+Alt+0 (⌘-Option-0 on the Mac). (That's a zero, not the letter *O*.)

✦ Double-click the zoom tool icon in the toolbox.

✦ Click the Actual Pixels button, which appears in the Options bar when the zoom tool is selected.

Fit on screen

When you first open an image, Photoshop displays it at the largest zoom ratio (up to 100 percent) that permits the entire image to fit on screen. Assuming you don't change the size of the image, you can return to this "fit-on-screen" view size in one of the following ways:

✦ Choose View ➪ Fit on Screen.

✦ Press Ctrl+0 (Win) or ⌘-0 (Mac).

✦ Double-click the hand tool icon in the toolbox.

✦ Select the zoom tool and then click the Fit on Screen button in the Options bar.

Strangely, any of these techniques may magnify the image beyond the 100-percent view size. When working on a very small image, for example, Photoshop enlarges the image to fill the screen, even if this means maxing out the zoom to 1,600 percent. Personally, I prefer to use the fit-on-screen view only when working on very large images.

Well, actually, I almost never use the fit-on-screen view because it's too arbitrary. Photoshop does the best job of previewing an image when you can see all pixels — that is, at 100-percent view size. Short of that, you want the screen pixels to divide evenly into the image pixels. This means view sizes like 50 percent or 25 percent, but not 75 percent or 66.7 percent. And you never know what it's going to be with the fit-on-screen view.

Print size

You can switch to yet another predefined view size by choosing View ➪ Print Size. This command theoretically displays the image on screen at the size it will print. (You set the print size using Image ➪ Image Size, as I explain in Chapter 3.) When the zoom tool is active, you also can click the Print Size button in the Options bar to turn on the print-size view.

In practice, "print-size" view isn't particularly reliable. Photoshop assumes that your monitor displays exactly 72 pixels per inch, even on the PC, where the accepted screen resolution is 96 pixels per inch. But it's all complete nonsense, whatever the assumption. Monitor resolutions vary all over the map. And high-end monitors let you change screen resolutions without Photoshop even noticing.

The long and the short of it is this: Don't expect to hold up your printed image and have it exactly match the print-size view on screen. It's a rough approximation, designed to show you how the image will look when imported into InDesign, QuarkXPress, PageMaker, or some other publishing program — nothing more.

The zoom tool

Obviously, the aforementioned zoom ratios aren't the only ones available to you. You can zoom in as close as 1,600 percent and zoom out to 0.2 percent.

The most straightforward way to zoom in and out of your image is to use the zoom tool:

✦ Click in the image window with the zoom tool to magnify the image in preset increments — from 33.33 percent to 50 to 66.67 to 100 to 200 and so on. Photoshop tries to center the zoomed view at the point where you clicked (or come as close as possible).

✦ Alt-click (Win) or Option-click (Mac) with the zoom tool to reduce the image incrementally — 200 to 100 to 66.67 to 50 to 33.33 and so on. Again, Photoshop tries to center the new view on the click point.

✦ Drag with the zoom tool to draw a rectangular marquee around the portion of the image you want to magnify. Photoshop magnifies the image so the marqueed area fits just inside the image window. (If the horizontal and vertical proportions of the marquee do not match those of your screen — for example, if you draw a tall, thin marquee or a really short, wide one — Photoshop favors the smaller of the two possible zoom ratios to avoid hiding any detail inside the marquee.)

✦ If you want Photoshop to resize the window when you click with the zoom tool, select the Resize Windows to Fit check box in the Options bar. The check box appears only when the zoom tool is the active tool.

✦ Turn off the Ignore Palettes check box in the Options bar if you want Photoshop to stop resizing the window when the window bumps up against a palette that's anchored against the side of the program window. Turn the option on to resize the window regardless of the palettes. The palettes then float over the resized window.

To access the zoom tool temporarily when some other tool is selected, press and hold the Ctrl (Win) or ⌘ (Mac) and spacebar keys. Release both keys to return control of the cursor to the selected tool. To access the zoom out cursor, press Alt (Win) or Option (Mac) with the spacebar. These keyboard equivalents work from inside many dialog boxes, enabling you to modify the view of an image while applying a filter or color correction.

The zoom commands

You can also zoom in and out using the following commands and keyboard shortcuts:

✦ Choose View ➪ Zoom In or press Ctrl+plus (+) (⌘-plus on the Mac) to zoom in. This command works exactly like clicking with the zoom tool except you can't specify the center of the new view size. Photoshop merely centers the zoom in keeping with the previous view size.

✦ Choose View ➪ Zoom Out or press Ctrl+minus (–) (⌘-minus on the Mac) to zoom out.

The General panel of the Photoshop 7 Preferences dialog box (that's Ctrl+K on the PC and ⌘-K on the Mac) includes an option called Keyboard Zoom Resizes Windows. If you select this option, Photoshop resizes the image window when you use the Zoom commands. (Despite the setting's name, it applies when you choose the zoom commands from the menu as well as when you use the keyboard shortcuts.) To override the setting temporarily, press Alt (Win) or Option (Mac) as you press the keyboard shortcut or select the menu command. Similarly, if you deselect the option in the Preferences dialog box, you can add Alt or Option to turn window-zooming on temporarily.

If Photoshop is unresponsive to these or any other keyboard shortcuts, it's probably because the image window has somehow become inactive. (It can happen in Windows if you so much as click the taskbar.) Just click the image-window title bar and try again.

The magnification box

Another way to zoom in and out without changing the window size is to enter a value into the magnification box, located in the lower-left corner of the Photoshop window (or image window on the Mac). Select the magnification value, enter a new one, and press Enter or Return. Photoshop zooms the view without zooming the window. (Neither the Resize Windows to Fit check box in the Options bar nor the Keyboard Zoom Resizes Windows option in the Preferences dialog box affect the magnification box.)

In Figure 2-13, I started with a specially sized window at 25 percent. I then entered two different zoom ratios into the magnification box — 57.8 percent and 18.9 percent — alternately enlarging and reducing the image within the confines of a static window.

You might like to know more about the magnification box:

✦ You can enter values in the magnification box as percentages, ratios, or "times" values. To switch to a zoom value of 250 percent, for example, you can enter *250%*, *5:2*, or *2.5x*.

✦ You can specify a zoom value in increments as small as 0.01 percent. So if a zoom value of 250.01 doesn't quite suit your fancy, you can try 250.02. I seriously doubt you'll need this kind of precision, but isn't it great to know it's there?

When you press Enter or Return after entering a magnification value, Photoshop changes the view size and returns focus to the image window. If you aren't exactly certain what zoom ratio you want to use, press Shift+Enter (Shift-Return on the Mac) instead. This changes the view size while keeping the magnification value active; this way you can enter a new value and try again.

Creating a reference window

In the ancient days, paint programs provided a cropped view of your image at the actual-pixels view size to serve as a reference when you worked in a magnified view. Because it's so doggone modern, Photoshop 7 does not, but you can easily create a second view of your image by choosing Window ⇨ Documents ⇨ New Window, as in Figure 2-14. Use one window to maintain a 100-percent view of your image while you zoom and edit inside the other window. Both windows track the changes to the image.

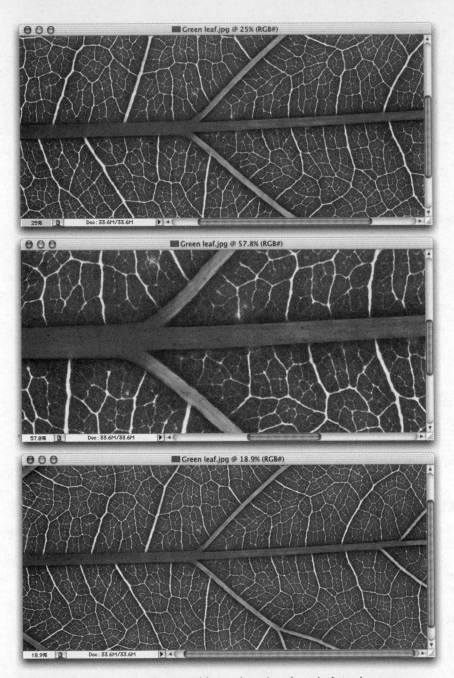

Figure 2-13: To zoom an image without changing the window size, enter a zoom ratio into the magnification box and press Enter or Return. Alternatively, deselect the Resize Windows to Fit check box in the Options bar when working with the zoom tool.

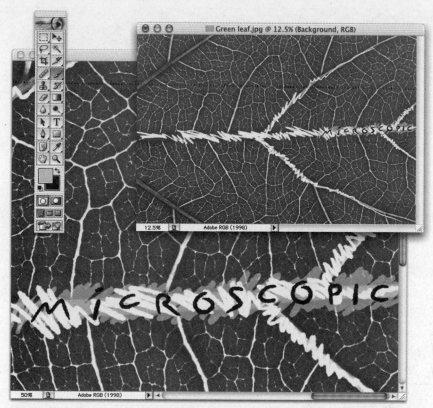

Figure 2-14: You can create multiple windows to track the changes made to a single image by choosing the New Window command from the Documents submenu of the Window menu.

Scrolling inside the window

In the standard window mode, you have access to scroll bars, as you do in just about every other major application. But as you become more proficient with Photoshop, you'll use the scroll bars less and less. One way to bypass the scroll bars is to use the keyboard equivalents listed in Table 2-1. If you're using a Mac that lacks the Page Up and Page Down keys — such as an older model PowerBook — try out the Control key equivalents in the third column. These may also come in handy when the Page Up and Page Down keys don't always behave properly, as on new PowerBook and iBook keyboards that require you to press a separate Fn key.

Table 2-1
Scrolling from the Keyboard

Scrolling Action	Keystroke	Alternate Keystroke (Mac only)
Up one screen	Page Up	Control-K
Up slightly	Shift+Page Up	Control-Shift-K
Down one screen	Page Down	Control-L
Down slightly	Shift+Page Down	Control-Shift-L
Left one screen	Ctrl+Page Up	⌘-Control-K (⌘-Page Up)
Left slightly	Ctrl+Shift+Page Up	⌘-Control-Shift-K (⌘-Shift-Page Up)
Right one screen	Ctrl+Page Down	⌘-Control-L (⌘-Page Down)
Right slightly	Ctrl+Shift+Page Down	⌘-Control-Shift-L (⌘-Shift-Page Down)
To upper-left corner	Home	Control-A
To lower-right corner	End	Control-D

I've heard tales of artists who use the Page Up and Page Down shortcuts to comb through very large images at 100-percent view size. This way, they can make sure all their pixels are in order before going to print.

Personally, however, I don't use the Page key tricks very often. I'm the kind of merry lad who prefers to scroll by hand. Armed with the grabber hand—as old timers call it—you can yank an image and pull it in any direction you choose. A good grabber hand is better than a scroll bar any day.

Tip

To access the hand tool temporarily when some other tool is selected, press and hold the spacebar. Releasing the spacebar returns the cursor to its original appearance. This keyboard equivalent even works from inside many dialog boxes.

The Navigator palette

I saved the best for last. Shown in Figure 2-15, the Navigator palette is the best thing to happen to zooming and scrolling since Photoshop was first introduced. If you routinely work on large images that extend beyond the confines of your relatively tiny screen, you'll want to get up and running with this palette as soon as possible.

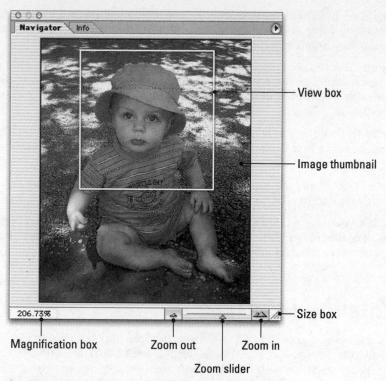

- View box
- Image thumbnail
- Size box
- Magnification box
- Zoom out
- Zoom in
- Zoom slider

206.73%

Figure 2-15: The Navigator palette is the best thing to happen to zooming and scrolling since Photoshop 1.0.

If the Navigator palette isn't visible, choose Window ➪ Navigator. You can then use the palette options as follows:

✦ **View box:** Drag the view box inside the image thumbnail to reveal some hidden portion of the photograph. Photoshop dynamically tracks your adjustments in the image window. Isn't it great?

But wait, it gets better. Press Ctrl (Win) or ⌘ (Mac) to get a zoom cursor in the Navigator palette. Then Ctrl-drag (Win) or ⌘-drag (Mac) to resize the view box and zoom the photo in the image window.

You can also Shift-drag to constrain dragging the view box to only horizontal or vertical movement.

✦ **Box color:** You can change the color of the view box by choosing the Palette Options command from the palette menu. My favorite setting is yellow, but it ultimately depends on the colors in your image. Ideally, you want something that stands out. To lift a color from the image itself, move the cursor outside the dialog box and click in the image window with the eyedropper.

✦ **Magnification box:** This value works like the one in the lower-left corner of the Photoshop window (or image window on the Mac). Just enter a new zoom ratio and press Enter or Return.

✦ **Zoom out:** Click the zoom out button to reduce the view size in the same pre-defined increments as the zoom tool. This button doesn't alter the size of the image window, regardless of any window resizing options you set for the other zoom controls.

✦ **Zoom slider:** Give the slider triangle a yank and see where it takes you. Drag to the left to zoom out; drag right to zoom in. Again, Photoshop dynamically tracks your changes in the image window. Dang, it's nice to zoom on-the-fly.

✦ **Zoom in:** Click the big mountains to incrementally magnify the view of the image without altering the window size.

✦ **Size box:** If you have a large monitor, you don't have to settle for that teeny thumbnail of the image. Drag the size box to enlarge both palette and thumbnail to a more reasonable size.

Customizing the Interface

Every program gives you access to a few core settings so you can modify the program to suit your personal needs. These settings are known far and wide as *preferences*. Photoshop ships with certain recommended preference settings already in force — known coast to coast as *factory defaults* — but just because these settings are recommended doesn't mean they're right. In fact, I disagree with quite a few of them. But why quibble when you can change the preferences according to your merest whim?

You can modify preference settings in two ways: You can make environmental adjustments in Windows and Mac OS 9 by using Edit ⇨ Preferences ⇨ General; in Mac OS X, that's Photoshop ⇨ Preferences ⇨ General. Or you can change the operation of specific tools by adjusting settings in the Options bar. Photoshop remembers environmental preferences, tool settings, and even the file format under which you saved the last image by storing this information to a file each time you exit the program.

To restore Photoshop's factory default settings, delete the Adobe Photoshop 7 Prefs.psp (or simply Prefs on the Mac) file when the application is *not* running. The next time you launch Photoshop, it creates a new preferences file automatically. On the PC, you can find the preferences file in the Application Data/Adobe/Photoshop/7.0/Adobe Photoshop 7.0 Settings folder. Under Windows 2000 and XP, the Application Data folder is located in the Documents and Settings/*User Name* folder. In earlier versions of Windows, the Application Data folder is found in the Windows folder. In Mac OS 9, the preferences file is located in the Preferences folder, which lives inside the System Folder. In Mac OS X, follow this path: Home folder ⇨ Library ⇨ Preferences ⇨ Adobe Photoshop 7.0 Settings. (Depending on your system setup, the program may choose a different storage folder.) You can also search for the preferences file by name using Sherlock on the Mac or Windows' built in search tool. Under Windows 2000 and XP, you must first turn on the visibility of hidden files. To do so, choose Tools ⇨ Folder Options, click the View tab, and turn on the Show hidden files and folders option.

Tip

You also can dump the preferences file using this trick: Close the program and then relaunch it. Immediately after you launch the program, press and hold Ctrl+Shift+Alt (⌘-Shift-Option on the Mac). Photoshop displays a dialog box asking for your okay to delete the preferences file. Click Yes.

Deleting the preferences file is also a good idea if Photoshop starts acting funny. Photoshop's preferences file has always been highly susceptible to corruption, possibly because the application writes to it so often. Whatever the reason, if Photoshop starts behaving erratically, trash that preferences file. You'll have to reset your preferences, but a smooth-running program is worth the few minutes of extra effort. It's a good thing that Photoshop saves actions, color settings, custom shapes, contours, and the like separately from the Prefs file. This means that you can delete your Prefs file without any worry about harming your scripts, color conversions, and other custom settings.

Tip

After you get your preferences set as you like them, you can prevent Photoshop from altering them further by locking the file. On the PC, right-click the Adobe Photoshop 7 Prefs.psp file in Windows Explorer and choose Properties from the pop-up menu. Then select the Read Only check box in the Properties dialog box and press Enter. On the Mac, go to the Finder desktop, track down the Adobe Photoshop 7 Prefs file, and choose File ⇨ Get Info in OS 9 or File ⇨ Show Info in OS X (⌘-I). Then select the Locked check box inside the Info dialog box. From now on, Photoshop will start up with a consistent set of default settings.

That's a good tip, and I include it in the name of comprehensive coverage. But personally, I don't lock my Prefs file because I periodically modify settings and I want Photoshop to remember the latest and greatest. Instead, I make a backup copy of my favorite settings. After a few weeks of working in the program and customizing it to a more or less acceptable level, copy the preferences file to a separate folder on your hard disk (someplace you'll remember!). Then if the preferences file becomes corrupt, you can replace it quickly with your backup.

The preference panels

In Windows and Mac OS 9, the Preferences command appears on the Edit menu. In Mac OS X, it's found on the Photoshop menu. Choosing the command displays a long submenu of commands, but you needn't ever use them if you remember a simple keyboard shortcut: Ctrl+K (⌘-K on the Mac).

This shortcut brings up the Preferences dialog box, which provides access to eight panels of options, representing every one of the Edit ⇨ Preferences commands. Select the desired panel from the pop-up menu in the upper-left corner of the dialog box, as demonstrated in Figure 2-16. Or press the Ctrl (Win) or ⌘ (Mac) key equivalent for the panel as listed in the pop-up menu. You can also click the Prev and Next buttons or press Alt+P and Alt+N, respectively (⌘-Option-P and ⌘-Option-N on the Mac) to cycle from one panel to the next.

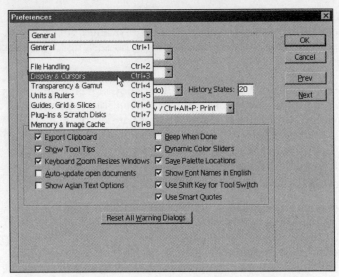

Figure 2-16: Select a panel of options from the pop-up menu, or click the Prev and Next buttons to advance from one panel to the next.

Tip   Photoshop always displays the first panel, General, when you press Ctrl+K (Win) or ⌘-K (Mac). If you prefer to go to the panel you were last using, press Ctrl+Alt+K (⌘-Option-K on the Mac).

To accept your settings and exit the Preferences dialog box, press Enter or Return. Or press Escape to cancel your settings. Okay, so you already knew that, but here's one you might not know: Press and hold Alt (Win) or Option (Mac) to change the Cancel button to Reset. Then click the button to restore the settings that were in force before you entered the dialog box.

The following sections examine the Preferences panels, in the order they appear in the Figure 2-16 pop-up menu. I explain how each option works, and include what I consider the optimal setting in parentheses. (The figures, however, show the default settings.) Out of context like this, Photoshop's preference settings can be a bit confusing. In later chapters, I try to shed some additional light on the settings you may find most useful.

General preferences

The General panel, shown in Figure 2-17, contains a miscellaneous supply of what are arguably the most important Preferences options.

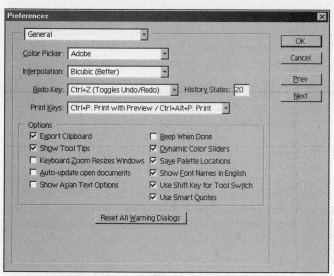

Figure 2-17: The General panel provides access to the most important environmental preference settings. I agree with many, but not all, of the default settings shown here.

✦ **Color Picker (Adobe):** When you click the foreground or background color control icon in the toolbox, Photoshop displays any color picker plug-ins that you may have installed plus one of two standard color pickers: the Adobe color picker or the one provided by the operating system. If you're familiar with other Windows graphics programs, the system's color picker may at first seem more familiar. But Photoshop's color picker is better suited to photographic work.

✦ **Interpolation (Bicubic):** When you resize an image using Image ⇨ Image Size or transform it using Edit ⇨ Free Transform or one of the commands in the Edit ⇨ Transform submenu, Photoshop has to make up — or *interpolate* — pixels to fill in the gaps. You can change how Photoshop calculates the interpolation by choosing one of three options from the Interpolation submenu.

If you select Nearest Neighbor, Photoshop simply copies the next-door pixel when creating a new one. This is the fastest setting (hence the label "Faster"), but it invariably results in jagged effects.

The second option, Bilinear, smoothes the transitions between pixels by creating intermediate shades. Photoshop averages the color of each pixel with four neighbors — the pixel above, the one below, and the two to the left and right. Bilinear takes more time but, typically, the softened effect is worth it.

Still more time intensive is the default setting, Bicubic, which averages the color of a pixel with its eight closest neighbors — one up, one down, two on the sides, and four in the corners. The Bicubic setting boosts the amount of contrast between pixels to offset the blurring effect that generally accompanies interpolation.

Tip

The moral is this: Select Bicubic to turn Photoshop's interpolation capabilities on and select Nearest Neighbor to turn them off. The Bilinear setting is a poor compromise between the two — too slow for roughing out effects, but too remedial to waste your time.

✦ **Redo Key (Ctrl+Z or Cmd-Z):** This option enables you to change the keyboard shortcuts assigned to the Undo, Redo, Step Back, and Step Forward commands. It's ultimately a personal preference, but I discourage you from changing this option from its default. Selecting something other than Ctrl+Z (Win) or Cmd-Z (Mac) makes Photoshop appear to match other programs that feature multiple undos — such as Adobe Illustrator and Macromedia FreeHand — but any resemblance is purely coincidental. The wonders of the History palette notwithstanding, Photoshop relies on a single-level Undo command. Setting it to match other programs' multilevel undos is misleading. If you haven't the vaguest idea of what I'm talking about, check out Chapter 7, "Retouching and Restoring."

✦ **History States (Your call):** This value controls how many steps you can undo via the History palette. The right value depends on the amount of RAM you're willing to devote to Photoshop. If you're working with limited memory, I suggest that you lower the value to 5 or 10. Otherwise, raise the value as you see fit, remembering that the more states the program retains, the more you strain your system.

Photoshop

7

✦ **Print Keys (Ctrl+P: Print with Preview / Ctrl+Alt+P: Print or Cmd-P: Print with Preview / Cmd-Opt-P: Print):** Even though it's a change to a long-standing keyboard shortcut, I think the Print with Preview dialog box is very helpful and don't mind seeing it when I press Ctrl+P or ⌘-P. You traditionalists can change this setting so that Ctrl+P or ⌘-P brings up the plain old Print dialog box as before.

✦ **Export Clipboard (off):** When selected, this option tells Photoshop to transfer a copied image from the program's internal clipboard to the operating system's clipboard whenever you switch applications. This enables you to paste the image into another running program. Turn this option off if you plan to use copied images only within Photoshop and you want to reduce the lag time that occurs when you switch from Photoshop to another program. Even with this option off, you can paste images copied from other programs into Photoshop.

✦ **Show Tool Tips (on):** When on, this option displays little labels and keyboard shortcuts when you hover your cursor over a tool or palette option. The tool tips don't impede Photoshop's performance, so I see no reason to turn off this option.

✦ **Keyboard Zoom Resizes Windows (on):** Select this option to force Photoshop to resize the image window when you zoom in or out on your image by choosing a Zoom command from the View menu or by using the keyboard shortcuts, Ctrl+plus (⌘-plus on the Mac) and Ctrl+minus (⌘-minus on the Mac). This one's really a matter of personal choice — I leave the option on (as it is by default on the Mac), but you'll do no harm to yourself or the planet if you turn it off. Either way, you can temporarily choose the opposite setting by pressing Alt (Win) or Option (Mac) as you choose the Zoom command.

✦ **Auto-update Open Documents (on):** This option creates and maintains a link between an open image and the image file on disk. Any time the image on disk updates, Photoshop updates the image on screen in kind. This feature is an amazing help when you're editing images with another artist over a network. Imagine that you and a coworker each have the same server file open in separate copies of Photoshop. Your coworker makes a change and saves it. Seconds later, your copy of Photoshop automatically updates the image on your screen. Then you make a change and save it, and Photoshop relays your modifications to your coworker's screen.

So what happens if you're both editing the image simultaneously? Whoever saves first gets the glory. If your coworker saves the image before you do, any changes that you haven't saved are overwritten by the other person's work.

Tip

However, you can snatch victory from the jaws of defeat simply by pressing Ctrl+Alt+Z (⌘-Option-Z on the Mac), which undoes your coworker's edits and retrieves yours. Quickly save your image to lob your changes over the net. Ooh, psych! With any luck, your coworker won't understand Photoshop well enough to know that your changes can be undone just as easily. But just to be safe, better hide this book from prying eyes.

✦ **Show Asian Text Options (off):** This option determines whether the Character and Paragraph palettes include options related to working with Chinese, Japanese, and Korean type. My recommendation here assumes that you're not adding text in those languages to your images.

✦ **Use System Shortcut Keys (Your call):** This Mac OS X-only option typically comes into play when trying to hide active selection edges. The longstanding keyboard shortcut for this has been ⌘-H. (More recently this command has also hidden other "Extras," such as the grid, slices, and annotations.) However, Mac OS X has appropriated ⌘-H as a system-wide keyboard shortcut for hiding the active application, whatever it might happen to be. In Photoshop, the Use System Shortcut Keys option is deselected by default, which allows Photoshop to steal ⌘-H for its traditional use, and assigns ⌘-Control-H for hiding Photoshop. Checking the option reverses this, making Photoshop keep its hands off OS X's reserved keyboard shortcuts. The downside to this is that you'll have to relearn ⌘-Control-H as the new shortcut for hiding the Extras. It's entirely your call; note, however, that for the duration of this book, I'm going to assume that you've kept this check box turned off, as is the default.

✦ **Beep When Done (off):** You can instruct Photoshop to beep at you whenever it finishes an operation that displays a Progress window. This option may be useful if you doze off during particularly time-consuming operations. But I'm a firm believer that computers should be seen and not heard.

✦ **Dynamic Color Sliders (on):** When selected, this option instructs Photoshop to preview color effects within the slider bars of the Color palette. When the option is turned off, the slider bars show the same colors regardless of your changes. Unless you're working on a slow computer, leave this option on. On a fast machine, Photoshop takes a billionth of a second longer to calculate the color effects and it's well worth it.

✦ **Save Palette Locations (on):** When this option is selected, Photoshop remembers the location of the toolbox and floating palettes from one session to the next. If you turn off this check box, Photoshop restores the default palette positions the next time you restart the program.

✦ **Show Font Names in English (on):** Check this box, and Photoshop displays foreign fonts in intelligible names in the Font menu in the Options bar and in the Character palette — well, assuming that English is intelligible to you, anyway.

✦ **Use Shift Key for Tool Switch (off):** When two or more tools share the same slot in the toolbox, you can press the keyboard shortcut associated with the tools to cycle through the tools. This Preferences option determines whether you must press Shift along with the shortcut. I recommend that you turn this option off — one extra keystroke per function adds up over the course of a day, you know.

In this book, I assume that you have this option turned off when I present tool shortcuts.

✦ **Use Smart Quotes (on):** Sometimes known as "curly quotes," smart quotes are simply more attractive, curved versions of quotation marks and apostrophes. If you're using fonts that include smart quotes, by all means turn this option on.

✦ **Reset All Warning Dialogs:** Every now and then, Photoshop displays a warning dialog box to let you know that the course you're on may have consequences you hadn't considered. Some dialog boxes include a check box that you can select to tell Photoshop that you don't want to see the current warning any more. If you click the Reset All Warning Dialogs button in the Preferences dialog box, Photoshop clears all the "don't show this warning again" check boxes so that you once again get all available warnings. Photoshop responds to your click of the reset button by displaying a warning dialog box that says that all warning dialog boxes will be enabled if you go forward. Don't ponder the irony too long before you click OK.

File Handling

When in the Preferences dialog box, press Ctrl+2 (Win) or ⌘-2 (Mac) to advance to the File Handling panel. Figures 2-18 and 2-19 show the panel as it appears on the PC and Mac, respectively. Every one of these options affects how Photoshop saves images to disk. The following list explains how the options work and the recommended settings:

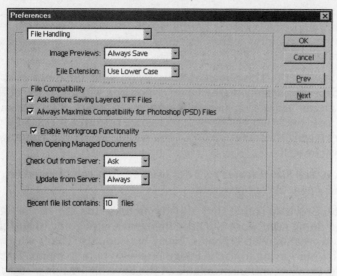

Figure 2-18: The File Handling panel as it appears on the PC.

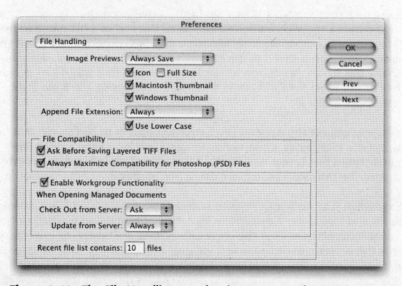

Figure 2-19: The File Handling panel as it appears on the Mac.

✦ **Image Previews (Ask When Saving):** When Always Save is active (as by default), Photoshop saves a postage-stamp preview so that you can see what an image looks like before opening or importing it. On the Mac, you can select as many as four kinds of image previews:

The Icon option creates a preview icon that you can view from the Finder desktop. In my opinion, this option is hardly worth the extra disk space it takes up, and too many custom icons can cause problems with older versions of the system software.

When you select one of the Thumbnail options, Photoshop creates a postage-stamp preview that displays inside the Open dialog box when you select a file. The Macintosh Thumbnail option saves the preview in a part of the file known as the resource fork, but Windows doesn't recognize resource forks. So if you ever plan on previewing the image on a PC, you should select the Windows Thumbnail option as well.

The fourth option, Full Size, creates a 72-dpi preview that can be used for placement inside a page-layout program.

The problem with previews is that they slightly increase the size of the file. This is fine when doing print work — a little thumbnail isn't going to add that much — but when creating Web graphics, every byte counts. That's why I prefer to select Ask When Saving from the Image Previews pop-up menu. This option makes the preview options available in the Save dialog box so that you can specify whether you want previews on a case-by-case basis when you save your images.

✦ **Append File Extension (Ask When Saving):** Available on the Mac only, this option appends a three-character extension to the end of a file name to make your Mac images compatible with Windows and DOS programs. For example, a layered composition saved in the Photoshop format gets a *.psd* extension. I personally like to set this option to Ask When Saving; that way, I can decide whether or not to include a PC-style extension from inside the Save dialog box on a file-by-file basis.

Actually, you can set the Append File Extension option to Never and still be able to access extensions when saving images. Just press the Option key when selecting a file format and Photoshop automatically slaps on an extension. I describe this process in more detail in Chapter 3.

✦ **File Extension (Use Lower Case)/Use Lower Case (on):** Called File Extension on the PC and Use Lower Case on the Mac, this option decides whether the three-character extensions at the end of file names are upper- or lowercase. Lower is the better choice because it ensures compatibility with other platforms, particularly UNIX, the primary operating system for Web servers. (UNIX is case-sensitive, so a file called *Image.psd* is different than *Image.PSD*. Lowercase extensions eliminate confusion.)

✦ **Ask Before Saving Layered TIFF Files (on):** If you add a layer to a TIFF file that formerly consisted of only a background layer and then try to save the file, having this option selected will bring up the TIFF Options dialog box. This dialog box lets you choose between JPEG, ZIP, and the traditional LZW compression for TIFFs, as well as other options discussed in Chapter 3. These are useful options, so I say leave this turned on.

✦ **Always Maximize Compatibility for Photoshop (PSD) Files (OFF!):** This option is pure evil. If you never change another preference setting, you should turn this one off. I know, I know, if it was so awful, Adobe wouldn't have it on by default. But believe me, this option should be named Double My File Sizes Because I'm an Absolute Fool, and even Adobe's designers will tell you that you probably want to go ahead and turn it off.

Okay, so here's the long tragic story: The check box ensures backward compatibility between Photoshop 7 and programs that support the Photoshop file format but don't recognize layers. It's a nice idea, but it comes at too steep a price. In order to ensure compatibility, Photoshop has to insert an additional flattened version of a layered image into every native Photoshop file. As you can imagine, this takes up a considerable amount of disk space, doubling the file size in the most extreme situations.

So turn this check box off. And when you want cross-application compatibility, save an extra TIFF version of your file (as explained in Chapter 3).

Actually, there is one instance when you might find this option useful. It permits older versions of After Effects or Illustrator to open files that contain layer effects that were added to Photoshop after those products shipped.

✦ **Enable Workgroup Functionality (Ask):** This grouping of preferences deals with the WebDAV technology, which is a means for multiple users to work on documents together over a network. While not currently a widely-implemented system, WebDAV (or just "DAV," as it's sometimes called) is expected to become a standard means of collaboration in the near future. And I'm not just talking about interoffice networks here; you might be able to work on a Photoshop image from the United States in collaboration with someone in Tokyo.

Both preferences here, Check Out from Server and Update from Server, give you three options: Never, Always, and Ask. If you're new to working over WebDAV (and you probably are), it can't hurt for Photoshop to give you a gentle reminder about what you're doing. So for the time being, set this to Ask.

✦ **Recent file list contains (10) Files (Your call):** This option determines how many file names appear when you choose the new Open Recent command, which displays a list of the images that you worked on most recently. You can simply click an image name to open the image. The default number of file names is ten, but you can raise it to 30. Raising the value doesn't use resources that would otherwise be useful to Photoshop, so enter whatever value makes you happy.

Display & Cursors

Press Ctrl+3 (⌘-3 on the Mac) to sidle up to the Display & Cursors options, which appear in Figure 2-20. These options affect the way colors and cursors appear on screen. Here's how the options work, along with recommended settings:

✦ **Color Channels in Color (off):** An individual color channel contains just 8 bits of data per pixel, which makes it equivalent to a grayscale image. Photoshop provides you with the option of colorizing the channel according to the primary color it represents. For example, when this option is turned on, the red color channel looks like a grayscale image viewed through red acetate. Most experts agree the effect isn't helpful, though, and it does more to obscure your image than make it easier for you to see what's happening. Leave this check box turned off and read Chapter 16 for more information.

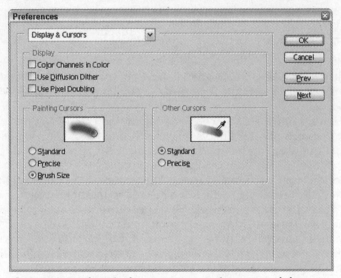

Figure 2-20: The Display & Cursors options control the way images and cursors look on screen. Shown here are the default settings, but I turn on Use Diffusion Dither.

✦ **Use Diffusion Dither (on):** Here's an option for you folks still working on 8-bit screens that display no more than 256 colors at a time. To simulate the 16-million-color spectrum on a 256-color screen, Photoshop automatically jumbles colored pixels using a technique called *dithering*. This option controls the pattern of dithered pixels. Photoshop offers a naturalistic "diffusion" dither that looks nice on screen. But because the diffusion dither follows no specific pattern, you sometimes see distinct edges between selected and deselected portions of your image after applying a filter or some other effect. You can eliminate these edges and resort to a more geometric dither pattern by turning off this check box.

Tip

Turning off the Use Diffusion Dither check box is an awfully drastic (not to mention ugly) solution, though. The better way to eliminate the occasional visual disharmony is to force Photoshop to redraw the entire image. You can press Ctrl+Alt+0 (⌘-Option-0 on the Mac) or perform some other zoom function.

✦ **Use Pixel Doubling (off):** This option can help speed up operations when you're editing huge images on a less-than-robust computer, but not by much. When you select the option, Photoshop displays selected areas using a low-resolution proxy. This option goes into effect both with selections and while moving layers.

✦ **Painting Cursors (Brush Size):** When you use a paint or edit tool, Photoshop can display one of three cursors. The Standard cursor looks like a paintbrush, airbrush, finger, or whatever tool you are using. These cursors are great if you have problems keeping track of what tool you selected, but otherwise they border on childish.

The Precise and Brush Size options are more functional. The Precise option displays a cross-shaped cursor — called a crosshair — regardless of which tool is active. The crosshair is great because it prevents the cursor from blocking your view as you edit. Meanwhile, the Brush Size option shows the actual size and shape of the active brush in the Brushes palette. The Brush Size option is the default setting in Photoshop 7, and that's a good thing. Most artists prefer this final setting to the others because it comes the closest to showing the cursor the way it really is.

When Standard or Brush Size is selected, you can access the crosshair cursor by pressing the Caps Lock key. When Precise is selected from the Painting Cursors options, pressing Caps Lock displays the brush size.

✦ **Other Cursors (Standard):** Again, you can select Standard to get the regular cursors or Precise to get crosshairs. I prefer to leave this option set to Standard because you can easily access the crosshair cursor by pressing Caps Lock. The Precise option locks you into the crosshair whether or not you like it.

Transparency & Gamut

Press Ctrl+4 (⌘-4 on the Mac) to switch to the Transparency & Gamut panel shown in Figure 2-21. The options in this panel change how Photoshop displays two conceptual items — transparent space behind layers and RGB colors that can't be expressed in CMYK printing.

The options are arranged into two groups — Transparency Settings and Gamut Warning — as explained in the following sections.

Transparency Settings

Just as the Earth spins around in empty space, a Photoshop image rests on a layer of absolute transparency. By default, Photoshop represents this transparency as a gray checkerboard pattern. (What better way to demonstrate nothingness? I might have preferred a few lines from a Jean-Paul Sartre play, but no matter.) You may get a brief glimpse of this checkerboard when you first open an image or switch to Photoshop from another application.

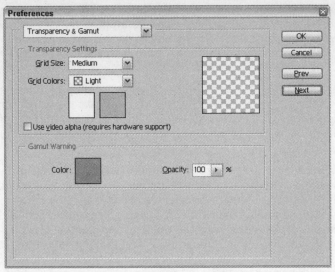

Figure 2-21: The options in this panel affect how Photoshop represents transparency and out-of-gamut colors. For the most part, you just want to select colors that you don't often see inside your images.

When you view a layer independently of others, Photoshop fills the see-through portions of the layer with the checkerboard. So having the checkerboard stand out from the layer itself is essential. You can customize the size of the checkers and the color of the squares using the Grid Size and Grid Colors pop-up menus. You can also click the color swatches to define your own colors.

To lift colors from the image window, move your cursor outside the Preferences dialog box to get the eyedropper. Click a color to change the color of the white checkers; Alt-click (Win) or Option-click (Mac) to change the gray ones.

If you own a TrueVision NuVista+ board or some other 32-bit device that enables chroma keying, you can select the Use Video Alpha check box to view a television signal in the transparent area behind a layer. Unless you work in video production, you needn't worry about this option.

Gamut Warning

If Photoshop can display a color on screen but can't accurately print the color, the color is said to be *out of gamut*. You can choose View ⇨ Gamut Warning to coat all out-of-gamut colors with gray. I'm not a big fan of this command — View ⇨ Proof Colors (Ctrl+Y or ⌘-Y) is much more useful — but if you use View ⇨ Gamut Warning, you don't have to accept gray as the out-of-gamut coating. Change the color by clicking the Gamut Warning Color swatch and lower the Opacity value to request a translucent coating.

Units & Rulers

The Units & Rulers panel is the fifth panel in the Preferences dialog box; hence, you reach the panel by pressing Ctrl+5 (⌘-5 on the Mac). Shown in Figure 2-22, this panel offers options that enable you to change the predominant system of measurement used throughout the program.

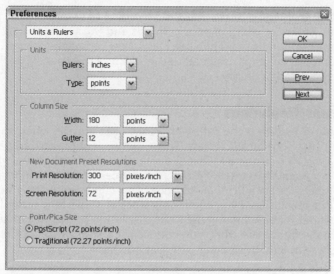

Figure 2-22: Go to the Units & Rulers panel to change the column and pica settings and set the unit of measurement. I prefer to use Pixels as opposed to Inches.

Tip

Whenever the rulers are visible, the Units & Rulers panel is only a double-click away. Choose View ⇨ Rulers (Ctrl+R or ⌘-R) to see the rulers on screen and then double-click either the horizontal or vertical ruler.

Rulers

You can set the unit of measurement via the Units option in the Preferences dialog box. But there's an easier way: Just right-click (Control-click on the Mac) anywhere on the ruler to display a pop-up menu of unit options and then click the unit you want to use. You can display the same pop-up menu by clicking the plus sign in the lower-left corner of the Info palette.

When you're first learning Photoshop, going with inches or picas is tempting, but experienced Photoshop artists use pixels. Because you can change the resolution of an image at any time, the only constant is pixels. An image measures a fixed number of pixels high by a fixed number of pixels wide — you can print those pixels as large or as small as you want. (To learn more about resolution, read Chapter 3.)

Type

Photoshop enables you to set the unit of measure used for the type tool independently of the ruler units. You can work in points, pixels, and millimeters; select your unit of choice from the Type pop-up menu. Check out Chapter 15 for more news about type in Photoshop.

Column Size

The Column Size options enable you to size images according to columns in a newsletter or magazine. Enter the width of your columns and the size of the gutter into the Width and Gutter option boxes. Then use File ⇨ New or Image ⇨ Image Size to specify the number of columns assigned to the width of the image. I explain these commands in more detail in Chapter 3.

New Document Preset Resolutions

One nifty new Photoshop 7 feature is the listing of preset sizes you get when you create a new document by choosing File ⇨ New. These convenient presets come in common sizes for creating Web banners (468×60) and for working with digital video (720×540). The New Document Preset Resolutions preferences let you set a default resolution for these presets for both Print and Screen. This can be especially helpful to set a different Print resolution if you commonly work at something other than the default of 300 pixels per inch. Adjusting the Print resolution preference changes the number of pixels in the document when you choose the Letter preset, for example. For general purposes though, the defaults are just fine here.

Point/Pica Size

The last option in the Units & Rulers panel may be the most obscure of all Photoshop options. In case you aren't familiar with points and picas, exactly 12 points are in a pica, and about 6.06 picas are in an inch.

Well, because picas are almost evenly divisible into inches, the folks who came up with the PostScript printing language decided to bag the difference and to define a pica as exactly $\frac{1}{6}$ inch. This makes a point exactly $\frac{1}{72}$ inch.

But a few purists didn't take to it. They found their new electronic documents weren't quite matching their old paste-up documents and, well, I guess life pretty much lost its meaning. So Adobe had to go back and add the Traditional (72.27 points/inch) option to keep everyone happy.

I prefer the nontraditional PostScript definition of points. This way, a pixel on screen translates to a point on paper when you print an image at 72 ppi (the standard screen resolution). Call me a soulless technodweeb, but computer imaging makes more sense when you can measure points and pixels without resorting to a calculator. The old ways are dead; long live the $\frac{1}{72}$-inch point!

Guides, Grid & Slices

Someone at Adobe said, "Let the preference settings continue." And, lo, there is Guides, Grid & Slices, which can be accessed by all who press Ctrl+6 (⌘-6 on the Mac) and viewed by all who cast an eye on Figure 2-23. This panel lets you modify the colors of the guides and specify the size of the grid.

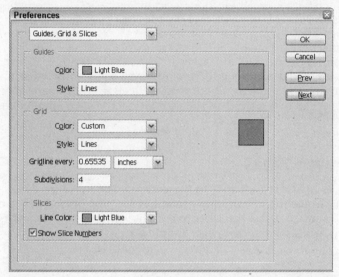

Figure 2-23: Use these options to adjust the size of the grid and change the way the grid, ruler guides, and slices appear on screen.

Tip

You can display the Preferences dialog box and go directly to the Guides, Grid & Slices panel by double-clicking a guide with the move tool or Ctrl-double-clicking (⌘-double-clicking on the Mac) with another tool. (To create a guide, drag from the horizontal or vertical ruler into the image.)

I explain these options in more detail in Chapter 12 but, for the moment, here are some brief descriptions.

Guides

Select a color for horizontal and vertical ruler guides from the Color pop-up menu. To lift a color from the image, move your cursor outside the Preferences dialog box and click in the image window with the eyedropper. You can also view guides as solid lines or dashes by selecting an option from the Style pop-up menu.

Grid

Choose a color for the grid from the Color menu, or Alt-click (Option-click on the Mac) in the image window to lift a color from the image. Then decide how the grid lines look by selecting a Style option. The Dots setting is the least intrusive.

The Gridline Every value determines the increments for the visible grid marks on screen. But the Subdivisions value sets the real grid. For example, if you request a grid mark every one inch with four subdivisions — as in Figure 2-23 — Photoshop snaps selections and layers in quarter-inch increments (one inch divided by four).

Slices

Like setting the color for guides and the grid, this preference lets you choose a color for the lines that illustrate exactly where you've sliced up your image for posting on the Web. You can turn on and off the visibility of the slice numbers here as well.

Plug-Ins & Scratch Disks

Press Ctrl+7 (Win) or ⌘-7 (Mac) to advance to the panel shown in Figure 2-24. Each time you launch Photoshop, the program searches for plug-in modules and identifies one or more scratch disks. You have to tell Photoshop where to find the plug-ins and where the temporary scratch files should go.

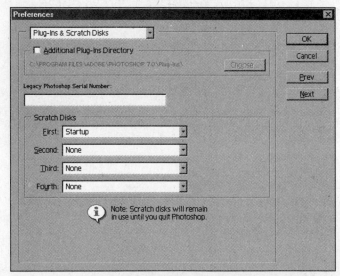

Figure 2-24: Tell Photoshop where to find plug-ins and where to put scratch files using these options.

Additional Plug-Ins Folder

By default, the plug-ins are located in a folder called Plug-Ins, which resides in the same folder as the Photoshop application. But you can tell Photoshop to also look for plug-ins in some other folder — a handy option if you install all your third-party plug-ins to some central location outside the Photoshop folders. To specify the second plug-ins location, select the check box and then click Choose to select the folder.

Legacy Photoshop Serial Number

As you might have noticed when you installed it, Photoshop 7 signals a new era in Adobe serial numbers. No longer are they a mixture of numbers and letters; it's all just numbers and dashes now. Some third-party plug-ins, however, serialize themselves to the old-style Photoshop serial number format. So if you're upgrading to Photoshop 7 and you've got an old serial number from Photoshop 6 or earlier, you can enter it here.

Scratch Disks

By default, Photoshop assumes you have only one hard disk, so Photoshop stores its temporary virtual memory documents — called *scratch files* — on the same disk that contains your system software. If you have more than one drive available, though, you might want to tell Photoshop to look elsewhere. In fact, Photoshop can use up to four drives.

For example, one of my Windows computers is equipped with two internal hard drives:

✦ A 60GB drive, C:, contains the system and most of the workaday documents I create.

✦ The other drive is a 40GB device partitioned into two 20GB segments. These are formatted as the D: and E: drives. D: contains all my applications while E: remains largely empty except for a few large miscellaneous files — QuickTime movies, digital camera snapshots, weird plug-ins — that I haven't gotten around to backing up yet.

E: has the most free space, so I set it as the First scratch disk. On the off chance that my images get so huge that Photoshop fills up E: and has to look elsewhere for scratch space, I select D: from the Second pop-up menu and my main system drive, C:, from the Third. That's the end of my drives, so Fourth remains set to None.

Adobe advises against using removable media — such as SyQuest, MO, and Zip drives — as a scratch disk. Removable media is typically less reliable and slower than a permanent drive. (A Jaz cartridge is more stable than Zip or the others, but still not as reliable as a fixed hard drive.) Using a removable drive on an occasional basis isn't the end of the world, but if you use it regularly you may end up crashing more often, in which case you'll probably want to add a new hard drive.

Changes affect the next session

As the note at the bottom of the Plug-ins & Scratch Disks panel warns, the settings in this panel don't take effect until the next time you launch Photoshop. This means you must quit Photoshop and restart the program.

There's nothing more frustrating than knowing that the options in this dialog box are set incorrectly before you've even started up Photoshop. It means you have to launch Photoshop, change the settings, quit Photoshop, and launch the program again. What a waste of time!

That is, it *would* be a waste of time if there wasn't a workaround. Fortunately, you can access the plug-ins and scratch disk settings during the launch cycle. After double-clicking on the Photoshop application icon or choosing Photoshop from the Windows Start menu, press and hold the Ctrl and Alt keys (⌘ and Option keys on the Mac). If you're using a Mac, Photoshop greets you with a message requesting that you locate the Plug-Ins folder. After you do so, press and hold the ⌘ and Option keys again. After a few seconds, a screen of the scratch disk options appears. Specify the disks as desired and press Enter or Return. Your new settings now work for the current session — no restarting necessary.

Memory & Image Cache

Photoshop sports a caching scheme that speeds operations at reduced view sizes. You can adjust this feature by pressing Ctrl+8 (Win) or ⌘-8 (Mac) in the Preferences dialog box to display the Memory & Image Cache panel shown in Figure 2-25.

This preference panel is called simply Image Cache in Macintosh OS 9, because that operating system doesn't feature dynamic memory allocation like Windows and Mac OS X do.

Cache Levels

Photoshop has been criticized for its lack of a "pyramid-style" file format capable of storing an image several times over at progressively smaller and smaller image sizes, called *downsamplings*. Photoshop's alternative is image caching. Rather than saving the downsamplings to disk, Photoshop generates the reduced images in RAM. By default, the Cache Levels value is set to 4, the medium value. This means Photoshop can cache up to four downsamplings — at 100, 50, 25, and 12.5 percent — which permits the program to apply operations more quickly at reduced view sizes. For example, if you choose a color correction command at the 50 percent view size, it previews much faster than normal because Photoshop has to modify a quarter as many pixels on screen.

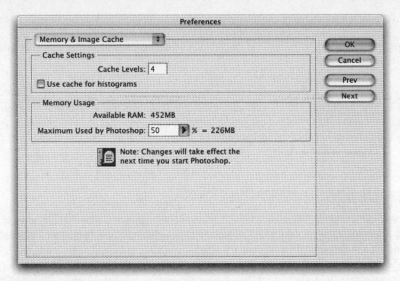

Figure 2-25: Photoshop's caching capabilities speed the processing of very large images. This is also where you specify how much memory goes to Photoshop.

However, Photoshop must cache downsamplings in RAM, which takes away memory that could be used to hold the image. If you have lots of RAM (say, 256MB or more) and you frequently work on large images (20MB or larger), you'll probably want to raise the value to the maximum, 8. The lost memory is worth the speed boost. If you have little RAM (say, 192MB or less) and you usually work on small images or Web graphics (4MB or smaller), you may want to reduce the Cache Levels value to 1 or 2. When files are small, RAM is better allocated to storing images rather than caching them.

Use cache for histograms

The Use Cache for Histograms check box tells Photoshop whether to generate the histograms that appear in the Levels and Threshold dialog boxes based on the cached sampling or the original image. As I explain in Chapter 17, a *histogram* is a bar graph of the colors in an image. When you choose a command such as Image ⇨ Adjustments ⇨ Levels, Photoshop must spend a few seconds graphing the colors. If you turn the Use Cache for Histograms check box on, Photoshop graphs the colors in the reduced screen view, which takes less time, but is also less accurate. Turn the check box off for slower, more accurate histograms.

Generally speaking, I say turn the option on. A histogram is merely a visual indicator and most folks are unable to judge the difference between a downsampled histogram and a fully accurate one.

Again, if you're working in very large images and you have the Cache Levels value maxed out at 8, you should probably leave this check box selected. But if you have to reduce the Cache Levels value, turn off the check box. Histograms are the first thing that can go.

Note This option is *not* responsible for the histogram irregularities that popped up in Photoshop 4. The fact that the Threshold dialog box sometimes lifted its histogram from the active layer only was a bug, not a function of Use Cache for Histograms. Even so, this option has received a lot of flack it did not deserve. My opinion is that, on balance, this is a positive feature that should be left on.

Memory Usage

Mac OS X, Windows 95, NT 4, and later offer dynamic memory allocation, which means that each application gets the memory it needs as it needs it. But Photoshop is something of a memory pig and has a habit of using every spare bit of RAM it can get its hands on. Left to its own devices, it might gobble up all the RAM and bleed over into the operating system's virtual memory space, which is less efficient than Photoshop's own scratch disk scheme.

The Memory Usage option helps you place some limits on Photoshop's ravenous appetites. The option lists the amount of RAM available to all applications after the operating system loads into memory. You can then decide how much of that memory should go to Photoshop. If you like to run lots of applications at the same time — your word processor, Web browser, spreadsheet, drawing program, and Photoshop, for example — then set the Maximum Used by Photoshop value to 50 percent or lower. But if Photoshop is the only program running — and if you have less than 192MB of RAM — raise the value to 70 to 80 percent.

Caution I recommend against taking the Maximum Used by Photoshop value any higher than 80 percent, particularly on a low-capacity machine (192MB or less). Doing so permits Photoshop to fill up RAM that the operating system might need, which makes for a less stable working environment. As I've said before, if Photoshop is going too slow for you and hitting scratch disk too often, buy more RAM — don't play dangerous games with the little RAM you do have.

✦   ✦   ✦

Image Management

How Images Work

Think of a bitmapped image as a mosaic made from square
tiles of various colors. When you view the mosaic up close, it
looks like something you might use to decorate your bath-
room. You see the individual tiles, not the image itself. But if
you back up a few feet, the tiles lose their definition and
merge to create a recognizable work of art, presumably
Medusa getting her head whacked off or some equally
appetizing thematic classic.

The colored pixels that make up an *image* work much like the
tiles in a mosaic. If you enlarge the pixels, they look like an
unrelated collection of colored squares. Reduce the size of the
pixels, and they blend together to form an image that looks to
all the world like a standard photograph. Photoshop deceives
the eye by borrowing from an artistic technique older than
Mycenae or Pompeii.

Of course, there are differences between pixels and ancient
mosaic tiles. Pixels come in 16 million distinct colors. Mosaic
tiles of antiquity came in your basic granite and sandstone
varieties, with an occasional chunk of lapis lazuli thrown in
for good measure. Also, you can resample, color separate,
and crop electronic images. We know from the timeworn
scribblings of Dionysius of Halicarnassus that these
processes were beyond the means of classical artisans.

But I'm getting ahead of myself. I won't be discussing resampling, cropping, or Halicarnassus for several pages. First, I
address the inverse relationship between image size and
resolution.

Size versus resolution

If you haven't already guessed, the term *image size* describes the physical dimensions of an image. *Resolution* is the number of pixels per linear inch in the final printed image. I say linear because you measure pixels in a straight line. If the resolution of an image is 72 *ppi* — that is, pixels per inch — you get 5,184 pixels per square inch (72 pixels wide × 72 pixels tall = 5,184).

Assuming the number of pixels in an image is fixed, increasing the size of an image decreases its resolution and vice versa. An image that looks good when printed on a postage stamp, therefore, probably looks jagged when printed as an 11×17-inch poster.

Figure 3-1 shows a single image printed at three different sizes and resolutions. The smallest image is printed at twice the resolution of the medium-sized image; the medium-sized image is printed at twice the resolution of the largest image.

One inch in the smallest image includes twice as many pixels vertically and twice as many pixels horizontally as an inch in the medium-sized image, for a total of four times as many pixels per square inch. Therefore, the smallest image covers one-fourth the area of the medium-sized image.

The same relationships exist between the medium-sized image and the largest image. An inch in the medium-sized image comprises four times as many pixels as an inch in the largest image. Consequently, the medium-sized image consumes one-fourth the area of the largest image.

Changing the printing resolution

When printing an image, a higher resolution translates to a sharper image with greater clarity. Photoshop lets you change the resolution of a printed image in one of two ways:

✦ Choose Image ➪ Image Size to access the controls that enable you to change the pixel dimensions and resolution of an image. Then enter a value into the Resolution option box, either in pixels per inch or pixels per centimeter.

A good idea (although not essential) is to turn off the Resample Image check box, as demonstrated in Figure 3-2. If you leave it on, Photoshop may add or subtract pixels, as discussed in the "Resampling and Cropping" section later in this chapter. (Of course, if you're shrinking down an image for posting on the Web, resampling the image will be necessary.) By turning it off, you instruct Photoshop to leave the pixels intact but merely change how many of them print per inch.

Figure 3-1: These three images contain the same number of pixels, but are printed at different resolutions. Doubling the resolution of an image reduces it to 25 percent of its original size.

✦ Alternatively, you can ask Photoshop to scale an image during the print cycle. You hand down this edict with the new Print with Preview command. Choose File ➪ Print with Preview or (assuming the default preference settings) press Ctrl+P (⌘-P on the Mac) to open the dialog box. You can enter specific Width and Height values or enter a percentage value into the Scale option box. Lower values reduce the size of the printed image and thereby increase the resolution; higher values lower the resolution. (Chapter 18 contains more information about scaling images as well as the other settings in the Print with Preview dialog box.)

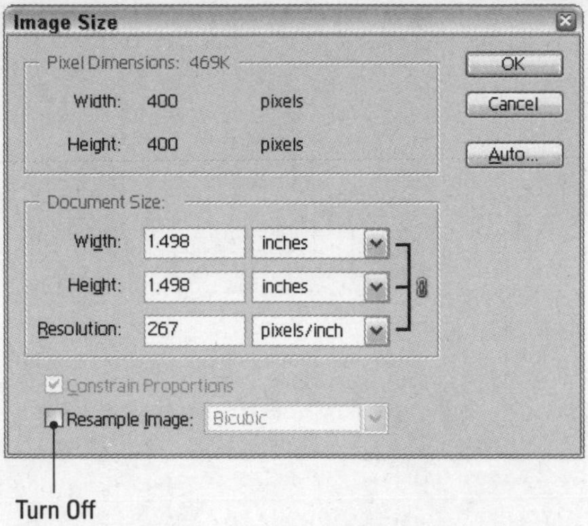

Image Size

Pixel Dimensions: 469K

Width: 400   pixels

Height: 400   pixels

Document Size:

Width: 1.498   inches

Height: 1.498   inches

Resolution: 267   pixels/inch

☑ Constrain Proportions

☐ Resample Image: Bicubic

OK

Cancel

Auto...

Turn Off

Figure 3-2: Turn off the Resample Image check box to maintain a constant number of pixels in an image and to change only the printed resolution.

Photoshop saves the Resolution setting with the image; the scale settings in the Print with Preview box affect the current print job only. Together, the two determine the printed resolution. Photoshop divides the Resolution value in the Image Size dialog box by the Scale percentage from the Print with Preview dialog box. For example, if the image resolution is set to 72 ppi and you reduce the image to 48 percent, the final printed image has a resolution of 150 ppi (72 divided by 0.48).

Note

At the risk of boring some of you, I briefly remind the math haters in the audience that whenever you use a percentage in an equation, you first convert it to a decimal. For example, 100 percent is 1.0, 64 percent is 0.64, and 5 percent is 0.05.

Tip

To avoid confusion, most folks rely exclusively on the Resolution value and leave the Print with Preview dialog box Scale value set to 100 percent. The only exception is when printing tests and proofs. Because inkjet and other consumer printers offer lower-resolution output than high-end commercial devices, you may find it helpful to proof images larger so that you can see more pixels. Raising the Scale value lets you accomplish this without upsetting the Resolution value. Just be sure to restore the value to 100 percent after you make your test print.

Changing the page-layout resolution

The Scale value in the Print with Preview dialog box value has no effect on the size and resolution of an image imported into an object-oriented application, such as QuarkXPress or Illustrator. But these same applications do observe the Resolution setting from the Image Size dialog box.

Specifying the resolution in Photoshop is a handy way to avoid resizing operations and printing complications in your page-layout program. For example, I preset the resolution of all the images in this book so the production team had only to import the images and print away.

 Tip

Always remember: Photoshop is as good or better at adjusting pixels than any other program with which you work. So prepare an image as completely as possible in Photoshop before importing the image into another program. Ideally, you should never resize, rotate, or crop an image in any other program; doing so can easily introduce problems when the image is processed, leading to the slowdown — or possible crash — of your system.

That tip is so important I'm going to repeat it: *Never* resize, rotate, or crop an image in Illustrator, FreeHand, CorelDraw, PageMaker, InDesign, or QuarkXPress. Get your image fully ready to go in Photoshop and then place it in the drawing or page-layout program, position it on the page, and leave it alone.

So, what's the perfect resolution?

After all this explanation of pixels and resolution, you might be thinking, "Okay, this is all very interesting, but what's my bottom line? What Resolution value should I use?" The answer is frustrating to some and freeing to others: Any darn resolution you like. It's true — there is no right answer, there is no wrong answer. The images in this book vary from 100 ppi for screen shots to 300 ppi for color plates. I've seen low-resolution art that looks great and high-resolution art that looks horrible. As with all things, quality counts for more than quantity. You take the pixels you're dealt and make the best of them.

That said, I'll share a few guidelines, but only if you promise to take them with a grain of salt:

✦ Most experts recommend that you set the Resolution value to somewhere between 150 percent and 200 percent of the screen frequency of the final output device. The *screen frequency* is the number of halftone dots per linear inch, measured in *lpi* (short for *lines per inch*). So ask your commercial printer what screen frequency he uses — generally 120 lpi to 150 lpi — and multiply that times 1.5 or 2.

✦ Want to be more specific? For high-end photographic print work, it's hard to go wrong with the standard Resolution value of 267 ppi. That's around 200 percent of 133 lpi, arguably the most popular screen frequency. When in doubt, most professionals aim for 267 ppi.

✦ If you're printing on a home or small-office printer, the rules change slightly. Different manufacturers recommend different optimum resolutions for their various models, but the average is 250 to 300 ppi. Experiment to see how low you can go, though — sometimes you can get by with fewer pixels than the manufacturer suggests. And don't forget that the quality of the paper you use may be more to blame than a lack of pixels for a lousy print.

✦ What if you don't have enough pixels for 267 ppi? Say that you shoot a digital snapshot that measures 768×1024 pixels and you want to print it at 6×8 inches. That works out to a relatively scant 128 ppi. Won't that look grainy? Probably. Should you add pixels with Image Size or some other command? No, that typically won't help. You have a finite number of pixels to work with, so you can print the image large and a little grainy, or sharp and small. The choice is yours.

✦ What if you have a photograph or slide and you can scan it at any resolution you want? Flatbed scanners typically offer two maximum resolutions, a true optical maximum and an interpolated digital enhancement. The lower of the two values is invariably the true optical resolution. Scan at this lower maximum setting. Then use Image ⇨ Image Size to resample the image down to the desired size and resolution, as explained in the "Resampling and Cropping" section near the end of this chapter.

Orson Welles claimed that he relied on his inexperience when creating *Citizen Kane*. He didn't know the rules of filmmaking, so they couldn't hamper him. I feel the same about resolution. Take the pixels you have and try to make them look the best you can. Then print the image at the size you want it to appear. If you focus on the function of your image first and fret about resolution and other technical issues second, you'll produce better art.

The Resolution of Screen Images

Regardless of the Resolution and Scale values, Photoshop displays each pixel on screen according to the zoom ratio (covered in Chapter 2). If the zoom ratio is 100 percent, for example, each image pixel takes up a single screen pixel. Zoom ratio and printer output are unrelated.

This same rule applies outside Photoshop as well. Other programs that display screen images — including multimedia development applications, presentation programs, and Web browsers — default to showing one image pixel for every screen pixel. This means that when you're creating an image for the screen, the Resolution value has no effect whatsoever. I've seen some very bright people recommend that screen images should be set to 72 ppi on the Mac or 96 ppi for Windows, and while there's nothing wrong with doing this, there's no benefit either. When publishing for the screen, the Resolution value is ignored.

So all that counts is the 100 percent view. That means you want the image to fit inside the prospective monitor when you choose View ⇨ Actual Pixels (Ctrl+Alt+0 on the PC or ⌘-Option-0 on the Mac) inside Photoshop. I say *prospective* monitor because although you may use a 17-inch monitor when you create the image, you may need the final image to fit on a 13-inch display. So even though your monitor probably displays at least 1,024×768 pixels, many Web and screen artists prepare for the worst-case scenario, 640×480 pixels. This is the 13-inch VGA standard, shared by some of the first color Macs and PCs, most laptops, an endless array of defunct computers, and even televisions.

Of course, a 640×480-pixel image would consume an entire 13-inch screen. If you want the image to share the page with text and other elements, the image needs to be smaller than that. A typical screen image varies from as small as 16×16 pixels for icons and buttons to 320×240 pixels for a stand-alone photograph. Naturally, these are merely guidelines. You can create images at any size you like.

How to Open, Duplicate, and Save Images

Before you can work on an image in Photoshop—whether you're creating a brand-new document or opening an image from disk—you must first load the image into an image window. Here are the four basic ways to create an image window:

✦ **File ➪ New:** Create a new window by choosing File ➪ New or by pressing Ctrl+N (⌘-N on the Mac). After you fill out the desired size and resolution specifications in the New dialog box, Photoshop confronts you by default with a stark, white, empty canvas. You then face the ultimate test of your artistic abilities—painting from scratch. Feel free to go nuts and cut off your ear.

✦ **File ➪ Open:** Choose File ➪ Open or press Ctrl+O (⌘-O on the Mac) to open images scanned in other applications, images purchased from stock photo agencies, slides and transparencies digitized to a Kodak Photo CD, or an image you previously edited in Photoshop.

✦ **File ➪ Browse:** When you first launch Photoshop 7, the file browser is lurking in the docking well in the Options bar. If you close or hide the browser, you can always bring it up again by choosing File ➪ Browse or pressing Ctrl+Shift+O (⌘-Shift-O on the Mac). The file browser lets you see thumbnails for multiple images at a time. After you find an image you like, double-click it to open it.

✦ **File ➪ Open Recent:** A variation on the Open command, Open Recent, displays a list of the images that you recently opened. Click an image name to crack open the image file without taking that tedious trip to the Open dialog box. You can set the number of files you want to appear in this list in the File Handling panel of the Preferences dialog box.

✦ **Edit ➪ Paste:** Photoshop automatically adapts a new image window to the contents of the Clipboard (provided those contents are bitmapped). So if you copy an image inside a different application or in Photoshop and then choose File ➪ New, Photoshop enters the dimensions and resolution of the image into the New dialog box. You can just accept the settings and choose Edit ➪ Paste to introduce the image into a new window. Photoshop pastes the Clipboard contents as a new layer. This technique is useful for editing screen shots captured to the Clipboard or for testing effects on a sample of an image without harming the original.

✦ **File ➪ Import:** If you own a scanner or a digital camera, it may include a plug-in module that lets you transfer an image directly into Photoshop. Just copy the module into Photoshop's Plug-Ins folder and then run or relaunch the Photoshop application. To initiate a scan or to load an image into Photoshop, choose the plug-in module from the File ➪ Import submenu.

After you choose the command, Photoshop launches the device's download software. If you're scanning, select the scanner settings and initiate the scan as usual; the scanned picture appears in a new image window inside Photoshop. If you're transferring images from a digital camera, the camera software typically creates thumbnail previews of images in the camera's memory so that you can select the ones you want to transfer to Photoshop. By way of example, Figure 3-3 shows an image captured with a 5-megapixel Olympus E-20N. Here I've selected to load the raw image data captured by the E-20N's CCD. This permits me to open the 30-bit data in Photoshop's 48-bit color space, which can be useful in certain high-end printing conditions.

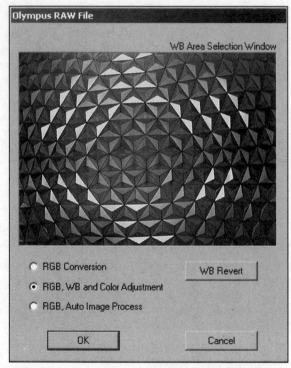

Figure 3-3: By loading an image directly from a scanner or digital camera into Photoshop, you may be able to bypass the hardware's automatic color correction and pixel interpolation. When loading the raw data from an Olympus camera, for example, I can choose to perform a simple white balance or leave the colors altogether unmodified.

Tip Save your images to disk immediately after you scan or download them; unlike some other programs, Photoshop doesn't automatically take this step for you. Also, if your digital camera stores images on removable memory cards (CompactFlash, SmartMedia, Memory Stick, and the like), do yourself a favor and invest in a card reader or adapter that enables your computer to see the memory card as just another hard drive. Then you can just drag and drop images from the memory card to your computer's hard drive — a much faster and more convenient option than transferring images via a cable connection. You'll spend between $10 and $75, depending on what type of reader or adapter you buy, but trust me, even if you wind up at the high end of that price range, you'll never regret the purchase.

Creating a new image

Whether you're creating an image from scratch or transferring the contents of the Clipboard to a new image window, choose File ➪ New or press Ctrl+N (⌘-N on the Mac) to bring up the New dialog box shown in Figure 3-4. If the Clipboard contains an image, the Width, Height, and Resolution option boxes show the size and resolution of this image. Otherwise, you can enter your own values in one of six units of measurement: pixels, inches, centimeters, millimeters, picas, or points. If you're uncertain exactly what size image you want to create, enter a rough approximation. You can always change your settings later.

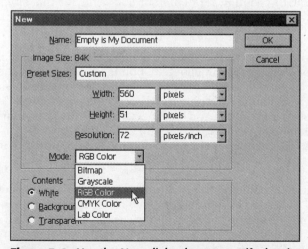

Figure 3-4: Use the New dialog box to specify the size, resolution, and color mode of your new image.

The new Preset Sizes pop-up menu gives you easy access to several popular document sizes, whether you're working in print, on the Web, or with digital video. And don't forget about the New Document Preset Resolutions settings in the Units & Rulers panel of the Preferences dialog box, which let you set a default resolution for print or screen; the resolutions you set in the preferences show up when you select an option from the Preset Sizes menu.

If you don't like Photoshop's preset document sizes, you can create your own. Inside the Presets folder of your Photoshop 7 application folder, you'll find a file entitled *New Doc Sizes.txt*, which contains complete instructions for adding custom document sizes to the Preset Sizes pop-up menu. You can't edit Adobe's presets, but you can follow the instructions and create your own at the bottom of the document. To experiment, just delete the semicolon and space at the beginning of the last line of the document, save and close the *.txt* file, and quit and relaunch Photoshop if it's currently running. Choose File ➪ New, scroll down to the bottom of the Preset Sizes pop-up menu, and you'll see an item called My Web Size, which is the preset you just created. This is a great new feature, and if you find yourself creating a large batch of identically sized files, it can be a huge timesaver.

Although Photoshop matches the contents of the Clipboard by default, you can also match the size and resolution of other images:

✦ Press Alt (Win) or Option (Mac) when choosing File ➪ New or press Ctrl+Alt+N (⌘-Option-N on the Mac) to override the contents of the Clipboard. Photoshop displays the size and resolution of the last image you created, whether or not it came from the Clipboard. Use this technique when creating many same-sized images in a row.

✦ You can also match the size and resolution of the new image to any other open image. While the New dialog box is open, choose the name of the image you want to match from the Window ➪ Documents submenu. It's that simple.

Units of measure

The Width and Height pop-up menus contain the six common units of measure mentioned earlier: pixels, inches, centimeters, millimeters, points, and picas. But the Width pop-up menu offers one more, called Columns. If you want to create an image that fits exactly within a certain number of columns when it's imported into a desktop publishing program, select this option. You can specify the width of a column and the gutter between columns by pressing Ctrl+K and Ctrl+5 (⌘-K and ⌘-5 on the Mac) to display the Units & Rulers preferences. Then enter values into the Column Size option boxes.

The Gutter value affects multiple-column images. Suppose you accept the default setting of a 15-pica column width and a 1-pica gutter. If you specify a one-column image in the New dialog box, Photoshop makes it 15 picas wide. If you ask for a two-column image, Photoshop adds the width of the gutter to the width of the two columns and creates an image 31 picas wide.

The Height pop-up menu in the New dialog box lacks a Column option because vertical columns have nothing to do with an image's height.

You can set the default unit of measurement for the Width and Height pop-up menus in the Units & Rulers panel of the Preferences dialog box. (Select the value from the Rulers pop-up menu; the Type menu sets the measurement unit for text-related controls.) But if the dialog box isn't already open, here are two quicker options:

✦ Press Ctrl+R (Win) or ⌘-R (Mac) to display the rulers, and then right-click (Win) or Control-click (Mac) anywhere in the rulers to display a pop-up menu of units. Click the unit you want to use.

✦ Display the same pop-up menu by pressing F8 to display the Info palette and then clicking or dragging on the cross icon (next to the X and Y coordinate values) in the palette's lower-left corner. Again, just click the unit you prefer.

New image size

In most cases, the on-screen dimensions of an image depend on your entries in the Width, Height, and Resolution option boxes. If you set both the Width and Height values to 10 inches and the Resolution to 72 ppi, the new image will measure 720×720 pixels. The exception occurs if you choose pixels as your unit of measurement. In this case, the on-screen dimensions depend solely on the Width and Height options, and the Resolution value determines the size at which the image prints.

Color mode

Use the Mode pop-up menu to specify the number of colors that can appear in your image. Choose Bitmap to create an image consisting of only black and white pixels, and choose Grayscale to access only gray values. RGB Color, CMYK Color, and Lab Color all provide access to the full range of 16 million colors, although their methods of doing so differ.

Cross-Reference

RGB stands for red-green-blue, CMYK for cyan-magenta-yellow-black, and Lab for luminosity and two abstract color variables: a and b. To learn how each of these color modes works, read the "Working in Different Color Modes" section of Chapter 4.

Background color

The New dialog box also provides three Contents radio buttons that enable you to change the color of the background for the new image. You can fill the new image with white, with the current background color (which might be white anyway, of course), or with no color at all. This last setting, Transparent, results in a floating layer with no background image whatsoever, which can be useful when editing one layer independently of the rest of an image or when preparing a layer to be composited with an image. (For an in-depth examination of the more nitty-gritty aspects of layering, see Chapter 12.)

If you do select a transparent background, you must later flatten the layer by choosing Layer ➪ Flatten Image if you want to save the image to a format that doesn't support layers (see the upcoming discussion "Saving an image to disk" for information about options for retaining layers when saving). The advantage of the Transparent setting, however, is that Photoshop doesn't create a new layer when you press Ctrl+V (⌘-V on the Mac) to paste the contents of the Clipboard. In the long run, you don't gain much — you still must flatten the image before you save it to some formats — but at least you needn't fuss with two layers, one of which is an unwanted background layer.

Incidentally, just because you create an image with a transparent background doesn't mean that you can automatically import a free-form image with transparency intact into an object-oriented program, such as Illustrator or QuarkXPress. To carve a transparent area out of the naturally rectangular boundaries of an image, you have to use the pen tool to create a clipping path. I explain how in the "Retaining transparent areas in an image" section of Chapter 8.

Naming the new image

The New dialog box provides a Name option. If you know what you want to call your new image, enter the name now. Or don't. It doesn't matter. Either way, when you choose File ⇨ Save, Photoshop asks you to specify the location of the file and confirm the file's name. So don't feel compelled to name your image anything. The only reason for this option is to help you keep your images organized on screen. Lots of folks create temporary images they never save; Photoshop offers a way to assign temporary images more meaningful names than *Untitled-4*, *Untitled-5*, *Untitled-6*, and so on.

Unlike some traditionalists, I whole-heartedly endorse using long file names under Windows 95, NT 4, and later. But naturally you should be aware of the implications. If you send a file to someone using Windows 3.1, DOS, or some other ancient operating system, the long file name gets truncated to eight characters with a tilde symbol (~) and number. (You can view the truncated DOS-style name at the desktop in Windows by right-clicking on the file and choosing Properties.) This can also happen when exchanging files between PCs and Macs, depending on how you do it. If you swap files to a Mac using a PC-formatted floppy disk, Zip disk, or the like, the file names get the ax when the disk is popped into the Mac. But if you network your PC to a Mac using Miramar Systems' (*www.miramarsys.com*) PC MACLAN or the like, the long file names come through swimmingly. In fact, this is precisely how I exchange files over my own cross-platform Ethernet LAN.

Opening an existing image

Photoshop provides a File menu command, Open Recent, which displays a list of the images you worked on in recent Photoshop sessions. Click the name of the image you want to open. You set the number of files that appear on the list by entering a value in the Recent File List Contains option box, found on the File Handling panel of the Preferences dialog box, which you access by pressing Ctrl+K and then Ctrl+2 (⌘-K and ⌘-2 on the Mac). The maximum value is 30.

Here are another couple of neat tricks for Mac folks: ⌘-click the title bar of an open image to display a pop-up menu showing the folder hierarchy for the image file. Click any folder to open it and display all image files therein. Then simply double-click the image file you want to open. (In Mac OS X, this trick works in any application, not just Photoshop.)

Also, the icon in the title bar gives you an instant hint as to whether or not your image has been edited since it was last saved. If there are unsaved changes to the image, the title bar icon will appear faded. (Mac OS X users can also look at the red close button in the title bar; if it contains a black dot, then the image has been edited since it was last saved.)

Of course, you can always open images the old-fashioned way, by choosing File ⇨ Open or pressing its keyboard shortcut, Ctrl+O (⌘-O on the Mac), to display the Open dialog box. On the PC, you also can double-click an empty spot in the Photoshop program window to open the dialog box.

The Open dialog box behaves just like the ones in other Windows and Macintosh applications, with a folder bar at top, a scrolling list of files, and the usual file management and navigation options. You can also open multiple files at one time. To select a range of files on the PC and in Mac OS X, click the first file name and Shift-click the last file in the range. Ctrl-click (⌘-click in Mac OS X) to add a single file to the group you want to open. Ctrl-click or ⌘-click again to deselect a file from the group. In Mac OS 9, the easiest way to select a large block of files is to marquee-drag around them. You can then Shift-click to add or remove single files.

The Photoshop Open dialog box also includes a few controls that most other programs lack. You can read about these options in the next sections. But first, a few other brief notes about opening files:

✦ When you choose File ⇨ Open, Photoshop displays the folder that contained the last file you opened. Similarly, when you save a file, the folder to which you saved last is selected automatically. (In Mac OS 9, you must first open the General Controls panel and select the Last Folder Used in the Application option to enable this behavior.)

✦ When you open an image, Photoshop may display a dialog box telling you that the color profile of the image doesn't match the default color profile you've established. You have the option of converting the image to the default profile or leaving well enough alone. See Chapter 16 for help with this issue.

Tip

✦ When opening an image, you may occasionally encounter a dialog box warning you that some data in the file cannot be read and will be ignored. If this happens to you, there's no cause for concern, just click OK to dismiss the warning and open the image as usual.

Viewing the thumbnail

To help you assess an image before you open it, Photoshop displays a thumbnail preview of the selected file at the bottom of the Open dialog box, as shown in Figure 3-5. In Mac OS 9, click the Show Preview button to display a thumbnail of the selected image. The button then changes to the Hide Preview button. If you click that button, the thumbnail disappears, and the file information expands to fill the empty area. In Mac OS X, the column view found in Open dialog boxes automatically displays a preview of graphic files. On the PC, Photoshop automatically displays thumbnails for any files saved in the native format (PSD). If you're running Windows 98 or Windows 2000, the operating system may generate thumbnails for files saved in other formats.

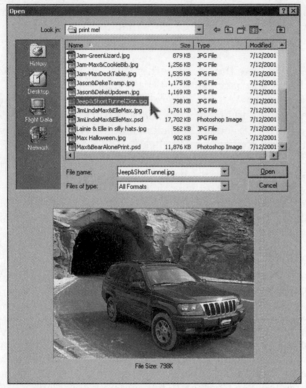

Figure 3-5: You can see a preview of an image if you previously saved it in Photoshop with the thumbnails option enabled.

In Mac OS 9, the thumbnail space may appear empty, which means the file does not contain a Photoshop-compatible preview. The file may have been created by a piece of hardware or software that doesn't support thumbnails, or the thumbnail feature may have simply been turned off when the image file was saved. To generate thumbnails when saving images in Photoshop, press Ctrl+K and then Ctrl+2 (⌘-K and ⌘-2 on the Mac) to display the File Handling panel of the Preferences dialog box. Then turn on the Macintosh Thumbnail check box if you're using a Mac or set the Image Previews pop-up menu to Always Save if you're using a PC. Alternatively, you can set the Image Previews pop-up menu to Ask When Saving, in which case Photoshop gives you the option of adding a thumbnail to the image inside the Save dialog box.

Previewing outside Photoshop

Tip

Under Windows 95 and later, the Open dialog box isn't the only place you can preview an image before you open it. In fact, provided you save the image in the native Photoshop (*.psd*) format, you can peek at an image without even opening the program.

Right-click a file with a *.psd* extension—either at the desktop, in a folder window, or in Windows Explorer—and choose Properties from the pop-up menu. When the Properties dialog box opens, click the Photoshop Image tab to look at your image. Again, you must have saved a thumbnail preview along with the image for this feature to work.

You can also see a tiny thumbnail in the General panel of the Properties dialog box. This same thumbnail appears at the desktop level, assuming that the folder is set to View ⇨ Large Icons. Using the other tabs in the Properties dialog box, you can view the caption, keywords, credits, and other information created by using Photoshop's File ⇨ File Info command (covered later in this chapter).

Unfortunately, this trick works only for images saved in the native Photoshop format. TIFF, JPEG, GIF, and other images can be previewed only from inside Photoshop's Open dialog box. Even so, it's a heck of a trick.

Note also that Mac OS X is pretty crafty about generating previews of graphic files all on its own. Depending on the file format, you can generally get a preview of a graphic file, no matter what the thumbnails saving settings were. Select an image in the Finder and press ⌘-O to access the Show Info command, as pictured in Figure 3-6.

Opening elusive files on a PC

The scrolling list in the Open dialog box contains the names of just those documents that Photoshop recognizes it can open. If you can't find a desired document on your PC, it may be because the Files of Type pop-up menu is set to the wrong file format. To view all supported formats, either select All Formats from the Files of Type pop-up or enter *.* into the File Name option box and press Enter.

If a file lacks any form of extension whatsoever, the Open dialog box won't be able to identify it. This unusual situation may arise in one of two ways. On rare occasions, a file transmitted electronically (via the Internet, for example) loses its extension en route. But more likely, the file comes from a Macintosh computer. The Mac doesn't need file extensions—the file type identification resides in the resource fork—therefore, many Mac users never give a thought to three-character extensions.

Figure 3-6: The Show Info command in Mac OS X can show previews of many different graphic file types.

You can solve this problem either by renaming the file and adding the proper extension or by choosing File ⇨ Open As (Ctrl+Alt+O). If you choose Open As, Photoshop shows you all documents in a directory, whether it supports them or not. Just click the extension-less file and select the correct file format from the Open As pop-up menu. Provided that the image conforms to the selected format option, Photoshop opens the image when you press Enter. If Photoshop gives you an error message instead, you need to either select a different format or try to open the document in a different application.

Opening elusive files on a Mac

If you can't find a document in the Open dialog box on your Mac, it may be because Photoshop doesn't recognize the document's four-character type code. The type code for a document created or last edited on a Macintosh computer corresponds to the file format under which the image was saved (as explained in the upcoming "File Format Roundup" section).

For example, TIFF is the type code for a TIFF image, JPEG is the code for a JPEG image, GIFf is the code for a GIF image, and so on. However, if you transferred a document from another platform, such as a Windows machine or a Unix worksta-tion, it probably lacks a type code. In the absence of a type code, Photoshop looks for a three-character extension at the end of the file name, such as *.tif* or *.jpg* or *.gif*. But if the extension is so much as a character off—*.tff* or *.jpe* or *.jif*—Photoshop won't know the file from Adam.

To see *all* documents regardless of type code or extension, select All Documents from the Show pop-up menu inside the Open dialog box, as shown in Figure 3-7. When you click on a document in the scrolling list, Photoshop displays the format that it thinks the file is saved in—if it has any thoughts to offer—in the Format option. If you disagree, click the Format option and select the correct file format from the pop-up menu. As long as the image conforms to the selected format option, Photoshop opens the image when you press Return. If you get an error message instead, either select a different format or try to open the document in a different application.

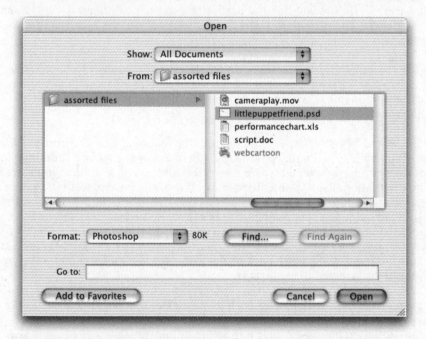

Figure 3-7: Select the All Documents option to access any document regardless of its four-character type code.

Tip

Normally, you can't see a file's four-character type code because it's socked away inside the resource fork. Unless, that is, you're willing to purchase a special utility, such as Prairie Group's (*www.prgrsoft.com*) DiskTop or Apple's (*www.apple.com*) ResEdit. Both are great, but DiskTop is more convenient for the simple day-to-day tasks of viewing and modifying type codes and other invisible resources.

Finding lost files on a Mac

If you know the name of a file—or at least part of the name—but you can't remember where you put it, click the Find button, enter some text in the resulting option box, and press the Return key. Photoshop searches the disk in a fairly random fashion and takes you to the first file name that contains the exact characters you entered.

If the first file name isn't the one you're looking for, click the Find Again button to find the next file name that contains your text. If you want to search for a different string of characters, click Find and enter some different text.

Using the file browser

Opening an image is like putting on a pair of socks. The actual operation of applying socks to one's feet is relatively easy. And most of us have more socks than we know what to do with. In fact, our feet would be eternally graced by elegant, matching socks if it weren't for the fact that the darned things are so difficult to find. Washing machines, dryers, and dresser drawers harbor vast collections of socks that we'll never see again.

Images are the same way. While easy to open, they're not so easy to find. Socked away (get it?) inside folders, on Zips and CDs, and among myriad digital camera cards, the common image is more abundant than lint and harder to locate than a clean dish towel.

Just as life would benefit from a sock browser, Photoshop 7 benefits from the file browser. Expressed as a floating palette, the file browser shows you thumbnail previews of every image contained inside a selected folder. The first time you start the program, Photoshop displays the browser docked to the palette well. Drag the File Browser tab away from the palette well to convert the palette into a free-floating window, as in Figure 3-8. This permits you to move the browser behind or in front of open image windows. Like any window, you can close or hide the browser. To again display it or bring it to front, choose File ➪ Browse or press Ctrl+Shift+O (⌘-Shift-O on the Mac). To send the palette back to the well, choose Dock to Palette Well from the palette menu (labeled in Figure 3-8).

Opening an image from the browser is simply a matter of navigating to its folder from the hierarchical list in the upper-left corner of the window (known as the *folder tree*) and then double-clicking a thumbnail. But there's much more to the file browser than may at first meet the eye. The best way to learn how it works is to run through a list of its parts. The following paragraphs explain the items labeled in Figure 3-8, ranked in rough order of importance:

✦ **Folder tree:** Adobe calls this the *desktop view*; I call it the *folder tree* because it shows folders branching off in various directions. Like the Explorer bar under Windows, the folder tree lets you dig several folders deep in search of images. Click the plus sign (or the "twirlie" triangle on the Mac) next to a folder name to view all subfolders inside it. Click a folder name to make it the so-called "current" folder and view thumbnails of the images contained therein.

Selected image

Folder tree   Up folder   Folder path menu   Thumbnails

Palette menu

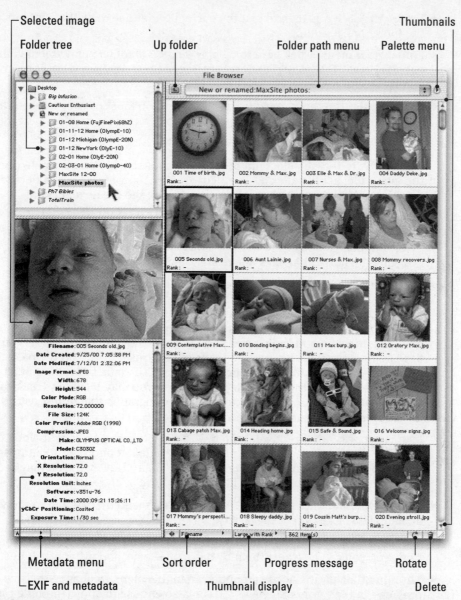

Figure 3-8: The file browser shows you thumbnail-sized previews of a folder full of images at a time. You can also change the sorting order and rotate vertical images to make them upright.

Metadata menu   Sort order   Progress message   Rotate

EXIF and metadata   Thumbnail display   Delete

Tip

To update the folder tree to show changes made to a networked volume, choose Refresh Desktop View from the palette menu. Under Windows, you can alternatively press F5. To hide the folder tree and other elements along the left sides of the browser, turn off the Expanded View command in the palette menu.

✦ **Up folder:** Click this icon to exit the current folder and view the contents of the folder one level up.

✦ **Folder path menu:** Click here to display a menu of folders and volumes that contain the current folder. Choose any one of them to make it the current folder.

✦ **Thumbnails:** The thumbnail view is where you do most of your work in the file browser. Click a thumbnail to select it. You can select multiple files by pressing Shift or Ctrl (⌘ on the Mac). Shift-clicking selects a range of files; Ctrl-clicking (⌘-clicking on the Mac) adds individual files to the selection. You can also Shift-drag to select multiple files. Double-click a thumbnail to open the image file; double-click a folder icon to view its contents. For a detailed discussion of the many other things you can do, see the next section, "Working with thumbnails."

✦ **Selected image:** The file browser sports a scalable preview of the selected image on the left side of the window. You can make it bigger or smaller by dragging the horizontal lines above and below the preview.

✦ **EXIF and metadata:** Of all the functions of the file browser, this may be my favorite. The Exchangeable Image File format (EXIF) is a standard for appending non-pixel information — known as *metadata* — to an image file. EXIF is most widely used by digital cameras to describe a photograph's history, including the date and time it was shot, the make and model of camera, the flash setting, the focal length, and loads of other useful stuff. In the past, Photoshop was capable of reading and saving EXIF data, but it did not let you view it. This means, thanks to the file browser, you may be able to find out all kinds of wonderful esoterica about digital photographs that you shot and edited years ago.

If an image was not directly captured with a digital camera, then it won't contain EXIF information. (For example, copying a digital photograph and pasting it into another image does not preserve EXIF data.) However, you may see more generic metadata, such as file size, file format, and so on.

✦ **Metadata menu:** Click the word All to display a menu that allows you to view all metadata or just the EXIF variety.

✦ **Sort order:** By default, the file browser sorts files alphabetically by file name. However, you can also sort them by date, rank, size, and other attributes.

✦ **Thumbnail display:** Choose an option from this menu to change the size of previews in the thumbnail view. You can also choose to show and hide ranking information.

✦ **Progress message:** The file browser often takes a while to generate thumbnails and perform other operations. As a result, it can seem like nothing's happening. If the browser keeps you waiting, take a peek at the progress message to find out what's going on.

✦ **Rotate:** Click this icon to rotate the selected thumbnail 90 degrees clockwise. Alt-click the icon (or Option-click on the Mac) to rotate 90 degrees counter-clockwise. Note that this does not change the image itself, just the thumbnail. If you double-click a thumbnail, Photoshop is smart enough to open the image and then rotate it in a separate operation. But you'll have to save this change to make it permanent.

✦ **Delete:** Click the trash icon to delete one or more selected images. You can also drag files to the trash icon to delete them. To delete the images without a warning, press the Alt key (or Option on the Mac) as you click the icon or drag the files.

Caution

Be aware, however, that this does move the selected images to the Recycle Bin or Trash, just as surely as if you had done it yourself at the desktop level.

✦ **Palette menu:** The palette menu contains a long list of commands that help you modify thumbnail orientations, rankings, and file names. Most duplicate functions already discussed in this list. But a few — specifically Batch Rename, Export Cache, and Purge Cache — are unique. I discuss these commands in the upcoming sections, "Managing the cache" and "Batch renaming."

Note that, for the most part, the file browser behaves the same whether it's a docked palette or free-floating window. The exception is when opening an image. If you open an image from the docked palette, Photoshop automatically hides the palette to get it out of the way. (Otherwise, like other palettes, it would always be in front.) However, if you open an image from the free-floating file browser window, Photoshop leaves the window open and brings the image to front. As a result, I prefer to work with the free-floating window. If it gets in the way, press Ctrl+W (⌘-W on the Mac) to close it. To bring it back, press Ctrl+Shift+O (⌘-Shift-O on the Mac).

Working with thumbnails

The file browser is a complex environment with more going on than you might imagine. And the thumbnail view is the hub of activity. You can select, rename, move, and even copy files from one folder to the next.

Photoshop generates thumbnail previews of all image files that it supports. If you saved a preview with the image (as explained in the section "Saving previews" later in this chapter), the file browser shows you that. Otherwise, it generates a new preview on the fly. This takes time, especially in the case of high-resolution or complex images. If a folder resides on a remote volume or contains lots of files — say, a few hundred — Photoshop may appear to hang for a few seconds while it gets its bearings. The progress message "Getting directory file list" tells you work is being done. If you're feeling impatient, you may be able to interrupt the process by switching to another folder.

All thumbnail previews and other browser-related data for a folder are saved to a cache that resides with other system-level settings on your computer's hard drive. The exact location of these cache files varies from operating system to system, but it's ultimately not important because you can access the cache more easily using commands, as I discuss shortly in "Managing the cache."

Like desktop icons and other cached picture libraries, thumbnails can get jumbled. Most common, a handful of thumbnails may be repeated or misassigned. To force a single thumbnail to redraw, just click it. If several thumbnails are messed up, press the right arrow key to advance from one thumbnail to the next.

Click the file name below a thumbnail to highlight the name and enter a new one. (Note that Photoshop protects the extension—*.jpg*, *.tif*, and so on—unless you specifically drag over it.) Click the Rank value to enter a grade for the image, useful for selecting a photograph from a group of proofs. Typical ranks are A through E, but you can enter other letters and numbers as you see fit.

To move an image to a different folder, drag its thumbnail and drop it into the desired folder in the folder tree. Press the Alt key (or Option on the Mac) when dragging a file to copy it. Right-click a thumbnail (or Control-click on the Mac) to display a shortcut menu of additional options, including ranking values, as shown in Figure 3-9.

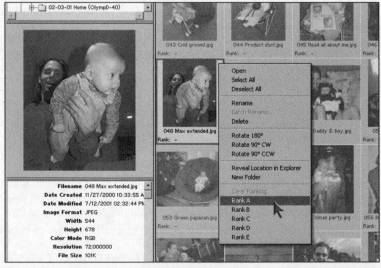

Figure 3-9: Right-click a thumbnail to select from a shortcut menu of common operations that you can apply inside the browser. (On the Mac, press the Control key and click.)

Managing the cache

You may spend several minutes generating previews, rotating thumbnails, and ranking images inside the file browser. And yet not a single one of these functions is saved with the image file. So how does Photoshop prevent you from losing your work? By saving a cache file that records all changes made to an entire folder full of images.

This all happens in the background without your aid or assistance, so you might assume there's no reason to worry about it. However, while Photoshop's approach works well when viewing pictures on a local hard drive, things get a little dicey when browsing images from a network or CD. Here are two possible problem scenarios:

✦ **Sharing images over a network.** There is one cache file per folder and each resides in a system folder on your computer. This is called a *local cache* because it resides locally on your machine. And a networked version of Photoshop running on a different computer cannot share a local cache file. For example, you and a coworker are browsing through images on a server. You rotate a few thumbnails, assign a few rankings, and naturally assume that the coworker can see what you've done. But she can't because her local cache is different than yours.

✦ **Browsing images on a CD.** You start with a folder of 200 images. After giving Photoshop a few minutes to generate the thumbnails, you rotate and rank the images as you see fit. Then you burn the images to a CD, having faith that the thumbnails, rotations, and ranks will be maintained. But when you put the CD in your drive and view it in the file browser, Photoshop starts generating the thumbnails all over again. Plus the rotation and ranks have been lost. The cache remains intact, but it's linked to the folder, not the CD. So Photoshop has to create a new cache for the CD. After you reperform your work, the CD will browse as expected from that point on — *but only on this one machine*. Other computers will require their own local caches.

Are you beginning to get a sense of how messy this can get? And that's not all. Any change to a folder — renaming it, moving it to a different location — likewise breaks the link and requires you to start over again.

So what's the solution? Fortunately, a very simple one. Just choose Export Cache from the file browser palette menu, as shown in Figure 3-10. Without any additional dialog with you, Photoshop exports two cache files to the folder itself. The files are *AdobePS7.td0*, which contains the thumbnails, and *AdobePS7.md0*, which contains the metadata, including rotation and ranking information. From that point on, the two cache files are available to other users on a network, you can burn them to a CD, or you can keep them with a folder on the off chance you move the folder or rename it.

Figure 3-10: Choose Export Cache to save thumbnails as well as rotation and ranking data to a networked folder or to burn to a CD.

Caution

Exporting is a manual process so don't expect Photoshop to update your changes. If you change a rotation or ranking and you want to make it available to other users or computers, then choose Export Cache again. When burning image CDs, get in the habit of choosing Export Cache immediately before writing the CD; this will ensure the cache is as up-to-date as possible.

Batch renaming

I'm not thrilled by the way the browser lets you rename files. It makes it difficult to select the extension and it can be slow when compared with renaming at the desktop level. However, Photoshop's browser gives you something the desktop doesn't — Batch Rename. This command lets you rename multiple files in one operation.

To rename a handful of specific files, click and Shift-click on their thumbnails to select them. To rename all files in a folder, choose Select All or Deselect All from the palette menu. Then choose Batch Rename to display the dialog box pictured in Figure 3-11. (The only time this command is dimmed is when just one thumbnail is selected.)

You have the option of renaming files in the folder where they currently reside (the most common choice) or moving them to a different folder. If you click Move to New Folder, the file browser will ask you to select a destination. Note that *moving* means just that — Photoshop relocates the files as opposed to copying them to the new location.

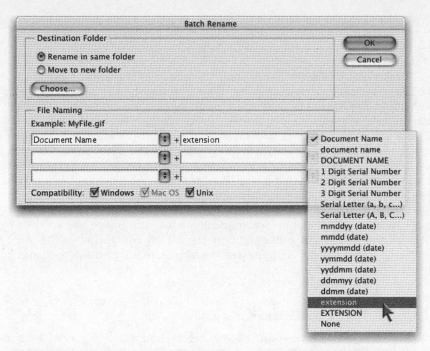

Figure 3-11: Use the Batch Rename command to rename multiple files in a single operation. You can select naming options from a pop-up menu, or enter your own name.

You can specify up to six File Naming variables, though two or three is generally sufficient. The three Document Name options retain or change the case of the name currently assigned to the file. Alternatively, you can enter your own name into an option box. In Figure 3-11, I've chosen to give all files a lowercase extension, useful for changing digital photographs with names like *PIC0301.JPG* to *PIC0301.jpg*. You can also append dates or serial numbers, as when tracking variations such as *SunnyDay001.jpg*, *SunnyDay002.jpg*, and so on.

To ensure that your images are named so that they'll work on any computer, select all three Compatibility check boxes. (Either Windows or Mac OS will already be selected, depending on your platform.) Then click OK to apply your changes. Note that, as with other file browser operations, renaming is not undoable. So be sure all settings are correct before you click OK. If you have any doubt how the command will work, experiment on a few trial images before renaming important files.

Duplicating an image

Have you ever wanted to try an effect without permanently damaging an image? Photoshop offers multiple undos, and you'll get a kick out of using the History palette to see before and after views of your image (as I explain in Chapter 7). But what if you want to apply a series of effects to an image independently and compare them side by side? And save the variations as separate files? Or perhaps even merge them? This is a job for image duplication.

To create a new window with an independent version of the foreground image, choose Image ➪ Duplicate. A dialog box appears, requesting a name for the new image. Just like the Name option in the New dialog box, the option is purely an organizational tool you can use or ignore. If your image contains multiple layers, Photoshop will, by default, retain all layers in the duplicate document. Or you can merge all visible layers into a single layer by selecting the oddly-named Duplicate Merged Layers Only check box. (Hidden layers are ignored.) Press Enter or Return to create your new, independent image. Bear in mind that this image is unsaved; you need to choose File ➪ Save to save any changes to disk.

Tip

If you're happy to let Photoshop automatically name your image and you don't care what it does with the layers, press and hold the Alt key (or Option on the Mac) and choose Image ➪ Duplicate. This bypasses the Duplicate Image dialog box and immediately creates a new window.

Saving an image to disk

The first rule of image editing — and of working on computers in general — is to save the file to disk frequently. If your computer or Photoshop crashes while you're working on an image, all edits made during the current editing session are lost.

To save an image for the first time, choose File ➪ Save or press Ctrl+S (⌘-S on the Mac) to display the Save dialog box. Name the image, select the drive and folder where you want to store the image file, select a file format, and press Enter or Return.

After you save the image once, choosing the Save command updates the file on disk without bringing up the Save dialog box. To save the image with a different name, location, or format, choose File ➪ Save As.

You also can issue the Save As command by pressing Ctrl+Shift+S (⌘-Shift-S on the Mac). As for the Save a Copy command found in some earlier versions of Photoshop, that function is provided through the As a Copy check box in the Save As dialog box. By the way, if your only reason for using Save As is to change the file format, it's perfectly acceptable to overwrite (save over) the original document, assuming you no longer need the previous copy of the image. Granted, your computer could crash during the Save As operation, but because Photoshop actually creates a new file during any save operation, your original document should survive the accident. Besides, the chance of crashing during a Save As is extremely remote — no more likely than crashing during any other save operation.

Tip

To speed the save process, I usually save an image in Photoshop's native format until I've finished working on it. Then, when the file is all ready to go, I choose File ➪ Save As and save the image in whatever compressed format is needed. This way, I compress each image only once during the time I work on it.

If you have multiple files open, you can close them in one step by choosing Window ⇨ Documents ⇨ Close All (or File ⇨ Close All on the Mac). Or better yet, press Ctrl+Shift+W (⌘-Shift-W on the Mac). Photoshop prompts you to save any images that haven't yet been saved and closes the others automatically.

Adding an extension to Mac files

On the Mac, the Preferences dialog box includes an option that lets you append a three-character file extension to the end of your files. (Again, this option is located in the File Handling panel, so press ⌘-K, ⌘-2 to get to it.) Here I have two recommendations. First, leave the Use Lower Case check box turned on. It ensures fewer conflicts if and when you post your images on the Web. Second, go ahead and append extensions to your file names.

Why add PC file extensions on a Mac? Obviously, it makes life easier when sharing images with PCs. More importantly, it's another form of insurance. If you're a Mac person and you ever find yourself using a PC, you're going to have tons and tons of old Macintosh image files that you'd like to open and reuse. With file extensions, you'll have no problem. Without them, good luck. The file extension is the only way a Windows application has to identify the file format. If there's no file extension, you have to tell the application which format to use. While I don't question the basic record-keeping capabilities of your brain, you probably have better things to remember than what file format you used five years ago.

Tip

As I mentioned in Chapter 2, you can automatically append an extension from the Save dialog box regardless of your preference settings. Press the Option key, choose an option from the Format pop-up menu, and there it is.

Saving previews

In Chapter 2, I recommended that you set the Image Previews option in the File Handling preferences panel (Ctrl+K, Ctrl+2 on the PC or ⌘-K, ⌘-2 on the Mac) to Ask When Saving. If you followed this sage advice, the Save dialog box on the PC offers a Thumbnail check box. On the Mac, it offers several Image Previews check boxes. For print work, I generally select the Thumbnail option on my PC and both the Macintosh and Windows Thumbnail options on my Mac. Previews consume extra disk space, but it's well worth it in exchange for being able to see files before opening them. Why save a Windows thumbnail on a Mac? If you ever swap files between platforms, it will come in handy.

The only reason *not* to save a thumbnail with an image is if you plan to post the picture on the Web. In that case, the file has to be as streamlined as possible, and that means shaving away the preview.

Choosing other save options

Certain save options that once upon a time were available only via the Save a Copy command now appear in the Save dialog box all the time. You also get access to these options when you choose Save As or press its keyboard shortcut, Ctrl+Shift+S (⌘-Shift-S on the Mac). Figure 3-12 shows the dialog box.

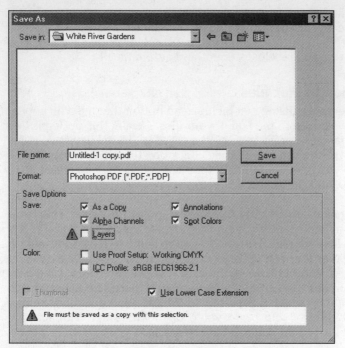

Figure 3-12: A look at the Save dialog box, which incorporates the old Save a Copy command as a save option

Note that the options you can select vary depending on the image file and the selected file format. If an option is grayed out, it either doesn't apply to your image or isn't supported by the file format you chose. And if your image includes features that won't be saved if you go forward with the current dialog box settings, Photoshop gives you the heads up by displaying a warning message at the bottom of the dialog box, as shown in Figure 3-12.

✦ **As a Copy:** Select this check box to save a copy of the image while leaving the original open and unchanged—in other words, to do what the Save a Copy command did in Photoshop 5.5 and earlier. The result is the same as duplicating an image, saving it, and closing the duplicate all in one step.

The whole point of this option is to enable you to save a flattened version of a layered image or to dump other extraneous data, such as masks. Just select the file format you want to use and let Photoshop do the rest for you.

✦ **Annotations:** Select this check box to include any annotations that you created using the notes and audio annotation tools. You can find out how to annotate your images in the section "Adding file information and annotations," later in this chapter.

✦ **Alpha Channels:** If your image contains an alpha channel—Photoshop's techy name for an extra channel, such as a mask (discussed in Chapter 9)—select the Alpha check box to retain the channel. Only a few formats—notably Photoshop, PDF, PICT, PICT Resource, TIFF, and DCS 2.0—support extra channels.

✦ **Spot Colors:** Did you create an image that incorporates spot colors? If so, select this option to retain the spot color channels in the saved image file. You must save the file in the native Photoshop, PDF, TIFF, or DCS 2.0 format to use this option.

✦ **Layers:** TIFF and PDF can retain independent image layers, as can the native Photoshop format. Select the check box to retain layers; deselect it to flatten the image.

If you're working with a layered image and select a file format that doesn't support layers, a cautionary message appears at the bottom of the dialog box. However, Photoshop doesn't prevent you from going through with the save, so be careful. All layers are automatically merged together when you save the file in a non-layer format. However, when you close the file, Photoshop reminds you that you haven't saved a version of the image that retains all data and gives you the opportunity to do so.

✦ **Use Proof Setup:** This option relates to Photoshop's color profile options. If the current view's proof setup is a "convert to" proof, Photoshop converts the image to the selected proofing space when saving.

✦ **ICC Profile (Win)/Embed Color Profile (Mac):** If you're saving your image in a file format that supports embedded ICC profiles, selecting this option embeds the profile. The current profile appears next to the option name. See Chapter 16 for advice about working with color profiles.

File Format Roundup

Photoshop 7 supports more than 20 file formats from inside its Open and Save dialog boxes. It can support even more through the addition of plug-in modules, which attach commands to the File ⇨ Save As, File ⇨ Import, and File ⇨ Export submenus.

File formats represent different ways to save a file to disk. Some formats provide unique image-compression schemes, which save an image in a manner that consumes less space on disk. Other formats enable Photoshop to trade images with different applications running under Windows, the Mac, or some other platform.

The native format

Like most programs, Photoshop offers its own native format — that is, a format optimized for Photoshop's particular capabilities and functions. This *.psd* format saves every attribute that you can apply in Photoshop — including layers, extra channels, file info, and so on — and is compatible with Versions 3 and later of the program. Of course, when you open files in earlier versions of Photoshop, you lose file attributes related to later versions, such as annotations, color proof options, and so on.

Note

Photoshop isn't the only application that uses *.psd* as its native format; *.psd* is also the native format used by Photoshop's close relatives ImageReady and Photoshop Elements.

Tip

Perhaps not surprisingly, Photoshop can open and save more quickly in its native format than in any other format. The native format also offers image compression. Like TIFF's LZW compression, the Photoshop compression scheme does not result in any loss of data. But Photoshop can compress and decompress its native format much more quickly than TIFF, and the compression scheme is better able to minimize the size of mask channels (as explained in Chapter 9).

The downside of the Photoshop format is that relatively few applications other than Photoshop support it, and those that do don't always do a great job. Some applications, such as Corel Photo-Paint and Adobe After Effects, can open a layered Photoshop image and interpret each layer independently. But most of the others limit their support to flat Photoshop files. To accommodate these programs, you can either (1) deselect the Layers check box in the Save dialog box to save a flattened version of the image or (2) activate the Always Maximize Compatibility check box in the Preferences dialog box.

However, I intensely dislike both of these options. (In fact, you should be sure to turn off Always Maximize Compatibility, for reasons explained in Chapter 2.) The native *.psd* format was never intended to function as an interapplication standard; it was meant for Photoshop alone. So use it that way. If you want to trade a flattened image with some other program, use TIFF, JPEG, or one of the other universal formats explained over the course of this chapter.

Special-purpose formats

With 20 file formats to choose from, you can imagine that most are not the kinds you'll be using on a regular basis. In fact, apart from the native Photoshop format, you'll probably want to stick with TIFF, JPEG, and GIF for Web images and EPS when preparing images for placement into InDesign, QuarkXPress, and other layout programs.

Many of the other formats are provided simply so that you can open an image created on another platform, saved from some antiquated paint program, or downloaded from the Web. In the spirit of sweeping away the chaff so we can move on to the good stuff, I cover these special-purpose formats first.

Microsoft Paint's BMP

BMP (*Windows Bitmap*) is the native format for Microsoft Paint (included with Windows) and is supported by a variety of Windows and DOS applications. Photoshop supports BMP images with up to 16 million colors. You also can use RLE (*Run-Length Encoding*), a lossless compression scheme specifically applicable to the BMP format.

Note

The term *lossless* refers to compression schemes that conserve space on disk without sacrificing any data in the image, such as BMP's RLE and TIFF's LZW (*Lempel-Ziv-Welch*). The only reasons not to use lossless compression are that it slows down the open and save operations and it may prevent less-sophisticated applications from opening an image. (Lossy compression routines, such as JPEG, sacrifice a user-defined amount of data to conserve even more disk space, as I explain later.)

The most common use for BMP is to create images for use in help files and Windows wallpaper. In fact, rolling your own wallpaper is a fun way to show off your Photoshop skills. For the best results, make sure you set your image to exactly the same pixel dimensions as your screen (which you can check from the Settings panel in the Display control panel). To conserve memory, you may want to reduce the number of colors in your wallpaper image to 256 using Image ⇨ Mode ⇨ Indexed Color.

When you save the wallpaper image, Photoshop displays the options shown in Figure 3-13. Generally, you'll want to select the Windows and Compress (RLE) options, but it really doesn't matter when creating wallpaper. Don't mess with the Depth options. Either you reduced the bit depth using the Indexed Color command as I directed previously or you didn't. There's no sense in changing the colors during the save process.

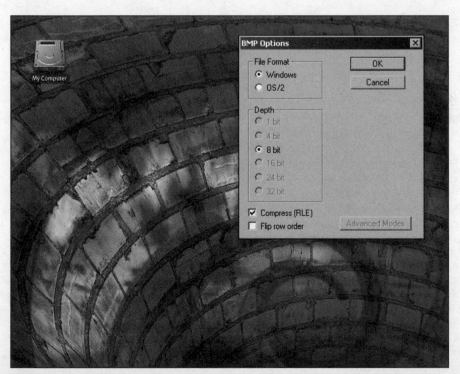

Figure 3-13: Select the options shown here when saving a BMP image for use as a desktop background. Leave the Depth setting alone.

To load the wallpaper onto your PC desktop, right-click anywhere on the desktop and choose the Properties command. This brings up the Display Properties dialog box shown in Figure 3-14. Click the Browse button and locate your BMP image on disk. Then click the Apply button to see how it looks.

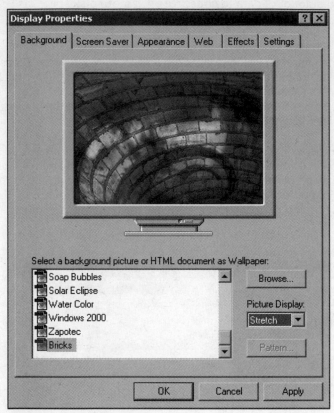

Figure 3-14: You can load a BMP file as desktop wallpaper using the Display Properties control panel provided with Windows 95 and later.

CompuServe's GIF

In the old days, the CompuServe online service championed GIF (short for *Graphics Interchange Format*) as a means of compressing files so you could quickly transfer photographs over your modem. Like TIFF, GIF uses LZW compression, but unlike TIFF, GIF is limited to just 256 colors.

With the advent of the World Wide Web, the GIF format has grown slightly more sophisticated. You can save an image with or without transparency by choosing File ⇨ Save and choosing CompuServe GIF from the Format pop-up menu. When you index (reduce) the image to 256 colors — which you can do either before or during the file save process — select the Transparency check box in the Indexed Color dialog box if you want any areas of the image that are transparent to remain transparent when you view the image file in a Web browser.

PC Paintbrush's PCX

PCX doesn't stand for anything. Rather, it's the extension PC Paintbrush assigns to images saved in its native file format. Although the format is losing favor, many PCX images are still in use today, largely because PC Paintbrush is the oldest painting program for DOS. Photoshop supports PCX images with up to 16 million colors. You can find an enormous amount of art, usually clip art, in this format. However, don't save files to PCX unless a client specifically demands it. Other formats are better.

Adobe's paperless PDF

The *Portable Document Format* (PDF) is a variation on the PostScript printing language that enables you to view electronically produced documents on screen. This means you can create a publication in QuarkXPress or PageMaker, export it to PDF, and distribute it without worrying about color separations, binding, and other printing costs. Using a program called Adobe Acrobat, you can open PDF documents, zoom in and out of them, and follow hypertext links by clicking highlighted words. Adobe distributes Mac, Windows, and UNIX versions of the Acrobat Reader for free, so almost anyone with a computer can view your stuff in full, natural color.

PDF files come in two flavors: those that contain just a single image and those that contain multiple pages and images. Photoshop can save only single-image PDF files, but it can open multipage files. The program rasterizes both types of files when it opens them.

You open PDF files in different ways depending on what elements of the file you want to access:

✦ Use File ⇨ Open to open a particular page in a multipage PDF file. After selecting the page you want to view, you can set the image size and resolution of the rasterized file. You also can choose File ⇨ Place to add a page as a new layer to an open image; in this case, you can't control size and resolution before adding the page. However, you can scale the page after the fact as you can any layer.

✦ Choose File ⇨ Import ⇨ PDF Image to bring up a dialog box that enables you to open a particular image in the PDF file.

✦ Choose File ⇨ Automate ⇨ Multi-Page PDF to PSD to turn each page in the PDF file into a separate Photoshop image file.

The real question, however, is why would you *want* to open or place a PDF file in Photoshop instead of viewing it in Acrobat, which provides you with a full range of document viewing tools not found in Photoshop? Furthermore, because you can save only single-page PDF files, why on earth would you save to PDF in Photoshop?

I can think of two scenarios where Photoshop's PDF functions may come in handy:

✦ You want to see how images in a PDF document will look when printed on a high-resolution printer. Open the PDF file using File ➪ Open, set the resolution to match that of the output device, and eyeball those images on screen. This "soft-proofing" technique enables you to spot defects that may not be noticeable in draft proofs that you output on a low-res printer.

✦ You need a convenient way to distribute images for approval or input. You can save an image as a PDF file and send it to clients and colleagues, who can view the image in Acrobat if they don't have Photoshop. You can even add text or voice annotations to your PDF file. In addition to annotations, Photoshop PDF supports layers, transparency, embedded color profiles, spot colors, duotones, and more. This enables you to route an image for approval without having to flatten the image or otherwise strip it of its Photoshop features. Of course, features not supported by Acrobat aren't accessible to the viewer.

When you save to PDF in Photoshop, you have a choice of two encoding options, as shown in Figure 3-15. Choose ZIP only for images that feature large expanses of a single color; otherwise, opt for JPEG. Keep the Quality option set to Maximum to maintain the best print quality, just as you do for regular JPEG files.

If you select JPEG encoding, you need a PostScript Level 2 or later printer to output your PDF file. Also be aware that separating files into individual plates can be problematic.

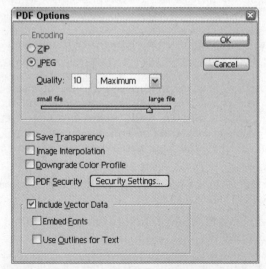

Figure 3-15: Photoshop 7 offers some new features in the PDF Options dialog box.

When saving to PDF, you also encounter several other options:

✦ **Save Transparency:** If your image has transparency and you're saving it as a PDF without layers, the Save Transparency check box determines whether or not the transparency will be maintained.

✦ **Image Interpolation:** Selecting this option enables other programs to interpolate the image when resampling to another size.

✦ **Downgrade Color Profile:** Here's an option you'll probably never use. PDF doesn't support Version 4 ICC profiles. Selecting this check box converts them to Version 2 profiles so that they'll work in PDF. The thing is, you probably don't have a Version 4 ICC profile anyway, in which case this option is grayed out. For more on ICC profiles, see Chapter 16.

✦ **PDF Security:** This option allows you to assign passwords to PDF documents — if the user doesn't know the password, she can't open the document. To set the security information, select the PDF Security check box and click the Security Settings button. You can set the user password here, along with a master password, which can prevent others from changing the user password. The Encryption Level options only take effect when the document is being opened with Adobe Acrobat; you can choose the version of Acrobat and determine whether options such as saving changes and printing are allowed.

✦ **Include Vector Data and Embed Fonts:** Select these two check boxes to retain any vector graphics and font data, respectively. Alternatively, you can select Use Outlines for Text to save text as character outlines that are editable in the PDF file.

Apple's PICT

PICT (*Macintosh Picture*) is the native graphics format for Mac OS 9. (Mac OS X has adopted PDF as its standard graphics file format.) Based on the QuickDraw display language that the system software uses to convey images on screen, PICT handles object-oriented artwork and bitmapped images with equal aplomb. It supports images in any bit depth, size, or resolution. PICT even supports 32-bit images, so that you can save a fourth masking channel when working in the RGB mode.

If you've installed QuickTime on the Mac, you can subject PICT images to JPEG compression. But while PICT's compression options may look similar to JPEG's, they are actually significantly inferior. The differences become especially noticeable if you open an image, make a change, and again save it to disk, effectively reapplying the compression.

In most cases, you'll want to use the JPEG format instead of PICT when compressing images. JPEG images are compatible with the Web; PICT images are not. Also, more Windows applications recognize JPEG than PICT, and it's extremely difficult to find a Windows program that can handle PICT files with QuickTime compression.

In fact, the only reason to use PICT is low-end compatibility. If you're trying to save an image in a format that your mom can open on her Mac, for example, PICT may be a better choice than JPEG. Heck, you can open PICT files inside a word processor, including everything from SimpleText to Microsoft Word. Just be sure mom has QuickTime loaded on her machine.

When you save a PICT image, Photoshop also lets you set the bit depth. You should always stick with the default option, which is the highest setting available for the particular image. Don't mess around with these options; they apply automatic pattern dithering, which is a bad thing.

If you're using a PC, you may need to open a PICT file a Mac friend sends you. Photoshop can do this, but one thing may trip you up: On the Mac, you have the option of saving PICT files with a variety of JPEG compressions supplied by Apple's QuickTime. Unless you have QuickTime installed on your PC — which you might if you do a lot of surfing on the Web — you won't be able to open compressed PICT images.

PICT resource #1, the startup screen

PICT resources are images contained in the resource fork of a Mac file in OS 9. (Windows programs can't recognize resource forks, so this and the following section are only relevant to Mac folks.) The only reason to save a PICT resource is to create an OS 9 startup screen, and the most likely reason to open one is to extract images from the Scrapbook.

The startup screen is that message that welcomes you to the great big wonderful Macintosh experience when you boot your computer. If you like to customize your system, you can create your own startup screen by saving an image in the PICT Resource file format under the name StartupScreen in the root directory of your System Folder.

PICT resource #2, the Scrapbook

To open a PICT resource other than the startup screen file, you bypass the Open command in favor of File ➪ Import ➪ PICT Resource. This command lets you open an application or other non-image file on disk and browse through any PICT resources it may contain.

The best use of File ➪ Import ➪ PICT Resource is to open images directly from the Scrapbook in OS 9. In fact, this function becomes phenomenally practical if you use a commercial or shareware screen-capture utility (such as Mainstay's Capture) that can store screen shots in the Scrapbook. You can process your screen shots en masse at your leisure.

Pixar workstations

Pixar has created some of the most memorable computer-animated short films and features in recent memory. From the desk lamps playing with a beach ball in *Luxo, Jr.,* to the artistic triumphs that were *Toy Story* and *Monsters, Inc.*, Pixar continues to blaze a trail in this spectacular new art form.

Pixar works its 3D magic using mondo-expensive workstations. Photoshop enables you to open a still image created on a Pixar machine or to save an image to the Pixar format so you can integrate it into a 3D rendering. The Pixar format supports grayscale and RGB images.

PNG for the Web

Pronounced *ping*, the PNG format enables you to save 16 million color images without compression for use on the Web. While PNG has been generally supported by Netscape Navigator and Microsoft Internet Explorer since 1997, these main two browsers still can't be counted to fully support all the features of PNG. Couple that info with the obvious fact that you can't count on the general public to have any-where near the most recent version of any software application, and using PNG begins to seem like a dicey proposition. It's a great format, though, offering full-color images without the pesky visual compression artifacts you get with JPEG. As time passes, I believe that PNG will one day be a big player.

Scitex image-processors

Some high-end commercial printers use Scitex printing devices to generate color separations of images and other documents. Photoshop can open images digitized with Scitex scanners and save the edited images to the *Scitex CT* (*Continuous Tone*) format. Because you need special hardware to transfer images from the PC to a Scitex drive, you'll probably want to consult with your local Scitex service bureau technician before saving to the CT format. The technician may prefer that you sub-mit images in the native Photoshop, TIFF, or JPEG format. The Scitex CT format supports grayscale, RGB, and CMYK images.

TrueVision's TGA

TrueVision's Targa and NuVista video boards enable you to overlay computer graphics and animation onto live video. The effect is called *chroma keying* because, typically, a key color is set aside to let the live video show through. TrueVision designed the TGA (*Targa*) format to support 32-bit images that include 8-bit alpha channels capable of displaying the live video. Support for TGA is widely imple-mented among professional-level color and video applications on the PC.

Interapplication formats

In the name of interapplication harmony, Photoshop supports a few software-spe-cific formats that permit you to trade files with popular object-oriented programs, such as Illustrator and QuarkXPress. Every one of these formats is a variation on EPS (*Encapsulated PostScript*), which is based in turn on Adobe's industry-standard PostScript printing language.

Rasterizing an Illustrator or FreeHand file

Photoshop supports object-oriented files saved in the EPS format. EPS is specifically designed to save object-oriented graphics that you intend to print to a PostScript output device. Just about every drawing and page-layout program on the planet (and a few on Mars) can save EPS documents.

Prior to Version 4, Photoshop could interpret only a small subset of EPS operations supported by Illustrator (including the native *.ai* format). But then Photoshop 4 came along and offered a full-blown EPS translation engine, capable of interpreting EPS illustrations created in FreeHand, CorelDraw, Deneba's Canvas, and more. You can even open EPS drawings that contain imported images, something else Version 3 could not do.

When you open an EPS or native Illustrator document, Photoshop *rasterizes* (or *renders*) the artwork — that is, it converts the artwork from a collection of objects to a bitmapped image. During the open operation, Photoshop presents the Rasterize Generic EPS Format dialog box (see Figure 3-16), which enables you to specify the size and resolution of the image, just as you can in the New dialog box. Assuming the illustration contains no imported images, you can render it as large or as small as you want without any loss of image quality.

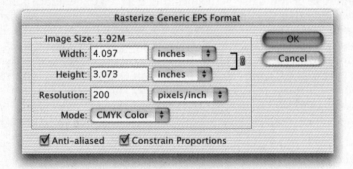

Figure 3-16: You can specify the size and resolution at which Photoshop renders an EPS illustration.

Tip If the EPS illustration does contain an imported image or two, you need to know the resolution of the images and factor this information into the Rasterize Generic EPS Format dialog box. Select anything but Pixels from both the Width and Height pop-up menus and leave the suggested values unchanged. Then enter the setting for the highest-resolution imported image into the Resolution option box. (If all the images are low-res, you may want to double or triple the Resolution value to ensure that the objects render smoothly.)

You should always select the Anti-aliased check box unless you're rendering a very large image — say, 300 ppi or higher. *Antialiasing* blurs pixels to soften the edges of the objects so they don't appear jagged. When you're rendering a very large image, the difference between image and printer resolution is less noticeable, so antialiasing is unwarranted.

Photoshop renders the illustration to a single layer against a transparent background. Before you can save the rasterized image to a format other than native Photoshop, you must eliminate the transparency by choosing Layer ⇨ Flatten Image. Or save a flattened version of the image to a separate file by choosing the As a Copy option in the Save dialog box.

Rendering an EPS illustration is an extremely useful technique for resolving printing problems. If you regularly work in Illustrator or FreeHand, you no doubt have encountered *limitcheck errors*, which occur when an illustration is too complex for an imagesetter or other high-end output device to print. If you're frustrated with the printer and tired of wasting your evening trying to figure out what's wrong (sound familiar?), use Photoshop to render the illustration at 300 ppi and print it. Nine times out of ten, this technique works flawlessly.

If Photoshop can't *parse* the EPS file — a techy way of saying Photoshop can't break down the individual objects — it attempts to open the PICT (Mac) or TIFF (Windows) preview. This exercise is usually futile, but occasionally you may wish to take a quick look at an illustration to, say, match the placement of elements in an image to those in the drawing.

Placing an EPS illustration

If you want to introduce an EPS graphic into the foreground image rather than to render it into a new image window of its own, choose File ⇨ Place. Unlike other File menu commands, Place supports only EPS illustrations and PDF files.

After you import the EPS graphic, it appears inside a box — which Photoshop calls a *bounding box* — with a great big X across it. You can move, scale, and rotate the illustration into position before rasterizing it to pixels. Drag a corner handle to resize the image; drag outside the image to rotate it. You can also nudge the graphic into position by pressing the arrow keys. When everything is the way you want it, press Enter (or Return on the Mac) or double-click inside the box to rasterize the illustration. If the placement isn't perfect, not to worry. The graphic appears on a separate layer, so you can move it with complete freedom. To cancel the Place operation, press Escape instead of Enter or Return.

Saving an EPS image

When preparing an image for placement inside a drawing or page-layout document that will be printed to a PostScript output device, many artists prefer to save the image in the EPS format. Converting the image to PostScript up front prevents the drawing or page-layout program from doing the work. The result is an image that prints more quickly and with less chance of problems. (Note that an image does not *look* any different when saved in EPS. The idea that the EPS format somehow blesses an image with better resolution is pure nonsense.)

A second point in the EPS format's favor is clipping paths. As explained graphically at the end of Chapter 8, a clipping path defines a free-form boundary around an image. When you place the image into an object-oriented program, everything outside the clipping path becomes transparent. While some programs — notably InDesign and PageMaker — recognize clipping paths saved with a TIFF image, many programs acknowledge a clipping path only when saved in the EPS format.

Third, although Illustrator has remedied the problems it had importing TIFF images, it still likes EPS best, especially where screen display is concerned. Thanks to the EPS file's fixed preview, Illustrator can display an EPS image on screen very quickly compared with other file formats. And Illustrator can display an EPS image both in the preview mode and in the super-fast artwork mode.

So if you want to import an image into Illustrator, QuarkXPress, or another object-oriented program, your best bet is EPS. On the downside, EPS is an inefficient format for saving images thanks to the laborious way that it describes pixels. An EPS image may be three to four times larger than the same image saved to the TIFF format with LZW compression. But this is the price we pay for reliable printing.

Caution

Absolutely avoid the EPS format if you plan on printing your final pages to a non-PostScript printer. This defeats the entire purpose of EPS, which is meant to avoid printing problems, not cause them. When printing without PostScript, use TIFF or JPEG.

To save an image in the EPS format, choose Photoshop EPS from the Format pop-up menu in the Save dialog box. After you press Enter or Return, Photoshop displays the dialog box shown in Figure 3-17. The options in this dialog box work as follows:

✦ **Preview:** Technically, an EPS document comprises two parts: a pure PostScript-language description of the graphic for the printer and a bitmapped preview so you can see the graphic on screen. On a PC, select the TIFF (8 bits/pixel) option from the Preview pop-up menu to save a 256-color TIFF preview of the image. On a Mac, select the Macintosh (8 bits/pixel) option from the Preview pop-up menu to save a 256-color PICT preview of the image. Or select the Macintosh (JPEG) option for a 24-bit preview (which in most cases takes up less room on disk, thanks to the JPEG compression). If you plan on passing off the image to a Windows colleague, select TIFF (8 Bits/Pixel). The 1-bit option provides a black-and-white preview only, which is useful if you want to save a little room on disk. Select None to include no preview and save even more disk space.

✦ **Encoding:** If you're saving an image for import into Illustrator, QuarkXPress, or some other established program, select the Binary encoding option (also known as *Huffman encoding*), which compresses an EPS document by substituting shorter codes for frequently used characters. The letter *a*, for example, receives the 3-bit code 010, rather than its standard 8-bit ASCII code, 01100001 (the binary equivalent of what we humans call 97).

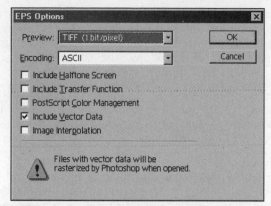

Figure 3-17: When you save an image in the EPS format, you can specify the type of preview and tack on some printing attributes.

Sadly, some programs and printers don't recognize Huffman encoding, in which case you must select the less efficient ASCII option. ASCII stands for *American Standard Code for Information Interchange*, which is fancy jargon for text-only. In other words, you can open and edit an ASCII EPS document in a word processor, provided you know how to read and write PostScript.

Tip

Actually, this can be a useful technique if you have a Mac file that won't open on a PC, especially if the file was sent to you electronically. Chances are that a Mac-specific header got into the works. Open the file in a word processor and look at the beginning. You should see the four characters *%!PS*. Anything that comes before this line is the Macintosh header. Delete the garbage before *%!PS*, save the file in text format, and try again to open the file in Photoshop.

Caution

The remaining Encoding options are JPEG settings. JPEG compression not only results in smaller files on disk but also degrades the quality of the image. Select JPEG (Maximum Quality) to invoke the least degradation. Better yet, avoid the JPEG settings altogether. These options work only if you plan to print your final artwork to a PostScript Level 2 or Level 3 device. Earlier PostScript printers do not support EPS artwork with JPEG compression and will choke on the code.

So to recap, ASCII results in really big files that work with virtually any printer or application. Binary creates smaller files that work with most mainstream applications but may choke some older-model printers. And the JPEG settings are compatible exclusively with Level 2 and later PostScript printers.

✦ **Include Halftone Screen:** Another advantage of EPS over other formats is that it can retain printing attributes. If you specified a custom halftone screen using the Screens button inside the Page Setup dialog box, you can save this setting with the EPS document by selecting the Include Halftone Screen check box. But be careful — you can just as easily ruin your image as help it. Read Chapter 18 before you select this check box.

✦ **Include Transfer Function:** As described in Chapter 18, you can change the brightness and contrast of a printed image using the Transfer button inside the Page Setup dialog box. To save these settings with the EPS document, select the Include Transfer Function check box. Again, this option can be dangerous when used casually. See Chapter 18 for more details.

✦ **PostScript Color Management:** Like JPEG compression, this check box is compatible with Level 2 and 3 printers only. It embeds a color profile, which helps the printer to massage the image during the printing cycle to generate more accurate colors. Unless you plan on printing to a Level 2 or later device, leave the option off. (For more information about color profiles, read Chapter 16.)

✦ **Include Vector Data:** Select this option if your file contains vector objects, including shapes, non-bitmap type, and layer clipping paths. Otherwise, Photoshop rasterizes the objects during the save process. When you select the option, Photoshop displays a warning in the dialog box to remind you that if you reopen the file in Photoshop, you rasterize any vector objects that you saved with the file.

✦ **Transparent Whites:** When saving bitmap mode images as EPS files in Photoshop, the four check boxes previously discussed drop away, replaced by Transparent Whites. Select this option to make all white pixels in the image transparent.

Although Photoshop EPS is the only format that offers the Transparent Whites option, many programs — including Illustrator and InDesign — treat white pixels in black-and-white TIFF images as transparent as well.

✦ **Image Interpolation:** Turn on this option if you want another program to be able to interpolate the image when resampling it to another size. For example, suppose you import an EPS image into InDesign and scale it to 400 percent. If Image Interpolation is turned off, then InDesign just makes pixels in the image four times larger, as if you had used the nearest neighbor interpolation inside Photoshop. If you turn Image Interpolation on, however, InDesign applies bicubic interpolation in order to generate new pixels. (For details on nearest neighbor and bicubic interpolation, see the "General preferences" section in Chapter 2.) Unless you have a reason for doing otherwise, turn this option on.

QuarkXPress DCS

Quark developed a variation on the EPS format called Desktop Color Separation (DCS). When you work in QuarkXPress, PageMaker, and other programs that support the format, DCS facilitates the printing of color separations. Before you can use DCS, you have to convert your image to the CMYK color space using Image ⇨ Mode ⇨ CMYK Color. (DCS 2.0 also supports grayscale images with spot-color channels.) Then bring up the Save dialog box and select Photoshop DCS 1.0 or 2.0 from the Format pop-up menu.

Photoshop 5 introduced support for DCS 2.0 to accommodate images that contain extra spot-color channels, as explained in Chapter 18. If you add a Pantone channel to an image, DCS 2.0 is the only PostScript format you can use. If your image doesn't contain any extra channels beyond the basic four required for CMYK, DCS 1.0 is the safer and simpler option.

After you press Enter or Return, Photoshop displays an additional pop-up menu of DCS options, which vary depending on whether you've selected DCS 1.0 or 2.0, as shown in Figure 3-18. The DCS 1.0 format invariably saves a total of five files: one master document (which is the file that you import into QuarkXPress) plus one file each for the cyan, magenta, yellow, and black color channels (which are the files that get printed). The DCS 2.0 format can be expressed as a single file (tidier) or five separate files (better compatibility).

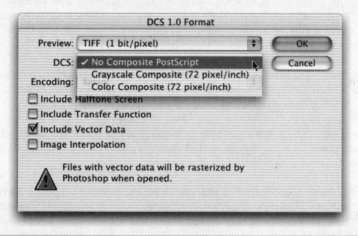

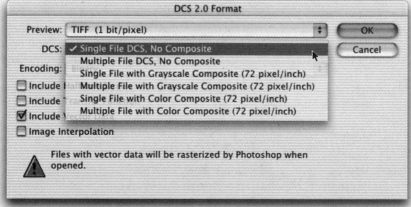

Figure 3-18: The extra options for the DCS 1.0 format (top) and those for the DCS 2.0 format (bottom).

Either way, the DCS pop-up menu gives you the option of saving a 72-ppi PostScript composite of the image inside the master document. Independent from the bitmapped preview—which you specify as usual by selecting a Preview option—the PostScript composite makes it possible to print a low-resolution version of a DCS image to a consumer-quality printer. If you're using a black-and-white printer, select the 72 pixel/inch grayscale option; if you're using a color printer, select the final option. Be forewarned, however, that the composite image significantly increases the size of the master document on disk. The two options at the bottom of the options dialog boxes for DCS 1.0 and 2.0, Include Vector Data and Image Interpolation, work just as described earlier for the Photoshop EPS format.

Premiere Filmstrip

Adobe Premiere is a popular QuickTime movie-editing application for both Macs and PCs. The program is a wonder when it comes to fades, frame merges, and special effects, but it offers no frame-by-frame editing capabilities. For example, you can neither draw a mustache on a person in the movie nor can you make brightly colored brush strokes swirl about in the background—at least, not inside Premiere.

You can export the movie to the Filmstrip format, though, which is a file-swapping option exclusive to Photoshop and Premiere. A Filmstrip document organizes frames in a long vertical strip, as shown on the left side of Figure 3-19. The right side of the figure shows the movie after I edited each individual frame in ways not permitted by Premiere. A boring movie of a cat stuck in a bag becomes an exciting movie of a cat-stuck-in-a-bag flying. If that doesn't sum up the miracle of digital imaging, I don't know what does.

A gray bar separates each frame. The number of each frame appears on the right; the SMPTE (Society of Motion Picture and Television Engineers) time code appears on the left. The structure of the three-number time code is minutes:seconds:frames, with 30 frames per second.

If you change the size of a Filmstrip document inside Photoshop in any way, you cannot save the image back to the Filmstrip format. Feel free to paint and apply effects, but stay the heck away from the Image Size and Canvas Size commands.

I don't really delve into the Filmstrip format anywhere else in this book, so I want to pass along a few quick Filmstrip tips right here and now:

✦ First, you can scroll up and down exactly one frame at a time by pressing Shift+Page Up or Shift+Page Down, respectively.

✦ Second, you can move a selection exactly one frame up or down by pressing Ctrl+Shift+up arrow (⌘-Shift-up arrow on the Mac) or Ctrl+Shift+down arrow (⌘-Shift-down arrow on the Mac).

✦ If you want to clone the selection as you move it, press Ctrl+Shift+Alt+up arrow (⌘-Shift-Option-up arrow on the Mac) or Ctrl+Shift+Alt+down arrow (⌘-Shift-Option-down arrow on the Mac).

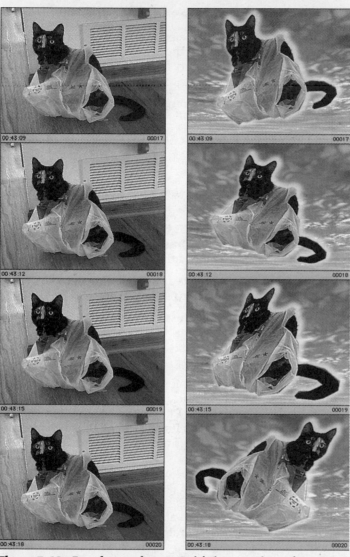

Figure 3-19: Four frames from a QuickTime movie as they appear in the Filmstrip format before (left) and after (right) editing the frames in Photoshop.

And finally—here's the great one—you can select several sequential frames and edit them simultaneously by following these steps:

STEPS: Selecting Sequential Frames in a Movie

1. **Select the first frame you want to edit.** Select the rectangular marquee tool by pressing the M key. Then drag around the area you want to edit in the movie. (This is the only step that takes any degree of care or coordination whatsoever.)

2. **Switch to the quick mask mode by pressing the Q key.** The areas around the selected frame are overlaid with pink.

3. **Set the magic wand Tolerance value to 0.** Select the magic wand tool. Then, in the Options bar, enter 0 for the Tolerance value and deselect the Anti-aliased check box.

4. **Click inside the selected frame (the one that's not pink) with the magic wand tool.** This selects the unmasked area inside the frame.

5. **Press Ctrl+Shift+Alt+down arrow (⌘-Shift-Option-down arrow on the Mac) to clone the unmasked area to the next frame in the movie.** When you exit the quick mask mode, both this frame and the one above it will be selected.

6. **Repeat several times.** Keep Ctrl+Shift+Alt+down arrowing until you're rid of the pink stuff on all the frames you want to select.

7. **Exit the quick mask mode by pressing the Q key again.** All frames appear selected.

8. **Edit the frames to your heart's content.**

Cross-Reference

If you're new to Photoshop, half of these steps, if not all of them, probably sailed over your head like so many low-flying cats stuck in bags. If you want to learn more about selections and cloning, see Chapter 8. In Chapter 9, I explore the quick mask mode and other masking techniques. After you finish reading those chapters, return to this section to see if it doesn't make a little more sense. Or don't. It's entirely up to you.

The process of editing individual frames as just described is sometimes called *rotoscoping*, named after the traditional technique of using live-action film as a source when creating animated sequences. You also can try out some scratch-and-doodle techniques, which is where an artist scratches and draws directly on frames of film. If this isn't enough, you can emulate *xerography,* in which an animator makes Xerox copies of photographs, enhances the copies using markers or whatever else is convenient, and shoots the finished artwork, frame by frame, on film. In a nutshell, Photoshop extends Premiere's functionality by adding animation to its standard supply of video-editing capabilities.

You can save an image in the Filmstrip format through the Save dialog box. But remember, you can save in this format only if you opened the image as a Filmstrip document and did not change the size of the image.

The mainstream formats

The formats discussed so far are mighty interesting and they all fulfill their own niche purposes. But two formats — JPEG and TIFF — are the all-stars of digital imagery. You'll use these formats the most because of their outstanding compression capabilities and almost universal support among graphics applications.

JPEG

The JPEG format is named after the folks who designed it, the Joint Photographic Experts Group. JPEG is the most efficient and essential compression format currently available and is likely to be the compression standard for years to come. JPEG is a lossy compression scheme, which means it sacrifices image quality to conserve space on disk. You can control how much data is lost during the save operation, however.

When you save an image in the JPEG format, you're greeted with the JPEG Options dialog box (see Figure 3-20). The most vital option in this dialog box is the Quality setting, which determines how much compression Photoshop applies to your image.

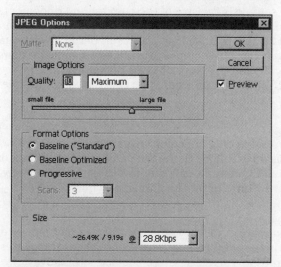

Figure 3-20: The JPEG Options dialog box provides a total of 13 compression settings, ranging from 0 (heaviest compression) to 12 (best quality).

Select an option from the Quality pop-up menu or drag the slider triangle from 0 to 12 to specify the quality setting. Of the named options, Low takes the least space on disk, but distorts the image rather severely; Maximum retains the highest amount of image quality, but consumes more disk space. Of the numbered options, 0 is the most severe compressor and 12 does the least damage.

JPEG evaluates an image in 8×8-pixel blocks, using a technique called *Adaptive Discrete Cosine Transform* (or ADCT, as in "Yes, I'm an acronym ADCT"). It averages the 24-bit value of every pixel in the block (or 8-bit value of every pixel in the case of a grayscale image). ADCT then stores the average color in the upper-left pixel in the block and assigns the remaining 63 pixels smaller values relative to the average.

Next, JPEG divides the block by an 8×8 block of its own called the *quantization matrix*, which homogenizes the pixels' values by changing as many as possible to zero. This process saves the majority of disk space, but loses data. When Photoshop opens a JPEG image, it can't recover the original distinction between the zero pixels, so the pixels become the same, or similar, colors. Finally, JPEG applies lossless Huffman encoding to translate repeating values to a single symbol.

In most instances, I recommend you use JPEG only at the Maximum Quality setting (10 or higher), at least until you gain some experience with it. The smallest amount of JPEG compression saves more space on disk than any non-JPEG compression format and still retains the most essential detail from the original image. Figure 3-21 shows a grayscale image saved at each of the four compression settings.

The samples are arranged from highest image quality (top) to lowest quality (bottom). At the top left of each sample is the size of the compressed document on disk. Saved in the only moderately compressed native Photoshop format, the image consumes 8.92MB on disk. From 8.92MB to 1.34MB — the result of the lowest-quality JPEG setting — is a remarkable savings, but it comes at a price of significant compression artifacts. The effect, incidentally, is more obvious on screen. Believe me, after you familiarize yourself with JPEG compression, you can spot other people's overly compressed JPEG images a mile away. This isn't something you want to exaggerate in your images.

To see the impact of JPEG compression on a full-color image, check out Color Plate 3-1. The original image consumes 9.45MB in the native Photoshop format, but 4.08MB when compressed at the JPEG module's Maximum setting. To demonstrate the differences between different settings better, I enlarged one portion of the image and oversharpened another.

JPEG is a *cumulative compression scheme*, meaning that Photoshop recompresses an image every time you save it in the JPEG format. There's no disadvantage to saving an image to disk repeatedly during a single session, because JPEG always works from the on-screen version. But if you close an image, reopen it, and save it in the JPEG format, you inflict a small amount of damage. Use JPEG sparingly. In the best of all possible worlds, you should save to the JPEG format only after you finish all work on an image. Even in a pinch, you should apply all filtering effects before saving to JPEG, because these have a habit of exacerbating imperfections in image quality.

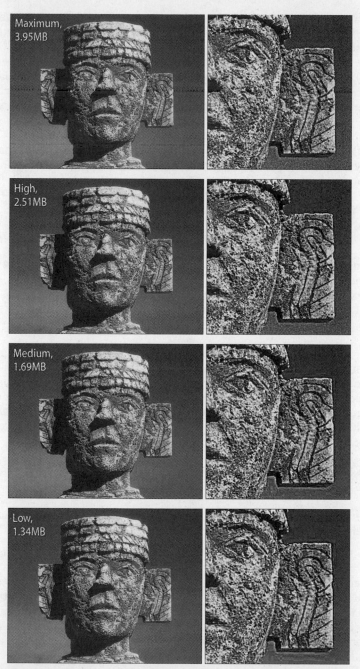

Figure 3-21: Four JPEG settings applied to a single image, with the highest image quality setting illustrated at the top and the lowest at the bottom.

JPEG is best used when compressing continuous-tone images (images in which the distinction between immediately neighboring pixels is slight). Any image that includes gradual color transitions, as in a photograph, qualifies for JPEG compression. JPEG is not the best choice for saving screen shots, line drawings (especially those converted from EPS graphics), and other high-contrast images. These are better served by GIF if you want to post them on the Web, or else by a lossless compression scheme, such as TIFF with LZW. The JPEG format is available when you are saving grayscale, RGB, and CMYK images.

Occupying the bottom half of the JPEG Options dialog box are three radio buttons, designed primarily to optimize JPEG images for the Web. If your image is destined for print, just select the first option, Baseline ("Standard"), and be done with it. For Web graphics, select Baseline Optimized to make images display on screen line-by-line or select the Progressive option to make images display in multiple passes.

TIFF

Developed by Aldus in the early days of the Mac to standardize an ever-growing population of scanned images, TIFF (*Tag Image File Format*) is the most widely supported image-printing format across both the Macintosh and PC platforms. Unlike EPS, it can't handle object-oriented artwork, but otherwise it's unrestricted. In fact, TIFF offers a few tricks of its own that make it very special.

In Photoshop, the TIFF format supports up to 24 channels, the maximum number permitted in any image. In fact, TIFF is the only format other than DCS 2.0, "raw," and the native Photoshop format that can save more than four channels. To save a TIFF file without extra mask channels, deselect the Alpha check box in the Save dialog box. (For an introduction to channels, read Chapter 16.) Even more impressive, TIFF supports multiple layers. If you want layers to remain independent when you save the file, you can select the Layers check box in the Save dialog box.

When you save an image as a TIFF file, Photoshop displays the TIFF Options dialog box (see Figure 3-22), which offers the following controls:

✦ **Compression:** You can choose between three different types of compression: LZW (Lempel-Ziv-Welch), ZIP, or JPEG. Here are the major differences:

  • **LZW:** Like Huffman encoding (previously described in the "Saving an EPS image" section), LZW digs into the computer code that describes an image and substitutes frequently used codes with shorter equivalents. But instead of substituting characters, as Huffman does, LZW substitutes strings of data. Because LZW doesn't so much as touch a pixel in your image, it's entirely lossless. Most image editors and desktop publishing applications — including Illustrator, FreeHand, InDesign, PageMaker, and QuarkXPress — import LZW-compressed TIFF images, but a few still have yet to catch on.

- **ZIP:** The problem with LZW (from a programming perspective) is that it's regulated by a patent. And whenever a bit of technology costs money to use, you can bet somebody out there is trying to come up with a free equivalent. Hence ZIP, a competing lossless compression scheme used in PDF documents. Why use it? Theoretically, it's a bit smarter than LZW and can on occasion deliver smaller image files. On the other hand, Photoshop is currently one of the few programs to support ZIP compression in a TIFF file. So unless you discover big savings when using ZIP, I'd stick with LZW until ZIP support becomes more widespread.

- **JPEG:** If two lossless compression schemes aren't enough options, the TIFF format also permits you to apply lossy JPEG compression. Long-time Photoshop users may balk at JPEG compression inside TIFF options. After all, one of the major benefits of TIFF is that it ensures optimum image quality; by applying JPEG compression, which results in loss of image data, you defeat the purpose. But now that TIFF supports layers, JPEG inside TIFF permits you a unique opportunity to cut the size of your layered image files in half. My experience shows that JPEG in TIFF results in only modest loss of data. And because the JPEG does not affect the transparency mask—which defines the outlines of the layers—the layers continue to exhibit nice, sharp edges.

Figure 3-22: Photoshop 7 offers a myriad of compression schemes for TIFF files.

If names such as Huffman, LZW, and ZIP ring a faint bell, it may be because these are the same compression schemes used by StuffIt, PKzip, WinZIP, and other file compression utilities. For this reason, using an additional utility to compress a TIFF image that you've already compressed using LZW, ZIP, or JPEG makes no sense. Neither do you want to compress a standard JPEG image, because JPEG takes advantage of Huffman encoding. You may shave off\ a few K, but this isn't enough space to make it worth your time and effort.

Also be aware that some programs may gag on compressed TIFF files, regardless of which compression scheme you apply. If an application balks at opening your Photoshop TIFF file, try resaving the file with no compression.

✦ **Byte Order:** Every once in a while, Photoshop chooses to name a straightforward option in the most confusing way possible. Byte Order is a prime example. No, this option doesn't have anything to do with how you eat your food. Instead, there are two variations of TIFF, one for the PC and the other for the Mac. I'm sure this has something to do with the arrangement of 8-bit chunks of data, but who cares? You want PC or you want Mac? It's that simple.

There may be a hermit somewhere who has a stone TIFF reader that baulks at this, but he probably can't run his 2 cycle per second wooden computer with Photoshop anyway!

✦ **Save Image Pyramid:** Choose this option to save *tiled* TIFF files. This variation of the standard TIFF file-saving algorithm divides your image into tiles and then stacks the tiles in a pyramid. Each level of the pyramid represents your image at a different resolution, with the highest-resolution version serving as the base of the pyramid. The idea is that an application can use the low-resolution tiles to perform certain image-processing tasks and dig down to the high-resolution version only when absolutely necessary. When you're working with very large image files, this approach not only speeds up certain editing tasks but also puts less strain on your computer's resources. (If you're familiar with the FlashPix format, the concept is the same.)

Unless you're saving your image for use in a program that you know supports tiled TIFF images, however, turn this option off. Photoshop itself can't take advantage of the tiled technology, and many applications can't open tiled images at all.

✦ **Save Transparency:** If the image contains transparent areas, select this check box to retain the transparency. Otherwise, transparent areas become white.

✦ **Layer Compression:** Not only can you decide whether you want to use lossless or lossy image compression, but Photoshop now lets you specify how you want to save the layers themselves. The choices speak for themselves; RLE saves faster but makes for bigger files, and the reverse is true for ZIP. Alternatively, you can choose to discard the layers altogether and save a flattened copy of your file.

If you've been working with Photoshop for a few years, you may be wondering what happened to the File ➪ Import ➪ QuickEdit command. This feature enabled you to open and edit just a small portion of a large TIFF file. QuickEdit can't deal with compressed TIFF files or properly process edits that you make to a layered TIFF file. So Adobe no longer provides QuickEdit on the Photoshop CD and strongly advises against using it to edit Photoshop TIFF files.

The oddball formats

Can you believe it? After plowing through a half-million formats, I still haven't covered them all. The last three are the odd men out. One format has a purpose so specific that Photoshop can open files saved in the format but it can't save to the format. One is less a format than a manual can opener that may come in handy for jimmying open a file from an unknown source. And the last one is the new kid on the block, signaling Photoshop's acknowledgment of the Wireless Age.

Photo CD YCC images

Photoshop can open Eastman Kodak's Photo CD and Pro Photo CD formats directly. A Photo CD contains compressed versions of every image in each of the five scan sizes provided on Photo CDs — from 128×192 pixels (72K) to 2,048×3,072 pixels (18MB).

The Pro Photo CD format can accommodate each of the five sizes included in the regular Photo CD format, plus one additional size — 4,096×6,144 pixels (72MB) — that's four times as large as the largest image on a regular Photo CD. As a result, Pro Photo CDs hold only 25 scans; standard Photo CDs hold 100. Like their standard Photo CD counterparts, Pro Photo CD scanners can accommodate 35mm film and slides. But they can also handle 70mm film and 4×5-inch negatives and transparencies. The cost might knock you out, though. While scanning an image to a standard Photo CD costs between $1 and $2, scanning it to a Pro Photo CD costs about $10. This goes to show you, as soon as you gravitate beyond consumerland, everyone expects you to start coughing up the big bucks.

Both Photo CD and Pro Photo CD use the YCC color model, a variation on the CIE (Commission Internationale d'Eclairage) color space, which I discuss in the next chapter. YCC provides a broader range of color — theoretically, every color your eye can see. By opening Photo CD files directly, you can translate the YCC images directly to Photoshop's Lab color mode, another variation on the CIE color space that ensures no color loss. When you open a Photo CD image, Photoshop displays the dialog box shown in Figure 3-23.

 Finding your photos on a Photo CD is a little harder than it should be. Look inside the Images folder in the Photo_CD folder. The files have friendly names, such as *Img0017.pcd*.

Figure 3-23: Use these options to select a resolution and to calibrate the colors in the Photo CD image.

The Photo CD dialog box is divided into three main sections: Image Info, Source Image, and Destination Image. The Image Info section simply tells you the type of film on which the image was shot and the type of scanner used to scan the image to CD. Selections that you make in the Source and Destination areas tell Photoshop how you want it to open the image. Here's what you need to know:

✦ **Pixel Size:** Select which of the available image sizes you want to use from this pop-up menu.

✦ **Profile:** Use this pop-up menu to select the kind of film from which the original photographs were scanned. You can select from one of the variations on Kodak's film brands — E-6 for Ektachrome or K-14 for Kodachrome — or settle for the generic Color Negative V3.0 Film option. Your selection determines the method Photoshop uses to transform the colors in the image.

✦ **Resolution:** This setting determines the output resolution and size at which Photoshop opens the image. You get the same number of image pixels no matter what — that's controlled by the Pixel Size option. In other words, changing this value is no different than changing the Resolution value in the Image Size dialog box with Resample Image turned off.

✦ **Color Space:** Select an option from this pop-up menu to specify the color model you want to use. Select RGB to open the image in the RGB mode; select LAB to open the image in the Lab mode. You can also select from 8 Bits/Channel to edit the image in 24-bit color or 16 Bits/Channel to open the image in 48-bit color.

✦ **Orientation:** The preview in the left side of the dialog box shows you the original orientation of the image. If you want to change that orientation, click the other Orientation radio button. The preview updates to show you the new orientation.

Photoshop cannot save to the Photo CD format. And frankly, there's little reason you'd want to do so. Photo CD is strictly a means for transferring slides and film negatives onto the world's most ubiquitous and indestructible storage medium, the CD-ROM.

Note

Kodak also offers a product called Picture CD, which is quite different from Photo CD — don't get the two confused. With Picture CD, consumers can drop off rolls of undeveloped film and receive both traditional prints and a CD containing scanned versions of their pictures. Picture CD images are provided in the JPEG format, so none of the Photo CD file-opening features discussed here apply. You open Picture CD images like any other JPEG file.

Opening raw documents

A *raw document* is a plain binary file stripped of all extraneous information. It contains no compression scheme, specifies no bit depth or image size, and offers no color mode. Each byte of data indicates a brightness value on a single color channel, and that's it. Photoshop offers this function specifically so you can open images created in undocumented formats, such as those created on mainframe computers.

To open an image of unknown origin on a PC, choose File ➪ Open As. On a Mac, choose File ➪ Open and select All Documents from the Show pop-up menu. Then select the desired image from the scrolling list and choose Raw (*.raw*) from the Open As pop-up menu (or Format pop-up menu on the Mac). After you press Enter or Return, the dialog box shown in Figure 3-24 appears, featuring these options:

✦ **Width, Height:** If you know the dimensions of the image in pixels, enter the values in these option boxes.

✦ **Swap:** Click this button to swap the Width value with the Height value.

✦ **Count:** Enter the number of color channels in this option box. If the document is an RGB image, enter 3; if it is a CMYK image, enter 4.

✦ **Interleaved:** Select this value if the color values are stored sequentially by pixels. In an RGB image, the first byte represents the red value for the first pixel, the second byte represents the green value for that pixel, the third the blue value, and so on. If you turn this check box off, the first byte represents the red value for the first pixel, the second value represents the red value for the second pixel, and so on. When Photoshop finishes describing the red channel, it describes the green channel and then the blue channel.

✦ **Depth:** Select the number of bits per color channel. Most images contain 8 bits per channel, but scientific scans from mainframe computers may contain 16.

✦ **Byte Order:** If you specify 16 bits per channel, you must tell Photoshop whether the image comes from a Mac or a PC.

✦ **Header:** This value tells Photoshop how many bytes of data at the beginning of the file comprise header information it can ignore.

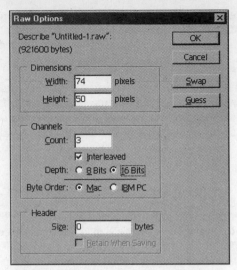

Figure 3-24: Photoshop requires you to specify the size of an image and the number of color channels when you open an image that does not conform to a standardized file format.

✦ **Retain When Saving:** If the Header value is greater than zero, you can instruct Photoshop to retain this data when you save the image in a different format.

✦ **Guess:** If you know the Width and Height values, but you don't know the number of bytes in the header — or vice versa — you can ask Photoshop for help. Fill in either the Dimensions or Header information and then click the Guess button to ask Photoshop to take a stab at the unknown value. Photoshop estimates all this information when the Raw Options dialog box first appears. Generally speaking, if it doesn't estimate correctly the first time around, you're on your own. But hey, the Guess button is worth a shot.

Tip

If a raw document is a CMYK image, it opens as an RGB image with an extra masking channel. To display the image correctly, choose Image ➪ Mode ➪ Multichannel to free the four channels from their incorrect relationship. Then recombine them by choosing Image ➪ Mode ➪ CMYK Color.

Saving a raw document

Photoshop also lets you save to the raw document format. This capability is useful when you create files you want to transfer to mainframe systems or output to devices that don't support other formats, such as the Kodak XL7700.

Caution

Do not save 256-color indexed images to the raw format or you will lose the color lookup table and, therefore, lose all color information. Be sure to convert such images first to RGB or one of the other full-color modes before saving.

When you save an image in the raw document format, Photoshop presents the dialog box shown in Figure 3-25. The dialog box options work as follows:

✦ **File Type:** This option defines information for the resource fork, so it's only pertinent to Mac folks. (Under Windows, the option is always dimmed. Feel free to ignore.) Enter the four-character file type code (TIFF, PICT, and so on) in this option box. (You should check the documentation for the application you plan to use to open the raw document.) If you plan to use this file on a computer other than a Mac, you can enter any four characters you like; only Macs use this code.

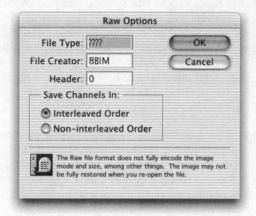

Figure 3-25: When saving a raw document on a Mac, enter the file type and creator codes and specify the order of data in the file.

✦ **File Creator:** Again, this option is only relevant on a Mac. Enter the four-character creator code, which tells the system software which application created the file. By default, the creator code is 8BIM, Photoshop's code. Ignore this option unless you have a specific reason for changing it — for example, to open the image in a particular Macintosh application. (You won't hurt anything by changing the code, but you will prevent Photoshop from opening the image when you double-click the document icon at the Finder desktop.). On Windows machines, the default code 8BIM is selected for you and the option is dimmed.

✦ **Header:** Enter the size of the header in bytes. If you enter any value but zero, you must fill in the header using a data editor, such as Norton Disk Editor.

✦ **Save Channels In:** Select the Interleaved Order option to arrange data sequentially by pixels, as described earlier. To group data by color channel, select Non-interleaved Order.

Wireless Bitmap

Hey, those crude little graphics found on handheld wireless devices have to come from somewhere, right? Why not Photoshop? Photoshop now can open and save in WBMP format, an up-and-coming standard for cell phones and personal digital assistants. Before the Wireless Bitmap option is available, the image must be in Bitmap mode, with only black-and-white pixels.

Still can't get that file open?

File format specs are continually evolving. As a result, programs that provide support for a particular format may not support the specific version of the format used to save the file you're trying to open. For example, JPEG is notorious for causing problems because there were several private implementations in the early days. As a result, some JPEG files can only be read by the originating application.

If you can't open a file in Photoshop, you may have another program that can read and write the problem format. Try the problem file in every program you have — and every program your friends have. After all, what are friends for?

You may also want to try a program such as HiJaak, TransverterPro, DeBabelizer Toolbox, or DeBabelizer Pro from Equilibrium (*www.equilibrium.com*). Absolutely the best format converter bar none, DeBabelizer Pro handles every format Photoshop handles, as well as Dr. Halo's CUT, Fractal Design Painter's RIFF, the animation formats PICS, FLI, and ANM, as well as UNIX workstation formats for Silicon Graphics, Sun Microsystems, and others.

Still out of it? Go online and check out such forums as ADOBEAPPS on CompuServe. The Usenet newsgroups *comp.graphics.apps.photoshop* and *rec.photo.digital* are other good resources. Post a question about your problem; chances are good someone may have an answer for you.

Adding File Information and Annotations

On top of pixels, alpha channels, color profiles, and all the other image data you can cram into your image files, you can add a variety of reference information — where you shot the picture, who owns the image copyright, and so on. This extra data can take the form of cataloging information that you enter in the File Info dialog box or text and audio annotations that you can view and play right from the image window. The next few sections explain these options.

Recording file information

If you work for a stock agency or distribute your work by some other means, you may be interested in Photoshop's File ⇨ File Info command. Using this command, you can record captions, credits, bylines, photo location and date, copyright, and other information as prescribed by the Newspaper Association of America (NAA) and the International Press Telecommunications Council (IPTC). We're talking official worldwide guidelines here.

Version 7 of Photoshop has seen some reorganization of the File Info command, redistributing the six different panels available in Photoshop 6 (Caption, Keywords, Categories, Credits, Origin, and Copyright & URL) into five panels (General, Keywords, Categories, Origin, and EXIF).

After you choose the File Info command, you see the five-paneled File Info dialog box, shown in Figure 3-26. You switch from one panel to another by pressing Ctrl+1 through Ctrl+5 (⌘-1 through ⌘-5 on the Mac) or choosing the panel name from the Section pop-up menu. On the PC, Alt+N and Alt+P also go to the next and previous panel, respectively. The first panel, the General panel, appears in Figure 3-26.

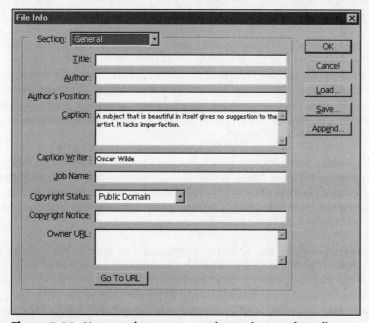

Figure 3-26: You can document your image in encyclopedic detail using the wealth of options in the File Info dialog box.

Although sprawling with options, this dialog box is pretty easy to master. For example, if you want to create a caption, travel to the General panel and enter your caption into the Caption option box, which can hold up to 2,000 characters. If you select Caption in the Print with Preview dialog box, the caption appears underneath the image when you print it from Photoshop. You can also add a copyright notice to your image. If you choose Copyrighted Work from the Copyright Status pop-up menu, a copyright symbol (©) will appear in the window title bar and in the information box at the bottom of the screen on the PC or at the bottom of the image window on the Mac. This symbol tells people viewing the image they can go to the General panel to get more information about the owner of the image copyright. Choose Public Domain if you want to make it clear that the work isn't copyrighted (an Unmarked image might actually be a neglected copyrighted one).

You can also include the URL for your Web site, if you have one. Then, when folks have your image open in Photoshop, they can come to this panel and click the Go to URL button to launch their Web browsers and jump to the URL.

Note   Because only people who open your image in Photoshop have access to the information in the File Info dialog box, you may want to embed a digital watermark into your image as well. Many watermarking programs exist, ranging from simple tools that merely imprint copyright data to those that build in protection features designed to prevent illegal downloading and reproduction of images. Photoshop provides a watermarking utility from Digimarc as a plug-in on the Filters menu; before using the plug-in, visit the Digimarc Web site (*www.digimarc.com*) to find out which, if any, of the Digimarc watermarking schemes best suits the type of work you do.

The Keywords panel enables you to enter a list of descriptive words that will help folks find the image if it's part of a large electronic library. Just enter the desired word and press Enter or Return or click the Add button to add the keyword to the list. Or you can replace a word in the list by selecting it, entering a new word, and pressing Enter (or Return on the Mac) or clicking Replace. Likewise, you can delete a selected keyword by clicking Delete. Browser utilities enable you to search images by keyword, as do some dedicated image servers.

The Categories panel may seem foreign to anyone who hasn't worked with a news service. Many large news services use a system of three-character categories to file and organize stories and photographs. If you're familiar with this system, you can enter the three-character code into the Category option box and even throw in a few supplemental categories up to 32 characters long.

You can use the Urgency pop-up menu in the Origin panel to specify the editorial timeliness of the photo. The High option tells editors around the world to hold the presses and holler for their copy boys. The Low option is for celebrity mug shots that can be tossed in the morgue to haul out only if the subject of the photograph decides to do something diverting, like lead police on a nail-biting tour of the Los Angeles freeway system.

The EXIF panel lets you view any EXIF metadata an image might contain if it originated in a digital camera. For more information about EXIF, see the "Using the file browser" section, earlier in this chapter.

Caution   On a PC, file information is only saved in file formats that support saving extra data with the file. This includes the native Photoshop (*.psd*) format, Encapsulated PostScript (*.eps*), PDF (*.pdf*), JPEG (*.jpg*), and TIFF (*.tif*). On a Mac, file information is saved with an image regardless of the format you use. Photoshop merely tacks the text onto the image's resource fork. Because you cannot format the text in the File Info dialog box, it consumes little space on disk—1 byte per character—meaning that you can fill in every option box without adding 1K.

You can also save the information from the File Info dialog box by clicking the Save button. Or open information saved to disk previously by clicking Load. To add the information from a saved file to the information you've already entered into the File Info dialog box, click the Append button.

Taping notes to your image

Photoshop enables you to slap the digital equivalent of a sticky note onto your image. The notes can be viewed in Adobe Acrobat (assuming that you save the image in the PDF format) as well as in Photoshop. You can jot down ideas that you want to remember later, for example. Or, if you're routing an image for approval, you can ask questions about a certain image element—or, more likely, explain why a part of the picture looks the way it does and why changing it would be an absolute *travesty* and *total* abdication of your artistic integrity.

The Photoshop notes tool works like its counterpart in Adobe Acrobat: Click in the image window to display a blank note, as shown in Figure 3-27, or drag to create a custom-sized note. If you don't want to use the name that appears in the note's title bar, type the desired name in the Author box in the Options bar. (By default, Photoshop displays the user name you entered when you installed the program.) Type your comments—all the standard text-editing techniques apply—and then click the close box in the upper-left corner of the note window. Your note shrinks to a little note icon, as shown in the figure. Double-click the icon to redisplay the note text.

When you save your image, be sure to save in the Photoshop native format or PDF and select the Annotations check box in the Save dialog box. Otherwise, you lose all your notes. For information on how to delete individual notes in an open image and how to customize and import notes, skip to the section "Managing annotations."

Voicing your opinions

If you like to speak your mind rather than put your thoughts in writing, check out the audio annotation tool. This tool works like the notes tool except that it inserts an audio recording of your voice rather than a text message into the file. Of course, you need a microphone, speakers, and a sound card installed in your computer to use this feature. Also, Photoshop retains audio annotations only when you save the image file using the Photoshop native format or PDF, as with text notes. Be aware, too, that audio files increase file size significantly.

Figure 3-27: After adding text-based notes or audio comments to an image, save the file in PDF so that others can access the annotations when viewing the image in Adobe Acrobat.

The audio annotation tool shares quarters with the notes tool in the toolbox. Press N to toggle between the two tools (or Shift+N, depending on the preference you established in the General panel of the Preferences dialog box). Click in your image at the spot where you want the icon representing your message to appear. When the Audio Annotation dialog box appears, click Start to begin your recording and then talk into the microphone. Click Stop when you've said all you have to say.

Photoshop represents your audio message with a little speaker icon in the image window. Double-click the icon to play the message.

Managing annotations

If you're a solo artist and the only approval of your work you need is your own, you may not have much reason to use the notes or audio annotation tools. Then again, you may be an easily distracted sort and find annotations a terrific way to remind yourself exactly what you're trying to accomplish in an image. And who's to say that your friends won't love being able to hear an audio clip of your dog Binky yapping at the vacuum cleaner when they view his picture in Acrobat?

Whether you're using annotations for fun or profit, employ the following strategies to manage audio and text annotations:

✦ Use the Font and Size controls in the Options bar to change the font and type size in an open note.

✦ Click the Color icon to change the color of the icon and title bar for any new note you create. This option comes in handy if several people will be reviewing the image and contributing their two cents' worth. You can assign a different color to each author. To change the color of an existing note, open the note and click the Color icon. This time, you affect only the open note — other notes by the same author don't change.

✦ You can move and copy annotations between image windows. Just click the icon and use the Cut, Copy, and Paste commands as you do to move and copy any selection.

✦ If an icon blocks your view of the image, you can drag it out of the way. However, when you open the note, its window appears in the icon's original location. Drag the size box in the lower-right corner of an open note to shrink the window if necessary.

✦ Choose View ➪ Show ➪ Annotations to toggle the display of annotation icons on and off. Alternatively, choose View ➪ Show ➪ All and View ➪ Show ➪ None to hide and display icons and other interface elements, such as selection marquees, guides, and so on.

✦ To delete a single annotation, click its icon and press Delete. Or right-click (Control-click on the Mac) the icon and choose Delete Note or Delete Audio Annotation. If you want to delete all annotations, choose Delete All Annotations or click the Clear All button in the Options bar.

Tip

If you send out several copies of the same image for approval, you don't have to open each copy individually to read the annotations. Instead, open just one copy and then import the annotations from the other files. Choose File ➪ Import ➪ Annotations, select the files containing the annotations, and click Open. Photoshop gathers up all the annotations and dumps them into your open image.

Caution

Remember to save your image in the PDF or Photoshop 7 file format to retain annotations in a file. And if you're sending an annotated file to other people for viewing, tell them that they need to use Adobe Acrobat 4.0 or higher to access the annotations.

Resampling and Cropping

After you bring up an image—whether you created it from scratch or opened an existing image stored in one of the five billion formats discussed in the preceding pages—its size and resolution are established. Neither size nor resolution is set in stone, however. Photoshop provides two methods for changing the number of pixels in an image: resampling and cropping.

Resizing versus resampling

Typically, when folks talk about *resizing* an image, they mean enlarging or reducing it without changing the number of pixels in the image, as demonstrated back in Figure 3-1. By contrast, *resampling* an image means scaling it so the image contains a larger or smaller number of pixels. With resizing, an inverse relationship exists between size and resolution—size increases when resolution decreases, and vice versa. But resampling affects either size or resolution independently. Figure 3-28 shows an image resized and resampled to 50 percent of its original dimensions. The resampled and original images have identical resolutions, but the resized image has twice the resolution of its companions.

Resizing an image

To resize an image, use one of the techniques discussed in the "Changing the printing resolution" section near the beginning of this chapter. To recap briefly, the best method is to choose Image ➪ Image Size, turn off the Resample Image check box, and enter a value into the Resolution option box. See Figure 3-2 to refresh your memory.

Figure 3-28: An image (top) resized (middle) and resampled (bottom) down to 50 percent. The resized image sports a higher resolution; the resampled one contains fewer pixels.

Resampling an image

You also use Image ➪ Image Size to resample an image. The difference is that you leave the Resample Image check box turned on, as shown in Figure 3-29. As its name implies, the Resample Image check box is the key to resampling.

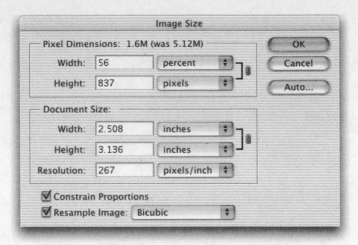

Figure 3-29: With the Resample Image check box turned on, you can modify the number of pixels in your image.

When Resample Image is selected, the Resolution value is independent of both sets of Width and Height values. (The only difference between the two sets of options is that the top options work in pixels and the bottom options work in relative units of measure, such as percent and inches.) You can increase the number of pixels in an image by increasing any of the five values in the dialog box; you can decrease the number of pixels by decreasing any value. Photoshop stretches or shrinks the image according to the new size specifications.

At all times, you can see the new number of pixels Photoshop will assign to the image, as well as the increased or decreased file size. In Figure 3-29, for example, I've changed the first Width value to 56 percent. The Pixel Dimensions value at the top of the dialog box reflects my change by reading *1.6M (was 5.12M)*, which shows that the file size has decreased.

To calculate the pixels in the resampled image, Photoshop must use its powers of interpolation, as explained in the "General preferences" section of Chapter 2. The interpolation setting defaults to the one chosen in the Preferences dialog box. But you can also change the setting right inside the Image Size dialog box. Simply select the desired method from the Resample Image pop-up menu. Bicubic results in the smoothest effects. Bilinear is faster. And Nearest Neighbor turns off interpolation so Photoshop merely throws away the pixels it doesn't need or duplicates pixels to resample up.

Here are a few more random items you should know about resampling with the Image Size dialog box:

✦ This may sound odd, but you generally want to avoid adding pixels. When you resample up, you're asking Photoshop to make up details from thin air, and the program isn't that smart. Simply put, an enlarged image almost never looks better than the original; it merely takes up more disk space and prints slower.

✦ Resampling down, on the other hand, is a useful technique. It enables you to smooth away photo grain, halftone patterns, and other scanning artifacts. One of the most tried-and-true rules is to scan at the maximum resolution permitted by your scanner and then resample the scan down to, say, 72 or 46 percent (with the interpolation set to Bicubic, naturally). By selecting a round value other than 50 percent, you force Photoshop to jumble the pixels into a regular, homogenous soup. You're left with fewer pixels, but these remaining pixels are better. And you have the added benefit that the image takes up less space on disk.

✦ To make an image tall and thin or short and fat, you must first turn off the Constrain Proportions check box. This enables you to edit the two Width values entirely independently of the two Height values.

✦ You can resample an image to match precisely the size and resolution of any other open image. While the Image Size dialog box is open, choose the name of the image you want to match from the Window menu.

✦ If you need help resampling an image to the proper size for a print job, choose Help ➪ Resize Image to bring up the Resize Image Wizard. The dialog box walks you through the process of resampling step-by-step. It's really for rank beginners, but you might find it helpful when you want to turn the old brain off and set Photoshop to autopilot. (Note that Adobe uses the word "resize" simply because it's friendlier than "resample." Whatever it's called, this command does indeed resample.)

If you ever get confused inside the Image Size dialog box and you want to return to the original size and resolution settings, press the Alt key (or Option key on the Mac) to change the Cancel button to Reset. Then click the Reset button to start from the beginning.

Photoshop remembers the setting of the Resample Image check box and uses this same setting the next time you open the Image Size dialog box. This can trip you up if you record an action in the Actions palette that uses the Image Size command. Suppose that you create an action to resize images, turning Resample Image off. If you later resample an image — turning on Resample Image — the check box stays selected when you close the dialog box. The next time you run the action, you end up resampling instead of resizing. Always check the status of the check box before you apply the Image Size command or run any actions containing the command.

Cropping

Another way to change the number of pixels in an image is to *crop* it, which means to clip away pixels around the edges of an image without harming the remaining pixels. (The one exception occurs when you rotate a cropped image or use the perspective crop feature, in which case Photoshop has to interpolate pixels to account for the rotation.)

Cropping enables you to focus on an element in your image. For example, the left side of Figure 3-30 shows an upstanding young lad standing up on a bus seat. This photo clearly captures his rakish charm, but the photo itself appears to have been taken at quite a rake. And did you notice that ghostly face reflected in the bus window? Creepy. Luckily, I can crop around the little fellow's head to delete the extraneous image elements and hone in on his noble visage, as shown in the right of Figure 3-30.

Figure 3-30: Starting with a crooked photograph shot with an Olympus C-3030 (left), I used the crop tool to straighten the image and hone in on the core subject of the piece (right).

Photoshop offers several cutting-edge cropping options — har har — including the capability to crop nonrectangular selections, automatically trim away transparent areas from the borders of an image, and correct perspective effects while cropping. You can read about all these features in the upcoming sections.

Changing the canvas size

One way to crop an image is to choose Image ➪ Canvas Size, which displays the Canvas Size dialog box shown in Figure 3-31. The options in this dialog box enable you to scale the imaginary canvas on which the image rests separately from the image itself.

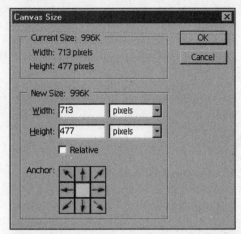

Figure 3-31: Choose Image ➪ Canvas Size to crop an image or to add empty space around the perimeter of an image.

If you enlarge the canvas of an image with a background layer, Photoshop surrounds the image with the background color. Enlarging the canvas of an image without a background layer will surround the image with transparent pixels. Either way, if you reduce the canvas, you crop the image. Just type the new desired pixel dimensions in the Width and Height boxes.

Selecting the new Relative check box allows you to change the height and/or width of the canvas by a specific pixel amount. For instance, enter 2 in each option box to change a 100×100-pixel image into a 102×102-pixel image; enter –2 to crop it down to a 98×98-pixel image. Not only can this save you from having to do a little math, but it can really come in handy when batch processing if you want to add the same number of pixels to a batch of different-sized files.

Click inside the Anchor grid to specify the placement of the image on the new canvas. For example, if you want to add space to the bottom of an image, enlarge the canvas size and then click inside the upper-middle square. If you want to crop away the upper-left corner of an image, create a smaller canvas size and then click the lower-right square. The Anchor grid offers little arrows to show how the canvas will shrink or grow.

To shrink the canvas so that it exactly fits the image, don't waste your time with the Canvas Size dialog box. Using a nifty command, Image ➪ Trim, you can automatically clip away empty canvas areas on the outskirts of your image. When you choose the command, the dialog box shown in Figure 3-32 appears. To snip away empty canvas, select the Transparent Pixels radio button. Then specify which edges of the canvas you want to slice off by using the four Trim Away check boxes. Alternatively, you can tell Photoshop to trim the image based on the pixel color in the top-left corner of the image or the bottom-right corner — just click the appropriate Based On radio button. For example, if you have a blue stripe running down the left edge of your image and you select the Top Left Pixel Color radio button, Photoshop clips away the stripe. No trimming occurs unless the entire edge of the image is bounded by the selected color.

Figure 3-32: To quickly snip away transparent areas from the edges of an image, use the Image ➪ Trim command.

 Tip   When you want to enlarge the canvas but aren't concerned with making it a specific size, try this time-saving trick: Drag with the crop tool to create a crop marquee and then enlarge the crop marquee beyond the boundaries of the image (see the next section if you need help). When you press Enter or Return to apply the crop, the canvas grows to match the size of the crop marquee.

Using the crop tool

Generally speaking, the Canvas Size command is most useful for enlarging the canvas or shaving a few pixels off the edge of an image. If you want to crop away a large portion of an image, using the crop tool is a better choice.

Press C or click the crop icon in the toolbox to activate the tool. To use the tool, you drag to create a rectangular marquee that surrounds the portion of the image you want to retain. But you can control what happens during and after you crop in two important ways:

✦ To help you distinguish the borders of the crop marquee, Photoshop displays a colored, translucent overlay on the area outside the crop box — similar to the way it indicates masked versus unmasked areas when you work in the quick mask mode. Hate the overlay? Deselect the Shield check box in the Options bar. You also can click the neighboring color box to change the overlay color and set the overlay opacity through the Opacity pop-up menu. Note that these controls don't appear in the Options bar until after you create your initial crop marquee.

✦ You have the option of permanently discarding the pixels you crop or simply hiding them from view. Before you drag with the crop tool, click the Delete or Hide radio button in the Options bar to signify your preference. If you choose Hide, you can bring the hidden regions back into view by enlarging the canvas or by using the Image ➪ Reveal All command.

As you drag, you can press the spacebar to move the crop boundary temporarily on the fly. To stop moving the boundary and return to resizing it, release the spacebar.

If you don't get the crop marquee right the first time, you can move, scale, or rotate it at will. Here's what you do:

✦ Drag inside the crop marquee to move it.

✦ Drag one of the square handles to resize the marquee. You can Shift-drag a handle to scale the marquee proportionally (the same percentage vertically and horizontally). You can also drag the sides of the marquee to resize it.

✦ Drag outside the crop marquee to rotate it, as explained in the next section. This may strike you as weird at first, but it works wonderfully.

✦ Drag the origin point (labeled in Figure 3-33) to change the center of a rotation.

✦ Select the Perspective check box in the Options bar, and you can drag corner handles to distort the image. What's the point? Well, the main reason to use this option is to correct convergence problems that occur when shooting images at an angle. For example, let's say you have a billboard in perspective, so that it declines toward the horizon. Using the Perspective check box, you can crop the billboard and remove its perspective so it appears flat.

But while a solid feature, it can prove confusing. For starters, you can't preview the results of your changes before applying the crop. Also, in any attempt to conserve important detail, Photoshop tends to stretch the image after applying the perspective. This is actually a good thing — better to stretch an image than trash data — but it requires you to reverse the stretch in a second operation. If this bothers you, you may be better off tackling perspective problems using the Free Transform command, covered in Chapter 12, and do your cropping afterwards.

Crop tool   Handles   Rotate cursor

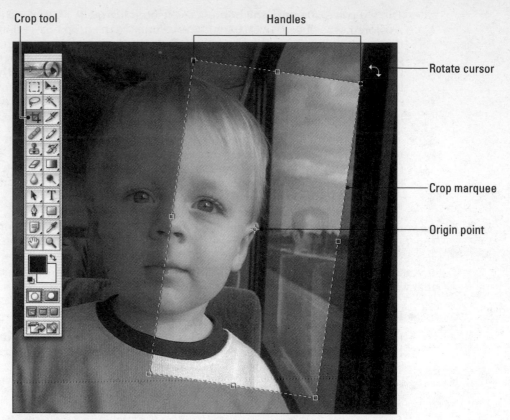

Crop marquee

Origin point

Figure 3-33: When rotating a crop boundary, align the marquee with an obvious axis in your image to determine the proper angle.

When the marquee surrounds the exact portion of the image you want to keep, apply the crop by pressing Enter (or Return on the Mac) or double-clicking inside the marquee. You also can click the OK button in the Options bar, which is the giant check mark at the right end of the bar.

If you change your mind about cropping, you can cancel the crop marquee by pressing Escape or clicking the Cancel button, the universal "no" symbol next to the check mark in the Options bar.

Rotating the crop marquee

As I said, you can rotate an image by dragging outside the crop marquee. Straightening a crooked image, however, can be a little tricky. I wish I had a certified check for every time I thought I had the marquee rotated properly, only to find the image was still crooked after I pressed Enter. If this happens to you, choose Edit ➪ Undo (Ctrl+Z or ⌘-Z) and try again. Do not try using the crop tool a second time to rotate the already rotated image. If you do, Photoshop sets about interpolating between already interpolated pixels, resulting in more lost data. Every rotation gets farther away from the original image.

A better solution is to do it right the first time. Locate a line or general axis in your image that should be straight up and down. Rotate the crop marquee so it aligns exactly with this axis. In Figure 3-33, I rotated my crop marquee so one edge bisects the innocent bus-stander's head. Don't worry, this isn't how you want to crop the image — you're just using the line as a reference. After you arrive at the correct angle for the marquee, drag the handles to size and position the boundary properly. As long as you don't drag outside the marquee, its angle remains fixed throughout.

Yet another solution is to use the measure tool. Just drag with the tool along the axis you want to make vertical. Choose Image ⇨ Rotate Canvas ⇨ Arbitrary, and, as if by magic, the angle of rotation you just sampled with the measure tool is automatically filled into the Rotate Canvas dialog box. Just click OK, and you're home free.

Cropping an image to match another

There are two ways to crop an image so it matches the size and resolution of another image:

✦ Bring the image you want to crop forward and choose Image ⇨ Canvas Size. Then, while inside the Canvas Size dialog box, select the name of the image you want to match from the Window ⇨ Documents menu.

This method doesn't give you much control when cropping an image, but it's a great way to enlarge the canvas and add empty space around an image.

✦ Better yet, use the crop tool in its fixed-size mode. First, bring the image you want to match to the front. Then select the crop tool and click the Front Image button in the Options bar. The Width, Height, and Resolution options automatically update to show the size and resolution of the front image.

Now bring the image you want to crop to the front and drag with the crop tool as normal. Photoshop constrains the crop marquee to the proportions of the targeted image. After you press Enter or Return, Photoshop crops, resamples, and rotates the image as necessary.

The next time you select the crop tool, it starts out in fixed-size mode. To return the tool to normal, click the Clear button in the Options bar.

Cropping a selection

Another way to crop an image is to create a selection and then choose Image ⇨ Crop. One advantage of the Crop command is that you needn't select the crop tool if the marquee tool is already active. One tool is all you need to select and crop. (If you're as lazy as I am, the mere act of selecting a tool can prove more effort than it's worth.) And, as with the crop tool, you can press the spacebar while you draw a marquee to move it on the fly. It's no trick to get the placement and size exactly right — the only thing you can't do is rotate.

Another advantage of the Crop command is flexibility. After drawing a selection, you can switch windows, apply commands, and generally use any function you like prior to choosing Image ⇨ Crop. The crop tool, by contrast, is much more limiting. After drawing a cropping marquee, you can't do anything but adjust the marquee until you press Enter or Return to accept the crop or Escape to dismiss it.

And finally, you can use the Crop command on selections of any shape, even feathered selections and multiple discontiguous selections. Of course, your image canvas remains rectangular no matter what the selection shape. Photoshop simply crops the canvas to the smallest size that can hold all selected areas.

✦   ✦   ✦

Painting and Retouching

Defining Colors

Selecting and Editing Colors

Color is so prevalent in computer graphics these days that you'd think the concept of a grayscale image, filled with only black, white, and gray pixels, would be a quaint, antiquated notion. Sadly, perhaps, this just isn't true. While every day we see more and more color in the world of print, it's still a fact that if this whomping-big book was printed fully in color, it would cost about three kazillion dollars, give or take a bazillion or two. Color may seem cooler, but black and white is still the bread and butter of many graphic artists.

Some of you Web graphics folks might be thinking, "Wait a second, what about the equalizing force of the Internet? It brings color to all of us!" Well, I concur wholeheartedly. Nearly everyone owns a color monitor, so we can all share color images freely.

Regardless of who you are—print person or Web head—color is always a prime concern. Even gray values, after all, are colors. Many folks have problems accepting this premise—I guess we're all so used to separating the worlds of grays and other colors in our minds that never the two shall meet. But gray values are only variations on what Noah Webster used to call "The sensation resulting from stimulation of the retina of the eye by light waves of certain lengths." (Give the guy a few drinks and he'd spout off 19 more definitions, not including the meanings of the transitive verb.) Just as black and white represent a subset of gray, gray is a subset of color. In fact, you'll find that using Photoshop involves a lot of navigating through these and other colorful subsets.

Specifying colors

First off, Photoshop provides four color controls in the toolbox, as shown in Figure 4-1. These icons work as follows:

✦ **Foreground color:** The foreground color icon indicates the color you apply when you use the paint bucket, pencil, brush, or one of the type tools, and also if you Alt-drag (Option-drag on the Mac) with the smudge tool. The foreground color also begins any gradation created with the gradient tool (assuming that you create a custom gradient, not one of the prefab gradients available through the gradient styles pop-up menu). Photoshop fills any shapes you create with the shape tools with the foreground color. You can apply the foreground color to a standard selection by choosing Edit ⇨ Fill or Edit ⇨ Stroke or by pressing Alt+Backspace (Option-Delete on the Mac).

To change the foreground color, click the foreground color icon to display the Color Picker dialog box, select a new color in the Color palette, or click an open image window with the eyedropper tool. You also can set the foreground color by clicking a swatch in the Swatches palette. (All are explained later in this chapter.)

By the way, Photoshop 7 introduces a lovely little addition to the eyedropper's powers. The tool can now sample colors not just within an image window, but anywhere on your computer screen. To take advantage of this, you first have to click within an image window, and then drag outside of the window. For complete details, see "The eyedropper tool" section later in this chapter.

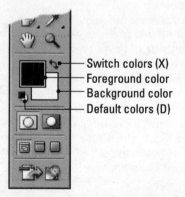

Switch colors (X)
Foreground color
Background color
Default colors (D)

Figure 4-1: The color controls provided with Photoshop (along with keyboard shortcuts in parentheses, where applicable).

✦ **Background color:** The active background color indicates the color you apply with the eraser tool when you're working on the background layer. By default, the background color also ends any custom gradation created with the gradient tool. To change the background color, click the background color icon to display the Color Picker dialog box. Or define the color by using the Color palette, clicking a swatch in the Swatches palette, or Alt-clicking (Option-clicking on the Mac) any open image window with the eyedropper tool. The new eyedropper trick about sampling outside an image window works here as well.

You can apply the background color to a selection by pressing Backspace or Delete. But if the selection is floating or exists on any layer except the background layer, pressing Backspace or Delete actually deletes the selection instead of filling it. For complete safety, use Ctrl+Backspace (⌘-Delete on the Mac) to fill a selection with the background color instead.

✦ **Switch colors:** Click this icon (or press X) to exchange the foreground and background colors.

✦ **Default colors:** Click this icon (or press D) to make the foreground color black and the background color white, according to their factory default settings. If you're editing a layer mask or an adjustment layer, the default colors are reversed, as explained in Chapter 12.

Using the Color Picker

When you click the foreground or background color icon in the toolbox or the Color palette, Photoshop displays the Color Picker dialog box. (This assumes that Adobe is the active option in the Color Picker pop-up menu in the General panel of the Preferences dialog box. If you select the Windows or Apple option, the generic Windows or Apple Color Picker appears; see Chapter 2 on why you shouldn't select these options.) Figure 4-2 labels the wealth of elements and options in the Color Picker dialog box, which work as follows:

✦ **Color slider:** Use the color slider to home in on the color you want to select. Drag up or down on either of the slider triangles to select a color from a particular 8-bit range. The colors represented inside the slider correspond to the selected radio button. For example, if you select the H (Hue) radio button, which is the default setting, the slider colors represent the full 8-bit range of hues. If you select S (Saturation), the slider shows the current hue at full saturation at the top of the slider, down to no saturation — or gray — at the bottom of the slider. If you select B (Brightness), the slider shows the 8-bit range of brightness values, from solid color at the top of the slider to absolute black at the bottom. You also can select R (Red), G (Green), or B (Blue), in which case the top of the slider shows you what the current color looks like when subjected to full-intensity red, green, or blue (respectively), and the bottom of the slider shows every bit of red, green, or blue subtracted.

Cross-Reference

For a proper introduction to the HSB and RGB color models, including definitions of specific terms, such as hue, saturation, and brightness, read the "Working in Different Color Modes" section later in this chapter.

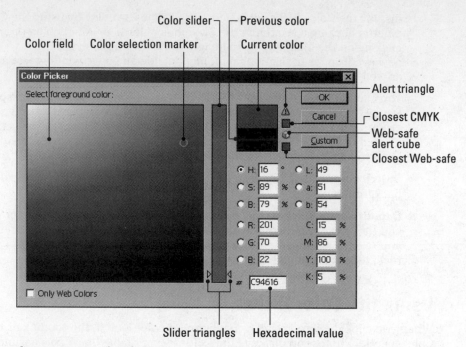

Figure 4-2: Use the elements and options in the Color Picker dialog box to specify a new foreground or background color from the 16-million-color range.

✦ **Color field:** The color field shows a 16-bit range of variations on the current slider color. Click inside it to move the color selection marker and, thereby, select a new color. The field graphs colors against the two remaining attributes not represented by the color slider. For example, if you select the H (Hue) radio button, the field graphs colors according to brightness vertically and saturation horizontally, as demonstrated in the first example of Figure 4-3. The other examples show what happens to the color field when you select the S (Saturation) and B (Brightness) radio buttons. Likewise, Figure 4-4 shows how the field graphs colors when you select the R (Red), G (Green), and B (Blue) radio buttons.

Slider and field always work together to represent the entire 16-million-color range. The slider displays 256 colors, and the field displays 65,000 variations on the slider color; 256 times 65,000 is roughly 16 million. No matter which radio button you select, you have access to the same colors; only your means of accessing them changes.

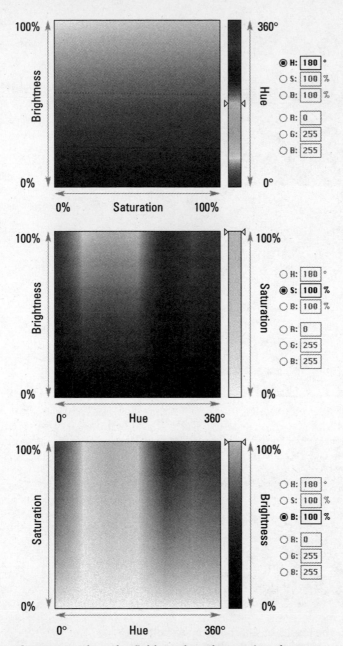

Figure 4-3: The color field graphs colors against the two attributes not represented in the slider. Here you can see how color is laid out when you select (top to bottom) the H (Hue), S (Saturation), and B (Brightness) radio buttons.

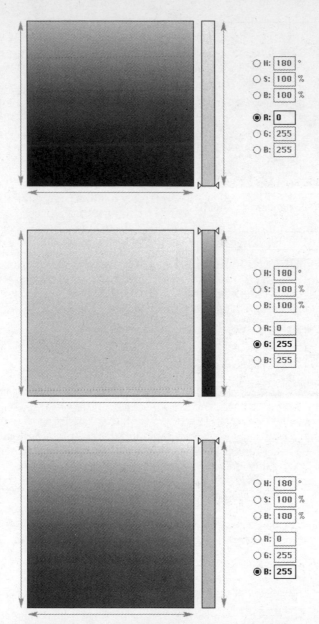

Figure 4-4: The results of selecting (top to bottom) the R (Red), G (Green), and B (Blue) radio buttons.

✦ **Current color:** The color currently selected from the color field appears in the top rectangle immediately to the right of the color slider. Click the OK button or press Enter or Return to make this the current foreground or background color (depending on which color control icon in the toolbox you originally clicked to display the Color Picker dialog box).

✦ **Previous color:** The bottom rectangle to the right of the color slider shows how the foreground or background color—whichever one you are in the process of editing—looked before you displayed the Color Picker dialog box. Click the Cancel button or press Escape to leave this color intact.

✦ **Alert triangle:** The alert triangle appears when you select a bright color that Photoshop can't print using standard process colors. The box below the triangle shows the closest CMYK equivalent, invariably a duller version of the color. Click either the triangle or the box to bring the color into the printable range. Pressing Ctrl+Shift+Y (⌘-Shift-Y on the Mac) or choosing View ➪ Gamut Warning automatically grays out any colors not allowed in the CMYK spectrum.

✦ **Web-safe alert cube:** This little cube appears if you select a color that's not included in the so-called Web-safe palette, a 216-color spectrum that's supposedly ideal for creating Web graphics. If you click either the cube or the swatch below, Photoshop selects the closest Web-safe equivalent to the color you originally selected.

Entering numeric color values

In addition to selecting colors using the slider and color field, you can enter specific color values in the option boxes in the lower-right region of the Color Picker dialog box. Novices and intermediates may find these options less satisfying to use than the slider and field. These options, however, enable artists and print professionals to specify exact color values, whether to make controlled adjustments to a color already in use or to match a color used in another document. The options fall into one of four camps:

✦ **HSB:** These options stand for hue, saturation, and brightness. Hue is measured on a 360-degree circle. Saturation and brightness are measured from 0 to 100 percent. These options permit access to more than 3 million color variations.

✦ **RGB:** You can change the amount of the primary colors red, green, and blue by specifying the brightness value of each color from 0 to 255. These options enable access to more than 16 million color variations.

✦ **Lab:** This acronym stands for luminosity, measured from 0 to 100 percent, and two arbitrary color axes, a and b, whose brightness values range from –120 to 120. These options enable access to more than 6 million color variations.

✦ **CMYK:** These options display the amount of cyan, magenta, yellow, and black ink required to print the current color. When you click the alert triangle, these are the only values that don't change, because they make up the closest CMYK equivalent.

At the bottom of the dialog box, the value next to the pound sign (#) shows you the hexadecimal value for the chosen color (see Figure 4-2). This value comes into play only if you're creating Web graphics — and maybe not even then.

In Web-land, every color is assigned a numeric value based on the hexadecimal numbering system. Each value includes a total of three pairs of numbers or letters, one pair each for the R, G, and B values. When you create a color tag in HTML code, you enter the hexadecimal value for the color you want to use. Fortunately, you can create a Web page without having to write your own HTML code; page-creation programs like GoLive and Macromedia Dreamweaver do the work for you. But if you prefer to do your own coding — you lovable geek, you — make note of the hexadecimal value in the Color Picker dialog box.

Tip   This option can also come in handy if you want to precisely match a color on an existing Web page. Just look at the HTML coding for the page, note the hexadecimal value in the appropriate color tag, and enter that value in the Color Picker dialog box.

In my opinion, the numerical range of these options is bewildering. For example, numerically speaking, the CMYK options enable you to create 100 million unique colors, whereas the RGB options enable the standard 16 million variations, and the Lab options enable a scant 6 million. Yet Lab is the largest color space, theoretically encompassing all colors from both CMYK and RGB. The printing standard CMYK provides by far the fewest colors, the opposite of what you might expect. What gives? Misleading numerical ranges. How do these weird color models work? Keep reading and you'll find out.

Working in Different Color Modes

The four sets of option boxes inside the Color Picker dialog box represent color models — or, if you prefer, color modes (one less letter, no less meaning, perfect for you folks who are trying to cut down in life). *Color models* are different ways to define colors both on screen and on the printed page.

Outside the Color Picker dialog box, you can work inside any one of these color models by choosing a command from the Image ➪ Mode submenu. In doing so, you generally change the colors in your image by dumping a few hundred, or even thousand, colors with no equivalents in the new color model. The only exception is Lab, which in theory encompasses every unique color your eyes can detect.

Rather than discuss the color models in the order in which they occur in the Mode submenu, I cover them in logical order, starting with the most common and widely accepted color model, RGB. Also, note that I don't discuss the duotone or multi-channel modes now. Image ⇨ Mode ⇨ Duotone represents an alternative method for printing grayscale images, so it is discussed in Chapter 18. The multichannel mode, meanwhile, is not even a color model. Rather, Image ⇨ Mode ⇨ Multichannel enables you to separate an image into independent channels, which you then can swap around and splice back together to create special effects. For more information, see the "Using multichannel techniques" section later in this chapter.

RGB

RGB is the color model of light. RGB comprises three primary colors — red, green, and blue — each of which can vary between 256 levels of intensity (called brightness values, as discussed in previous chapters). The RGB model is also called the *additive primary model*, because a color becomes lighter as you add higher levels of red, green, and blue light. All monitors, projection devices, and other items that transmit or filter light — including televisions, movie projectors, colored stage lights, and even stained glass — rely on the additive primary model.

Red, green, and blue light mix as follows:

✦ **Red and green:** Full-intensity red and green mix to form yellow. Subtract some red to make chartreuse; subtract some green to make orange. All these colors assume a complete lack of blue.

✦ **Green and blue:** Full-intensity green and blue with no red mix to form cyan. If you try hard enough, you can come up with 65,000 colors in the turquoise/jade/sky blue/sea green range.

✦ **Blue and red:** Full-intensity blue and red mix to form magenta. Subtract some blue to make rose; subtract some red to make purple. All these colors assume a complete lack of green.

✦ **Red, green, and blue:** Full-intensity red, green, and blue mix to form white, the absolute brightest color in the visible spectrum.

✦ **No light:** Low intensities of red, green, and blue plunge a color into blackness.

As far as image editing is concerned, the RGB color model is ideal for editing images on screen because it provides access to the entire range of 24-bit screen colors. Furthermore, you can save an RGB image in every file format supported by Photoshop except GIF and the two DCS formats. As shown in Table 4-1, grayscale is the only other color mode compatible with a wider range of file formats.

	Bitmap	Grayscale	Duotone	Indexed	RGB	CMYK	Lab
Photoshop	Yes	Yes	Yes	Yes	Yes	Yes	Yes
BMP	Yes	Yes	No	Yes	Yes	No	No
DCS 1.0	No	No	No	No	No	Yes	No
DCS 2.0	Yes	Yes	Yes*	No	No	Yes	No
EPS	Yes	Yes	Yes	Yes	Yes	Yes	Yes
GIF	Yes	Yes	No	Yes	No	No	No
JPEG	No	Yes	No	No	Yes	Yes	No
PCX	Yes	Yes	No	Yes	Yes	No	No
PDF	Yes	Yes	No	Yes	Yes	Yes	Yes
PICT	Yes	Yes	No	Yes	Yes	No	No
PNG	Yes**	Yes	No	Yes	Yes	No	No
Scitex CT	No	Yes	No	No	Yes	Yes	No
TIFF	Yes	Yes	No	Yes	Yes	Yes	Yes

Table 4-1
File-Format Support for Photoshop 7 Color Models

Note

Table 4-1 lists color models in the order they appear in the Image ➪ Mode submenu. Again, I left out the multichannel mode because it is not a true color model. The one exception is with duotones. Notice how I've included an asterisk (*) to DCS 2.0 support for duotones. This is because you can save a duotone in DCS 2.0 only after first converting the image to the multichannel mode. For more information, consult Chapter 18. As for the double asterisk (**) with PNG in the Bitmap column: PNG supports Bitmap mode only on the Mac OS.

On the negative side, the RGB color model provides access to a wider range of colors than you can print. If you are designing an image for full-color printing, therefore, you can expect to lose many of the brightest and most vivid colors in your image. The only way to avoid any color loss whatsoever is to have a professional scan your image to CMYK and then edit it in the CMYK mode, but then you're working inside a limited color range. Colors can get clipped when you apply special effects, and the editing process can be exceptionally slow. The better solution is to scan your images to RGB and edit them in the Lab mode, as explained in the upcoming "CIE's Lab" section.

HSB

Back in Photoshop 2, the Modes submenu provided access to the HSB — hue, saturation, brightness — color model, now relegated to the Color Picker dialog box and the Color palette (discussed later in this chapter). *Hue* is pure color, the stuff rainbows are made of, measured on a 360-degree circle. Red is located at 0 degrees, yellow at 60 degrees, green at 120 degrees, cyan at 180 degrees (midway around the circle), blue at 240 degrees, and magenta at 300 degrees. This is basically a pie-shaped version of the RGB model at full intensity.

Saturation represents the purity of the color. A zero saturation value equals gray. White, black, and any other colors you can express in a grayscale image have no saturation. Full saturation produces the purest version of a hue.

Brightness is the lightness or darkness of a color. A zero brightness value equals black. Full brightness combined with full saturation results in the most vivid version of any hue.

CMYK

In nature, our eyes perceive pigments according to the *subtractive color model.* Sunlight contains every visible color found on Earth. When sunlight is projected on an object, the object absorbs (subtracts) some of the light and reflects the rest. The reflected light is the color you see. For example, a fire engine is bright red because it absorbs all non-red — meaning all blue and green — from the white-light spectrum.

Pigments on a sheet of paper work the same way. You can even mix pigments to create other colors. Suppose you paint a red brush stroke, which absorbs green and blue light, over a blue brush stroke, which absorbs green and red light. You get a blackish mess with only a modicum of blue and red light left, along with a smidgen of green because the colors weren't absolutely pure.

But wait — every child knows red and blue mix to form purple. So what gives? What gives is that what you learned in elementary school is only a rude approximation of the truth. Did you ever try mixing a vivid red with a canary yellow only to produce an ugly orange-brown glop? The reason you didn't achieve the bright orange you wanted is because red starts out darker than bright orange, which means you must add a great deal of yellow before you arrive at orange. And even then, the yellow had better be an incredibly bright lemon yellow, not some deep canary yellow with a lot of red in it.

Commercial subtractive primaries

The subtractive primary colors used by commercial printers — cyan, magenta, and yellow — are for the most part very light. Cyan absorbs only red light, magenta absorbs only green light, and yellow absorbs only blue light. On their own, these colors unfortunately don't do a good job of producing dark colors. In fact, at full intensities, cyan, magenta, and yellow all mixed together don't get much beyond a muddy brown. That's where black comes in. Black helps to accentuate shadows, deepen dark colors, and, of course, print real blacks.

In case you're wondering how colors mix in the CMYK model, it's basically the opposite of the RGB model. Because pigments are not as pure as primary colors in the additive model, though, some differences exist:

✦ **Cyan and magenta:** Full-intensity cyan and magenta mix to form a deep blue with a little violet. Subtract some cyan to make purple; subtract some magenta to make a dull medium blue. All these colors assume a complete lack of yellow.

✦ **Magenta and yellow:** Full-intensity magenta and yellow mix to form a brilliant red. Subtract some magenta to make vivid orange; subtract some yellow to make rose. All these colors assume a complete lack of cyan.

✦ **Yellow and cyan:** Full-intensity yellow and cyan mix to form a bright green with a hint of blue. Subtract some yellow to make a deep teal; subtract some cyan to make chartreuse. All these colors assume a complete lack of magenta.

✦ **Cyan, magenta, and yellow:** Full-intensity cyan, magenta, and yellow mix to form a muddy brown.

✦ **Black:** Black pigmentation added to any other pigment darkens the color.

✦ **No pigment:** No pigmentation results in white (assuming white is the paper color).

Editing in CMYK

If you're used to editing RGB images, editing in the CMYK mode can require some new approaches, especially when editing individual color channels. When you view a single color channel in the RGB mode (as discussed later in this chapter), white indicates high-intensity color, and black indicates low-intensity color. It's the opposite in CMYK. When you view an individual color channel, black means high-intensity color, and white means low-intensity color.

This doesn't mean RGB and CMYK color channels look like inverted versions of each other. In fact, because the color theory is inverted, they look much the same. But if you're trying to achieve the full-intensity colors mentioned in the preceding section, you should apply black to the individual color channels, not white as you would in the RGB mode.

Should I edit in CMYK?

RGB doesn't accurately represent the colors you get when you print an image because the RGB color space contains many colors — particularly very bright colors — that CMYK can't touch. This is why when you switch from RGB to CMYK, the colors appear duller. (If you're familiar with painting, RGB is like oils and CMYK is like acrylics. The latter lacks the depth of color provided by the former.)

For this reason, many folks advocate working exclusively in the CMYK mode, but I do not. Although working in CMYK eliminates color disappointments, it is also much slower because Photoshop has to convert CMYK values to your RGB screen on-the-fly.

Furthermore, your scanner and monitor are RGB devices. No matter how you work, a translation from RGB to CMYK color space must occur at some time. If you pay the extra bucks to purchase a commercial drum scan, for example, you simply make the translation at the beginning of the process — Scitex has no option but to use RGB sensors internally — rather than at the end. Every color device on Earth, in fact, is RGB except the printer.

You should wait to convert to the CMYK mode until right before you print. After your artwork is finalized, choose Image ➪ Mode ➪ CMYK Color and make whatever edits you deem necessary. For example, you might want to introduce a few color corrections, apply some sharpening, and even retouch a few details by hand. Photoshop applies your changes more slowly in the CMYK mode, but at least you're only slowed down at the end of the job, not throughout the entire process.

Before converting an image to the CMYK color space, make certain Photoshop is aware of the monitor you're using and the printer you intend to use. These two items can have a pronounced effect on how Photoshop generates a CMYK image. I discuss how to set up your personal RGB and CMYK color spaces in Chapter 16.

The above advice about converting to CMYK before printing applies to professional printing situations only. If you're just in your home office printing to your inkjet printer, you should leave your image in RGB mode when you print. Your printer will handle the CMYK conversion internally, with no muss and fuss on your part.

Previewing the CMYK color space

While you're editing in RGB mode, you can *soft proof* your image — display a rough approximation of what the image will look like when converted to CMYK and printed. To display colors in the CMYK color space, choose View ➪ Proof Colors. You also can press Ctrl+Y (⌘-Y on the Mac).

But before you do either, select the output you want to preview from the View ➪ Proof Setup submenu. Photoshop creates the proof display based on your selection. You can preview the image using the current CMYK working space, choose Custom to specify a particular output device, or preview the individual cyan, magenta, yellow, and black plates. The plates appear as grayscale images unless you colorize them by selecting the Color Channels in Color option in the Display & Cursors panel of the Preferences dialog box (that's Ctrl+K, Ctrl+3 on the PC and ⌘-K, ⌘-3 on the Mac). If you work with an older model color inkjet printer that prints using just cyan, magenta, and yellow, you can choose the Working CMY Plates option to see what your image will look like when printed without black ink.

View ⇨ Gamut Warning (Ctrl+Shift+Y on the PC or ⌘-Shift-Y on the Mac) is a companion to Photoshop's CMYK preview commands that covers so-called out-of-gamut colors — RGB colors with no CMYK equivalents — with gray. I find this command less useful because it demonstrates a problem without suggesting a solution. You can desaturate the grayed colors with the sponge tool (which I explain in Chapter 5), but this accomplishes little that Photoshop won't do automatically. A CMYK preview is much more serviceable and representative of the final CMYK image.

CIE's Lab

RGB isn't the only mode that responds quickly and provides a bountiful range of colors. Photoshop's Lab color space comprises all the colors from RGB and CMYK and is every bit as fast as RGB. Many high-end users prefer to work in this mode, and I certainly advocate this if you're brave enough.

Whereas the RGB mode is the color model of your luminescent computer screen and the CMYK mode is the color model of the reflective page, Lab is independent of light or pigment. Perhaps you've already heard the bit about how, in 1931, an international color organization called the Commission Internationale d'Eclairage (CIE) developed a color model that, in theory, contains every single color the human eye can see. (Gnats, iguanas, fruit bats, go find your own color models; humans, you have CIE. Mutants and aliens — maybe CIE, maybe not, too early to tell.) Then, in 1976, the CIE came up with two additional color systems. One of those systems was Lab, and the other was shrouded in secrecy. Well, at least I don't know what the other one was. Probably something that measures how, when using flash photography, the entire visible spectrum of color can bounce off your retina and come out looking the exact shade of red one normally associates with lab (not Lab) rabbits. But this is just a guess.

The beauty of the Lab color model is it fills in gaps in both the RGB and CMYK models. RGB, for example, provides an overabundance of colors in the blue-to-green range but is stingy on yellows, oranges, and other colors in the green-to-red range. Meanwhile, the colors missing from CMYK are as numerous as the holes in the Albert Hall. Lab gets everything right.

Understanding Lab anatomy

The Lab mode features three color channels, one for luminosity and two others for color ranges, known simply by the initials a and b. (The Greeks would have called them alpha and beta, if that's any help.) Upon hearing luminosity, you might think, "Ah, just like HSL." Well, to make things confusing, Lab's *luminosity* is like HSB's brightness. White indicates full-intensity color.

Meanwhile, the a channel contains colors ranging from deep green (low-brightness values) to gray (medium-brightness values) to vivid pink (high-brightness values). The b channel ranges from bright blue (low-brightness values) to gray to burnt yellow (high-brightness values). As in the RGB model, these colors mix together to produce lighter colors. Only the brightness values in the luminosity channel darken the colors. So you can think of Lab as a two-channel RGB with brightness thrown on top.

To get a glimpse of how it works, try the following simple experiment.

STEPS: Testing Out the Lab Mode

1. **Create a new image in the Lab mode—say, 300×300 pixels, setting the Contents option to White.**

2. **Press D to return the default colors to the toolbox.** The foreground color is now black and the background color is white.

3. **Press Ctrl+2 (⌘-2 on the Mac).** This takes you to the *a* channel.

4. **Click the gradient tool in the toolbox.** In the Options bar, select the Foreground to Background option from the gradient pop-up menu, select the Linear gradient style, and select Normal from the Mode pop-up menu. (See Chapter 6 if you need help using these controls in the Options bar.)

5. **Shift-drag with the gradient tool from the top to the bottom of the window.** This creates a vertical black-to-white gradation.

6. **Press Ctrl+3 (⌘-3 on the Mac).** This takes you to the *b* channel.

7. **Shift-drag from left to right with the gradient tool.** Photoshop paints a horizontal gradation.

8. **Press Ctrl+tilde (~) (⌘-tilde on the Mac) to return to the composite display.** Now you can see all channels at once. If you're using a 24-bit monitor, you should be looking at a window filled with an incredible array of super bright colors. In theory, these are the brightest shades of all the colors you can see. In practice, however, the colors are limited by the display capabilities of your RGB monitor.

Using Lab

Because it's device independent, you can use the Lab mode to edit any image. Editing in the Lab mode is as fast as editing in the RGB mode and several times faster than editing in the CMYK mode. If you plan on printing your image to color separations, you may want to experiment with using the Lab mode instead of RGB, because Lab ensures no colors are altered when you convert the image to CMYK, except to change colors that fall outside the CMYK range. In fact, any time you convert an image from RGB to CMYK, Photoshop automatically converts the image to the Lab mode as an intermediate step.

 Tip If you work with Photo CDs often, open the scans directly from the Photo CD format as Lab images. Kodak's proprietary YCC color model is nearly identical to Lab, so you can expect an absolute minimum of data loss; some people claim no loss whatever occurs.

Indexed Color

Choose Image ➪ Mode ➪ Indexed Color to display the dialog box shown in Figure 4-5. This command permits you to strip an image of all but its most essential colors, a necessary step when saving GIF images and other graphics for display on the Web. Photoshop then generates a color look-up table (LUT), which describes the few remaining colors in the image. The LUT serves as an index, which is why the process is called *indexing*.

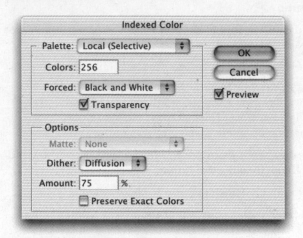

Figure 4-5: Use the Palette options to select the kinds of colors that remain in the image. Use the Colors option to specify how many colors remain.

For some reason, Photoshop doesn't let you apply the Indexed Color command to Lab or CMYK images. And although you can apply Indexed Color to a grayscale image, you don't get any control over the indexing process; Photoshop doesn't let you reduce the image to fewer than 256 colors, for example. So if you want to index a Lab or CMYK image or custom-prepare a grayscale image, choose Image ➪ Mode ➪ RGB Color to convert the image to the RGB mode and then choose Image ➪ Mode ➪ Indexed Color.

Tip
Don't expect to be able to edit your image after indexing it. Most of Photoshop's functions — including the gradient tool, all the edit tools, and the filters — refuse to work. Others, like feathering and the brush tool, produce undesirable effects. If you plan on editing an 8-bit image much in Photoshop, convert it to the RGB mode, edit it as desired, and then switch back to the indexed color mode when you finish.

Now that I've gotten all the warnings and special advice out of the way, the following list provides a brief rundown of the options inside the Indexed Color dialog box along with some recommended settings for Web graphics:

✦ **Palette:** This pop-up menu tells Photoshop how to compute the colors in the look-up table. You have lots of options here, but only a handful are really useful. If your image already contains fewer than 256 colors, the Exact option appears by default, in which case you should just press Enter or Return and let the command do its stuff. The Web option converts your image to the 216 so-called "Web-safe" colors. The Adaptive option selects the most frequently used colors in your image, which typically delivers the best possible results. The Perceptual and Selective options are variations on Adaptive. But where Adaptive maintains the most popular colors, Perceptual is more intelligent, sampling the colors that produce the best transitions. The Selective option tries to maintain key colors, including those in the "Web-safe" palette. The Adaptive, Perceptual, and Selective options each come in two flavors, Local and Master. Choose Local if you want Photoshop to consider the colors in the current image only. If you have several images open and want to create a palette based on all the images, choose Master.

Tip

Here's some advice: Select Perceptual for images where smooth transitions are more important than color values. Use Selective when an image contains bright colors or sharp, graphic transitions. And if an image contains relatively few colors — and you want to maintain those colors as exactly as possible, go for Adaptive.

✦ **Colors:** You can specify the actual number of colors in the palette by entering a number in this option box. As you can guess, fewer colors result in smaller files. For GIF images, I generally start with 64 colors. If the image looks okay, I try going even lower.

✦ **Forced:** This option enables you to lock in important colors so that they don't change. Black and White locks in black and white. Primaries protects eight colors — white, red, green, blue, cyan, magenta, yellow, and black. And Web protects the 216 colors in the Web-safe palette. If you choose Custom, you can select the colors that you want to lock in.

✦ **Transparency:** If an image is set on a layer against a transparent background, selecting this check box maintains that transparency. Bear in mind, however, that transparency in a GIF file is either on or off; there are no soft transitions as in a Photoshop layer.

✦ **Matte:** The Matte option works in collaboration with the Transparency check box. (If there is no transparency in an image — that is, all layers cover one another to create a seamless opacity — the Matte option is dimmed.) When you select Transparency, the specified Matte color fills the translucent pixels in the image. When Transparency is turned off, the Matte color fills all translucent and transparent areas.

✦ **Dither:** This option controls how Photoshop mimics the colors that you asked it to remove from an image. None maps each color in the image to its closest equivalent in the look-up table, pixel for pixel. This results in the harshest color transitions, but it is frequently the preferable option. Diffusion dithers colors randomly to create a naturalistic effect. Pattern dithers colors in a geometric pattern, which is altogether ugly. Noise mixes pixels throughout the image, not merely in areas of transition.

✦ **Amount:** When you choose Diffusion as the dithering mode, you can modify the amount of dithering by raising or lowering this value. Lower values produce harsher color transitions, but lower the file size. It's a trade-off. Keep an eye on the image window to see how low you can go.

✦ **Preserve Exact Colors:** This check box is available only when the Diffusion option is selected from the Dither pop-up menu. When turned on, this option turns off dithering inside areas of flat color that exactly match a color in the active palette. As I mentioned before, you may often get better looking images if you apply no dithering. But if you decide to dither, turn Preserve Exact Colors on. Even if you can't see a difference on your screen, it may show up on another screen.

Grayscale

Grayscale is possibly my favorite color mode. Grayscale frees you from all the hassles and possible expense of working with color and provides access to every bit of Photoshop's power and functionality. Anyone who says you can't do as much with grayscale as you can with color missed out on *Citizen Kane*, *Grapes of Wrath*, *Manhattan*, and *Raging Bull*. You can print grayscale images to any laser printer, reproduce them in any publication, and edit them on nearly any machine. Besides, they look great, they remind you of old movies, and they make a hefty book such as this one affordable. What could be better?

Other than extolling its virtues, however, there isn't a whole lot to say about grayscale. You can convert an image to the grayscale mode regardless of its current mode, and you can convert from grayscale to any other mode just as easily. In fact, choosing Image ⇨ Mode ⇨ Grayscale is a necessary step in converting a color image to a duotone or black-and-white bitmap. (You also can use the Channel Mixer command to create a custom grayscale version of a color image, as I discuss near the end of this chapter.)

Search your channels before converting

When you convert an image from one of the color modes to the grayscale mode, Photoshop normally weights the values of each color channel in a way that retains the apparent brightness of the overall image. For example, when you convert an image from RGB, Photoshop weights red more heavily than blue when computing dark values. This is because red is a darker-looking color than blue (much as that might seem contrary to popular belief).

Tip

If you choose Image ⇨ Mode ⇨ Grayscale while viewing a single color channel, though, Photoshop retains all brightness values in that channel only and abandons the data in the other channels. This can be an especially useful technique for rescuing a grayscale image from a bad RGB scan.

So before switching to the grayscale mode, be sure to look at the individual color channels — particularly the red and green channels (the blue channel frequently contains substandard detail) — to see how each might look on its own. To browse the channels, use the following shortcuts (on the Mac, substitute the ⌘ key for Ctrl): Press Ctrl+1 for red, Ctrl+2 for green, and Ctrl+3 for blue. Or Ctrl+1 for cyan, Ctrl+2 for magenta, Ctrl+3 for yellow, and Ctrl+4 for black. Or even Ctrl+1 for luminosity, Ctrl+2 for *a*, and Ctrl+3 for *b*. I describe color channels in more detail later in this chapter.

Black-and-white (bitmap)

Choose Image ➪ Mode ➪ Bitmap to convert a flattened grayscale image to exclusively black-and-white pixels. This may sound like a boring option, but it can prove useful for gaining complete control over the printing of grayscale images. After all, output devices, such as laser printers and imagesetters, render grayscale images as a series of tiny dots. Using the Bitmap command, you can specify the size, shape, and angle of those dots.

When you choose Image ➪ Mode ➪ Bitmap, Photoshop displays the Bitmap dialog box, shown in Figure 4-6. Here you specify the resolution of the black-and-white image and select a conversion process. The options work as follows:

✦ **Output:** Specify the resolution of the black-and-white file. If you want control over every single pixel available to your printer, raise this value to match your printer's resolution. As a rule of thumb, try setting the Output value somewhere between 200 to 250 percent of the Input value.

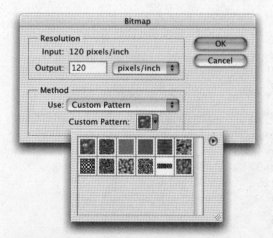

Figure 4-6: The Bitmap dialog box converts images from grayscale to black and white.

✦ **50% Threshold:** Select this option from the Use pop-up menu to change every pixel that is darker than 50 percent gray to black and every pixel that is 50 percent gray or lighter to white. Unless you are working toward some special effect — for example, overlaying a black-and-white version of an image over the original grayscale image — this option most likely isn't for you. (And if you're working toward a special effect, Image ⇨ Adjustments ⇨ Threshold is the better alternative.)

✦ **Pattern Dither:** To *dither* pixels is to mix them up to emulate different colors. In this case, Photoshop mixes up black and white pixels to produce shades of gray. The Pattern Dither option dithers an image using a geometric pattern. Unfortunately, the results are pretty ugly, as demonstrated in the top example in Figure 4-7. And the space between dots has a tendency to fill in, especially when you output to a laser printer.

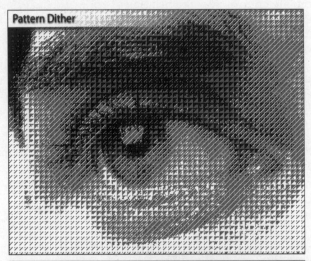

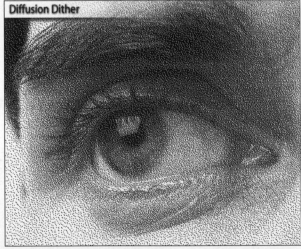

Figure 4-7: The results of selecting the Pattern Dither option (top) and the much-more-acceptable Diffusion Dither option (bottom).

✦ **Diffusion Dither:** Select this option from the Use pop-up menu to create a mezzotint-like effect, as demonstrated in the bottom example in Figure 4-7. Again, because this option converts an image into thousands of stray pixels, you can expect your image to darken dramatically when output to a low-resolution laser printer and when reproduced. So be sure to lighten the image with something like the Levels command (as described in Chapter 17) before selecting this option.

✦ **Halftone Screen:** When you select this option from the Use pop-up menu and press Enter or Return, Photoshop displays the dialog box shown in Figure 4-8. These options enable you to apply a dot pattern to the image, as demonstrated in Figure 4-9. Enter the number of dots per inch in the Frequency option box and the angle of the dots in the Angle option box. Then select a dot shape from the Shape pop-up menu. Figure 4-9 shows examples of four shapes, each with a frequency of 24 lines per inch.

Cross-Reference

I cover screen patterns and frequency settings in more depth in the "Changing the halftone screen" section of Chapter 18.

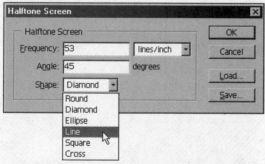

Figure 4-8: This dialog box appears when you select the Halftone Screen option in the Bitmap dialog box.

✦ **Custom Pattern:** To use a custom dither pattern, choose this option from the Use pop-up menu and open the Custom Pattern palette, as shown in Figure 4-6. The palette includes a number of predefined patterns that ship with Photoshop as well as any custom preset patterns that you may have defined using Edit ➪ Define Pattern. Simply click the icon for the pattern you want to use. Figure 4-10 shows two examples of predefined patterns (Metal Landscape and Herringbone 2) used as custom halftoning patterns.

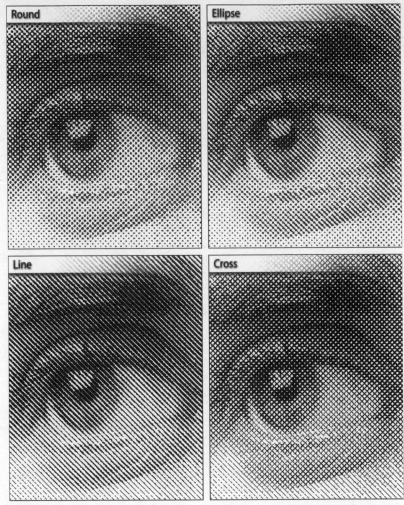

Figure 4-9: Four random examples of halftone cell shapes. In all cases, the Frequency value was set to 24.

Tip   To access additional preset patterns, choose Load from the palette menu (click the right-pointing triangle in the upper-right corner of the palette to display the menu). You can find the patterns in the Patterns folder, which lives inside the Presets folder. To delete a pattern from the palette, click its icon and choose Delete Pattern from the palette menu.

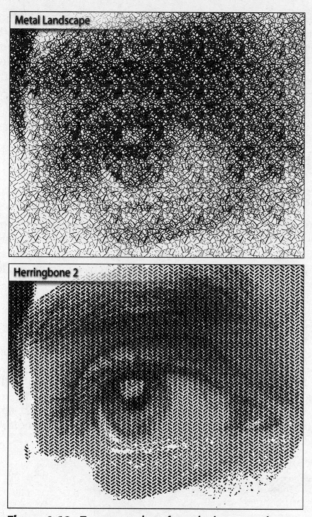

Metal Landscape

Herringbone 2

Figure 4-10: Two examples of employing repeating patterns as custom halftoning patterns.

Cross-Reference For a complete guide to creating and defining patterns in Photoshop, see the "Applying Repeating Patterns" section of Chapter 7.

Photoshop lets you edit individual pixels in the so-called bitmap mode, but that's about the extent of it. After you go to black-and-white, you can neither perform any serious editing nor expect to return to the grayscale mode and restore your original pixels. So be sure to finish your image editing before choosing Image ➪ Mode ➪ Bitmap. Even more important, make certain to save your image before converting it to black-and-white. Frankly, saving is a good idea prior to performing any color conversion.

Using Photoshop's Other Color Selection Methods

In addition to the Color Picker dialog box, Photoshop provides a handful of additional techniques for selecting colors. The next several sections explain how to use the Custom Colors dialog box, the Color palette, and the eyedropper tool. None of this information is terribly exciting, but it will enable you to work more efficiently and conveniently.

Predefined colors

If you click the Custom button inside the Color Picker dialog box, Photoshop displays the Custom Colors dialog box shown in Figure 4-11. In this dialog box, you can select from a variety of predefined colors by choosing the color family from the Book pop-up menu, moving the slider triangles up and down the color slider to specify a general range of colors, and ultimately, selecting a color from the color list on the left. If you own the swatchbook for a color family, you can locate a specific color by entering its number on the keyboard.

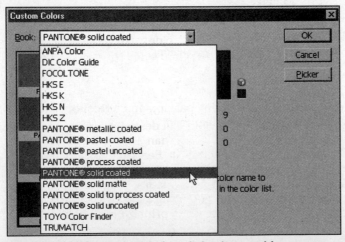

Figure 4-11: The Custom Colors dialog box enables you to select predefined colors from brand-name libraries.

The color families represented in the Book pop-up menu fall into seven brands: ANPA (now actually NAA, as I explain shortly), DIC, Focoltone, HKS, Pantone, Toyo, and Trumatch, all of which get a big kick out of capitalizing their entire names in dialog boxes, whether or not those names are acronyms. I honestly think one of these companies would stand out better if its name weren't capitalized. Anyway, at the risk of offending a few of these companies, you're likely to find certain brands more useful than others. The following sections briefly introduce the brands in order of their impact on the American market — forgive me for being ethnocentric in this regard — from smallest to greatest impact.

Tip

The number-one use for predefined colors in Photoshop is in the creation of duotones, tritones, and quadtones (described in Chapter 18). You can also use predefined colors to match the colors in a logo or some other important element in an image to a commercial standard. And you can add an independent channel for a predefined color and print it to a separate plate, as discussed later in this chapter.

Focoltone, DIC, Toyo, and HKS

Focoltone, Dianippon Ink and Chemical (DIC), Toyo, and HKS fall into the negligible impact category. All are foreign color standards with followings abroad. Focoltone is an English company; not English speaking (although they probably do), but English living, as in commuting-to-France-through-the-Channel England. DIC and Toyo are popular in the Japanese market, but have next to no subscribers outside Japan. HKS formerly was provided only in the German and French versions of Photoshop, but enough people asked for it to be included in other languages that it now is available in all versions of the program.

Newspaper Association of America

American Newspaper Publishers Association (ANPA) is now part of NAA, which stands for Newspaper Association of America, and has updated its color catalog. NAA provides a small sampling of 45 process colors (mixes of cyan, magenta, yellow, and black ink) plus 5 spot colors (colors produced by printing a single ink). The idea behind the NAA colors is to isolate the color combinations that reproduce most successfully on inexpensive newsprint and to provide advertisers with a solid range of colors from which to choose, without allowing the color choices to get out of hand.

Trumatch

Trumatch remains my personal favorite process-color standard. Designed entirely using a desktop system and created especially with desktop publishers in mind, the Trumatch Colorfinder swatchbook features more than 2,000 process colors, organized according to hue, saturation, and brightness. Each hue is broken down into 40 tints and shades. Reducing the saturation in 15-percent increments creates tints; adding black ink in 6-percent increments creates shades. The result is a guide that shows you exactly which colors you can attain using a desktop system. If you're wondering what a CMYK blend will look like when printed, you need look no further than the Trumatch Colorfinder.

As if the Colorfinder weren't enough, Trumatch provides the ColorPrinter Software utility, which automatically prints the entire 2,000-color library to any PostScript-compatible output device. The utility integrates EfiColor and PostScript Level 2, thereby enabling design firms and commercial printers to test the entire range of capabilities available to their hardware. Companies can provide select clients with swatches of colors created on their own printers, guaranteeing what you see is darn well what you'll get.

Pantone

On the heels of Trumatch, Pantone released a 3,006-color Process Color System Guide (labeled Pantone Process in the Book pop-up menu) priced at $85. Pantone also produces the foremost spot color swatchbook, the Color Formula Guide. Then there's the Solid to Process Guide, which enables you to figure out quickly if you can closely match a Pantone spot color using a process-color blend or if you ought to give it up and stick with the spot color.

Pantone spot colors are ideal for creating duotones and adding custom colors to an image for logos and the like, both discussed in Chapter 18. Furthermore, Pantone is supported by every computer application that aspires to the color prepress market. As long as the company retains the old competitive spirit, you can, most likely, expect Pantone to remain the primary color printing standard for years to come.

The Color palette

Another means of selecting colors in Photoshop is to use the Color palette, shown in Figure 4-12. The Color palette is convenient, it's always there, and it doesn't hog your screen like the Color Picker dialog box. Frankly, this is the tool I use most often to select colors in Photoshop.

To display the palette, choose Window ➪ Color or press the F6 key. If you want, you can dock the palette in the Options bar palette well. For details on that intriguing offer, flip back to Chapter 2. Either way, you use the elements and options inside the palette as follows:

✦ **Foreground color/background color:** Click the foreground or background color icon in the Color palette to specify the color you want to edit. If you click the foreground or background color icon when it's already highlighted — as indicated by a double-line frame — Photoshop displays the Color Picker dialog box.

✦ **Sliders:** Drag the triangles in the slider controls to edit the highlighted color. By default, the sliders represent the red, green, and blue primary colors when a color image is open. You can change the slider bars by choosing a different color model from the palette menu.

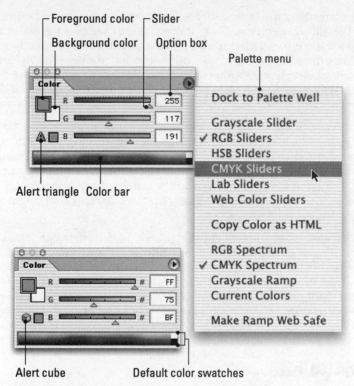

Figure 4-12: The Color palette as it appears normally (top) and with the Web Color Sliders option selected (bottom).

✦ **Option boxes:** Alternatively, you can enter numerical values into the option boxes to the right of the sliders. Press Tab to advance from one option box to the next; press Shift+Tab to go to the previous option.

✦ **Alert triangle and cube:** Photoshop displays the alert triangle when a color falls outside the CMYK color gamut. The color swatch to the right of the triangle shows the closest CMYK equivalent. Click the triangle or the color swatch to replace the current color with the CMYK equivalent.

If you select the Web Color Sliders option from the palette menu, the alert cube appears to indicate colors that aren't included in the Web-safe palette. The palette also displays the hexadecimal values for the color, as shown in Figure 4-12. And as you drag the sliders, they automatically snap to Web-safe hues. To limit the palette so that it displays Web-safe colors only, choose Make Ramp Web Safe from the palette menu.

Tip

After you define a Web color, choose Copy Color as HTML from the palette menu to save the hexadecimal code for the color to the Clipboard. You can then paste the code into an HTML file by choosing Edit ➪ Paste in the Web application.

✦ **Color bar:** The bar along the bottom of the Color palette displays all colors contained in the CMYK spectrum. Click or drag inside the color bar to lift a color and make it the current foreground or background color (depending on whether the foreground or background icon is selected above). The sliders update as you drag. Alt-click (Option-click on the Mac) or drag to lift the background color if the foreground icon is selected or the foreground color if the background color is selected.

You needn't accept the CMYK spectrum in the color bar, however. To change to a different spectrum, just choose the spectrum from the palette menu. Or Shift-click the color bar to cycle through the available spectrums. You can opt for the RGB spectrum, a black-to-white gradation (Grayscale Ramp), or a gradation from the current foreground color to the current background color (Current Colors). The color bar continuously updates to represent the newest foreground and background colors.

Notice the black and white squares at the right end of the color bar? You can click 'em to set a color to absolute black or white. But if all you want to do is set the foreground color to black, don't bother with the Color palette — just press D. For white, press D and then X. The first shortcut restores the foreground and background colors to black and white, respectively; pressing X swaps the colors to make white the foreground color and black the background color.

The Swatches palette

Choose Window ⇨ Swatches to display the Swatches palette, shown in Figure 4-13, which lets you collect colors for future use, sort of like a favorite color reservoir. You can use the palette also to set the foreground and background colors.

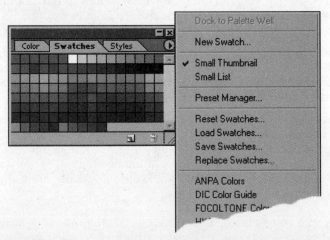

Figure 4-13: You can create custom swatch collections in the Swatches palette.

Here's how to take advantage of the Swatches palette:

✦ Click a color swatch to make that color the foreground color. Alt-click (Option-click on the Mac) to set the background color.

✦ To add the current foreground color to the reservoir, Shift-click an existing color swatch to replace the old color or click an empty swatch to append the new color. In either case, your cursor temporarily changes to a paint bucket. After you click, you're asked to give the swatch a name. Type the name and click OK. If you later want to change the name, just double-click the swatch to redisplay the name dialog box.

You can bypass the dialog box and add an unnamed color to the palette by Alt-clicking (Option-clicking on the Mac) an empty space in the palette.

✦ To delete a color from the palette, Alt-click (Option-click on the Mac) a color swatch. Your cursor changes to a pair of scissors and cuts the color away.

✦ The Swatches palette includes a new icon and trash icon, similar to those you find in the Layers palette. The icons provide alternative methods of adding and deleting colors: Click the new icon (it's the one that looks like a page) to add a new swatch in the current foreground color; Alt-click (Win) or Option-click (Mac) to display the name dialog box and then add the color. Drag a swatch to the trash icon to delete it from the palette.

You can also save and load color palettes on disk using options in the pop-up menu. Load Swatches appends swatches stored in a swatches file to the current set of swatches; Replace Swatches replaces the current swatches with the ones in the file. Save Swatches lets you create a new swatch collection and save it to disk.

The Presets folder, located inside the main Photoshop folder, contains folders for all the available preset items, tool presets (see Chapter 2) and color swatches being only two of them. The Color Swatches folder, found inside the Photoshop Only folder of the Presets folder, contains palettes for the major color libraries from Pantone, Trumatch, and others. You can load these palettes by simply selecting them from the palette pop-up menu. You're then given the choice of appending the swatches to the existing swatches or replacing the current swatches altogether. Custom swatch sets that you create also appear on the palette menu, but only after you close and restart Photoshop.

When a color library palette is loaded, positioning your cursor over a color swatch displays a tool tip showing the name of that color. If you prefer to select colors by using the color names, select Small List from the palette menu. Now you see a scrolling list of colors instead of just the swatches.

Swatches presets

You can also create and manage swatch collections using the Preset Manager. Choose Preset Manager from the Swatches palette menu, choose Edit ⇨ Preset

Manager and then choose Swatches from the Preset Type pop-up menu, or choose Edit ⇨ Preset Manager and then press Ctrl+2 (⌘-2 on the Mac) to display the Swatches presets panel, shown in Figure 4-14. The presets panel shows the current swatch set.

Click for palette menu

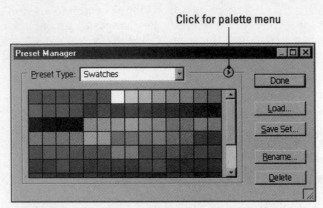

Figure 4-14: To easily create a new swatch collection using just some colors from an existing collection, head for the Preset Manager.

Many functions in the Swatches panel of the Preset Manager duplicate those offered by the Swatches palette. If you click the arrow to the left of the Done button (see the figure), you display a pop-up menu that's nearly identical to the Swatches palette menu. You can choose the Replace Swatches command on the pop-up menu to replace the current swatch collection with another or choose Reset Swatches to return to the default swatch collection. To append a collection, click the Load button. Alternatively, click a collection name in the pop-up menu, in which case you have the choice of appending or replacing the current collection with the new one. To create a new swatch collection comprised of colors from an existing set, Shift-click the swatches you want to include and click Save Set. Then name the collection and store it in the Color Swatches folder.

Cross-Reference
For complete details on using the Preset Manager, see "The Preset Manager" section in Chapter 2.

The eyedropper tool

The eyedropper tool—which you can select by pressing I—provides the most convenient and straightforward means of selecting colors in Photoshop. This is so straightforward, in fact, it's hardly worth explaining. But quickly, here's how the eyedropper tool works:

✦ **Selecting a foreground color:** To select a new foreground color, click the desired color inside any open image window with the eyedropper tool. (This assumes the foreground icon in the Color palette is selected. If the background icon is selected, Alt-click or Option-click with the eyedropper tool to lift the foreground color.) You can even click inside a background window to lift a color without bringing that window to the foreground.

To select a color on your computer screen that isn't contained in one of Photoshop's image windows, click inside an image window with the eyedropper and then drag the tool outside of the window.

✦ **Selecting a background color:** To select a new background color, Alt-click (Option-click on the Mac) the desired color with the eyedropper tool. (Again, this assumes the foreground icon is selected in the Color palette. If the background icon is selected, click with the eyedropper to lift the background color.)

✦ **Skating over the color spectrum:** You can animate the foreground color control box by dragging with the eyedropper tool. As soon as you achieve the desired color, release your mouse button. To animate the background color icon, Alt-drag (Win) or Option-drag (Mac) with the eyedropper tool. The icon color changes as you move the eyedropper tool. Again, swap these procedures if the background color icon is selected in the Color palette.

✦ **Sampling multiple pixels:** Normally, the eyedropper tool selects the color from the single pixel on which you click. If you prefer to average the colors of several neighboring pixels, however, choose either the 3 by 3 Average or 5 by 5 Average option from the Sample Size pop-up menu in the Options bar. Or right-click (Control-click on the Mac) with the eyedropper to display a pop-up menu of sampling options near the cursor. In this case, you get one additional choice, Copy Color as HTML, which works just as it does when you select it from the Color palette pop-up menu. Photoshop determines the hexadecimal code for the color and sends the code to the Clipboard so that you can use Edit ➪ Paste to dump the code into an HTML file.

Tip

To access the eyedropper tool temporarily when using a type, paint bucket, gradient, line, pencil, or brush tool, press and hold the Alt key (or Option key on the Mac). The eyedropper cursor remains in force for as long as the Alt or Option key is down. The eyedropper lifts whatever color is active in the Color palette (foreground or background). To lift the other color, switch to the eyedropper tool by pressing the I key and then Alt-click (Option-click on the Mac) in an image window.

The color sampler tool

Found in the same toolbox flyout as the eyedropper, the color sampler tool looks like the eyedropper with a little crosshair target. But where the eyedropper lifts foreground and background colors, the color sampler merely measures the colors of pixels so that you can monitor how the pixels react to various color changes.

Select the color sampler and click somewhere inside the image window. Photoshop adds a crosshair target to indicate the point you clicked. The program also brings up the Info palette (if it isn't up already) and adds a new color measurement item labeled #1. This item corresponds to the target in the image, which is likewise labeled #1. Click again and you add a second target and a corresponding item #2 in the Info palette. You can add up to four targets to an image, as demonstrated in Figure 4-15.

Figure 4-15: The color sampler tool lets you measure the colors of four points in your image, as indicated by the black arrows. You can also measure a fifth point by merely moving the cursor around.

The color sampler is primarily intended for printers and technicians who want to monitor the effects of color corrections on specific points in an image. If you apply Image ➪ Adjustments ➪ Levels, for example, Photoshop constantly updates the items in the Info palette to reflect your changes (as I explain in more detail in Chapter 17). But you can also sample points in an image to monitor the effects of filters (Chapters 10 and 11), blend modes (Chapter 13), and edit tools, such as dodge and burn (Chapter 5). The color sampler is just another way to monitor changes to an image.

Here are a few more techniques of interest when color sampling:

✦ Photoshop limits you to four color targets. If you try to create a fifth one, the program generates an error message. If you want to measure a different point in the image, you can either hover your cursor over the point and note the top set of color values in the Info palette (as in Figure 4-15) or move one of the targets.

✦ To move a target inside the image window, drag it with the color sampler tool. You can also move a target by pressing Ctrl (Win) or ⌘ (Mac) and dragging it with the eyedropper tool. Hold down the Shift key to constrain the drag to a 45-degree angle.

✦ To delete a target, Alt-click (Win) or Option-click (Mac) it. To delete all targets, click the Clear button in the Options bar.

✦ The Info palette grows to more than twice its normal size when you start clicking with the color sampler. To hide the sampler information without deleting targets, click the Info palette's collapse box or choose Hide Color Samplers from the palette menu. If you go the second route, you have to choose Show Color Samplers to bring the samples back.

✦ By default, the sampler items in the Info palette measure colors in the active color space. If you want to track a target in a different color space, click the item's eyedropper icon in the Info palette or right-click (Control-click on the Mac) the target in the image window. Either way, you get a pop-up menu of color space alternatives, including Grayscale, RGB, and several others that you may recall from previous explanations in this chapter.

Tip

To select the color sampler, press I when the eyedropper is active or Alt-click (Option-click on the Mac) the eyedropper icon. Or press I repeatedly to cycle between the eyedropper, color sampler, and measure tool (add Shift if you activated the Use Shift Key for Tool Switch option in the Preferences dialog box). You can also temporarily access the color sampler any time the eyedropper is active by pressing Shift. This little trick also works when a color correction dialog box such as Levels or Curves is open, as explained in Chapter 17. It's just the ticket when you're in the middle of an adjustment and you need to know how it's affecting specific portions of the image.

Introducing Color Channels

After I've droned on for pages about color in Photoshop, it might surprise you when I say that Photoshop is at its heart a grayscale editor. Oh sure, it offers an array of color conversion features and it displays and prints spectacular full-color images. But when it comes to editing the image, everything happens in grayscale.

This is because Photoshop approaches every full-color image not as a single collection of 24-bit pixels, but as three or four bands of 8-bit (grayscale) pixels. An RGB file contains a band of red, a band of green, and a band of blue, each of which functions as a separate grayscale image. A Lab image likewise contains three bands, one corresponding to luminosity and the others to the variables *a* and *b*. A CMYK file contains four bands, one for each of the process-color inks. These bands are known as *channels*.

Channels frequently correspond to the structure of an input or output device. Each channel in a CMYK image, for example, corresponds to a different printer's plate when the document goes to press. The cyan plate is inked with cyan, the magenta plate is inked with magenta, and so on. Each channel in an RGB image corresponds to a pass of the red, green, or blue scanner sensor over the original photograph or artwork. Only the Lab mode is device independent, so its channels don't correspond to any piece of hardware.

Why you should care

But so what, right? Who cares how many planes of color an image comprises? You want to edit the photograph, not dissect it. "Dammit, Jim, I'm an artist, not a doctor!" Well, even if you don't like to poke preserved frog entrails with sharp knives, you'll get a charge out of editing channels. The fact is, channels provide you with yet another degree of selective control over an image.

Consider this example: Your client scanned a photograph of his gap-toothed daughter that he wants you to integrate into some goofy ad campaign for his car dealership. Unfortunately, the scan is downright rotten. You don't want to offend the guy, so you praise him on his fine offspring and say something to the effect of, "No problem, boss." But after you take it back to your office and load it into Photoshop, you break out in a cold sweat. You try swabbing at it with the edit tools, applying a few filters, and even attempting some scary-looking color correction commands, but the image continues to look like the inside of a garbage disposal. (Not that I've ever seen the inside of a garbage disposal, but it can't be attractive.)

Suddenly, it occurs to you to look at the channels. What the heck, it can't hurt. With very little effort, you discover that the red and green channels look okay, but the blue channel looks like it's melting. Her mouth is sort of mixed in with her teeth, her eyes look like an experiment in expressionism, and her hair has taken on a slightly geometric appearance. (If you think that this is a big exaggeration, take a look at a few blue channels from a low-end scanner or digital camera. They're frequently rife with tattered edges, random blocks of color, stray pixels, and other so-called digital artifacts.)

The point is, you've located the cancer. You don't have to waste your time trying to perform surgery on the entire image; in fact, doing so may very well harm the channels that are in good shape. You merely have to fix this one channel. A wave of the Gaussian Blur filter here, an application of the Levels command there, and some selective rebuilding of missing detail borrowed from the other channels — all of which I'll get to in future sections and chapters—result in an image that resembles a living, breathing human being. Granted, she still needs braces, but you're an artist, not an orthodontist.

How channels work

Photoshop devotes 8 bits of data to each pixel in each channel, thus permitting 256 brightness values, from 0 (black) to 255 (white). Therefore, each channel is actually an independent grayscale image. At first, this may throw you off. If an RGB image is made up of red, green, and blue channels, why do all the channels look gray?

Photoshop provides an option in the Display & Cursors panel of the Preferences dialog box (that's Ctrl+K, Ctrl+3 on the PC and ⌘-K, ⌘-3 on the Mac) called Color Channels in Color. When selected, this function displays each channel in its corresponding primary color. But although this feature can be reassuring—particularly to novices—it's equally counterproductive.

When you view an 8-bit image composed exclusively of shades of red, for example, it's easy to miss subtle variations in detail that may appear obvious when you print the image. You may have problems accurately gauging the impact of filters and tonal adjustments. I mean, face it, red isn't a friendly shade to stare at for a half hour of intense editing. So leave the Color Channels in Color option off and temporarily suspend your biological urge for on-screen color. With a little experience, you'll be able to better monitor your adjustments and predict the outcome of your edits in plain old grayscale.

Images that include 256 or fewer colors can be expressed in a single channel and therefore do not include multiple channels that you can edit independently. A grayscale image, for example, is just one channel. A black-and-white bitmap permits only one bit of data per pixel, so a single channel is more than enough to express it.

Cross-Reference

You can add channels above and beyond those required to represent a color or grayscale image for the purpose of storing masks, as described in Chapter 9. But even then, each channel is typically limited to 8 bits of data per pixel—meaning that it's just another grayscale image. Mask channels do not affect the appearance of the image on screen or when it is printed. Rather, they serve to save selection outlines, as Chapter 9 explains.

How to switch and view channels

To access channels in Photoshop, display the Channels palette by choosing Window ➪ Channels. Every channel in the image appears in the palette—including any mask channels—as shown in Figure 4-16. Photoshop even shows little thumbnail views of each channel so that you can see what it looks like.

To switch to a different channel, click a channel name in the Channels palette. The channel name becomes selected — like the Blue channel in Figure 4-16 — showing that you can now edit it independently of other channels in the image.

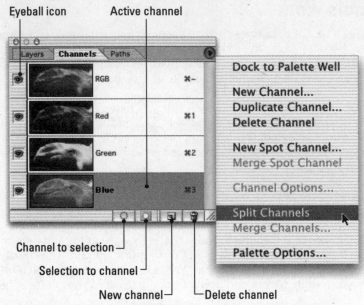

Figure 4-16: Photoshop displays tiny thumbnails of each color channel in the Channels palette.

Tip

To edit more than one channel at a time, click one channel name and then Shift-click another. You can also Shift-click an active channel to deactivate it independently of any others.

When you select a single channel, Photoshop displays just that one channel on screen. However, you can view additional channels beyond those that you want to edit. To specify which channels appear and which remain invisible, click in the far-left column of the Channels palette. Click an eyeball icon to make it disappear and hence hide that channel. Click where there is no eyeball to create one and thus display the channel.

When only one channel is visible, that channel appears as a grayscale picture in the image window (possibly colorized in accordance with the Color Channels in Color check box in the Preferences dialog box). However, when more than one channel is visible, you always see color. If both the blue and green channels are visible, for example, the image appears blue-green. If the red and green channels are visible, the image has a yellow cast, and so on.

In addition to the individual channels, Photoshop provides access to a *composite view* that displays all colors in an RGB, CMYK, or Lab image at once. (The composite view does not show mask channels; you have to specify their display separately.) The composite view is listed first in the Channels palette and is displayed by default. Notice that when you select the composite view, all the names of the individual color channels in the Channels palette turn gray along with the composite channel. This shows that all the channels are active. The composite view is the default in which you will perform the majority of your image editing.

Press Ctrl (Win) or ⌘ (Mac) plus a number key to switch between color channels. Depending on the color mode you're working in, Ctrl+1 (⌘-1 on the Mac) takes you to the red (RGB), cyan (CMYK), or luminosity (Lab) channel; Ctrl+2 takes you to the green, magenta, or *a* channel; and Ctrl+3 takes you to the blue, yellow, or *b* channel. In the CMYK mode, Ctrl+4 displays the black channel. Other Ctrl-key equivalents — up to Ctrl+9 — take you to mask or spot-color channels (if there are any). To go to the composite view, press Ctrl+tilde (~) — that's ⌘-tilde on the Mac, of course. Tilde is typically the key to the left of 1, or on some keyboards, to the right of the spacebar.

When editing a single channel, you may find it helpful to monitor the results in both grayscale and full-color views. Choose Window ⇨ Documents ⇨ New Window to create a new window for the image, which automatically sets to the color composite view. Then return to the first window and edit away on the individual channel. One of the amazing benefits to creating multiple views in Photoshop is that the views may show entirely different channels, layers, and other image elements.

The shortcuts are slightly different when you're working on a grayscale image. You access the image itself by pressing Ctrl+1 (⌘-1 on the Mac). Ctrl+2 (⌘-2 on the Mac) and higher take you to extra spot-color and mask channels.

Trying Channels on for Size

Feeling a little mystified? Need some examples? Fair enough. The top image in Color Plate 4-1 shows what is apparently a beluga whale in its natural habitat — the water. As you'd expect, this underwater image contains lots of greens and blues. These colors, along with yellow and red, cover the four corners of the color spectrum. Therefore, you can expect to see a good bit of variation between the images in the independent color channels.

RGB channels

Suppose that the beluga whale is an RGB image. Figure 4-17 compares a grayscale composite of this same image (created by choosing Image ⇨ Mode ⇨ Grayscale) compared with the contents of the red, green, and blue color channels from the original color image. The green channel is closest to the grayscale composite because green is such a dominant color in the image. The red channel differs the most from the grayscale composite, because there simply isn't much red in the image. The overall darkness of the red channel bears this out. The pixels in the blue channel are lightest in the water because — you guessed it — the water is rich with blue.

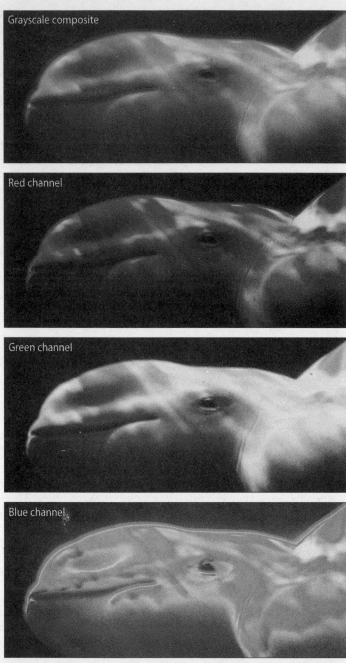

Grayscale composite

Red channel

Green channel

Blue channel

Figure 4-17: A grayscale composite of the original image from Color Plate 4-1 followed by the contents of the red, green, and blue color channels.

Notice how the channels in Figure 4-17 make interesting grayscale images in and of themselves? The red channel, for example, makes the whale look like he's much deeper underwater; we can see the sun streaming through, but it seems to be filtered through a great mass of water.

I mentioned this as a tip earlier, but it bears a bit of casual drumming into the old noggin. When converting a color image to grayscale, you have the option of calculating a grayscale composite or simply retaining the image exactly as it appears in one of the channels. To create a grayscale composite, choose Image ⇨ Mode ⇨ Grayscale when viewing all colors in the image in the composite view, as usual. To retain a single channel only, switch to that channel and then choose Image ⇨ Mode ⇨ Grayscale. Instead of the usual *Discard color information?* message, Photoshop displays the message *Discard other channels?* If you click the OK button, Photoshop chucks the other channels into the electronic abyss.

When the warning dialog box appears, select the Do Not Show Again check box if you don't want Photoshop to ask for permission to dump color information or channels when you convert to grayscale. If you grow to miss the warning, click the Reset All Warning Dialogs button on the General panel of the Preferences dialog box.

CMYK channels

In the name of fair and unbiased coverage, Figures 4-18 and 4-19 show the channels from the image after it was converted to other color modes. In Figure 4-18, I converted the image to the CMYK mode and examined its channels. Here, the predominant color is cyan, due to the blues and greens in the image. Because this color mode relies on pigments rather than light, as explained in the "CMYK" section earlier in this chapter, dark areas in the channels represent high color intensity. For that reason, the whale is dark in the cyan channel, whereas it's light in the blue channel back in Figure 4-17.

Notice that the cyan channel in Figure 4-18 is similar to its red counterpart in Figure 4-17. Same with the magenta and green channels, and the yellow and blue channels. The CMY channels have more contrast than their RGB pals, but the basic brightness distribution is the same. Here's another graphic demonstration of color theory. In a perfect world, the CMY channels would be identical to the RGB channels — one color model would simply be the other turned on its head. But because this is not a perfect world (you might have noticed that as you've traveled life's bitter highway), Photoshop has to boost the contrast of the CMY channels and throw in black to punch up those shadows.

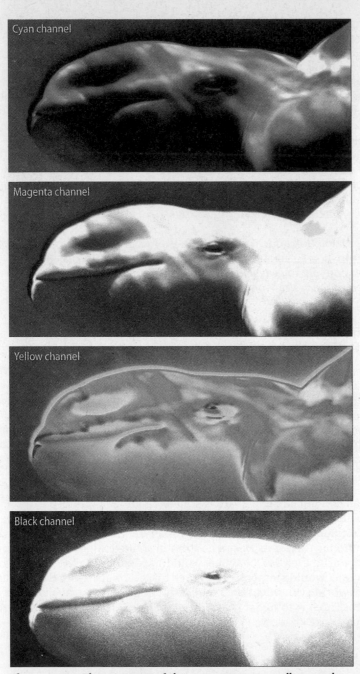

Figure 4-18: The contents of the cyan, magenta, yellow, and black channels from the original image shown in Color Plate 4-1.

Lab channels

To create Figure 4-19, I converted the original image in Color Plate 4-1 to the Lab mode. The image in the luminosity channel looks very similar to the grayscale composite in Figure 4-17 because it contains the lightness and darkness values for the image. The *a* channel maps the greens and magentas, while the *b* channel maps the yellows and blues, so both channels are working hard to provide color information for this photograph. Certainly there are differences — the whale is much darker in the *a* channel, and its glowing halo appears dark in the *b* channel — but the two channels carry roughly equivalent amounts of color information.

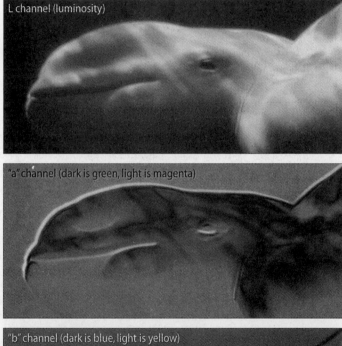

Figure 4-19: The contents of the luminosity channel and the *a* and *b* color channels after converting the original image shown in Color Plate 4-1 to the Lab mode.

You can achieve some entertaining effects by applying commands from the Image ⇨ Adjustments submenu to the *a* and *b* color channels. For example, if I go to the *a* channel in Figure 4-19 and reverse the brightness values by choosing Image ⇨ Adjustments ⇨ Invert or pressing Ctrl+I (⌘-I on the Mac), the whale turns a sort of light violet, as demonstrated in the second example of Color Plate 4-1. If I apply Image ⇨ Adjustments ⇨ Auto Levels (that's Ctrl+Shift+L on the PC and ⌘-Shift-L on the Mac) to the *b* channel, the whale assumes a groovy mottled lemon-green and blue appearance. The bottom example in Color Plate 4-1 shows what happens when I combine the inverted *a* channel with the Auto Leveled *b* channel. There's only one word to describe this dude—*orcadelic*.

Other Channel Functions

In addition to viewing and editing channels using any of the techniques discussed in future chapters of this book, you can choose commands from the Channels palette menu and select icons along the bottom of the palette (labeled back in Figure 4-16). The following items explain how the commands and icons work.

You'll notice that I say "see Chapter 9" every so often when explaining these options, because many of them are specifically designed to accommodate masks. This list is designed to introduce you to *all* the options in the Channels palette, even if you'll need more background to use a few of them. After I introduce the options, we'll revisit the ones that have a direct effect on managing the colors in your image.

✦ **Palette Options:** Even though this is the last command in the menu, it's the easiest, so I'll start with it. When you choose Palette Options, Photoshop displays four Thumbnail Size radio buttons, enabling you to change the size of the thumbnail previews that appear along the left side of the Channels palette. Figure 4-20 shows the four thumbnail settings—nonexistent, small, medium, and large.

Have you ever wondered what those thumbnail icons in the Palette Options dialog box are supposed to show? They're silhouettes of tiny Merlins on a painter's palette. How do I know that? Switch to the Layers palette and choose Palette Options and you'll see them in color. But how do I know they're specifically Merlins? Press Alt (Option on the Mac) when choosing Palette Options to see the magician up close. We're talking vintage Easter egg, here—circa Photoshop 2.5.

✦ **New Channel:** Choose this command to add a mask channel to the current image. The Channel Options dialog box appears, requesting that you name the channel. You also can specify the color and translucency that Photoshop applies to the channel when you view it with other channels. I explain how these options work in the "Changing the red coating" section of Chapter 9. An image can contain up to 24 total channels, regardless of color mode.

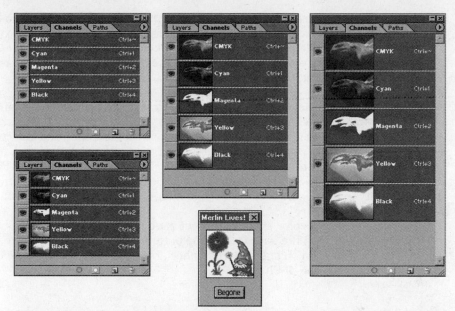

Figure 4-20: The Palette Options command lets you select between four thumbnail preview options and a Merlin.

You can also create a new channel by clicking on the new channel icon at the bottom of the Channels palette. (It's the one that looks like a little page.) Photoshop creates the channel without displaying the dialog box. To force the dialog box to appear on screen, Alt-click (Option-click on the Mac) the page icon.

✦ **Duplicate Channel:** Choose this command to create a duplicate of the selected channel, either inside the same document or as part of a new document. (If the composite view is active, the Duplicate Channel command is dimmed, because you can only duplicate one channel at a time.) The most common reason to use this command is to convert a channel into a mask. Again, you can find real-life applications in Chapter 9.

You can also duplicate a channel by dragging the channel name onto the new channel icon. No dialog box appears; Photoshop merely names the channel automatically. To copy a channel to a different document, drag the channel name and drop it into an open image window. Photoshop automatically creates a new channel for the duplicate.

✦ **Delete Channel:** To delete a channel from an image, click the channel name in the palette and choose this command. You can delete only one channel at a time. The Delete Channel command is dimmed when any essential color channel is active, or when more than one channel is selected.

Tip

If choosing a command is too much effort, just drag the channel onto the delete channel icon (which is the little trash icon in the lower-right corner of the Channels palette). Or you can just click the trash icon, in which case Photoshop asks you if you really want to delete the channel. To bypass this warning, Alt-click (Option-click on the Mac) the trash icon.

✦ **New Spot Channel:** Photoshop lets you add spot color channels to an image. Each spot color channel prints to a separate plate, just like spot colors in Illustrator or QuarkXPress. When you choose the New Spot Channel command, Photoshop asks you to specify a color and a Solidity. Click the color square to bring up the Custom Colors dialog box, from which you can select a Pantone or other spot color (see Figure 4-21). The Solidity option lets you increase the opacity of the ink, perfect for Day-Glo fluorescents and metallic inks.

Tip

To create a spot color channel without choosing a command, Ctrl-click (⌘-click on the Mac) the page icon at the bottom of the Channels palette. For more information on spot-color channels, read the "Spot-Color Separations" section at the end of Chapter 18.

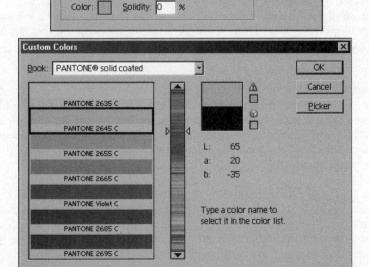

Figure 4-21: When creating a spot-color channel, Photoshop asks you to select a color and specify the degree to which the spot color will cover up other inks in the printed image.

✦ **Merge Spot Channel:** Select a spot-color channel and choose this command to merge the spot color with the RGB, Lab, or CMYK colors in the image. Most spot colors don't have precise RGB or CMYK equivalents, so you will lose some color fidelity in the merge. Adobe includes this command to enable you to proof an image to a typical midrange color printer.

✦ **Channel Options:** Choose this command or double-click the channel name in the palette's scrolling list to change the settings assigned to a spot-color or mask channel. The Channel Options command is dimmed when a regular, everyday color channel is active.

✦ **Split Channels:** When you choose this command, Photoshop splits off each channel in an image to its own independent grayscale image window. As demonstrated in Figure 4-22, Photoshop automatically appends the channel color to the end of the window name. The Split Channels command is useful as a first step in redistributing channels in an image prior to choosing Merge Channels, as I will demonstrate later in this same chapter.

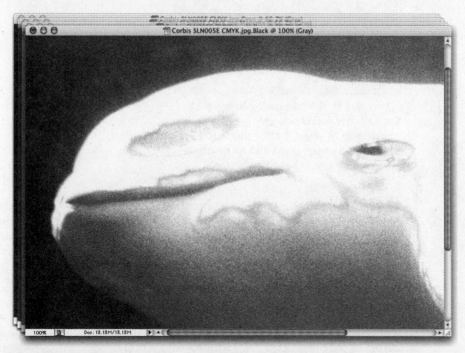

Figure 4-22: When you choose the Split Channels command, Photoshop relocates each channel to an independent image window.

✦ **Merge Channels:** Choose this command to merge several images into a single multichannel image. The images you want to merge must be open, they must be grayscale, and they must be absolutely equal in size — the same number of pixels horizontally and vertically. When you choose Merge Channels, Photoshop displays the Merge Channels dialog box, shown in Figure 4-23. It then assigns a color mode for the new image based on the number of open grayscale images that contain the same number of pixels as the foreground image.

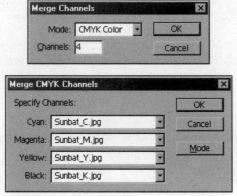

Figure 4-23: The two dialog boxes that appear after you choose Merge Channels enable you to select a color mode for the merged image (top) and to associate images with color channels (bottom).

You can override Photoshop's choice by selecting a different option from the Mode pop-up menu. (Generally, you won't want to change the value in the Channels option box because doing so causes Photoshop to automatically select Multichannel from the Mode pop-up menu. I explain multichannel images in the upcoming "Using multichannel techniques" section.)

After you press Enter or Return, Photoshop displays a second dialog box, which also appears in Figure 4-23. In this dialog box, you can specify which grayscale image goes with which channel by choosing options from pop-up menus. When working from an image split with the Split Channels command, Photoshop automatically organizes each window into a pop-up menu according to the color appended to the window's name. For example, Photoshop associates the window *Sunbat_C.jpg* with the Cyan pop-up menu.

Color Channel Effects

Now that you know how to navigate among channels and apply commands, permit me to suggest a few reasons for doing so. The most pragmatic applications for channel effects involve the restoration of bad color scans. If you use a color scanner, know someone who uses a color scanner, or just have a bunch of color scans lying around, you can be sure that some of them look like dog meat. (Nothing against dog meat, mind you. I'm sure that Purina has some very lovely dog meat scans in their advertising archives.) With Photoshop's help, you can turn those scans into filet mignon — or at the very least, into an acceptable Sunday roast.

Improving the appearance of color scans

The following are a few channel-editing techniques you can use to improve the appearance of poorly scanned full-color images. Keep in mind that these techniques don't work miracles, but they can retrieve an image from the brink of absolute ugliness into the realm of tolerability.

Don't forget that you can choose Window ➪ Documents ➪ New Window to maintain a constant composite view. Or you can click the eyeball icon in front of the composite view in the Channels palette to view the full-color image, even when editing a single channel.

- ✦ **Aligning channels:** Every so often, a scan may appear out of focus even after you use Photoshop's sharpening commands to try to correct the problem, as discussed in Chapter 10. If, on closer inspection, you can see slight shadows or halos around colored areas, one of the color channels probably is out of alignment. To remedy the problem, switch to the color channel that corresponds to the color of the halos. Then select the move tool (by pressing V) and use the arrow keys to nudge the contents of the channel into alignment. Use the separate composite view (created by choosing Window ➪ Documents ➪ New Window) or click the eyeball in front of the composite channel to monitor your changes.

- ✦ **Channel focusing:** If all channels seem to be in alignment (or, at least, as aligned as they're going to get), one of your channels may be poorly focused. Use the Ctrl-key (Win) or ⌘-key (Mac) equivalents to search for the responsible channel. When and if you find it, use the Unsharp Mask filter to sharpen it as desired. You may also find it helpful to blur a channel, as when trying to eliminate moiré patterns in a scanned halftone. (For a specific application of these techniques, see the "Cleaning up Scanned Halftones" section in Chapter 10.)

- ✦ **Bad channels:** In your color channel tour, if you discover that a channel is not so much poorly focused as simply rotten to the core — complete with harsh transitions, jagged edges, and random brightness variations — you may be able to improve the appearance of the channel by mixing other channels with it.

  Suppose that the blue channel is awful, but the red and green channels are in fairly decent shape. The Channel Mixer command lets you mix channels together, whether to repair a bad channel or achieve an interesting effect. Choose Image ⇨ Adjustments ⇨ Channel Mixer and press Ctrl+3 (⌘-3 on the Mac) to switch to the blue channel. Then raise the Red and Green values and lower the Blue value to mix the three channels together to create a better blue. To maintain consistent brightness levels, it's generally a good idea to use a combination of Red, Green, and Blue values that adds up to 100 percent, as in Figure 4-24. If you can live with the inevitable color changes, the appearance of the image should improve dramatically.

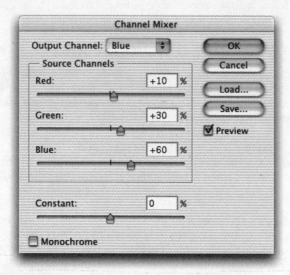

Figure 4-24: Here I use the Channel Mixer command to repair the blue channel by mixing in 10 percent of the red channel and 30 percent of the green channel. The red and green channels remain unaffected.

Note that Channel Mixer is also a great command for creating custom grayscale images. Rather than choosing Image ⇨ Mode ⇨ Grayscale and taking what Photoshop gives you, you can choose the Channel Mixer command and select the Monochrome check box. Then adjust the Red, Green, and Blue values to mix your own grayscale variation.

Incidentally, the Constant slider simply brightens or darkens the image across the board. Usually, you'll want to leave it set to 0. But if you're having problems getting the color balance right, give it a tweak.

Note   Although the Channel Mixer didn't arrive until Photoshop 5, I created my own channel mixing filter quite a few years ago. Created in Photoshop's Filter Factory, this filter coincidentally went by the name . . . *Channel Mixer!* I submit Figure 4-25

as Exhibit A. "But Deke," you say, "your filter doesn't look anything like Adobe's Channel Mixer, and your sliders don't make nearly as much sense." Yes, I imagine that's precisely what they want you to think. Perhaps now you're beginning to understand how diabolically crafty these Photoshop programmers can be.

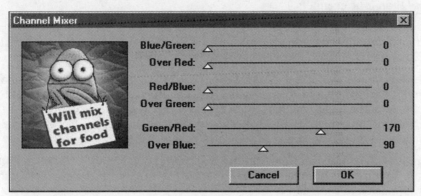

Figure 4-25: An early version of the Channel Mixer invented by yours truly. Has Adobe gone and swiped my visionary idea? You be the judge.

Using multichannel techniques

The one channel function I've so far ignored is Image ⇨ Mode ⇨ Multichannel. When you choose this command, Photoshop changes your image so that channels no longer have a specific relationship to one another. They don't mix to create a full-color image; instead, they exist independently within the confines of a single image. The multichannel mode is generally an intermediary step for converting between different color modes without recalculating the contents of the channels.

For example, normally when you convert between the RGB and CMYK modes, Photoshop maps RGB colors to the CMYK color model, changing the contents of each channel as demonstrated back in Figures 4-17 and 4-18. But suppose, just as an experiment, that you want to bypass the color mapping and instead transfer the exact contents of the red channel to the cyan channel, the contents of the green channel to the magenta channel, and so on. You convert from RGB to the multi-channel mode and then from multichannel to CMYK as described in the following steps.

STEPS: Using the Multichannel Mode as an Intermediary Step

1. **Open an RGB image.** If the image is already open, make sure that it is saved to disk.

2. **Choose Image ⇨ Mode ⇨ Multichannel.** This eliminates any relationship between the formerly red, green, and blue color channels.

3. **Click the new channel icon at the bottom of the Channels palette.** Or choose the New Channel command from the palette menu and press Enter or Return to accept the default settings. Either way, you add a mask channel to the image. This empty channel will serve as the black channel in the CMYK image. (Photoshop won't let you convert from the multichannel mode to CMYK with less than four channels.)

4. **Press Ctrl+I (⌘-I on the Mac).** Unfortunately, the new channel comes up black, which would make the entire image black. To change it to white, press Ctrl+I (⌘-I on the Mac) or choose Image ➪ Adjustments ➪ Invert.

5. **Choose Image ➪ Mode ➪ CMYK Color.** The image looks washed out and a tad bit dark compared to its original RGB counterpart, but the overall color scheme of the image remains more or less intact. This is because the red, green, and blue color channels each have a respective opposite in the cyan, magenta, and yellow channels.

6. **Press Ctrl+Shift+L (⌘-Shift-L on the Mac).** Or choose Image ➪ Adjustments ➪ Auto Levels. This punches up the color a bit by automatically correcting the brightness and contrast.

7. **Convert the image to RGB and then back to CMYK again.** The problem with the image is that it lacks any information in the black channel. So although it may look okay on screen, it will lose much of its definition when printed. To fill in the black channel, choose Image ➪ Mode ➪ RGB Color, and then choose Image ➪ Mode ➪ CMYK Color. Photoshop automatically generates an image in the black channel in keeping with the standards of color separations (as explained in Chapter 18).

Keep in mind that these steps are by no means a recommended procedure for converting an RGB image to a CMYK image. Rather, they are merely intended to suggest one way to experiment with channel conversions to create a halfway decent image. You can likewise experiment with converting between the Lab, multichannel, and RGB modes, or Lab, multichannel, and CMYK.

Replacing and swapping color channels

If you truly want to abuse the colors in an RGB or CMYK image, there's nothing like replacing one color channel with another to produce spectacular effects. Color Plate 4-2 shows a few examples applied to an RGB image.

✦ In the first example, I used the Channel Mixer to replace the red channel with the green. I did this by setting the Output Channel to Red, changing the Red value to 0 percent and the Green value to 100 percent. The result is a yellow whale in a violet-blue sea.

✦ To achieve the next example, I again started from the original RGB image and used the Channel Mixer to replace the blue channel with the green. The result this time is a blue whale against a deep blue background.

You can create more interesting effects by using the Channel Mixer to swap the contents of color channels. For example, in the third example of Color Plate 4-2, I swapped the contents of the red and blue channels to create a green whale in a burnt orange sea. To accomplish this, I set the Output Channel to Red, set the Red value to 0 and the Blue to 100. Then I switched to the blue channel by pressing Ctrl+3 (⌘-3 on the Mac) and set the Red value to 100 and the Blue to 0.

As a final test, I did the same sort of swap to the original image as described in the last paragraph, but substituted the green channel for the blue. I then skipped over to the blue channel by pressing Ctrl+3 (⌘-3 on the Mac) and dropped the Blue value down to 50 percent, giving me the fuchsia and yellow fellow pictured in the bottom example of Color Plate 4-2.

✦   ✦   ✦

Painting and Brushes

Photoshop Paints Like a Pro

Once upon a time, there used to be gobs of digital painting programs. And when I say gobs, I mean bucket loads. And when I say bucket loads, I mean squillions. They had names like Lumina and Studio/32 and Deluxe Paint and Color MacCheese and — well, I really haven't the time to list them all. Suffice it to say, in the last dozen years, there have been more than 100 of them. At one time, there were more painting applications in circulation than word processors, spreadsheet programs, and database managers combined.

Their astonishing abundance is made all the more amazing by the fact that virtually every one of them is now stone, cold dead. The one notable exception is Procreate's powerful Painter (*www.procreate.com*), which enjoys a loyal but tiny following. There's also Paint Shop Pro from Jasc Software (*www.jasc.com*). But while it has the word Paint in its title, it's more of a general purpose image editor, in many ways a lesser, not to mention less expensive, version of Photoshop.

What killed them all? Photoshop. If painting programs used to roam software shelves like bison roamed the plains, then Photoshop was the drunken cowboy perched on a train car and filling the colorful software boxes with so much virtual lead. Okay, that metaphor might be a bit extreme, but it makes my point: This one program made mincemeat of everything around it.

This is ironic because Photoshop never was a painting program. Traditionally, Adobe has concentrated its efforts on making Photoshop a terrific image editor. Oh, sure, Photoshop has always provided a few very basic painting tools, but most of the now-dead applications offered better. The fact that artists abandoned other painting programs in favor of Photoshop largely seems to be an indication that folks preferred image editing to painting. So if Photoshop was a drunken cowboy, it was unintentional. Adobe was shooting at something much larger, and the painting programs just got in the way.

The fact that Version 7 greatly expands Photoshop's range of painting options — making it one of the most powerful painting applications in history — doubles the irony. Several years after most painting programs are gone, Photoshop competes with them head on. It's a case of predator emulating its prey.

Taken at face value, Photoshop's enhanced brush options may not make much sense. Why should Photoshop want to integrate capabilities from an unsuccessful category of software? The answer is timing. Although the painting programs of yore provided a wealth of amazing tools and color selection options, the hardware of the time was only barely able to keep up with them. Memory was expensive, hard drives were small, and 24-bit video was rare. As a result, painting programs tended to be slow and capable of producing low-resolution artwork. Software has long been judged by whether it will save you time or make you money, and painting programs could do neither. They were therefore clever playthings and nothing more.

Photoshop has long since proven itself a capable, practical application, with a loyal following among professional designers. Meanwhile, the hardware has grown several times more powerful. Memory is cheap, hard drives are spacious and fast, and a modern video card can render anything Photoshop can send it in a matter of nanoseconds. So now seems a perfect time to rediscover the lost art of painting, as you and I will do throughout the following pages.

Meet the Paint and Edit Tools

Photoshop provides two basic varieties of brush tools. There are paint tools, which allow you to apply colors to an image. Then there are edit tools, which modify existing colors in an image. Either way, you operate the tool by dragging the cursor inside the image, much as you might drag a real brush across a real sheet of paper.

This might lead you to think that the paint and edit tools require artistic talent. In truth, each tool provides options for almost any level of proficiency or experience. Photoshop offers get-by measures for novices who want to make quick edits and put the tool down before they make a mess of things. It also provides a wealth of features so complex and powerful that only the most capable artist will want to approach them. But no matter who you are, you'll find the tools more flexible, less messy, and more forgiving than their traditional counterparts.

In all, Photoshop 7 provides two paint tools: the brush and the pencil. You also get six edit tools: blur, sharpen, smudge, dodge, burn, and sponge. Figure 5-1 shows all the tools along with the keyboard shortcuts for selecting them.

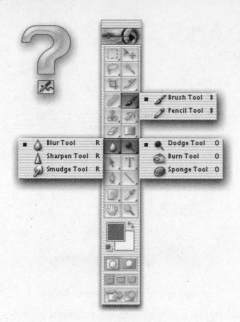

Figure 5-1: Here we see the two paint tools and six edit tools, all available from flyout menus. But where, oh where, has the airbrush gone?

Tip

When two or more tools share a slot in the toolbox, click and hold on the tool icon to display a flyout menu of all the tools, as illustrated in Figure 5-1. Or you can just press the keyboard shortcut listed in the menu to switch from one tool to the next. For example, repeatedly pressing B cycles between the brush and pencil tools. (This assumes you turned off the Use Shift Key for Tool Switch check box in the General panel of the Preferences dialog box, as I recommended in Chapter 2. Otherwise, you must press Shift and the shortcut to switch tools.)

You can vary the performance of the active tool by using the controls in the Options bar along the top of your screen. If you don't see the Options bar, choose Window ➪ Options or double-click a tool icon in the toolbox.

Photoshop
7

I explore how to use the specific settings in the Options bar in upcoming sections. But those of you experienced with previous versions of Photoshop will want to note three things right away, each labeled in Figure 5-2:

✦ **The airbrush:** A staple of Photoshop since Version 1, the airbrush has been moved from the toolbox to the Options bar. That's because it's no longer a tool; it's now a setting that affects other tools. To invoke the old airbrush, select the brush tool and turn on the airbrush setting. But you can also use the airbrush with the dodge and burn tools, the history brush, the clone stamp tool, and more.

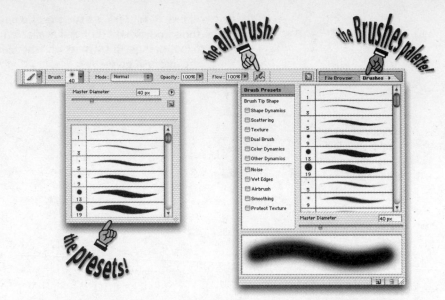

Figure 5-2: Artists familiar with Photoshop 6 will notice three additions to the Options bar in Version 7.

✦ **The Brushes palette:** Removed from Photoshop 6, the Brushes palette is back and better than ever. You can get to it by pressing the F5 key or choosing Window ➪ Brushes. If your monitor's resolution is set to display 1024 or more pixels horizontally, you can also click the Brushes tab in the docking well on the far right side of the Options bar. If not, click the little palette icon on the right side of the Options bar. In any case, the brushes palette is where most of the new painting capabilities are concentrated, so you can be sure we'll be visiting it several times throughout this chapter.

✦ **The presets:** Right-click (Control-click on the Mac) in the image window to display a miniature version of the Brushes palette, which shows a list of preset brushes. You can also display the mini palette by clicking the Brush icon in the Options bar. To see a shortcut menu of blend modes, as in Photoshop 6.0 and earlier, press Shift and right-click (Shift-Control-click on the Mac). To hide either the presets palette or shortcut menu, just press Enter or Return.

The paint tools

The paint tools apply strokes of color. In most cases, you'll be painting with the foreground color, though you can also create multicolored brushstrokes using the Color Dynamics options in the Brushes palette, as we'll see later. Here's how the paint tools work:

✦ **Brush:** Formerly called the *paintbrush*, Photoshop 7's brush tool paints a line of any thickness that you specify. You can make the line sharp or blurry, but it's always slightly soft — that is to say, the edges of the brushstroke blend to some extent with the background. Known as *antialiasing*, this softness produces halftone dots when printing, ensuring smooth transitions between a brushstroke and its surroundings.

Normally, the brush tool applies a continuous stream of color and stops applying paint whenever you stop dragging. However, if you activate the airbrush function by clicking the airbrush icon in the Options bar (labeled in Figure 5-2), the color continues to build up so long as you press the mouse button, even when you hold the cursor still. In Figure 5-3, the first line was painted with a 65-pixel soft brush and the airbrush option off. To make the second line, I turned on the airbrush setting and reduced the Flow value (also in the Options bar) to 50 percent. The result is a build up of color at the corners and at the end of the stroke.

To invoke the airbrush function from the keyboard, press Shift+Alt+P (or Shift-Option-P on the Mac). Pressing Shift+Alt+P again turns the function off. For those of you who are wondering where this keystroke comes from, it's P for paint, baby, paint.

✦ **Pencil:** Like the brush tool, the pencil paints a line of any thickness in the foreground color. However, whereas brush tool lines are always soft, pencil lines are always hard edged, with no interaction between the pencil line and background colors. Figure 5-3 shows a 45-pixel pencil line printed at 300 ppi. At such high resolutions, pencil lines appear sharp. At low resolutions, pencil lines have jagged edges.

When you select the pencil tool, a unique check box, Auto Erase, appears in the Options bar. When selected, this option instructs Photoshop to paint with the background color, thereby erasing, whenever you begin painting on an area already colored with the foreground color. A throwback to old black-and-white painting programs such as MacPaint, this option is useful when editing screen shots, custom icons, and the occasional Web graphic.

As when painting in real life, one of the imperatives of painting in Photoshop is switching out the color of your brush. The Color palette is handy, but it's not immediate enough. You need something that can keep up with the speed of your creative ideas. The solution is the eyedropper. As introduced in "The eyedropper" section of Chapter 4, you can sample colors from an image by Alt-clicking (Option-clicking on the Mac) when using either the brush or pencil tool. It's so useful that those of you who do a lot of painting with the brush tool may find yourselves Alt-clicking almost as often as you drag.

Figure 5-3: Three lines painted in black with the brush and pencil tools. To create the second stroke, I turned on the airbrush setting. I created the color buildup at the bottom of the line by slowing my stroke and, at the very end, holding the cursor in place for a moment.

The edit tools

The edit tools don't apply color; rather, they influence existing colors in an image. Figure 5-4 shows the effect of dragging with each of the edit tools except the sponge, which works best with color images. Future sections cover the tools in more detail, but here's a brief introduction:

✦ **Blur:** The first of the two focus tools, the blur tool blurs an image by lessening the amount of color contrast between neighboring pixels.

✦ **Sharpen:** The second focus tool selectively sharpens by increasing the contrast between neighboring pixels.

Generally speaking, neither the blur nor sharpen tool is as useful as its command counterparts in the Filters menu. Each provides little control and requires scrubbing at the image. The sharpen tool is especially ineffective, tending toward too much sharpening or no sharpening at all. I might use it to dab at the occasional edge, but that's about it.

✦ **Smudge:** The smudge tool smears colors in an image. The effect is rather like dragging your finger across wet paint. Although simple, this tool can be effective for smoothing out colors and textures. See "Painting with the smudge tool" later in this chapter for more information.

Figure 5-4: The effects of dragging with five of Photoshop's edit tools. The boundaries of each line are highlighted so you can clearly see the distinctions between line and background.

Obviously doesn't go to Brasil

✦ **Dodge:** The first of three toning tools, the dodge tool lets you lighten a portion of an image by dragging across it. Named after a traditional darkroom technique, the dodge tool is supposed to look like a little paddle. Before computers, a technician would wave such a paddle (or anything, really) over photographic paper to prevent light from hitting the paper and thereby leave areas less exposed. Thank golly, we no longer have to wave little paddles in our modern age.

✦ **Burn:** The burn tool is the dodge tool's opposite, darkening an area as you drag over it. Returning once again to the dark room, the technician would create a mask by, say, cutting a hole in a piece of paper or cupping his hand. This would protect areas of photographic paper that had already been exposed and darken the area inside the hole. Photoshop's metaphor for this is a hand in the shape of an O, kind of a lazy man's mask. I can't testify how well that would work—never tried it myself—but I imagine the burn tool is a lot easier and more effective than the old hand trick.

Tip

If you're like most folks, you have difficulty remembering which tool lightens and which one darkens. But think of them in terms of toast, and suddenly, everything falls into place. For example, that little hand icon looks like it could be holding a piece of toast. And when you *burn* toast, it gets *darker*. Hand, toast, burn, darker. That other tool, the little paddle, is not so deft at holding toast. The toast would fall off, in which case, a small person standing below the paddle would have to *dodge* the toast. Suddenly, your load as the bearer of toast gets *lighter*. Paddle, falling toast, dodge, lighter. With these two strained but handy metaphors in mind, you'll never have problems again.

✦ **Sponge:** The final toning tool, the sponge tool, robs an image of saturation when working inside a color image or contrast when working in grayscale. Or you can set the tool so it boosts saturation or adds contrast. For more information, stay tuned for the upcoming section, "Mopping up with the sponge tool."

Tip

To access the sharpen tool temporarily when the blur tool is selected, press and hold Alt (Win) or Option (Mac) while using the tool. The sharpen tool remains available only as long as you press Alt or Option. Likewise, you can press Alt (Win) or Option (Mac) to access the blur tool when the sharpen tool is selected, to access the burn tool when the dodge tool is selected, or to access the dodge tool when the burn tool is selected. This can be a real timesaver. Say, for example, that you want to burn the image using the settings configured for the dodge tool. Rather than switching to the burn tool and changing its settings, you could select the dodge tool and Alt-drag (or Option-drag).

You can replace the blur tool with the sharpen tool in the toolbox by Alt-clicking (Option-clicking on the Mac) on the tool's icon. Alt-click (or Option-click) again to select the smudge tool and yet again to cycle back to the blur tool. Likewise, you can Alt-click (Option-click on the Mac) the dodge tool icon to cycle between the dodge, burn, and sponge tools.

The keyboard shortcut for the blur tool is R; the shortcut for the dodge tool is O (the letter shared by "dodge" and "toning tools"). These keys also toggle between the tools. When the blur tool is selected, press R to switch to the sharpen tool. Repeated pressings of R take you to the smudge tool and back to the blur tool. When the dodge tool is selected, press O to toggle to the burn tool; press O again to get the sponge.

Note

If these shortcuts don't work for you, press Ctrl+K (⌘-K on the Mac) to display the General panel of the Preferences dialog box. Chances are, the Use Shift Key for Tool Switch check box is selected, which means that you have to press Shift plus the keyboard shortcut to cycle through tools. Turn the check box off to give your Shift finger a rest.

Basic Techniques

I know several people who claim that they can't paint, and yet they create beautiful work in Photoshop. Even though they don't have sufficient hand-eye coordination to write their names on screen, they have unique and powerful artistic sensibilities, and they know many tricks that enable them to make judicious use of the paint and edit tools. I can't help you in the sensibilities department, but I can show you a few tricks to boost your ability and inclination to use the paint and edit tools.

Painting a straight line

Photoshop provides a line tool that lets you draw straight lines. It's a surprisingly flexible tool, permitting you to draw vector-based layers or pixel-based lines, and you can even add arrowheads. If you'd like to learn about it, I explain the line tool and others like it in Chapter 14, "Shapes and Styles."

The main reason I use the line tool is to fashion arrows (as I explain in the "Applying Strokes and Arrowheads" section of the next chapter). If I don't want arrows, I usually take advantage of Photoshop's other means for creating straight lines: the Shift key. By Shift-clicking with any of the tools introduced in this chapter, you can paint or edit in straight lines.

Try this: Using the brush tool, click at one point in the image and then press Shift and click at another point. Photoshop connects the start and end points with a straight stroke of paint. You can use this same technique with the pencil, or to blur, smudge, dodge, or otherwise edit pixels in a straight line.

To create free-form polygons, continue to Shift-click with the tool. Figure 5-5 features a photograph and a tracing I made by Shift-clicking with the brush tool. Note that I experimented with different brush sizes, as explained later in the "Brush Size and

Figure 5-5: Starting from an image by photographer Barbara Penoyar (left), I created a stylized tracing (right) by clicking and Shift-clicking with the brush tool on a separate layer.

Shape" section. I also used a variety of colors sampled from the image by Alt-clicking (Option-clicking on the Mac). Most importantly, I painted the image on a separate layer. This served two purposes: I was able to protect my original image from harm, and I could erase mistakes along the way by clicking and Shift-clicking with the eraser tool. (I discuss layers in Chapter 12; I discuss the eraser in Chapter 7.) But as a matter of principal, I only Shift-clicked with the brush tool; I never dragged.

The Shift key makes the blur tool and even the sharpen tool halfway useful as well. Suppose that I wanted to edit the perimeter of the knife shown in Figure 5-6. The arrows in the figure illustrate the path my Shift-clicks should follow. Figure 5-7 shows the effect of Shift-clicking with the blur tool; Figure 5-8 demonstrates the effect of Shift-clicking with the sharpen tool.

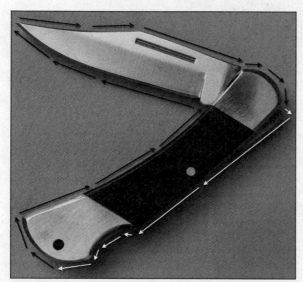

Figure 5-6: It takes one click and 21 Shift-clicks to soften or sharpen the edges around this knife using the blur or sharpen tool.

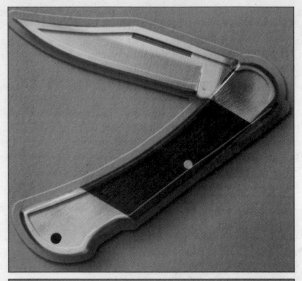

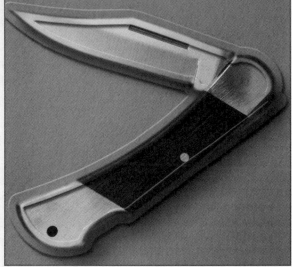

Figure 5-7: These are the results of blurring the knife's perimeter with the Strength value in the Options bar set to 50 percent (top) and 100 percent (bottom).

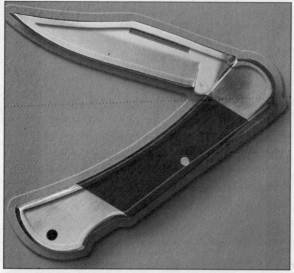

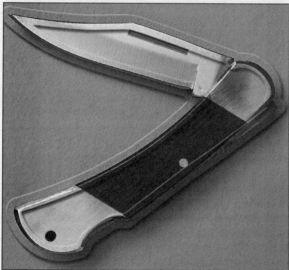

Figure 5-8: The results of sharpening the knife with the Strength value set to 35 percent (top) and 70 percent (bottom). Anything higher produced an oversharpening effect.

Painting a perpendicular line

To create a perpendicular line—that is, a line that is either vertical or horizontal—with any of the paint tools, press Shift while dragging with a paint or edit tool. Releasing Shift returns the line to freeform, as illustrated in Figure 5-9. Press Shift in mid-drag to snap the line back into perpendicular alignment.

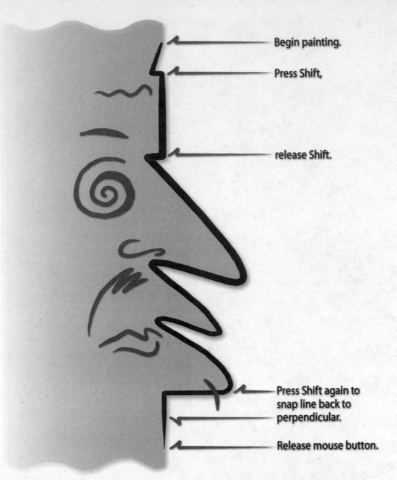

Begin painting.

Press Shift,

release Shift.

Press Shift again to
snap line back to
perpendicular.

Release mouse button.

Figure 5-9: Pressing Shift after you start to drag with a paint or edit
tool results in a perpendicular line for as long as the key is pressed.

One way to exploit the Shift key's penchant for snapping to the perpendicular is to
draw "ribbed" structures. To create the central outlines around the skeleton that
appear at the top of Figure 5-10, I dragged from right to left with the brush tool. I
painted each rib by periodically pressing and releasing Shift as I dragged. In each
case, pressing Shift snapped the line to the horizontal axis, the location of which
was established by the beginning of the drag.

After establishing the basic skeletal form, I added some free-form details with the
brush and pencil tools, as shown in the middle image in Figure 5-10. Having painted
the skeleton on a separate layer, I set it against Black Marble, one of Photoshop's
predefined patterns, and applied a Bevel and Emboss layer effect. (See Chapters 7
and 14, respectively, for complete information on patterns and layer effects.)
Nobody's going to mistake my painting for a bona fide fossil, but it's not too shabby
for a cartoon.

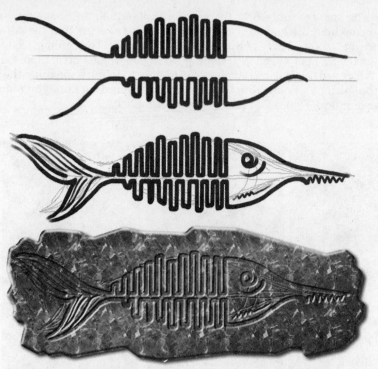

Figure 5-10: To create the basic structure for our bony pal, I periodically pressed and released Shift while dragging with the brush tool (top). Then I embellished the fish using the brush and pencil (middle). Finally, I applied a Bevel and Emboss layer effect and set the fossil against a patterned background (bottom).

Note

It's no accident Figure 5-10 features a swordfish instead of your everyday round-nosed carp. To snap to the horizontal axis, I had to establish the direction of my drag as being more or less horizontal from the get go. If I had instead dragged in a fish-faced convex arc, Photoshop would have interpreted my drag as vertical and snapped to the vertical axis.

Painting with the smudge tool

Many first-time Photoshop artists misuse the smudge tool to soften color transitions, which is the purpose of the blur tool. The smudge tool is designed to smear colors by shoving them into each other. The process bears more resemblance to finger painting than to any traditional photographic-editing technique.

In Photoshop, the performance of the smudge tool depends in part on the settings of the Strength and Finger Painting controls in the Options bar. Here's what you need to know about these options:

✦ **Strength:** The smudge tool works by repeatedly stamping the image hundreds of times throughout the length of a brushstroke. The effect is that the color appears to get "pushed" across the length of the stroke. The Strength value determines the intensity of each stamping. So higher values push colors the farthest. A Strength setting of 100 percent equates to infinity, meaning the smudge tool pushes a color from the beginning of your drag until you release your mouse button. Figure 5-11 shows a few examples.

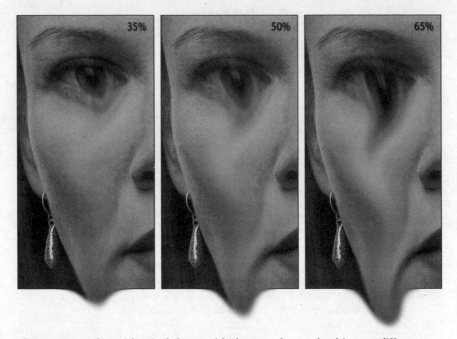

Figure 5-11: Three identical drags with the smudge tool subject to different Strength settings. In each case, I began the brushstroke at the eye and dragged downward.

✦ **Finger Painting:** Back in the old days, the folks at Adobe called this effect *dipping*, which I think more accurately expressed how it works. When you select this option, the smudge tool begins by applying a smidgen of foreground color, which it eventually blends in with the colors in the image. It's as if you dipped your finger in a color and then dragged it through an oil painting. Use the Strength setting to specify the amount of foreground color applied. If you turn on Finger Painting and set the Strength to 100 percent, the smudge tool behaves like the brush tool. Figure 5-12 shows examples of finger painting with the smudge tool when the foreground color is set to white.

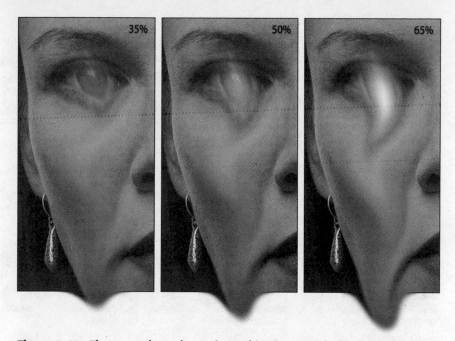

Figure 5-12: The same three drags pictured in Figure 5-11, this time with the Finger Painting option turned on and the foreground color set to white.

Tip

You can reverse the Finger Painting setting by pressing the Alt key (Option on the Mac) and dragging. If the option is off, Alt-dragging dips the tool into the foreground color. If Finger Painting is turned on, Alt-dragging smudges normally.

The Use All Layers option instructs the smudge tool to grab colors in all visible layers and smudge them into the current layer. Whether the option is on or off, only the current layer is affected; the background and other layers remain intact.

For example, suppose the mask around the woman's eye on the left side of Figure 5-13 is on a different layer than the rest of the face. If I use the smudge tool on this mask layer with Use All Layers turned off, Photoshop ignores the face layer when smudging the mask. As a result, details such as the eye and skin remain unsmudged, as in the middle example in the figure. If I turn Use All Layers on, Photoshop lifts colors from the face layer and mixes them with the mask layer, as shown in the right-hand example.

Tip

In the case of Figure 5-13, the mask appears to smudge better when the Use All Layers check box is turned off. But this isn't always the case. In fact, turning the check box on is a great way to smudge without harming a single pixel in your image. Just make a new, empty layer in the Layers palette. Then select the smudge tool and turn Use All Layers on. Now smudge to your heart's content. Even though the active layer is empty, Photoshop is able to draw colors from other layers. Meanwhile, the colors in the underlying layers remain unharmed.

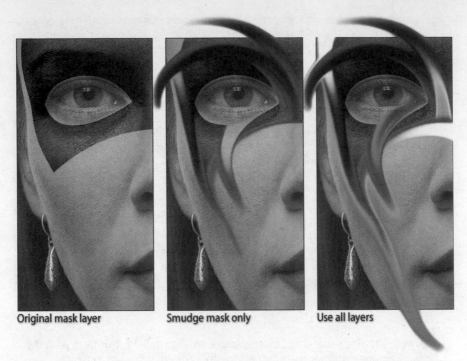

Original mask layer   Smudge mask only   Use all layers

Figure 5-13: The original image (left) features a mask on an independent layer in front of the rest of the face. I first smudged the mask with Use All Layers turned off (middle) and then with the option turned on (right). In both cases, the Strength setting was set to 80 percent; the brushstrokes were identical.

Mopping up with the sponge tool

The sponge tool is actually a pretty simple tool, hardly worth expending valuable space in a book as tiny as this one. But I'm a compulsive explainer, so here's the deal—when the sponge tool is active, you can select either Desaturate or Saturate from the Mode pop-up menu in the Options bar. Here's what they do:

✦ **Desaturate:** When set to Desaturate, the tool reduces the saturation of the colors over which you drag. When you're editing a grayscale image, the tool reduces contrast.

✦ **Saturate:** If you select Saturate, the sponge tool increases the saturation of the colors over which you drag or increases contrast in a grayscale image.

You can switch between the Desaturate and Saturate modes from the keyboard. Press Shift+Alt+D (Shift-Option-D on the Mac) to select the Desaturate option. Press Shift+Alt+S (Shift-Option-S on the Mac) for Saturate. No matter which mode you choose, higher Flow settings produce more dramatic results.

To see the sponge tool in action, take a look at Color Plate 5-1. The first example shows a photograph of a delicately featured woman from the Corbis image library. The rest of the color plate shows me adding a virtual face-paint mask around the woman's eyes, a technique that relied heavily on the burn and sponge tools. The following steps explain how I did it.

STEPS: Sponging In and Away Color Saturation

1. **Draw the mask.** To make the mask, I drew the mask outline using the pen tool set to the Paths mode. For more information about this wonderful tool, read the section "How to Draw and Edit Paths," in Chapter 8.

2. **Convert the path to a selection outline.** After drawing the mask outline and eyeholes, I converted the path to a selection outline by Ctrl-clicking on it in the Paths palette. If you're intimidated by the pen tool and Paths palette, you could create a similar selection using the lasso tool, it just wouldn't look as smooth. Chapter 8 tells more.

3. **Jump the selection to a layer.** I next pressed Ctrl+J (⌘-J on the Mac) to copy the selection to an independent layer. This protected the image so that any edits I applied to the mask would not harm the face.

4. **Burn the mask.** Thus far, mask and face were the same colors. To set the mask apart, I darkened it with the burn tool. This involved multiple drags with the Strength set to 50 percent, focusing primarily on the outer edges. The result is the second image in Color Plate 5-1. (Note that no other tools or commands were used to darken the mask—that's 100 percent burn tool. See what I meant by my earlier toast analogy? That burn tool makes some tasty looking toast.)

5. **Sponge away saturation.** The mask had a nice tone to it. But to get more of a Mardi Gras effect, I wanted to introduce some difference in saturation values. I began by painting around the eyes inside the mask. Because the Mode option in the Options bar was set to Desaturate, this sucked away the color around the eyes, leaving mostly gray.

6. **Sponge in saturation.** Still armed with the sponge tool, I changed the Mode setting to Saturate and painted along the forehead of the mask and bridge of the nose. This drew out some vivid oranges. Then I switched to the face layer and painted the eyes, lips, and hair to increase their saturation as well.

7. **Dodge the eyes.** Want to make a person look better? Use the dodge tool on her eyes. Just a click or two on each eye brightens the irises and gives the person an almost hypnotic stare. A little bit of extra dodging makes her look downright freaky, like some kind of radioactive X-Men character. Which is a good thing, needless to say.

The finished image appears at the bottom of Color Plate 5-1. Note that while the woman now appears more brightly colored, she does not look more made up. That's because the sponge doesn't add color to an image; it merely enhances the colors that are already there. This makes the tool a bit unpredictable at times as well. For my part, I was surprised to see the hair turn a fiery orange and the tips of the earrings go purple. You never know what you'll find when you raise saturation values.

The sponge tool works inside grayscale images, but its effects are much more subtle, reducing and enhancing the contrast between neighboring pixels. The first image in Figure 5-14 shows a grayscale version of the middle image from Color Plate 5-1. To create the second image in Figure 5-14, I started by lightening the eyes and skin with the dodge tool. Then I set the sponge to Saturate and dragged all over the place. The result was a pumped up image with a lot more depth and contrast.

Tip

I find it very helpful to turn on the airbrush setting in the Options bar when using the sponge tool (as well as the other toning tools, dodge and burn). This way, you can gradually build up effects on the fly. When you find a section of an image that needs more sponging than most, hold your cursor in place, watch Photoshop airbrush in the effect, and then move the cursor when you've had enough.

Undoing the damage that you've done

If you make a mistake in the course of painting an image, stop and choose Edit ⇨ Undo or press Ctrl+Z (⌘-Z on the Mac). If this doesn't work, press Ctrl+Alt+Z (⌘-Option-Z on the Mac) to step back through a sequence of paint strokes. Note that both shortcuts assume that you haven't changed the default Redo Key setting in the Preferences dialog box, explained back in Chapter 2.

Cross-Reference

You can also undo a brushstroke by selecting a previous state in the History palette. As explained in Chapter 7, the History palette lists brushstrokes and other changes according to the tool you used to create them.

If you like the basic look of a brushstroke but you'd like to fade it back a bit, choose Edit ⇨ Fade or press Ctrl+Shift+F (⌘-Shift-F on the Mac). The Fade command let's you reduce the Opacity or change the blend mode of the brushstroke you just finished painting. (If you have since clicked with another tool, the command may appear dimmed, indicating that you've lost your chance.) The Fade command is applicable to all paint and edit tools, as well as other operations inside Photoshop, so we'll be seeing a lot of it throughout this book.

Figure 5-14: The middle image from Color Plate 5-1 (top) followed by that same image enhanced with the dodge and sponge tools in Photoshop's grayscale mode (bottom).

Brush Size and Shape

Now that we've gotten a feeling for the basics of using the paint and edit tools, let's take a broader look at how you modify the performance of the tools. For example, every tool behaves differently according to the size and shape of your cursor, known as the *brush tip*. Different styles of brush tips are known as *brush shapes*, or just plain *brushes* (not to be confused with the brush tool, which folks sometimes call "the brush" as well). But while there's a lot of nomenclature at work here, the concept behind the brush shape is very simple. A big, round brush paints in broad strokes. A small, elliptical brush is useful for performing hairline adjustments. And if that's not enough — which it clearly isn't — you've a world of options in between and many more besides.

Selecting a brush shape

Provided that a paint or edit tool is active, there are a handful of ways to modify the brush shape in Photoshop 7:

✦ **Right-click:** Right-click anywhere inside the image window (Control-click on the Mac) to display a small palette of preset brush shapes, complete with a menu of additional options, as pictured in Figure 5-15. Scroll through the list of brush shapes, click on the one you want to use, then press Enter or Return to hide the palette. You can also press Esc to hide the palette and leave the brush shape unchanged.

The presets palette previews how the brush looks both when you click and when you drag. If your computer includes a pressure-sensitive drawing tablet, then the strokes will appear to taper, as in the figure; otherwise, they will appear uniform. To dispense with the stroke previews, choose Large Thumbnail from the palette menu. To restore the stroke previews, choose Stroke Thumbnail.

✦ **The Brushes palette:** Choose Window ➪ Brushes or press F5 to display the Brushes palette, which appears on the left side of Figure 5-16. Click the word Brush Presets in the top-left corner of the palette to see a list of predefined brush shapes. You also get a large preview of the active brush shape at the bottom of the palette. Bear in mind, it will only appear tapered if you turn on the Shape Dynamics check box along the left side of the palette.

The primary advantage of the Brushes palette is that you can define your own brush shapes and adjust various exciting dynamics, as I discuss in the next section. If all you want to do is select a predefined brush, right-clicking (or Control-clicking) is generally simpler.

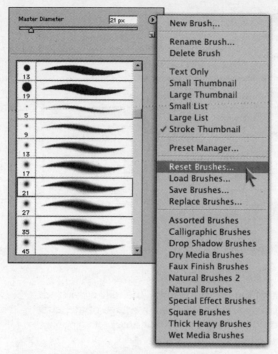

Figure 5-15: The new presets palette lets you select from a list of predefined brush shapes and load other ones from disk.

Tip

By default, the Brushes palette is wider than Photoshop's other palettes, which means it doesn't stack well on the right side of your screen. You have two ways of working around this: One is to get in the habit of pressing F5 to show and hide the palette at a moment's notice. The other is to turn off the Expanded View command in the Brushes palette menu, which lets you shrink the preset brush list to Photoshop's standard palettes width, as in the right example in Figure 5-16.

✦ **Master diameter:** With the preset palette or Brushes palette on screen, you can change the size of the brush by adjusting the Master Diameter value. Measured in pixels, this value represents the thickest stroke the brush will paint. (It can get thinner based on the Shape Dynamic settings, as I explain later in this chapter.) This means you're never locked into a preset brush diameter, even when painting with custom (non-round) brushes.

Tip

Changing the brush diameter is so useful you can do it from the keyboard. Press the left bracket key, which looks like [, to make the brush smaller. Press the right bracket key, or], to make the brush bigger. (Both keys are to the right of the P key on most keyboards.) Keep an eye on the brush icon in the Options bar to see how much smaller or larger the brush diameter gets.

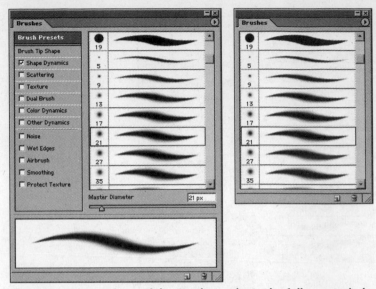

Figure 5-16: Two views of the Brushes palette, the fully expanded view (left) and the reduced view (right). The advantage of the latter is that it stacks well with Photoshop's other palettes.

Tip

✦ **Preset shortcuts:** You can cycle between presets even when no palette is visible. Press the comma key to toggle to the previous brush shape in the list. Press the period key to select the next brush shape. You also can press Shift+comma to select the first brush shape in the list (1-pixel wide) and Shift+period to select the last brush.

By default, your cursor outline reflects the active brush shape. If your cursor instead looks like a crosshair or tool icon, press Ctrl+K (⌘-K on the Mac) to bring up the Preferences dialog box and press Ctrl+3 (⌘-3 on the Mac) for the Display & Cursors panel. Then select Brush Size from the Painting Cursors radio buttons. Now you can create a brush as big as 2,500 pixels in diameter and have your cursor grow accordingly.

Tip

When you use a very small brush, four dots appear around the cursor perimeter, making the cursor easier to locate. If you need a little more help, press the Caps Lock key to access the more obvious crosshair cursor.

Making your own brush shape

To create a custom brush shape, click the item named Brush Tip Shape inside the Brushes palette, which displays the options shown in Figure 5-17. Photoshop displays thumbnails for the predefined brushes in the top right quadrant of the palette. Select a brush to serve as a starting point for your custom creation, and then tweak away:

Caution

✦ **Diameter:** This option determines the width of the brush. If the brush shape is elliptical instead of circular, the Diameter value determines the longest dimension. You can enter any value from 1 to 2,500 pixels.

A small word of warning: Brush shapes with diameters of 15 pixels or higher are too large to display accurately in the Options bar; the stroke preview at the bottom of the Brushes palette is accurate no higher than 50 pixels. So regard the previews with a grain of salt.

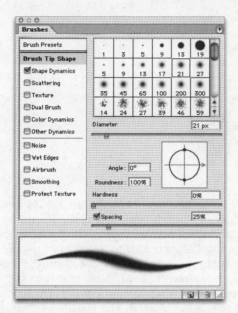

Figure 5-17: To change the size, shape, and hardness of a brush, click the item named Brush Tip Shape in the Brushes palette.

✦ **Angle:** This option pivots a brush shape on its axes. Unless the brush is elliptical, though, you won't see a difference. So it's best to first adjust the Roundness value and then adjust the Angle.

✦ **Roundness:** Enter a Roundness value of less than 100 percent to create an elliptical brush shape. The value modifies the height of the brush as a percentage of the Diameter value, so a Roundness of 50 percent results in a short, fat brush.

Tip

You can adjust the angle of the brush dynamically by dragging the gray arrow inside the box to the right of the Angle and Roundness options. Drag the handles on either side of the black circle to make the brush shape elliptical, as demonstrated in Figure 5-18. Drag the arrow tip to angle the brush. Or try this trick: Click anywhere in the white box to move the arrow to that point.

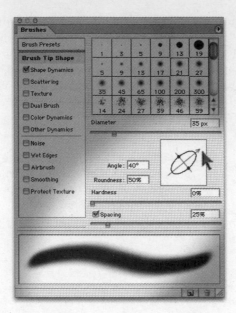

Figure 5-18: Drag the black handles and gray arrow to change the roundness and angle of the brush, respectively. The Roundness and Angle values update automatically, as does the preview of the brushstroke at the bottom of the palette.

✦ **Hardness:** Except when using the pencil tool, brushes are always antialiased. You can further soften the edges of a brush by dragging the Hardness slider bar away from 100 percent. The softest setting, 0 percent, gradually tapers the brush from a single solid color pixel at its center to a ring of transparent pixels around the brush's perimeter. Figure 5-19 shows how low Hardness percentages expand the size of a 200-pixel brush beyond the Diameter value (as demonstrated by the examples in the bottom row). Even a 100-percent hard brush shape expands slightly because it is antialiased. The Hardness setting is ignored when you use the pencil tool.

Tip

Like Diameter, Hardness is one of those settings that you need regular access to. So the ever-helpful Photoshop lets you change the Hardness from the keyboard. Press Shift+[(Shift+left bracket) to make the brush softer; press Shift+] (Shift+right bracket) to make the brush harder. Both shortcuts work in 25 percent increments. For example, you have to press Shift+] four times to go from 0 percent Hardness to 100 percent.

✦ **Spacing:** In real life, a brush lays down a continuous coat of paint. But that's not how it works on the computer. Photoshop actually blasts out a stream of colored spots. The Spacing option controls how frequently the spots are emitted, measured as a percentage of the brush shape. For example, suppose the Diameter of a brush is 40 pixels and the Spacing is set to 25 percent (the default setting for all predefined brushes). For every 10 pixels (25 percent of 40) you drag with the brush tool, Photoshop lays down a 40-pixel wide spot of color. A Spacing of 1 percent provides the most coverage but also slows down the performance of the tool. If you deselect the Spacing check box, the effect of the tool is wholly dependent on the speed at which you drag; this can be useful for creating splotchy or oscillating lines. Figure 5-20 shows examples.

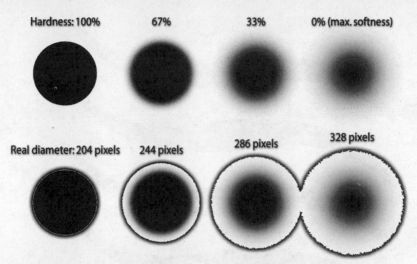

Figure 5-19: A 200-pixel brush shown as it appears when set to each of four Hardness percentages. In the bottom row, I placed the brushes on a separate layer and applied a black fringe so that you can see the effective diameter of each Hardness value.

Tip

In my experience, ridges generally begin to appear at the default Spacing value of 25 percent, especially when painting with a mouse. If you notice lumps in your brushstrokes, lower the Spacing to 15 percent, which (as illustrated in the second example in Figure 5-20) ensures a good mix of speed and smoothness.

After you edit a brush, you can save the brush for later use by clicking the tiny page icon at the bottom of the palette. Photoshop suggests a name, which you can then change. To save a brush without being asked to name it, Alt-click the page icon (or Option-click on the Mac). Photoshop stores the brush with your program preferences so that it's preserved between editing sessions.

Caution

Note that if you delete the preferences file (as discussed in Chapter 2), you lose your custom brushes. To ensure that your custom brushes are saved in case you delete the preferences file or for use on another machine, choose Save Brushes from the palette menu. See the upcoming section "Saving and loading brush sets" for more information.

To delete a brush from the list, switch back to the Brushes Presets view and drag the brush to the trash icon at the bottom of the palette.

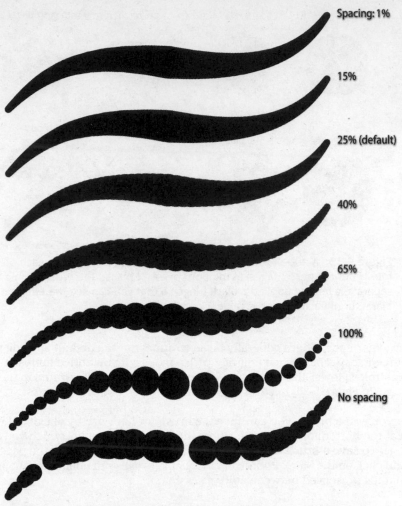

Figure 5-20: Examples of lines drawn with the brush tool subject to different Spacing values. Values greater than 100 percent are useful for creating dotted line effects. The final line was created by turning off the Spacing option.

Defining a custom brush

Photoshop allows you to not only modify the size and roundness of a brush, but define a custom brush as well. Start by making a new image and doodling the shape of your brush tip. For now, any squiggle will do. Then use the rectangular marquee tool to select the doodle. (The rectangular marquee is discussed in "Geometric selection outlines," in Chapter 8). You don't have to be particularly careful; just select the general area around the doodle, as I've done in Figure 5-21. Photoshop is smart enough to distinguish the confines of the brush from its background.

Next, choose the Define Brush command from the Edit menu. Photoshop invites you to give your brush a name; if you're not feeling inspired, just press Enter or Return and accept the default name, Sampled Brush #1.

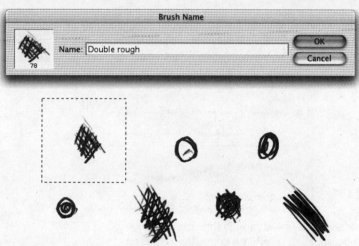

Figure 5-21: After selecting a doodle against a white background, choose Edit ⇨ Define Brush and enter a name to turn the doodle into a custom brush.

After you define a custom brush, you can tweak it just like any other brush inside the Brush Tip Shape panel of the Brushes palette. Whereas Photoshop 6 and earlier let you modify the Spacing of a custom brush and that's about it, Version 7 lets you adjust the Diameter, Angle, and Roundness (height versus width) as well. As shown in Figure 5-22, the only option that appears dimmed is Hardness; you have to accept the sharpness of the brush as it was originally defined. A custom brush will even grow and shrink according to stylus pressure.

To restore a custom brush to its original size, click the Use Sample Size button in the Brush Tip Shape panel of the Brushes palette.

Saving and loading brush sets

After you define a handful of brushes — custom or otherwise — you may want to save them to avoid losing them in the event of a hard drive crash or if you want to be able to use the brushes on a different computer. Photoshop saves multiple brushes at a time to libraries. The program also ships several predefined libraries, found in the Presets/Brushes folder inside the folder that contains the Photoshop application. Brush libraries have the file extension *.abr*.

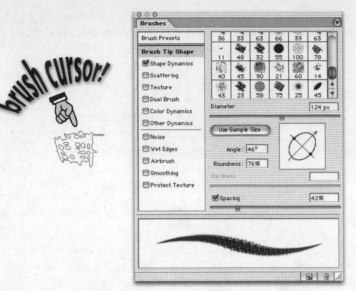

Figure 5-22: Photoshop 7 lets you modify the size, shape, and angle of a custom brush, all of which are accurately reflected by the brush cursor.

You can save brush sets — as well as load and edit them — by choosing commands from the Brushes palette menu when the Brush Presets panel is displayed. Or choose commands from the presets palette that you get when right-clicking with a paint or edit tool. You can also manage libraries by choosing Edit ⇨ Preset Manager. Figure 5-23 gives you a look at the Preset Manager with the Brushes panel at the forefront. If you're already working in the Preset Manager, press Ctrl+1 (⌘-1 on the Mac) to get to the Brushes panel.

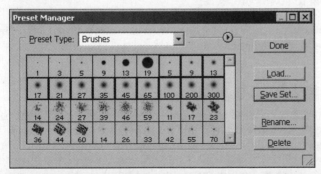

Figure 5-23: Choose Edit ⇨ Preset Manager to display the central headquarters for loading, saving, and editing brush sets.

By default, the Brushes palette displays a list of nearly 70 predefined brushes, including both elliptical and custom varieties. You can't delete this brush set, but you can prevent brushes you don't use from taking up space in the palette. You also can load or create a different set, combine two or more sets, and add or delete brushes from your custom brush sets. Here's the drill:

✦ **Save a brush set:** To save all brushes currently displayed in the Brushes palette, choose Save Brushes from the palette menu. If you want to save only some of the brushes as a set, however, choose Edit ➪ Preset Manager. Shift-click the brushes you want to save and then click the Save Set button.

Regardless of where you initiate the save, Photoshop takes you to the Save dialog box, where you can name your brush set. By default, brushes are saved in the Presets/Brushes folder, which is a darn good place for them. The next time you start Photoshop, your new brush set appears on the Brushes palette menu along with other available sets.

✦ **Use a different brush set:** If you want to put the current brush set away and use a different set, choose Replace Brushes from the Brushes palette menu and select the brush set you want to use. Alternatively, click the arrowhead at the top of the scrolling list of icons in the Preset Manager dialog box to display a similar menu, and then choose Replace Brushes from that menu.

✦ **Load multiple brush sets:** You can keep multiple brush sets active if you want. After loading the first set, choose Load Brushes from the Brushes palette menu or click the Load button in the Preset Manager dialog box. Photoshop appends the second brush set onto the first. If you want to keep using the two sets together, you may want to save them as a new, custom brush set.

✦ **Delete a brush:** To delete a brush from the current brush set, select it from the Brush Presets panel of the Brushes palette and click the trash icon. Or choose Delete Brush from the palette menu.

Want to give a bunch of brushes the boot? Do the job in the Preset Manager dialog box. Shift-click the brushes you no longer want and then click the Delete button.

✦ **Restore default brushes:** To return to the default Photoshop brush set, choose Reset Brushes from the menu in the palette or the dialog box. You then have the option of either replacing the existing brushes with the default brushes or simply adding them to the end of the palette.

✦ **Rename a brush:** If you ever want to rename a brush, select it in the Preset Manager dialog box and click the Rename button. Or, even easier, double-click the brushstroke in the Brush Presets panel of the Brushes palette.

If you want your new brush names to live in perpetuity, resave the brush set. Otherwise, the names will revert to their original labels when and if you replace the brush set.

Brush Dynamics

Photoshop has long permitted you to vary the size, opacity, and color of paint according to input from a pressure-sensitive drawing tablet. Available from companies such as Wacom (*www.wacom.com*), pressure-sensitive drawing tablets respond to how hard you press on the stylus, as well as the angle of the stylus and other attributes.

I happen to be an old fan of drawing tablets. I believe I have roughly a dozen sitting around in one form or other. So it's hardly surprising that I consider them every bit as essential as mice and keyboards. Alas, despite my advice, you may not own a tablet. Fortunately, Photoshop permits mouse users to enjoy much of the same flexibility as their stylus-wielding colleagues. Whether you use a stylus, a mouse, or even a finger on a notebook trackpad, you can introduce an element of spontaneity into what seems at times like an absolute world of computer imaging.

Photoshop calls these imaginative options *brush dynamics*, and they've gotten a heck of a lot better in Version 7. For example, you can make a brush shape twirl as you paint. You can add noise to the edges of a stroke. You can spray shapes, add texture, combine brushes, or even paint in rainbows. And most of the settings work every bit as well with, say, the sponge as they do with the brush tool. If you're a creative type, prepare to get lost inside Photoshop and lose track of reality for a few hours, maybe even days.

Brush dynamic basics

To access Photoshop's brush dynamics when a paint or an edit tool is active, bring up the Brushes palette (press F5 if it's hidden) and click the item labeled Shape Dynamics on the left side of the palette. This simultaneously activates and displays the first of six panels — including Scattering, Texture, and so on — devoted to brush dynamics. Photoshop also provides a series of check boxes in the central portion of the palette (starting with Noise and ending with Protect Texture) that apply minor effects without displaying additional panels of options.

Note that all check boxes and options are available when using the brush tool, but they come and go for the other paint and edit tools. For example, the Wet Edges check box is unavailable when using the pencil tool, Color Dynamics is dimmed when using the dodge and burn tools, and so on. Even so, the sheer amount of options available for even the most limited of the edit tools verges on fantastic, especially when compared with older versions of Photoshop. Also, each tool observes an independent set of defaults. So activating, say, Shape Dynamics, Texture, and Smoothing for the brush tool does not turn them on for other tools. However, they will again be turned on the next time you return to the brush tool.

If you want to save a group of brush dynamics for use with a variety of tools, then click the page icon along the bottom of the Brushes palette. Brush dynamics are considered to be part of a saved brush shape, and transfer from one tool to another. To save a group of brush dynamics for use with a single tool, visit the Tool Presets palette (Window ⇨ Tool Presets) and choose New Tool Preset from the palette menu. It's equivalent to designing your own custom tool that you can select from the Options bar, as discussed back in Chapter 2.

Tip

So there's your general overview; now let's plunge headlong into the specifics. To give you a sense of what's going on, we start with a detailed look at the options in the Shape Dynamics panel, which are arguably the most interesting, useful, and representative of all the brush dynamics. Then we take a more cursory look at the other options, which often follow in the same vein. After that, I encourage you to explore the options on your own. And as you do, don't forget to keep one eye on the big stroke preview at the bottom of the palette. It really is useful, especially when trying out settings that you haven't used before or combining options to achieve specific effects.

So have fun. And when I say "have fun," I mean, have a blast, go nuts. By which I mean, wowsers, this stuff rocks. Goodness, how I envy you, so young and naive, embarking upon brush dynamics for the very first time. You're about to be amazed, astonished, and then once again amazed. Or, after this build up, horribly disappointed. I guess it all depends on how much of a thrill you get from drawing wiggly, splattery, rough, colorful brushstrokes. Me, I love it. But you, who knows? Okay, I'll shut up now.

Shape dynamics

Inside the Brushes palette, click the Shape Dynamics option—the name, not the check box—to display the panel of options illustrated in Figure 5-24. Notice that the panel is divided into three sections, which start with the words Size Jitter, Angle Jitter, and Roundness Jitter. These options permit you to vary the diameter, angle, and roundness of the brush over the course of a single stroke. But the repetition of the word "Jitter" may be misleading. It implies (to me, at least) that each group of options is related to jittering—Photoshop's word for random brush shape fluctuations—when in fact, jittering is a minor element of shape dynamics.

If I had designed this panel, it would look more like the one in Figure 5-25, with clear headlines for each section followed by the single most important option, the Control pop-up menu. Meanwhile, I'd put the least important option, Jitter, at the end. Because I believe this is the most logical way to present these options, I will explain them in this order as well.

Figure 5-24: The Shape Dynamics panel along with a quick cartoon I drew using the brush shape described in the palette and a Wacom Intuos II tablet.

Figure 5-25: My suggestion for a redesign of this panel that would help it to make more sense. (It seems to make more sense to my cartoon, anyway.)

The diameter settings

The first group of options control the thickness of the brushstroke. Most important of these is the Control pop-up menu, which links the diameter of the brush to one of several variables. If you own a pressure-sensitive tablet, the most obvious setting is Pen Pressure, which is the default. This turns the brush into a traditional, pressure-sensitive painting tool, growing when you bear down on the stylus and shrinking with you let up.

Note

Three settings, Pen Pressure, Pen Tilt, and Stylus Wheel, require compatible hardware. If your only pointing device is a standard mouse, as is typical, selecting one of these options displays a triangular warning icon. This is Photoshop's way of telling you that, although you are welcome to select the option, it isn't really going to work. If you get the message in error — say, you get a warning for Pen Pressure even though you have a tablet installed — try clicking with the stylus on the Brushes palette. If that doesn't work, open the control panel or utility that manages the tablet to make sure the tablet is properly installed.

Cross-Reference

But as it turns out, you can take advantage of the Pen Pressure option, even if you don't own a pressure-sensitive tablet. In Photoshop 7, you can simulate pressure by stroking a paint or edit tool along a path. For complete information, see the "Painting along a path" section of Chapter 8.

In addition to Pen Pressure, the Control pop-up menu lets you select between the following options:

✦ **Off:** Select this option to turn off your control over varying the thickness of the brushstroke. You can still add random variations to the thickness using the Size Jitter value.

✦ **Fade:** This option works every bit as well whether you use a mouse or tablet. Select Fade to reduce the size of the brush over the course of the drag, and then enter a value in the option box on right to specify the distance over which the fading should occur. This distance is measured in steps — that is, the number of spots of color the brush plops down before reducing the size of the brush to its minimum (defined by the Minimum Diameter setting). The default value is 25#, which means 25 spots of color. Exactly how long such a stroke is in, say, inches depends on the Diameter and the Spacing values in the Brush Tip Shape panel. In other words, be prepared to experiment.

The Fade option can be most useful in the creation of a specular reflection, or in layman's terms, a sparkle. Figure 5-26 shows a highly polished, gold-painted egg. To add the sparkle in the second example, I painted a series of white strokes outward from the center using the brush tool. I Shift-dragged to make each of the four horizontal and vertical strokes, using a soft brush with a diameter of 20 pixels and a Fade value of 100 steps. To make each of the diagonal strokes, I clicked in the center and Shift-clicked farther out, using a diameter of 10 pixels and a Fade value of 50 steps. To complete the effect, I clicked once in the center of the sparkle with a very large, very soft brush.

Figure 5-26: A shiny golden egg from the Corbis library (top), and that same egg with a sparkle created using the Fade setting (bottom).

✦ **Pen Tilt:** As illustrated in Figure 5-27, the tilt of a pen is its angle with respect to the tablet. Straight up and down, the pen communicates no tilt; at a severe angle, the pen communicates maximum tilt. When you set the Control option to Pen Tilt, you do two things. First, you vary the size of the brush according to pressure, just as you do when using Pen Pressure. Second, you add an element of vertical scaling so that the brush shape is oblong during a tilt. This scaling is defined by the Tilt Scale slider. All in all, it's an interesting idea, but for my money, Pen Tilt works more predictably when applied to roundness.

JPEG Compression

Color Plate 3-1

Taken from the Corbis Royalty Free image library, this photograph shows the effects of four different JPEG compression settings, starting with maximum quality, minimum compression (top) and ending with minimum quality, maximum compression (bottom). The images in the left-hand column show each compressed photo at the standard print resolution of 300 pixels per inch.

Even with the Quality option set to Low (or a value of 3), the effects of lossy compression can be subtle and difficult to see, which is why I performed a few modifications to exaggerate the compression artifacts. First, because JPEG compression produces the most pronounced effects on highly saturated colors and super-sharp edges, I used Image ⇨ Adjustments ⇨ Hue/Saturation (discussed in Chapter 17) to recolor half the face a vivid blue and then applied Filter ⇨ Sharpen ⇨ Unsharp Mask (Chapter 10) to sharpen the focus. Second, because JPEG compression becomes easier to see at low resolutions, I magnified details from the original and colorized images to 200 percent (or 150 ppi) in the right-hand column. Throughout these examples, images toward the top of the page look better than those toward the bottom, but they likewise take up more room on disk.

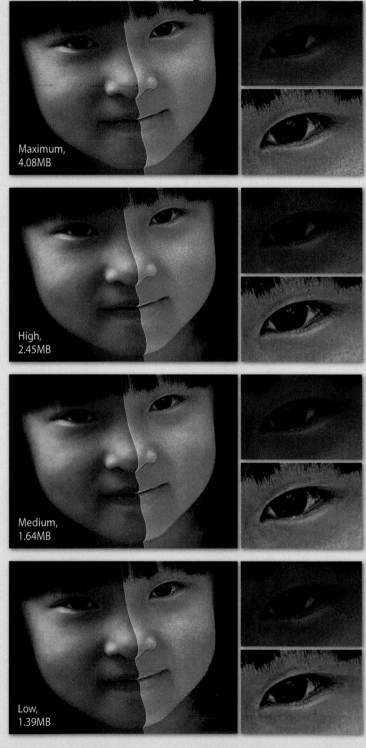

Maximum, 4.08MB

High, 2.45MB

Medium, 1.64MB

Low, 1.39MB

Lab Channel Effects

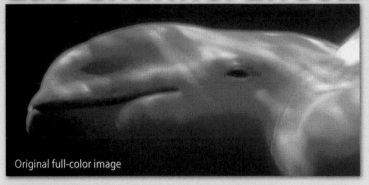

Original full-color image

Invert "a" channel

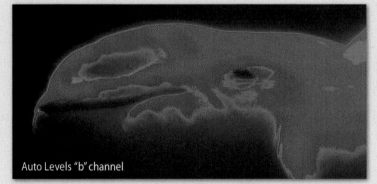

Auto Levels "b" channel

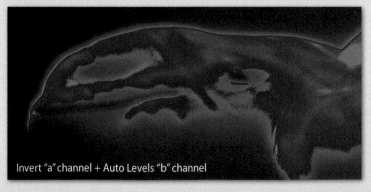

Invert "a" channel + Auto Levels "b" channel

Color Plate 4-1

One of the wonderful advantages to Photoshop's Lab mode is that it permits you to edit colors in an image independently of the brightness values. By way of demonstration, the top image shows an unedited photograph of a beluga whale. After converting the photo to Lab (Image ⇨ Mode ⇨ Lab Color), I switched to the *a* channel and pressed Ctrl+I (⌘-I on the Mac) to invert it. Because the *a* channel carries the green and pink colors in the image, inverting it swapped the greens inside the whale with pinks, as in the second example. In the third example, I started once again with the original Lab image, switched to the *b* channel, and chose Image ⇨ Adjustments ⇨ Auto Levels. This enhanced the contrast of the *b* channel, thus boosting the blues and yellows inside the beluga. In the final example, I combined the two effects, inverting the *a* channel and enhancing the *b* channel. Using some very simple commands, I was able to dramatically alter the colors in the image without harming a smidgen of detail.

The Channel Mixer

Color Plate 4-2

Another way to wreak some pretty interesting havoc on colors without upsetting the detail in an image is to replace one color channel with another or swap the contents of two or more channels using Image ⇨ Adjustments ⇨ Channel Mixer. Starting with an RGB version of the beluga, I replaced the Red channel with the contents of the Green channel. The result of cloning the bright greens into the Red channel was to make the beluga yellow, as in the top example. Restoring the Red channel and cloning the Green channel into the Blue channel turns the whale vivid cyan, as in the second example. In the third example, I copied the contents of the Blue channel into the Red channel and vice versa, thus exaggerating the reds and muting the blues to almost nothing. In the final example, I swapped the contents of the Red and Green channels, which turned the previously greenish beluga a vivid magenta. Then I dimmed the Blue channel to 50 percent, leaving the whale a vivid orange.

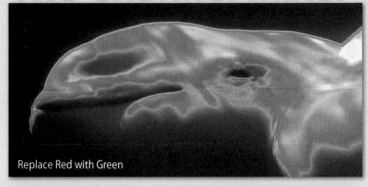

Replace Red with Green

Replace Blue with Green

Swap Red and Blue

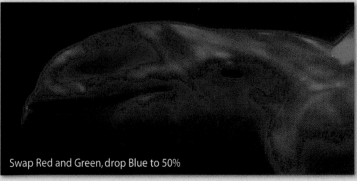

Swap Red and Green, drop Blue to 50%

The Sponge Tool

Original image

Select mask area,
darken with burn tool

Sponge applied to
mask, eyes, lips, and hair

Color Plate 5-1

Although the edit tools are less powerful than many of Photoshop's filters and color adjustment commands, they can be useful for applying spontaneous creative effects. In this sequence of images, for example, I added a mask to the woman's face shown at top using just two edit tools, the burn tool and the sponge. I started by selecting an area around the woman's eyes using the pen tool (which I discuss at length in Chapter 8). Then I painted inside the selection with the burn tool, toasting the skin to achieve a rich umber tone (middle). I painted additional strokes under the eyebrows and around the edges of the mask to deepen the shadows. Next, I painted inside the mask with the sponge tool to alternatively dim colors and saturate them. With the sponge set to Desaturate, I painted under the eyes, making the mask more gray. Then I changed the Mode setting to Saturate and painted over the forehead and the bridge of the nose, turning these areas a vivid orange. Finally, I deselected the image and painted inside the irises, lips, and hair to increase the saturation of these areas as well (bottom).

Brush Modes

Color Plate 5-2

These images show a series of brushstrokes applied using a handful of brush modes. In each case, I painted the lines with the brush tool. The lines are identical from one image to the next; only the mode and the Opacity setting change (as indicated by the labels). The bottom image gives you the best idea of what the brushstrokes themselves look like.

Each of the six major groups of brush modes is represented. The default Normal mode produces an even mix of brushed color and underlying original pixel. So at 30 percent Opacity, I got 30 percent brushed color mixed with 70 percent underlying (top). The next image shows an example of a darkening mode, Multiply, which causes the brush to burn and color at the same time. The image after that shows a lightening mode, Lighten, which applies a brushed color only when it's lighter than the underlying colors. New to Photoshop 7, Vivid Light darkens the darkest colors and lightens the lightest ones while enhancing color saturation. The Exclusion mode subtracts the brush colors from the underlying color values, in effect inverting as you paint. And finally, Luminosity preserves the brightness values of the brushed colors and mixes them with the colors from the pixels over which you paint.

Normal, 30% Opacity

Multiply, 65% Opacity

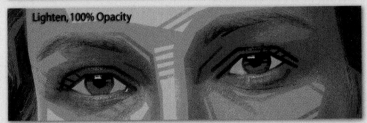

Lighten, 100% Opacity

Vivid Light, 50% Opacity

Exclusion, 80% Opacity

Luminosity, 100% Opacity

The Paint Bucket

Original map outlines

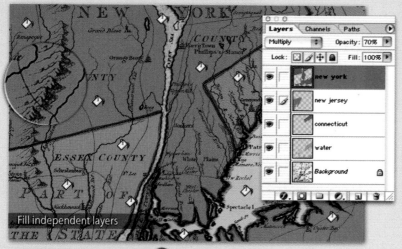

Fill independent layers

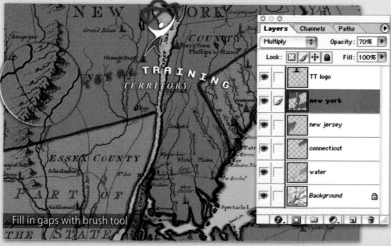

Fill in gaps with brush tool

Color Plate 6-1

Used properly, the paint bucket can be a powerful tool for coloring scanned line art like this 18th-century map (top). Start by creating an independent layer for each color in the image, as I did for New York, New Jersey, Connecticut, and the water. Next, select the paint bucket tool and turn on the All Layers check box in the Options bar. This allows you to fill one layer based on the contents of others.

In filling my map, a Tolerance value of 120 seemed to work best. I selected the New York layer, set the foreground color to green, and clicked with the paint bucket until I had covered most of the state. Then I repeated the process for the other layers. The paint bucket cursors in the middle image show the locations of my clicks. Finally, I set each layer to the Multiply blend mode, which forced the fill colors to transition smoothly into the map.

Even after clicking 20 or so times with the paint bucket, the image was not completely filled, as demonstrated by the gaps inside the mountain range (enlarged on left). So I used the brush tool to fill in these gaps where they appeared on each layer. Note that I didn't have to set the brush to any special mode — because Multiply was in force for each layer, Photoshop blended the colors automatically (bottom).

Gradients

Two overlapping gradients

Color Plate 6-2

At top, I designed two gradients, each on separate layers, that fade several times into translucency or complete transparency, indicated by the checkerboard pattern. The rear layer contains a linear gradient that flows from blue to orange to red, each time fading to 50 percent Opacity midway from one color to the next. The front layer contains a radial gradient that begins opaque and yellow in the center and then fades out, in, and back out twice as it transitions to white.

Such gradations are meant to be blended with an image, such as this intricately carved tunnel interior that I shot in Zion National Park (middle). Then I laid each of the gradients on top of the image, setting the linear blue-orange-red gradient to the Color blend mode and the radial yellow-to-white gradient to Linear Dodge (bottom). For complete information on blend modes, read Chapter 13.

Original photograph

Color and Linear Dodge

Heal, Patch,…

A face composed entirely of acne scars, renegade oil glands, crow's feet, chapped lips, and razor stubble

Alt-click (Option-click)

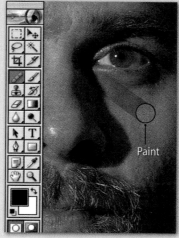

Paint

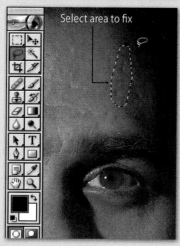

Select area to fix

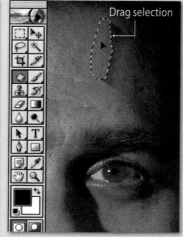

Drag selection

Color Plate 7-1

In creating a promotional piece for a training video (opposite page), I started with a simple digital photo of myself (top). I hadn't shaved, my lips were chapped, I wasn't wearing makeup — in short, I was a mess. So before I could begin work, I had to fix my face.

I was hoping to eliminate the scaly bumps under my eye. So I selected the healing brush, pressed Alt (Option on the Mac), and clicked in the shadow to the side of my nose, where the skin appeared smoother (middle left). Having set the source point, I began my brushstroke inside the shadow just below my eye. This ensured that the shadows from the source and destination areas aligned properly. By sampling texture and color independently, the healing brush fixed my scaly eye bumps in the first pass (middle right).

For larger areas, give the patch tool a try. First, select the area that you want to fix, such as the lovely cluster of scars on my forehead (bottom left). I also feathered the selection slightly to soften the transitions. Then drag the selection outline over the texture you want to emulate (bottom right). The moment I released, Photoshop healed the scars using the texture from the new area and the colors that surrounded the selection outline.

...& Lots of Makeup

Color Plate 7-2

Having healed a few of my most alarming facial defects — I'm not looking for sympathy or anything, I'm just saying, no tool can heal everything that's wrong with my mug — I set about building up some of the makeup I now regret I wasn't wearing. Because a nice duotone helps make even a troll look presentable, I colorized my face blue using Image ⇨ Adjustments ⇨ Hue/Saturation (discussed in Chapter 17). To give my skin a haunting glow, I used Select ⇨ Color Range (Chapter 8) to select the highlights in the image. Then I feathered the selection and filled it with white, as shown on top.

To complete the ad, I enlarged my eyes slightly, painted in new irises and pupils, painted away some of my beard, and drew a pacifier using the shape tools and a few layer effects (Chapter 14). The result is an image that makes me look remotely handsome. If I also happen to look a trifle insane, well, that's the price I pay. Anything for vanity, after all.

Colorize image blue, select highlights with Select ⇨ Color Range, fill with white

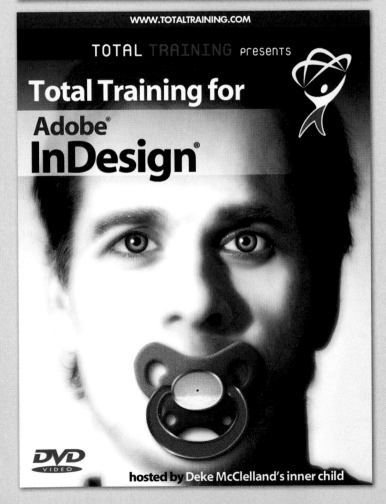

WWW.TOTALTRAINING.COM

TOTAL TRAINING presents

Total Training for

Adobe®
InDesign®

DVD
VIDEO

hosted by Deke McClelland's inner child

Masking Defined

Marching ants-style selection outline

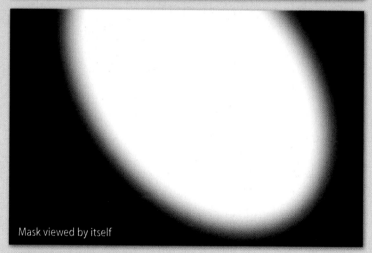

Mask viewed by itself

Mask & image viewed together

Color Plate 9-1

The top image shows an elliptical selection outline rotated a few degrees counter-clockwise and feathered by a Radius value of 64 pixels. But you wouldn't know any feathering had occurred by the marching ants-style selection outline, which appears as hard-edged as ever.

But if you express the selection outline as a mask (middle), you can see it for what it really is — a feathered ellipse. White represents the selected area; black represents the deselected, or masked, area.

From the Channels palette, you can choose to view any kind of mask — quick mask, layer mask, or independent alpha channel — by itself or along with the image. If you choose the latter, Photoshop shows you the mask as a traditional rubylith (bottom). Red-tinted areas are masked; untinted areas are unmasked, and thus represent selections. If an image already contains a preponderance of red, you can change the red overlay to any color you like.

Gradient Quick Mask

Color Plate 9-2

Among other things, the quick mask mode affords you the option of feathering one portion of a selection independently of another. For example, let's say that I wanted to take this native African mask (upper left) and make it appear as if it were emerging from the ground like a giant totem. I began by selecting the mask using the pen tool and then switching to the quick mask mode by pressing the Q key. Then I drew a black-to-transparent gradient from the chin of the mask upward (upper right). This feathers the bottom of the selection while leaving the rest of it unharmed.

I pressed Q again to switch out of the quick mask mode and Ctrl+C (⌘-C on the Mac) to copy the selection. I next switched to a different image that featured grassy plains against a clouded sky and pressed Ctrl+V (⌘-V) to paste the mask into its new background (lower left). Finally, I pressed Ctrl+T (⌘-T) to enter the Free Transform mode. Then I scaled and distorted the image by Ctrl-dragging (⌘-dragging) the corner handles (lower right).

Original image

Gradient in quick mask mode

Paste image into new background

Distort with Free Transform

Photorealistic Mask

Original image

Final mask

Color Plate 9-3

What do you do when you want to composite a complex image — with hair and everything (top left) — against a new background? The solution is to create a complex mask. Using the technique outlined in the section "Building a Mask from an Image" in Chapter 9 — which hinges on Filter ⇨ Other ⇨ High Pass and Image ⇨ Adjustments ⇨ Levels — I arrived at the highly detailed mask shown above right. I used this mask to copy the girl and paste her against a new background. But while the edges were accurate, I still had a ways to go to make the composition look natural.

So I painted in colors from the background using the brush tool set to the Color mode. Finally, I used the brush tool set to Normal with the foreground color set to black to paint in a few very fine hairs. Here, it helped to have a Wacom pressure-sensitive drawing tablet. As it turns out, these painted hairs never occurred in the original image, but they helped sell the effect (bottom).

Image composited against new background

Unsharp Mask

Color Plate 10-1

Arguably Photoshop's most useful filter, Unsharp Mask sharpens the focus of an image by increasing the contrast of edge details. You can apply the filter to an entire image or to independent color channels to achieve different effects. Starting with an image from the Corbis Royalty Free library (upper left), I applied Unsharp Mask with an Amount of 500 percent, a Radius of 4.0 pixels, and a Threshold of 0. The result is an exaggerated sharpening effect with very thick edges, creating the appearance of deep grooves in the cream on the woman's face (upper right).

The remaining examples show what happens if I alternatively apply these same settings to a single color channel or a pair of channels. The results are relatively predictable once you understand what's going on. Unsharp Mask highlights edges by tracing light and dark lines along them. So if you apply the filter in just the red channel, for example, the edges become red where Unsharp Mask traces its light lines and turquoise (the inverse of red) where the lines are dark.

Beyond special effects, you can apply Unsharp Mask to independent channels to accommodate an image that has different focus problems in each channel (see Color Plate 10-3).

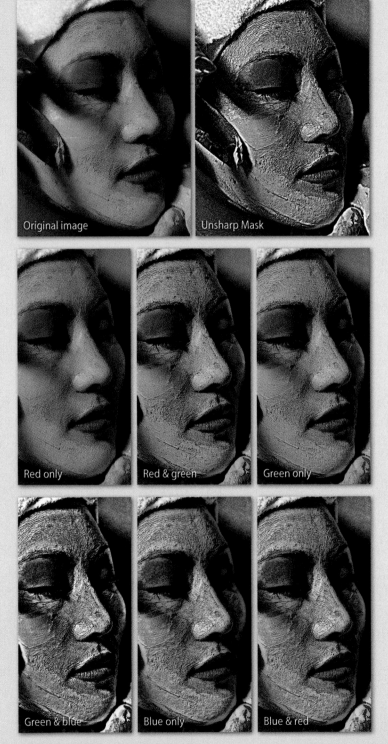

Original image

Unsharp Mask

Red only

Red & green

Green only

Green & blue

Blue only

Blue & red

Gaussian Blur

Gaussian Blur, Radius: 12 pixels

Edit ➪ Fade Gaussian Blur, Mode: Darken

Repeat Gaussian Blur, Edit ➪ Fade, Mode: Linear Dodge, Opacity: 80%

Color Plate 10-2

The Gaussian Blur filter ranks among Photoshop's most useful functions, essential for building masks, creating depth effects, and more. In the examples on left, I used Gaussian Blur to simulate a soft diffused glow. The first image shows the result of applying the filter with a Radius of 12 pixels. The image appears out of focus, as if in the background. The problem is, this woman is our foreground subject, so she needs to look sharp and clear. To bring back some of the detail, I chose Edit ➪ Fade and set the Mode to Darken, which kept only those pixels from the blur effect that were darker than their counterparts in the original image (middle). The result is an overall darkening of the image, with blurry transitions most evident in the highlights like the cheeks, eyes, and teeth.

To restore some of the lightness to the image, I pressed Ctrl+F (⌘-F) to reapply the Gaussian Blur filter using the same Radius setting. Then I again chose Edit ➪ Fade, this time changing the Mode to Linear Dodge and reducing the Opacity value to 80 percent. The effect is one of an image shot in soft focus under powerful direct light (bottom), but with the pivotal details in the image fully intact.

Descreen a Halftone

Color Plate 10-3

This image I created for Macworld magazine more than ten years ago illustrates a
common problem with scanned images.
Where you see a continuous-tone image,
your scanner sees and captures a collection
of colored dots. If you commercially reproduce that scanned image — as I've done at
top — you're adding new halftone to old
halftone, which invariably produces moiré
patterns.

How do you get rid of the halftone pattern
without harming the image? The easy way
is to apply the Dust & Scratches filter. But as
demonstrated by the second image, in
averaging away the pattern, Dust &
Scratches has averaged away the detail in
the image as well.

The final image appears miraculous by
comparison, and yet it's the result of about
10 minutes of work on the original scan. I
used three filters — Median, Gaussian Blur,
and Unsharp Mask — each applied to a
single color channel at a time. As is typical,
the blue channel was in the worst shape, so
I applied the highest Radius amounts
there. I was more careful with the green
and red channels, which carry the majority
of the detail and color information,
respectively. For a full account of the
procedure, read the last section of
Chapter 10.

Scanned image, printed in *Macworld* magazine, Feb. 1991

Dust & Scratches, Radius: 2 pixels, Threshold: 20

Gaussian Blur, Median, & USM applied to individual channels

Sketch Filters

Original image

Halftone Pattern, Size: 2, Contrast: 18, Pattern Type: Line

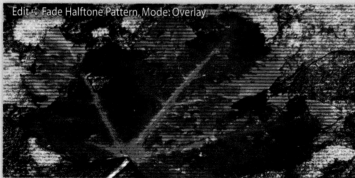
Edit ⇨ Fade Halftone Pattern, Mode: Overlay

same, Mode: Luminosity

Color Plate 11-1

Most of Photoshop's Sketch filters — those that appear under the Filter ⇨ Sketch sub-menu — recolor an image entirely in the foreground and background colors. (The exceptions are Chrome, which converts the image to shades of gray, and Water Paper, which retains the image's original colors.) For example, starting with the photograph shown at top, I set the foreground and background colors to medium green and light turquoise, respectively, and then applied Filter ⇨ Sketch ⇨ Halftone Pattern using the settings listed in the second image. The result is a photo that looks as if it were projected on an old-style computer monitor.

That's fine, but what if you want to combine the texture from the filtered image with the colors from the original? Fade the filter. Immediately after applying the Halftone Pattern filter, I pressed Ctrl+Shift+F (⌘-Shift-F on the Mac) to invoke the Fade command and changed the blend mode to Overlay. Shown in the third image, the result brings back the reds and yellows inside the leaf but keeps the filtered greens inside the previously gray background. If you'd prefer to forsake all color from the filtered image, set the blend mode to Luminosity, as in the last example.

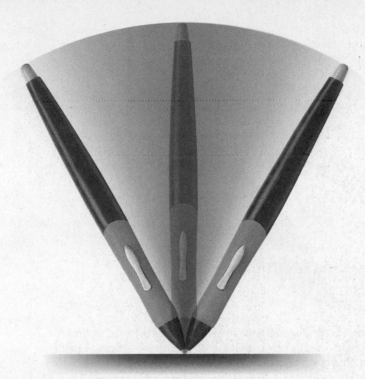

Figure 5-27: Most Wacom tablets are sensitive not only to how much pressure you apply to a stylus, but also the angle of the stylus with respect to the tablet, known as the tilt.

✦ **Stylus Wheel:** If tablet owners account for 10 percent of Photoshop users, then airbrush owners account for about 1 percent of tablet users. But heck, that's still enough folks to populate a small town, so might as well support them. For those of you who have never seen an electronic airbrush, Figure 5-28 shows what one looks like, complete with stylus wheel. Unlike the scroll wheels included with many PC mice—which are exceptionally useful for scrolling Web pages and Word documents—the wheel on an airbrush locks into position. This means you can nudge it higher or lower and leave it there. While typically associated with properties such as Flow (which you can set from the Other Dynamics panel), the airbrush wheel is surprisingly useful for diameter as well. Move the wheel up, the brush gets thick and stays thick; move the wheel down, and you lock in a fine line, all in the middle of painting a brushstroke. Downside: a Wacom airbrush costs $99, not including the tablet. So it's a stocking stuffer. She gets earrings, he gets an airbrush. Or vice versa. Heck, send *me* the earrings—I already have an airbrush. And no, I'm not interested in a trade, just give me the earrings!

stylus wheel!

Figure 5-28: The airbrush stylus includes a wheel that you can permanently set to increase or decrease the flow of paint, as with a traditional airbrush.

Accompanying the Control pop-up menu are three slider bars:

✦ **Minimum Diameter:** Use this option to determine the thinnest a brushstroke can go. Me, I say go all the way, 1 percent baby. Why settle for more?

✦ **Tilt Scale:** I don't admit this very often, but this option puzzles me. Yes, it's only available when you set the Control option to Pen Tilt, and yes, it stretches the height of the brush to make it elliptical when you tilt the stylus. But why? You can do this just as well with the roundness options, as I explain shortly. My guess: A thoughtful engineer at Adobe wanted you to get confused by this option so you'd go out and buy this book. Really, that's my best guess. Now for those of you who did buy this book for a lucid description of the Tilt Scale option, sorry I couldn't help. Check out the other pages, though — they're really great.

✦ **Size Jitter:** Use this slider to add an element of pure randomness to the thickness of a brushstroke. It doesn't matter whether you use a mouse or a stylus; the brush will jitter every bit as well either way. Higher values produce a wider range of jitter. Keep an eye on the preview at the bottom of the palette to get a sense of what different settings will do.

Angle and roundness

Now that you understand the diameter settings, the angle and roundness settings are pretty simple stuff. But to confirm your knowledge and ensure that we're all on the same page, here's how they work:

✦ **Angle Control:** As with diameter, you can link the angle of the brush to such variables as Pen Pressure, Pen Tilt, and Stylus Wheel. More pressure or tilt equals more rotation of the brush. Naturally, the changes show up best with elliptical or asymmetrical brushes. You can also link the angle to Fade, which rotates the brush over the course of a specific number of steps, and then returns the brush to its normal angle (as specified in the Brush Tip Shape panel).

But this Control pop-up menu adds in two more settings, Direction and Initial Direction. The first rotates the brush according to the direction of your drag. A horizontal drag is considered the normal angle; when dragging vertically, the brush rotates 90 degrees. For maximum effect, after setting this option to Direction, go to the Brush Tip Shape panel and set the Angle value to 90 degrees (or something close) with an elliptical brush. Then raise the Spacing value to something higher than 100 percent.

Meanwhile, the Initial Direction option rotates the brush according to the very start of your drag and then locks it into position. It's a nice idea, but the angle is locked down about 2 pixels into your drag, which means Photoshop is aware of your initial direction before you are.

✦ **Angle Jitter:** This option rotates the brush randomly as you paint. As always, be sure to adjust the roundness of the brush so you can see the randomness at work.

✦ **Roundness Control:** Set this option to Fade to reduce the roundness to its minimum over the course of a specified number of steps. You can also associate the roundness with Pen Pressure, Pen Tilt, or Stylus Wheel. Of these, Pen Tilt makes by far the most sense to me, because that's what pen tilt does in real life.

✦ **Minimum Roundness:** This value determines the minimum roundness, or maximum flatness, of the brush available to the Control and Jitter settings. If the Control option is set to Off and the Roundness Jitter is 0 percent, then the Minimum Roundness slider is dimmed.

✦ **Roundness Jitter:** Use this option to introduce random variations in roundness to your brushstroke.

Additional brush dynamics

For many, the Shape Dynamic settings will be enough. And certainly, they permit you to achieve an enormous range of effects. But if you're feeling ambitious, you can venture deeper, much deeper. Fortunately, the other panels of options — Scattering, Texture, and so on — follow the same logic we've seen thus far. So I'll breeze through them fairly quickly.

Figure 5-29 demonstrates several dynamic permutations as applied to the predefined custom brush Scattered Leaves. Here's how these options work:

✦ **Scattering:** Highlight the Scattering option to spread the position of the spots of color around the brushstroke. When using a custom brush, like Scattered Leaves in Figure 5-29, the effect is like spraying a pattern of images. Raise the Scatter value to increase the spread. Select Both Axes to scatter the brush spots along the stroke as well as perpendicularly to it. Use the Control pop-up menu to link it to stylus pressure or some other variable. Finally, use the Count options to increase the population of brush spots.

Scatter: 75%
Count: 2

Texture: Metal Landscape
Mode: Overlay
Depth: 100%

Texture: Op Checkerboard
Texture Each Tip
Mode: Color Dodge

Dual Brush: Maple
Mode: Overlay
Scatter: 100%

Dual Brush: Grass
Mode: Color Dodge
Scatter: 35%

Fore/Background
Jitter: 100%

Opacity Control:
Pen Pressure

Figure 5-29: Several brush dynamics applied to Scattered Leaves, one of Photoshop 7's predefined custom brushes.

✦ **Texture:** Select this option to apply a texture to a brushstroke, useful for conveying a surface such as paper or canvas. After selecting a predefined texture, set the Scale and Depth values to determine the size and degree of texture applied. Use the Mode option to define how brush and texture mix. (I discuss modes in the "Brush Modes" section near the end of this chapter, but for now, just experiment with an eye on the preview.)

If you want to vary the depth of texture throughout a stroke, turn on the Texture Each Tip check box. Then use the Control option to vary the depth according to, say, stylus pressure, or add some random Depth Jitter.

✦ **Dual Brush:** The Dual Brush panel lets you mix two brushes together. Select the second brush from the list of thumbnails and use the Mode option to specify how the brushes intermix. You can also throw in settings such as Spacing, Scatter, and Count, all of which affect the second brush.

Figure 5-29 includes a couple of examples, mixing the Scattered Leaves brush with the Maple Leaves and Grass brushes, respectively. Figure 5-30 shows another example, complete with settings in the Brushes palette. Notice how by mixing a standard round brush with one of Photoshop's predefined Dry Brush options, I'm able to generate a complex brush that imparts its own texture. Nothing like this has been possible inside Photoshop before.

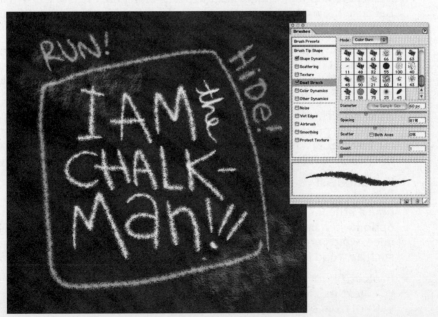

Figure 5-30: I used the Dual Brush options to combine a soft round brush and a predefined custom brush to create a fairly convincing chalk effect. I also scaled and rotated the brushes to create the light eraser stamps in the upper-left and lower-right corners.

✦ **Color Dynamics:** Use these options to vary the color of the stroke between the foreground and background colors depending on a fade or stylus pressure. You can also apply random changes to the hue, saturation, and brightness, or all three. The final slider bar, Purity, increases or decreases the saturation of colors throughout the brushstroke.

✦ **Other Dynamics:** The final set of brush dynamics permit you to associate the opacity, strength, flow, or exposure of the brush, depending on what tool you're using. I discuss each of these attributes in more detail in the upcoming section, "Opacity and Strength, Flow and Exposure." If you happen to own an airbrush, settings such as the Flow and Exposure are what the wheel was originally designed for.

Noise, Wet Edges, and the rest

The list along the left side of the Brushes palette ends with five check boxes that you can use to add highlights and constraints to your brushstrokes. Not all options work with all tools — none are compatible with the smudge tool, for example — but when available, they're as effective as they are easy to use. And they work equally well with mouse or tablet.

✦ **Noise:** This option randomizes the pixels along the edge of a brushstroke. Because the option affects the edge only, softer brushes result in more noise. The middle line in Figure 5-31 shows an example.

✦ **Wet Edges:** When you select the Wet Edges check box, the brush creates a translucent line with darkened edges, much as if you were painting with watercolors. Soft brush shapes produce more naturalistic effects. The final example in Figure 5-31 shows a soft brushstroke painted in black.

✦ **Airbrush:** This check box duplicates the airbrush icon in the Options bar. When turned on, paint builds up even when you hold the cursor in place, as if spraying color from a real airbrush. The Airbrush option is not available when using the pencil tool or any of the three focus tools (blur, sharpen, and smudge).

✦ **Smoothing:** If you have difficulty drawing smooth lines and curves, turn this check box on to even out the rough spots. It slows down Photoshop's tracking time a little, but in many cases, it may be worth it. Adobe recommends this option when using a stylus, but I've found it most helpful when using optical mice, which are notoriously bad at tracking evenly on patterned surfaces, such as wood tabletops.

✦ **Protect Texture:** If you plan on painting a lot of textured lines and you want your textures to match, then select this check box. It maintains a consistent pattern from one brushstroke to the next. The effect can be subtle, but I usually advise working with the option turned on.

Figure 5-31: Three lines painted in black with the brush tool. The first was painted without dynamics; the second was painted with Noise and the third with Wet Edges. The enlarged details show how the edges of the strokes compare.

Undoing pressure-sensitive lines

In the old days, pressure-sensitive lines were a pain to undo. Because a stylus is so sensitive to gradual pressure, you can unwittingly let up and repress the stylus during what you perceive as a single drag. If, after doing so, you decide you don't like the line and press Ctrl+Z (⌘-Z on the Mac), Photoshop deletes only the last portion of the line because it detected a release midway.

This is why it's a good idea to get in the habit of using Ctrl+Alt+Z (⌘-Option-Z on the Mac), if you haven't already. Each time you press this shortcut, you take another step back in the history of your image, permitting you to eliminate every bit of a line regardless of how many times you let up on the stylus. (See Chapter 7 for complete information on Photoshop's multiple undos.)

Note that the shortcuts I mention here assume that you set the Redo Key option on the General panel of the Preferences dialog box to its default setting, Ctrl+Z (Cmd-Z on the Mac). Check out Chapter 2 for more information on your other Redo Key options.

Better yet, create a new layer (by pressing Ctrl+Shift+N on the PC or ⌘-Shift-N on the Mac) before you paint with or without a stylus. Then you can refine your lines and erase them without harming the original appearance of your image. (You can do this without layers using the history brush, again explained in Chapter 7, but a relatively old-fashioned layer tends to be less hassle.)

Opacity and Strength, Flow and Exposure

Another way to change the performance of a paint or an edit tool is to adjust the Opacity and Flow values, which also go by Strength and Exposure, respectively, depending on the tool you're using. When available, these controls appear in the Options bar. Regardless of which setting you want to change, you click the triangle to display a slider bar, drag the slider to raise or lower the value, and then press Enter or Return. Alternatively, you can double-click the option box, type a value, and press Enter.

Here's a look at how these options work:

✦ **Opacity:** The Opacity value determines the translucency of colors applied with the brush or pencil tool. The option is also available when using the gradient tool, paint bucket, history brush, both stamp tools, and the eraser, all of which I discuss in future chapters. At 100 percent, the applied colors appear opaque, completely covering the image behind them. (Exceptions occur when using the brush tool with Wet Edges active, which produces a translucent stroke, and when applying Mode options, discussed in the upcoming "Brush Modes" section.) At lower settings, the applied colors mix with the existing colors in the image.

You can change the opacity of brushstrokes or edits that you just applied by choosing Edit ⇨ Fade or pressing Ctrl+Shift+F (⌘-Shift-F on the Mac). Then drag the Opacity slider in the Fade dialog box. While you're in the dialog box, you can apply one of Photoshop's brush modes to further change how the modified pixels blend with the original ones.

✦ **Strength:** When using the blur or sharpen tool, the Opacity option changes to Strength. The value determines the degree to which the tool changes the focus of the image, 1 percent being the minimum and 100 percent being the maximum. Strength also appears when using the smudge tool, in which case it governs the distance the tool drags colors in the image. Another difference between Strength and Opacity: Whereas the default Opacity value for each tool when you begin using Photoshop is 100 percent, the default Strength value is 50 percent. Whether Strength is stronger than Opacity or these tools merely happen to know their own Strength is uncertain; but 50 percent is the baseline.

✦ **Flow:** New to Photoshop 7, the Flow option appears when using the brush tool, sponge, history brush, both stamp tools, and the eraser. Although it is always accompanied by the airbrush icon, you can use Flow and airbrush independently. The Flow value controls the opacity of each spot of color a tool delivers. So as a tool lays each spot of color onto the previous spot, the spots mix together and become more opaque. This means three things: First, a particular Flow setting will produce a more opaque line than an equivalent Opacity setting. In Figure 5-32, for example, a Flow value of 20 percent comes in slightly darker than an Opacity value of 50 percent. Second, Flow results in a progressive effect that compounds as a brushstroke overlaps itself, also demonstrated in the figure. Third, because Flow works on a spot-by-spot basis, you can increase or decrease the opacity of a line further by lowering or raising, respectively, the Spacing value in the Brush Tip Shape panel.

When using the brush, history, stamp, and eraser tools, you can combine Opacity and Flow values to achieve unique effects. You can also add in the airbrush, which compounds Flow further by adding spots of color when you slow down a brushstroke or hold the cursor still.

✦ **Exposure:** Available when using the dodge or burn tool, Exposure controls how much the tools lighten or darken the image, respectively. As with Flow, Exposure compounds when you corner or overlap a brushstroke, and includes an airbrush variation. A setting of 100 percent applies the maximum amount of lightening or darkening, which is still far short of either absolute white or black. As with Strength, the default is 50 percent.

Tip

You can change the Opacity, Strength, or Exposure setting for the active tool in 10-percent increments by pressing a number key on the keyboard or keypad. Press 1 to change the setting to 10 percent, press 2 for 20 percent, and so on, all the way up to 0 for 100 percent.

Want to change the Opacity, Strength, or Exposure setting in 1-percent increments? No problem—just press two keys in a row. Press 4 twice for 44 percent, 0 and 7 for 7 percent, and so on. This tip and the preceding one work whether or not the Options bar is visible. Get in the habit of using the number keys and you'll thank yourself later.

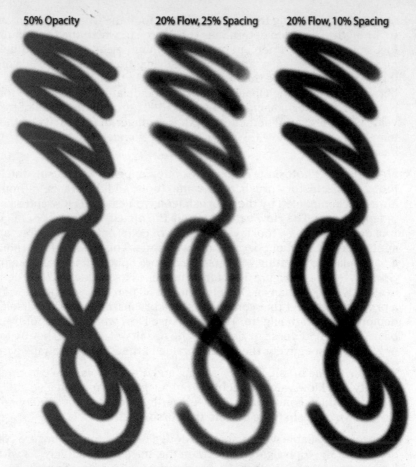

50% Opacity   20% Flow, 25% Spacing   20% Flow, 10% Spacing

Figure 5-32: Here we see the difference between Opacity, which controls an entire brushstroke, and Flow, which affects individual spots of paint. Where Opacity is consistent (left), Flow compounds wherever the stroke overlaps itself (middle). Tighter Spacing values also heighten the effect of Flow (right).

Changing the Flow value on the fly is trickier, but still possible. When the sponge tool is active, Flow works just like Opacity: Type a number to change the value in 10-percent increments; type two numbers to enter a specific value. But what about the brush tool and others that offer both Opacity and Flow? Typing a number changes the Opacity value *unless* the airbrush icon is active, in which case typing a number changes Flow. If the airbrush is turned off, press Shift plus a number key to change the Flow value. When the airbrush is turned on, pressing Shift plus a number key changes the Opacity value.

Brush Modes

When certain painting or editing tools are active, the Options bar provides access to Photoshop's brush modes, which control how the colors applied by the tool mix with existing colors inside an image or layer. Figure 5-33 shows which brush modes are available when you select various tools.

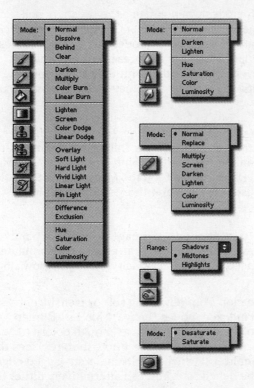

Figure 5-33: The specific Mode settings in the Options bar vary depending on which tool is active. The Mode pop-up menu changes to Range when using the dodge or burn tool.

With the exception of the specialized modes available for the dodge, burn, and sponge tools, these brush modes are merely variations on the blend modes that are available in the Layers palette, which I examine in Chapter 13, "The Wonders of Blend Modes." The difference is that the blend modes in the Layers palette mix colors between layers; meanwhile, the brush modes in the Options bar mix colors inside a single layer. Because of this subtle distinction, I describe the modes twice, once in the following section and again in Chapter 13. The latter discussion is more detailed, so if you don't get all the info you need here, feel free to read Chapter 13 to find out more.

You can change brush modes from the keyboard by pressing Shift+plus (+) or Shift+minus (–). Shift+plus takes you to the next brush mode listed in the pop-up menu; Shift+minus selects the previous brush mode. It's a great way to cycle through the brush modes without losing your place in the image.

The 24 paint tool modes

Photoshop 7 offers a total of 24 brush modes when you use the brush, pencil, or any of the other tools shown along the left side of Figure 5-33. (An additional mode, Threshold, is an alternative to Normal in certain color modes.) The brush modes are organized into six groups. Color Plate 5-2 shows a representative from each group, as applied to the strokes I drew by Shift-clicking with the brush tool way back in Figure 5-5. I also varied the Opacity settings to achieve what I considered to be optimal results.

Just as you can cycle from one brush mode to the next from the keyboard, you can jump directly to a specific brush mode as well. Just press Shift+Alt (Win) or Shift-Option (Mac) and a letter key. For example, Shift+Alt+N (Shift-Option-N on the Mac) selects the Normal mode, Shift+Alt+C (Shift-Option-C on the Mac) selects the Color mode. I list the letter key for each brush mode in parentheses along with its description:

✦ **Normal (N):** Choose this mode to paint or edit an image normally. A paint tool coats the image with the foreground color, and an edit tool manipulates the existing colors in an image according to the Opacity, Strength, Flow, and Exposure values.

Two color modes prevent Photoshop from rendering soft or translucent edges. The black-and-white and indexed modes (Image ➪ Mode ➪ Bitmap and Image ➪ Mode ➪ Indexed Color) simply don't have enough colors to go around. When painting in such a low-color image, Photoshop replaces the Normal brush mode with Threshold (L), which results in harsh, jagged edges, just like a stroke painted with the pencil tool. You can alternatively dither the soft edges by selecting the Dissolve mode, as described next.

✦ **Dissolve (I):** Dissolve scatters a random pattern of colors to simulate translucency. The pattern shows up along the edges of opaque brushstrokes or inside translucent strokes, like those in Figure 5-34. Note that this mode and the two that follow are not applicable to the edit tools. To get something resembling Dissolve with, say, the smudge tool, try applying the Noise setting in the Brushes palette.

✦ **Behind (Q):** This mode is applicable exclusively to layers with transparency. When Behind is selected, the paint tools apply color behind the image on the active layer, showing through only in the transparent and translucent areas. Figure 5-35 shows how I created the Shift-click painting from Figure 5-5 by applying each coat of lighter color behind the last. Note that when working on an image without layers or on the background layer of a multi-layered image, the Behind mode is dimmed.

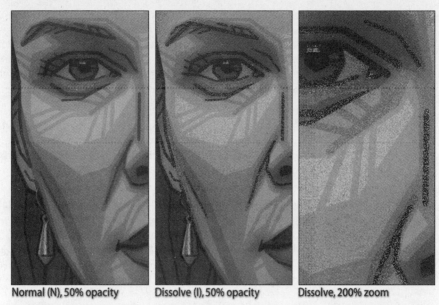

Normal (N), 50% opacity   Dissolve (I), 50% opacity   Dissolve, 200% zoom

Figure 5-34: Lines painted with the Normal (left) and Dissolve (middle) mode set to 50 percent opacity. Dissolve dithers colors to simulate translucency, as the magnified detail shows (right).

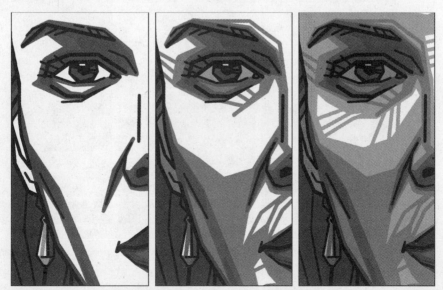

Figure 5-35: To build up the layers of color in this painting, I drew the darkest colors first and then applied progressively lighter colors using the brush tool set to the Behind mode.

✦ **Clear (R):** When working on a layer other than *Background*, the Clear mode turns the brush tool, pencil, or paint bucket into an erasing tool, clearing away pixels. Given that the eraser already emulates the behavior of both the brush and pencil tools (as I explain in Chapter 7), there's not a lot of reason to use Clear with either of these tools. However, it creates a unique effect when combined with the paint bucket, as explained in the next chapter.

✦ **Darken (K):** The first of the four darkening modes, Darken applies a new color to a pixel only if that color is darker than the pixel's present color. Otherwise, the pixel is left unchanged. The mode works on a channel-by-channel basis, so it might change a pixel in the green channel, for example, without changing the pixel in the red or blue channel.

✦ **Multiply (M):** The Multiply mode combines the foreground color with an existing color in an image to create a third color, darker than the other two. Using the multiply analogy, cyan times magenta is blue, magenta times yellow is red, yellow times cyan is green, and so on. Discussed in Chapter 4, this is the subtractive (CMYK) color theory at work. The effect is almost exactly like drawing with felt-tipped markers, except the colors don't bleed. The second examples in Figure 5-36 and Color Plate 5-2 show the Multiply mode in action.

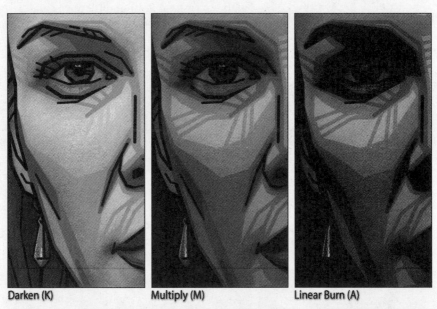

Darken (K)   Multiply (M)   Linear Burn (A)

Figure 5-36: Examples of three of the four darkening modes applied to grayscale versions of my Shift-click painting. In all cases, the Opacity setting is 100 percent.

Photoshop 7

✦ **Color Burn (B)** and **Linear Burn (A):** The two Burn modes are designed to simulate colored versions of the burn tool. Typically (though not always), Color Burn results in a darker, more colorful stroke than Multiply; new to Photoshop 7, Linear Burn is darker still and more muted, as shown in the last example in Figure 5-36. When combined with low Opacity values, the two modes can be interesting, but I wouldn't go so far as to call them particularly helpful.

✦ **Lighten (G):** Leading the lightening modes is the appropriately named Lighten, which ensures that Photoshop applies a new color to a pixel only if the color is lighter than the pixel's present color. See the first image in Figure 5-37 and the third image in Color Plate 5-2 for examples.

✦ **Screen (S):** The inverse of the Multiply mode, Screen combines the foreground color with each colored pixel you paint to create a third color, lighter than the other two. Red on green is yellow, green on blue is cyan, blue on red is magenta. In other words, Screen obeys the rules of the additive (RGB) color theory.

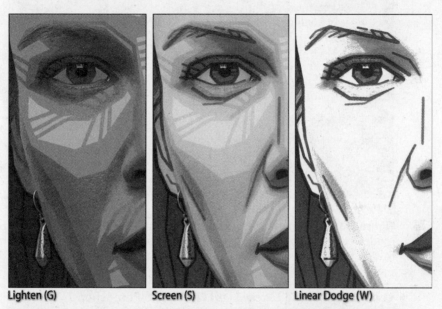

Lighten (G)   Screen (S)   Linear Dodge (W)

Figure 5-37: Three of the four lightening modes. Note that Linear Dodge has a tendency to send a large portion of the colors to white. The same is true of Color Dodge as well.

✦ **Color Dodge (D)** and **Linear Dodge (W):** Intended to emulate the dodge tool, these modes radically lighten an image. Color Dodge produces the more colorful effect; Linear Dodge works out to be the lightest (see the last image in Figure 5-37 for an example). As with the Burn modes, you're likely to have the most luck with the two Dodge modes at low Opacity values.

✦ **Overlay (O):** The six modes starting with Overlay are cousins, each multiplying the dark pixels in an image and screening the light pixels. Of the six, Overlay is the kindest and arguably the most useful. It enhances contrast and boosts the saturation of colors, rather like a colored version of the sponge tool set to Saturate. The first image in Figure 5-38 shows the Overlay mode in action.

✦ **Soft Light (F)** and **Hard Light (H):** The Soft Light mode applies a subtle glazing of color to an image. Even black or white applied at 100 percent Opacity does no more than darken or lighten the image, but it does slightly diminish contrast, as you can see in the middle image in Figure 5-38. Meanwhile, Hard Light produces a much stronger effect, even stronger than Overlay. Of the modes we've seen so far, only Normal is more opaque.

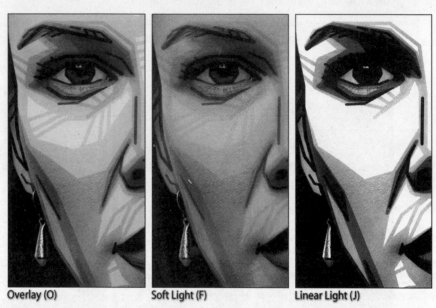

Overlay (O) Soft Light (F) Linear Light (J)

Figure 5-38: The medium Overlay, subtle Soft Light, and extreme Linear Light modes each mix brushstrokes to darken the darkest colors in an image and lighten the lightest colors.

✦ **Vivid Light (V)** and **Linear Light (J):** New to Photoshop 7, Vivid Light works like a more colorful variation on the Hard Light mode, much like a Color Burn and Color Dodge effect combined. (Color Plate 5-2 shows an example.) Linear Light produces an even higher contrast effect, as shown in the last image in Figure 5-38. Try one of these modes when you want to simultaneously burn the darkest colors in an image and dodge the lightest ones.

✦ **Pin Light (Z):** This peculiar mode drops out all but the so-called "high frequency" colors, which are the lightest, darkest, and most saturated color values, as illustrated in the first example in Figure 5-39. It is almost never useful for brushing, though it can come in very handy when applied to layers, as I discuss in Chapter 13.

✦ **Difference (E):** When a paint tool is set to the Difference mode, Photoshop subtracts the brightness value of the foreground color from the brightness value of the pixels in the image. If the result is a negative number, Photoshop simply makes it positive. The result of this complex-sounding operation is an inversion effect. Painting with black has no effect on an image; painting with white inverts it completely.

Tip

Because the Difference mode inverts an image, it results in an outline around the brushstroke. You can make this outline thicker by using a softer brush shape (which you get by pressing Shift+left bracket).

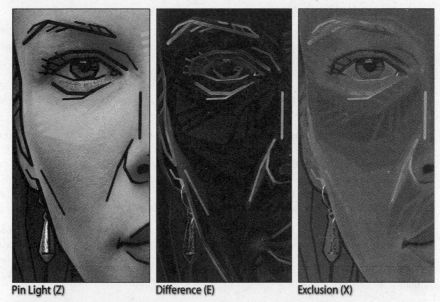

Pin Light (Z)   Difference (E)   Exclusion (X)

Figure 5-39: The Pin Light mode preserves only high frequency colors, turning less vividly colored brushstrokes invisible. Difference and Exclusion modes subtract color values, resulting in colorful inversion effects.

✦ **Exclusion (X):** When I first asked Mark Hamburg, lead programmer for Photoshop, for his definition of Exclusion, he kindly explained, "Exclusion applies a probabilistic, fuzzy-set-theoretic, symmetric difference to each channel." Ouch, copying and pasting that text hurt my head. In any case, I'm not sure, but I think what he meant was that Exclusion inverts an image in much the same way as Difference, except colors in the middle of the spectrum mix to form lighter colors, as in the case of the second-to-last image in Color Plate 5-2.

✦ **Hue (U):** Understanding this and the next few modes requires a color theory recap. Remember how the HSL color model calls for three color channels? One is for hue, the value that explains the colors in an image; the second is for saturation, which represents the intensity of the colors; and the third is for luminosity, which explains the lightness and darkness of colors. If you choose the Hue brush mode, therefore, Photoshop applies the hue from the foreground color without changing any saturation or luminosity values in the existing image.

Note that all of the HSL brush modes — Hue, Saturation, Color, or Luminosity — are exclusively applicable to color, and are therefore unavailable when painting within grayscale images.

✦ **Saturation (T):** If you choose this mode, Photoshop changes the intensity of the colors in an image without changing the colors themselves or the lightness and darkness of individual pixels.

✦ **Color (C):** This mode combines Hue and Saturation to change the colors in an image and the intensity of those colors without changing the lightness and darkness of individual pixels.

In concert with the brush tool, the Color mode is most often used to colorize grayscale photographs. Here's how it works: Open a grayscale image and then choose Image ⇨ Mode ⇨ RGB Color to convert the image to the RGB mode. Then select the brush tool — with or without the airbrush turned on — and set the Mode pop-up menu to Color. From that point on, you have only to select the colors you want to use and start painting.

✦ **Luminosity (Y):** The opposite of the Color mode, Luminosity changes the lightness and darkness of pixels, but leaves the hue and saturation values unaffected. The final example in Color Plate 5-2 shows how I was able to use the Luminosity mode to trace lines and shadows without altering the color values in the original image.

The three dodge and burn modes

That takes care of the brush modes available to the paint tools, the smudge tool, and the two focus tools. I explained the Desaturate and Saturate modes available to the sponge tool in the section, "Mopping up with the sponge tool." That leaves the three brush modes available to the dodge and burn tools.

You access these modes from the Range pop-up menu in the Options bar. As with other brush modes, you can select the dodge and burn modes from the keyboard. Just press Shift+Alt (Win) or Shift-Option (Mac) and the letter in parentheses as follows:

✦ **Midtones (M):** Selected by default, the Midtones mode applies the dodge or burn tool equally to all but the very lightest or darkest pixels in an image. Midtones enables you to adjust the brightness of colors without blowing out highlights or filling in shadows.

✦ **Shadows (S):** When you select this mode, the dodge or burn tool affects dark pixels in an image more dramatically than light pixels. As illustrated in Figure 5-40, medium values are likewise affected, so the Shadows option modifies a wider range of colors than Midtones.

✦ **Highlights (H):** This option lets you lighten or darken the midtones and lightest colors in an image.

Figure 5-40: The dodge and burn tools applied at 100-percent Exposure settings subject to each of the three applicable brush modes.

Selecting Shadows when using the dodge tool or Highlights when using the burn tool has an equalizing effect on an image. For example, the first brushstroke in Figure 5-40 shows the Shadows option combined with the dodge tool. As a result, Photoshop paints an almost consistent brightness value across the course of a white-to-black gradient. The same is true for the last brushstroke, which combines Highlights with the burn tool.

✦   ✦   ✦

Filling and Stroking

Filling Portions of an Image

No explanation of filling and stroking would be complete without a definition, so here goes: To *fill* a selection or a layer is to put color inside it; to *stroke* a selection or a layer is to put color around it. Some folks prefer the term *outline* to *stroke*, but I defer to PostScript terminology because that's where this whole desktop graphics thing started. Besides, when I think outline, I think perimeter, boundary, enclosure, prison, let me out of here. Stroke is more like brush, caress, pet, puppy, warm fire, glad heart. I'm a joker, I'm a smoker, I'm a midnight stroker. I'd rather be stroking. Stop me before I stroke again. And, that timeless favorite, keep on strokin'. So you see, people who prefer the word "outline" have no soul.

But whatever you call them, Photoshop's fill and stroke functions are so straightforward that you may have long since dismissed them as wimpy little tools with remarkably limited potential. But the truth is, you can do a world of stuff with them. In this chapter, for example, I show you how to fill selections using nifty keyboard shortcuts, how to create an antique framing effect, how to make the most of Photoshop's gradient options, and how to add an arrowhead to a curving line — all in addition to the really basic stuff every Photoshop user needs to know.

As the poet said, "Teacher don't you *fill* me up with your rules, I know *strokin's* not allowed in school." I'd love to share the entire transcript from "Strokin' in the Boy's Room," but this is, after all, a family book.

Filling Selections with Color or Patterns

You can fill an area of an image in the following ways:

✦ **The paint bucket tool:** Also known as the fill tool, the paint bucket resides in the same flyout as the gradient tool in the toolbox. You can apply the foreground color or a repeating pattern to areas of related color in an image by clicking in the image window with the tool. For example, if you want to turn all midnight blue pixels in an image into red pixels, set the foreground color to red and then click one of the blue pixels. Note that you can't use this tool on images that you converted to Bitmap mode.

✦ **The Fill command:** Choose Edit ⇨ Fill to fill a selection with the foreground color or a repeating pattern. You don't need to select a portion of the image to access the Fill command. If you choose the command while no selection is active, Photoshop fills the entire layer.

To choose the Fill command without so much as moving the mouse, press Shift+Backspace (Shift-Delete on the Mac).

✦ **Backspace (Win) and Delete (Mac) key techniques:** After selecting part of a single-layer image—or part of the background layer in a multi-layered image—you can fill the selection with the background color by pressing Backspace (Win) or Delete (Mac). You can also fill any layer with the background color without a selection by pressing Ctrl+Backspace (Win) or ⌘-Delete (Mac). To fill with the foreground color, press Alt+Backspace (Win) or Option-Delete (Mac).

✦ **The gradient tool:** Drag across a layer or selection with a gradient tool to fill it with a multi-color gradation in one of five gradient styles. You choose a gradient style by clicking an icon in the Options bar. Shift+G toggles the gradient and paint bucket tools, which occupy the same flyout menu in the toolbox. If you turn off the Use Shift Key for Tool Switch check box in the Preferences dialog box (Ctrl+K on the PC or ⌘-K on the Mac), you need only press G to toggle the tools.

✦ **Layer fills:** Photoshop provides two additional ways to fill an entire layer. You can use the Dynamic Fill and Layer Style features to fill a layer with a solid color, gradient, or pattern.

The next sections explain the first four fill options. To find out more about dynamic fills and layer styles, trek off to Chapter 14.

The paint bucket tool

Unlike remedial paint bucket tools in other painting programs, which apply paint exclusively within outlined areas or areas of solid color, the Photoshop paint bucket tool offers several useful adjustment options. You access the paint bucket controls in the Options bar, as with all tools. When you select the paint bucket, the Options bar automatically updates to show the available controls. If you don't see the Options bar, press Enter or Return, double-click the paint bucket icon in the toolbox, or choose Window ➪ Options. The paint bucket and gradient tools share a flyout menu in the toolbox; press G or Shift+G to toggle between the two tools.

Here's a look at the paint bucket options:

✦ **Fill:** In this pop-up menu, choose whether you want to apply the foreground color or a repeating pattern created using Edit ➪ Define Pattern. The Define Pattern command is covered in the "Applying Repeating Patterns" section of Chapter 7.

✦ **Pattern:** If you select Pattern from the Fill pop-up, click the Pattern icon (or the adjacent triangle) to display the Pattern drop-down palette, as shown in Figure 6-1. The palette contains icons representing the patterns in the current preset. Click the pattern you want to use.

You load, replace, edit, and create pattern presets just as you do tool and brush presets (see Chapters 2 and 5, respectively), working either in the Preset Manager dialog box or the Pattern palette menu, which you display by clicking the triangle labeled in Figure 6-1. Photoshop lets you create multiple patterns; you're not limited to one custom pattern.

Click to display palette menu

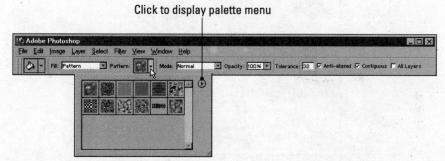

Figure 6-1: These options govern the performance of the paint bucket tool.

✦ **Tolerance:** Raise or lower the Tolerance value to increase or decrease the number of pixels affected by the paint bucket tool. The Tolerance value represents a range in brightness values, as measured from the pixel that you click with the paint bucket.

Immediately after you click a pixel, Photoshop reads the brightness value of that pixel from each color channel. Next, the program calculates a color range based on the Tolerance value — which can vary from 0 to 255. The program adds the Tolerance to the brightness value of the pixel you clicked to determine the top of the range and subtracts the Tolerance from the pixel's brightness value to determine the bottom of the range. For example, if the pixel's brightness value is 100 and the Tolerance value is 32, the top of the range is 132 and the bottom is 68.

Figure 6-2 shows the result of clicking on the same pixel three separate times, each time using a different Tolerance value. It takes a dizzingly high Tolerance value of 160 to fill Morris County. And even then, I'll have to click several times to fill all of New York state. The moral is, don't get too hung up on getting the Tolerance exactly right—no matter how you paint it, the bucket is not a precise tool.

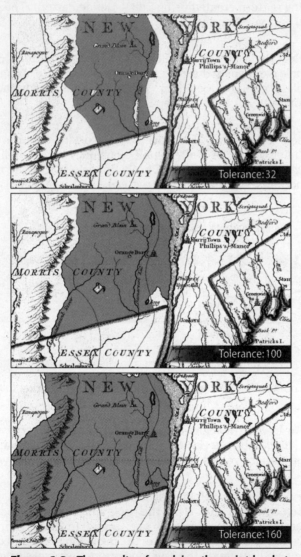

Figure 6-2: The results of applying the paint bucket tool to the same pixel on an antique map of New York after setting the Tolerance value to 32 (top), 100 (middle), and 160 (bottom). In each case, the foreground color was light gray.

✦ **Anti-aliased:** Select this option to soften the effect of the paint bucket tool. As demonstrated in the left example of Figure 6-3, Photoshop creates a border of translucent color between the filled pixels and their unaffected neighbors. If you don't want to soften the transition, turn off the Anti-aliased check box. Photoshop then fills only those pixels that fall inside the Tolerance range, as demonstrated in the right example of the figure.

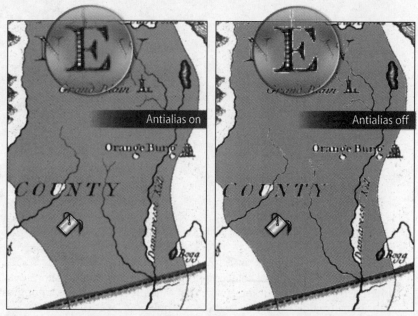

Figure 6-3: The results of turning on (left) and off (right) the Anti-aliased check box before using the paint bucket tool. Antialiasing is better for soft transitions, while turning the option off works best in high-contrast situations.

✦ **Contiguous:** When you select this check box, Photoshop fills only contiguous pixels — that is, pixels that both fall inside the Tolerance range and touch another affected pixel. If you instead want to fill all pixels that fall within the Tolerance range — regardless of where those pixels lie — deselect the check box. For what it's worth, I left the option on when creating Figure 6-2 and Color Plate 6-1.

✦ **All Layers:** Select this option to make the paint bucket see beyond the current layer. When the option is selected, the tool takes all visible layers into account when calculating the area to fill. Mind you, it only fills the active layer, but the way it fills an area is dictated by all layers.

✦ **Mode:** This menu offers a selection of blend modes, which determine how and when color is applied. As demonstrated in Figure 6-4, the Normal mode can result in sharp transitions between fill color and outline. To create a smoother transition, try choosing the Multiply mode instead (as in the second example).

Figure 6-4 also shows the Clear mode, which deletes pixels in a layer to create a hole, useful for deleting backgrounds. (Note that Clear is dimmed when working on a flat image or Background layer.)

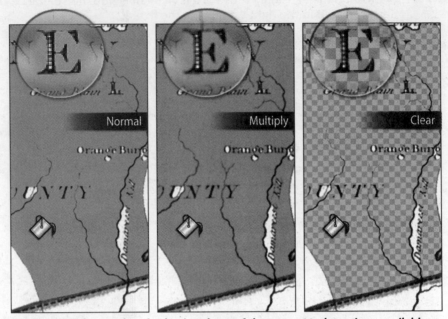

Figure 6-4: The results of selecting three of the many Mode options available when using the paint bucket. Notice that Multiply results in the smoothest edge transitions (middle) while Clear creates a hole in a layer (right).

Cross-Reference

For a thorough rundown of blend modes, see Chapter 13.

✦ **Opacity:** This option works just like when you paint with the paintbrush. Enter a new value or press a number key to change the translucency of a color applied with the paint bucket. (Press 0 for full opacity, 9 for 90 percent opacity, and so on.)

I feel the need at this point to expound a bit more on the All Layers option. For an example of how this feature works, look no further than Figure 6-5. The first image shows a flat version of the map with no fill colors. I could have set right in filling the state and seas, but then I would have made permanent changes to the map that might have been difficult to edit later on. So instead, I created independent layers for each state — New York, New Jersey, and Connecticut — and a fourth for the water. To fill each layer, I turned on the All Layers check box and then used the paint bucket as normal. This way, Photoshop respected the outlines of the background map when coloring the various layers.

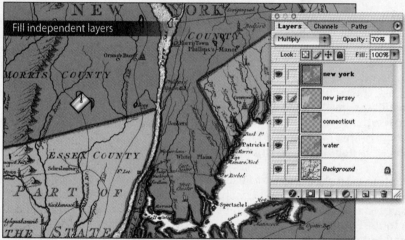

Figure 6-5: To avoid harming this antique map from the Corbis image library (top), I turned on the All Layers option and applied my fill colors to independent layers (bottom). This permitted me to fill an area of the map even though another layer was active.

For a color version of this same project, see Color Plate 6-1. The middle image in the color plate shows all the points at which I clicked with the paint bucket to fill the map. But even after all that work, I still had to paint in a few gaps with the brush tool. Note that in the cases of Figure 6-5 and Color Plate 6-1, I set the Mode option for the paint bucket tool to Normal, and then I set the blend mode for each layer to Multiply.

Tip

To limit the area affected by the paint bucket, select a portion of the image before using the tool. As when using a paint or edit tool, the region outside the selection outline is protected from the paint bucket. To see an interesting application of this, skip ahead to the "Using the paint bucket inside a selection" section, later in this chapter.

When working on a layer, you can protect pixels by locking the layer's transparency in the Layers palette. Like all layering issues, I cover the locking options in Chapter 12.

Tip

Here's one more paint bucket tip for good measure: You can use the paint bucket to color the empty window area around your image. First, make your image window larger than your image, so you can see some gray canvas area around the image. Now Shift-click with the paint bucket to fill the canvas area with the foreground color. This technique can come in handy if you're creating a presentation or you simply don't care for the default shade of gray.

The Fill command

The one problem with the paint bucket tool is its lack of precision. Although the tool is undeniably convenient, the effects of the Tolerance value are so difficult to predict that you typically have to click with the tool, choose Edit ➪ Undo when you don't like the result, adjust the Tolerance value, and reclick several times more before you fill the image as desired. For my part, I rarely use the paint bucket for any purpose other than filling same-colored areas. On my machine, the Tolerance option is nearly always set to 0 and Anti-aliased is generally off, which puts me right back in the all-the-subtlety-of-dumping-paint-out-of-a-bucket camp.

A better option is to choose Edit ➪ Fill or press Shift+Backspace (Shift-Delete on the Mac). (If you prefer function keys, try Shift+F5.) In this way, you can define the exact area of the image you want to color using the entire range of Photoshop's selection tools. For example, instead of putting your faith in the paint bucket tool's Anti-aliased option, you can draw a selection outline that features hard edges in one area, antialiased edges elsewhere, and downright blurry edges in between.

If you want to fill an entire layer, you don't need to create a selection outline before choosing Fill. The program assumes that you want to fill the whole layer if it doesn't see a selection outline. (Dynamic fills and layer styles provide additional ways to fill a layer; see Chapter 14 for details on how these fills differ from those you create with the Fill command.)

Whether or not you've created a selection outline, choosing the Fill command displays the dialog box shown in Figure 6-6. In this dialog box, you can apply a translucent color or pattern by entering a value in the Opacity option box. You can also choose a brush mode from the Mode pop-up menu. In addition to its inherent precision, the Fill command provides all the functionality of the paint bucket tool — and then some.

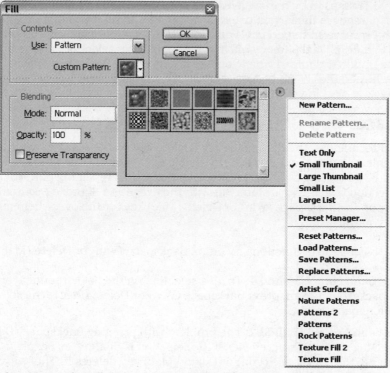

Figure 6-6: The Fill dialog box combines the opacity and brush mode options available for the paint bucket with an expanded collection of fill content options.

If you display the Use pop-up menu, you see a collection of fills that you can apply. Foreground Color and Pattern behave the same as they do for the paint bucket tool. When you select Pattern, the Custom Pattern option becomes available, as shown in Figure 6-6. Click the icon to display the Pattern drop-down palette, which also works just as described in the preceding section. Click an icon to select a pattern; click the right-pointing arrow to display the palette menu and load a different pattern preset.

Cross-Reference

To find out how to load, save, edit, and create custom pattern presets, see "Saving and loading brush sets" in Chapter 5. You use the same techniques for brush presets and pattern presets.

You can also fill a selection with the background color and such monochrome options as Black, White, and 50% Gray. Black and White are useful if the foreground and background colors have been changed from their defaults; 50% Gray fills the selection with the absolute medium color without having to mess around with the Color palette. History enables you to revert the selected area to a previous appearance, as I discuss at length in Chapter 7.

The Preserve Transparency option gives you the same result as locking the active layer's transparency in the Layers palette, which you can read about in Chapter 12. If you select Preserve Transparency, you can't fill transparent pixels in the active layer. Turn Preserve Transparency off, and you can fill the selection outline uniformly. (The option is dimmed when you're working on the background layer or if you already locked the layer's transparency in the Layers palette.)

Backspace- and Delete-key techniques

Of all the fill techniques, the Backspace key (Delete key on the Mac) is by far the most convenient and, in most respects, every bit as capable as the others. The key's only failing is that it can neither fill a selection with a repeating pattern nor revert a selection to a previous state. But with the exception of those two items, you can rely on the Backspace (Win) or Delete (Mac) key for the overwhelming majority of your fill needs.

Here's how to get a ton of functionality out of Backspace (Win) or Delete (Mac):

Caution

✦ **Background color, method 1:** To fill a selection on the background layer with solid background color, press Backspace (Win) or Delete (Mac). The selection outline remains intact.

✦ **Background color, method 2:** The problem with pressing Backspace (Delete on the Mac) is that it's unreliable. If the selection is floating, as I explain in Chapter 8, the Backspace (Win) or Delete (Mac) key deletes it. The key also erases pixels on a layer. So there's no time like the present to get into a new habit — press Ctrl+Backspace (⌘-Delete on the Mac) instead. Ctrl+Backspace (Win) or ⌘-Delete (Mac) fills the selection with the background color, no matter where it is.

✦ **Foreground color:** To fill a selection or a layer with solid foreground color, press Alt+Backspace (Win) or Option-Delete (Mac). This works when filling floating and nonfloating selections alike.

✦ **Black or white:** To fill an area with black, press D to get the default foreground and background colors and then press Alt+Backspace (Option-Delete on the Mac). To fill an area with white, press D for the defaults and then Ctrl+Backspace (⌘-Delete on the Mac).

✦ **Preserve transparency:** Add the Shift key and you get two more key tricks that make more sense when you read Chapter 12. (Don't worry, I'll repeat the tricks then.) You can fill only the opaque pixels in a layer — regardless of whether you locked the layer's transparency in the Layers palette — by pressing Shift. Press Shift+Alt+Backspace (Shift-Option-Delete on the Mac) to fill a selection with the foreground color while preserving transparency. Press Ctrl+Shift+Backspace (⌘-Shift-Delete on the Mac) to fill the opaque pixels with the background color.

Using the paint bucket inside a selection

So far, I've come up with two astounding generalizations: The paint bucket tool is mostly useless, and you can fill anything with the Backspace key (Delete key on the Mac). Well, just to prove you shouldn't believe everything I say — some might even suggest you dismiss everything I say — the following steps explain an effect you can create only with the paint bucket tool. Doubtless, it's the only such example you'll ever discover using Photoshop — after all, the paint bucket is mostly useless and you can fill anything with the Backspace (Win) or Delete (Mac) key — but I'm man enough to eat my rules this once.

The following steps explain how to create an antique photographic frame effect, such as the one shown in Figure 6-7.

STEPS: Creating an Antique Framing Effect

1. **Use the rectangular marquee tool to select the portion of the image you want to frame.** Make certain the image extends at least 20 pixels outside the boundaries of the selection outline; and be sure to use a photo — this effect won't look right against a plain white background.

2. **Choose Select ⇨ Feather.** Or press Ctrl+Alt+D (⌘-Option-D on the Mac). Then specify a Radius value somewhere in the neighborhood of 6 to 12 pixels. I've found these values work for nearly any resolution of image. (If you enter too high a value, the color you'll add in a moment with the paint bucket will run out into the image.)

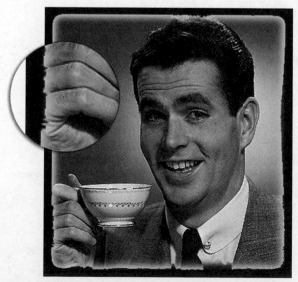

Figure 6-7: I created this antique frame effect by filling a feathered selection with the paint bucket tool.

3. **Choose Select ➪ Inverse.** Or press Ctrl+Shift+I (⌘-Shift-I on the Mac). This exchanges the selected and deselected portions of the image.

4. **Press D to make certain the background color is white.** Then press Ctrl+Backspace (⌘-Delete on the Mac) to fill the selected area with the background color.

5. **Select the paint bucket tool.** If the Options bar isn't visible, press Enter or Return to display it. Then enter 20 or 30 in the Tolerance option box and turn on the Anti-aliased check box. (You can also experiment with turning off this last option.)

6. **Click inside the feathered selection to fill it with black.** The result is an image fading into white and then into black, like the edges of a worn slide or photograph, as shown in Figure 6-7.

Figure 6-8 shows a variation on this effect that you can produce using the Dissolve brush mode. Rather than setting the Tolerance value to 20, raise it to around 60. Then select the Dissolve option from the Mode pop-up menu in the Options bar. When you click inside the feathered selection with the paint bucket tool, you create a frame of random pixels, as illustrated in the figure.

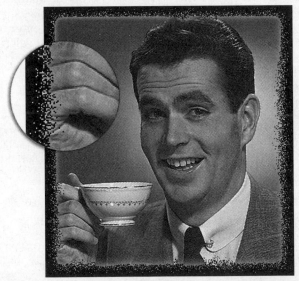

Figure 6-8: Select Dissolve from the Mode pop-up menu in the Options bar to achieve a speckled frame effect.

Applying Gradient Fills

The three previous versions of Photoshop made great strides in the gradation department. Version 4 introduced the Edit button into the Gradient Options palette. This one button made it possible to create a gradient with as many as 32 colors, name gradients and save them to disk, and adjust the transparency of colors so that they fade in and out over the course of the fill. Version 5 widened the range of gradient styles, removed the limit on colors per gradient, and enabled you to reverse the foreground and background colors from within the Gradient Options palette, a nice convenience when applying radial and diamond fills. Version 6 added even more gradient features, enabling you to create and save collections of your favorite gradients as presets, just as you can with patterns and brushes. In addition, you can create noise gradients, create a gradient as a dynamic fill layer, and use the Layer Style command to add a gradient overlay to a layer. (I explain dynamic fills and layer styles in Chapter 14.)

Note

If you're accustomed to using gradients in a drawing program — such as Illustrator or FreeHand — you'll find that Photoshop is better. Because Photoshop is a pixel editor, it lets you blur and mix colors in a gradation if they start *banding* — that is, if you can see a hard edge between one color and the next when you print the image; and Photoshop's gradations never choke the printer or slow it down, no matter how many colors you add. While in Illustrator each band of color in an object-oriented gradation is expressed as a separate shape — so that one gradation can contain hundreds, or even thousands, of objects — gradations in Photoshop are plain old colored pixels, the kind we've been editing for five and a half chapters.

Using the gradient tool

First, the basics. A *gradation* (also called a *gradient fill*) is a progression of colors that fade gradually into one another, as demonstrated in Figure 6-9. You specify a few key colors in the gradation, and Photoshop automatically generates the hundred or so colors in between to create a smooth transition.

The gradient tool and paint bucket share a toolbox slot and keyboard shortcut — press G to toggle between the two tools (or Shift+G, depending on whether you selected the Use Shift Key for Tool Switch check box in the Preferences dialog box, as discussed in Chapter 2). But unlike the paint bucket, which fills areas of similar color according to the Tolerance setting, the gradient tool affects all colors within a selection. If you don't select a portion of your image, Photoshop applies the gradation to the entire layer.

To use the tool, drag inside the selection, as shown in the left example of Figure 6-9. The point at which you begin dragging (the upper-left corner in the figure) defines the location of the first color in the gradation. The point at which you release (the lower-right corner) defines the location of the last color. If multiple portions of the image are selected, the gradation fills all selections continuously, as demonstrated by the right example of Figure 6-9.

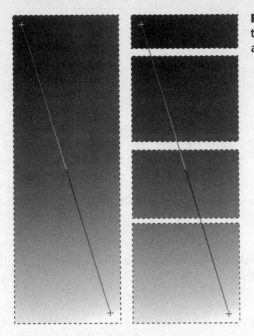

Figure 6-9: Dragging with the gradient tool within a single selection (left) and across multiple selections (right).

Gradient options

As with other tools in Photoshop, the Options bar contains the gradient tool controls, which you can examine in Figure 6-10. If you don't see the Options bar, press Enter or Return when the gradient tool is active or double-click the tool icon in the toolbox.

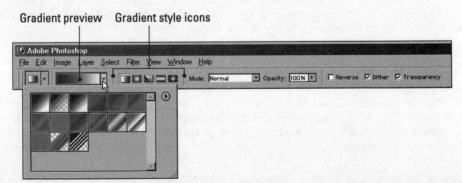

Figure 6-10: The Options bar gives you quick access to all the gradient tool options.

The following list explains how the controls in the Options bar work. In all cases, you must adjust the options before using the gradient tool. They do not affect existing gradations.

✦ **Gradient preview:** The selected gradient appears in the gradient preview, labeled in Figure 6-10. Click the preview to open the Gradient Editor dialog box, discussed in the upcoming section, "Creating custom gradations."

✦ **Gradient drop-down palette:** Click the triangle adjacent to the preview to display the Gradient palette, which contains icons representing gradients in the current gradient presets. Click the icon for the gradient you want.

Note

In the default gradient preset, the first two gradations are dependent on the current foreground and background colors. The others contain specific colors bearing no relationship to the colors in the toolbox.

You load gradient presets using the same techniques that I describe in detail in the brush preset discussion in Chapter 5. Here's a brief recap:

• Click the triangle near the top of the drop-down palette to display the palette menu. The Photoshop collection of presets and any presets that you define appear at the bottom of the palette menu. Click a preset name to use the preset instead of the current preset or append the new preset to the current one.

• To append a preset from disk — such as when a coworker gives you a preset file — choose Load Gradients from the palette menu or click Load in the Preset Manager dialog box. If you want to replace the current preset instead, choose Replace Gradients from the palette menu or click Replace in the dialog box. To return to the default gradients, choose Reset Gradients from the palette menu, either from the Options bar palette or the one in the Preset Manager dialog box.

Tip

You can edit a gradient and perform the aforementioned preset juggling acts from within the Gradient Editor dialog box, too. The upcoming section, "Creating custom gradations," covers this dialog box.

✦ **Gradient style:** Click an icon to select the gradient style — a function that you formerly accomplished by choosing a specific gradient tool. The next section explains these five styles.

✦ **Mode and Opacity:** These options work as they do for the paint and edit tools, the Fill command, and every other tool or command that offers them as options. Select a different brush mode to change how colors are applied; lower the Opacity value to make a gradation translucent. Remember that you can change the Opacity value by pressing number keys as well as by using the Opacity control in the Options bar. Press 0 for 100 percent opacity, 9 for 90 percent, and so on.

✦ **Reverse:** When active, this check box begins the gradation with the background color and ends it with the foreground color. Use this option when you want to start a radial or other style of gradation with white, but you want to keep the foreground and background colors set to their defaults.

✦ **Dither:** In the old days, Photoshop drew its gradients one band at a time. Each band was filled with an incrementally different shade of color. The potential result was banding, in which you could clearly distinguish the transition between two or more bands of color. The Dither check box helps to eliminate this problem by mixing up the pixels between bands (much as Photoshop dithers pixels when converting a grayscale image to black and white). You should leave this option turned on unless you want to use banding to create a special effect.

✦ **Transparency:** You can specify different levels of opacity throughout a gradation. For example, the Soft Stripes effect (available from the Gradient palette when the Special Effects preset is loaded) lays down a series of alternately black and transparent stripes. But you needn't use this transparency information. If you prefer to apply a series of black and white stripes instead, you can make all portions of the gradation equally opaque by turning off the Transparency check box.

For example, in Figure 6-11, I applied Soft Stripes as a radial gradation in two separate swipes (middle and bottom). Both times, I changed the Opacity setting to 50 percent, so the eye would never be completely obscured. (The Opacity setting works independently of the gradation's built-in transparency, providing you with additional flexibility.) In the top gradation (middle example), the Transparency check box is on, so the white stripes are completely transparent. In the bottom gradation, Transparency is turned off, so the white stripes become 50 percent opaque (as prescribed by the Opacity setting).

Gradient styles

You select the gradient style by clicking the gradient style icons in the Options bar (refer back to Figure 6-10). Illustrated in Figure 6-12, the five styles are as follows:

✦ **Linear:** A linear gradation progresses in bands of color in a straight line between the beginning and end of your drag. The top two examples in Figure 6-12 show linear gradations created from black to white, and from white to black. The point labeled B marks the beginning of the drag; E marks the end.

✦ **Radial:** A radial gradation progresses outward from a central point in concentric circles, as in the second row of examples in Figure 6-12. The point at which you begin dragging defines the center of the gradation, and the point at which you release defines the outermost circle. This means the first color in the gradation appears in the center of the fill. So to create the gradation on the right side of Figure 6-12, you must set the foreground color to white and the background color to black (or select the Reverse check box in the Options bar).

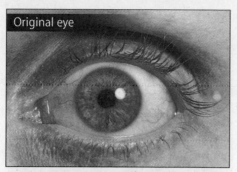

Original eye

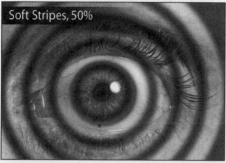

Soft Stripes, 50%

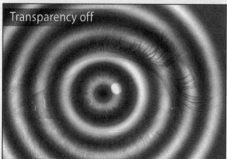

Transparency off

Figure 6-11: With the Opacity value set to 50 percent, I applied the Soft Stripes gradation with Transparency on (middle) and off (bottom). When Transparency is off, the white stripes obscure the view of the underlying image.

✦ **Angle:** The angle gradient style creates a fountain of colors flowing in a counter-clockwise direction with respect to your drag, as demonstrated by the middle two examples of Figure 6-12. This type of gradient is known more commonly as a *conical gradation*, because it looks like the bird's eye view of the top of a cone.

Of course, a real cone doesn't have the sharp edge between black and white that you see in Photoshop's angle gradient. To eliminate this edge, create a custom gradation from black to white to black again, as I explain in the "Adjusting colors in a solid gradation" section later in this chapter. (Take a peek at Figure 6-17 later in this chapter if you're not sure what I'm talking about.)

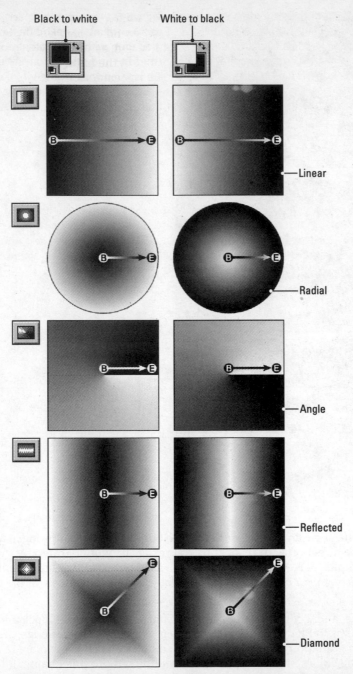

Figure 6-12: Examples of each of the five gradient styles created using the default foreground and background colors (left column) and with the foreground and background colors reversed (right column). B marks the beginning of the drag; E marks the end.

✦ **Reflected:** The fourth gradient style creates a linear gradation that reflects back on itself. Photoshop positions the foreground color at the beginning of your drag and the background color at the end, as when using the linear gradient style. But it also repeats the gradient in the opposite direction of your drag, as demonstrated in Figure 6-12. It's great for creating natural shadows or highlights that fade in two directions.

✦ **Diamond:** The last gradient style creates a series of concentric diamonds (if you drag at a 90-degree angle) or squares (if you drag at a 45-degree angle, as in Figure 6-12). Otherwise, It works exactly like the radial gradient style.

Creating custom gradations

The secret passageway to the Gradient Editor dialog box shown in Figure 6-13 — as you already know if you read the "Gradient options" section earlier in this chapter — is the color preview that appears at the left end of the Options bar. If you click the preview, you display the Gradient Editor dialog box; if you click the neighboring triangle, you display the Gradient palette, as shown earlier in Figure 6-10.

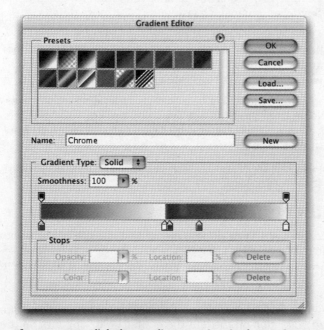

Figure 6-13: Click the gradient preview in the Options bar to display the Gradient Editor dialog box, which enables you to design custom gradations.

Here are some important points about the Gradient Editor:

✦ The scrolling list at the top of the dialog box mirrors the Gradient drop-down palette in the Options bar and the Gradients panel of the Preset Manager dialog box; if you click the triangle at the top of the scrolling list, you display a virtual duplicate of the palette menu.

If you want to see gradient names instead of icons in the list, choose Text Only from the dialog box menu. Or choose Small List or Large List to see both icon and gradient name.

✦ To create a new gradient, find an existing gradient that's close to what you have in mind. Then type a name for the gradient in the Name option box and click the New button. The new gradient appears in the scrolling list, and you can edit the gradient as you see fit.

Even though the gradient appears in the dialog box (as well as in the Gradient palette and Preset Manager dialog box), it's vulnerable until you save it as part of a preset. If you make further edits to the gradient or replace the current gradient preset, the original gradient is a goner. Deleting your main Photoshop preferences file also wipes out an unsaved gradient. See the upcoming section, "Saving and managing gradients," for more details.

✦ You can create *noise gradients* as well as solid-color gradations. If you select Noise from the Gradient Type pop-up menu, Photoshop introduces random color information into the gradient, the result of which is a sort of special-effect gradient that would be difficult to create manually.

✦ The options at the bottom of the dialog box change depending on whether you select Solid or Noise from the Gradient Type pop-up. For solid gradients, Photoshop provides a Smoothness slider, which you can use to adjust how abrupt you want to make the color transitions in the gradient.

✦ You can resize the dialog box by dragging the size box in the lower-right corner.

Editing solid gradients

If you select Solid from the Gradient Type pop-up menu, you use the options shown in Figure 6-14 to adjust the gradient. (Note that this is a doctored screen shot — I made all the options visible in the figure, but normally, only some of these options are available at a time.)

The *fade bar* (labeled in Figure 6-14) shows the active gradient. The starting color appears as a house-shaped *color stop* on the left; the ending color appears on the far right. The upside-down houses on the top of the fade bar are *opacity stops*. These stops determine where colors are opaque and where they fade into translucency or even transparency.

Fade bar   Active opacity stop   Midpoint marker

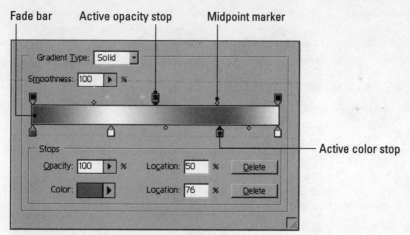

Active color stop

Figure 6-14: Use these controls to adjust the colors and transparency in a solid gradient.

To select either type of stop, click it. The triangle portion of the stop appears black to show you which stop is active. After you select a stop, diamond-shaped *midpoint markers* appear between the stop and its immediate neighbors. On the color-stop side of the fade bar, the midpoint marker represents the spot where the two colors mix in exactly equal amounts. On the transparency side, a marker indicates the point where the opacity value is midway between the values that you set for the stops on either side of the marker.

You can change the location of any stop or marker by dragging it. Or you can click a stop or marker to select it and then enter a value in the Location option box below the fade bar:

✦ When numerically positioning a stop, a value of 0 percent indicates the left end of the fade bar; 100 percent indicates the right end. Even if you add more stops to the gradation, the values represent absolute positions along the fade bar.

✦ When repositioning a midpoint marker, the initial setting of 50 percent is smack dab between two stops; 0 percent is all the way over to the left stop, and 100 percent is all the way over to the right. Midpoint values are, therefore, measured relative to stop positions. In fact, when you move a stop, Photoshop moves the midpoint marker along with it to maintain the same relative positioning.

Figure 6-15 shows four black-to-white radial gradations that I created by setting the midpoint between the black and white color stops to four different positions. The midpoint settings range from the minimum to maximum allowable Location values. If you enter a value below 5 percent or over 95, Photoshop politely ignores you. In all cases, I set the opacity to 100 percent along the entire gradient.

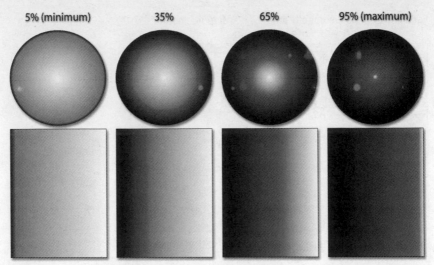

5% (minimum)   35%   65%   95% (maximum)

Figure 6-15: Four sets of white-to-black gradations — radial on top and linear at bottom — subject to different midpoint settings.

Tip

Pressing Enter or Return after you enter a value into the Location option box is tempting, but don't do it. If you do, Photoshop dumps you out of the Gradient Editor dialog box.

Adjusting colors in a solid gradation

When editing a solid gradation, you can add colors, delete colors, change the positioning of the colors within the gradient, and control how two colors blend together. After clicking a color stop to select it, you can change its color in several ways:

✦ To change the color to the current foreground color, open the Color pop-up menu, as shown in Figure 6-16, and select Foreground. Select Background to use the background color instead.

When you select Foreground or Background, the color stop becomes filled with a grayscale pattern instead of a solid color. If you squint real hard and put your nose to the screen, you can see that the pattern is actually a representation of the Foreground and Background color controls in the toolbox. The little black square appears in the upper-left corner when the foreground color is active, as shown in the first stop on the fade bar in Figure 6-16; the black square moves to the bottom-right corner when the background color is active, as shown in the end stop in the figure.

If you change the foreground or background color after closing the Gradient Editor, the gradient changes to reflect the new color. When you next open the Gradient Editor, you can revert the stop to the original foreground or background color by selecting User Color from the pop-up menu.

Foreground color stop   Color midpoint marker   Background color stop

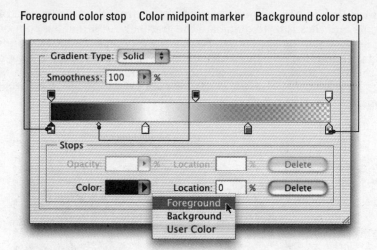

Figure 6-16: A look at the color stop options in the Gradient Editor dialog box.

✦ To set the color stop to some other color, click the Color swatch or double-click the color stop to open the Color Picker and define the new color. Select your color and press Enter or Return.

✦ You may have noticed that when you opened the Gradient Editor dialog box, Photoshop automatically selected the eyedropper tool for you and displayed that tool's controls in the Options bar. Here's why: You can click with the eyedropper in an open image window to lift a color from the image and assign the color to the selected color stop. You can also sample a color from anywhere on screen by first clicking with the eyedropper in an image window and then dragging outside of it.

To change the point at which two colors meet, drag the midpoint marker between the two stops. Or click the midpoint marker and enter a new value into the Location box. As I mentioned earlier, a value of 0 puts the midpoint marker smack up against the left color stop; a value of 100 scoots the stop all the way over to the right stop.

You add or delete stops as follows:

✦ To add a color stop, click anywhere along the bottom of the fade bar. A new stop appears where you click. Photoshop also adds a midpoint marker between the new color stop and its neighbors. You can add as many color stops as your heart desires. (But if your goal is a gradient featuring tons of random colors, you may be able to create the effect you want more easily by using the Noise gradient option, discussed shortly.)

✦ To duplicate a color stop, Alt-drag (Option-drag on the Mac) it to a new location along the fade bar. One great use for this is to create a reflecting gradation.

For example, select Foreground to Background from the scrolling list of gradients and click New to duplicate the gradient. After naming your new gradient — something like Fore to Back to Fore — click the background color stop and change the Location value to 50. Then Alt-drag (Option-drag on the Mac) the foreground color stop all the way to the right. This new gradient is perfect for making true conical gradations with the angle gradient style, as demonstrated in Figure 6-17.

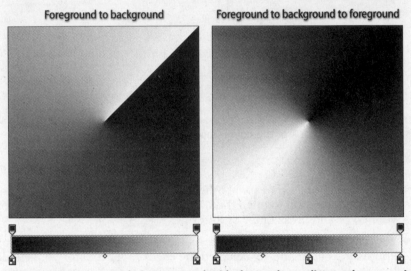

Foreground to background   Foreground to background to foreground

Figure 6-17: Two gradations created with the angle gradient style, one using the standard Foreground to Background gradient (left) and the other with my reflected Fore to Back to Fore style (right). Which looks better to you?

✦ To remove a color stop, drag the stop away from the fade bar. Or click the stop and click the Delete button. The stop icon vanishes and the fade bar automatically adjusts as defined by the remaining color stops.

Adjusting the transparency mask

If you like, you can include a *transparency mask* with each gradation. The mask determines the opacity of different colors along the gradation. You create and edit this mask independently of the colors in the gradation.

To create a transparency mask, you play with the opacity stops across the top of the fade bar. When you click an opacity stop, the transparency options become available beneath the fade bar and the color options dim, as shown in Figure 6-18.

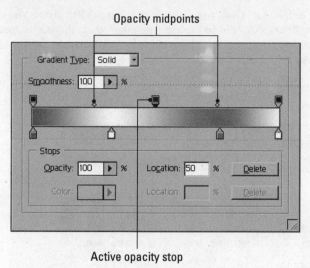

Opacity midpoints

Active opacity stop

Figure 6-18: Click a stop along the top of the fade bar to adjust the opacity of the gradient at that location.

To add an opacity stop, click above the fade bar. By default, each new stop is 100 percent opaque. You can modify the transparency by selecting a stop and changing the Opacity value. The fade bar updates to reflect your changes. To reposition a stop, drag it or enter a value in the Location option box.

Midpoint markers represent the spot where the opacity value is half the difference between the opacity values of a pair of opacity stops. In other words, if you set one opacity stop to 30 percent and another to 90 percent, the midpoint marker shows you where the gradient reaches 60 percent opacity. You can relocate the midpoint marker, and thus change the spot where the gradient reaches that mid-range opacity value, by dragging the marker or entering a new value in the Location box.

Color Plate 6-2 demonstrates the effect of applying two gradations to a photograph. The first linear gradation fades from red to transparency to orange to transparency and, finally, to blue. The second gradation is radial, starting with yellow, fading to transparency, then fading back up twice to create a couple of white rings. I applied these two gradients with special blend mode settings to make their pixels meld into the underlying photo; the linear gradient was applied using the Color blend mode, and the radial gradient uses the Linear Dodge mode.

Creating noise gradients

Adobe describes a noise gradient as a gradient that "contains random components along with the deterministic ones that create the gradient." Allow me to translate: Photoshop adds random colors to the parameters that you set in the Gradient

Editor dialog box. Did that help? No? Then take a look at Figure 6-19, which shows examples of three noise gradients. You could create these same gradients using the regular Solid gradient controls, of course, but it would take you forever to add all the color and midpoint stops required to produce the same effect.

Figure 6-19: Here you see three gradients created using the Noise option in the Gradient Editor dialog box. I created the first two using two different Roughness values; for the bottom example, I used the same Roughness value as in the middle example but selected the Add Transparency option.

To create a noise gradient, select Noise from the Gradient Type menu in the Gradient Editor dialog box, as shown in Figure 6-20. You can adjust the gradient as follows:

✦ Raise the Roughness value to create more distinct bands of color, as in the middle example in Figure 6-19. Lowering the Roughness value results in softer color transitions, as you can see from the top example, which I set at one half the Roughness value of the middle example.

✦ Use the color sliders at the bottom of the dialog box to define the range of allowable colors in the gradient. You can work in one of three color modes: RGB, HSB, or Lab. Select the mode you want from the pop-up menu above the sliders.

✦ The Restrict Colors option, when selected, adjusts the gradient so that you don't wind up with any oversaturated colors. Deselect the option for more vibrant hues.

✦ If you select Add Transparency, Photoshop adds random transparency information to the gradient, as if you had added scads of opacity stops to a regular gradient. In the bottom example of Figure 6-19, I started with the gradient from the middle example, selected the Add Transparency check box, and left the Roughness value at 100.

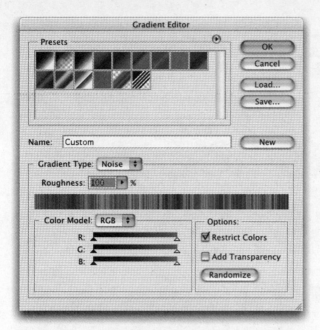

Figure 6-20: Use the Noise gradient option to create gradients like the ones you see in Figure 6-19.

✦ Click the Randomize button, and Photoshop shuffles all the gradient colors and transparency values to create another gradient. If you don't like what you see, just keep clicking Randomize until you're satisfied. Note that each click of the Randomize button produces a radically different gradient, so if you find a gradient that's close to what you're looking for, you might want to save it as a preset and continue tweaking it by hand.

Tip For some really cool effects, try applying special effects filters to a noise gradient. Figure 6-21 shows the results of applying the Gaussian Blur, Twirl, and Ripple filters on the original noise gradient shown in the upper-left example.

Saving and managing gradients

When you define a new gradient, its icon appears in the palette, the Preset Manger dialog box, and the Gradient Editor dialog box. But if you replace the current gradient set or edit the gradient, the original gradient gets trashed. You also lose the gradient if you delete your Photoshop 7 preferences file because that's where the temporary gradient information is stored.

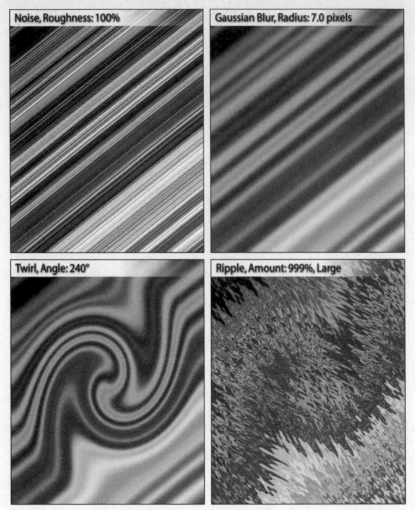

Figure 6-21: I applied three effects filters to the original noise gradient to create some interesting random patterns.

If you want to preserve a gradient, you must save it as part of a preset — which is nothing more than a collection of gradients. As I mentioned earlier, Photoshop ships with several gradient presets that are stored in the Gradients folder, which lives inside the Presets folder in the main Photoshop program folder. You also can create as many custom presets as you like. Gradient presets have the file extension *.grd*.

You can save all the gradients in the active preset — including any custom gradients that you define — by clicking Save in the Gradient Editor dialog box or by choosing Save Gradients from the Gradient palette pop-up menu. But if you want to save only some of the current gradients as a preset, choose Preset Manager from the Gradient palette pop-up menu and then display the Gradients panel, shown in Figure 6-22, by pressing Ctrl+3 (⌘-3 on the Mac) or by choosing Gradients from the Preset Type pop-up menu. Shift-click the gradients you want to save and then click Save Set. If you want to dump the selected gradients into an existing preset, select the preset file and press Enter or Return. Alternatively, you can enter a new preset name to create a brand new preset that contains only the selected gradients.

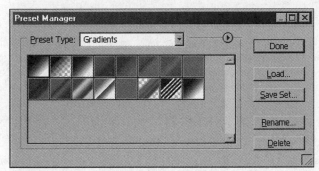

Figure 6-22: To select specific gradients and save them as a new preset, use the Preset Manager.

To delete a gradient, Alt-click (Option-click on the Mac) its icon in the palette, the Preset Manager, or the Gradient Editor dialog box. To delete multiple gradients, Shift-click the gradients in the Preset Manager and then click the Delete button. Save the preset immediately if you want the deleted gradients gone for good; otherwise, it remains an official part of the preset and reappears the next time you load the preset.

Gradations and brush modes

All the standard brush modes are available when you apply gradations, and they make a tremendous impression on the performance of the gradient tool. This section examines one way to apply a brush mode in conjunction with the tool. Naturally, it barely scrapes the surface of what's possible, but it may inspire you to experiment and discover additional effects on your own.

The following steps tell you how to use the Dissolve mode with a radial gradation to create a supernova explosion. (At least, it looks like a supernova to me—not that I've ever seen one up close, mind you.) Figures 6-23 through 6-25 show the nova in progress. The steps offer you the opportunity to experiment with a brush mode setting and some general insight into creating radial gradations.

These steps involve the use of the elliptical marquee tool. Generally speaking, it's an easy tool to use. But if you find you have problems making it work according to my instructions, you may want to read the "Geometric selection outlines" section of Chapter 8. It's only a few pages long.

STEPS: Creating a Gradient Supernova

1. **Create a new image window.** Make it 500×500 pixels. A grayscale image is fine for this exercise.

2. **Use guides to pinpoint the center of your image.** If rulers aren't already visible, press Ctrl+R (⌘-R on the Mac) to turn them on. Right-click (Control-click on the Mac) on a ruler and make sure that the unit of measurement is set to pixels. Then drag from each ruler to set a guide at the 250-pixel point. The intersection of the two guides will be in the exact center of your image.

3. **Alt-drag (Option-drag on the Mac) from the center point with the elliptical marquee tool to draw the marquee outward from the center.** While dragging with the tool, press and hold Shift to constrain the marquee to a circle. Release Shift after you release the mouse button. Draw a marquee that fills about ¾ of the window.

4. **Choose Image ➪ Adjustments ➪ Invert.** Or press Ctrl+I (⌘-I on the Mac). This fills the marquee with black.

5. **Choose Select ➪ Deselect.** Or press Ctrl+D (⌘-D on the Mac). As the command name suggests, this deselects the circle.

6. **Again, Alt-drag (Option-drag on the Mac) from the center point with the elliptical marquee tool.** And, again, press Shift to constrain the shape to a circle. Create a marquee roughly 20 pixels larger than the black circle.

7. **Alt-drag (Option-drag on the Mac) from the center point with the elliptical marquee tool.** This subtracts a hole from the selection. After you begin dragging, release Alt (Win) or Option (Mac), but keep that mouse button down. Then press and hold both Shift and Alt (Win) or Option (Mac) together and keep them down. Draw a marquee roughly 20 pixels smaller than the black circle. Release the mouse button and finally release the keys. The result is a doughnut-shaped selection — a large circle with a smaller circular hole — as shown in Figure 6-23.

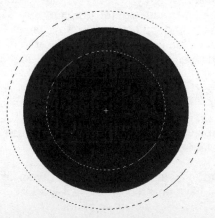

Figure 6-23: The result of creating a black circle and two circular marquees, all centered about a single point (represented here by a small crosshair).

8. **Choose Select ⇨ Feather and enter 10 for the Radius value.** Then press Enter or Return to feather the section outline.

9. **Press D and then press X.** This makes the foreground color white and the background color black.

10. **Select the gradient tool and click the radial gradient icon in the Options bar.** That's the second icon from the left with the white circle at its center. (Flip back to Figure 6-12 if you still don't know what I mean.)

11. **Open the Gradient palette and select the Foreground to Background gradient.** Assuming that you have the default gradients preset loaded and haven't altered the preset, the icon is the first one in the palette.

12. **Select Dissolve from the Mode menu in the Options bar.**

13. **Drag from the center point in the image window to anywhere along the outer rim of the largest marquee.** The result is the fuzzy gradation shown in Figure 6-24.

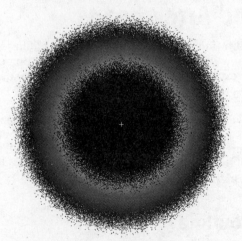

Figure 6-24: The Dissolve brush mode option randomizes the pixels around the feathered edges of the selection outlines.

14. **Choose Select ⇨ Deselect to deselect the image.** Or press Ctrl+D (⌘-D on the Mac).

15. **Choose Image ⇨ Adjustments ⇨ Invert to invert the entire image.** Or press Ctrl+I (⌘-I on the Mac).

16. **Press D to restore black and white as foreground and background colors, respectively.** Then choose View ⇨ Clear Guides. The finished supernova appears in Figure 6-25.

Figure 6-25: By inverting the image from the previous figure, you create an expanding series of progressively lighter rings dissolving into the black void of space, an effect better known to its friends as a supernova.

Applying Strokes and Arrowheads

Photoshop is nearly as adept at drawing lines and outlines as it is at filling selections. The following sections discuss how to apply a border around a selection outline — which is practical, if not terribly exciting — and how to create arrowheads — which can yield more interesting results than you might think.

When I mention lines here, I'm talking about *raster* lines — that is, lines made of pixels that you create with the line tool set to the Fill Pixels mode. To find out how to use the tool to produce vector lines and work paths, see Chapters 14 and 8, respectively. Some, but not all, line tool techniques discussed here apply to the line tool also when it's set to vector or work path mode.

Stroking a selection outline

Stroking is useful for creating frames and outlines. Generally speaking, you can stroke an image in Photoshop in four ways:

✦ **The Stroke command:** Select the portion of the image you want to stroke and choose Edit ➪ Stroke to display the Stroke dialog box shown in Figure 6-26. Or, if you're working on a multilayered image, you can choose the Stroke command without making a selection; Photoshop then applies the stroke to the entire layer.

In the Stroke dialog box, enter the thickness of the stroke in the Width option box. The default unit of measurement here is pixels, but you can use inches and centimeters as well. Just type the value and then the unit abbreviation (*px* for pixels, *in* for inches, or *cm* for centimeters).

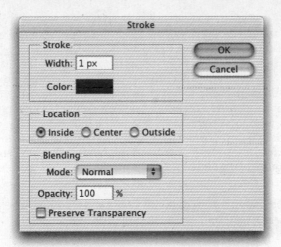

Figure 6-26: Use the options in the Stroke dialog box to specify the thickness of a stroke and its location with respect to the selection outline.

You can set the stroke color from within the dialog box. Click the color swatch to select a color from the Color Picker — don't forget that you have full access to the eyedropper tool while the Color Picker is open. Press Enter or Return to close the Color Picker and return to the Stroke dialog box.

Select a Location radio button to specify the position of the stroke with respect to the selection outline. When in doubt, select Inside from the Location radio buttons. This setting ensures that the stroke is entirely inside the selection outline in case you decide to move the selection. If you select Center or Outside, Photoshop applies part or all of the stroke to the deselected area around the selection outline — unless, of course, your selection extends to the edge of the canvas, in which case you wind up with no stroke at all for Outside and half a stroke inside the selection outline for Center.

The Stroke dialog box also includes Mode, Opacity, and Preserve Transparency options that work like those in the Fill dialog box.

✦ **The Border command:** Select a portion of the image and choose Select ➪ Modify ➪ Border to retain only the outline of the selection. Specify the size of the border by entering a value in pixels in the Width option box and press Enter or Return. To fill the border with the background color, press Ctrl+Backspace (⌘-Delete on the Mac). To fill the border with the foreground color, press Alt+Backspace (Option-Delete on the Mac). To apply a repeating pattern to the border, choose Edit ➪ Fill and select the Pattern option from the Use pop-up menu. You can even apply a command under the Filter menu or some other special effect.

✦ **Layer Style effects:** If you want to stroke an entire layer, also check out the options provided by the Layer Style feature. Choose Layer ➪ Layer Style ➪ Stroke to display the dialog box shown in Figure 6-27. At first glance, the options here appear to mirror those you find in the regular Stroke dialog box; and they do, as long as you select Color from the Fill pop-up menu. But if you crack open that pop-up menu, you discover two goodies. First, you can fill the stroke with a gradient or a pattern. Second, you can adjust the pattern and gradient on the fly and preview the results inside the dialog box. For example, you can scale the gradient and change its angle — two things you can't do inside the regular Gradient Editor dialog box, I might add. By using the settings shown in the figure, I adapted a plain old black-to-white gradient to produce the shadowed frame effect you see in the preview.

I cover the Layer Style dialog box in detail in Chapter 14, so if you have trouble figuring out the stroke options, look there for help.

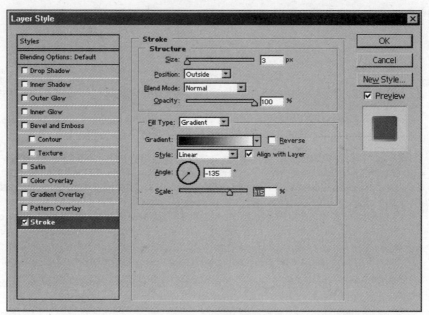

Figure 6-27: With the Stroke options in the Layer Style dialog box, you can stroke a layer with a solid color, gradient, or pattern. You also can adjust the angle and scale of gradients, as I did to create the effect shown in the preview.

✦ **The Canvas Size trick:** Okay, so this one is a throwaway, but I use it all the time. To create an outline around the entire image, change the background color (yes, the background color) to the color you want to apply to the outline. Then choose Image ➪ Canvas Size, check the Relative check box and enter twice the desired border thickness in pixels into the Width and Height options.

For example, to create a 1-pixel border all the way around, enter 2 pixels for the Width value (1 for the left side and 1 for the right) and 2 pixels for the Height value (1 for the top and 1 for the bottom). (You could also deselect the Relative check box and add 2 pixels to the existing Width and Height values, if you're inordinately fond of doing math.) Leave the Anchor option set to the center tile. When you press Enter or Return, Photoshop enlarges the canvas size according to your specifications and fills the new pixels around the perimeter of the image with the background color. Simplicity at its best.

Applying arrowheads to straight lines

The one function missing from all the operations in the preceding list is applying arrowheads. The fact is, in Photoshop, you can apply arrowheads only to straight lines drawn with the line tool.

The line tool is grouped with the drawing tools. You can cycle between the tools by pressing U (or Shift+U, depending on whether you select the Use Shift for Tool Switch check box in the Preferences dialog box). As I mentioned previously, the line tool can create three different kinds of shapes. You can paint raster lines — that is, lines made up of pixels. Or you can draw vector-based lines on a new shape layer, as explained in Chapter 14. Finally, you can create a work path using the line tool, as I discuss in Chapter 8.

You specify which type of line you want to create by clicking one of the three icons near the left end of the Options bar, which I labeled in Figure 6-28. If you don't see the Options bar on screen, press Enter or Return or double-click the line tool icon in the toolbox.

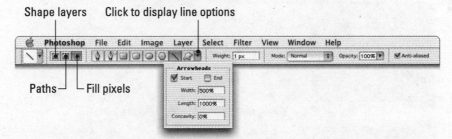

Figure 6-28: The arrowhead options appear in this drop-down palette.

Regardless of which type of line you're creating, you set the width of the line by entering a value into the Weight box in the Options bar. Then you add arrowheads via the drop-down options palette shown in the figure. To display the options, click the triangle at the end of the strip of shape icons (again, see the figure). Use the Arrowheads options as follows:

✦ **Start:** Select this check box to append an arrowhead to the beginning of a line drawn with the line tool.

✦ **End:** Select this check box to append an arrowhead to the end of a line. (Like you needed me to tell you this.)

✦ **Width:** Enter the width of the arrowhead in this option box. The width is measured as a percentage of the line weight, so if the Weight is set to 6 pixels and the Width value is 500 percent, the width of the arrowhead will be 30 pixels. Math in action.

✦ **Length:** Enter the length of the arrowhead, measured from the base of the arrowhead to its tip, again as a percentage of the line weight.

✦ **Concavity:** You can specify the shape of the arrowhead by entering a value between negative and positive 50 percent in the Concavity option box. Figure 6-29 shows examples of a few Concavity settings applied to an arrowhead 50 pixels wide and 100 pixels long.

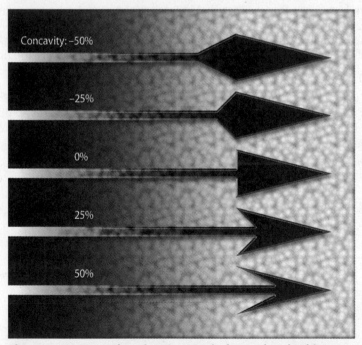

Figure 6-29: Examples of a 50×100-pixel arrowhead subject to five different Concavity values

Appending arrowheads to curved lines

Applying arrowheads to straight lines is a simple matter. Applying an arrowhead to a stroked selection outline is a little trickier, but still possible. The following steps explain the process.

For the effect shown in this example, you need raster arrowheads, so click the Fill Pixels icon in the Options bar (see Figure 6-28). Now your line tool creates raster lines rather than vector lines or work paths.

STEPS: Adding an Arrowhead to a Free-form Stroke

1. **Create a new layer.** Display the Layers palette by pressing the F7 key. Then click the little page icon at the bottom of the palette to create a new layer.

2. **Draw and stroke a selection.** Draw any selection outline you like. Stroke it by choosing Edit ➪ Stroke and applying whatever settings strike your fancy. Remember the value you enter in the Width option. In Figure 6-30, I drew a wiggly line with the lasso tool and applied a 4-pixel black stroke set to 30 percent Opacity.

Figure 6-30: Here I created a new layer, drew a free-form shape with the lasso tool, and stroked it with a 4-pixel black outline at 30 percent Opacity.

3. **Press Ctrl+D (⌘-D on the Mac).** This deselects all portions of the image.

4. **Erase the portions of the stroke you don't need.** Select the eraser tool by pressing E. Then drag to erase through the stroke layer without harming the layer below. Erase the areas of the stroke where you want to add arrowheads. I wanted to add an arrowhead behind the fly, so I erased around the fly.

5. **Select the line tool and click the Fill Pixels icon in the Options bar.**

6. **Specify the line weight and arrowhead settings.** Enter the line weight you used when stroking the selection outline into the Weight option box (in my case, 4 pixels). Next, display the line options drop-down palette. Just click the triangle at the end of the strip of shape icons, as shown previously in Figure 6-28. Select the End check box and deselect the Start check box. Then specify the width, length, and concavity of the arrowhead as desired.

7. **Set the foreground color as needed.** I applied a black stroke at 30 percent Opacity, so I set the foreground color to 30 percent gray. (Click the stroke with the eyedropper to change the foreground color to the stroke color.)

8. **Zoom in to the point in the image where you want to add the arrowhead.** You have to get in close enough to see what you're doing, as in Figure 6-31.

9. **At the tip of the stroke, draw a very short line exactly the length of the arrowhead.** Figure 6-31 illustrates what I mean. This may take some practice to accomplish. Start the line a few pixels in from the end of the stroke to make sure the base of the arrowhead fits snugly. If you mess up the first time, choose Edit ➪ Undo or press Ctrl+Z (⌘-Z on the Mac) and try again.

Figure 6-31: Use the line tool to draw a line no longer than the arrowhead. This appends the arrow to the end of the stroke. The view size of this image is magnified to 300 percent.

That's all there is to it. From then on, you can continue to edit the stroke as you see fit. In Figure 6-32, for example, I erased a series of scratches across the stroke to create a dashed-line effect, all the rage for representing cartoon fly trails. I then set the eraser brush size to the largest, fuzziest setting and erased the end of the stroke (above the dog's head) to create a gradual trailing off. That crazy fly is now officially distracting our hero from his appointed rounds.

Figure 6-32: I finished by erasing dashes into the line and softening the end of the trail with a large, fuzzy eraser.

✦ ✦ ✦

Retouching and Restoring

Four of the Best

So far in Part II, we've looked at a host of editing disciplines — smearing and sponging, filling and stroking, and the powerful art of painting. Although most of these tools perform splendidly, they represent just the tip of the image-manipulation iceberg. And having melted that tip away, we come to the next strata in the pixel-based glacier, the retouchers — the stamp, healing tool, eraser, and history brush. Together with variations like the patch tool and art history brush, these remarkable tools permit you to repair damaged images, create and apply repeating patterns, erase away mistakes, and restore operations from your recent past. In short, they permit you to perform the sorts of miracles that simply weren't possible in the days before computer imaging, all without the slightest fear of damaging your artwork.

Very briefly, here's how each tool works:

✦ **Clone stamp** and **pattern stamp:** Use the clone stamp to replicate pixels from one area in an image to another. This one feature makes the clone stamp ideally suited to removing dust, repairing minor defects, and eliminating distracting background elements. Alt-click (Option-click on the Mac) the clone stamp icon in the toolbox or press S or Shift+S to switch to the pattern stamp tool, which paints with a repeating image tile selected from Photoshop's library of predefined patterns or defined using Edit ➪ Define Pattern or Filter ➪ Pattern Maker.

✦ **Healing brush** and **patch tool:** The healing brush is an expanded version of the clone stamp tool that merges texture detail from one portion of an image with color and brightness values from another. This permits you more flexibility when retouching imperfections, particularly when repairing tricky defects, such as scratches and wrinkles. Mouse down on the healing brush icon to display the flyout menu, or press J or Shift+J to switch to the patch tool, which allows you to repair entire selections at a time. Like the stamp tool, the healing brush and patch tool alternatively let you retouch with a pattern.

✦ **Eraser:** When used in a single-layer image or on the background layer, the eraser paints in the background color. When applied to a layer, it erases pixels to reveal the layers below.

The eraser tool includes two variations, the background eraser and magic eraser (dimmed in Figure 7-1), which automatically extract background details from a layer. Because they're specific purpose is to extract and they work only with layered images, I discuss them independently of the standard eraser tool in Chapter 9, "Masks and Extractions."

Figure 7-1: By using these tools and the History palette, you can retouch an image and restore portions to an earlier or even later state.

✦ **History brush** and **art history brush:** The history brush selectively reverts to any of several states listed in the History palette. To select the *source state* that you want to paint with, click in the first column of the History palette. A brush icon identifies the source state, as illustrated by the Lasso item in Figure 7-1. If Photoshop displays a little "not-allowed" cursor when you try to use the history brush, it means you can't paint from the selected state. Click another state in the History palette and try again.

Alt-click on the history brush icon or press Y or Shift+Y to switch to the art history brush, which lets you apply impressionistic effects based on the active source state in the History palette. I wouldn't go so far as to call it a terribly useful tool, but it can be a lot of fun.

Obviously, these are but the skimpiest of introductions, every bit as stingy with information as a 19th-century headmaster might have been with his Christmas gruel and treacle. But fear not, my hungry one. This chapter doles out so many courses of meaty facts, fibrous techniques, and sweet, buttery insights that you'll need a whole box of toothpicks to dislodge the excess tips from your incisors.

Cloning and Healing

One of the most venerable, most practical tools in all of Photoshop is the clone stamp, which duplicates portions of an image. After selecting the tool — which you can do by pressing the S key — press the Alt key (or Option on the Mac) and click in the image window to specify the portion of the image you want to clone. This is termed the *source point*. Then paint with the tool to copy colors from that source point to another part of the image.

Closely related to the clone stamp tool is the healing brush, which clones multiple attributes of an image at a time. Press J to select the tool. Then, as with the clone stamp, Alt-click in the image (or Option-click on the Mac) to set the source of the clone. Note that the clone stamp and healing brush share a common source point, so setting the source for one tool sets it for both. Drag with the healing brush to mix the texture from the source point with the highlights, shadows, and colors of pixels that neighbor the brushstroke.

"Fascinating stuff," I hear you saying, "And by all means, I'll want you to elaborate. But why in the world would I want to clone pixels? I mean if these tools could clone, say, sheep, they'd be no-brainers. This weary world could always use a few more sheep. But pixels, I just don't get it." Clearly, if this is your first experience with cloning, it might sound peculiar. But as any dyed-in-the-wool Photoshop user will tell you, the clone stamp and healing brush are nothing short of invaluable for touching up images. You can remove dust, hairs, and other impurities; rebuild scratched, creased, or torn photographs; and even eliminate elements that wandered into your picture when you weren't looking. They are very simple, very useful tools.

The clone stamp tool

Let's start things off with a brief examination of the simpler of the two tools, the clone stamp. Although easy to use, it can be a little tricky at first. If you just start in dragging, Photoshop warns you that you must first define a source point. And it doesn't warn you politely. No "Sorry 'bout that," or "Ahem, pardon me, but . . . ." Just an abrupt, "Holy cow, you sorry excuse for a user! Don't you even know you have to Alt-click to define a source point to be used to repair the image? Honestly, get a grip or I'll shut down and bar you from ever launching me again!" or words to that effect. But while you may not like its tone, Photoshop's message is accurate. You have to set a source point before you can proceed.

How cloning works

Here's how it works: To clone part of an image, Alt-click (Option-click on the Mac) in the image window to specify a point of reference in the portion of the image you want to clone. Then click or drag with the tool in some other region of the image to paint a cloned spot or line. In Figure 7-2, for example, I pressed Alt (or Option) and clicked to the right of my sporty wife's head, as demonstrated by the appearance of the target cursor. I then painted the line shown on right. The stamp brush cursor shows the end of my drag; the clone source crosshair shows the corresponding point in the original image.

It's worth noting that the clone stamp clones the image as it existed before you began using the tool. Even when you drag over an area that contains a clone, the tool references the original appearance of the image. This means there may be a visual disconnect between what the clone tool seems to be sourcing and what it paints, as illustrated in Figure 7-3. This is actually a good thing, however, because it avoids repetition of detail, a dead giveaway of poor retouching.

Tip

Photoshop lets you clone not only within the image you're working on but from a separate image window as well. This technique makes it possible to merge two different images, as demonstrated in Figure 7-4. To achieve this effect, Alt-click (Option-click) in one image, bring a second image to the foreground, and then drag with the clone stamp tool to copy from the first image. You can also clone between layers. Just Alt-click (Option-click) one layer and then switch to a different layer and drag.

Alt-click (Option-click) to set the source point … and then paint away.

The clone stamp tool copies pixels from one location … to another.

Clone source crosshair   Stamp brush cursor

Figure 7-2: After Alt-clicking (Option-clicking on the Mac) at the point indicated by the target cursor, I dragged with the clone stamp tool to paint with the image. I painted inside a white area to make the brushstroke easier to see.

Clone source crosshair   Stamp brush cursor

Throughout a drag, the clone tool copies from the original image.

Figure 7-3: During the course of a single drag, the clone tool continues to clone from the image as it appeared before you began painting. This prevents you from creating more than one clone during a single drag.

Figure 7-4: Here I used the clone stamp tool to merge my wife with a NASA photo. I employed the Multiply brush mode to achieve the shadowy edge. I also added some extra length to the snow-covered ground by cloning and recloning areas with the stamp tool. If you've ever seen *The Honeymooners*, you have to wonder, is this what Ralph Kramden had in mind?

Cloning options

When the clone stamp is active, the Options bar gives you access to the standard Brush, Mode, and Opacity settings that you get when using the brush tool. These permit you to mix the cloned image with the original to get different effects, as I explained at length in Chapter 5. New to Photoshop 7, you also get the Flow value and airbrush icon, which permit you to build up brushstrokes where they overlap and at points where you mouse down without moving the cursor.

You'll also find the Use All Layers check box, which lets you clone from multiple layers at a time, very useful for cloning from the composite image onto a new layer. For more information on this option, read the "Painting with the smudge tool" section of Chapter 5.

The only option associated with the stamp tool that's a complete departure from what we've seen so far is the Aligned check box, which locks down the relative source of a clone from one Alt- or Option-click to the next. To understand how this option works, think of the locations where you Alt-click (Option-click on the Mac) and begin dragging with the stamp tool as opposite ends of an imaginary straight line, as illustrated in Figure 7-5. When Aligned is turned on, the length and angle of this imaginary line remains fixed until the next time you Alt-click. As you drag, Photoshop moves the line, cloning pixels from one end of the line and laying them down at the other. The upshot is that regardless of how many times you start and stop dragging with the stamp tool, all brushstrokes match up as seamlessly as pieces in a puzzle.

If you want to clone from a single portion of an image repeatedly, deselect the Aligned check box. Figure 7-6 shows how, with Aligned turned off, Photoshop clones from the same point every time you paint a new line with the clone stamp tool. As a result, each of the brushstrokes features some fragment of my wife's face or hair but none line up with each other. In these examples, it may appear as if having Aligned selected is the superior setting. But as you'll see in later sections, both turning the option on and off serve specific purposes.

The healing brush

I was first introduced to the healing brush in June 2001 at an Adobe-sponsored event called the Design Invitational. This was ten months before Photoshop 7 hit the shelves, and at the time, Adobe's plan was to introduce the healing brush as the central feature in the next bold upgrade to the software, the never released Photoshop 6.5. And to be honest, I was profoundly impressed. Finally, after 11 years cloning with the stamp tool, Adobe planned to release an upgrade that did more than simply duplicate pixels.

Source point

aligned on!

Clones in alignment

Figure 7-5: Here I've set the stamp tool's blend mode to Hard Light to mix the moon image with the texture on right. I've also turned on the Aligned check box to instruct Photoshop to clone the image continuously, no matter how many times I paint a new brushstroke.

Source point

aligned off?

Figure 7-6: If you turn off the Aligned check box, Photoshop clones each new line from the point at which you Alt- or Option-click.

Naturally, the fellow who demoed the tool made it look like magic. The difference is that this time, magic isn't far from the truth. To get a feel for the tool, open a picture of a person's face that needs some work. For my part, I opened the picture shown in

Figure 7-7. That's me, by the way, in case you were wondering what I look like. If not, my apologies — after all, you've done nothing to deserve such a gruesome image — but the picture well illustrates the healing brush because it suffers myriad irregularities, not the least of which is a field of divots emblazoned across my forehead. I can only guess that these scars were the result of a bombardment of very tiny meteorites. As suggested in Figure 7-8, my forehead and the surface of the moon bear too close a resemblance to be written off as pure chance.

Isn't there enough pain in the world without this?

Figure 7-7: I am told that this is a really good picture of me. As I'm sure you can understand, that depresses me to no end. Fortunately, I can make it appear a bit more human using the healing brush.

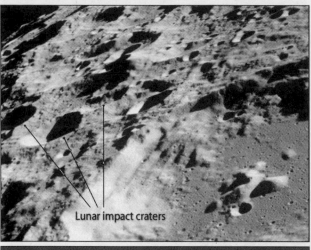

Lunar impact craters

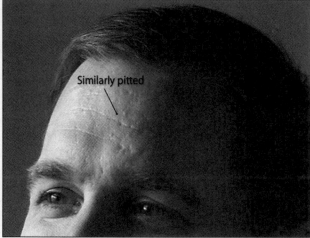

Similarly pitted

Figure 7-8: No, I didn't accidentally switch the labels on these two images. Hard as it is to believe, my forehead is indeed more dented than the lunar surface. You should see me when I sweat — my head illuminates the night sky.

If you can locate an image this hideous, God bless you. If not, hunt down something, say, half as bad. Select the healing brush by pressing the J key, which you can remember because it's the only letter missing from the words *heal*, *patch*, *mend*, *fix*, *knit*, *remedy*, *salvage*, *cobble*, *requite*, and the antonym *wizen*. Then press Alt (or Option) and click in the image to identify the texture that you want to match. Paint over a spot, scratch, pimple, wrinkle, or scar to miraculously heal that portion of the image. And it's fast, too. It took me about five minutes to retouch every defect on my forehead. As shown in Figure 7-9, the result is a virtual skin graft of newborn flesh, but without the cost or controversy.

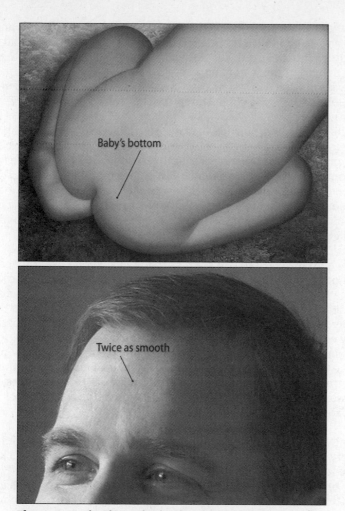

Figure 7-9: Thanks to the healing brush, my once-blemished brow is now the envy of men, women, and infants alike. You won't see any more kiddo keisters kicking sand in my face.

In case you can't get enough of watching me heal my own face—admittedly an act of vanity, but given the general state of my flesh, someone's got to do it—then check out Color Plates 7-1 and 7-2. The former shows the healing brush and patch tool in action. The latter shows a bit of extra retouching performed the old fashioned way, using any old tool in Photoshop's arsenal.

How healing works

In dabbling with the healing brush, you'll quickly discover two things. When it works, it works incredibly well, better than any other retouching technique available inside

Photoshop. But when it doesn't work, it *really* doesn't work, introducing colors and shades that appear clearly at odds with their surroundings. My experience is that, even when used carelessly, the tool produces desirable results slightly more often than it doesn't, so you may be content to paint and hope for the best. However, if you take a little time to learn what it is the healing brush is doing, you'll figure out how best to use it and when to use the clone stamp tool instead.

Naturally, I advocate the latter route, so with your approval, I'll take a moment and peel away some of the magic. The healing brush blends the pixels from the source point with the original pixels of your brushstroke. In that respect, it works a little bit like the clone stamp combined with a brush mode. But rather than blending two pixels at a time — cloned and underlying original, as a brush mode does — the healing brush blends cloned pixels with those just outside the brushstroke. The idea is that the pixels that you're painting over are messed up, but the pixels just beyond the brushstroke are in good shape and should be emulated.

Figure 7-10 illustrates what I mean. Here you see what happens when I use the healing brush to clone a photo of my son onto the slightly embossed background shown on right. Notice also that the left edge of the background is shadowed while the right edge is lit. I applied a slight bevel to the brushstroke to make it easier to see. As the healing brush clones my son, it blends the colors from the photograph and embossed background in roughly equal amounts. This is a grayscale figure, so you'll have to take my word for that part, but this next part you can see for yourself: Photoshop dodges the brushstroke to match the light edges of the background and burns the brushstroke to match the dark edges. And it does all this according to the colors, highlights, and shadows that it encounters in tracing the very outer perimeter of the brushstroke, indicated by the dashed line on the right side of Figure 7-10.

Despite all this coloring and shading, bear in mind that the healing brush transfers the texture in its entirety from source point to brushstroke. In Figure 7-11, I Alt-clicked (Option-clicked) in the top image and dragged five times in the bottom image. In each case, the healing brush entirely replaced the pattern texture with my son's ear and eyes. At the same time, each brushstroke gets progressively darker to match the shade of the gradient in the background.

What can you deduce from this?

✦ **First, the healing brush replaces the texture as you paint just as surely as if you were using the clone stamp tool.** If you want to mix textures, you'll need to employ a brush mode, as I explain in the next section.

Tip

✦ **Second, the manner in which the color and shading are mixed is directly linked to the size and hardness of your brush.** Bear in mind Photoshop is looking at the outside edge of the brushstroke. As illustrated way back in Figure 5-19 (see Chapter 5), the outer edge of the brush grows as the Hardness value shrinks. So soft brushes cause the healing brush to factor in more surrounding colors and shading.

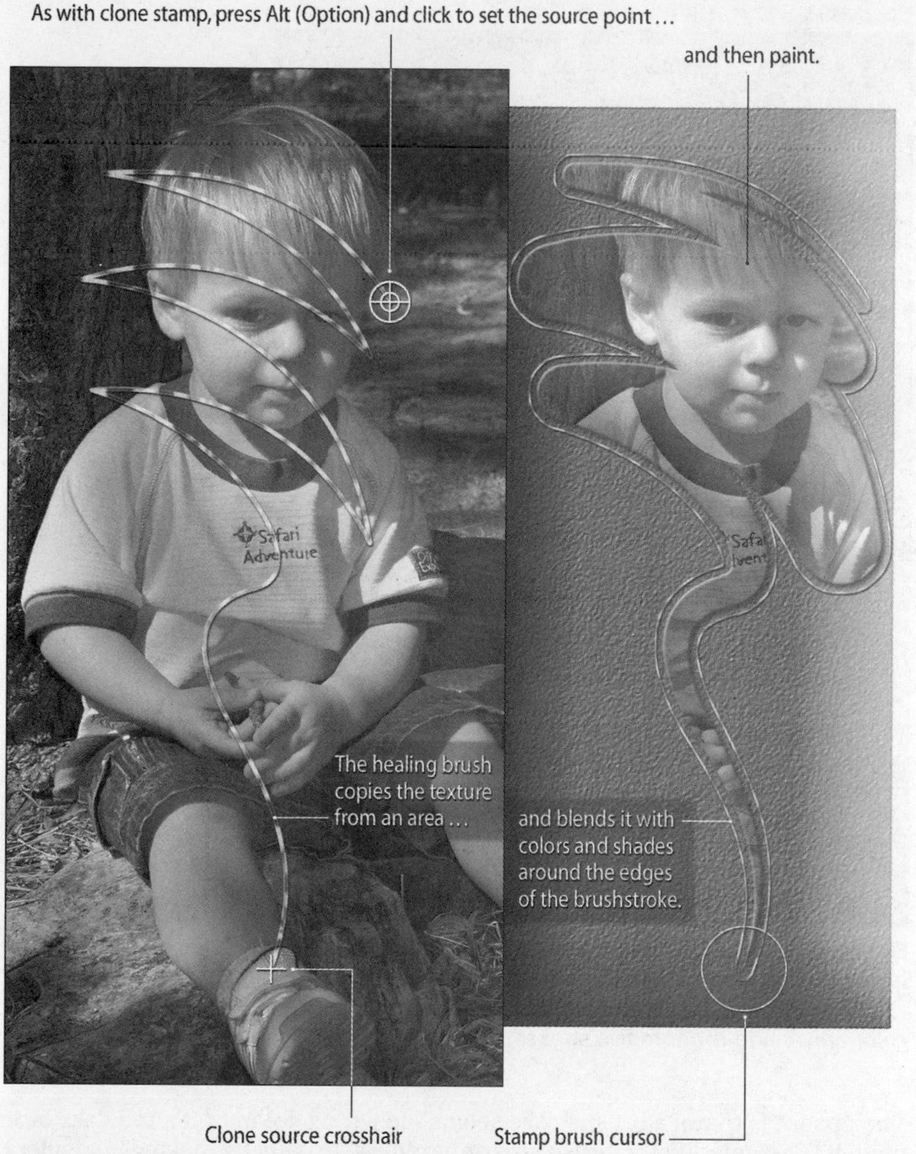

As with clone stamp, press Alt (Option) and click to set the source point ...

and then paint.

The healing brush copies the texture from an area ...

and blends it with colors and shades around the edges of the brushstroke.

Clone source crosshair

Stamp brush cursor

Figure 7-10: Here I used the healing brush to clone my son (left) onto an embossed background (right). The dashed line on left shows the path of the source point throughout the brushstroke. The dashed line that surrounds the brushstroke on right indicates the outer edge of the brushstroke, which serves as the source for the additional coloring and shading that the healing brush performs.

Sourced image

Healing brushstrokes

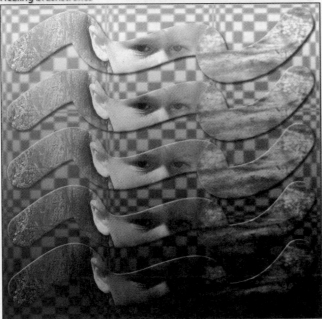

Figure 7-11: When set to the Normal brush mode, the healing brush clones the texture from the source image (above) in its entirety. The only thing that changes is the color and shade (bottom five strokes).

The upshot is that if a brushstroke seems the wrong color, or it's too dark or light, undo it. Then modify the brush size or hardness, usually by making it smaller or harder. And try again.

Healing options

In contrast to its astonishing editing powers, there's little you can do to customize the behavior of the healing brush. It permits you neither to use custom brushes nor apply any of the settings inside the Brushes palette. To modify a brush, you have to click the Brush icon in the Options bar. This gives you access to Photoshop 6-style brush tip settings along with a single dynamic, which lets you link brush size to pen pressure or airbrush wheel.

You have no control over Opacity or Flow. (It's a shocking omission, frankly, but you can work around this problem using Edit ➪ Fade, as I'll discuss later.) Meanwhile, the brush modes are limited to just eight. In each case, the mode merges cloned and original pixels, and then performs the additional healing blending. By way of example, Figure 7-12 shows five of the eight modes when painted over a horizontal gradient. Thanks to the dodging and burning applied by the healing brush, dark modes like Multiply and light modes such as Screen can be substantially compromised. In fact, truth be told, most of the brush modes have little effect.

Source image

Healing brush modes

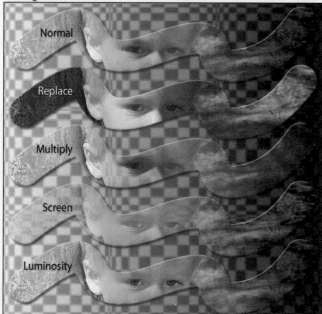

Figure 7-12: Examples of the healing brush combined with five brush modes across a light-to-dark gradient. Due to Photoshop's healing algorithms, many portions of the Multiply brushstroke are lighter than those of the Screen stroke.

Tip

The exception is Replace. Unique to the healing brush, the Replace mode clones pixels without any blending, just as if you were painting with the clone stamp tool set to Normal. The question is, why in the world would you want to do this, particularly when the healing brush set to Replace offers far fewer options than the highly customizable clone stamp tool? The answer is to test effects. Thanks to its blending routine, the healing brush sometimes takes several seconds to apply. But when set to Replace, it takes no time at all. You can test a brushstroke, make sure it's cloning the right area, undo it, switch back to Normal, and paint the real thing. Replace is so useful that it's worth remembering its shortcut, Shift+Alt+Z (Shift-Option-Z on the Mac). Press Shift+Alt+N (Shift-Option-N) to return to Normal.

Other options include the Source buttons, which determine whether the healing brush clones pixels (Sampled) or paints with a predefined texture (Pattern). I explore the Pattern setting in the section "Applying Repeating Patterns," later in this chapter.

You also have the Aligned check box, which aligns multiple brushstrokes to a fixed source point, as described previously in the "Cloning options" section. The Aligned check boxes for the healing brush and clone stamp tools are linked, so selecting one selects the other as well.

Finally, the healing brush lets you clone between different images or layers, but because it requires pixels on the active layer to work, painting on an empty layer produces no results. Also limiting, the healing brush gives you no way to clone from multiple layers at a time. To clone from a composite, you must first merge the layers, as discussed in Chapter 12.

The patch tool

If you prefer to heal a selected area all at once, choose the patch tool from the healing brush flyout menu in the toolbox. You can also press the J key — or if you did not turn off the Use Shift Key for Tool Switch check box in the Preferences dialog box, press Shift+J instead.

You can use the patch tool in one of two ways:

✦ **Define destination, drag onto source:** Assuming the Source option is selected in the Options bar, as by default, use the patch tool to draw an outline around the portion of the image you want to heal. This creates a selection outline. In Figure 7-13, for example, I selected my eyes. Next, drag inside the selection outline to move it to a new location. The middle image in Figure 7-13 finds me dragging the selection over my forehead. The spot at which you release the mouse button determines the source for the clone. When I dropped the selection on my forehead, Photoshop healed the forehead onto my eyes, as the final image in the figure shows.

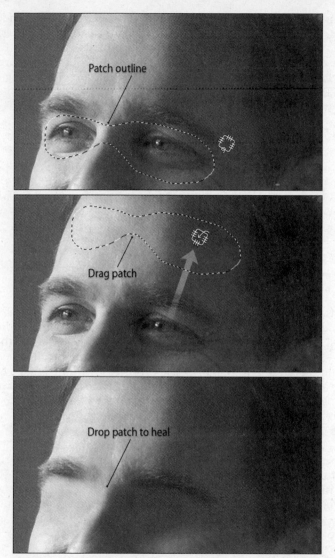

Figure 7-13: Armed with the patch tool, draw a selection outline around the portion of the image you want to heal (top), drag the selection over the clone source (middle), and release to watch the original selection heal away (bottom).

✦ **Define source, drag onto destination:** If dragging the thing you want to heal onto the thing you want to clone seems backwards to you, flip it. Select the Destination radio button in the Options bar. Then use the patch tool to select the portion of the image that you want to clone. Drag the selection over the area you want to heal and release your mouse button.

Insofar as selecting is concerned, the patch tool behaves just like the standard lasso tool. You can add to a selection by Shift-dragging or delete by Alt-dragging (Option-dragging on the Mac). You can even soften a patch using Select ➪ Feather or modify it in the quick mask mode, thus giving the patch tool more room along the edge of the selection to sample colors and shades. And there's nothing that says you have to draw a selection with the patch tool. Feel free to define the selection any way you want, then use the patch tool to move it over the source or destination area. For complete information on creating and editing selections, read Chapter 8, "Selections and Paths."

The patch tool lacks Opacity and brush mode controls, and you can't use it between layers or between different images. All work has to be done on a single layer, which ultimately limits its potential. On the plus side, you can patch a selection with a predefined pattern by clicking the Use Pattern button in the Options bar. The upcoming "Applying Repeating Patterns" section tells more.

Retouching Photographs

Having seen how the clone stamp tool and healing brush work, the following sections examine a few sample uses for the tools. For example, let's say you're confronted by the worst image in the world, shown in Figure 7-14. It's not the subject of the photo that's a problem — that's my son, after all, whom I consider to be beautiful even when shot from a distance of a few inches. Rather the problems with this image are ones of technique. The autofocus locked down a couple of seconds before the shutter release fired, giving my son ample time to rush the camera as he is wont to do. The image was shot to film and then scanned from a 35mm negative, which introduced a wealth of dust particles, hairs, and other fibers.

So the question becomes, what's a person to do when confronted with such an abomination? Naturally, one answer is to reshoot the photo using manual focus if necessary. You might also want to take a moment to clean the glass on your scanner. And come to think of it, I probably would've done well to avoid rubbing the negative in dirt, an extra step I performed to make the image as filthy as possible for purposes of this example.

But let's say none of that is an option. Let's say, my son's all grown up, I lost the original negative, and my scanner blew up and burst into flames. In a nutshell, this is the only picture I have to work with. What am I to do?

After taking a moment to allow that mad feeling of panic to pass, I investigate my tools. And as luck would have it, Photoshop actually offers an automatic function for images such as this. It's called Dust & Scratches, and it's located under the Filter menu in the Noise submenu. Described in more detail in Chapter 10, this filter averages the colors of neighboring pixels with the intent of smearing away imperfections. Unfortunately, as it does so it smears away photographic detail as well. However, in the case of this image, there's not much detail to work with in the first place, so it's not that big of a deal. And so it comes to pass that I apply Dust & Scratches using the settings indicated in the left example of Figure 7-15. In the matter of a few seconds, the filter gets rid of every single dust and scratch in the photo. But in doing so, it gums up a few details more than I would have liked, most notably reducing the size of the pupil and reflected light in my son's eye.

Original dusty, scratchy 35mm negative

Figure 7-14: A very bad photograph, made worse by a bad scanning process. How does one fix such a wretched image inside Photoshop?

Filter ➡ Noise ➡ Dust & Scratches
(Radius: 20 pixels, Threshold: 10 levels)

30 minutes of mind-numbing
manual labor with healing brush
and clone stamp tools

Figure 7-15: I have one of two options with this photo — apply Dust & Scratches, which takes just a few seconds but results in some pretty blobby detail (left), or fix the image manually, which takes forever but produces better results (right).

So being a good father, I undo the automatic fix and set about correcting the photo manually with the healing brush and a bit of clone stamp tool. The healing brush fares well in flat areas of flesh, like the cheeks, nose, and forehead. But it introduces incongruous colors around the lips, eyes, and other edges, which is where I use the clone stamp tool instead. A half hour later, I finally arrive at the image shown on the right side of Figure 7-15. Mind you, I'm kicking myself a little bit because, while the right-hand image is an improvement, it's not what I would call vastly superior. So in purely practical terms, it hardly justifies the effort. Then again, it's a daddy's job to toil away on pointless exercises that his kids will never appreciate, so I feel a warm glow for that.

As a final step, I apply Filter ⇨ Sharpen ⇨ Unsharp Mask (another feature discussed in Chapter 10), which firms up some of the detail to produce the image shown in Figure 7-16.

Figure 7-16: The final touch is to sharpen the image using the Unsharp Mask filter. The result is by no means perfect — Photoshop can't produce detail out of thin air — but it's adorable, and that's good enough for me.

The lesson to draw from all this is that, while Dust & Scratches may suffice for purging fibers and defects from a low-quality photo like this one, it's hardly a professional-level tool. In fact, and I'm going to be painfully blunt here, Dust & Scratches is, generally speaking, a worthless wad of goober-covered tooth decay. In almost all cases, the better alternative is to roll up your sleeves, get real with your image, and fix its flaws manually — not to mention lovingly — with the healing brush and clone stamp tools. You'll be glad you did.

Restoring an old photograph

Dust, hairs, gloops, and other blemishes are introduced during the scanning process. But what about more severe problems that trace back to the original image? Figure 7-17 is a prime example. This photograph was shot sometime before 1910. It's a wonderful photo, but 90 years is a long time for something as fragile and transient as a scrap of paper. It's torn, faded, stained, creased, and flaking. The normally simple act of extracting it from its photo album took every bit as long as scanning it.

Figure 7-17: This photo has seen better days. Then again, I hope to look as good when I'm 90 years old.

But despite the photo's rough condition, I was able to restore it in Photoshop, as evidenced by Figure 7-18. After about an hour and a few hundred brushstrokes, I had the image well in hand. If an hour sounds like a long time to fix a few rips and scrapes, bear in mind that photographic restoration is a labor-intensive activity that relies heavily on your talents and your mastery of Photoshop. The job of the clone stamp and healing brush tools is to make your edits believable, but they do little to automate the process. Retouching calls for a human touch, and that's where you come in.

Figure 7-18: The same image after about an hour of work with the clone stamp tool and healing brush.

The main trick in all this is to Alt-click (Option-click on the Mac) in an area that looks like it'd do a good job of covering up a blemish and then drag over the blemish. Repeat about 250 times, and you're done. So rather than document every single brushstroke — which would be tedious and, I fear, about as enlightening as a day at the box factory — I'll share some advice that specifically addresses the art of photo restoration:

✦ **Toss the bad channels:** Most images in this kind of condition are black-and-white. Scan them in color and then peruse the color channels to see which grayscale version of the image looks best. In my case, the original image had lots of yellow stains around the tears. So when I viewed the individual color channels, as illustrated in Figure 7-19, I was hardly surprised to see dark blotches in the blue channel. (Blue is the opposite of yellow, so where yellow is prominent, the blue channel was dark.) The red channel turned out to be in the best shape, so I switched to the red channel and disposed of the other two by choosing Image ➪ Mode ➪ Grayscale. The simple act of trashing the green and blue channels went a long way toward getting rid of the splotches.

✦ **View actual pixels:** When possible, work at 100 percent view size or larger. It's difficult to judge scratches and other defects accurately at smaller zoom ratios, but if you must, stick with the "smooth views" 50 percent and 25 percent.

✦ **Keep an eye on the source:** Keep the original photo next to you as you work. What looks like a scratch on screen may actually be a photographic element, and what looks like an element may be a scratch. Only by referring to the original image can you be sure.

✦ **Wait to crop:** Don't crop until you're finished retouching the image. You'd be surprised how useful that extra garbage around the perimeter is when it comes to covering up really big tears.

✦ **Vary the brush hardness:** Use hard brush shapes against sharp edges. But when working in general areas such as the shadow, the ground, and the wall, mix it up between soft and hard brushes using the shortcuts Shift+[and Shift+]. Staying random is the best way to avoid harsh transitions, repeating patterns, and other digital giveaways.

✦ **Short is beautiful:** Paint in short strokes. This helps keep things random, but it also means you don't have to redraw a big long brushstroke if you make a mistake.

✦ **Use your history:** When you *do* make a mistake, don't automatically press Ctrl+Z (⌘-Z for you Mac folks). In many cases, you'll be better off using the history brush to paint back the image as it appeared before the last healing brush or clone stamp operation. As luck would have it, I explain more about the history brush in the "Stepping Back through Time," section later in this chapter.

Red channel   Green channel   Blue channel

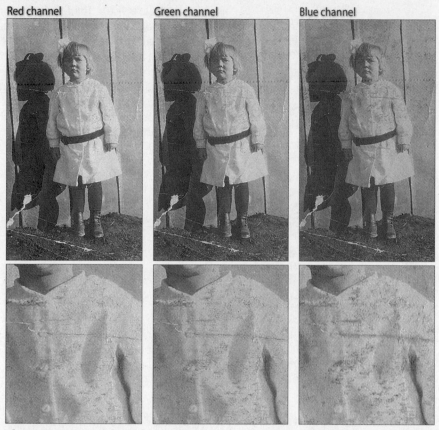

Figure 7-19: A quick peek through the color channels shows the red channel (left) to be my best choice. The blotches are most evident in the girl's blouse, enlarged in the bottom row.

✦ **Turn Aligned off:** Another way to stay random is to change the source of your clone frequently. That means Alt-clicking (Option-clicking) after every second or third brushstroke. And keep the Aligned check box turned off. An aligned clone is not a random one.

✦ **Try out brush modes:** Feel free to experiment with the brush modes and, when using the clone stamp tool, the Opacity setting. For example, magnified in Figure 7-20, the girl has a scratch on the left eye (her right). I corrected this by cloning the right eye with the healing brush, but while the detail looked great, the healing brush over-burned the effect, as in the middle image. To fix this, I set the brush mode for the healing brush to Screen. Then I cloned a bit of the shadowed flesh onto the eye to get the finished effect.

Left eye scratched

Heal right eye onto left

Heal flesh onto left eye, Screen mode

Figure 7-20: The left eye in the original image was scratched (top). I used the healing brush to copy the right eye onto the left (middle), but in trying to match the shadows on the left half of the face, Photoshop took the eye too dark. So I set the brush mode to Screen and healed a little flesh over the eye to even things out (bottom).

Tip

Fade the clone: You also can try applying Edit ➪ Fade to change the opacity and brush mode of the pixels you just cloned. This little trick can be extremely useful when using the healing brush, because it means you can introduce an Opacity value into the proceedings where none existed previously. Curious? After applying a healing brushstroke, choose Edit ➪ Fade or press Ctrl+Shift+F (⌘-Shift-F on the Mac). You get an Opacity value and no Mode option, exactly the opposite of what you see in the Options bar when using the tool.

✦ **Grain is good:** Don't attempt to smooth out the general appearance of grain in the image. Grain is integral to an old photo and hiding it usually makes the image look faked. If your image gets too smooth, or if your cloning results in irregular patterns, select the problem area and apply Filter ➪ Noise ➪ Add Noise. Enter very small Amount values (2 to 6 percent). Monochromatic noise tends to work best. If necessary, press Ctrl+F (⌘-F on the Mac) to reapply the filter one or more times.

With Photoshop's history brush at your side, there's really no way to permanently harm an image. You can even let four or five little mistakes go and then correct them *en masse* with the history brush. Just click to the left of the state in the History palette that directly precedes your first screw-up and then drag with the history brush. It's easy, satisfying, and incredibly freeing. To paint back to the original scanned image, click in front of the very top item in the History palette. For more information, check out "Stepping Back through Time" later in this chapter.

Eliminating distracting background elements

The stamp and healing tools also come in handy for eliminating background action that competes with the central elements in an image. For example, Figure 7-21 shows a nifty news photo from the Reuters image library. Although the image is well-photographed and historic and all that good stuff, that rear workman doesn't contribute anything to the scene; in fact, he draws your attention away from the foreground drama. I mean, hail to the worker and everything, but the image would be better off without him. The following steps explain how I eradicated the offending workman from the scene.

Hey there, you with the bolts in your head

Michael Probst, Reuters

Figure 7-21: You have to love that old Soviet state-endorsed art. So bold, so angular, so politically intolerant. But you also have to lose that rear workman.

Note Remember as you read these steps that cloning away an image element is something of an inexact science. It requires considerable patience and a dash of trial and error. So regard the following steps as an example of how to approach the process of editing your image rather than as a specific procedure that works for all images. You will undoubtedly need to adapt the process to suit the specific needs of your image.

On the other hand, any approach that eliminates an element as big as the workman can also correct the most egregious of photographic flaws, including mold, holes, and fire damage. You can even restore photos that have been ripped into pieces, a particular problem for pictures of ex-boyfriends, current boyfriends, and potential boyfriends of the future. These steps qualify as major reconstructive surgery.

STEPS: Eliminating Distracting Elements from an Image

1. **My first step was to clone the area around the neck of the statue with a soft brush shape.** Abandoning the controlled clicks I recommended in the last section, I permitted myself to drag with the clone stamp tool — which generally fares better than the healing brush for this kind of work — because I needed to cover relatively large portions of the image. The apartment building (or whatever that structure is) behind the floating head is magnificently out of focus, just the thing for hiding any incongruous transitions I might create with the stamp tool. So I warmed up to the image by retouching this area first. Figure 7-22 shows my progress.

   I covered the workman's body by cloning pixels from both his left and right sides. I also added a vertical bar where the workman's right arm used to be to maintain the rhythm of the building. Remember, variety is the key to using the clone stamp tool: If you consistently clone from one portion of the image, you create an obvious repetition the viewer can't help but notice.

2. **The next step was to eliminate the workman's head.** This was a little tricky because it involved rubbing up against the focused perimeter of Lenin's neck. I had to clone some of the more intricate areas using a hard-edged brush. I also ended up duplicating some of the neck edges to maintain continuity. In addition, I touched up the left side of the neck (your left, not Lenin's) and removed a few of the white spots from his face. You see my progress in Figure 7-23.

3. **Now for the hard part: eliminating the worker's legs and lower torso.** See that metal fragment that the foreground worker is holding? What a pain. Its edges were so irregular, there was no way I could restore it if I messed up while trying to eradicate the background worker's limbs. So I lassoed around

the fragment to select it and chose Select ⇨ Inverse to protect it. I also chose Select ⇨ Feather and gave the selection a Radius value of 1 to soften its edges slightly. (The next chapter explains the lasso tool and the Inverse and Feather commands in more detail.) This prevented me from messing up the metal no matter what edits I made to the background worker's remaining body parts.

Clone away rear workman's torso

Figure 7-22: Cloning over the background worker's upper torso was fairly easy. Because the background building is so regular and out of focus, it provided me with a wealth of material from which to clone.

Clone into oblivion rear workman's head

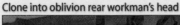

Figure 7-23: I eliminated the workman's head and touched up details around the perimeter of Lenin's neck.

4. **From here on, it was just more cloning.** Unfortunately, I barely had anything from which to clone. See the little bit of black edging between the two "legs" of the metal fragment? That's it. This was all I had to draw the strip of edging to the right of the fragment that eventually appears in Figure 7-24. To pull off this feat, I made sure that the Aligned check box was turned off in Options bar. Then I Alt-clicked (or Option-clicked) on the tiny bit of edging and click-click-clicked my way down the street.

The completed, cropped image

Figure 7-24: After about 45 minutes of monkey-ing around with the clone stamp tool — a practice declared illegal during Stalin's reign — the rear workman is gone, leaving us with an unfettered view of the dubious V. I. Lenin himself.

5. **Unfortunately, the strip I laid down in Step 4 appeared noticeably blobular — it looked for all the world like I clicked a bunch of times.**
Darn. To fix this problem, I clicked and Shift-clicked with the smudge tool set to about 30 percent pressure. This smeared the blobs into a continuous strip but, again, the effect was noticeable. It looked as if I had smeared the strip. So I went back and cloned some more, this time with the Opacity value set to 50 percent.

6. **To polish the image off, I chose Select ⇨ Deselect and ran the sharpen tool along the edges of the metal fragment.** This helped to hide my retouching around it and further distinguished the fragment from the unfocused background. I also cropped away 120 or so pixels from the right side of the image to correct the balance.

What I hope I demonstrated in these steps is this: Cloning with the stamp tool requires you to alternate between patching and whittling away. There are no rights and wrongs, no hard and fast rules. Anything you can find to clone is fair game. As long as you avoid mucking up the foreground image, you can't go wrong (so I guess there is *one* hard and fast rule). If you're careful and diligent, no one but you will notice your alterations.

Any time you edit the contents of a photograph, you tread on sensitive ground. Although some have convincingly argued that electronically retouching an image is, theoretically, no different than cropping a photograph—a technique available and in use since the first daguerreotype—photographers have certain rights under copyright law that cannot be ignored. A photographer may have a reason for including an element you want to eliminate. So, before you edit any photograph, be sure to get permission either from the original photographer or from the copyright holder, as I did for this photo.

Applying Repeating Patterns

The clone stamp tool shares a slot with the pattern stamp tool, which you can get by pressing the S key or Shift+S. Unlike the clone stamp tool, the pattern stamp tool doesn't require you to Alt-click to set a source. Instead, it paints with a repeating pattern that you select from the Pattern pop-up palette in the Options bar, as shown in Figure 7-25. You can use the pattern stamp to create frames, paint wallpaper-type patterns, or retouch patches of grass, dirt, sky, and so on.

Even better for retouching is the healing brush with the Source option set to Pattern, as shown in the bottom half of Figure 7-25. Select the pattern that you want to use from the Pattern pop-up palette. Then paint to merge the texture of the pattern with the colors and shades around the edge of the brushstroke. Again, no Alt-clicking is needed.

You can likewise apply a pattern with the patch tool. To do so, draw a selection with the tool or start with a selection defined earlier. Then select a pattern from the Pattern pop-up palette in the Options bar and click the Use Pattern button. In many ways, the effect is similar to filling a selection with a pattern using the paint bucket or Edit ⇨ Fill (see "Filling Selections with Colors or Patterns," in Chapter 6). The difference is that the patch tool mixes the texture of the pattern with the colors and shades of the pixels around the outside edge of the selection.

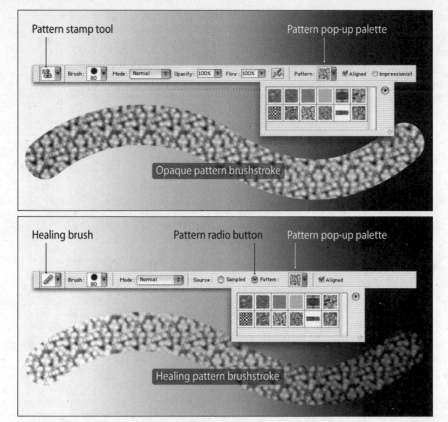

Figure 7-25: Both the stamp tool and the healing brush offer variations for painting with repeating patterns.

Retouching with a pattern

Figure 7-26 begins our look at how and why you might apply a repeating pattern with the healing brush. The figure starts out with my face, free of meteorite craters but rife with a handful of jolly wrinkles. I rather like my wrinkles — they convey a false sense of wisdom — but in the name of higher learning, I will demonstrate how I removed them.

Tip

I first had to establish the neutral noise pattern shown magnified to 700 percent on the right side of Figure 7-26. Combined with the healing brush, this neutral noise pattern allowed me to smooth over imperfections while matching the grain of my image. Given the repeated success I've had with it, I'm guessing it'll work for your images as well.

My semi-wrinkly face
(certain to be wrinklier in future installments)

Enlarged view of neutral noise pattern created
by applying Add Noise at 6% to solid gray

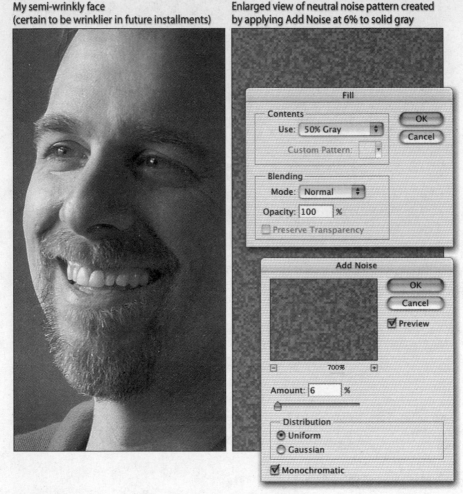

Figure 7-26: The starting point for my face (left) flanked by a 64 by 64-pixel neutral noise pattern magnified to 700 percent view size (right). I created this pattern by filling the image with medium gray and then applying the Add Noise filter with an Amount value of 6 percent and Monochromatic turned on.

I created a new image measuring 64 by 64 pixels. (The exact size isn't important, but 64 by 64 pixels is big enough to hide repetition and small enough to require little processing on the part of Photoshop.) Then I chose Edit ⇨ Fill and set the Use option to 50% Gray. After clicking OK, I chose Filter ⇨ Noise ⇨ Add Noise, entered an Amount value of 6 percent, and selected the Monochromatic check box. This is about the right amount of noise to match the grain in a high-quality photograph.

To turn the gray noise into a pattern, I chose Edit ⇨ Define Pattern. Photoshop asked me to name the pattern, and I called it Neutral Noise 6%.

I was now ready to paint with the pattern using the healing brush. For the sake of demonstration, the first image in Figure 7-27 shows what would have happened if I had applied the Neutral Noise 6% pattern using the pattern stamp tool. This way, you can see every one of the 42 brushstrokes I used to retouch the image. The second image shows what happened when I painted these exact same brushstrokes using the healing brush instead. Photoshop applied the noise to the image and fused together the wrinkles to match the surrounding skin. It may sound too good to be true, but it works like a dream.

Lines painted with pattern stamp tool set to the Neutral Noise 6% pattern

Same lines painted with healing brush, again using the Neutral Noise 6% pattern

Figure 7-27: Here you see what would happen if I used the pattern stamp tool to paint a series of Neutral Noise 6% strokes over the most prominent wrinkles in my semi-craggy semi-young face (left). But I didn't do that. Instead, I painted these exact same brushstrokes using the healing brush. Happily, that's all it took to make my wrinkles go away (right).

At this point, I was having such a grand time that I just kept on painting. Pretty soon, I had painted away everything but my eyes, nose, and mouth. As the first image in Figure 7-28 shows, some might mistake this for overkill, as it pretty much gooed away my world. But creative experiment is never overkill, and every road wandered is worth seeing to the end. So I switched to the burn tool and painted a series of shadows and dark lines. Then I used the dodge tool to lighten my eyes. I also used Filter ➪ Liquify (discussed in Chapter 11) to extend my eyeteeth into fangs. Now you're probably thinking, "That Deke, he's a demon," but for me, it was just a subconscious expression of my state of mind screaming like the devil to get out. I mean, you try writing a 900-page book and see if you don't feel a little possessed at some point in the process.

Of course, there is such
a thing as too much healing.   Or is there?

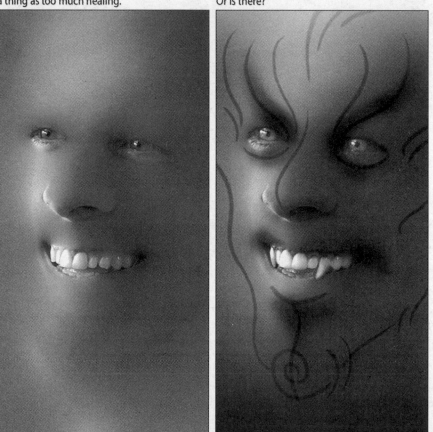

Figure 7-28: With the help of the Neutral Noise 6% pattern, the healing brush becomes a truly effective blur tool (left). Add a few strokes of the burn tool, dab the dodge tool on the eyes, and stretch the fangs, and you have yourself a serviceable netherworld villain (right).

Pattern painting options

The pattern painting tools offer the usual group of settings in the Options bar that we saw when using the clone stamp tool and healing brush. For example, there's the Aligned check box. When turned off, Photoshop begins and ends patterns in different brushstrokes at different locations. This means that the patterns clash when they overlap. In Figure 7-29, I painted a series of strokes using the Optical Checkerboard pattern (one of Photoshop's defaults) and the pattern stamp tool. In the first image, the Aligned option was turned off.

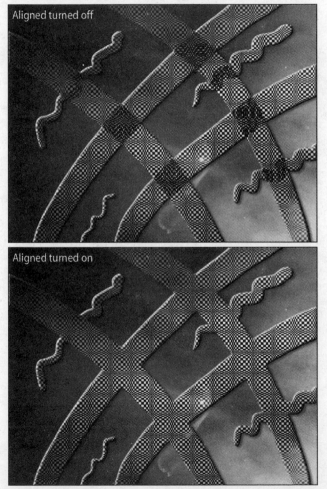

Figure 7-29: If you turn off the Aligned check box, Photoshop starts each pattern with the beginning of the brushstroke (top), so that overlapping brushstrokes clash. Select the Aligned check box to align the patterns in all brushstrokes to match up perfectly (bottom).

If you select the Aligned check box, Photoshop aligns all patterns you apply with the stamp tool, regardless of how many times you start and stop dragging. As in the bottom example in Figure 7-29, all elements in the pattern remain exactly aligned throughout all the brushstrokes.

An option that's utterly unique to the pattern stamp tool is the Impressionist check box. A very old and, I would argue, archaic feature, Impressionist adds an element of color jitter to the brushstroke. If you select the Impressionist check box, the pattern stamp tool paints a series of spots, randomly colored according to colors inside the active pattern. If this sounds peculiar at best and useless at worst, then our minds are as one. Besides, the Color Dynamics options inside the Brushes palette (discussed in Chapter 5) render Impressionist largely redundant.

Creating patterns and textures

Now that you know how to apply patterns, the question becomes, where do you find patterns and how do you go about making your own? The answers, it turns out, are numerous. Artists and designers generally think of Photoshop as an image editor, but it lives a secret life as a frustrated pattern laboratory. Since Version 1, Photoshop has shipped with highly specialized varieties of pattern libraries, and new patterning features are added with just about every upgrade.

The simplest way to access a pattern is from the Options bar. The Pattern option makes itself available when using the healing brush, patch tool, pattern stamp tool, or paint bucket. Click the down-pointing arrowhead to display a pop-up palette of pattern thumbnails, numbering 12 by default, some of which appear in Figure 7-30. You can also access these patterns from the Texture panel of the Brushes palette (as discussed in Chapter 5), by choosing Edit ⇨ Fill (Chapter 6), or by choosing either the Pattern Overlay or Pattern command from one of the icons at the bottom of the Layers palette (see Chapter 14). To restore the default dozen patterns at any time in the future, click the right-pointing arrowhead in the Pattern palette and choose Reset Patterns. To clean out all patterns but the default dozen, click OK. To add the default dozen to your existing patterns (which may result in duplicates), click Append.

Default dozen patterns

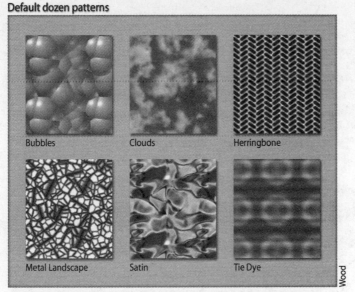

Bubbles   Clouds   Herringbone

Metal Landscape Satin   Tie Dye   Wood

Figure 7-30: Seven samples from the dozen predefined patterns that Photoshop loads by default the first time you launch the program (and thereafter until you make changes). The seventh sample, Wood, appears in the background.

But these dozen are just the beginning. Here are some other ways to access Photoshop's predefined patterns, and create your own:

✦ **Add a preset library:** In all, Photoshop 7 installs a total of seven pattern libraries that you can load at will. With the Pattern pop-up palette visible, click the right-pointing arrowhead to display the palette menu. There at the bottom of the menu are seven options, each of which loads a different library. The library called Patterns comprises the default dozen plus 12 more, so if you choose this option (which I recommend you do), click OK rather than Append to avoid repetition. Most of the other libraries include unique sets of patterns, the exception being the mostly redundant Pattern 2, which calls up patterns that you can find elsewhere. Figure 7-31 shows a few examples.

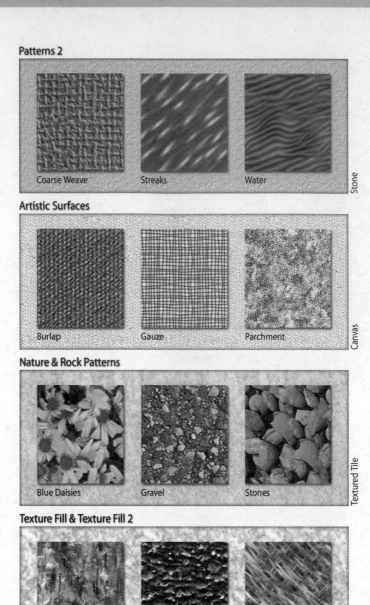

Figure 7-31: A handful of preset patterns from Photoshop's other pattern libraries. To open any one of these patterns, choose its library name from the bottom of the Pattern palette menu.

✦ **Define a pattern tile:** You can save any rectangular area as a tile that will repeat over and over inside a pattern. Just select the area with the rectangular marquee tool — no other tool will do. Then choose Edit ⇨ Define Pattern. Photoshop asks you to name the pattern and then makes it available to all the Pattern pop-up palettes until you delete the pattern or replace the active library with another one. Obviously, not every rectangular selection repeats well, which is why it's so important to know how to design seamless tiles that blend to form continuous patterns, as I explain shortly.

✦ **Load a displacement map:** A *displacement map* is a special kind of pattern that refracts colors inside an image as if you're looking through textured glass. Consider Figure 7-32. In the top row, you see each of three patterns. In the bottom row, you see the demon face from Figure 7-28 as it looks when viewed through each of the patterns expressed as a displacement map. To get one of these effects, choose Filter ⇨ Distort ⇨ Displace and enter the percentage values shown in the figure. Also make sure the Displacement Map option is set to Tile. Then click OK and open one of the pattern files, Cees, Random Strokes, or Schnable Effect. You'll find these patterns as well as nine others inside a folder called Displacement Maps that's inside the Plug-Ins folder, which is inside the same folder as the Photoshop application. Naturally, every one of these images doubles as a repeating pattern. Just open it inside Photoshop and choose Edit ⇨ Define Pattern.

Plug-ins\Displacement maps

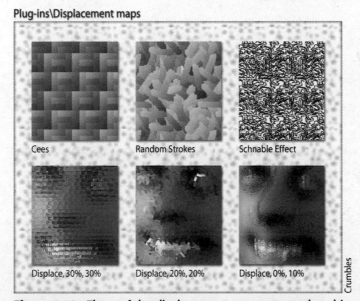

Figure 7-32: Three of the displacement map patterns that ship with Photoshop as they appear when viewed as repeating patterns (top row) and when applied to the demon image using the Displace filter (bottom).

To find still more displacement map patterns, open the folder that contains the Photoshop application file, and then open the Presets folder, the Patterns folder, and finally Adobe ImageReady Only. You'll find 15 images representing Photoshop's dozen default patterns plus three more.

✦ **The Texturizer:** To emboss an image with a pattern file stored on disk, choose Filter ⇨ Texture ⇨ Texturizer, select Load Texture from the Texture pop-up menu, and open one of the pattern files stored in the Displacement Maps or Adobe ImageReady Only folder. For a demonstration of the Texturizer filter, see Figure 11-3 in Chapter 11.

✦ **Illustrator patterns:** If you open the Presets folder, then the Patterns folder, and then the PostScript Patterns folder, you will find more than 40 Adobe Illustrator files that contain pattern tiles. The patterns, some of which appear in Figure 7-33, are all seamless repeaters. Open one of them in Photoshop and rasterize it to any size you like. Then choose Edit ⇨ Define Pattern to convert it to a Photoshop pattern. Notice that two of Photoshop's default dozen, Optical Checkerboard (bottom left in Figure 7-33) and Herringbone, are based on these Illustrator files. This means you can render these patterns at higher resolutions using the Illustrator files that bear the same names. Also notice that some Illustrator files, such as Weave-Y, include transparent areas, permitting you to merge the pattern into underlying image elements.

Presets\Patterns\PostScript Patterns

Blossoms   Diamond-Cubes   Mexican Tile

Optical Checkerboard   Scales   Weave-Y

Flowers 2

Figure 7-33: A random sampling of the Illustrator files included in the PostScript Patterns folder. Every one of these files can be opened inside Photoshop and converted to a repeating pattern.

✦ **Designing patterns with filters:** That's it for Photoshop's predefined patterns, but it's just the beginning of Photoshop's patterning capabilities. Like so many things in the program, you can create your own. And as luck would have it, you can do so without painting a single line. In fact, you can create a nearly infinite variety of background textures by applying several filters to a blank document.

Figure 7-34 presents four examples. Note that none of these textures repeats seamlessly like the pattern tiles we've looked at so far — they're each intended to fill an entire background with very little effort. To create the texture shown in the top row of the figure, I started with a blank image. Then I chose Filter ⇨ Noise ⇨ Add Noise, entered a value of 100 percent, and selected the Monochromatic check box. After clicking OK, I pressed Ctrl+F (⌘-F on the Mac) twice, each time repeating the filter, so that I had applied Add Noise three times in a row. Next, I chose Filter ⇨ Noise ⇨ Median and entered a value of 2 pixels, which averaged the noise into clumps. Finally, I chose Filter ⇨ Stylize ⇨ Emboss and entered 45 degrees in the Angle option box, 2 pixels for the Height value, and 100 percent for the Amount. The result is a bumpy surface that looks a bit like stucco.

To get the second row of effects in Figure 7-34, I started at the point labeled "Add Noise (100%) x 3" in the first row and applied Filter ⇨ Pixelate ⇨ Crystallize with a Cell Size of 20 pixels. Then I blurred the cells using Filter ⇨ Blur ⇨ Gaussian Blur and a Radius of 3 pixels. And finally, I again applied the Add Noise filter, this time at 25 percent, and the Emboss filter, using the same settings as before.

To create the third row of textures, I started with a blank image, pressed the D key to make the foreground and background colors black and white, and chose Filter ⇨ Render ⇨ Clouds. Then I applied Filter ⇨ Render ⇨ Difference Clouds and repeated the filter by pressing Ctrl+F (⌘-F) seven times in a row. In the last image, I once again applied the Emboss filter with an Amount value of 350 percent.

In the fourth row, I took up from the second effect in the third row, the one labeled "Difference Clouds x 8." Then I applied Filter ⇨ Sketch ⇨ Chrome with a Detail value of 4 and a Smoothness setting of 10. Next, I applied Emboss using the same Amount value of 350 percent as before. And finally, deciding I had gone a bit too far, I chose Edit ⇨ Fade Emboss and selected Pin Light from the Mode pop-up menu. This blended the Chrome and Emboss effects into a frothy, plastery soup.

Cross-Reference

Obviously, I could go on like this for days. To learn more about filters so you can make up your own textures, read Chapters 10 and 11. Chapter 10 covers Add Noise, Median, Gaussian Blur, and the Fade command; Chapter 11 talks about Emboss, Crystallize, Clouds, Difference Clouds, and Chrome.

Noise, Median, & Emboss

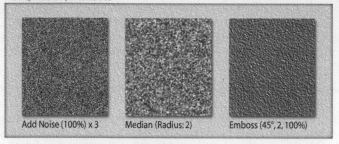

Add Noise (100%) x 3   Median (Radius: 2)   Emboss (45°, 2, 100%)

Noise, Crystallize, GBlur, Noise, & Emboss

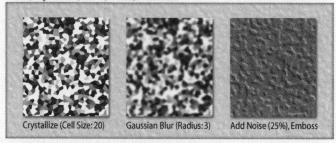

Crystallize (Cell Size: 20)   Gaussian Blur (Radius: 3)   Add Noise (25%), Emboss

Clouds, Difference Clouds, Emboss

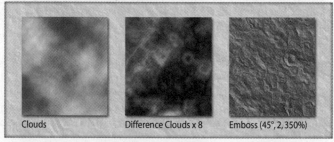

Clouds   Difference Clouds x 8   Emboss (45°, 2, 350%)

Clouds, Difference Clouds, Chrome, Emboss, Fade

Chrome (4, 10)   Emboss (45°, 2, 350%)   Edit ➪ Fade, Pin Light

Figure 7-34: A series of four different background textures created using commands under the Filter menu, including Add Noise, Median, Crystallize, Gaussian Blur, Clouds, Difference Clouds, Chrome, and a heaping helping of Emboss.

✦ **The Pattern Maker:** Photoshop 7's addition to the fine art of patterning is the Pattern Maker under the Filter menu. This command generates repeating tiles at the click of a button and is responsible for most of the patterns I showed back in Figure 7-31. More often than not, it still results is some harsh edges, but if you tough it out, you can get some interesting results. I explain how to use this command in the next section, "Using the Pattern Maker."

✦ **Marquee and clone:** Not happy with any of these solutions? Interested in creating the best seamlessly repeating pattern ever made? Well, it's a fair amount of work, but you can use the rectangular marquee and pattern stamp tools to transform an image into a custom pattern. Because this technique is more complicated as well as more rewarding than the others, I explain it in detail in the section, "Building your own seamless pattern."

Using the Pattern Maker

Located under the Filter menu, the Pattern Maker is a repeating tile generator. It permits you to fill an entire image or layer with a repeating pattern — or even one massive texture — or save a pattern to Photoshop's presets for later use.

Unlike other patterning tools on the market, it does not blur the edges of an image or create reflections to ensure seamless transitions. Rather, it chops an image into random clumps, pieces those clumps together in random formation, and does its best to make a sort of chopped salad of the image so it resembles the sorts of random repetitions you see in the natural world. In most cases, the results are only marginally successful and they often exhibit unacceptably defined edges. But every so often, you get something you can actually use. If that sounds like a backhanded compliment, then bear in mind that the upside is that the Pattern Maker requires very little effort to use. It works like a free slot machine, so even though the odds are against you, you can take as many chances as you like. Just keep pulling the crank and sooner or later, you'll come up with a winner.

Generating a pattern

Start with an image that contains some basic texture like gravel or grass or something else that you'd want to repeat over a large image area. If you don't have such an image, you're in luck — Photoshop has already gone ahead and given you some. Inside the folder that contains the Photoshop 7 application, open the Presets folder, and then open the Textures folder. Inside you should find close to 30 images with names like Leafy Bush and Snake Skin. These are photographic textures provided specifically for use with the Pattern Maker filter. For my part, I opened the image called Yellow Green Chalk.

To give myself room to work, I expanded the canvas size by choosing Image ➪ Canvas Size, turning on the Relative check box, and entering 200 for both the Width and Height options. This way, I'll have space to see my tile repeated a few times and see how it holds up as a pattern.

Next, choose Filter ⇨ Pattern Maker. This displays the commodious dialog box pictured in Figure 7-35. From here, creating a texture is the three-step process outlined in the figure. First, outline the portion of the image upon which you want to base the pattern. (If you prefer, you can select the area before entering the Pattern Maker dialog box. Or copy an image and select the Use Clipboard as Sample check box to base the pattern on that.) Second, click the Generate button to fill the image area with a random repeating pattern. If that looks beautiful, you're in luck. But more likely, it won't look very good and you'll want to click Generate Again. And again. And again. Imagine yourself to be a crazy woodpecker and there's a yummy bug under the Generate Again button. You'll have more fun with it that way.

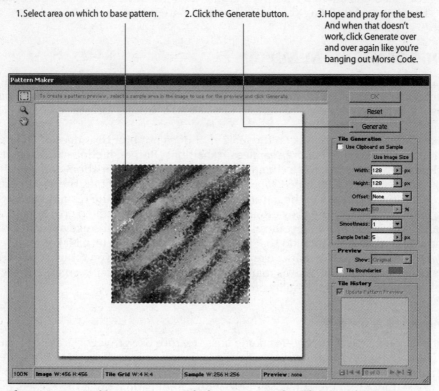

Figure 7-35: Crafting a pattern with the Pattern Maker filter is a three-step process, provided of course that you regard repeatedly clicking the Generate button as a single step.

That's really the gist of it. Some might argue that there's more to using the Pattern Maker than clicking the Generate button like a couch potato searching for a good TV show, but of course they'd be wrong. Still, at the risk of overcomplicating the topic, here are a few things you might want to know:

✦ **Tweaking the settings:** If the filter consistently falls short of spawning a satisfactory effect, you can modify the Tile Generation options — Width, Height, Offset, and so on, all of which I discuss in the following section — then click Generate Again to see what kind of difference your new settings make. You may want to click Generate Again two or three times before giving up on a setting and moving on.

✦ **History is now full:** The Pattern Maker saves your last 20 tiles to a temporary *history buffer* so that you can go back and compare them. After you generate your 20th tile, Photoshop warns you that the history buffer is full. After that point, an old tile drops off into the pit of pattern despair every time you generate a new one.

✦ **Managing your tiles:** Fortunately, you can manage the tiles in the history buffer so you don't lose your best tiles. You do this using the Tile History options in the lower-right corner of the dialog box, magnified in Figure 7-36. So when you get the "History is now full" error message, go down to the Tile History options and browse through the tiles you've created so far by clicking the arrowhead icons. You can also click inside the tile number — 15 of 20, for example — and enter a different tile number. When you come across a bad pattern, click the trash can icon to delete it.

✦ **Saving a tile:** Once you arrive at a tile that you deem satisfactory, don't just click the OK button. Instead, click the little disk icon under the tile preview, labeled *Save pattern* in Figure 7-36. This saves the pattern to Photoshop's presets for later use. In fact, you may want to save several patterns. They take up very little room, so you might as well.

When you're finished and you've saved the pattern or patterns you want to use, click Cancel. Yes, you read that right, click Cancel. Clicking OK fills the entire image or active layer with the pattern, even if you have a selection active, which is almost never what you want. (The one exception occurs when using the Offset option, which only the Pattern Maker supports, as explained in the next section.) With the pattern saved to the presets, you can apply it with more precision using the pattern stamp tool, history brush, Fill command, or other function. So clicking Cancel opens up a wider world of options.

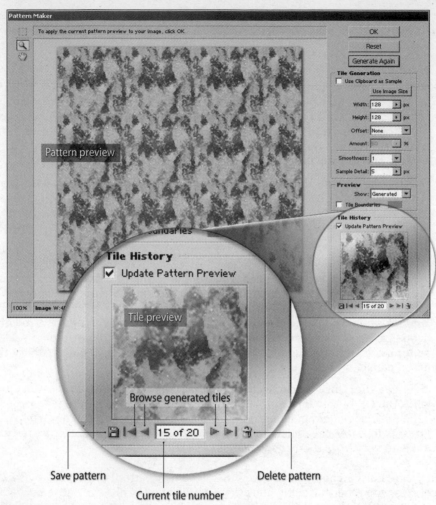

Figure 7-36: The Tile History area lets you peruse the last 20 patterns that you've created. Any time you see a pattern you like, be sure to click the disk icon to save the pattern with Photoshop's presets.

Tile Generation options

The options in the Tile Generation section of the dialog box allow you to change the size of the repeating tile and adjust other parameters that affect how the Pattern Maker calculates patterns. To make a modified setting take effect, you must click the Generate Again button. In order, here's how the options work:

✦ **Use Clipboard as Sample:** When selected, this check box generates the pattern from an image you copied to the Clipboard rather than the selected area in the image window.

✦ **Use Image Size:** Nothing says that you have to generate a repeating tile pattern. You can fill the image with one enormous texture. To do so, click the Use Image Size button to load the size of the foreground image into the Width and Height option boxes. Then click Generate Again. It takes several seconds to generate a very large tile, so be patient.

✦ **Width** and **Height:** By default, the Pattern Maker creates 128 by 128-pixel tiles, a common standard for background patterns inside your computer's operating system and on the Web. However, you can enter any values you like. And they can be different — rectangular tiles are completely acceptable.

✦ **Offset** and **Amount:** Use the Offset option to offset rows or columns of tiles in the final pattern. The Horizontal setting offsets the rows; Vertical offsets the columns. Then use the Amount value to determine the amount of offset, measured as a percentage of the tile dimensions. Figure 7-37 shows the results of applying different Offset options to a single tile. The bottom examples show the same settings, but with tile boundaries visible. To see these boundaries, turn on the Tile Boundaries check box in the Preview area of the dialog box.

Caution

Note that the Offset values only work when you apply the pattern directly from the Pattern Maker by clicking the OK button. The Offset data is not saved with a pattern and cannot be accessed from other pattern functions inside Photoshop.

Offset variations

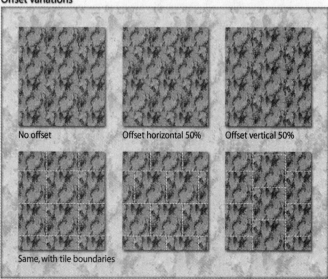

No offset   Offset horizontal 50%   Offset vertical 50%

Same, with tile boundaries

Figure 7-37: Examples of each of the three possible Offset settings, with tile boundaries hidden (top) and visible (bottom).

✦ **Smoothness:** If you keep seeing sharp edges inside your pattern, no matter how many times you regenerate it, try raising the Smoothness value. The value can only vary from 1 to 3, but higher values generally result in smoother transitions.

✦ **Sample Detail:** I mentioned earlier that the Pattern Maker works by chopping up an image and reassembling its parts. The size of those chopped up bits is determined by the Sample Detail value. Very small details result in faster pattern generation, with the potential for more cut lines and harsh transitions. A higher Sample Detail value creates a chunkier pattern, with better detail and more natural transitions, but it takes longer to generate as well. I recommend trying this value at its minimum and maximum settings, 3 and 21, to see if it makes much of a difference. If so, endure the delays and play with the value to get the desired results. If not, crank it down to 5 and focus on the other settings instead.

Bear in mind that, as you work on a pattern, you can zoom in and out of the preview area in the central portion of the dialog box to get a better idea of how the pattern will look. The Pattern Maker provides specific tools for this purpose, but it's generally easiest to rely on the keyboard shortcuts Ctrl+plus and minus (⌘-plus and minus on the Mac).

Building your own seamless pattern

Now don't get me wrong, the Pattern Maker is all very well and good for what it is — that is, a filter that slices your image into a bunch of bacon strips and throws them all over the floor in a big pile. That works for random patterns, but it doesn't work well for regular, smooth transitions between recognizable elements. For example, let's say I want to make a pattern based on the Toltec statue shown at the top of Figure 7-38. If I applied the Pattern Maker to it, I'd get something like the image shown on bottom. If I want to simulate petrified Toltec bacon strips, then that's exactly the kind of effect I want. But I don't. So what do I do?

The following steps describe how to change a scanned image into a seamless, repeating pattern the old-fashioned way — by hand. To illustrate how this process works, Figures 7-39 through 7-42 show various stages in the creation of my Toltec pattern. You need only two tools to carry out these steps: the rectangular marquee tool and the clone stamp tool. And a bit of manual dexterity doesn't hurt.

Cross-Reference

Those of you reading sequentially may notice that these steps involve a few selection and layering techniques I haven't yet discussed. If you become confused, you can find out more about selecting, moving, and cloning images in Chapter 8.

Original image

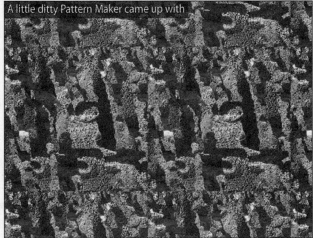

A little ditty Pattern Maker came up with

Figure 7-38: This Toltec statue from ancient Mexico seems a perfect starting point for a repeating pattern (top). But surely I can design something better than what the Pattern Maker comes up with (bottom).

STEPS: Building a Repeating Pattern from an Image

1. **Open the image that you want to convert into a pattern.** I started with the Toltec statue from Figure 7-38. The top one, not the bacon.

2. **Select the rectangular marquee tool.** In the Options bar, select Fixed Size from the Style pop-up menu and enter specific values in the Width and Height option boxes. This way, you can easily reselect a portion of the pattern in the steps that follow, as well as use the fixed-size marquee to define the pattern when you finish. To create the patterns shown in the figures, I set the marquee to 450 by 450 pixels.

3. **Select the portion of the image you want to feature in the pattern.** Because you've specified an exact marquee size, Photoshop selects a fixed area whenever you click. You can drag to move the marquee around in the window.

4. **Press Ctrl+C (⌘-C on the Mac).** This copies the selection to the Clipboard.

5. **Press Ctrl+N (⌘-N on the Mac) to make a new image and triple the Width and Height values.** In my case, Photoshop suggested a new image size of 450 by 450 pixels, which matches the size of the selection I copied to the Clipboard. By tripling these values, I arrived at a new image size of 1350 by 1350 pixels.

6. **Press Ctrl+V (⌘-V on the Mac).** Photoshop pastes the copied selection smack dab in the center of the window, which is exactly where you want it. This image will serve as the central tile of your repeating pattern.

7. **Ctrl-click (⌘-click on the Mac) the item labeled Layer 1 in the Layers palette.** Photoshop pasted the image on a new layer. But to duplicate the image and convert it into a pattern, you need to select it, and the easiest way to do that is to Ctrl-click (or ⌘-click) the layer name to select the pasted pixels.

8. **Press Ctrl+E (⌘-E on the Mac).** This merges the layer with the background, thereby flattening it. Or you can choose Layer ⇨ Flatten Image. Either way, the selection outline remains intact.

9. **Choose Edit ⇨ Define Pattern.** This establishes the selected image as a pattern tile. Give the pattern a name when Photoshop prompts you.

10. **Press Ctrl+D (⌘-D on the Mac) to deselect the image.** You neither need nor want the selection outline any more. You'll need to be able to fill and clone freely without a selection outline getting in the way.

11. **Press Shift+Backspace (Shift-Delete on the Mac) or choose Edit ⇨ Fill.** Then select Pattern from the Use pop-up menu, select your new pattern from the Custom Pattern palette, and press Enter or Return. This fills the window with a 3 by 3-tile grid, as shown in Figure 7-39.

12. **Drag the title bar of the new image window to position it so you can see the portion of the image you copied in the original image window.** You want to be able to see both images at once, because you'll be cloning from one into the other. After you have your windows arranged, click the title bar of the new image, the one in Figure 7-39, to make it the active window.

13. **Select the clone stamp tool.** Press the S key, or press S twice if the pattern stamp tool is active.

14. **Turn off the Aligned check box in the Options bar.** Ironic as it may sound, it's easier to get the alignment between the clone-from and clone-to points established with Aligned turned off.

15. **Specify the image you want to clone by pressing Alt (Option on the Mac) and clicking in the original image window.** No need to switch out of the

new window. Alt-click (or Option-click) an easily identifiable pixel that belongs to the portion of the image you copied. The exact pixel you click is very important. In my case, I clicked the corner of the Toltec statue's mouth.

Figure 7-39: To build the repeating pattern shown in Figure 7-42, I started by creating a grid of nine image tiles. As you can see, the seams between the tiles are harsh and unacceptable.

16. **Now click with the stamp tool on the matching pixel in the central tile of the new window.** If you clicked the correct pixel, the tile should not change one iota. If it shifts at all, press Ctrl+Z (⌘-Z on the Mac) and try again. Because Aligned is turned off, you can keep undoing and clicking over and over again without resetting the clone-from point in the original image.

17. **Turn on the Aligned check box.** After you click in the image without seeing any shift, select the Aligned option to lock in the alignment between the clone-from and clone-to points.

18. **Use the stamp tool to fill in portions of the central tile.** For example, in Figure 7-40, I extended the Toltec statue's face outward both to the left and to the right. I also extended his headdress upward into the upper Toltec's neck.

Figure 7-40: I used the clone stamp tool to copy pixels from the original image into the central tile, extending the statue's headdress and jaw line.

19. **Select a portion of the modified image.** After you establish one continuous transition between two tiles in any direction — up, down, left, or right — click with the rectangular marquee tool to select an area that includes the transition. In my case, I decided my best transitions were between the central and top tiles. Therefore, I selected a region that includes half the central tile and half the tile above it.

20. **Repeat Steps 9 through 11.** That is, choose Edit ⇨ Define Pattern, press Ctrl+D (or ⌘-D), choose Edit ⇨ Fill, select the pattern you just defined, and press Enter or Return. This fills the image with your new transition. Don't worry if the tiles shift around a bit — that's to be expected.

21. **If you started by creating a vertical transition, use the clone stamp tool to create a horizontal transition.** Likewise, if you started horizontally, now go vertically. You'll need to turn off the Aligned check box again to establish the proper alignment between clone-from and clone-to points. In my case, I shifted the clone-to point several times — alternatively building on the central statue, the one to the left of it, and the one directly above. Each time you get the clone-to point properly positioned, turn the Aligned check box back on to lock in the alignment. Then clone away.

Note

As long as you get the clone-from and clone-to points properly aligned, you can't make a mistake. If you change your mind, realign the clone points and try again. In my case, I cloned the left side of the headdress into the cheek of the head to the left. I also cloned the bottom-left edge of the headdress from the statue above, ultimately achieving the effect shown in Figure 7-41.

Figure 7-41: After completing a smooth transition between the upper central tile and the tiles above and to the left of it, I selected a portion of the image and chose Edit ⇨ Define Pattern.

22. **After you build up one set of both horizontal and vertical transitions, click with the rectangular marquee tool to select the transitions.** Figure 7-41 shows where I positioned my 450 by 450-pixel selection boundary. This includes parts of each of four neighboring heads, mostly focusing on the horizontal transition. Don't worry if the image doesn't appear centered inside the selection. What counts is that the image flows seamlessly inside the selection outline.

23. **Repeat Steps 9 through 11 again.** If the tiles blend together seamlessly, as in Figure 7-42, you're finished. If not, clone some more with the clone stamp tool and try again.

Figure 7-42: This south-of-the-border montage is the result of applying the finished Toltec pattern with the Fill command. The result is a solid wall of Toltec totems.

Stepping Back through Time

Since roughly the dawn of recorded time, folks begged, pleaded, and screamed at the top of their lungs for multiple undos in Photoshop. But it wasn't until Photoshop 5 that Adobe delivered what the masses craved. The payoff for the long wait was huge: Version 5 offered up the History palette, which remains the best implementation of multiple undos I've seen to this day.

Moving beyond simple backstepping, the History palette takes the whole reversion metaphor into *Slaughterhouse Five* territory. If you've never read the novel (or you've somehow forgotten), Kurt Vonnegut, Jr. suggested that humans live from one moment to the next like a person strapped to a boxcar, unable to change the speed or direction of the train as it hurtles through time. In most programs that offer multiple undos, you can make the train stop and back up, but you're still strapped to it. The History palette is the first tool that lets you get off the train and transport to any point on the track—instantaneously. In short, we now have a digital version of time travel.

Here are just a few of the marvelous innovations of the History palette:

✦ **Undo-independent stepping:** Step backward by pressing Ctrl+Alt+Z (⌘-Option-Z on the Mac); step forward by pressing Ctrl+Shift+Z (⌘-Shift-Z). Every program with multiple undos does this, but Photoshop's default keyboard equivalents are different. Why? Because you can backstep independently of the Undo command, so that even backstepping is undoable.

As discussed in Chapter 2, Photoshop lets you change the keys assigned to the step forward, step backward, and Undo/Redo actions. Press Ctrl+K (Win) or ⌘-K (Mac) to open the Preferences dialog box and then look for the Redo Key pop-up menu. While it might be tempting to change the forward and backstepping operations so they better match other programs, I personally consider it a mistake because, simply put, Photoshop does it better.

The shortcuts that I mention in this book assume that you leave the Redo Key option set to the default, which makes Ctrl+Z (⌘-Z on the Mac) the shortcut to toggle between the Undo and Redo commands.

✦ **Before and after:** Revert to a point in history to see a "before" view of your image and then fly forward to see the "after" view. From then on, Ctrl+Z (⌘-Z on the Mac) becomes a super-undo, toggling between the before and after views. The opportunities for comparing states and changing your mind are truly colossal.

✦ **Dynamic time travel:** If before and after aren't enough, how about animated history? You can drag a control to slide dynamically forward and backward through operations. It's as if you recorded the operations to videotape, and now you're rewinding and fast-forwarding through them.

✦ **Sweeping away the mistakes:** Select a point in the history of your image and paint back to it using the history brush. You can let the mistakes pile up and then brush them away. This brush isn't a paintbrush; it's a hand broom. Want even more variety? Use the art history brush to paint back to the image using various artistic styles.

✦ **Take a picture, it'll last longer:** You can save any point in the History palette as a snapshot. That way, even several hundred operations after that point in history are long gone, you can revisit the snapshot.

✦ **This is your life, Image A:** Each and every image has its own history. So after performing a few hundred operations on Image A, you can still go back to Image B and backstep through operations you performed hours ago. The caveat is that the history remains available only as long as an image is open. Close the image, and its history goes away.

✦ **Undo the Revert command:** Back in the days before Photoshop 5.5, you couldn't undo the Revert command. Now, the History palette tracks Revert. So if you don't like the image that was last saved to disk, you can undo the reversion and get back to where you were. Also notice that when you choose File ⇨ Revert, Photoshop does not ask you to confirm the reversion. There's no reason for a warning because Revert is fully undoable.

The only thing you can't do through the History palette is travel forward into the future — say, to about three days from now when you've finished your grueling project, submitted it to your client, and received your big fat paycheck. Believe it or not, that's actually good news. The day Adobe can figure out how to do your work for you, your clients will hire Photoshop and stop hiring you.

So I ask you — Photoshop, *Slaughterhouse Five*, just a coincidence? Well, yes, I suppose it is. But the fact remains, you have the option of getting off the boxcar. How you make use of your freedom is up to you.

Using the traditional undo functions

Before I dive into the History palette, I should take a moment to summarize Photoshop's more traditional reversion functions. (If you already know about this stuff, skip to the next section.)

✦ **Undo:** To restore an image to the way it looked before the last operation, choose Edit ➪ Undo or press Ctrl+Z (⌘-Z on the Mac). You can undo the effect of a paint or edit tool, a change made to a selection outline, or a special-effect or color-correction command. You can't undo disk operations, such as opening or saving. Photoshop does enable you to undo an edit after printing an image, though. You can test an effect, print the image, and then undo the effect if you think it looks awful. But to perform such an undo, you have to press Ctrl+Alt+Z (⌘-Option-Z on the Mac) to backstep through history.

✦ **Revert:** Choose File ➪ Revert to reload an image from disk. In most programs, this is the last-resort function, the command you choose after everything else has failed. But in Photoshop, it's a very useful tool. Forget what the image looked like last time you saved it? Choose the Revert command. Don't like it? Press Ctrl+Z (⌘-Z on the Mac) to undo it. That's right, you can undo a reversion — what'll they think of next?

To restore the image to the way it looked when you originally opened it — which may precede the last-saved state — scroll to the top of the History palette and click the topmost item. (This assumes that you haven't turned off the Automatically Create First Snapshot check box in the History Options dialog box.)

✦ **Selective reversion:** To revert a selected area to the way it appeared when it was first opened — or some other source state identified in the History palette — choose Edit ➪ Fill or press Shift+Backspace (Shift-Delete on the Mac). Then select History from the Use pop-up menu and press Enter or Return.

Better yet, just press Ctrl+Alt+Backspace (⌘-Option-Delete on the Mac). This one keystroke fills the selection with the source state in a jiffy. Either way, you set the source state for the reversion by clicking in the left column of the History palette, as I explain in the very next section.

✦ **The erasers:** Drag in the background layer with the eraser tool to paint in the background color. You're essentially erasing the image back to bare canvas. Or apply the eraser to a layer to delete pixels and expose underlying layers.

Tip You can also Alt-drag (Option-drag on the Mac) with the eraser to revert to the targeted state in the History palette. Or select Erase to History in the Options bar and just drag. But you're better off using the history brush for this purpose. The history brush offers more capabilities, including most notably brush modes.

Where warranted, I explain these functions in greater detail in the following sections. But first, the next few paragraphs look at the central headquarters for reversion in Photoshop, the History palette.

The History palette

Choose Window ⇨ History to view the History palette, annotated with the palette menu in full view in Figure 7-43. The History palette records each significant operation — everything other than settings and preferences (for example, selecting a new foreground color) — and adds it to a list. The oldest operations appear at the top of the list with the most recent operations at the bottom.

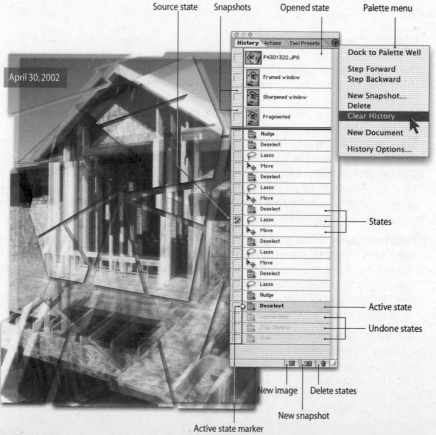

Figure 7-43: The History palette records each significant event as an independent state. To return to a state, just click on it.

Each item in the list is called a *state*. That's not my word, it's Adobe's, and several have voiced the opinion that the term is too stiff and formal. But I think it's dead on. Each item in the palette represents a stepping-stone in the progression of the image, a condition at a moment in time—in other words, a state.

Photoshop automatically names each item according to the tool, command, or operation used to arrive at the state. The icon next to the name helps to identify the state further. But the best way to find out what a state is like is to click it. Photoshop instantaneously undoes all operations performed after that state and returns you to the state so that you can inspect it in detail. To redo all the operations you just did in one fell swoop, press Ctrl+Z (⌘-Z on the Mac) or choose Edit ⇨ Undo State Change.

That one action—clicking on a state—is the gist of what you need to know to travel forward and backward through time in Photoshop. If that's all you ever learn, you'll find yourself working with greater speed, freedom, and security than is possible in virtually any other graphics application. But this represents only the first in a long list of the History palette's capabilities. Here's the rest of what you might want to know:

✦ **Changing the number of undos:** By default, Photoshop records the last 20 operations in the History palette. When you perform the 21st operation, the first state is shoved off the list. To change this behavior, choose Edit ⇨ Preferences ⇨ General or press Ctrl+K (⌘-K on the Mac), which opens the Preferences dialog box, then enter your preferred number of undoable operations in the History States option box. If your computer is equipped with 128MB or less of RAM, you might want to lower the value to 5 or 10 to maintain greater efficiency. On the other hand, if you become a time-traveling freak (like me) and have plenty of RAM—say, 1GB or more—turn it up, baby. Should you be so inclined, the History palette can hold up to 1,000 states. That's probably more than you want to use—after all, some states take up an awful lot of memory—but when working on a single image, 100 states may on rare occasions be comfortable.

✦ **Undone states:** When you revert to a state by clicking on it, every subsequent state turns gray to show that it's been undone. You can redo a grayed state simply by clicking on it. But if you perform a new operation, all grayed states disappear. You have one opportunity to bring them back by pressing Ctrl+Z (⌘-Z); if you perform another new operation, the once-grayed states are gone for good. For an exception to this behavior, see the very next paragraph.

✦ **Working with non-sequential states:** If you don't like the idea of losing your undone states—every state is sacred, after all—choose the History Options command in the palette menu and select the Allow Non-Linear History check box (see Figure 7-44). Undone states no longer drop off the list when you perform a new operation. They remain available on the off chance that you might want to revisit them. It's like having multiple possible time trails.

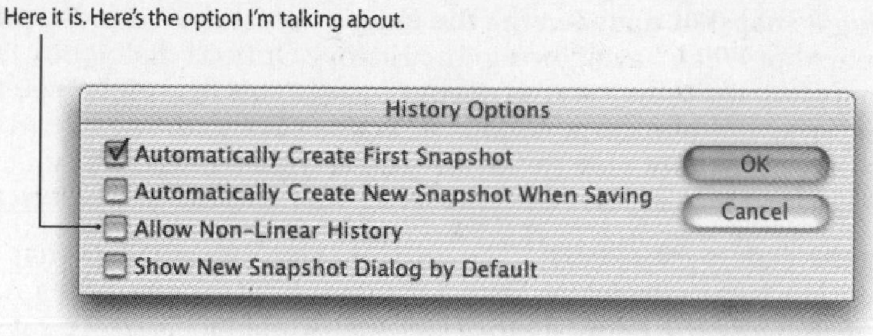

Here it is. Here's the option I'm talking about.

History Options

☑ Automatically Create First Snapshot

☐ Automatically Create New Snapshot When Saving

☐ Allow Non-Linear History

☐ Show New Snapshot Dialog by Default

OK

Cancel

Figure 7-44: Choose History Options from the History palette menu and select Allow Non-Linear History to permit Photoshop to keep states that you have undone.

Note

The Allow Non-Linear History check box does not permit you to undo a single state without affecting the subsequent states. For example, let's say you paint with the airbrush, smear with the smudge tool, and then clone with the clone stamp. You can revert back to the airbrush state and then apply other operations without losing the option of restoring the smudge and clone. But you can't undo the smudge and leave the clone intact. Operations can only occur in the sequence they were applied.

✦ **Stepping through states:** As I mentioned earlier, you can press Ctrl+Alt+Z (⌘-Option-Z) to undo the active step or Ctrl+Shift+Z (⌘-Shift-Z) to redo the next step in the list. Backstepping goes up the list of states in the History palette; forward stepping goes down. So bear in mind that if the Allow Non-Linear History check box is active, backstepping may take you to a state that was previously inactive.

✦ **Flying through states:** Drag the right-pointing active state marker (labeled in Figure 7-43) up and down the list to rewind and fast-forward, respectively, through time. If the screen image doesn't appear to change as you fly by certain states, it most likely means those states involve small brushstrokes or changes to selection outlines. Otherwise, the changes are quite apparent.

✦ **Taking a snapshot:** Every once in a while, a state comes along that's so great, you don't want it to fall by the wayside 20 operations from now. To set a state aside, choose New Snapshot or click the little page icon at the bottom of the History palette. To rename a snapshot after you create it, just double-click on its name at the top of the History palette and enter a new one. Or you can name a snapshot as you create it by pressing the Alt key (or Option on the Mac), clicking the little page icon, and entering a name in the dialog box.

Photoshop lets you store as many snapshots as your computer's RAM permits. Also worth noting, the program automatically creates a snapshot of the image as it appears when it's first opened. If you don't like this opening snapshot, you can change this behavior by turning off Automatically Create First Snapshot inside the History Options dialog box.

✦ **Creating a snapshot upon saving the image:** Select the Automatically Create New Snapshot When Saving box in the History Options dialog box to create a new snapshot every time you save your image. This is useful if you find yourself venturing down uncertain roads from one save to the next, and want the ability to backstep not only to the last saved state (which you can do by choosing File ➪ Revert), but the one before that and the one before that.

✦ **Saving the state permanently:** The problem with snapshots is that they last only as long as the current session. If you quit Photoshop or the program crashes, you lose the entire history list, snapshots included. To save a state so you can refer to it several days from now, choose the New Document command or click the leftmost icon at the bottom of the History palette. You can also drag and drop a state onto the icon. Either way, Photoshop duplicates the state to a new image window. Then you can save the state to the format of your choice.

✦ **Setting the source:** Click to the left of a state to identify it as the *source state*. The history brush icon appears where you click. The source state affects the performance of the history brush, art history brush, Fill command, and eraser, if you select Erase to History. The keystroke Ctrl+Alt+Backspace (⌘-Option-Delete on the Mac) fills a selection with the source state.

✦ **Trashing states:** If your machine is equipped with little RAM or you're working on a particularly large image, Photoshop may slow down as the states accumulate. If it gets too slow, you may want to purge the History palette. To delete any state as well as those before it, drag the state to the trash icon at the bottom of the palette. Your image updates accordingly. If the Allow Non-Linear History check box is on, clicking the trash can deletes just the active state.

Tip

To clear all states from the History palette, choose the Clear History command from the palette menu. This doesn't immediately empty the RAM, just in case you change your mind and decide you want to undo. After you perform another operation, only then does Photoshop purge the memory for real. If you want the memory emptied right away — and you're *positive* that you have no desire whatsoever to undo — press the Alt key (Option on the Mac) and choose the Clear History command. And if you're really hankering to purge, choose Edit ➪ Purge ➪ Histories — this gets rid of *all* states for *all* open documents.

Painting away the past

The History palette represents the regimental way to revert images inside Photoshop. You can retreat, march forward, proceed in linear or non-linear formation, capture states, and retire them. Every state plays backward in the same way it played forward. It's precise, predictable, and positively by the book.

But what if you want to get free-form? What if you want to brush away the present and paint in the past? In that case, a palette isn't going to do you any good. What you need is a pliable, emancipated, free-wheeling tool.

As luck would have it, Photoshop offers three candidates — the eraser, the history brush, and the art history brush. The eraser washes away pixels to reveal underlying pixels or exposed canvas. The history brush takes you back to a kinder, simpler state; the art history brush does the same but enables you to paint using special artistic effects. Although the functions of these tools overlap slightly, they each have a very specific purpose, as becomes clear in the following sections.

As you work with any of these tools, remember that you can use the Edit ➪ Fade command to blend the altered pixels with the originals, just as you can when applying a filter. You can adjust both the opacity and blend mode of the erased or painted pixels. Chapter 17 explores the Fade command in detail.

The eraser tool

When you work with the eraser, you can select from three eraser styles, all available from the Mode pop-up menu in the Options bar, pictured in Figure 7-45. These are Brush, Pencil, and Block. Block is the ancient 16×16-pixel square eraser that's great for hard-edged touch-ups. The other options work exactly like the tools for which they're named.

In addition to the Mode settings, the Options bar provides access to the Brush option, the Opacity and Flow values, and the airbrush icon, all of which work as described in Chapter 5. All options are available when using the Brush-style eraser, none are applicable to the Block style, and Flow and airbrush dim when painting with a Pencil-style eraser.

Figure 7-45: When the eraser is selected, the Mode pop-up menu offers a choice of eraser styles rather than the brush modes available to the painting and editing tools.

Although the eraser is pretty straightforward, there's no sense in leaving any stone unturned. So here's everything you ever wanted to know about the art of erasing:

✦ **Erasing on a layer:** When you're working on the Background layer, the eraser merely paints in the background color. Big whoop. What distinguishes the eraser tool from the other brushes is layers. If you drag on a layer and deselect the Lock buttons for transparency and image pixels in the Layers palette, the eraser tool removes paint and exposes portions of the underlying image. The eraser tool suddenly performs like a real eraser.

If you select the transparency Lock button in the Layers palette, Photoshop won't let the eraser bore holes in the layer or alter areas that are already transparent. Instead, the eraser paints opaque pixels in the background color. If you select the option for locking image pixels, you can't erase or paint any part of the layer. For more information on locking layers, see Chapter 12.

✦ **Erasing lightly:** Change the Opacity setting in the Options bar to make portions of a layer translucent in inverse proportion to the Opacity value. For example, if you set the Opacity to 90 percent, you remove 90 percent of the opacity from the layer and, therefore, leave 10 percent of the opacity behind. The result is a nearly transparent stroke through the layer.

✦ **Erasing versus using layer masks:** As described in the "Creating layer-specific masks" section of Chapter 12, you can also erase holes in a layer using a layer mask. But unlike the eraser—which eliminates pixels for good—a layer mask doesn't do any permanent damage. On the other hand, using the eraser tool doesn't increase the size of your image as much as a layer mask does. (You can argue that *any* operation—even a deletion—increases the size of the image in RAM because the History palette has to track it. But even so, the eraser remains more memory-efficient than a layer mask.) So it's a trade-off.

✦ **Erasing with the pencil:** When you work with the pencil tool—not the Pencil mode but the actual pencil tool—Photoshop presents you with an Auto Erase check box in the Options bar. Turn it on to draw in the background color any time you click or drag on a pixel that is already colored in the foreground color. This technique can be useful when you're drawing a line against a plain background. Set the foreground color to the color of the line; set the background color to the color of the background. Then use the pencil tool to draw and erase the line until you get it just right. I use this feature all the time when preparing screen shots. Adobe engineers once called the Auto Erase check box their "ode to Fatbits," from the ancient MacPaint zoom function.

Unlike the eraser, the pencil tool always draws either in the foreground or background color, even when used on a layer.

✦ **Erasing to history:** Press Alt (Option on the Mac) as you drag with the eraser to paint with the source state identified by the history brush icon in the History palette. It's like scraping away the paint laid down by the operations following the source state. For example, in Figure 7-46, I used the rectangular marquee tool along with the eraser to paint a frame around a frame job inside this picture of a picture window. I began by creating a new layer and then selecting various rectangular areas and filling them with black or gray. In the second image, I selected a few more areas and filled them with white. At this point, however, I decided the white was too garish and elected to erase portions of it away using history. I clicked in front of the last state before I added the white to make it the source state. Then I pressed Alt (or Option) and painted with the eraser to erase through the white rectangles while leaving the black and gray rectangles unchanged.

Figure 7-46: I created a geometric frame by selecting areas with the rectangular marquee tool and filling them with black or gray (left). Then I added a series of white rectangles (middle). By identifying the state just before the first white rectangle as the source state, I was then able to use the history eraser function to erase away the white and leave the black and gray unharmed.

Instead of pressing Alt, you can select the Erase to History check box in the Options bar. In this case, dragging with the eraser reverts and Alt-dragging (Option-dragging on the Mac) paints in the background color or erases away the active layer.

Note

In the old days, folks used the term "magic eraser" to mean the eraser set to the revert mode. But when Photoshop 5.5 introduced the official magic eraser, which deletes a range of similarly colored pixels each time you click in the image window (see Chapter 9), this use of the term died away. So the old magic eraser is the modern history eraser — don't you dare get the two confused.

The history brush

Painting with the history brush tool — which you can select from the keyboard by pressing the Y key — is like painting with the eraser when Erase to History is turned on. Just drag with the history brush to selectively revert to the source state targeted in the History palette. You also can vary the translucency of your strokes using the Opacity setting in the Options bar. But that's where the similarities end. Unlike the part-time history eraser, the dedicated history brush lets you take advantage of brush modes. By choosing a different brush mode from the Mode pop-up menu in the Options bar, you can mix pixels from the changed and saved images to achieve interesting and sometimes surprising, effects.

I advise you to get in the habit of using the history brush instead of using the eraser's Erase to History function. Granted, with Pencil and Block, the eraser offers more styles. But when weighed against brush modes, these styles aren't much of an advantage. The history brush is also more intuitive because its icon matches the source state icon in the History palette.

Tip

As you play with the history brush, keep in mind that you don't have to limit yourself to painting into the past. Just as the History palette lets you skip back and forth along the train track of time, the history brush lets you paint to any point in time. The following steps provide an example of how you can use the History palette to establish an alternative reality and then follow up with the history brush to merge that reality with the present. It can be a lot to keep track of, but I'm confident that with a little effort, you can give that post-modern brain of yours a half twist and wrap it around these steps like a big, mushy Möbius strip.

STEPS: Brushing to a Parallel Time Line

1. **Open the image you want to warp into the fourth dimension.** I began with an embellished map of Japan shown in Figure 7-47. Japan is a wacky combination of 17th-century cultural uniformity, 1950's innocence, and 21st-century corporate imperialism, so it struck me as a perfect subject for my compound-time experiment.

Figure 7-47: I created this image by compositing a stock art image of Japan against a soft cloud background.

2. **Apply a couple of filters.** I chose Filter ⇨ Pixelate ⇨ Mosaic and set the Cell Size value to 20 pixels. Then I applied Filter ⇨ Stylize ⇨ Emboss with a Height of 5 pixels and an Amount of 200 percent. Figure 7-48 shows the results of each.

Filter ⇨ Pixelate ⇨ Mosaic (Cell Size: 20)   Filter ⇨ Stylize ⇨ Emboss (45°, 5 pixels, 200%)

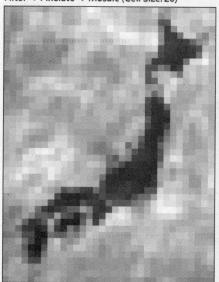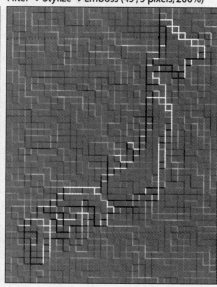

Figure 7-48: The results of applying the Mosaic (left) and Emboss (right) filters. Both effects are overstated, so I decided to undo them and then paint them back in with the history brush.

3. **Choose the History Options command from the History palette menu.** Then turn on the Allow Non-Linear History check box and press Enter or Return.

4. **Click the Open item in the History palette.** This reverts the image to the state at which it existed when you first opened it. But thanks to non-linear history, Photoshop retains the filtered versions of the image just in case you'd like to revisit this timeline in the future.

5. **Click in front of the first filter effect in the History palette to make it the source state.** In my case, I clicked in front of the Mosaic item.

6. **Select the history brush and start painting.** As you do, you'll paint with the filtered version of the image. For my part, I set the blend mode to Darken and painted around the island country to give it a chunky digital edge, as in the first example of Figure 7-49.

Source state: Mosaic, brush mode: Darken   Source state: Emboss, brush mode: Overlay

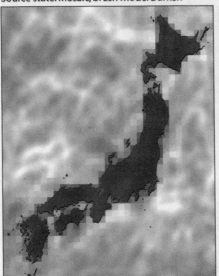 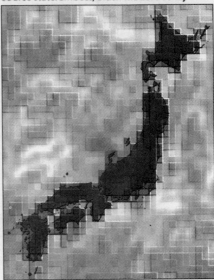

Figure 7-49: Having restored the unfiltered version of the image, I set the brush mode to Darken and painted in the Mosaic state with the history brush (left). Then I changed the brush mode to Overlay and brushed in the Emboss state (right).

7. **Switch the source state by clicking in front of the second filter effect.** Naturally, I clicked in front of the Emboss item.

8. **Paint again with the history brush.** This time, I changed the brush mode to Overlay and painted randomly over Japan and the surrounding ocean. The result appears in the second example of Figure 7-49.

After you finish, you can toss the filtered states. This alternate timeline has served its purpose. Or keep it around as a snapshot to come back to later.

The art history brush

The art history brush lets you create impressionistic effects with the aid of the History palette. To get a sense for how it works, open any old file. Me, I opened the simple still life featured in Figure 7-50. Press D to get the default foreground and background colors, select the standard brush tool, and paint willy nilly all over your image. That's right, make a total mess of it, as I did in the first example in Figure 7-51. You think it's ruined? Ah ha, but it is not. It is now ready for you to turn into an impressionistic masterpiece.

Figure 7-50: A simple still life that I shot a few years back using what was then a state-of-the-art digital camera, but is now considered so low-res, it makes the digital angels cry.

Select the art history brush, which shares a flyout menu and keyboard shortcut (Y) with the history brush. Bring up the History palette and make sure the first snapshot is identified as the source state (assuming that you haven't made any unauthorized changes to the image since you opened it). Now paint inside your black image. Each stroke reveals a bit of your original photograph in painterly detail, as illustrated in the second image in Figure 7-51.

Tip

Hoping to punch home the effect a little more? Well, you're in luck, because I have just the recipe. First, choose Filter ➪ Distort ➪ Displace, enter 10 percent for both of the Scale values, select the Tile radio button, click OK, and load the Random Strokes pattern (discussed in the section "Creating patterns and textures" earlier in this chapter). Photoshop adds a little bit of extra brushwork, as in the first example of Figure 7-52. Next, choose Filter ➪ Texture ➪ Texturizer, select the Canvas texture, and fiddle with the Scaling and Relief options to get the desired effect. Regardless of your settings, you'll get a painted canvas look, as shown on the right side of Figure 7-52. If that's not art, then my name's not Dekebrandt McVinci.

Scribble a bunch of black with the brush tool   Restore original image using art history brush

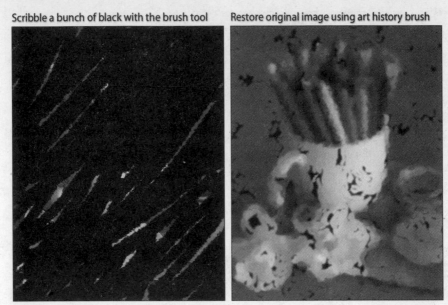

Figure 7-51: After painting a random series of black brushstrokes all over my image (left), I selected the art history brush and painted in a rough translation of the original (right).

Displace (10%, 10%, Random Strokes)   Texturizer (Canvas, 140%, 5, Top Left)

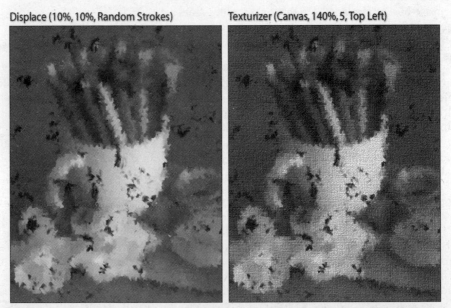

Figure 7-52: My art wasn't artsy enough, so I applied the Displace filter (left) and then added some canvas texture with the Texturizer filter (right). It took me just two minutes to create and it's suitable for hanging in a dentist's waiting room, just like art is supposed to be.

Like the history brush, the art history brush paints from the source state specified in the History palette. But it does so by painting tens or even hundreds of tiny brushstrokes at a time, swirling and gyrating according to settings you select in the Options bar. Many of these settings you've seen several times before. As shown in Figure 7-53, you have the standard Brush controls, a reduced Mode option, and the tried and true Opacity value. But starting with the Style option, the art history brush goes its own way:

✦ **Style:** The art history brush paints with randomly generated worms and corkscrews of color. You can decide the basic shapes of the creepy crawlies by selecting an option from the Style pop-up menu, displayed in Figure 7-53. Combine these options with different brush sizes to vary the detail conveyed by the impressionistic image. Tight styles and small brushes give you better detail; Loose styles and big brushes produce less detail.

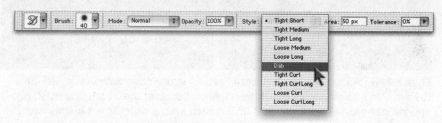

Figure 7-53: Choose an option from the Style menu to change the type of strokes applied by the art history brush.

✦ **Area:** This value defines the area covered by a single spot of corkscrews. Larger values generally mean more corkscrews are laid down at a time; reduce the value for a more sparse look. You can get some very interesting effects by raising the Area value to its maximum, 500 pixels, and mousing down inside the image without moving the cursor. Watch those worms writhe.

✦ **Tolerance:** Previously called Spacing, this value limits where the art history brush can paint. A value of 0 lets the brush paint anywhere; higher values let the brush paint only in areas where the current state and source state differ dramatically in color. High Tolerance values are especially useful for achieving the black velvet look that's always in vogue because it's perpetually on the verge of experiencing a major revival. Figure 7-54 shows a couple of examples painted against black using different Style settings, namely Dab and Tight Long, combined with high Area and Tolerance values. For effect, I applied the Texturizer filter set to Bricks to the second image.

If impressionism interests you, I encourage you to experiment. If not, give this brush the slip. I happen to think it's pretty nifty (and surprisingly well implemented), but it definitely falls under the heading of Whimsical Creative Tools to Play with When You're Not under Deadline.

Area: 300 pixels, Tolerance: 60%, Style: Dab   same, Style: Tight Long

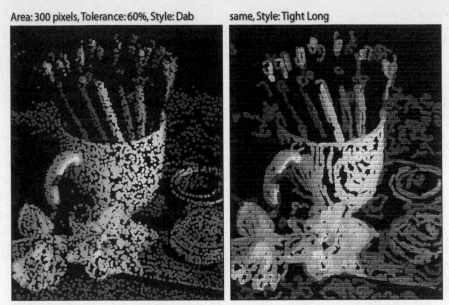

Figure 7-54: To get the black velvet effect, fill your image with black and raise the Area and Tolerance values in the Options bar. I set the brush size to 10 pixels and clicked maybe a dozen times inside each image with the art history brush.

Source state limitations

Photoshop displays the cancel cursor if you try to paint with the history brush or art history brush using a source state that's a different width or height than the current image. One pixel difference, and the source state is a moot point. This same restriction applies to Edit ⇨ Fill, Ctrl+Alt+Backspace (⌘-Option-Delete on the Mac), and any other history technique.

You may also see the cancel cursor if the layer is locked, or if the source state lacks an equivalent layer. To find out exactly what the problem is, click the image with the cancel cursor to display an explanatory alert message. If the problem relates to the source state, move the source state icon in the History palette to a point after you modified the width or the height of the image. The crop tool and the Image ⇨ Image Size, Canvas Size, Rotate Canvas, and Crop commands can mix up the history brush. If you applied one of these operations in the very last state, you either have to back-step before that operation or find some alternative to the history brush.

It's not a big deal, though. Give it some time and you'll learn to anticipate this problem. In the case of my experiment with Japan a couple sections ago, I made sure to resample and crop the image before I began applying filters. Get the dimensions ironed out, and then start laying down your time trails.

✦   ✦   ✦

Selections, Masks, and Filters

Selections and Paths

Selection Fundamentals

Selections direct and protect. If it weren't for Photoshop's selection capabilities, you and I would be flinging paint on the canvas for all we're worth, like so many Jackson Pollock and Vasily Kandinsky wannabes, without any means to constrain, discriminate, or otherwise regulate the effects of our actions. Without selections, there'd be no filters, no color corrections, and no layers. In fact, we'd all be dangerously close to real life, that dreaded environment we've spent so much time and money to avoid.

No other program gives you as much control over the size and shape of selections as Photoshop. You can finesse selection outlines with unparalleled flexibility, alternatively adding to and subtracting from selected areas and moving and rotating selections independently of the pixels inside them. You can even mix masks and selection outlines together, as covered in Chapter 9.

That's why this chapter and the one that follows are the most important chapters in this book.

Pretty cool, huh? You put a provocative sentence like that on a line by itself and it resonates with authority. Granted, it's a little overstated, but can you blame me? I mean, I can't have a sentence like, "If you want my opinion, I think these are some pretty doggone important chapters — at least, that's the way it seems to me; certainly, you might have a different opinion," on a line by itself. The other paragraphs would laugh at it.

At any rate, I invite you to pay close attention to the fundamental concepts and approaches documented throughout this chapter. Although I wouldn't characterize each and every technique as essential—lots of artists get by without paying much attention to paths, for example, while other artists swear by them—a working knowledge of selection outlines is key to using Photoshop successfully.

How selections work

If you want to edit a portion of an image without fear that you might accidentally muck up another portion of the image, you must first *select* it, which is computerese for indicating the boundaries of the area you want to edit. To select part of an image in a painting program, you surround it with a selection outline or a marquee, which tells Photoshop where to apply your editing instructions. The selection outline appears as a moving pattern of dash marks, lovingly termed *marching ants* by doughheads who've been using computers too long. (See Figure 8-1 for the inside story.)

Figure 8-1: A magnified view of a dash mark in a selection outline reveals a startling discovery.

Visible selection outlines can be helpful sometimes, but they can as readily impede your view of an image. When they annoy you, you can press Ctrl+H (⌘-H on the Mac) to shoo them away. Pressing Ctrl+H (Win) or ⌘-H (Mac) toggles the View ➪ Extras command, which hides and displays all on-screen aids, not just those pesky ants. So you also lose guides, the grid, note icons, slices, and target paths. If you want to hide just the ants, choose View ➪ Show ➪ Selection Edges to toggle the command off. Choose the command again to toggle the ants back on. You also can control which items disappear when you press Ctrl+H (⌘-H on the Mac) by choosing View ➪ Show ➪ Show Extras Options. In the resulting dialog box, check the items that you want Photoshop to display at all times.

As for creating selections, you have at your disposal a plethora of tools, all shown in Figure 8-2 and described briefly in the following list. You can access most of the tools by using keyboard shortcuts, which appear in parentheses.

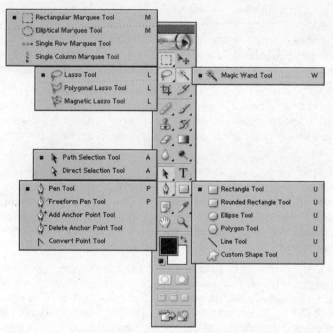

Figure 8-2: Photoshop offers a bounty of selection tools.

When multiple tools share the same shortcut, you press the key once to activate the tool that's visible in the toolbox and press the key repeatedly to cycle through the other tools. This assumes that you turn off the Use Shift Key for Tool Switch check box in the Preferences dialog box. Otherwise, press Shift and the shortcut key to cycle through the following tools:

✦ **Rectangular marquee (M):** Long a staple of painting programs, this tool enables you to select rectangular or square portions of an image.

✦ **Elliptical marquee (M):** The elliptical marquee tool works like the rectangular marquee except it selects elliptical or circular portions of an image.

✦ **Single-row and single-column:** The single-row and single-column tools enable you to select a single row or column of pixels that stretches the entire width or height of the image. These tools are so seldom used that Adobe didn't give them keyboard shortcuts.

✦ **Lasso (L):** Drag with the lasso tool to select a free-form portion of an image. Unlike the lasso tools in most painting programs, which shrink selection outlines to disqualify pixels in the background color, Photoshop's lasso tool selects the exact portion of the image you enclose in your drag.

✦ **Polygonal lasso (L):** Click different points in your image to set corners in a straight-sided selection outline. This is a great way to select free-form areas if you're not good at wielding the mouse or your wrists are a tad sore. (You can achieve this same effect by Alt-clicking or Option-clicking with the lasso tool; I explain this more in the "Free-form outlines" section later in this chapter.)

✦ **Magnetic lasso (L):** Click with the magnetic lasso along the edge of an image element that you want to select independently from its background. Then move (you don't have to drag) the magnetic lasso around the edge of the element. It's a tricky tool to use, so you can be sure I describe it in excruciating detail in the coming pages.

✦ **Magic wand (W):** First introduced by Photoshop, this tool lets you select a contiguous region of similarly colored pixels by clicking inside the region. For example, you might click inside the boundaries of a face to isolate it from the hair and background elements. Novices tend to gravitate toward the magic wand because it seems like such a miracle tool, but, in fact, it's the least predictable and ultimately the least useful of the bunch.

✦ **Pen (P):** The pen tool is difficult to master, but it's the most accurate and versatile of the selection tools. You use the pen tool to create a *path*, which is an object-oriented breed of selection outline. You click and drag to create individual points in the path. You can edit the path after the fact by moving, adding, and deleting points. You can even transfer a path by dragging and dropping between Photoshop, Illustrator, and FreeHand. For a discussion of the pen tool, read the "How to Draw and Edit Paths" section, later in this chapter.

✦ **Freeform pen and magnetic pen (P):** If you hate setting points but you need to create a clipping path, the freeform pen is the tool for you. You just drag with the tool as if you were selecting with the lasso tool and let Photoshop define the points automatically. Obviously, you can't expect the same level of accuracy that you get from the standard pen tool, but it's child's play to use.

Selecting the Magnetic check box in the Options bar transforms the freeform pen into the magnetic pen, which once upon a time was a tool in its own right. The magnetic pen is basically an object-oriented version of the magnetic lasso tool. Click to set the first point and then move your mouse and watch Photoshop create the other points automatically. It's not a great tool, but it can prove handy when selecting image elements that stand out very clearly from their backgrounds.

✦ **Shape tools (U):** To draw paths in simple geometric shapes — rectangles, polygons, and so on — give the shape tools a whirl. First, put the tools into path mode by clicking the Paths icon at the left end of the Options bar. Then simply drag to create the path. To find out more about working with these tools, visit Chapter 14.

✦ **Path and shape selection tools:** Use the path selection tool (the black arrow) and the direct selection tool (the white arrow) to select and edit paths and vector shapes. You can read more about these tools later in this chapter, in the section, "How to Draw and Edit Paths."

Photoshop's horizontal type mask tool and vertical type mask tool are also technically selection tools because Photoshop converts each character of type to a selection outline. But type involves other issues that would merely confuse the contents of this chapter, so I've awarded type its own chapter (Chapter 15). Also, if your purpose for selecting an area is to separate it from its background, you should investigate the Extract command and the magic eraser and background eraser (Chapter 9).

If this were all you needed to know to use the selection tools in Photoshop, the application would be on par with the average paint program. Part of what makes Photoshop exceptional, however, is that it provides literally hundreds of little tricks to increase the functionality of every selection tool. Furthermore, all of Photoshop's selection tools work together in perfect harmony. You can exploit the specialized capabilities of the selection tools to create a single selection boundary. After you understand which tool best serves which purpose, you can isolate any element in an image, no matter how complex or how delicate its outline.

Geometric selection outlines

Tools for creating simple geometric selection outlines occupy the very first slot in the Photoshop toolbox. By default, the rectangular marquee tool has the stage. You select the elliptical, single-row, and single-column marquee tools from the flyout menu that appears when you drag from the marquee tool icon.

Press M to select the tool that's currently visible in the toolbox. Press M again to toggle between the rectangular and elliptical marquee tools. Alternatively, Alt-click (Win) or Option-click (Mac) the tool icon to toggle between the rectangular and elliptical marquee tools.

The marquee tools are more versatile than they may appear at first glance. You can adjust the performance of each tool as follows:

✦ **Constraining to a square or circle:** Press and hold Shift *after* beginning your drag to draw a perfect square with the rectangular marquee tool or a perfect circle with the elliptical marquee tool. (Pressing Shift *before* dragging also works if no other selection is active; otherwise, this adds to a selection, as I explain later in the "Ways to Change Selection Outlines" section.)

✦ **Drawing a circular marquee:** When I was perusing an online forum a while back, someone asked how to create a perfect circular marquee. Despite more than a month of helpful suggestions — some highly imaginative — no one offered the easiest suggestion of all (well, I ultimately did, but I'm a know-it-all). So remember to press Shift after you begin to drag and you'll be one step ahead of the game.

✦ **Drawing out from the center:** Press and hold Alt (Option on the Mac) after you begin dragging to draw the marquee from the center outward instead of from corner to corner. (Again, pressing Alt or Option before dragging works if no selection outline is active; otherwise, this subtracts from the selection.) This technique is especially useful when you draw an elliptical marquee. Locating the center of the area you want to select is frequently easier than locating one of its corners — particularly because ellipses don't have corners.

✦ **Moving the marquee on the fly:** While drawing a marquee, press and hold the spacebar to move the marquee rather than resize it. When you get the marquee in place, release the spacebar and keep dragging to modify the size. The spacebar is most helpful when drawing elliptical selections or when drawing a marquee out from the center — this eliminates the guesswork, so you can position your marquees exactly on target.

✦ **Selecting a single-pixel line:** Use the single-row or single-column tools to select a single row or column (respectively) of pixels stretching across the width or length of your image. I use these tools to fix screw-ups such as a missing line of pixels in a screen shot, to delete random pixels around the perimeter of an image, or to create perpendicular lines in a fixed space.

✦ **Constraining the aspect ratio:** If you want to create an image that conforms to a certain aspect ratio, you can constrain either a rectangular or an elliptical marquee so that the ratio between height and width remains fixed, no matter how large or small a marquee you create. To accomplish this, select Fixed Aspect Ratio from the Style pop-up menu in the Options bar, as shown in Figure 8-3. Enter the desired ratio values into the Width and Height option boxes.

If you work with a digital camera, you may find this feature especially helpful. Digital cameras typically produce images that fit the 4×3 aspect ratio used by computer screens and televisions. If you want to crop an image to a standard photo size — say, 6×4 inches — enter 6 and 4, respectively, in the Width and Height option boxes. Then drag the marquee around to select the portion of the picture you want to retain, as shown in the figure, and choose Image ➪ Crop.

Remember that you're just establishing the image aspect ratio here, not setting the output width and height. So you could just as easily enter 2 and 3 in the Width and Height option boxes. The size of the final, cropped image depends on how large you draw the marquee and the Resolution value you set in the Image Size dialog box.

✦ **Sizing the marquee numerically:** If you're editing a screen shot or some other form of regular or schematic image, you may find it helpful to specify the size of the marquee numerically. To do so, select Fixed Size from the Style pop-up menu and enter size values in the Width and Height option boxes. To match the selection to a 640×480-pixel screen, for example, change the Width and Height values to 640 and 480, respectively. Then click in the image to create the marquee.

Fixed aspect ratio: 6 x 4

Cropped image

Figure 8-3: Select Fixed Aspect Ratio from the Style pop-up menu in the Options bar to constrain the width and height of a rectangular selection outline.

Note

You can set the marquee size in any unit of measurement you like. Just type the number followed by one of these units: px (pixels), in, mm, cm, pt (points), pica, or %.

✦ **Drawing feathered selections:** A Feather option box is available in the Options bar when you use any of the marquee tools. To *feather* a selection is to blur its edges beyond the automatic antialiasing afforded by most tools. For more information on feathering, refer to the "Softening selection outlines" section, later in this chapter.

✦ **Creating jagged ellipses:** By default, elliptical selection outlines are antialiased. If you don't want antialiasing—you might prefer harsh edges when editing screen shots or designing screen interfaces—deselect the Anti-aliased check box. (This option is dimmed when you use the rectangular marquee because antialiasing is always off for this tool.)

Photoshop novices often misunderstand the rectangular and elliptical marquee tools and expect them to create filled and stroked shapes. For this purpose Photoshop provides the shape tools, which can create filled vector and raster shapes. You can apply strokes and other effects to these shapes if you like. Chapter 14 takes you on a guided tour of the shape tools.

Free-form outlines

In comparison to the rectangular and elliptical marquee tools, the lasso tool provides a rather limited range of options. Generally speaking, you drag in a free-form path around the image you want to select. The few special considerations are as follows:

✦ **Feathering and antialiasing:** Just as you can feather rectangular and elliptical marquees, you can feather selections drawn with the lasso tool by first selecting the Feather check box in the Options bar. To soften the edges of a lasso outline, select the Anti-aliased check box.

Although you can adjust the feathering of any selection after you draw it by choosing Select ➪ Feather, you must specify antialiasing before you draw a selection. Unless you have a specific reason for doing otherwise, leave the Anti-aliased check box turned on (as it is by default).

✦ **Drawing polygons:** When you press and hold Alt (Option on the Mac), the lasso tool functions like (and the icon even looks like) the polygonal lasso tool. (*Polygon*, incidentally, means a shape with multiple straight sides.) With the Alt or Option key down, click to specify corners in a free-form polygon, as shown in Figure 8-4. If you want to add curves to the selection outline, drag with the tool while still pressing Alt or Option. Photoshop closes the selection outline the moment you release both the Alt or Option key and the mouse button.

You can extend a polygon selection outline to the absolute top, right, or bottom edges of an image. If the image window is larger than the image, you can Alt-click (Win) or Option-click (Mac) with the lasso tool on the background canvas surrounding the image. You can even click on the scroll bars. Figure 8-4 illustrates the idea.

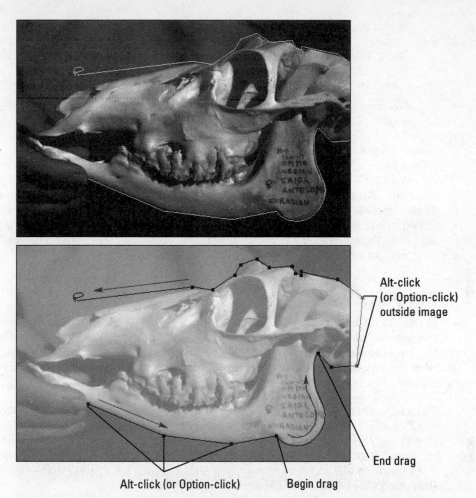

Figure 8-4: Alt-click (Win) or Option-click (Mac) with the lasso tool to create corners in a selection outline, shown as black squares in the bottom image. Drag to create free-form curves. Surprisingly, you can Alt-click or Option-click anywhere within the image window, even on the scroll bars, to add corners outside the boundaries of the image.

✦ **The polygonal lasso tool:** If you don't want to bother with pressing Alt (Win) or Option (Mac), select the polygonal lasso. When the lasso is active, you can switch to the polygonal lasso by pressing L or Shift+L, depending on your Use Shift Key for Tool Switch setting in the Preferences dialog box. Or drag from the lasso tool icon to display the lasso flyout menu and select the polygonal lasso that way. Then click inside the image to set corners in the selection. Click the first point in the selection or double-click with the tool to complete the selection outline.

Tip

If you make a mistake while creating a selection outline with the polygonal lasso, press Backspace (Delete on the Mac) to eliminate the last segment you drew. Keep pressing Backspace or Delete to eliminate more segments in the selection outline. This technique works until you close the selection outline and it turns into marching ants.

To create free-form curves with the polygonal lasso tool, press Alt (Win) or Option (Mac) and drag.

Adobe added the polygonal lasso for those times when Alt-clicking (Option-clicking on the Mac) isn't convenient. If no portion of the image is selected, it's no trick to Alt-click (Win) or Option-click (Mac) with the standard lasso to draw a straight-sided selection. But if some area in the image is selected, pressing Alt or Option tells Photoshop that you want to subtract from the selection outline. For this reason, it's often easier to use the polygonal lasso (although you still can make it work by pressing Alt or Option *after* you click with the lasso tool, as I explain in the "Using Shift and Alt or Option like a pro" section later in this chapter).

Magnetic selections

In the old days of black-and-white painting programs — most notably MacPaint on the Mac — black pixels were considered foreground elements and white pixels were the background. To select a black element, you had only to vaguely drag around it with the lasso tool and the program would automatically omit the white pixels and "shrink" the selection around the black ones.

The magnetic lasso tool is Adobe's attempt to transfer shrinking into the world of color. Under ideal conditions — very ideal conditions, I might add — a selection drawn with the magnetic lasso automatically shrinks around the foreground element and omits the background. Naturally, it rarely works this miraculously, but it does produce halfway decent selection outlines with very little effort — provided that you know what you're doing.

Using the magnetic lasso tool

Typically, when people have a problem using the magnetic lasso tool, it's because they're trying to make the process too complex. Work less, and the tool works better. Here are the basic steps for using this unusual tool:

STEPS: Making Sense of the Magnetic Lasso Tool

1. **Select an image with very definite contrast between the foreground image and its background.** The skull in Figure 8-5 is a good example: a light gray skull against a dark gray background. Here's something that Photoshop can really sink its teeth into.

2. **Select the magnetic lasso.** If any tool but a lasso tool is active, press L to grab the lasso that's showing in the toolbox. Then press L as necessary to cycle to the magnetic lasso.

3. **Click anywhere along the edge of the foreground element.** I clicked at the top of the skull, as labeled in Figure 8-5.

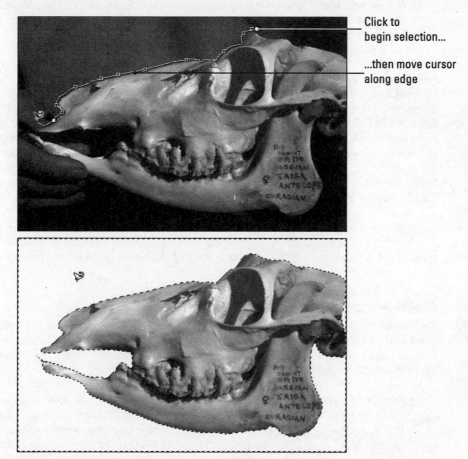

Click to
begin selection...

...then move cursor
along edge

Figure 8-5: After clicking to set the start point (top), I moved the magnetic lasso cursor along the edge of the skull. Then I reversed the completed selection by pressing Ctrl+Shift+I (⌘-Shift-I on the Mac) and pressed Backspace (Delete on the Mac) to fill it with white (bottom).

4. **Move the cursor around the edge of the foreground element.** Just *move* the mouse, don't drag — that is, there's no need to press the mouse button. As your cursor passes over the image, Photoshop lays down a line along the

edge of the element, as Figure 8-5 shows. If you don't like the placement of the line, back up the cursor and try moving along the edge again. The magnetic lasso also lays down anchor points at significant locations around the image. If you don't like where the program puts a point, press Backspace (Win) or Delete (Mac). Each time you press Backspace or Delete, Photoshop gets rid of the most recent point along the line. To set your own anchor points, just click.

5. **When you make it all the way around to the beginning of the shape, click the first point in the outline to close the selection.** Or just double-click to close with a straight edge.

As I mentioned before, the magnetic lasso does not perform miracles. It almost never selects an image exactly the way you would like it to. After moving the cursor around the skull, I reversed the selection by choosing Select ➪ Inverse and then I pressed Backspace (Delete on the Mac) to fill the background with white. The result appears in the second example in Figure 8-5. As you can see, the magnetic lasso did a very nice job of isolating the skull — much better than I could have done with the lasso alone — but the selection isn't perfect. Notice the gap on the right side of the skull and the clumsy treatment of the tip of the pointy lower jaw on left. Okay, no automated selection tool is perfect, but the magnetic lasso makes as few mistakes as any I've seen.

To create a straight segment while working with the magnetic lasso tool, press Alt (Option on the Mac), click to set the start of the segment, and click again at the end point. The next time you click without holding down Alt or Option, the tool reverts to its normal magnetic self.

Modifying the magnetic lasso options

You modify the performance of the magnetic lasso tool by adjusting the values in the Options bar. The Feather and Anti-aliased options define the softness of the final selection outline, just as they do for the standard lasso tool. The others control how the magnetic lasso positions lines and lays down points:

✦ **Width:** I might have named this option Sloppiness Factor. It determines how close to an edge you have to move the cursor for Photoshop to accurately see the image element. Large values are great for smooth elements that stand out clearly from their backgrounds. If I raise the Width to 20 when selecting the top of the skull, for example, I can move the cursor 20 pixels away from the skull and Photoshop still shrinks the selection tight around the skull's edge. That's a lot of wiggle room and makes my life easier. But when you're selecting narrow passageways, you need a low value to keep Photoshop from veering off to the wrong edge. The spot where the pointy jaw meets with the snout is a good example of a place where I need to set a small Width and move very carefully around the edge.

The great advantage to the Width value is that you can change it on the fly by pressing a bracket key. Press the [key to lower the Width value; press the] key to raise the value. Shift+[lowers the value to its minimum, 1, and Shift+] raises it to the maximum, 256.

If you have a pressure-sensitive tablet and select the Pen Pressure check box, you can control the sloppiness factor dynamically according to how hard you press on the pen. Bear down to be careful; let up to be sloppy. Because this is the way you probably work naturally, you'll be able to adjust the width as needed without even thinking much about it.

✦ **Edge Contrast:** This is the simplest of the options. It tells Photoshop how much contrast there has to be between the element you're trying to select and its background to even be recognized. If the foreground element stands out clearly, you may want to raise the Edge Contrast value to avoid selecting random flack around the edges. If the contrast between foreground and background is subtle, lower the value.

✦ **Frequency:** This option tells the magnetic lasso when to lay down points. As you drag with the tool, the line around the image changes to keep up with your movements. When some point in the line stays still for a few moments, Photoshop decides it must be on target and anchors it down with a point. If you want Photoshop to anchor points more frequently, raise the value. For less frequent anchoring, lower the option. High values tend to be better for rough edges; lower values are better for smooth edges.

Most of the time, you can rely on the bracket keys to adjust the Width and leave the Frequency and Edge Contrast values set to their defaults. When dealing with a low-contrast image, lower the Edge Contrast value to 5 percent or so. And when selecting unusually rough edges, raise the Frequency to 70 or more. But careful movements with the magnetic lasso tool go farther than adjusting any of these settings.

The world of the wand

Using the magic wand tool is a no-brainer, right? You just click with the tool and it selects all colors that fall within a selected range. The problem is getting the wand to recognize the same range of colors that you see on screen. For example, if you're editing a photo of a red plate against a pink tablecloth, how do you tell the magic wand to select the plate and leave the tablecloth alone?

Sadly, adjusting the wand is pretty tricky and frequently unsatisfying. When the magic wand is active, you'll see the following four controls in the Options bar:

✦ **Tolerance:** This option determines the range of colors the tool selects when you click with it in the image window.

✦ **Anti-aliased:** This check box softens the selection, just as it does for the lasso tools.

✦ **Contiguous:** When selected, this option tells Photoshop to select a contiguous region of pixels emanating from the pixel on which you click. If you're trying to select landmasses on a globe, for example, clicking on St. Louis selects everything from Juneau to Mexico City. It doesn't select London, though, because an ocean of water that doesn't fall within the tolerance range separates the cities. To select all similarly colored pixels throughout the picture, deselect the option.

✦ **Use All Layers:** Turn this option on to take all visible layers into account when defining a selection.

You now know all you need to know about the Anti-aliased and Contiguous options; the next two sections explain Tolerance and Use All Layers.

Adjusting the tolerance

You may have heard the standard explanation for adjusting the Tolerance value: You can enter any number from 0 to 255 in the Tolerance option box. Enter a low number to select a small range of colors; increase the value to select a wider range of colors.

Nothing is wrong with this explanation—it's accurate, in its own small way—but it doesn't provide one iota of information you couldn't glean on your own. If you really want to understand this option, you have to dig a little deeper.

When you click a pixel with the magic wand tool, Photoshop first reads the brightness value that each color channel assigned to that pixel. If you're working with a grayscale image, Photoshop reads a single brightness value from the one channel only; if you're working with an RGB image, it reads three brightness values, one each from the red, green, and blue channels; and so on. Because each color channel permits 8-bits of data, brightness values range from 0 to 255.

Next, Photoshop applies the Tolerance value, or simply *tolerance*, to the pixel. The tolerance describes a range that extends in both directions—lighter and darker—from each brightness value.

Suppose you're editing a standard RGB image. The tolerance is set to 32 (as it is by default); you click with the magic wand on a turquoise pixel, whose brightness values are 40 red, 210 green, and 170 blue. Photoshop subtracts and adds 32 from each brightness value to calculate the magic wand range that, in this case, is 8 to 72 red, 178 to 242 green, and 138 to 202 blue. Photoshop selects any pixel that both falls inside this range and can be traced back to the original pixel through an uninterrupted line of other pixels, which also fall within the range.

From this information, you can draw the following basic conclusions about the magic wand tool:

✦ **Clicking on midtones maintains a higher range:** Because the tolerance range extends in two directions, you cut off the range when you click a light or dark pixel, as demonstrated in Figure 8-6. Consider the two middle gradations: In both cases, I selected the Contiguous check box and set the Tolerance value to 60. In the top gradation, I clicked on a pixel with a brightness value of 140, so Photoshop calculated a range from 80 to 200. But when I clicked on a pixel with a brightness value of 10, as in the bottom gradation, the range shrank to 0 to 70. Clicking on a medium-brightness pixel, therefore, permits the most generous range.

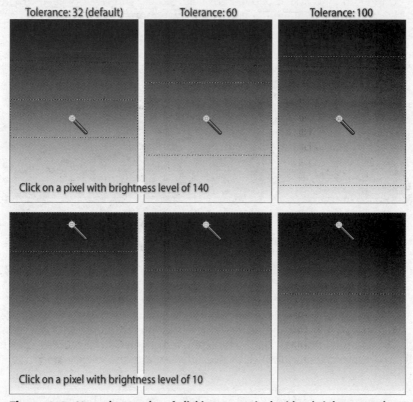

Figure 8-6: Note the results of clicking on a pixel with a brightness value of 140 (top row) and a brightness value of 10 (bottom row) with the tolerance set to three different values.

✦ **Selecting brightness ranges:** Many people have the impression that the magic wand selects color ranges. The magic wand, in fact, selects brightness ranges within color channels. So if you want to select a flesh-colored region — regardless of shade — set against an orange or a red background that is roughly equivalent in terms of brightness values, you probably should use a different tool.

✦ **Selecting from a single channel:** If the magic wand repeatedly fails to select a region of color that appears unique from its background, try isolating that region inside a single-color channel. You'll probably have the most luck isolating a color on the channel that least resembles it. For example, to select the sky shown in Figure 8-7, I examined each color channel closely to see which provided the greatest contrast between the sky and the lighthouse. Although at first glance the red and green channels both looked promising, on closer inspection I noted that only in the red channel does the red flag at the top of the lighthouse stand out against the sky. If I use the red channel, the magic wand can distinguish between the lighthouse and the sky easily. Experiment with this technique and it will prove even more useful over time.

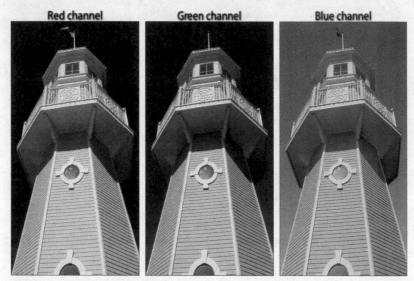

Figure 8-7: Because the sky contains almost no red, it appears most clearly distinguished from the lighthouse in the red channel. So the red channel is the easiest channel in which to select the sky with the magic wand.

Here's one more important twist to the Tolerance story: The magic wand is affected by the Sample Size option that you select for the eyedropper tool. If you select Point Sample, the wand bases its selection solely on the single pixel that you click. But if you select 3 by 3 Average or 5 by 5 Average, the wand takes into account 9 or 25 pixels, respectively. As you can imagine, this obscure option can have a noticeable impact on the extent of the selection that you get from the wand. Try clicking the same spot in your image using each of these Sample Size settings, using the same Tolerance value throughout, to see what I mean.

Making the wand see beyond a single layer

The Use All Layers option enables you to create a selection based on pixels from different layers (see Chapter 12 for more about layers). Returning to my previous landmass example, suppose you set Europe on one layer and North America on the layer behind it so that the two continents overlap. Normally, if you clicked inside Europe with the magic wand, it would select an area inside Europe without extending out into the area occupied by North America on the other layer. Because the wand doesn't even see the contents of other layers, anything outside Europe is an empty void. We're talking pre-Columbus Europe here.

If you select Use All Layers, though, the situation changes. Suddenly, the wand can see all the layers you can see. If you click on Europe, and if North America and Europe contain similar colors, the wand selects across both shapes.

Mind you, while the Use All Layers option enables the wand to consider pixels on different layers when creating a selection, it does not permit the wand to actually select images on two separate layers. Strange as this may sound, no selection tool can pull off this feat. Every one of the techniques explained in this chapter is applicable to only a single layer at a time. Use All Layers merely allows the wand to draw selection outlines that appear to encompass colors on many layers.

What good is this? Well, suppose you want to apply an effect to both Europe and North America. With the help of Use All Layers, you can draw a selection outline that encompasses both continents. After you apply the effect to Europe, you can switch to the North America layer — the selection outline remains intact — and then reapply the effect.

Ways to Change Selection Outlines

If you don't draw a selection outline correctly the first time, you have two options. You can either draw it again from scratch, which is a real bore, or you can change your botched selection outline, which is likely to be the more efficient solution. You can deselect a selection, add to a selection, subtract from a selection, and even select the stuff that's not selected and deselect the stuff that is. (If this sounds like a load of nonsense, keep reading.)

Quick changes

Some methods of adjusting a selection outline are automatic: You choose a command and you're finished. The following list explains how a few commands — all members of the Select menu — work:

✦ **Deselect (Ctrl+D or ⌘-D):** You can deselect the selected portion of an image in three ways. You can select a different portion of the image; click anywhere in the image window with the rectangular marquee tool, the elliptical marquee tool, or the lasso tool; or choose Select ➪ Deselect. Remember, though, when no part of a layer is selected, the entire layer is susceptible to your changes. If you apply a filter, choose a color-correction command, or use a paint tool, you affect every pixel of the layer.

✦ **Reselect (Ctrl+Shift+D or ⌘-Shift-D):** If you accidentally deselect an image, you can retrieve the most recent selection outline by choosing Select ➪ Reselect. It's a great function that operates entirely independently of the Undo command and History palette, and it works even after performing a long string of selection-unrelated operations. (You can restore older selections from the History palette, but that usually means undoing operations along the way.)

✦ **Inverse (Ctrl+Shift+I or ⌘-Shift-I):** Choose Select ➪ Inverse to reverse the selection. Photoshop deselects the portion of the image that was previously selected and selects the portion of the image that was not selected. This way, you can begin a selection by outlining the portion of the image you want to protect, rather than the portion you want to affect. To select the lighthouse in Figure 8-7, for example, it's easier to first select the sky in the red channel and then inverse the selection so that the lighthouse becomes selected.

You can also access the Inverse and Deselect commands from a shortcut menu in the image window. Right-click (Control-click on the Mac) to make the menu appear underneath your cursor.

Manually adding and subtracting

Ready for some riddles? When editing a portrait, how do you select both eyes without affecting any other portion of the face? Answer: By drawing one selection and then tacking on a second selection. How do you select a doughnut and leave the hole behind? Answer: Encircle the doughnut with the elliptical marquee tool, and then use the same tool to subtract the center.

Photoshop permits you to whittle away at a selection, add pieces on again, whittle away some more, ad infinitum, until you get it exactly right. Short of sheer laziness or frustration, there's no reason why you can't eventually create the selection outline of your dreams:

✦ **Adding to a selection outline:** To increase the area enclosed in an existing selection outline, Shift-drag with one of the marquee or lasso tools. You also can Shift-click with the magic wand tool or Shift-click with one of the marquee tools when the Fixed Size option is active (as described in the "Geometric selection outlines" section earlier in this chapter).

✦ **Subtracting from a selection outline:** To take a bite from an existing selection outline, press Alt (Win) or Option (Mac) while using one of the selection tools.

✦ **Intersecting one selection outline with another:** Another way to subtract from an existing selection outline is to Shift+Alt-drag (Shift-Option-drag on the Mac) around the selection with the rectangular marquee, elliptical marquee, or lasso tool. You also can Shift+Alt-click (Shift-Option-click on the Mac) with the magic wand tool. Shift+Alt-dragging instructs Photoshop to retain only the portion of an existing selection that also falls inside the new selection outline. I frequently use this technique to confine a selection within a rectangular or elliptical border.

If the key-press techniques seem bothersome, use the selection state buttons (labeled in Figure 8-8) at the left end of the Options bar to set your selection tool to add, subtract, or intersect mode. After clicking a button, simply drag to alter the selection outline. To toggle the tool back to normal operating mode, click the first button in the bunch. Note that the keyboard techniques described in the preceding list work no matter what button you select in the Options bar. For example, if you click the Intersect button, Alt-dragging (Option-dragging on the Mac) still subtracts from the selection outline.

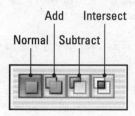

Figure 8-8: You can use the selection state buttons as well as the Shift and Alt keys (Shift and Option keys on the Mac) when modifying a selection outline.

When you're working with the magic wand, you can right-click (Control-click on the Mac) to display a shortcut menu that contains the add, subtract, and intersect mode options. Click the mode you want to use.

Photoshop displays special cursors to help you keep track of a tool's selection state. Suppose that you select part of an image and the lasso tool is active. When you press Shift or click the Add button in the Options bar, Photoshop appends a little plus sign to the lasso cursor to show you're about to add. A minus sign indicates that you're set to subtract from the selection outline; a multiply sign appears when you work in intersect mode. If you're pressing keys to switch tool modes, Photoshop temporarily selects the corresponding selection state button in the Options bar as well.

Using Shift and Alt (or Shift and Option) like a pro

The roles of the Shift and Alt keys (or Shift and Option keys on the Mac) in adding, subtracting, and intersecting selection outlines can interfere with your ability to take advantage of other functions of the selection tools. For example, when no portion of an image is selected, you can Shift-drag with the rectangular marquee tool to draw a square. But after a selection is active, Shift-dragging adds a rectangle—not a square—to the selection outline.

This is one reason for the selection state buttons in the Options bar. After you click a button, the tool adds, subtracts, or intersects, with no additional key presses on your part, depending on which button you click. But if you want to hide the Options bar or you just prefer pressing keys to clicking buttons, you can control the selection tools from the keyboard without giving up any selection flexibility.

The trick is to learn when to press Shift and Alt (or Option on the Mac). Sometimes you have to press the key before you begin your drag; other times you must press the key after you begin the drag but before you release. For example, to add a square to a selection outline with the rectangular marquee tool, Shift-drag, release Shift while keeping the mouse button pressed, and press Shift again to snap the rectangle to a square. The same goes for adding a circle with the elliptical marquee tool.

The following list introduces you to a few other techniques. They sound pretty elaborate, I admit, but with a little practice, they become second nature (so does tightrope walking, but don't let that worry you). Before you try any of them, be sure to select Normal from the Style pop-up menu in the Options bar.

To keep things simple, the following list is geared toward Windows users. If you use a Macintosh, press Option instead of Alt.

✦ To subtract a square or a circle from a selection, Alt-drag, release Alt, press Shift, drag until you get it right, release the mouse button, and then release Shift.

✦ To add a rectangle or an ellipse by drawing from the center outward, Shift-drag, release Shift, press Alt, and hold Alt until after you release the mouse button. You can even press the spacebar during the drag to move the marquee around, if you like.

✦ To subtract a marquee drawn from the center outward, Alt-drag, release Alt, press Alt again, and hold the key down until after you release.

✦ What about drawing a straight-sided selection with the lasso tool? To add a straight-sided area to an existing selection, Shift-drag with the tool for a short distance. With the mouse button still down, release Shift and press Alt. Then click around as you normally would, while keeping the Alt key down.

✦ To subtract a straight-sided area, Alt-drag with the lasso, release Alt, press Alt again, and click around with the tool.

If you can't manage the last two lasso-tool techniques, switch to the polygonal lasso instead. In fact, the reason Adobe provided the polygonal lasso tool was to accommodate folks who don't want to deal with pressing Alt or Option seven times during a single drag (which I strangely quite enjoy).

Adding and subtracting by command

Photoshop provides several commands under the Select menu that automatically increase or decrease the number of selected pixels in an image according to numerical specifications. The commands in the Select ➪ Modify submenu work as follows:

✦ **Border:** This command selects an area of a specified thickness around the perimeter of the current selection outline and deselects the rest of the selection. For example, to select a 6-point-thick border around the current selection, choose Select ➪ Modify ➪ Border, enter 6 in the Width option box, and press Enter or Return. But what's the point? After all, if you want to create an outline around a selection, you can accomplish this in fewer steps by choosing Edit ➪ Stroke, right? The Border command, however, broadens your range of options. You can apply a special effect to the border, move the border to a new location, or even create a double-outline effect by first applying Select ➪ Modify ➪ Border and then applying Edit ➪ Stroke.

✦ **Smooth:** This command rounds off the sharp corners and weird anomalies in the outline of a selection. When you choose Select ➪ Modify ➪ Smooth, the program asks you to enter a Sample Radius value. Photoshop smoothes out corners by drawing little circles around them; the Sample Radius value determines the radius of these circles. Larger values result in smoother corners.

The Smooth command is especially useful in combination with the magic wand. After you draw one of those weird, scraggly selection outlines with the wand tool, use Select ➪ Modify ➪ Smooth to smooth out the rough edges.

✦ **Expand and Contract:** Both of these commands do exactly what they say, either expanding or contracting the selected area by a specified amount. For example, if you want an elliptical selection to grow by 8 pixels, choose Select ➪ Modify ➪ Expand, enter 8, and call it a day. These are extremely useful commands; I refer to them several times throughout the book.

Both Expand and Contract have a flattening effect on a selection. To round things off, apply the Smooth command with a Sample Radius value equal to the number you just entered into the Expand Selection or Contract Selection dialog box. You end up with a pretty vague selection outline, but what do you expect from automated commands?

In addition to the Expand command, Photoshop provides two other commands — Grow and Similar — that increase the area covered by a selection outline. Both commands resemble the magic wand tool because they measure the range of eligible pixels by way of a Tolerance value. In fact, the commands rely on the same Tolerance value (in the Options bar) that you set for the magic wand. So if you want to adjust the impact of either command, you must first select the magic wand and then apply the commands:

✦ **Grow:** Choose Select ➪ Grow to select all pixels that both neighbor an existing selection and resemble the colors included in the selection, in accordance with the Tolerance value. In other words, Select ➪ Grow is the command equivalent of the magic wand tool. If you feel constrained because you can only click one pixel at a time with the magic wand tool, you may prefer to select a small group of representative pixels with a marquee tool and then choose Select ➪ Grow to initiate the wand's magic.

✦ **Similar:** Another member of the Select menu, Similar works like Grow, except the pixels needn't be adjacent. When you choose Select ➪ Similar, Photoshop selects any pixel that falls within the tolerance range, regardless of the location of the pixel in the foreground image.

Although both Grow and Similar respect the magic wand's Tolerance value, they pay no attention to the other wand options — Contiguous, Use All Layers, and Anti-aliased. Grow always selects contiguous regions only; Similar selects noncontiguous areas. Neither can see beyond the active layer nor produce antialiased selection outlines.

One of the best applications for the Similar command is to isolate a complicated image set against a consistent background whose colors are significantly lighter or darker than the image. Consider Figure 8-9, which features a light and relatively complex foreground image set against a continuous background of medium brightness values. The following steps explain how to separate this image using the Similar command in combination with a few other techniques I've described thus far.

STEPS: Isolating a Complex Image Set against a Plain Background

1. **Use the rectangular marquee tool to select some representative portions of the background.** In Figure 8-9, I selected the lightest and darkest portions of the background along with some representative shades in between. Remember, you make multiple selections by Shift-dragging with the tool.

Figure 8-9: Before choosing Select ➪ Similar, select a few sample portions of the background for Photoshop to base its selection range.

2. **Double-click the magic wand tool icon to display the Tolerance option box in the Options bar.** For my image, I entered a Tolerance value of 16, a relatively low value, in keeping with the consistency of the background. If your background is less homogenous, you may want to enter a higher value. Make certain you turn on the Anti-aliased check box.

3. **Choose Select ⇨ Similar.** Photoshop should select the entire background. If Photoshop fails to select all the background, choose Edit ⇨ Undo and use the rectangular marquee tool to select more portions of the background. You may also want to increase the magic wand's Tolerance value. If Photoshop's selection bleeds into the foreground image, try reducing the Tolerance value.

4. **Choose Select ⇨ Inverse.** Or press Ctrl+Shift+I (⌘-Shift-I on the Mac). Photoshop selects the foreground image and deselects the background, as shown in Figure 8-10.

Figure 8-10: After selecting the entire background, press Ctrl+Shift+I (⌘-Shift-I on the Mac) to reverse what's selected and what's not.

5. **Modify the selection as desired.** If too few pixels are selected, try choosing the Similar command again. You might also have luck with Select ⇨ Grow. Or you can modify the selection using the Shift and Alt keys (Shift and Option keys on the Mac).

6. **Congratulations, you've isolated your complex image.** Now you can filter your image, colorize it, or perform whatever operation inspired you to select this image in the first place. I wanted to superimpose the image onto a different background, so I copied the image to the Clipboard (Ctrl+C or ⌘-C), opened the desired background image, and then pasted the first image into place (Ctrl+V or ⌘-V). The result, shown in Figure 8-11, still needs some touching up with the paint and edit tools, but it's not half bad for an automated selection process.

Figure 8-11: The completed selection superimposed onto a new background.

Whenever you introduce a selection into another image — by copying and pasting or by dragging the selection and dropping it into another image window — Photoshop automatically assigns the selection to a new layer. This is a great safety mechanism because it prevents you from permanently affixing the selection to its new background. But it also limits your file format options when saving an image; you can't save in a format other than the native Photoshop format, PDF, or TIFF without first flattening the image. For the big story on layers, read Chapter 12.

Softening selection outlines

You can soften a selection in two ways. The first method is antialiasing, introduced in Chapter 5. Antialiasing is an intelligent and automatic softening algorithm that mimics the appearance of edges you'd expect to see in a sharply focused photograph.

Note

Where did the term *antialias* originate? Anytime you try to fit the digital equivalent of a square peg into a round hole — say, by printing a high-resolution image to a low-resolution printer — the data gets revised during the process. This revised data, called an *alias*, is frequently inaccurate and undesirable. Antialiasing is the act of revising the data ahead of time, essentially rounding off the square peg so it looks nice as it goes into the hole. According to a reader who spent time at MIT's Architecture Machine Group, "We did the first work with displaying smooth lines. We called the harsh transitions *jaggies* and the display process *dejaggying*. Somehow, this easy-to-understand term slid sideways into 'alias' (which it isn't, really, but it's too late to change)." Now you know.

When you draw an antialiased selection outline in Photoshop, the program calculates the hard-edged selection at twice its actual size. The program then shrinks the selection in half using bicubic interpolation (described in Chapter 2). The result is a crisp image with no visible jagged edges.

The second softening method, feathering, is more dramatic. Feathering gradually dissipates the selection outline, giving it a blurry edge. Photoshop accommodates partially selected pixels; feathering fades the selection both inward and outward from the original edge.

You can specify the number of pixels affected either before or after drawing a selection. To feather a selection before you draw it with a marquee or lasso tool, enter a value in the Feather option box, found in the Options bar. To feather a selection after drawing it, choose Select ➪ Feather or press Ctrl+Alt+D (⌘-Option-D on the Mac). You also can right-click (Control-click on the Mac) in the image window and then choose Feather from the pop-up menu that appears next to your cursor.

The Feather Radius value determines the approximate distance over which Photoshop fades a selection, measured in pixels in both directions from the original selection outline. Figure 8-12 shows the effects of feathering a selection. In the first example, the elliptical window showing the close-up of the young lovers comes from a selection that was antialiased only; no feathering was used. In the second example, before pasting the elliptical selection into the new image, I first feathered the selection, assigning a relatively high Feather Radius value of 24. As you can see, a large feather radius makes a selection fade into view.

Antialiased, no feather

Feather, Radius: 24 pixels

Figure 8-12: Two ways of using the elliptical marquee tool to place an inset close-up into an image. The selection in the top image was antialiased and not feathered, and the selection in the bottom image was feathered with a radius of 24 pixels.

The math behind the feather

A few eagle-eyed readers have written to ask me why feathering blurs a selection outline more than the number of pixels stated in the Feather Radius value. A radius of 4 pixels actually affects a total of 20 pixels: 10 inward and 10 outward. The reason revolves around Photoshop's use of a mathematical routine called the *Gaussian bell curve*, which exaggerates the distance over which the selection outline is blurred.

Figure 8-13 demonstrates the math visually. The top-left image shows a hard-edged elliptical selection filled with white against a black background. To its right is a side view of the ellipse, in which black pixels are short and white pixels are tall. (Okay, so it's really a graph, but I didn't want to scare you.) Because no gray pixels are in the ellipse, the side view has sharp vertical walls.

The bottom-left image shows what happens if I first feather the selection with a radius of 24 pixels and then fill it with white. The side view (bottom-right) now graphs a range of gray values, which taper gradually from black to white. See those dark gray areas labeled "2 x Radius"? Those are the pixels that fall into the 48-pixel area measured 24 pixels in and out from the pre-feathered selection outline. These gray areas slope in straight lines.

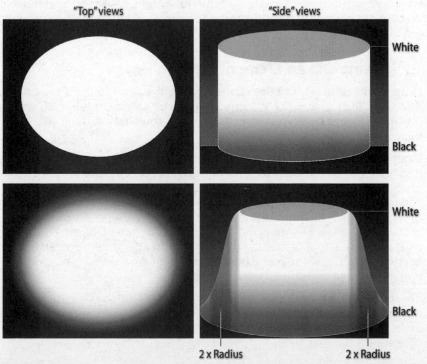

Figure 8-13: Here are some graphic demonstrations of what happens when you feather a selection. Photoshop tapers the ends of the feathered selections to prevent your eye from easily detecting where the feathering starts and stops.

The rounded areas of the side view are the Gaussian bell curves. These are appended to the radius of the feather to ensure smooth transitions between the blurry edges and the selected and deselected pixels. Programs that do not include these extra Gaussian curves end up producing ugly feathered selections that appear to have sharp, incongruous edges.

Tip

If exact space is an issue, you can count on the Feather command affecting about 2.7 times as many pixels as you enter into the Feather Radius option box, both in and out from the selection. That's a total of 5.4 times as many pixels as the radius in all.

If this was more than you wanted to know, cast it from your mind. Feathering makes the edges of a selection fuzzy — 'nuff said.

Putting feathering to use

You can use feathering to remove an element from an image while leaving the background intact, a process described in the following steps. The image described in these steps, shown in Figure 8-14, is a photo of yours truly (pardon the trousers) and my son Max (third pumpkin from the right) on a recent Allhallows Eve. While no amount of feathering could fix my pants, I can use it to do a little home remodeling. As you can see in the image, I've notated the three elements I need to remove in order to turn my home into the impenetrable fortress of solitude that I've always dreamed of.

STEPS: Removing an Element from an Image

1. **Draw a selection around the element using the lasso tool.** I'll start with my door handle and lock. The selection needn't be an exact fit; in fact, you want it rather loose, so allow a comfortable buffer zone between the edges of the image and the selection outline.

2. **Drag the selection outline over a patch in the image.** Now that you've specified the element you want to remove, you must find a patch — that is, some portion of the image to cover the element in a manner that matches the surroundings. In Figure 8-15, the best match was clearly from the middle section of my door. To select this area, move the selection outline independently of the image merely by dragging it with the lasso tool. (Dragging a selection with a selection tool moves the outline without affecting the pixels.) Make certain you allow some space between the selection outline and the element you're trying to cover.

3. **Choose Select ⇨ Feather.** Or press Ctrl+Alt+D (⌘-Option-D on the Mac). Enter a small value (8 or less) in the Feather Radius option box — just enough to make the edges fuzzy. (I entered 2.) Then press Enter or Return to initiate the operation.

Figure 8-14: The trick—or treat—is to remove various components from my front door by covering them with selections cloned from other areas.

Figure 8-15: After drawing a loose outline around the lock and handle with the lasso tool, I dragged the outline to select another portion of the door. Then I feathered the selection.

4. **Clone the patch onto the area you want to cover.** Select the move tool by pressing V. Then Alt-drag (Option-drag on the Mac) the feathered selection to clone the patch and position it over the element you want to cover, as shown in Figure 8-16. To align the patch correctly, choose Select ➪ Hide Extras or press Ctrl+H (⌘-H on the Mac) to hide the marching ants and then nudge the patch into position with the arrow keys.

Figure 8-16: Next, I used the move tool to Alt-drag (Option-drag on the Mac) the feathered selection over the lock and handle.

5. **Repeat as desired.** I used the same technique to eliminate the other undesired elements from the image, selecting from the same area of the door to get rid of the door seam, and selecting a bit of the brick wall to wipe out my doorbell. Figure 8-17 shows the details.

6. **It's all déjà vu from here.** After some more feathering, Alt-dragging, and nudging, my mission was complete, as you can see in Figure 8-18. No more points of entry. Nowhere for delivery guys to lodge take-out menus. Not even a doorbell. That'll thwart those pesky trick-or-treaters.

Figure 8-17: I used the lasso tool to draw a new outline around the seam and then dragged the outline over another portion of the door. Then I did the same for the doorbell, using the brick wall as a patch.

Figure 8-18: The final result. Even the pumpkins are pleased.

Moving and Duplicating Selections

In the preceding steps, I mentioned that you can move either the selected pixels or the empty selection outline to a new location. Now it's time to examine these techniques in greater depth.

The role of the move tool

To move selected pixels, you have to use the move tool. No longer is it acceptable merely to drag inside the selection with the marquee, lasso, or wand tool, as it was way back in Photoshop 3 and earlier. If you haven't gotten used to it yet, now is as good a time as any. The move tool is here to stay.

You can select the move tool at any time by pressing V (for *mooV*). The advantage of using the move tool is that there's no chance of deselecting an image or harming the selection outline. Drag inside the selected area to move the selection; drag outside the selection to move the entire layer, selection included. I explain layers in more detail in Chapter 12.

Tip

To access the move tool on a temporary basis, press and hold Ctrl (⌘ on the Mac). The move tool remains active as long as you hold Ctrl or ⌘. This shortcut works when any tool except the hand, direct selection, path selection, or any pen, shape, or slice tool is active. Assign this shortcut to memory at your earliest convenience. Believe me, you spend a lot of time Ctrl-dragging (⌘-dragging on the Mac) in Photoshop.

Making precise movements

Photoshop provides three methods for moving selections in prescribed increments. In each case, the move tool is active, unless otherwise indicated:

✦ First, you can nudge a selection in 1-pixel increments by pressing an arrow key on the keyboard or nudge in 10-pixel increments by pressing Shift with an arrow key. This technique is useful for making precise adjustments to the position of an image. Note that a series of consecutive nudges is recorded in the History palette (see Chapter 7) as only one history state, regardless of how much you move the selection. Choosing Undo will take the selection back to its original position in the image.

Tip

To nudge a selected area when the move tool is not active, press Ctrl (Win) or ⌘ (Mac) with an arrow key. Press Ctrl+Shift (Win) or ⌘-Shift (Mac) with an arrow key to move in 10-pixel increments. After the selection is floating—that is, after your first nudge—you can let up on the Ctrl or ⌘ key and use only the arrows (assuming a selection tool is active).

✦ Second, you can press Shift during a drag to constrain a move to a 45-degree direction—that is, horizontally, vertically, or diagonally.

✦ And third, you can use the Info palette to track your movements and to help locate a precise position in the image.

To display the Info palette, shown in Figure 8-19, choose Window ➪ Info or press F8. The first section of the Info palette displays the color values of the image area beneath your cursor. When you move a selection, the other eight items in the palette monitor movement, as follows:

✦ **X, Y:** These values show the coordinate position of your cursor. The distance is measured from the upper-left corner of the image in the current unit of measure. The unit of measure in Figure 8-19 is pixels.

✦ **ΔX, ΔY:** These values indicate the distance of your move as measured horizontally and vertically.

✦ **A, D:** The A and D values reflect the angle and direct distance of your drag.

✦ **W, H:** These values reflect the width and height of your selection.

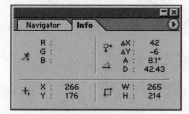

Figure 8-19: The Info palette provides a world of numerical feedback when you move a selection.

Cloning a selection

When you move a selection, you leave a hole in your image in the background color, as shown in the top half of Figure 8-20. If you prefer to leave the original in place during a move, you have to *clone* the selection—that is, create a copy of the selection without upsetting the contents of the Clipboard. Photoshop offers several ways to clone a selection:

✦ **Alt-dragging (Option-dragging on the Mac):** When the move tool is active, press Alt (Option on the Mac) and drag a selection to clone it. The bottom half of Figure 8-20 shows a selection I Alt-dragged three times. (Between clonings, I changed the gray level of each selection to set them apart a little more clearly.)

✦ **Ctrl+Alt-dragging (⌘-Option-dragging on the Mac):** If some tool other than the move tool is active, press Ctrl+Alt (⌘-Option on the Mac) and drag the selection to clone it. This is probably the technique you'll end up using most often.

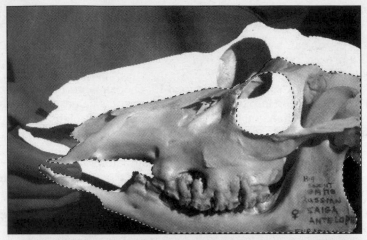

Figure 8-20: When you move a selection, you leave a gaping hole in the selection's wake (top). When you clone an image, you leave a copy of the selection behind. To illustrate this point, I cloned the selection in the bottom image three times.

✦ **Alt+arrowing (Option-arrowing on the Mac):** When the move tool is active, press Alt (Win) or Option (Mac) in combination with one of the arrow keys to clone the selection and nudge it one pixel away from the original. If you want to move the image multiple pixels, press Alt+arrow (Option-arrow on the Mac) the first time only. Then nudge the clone using the arrow key alone. Otherwise, you'll create a bunch of clones, which probably isn't what you want to do.

✦ **Ctrl+Alt+arrowing (⌘-Option-arrowing on the Mac):** If some other tool is active, press Ctrl and Alt (⌘ and Option on the Mac) with an arrow key. Again, press only Alt (Win) or Option (Mac) the first time, unless you want to create a string of clones.

✦ **Drag-and-drop:** Like about every other program on the planet, Photoshop lets you clone a selection between documents by dragging it with the move tool from one open window and dropping it in another, as demonstrated in Figure 8-21. As long as you manage to drop into the second window, the original image remains intact and selected in the first window. My advice: Don't worry about exact positioning during a drag-and-drop; first get it into the second window and then worry about placement.

You can drag-and-drop multiple layers if you link the layers first. For more information on this subject, see Chapter 12.

✦ **Shift-drop:** If the two images are exactly the same size — pixel for pixel — press Shift when dropping the selection to position it in the same spot it occupied in the original image. This is called *registering* the selection.

If an area is selected in the destination image, Shift-dropping positions the selection you're moving in the center of the selection in the destination image. This tip works regardless of whether the two images are the same size.

✦ **Ctrl-drag-and-drop (⌘-drag-and-drop on the Mac):** Again, if some other tool than the move tool is selected, you must press Ctrl (Win) or ⌘ (Mac) when you drag to move the selected pixels from one window to the other.

Moving a selection outline independently of its contents

After all this talk about the move tool and the Ctrl key (⌘ key on the Mac), you may be wondering what happens if you drag a selection with the marquee, lasso, or wand. The answer is, you move the selection outline independently of the image. This technique, which I used earlier in this chapter in the steps, "Removing an Element from an Image," serves as yet another means to manipulate inaccurate selection outlines. It also enables you to mimic one portion of an image inside another portion of the image or inside a completely different image window.

In the top image in Figure 8-22, I used the marquee tool to drag the skull outline down and to the right, so that it only partially overlapped the skull. I then lightened the new selection, applied a few strokes to set it off from its background, and gave it stripes, as shown in the bottom image. For all I know, this is exactly what a female Russian Saiga antelope looks like.

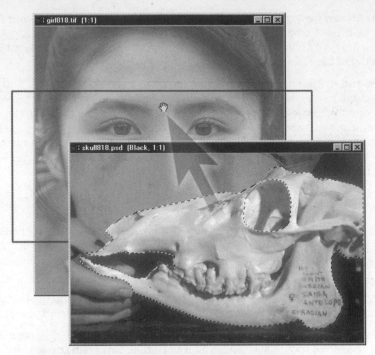

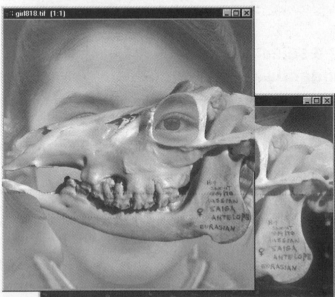

Figure 8-21: Use the move tool to drag a selection from one open window and drop it into another (top). This creates a clone of the selection in the receiving window (bottom).

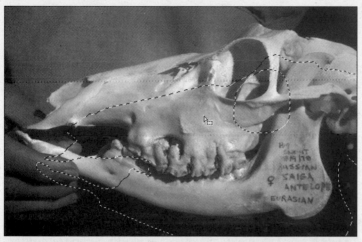

Figure 8-22: Drag a selection with a selection tool to move the outline independently of its image (top). Wherever you drag the selection outline becomes the new selection (bottom).

Tip

You can nudge a selection outline independently of its contents by pressing an arrow key when a selection tool is active. Press Shift with an arrow key to move the outline in 10-pixel increments.

For even more selection fun, you can drag-and-drop empty selection outlines between images. Just drag the outline from one image and drop it into another, as demonstrated in the first example of Figure 8-21. The only difference is that only the selection outline gets cloned; the pixels remain behind. This is a great way to copy pixels back and forth between images. You can set up an exact selection outline in Image A, drag it into Image B with the marquee tool, move it over the pixels you want to clone, and Ctrl-drag-and-drop (⌘-drag-and-drop on the Mac) the selection back into Image A. This is slick as hair grease, I'm telling you.

So remember: The selection tools affect the selection outline only. The selection tools never affect the pixels themselves; that's the move tool's job.

Scaling or rotating a selection outline

In case you fell asleep during the last two sentences, let me repeat the important part: Selection outlines stay independent — and entirely changeable — as long as a selection tool is active. In addition to moving a selection outline, you can transform it by choosing Select ⇨ Transform Selection.

When you select this command, Photoshop displays a transformation boundary framed by eight handles, as shown in Figure 8-23. You can drag the handles to adjust the outline as described in the upcoming list. In addition, the Options bar gives you access to a slew of mysterious option boxes, as shown at the top of the figure. You can enter specific values to relocate, size, rotate, and skew the selection outline precisely.

The handles and Options bar controls work just as they do for the Edit ⇨ Free Transform command, which I cover in gripping detail in Chapter 12. To save you the backbreaking chore of flipping ahead four chapters, though, here's the short course:

✦ **Scale:** Drag any of the handles to scale the selection, as shown in Figure 8-23. Shift-drag to scale proportionally, Alt-drag (Option-drag on the Mac) to scale with respect to the origin (labeled in the figure). You can move the origin just by dragging it.

Alternatively, enter a scale percentage in the W (width) and H (height) boxes in the Options bar. By default, Photoshop maintains the original proportions of the outline. If that doesn't suit you, click the Constrain Proportions button between the two boxes.

See that little replica of the transformation boundary near the left end of the Options bar? The black square represents the current origin. You can click the boxes to relocate the origin to one of the handles. Use the X and Y values to change the position of the origin numerically. Click the triangular delta symbol, labeled in Figure 8-23, to measure positioning relative to the transformation origin.

✦ **Rotate:** Enter a value in the Rotate box or drag outside the transformation boundary to rotate the selection, as in the second example in Figure 8-23. The rotation always occurs with respect to the origin.

To rotate the outline by 90 or 180 degrees, right-click (Control-click on the Mac) the image window and choose the rotation amount you want from the resulting pop-up menu.

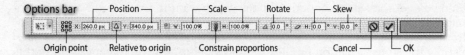

Options bar — Position — — Scale — Rotate — Skew

Origin point   Relative to origin   Constrain proportions   Cancel — — OK

Drag handle to scale

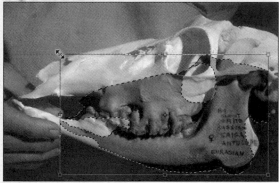

Drag outside to rotate

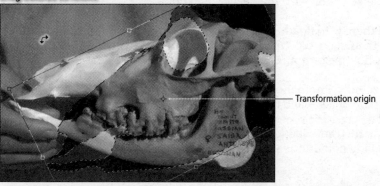

Transformation origin

Figure 8-23: After choosing Select ⇨ Transform Selection, you can scale the selection outline (top) and rotate it (bottom), all without harming the image in the slightest.

✦ **Flip:** You can flip a selection outline by dragging one handle past its opposite handle, but this is a lot of work. The easier way is to right-click (Control-click on the Mac) inside the image window and choose Flip Horizontal or Flip Vertical from the pop-up menu.

✦ **Skew and distort:** To skew the selection outline, Ctrl-drag (⌘-drag on the Mac) a side, top, or bottom handle. Or enter values in the H (horizontal) and V (vertical) skew boxes in the Options bar. To distort the selection, Ctrl-drag (Win) or ⌘-drag (Mac) a corner handle.

When you get the selection outline the way you want it, press Enter or Return or double-click inside the boundary. To cancel the transformation, press Escape. Alternatively, click the checkmark button near the right end of the Options bar to apply the transformation or click the "no symbol" button to cancel out of the operation.

The untimely demise of floating selections

As you may (or may not) recall, Photoshop 4 bludgeoned floating selections into a state of unconsciousness. While Version 5 didn't entirely kill them, it moved them to the critical list. Version 6 saw them in critical but stable condition, and that's where they remain in Version 7.

In case you're unsure what I'm talking about, a *floating selection* is an element that hovers above the surface of the image. Any time you move a selection or clone it, Photoshop floats the selection onto a temporary layer. This way, you can move the selection or nudge it into position without harming the underlying image. And if you press Backspace (Win) or Delete (Mac), Photoshop deletes the floater rather than filling the selection with the background color.

But that's all there is to floating selections now. The Floating Selection item that used to appear in the Layers palette is a thing of the past, so you don't even know when a selection is floating or not. And the only way to defloat a floater is to deselect it.

Tip   Quite unexpectedly, Photoshop still lets you mix a floater with the image behind it by modifying the opacity and blend mode settings. After dragging a selection to float it, choose Edit ⇨ Fade or press Ctrl+Shift+F (⌘-Shift-F on the Mac). Then modify the settings inside the Fade dialog box to mix the floater with the background. The process is incredibly nonintuitive, but it works.

How to Draw and Edit Paths

Photoshop's path tools provide the most flexible and precise ways to define a selection short of masking. However, while a godsend to the experienced user, the path tools represent something of a chore to novices and intermediates. Most people take some time to grow comfortable with the pen tool, for example, because it requires you to draw a selection outline one point at a time.

Note   If you're familiar with Illustrator's pen tool and other path-editing functions, you'll find Photoshop's tools nearly identical. Photoshop doesn't provide the breadth of options available in Illustrator, but the basic techniques are the same. Photoshop also includes a set of path-drawing tools to help smooth out the learning curve for inexperienced users. You can use any of the shape tools — rectangle, rounded rectangle, line, ellipse, polygon, and custom shape — to draw a simple geometric path.

The following pages get you up and running with all the path features. I explain how to draw a path, edit it, convert it to a selection outline, and stroke it with a paint or edit tool. All in all, you learn more about paths than you ever wanted to know.

Paths overview

You create and edit paths from scratch by using the various pen tools or shape tools. (Figure 8-2, earlier in this chapter, shows all the path-related tools along with their selection tool counterparts.) Path management options — which enable you to convert paths to selections, fill and stroke paths, and save and delete them — reside in the Paths palette, shown in Figure 8-24.

Stroke path | Make path | Delete path
Fill path | Make selection | New path

Figure 8-24: To save and organize your paths, display the Paths palette by choosing Window ➪ Paths.

How paths work

Paths differ from normal selections because they exist on the equivalent of a distinct, object-oriented layer that sits in front of the bitmapped image. This setup enables you to edit a path with point-by-point precision with no fear that you'll accidentally mess up the image, as you can when you edit ordinary selection outlines. After you get a path just so, you convert it into a standard selection outline, which you can then use to edit the contents of the image. (I detail this part of the process in the section "Converting and saving paths," later in this chapter.)

The following steps explain the basic process of drawing a selection outline with the path tools. I explain each step in more detail throughout the remainder of this chapter.

STEPS: Creating a Selection with the Path Tools

1. **Draw the path.** Use a pen tool or a shape tool to draw the outline of your prospective selection.

   If your goal is to select multiple areas of the image, draw outlines around all of them. A path can include as many separate segments as you like. Technically, the individual segments in a path are called *subpaths*.

2. **Edit the path.** If the path requires some adjustment, reshape it using the other path tools.

3. **Save the path.** When you get the path exactly as you want it, save the path by choosing the Save Path command from the Paths palette menu. Or double-click the *Work Path* item in the scrolling list.

4. **Convert the path to a selection.** You can make the path a selection outline by choosing the Make Selection command or by pressing Enter on the numeric keypad when a path or selection tool is active.

That's it. After you convert the path to a selection, it works like any of the selection outlines described earlier. You can feather a selection, move it, copy it, clone it, or apply one of the special effects described in future chapters. The path remains intact in case you want to do further editing or use it again.

Sorting through the path tools

Before I get into my long-winded description of how you draw and edit paths, here's a quick introduction to the path tools. First up, the tools on the pen tool flyout:

Pen: Use the pen tool to draw paths in Photoshop one point at a time. Click to create a corner in a path; drag to make a smooth point that results in a continuous arc. (Never fear, I explain this tool *ad nauseam* in the "Drawing paths with the pen tool" section later in this chapter.) You can select the pen tool by pressing P; press P again to toggle to the freeform pen, described next. (As always, the shortcuts assume that you turned off the Use Shift Key for Tool Switch option in the Preferences dialog box.)

Freeform pen: Drag with this tool to create a path that automatically follows the twists and turns of your drag. Simplicity at its best; control at its lowest. Luckily, you can turn around and edit the path after you initially draw it.

The magnetic pen, doesn't actually appear in the toolbox. But if you select the freeform pen and then select the Magnetic check box in the Options bar, the freeform pen dashes into a phone booth and becomes the magnetic pen. Click the edge of the foreground element you want to select and then move the cursor along the edge of the shape. Photoshop automatically assigns points as it deems appropriate.

Add anchor point: Click an existing path to add a point to it.

 Delete anchor point: Click an existing point in a path to delete the point without creating a break in the path's outline.

Convert point: Click or drag a point to convert it to a corner or smooth point. You also can drag a handle to convert the point. To access the convert point tool, press Alt (Win) or Option (Mac) when the pen is active. Press Ctrl+Alt (⌘-Option on the Mac) when an arrow tool (explained in the next section) is active. (The terms *anchor point*, *smooth point*, and others associated with drawing paths are explained in the upcoming section.)

You can use the pen tool to add, delete, and convert points, too, providing that you turn on the Auto Add/Delete check box in the Options bar. Pass the cursor over a segment in a selected path to toggle to the add anchor point tool; move the cursor over a point to get the delete anchor point tool. Press Alt (Option on the Mac) over a point to get the convert point tool.

If all you need is a simple, geometric path, you can save time by creating the path with the shape tools. I cover these tools in detail in Chapter 14, so I won't repeat everything here. Just know that after you select a shape tool, you shift it into path-drawing mode by clicking the Paths button in the Options bar, labeled in Figure 8-25. (The pen that appears on the button face serves as a reminder that you're in path country.) Photoshop sets the shape tools to that mode automatically if you select them while working on an existing path.

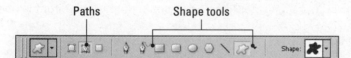

Figure 8-25: Click the Paths button in the Options bar to draw paths with the shape tools.

As you draw, Photoshop automatically adds whatever points are needed. You only need to worry about selecting a path overlap button, which determines how paths intersect and interact. See the next section to find out which button to choose when.

After you create a path, you can select it or edit it by using the two tools on the flyout directly above the pen tools flyout:

Path selection tool (black arrow): This tool selects an entire path. Just click inside the path to select it. If you created subpaths, the tool selects only the one underneath your cursor. You also use this tool to select vector objects, as explained in Chapter 14.

Direct selection tool (white arrow): This tool permits you to drag points and handles to reshape a path. You can access the tool when any other path tool is active by pressing and holding Ctrl (⌘ on the Mac). And you can Alt-click (Option-click on the Mac) inside a path to select the entire path without switching to the path selection (black arrow) tool.

Note

From this point on, I refer to these two tools as the black arrow and white arrow. First off, because we Photoshop users are a visually oriented lot, I'm guessing that you can find the right tool more quickly if I say "click with the black arrow" or "drag with the white arrow" than if I use the technical tool names. Second, the nicknames save some page space, enabling me to fill your head with even more jaw-dropping insights than would otherwise be possible.

You can access the arrow tools from the keyboard by pressing A. You know the drill: Press A to switch to the tool that's currently active; press A again to toggle to the other tool. (Add Shift if you turned on the Use Shift Key for Tool Switch option in the Preferences dialog box.)

Drawing paths with the pen tool

When drawing with the regular pen tool, you build a path by creating individual points. Photoshop automatically connects the points with segments, which are simply straight or curved lines.

Note

Adobe prefers the term *anchor points* rather than *points* because the points anchor the path into place. But most folks just call 'em points. I mean, *all* points associated with paths are anchor points, so it's not like there's some potential for confusion.

All paths in Photoshop are *Bézier* (pronounced bay-zee-ay) paths, meaning they rely on the same mathematical curve definitions that make up the core of the PostScript printer language. The Bézier curve model allows for zero, one, or two levers to be associated with each point in a path. These levers, labeled in Figure 8-26, are called *Bézier control handles* or simply *handles.* You can move each handle in relation to a point, enabling you to bend and tug at a curved segment like it's a piece of soft wire.

The following list summarizes how you can use the pen tool to build paths in Photoshop:

✦ **Adding segments:** To build a path, create one point after another until the path is the desired length and shape. Photoshop automatically draws a segment between each new point and its predecessor. (The next section gets specific about how you use the tool to create points.)

Smooth points

Bézier
control
handles

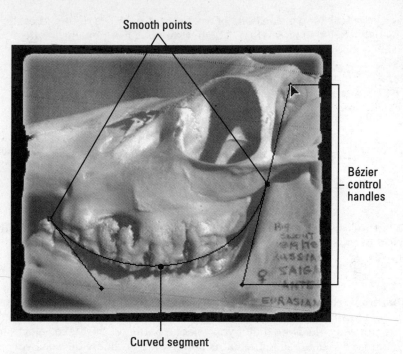

Curved segment

Figure 8-26: Drag with the pen tool to create a smooth point flanked by two Bézier control handles.

✦ **Closing the path:** If you plan to convert the path to a selection outline, you need to complete the outline by clicking again on the first point in the path. Every point will then have one segment entering it and another segment exiting it. Such a path is called a *closed path* because it completely encloses the desired area.

✦ **Leaving the path open:** If you plan to apply the Stroke Path command (explained later), you may not want to close a path. To leave the path open, so it has a specific beginning and ending, deactivate the path by saving it (choose the Save Path command from the Paths palette menu).

✦ **Extending an open path:** To reactivate an open path, click or drag one of its endpoints. Photoshop draws a segment between the endpoint and the next point you create.

✦ **Joining two open subpaths:** To join one open subpath with another, click or drag an endpoint in the first subpath and then click or drag an endpoint in the second.

✦ **Specifying path overlap:** You can set the path tools to one of four settings, which control how Photoshop treats overlapping areas in a path when you convert the path to a selection.

To make your will known, click one of the buttons near the right end of the Options bar, labeled in Figure 8-27. The button you click remains in effect until you choose another button.

Add   Intersect

Subtract   Exclude

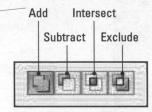

Figure 8-27: Click one of these buttons in the Options bar to control how Photoshop treats overlapping areas when you convert a path to a selection.

These buttons also appear when you draw paths with the shape tools. With either set of tools, your choices are as follows:

- **Add to path area:** Select this button if you want all areas, overlapping or not, to be selected.

- **Subtract from path area:** Select this button to draw a subpath that eats a hole in an existing path. Any areas that you enclose with the subpath are not selected. Note that if you select a path and the Make Selection command is dimmed in the Paths palette, it's probably because you drew the path with the subtract option in force.

- **Intersect path areas:** The opposite of Exclude, this option selects *only* overlapping areas.

- **Exclude overlapping path areas:** Any overlapping regions are not included in the selection.

You can change the overlap setting for a subpath after you draw it if necessary. Select the paths with the black arrow tool and then click the overlap button for the setting you want to use.

✦ **Deactivating paths:** At any time, you can press Enter or Return to *dismiss* — deactivate — the path. When you do, Photoshop hides the path from view. To retrieve the path, click its name in the Paths palette. Be careful with this one, though: If you dismiss an unsaved path and then start drawing a new path, you can lose the dismissed one. For more details, see "Converting and saving paths," later in this chapter.

✦ **Hiding paths:** If you merely want to hide paths from view, press Ctrl+H (⌘-H on the Mac), which hides selections, guides, and other screen elements as well. You can also press Ctrl+Shift+H (⌘-Shift-H on the Mac) or choose View ⇨ Show ⇨ Target Path to toggle the path display on and off. To select which items you want to hide with Ctrl+H (Win) or ⌘-H (Mac), choose View ⇨ Show ⇨ Show Extras Options.

To get a better sense of how the pen tool works, click the arrow button at the right end of the row of path drawing icons to access the Pen Options (or "Option," in this case). Here you can enable the Rubber Band check box. This tells Photoshop to draw an animated segment between the last point drawn and the cursor. Unless you're an old pro and the connecting segment gets in your face, there's no reason not to select Rubber Band. (Besides, what with the '70s being so hot with the tee-nies, the Rubber Band check box makes the pen tool seem, well, kind of funky. Consider it another chance to bond with today's youth.)

The anatomy of points and segments

Points in a Bézier path act as little road signs. Each point steers the path by specifying how a segment enters it and how another segment exits it. You specify the identity of each little road sign by clicking, dragging, or Alt-dragging (Option-dragging on the Mac) with the pen tool. The following items explain the specific kinds of points and segments you can create in Photoshop. See Figure 8-28 for examples.

✦ **Corner point:** Click with the pen tool to create a *corner point*, which represents the corner between two straight segments in a path.

✦ **Straight segment:** Click at two different locations to create a straight segment between two corner points. Shift-click to draw a 45-degree-angle segment between the new corner point and its predecessor.

✦ **Smooth point:** Drag to create a smooth point with two symmetrical Bézier control handles. A *smooth point* ensures that one segment meets with another in a continuous arc.

✦ **Curved segment:** Drag at two different locations to create a curved segment between two smooth points.

✦ **Straight segment followed by curved:** After drawing a straight segment, drag from the corner point you just created to add a Bézier control handle. Then drag again at a different location to append a curved segment to the end of the straight segment.

✦ **Curved segment followed by straight:** After drawing a curved segment, Alt-click (Option-click on the Mac) the smooth point you just created to delete the forward Bézier control handle. This converts the smooth point to a corner point with one handle. Then click at a different location to append a straight segment to the end of the curved segment.

✦ **Cusp point:** After drawing a curved segment, Alt-drag (Option-drag on the Mac) from the smooth point you just created to redirect the forward Bézier control handle, converting the smooth point to a corner point with two independent handles, sometimes known as a *cusp point*. Then drag again at a new location to append a curved segment that proceeds in a different direction than the previous curved segment.

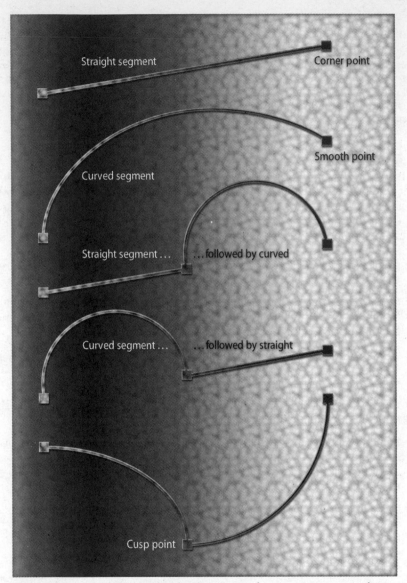

Figure 8-28: The different kinds of points and segments you can draw with the pen tool.

Going freeform

If the pen tool is too much work, try the freeform pen tool, which is just a press of the P key away from the standard pen. As you drag, Photoshop tracks the motion of the cursor with a continuous line. After you release the mouse button, the program automatically assigns and positions the points and segments needed to create the Bézier path.

Tip

You can draw straight segments with the freeform pen: As you're dragging, press and hold Alt (Win) or Option (Mac). Then click around to create points. When you're finished drawing straight segments, drag again and release Alt (Option on the Mac).

Alas, automation is rarely perfect. (If it were, what need would these machines have for us?) When the program finishes its calculations, a path may appear riddled with far too many points or equipped with too few.

Fortunately, you can adjust the performance of the freeform pen to accommodate your personal drawing style using the Curve Fit control, which you can access by clicking the arrow at the end of the row of path drawing tool icons in the Options bar. You can enter any value between 0.5 and 10, which Photoshop interprets in screen pixels. The default value of 2, for example, instructs the program to ignore any jags in your mouse movements that do not exceed 2 pixels in length or width. Setting the value to 0.5 makes the freeform pen extremely sensitive; setting the value to 10 smoothes the roughest of gestures.

A Curve Fit from 2 to 4 is generally adequate for most folks, but you should experiment to determine the best setting. Like the magic wand's Tolerance setting, you can't alter the Curve Fit value for a path after you've drawn it. Photoshop calculates the points for a path only once, after you release the mouse button.

Going magnetic

To use the magnetic pen tool, first select the freeform pen tool and then select the Magnetic check box in the Options bar. The magnetic pen works like a combination of the magnetic lasso and the freeform pen. As with the magnetic lasso, you begin by clicking anywhere along the edge of the image element you want to select. (For a pertinent blast from the past, see Figure 8-5.) Then move the cursor — no need to drag — around the perimeter of the element and watch Photoshop do its work. To set an anchor point, click. When you come full circle, click the point where you started to complete the path.

You can create straight segments by Alt-clicking (Option-clicking on the Mac), just as you can when using the freeform pen without Magnetic turned on. And the Curve Fit option (in the Freeform Pen Options drop-down palette shown in Figure 8-29) controls the smoothness of the path. Lower values trace the edges more carefully; higher values result in fewer points and smoother edges. The other options here give you access to the Width, Contrast, Frequency, and Pen Pressure, all of which are lifted right out of the magnetic lasso playbook. Read "Modifying the magnetic lasso options" near the beginning of this chapter for complete information.

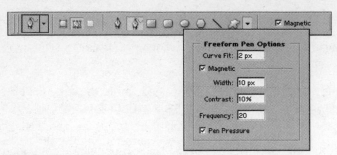

Figure 8-29: While the freeform pen is active, select the Magnetic check box in the Options bar to access the magnetic pen. Click the arrow at the left of the check box to display additional options.

Editing paths

If you take time to master the default pen tool, you'll find yourself drawing accurate paths more and more frequently. But you'll never get it right 100 percent of the time—or even 50 percent of the time. And when you rely on the freeform or magnetic pen tools, the results are never dead on. From your first timid steps until you develop into a seasoned pro, you'll rely heavily on Photoshop's capability to *reshape* paths by moving points and handles, adding and deleting points, and converting points to change the curvature of segments. So don't worry too much if your path looks like an erratic stitch on the forehead of Frankenstein's monster. The path-edit tools provide all the second chances you'll ever need.

Reshaping paths

The white arrow tool—known in official Adobe circles as the direct selection tool—represents the foremost path-reshaping function in Photoshop. To select this tool from the keyboard, first press A to select the black arrow tool and then press A again to toggle to the white arrow. Or just Alt-click (Win) or Option-click (Mac) the black arrow tool in the toolbox. (You use the black arrow to select, relocate, and duplicate entire paths or subpaths, as explained in the upcoming section "Moving and cloning paths.")

Tip

Press and hold Ctrl (Win) or ⌘ (Mac) to access the white arrow tool temporarily when one of the pen or path-edit tools is selected. When you release Ctrl or ⌘, the cursor returns to the selected tool. This is a great way to edit a path while you're drawing it.

However you put your hands on the white arrow, you can perform any of the following functions with it:

✦ **Selecting points:** Click a point to select it independently of other points in a path. Shift-click to select an additional point, even if the point belongs to a different subpath than other selected points. Alt-click (Win) or Option-click (Mac) a path to select all its points in one fell swoop. You can even marquee points by dragging in a rectangle around them. You cannot, however, apply commands from the Select menu, such as All or Deselect, to the selection of paths.

✦ **Drag selected points:** To move one or more points, select them and then drag one of the selected points. All selected points move the same distance and direction. When you move a point while a neighboring point remains stationary, the segment between the two points shrinks, stretches, and bends to accommodate the change in distance. Segments located between two selected or deselected points remain unchanged during a move.

You can move selected points in 1-pixel increments by pressing arrow keys. If both a portion of the image and points in a path are selected, the arrow keys move the points only. Because paths reside on a higher layer, they take precedence in all functions that might concern them.

✦ **Drag a straight segment:** You also can reshape a path by dragging its segments. When you drag a straight segment, the two corner points on either side of the segment move as well. As illustrated in Figure 8-30, the neighboring segments stretch, shrink, or bend to accommodate the drag.

This technique works best with straight segments drawn with the default pen tool. Segments created by Alt-clicking (Option-clicking on the Mac) with the freeform or magnetic pen may include trace control handles that make Photoshop think the segment is actually curved.

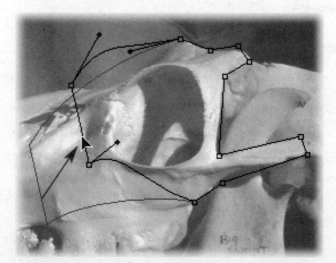

Figure 8-30: Drag a straight segment to move the segment and change the length, direction, and curvature of the neighboring segments.

✦ **Drag a curved segment:** When you drag a curved segment, you stretch, shrink, or bend that segment, as demonstrated in Figure 8-31.

When you drag a curved segment, drag from the middle of the segment, approximately equidistant from both its points. This method provides the best leverage and ensures that the segment doesn't go flying off in some weird direction you hadn't anticipated.

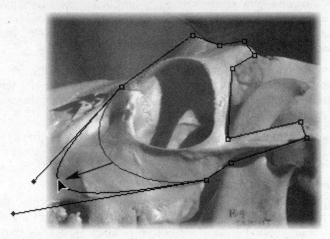

Figure 8-31: Drag a curved segment to change the curvature of that segment only and leave the neighboring segments unchanged.

✦ **Drag a Bézier control handle:** Select a point and drag either of its Bézier control handles to change the curvature of the corresponding segment without moving any of the points in the path. If the point is a smooth point, moving one handle moves both handles in the path. If you want to move a smooth handle independently of its partner, you must use the convert point tool, as discussed in the "Converting points" section, later in this chapter.

Adding and deleting points and segments

The quantity of points and segments in a path is forever subject to change. Whether a path is closed or open, you can reshape it by adding and deleting points, which, in turn, forces the addition or deletion of a segment:

✦ **Appending a point to the end of an open path:** If a path is open, you can activate one of its endpoints by clicking or dragging it with the pen tool, depending on the identity of the endpoint and whether you want the next segment to be straight or curved. Photoshop is then prepared to draw a segment between the endpoint and the next point you create.

✦ **Closing an open path:** You also can use the technique I just described to close an open path. Select one endpoint, click or drag it with the pen tool to activate it, and then click or drag the opposite endpoint. Photoshop draws a segment between the two endpoints, closing the path and eliminating both endpoints by converting them to *interior points*, which simply means the points are bound on both sides by segments.

✦ **Joining two open subpaths:** You can join two open subpaths to create one longer open path. To do so, activate an endpoint of the first subpath and then, using the pen tool, click or drag an endpoint of the second subpath.

✦ **Inserting a point in a segment:** Using the add point tool, click anywhere along an open or closed path to insert a point and divide the segment into two segments. Photoshop automatically inserts a corner or smooth point, depending on its reading of the path. If the point does not exactly meet your needs, use the convert point tool to change it. In addition to using the add point tool, you can select the Auto Add/Delete check box in the Options bar. Then, whenever you pass the pen tool cursor over a segment, you see the little plus sign next to your cursor, indicating that the add point tool is temporarily in the house. This trick works only if the path is selected, however.

✦ **Deleting a point and breaking the path:** The simplest way to delete a point and break the path is to select it with the white arrow and press Delete or Clear. (You also can choose Edit ⇨ Clear, though why you would want to expend so much effort is beyond me.) When you delete an interior point, you delete both segments associated with that point, resulting in a break in the path. If you delete an endpoint from an open path, you delete the single segment associated with the point.

✦ **Removing a point without breaking the path:** Select the delete point tool and click a point in an open or closed path to delete the point and draw a new segment between the two points that neighbor it. The delete point tool ensures that no break occurs in a path.

Tip

To access the delete point tool when using the pen tool, select the Auto Add/ Delete check box in the Options bar and then hover your cursor over a selected interior point in an existing path. You see the minus sign next to the cursor, indicating that the delete point tool is active. Click the point and it goes away. Alternately, you can remove a point when the add point tool is active by Alt-clicking (Option-clicking on the Mac), and vice versa.

✦ **Deleting a segment:** You can delete a single interior segment from a path without affecting any point. To do so, first click outside the path with the white arrow tool to deselect the path. Then click the segment you want to delete and press Delete. When you delete an interior segment, you create a break in your path.

Converting points

Photoshop lets you change the identity of an interior point. You can convert a corner point to a smooth point and vice versa. You perform all point conversions using the convert point tool as follows:

✦ **Smooth to corner:** Click an existing smooth point to convert it to a corner point with no Bézier control handle.

✦ **Smooth to cusp:** Drag one of the handles of a smooth point to move it independently of the other, thus converting the smooth point to a cusp.

✦ **Corner to smooth:** Drag from a corner point to convert it to a smooth point with two symmetrical Bézier control handles.

✦ **Cusp to smooth:** Drag one of the handles of a cusp point to lock both handles back into alignment, thus converting the cusp to a smooth point.

Press Alt (Win) or Option (Mac) to access the convert point tool temporarily when one of the three pen tools is active and positioned over a selected point. To do the same when an arrow tool is active, press Ctrl+Alt (⌘-Option on the Mac).

Transforming paths

In addition to all the aforementioned path-altering techniques, you can scale, rotate, skew, and otherwise transform paths using the following techniques:

✦ To transform all subpaths in a group — such as both the eye and skull outline in the first example of Figure 8-32 — select either arrow tool and click off a path to make sure all paths are deselected. Then choose Edit ➪ Free Transform Path.

✦ To transform a single subpath independently of others in a group, click it with the black arrow and then select the Show Bounding Box check box in the Options bar. Or click the path with the white arrow and choose Edit ➪ Free Transform Path.

✦ Photoshop even lets you transform some points independently of others inside a single path, as demonstrated in the second example of Figure 8-32. Just use the white arrow to select the points you want to modify and then choose Edit ➪ Free Transform Points.

The keyboard shortcut for all of these operations is Ctrl+T (⌘-T on the Mac). If you select an independent path — or specific points inside a path — press Ctrl+Alt+T (⌘-Option-T on the Mac) to transform a duplicate of the path and leave the original unaffected.

Rotate cursor   Transformation origin

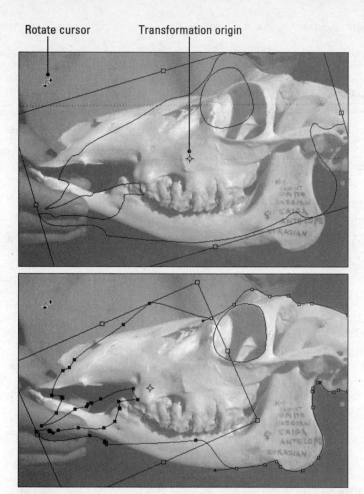

Figure 8-32: To transform multiple paths at once (top), deselect all paths and press Ctrl+T (⌘-T on the Mac). Alternatively, you can transform independent paths or points by selecting them and pressing Ctrl+T (bottom).

In an attempt to conserve tree matter — which is being wasted liberally enough in this tome — I explain the larger topic of transformation in one central location, the "Applying Transformations" section of Chapter 12. Even so, here's a brief rundown of your transformation options after you press Ctrl+T (⌘-T on the Mac):

✦ **Scale:** To scale a path, drag one of the eight square handles that adorn the transformation boundary. Alt-drag (Win) or Option-drag (Mac) a handle to scale with respect to the origin point. You can move the origin by dragging it or by clicking one of the boxes in the little bounding box icon at the left end of the Options bar.

✦ **Rotate:** Drag outside the boundary to rotate the paths or points, as demonstrated in Figure 8-32.

✦ **Flip:** Right-click (Control-click on the Mac) to access a pop-up menu of transformation options. Choose Flip Horizontal or Flip Vertical to create a mirror image of the path.

✦ **Skew:** Ctrl-drag (Win) or ⌘-drag (Mac) one of the side handles to slant the paths. Press Shift along with Ctrl or ⌘ to constrain the slant along a consistent axis.

✦ **Distort:** Ctrl-drag (Win) or ⌘-drag (Mac) one of the corner handles to distort the paths.

✦ **Perspective:** Press Ctrl+Shift+Alt (⌘-Shift-Option on the Mac) and drag a corner handle to achieve a perspective effect.

Note

You can't take advantage of the distortion or perspective feature when individual points are selected. These techniques apply to whole paths only.

✦ **Numerical transformations:** If you need to transform a path by a very specific amount, use the controls in the Options bar, which are the same ones you get when transforming a regular selection. Modify the values as desired and press Enter or Return. (Figure 8-23 earlier in this chapter labels the options.)

When you finish stretching and distorting your paths, press Enter or Return or double-click inside the boundary to apply the transformation. You also can click the check-mark button at the right end of the Options bar. To undo the last transformation inside the transform mode, press Ctrl+Z (⌘-Z on the Mac). Or bag the whole thing by pressing Escape.

Tip

To repeat the last transformation on another path, press Ctrl+Shift+T (⌘-Shift-T on the Mac).

Moving and cloning paths

You can relocate and duplicate paths as follows:

✦ **Clone a path:** Click inside the path with the black arrow tool to select it. To select multiple subpaths, Shift-click them, or marquee-drag around them. Then Alt-drag (Option-drag on the Mac) to clone all selected paths.

✦ **Move a path:** After selecting the path with the black arrow, drag the path to its new home.

✦ **Align and distribute paths:** You can align two or more paths by selecting them with the black arrow and then clicking an alignment button in the Options bar. To space the paths evenly across the image, click one of the distribution buttons, which are shown in Figure 8-33. Press Enter or Return or click the check-mark button in the Options bar to apply the transformation.

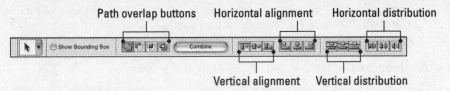

Figure 8-33: You can align and distribute multiple selected paths, just as you can layers and vector objects.

Merging and deleting paths

When the black arrow is selected, the Options bar contains a Combine button (see Figure 8-33). Clicking this button merges all selected subpaths into one. When Photoshop combines the subpaths, it does so according to which path overlap options were active when you drew the subpaths. Remember, you can select a subpath with the black arrow to change its overlap setting if necessary. Just select the subpath and then click the appropriate overlap button in the Options bar (see Figure 8-33). Refer to the earlier section, "Drawing paths with the pen tool," for more information about overlap options.

To get rid of a path, click inside it with the black arrow or drag around it with the white arrow. Then press Delete. That path is outta here.

Filling paths

After you finish drawing a path, you can convert it to a selection outline — as described in the upcoming "Converting paths to selections" section — or you can paint it. You can paint the interior of the path by choosing the Fill Path command from the Paths palette menu, or you can paint the outline of the path by choosing Stroke Path. In either case, Photoshop applies the fill on the active image layer.

The Fill Path command works much like Edit ⇨ Fill. After drawing a path, choose the Fill Path command or Alt-click (Option-click on the Mac) the fill path icon in the lower-left corner of the palette (the one that looks like a filled circle). Photoshop displays a slight variation of the Fill dialog box discussed in Chapter 6; the only difference is the inclusion of two Rendering options. Enter a value in the Feather Radius option box to blur the edges of the fill, as if the path were a selection with a feathered outline. Select the Anti-aliased check box to slightly soften the outline of the filled area. If you simply click the fill path icon without holding down a modifier key, the path is automatically filled with the foreground color.

If you select one or more subpaths, the Fill Path command changes to Fill Subpaths, enabling you to fill the selected subpaths only. The fill path icon also affects only the selected subpaths.

When applying the fill, Photoshop adheres to the overlap option you used when creating the path. Suppose that you draw two round paths, one fully inside the other. If you drew both circles with the Add overlap option active, both circles get filled. If you drew the interior circle with the Invert option active, Photoshop fills only the area between the two paths, resulting in the letter *O*.

If the Fill Path command fills only part or none of the path, the path probably falls outside a selection outline. Choose Select ➪ Deselect or press Ctrl+D (⌘-D on the Mac) to deselect the image and then choose the Fill Path command again.

Painting along a path

Unlike the Fill Path command, which bears a strong resemblance to Edit ➪ Fill, the Stroke Path command is altogether different from Edit ➪ Stroke. Edit ➪ Stroke creates outlines on an active selection, whereas the Stroke Path command enables you to paint a brush stroke along the contours of a path. This may not sound like a big deal at first, but this feature enables you to combine the spontaneity of the paint and edit tools with the structure and precision of a path.

To paint a path, choose the Stroke Path command from the Paths palette menu to display the Stroke Path dialog box shown in Figure 8-34. In this dialog box, you can choose the paint or edit tool with which you want to stroke the path (which only means to paint a brush stroke along a path). Photoshop drags the chosen tool along the exact route of the path, retaining any tool or brush shape settings that were in force when you chose the tool.

The Stroke Path dialog box includes a nifty new Simulate Pressure check box, which is a gem, particularly to those who don't have a pressure-sensitive tablet. Provided you use appropriate settings in the Brushes palette, this option begins your stroke with a thin line, fattens it up as it reaches the middle, and then tapers it off as it reaches the end. The effect is very similar to what you could achieve with a pressure-sensitive drawing tablet. For experimentation, try these settings: Choose a large brush (around 20 pixels or so), turn on Shape Dynamics in the Brushes palette, set the first Control to Pen Pressure and the other controls to Off, and set all the sliders as low as they will go. Now when you stroke your path, choose Brush as the tool, and turn on Simulate Pressure. Tres elegant, non?

You can also display the Stroke Path dialog box by Alt-clicking (Win) or Option-clicking (Mac) on the stroke path icon, the second icon at the bottom of the Paths palette (labeled back in Figure 8-24). If you prefer to bypass the dialog box, select a paint or an edit tool and then either click the stroke path icon or simply press Enter or Return. Instead of displaying the dialog box, Photoshop assumes that you want to use the selected tool and strokes away. If any tool but a paint or an edit tool is active, Photoshop strokes the path using the tool you previously selected in the Stroke Path dialog box.

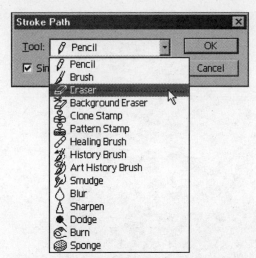

Figure 8-34: Select the paint or edit tool that you want Photoshop to use to stroke the path.

If you select one or more subpaths, the Stroke Path command becomes a Stroke Subpath command. Photoshop then strokes only the selected path, rather than all paths saved under the current name.

The following steps walk you through a little project I created by stroking paths with the brush tool. Figures 8-35 through 8-39 show the progression and eventual outcome of the image.

STEPS: Stroking Paths with Paint Tools

1. **After opening a high-resolution image of Saturn, I clicked the Paths button in the Options bar and drew the curvy path shown in Figure 8-35.** As you can see, the path extends from the bottom of Saturn. I drew the path working downward, which is important to know because Photoshop strokes a path in the same direction as you draw the path.

2. **I saved the path.** I double-clicked the *Work Path* item in the Paths palette, entered a name for my path, and pressed Enter (or Return on the Mac).

3. **I used the Brushes palette to create a custom brush.** In the Brushes palette I selected the preset 59-pixel spatter brush, cranked the diameter up to 100 pixels, then jumped over to Shape Dynamics and gave the brush high jitter settings. I Alt-clicked (Option-clicked on the Mac) on the stroke path icon at the bottom of the Paths palette, turned on Simulate Pressure, and let Photoshop stroke the path using a medium gray color. The results are shown in Figure 8-36.

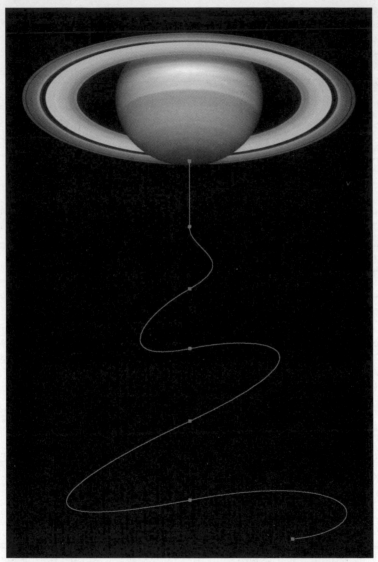

Figure 8-35: I drew this path starting at the bottom of the planet and working my way downward.

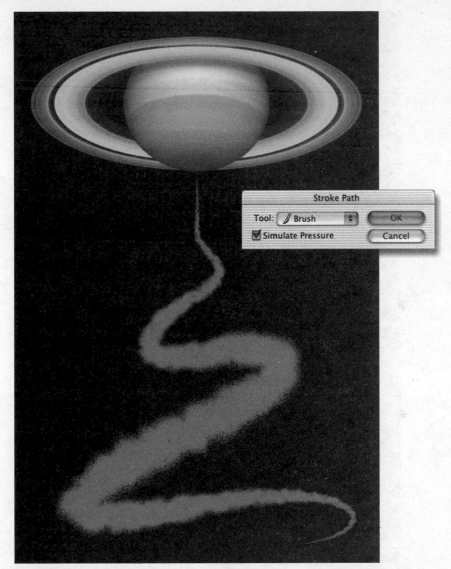

Figure 8-36: My path with a stroke applied. Turning on Simulate Pressure creates a tapered effect, similar to what you could achieve with a pressure-sensitive tablet.

4. **I stroked the path three more times using the Stroke Path command.**
   Repeating step three, I stroked the path again in dark gray, light gray, and white, using progressively smaller brush diameters (70, 45, and 20 pixels, respectively). The result of all this stroking is shown in Figure 8-37.

Figure 8-37: I stroked the path three more times, with diminishing brush sizes and different shades of gray.

5. **Next, I drew three more paths.** After drawing the first one, I double-clicked the new work path to save it, and then added two more paths to the one I just drew. I clicked in an empty portion of the image window with the black arrow tool to deselect all paths, so they appeared as shown in Figure 8-38. This enabled me to stroke them all simultaneously in Step 6.

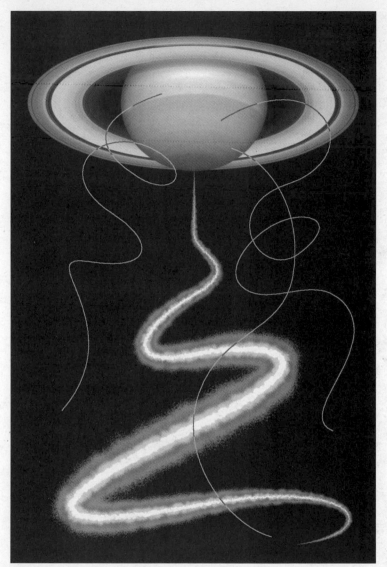

Figure 8-38: I drew another path, saved it, and then repeated the process to add two more paths.

6. **Using a 20-pixel brush, I stroked the three paths with black, reduced the brush diameter, and then stroked with medium gray.** A little more path drawing, a little more pressure-simulated stroking, and the intergalactic advertising masterpiece shown in Figure 8-39 emerged. Pretty spectacular, huh? Beats some guy pounding the sidewalks wearing a sandwich board any day.

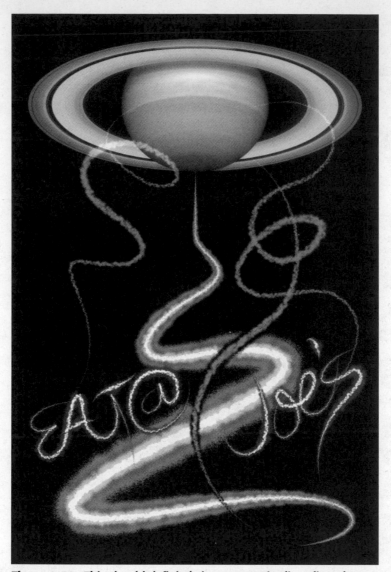

Figure 8-39: This should definitely increase Joe's alien clientele.

Tip

If you're feeling really precise — I think they have a clinical term for that — you can specify the location of every single blob of paint laid down in an image. When you deselect the Spacing value in the Brush Tip Shape Options of the Brushes palette, Photoshop applies a single blob of paint for each point in a path. If this isn't sufficient control, I'm a monkey's uncle. (What a terrible thing to say about one's nephew!)

Converting and saving paths

Photoshop provides two commands to switch between paths and selections, both of which are located in the Paths palette menu. The Make Selection command converts a path to a selection outline; the Make Work Path command converts a selection to a path. Regardless of how you create a path, you can save it with the current image, which enables you not only to reuse the path, but also to hide and display it at will.

Converting paths to selections

When you choose the Make Selection command or Alt-click (Option-click on the Mac) the make selection icon (which looks like a dotted circle, as shown back in Figure 8-24), Photoshop displays the dialog box shown in Figure 8-40. You can specify whether to antialias or feather the selection and to what degree. You can also instruct Photoshop to combine the prospective selection outline with any existing selection in the image. The Operation options correspond to the keyboard functions discussed in the "Manually adding and subtracting" section, earlier in this chapter.

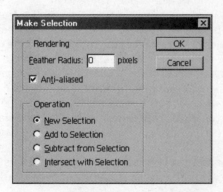

Figure 8-40: When you choose the Make Selection command, you have the option of combining the path with an existing selection.

Photoshop offers several alternative ways to convert a path to a selection outline, all of which are more convenient than the Make Selection command:

✦ **Press Ctrl+Enter (Win) or ⌘-Return (Mac):** As long as a path, shape, or selection tool is active, this keyboard shortcut converts the path to a selection.

✦ **Ctrl-click (Win) or ⌘-click (Mac) the path name:** If a tool other than a path, shape, or selection tool is active, you can Ctrl-click (Win) or ⌘-click (Mac) the name of a path in the Paths palette. The path needn't be active.

✦ **Ctrl+Shift+Enter or Ctrl+Shift-click (⌘-Shift-Return or ⌘-Shift-click on the Mac):** To add the path to an existing selection, press Shift with one of the previous techniques.

✦ **Alt+Enter or Ctrl+Alt-click (Option-Return or ⌘-Option-click on the Mac):** Naturally, if you can add, you can subtract.

✦ **Shift+Alt+Enter or Ctrl+Shift+Alt-click (Shift-Option-Return or ⌘-Shift-Option-click on the Mac):** Now we're starting to get into some obscure stuff, but what's possible is possible. You select the intersection of a path and a selection outline by pressing a whole mess of keys.

All these techniques offer the advantage of hiding the path when converting the path to a selection, giving you full, unobstructed access to your selection outline.

Caution By contrast, the Make Selection command leaves the path on screen in front of the converted selection. If you try to copy, cut, delete, or nudge the selection, you perform the operation on the path instead.

Converting selections to paths

You turn a selection into a path by choosing the Make Work Path command from the Paths palette. When you choose the command, Photoshop produces a dialog box containing a single option, Tolerance. Unlike the Tolerance options you've encountered so far, this one is accurate to $\frac{1}{10}$ pixel and has nothing to do with colors or brightness values. Rather, it works like the Curve Fit option for the freeform pen and magnetic pen. That is, it permits you to specify Photoshop's sensitivity to twists and turns in a selection outline. The value you enter determines how far the path can vary from the original selection. The lowest possible value, 0.5, not only ensures that Photoshop retains every nuance of the selection, but also can result in overly complicated paths with an abundance of points. If you enter the highest value, 10, Photoshop rounds the path and uses few points. If you plan on editing the path, you probably won't want to venture any lower than 2.0, the default setting.

To bypass the Make Work Path dialog box and turn your selection into a path using the current Tolerance settings, click the make path icon at the bottom of the Paths palette. (It's labeled back in Figure 8-24.)

Saving paths with an image

As I mentioned at the beginning of the paths discussion, saving a path is an integral step in the path-creation process. You can store every path you draw and keep it handy in case you decide later to reselect an area. Because Photoshop defines paths as compact mathematical equations, they take up virtually no room when you save an image to disk.

You save one or more paths by choosing the Save Path command from the Paths palette menu or by simply double-clicking the italicized *Work Path* item in the scrolling list. After you perform the save operation, during which you name the path, the path name appears in non-italicized characters in the palette. A path listed in the palette can include any number of separate paths. In fact, if you save a path and then set about drawing another one, Photoshop automatically adds the new path in with the saved path. To start a new path under a new name, you first must hide the existing path. Or click the new path icon—the little page at the bottom of the Paths palette—to establish an independent path. To hide paths, you can click the empty portion of the scrolling list below the last saved path name. You can even hide unsaved paths in this way. If you hide an unsaved path and then begin drawing a new one, however, the unsaved path is deleted, never to return again.

Importing and Exporting Paths

Paths come in handy not only for working inside Photoshop, but also for importing images into drawing programs, such as Illustrator and FreeHand, and into page-layout programs, such as InDesign and QuarkXPress. By saving a path as a clipping path, you can mask regions of an image so that it appears transparent when placed in other programs that support clipping paths.

In addition, you can swap paths directly with the most recent versions of Illustrator and FreeHand. That way, you can take advantage of the more advanced path-creation features found in those programs.

The last few sections of this chapter explain these added uses for your Photoshop paths.

Swapping paths with Illustrator

You can exchange paths between Photoshop and Illustrator or FreeHand by using the Clipboard. This special cross-application compatibility feature expands and simplifies a variety of path-editing functions.

To avoid having problems transferring data between Photoshop and Illustrator, go into Illustrator, choose Edit ⇨ Preferences ⇨ Files & Clipboards, and turn on the AICB check box. I also recommend that you turn on the Preserve Paths radio button when using Illustrator to alter Photoshop paths.

Suppose that you want to scale and rotate a path. Select the path in Photoshop with the black arrow tool and copy it to the Clipboard by pressing Ctrl+C (⌘-C on the Mac). Then switch to Illustrator, paste the path, and edit as desired. About 95 percent of Illustrator's capabilities are devoted to the task of editing paths, so you have many more options at your disposal in Illustrator than in Photoshop. When you finish modifying the path, copy it again, switch to Photoshop, and paste.

When you paste an Illustrator path into Photoshop, the dialog box shown in Figure 8-41 gives you the option of rendering the path to pixels (just as you can render an Illustrator EPS document using File ⇨ Open), keeping the path information intact, or creating a new shape layer. Select the Paths radio button to add the copied paths to the selected item in the Paths palette. (If no item is selected, Photoshop creates a new *Work Path* item.) You can then use the path to create a selection outline or whatever you want.

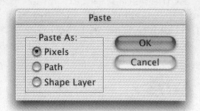

Figure 8-41: When pasting a path copied from Illustrator, Photoshop greets you with this dialog box.

 Things can get pretty muddled in the Clipboard, especially when you're switching applications. If you copy something from Illustrator, but the Paste command is dimmed inside Photoshop, you may be able to force the issue a little. If you're using a PC, you may simply need to wake up the Clipboard by opening the Windows Clipbook Viewer (Start ➪ Programs ➪ Accessories ➪ System Tools ➪ Clipbook Viewer). Don't worry if you see a message about an unsupported format, or if the image looks a complete mess. Just minimize the viewer window and try to paste again. If you're using Macintosh OS 9, press the Option key inside Illustrator and choose Edit ➪ Copy. This is intended to copy a PICT version of the path, but it sometimes has the added benefit of waking up the Clipboard to the fact that, yes indeed, there is something in here that Photoshop can use. (Computers are kind of slow sometimes. Every once in a while you must give them a kick in the pants.)

 You can copy paths from Photoshop and paste them into Illustrator or some other drawing program regardless of the setting of the Export Clipboard check box in the Preferences dialog box. That option affects pixels only. Paths are so tiny, Photoshop always exports them.

Exporting to Illustrator

If you don't have enough memory to run both Illustrator and Photoshop at the same time, you can export Photoshop paths to disk and then open them in Illustrator. To export all paths in the current image, choose File ➪ Export ➪ Paths to Illustrator. Photoshop saves the paths as a fully editable Illustrator document. This scheme enables you to trace images exactly with paths in Photoshop and then combine those paths as objects with the exported EPS version of the image inside Illustrator. Whereas tracing an image in Illustrator can prove a little tricky because of resolution differences and other previewing limitations, you can trace images in Photoshop as accurately as you like.

Unfortunately, Illustrator provides no equivalent function to export paths for use in Photoshop, nor can Photoshop open Illustrator documents from disk and interpret them as paths. This means the Clipboard is the only way to take a path created or edited in Illustrator and use it in Photoshop.

Only about half of Photoshop users own Illustrator. Meanwhile, close to 90 percent of Illustrator users own Photoshop. This is why I cover the special relationship between Illustrator and Photoshop in depth in my Illustrator book, *Real World Illustrator 10* (Berkeley, CA: Peachpit Press, 2002).

Retaining transparent areas in an image

Adobe's object-oriented design programs, InDesign 2 and Illustrator 10 (and later), can read transparency straight from a native Photoshop (PSD) file. However, this is hardly the norm. In virtually every other program—including the likes of QuarkXPress 5 and FreeHand 10—any image file, whether it contains transparent pixels or not, comes in as a fully opaque rectangle. Even if the image appeared partially transparent in Photoshop—on a layer, for example—the pixels will be filled with white or some other color. In cases like this, you need to establish a *clipping path* to mask portions of an image that you want to appear transparent. Elements that lie inside the clipping path are opaque; elements outside the clipping path are transparent. Photoshop enables you to export an image in the EPS format with an object-oriented clipping path intact. When you import the image, it appears premasked with a perfectly smooth perimeter, as illustrated by the clipped image in Figure 8-42.

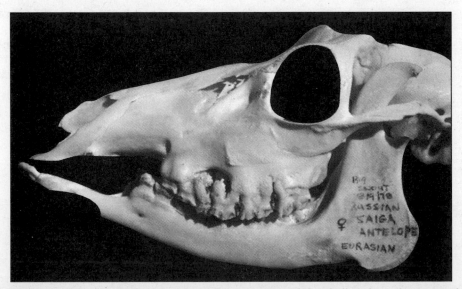

Figure 8-42: I drew one path around the perimeter of the skull and another around the eye socket. After defining the paths as clipping paths, I exported the image in the EPS format, imported it into Illustrator, and set it against a black background for contrast.

The following steps explain how to assign a set of saved paths as clipping paths.

STEPS: Saving an Image with Clipping Paths

1. **Draw one or more paths around the portions of the image that you want to appear opaque.** Areas outside the paths will be transparent.

2. **Save the paths.** Double-click the *Work Path* item in the Paths palette, enter a path name, and press Enter or Return. (Try to use a name that will make sense three years from now when you have to revisit this document and determine what the heck you did.)

3. **Choose the Clipping Path command from the Paths palette menu, as shown in Figure 8-43.** Photoshop displays the dialog box shown at the top of the figure, asking you to select the saved paths you want to assign as the clipping path. Remember, you can't make the *Work Path* a clipping path; you must save it as a named path first.

If you like, enter a value in the Flatness option box. This option enables you to simplify the clipping paths by printing otherwise fluid curves as polygons. The Flatness value represents the distance — between 0.2 and 100, in printer pixels — that the polygon may vary from the true mathematical curve. A higher value leads to a polygon with fewer sides. This means it looks chunkier, but it also prints more quickly. I recommend a value of 3. Many experts say you can go as high as 7 when printing to an imagesetter without seeing the straight edges. But I strongly suspect it depends on how much of a perfectionist you are. Me? I like 3.

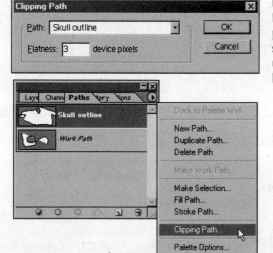

Figure 8-43: Choose the Clipping Path command from the Paths palette menu (bottom), and then select the path that you want to use from the Clipping Path dialog box (top).

4. **Choose File ⇨ Save As and select Photoshop EPS from the Format pop-up menu.** Select the desired Preview and Encoding settings and then press Enter or Return. Photoshop saves the EPS image with masked transparencies to disk.

Note

InDesign and PageMaker support clipping paths saved in the TIFF format. So if you plan on placing the image in one of those programs, you can save the image in TIFF instead of EPS in Step 4.

Figure 8-44 shows an enhanced version of the clipped skull from Figure 8-42. In addition to exporting the image with clipping paths in the EPS format, I saved the paths to disk by choosing File ⇨ Export ⇨ Paths to Illustrator. Inside Illustrator, I used the exported paths to create the outline around the clipped image. I also used them to create the shadow behind the image. The white of the eyeball is a reduced version of the eye socket, as are the iris and pupil. The background features a bunch of flipped and reduced versions of the paths. This may look like a lot of work, but the only drawing required was the creation of the two initial Photoshop paths.

Figure 8-44: It's amazing what you can accomplish by combining scans edited in a painting program with smooth lines created in a drawing program.

Be prepared for your images to grow by leaps and bounds when imported into Illustrator. The EPS illustration shown in Figure 8-44 consumes six times as much space on disk as the original Photoshop image saved in the TIFF format.

When used in excess, clipping paths can present problems for the most sophisticated printing devices. You should use a clipping path only when it's absolutely
necessary and can't be avoided. If you want to place an image against a bitmapped
background, for example, do it in Photoshop, not in Illustrator, QuarkXPress, or any
other application. This invariably speeds printing and may mean the difference
between whether or not a file prints successfully.

✦   ✦   ✦

Masks and Extractions

Selecting via Masks

Most Photoshop users don't use masks. If my personal experience is any indication, it's not only because masks seem complicated but also because they strike most folks as being more trouble than they're worth. Like nearly everyone, when I first started using Photoshop, I couldn't even imagine a possible application for a mask. I have my lasso tool and my magic wand. If I'm really in a rut, I can pull out my pen tool. What more could I possibly want?

Quite a bit, as it turns out. Every one of the tools I just mentioned is only moderately suited to the task of selecting images. The lasso tools let you create free-form selections, but none of the tools — not even the magnetic lasso — can account for differences in focus levels. The magic wand selects areas of color, but it usually leaves important colors behind, and the edges of its selection outlines often appear ragged and ugly. The pen tool is extremely precise, but it results in mechanical outlines that may appear incongruous with the natural imagery they contain.

Masks offer all the benefits of the other tools. With masks, you can create free-form selections, select areas of color, and generate amazingly precise selections. Masks also address all the deficiencies associated with the selection tools. They can account for different levels of focus, they give you absolute control over the look of the edges, and they create selections every bit as natural as the image itself.

In fact, a mask *is* the image itself. Masks use pixels to select pixels. Masks are your way to make Photoshop see what you see using the data inherent in the photograph. Masks enable you to devote every one of Photoshop's powerful capabilities to the task of creating a selection outline. Masks are, without a doubt, the most accurate selection mechanism available in Photoshop.

Masking defined

If you're not entirely clear about what I mean by the term *mask*, I'll tell you: A mask is a selection outline expressed as a grayscale image.

✦ Selected areas appear white.

✦ Deselected areas appear black.

✦ Partially selected parts of the image appear in gray. Feathered edges are also expressed in shades of gray, from light gray near the selected area to dark gray near the deselected area.

Figure 9-1 shows a selection outline and its equivalent mask. The top example shows an elliptical selection outline that I feathered by choosing Select ➪ Feather. Below this example is the same selection expressed as a mask. The selected area is white and is said to be *unmasked*; the deselected area is black, or *masked*. Note that while you can't see the feathering effect in the selection outline — marching ants can't accurately express softened edges — in the equivalent mask it's completely visible.

When you look at the mask at the bottom of Figure 9-1, you may wonder where the heck the image went. One of the wonderful things about masks is that you can view them independently of an image, as in Figure 9-1, or with an image, as in Figure 9-2. In the second figure, the mask is expressed as a color overlay. By default, the color of the overlay is a translucent red, like a sheet of rubylith film used in printing. (To see the overlay in its full, natural color, see Color Plate 9-1.) Areas covered with the rubylith are masked (deselected); areas that appear normal — without any red tint — are unmasked (selected). When you return to the standard marching ants mode, any changes you make to your image affect only the unmasked areas.

Now that you know roughly what masks are (the definition becomes progressively clearer throughout this chapter), the question remains what good are they? Because a mask is essentially an independent grayscale image, you can edit the mask using paint and edit tools, filters, color correction options, and almost every other Photoshop function. You can even use the selection tools, as discussed in the previous chapter. With all these features at your disposal, you can't help but create a more accurate selection outline in a shorter amount of time.

Figure 9-1: A feathered selection outline (top) and its equivalent mask (bottom).

Figure 9-2: Here is the mask from Figure 9-1, shown as it appears when viewed along with the image.

Painting and Editing Inside Selections

Before we immerse ourselves in masking techniques, let's start with a warm-up topic: *selection masking*. When you were in grade school, you may have had a teacher who nagged you to color within the lines. (I didn't. My teachers were more concerned about preventing me from writing on the walls and coloring on the other kids, or so I'm told.) If so, your teacher would have loved this incredibly straightforward feature. In Photoshop, all selection outlines act as masks — hence the term *selection masking*. (And you thought this chapter was going to be hard.) Regardless of which tool you use to create the selection — marquee, lasso, magic wand, or pen — Photoshop permits you to paint or edit only the selected area. The paint can't enter the deselected (or protected) portions of the image, so you can't help but paint inside the lines. If you dread painting inside an image because you're afraid you'll screw it up, selection masking is the answer.

Figures 9-3 through 9-6 show a sculpted head subject to some pretty free-and-easy use of the paint and edit tools. (In case this whole book-writing thing falls through, I plan to look for work as a hairdresser.) The following steps describe how I created these images using a selection mask.

STEPS: Painting and Editing inside a Selection Mask

1. **I selected the sculpted head.** You can see the selection outline in the right example of Figure 9-3. For the record, I drew this selection outline using the pen tool, explained in Chapter 8.

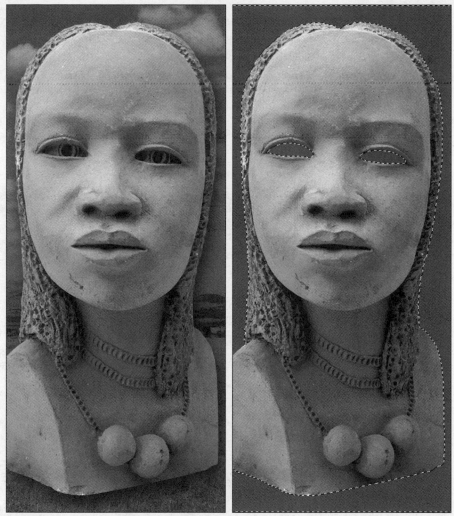

Figure 9-3: Starting with the image shown at left, I drew a selection outline around the sculpted head, inversed the selection, and deleted the background, as you can see in the right-hand image.

2. **I reversed the selection with the Inverse command.** I wanted to edit the area surrounding the head, so I chose Select ⇨ Inverse (that's Ctrl+Shift+I under Windows or ⌘-Shift-I on the Mac) to reverse which areas were selected and which were not.

3. **I pressed Ctrl+Backspace (⌘-Delete on the Mac) to fill the selected area with the background color.** In this case, the background color was gray — as shown in the right half of Figure 9-3.

4. **I painted inside the selection mask.** But before I began, I chose View ⇨ Extras (Ctrl+H or ⌘-H). This toggled off those infernal marching ants, which enabled me to paint without being distracted. (In fact, this is one of the most essential reasons for toggling the Extras command.)

5. **I selected the brush tool and expressed myself.** I chose a 150-pixel brush in the Brushes palette. With the foreground color set to black, I dragged around the perimeter of the head to set it apart from its gray background, then roughed in an outline around the black using white, as shown in Figure 9-4. I also painted inside the eye sockets of the head. Even though the brush was wider than the eye sockets, the head remained unscathed.

Figure 9-4: I painted inside the selection mask with a 150-pixel brush.

6. I selected and used the smudge tool. I set the tool's Strength value to 80 percent by pressing the 8 key. I dragged from inside the head outward 20 or so times to create a series of curlicues. As shown in Figure 9-5, the smudge tool can smear colors from inside the protected area, but it does not apply these colors until you go inside the selection. This is an important point to remember because it demonstrates that although the protected area is safe from all changes, the selected area may be influenced by colors from protected pixels.

Figure 9-5: Dragging with the smudge tool smeared colors from pixels outside the selection mask without changing the appearance of those pixels.

7. I added some additional embellishments. Okay, as you can see in Figure 9-6, I got a little carried away here. The selection mask came in handy when I used the burn tool to darken the background around the base of the head, and I inversed the mask again so I could burn some dark areas into the face. But in my zeal to create fabulous hair, I went a little beyond the bounds of this exercise: I created a separate layer and used the smudge tool set to All Layers to help blend the wild background in with the head.

Figure 9-6: Pretty wild effect, huh? This actually reminds me a little of my Godspell Original Cast Album cover.

Working in Quick Mask Mode

Selection masks give you an idea of what masks are all about, but they only scrape the surface. The rest of this chapter revolves around using masks to define complex selection outlines.

The most straightforward environment for creating a mask is the *quick mask mode*. In the quick mask mode, a selection is expressed as a rubylith overlay. All dese-lected areas appear coated with red, and selected areas appear without red coating, as shown in the bottom example of Color Plate 9-1. You can then edit the mask as desired and exit quick mask mode to return to the standard selection outline. The quick mask mode is — as its name implies — expeditious and convenient, with none of the trappings or permanence of more conventional masks. It's kind of like a fast food restaurant — you use it when you aren't overly concerned about quality and you want to get in and out in a hurry.

How the quick mask mode works

Typically, you'll at least want to rough out a selection with the standard selection tools before entering the quick mask mode. Then you can concentrate on refining and modifying your selection inside the quick mask, rather than having to create the selection from scratch. (Naturally, this is only a rule of thumb. I violate the rule several times throughout this chapter, but only because the quick mask mode and I are such tight friends.)

To enter the quick mask mode, click the quick mask mode icon in the toolbox, as I've done in Figure 9-7. Or press Q. Starting with the same selection I used on the sculpted head in the previous steps section (I inversed the selection yet again so that the background was selected), I pressed Q and got the image shown in Figure 9-7. The head receives the mask because it is not selected. (In Figure 9-7, the mask appears as a light gray coating; on your color screen, the mask appears in red.) The area outside the head looks the same as it always did because it's selected and, therefore, not masked.

Notice that the selection outline disappears when you enter the quick mask mode. This happens because the outline temporarily ceases to exist. Any operations you apply affect the mask itself and leave the underlying image untouched. When you click the marching ants mode icon (to the left of the quick mask mode icon) or press Q, Photoshop converts the mask back into a selection outline and again enables you to edit the image.

Figure 9-7: Click the quick mask mode icon to instruct Photoshop to express the selection temporarily as a grayscale image.

If you click the quick mask mode icon and nothing changes on screen, your computer isn't broken; you simply didn't select anything before you entered quick mask mode. When nothing is selected, Photoshop makes the whole image open for editing. In other words, everything's selected. (Only a smattering of commands under the Edit, Layer, and Select menus require something to be selected before they work.) If everything is selected, the mask is white; therefore, the quick mask overlay is transparent and you don't see any difference on screen. This is another reason why it's better to select something before you enter the quick mask mode — you get an immediate sense you're accomplishing something.

Also, Photoshop enables you to specify whether you want the red mask coating to cover selected areas or deselected areas. For information on how to change this setting, see "Changing the red coating," later in this chapter.

In quick mask mode, you can edit the mask in the following ways:

✦ **Subtracting from a selection:** Paint with black to add red coating and, thus, deselect areas of the image. This means you can selectively protect portions of your image by merely painting over them.

✦ **Adding to a selection:** Paint with white to remove red coating and, thus, add to the selection outline, as demonstrated in the left half of Figure 9-8. You can use the eraser tool to whittle away at the masked area (assuming the background color is set to white). Or you can swap the foreground and background colors so you can paint in white with one of the painting tools.

✦ **Adding feathered selections:** If you paint with a shade of gray, you add feathered selections. You also can feather an outline by painting with black or white with a soft brush shape, as shown in the left image in Figure 9-8. Here, I'm painting in white with a soft-edged brush, adding a nice feathered edge to the top of the selection. Then after re-entering the world of the marching ants, a little more painting and smudging creates the image on the right in Figure 9-8.

✦ **Cloning selection outlines:** If you have a selection outline that you want to repeat in several locations throughout the image, the quick mask is your friend. Select the transparent area with one of the standard selection tools, press and hold Ctrl+Alt (⌘-Option on the Mac), and drag it to a new location in the image, as shown in Figure 9-9. Although I use the rectangular marquee tool in the figure, the magic wand tool also works well for this purpose. To select an antialiased selection outline with the wand tool, set the Tolerance value to about 10 and be sure the Anti-aliased check box is active. Then click inside the selection. It's that easy.

Figure 9-8: I painted in white with a soft-edged brush to enlarge the selected area (left). After switching out of quick mask mode I went a little crazier with the brush and smudge tools (right).

✦ **Transforming selection outlines:** You can scale or rotate a selection independently of the image, just as you can with the Transform Selection command (covered in Chapter 8). Enter the quick mask mode, select the mask using one of the standard selection tools, and choose Edit ⇨ Free Transform or press Ctrl+T (⌘-T on the Mac). (See Chapter 12 for more information on Free Transform and related commands.)

Figure 9-9: To clone the eye sockets selection, I marquee-dragged around it. Then I pressed Ctrl+Alt (⌘-Option on the Mac) and dragged it first to the top, and then to the bottom (left). This enabled me to switch out of quick mask mode and paint details into the new eye sockets (right).

These are only a few of the unique effects you can achieve by editing a selection in the quick mask mode. Others involve tools and capabilities I haven't yet discussed, such as filters and color corrections.

When you finish editing your selection outlines, click the marching ants mode icon (to the left of the quick mask mode icon) or press Q again to return to the marching ants mode. Your selection outlines again appear flanked by marching ants, and all tools and commands return to their normal image-editing functions. Figure 9-10 shows the results of switching to the marching ants mode and pressing Ctrl+J (⌘-J on the Mac) to float the selection to a new layer. I then filled the background layer with white and threw in a drop shadow for good measure.

Figure 9-10: The results of creating new layers from the selected areas in the right examples of Figures 9-8 (left) and 9-9 (right).

As demonstrated in the left example of Figure 9-10, the quick mask mode offers a splendid environment for feathering one selection outline, while leaving another hard-edged or antialiased. Granted, because most selection tools offer built-in feathering options, you can accomplish this task without resorting to the quick mask mode. But the quick mask mode enables you to change feathering selectively after drawing selection outlines, something you can't accomplish with Select ➪ Feather. The quick mask mode also enables you to see exactly what you're doing. Kind of makes those marching ants look piddly and insignificant, huh?

Changing the red coating

By default, the protected region of an image appears in translucent red in the quick mask mode, but if your image contains a lot of red, the mask can be difficult to see. Luckily, you can change it to any color and any degree of opacity that you like. To do so, double-click the quick mask icon in the toolbox (or double-click the *Quick Mask* item in the Channels palette) to display the dialog box shown in Figure 9-11.

✦ **Color Indicates:** Choose Selected Areas to reverse the color coating so that the translucent red coating covers selected areas, and deselected areas appear normally. Choose Masked Areas (the default setting) to cover deselected areas in color.

You can reverse the color coating without ever entering the Quick Mask Options dialog box. Simply Alt-click (Win) or Option-click (Mac) the quick mask icon in the toolbox to toggle between coating the masked or selected portions of the image. The icon itself changes to reflect your choice.

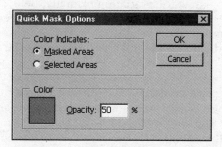

Figure 9-11: Double-click the quick mask mode icon to access the Quick Mask Options dialog box. You then can change the color and opacity of the protected or selected areas when viewed in the quick mask mode.

✦ **Color:** Click the Color icon to display the Color Picker dialog box and select a different color coating. (If you don't know how to use this dialog box, see the "Using the Color Picker" section of Chapter 4.) You can lift a color with the eyedropper after the Color Picker dialog box comes up; just keep in mind that you probably want to use a color that isn't in the image so that you can better see the mask.

✦ **Opacity:** Enter a value to change the opacity of the translucent color that coats the image. A value of 100 percent makes the coating absolutely opaque.

Change the color coating to achieve the most acceptable balance between being able to view and edit your selection and being able to view your image. For example, the default red coating shows up poorly on my grayscale screen shots, so I changed the color of the coating to light blue and the Opacity value to 65 percent before shooting the screens featured in Figures 9-7 through 9-9.

Gradations as masks

If you think that the Feather command is a hot tool for creating softened selection outlines, wait until you get a load of gradations in the quick mask mode. There's no better way to create fading effects than selecting an image with the gradient tools.

Fading an image

Just to make this explanation more difficult, I'm going to show you how to create a gradient mask by using an image of an actual mask, shown in Figure 9-12. This is no doubt some primitive sacred relic from a bygone civilization, but that won't stop me from turning it into a towering monolith like you might find on Easter Island. Here we go:

Switch to the quick mask mode by pressing Q. Then use the gradient tool to draw a linear gradation from black to white. (Chapter 6 explains exactly how to do so.) The white portion of the gradation represents the area you want to select. I wanted to select the top portion of the mask, so I drew the gradation from just below the lower lip to the bottom of the nose, as shown in the first example of Figure 9-13. Because the gradient line is a little hard to see, I've added an arrow to show the direction of the drag. (To see the gradient mask in full color, check out the second image in Color Plate 9-2.)

Banding can be a problem when you use a gradation as a mask. To eliminate the banding effect, therefore, apply the Add Noise filter at a low setting several times. To create the right example in Figure 9-13, I applied Add Noise using an Amount value of 10 and the Uniform distribution option.

In the right example of Figure 9-13, I hid the image so that only the gradient mask is visible. As the figure shows, the Channels palette lists the *Quick Mask* item in italics. This is because Photoshop regards the quick mask as a temporary channel. You can hide the image and view the gradient mask in black and white by clicking the eyeball in front of the color composite view, in this case RGB. Or just press the tilde key (~) to hide the image. Press tilde again to view gradient mask and image together.

Figure 9-12: You can create a linear gradient in the quick mask mode to make the mask (left) rise from the middle of the field (right).

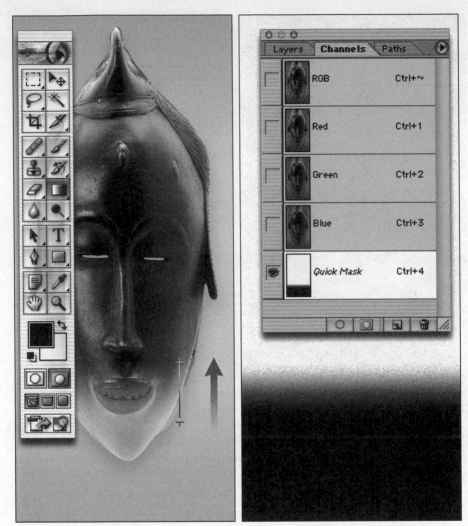

Figure 9-13: After drawing a linear gradation in the quick mask mode over the bottom of the image (left), I hid the image and applied the Add Noise filter with an Amount of 10 (right).

To apply the gradation as a selection, I returned to the marching ants mode by again pressing Q. I then Ctrl-dragged (⌘-dragged on the Mac) the selected portion of the mask and dropped it into the open field, as seen in the left half of Figure 9-14. Not content with this level of desecration, I also used a liberal amount of the Free Transform command (see Chapter 12), scorched the mask with the burn tool (see Chapter 5), and added dramatic lighting effects. The end result is shown on the right in Figure 9-14. For the color version of this splendid image, and more on those dramatic lighting effects, see Color Plate 9-2.

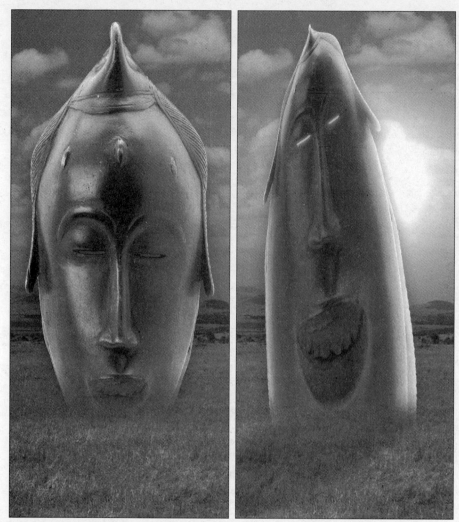

Figure 9-14: The result of selecting the top portion of the mask using a gradient mask and then Ctrl-dragging (⌘-dragging on the Mac) and dropping the selection into the field (left). Throw in a little more tweaking, and you've got your own personal Easter Island (right) — minus the bunnies, of course.

Applying special effects gradually

You also can use gradations in the quick mask mode to fade the outcomes of filters and other automated special effects. For example, I wanted to apply a filter around the edges of the image that appears in Figure 9-15. I began by deselecting everything in the image by pressing Ctrl+D (⌘-D on the Mac) and switching to the quick mask mode. Then I selected the gradient tool, selected the linear gradient style icon in the Options bar, and selected the Foreground to Transparent gradient from the Gradient drop-down palette. I also selected the Transparency check box in the Options bar.

Figure 9-15: This time around, my intention is to surround the foreground image with a gradual filtering effect.

I pressed D to make the foreground color black. Then I dragged with the linear gradient tool from each of the four corners of the image inward to create a series of short gradations that trace around the focal point of the image, as shown in Figure 9-16. (As you can see, I've hidden the image so that you see the mask in black and white.) Because I've selected the Foreground to Transparent option, Photoshop adds each gradation to the previous gradation.

To jumble the pixels in the mask, I applied Filter ⇨ Noise ⇨ Add Noise with an Amount value of 24. You see the effect in Figure 9-16.

Figure 9-16: Inside the quick mask mode, I dragged from each of the four corners with the gradient tool (as indicated by the arrows).

Tip

The only problem is that I want to select the outside of the image, not the inside. So I need the edges to appear white and the inside to appear black, the opposite of what you see in Figure 9-16. No problem. All I do is press Ctrl+I (⌘-I on the Mac) to invert the image. Inverting inside the quick mask mode produces the same effect as applying Select ⇨ Inverse to a selection.

Finally, I switched back to the marching ants mode by again pressing Q. Then I applied Filter ⇨ Render ⇨ Clouds to get the atmospheric effect you see in Figure 9-17.

Figure 9-17: After switching back to the marching ants mode,
I chose Filter ➪ Render ➪ Clouds to create the foggy effect
shown here.

Tip

Notice the corners in the mask in Figure 9-16? These corners are soft and rounded,
but you can achieve all kinds of corner effects with the linear gradient tool. For
harsher corners, select the Foreground to Background gradient and select Lighten
from the Mode pop-up menu in the Options bar. For some *really* unusual corner
treatments, try out the Difference and Exclusion brush modes. Wild stuff.

Creating gradient arrows

The following steps explain how to add cool fading arrows to any image, similar to the one shown back in Figure 9-13. Photoshop not only makes it easy to use gradients for fading effects, it's also a breeze to create dramatic drop shadows for image elements, as demonstrated in Figures 9-18 and 9-19. The steps involve a gradient layer mask, the Free Transform command, the line tool, and a little old-fashioned layer opacity.

STEPS: Creating Fading Arrows with Drop Shadows

1. **Draw an arrow with the line tool, creating a shape layer.** First, select the line tool and make sure the Shape Layers button is selected in the Options bar. Click on the Geometry Options and give your line an arrowhead at the end. No doubt a bit of trial and error will be necessary to get the right settings. (To create the arrow in the top example of Figure 9-18, I used a Weight of 25, both a Width and Length of 400 percent, and a Concavity setting of 25 percent.) Set the foreground color to white and then drag to draw your arrow in the desired direction.

   For the straight dope on using the shape tools, check out Chapter 14.

2. **Use rotation to create a perspective effect for the arrow.** I switched to the direct selection tool and selected the three points on the left side of the arrow. Next I chose Edit ➪ Free Transform Points, moved the rotation point from the center to the upper-right corner by adjusting the reference point location control in the Options bar, and rotated the selected points.

3. **Apply a drop shadow.** I clicked the layer style icon at the bottom of the Layers palette and selected Drop Shadow. I accepted the default settings, but you can tweak as you wish. The bottom image in Figure 9-18 shows the result.

4. **Create a layer mask.** Choose Layer ➪ Add Layer Mask ➪ Reveal All.

5. **Draw a gradient mask.** Select the gradient tool and make sure the Black to White gradient is selected in the Options bar. Then draw a gradient on the arrow, starting at the end of the arrow and extending to around the middle, as shown in the top example of Figure 9-19.

6. **Lower the overall opacity of the arrow.** Now I've got a nice fade to transparency within the arrow, but it seems that the top of the arrow is obscuring too much of the image. No problem; I just reduce the Opacity of the arrow layer in the Layers palette to 70 percent. The bottom image in Figure 9-19 shows the result. Isn't it neat how you can combine the sharp edges of the vector shape tools with the soft edges of the layer mask?

Figure 9-18: Use the line tool with appropriate arrowhead settings to draw an arrow (top). To create the perspective distortion effect, select the points on the left side of the arrow and rotate them using Free Transform. Add a drop shadow layer style for extra dimension (bottom).

Figure 9-19: Drag from the end of the arrow upward to create a gradient layer mask that makes the arrow seem to fade into view (top). Lower the layer's Opacity value, and the result makes it much easier to keep your eye on the ball (bottom).

Generating Masks Automatically

In addition to the quick mask mode and selection masking, Photoshop offers a few tools that automate the masking process — well, automate *some* parts of the process. You still need to provide some input to tell the program exactly what you're trying to mask. These tools are the magic eraser, background eraser, and Extract command. We've already taken a look at the standard eraser tool (Chapter 7), but in case you're skipping around, the eraser paints in the background color when used on the background layer. When applied to a layer, it erases pixels to reveal the layers below. The magic eraser works like the fill tool but in reverse. When you click with the magic eraser, you delete a range of similarly colored pixels. The background eraser, as its name implies, erases the background from an image and leaves the foreground intact — or at least, that's what happens if you use the tool correctly. Otherwise, it just erases everything.

Tip

You can cycle through the erasers by Alt-clicking (Option-clicking on the Mac) the eraser icon in the toolbox or by pressing E (or Shift+E).

The magic eraser

As I just mentioned, the magic eraser, found on the same flyout as the regular eraser, erases similarly colored pixels. If you're familiar with the magic wand, which I cover in Chapter 8, using the magic eraser is a cinch. The two tools operate virtually identically, except that the wand selects and the magic eraser erases.

When you click a pixel with the magic eraser, Photoshop identifies a range of similarly colored pixels, just as it does with the magic wand. But instead of selecting the pixels, the magic eraser makes them transparent, as demonstrated in Figure 9-20. Bear in mind that in Photoshop, transparency requires a separate layer. So if the image consists only of the background, Photoshop automatically converts the background into a layer with nothing underneath. Hence the checkerboard pattern shown in the second example in the figure — transparency with nothing underneath.

Note

The Lock buttons in the Layers palette affect the magic eraser. When you have no buttons selected, the magic eraser works as I just described it. But if you lock transparent pixels, the magic eraser paints opaque pixels in the background color and leaves transparent areas untouched. You can't use the magic eraser at all on a layer for which you've locked image pixels.

You can further alter the performance of the magic eraser through the controls in the Options bar, shown in Figure 9-21 and described in the following list. Except for the Opacity value, these options work the same way as the options for the magic wand:

✦ **Tolerance:** Just like the magic wand's Tolerance value, this one determines how similar a neighboring color has to be to the clicked color to be made transparent. A higher value affects more colors; a lower value affects fewer colors. (Remember, any change to the Tolerance value affects the *next* click you make; it does not affect the existing transparent area.)

Figure 9-20: To delete a homogeneously colored background, such as the sky in this picture, click inside it with the magic eraser (bottom).

✦ **Anti-aliased:** To create a soft fringe around the outline of your transparent area, leave this option turned on. If you'd prefer a hard edge — as when using a very low Tolerance value, for example — turn this check box off.

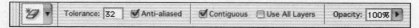

Figure 9-21: The magic eraser options are nearly identical to the options for the magic wand.

✦ **Contiguous:** Select this check box, and the magic eraser deletes *contiguous* colors only — that is, similar colors that touch each other. If you prefer to delete all pixels of a certain color — such as the background pixels in Figure 9-20 that are divided from the rest of the sky by the lion — turn the Contiguous check box off.

✦ **Use All Layers:** When turned on, this check box tells Photoshop to factor in all visible layers when erasing pixels. The tool continues to erase pixels on the active layer only, but it erases them according to colors found across all layers.

✦ **Opacity:** Lower this value to make the erased pixels translucent instead of transparent. Low values result in more subtle effects than high ones.

The more-magical background eraser

The magic eraser is as simple to use as a hammer, and every bit as indelicate. It pounds away pixels, but it leaves lots of color fringes and shredded edges in its wake. You might as well select an area with the magic wand and press Backspace (Win) or Delete (Mac). The effect is the same.

The more capable, more scrupulous tool is the background eraser. As demonstrated in Figure 9-22, the background eraser deletes background pixels as you drag over them. (Again, if the image consists only of a background, Photoshop converts the background into a new layer to accommodate the transparency.) The tool is intelligent enough to erase background pixels and retain foreground pixels provided that — and here's the clincher — you keep the cross in the center of the eraser cursor squarely centered on a background-color pixel. Move the cross over a foreground pixel, and the background eraser deletes foreground pixels as well. As Figure 9-23 demonstrates, it's the position of the cross that counts.

Figure 9-22: Drag around the edge of an image with the background eraser to erase the background but leave the foreground intact.

Figure 9-23: Keep the cross of the background eraser cursor over the background you want to erase (top). If you inadvertently move the cross over the foreground, the foreground gets erased (bottom).

Note

As is the case when you work with the magic eraser, the Lock buttons in the Layers palette affect the background eraser. In this case, locking image pixels prevents you from using the background eraser. Be aware that if you drag over a selection that's already partially transparent, locking transparent pixels does not protect the selection from the background eraser.

You can also modify the performance of the background eraser using the Options bar controls, pictured in Figure 9-24. These options are a bit intimidating at first, but they're actually pretty easy to use:

✦ **Limits:** Choose Contiguous from this pop-up menu, and the background eraser deletes colors inside the cursor as long as they are contiguous with the color immediately under the cross. To erase all similarly colored pixels, whether contiguous or not, select Discontiguous. One additional option, Find Edges, searches for edges as you brush and emphasizes them. Although interesting, Find Edges has a habit of producing halos and is rarely useful.

✦ **Tolerance:** Raise the Tolerance value to erase more colors at a time; lower the value to erase fewer colors. Low Tolerance values are useful for erasing around tight and delicate details, such as hair.

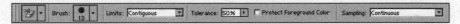

Figure 9-24: The seemingly intimidating background eraser options are actually pretty intuitive.

✦ **Protect Foreground Color:** Select this check box to prevent the current foreground color (by default, black) from ever being erased. Stupid, really, but there it is.

✦ **Sampling:** This pop-up menu determines how the background eraser determines what it should and should not erase. The default setting, Continuous, tells the erasers to continuously reappraise which colors should be erased as you drag. If the background is pretty homogenous, you might prefer to use the Once option, which samples the background color when you first click and erases only that color throughout the drag. Select Background Swatch to erase only the current background color (by default, white).

The still-more-magical Extract command

Like the magic eraser and background eraser, the Extract command aims to separate—extract, if you will—an image element from its surroundings. After you draw a rough highlight around the subject you want to retain, Photoshop analyzes the situation and automatically deletes everything but the subject. In my estimation, though, Extract is only slightly more powerful than the background eraser and several times more complex. Some images respond very well to the command, others do not. That said, Extract can produce reasonably good results if you get the steps right. So take Extract for a test drive, as follows:

1. **Choose Extract from its new home in the Filter menu.** Or press Ctrl+Alt+X (⌘-Option-X on the Mac). Either way, Photoshop displays the large Extract window shown in Figure 9-25.

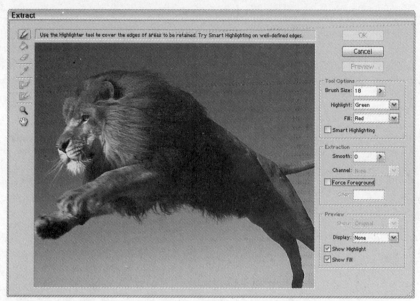

Figure 9-25: The Extract window serves as a miniature masking laboratory, complete with a toolbox and options.

2. **Select the edge highlighter tool.** Most likely, this tool is already active, but if not, press B to select it.

3. **Outline the subject that you want to retain.** In my case, I want to delete the background, so I traced around the lion, as shown in Figure 9-26. Be sure to either completely encircle the subject or, if the subject is partially cropped, trace all the way up against the outer boundaries of the photograph.

Often, it's easier to Shift-click around the perimeter of an image than drag manually. Shift-clicking creates a straight highlight from one click point to the next. As long as you do a reasonably careful job, the performance of the Extract command won't be impaired.

Turn on the Smart Highlighting check box in the Tool Options section of the Extract dialog box to get some assistance in drawing your outline. Smart Highlighting seeks out edges in the image and places the highlight along them. When you turn on Smart Highlighting, your cursor becomes a circle with four inward-pointing lines. Keep the center of the circle over the edge between the subject and the background as you drag. This feature works best when your subject has well-defined edges, of course. Note that you can't Shift-click with the tool to draw straight segments when Smart Highlighting is active.

Eraser

Fill

Edge highlighter

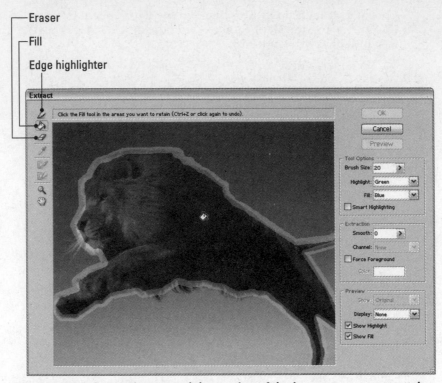

Figure 9-26: After tracing around the portion of the image you want to retain, click inside the outline with the fill tool.

Tip

Ctrl-drag (Win) or ⌘-drag (Mac) to temporarily turn off Smart Highlighting without deselecting the check box. Or go the opposite direction: Deselect the check box and then Ctrl-drag (Win) or ⌘-drag (Mac) to temporarily take advantage of Smart Highlighting.

4. **As you trace, use the bracket keys, [and], to make the brush larger or smaller.** When you work with brushes from 1 to 9 pixels in diameter, each press of [or] changes the brush size by 1 pixel. The increment of change gets larger as you increase the brush size.

Tip

Small brush sizes result in sharper edges. Larger brush sizes are better for fragile, intricate detailing, such as hair, foliage, wispy fabric, bits of steel wool, thin pasta—you get the idea.

5. **If you make a mistake, press Ctrl+Z (⌘-Z on the Mac).** You get only one Undo level here—you can only undo and redo your last stroke with the highlighter tool.

   If you want to erase more of the highlight, drag over the botched region with the eraser tool (press E to access it from the keyboard) or press Alt (Option on the Mac) and drag with the edge highlighter tool. To delete the entire highlight and start over, press Alt+Backspace (Win) or Option-Delete (Mac).

6. **Navigate as needed.** If you can't see all of your image, you can access the hand tool by pressing the spacebar or clicking the hand tool icon. You can also zoom by pressing Ctrl+plus or Ctrl+minus (⌘-plus or ⌘-minus on the Mac), or by using the zoom tool.

7. **Select the fill tool.** It's the one that looks like a paint bucket. To select the fill tool from the keyboard, press G, same as you do to select the paint bucket in the regular Photoshop toolbox.

8. **Click inside the subject of the image.** The highlighted outline should fill with color. If the fill color spills outside the outline, then there's probably a break in your outline someplace. Press Ctrl+Z (⌘-Z on the Mac) to undo the fill and then scroll the image with the hand tool to find the break. Patch it with the edge highlighter and then click with the fill tool again.

   You also can click inside a filled area with the fill tool or eraser to remove the fill.

9. **Click the Preview button.** Before you can apply your prospective mask, you need to preview it so you can gauge the finished effect, as in Figure 9-27.

   If you Shift-click with the fill tool in Step 8, Photoshop fills the outline and processes the preview automatically, saving you the trouble of clicking the Preview button.

10. **Edit the mask as needed.** You have several tools at your disposal. The tools are labeled in Figure 9-27, and you can read about them in the list following these steps.

11. **Click the OK button to delete the masked portion of the image.** If the image consisted only of a background, Photoshop converts it into a separate layer. You can then use the move tool to drag the layer against a different background. In Figure 9-28, I set my lion against an Italian landscape. The composite isn't perfect, but it's not half bad for five to ten minutes of work.

12. **After you exit the Extract window, fix any problems using the background eraser and history brush.** Use the background eraser to erase stray pixels that you wish the Extract command had deleted. Use the history brush to restore details that you wish the Extract command hadn't deleted.

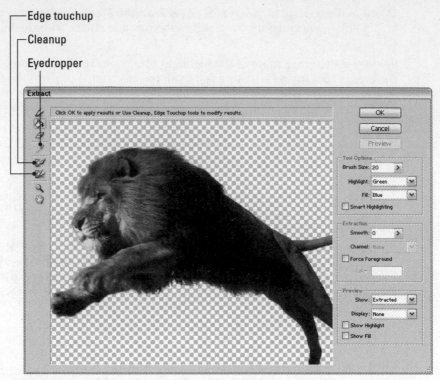

Figure 9-27: Click the Preview button to gauge the appearance of the final masked image.

Back in Step 10, I alluded to ways that you can refine the mask within the Extract dialog box. You can use the following techniques to touch up the mask before clicking OK to create it:

✦ **Drag with the cleanup tool (C) to change mask opacity.** Press the number keys to adjust the pressure of the tool and thus alter the amount of opacity that the tool subtracts. To erase to full transparency, press 0, as you do when working with the eraser on a layer. Press 9 for 90 percent transparency, 8 for 80 percent, and so on. Alt-drag (Win) or Option-drag (Mac) to add opacity.

✦ **Drag along the boundaries of the mask with the edge touchup tool (T) to sharpen the mask edges.** If the boundary between mask and subject isn't well defined, dragging with this tool adds opacity to the subject and removes it from the mask. In other words, it turns soft, feathery edges into crisp, clearly defined edges. Again, you can press the number keys to adjust the impact of the tool.

✦ **Raise the Smooth value to remove stray pixels from the mask.** A high value smoothes out the edges around the image and fills in holes. Basically, if your edges are a big mess, give this option a try.

Figure 9-28: I believe this particular lion is stuffed, but even a dead creature may enjoy a change in its diorama.

✦ **Drag with the edge highlighter or eraser tools to edit the mask boundary.**
When you select either tool, the original mask highlight reappears, and the tools work as they do when you initially draw the highlight. After you adjust the highlight, Shift-click inside it to redraw and preview the adjusted mask.

✦ **Choose an option from the Show pop-up menu to toggle between the original highlight and the extracted image preview.** You can press X to toggle between the two views without bothering with the pop-up menu.

That's 99 percent of what you need to know about the Extract command. For those of you who care to learn the other 1 percent, here's a quick rundown of the remaining options that appear along the right side of the Extract window.

✦ **Highlight, Fill:** Use these pop-up menus to change the highlighter and fill colors. It doesn't matter what colors you use, so long as they show up well against the image.

✦ **Channel:** Advanced users may prefer to prepare the highlighter work by tracing around the image inside an independent mask channel, which you can create in the Channels palette prior to choosing the Extract command. Then load the mask by selecting it from the Channel pop-up menu. You can further modify the highlight using the edge highlight and eraser tools. One weirdness: When loading a mask, black in the mask channel represents the highlighted area, white represents the nonhighlighted area. Strikes me as upside-down, but that's how it goes.

✦ **Force Foreground:** If the subject of your image is predominantly a single color, select Force Foreground and use the eyedropper to sample the color in the image that you want to preserve. (Alternatively, you can define the color using the Color swatch, but it's much more work.) Then use the edge highlighter tool to paint over all occurrences of the foreground color. (Note that this check box is an alternative to the fill tool. When Force Foreground is selected, the fill tool is dimmed.)

✦ **Display:** You don't have to preview the image against the transparent checkerboard background. You can also view it against white (White Matte) or some other color. Or you can view it as a mask, where white represents the opaque area and black the transparent area. (Ironically, you can't export the extraction as a mask — go figure.)

Press F to select the next display mode in the menu; press Shift+F to switch to the previous mode in the menu.

✦ **Show Highlight, Show Fill:** Use these check boxes to hide and show the highlight and fill colors.

One final tip: Before using the Extract command — or the magic eraser or background eraser, for that matter — you may want to copy the image to a separate layer or take a snapshot of the image in the History palette. Either way, you have a backup in case things don't go exactly according to plan.

Using the Color Range command

Another convenient method for creating a mask is the Color Range command under the Select menu. This command enables you to generate selections based on color ranges. Use the familiar eyedropper cursor to specify colors that should be considered for selection and colors that you want to rule out. The Color Range command is a lot like the magic wand tool, except that it enables you to select colors with more precision and to change the tolerance of the selection on-the-fly.

When you choose Select ➪ Color Range, Photoshop displays the Color Range dialog box shown in Figure 9-29. Like the magic wand with the Contiguous option turned off, Color Range selects areas of related color all across the image, whether or not the colors are immediate neighbors. Click in the image window to select and deselect colors, as you do with the wand. But rather than adjusting a Tolerance value before you use the tool, you adjust a Fuzziness option any old time you like. Photoshop dynamically updates the selection according to the new value. Think of Color Range as the magic wand on steroids.

So why didn't the folks at Adobe merely enhance the functionality of the magic wand instead of adding this strange command? The Color Range dialog box offers a preview of the mask — something a tool can't do — which is pretty essential for gauging the accuracy of your selection. And the magic wand is convenient, if nothing else. If Adobe were to combine the two functions, you would lose functionality.

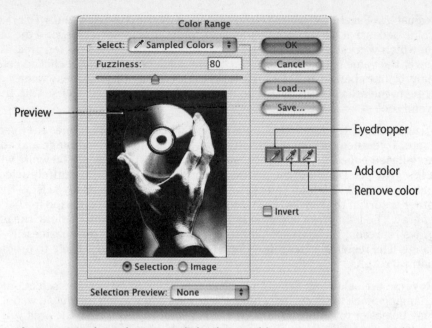

Preview —

Eyedropper

Add color

Remove color

Figure 9-29: The Color Range dialog box enables you to generate a mask by dragging with the eyedropper tool and adjusting the Fuzziness option.

When you move your cursor outside the Color Range dialog box, it changes to an eyedropper. Click to specify the color on which you want to base the selection — I call this the base color — as if you were using the magic wand. Or click inside the preview, labeled in Figure 9-29. In either case, the preview updates to show the resulting mask.

You can also do the following:

✦ **Add colors to the selection:** To add base colors to the selection, select the add color tool inside the Color Range dialog box and click inside the image window or preview. You can access the tool while the standard eyedropper is selected by Shift-clicking (just as you Shift-click with the magic wand to add colors to a selection). You can even Shift-drag with the eyedropper to add multiple colors in a single pass, something you can't do with the magic wand.

✦ **Remove colors from the selection:** To remove base colors from the selection, click with the remove color tool or Alt-click (Option-click on the Mac) with the eyedropper. You can also drag or Alt-drag (Option-drag on the Mac) to remove many colors at a time.

If adding or removing a color sends your selection careening in the wrong direction, press Ctrl+Z (⌘-Z on the Mac). Yes, the Undo command works inside the Color Range dialog box as well as out of it.

✦ **Adjust the Fuzziness value:** This option resembles the magic wand's Tolerance value because it determines the range of colors to be selected beyond the ones on which you click. Raise the Fuzziness value to expand the selected area; lower the value to contract the selection. A value of 0 selects the clicked color only. Unlike changes to Tolerance, however, changing the Fuzziness value adjusts the selection on the fly; no repeat clicking is required, as it is with the wand tool.

Fuzziness and Tolerance also differ in the kind of selection outlines they generate. Tolerance entirely selects all colors within the specified range and adds antialiased edges. If the selection were a mask, most of it would be white with a few gray pixels around the perimeter. By contrast, Fuzziness entirely selects only the colors on which you click and Shift-click, and it partially selects the other colors in the range. That's why most of the mask is expressed in shades of gray. The light grays in the mask represent the most similar colors; the dark grays represent the least similar pixels that still fall within the Fuzziness range. The result is a tapering, gradual selection, much more likely to produce natural results.

✦ **Reverse the selection:** Select the Invert check box to reverse the selection, changing black to white and white to black. As when using the magic wand, it may be easier to isolate the area you don't want to select than the area you do want to select. When you encounter such a situation, select Invert.

✦ **Toggle the preview area:** Use the two radio buttons below the preview area to control the preview's contents. If you select the first option, Selection, you see the mask that will be generated when you press Enter (Win) or Return (Mac). If you select Image, the preview shows the image.

Press and hold Ctrl (Win) or ⌘ (Mac) to toggle between the two previews. My advice is to leave the option set to Selection and press Ctrl or ⌘ when you want to view the image.

✦ **Control the contents of the image window:** The Selection Preview pop-up menu at the bottom of the dialog box enables you to change what you see in the image window. Leave the option set to None—the default setting—to view the image normally in the image window. Select Grayscale to see the mask on its own. Select Quick Mask to see the mask and image together. Select Black Matte or White Matte to see what the selection would look like against a black or white background.

Although they may sound weird, the Matte options enable you to get an accurate picture of how the selected image will mesh with a different background. Figure 9-30 shows an original image at the top left with the grayscale mask on the right. The mask calls for the shadows in the disc, fingers, and wrist to be selected, with the highlights deselected. The two Matte views help you see how this particular selection looks against two backgrounds as different as night and day. Use the Fuzziness option in combination with Black Matte or White Matte to come up with a softness setting that will ensure a smooth transition.

Selection Preview:

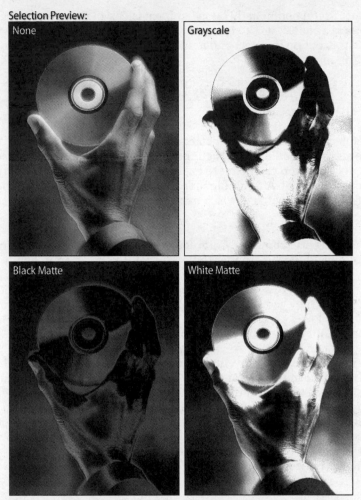

Figure 9-30: The options in the Selection Preview pop-up menu change the way the Color Range command previews the selection in the image window.

✦ **Select by predefined colors:** Choose an option from the Select pop-up menu at the top of the dialog box to specify the means of selecting a base color. If you choose any option besides Sampled Colors, the Fuzziness option and eye-dropper tools become dimmed to show they are no longer operable. Instead, Photoshop selects colors based on their relationship to a predefined color. For example, if you select Red, the program entirely selects red and partially selects other colors based on the amount of red they contain. Colors composed exclusively of blue and green are not selected.

The most useful option in this pop-up menu is Out of Gamut, which selects all the colors in an RGB or Lab image that fall outside the CMYK color space. You can use this option to select and modify the out-of-gamut colors before converting an image to CMYK.

✦ **Load and save settings:** Click the Save button to save the current settings to disk. Click Load to open a saved settings file. To use a settings file on a PC, it must end in the extension .*axt*.

After you define the mask to your satisfaction, click OK or press Enter or Return to generate the selection outline. Although the Color Range command is more flexible than the magic wand, you can no more expect it to generate perfect selections than any other automated tool. After Photoshop draws the selection outline, therefore, you'll probably want to switch to quick mask mode and paint and edit the mask to taste.

If you learn nothing else about the Color Range dialog box, at least learn to use the Fuzziness option and the eyedropper tools. Basically, you can approach these options in two ways. If you want to create a diffused selection with gradual edges, set the Fuzziness option to a high value — 60 or more — and click and Shift-click two or three times with the eyedropper. To create a more precise selection, enter a Fuzziness of 40 or lower and Shift-drag and Alt-drag (Option-drag on the Mac) with the eyedropper until you get the exact colors you want.

Figure 9-31 shows some sample results. To create the left images, I clicked with the eyedropper tool once in the disc and set the Fuzziness value to 40. To create the right images, I raised the Fuzziness value to 180; then I clicked, Shift-clicked, and Alt-clicked with the eyedropper to lift exactly the colors I wanted. The top examples show the effects of filling the selections with white. In the two bottom examples, I copied the selections and pasted them against an identical cloud background. In all four cases, the higher Fuzziness value yields more generalized and softer results; the lower value produces a more exact but harsher selection.

A few helpful Color Range hints

Tip

You can limit the portion of an image that Select ⇨ Color Range affects by selecting part of the image before choosing the command. When a selection exists, the Color Range command masks only those pixels that fall inside it. Even the preview area reflects your selection.

You also can add or subtract from an existing selection using the Color Range command. Press Shift when choosing Select ⇨ Color Range to add to a selection. Press Alt (Win) or Option (Mac) when choosing Color Range to subtract from a selection.

Fuzziness: 40   Fuzziness: 180
Filled with white

Against cloud background

Figure 9-31: After creating two selections with the Color Range command — one with a low Fuzziness value (left) and one with a high one (right) — I alternately filled the selections with white (top) and pasted them against a different background (bottom).

If you get hopelessly lost when creating your selection and you can't figure out what to select and what to deselect, click with the eyedropper tool to start over. This clears all the colors from the selection except the one you click. Or you can press Alt (Option on the Mac) to change the Cancel button to a Reset button, which returns the settings inside the dialog box to those in force when you first chose Select ➪ Color Range.

Creating an Independent Mask Channel

The problem with masks generated via the quick mask mode and Color Range command is that they're here one day and gone the next. Photoshop is no more prepared to remember them than it is a lasso or wand selection.

Most of the time, that's okay. You'll only use the selection once, so there's no rea-son to sweat it. But what if the selection takes you a long time to create? What if, after a quarter hour of Shift-clicking here and Alt-dragging there, adding a few strokes in the quick mask mode, and getting the selection outline exactly right, your boss calls a sudden meeting or the dinner bell rings? You can't just drop everything; you're in the middle of a selection. But nor can you convey your predicament to non-Photoshop users because they'll have no idea what you're talking about and no sympathy for your plight.

The simplest solution is to back up your selection, save your file, and move on to the next phase of your life. In fact, anytime that you spend 15 minutes or more on a selection, save it. After all, you never know when all heck is going to break loose, and 15 minutes is just too big a chunk of your life to repeat. (The average person racks up a mere 2.5 million quarter hours, so use them wisely!) You wouldn't let 15 minutes of image-editing go by without saving, and the rules don't change just because you're working on a selection.

Saving a selection outline to a mask channel

The following steps describe how to back up a selection to an independent mask channel, which is any channel above and beyond those required to represent a grayscale or color image. Mask channels are saved along with the image itself, making them a safe and sturdy solution.

STEPS: Transferring a Selection to an Independent Channel

1. **Convert the selection to a mask channel.** One way to do this is to choose Select ➪ Save Selection or right-click (Control-click on the Mac) in the image window and choose Save Selection from the pop-up menu, which saves the selection as a mask. The dialog box shown in Figure 9-32 appears, asking you where you want to put the mask. In most cases, you'll want to save the mask to a separate channel inside the current image. To do so, make sure that the name of the current image appears in the Document pop-up menu. Then select New from the Channel pop-up menu, enter any name for the channel that you like, and press Enter or Return.

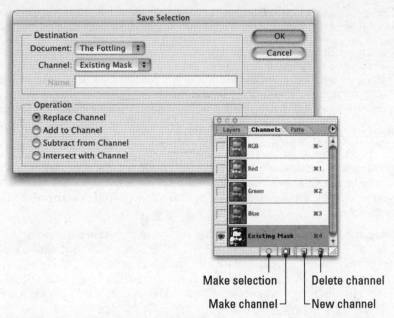

Make selection   Delete channel

Make channel   New channel

Figure 9-32: The Save Selection dialog box enables you to convert your selection outline to a mask and save it to a new or existing channel.

If you have an old channel you want to replace, select the channel's name from the Channel pop-up menu. The radio buttons at the bottom of the dialog box become available, permitting you to add the mask to the channel, subtract it, or intersect it. These radio buttons work like the equivalent options that appear when you make a path into a selection outline (as discussed in the previous chapter), but they blend the masks together, instead. The result is the same as if you were adding, subtracting, or intersecting selection outlines, except it's expressed as a mask.

Alternatively, you can save the mask to a new multichannel document all its own. To do this, choose New from the Document pop-up menu and press Enter or Return.

Tip

Man, what a lot of options! If you only want to save the selection to a new channel and be done with it, you needn't bother with the Save Selection command or dialog box. Just click the make channel icon at the bottom of the Channels palette (labeled in Figure 9-32). Photoshop automatically creates a new channel, converts the selection to a mask, and places the mask in the channel.

Regardless of which of these many methods you choose, your selection outline remains intact.

2. **View the mask in the Channels palette.** To do so, click the appropriate channel name in the Channels palette—automatically named *Alpha 1* unless you assigned a name of your own. In Figure 9-32, I replaced the contents of a channel called Existing Mask, so this is where my mask now resides.

This step isn't the least bit mandatory. It just lets you see your mask and generally familiarize yourself with how masks look. Remember, white represents selection, black is deselected, and gray is partial selection.

Tip

If you didn't name your mask in Step 1 and you want to name it now, double-click the Alpha 1 name in the Channels palette and enter a new name.

3. **Return to the standard image-editing mode by clicking the first channel name in the Channels palette.** Better yet, press Ctrl+1 (⌘-1 on the Mac) if you're editing a grayscale image or Ctrl+tilde (⌘-tilde on the Mac) if the image is in color.

4. **Save the image to disk to store the selection permanently as part of the file.** A handful of formats—PICT, Pixar, PNG, TIFF, Targa, PDF, and native Photoshop—accommodate RGB images with an extra mask channel. But only TIFF, PDF, and the native Photoshop format can handle more than four channels, all saving up to 24 channels in all. I generally use the TIFF format with LZW compression when saving images with masks. Because TIFF supports layers, you aren't restricted to the Photoshop format for multilayered images with masks. (See Chapter 3 for more on that topic.)

Both the native Photoshop format and TIFF can compress masks so that they take up substantially less room on disk. The Photoshop format does this automatically. When saving a TIFF image, be sure to turn on the LZW Compression check box. In both cases, this run-line compression is entirely safe. It does not change a single pixel in the image; it merely writes the code in a more efficient manner.

Tip

If you performed the steps in the "Creating gradient arrows" section, earlier in this chapter, you know that you can also save a quick mask to its own channel for later use. But in case you missed those steps, or you're saving them for a special occasion, here's how it works. When you enter the quick mask mode, the Channels palette displays an item called *Quick Mask*. The italic letters show the channel is temporary and will not be saved with the image. (To clone it to a permanent channel, drag the *Quick Mask* item onto the page icon at the bottom of the Channels palette.) Now save the image to the TIFF or Photoshop format, and you're backed up.

Converting a mask to a selection

To retrieve your selection later, choose Select ➪ Load Selection. A dialog box nearly identical to the one shown in Figure 9-32 appears except for the addition of an Invert check box. Select the document and channel that contain the mask you want to use. You can add it to a current selection, subtract it, or intersect it. Select the Invert option if you want to reverse the selected and deselected portions of the mask.

Want to avoid the Load Selection command? Ctrl-click (Win) or ⌘-click (Mac) the channel name in the Channels palette that contains the mask you want to use. For example, if I Ctrl-clicked the Existing Mask item in Figure 9-32, Photoshop would load the equivalent selection outline into the image window.

But wait, there's more:

- ✦ You can press Ctrl+Alt (⌘-Option on the Mac) plus the channel number to convert the channel to a selection. For example, Ctrl+Alt+4 would convert the Existing Mask channel shown in Figure 9-32.

- ✦ You can also select the channel and click the far-left mask selection icon at the bottom of the Channels palette. But for my money, this takes too much effort.

- ✦ To add a mask to the current selection outline, Ctrl+Shift-click (⌘-Shift-click on the Mac) the channel name in the Channels palette.

- ✦ Ctrl+Alt-click (⌘-Option-click on the Mac) a channel name to subtract the mask from the selection.

- ✦ And Ctrl+Shift+Alt-click (⌘-Shift-Option-click on the Mac) to find the intersection.

You can convert color channels to selections, as well as mask channels. For example, if you want to select the black pixels in a piece of scanned line art in grayscale mode, Ctrl-click (Win) or ⌘-click (Mac) the first item in the Channels palette. This selects the white pixels; press Ctrl+Shift+I (⌘-Shift-I on the Mac) or choose Select ➪ Inverse to reverse the selection to the black pixels.

Viewing mask and image

Photoshop lets you view any mask channel along with an image, just as you can view mask and image together in the quick mask mode. To do this, click in the first column of the Channels palette to toggle the display of the eyeball icon. An eyeball in front of a channel name indicates you can see that channel. If you are currently viewing the full-color image, for example, click in front of the mask channel name to view the mask as a translucent color coating, again as in the quick mask mode. Or if the contents of the mask channel appear by themselves on screen, click in front of the composite name (RGB, CMYK, or LAB) to display the image as well.

When the mask is active, you can likewise toggle the display of the image by pressing the tilde (~) key. Few folks know about this shortcut, but it's a good one to assign to memory. It works whether the Channels palette is open or not, and it permits you to focus on the mask without moving your mouse all over the screen.

Using a mask channel is different from using the quick mask mode in that you can edit either the image or the mask channel when viewing the two together. You can even edit two or more masks at once. To specify which channel you want to edit, click the channel name in the palette. To edit two channels at once, click one and Shift-click another. All active channel names appear highlighted.

You can change the color and opacity of each mask independently of other mask channels and the quick mask mode. Double-click the mask channel thumbnail or choose the Channel Options command from the Channels palette menu. (This command is dimmed when editing a standard color channel, such as Red, Green, Blue, Cyan, Magenta, Yellow, or Black.) A dialog box similar to the one shown back in Figure 9-11 appears, but this one contains a Name option box so you can change the name of the mask channel. You can then edit the color overlay as described in the "Changing the red coating" section, earlier in this chapter.

Tip

If you ever need to edit a selection outline inside the mask channel using paint and edit tools, click the quick mask mode icon in the toolbox. It may sound a little like a play within a play, but you can access the quick mask mode even when working within a mask channel. Make sure the mask channel color is different from the quick mask color so you can tell what's happening.

Building a Mask from an Image

So far, everything I've discussed in this chapter has been pretty straightforward. Now it's time to see how the professionals do things. This final section explains every step required to create a mask for a complex image. Here's how to select the image you never thought you could select, complete with wispy little details such as leaves, stray pieces of string, very small rocks, and hair.

Take a gander at Figure 9-33 and see what I mean. This little cutey presents us with three big challenges: the stray bits of hair roaming about her head and shoulders, the veritable rainbow of colors in her dress, and the wide range of brightness levels in the background. (To fully appreciate the dress and background, see Color Plate 9-3.) Can you imagine selecting any one of them with the magnetic lasso or magic wand? No way. As demonstrated in Figure 9-33, these tools lack sufficient accuracy to do any good. The dress and background share too many colors for the background eraser to work. Meanwhile, you'd be fit for an asylum by the time you finished selecting the hairs with the pen tools, and the edges aren't definite enough for Select ⇨ Color Range to latch onto.

So, what's the solution? Manual masking. Although masking styles vary as widely as artistic styles, a few tried-and-true formulas work for just about everyone. First, you peruse the channels in an image to find the channel that lends itself best to a mask. You're looking for high degrees of contrast, especially around the edges. Next, you copy the channel and boost the level of contrast using Image ⇨ Adjustments ⇨ Levels. (Some folks prefer Image ⇨ Adjustments ⇨ Curves, but the Levels command is more straightforward.) Then you paint or edit the mask until you get it just the way you want it.

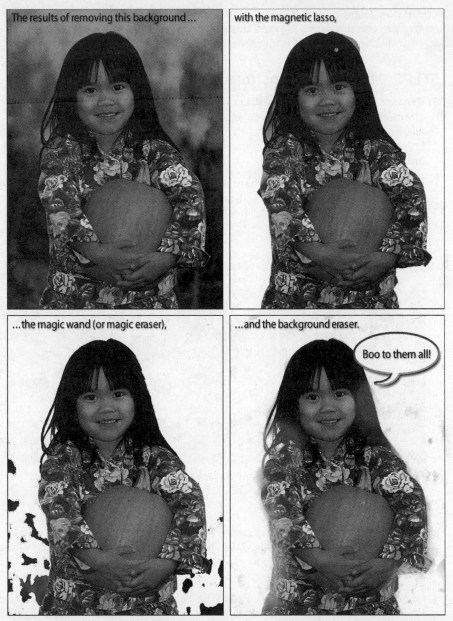

Figure 9-33: She may look like a sweetheart, but this kid's elaborate details and indistinct transitions are too much for Photoshop's selection and extraction tools. This is a job for manual masking.

The only way to get a feel for masking is to try it out for yourself. The following steps explain exactly how I masked this girl and pasted her against a different background. The final result is so realistic, you'd think she was born there.

STEPS: Masking a Monstrously Complicated Image

1. **Browse the color channels.** Press Ctrl+1 (⌘-1 on the Mac) to see the red channel, Ctrl+2 (⌘-2) for green, and Ctrl+3 (⌘-3) for blue. Note that this assumes you're working inside an RGB image. You can also peruse CMYK and Lab images. If you're editing a grayscale image, you have only one channel, and that's Black, Jack.

   Figure 9-34 shows the three channels in my RGB image. Of the three, the green channel offers the most contrast between the hair, the dress, and the background. Hey, it ain't much, but it's better than nothing.

Red   Green   Blue

Figure 9-34: Of the three color channels, the green channel offers the best contrast between hair, dress, and background. Take my word for it.

2. **Clone the channel.** Drag the channel onto the little page icon at the bottom of the Channels palette to create a duplicate of the channel. Naturally, I clone the green channel. Now you can work on the channel without harming the image itself.

3. **Choose Filter ⇨ Other ⇨ High Pass.** The next thing you want to do is to force Photoshop to bring out the edges in the image so you don't have to hunt for them manually. And when you think edges, think filters. All of Photoshop's edge-detection prowess is packed into the Filter menu. Several edge-detection filters are available to you — Unsharp Mask, Find Edges, and many others that I discuss in Chapters 10 and 11. But the best filter for finding edges inside a mask is Filter ⇨ Other ⇨ High Pass.

High Pass selectively turns an image gray. High Pass may sound strange, but it's quite useful. The filter turns the non-edges completely gray while leaving the edges mostly intact, thus dividing edges and non-edges into different brightness camps, based on the Radius value in the High Pass dialog box. Unlike in most filters, a low Radius value produces a more pronounced effect than a high one, in effect locating more edges.

Figure 9-35 shows the cloned green channel on left with the result of the High Pass filter on right. I used a Radius of 10, which is a nice, moderate value. The lower you go, the more edges you find and the more work you make for yourself. A Radius of 3 is accurate, but it'll take you an hour to fill in the mask. Granted, 10 is less accurate, but if you value your time, it's more sensible.

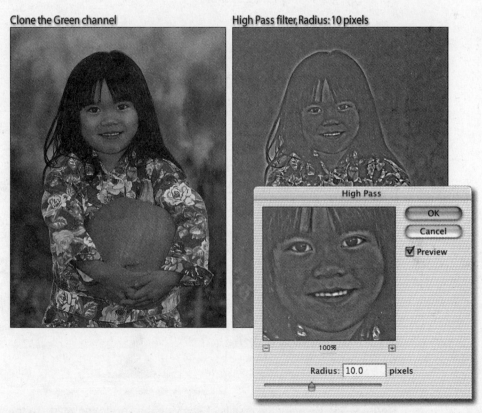

Figure 9-35: After cloning the green channel (left), I applied the High Pass filter with a Radius value of 10 to highlight the edges in the image (right).

4. **Choose Image ➪ Adjustments ➪ Levels or press Ctrl+L (⌘-L on the Mac).**
   After adding all that gray to the image, follow it up by increasing the contrast. And the best command for enhancing contrast is Levels. Although I discuss

this command in depth in Chapter 17, here's the short version: Inside the Levels dialog box, raise the first Input Levels value to make the dark colors darker, and lower the third Input Levels value to make the light colors lighter. (For now you can ignore the middle value.)

Figure 9-36 shows the result of raising the first Input Levels value to 110 and lowering the third value to 155. As you can see in the left-hand image, this gives me some excellent contrast between the white hairs and black background.

To demonstrate the importance of the High Pass command in these steps, I've shown what would happen if I had skipped Step 3 in the right-hand image in Figure 9-36. I applied the same Levels values as in the left image, and yet the image is overly dark and quite lacking in edges. Look at that wishy washy hair. I'm sorry, it's simply unacceptable.

Levels after High Pass

Levels only

Input Levels: 110   1.00   155

Figure 9-36: Here are the results of applying the Levels command to the mask after the High Pass step (left) and without High Pass (right). As you can see, High Pass has a very positive effect on the edge detail.

5. **Identify the edges.** By way of High Pass and Levels, Photoshop has presented you with a complex coloring book. From here on, it's a matter of coloring inside the lines. But you have to make sure your lines are coherent. In my case, the hair edges showed up as black lines against white, but the dress

showed up as white lines against black. To keep things consistent, I selected the general region of the dress using the lasso tool and then chose Image ⇨ Adjustments ⇨ Invert (Ctrl+I under Windows, ⌘-I on the Mac) to swap the blacks and whites. As shown in the first example in Figure 9-37, the image looks the worse for this change, but the outlines are easier to follow.

Invert dress region   Select along edges & fill black

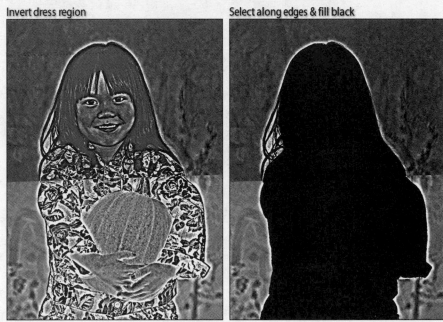

Figure 9-37: To ensure a consistent line between foreground and background, I selected the area around the dress with the lasso tool and inverted it (left). Then I selected the area inside the girl and filled it with black (right).

6. **Use the lasso tool to remove the big stuff you don't need.** To simplify things, get rid of the stuff you know you don't need. All you care about is the area where the girl meets her background — mostly around the hair and dress. Everything else goes to white or black.

   In the second example in Figure 9-37, I selected a general area inside the girl by Alt-clicking with the lasso tool (or Option-clicking on the Mac). Then I filled it with black by pressing Alt+Backspace (Option-Delete on the Mac).

   In Figure 9-38, I selected the area outside the girl and filled it with white by pressing Ctrl+Backspace (⌘-Delete on the Mac). Notice I was able to accomplish a lot with the lasso tool, but not everything is as it should be. The areas inside the hair and around the right sleeve, in particular, will require some careful attention with the brush tool.

   Incidentally, be sure to press Ctrl+D (⌘-D on the Mac) to eliminate the selection before continuing to the next step.

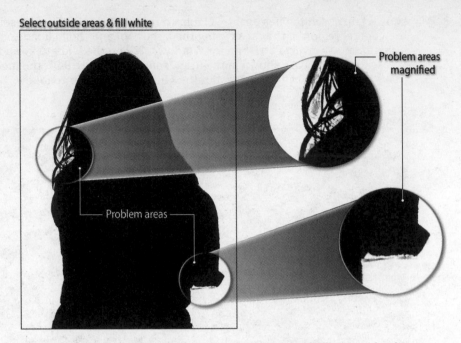

Select outside areas & fill white

Problem areas
magnified

Problem areas

Figure 9-38: By selecting the area outside the girl and filling it with white, I was able to clearly distinguish between foreground and background. But that still left a few messy edges, identified by the circles.

7. **Paint inside the lines with the brush tool.** This tends to be the most time-consuming part. Now you have to paint inside the lines to make the edge pixels black or white. For this image, I used the brush tool with a hard brush size of about 5 to 10 pixels. I used the X key to switch between painting with black and white. The first image in Figure 9-39 shows the fruits of my labors. As you can see, I made a few judgment calls and decided — sometimes arbitrarily — where the hair got so thick that background imagery wouldn't show through. You may even disagree with some of my brushstrokes. But you know what? It doesn't matter. Despite whatever flaws I may have introduced, my mask is more than accurate enough to select the girl, as I will soon demonstrate.

8. **Invert the mask.** You may or may not need to perform this step. Based on the condition of the edges after I chose the High Pass command, my girl ended up black against a white background. But I want to select the girl, so she needs to be white. Therefore, I pressed Ctrl+I (⌘-I on the Mac) to swap the blacks and whites. If your foreground image ends up white after Step 7, then skip this step.

Clean up edges   Invert for final mask

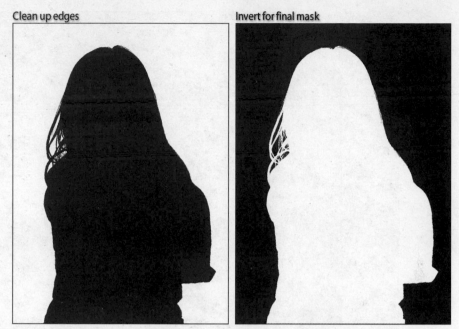

Figure 9-39: I fixed the problem areas by hand using the brush tool (left). Then I inverted the entire mask so the area inside the girl was white and the area outside was black (right). Depending on how you paint your mask, you may be able to skip this last step.

9. **Switch to the color composite view.** Press Ctrl+tilde (⌘-tilde on the Mac). Or if you're working in a grayscale image, press Ctrl+1 (⌘-1). By the way, now is a good time to save the image if you haven't already done so. Remember, TIFF is a terrific format for this purpose.

10. **Ctrl-click (Win) or ⌘-click (Mac) the mask channel to convert it to a selection.** This mask is ready to go prime time.

11. **Ctrl-drag (Win) or ⌘-drag (Mac) the selection and drop it into a different image.** Figure 9-40 shows the result of dropping the girl into a background of giant orange squash not unlike the one she holds in her arms. Thanks to my mask, she looks as natural in her new environment as she did in her previous one. In fact, an uninitiated viewer might have difficulty believing this isn't how she was originally photographed. But if you take a peek at Figure 9-33, you can confirm that Figure 9-40 is indeed an artificial composite. I painted in a few extra hairs to sell the composition, but that's because I'm an obsessive fussbudget. In most cases, you won't need to bother.

Figure 9-40: Thanks to masking, our girl has found a new life in a more sincere pumpkin patch. The prodigal daughter has returned.

The grayscale Figure 9-40 looks great, but your compositions may not fare quite so well in color where fringing is a common problem. The solution may be to brush in color from the new background. In Color Plate 9-3, I set the brush tool to the Color mode. Then I Alt-clicked (or Option-clicked on the Mac) in the Background layer to lift colors from the new background and dragged to paint them into the hair. After a minute or two of this color painting, I arrived at the final composition in the color plate. Now if that isn't compositing perfection, well, gee whiz, I don't know what is.

✦   ✦   ✦

Corrective Filtering

Filter Basics

In Photoshop, filters enable you to apply automated effects to an image. Though named after photographers' filters, which typically correct lighting fluctuations and perspective, Photoshop's filters can accomplish a great deal more. You can slightly increase the focus of an image, introduce random pixels, add depth to an image, or completely rip it apart and reassemble it into a hurky pile of goo. Any number of special effects are made available via filters.

At this point, a little bell should be ringing in your head, telling you to beware of standardized special effects. Why? Because everyone who has Photoshop — or its cocky young offspring Photoshop Elements — has access to the same filters that you do. If you rely on filters to edit your images for you, your audience will quickly recognize your work as poor or at least unremarkable art.

Imagine this scenario: You're wasting away in front of your TV, flipping aimlessly through the channels. Just as your brain is about to shrivel and implode, you stumble across that really cool commercial for an SUV where it keeps on rolling along implacably as the background behind it changes something like 17 times. Really eye-catching, unusual stuff, and I would say it was a terrific commercial if only I could remember precisely which SUV it was selling. Ah, well.

The commercial ends, and you're so busy basking in the glow that you neglect for a split second to whack the channel-changer. Before you know it, you're midway through an advertisement for a monster truck rally. Like the SUV commercial, this ad is riddled with special effects — spinning letters, a reverberating voice-over slowed down to an octave below the narrator's normal pitch, and lots of big machines filled with little men filled with single brain cells working overtime. Watching this obnoxious commercial is like being beaten over the head with a sledgehammer, and then run over several times by a steamroller for good measure.

You see, in and of themselves, special effects aren't bad. It's all in how you use them. The SUV commercial manages to entice your eye and draw you into its constantly morphing world, making the vehicle look very hip and cool. The monster truck rally's effects are more of the hard-sell, hit-you-over-the-head variety. Not only are these effects devoid of substance, but, more importantly, they're devoid of creativity.

This chapter and the next, therefore, are about the creative application of special effects. Rather than trying to show an image subject to every single filter—a service already performed quite adequately by the manual included with your software— these chapters explain exactly how the most important filters work and offer some concrete ways to use them.

You also learn how to apply several filters in tandem and how to use filters to edit images and selection outlines. My goal is not so much to teach you what filters are available—you can find that out by tugging on the Filter menu—but how and when to use filters.

A first look at filters

You access Photoshop's special effects filters by choosing commands from the Filter menu. These commands fall into two general camps—*corrective* and *destructive*.

Corrective filters

Corrective filters are workaday tools that you use to modify scanned or otherwise captured images and prepare an image for printing or screen display. In many cases, the effects are subtle enough that the viewer won't even notice that you applied a corrective filter. As demonstrated in Figure 10-1, these filters include those that change the focus of an image, enhance color transitions, and average the colors of neighboring pixels. Find these filters in the Filter ⇨ Blur, Noise, Sharpen, and Other submenus.

Many corrective filters have direct opposites. Blur is the opposite of Sharpen, Add Noise is the opposite of Median, and so on. This is not to say that one filter entirely removes the effect of the other; only reversion functions such as the History palette provide that capability. Instead, two opposite filters produce contrasting effects.

Corrective filters are the subject of this chapter. Although they number fewer than their destructive counterparts, I spend more time on them because they represent the functions you're most likely to use on a day-to-day basis.

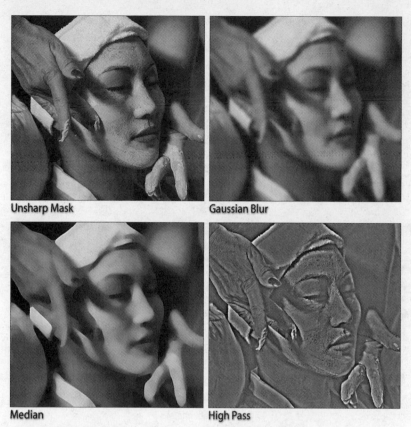

Unsharp Mask

Gaussian Blur

Median

High Pass

Figure 10-1: A woman getting a facial subject to four corrective filters, including one each from the Sharpen, Blur, Other, and Noise submenus (reading clockwise from upper left).

Destructive filters

The destructive filters produce effects so dramatic that they can, if used improperly, completely overwhelm your artwork, making the filter more important than the image itself. For the most part, destructive filters reside in the Filter ➪ Distort, Pixelate, Render, and Stylize submenus. A few examples of overwhelmed images appear in Figure 10-2.

Destructive filters produce way-cool effects, and many people gravitate toward them when first experimenting with Photoshop. But the filters invariably destroy the original clarity and composition of the image. Granted, every Photoshop function is destructive to a certain extent, but destructive filters change your image so extensively that you can't easily disguise the changes later by applying other filters or editing techniques.

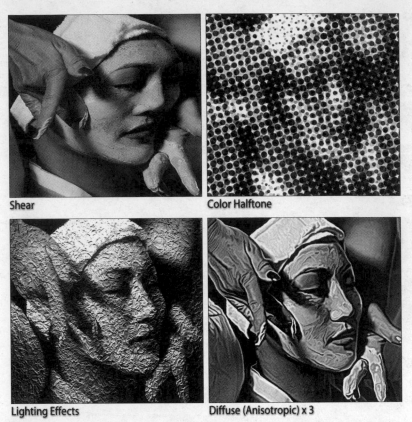

Shear

Color Halftone

Lighting Effects

Diffuse (Anisotropic) x 3

Figure 10-2: The effects of applying four destructive filters, one each from the Distort, Pixelate, Stylize, and Render submenus (clockwise from upper left). Note that Lighting Effects is applicable to color images only, so I had to convert this woman to the RGB mode before applying the filter.

Destructive filters are the subject of Chapter 11. Rather than explaining every one of these filters in detail, I try to provide a general overview.

Effects filters

Photoshop also provides a subset of 47 destructive filters called the *effects* filters. These filters originally sire from the Gallery Effects collection, developed by Silicon Beach, which got gobbled up by Aldus (of PageMaker fame), and finally acquired by Adobe Systems. Not knowing what exactly to do with this grab bag of plug-ins, Adobe integrated them into Photoshop.

Little about these filters has changed since Gallery Effects 1.5 came out in 1993. A couple of filters have been renamed — the old GE Ripple filter is now Ocean Ripple to avoid confusion with Photoshop's own Ripple filter. And one filter, GE Emboss, is gone, presumably because it detracted from the popular Filter ➪ Stylize ➪ Emboss.

But Adobe hasn't bothered with any meaningful retooling. You can't preview the effect in the image window and a few filters are dreadfully slow.

As a result, I devote only passing attention to the effects filters, explaining those very few that fulfill a real need. Of course, I encourage you to experiment and derive your own conclusions. After all, as Figure 10-3 illustrates, these filters do produce intriguing special effects. I mean, that Plastic Wrap effect is just plain cool. For the record, most of the effects filters reside in the Filter ➪ Artistic, Brush Strokes, Sketch, and Texture submenus. A few have trickled out into other submenus, including Filter ➪ Distort ➪ Diffuse Glow, Glass, and Ocean Ripple; and Filter ➪ Stylize ➪ Glowing Edges.

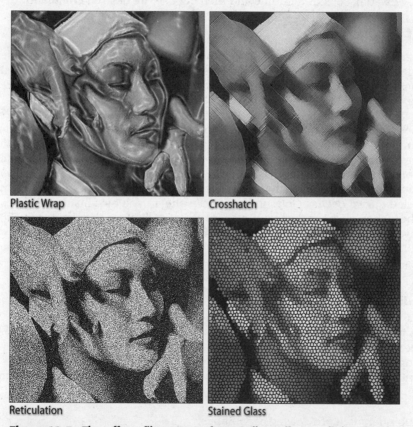

Plastic Wrap   Crosshatch

Reticulation   Stained Glass

Figure 10-3: The *effects* filters come from Gallery Effects, a little toy surprise that Adobe accidentally acquired when it purchased Aldus Corporation. Here we see the impact of one filter each from the Filter ➪ Artistic, Brush Strokes, Texture, and Sketch submenus (clockwise from upper left).

If your experimentation leads you to the same conclusion as it did me — that you can live through most days without the effects filters — you can turn them off. All the effects filters are stored in the Effects folder inside the Plug-Ins folder on your hard drive. Rename the Effects folder ~Effects, and all 47 filters will be turned off.

How filters work

When you choose a command from the Filter menu, Photoshop applies the filter to the selected portion of the image on the current layer. If no portion of the image is selected, Photoshop applies the filter to the entire layer. Therefore, if you want to filter every nook and cranny of the current layer, press Ctrl+D (⌘-D on the Mac) to cancel any existing selection outline and then choose the desired command.

External plug-ins

Some filters are built into the Photoshop application. Others are external modules that reside in the Plug-Ins folder. This enables you to add functionality to Photoshop by purchasing additional filters from third-party collections. Gallery Effects used to be such a collection. Eye Candy, from Alien Skin, is another popular collection.

If you open the Plug-Ins folder inside the Photoshop folder, you see that it contains several subfolders. By default, Photoshop places the filters in the Filters and Effects subfolders, but you can place additional filters anywhere inside the Plug-Ins folder. Even if you create a new folder inside the Plug-Ins folder and call it *No Filters Here*, create another folder inside that called *Honest, Fresh Out of Filters*, toss in one more folder called *Carpet Beetles Only*, and put every plug-in you own inside this latest folder, Photoshop sees through your clever ruse and displays the exact same filters you always see under their same submenus in the Filter menu. The only purpose of the subfolders is to keep things tidy, so that you don't have to look through a list of 6,000 files.

Previewing filters

For years, the biggest problem with Photoshop's filters was that none offered previews to help you predict the outcome of an effect. You just had to tweak your 15,000 meaningless settings and hope for the best. But today, life is much better. Photoshop 3 introduced previews, Version 4 made them commonly available to all but the most gnarly filters, and subsequent versions have had the good sense to leave well enough alone.

Photoshop offers two previewing capabilities:

✦ **Dialog box previews:** Labeled in Figure 10-4, the 100×100-pixel preview box is now a common feature to all filter dialog boxes. Drag inside the preview box to scroll the portion of the image you want to preview. Move the cursor outside the dialog box to get the square preview cursor (labeled in the figure). Click with the cursor to center the contents of the preview box at the clicked position in the image.

Click the zoom buttons (+ and –) to change the view of the image inside the preview box. You can even take advantage of the standard zoom tool by pressing Ctrl+spacebar or Alt+spacebar (⌘-spacebar or Option-spacebar on the Mac), depending on whether you want to zoom in or out.

Preview box   Zoom buttons   Progress line   Preview cursor   Image window

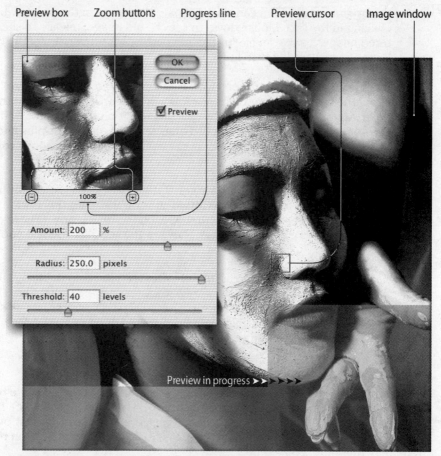

Figure 10-4: Most filter dialog boxes let you preview the effects of the filter both inside the dialog box and in the image window.

Tip

✦ **Image window previews:** Most corrective filters—as well as a couple of destructives such as Mosaic and Emboss—also preview effects in the full image window. Just select the Preview check box to activate this function. While the effect is previewing, a blinking progress line appears under the zoom value in the dialog box. In Figure 10-4, for example, you can see that the bottom of the image still hasn't finished previewing, so the progress line strobes away. If you're working on a relatively poky computer, you'll probably want to turn the Preview check box off to speed up the pace at which the filter functions.

Incidentally, the Preview check box has no affect on the contents of the pre-view box. The latter continually monitors the effects of your settings, whether you like it or not.

Use the Preview check box to compare the before and after effects of a correc-tive filter in the image window. Turn it on to see the effect; turn it off to see the original image. You can also compare the image in the preview box by clicking in the box. Mouse down to see the old image; release to see the fil-tered image. It's like an electronic, high-priced, adult version of peek-a-boo. But not nearly as likely to induce giggles.

Even though a dialog box is on screen and active, you can zoom and scroll the contents of the image window. Ctrl+spacebar-click (⌘-spacebar-click on the Mac) to zoom in; Alt+spacebar-click (Option-spacebar-click on the Mac) to zoom out. Or you can zoom in and out by pressing Ctrl+plus and Ctrl+minus (⌘-plus and ⌘-minus on the Mac), respectively. Spacebar-drag to scroll. You can also choose commands from the View and Window menus.

One more tip: When you press Alt (Win) or Option (Mac), the Cancel button changes to a Reset button. Alt-click (Option-click on the Mac) this button to restore the settings that appeared when you first opened the dialog box. (These are not necessarily the factory default settings; they are the settings you last applied to an image.)

Most destructive filters make no attempt to preview effects in the image window. And seven filters continue to offer no previews whatsoever: Radial Blur, Displace, Color Halftone, Extrude, Tiles, De-Interlace, and Offset. Of course, single-shot filters — the ones that don't bring up dialog boxes — don't need previews because there aren't any settings to adjust.

Reapplying the last filter

To reapply the last filter used in the current Photoshop session, choose the first command from the Filter menu or simply press Ctrl+F (⌘-F on the Mac). If you want to reapply the filter subject to different settings, press Alt (Win) or Option (Mac) and choose the first Filter command or press Ctrl+Alt+F (⌘-Option-F on the Mac) to redisplay that filter's dialog box.

Both techniques work even if you undo the last application of a filter. However, if you cancel a filter while in progress, pressing Ctrl+F or Ctrl+Alt+F (⌘-F or ⌘-Option-F on the Mac) applies the last uncanceled filter.

Nudging numerical values

In addition to entering specific numerical values inside filter dialog boxes, you can nudge the values using the up and down arrow keys. When working with percentage values, press an arrow key to raise or lower the value by 1. Press Shift-up or -down arrow to change the value in increments of 10. Note that with some of the destruc-tive filters, most notably those associated with the old Gallery Effects filters, you must use the arrow keys on the numeric keypad; the regular navigation arrow keys don't work.

If the value accommodates decimal values, it's probably more sensitive to the arrow key. Press an arrow for a 0.1 change; press Shift+arrow for 1.0.

Fading a filter

In many cases, you apply filters to a selection or image at full intensity—meaning that you marquee an area using a selection tool, choose a filter command, enter whatever settings you deem appropriate if a dialog box appears, and sit back and watch the fireworks.

What's so full intensity about that? Sounds normal, right? Well, the fact is, you can reduce the intensity of the last filter applied by choosing Edit ➪ Fade or pressing Ctrl+Shift+F (⌘-Shift-F on the Mac). This command permits you to mix the filtered image with the original, unfiltered one.

As shown in Figure 10-5, the Fade dialog box provides you with the basic tools of image mixing—an Opacity value and a blend mode pop-up menu. To demonstrate the wonders of Edit ➪ Fade, I've applied two particularly destructive Gallery Effects filters to the woman getting a facial—Filter ➪ Stylize ➪ Glowing Edges and Filter ➪ Sketch ➪ Bas Relief. The right-hand images show the effects of pressing Ctrl+Shift+F and applying two blend modes, Screen and Vivid Light, with the Opacity value set to 100 and 65 percent, respectively.

Creating layered effects

Caution

The drawback of the Fade command is that it's only available immediately after you apply a filter (or other applicable edit). If you so much as modify a selection outline after applying the filter, the Fade command dims, only to return when you apply the next filter.

Therefore, you may find it more helpful to copy a selection to a separate layer (by pressing Ctrl+J on the PC or ⌘-J on the Mac) before applying a filter. This way, you can perform other operations, and even apply many filters in a row, before mixing the filtered image with the underlying original.

Filtering inside a border

And here's another reason to layer before you filter: If your image has a border around it—like the ones shown in Figure 10-6—you don't want Photoshop to factor the border into the filtering operation. To avoid this, select the image inside the border and press Ctrl+J (Win) or ⌘-J (Mac) to layer it prior to applying the filter. The reason is that most filters take neighboring pixels into consideration even if they are not selected. By contrast, when a selection floats, it has no neighboring pixels, and therefore the filter affects the selected pixels only.

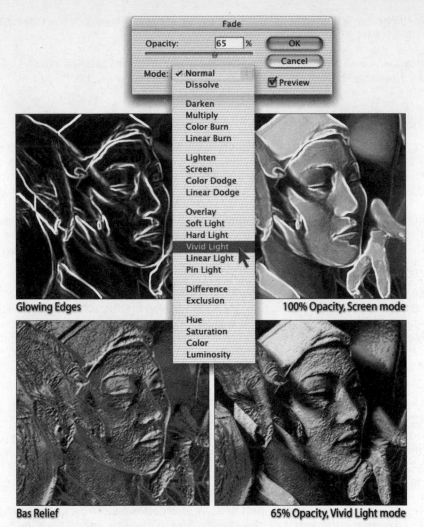

Figure 10-5: Press Ctrl+Shift+F (⌘-Shift-F on the Mac) to mix the filtered image with the unfiltered original. I don't know about you, but I'd take a Glowing Edges facial over a Bas Relief one any day.

Figure 10-6 shows the results of applying two filters discussed in this chapter — Unsharp Mask and Motion Blur — when the image is anchored in place and when it's layered. In all cases, the 2-pixel border was not selected. In the left examples, the Unsharp Mask filter leaves a high-contrast residue around the edge of the image, while Motion Blur duplicates the left and right edges of the border. Both problems vanish when the filters are applied to layered images, as seen on the right.

Even if the area outside the selection is not a border per se — perhaps it's just a comparatively dark or light area that serves as a visual frame — layering comes in handy. You should always layer the selection unless you specifically want edge pixels to be calculated by the filter.

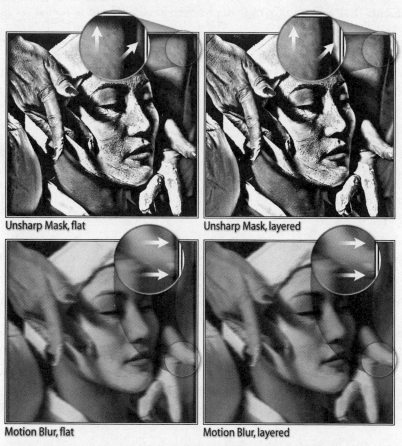

Unsharp Mask, flat   Unsharp Mask, layered

Motion Blur, flat   Motion Blur, layered

Figure 10-6: The results of applying two sample filters to images surrounded by borders. In each case, only the image was selected; the border was not. Layering the right examples prevented the borders from affecting the performance of the filters.

Undoing a sequence of filters

Okay, here's one last reason to layer before you filter. Copying an image to a layer protects the underlying image. If you just want to experiment a little, pressing Ctrl+J (⌘-J on the Mac) is often more convenient than restoring a state in the History palette. After applying four or five effects to a layer, you can undo all that automated abuse by Alt-clicking (Win) or Option-clicking (Mac) the trash icon at the bottom of the Layers palette, which deletes the layer. The underlying original remains unharmed.

Heightening Focus and Contrast

If you've experimented at all with Photoshop, you've no doubt had your way with many of the commands in the Filter ➪ Sharpen submenu. By increasing the contrast between neighboring pixels, the sharpening filters enable you to compensate for image elements that were photographed or scanned slightly out of focus.

The Sharpen, Sharpen More, and Sharpen Edges commands are easy to use and immediate in their effect. However, you can achieve better results and widen your range of sharpening options if you learn how to use the Unsharp Mask and High Pass commands, which I discuss at length in the following pages.

Using the Unsharp Mask filter

The first thing you need to know about the Unsharp Mask filter is that it has a weird name. The filter has nothing to do with unsharpening—whatever that is—nor is it tied into Photoshop's masking capabilities. Unsharp Mask is named after a traditional film compositing technique (which is also oddly named) that highlights the edges in an image by combining a blurred film negative with the original film positive.

That's all very well and good, but the fact is most Photoshop artists have never touched a stat camera (an expensive piece of machinery, roughly twice the size of a washing machine, used by image editors of the late Jurassic, pre-Photoshop epoch). Even folks like me who used to operate stat cameras professionally never had the time to delve into the world of unsharp masking. In addition—and much to the filter's credit—Unsharp Mask goes beyond traditional camera techniques.

To understand Unsharp Mask—or Photoshop's other sharpening filters, for that matter—you first need to understand some basic terminology. When you apply one of the sharpening filters, Photoshop increases the contrast between neighboring pixels. The effect is similar to what you see when you adjust a camera to bring a scene into sharper focus.

Two of Photoshop's sharpening filters, Sharpen and Sharpen More, affect whatever area of your image is selected. The Sharpen Edges filter, however, performs its sharpening operations only on the *edges* in the image—those areas that feature the highest amount of contrast.

Unsharp Mask gives you both sharpening options. It can sharpen only the edges in an image or it can sharpen any portion of an image according to your exact specifications, whether it finds an edge or not. It fulfills the exact same purposes as the Sharpen, Sharpen Edges, and Sharpen More commands, but it's much more versatile. Simply put, the Unsharp Mask tool is the only sharpening filter you'll ever need.

When you choose Filter ➪ Sharpen ➪ Unsharp Mask, Photoshop displays the Unsharp Mask dialog box, shown in Figure 10-7, which offers the following options:

✦ **Amount:** Enter a value between 1 and 500 percent to specify the degree to which you want to sharpen the selected image. Higher values produce more pronounced effects.

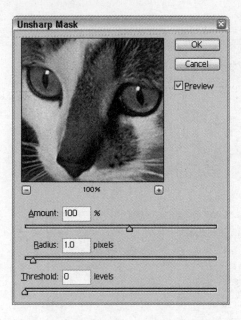

Figure 10-7: Despite any conclusions you may glean from its bizarre name, the Unsharp Mask filter sharpens images according to your specifications in this dialog box.

✦ **Radius:** This option determines the thickness of the sharpened edge. Low values produce crisp edges. High values produce thicker edges with more contrast throughout the image.

✦ **Threshold:** Enter a value between 0 and 255 to control how Photoshop recognizes edges in an image. The value indicates the numerical difference between the brightness values of two neighboring pixels that must occur if Photoshop is to sharpen those pixels. A low value sharpens lots of pixels; a high value excludes most pixels from the running.

The preview options offered by the Unsharp Mask dialog box are absolutely essential visual aids that you're likely to find tremendously useful throughout your Photoshop career. Just the same, you'll be better prepared to experiment with the Amount, Radius, and Threshold options and less surprised by the results if you read the following sections, which explain these options in detail and demonstrate the effects of each.

Specifying the amount of sharpening

If Amount were the only Unsharp Mask option, no one would have any problems understanding this filter. If you want to sharpen an image ever so slightly, enter a low percentage value. Values between 25 and 50 percent are ideal for producing subtle effects. If you want to sharpen an image beyond the point of good taste, enter a value somewhere in the 300 to 500 percent range. And if you're looking for moderate sharpening, try out some value between 50 and 300 percent. Figure 10-8 shows the results of applying different Amount values while leaving the Radius and Threshold values at their default settings of 1.0 and 0, respectively.

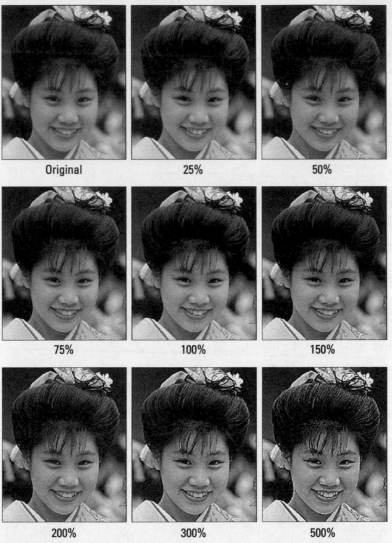

Figure 10-8: The results of sharpening an image with the Unsharp Mask filter using eight different Amount values. The Radius and Threshold values used for all images were 1.0 and 0, respectively (the default settings).

If you're not sure how much you want to sharpen an image, try out a small value in the 25 to 50 percent range. Then reapply that setting repeatedly by pressing Ctrl+F (⌘-F on the Mac). As you can see in Figure 10-9, repeatedly applying the filter at a low setting produces a nearly identical result to applying the filter once at a higher setting. For example, you can achieve the effect shown in the middle image in the figure by applying the Unsharp Mask filter three times at 50 percent or once at 250 percent. I created the top-row results in Figure 10-9 using a constant Radius value of 1.0. In the second row, I lowered the Radius progressively from 1.0 (left) to 0.8 (middle) to 0.6 (right).

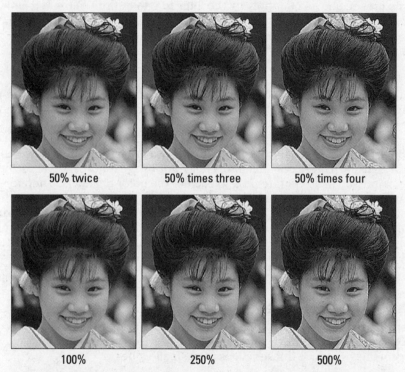

Figure 10-9: Repeatedly applying the Unsharp Mask filter at 50 percent (top row) is nearly equivalent on a pixel-by-pixel basis to applying the filter once at higher settings (bottom row).

The benefit of using small values is that they enable you to experiment with sharpening incrementally. As the figure demonstrates, you can add sharpening bit by bit to increase the focus of an image. You can't, however, reduce sharpening incrementally if you apply too high a value; you must press Ctrl+Z (Win) or ⌘-Z (Mac) and start again.

Just for fun, Color Plate 10-1 shows the results of applying the Unsharp Mask filter to each of the color channels in an RGB image independently, as well as in pairs. In each case, I maxed out the Amount value to 500 percent and set the Radius and Threshold to 4.0 and 0 respectively. The top row shows the original image on the left and Unsharp Mask applied to all three channels at once on the right. In the remaining rows, I alternated single channel applications with applications to pairs of channels. You can see how the filter creates a crisp halo of color, especially around the outside edge of the lady's face. Sharpening the red channel creates a red halo on the face and brings out blue-green details in the facial cream; sharpening the red and green channels together creates a yellow halo on the face and bluish details in the cream; and so on. Applying the filter to one or both of the red and green channels produced the most noticeable effects because these channels contain the lion's share of the image detail. The blue channel contained the least detail — as is typical — so sharpening this channel produced the least dramatic results.

If you're a little foggy on how to access individual color channels, read Chapter 4. Incidentally, you can achieve similar effects by sharpening the individual channels in a Lab or CMYK image.

As I mentioned in Chapter 4, Photoshop is ultimately a grayscale editor, so when you apply the Unsharp Mask command to a full-color image, Photoshop actually applies the command in a separate pass to each of the color channels. Therefore, the command always results in the color halos shown in Color Plate 10-1 — it's just that the halos get mixed together, minimizing the effect. To avoid any haloing what-soever, convert the image to the Lab mode (Image ➪ Mode ➪ Lab Color) and apply Unsharp Mask to only the Lightness channel in the Channels palette. (Do not filter the *a* and *b* channels.) This sharpens the brightness values in the image and leaves the colors 100 percent untouched.

Setting the thickness of the edges

The Unsharp Mask filter works by identifying edges and increasing the contrast around those edges. The Radius value tells Photoshop how thick you want your edges. Large values produce thicker edges than small values.

The ideal Radius value depends on the resolution of your image and the quality of its edges:

✦ When creating screen images — such as Web graphics — use a very low Radius value, such as 0.5. This results in terrific hairline edges that look so crisp, you'll think you washed your bifocals.

✦ If a low Radius value brings out weird little imperfections — such as grain, scan lines, or JPEG compression artifacts — raise the value to 1.0 or higher. If that doesn't help, don't fret. I include two different sure-fire image-fixing techniques later in this chapter, one designed to sharpen grainy old photos, and another that accommodates compressed images.

✦ When printing an image at a moderate resolution—anywhere from 120 to 180 ppi—use a Radius value of 1.0. The edges will look a little thick on screen, but they'll print fine.

✦ For high-resolution images—around 300 ppi—try a Radius of 2.0. Because Photoshop prints more pixels per inch, the edges have to be thicker to remain nice and visible.

If you're looking for a simple formula, I recommend 0.1 of Radius for every 15 ppi of final image resolution. That means 75 ppi warrants a Radius of 0.5, 120 ppi warrants 0.8, 180 ppi warrants 1.2, and so on. If you have a calculator, just divide the intended resolution by 150 to get the ideal Radius value.

You can of course enter higher Radius values—as high as 250, in fact. Higher values produce heightened contrast effects, almost as if the image had been photocopied too many times, generally useful for producing special effects.

But don't take my word for it; you be the judge. Figure 10-10 demonstrates the results of specific Radius values. In each case, the Amount and Threshold values remain constant at 100 percent and 0, respectively.

Figure 10-11 shows the results of combining different Amount and Radius values. You can see that a large Amount value helps to offset the softening of a high Radius value. For example, when the Amount is set to 200 percent, as in the first row, the Radius value appears to mainly enhance contrast when raised from 0.5 to 2.0. However, when the Amount value is lowered to 50 percent, the higher Radius value does more to distribute the effect than boost contrast.

Recognizing edges

By default, the Unsharp Mask filter sharpens every pixel in a selection. However, you can instruct the filter to sharpen only the edges in an image by raising the Threshold value from zero to some other number. The Threshold value represents the difference between two neighboring pixels—as measured in brightness levels—that must occur for Photoshop to recognize them as an edge.

Suppose that the brightness values of neighboring pixels are 10 and 20. If you set the Threshold value to 5, Photoshop reads both pixels, notes that the difference between their brightness values is more than 5, and treats them as an edge. If you set the Threshold value to 20, however, Photoshop passes them by. A low Threshold value, therefore, causes the Unsharp Mask filter to affect a high number of pixels, and vice versa.

Original   0.5   1.0

1.5   2.5   5.0

10.0   50.0   100.0

Figure 10-10: The results of applying eight different Radius values, ranging from precise edges to very gooey.

200%, 0.5   200%, 2.0   200%, 10.0

100%, 0.5   100%, 2.0   100%, 10.0

50%, 0.5   50%, 2.0   50%, 10.0

Figure 10-11: The effects of combining different Amount and Radius settings. The Threshold value for each image was set to 0, the default setting.

In the top row of images in Figure 10-12, the high Threshold values result in tiny slivers of sharpness that outline only the most substantial edges in the woman's face. As I lower the Threshold value incrementally in the second and third rows, the sharpening effect takes over more and more of the face, ultimately sharpening all details uniformly in the lower-right example.

Figure 10-12: The results of applying nine different Threshold values. To best show off the differences between each image, I set the Amount and Radius values to 500 percent and 2.0 respectively.

Using the preset sharpening filters

So how do the Sharpen, Sharpen Edges, and Sharpen More commands compare with the Unsharp Mask filter? First of all, none of the preset commands permit you to vary the thickness of your edges, a function provided by Unsharp Mask's Radius option. Second, only the Sharpen Edges command can recognize high-contrast areas in an image. And third, all three commands are set in stone — you can't adjust their effects in any way (except, of course, to fade the filter after the fact). Figure 10-13 shows the effect of each preset command and the nearly equivalent effect created with the Unsharp Mask filter.

Sharpen   Sharpen Edges   Sharpen More

100%, 0.5, 0   100%, 0.5, 5   300%, 0.5, 0

Figure 10-13: The effects of the three preset sharpening filters (top row) compared with the Unsharp Mask equivalents (bottom row). Unsharp Mask values are listed in the following order: Amount, Radius, Threshold.

Sharpening grainy photographs

Having completed my neutral discussion of Unsharp Mask, king of the Sharpen filters, I hasten to interject a little bit of commentary, along with a helpful solution to a common sharpening problem.

First, the commentary: While Amount and Radius are the kinds of superior options that will serve you well throughout the foreseeable future, I urge young and old to observe Threshold with the utmost scorn and rancor. The idea is fine—we can all agree that you need some way to draw a dividing line between those pixels that you want to sharpen and those that you want to leave unchanged. But the Threshold setting is nothing more than a glorified on/off switch that results in harsh transitions between sharpened and unsharpened pixels.

Consider the picture of Frederick Douglass in Figure 10-14. Like so many vintage photographs, this particular image of the famed abolitionist is a little softer than we're used to seeing these days. But if I apply a heaping helping of Unsharp Mask—as in the second example in the figure—I bring out as much film grain as image detail. The official Photoshop solution is to raise the Threshold value, but the option's intrinsic harshness results in a pockmarked effect, as shown on the right. Photoshop has simply replaced one kind of grain with another.

Soft vintage image   Sharpened, Threshold: 0   Sharpened, Threshold: 20

Figure 10-14: The original photograph is a bit soft (left), a condition I can remedy with Unsharp Mask. Leaving the Threshold value set to 0 brings out the film grain (middle), but raising the value results in equally unattractive artifacts (right).

These abrupt transitions are quite out of keeping with Photoshop's normal approach. Paintbrushes have antialiased edges, selections can be feathered, the Color Range command offers Fuzziness—in short, everything mimics the softness found in real life. Yet right here, inside what is indisputably Photoshop's most essential filter, we find no mechanism for softness whatsoever.

While we wait for Photoshop to give us a better Threshold — one with a Fuzziness slider or similar control — you can create a better Threshold using a very simple masking technique. Using a few filters that I explore at greater length throughout this chapter and the next, you can devise a selection outline that traces the essential edges in the image — complete with fuzzy transitions — and leaves the non-edges unmolested. So get out your favorite old vintage photograph and follow along with these steps.

STEPS: Creating and Using an Edge Mask

1. **Duplicate one of the color channels.** Bring up the Channels palette and drag one of the color channels onto the little page icon. Mr. Douglass is a grayscale image, so I duplicate the one and only channel.

2. **Choose Filter ⇨ Stylize ⇨ Find Edges.** As I explain in Chapter 11, the Find Edges filter automatically traces the edges of your image with thick, gooey outlines that are ideal for creating edge masks.

3. **Press Ctrl+I (⌘-I on the Mac).** Or choose Image ⇨ Adjustments ⇨ Invert. Find Edges produces black lines against a white background, but in order to select your edges, you need white lines against a black background. The Invert command reverses the lights and darks in the mask, as in the first example in Figure 10-15.

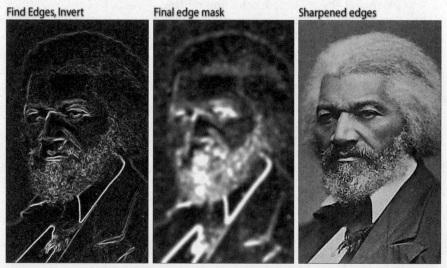

Find Edges, Invert   Final edge mask   Sharpened edges

Figure 10-15: I copy a channel, find the edges, and invert (left). I then apply a string of filters to expand and soften the edges (middle). After converting the mask to a selection outline, I reapply Unsharp Mask with winning results (right).

4. **Choose Filter ➪ Other ➪ Maximum.** The next step is to thicken up the edges. The Maximum filter expands the white areas in the image, serving much the same function in a mask as Select ➪ Modify ➪ Expand serves when editing a selection outline. Enter a Radius value and press Enter or Return. In my case, a Radius of 4 pixels worked nicely, but for best results you should experiment with different values based on the resolution of your image.

5. **Choose Filter ➪ Noise ➪ Median.** You need fat, gooey edges, and the current ones are a bit tenuous. To firm up the edges, choose the Median filter, enter the same Radius value you did for the Maximum filter, in my case 4, and press Enter or Return.

6. **Choose Filter ➪ Blur ➪ Gaussian Blur.** Unfortunately, the Maximum filter results in a bunch of little squares that don't do much for our cause. You can merge the squares into a seamless line by choosing the Gaussian Blur command and entering 4, the same radius you entered for Maximum. Then press Enter or Return.

   The completed mask is pictured in the second example of Figure 10-15. Though hardly an impressive sight to the uninitiated eye, you're looking at the perfect edge mask — soft, natural, and extremely accurate.

7. **Return to the standard composite view.** Press Ctrl+tilde (Win) or ⌘-tilde (Mac) in a color image. In a grayscale image, press Ctrl+1 (Win) or ⌘-1 (Mac).

8. **Convert the mask to a selection outline.** Ctrl-click (Win) or ⌘-click (Mac) the mask name in the Channels palette. Photoshop selects the most essential edges in the image without selecting the grain.

9. **Choose Filter ➪ Sharpen ➪ Unsharp Mask.** In the last example in Figure 10-15, I applied the highest permitted Amount value, 500 percent, and a Radius of 2.0.

10. **Whatever values you use, make sure the Threshold is set to 0.** And always leave it at 0 from this day forward.

In case Figures 10-14 and 10-15 are a little too subtle, I include enlarged views of the great abolitionist's face in Figure 10-16. The top image shows the result of using the Threshold value, the bottom image was created using the edge mask. Which one appears sharper and less grainy to you?

Sharpened, Threshold: 20 (speckled)

Sharpened with edge mask (smooth)

Figure 10-16: Enlarged views of the last examples from Figures 10-14 (top) and 10-15 (bottom). A good edge mask beats the Threshold value every time.

Using the High Pass filter

The High Pass filter falls more or less in the same camp as the sharpening filters but is not located under the Filter ⇨ Sharpen submenu. This frequently overlooked gem enables you to isolate high-contrast image areas from their low-contrast counterparts.

When you choose Filter ⇨ Other ⇨ High Pass, Photoshop offers a single option: the familiar Radius value, which can vary from 0.1 to 250.0. As demonstrated in Figure 10-17, high Radius values distinguish areas of high and low contrast only slightly. Low values change all high-contrast areas to dark gray and low-contrast areas to a slightly lighter gray. A value of 0.1 (not shown) changes all pixels in an image to a single gray value and is therefore useless.

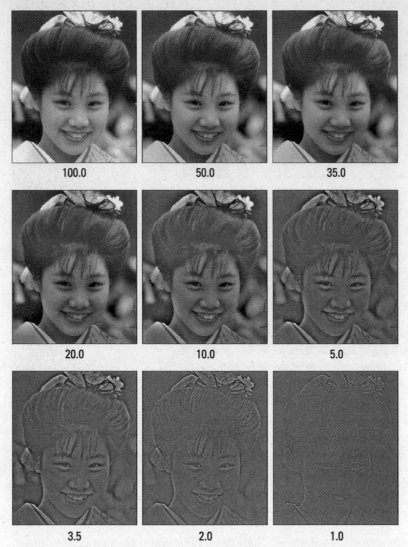

Figure 10-17: The results of separating high- and low-contrast areas in an image with the High Pass filter set at nine different Radius values.

Converting an image into a line drawing

The High Pass filter is especially useful as a precursor to Image ⇨ Adjustments ⇨ Threshold (covered in Chapter 17), which converts all pixels in an image to black and white. As illustrated in Figure 10-18, the Threshold command produces entirely different effects on images before and after you alter them with the High Pass filter. In fact, applying the High Pass filter with a low Radius value and then issuing the Threshold command converts your image into a line drawing.

Mezzotint Filter

Color Plate 11-2

Here I've applied Filter ⇨ Pixelate ⇨ Mezzotint with the Type option set to Long Strokes to the photograph featured at the top of Color Plate 11-1. The left-hand column of images shows the results of applying the filter in each of the three main color modes, RGB, Lab, and CMYK. In each case, Photoshop has changed all pixels in each and every channel to either black or white, resulting in some very high-contrast images. To temper the effect slightly, I chose Edit ⇨ Fade Mezzotint after the application of each filter and changed the Mode setting to Overlay and the Opacity value to 40 percent. As you can see in the right-hand column, fading Mezzotint permits me to achieve more subtle and functional effects.

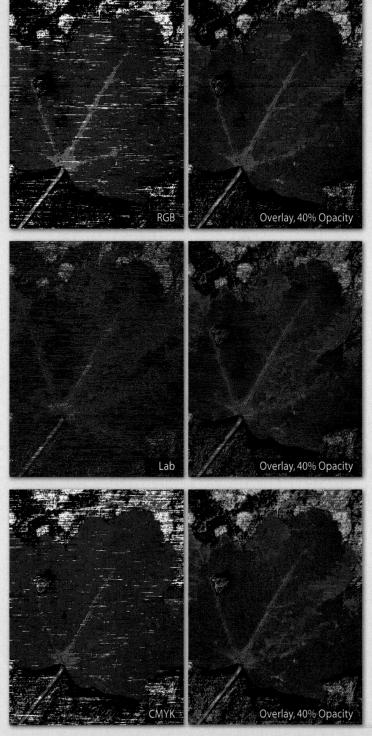

Emboss Filter

Normal, 30% Opacity

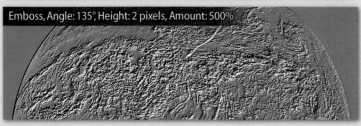

Emboss, Angle: 135°, Height: 2 pixels, Amount: 500%

Overlay blend mode, 85% Opacity

Color Dodge blend mode, 60% Opacity

Luminosity blend mode, 100% Opacity

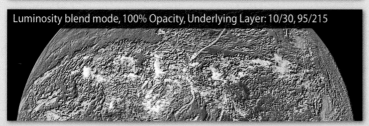

Luminosity blend mode, 100% Opacity, Underlying Layer: 10/30, 95/215

Color Plate 11-3

At first glance, the Emboss filter may seem like one of Photoshop's most destructive commands. It takes a full-color image and makes it look as if it were chiseled out of a slab of neutral gray slate. But by virtue of its complete neutrality, it lends itself well to blend mode experimentations.

The top example shows a satellite view of the Earth. Apply the Emboss filter with the settings listed in the second example, and details like earth and clouds are replaced with a swirling mass of engraved edges.

The trick is, before applying Emboss, I floated the image to an independent layer. This way, I was free to experiment with the Opacity and blend mode settings. The third, fourth, and fifth examples illustrate the effects of different blend mode and Opacity combinations. Of the three, the Luminosity mode preserves the colors from the land and ocean, but chokes out the black sky and white clouds with gray. To fix this, I opened the Layer Style dialog box. Then I dragged and Alt-dragged (or Option-dragged) the triangles in the Underlying Layer slider bar to the settings listed in the final example, thus permitting the blacks and whites to show through. For more on the Underlying Layer slider, read "Dropping Out and Forcing Through" in Chapter 13.

Twirl Drops

Color Plate 11-4

One of my favorite things about Photoshop's distortion filters is that they permit you to create glittering op art, which I call synthetic effects, out of thin air. These particular synthetic effects are a result of the steps outlined in the "Twirling spirals" section of Chapter 11. Starting with the Blue, Red, Yellow predefined gradient, I applied the Twirl filter with an Angle value of –360 degrees. Then I pressed Ctrl+F (⌘-F on the Mac) twice to apply the filter a total of three times (upper left). Next, I cloned the image to a separate layer, chose Edit ➪ Transform ➪ Flip Horizontal, and applied the Difference blend mode (upper right).

From there, it was largely a matter of cloning the layer and applying more transformations, as noted in the middle examples. Because the Difference mode remains in effect for each new layer, the bright colors from one layer invert the colors from the layers below, producing a wild array of colors that go well beyond the original blue, red, and yellow.

To produce the final effect, I applied a series of filters to the top layer only. The specific filters and settings I used are listed in order in the figure. With its colorful bubbles and deeply etched concentric rings, the resulting image is perhaps the ultimate embodiment of groovy.

Blue, Red, Yellow; Twirl: –360° x 3

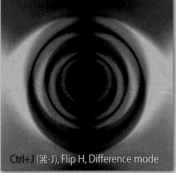

Ctrl+J (⌘-J), Flip H, Difference mode

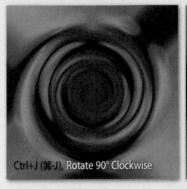

Ctrl+J (⌘-J), Rotate 90° Clockwise

Ctrl+J (⌘-J), Rotate 180°

Spherize (100%), ZigZag (100%, 10), Lens Flare (170%), Unsharp Mask (500%, 20, 0)

Polar to Rectangular

From 10 pinches & seven twirls ...

we get a wavy pattern.

A crazy guy in a circle ...

turns into a manatee!

Color Plate 11-5

If I had to name the wackiest filter in all of Photoshop, after much pain and inner turmoil, I believe I would ultimately choose Filter ⇨ Distort ⇨ Polar Coordinates. Why? Because you can select the Polar to Rectangular option to tear a perfectly harmless image inside out. This can be especially useful for examining the composition of a spiraling effect, as in the top examples. Or if you're feeling ornery, try it out on a guy's face. As the second examples illustrate, the Polar to Rectangular setting makes a person's eyes slide down his cheeks and gives you a once-in-a-lifetime opportunity to look up his nose.

But I guess my favorite use for this setting is to expand synthetic effects. The final example shows the Polar to Rectangular option applied to the final twirl drops image from Color Plate 11-4. Notice that the right side of each of the filtered images matches up perfectly with its left side. In the rainbow pool, for example, that subtle cyan splash flows from the right edge of the image into the left edge. This means the image will transition seamlessly when repeated horizontally, perfect for building patterns (as discussed in Chapter 7).

Where once there were twirl drops ...there is now a rainbow pool.

Blend Modes

Color Plate 13-1

Simply put, blend modes permit you to mix colors and brightness values between independent layers. In the examples on right, I start with just two layers, a face painstakingly rendered by Michelangelo against a tranquil background. The face is set to the Normal blend mode and an Opacity value of 100 percent, so with the exception of some feathered edges, it is fully opaque. In the second image, I introduce three additional layers: an opaque black-to-white gradient behind the face, a 1946 vertical coil postage stamp directly above that, and the Blistered Paint pattern (one of Photoshop's presets) set to the Overlay blend mode and 30 percent Opacity at the very front of the stack. In the final image, I changed the gradient layer to the Screen mode and reduced the Opacity setting to 60 percent. Then I combined the face and stamp layers into a layer set and assigned the Luminosity blend mode to the set. By assigning the Luminosity mode to the set instead of the individual layers, I instructed Photoshop to blend the two layers as if they were one, so the face and stamp interact with other layers but not with each other.

Original foreground & background

Three new layers (back to front):
Black, White gradient (100% Normal), postage
stamp (70% Normal), & Blistered Paint pattern (30% Overlay)

Change blend mode for gradient (60% Screen),
combine face & stamp into set (100% Luminosity)

Difference Sandwich

Unsharp Mask
(300%, Radius: 40)

Radial Blur
(Amount: 50,
Zoom, Draft)

Stamp (Light/Dark
Balance: 25,
Smoothness: 5)

Filtered image layered in front of original and set to Difference blend mode

Clone original image and move to top of stack to make Difference sandwich

Color Plate 13-2

Hungry for a fistful of yummy eye victuals? Then a Difference sandwich is sure to satisfy. Start with a flat image and press Ctrl+J (⌘-J on the Mac) to clone it to an independent layer. This new layer will serve as the meat of your sandwich. The meat holds the effect, so apply the filter of your choice. In my case, I was feeling rather famished, so I decided to fix three sandwiches. The top row shows my tray of meats, subject to three random filters — Unsharp Mask, Radial Blur, and Stamp. When you're finished filtering, select the Difference blend mode in the Layers palette. The middle row of images shows the effect of applying Difference to each of my meats.

Now for the top slice of bread. Return to the original Background layer and press Ctrl+J (or ⌘-J) to again clone it. Then press Ctrl+Shift+] (⌘-Shift-] on the Mac) to move the bread to the top of the stack. Now choose the Difference blend mode. That's all there is to it. In less time than it takes to say "baloney," I slapped together the bottom row of Difference sandwiches.

Layer Effects

Color Plate 14-1

In addition to enabling you to define drop shadows and glows, layer effects let you devise libraries of graphic styles. They are, in fact, Photoshop's answer to parametric effects, which are forever editable formatting attributes painted on with numerical values.

Consider the white 7 and black S in the upper-left image. I painted each on an independent layer using the brush tool. The layers have interesting shapes, but flat fills. So I set about applying layer effects. In the upper-right image, I applied a drop shadow and inner bevel to the 7 and an inner bevel and outer glow to the S. The middle-left image shows the effect of adding gradient and pattern overlays. To create the middle-right image, I added a satin effect to the 7 and color overlays to both the 7 and S with the blend mode set to Overlay.

Next, I applied blend modes to the overall layers, but my settings had no effect. This is because the blend modes assigned to the interior effects take precedence over those assigned to the layers themselves. To change this, I double-clicked on each layer and turned on the Blend Interior Effects as Group check box. Now, all interior effects were governed by the layers' blend modes, as shown in the final image.

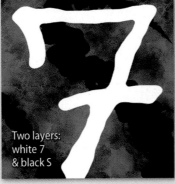

Two layers: white 7 & black S

Shadows, glows, & bevels

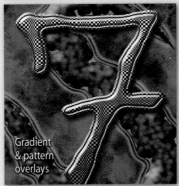

Gradient & pattern overlays

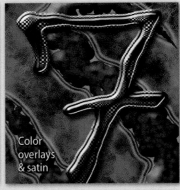

Color overlays & satin

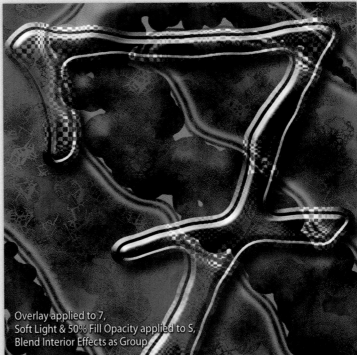

Overlay applied to 7,
Soft Light & 50% Fill Opacity applied to S,
Blend Interior Effects as Group

Threshold Tricks

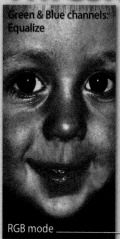

Green & Blue channels: Equalize

RGB mode

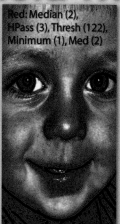

Red: Median (2), HPass (3), Thresh (122), Minimum (1), Med (2)

Green: Median (6), Threshold (126)

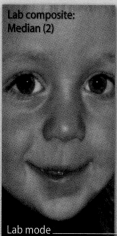

Lab composite: Median (2)

Lab mode

L channel: HPass (3), Thresh (124), Minimum (1), Med (2)

a & b channels: Threshold (132)

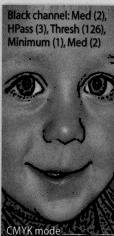

Black channel: Med (2), HPass (3), Thresh (126), Minimum (1), Med (2)

CMYK mode

Magenta & Yellow: Gaussian Blur (4), Threshold (120)

Cyan channel: Gaussian Blur (6), Thresh (200), Invert

Color Plate 17-1

Here we see three sets of tricks pulled off by applying the Threshold command to independent color channels when working in the RGB (top row), Lab (middle), and CMYK (bottom) modes. The techniques are largely experimental, but they show you the kinds of high-contrast, graphic effects you can achieve using Threshold. The labels explain the specifics, but just so everything's crystal clear, I'll walk through one of the techniques:

In the top row, I began by selecting the Green and Blue channels and choosing the Equalize command (upper left). Next, I clicked on the Red channel, applied the Median filter with a Radius of 2 pixels, the High Pass filter with a Radius of 3, and Threshold with a Threshold Level value of 122. Then I thickened the lines with the Minimum filter using a Radius of 1, and I smoothed out the edges by again applying Median with a Radius of 2 (upper middle). Finally, I switched to the Green channel, applied Median with a Radius of 6, and followed that with Threshold set to 126.

I experimented quite a bit before arriving at these specific techniques. In the end, I was able to achieve vivid silk-screen effects, and with any luck, so will you.

Auto Adjustments

Color Plate 17-2

Here we see the results of correcting the seemingly snooty Giuliano de' Medici as rendered by 15th-century master artist Sandro Botticelli, the same deft daddy-o responsible for *The Birth of Venus*, which later gained so much fame as the logo for Adobe Illustrator. In each case, I corrected the image using one of Photoshop's automatic adjustment operations: Auto Levels, Auto Contrast, and Auto Color, all under the Image ⇨ Adjustments submenu.

Auto Levels enhances the contrast of an image on a channel-by-channel basis, which may result in a color shift. In the case of good old Giuliano, the painting shifts from a green background to cool blue. If a color shift is not desired, use Auto Contrast instead. As the third image demonstrates, we now have sharper contrast, but the green background stays green. The Auto Color command seeks to neutralize the highlights, shadows, and midtones in an image, producing in the last example a gray background and perhaps the most naturalistic skin tones of the bunch.

Rumor has it, Giuliano may have been painted posthumously. So perhaps his skin should be gray and the background a fleshy peach. Only my homey Sandro knows for sure.

Uncorrected painting

Auto Levels

Auto Contrast

Auto Color

Hue/Saturation

Original Little Puppet Friend

Edit: Master, Hue: +120°

Edit: Master, Hue: +120° Saturation: +40%

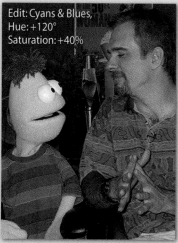
Edit: Cyans & Blues, Hue: +120° Saturation: +40%

Colorize, Hue: 340° Saturation: 25%

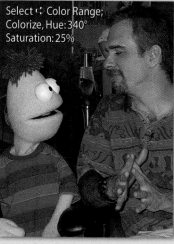
Select ➪ Color Range; Colorize, Hue: 340° Saturation: 25%

Color Plate 17-3

The Hue/Saturation command permits you to shift the colors in an image or altogether replace them. By way of example, consider this image of me and my Little Puppet Friend (as played by my *Photoshop Elements For Dummies* coauthor, Galen Fott). In the upper-right example, I entered a Hue value of 120 degrees, which rotated the colors one-third the way around the rainbow, shifting the flesh tones to green, the puppet tones to pink, and so on. In the middle-left example, I performed the same Hue shift, but also increased the Saturation value to +40 percent, making the colors slightly more vivid. But let's say I wanted to alter the colors inside LPF only. Using the Edit pop-up menu, I adjusted the settings for the Cyans and Blues only — those colors that make up LPF's flesh — changing my buddy's skin from bluish to pinkish while leaving my own flesh unchanged (middle right).

If you select the Colorize check box, Hue/Saturation replaces the colors in the image (lower left), but you can't limit the colorized areas as you can when Hue shifting. So if I wanted to colorize LPF's skin only (lower right), I would have to first select the cyans and blues using Select ➪ Color Range or the like, and then apply the Hue/Saturation command.

Variations

Color Plate 17-4

The results of applying each of the thumbnails offered inside the Variations dialog box (Image ➪ Adjustments ➪ Variations) to myself and Little Puppet Friend. In each case, the slider bar was set to its default position midway between Fine and Coarse, with the Midtones radio button selected.

Notice that each of the More buttons along the left and right columns not only adds the specified color to an image but simultaneously subtracts the complementary color. For example, clicking the More Yellow button adds yellow and subtracts blue, clicking More Red adds red and subtracts cyan, and so on, just as surely as clicking Lighter adds lightness and subtracts darkness.

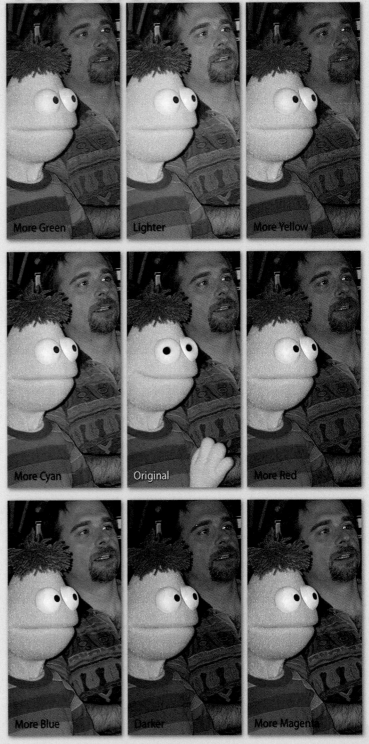

More Green • Lighter • More Yellow

More Cyan • Original • More Red

More Blue • Darker • More Magenta

Boost JPEG Colors

Heavily JPEG'ed digital photograph

Hue/Saturation (Saturation: +80%)

Median (Radius: 6), Gaussian Blur (Radius: 4)

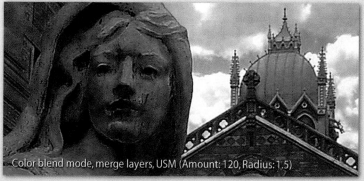

Color blend mode, merge layers, USM (Amount: 120, Radius: 1.5)

Color Plate 17-5

Sharpening or increasing the saturation values of an image can draw out JPEG compression artifacts. So correcting a heavily compressed photograph requires some extra work. I began with a washed out image that I shot several years ago with a Kodak DC50 digital camera (top). While the composition is nice, the focus is soft and the colors are drab. So I copied the image to a new layer and boosted the saturation using Hue/Saturation. While the resulting image (second from top) is much more colorful, it's also rife with noise, grain, and rough edges.

But that's okay. Because I have my original image in the Background layer, I can clear away the noise and still retain the clear edges I started with. So I averaged the colors in the high-saturation layer by applying the Median filter. Because Median generates its own displaced edges, I followed up with Gaussian Blur (third image). Next, I mixed the filtered layer with the underlying original by selecting the Color blend mode. Lastly, I merged the layers and then enhanced the edges by applying Unsharp Mask. The final image is sharper than the original and more colorful, all without amplifying the JPEG compression artifacts (bottom).

Levels Corrections

If I were stranded on a desert island and had to pick one color adjustment command over all others — an unlikely scenario, but bear with me — it would be Image ⇨ Adjustments ⇨ Levels. The Levels command permits you to modify the black point, white point, and midtone, all independently, and on a channel-by-channel basis. This means you can fix brightness, contrast, and color balance from a central dialog box.

Starting with the photograph shown at top, I modified the settings for the Red channel (second), Green channel (third), and Blue channel (fourth), according to the feedback provided to me by the histogram and the image preview. Finally, I returned to the RGB composite view and increased the gamma value to 1.40, which lightened the midtones. This increases the likelihood of the image printing successfully, without the shadowed areas filling in and becoming black.

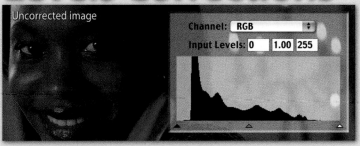

Uncorrected image

Channel: RGB
Input Levels: 0 1.00 255

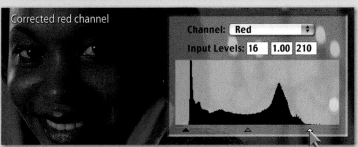

Corrected red channel

Channel: Red
Input Levels: 16 1.00 210

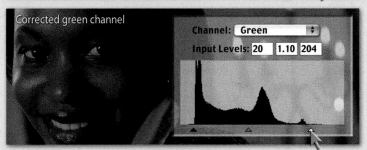

Corrected green channel

Channel: Green
Input Levels: 20 1.10 204

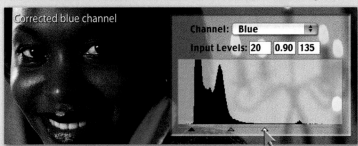

Corrected blue channel

Channel: Blue
Input Levels: 20 0.90 135

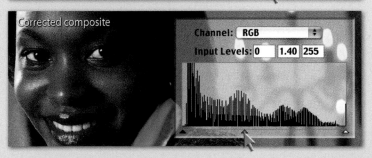

Corrected composite

Channel: RGB
Input Levels: 0 1.40 255

Gradient Map

Original painting

Violet, Orange

Chrome

Gaussian Blur (4)

Blue, Red, Yellow

Copper (Reverse)

Chrome

Color blend mode

Blue, Red, Yellow

Copper (Reverse)

Chrome

Color Plate 17-7

The Gradient Map command maps brightness values in an image to colors inside a gradient, effectively turning an image into a kind of duotone, tritone, or better, depending on the number of colors inside the gradient. In the top row, I started with the classic *Portrait of a Young Woman* by 19th century Italian artist Pelagio Palagi. It's a wonderful composition, but that crazy Pelagio got the colors all wrong, so I decided to fix that by applying Image ➪ Adjustments ➪ Gradient Map and experimenting with two of Photoshop's predefined gradients: Violet, Orange and Chrome. The first of the two effects looks swell because the Violet, Orange gradient transitions evenly from first color to last. But Chrome is more elaborate, and therefore results in harsh edges when expressed as a map.

So I decided to change my approach. Before applying the Gradient Map command, I copied the image to a new layer and then applied Gaussian Blur. Next, I experimented with applying each of three gradient maps, as shown in the second row. The results are blurry but smooth. To complete the effect, I mixed each of the mapped images with its underlying original by applying the Color blend mode (bottom row).

Curves Corrections

Color Plate 17-8

If you can't quite correct the colors in an image using Levels, try the Curves command, which permits you to adjust points on a brightness curve beyond the blacks, whites, and midtones. The left half of the top image shows the original uncorrected image; the right half shows the image after my Curves correction.

After choosing Curves, I switched to the Green channel and lightened it by clicking at two points in the brightness graph and dragging up on the curve (second). Then I switched to the Blue channel, clicked at four points in the graph, and dragged the first point down to darken the darkest colors and the remaining three points up to lighten the lightest colors. The result was to increase the contrast of the channel (third).

To complete the correction (upper right), I only needed to switch to the Red channel and lift the center of the curve slightly. But instead, I decided to finish things off with an arbitrary map. So I switched to the Red channel, added three points to the graph, dragged the first and last points up and the middle point down. This lightened the shadows and highlights while darkening the midtones, resulting in a couple of brightly colored red hats (bottom).

Corrected with Curves

Uncorrected image

Green channel: lighten

Channel: Green
Input: 184
Output: 245

Blue channel: increase contrast

Channel: Blue
Input: 63
Output: 131

Red channel: arbitrary map

Channel: Red
Input: 79
Output: 6

Duotones

Monotone, navy blue

Duotone, orange

Tritone, teal

Quadtone, deep red

Color Plate 18-1

A duotone is an image created by blending two or more inks. But the term is also used to indicate any image created by blending colored inks, whether it contains a single ink (monotone), three inks (tritone), or four (quadtone). Printing two or more inks increases the dynamic range of an otherwise grayscale image, producing darker blacks and richer midtones.

The examples on left show the process of building up a formerly grayscale image — scanned from an imperforate souvenir sheet of postage stamps issued in 1936 and captured nearly 70 years later with a Umax PowerLook 3000 desktop scanner — into first a Navy Blue monotone and finally a richly colored quadtone. Each example lists the new ink added to the mix. The swatches show the curve for the ink and the color of the ink when printed on its own. Notice that I have to adjust the curve for each ink every time I add a new one. The Navy Blue ink in particular declines radically as the inks build up. This prevents overinking or, since I'm ultimately printing to CMYK, overdarkening and ensures smooth transitions from one brightness value to the next.

In the second row of examples in the figure, I followed Threshold with Filter ⇨ Blur ⇨ Gaussian Blur (the subject of the next section). I set the Gaussian Blur Radius value to 1.0. Like the Threshold option in the Unsharp Mask dialog box, the Threshold command results in harsh transitions; Gaussian Blur softens them to produce a more natural effect.

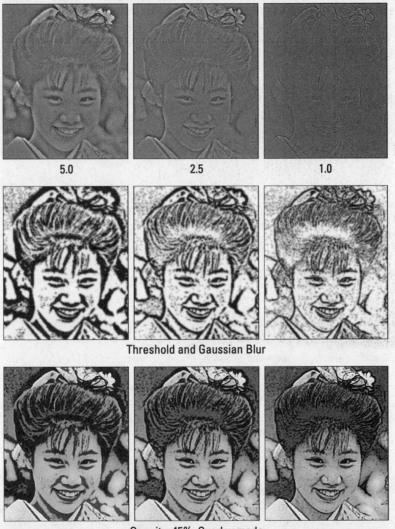

5.0   2.5   1.0

Threshold and Gaussian Blur

Opacity: 45%, Overlay mode

Figure 10-18: Several applications of the High Pass filter with low Radius values (top row), followed by the same images subject to Image ⇨ Adjustments ⇨ Threshold and Filter ⇨ Blur ⇨ Gaussian Blur (middle). I then layered the second row onto the first and modified the Opacity and blend mode settings to create the third row.

Why change your image to a bunch of slightly different gray values and then apply a command such as Threshold? One reason is to create a mask, as discussed at length in the "Building a Mask from an Image" section of Chapter 9. (In Chapter 9, I used Levels instead of Threshold, but both are variations on the same theme.)

You might also want to bolster the edges in an image. For example, to achieve the last row of examples in Figure 10-18, I layered the images prior to applying High Pass, Threshold, and Gaussian Blur. Then I monkeyed around with the Opacity setting and the blend mode to achieve an edge-tracing effect.

I should mention that Photoshop provides several automated edge-tracing filters — including Find Edges, Trace Contour, and the Gallery Effects acquisition, Glowing Edges. But High Pass affords more control than any of these commands and permits you to explore a wider range of alternatives. Also worth noting, several Gallery Effects filters — most obviously Filter ⇨ Sketch ⇨ Photocopy — lift much of their code directly from High Pass. Although it may seem at first glance a strange effect, High Pass is one of the seminal filters in Photoshop.

Blurring an Image

The commands under the Filter ⇨ Blur submenu produce the opposite effects of their counterparts under the Filter ⇨ Sharpen submenu. Rather than enhancing the amount of contrast between neighboring pixels, the Blur filters diminish contrast to create softening effects.

Applying the Gaussian Blur filter

The preeminent Blur filter, Gaussian Blur, blends a specified number of pixels incrementally, following the bell-shaped Gaussian distribution curve I touched on earlier. When you choose Filter ⇨ Blur ⇨ Gaussian Blur, Photoshop produces a single Radius option box, in which you can enter any value from 0.1 to 250.0. (Beginning to sound familiar?) As demonstrated in Figure 10-19, Radius values of 1.0 and smaller blur an image slightly; moderate values, between 1.0 and 5.0, turn an image into a rude approximation of life without my glasses on; and higher values blur the image beyond recognition.

Moderate to high Radius values can be especially useful for creating that hugely amusing *Star Trek* Iridescent Female effect. (This is the old *Star Trek*, of course.) Captain Kirk meets some bewitching ambassador or scientist who has just beamed on board. He takes her hand in sincere welcome as he gives out with a lecherous grin and explains how truly honored he is to have such a renowned guest in his transporter room, and so charming to boot. Then we see it — the close-up of the fetching actress shrouded in a kind of gleaming halo that prevents us from discerning if her lips are chapped or perhaps she's hiding an old acne scar, because some cockeyed cinematographer smeared Vaseline all over the camera lens. I mean, what *wouldn't* you give to be able to recreate this effect in Photoshop?

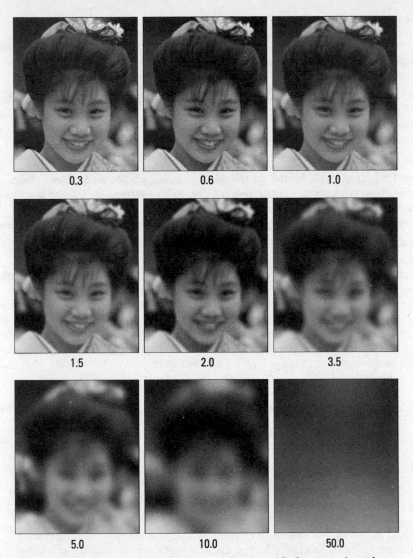

0.3 0.6 1.0

1.5 2.0 3.5

5.0 10.0 50.0

Figure 10-19: The results of blurring an image with the Gaussian Blur filter using nine different Radius values, ranging from slightly out of focus to Bad Day at the Ophthalmologist's Office.

Figure 10-20 and Color Plate 10-2 show a suitably comely lass — for the sake of this example, we'll assume she has her pointy ears tucked up into her hat, and some intergalactic beautician has tweezed her eyebrows into a more humanoid shape. The following steps explain how to give her that glorious Kirk-O-Vision glow.

STEPS: The Captain Kirk Myopia Effect

1. **Select a portion of the image if desired.** If you only want to apply the effect to a portion of the image, feather the selection with a Radius in the neighborhood of 5 to 8 pixels.

2. **Choose Filter ➪ Blur ➪ Gaussian Blur.** Enter some unusually large value into the Radius option box — say, 8.0 — and press Enter or Return. The results are shown in the first example of Figure 10-20. I upped the Radius value to 12 in the first example of Color Plate 10-2, because the pixel dimensions of that image are about twice those of the black and white example.

3. **Press Ctrl+Shift+F (⌘-Shift-F on the Mac) to bring up the Fade dialog box.** To achieve the effect shown in the second example of Figure 10-20, I reduced the Opacity value to 65 percent, making the blurred image slightly translucent. This way, you can see the hard edges of the original image through the filtered one.

4. **You can achieve additional effects by selecting options from the Mode pop-up menu.** For example, I created the third example in Figure 10-20 (also seen in the second example of Color Plate 10-2) by raising the Opacity back up to 100 percent and selecting the Darken mode option, which uses the colors in the filtered image to darken the original. I built upon this effect by pressing Ctrl+F (⌘-F on the Mac) to reapply my Gaussian Blur settings, pressing Ctrl+Shift+F (⌘-Shift-F on the Mac) to bring back the Fade command, lowering the Opacity to 80 percent, and choosing the Linear Dodge mode, as seen in the last example of Figure 10-20. The final example of Color Plate 10-2 shows this in color.

You know, though, as I look at this woman, I'm beginning to have my doubts about her and Captain Kirk. I mean, she has Scotty written all over her.

The preset blurring filters

Neither of the two preset commands in the Filter ➪ Blur submenu, Blur and Blur More, can distribute its blurring effect over a bell-shaped Gaussian curve. For that reason, these two commands are less functional than the Gaussian Blur filter. However, just so you know where they stand in the grand Photoshop focusing scheme, Figure 10-21 shows the effect of each preset command and the nearly equivalent effect created with the Gaussian Blur filter.

Gaussian Blur, Radius: 8 pixels

Normal, 65% Opacity

Darken, 100% Opacity

...plus Linear Dodge, 80% Opacity

Figure 10-20: After applying Gaussian Blur (top left), I used the Fade command to lower the Opacity to 65 percent (top right) and to apply the Darken mode with 100 percent Opacity (bottom left). Overlaying another application of Gaussian Blur with Opacity at 80 percent and Linear Dodge mode in force created the final example in the figure.

Antialiasing an image

If you have a particularly jagged image, such as a 256-color GIF file, there's a better way to soften the rough edges than applying the Gaussian Blur filter. The best solution is to antialias the image. How? After all, Photoshop doesn't offer an Antialias filter. Well, think about it. Back in the "Softening selection outlines" section of Chapter 8, I described how Photoshop antialiases a brushstroke or selection outline at twice its normal size and then reduces it by 50 percent and applies bicubic interpolation. You can do the same thing with an image.

Blur   Blur More

0.3   0.7

Figure 10-21: The effects of the two preset blurring filters (top row) compared with their Gaussian Blur equivalents (bottom row), which are labeled according to Radius values.

Choose Image ➪ Image Size and enlarge the image to 200 percent of its present size. Make sure that the Resample Image check box is turned on and set to Bicubic. (You can also experiment with Bilinear for a slightly different effect, but don't use Nearest Neighbor.) Next, turn right around and choose Image ➪ Image Size again, but this time shrink the image by 50 percent.

Figure 10-22 shows an odd doodle I did in a fit of torpor. The top-left example in Figure 10-23 shows an enlarged detail from my masterpiece badly in need of some smoothing. To the right is a detail from the same image subject to Gaussian Blur with a very low Radius value of 0.5. Rather than appearing softened, the result is just plain fuzzy.

Figure 10-22: A doodle by yours truly. Read into it what you will.

However, if I instead enlarge and reduce the image with the Image Size command, I achieve a true softening effect, as shown in the lower-left example in the figure, commensurate with Photoshop's antialiasing options. Even after enlarging and reducing the image four times in a row—as in the bottom-right example—I don't make the image blurry, I simply make it softer.

Directional blurring

In addition to its everyday blurring functions, Photoshop provides two *directional blurring* filters, Motion Blur and Radial Blur. Instead of blurring pixels in feathered clusters like the Gaussian Blur filter, the Motion Blur filter blurs pixels in straight lines over a specified distance. The Radial Blur filter blurs pixels in varying degrees depending on their distance from the center of the blur. The following pages explain both of these filters in detail.

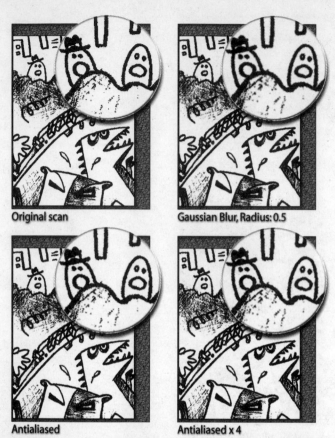

Original scan   Gaussian Blur, Radius: 0.5

Antialiased   Antialiased x 4

Figure 10-23: A detail from Figure 10-22 (top left) followed by the image blurred using a filter (top right). By enlarging and reducing the image one or more times (bottom left and right), I soften the pixels without making them appear blurry. The enlarged details show each operation's effect on the individual pixels.

Motion blurring

The Motion Blur filter makes an image appear as if either the image or camera was moving when you shot the photo. When you choose Filter ⇨ Blur ⇨ Motion Blur, Photoshop displays the dialog box shown in Figure 10-24. You enter the angle of movement into the Angle option box. Alternatively, you can indicate the angle by dragging the straight line inside the circle to the right of the Angle option, as shown in the figure. (Notice that the arrow cursor actually appears outside the circle. After you begin dragging on the line, you can move the cursor anywhere you want and still affect the angle.)

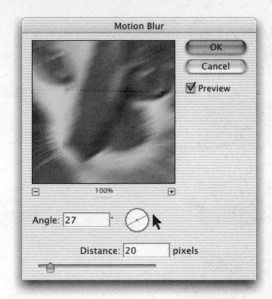

Figure 10-24: Drag the line inside the circle to change the angle of the blur.

You then enter the distance of the movement in the Distance option box. Photoshop permits any value between 1 and 999 pixels. The filter distributes the effect of the blur over the course of the Distance value, as illustrated by the examples in Figure 10-25.

Mathematically speaking, Motion Blur is one of Photoshop's simpler filters. Rather than distributing the effect over a Gaussian curve — which one might argue would produce a more believable effect — Photoshop creates a simple linear distribution, peaking in the center and fading at either end. It's as if the program took the value you specified in the Distance option, created that many clones of the image, offset half the clones in one direction and half the clones in the other — all spaced 1 pixel apart — and then varied the opacity of each.

Using the Wind filter

The problem with the Motion Blur filter is that it blurs pixels in two directions. If you want to distribute pixels in one absolute direction or the other, try the Wind filter, which you can use either on its own or in tandem with Motion Blur.

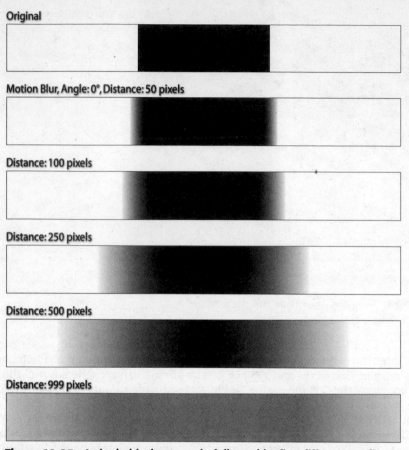

Original

Motion Blur, Angle: 0°, Distance: 50 pixels

Distance: 100 pixels

Distance: 250 pixels

Distance: 500 pixels

Distance: 999 pixels

Figure 10-25: A single black rectangle followed by five different applications of the Motion Blur filter. Only the Distance value varied, as labeled.
A 0-degree Angle value was used in all five examples.

When you choose Filter ➪ Stylize ➪ Wind, Photoshop displays the Wind dialog
box shown in Figure 10-26. You can select from three methods and two directions to
distribute the selected pixels. Figure 10-27 compares the effect of the Motion Blur
filter to each of the three methods offered by the Wind filter. Notice that the Wind
filter does not blur pixels. Rather, it evaluates a selection in 1-pixel-tall horizontal
strips and offsets the strips randomly inside the image.

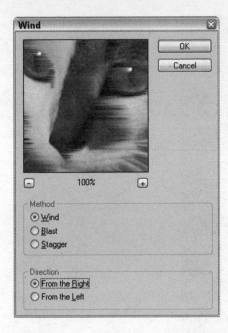

Figure 10-26: Use the Wind filter to randomly distribute a selection in 1-pixel horizontal strips in one of two directions.

To get the best results, try combining the Motion Blur and Wind filters with a blending mode. For example, as shown in Figure 10-28, I cloned the entire image to a new layer and applied the Wind command twice to the topmost layer, first selecting the Stagger option and then selecting Blast (top example). Next, I applied the Motion Blur command with a 0-degree Angle and a Distance value of 100 (second example). I then selected Lighten from the blend mode pop-up menu (third example). Finally, to keep the front of the truck from being obscured by the blurring effect, I added a layer mask and filled it with a gradient starting on the right with black and ending in white near the middle. I also did a little painting in the mask to control exactly where the motion streaks appeared in the image. (For the full monty on layer masks, turn to Chapter 12.)

The result is a perfect blend between two worlds. The motion effect at the bottom of Figure 10-28 doesn't obliterate the image detail, as the Wind filter does in Figure 10-27. And thanks to the layer mask, the motion appears to run in a single direction—to the left—something you can't accomplish using Motion Blur on its own.

Figure 10-27: The difference between the effects of the Motion Blur filter (top) and the Wind filter (other three). In each case, I selected From the Right from the Direction radio buttons.

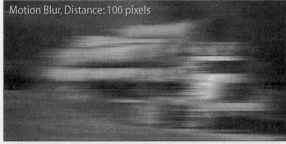

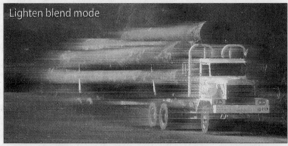

Figure 10-28: Combining the Wind filter (top) with Motion Blur (second image), the Lighten blend mode (third image), and a layer mask (bottom).

Radial blurring

Choosing Filter ⇨ Blur ⇨ Radial Blur displays the Radial Blur dialog box shown in Figure 10-29. The dialog box offers two Blur Method options: Spin and Zoom.

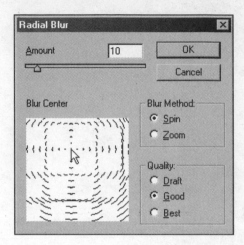

Figure 10-29: Drag inside the Blur Center grid to change the point about which the Radial Blur filter spins or zooms the image.

If you select Spin, the image appears to be rotating about a central point. You specify that point by dragging in the grid inside the Blur Center box (as demonstrated in the figure). If you select Zoom, the image appears to rush away from you, as if you were zooming the camera while shooting the photograph. Again, you specify the central point of the Zoom by dragging in the Blur Center box. Figure 10-30 features examples of both settings.

After selecting a Blur Method option, you can enter any value between 1 and 100 in the Amount option box to specify the maximum distance over which the filter blurs pixels. (You can enter a value of 0, but doing so merely causes the filter to waste time without producing an effect.) Pixels farthest away from the center point move the most; pixels close to the center point barely move at all. Keep in mind that large values take more time to apply than small values. The Radial Blur filter, incidentally, qualifies as one of Photoshop's most time-consuming operations.

Select a Quality option to specify your favorite time/quality compromise. The Good and Best Quality options ensure smooth results by respectively applying bilinear and bicubic interpolation (as explained in the "General preferences" section of Chapter 2). However, they also prolong the amount of time the filter spends calculating pixels in your image.

The Draft option *diffuses* an image, which leaves a trail of loose and randomized pixels but takes less time to complete. I used the Draft setting to create the top-right and bottom-left images in Figure 10-30; I selected the Good option to create the middle-left image and the Best option to create the middle and bottom images on the right.

Original Corbis image

Radial Blur, Spin, Amount: 10, Draft

Spin, Amount: 10, Good

Spin, Amount: 10, Best

Zoom, Amount: 30, Draft

Zoom, Amount: 30, Best

Figure 10-30: Five examples of the Radial Blur filter set to both Spin and Zoom, subject to different Quality settings. I specified Amount values of 10 pixels for the Spin examples and 30 for the Zooms. Each effect is centered about the bridge of the woman's nose.

Blurring with a threshold

The purpose of Filter ➪ Blur ➪ Smart Blur is to blur the low-contrast portions of an image while retaining the edges. This way, you can downplay photo grain, blemishes, and artifacts without harming the real edges in the image. (If you're familiar with Filter ➪ Pixelate ➪ Facet, it may help to know Smart Blur is essentially a customizable version of that filter.)

The two key options inside the Smart Blur dialog box (see Figure 10-31) are the Radius and Threshold slider bars. As with all Radius options, this one expands the number of pixels calculated at a time as you increase the value. Meanwhile, the Threshold value works just like the one in the Unsharp Mask dialog box, specifying how different two neighboring pixels must be to be considered an edge.

Figure 10-31: The Smart Blur filter lets you blur the low-contrast areas of an image without harming the edges.

But the Threshold value has a peculiar and unexpected effect on the Radius. The Radius value actually produces more subtle effects if you raise the value beyond the Threshold. For example, take a look at Figure 10-32. Here we have a grid of images subject to different Radius and Threshold values. (The first value below each image is the Radius.) In the top row of the figure, the 5.0 Radius actually produces a more pronounced effect than its 20.0 and 60.0 cousins. This is because 5.0 is less than the 10.0 Threshold, while 20.0 and 60.0 are more.

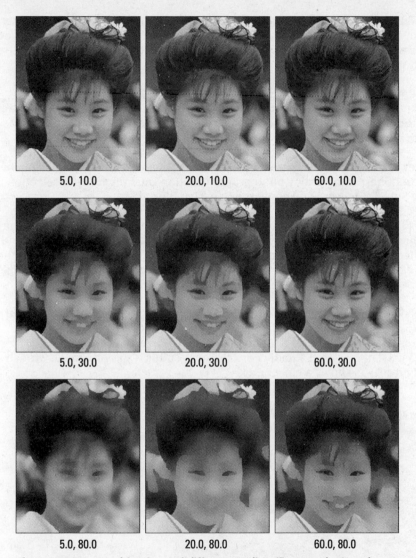

5.0, 10.0 20.0, 10.0 60.0, 10.0

5.0, 30.0 20.0, 30.0 60.0, 30.0

5.0, 80.0 20.0, 80.0 60.0, 80.0

Figure 10-32: Combinations of different Radius (first number) and Threshold (second) values. Notice that the most dramatic effects occur when the Radius is equal to about half the Threshold.

The Quality settings control the smoothness of the edges. The High setting takes more time than Medium and Low, but it looks smoother as well. (I set the value to High to create all the effects in Figure 10-32.) The two additional Mode options enable you to trace the edges defined by the Threshold value with white lines.

Overlay Edge shows image and lines, while Edge Only shows just the traced lines. About the only practical purpose for these options is to monitor the precise effect of the Threshold setting in the preview box. Otherwise, the Edge options are clearly relegated to special effects.

Frankly, I'm not convinced that Smart Blur is quite ready for prime time. You already know what I think of the Threshold option, and it hasn't gotten any better here. Without control over the transitions between focused and unfocused areas, things are going to look pretty strange.

Tip

The better way to blur low-contrast areas is to create an edge mask, as I explained back in the "Sharpening grainy photographs" section. Just reverse the selection by choosing Select ⇨ Inverse and apply the Gaussian Blur filter.

Figure 10-33 shows how the masking technique compares with Smart Blur. In the first image, I applied Unsharp Mask with a Threshold of 20. Then I turned around and applied Smart Blur with a Radius of 2.0 and a Threshold of 20.0, matching the Unsharp Mask value. The result makes the venerable Frederick Douglass look like he just sneezed while peppering his food.

In the second image, I created an edge mask—as explained in the "Creating and Using an Edge Mask" steps—and applied Unsharp Mask with a Threshold of 0. Then I pressed Ctrl+Shift+I (⌘-Shift-I on the Mac) to reverse the selection and applied Gaussian Blur with a Radius of 2.0. The result is a smooth image with sharp edges; Figure 10-34 shows a closer look.

USM+Smart Blur, Threshold: 20   USM+GBlur, edge mask

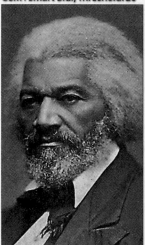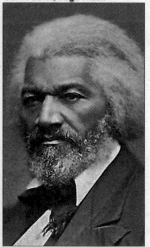

Figure 10-33: The difference between relying on Photoshop's automated Threshold capabilities (left) and sharpening and blurring with the aid of an edge mask (right). A little manual labor (even if it's performed on the computer) still wins out over total automation.

Threshold settings infect image with hideous skin disease.

Edge mask cures all. "Good lord, I'm handsome," thinks Fred.

Figure 10-34: A closer look at the "Smart Blur versus Edge Mask" debate.

Softening a selection outline

Gaussian Blur and other Blur filters are equally as useful for editing masks as they are for editing image pixels. As I mentioned earlier, applying Gaussian Blur to a mask has the same effect as applying Select ➪ Feather to a selection outline. But Gaussian Blur affords more control. Where the Feather command affects all portions of a selection outline uniformly, you can apply Gaussian Blur selectively to a mask, permitting you to easily mix soft and hard edges within a single selection outline.

Another advantage to blurring a mask is that you can see the results of your adjustments on screen, instead of relying on the seldom-helpful marching ants. For example, suppose that you want to create a shadow that recedes away from a subject in your composition. You've managed to accurately select the foreground image — how do you now feather the selection exclusively inward, so that it appears smaller than the object that casts it? Although you can pull off this feat using selection commands such as Contract and Feather, it's much easier to apply filters such as Minimum and Gaussian Blur inside a mask. But before I go any farther, I need to back up and explain how Minimum and its pal Maximum work.

Minimum and Maximum

Filter ➪ Other ➪ Minimum expands the dark portions of an image, spreading them outward into other pixels. Its opposite, Filter ➪ Other ➪ Maximum, expands the light portions of an image. In traditional stat photography, these techniques are known, respectively, as *choking* and *spreading*.

When you are working in the quick mask mode or an independent mask channel, applying the Minimum filter has the effect of incrementally contracting the selected area, subtracting pixels uniformly around the edges of the selection outline. The Minimum dialog box presents you with a single Radius value, which tells Photoshop how many edge pixels to delete. Just the opposite, the Maximum filter incrementally increases the size of white areas, which adds pixels uniformly around the edges of a selection.

Adding a cast shadow to a layer

The following steps describe how to use the Minimum and Gaussian Blur filters to contract and feather an existing selection outline to create a shadow that leans away from the foreground subject of a composition. Figures 10-35 through 10-37 illustrate the steps in the project. Figure 10-38 shows the final cast shadow.

STEPS: Filtering a Selection Outline in the Quick Mask Mode

1. **Select the foreground image.** My foreground image was the screwball character from the Corbis image library pictured in Figure 10-35. I had already set him up on an independent layer from the background. These steps work best if you do the same. (To learn how, see Chapter 12, "Working with Layers.") To select this scary fellow, I converted the layer's transparency mask to a selection outline by Ctrl-clicking (⌘-clicking on the Mac) on the layer's name in the Layers palette.

2. **If you're working on a layer, switch to the background image.** The quickest route is Shift+Alt+[(that's Shift-Option-[on the Mac).

3. **Press Q to enter the quick mask mode.** You can create a new mask channel if you prefer, but the quick mask mode is more convenient.

4. **Choose Filter ➪ Other ➪ Minimum.** Enter a Radius value to expand the transparent area into the rubylith. In Figure 10-36, I entered a Radius value of 20 pixels. This expanded the size of the black, or masked, area and made the selection smaller.

5. **Choose Filter ➪ Blur ➪ Gaussian Blur.** To create a soft shadow, I entered a Radius equal to the Radius I used in the Minimum dialog box, which was 20 pixels. Smaller values are likewise acceptable. The only potential problem with larger values is that they expand the shadow beyond the boundaries of the image, which in all probability is not the effect you want. When you click OK, Photoshop blurs the transparent area.

Figure 10-35: This artificially gleeful human resides on an independent layer. To select him, I Ctrl-clicked (or ⌘-clicked) on his layer in the Layers palette.

6. **Press Q to exit the quick mask mode.** Ah, back in the workaday world of marching ants.

7. **Send the selection to an independent layer.** The easiest way to do this is to press Ctrl+J (⌘-J on the Mac). You now have a shadow filled with colors from the background layer.

8. **Choose the Multiply mode.** You can choose Multiply from the pop-up menu at the top of the Layers palette, or press Shift+Alt+M (Shift-Option-M on the Mac). As discussed in Chapter 13, this burns the shadow into its background, so it looks darker, as a shadow should. Because your foreground image is in the way, you may not be able to see the effect of this step, but don't worry — you will soon.

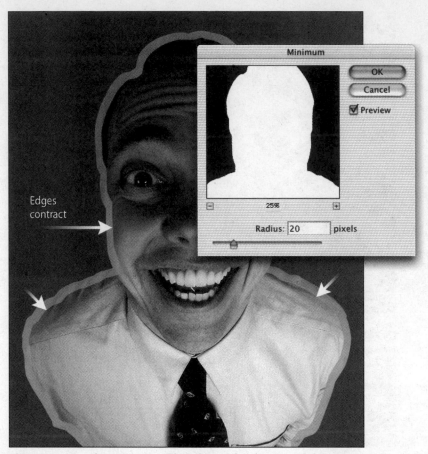

Edges contract

Figure 10-36: The Minimum filter decreases the size of the transparent area inside the quick mask mode, thereby choking the selection outline.

9. **Scale and distort the shadow.** Press Ctrl+T (⌘-T on the Mac) to invoke the Free Transform command. Then drag the top handles in the bounding box to scale the shadow; press Ctrl (⌘ on the Mac) and drag a handle to distort the shadow. For the best effect, you'll need a big distortion. As demonstrated in Figure 10-37, you may have to zoom out and expand the size of the image window to give yourself lots of room to work. When you get the effect you want, press Enter or Return to apply the distortion.

Figure 10-37: Press Ctrl+T (⌘-T on the Mac) to enter the Free Transform mode. Then Ctrl-drag (⌘-drag) a corner handle to distort the shadow.

Thanks to the fact you applied the Multiply blend mode to the shadow, it appears darker than the rest of the background. You can adjust its opacity or fill it with a different color if you like. I elected to fill my background with one of Photoshop's predefined patterns, called Molecular. As shown in Figure 10-38, this permitted me to transform the subject of my montage from an overly enthusiastic sycophant into an overly enthusiastic tour guide. As I said, you could have achieved a similar effect using Select ⇨ Modify ⇨ Contract and Select ⇨ Feather, but unless you have a special aversion to the quick mask mode, it's easier to be sure of your results when you can see exactly what you're doing using filters.

Figure 10-38: Suddenly, he's not scary anymore, he's just passionate about his work. No doubt, we could all learn a lesson from this plainly insane man.

Noise Factors

Photoshop offers four loosely associated filters in its Filter ⇨ Noise submenu. One filter adds random pixels — known as *noise* — to an image. The other three, Despeckle, Dust and Scratches, and Median, average the colors of neighboring pixels in ways that theoretically remove noise from poorly scanned images. But in fact, they function nearly as well at removing essential detail as they do at removing extraneous noise. In the following sections, I show you how the Noise filters work, demonstrate a few of my favorite applications, and leave you to draw your own conclusions.

Adding noise

Noise adds grit and texture to an image. Noise makes an image look like you shot it in New York on the Lower East Side and were lucky to get the photo at all because someone was throwing sand in your face as you sped away your chauffeur-driven, jet-black Maserati Bora, hammering away at the shutter release. In reality, of course, a guy over at Sears shot the photo for you, after which you toodled around in your minivan trying to find a store that sold day-old bread. But that's the beauty of Noise. It makes you look cool, even when you aren't.

You add noise by choosing Filter ➪ Noise ➪ Add Noise. Shown in Figure 10-39, the Add Noise dialog box features the following options:

✦ **Amount:** This value determines how far pixels in the image can stray from their current colors. The value represents a color range rather than a brightness range and is expressed as a percentage. You can enter a value as high as 400 percent. The percentage is based on 256 brightness values per channel if you're working with a 24-bit image and 32,768 brightness values for 16-bit images. So with a 24-bit image (8-bit channels), the default value of 12.5 percent is equivalent to 32 brightness levels, which is 12.5 percent of 256.

For example, if you enter a value of 12.5 percent for a 24-bit image, Photoshop can apply any color that is 32 shades more or less red, more or less green, *and* more or less blue than the current color. If you enter 400 percent, Photoshop theoretically can go 1024 brightness values lighter or darker. But that results in colors that are out of range; therefore, they get clipped to black or white. The result is higher contrast inside the noise pixels.

Figure 10-39: The Add Noise dialog box asks you to specify the amount and variety of noise you want to add to the selection.

✦ **Uniform:** Select this option to apply colors absolutely randomly within the specified range. Photoshop is no more likely to apply one color within the range than another, thus resulting in an even color distribution.

✦ **Gaussian:** When you select this option, you instruct Photoshop to prioritize colors along the Gaussian distribution curve. The effect is that most colors added by the filter either closely resemble the original colors or push the boundaries of the specified range. In other words, this option results in more light and dark pixels, thus producing a more pronounced effect.

✦ **Monochromatic:** When working on a full-color image, the Add Noise filter distributes pixels randomly throughout the different color channels. However, when you select the Monochrome check box, Photoshop distributes the noise in the same manner in all channels. The result is grayscale noise. (This option does not affect grayscale images; the noise can't get any more grayscale than it already is.)

Figure 10-40 compares three applications of Gaussian noise to identical amounts of Uniform noise.

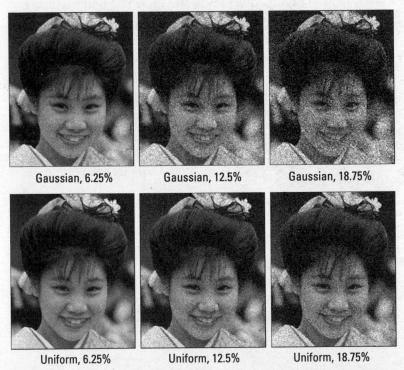

Gaussian, 6.25%   Gaussian, 12.5%   Gaussian, 18.75%

Uniform, 6.25%   Uniform, 12.5%   Uniform, 18.75%

Figure 10-40: The Gaussian option produces more pronounced effects than the Uniform option at identical Amount values.

Noise variations

Normally, the Add Noise filter adds both lighter and darker pixels to an image. If you prefer, however, you can limit the effect of the filter to strictly lighter or darker pixels. To do so, apply the Add Noise filter, and then apply the Fade command (Ctrl+Shift+F on the PC or ⌘-Shift-F on the Mac) and select the Lighten or Darken blend mode. Or you can copy the image to a new layer, apply the filter, and merge the filtered image with the underlying original.

Figure 10-41 shows sample applications of lighter and darker noise. After copying the image to a separate layer, I applied the Add Noise filter with an Amount value of 40 percent, and selected Gaussian. To create the upper-left example in the figure, I selected Lighten from the blend mode pop-up menu. To create the upper-right example, I selected the Darken mode. In each case, I added a layer of strictly lighter or darker noise while at the same time retaining the clarity of the original image.

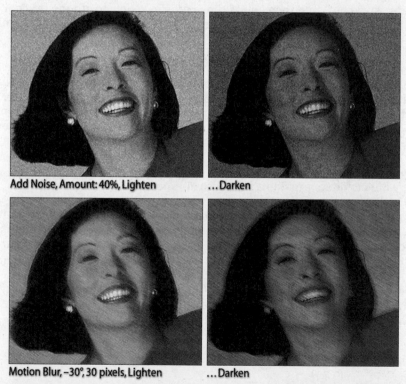

Add Noise, Amount: 40%, Lighten   …Darken

Motion Blur, –30°, 30 pixels, Lighten   …Darken

Figure 10-41: You can limit the Add Noise filter to strictly lighter (left) or darker (right) noise by applying the filter to a layered clone. To create the rainy and scraped effects (bottom examples), I applied Motion Blur and Unsharp Mask to the noise layers.

To achieve the streaked noise effects in the bottom examples of Figure 10-41, I applied Motion Blur and Unsharp Mask to the layered images. Inside the Motion Blur dialog box, I set the Angle value to –30 degrees and the Distance to 30 pixels. Then I applied Unsharp Mask with an Amount value of 200 percent and a Radius of 1. Naturally, the Threshold value was 0.

Chunky noise

My biggest frustration with the Add Noise filter is that you can't specify the size of individual specks of noise. No matter how you cut it, noise only comes in 1-pixel squares. It may occur to you that you can enlarge the noise dots in a layer by applying the Maximum or Minimum filter. But in practice, doing so simply fills in the image, because there isn't sufficient space between the noise pixels to accommodate the larger dot sizes.

Luckily, Photoshop provides several alternatives. One is the Pointillize filter, which adds variable-sized dots and then colors those dots in keeping with the original colors in the image. Though Pointillize lacks the random quality of the Add Noise filter, you can use it to add texture to an image.

To create the top-left image in Figure 10-42, I chose Filter ➪ Pixelate ➪ Pointillize and entered 5 into the Cell Size option box. After pressing Enter (or Return on the Mac) to apply the filter, I pressed Ctrl+Shift+F (⌘-Shift-F on the Mac) to fade the filter, changing the Opacity value to 50 percent. The effect is rather like applying chunky bits of noise. The top-right image is similar, but with the Opacity value at 100 percent and with the Pin Light blend mode applied. (For more on blend modes, see Chapter 13.)

The Gallery Effects filters provide a few noise alternatives. Filter ➪ Sketch ➪ Halftone Pattern adds your choice of dot patterns, as shown in the two middle examples in Figure 10-42 (Size and Contrast settings were the same for both examples). But like all filters in the Sketch submenu, it replaces the colors in your image with the foreground and background colors. Filter ➪ Texture ➪ Grain is a regular noise smorgasbord, permitting you to select from 10 different Grain Type options, each of which produces a different kind of noise. The bottom examples in Figure 10-42 show off two of the Grain options, Clumped and Speckle. The Intensity and Contrast remained the same in each; I added a Soft Light blend mode in the Speckle example.

Pointillize, Cell Size: 5, 50% Opacity   Pointillize, Pin Light blend mode

Halftone Pattern, Size: 2, Contrast: 3   Halftone Pattern, Pin Light blend mode

Grain, Intensity: 80, Contrast: 50, Clumped   Grain, Speckle, Soft Light blend mode

Figure 10-42: The results of applying several different Add Noise–like filters, including Pointillize, Halftone Pattern, and Grain.

Removing noise with Despeckle

Now for the noise removal filters. Strictly speaking, the Despeckle command probably belongs in the Filter ⇨ Blur submenu. It blurs a selection while at the same
time preserving its edges — the idea being that unwanted noise is most noticeable
in the continuous regions of an image. In practice, this filter is nearly the exact
opposite of the Sharpen Edges filter.

The Despeckle command searches an image for edges using the equivalent of an
Unsharp Mask Threshold value of 5. It then ignores the edges in the image and
blurs everything else with the force of the Blur More filter, as shown in the upper-
left image in Figure 10-43.

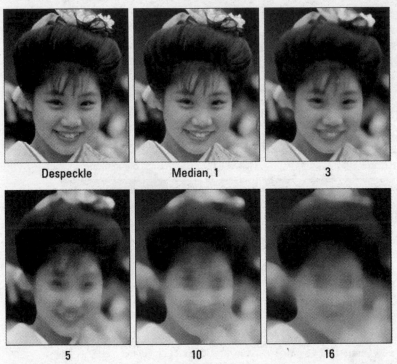

Figure 10-43: The effects of the Despeckle filter (upper left) and Median
filter. The numbers indicate Median filter Radius values.

Averaging pixels with Median

Another command in the Filter ⇨ Noise submenu, Median removes noise by averaging the colors in an image, one pixel at a time. When you choose Filter ⇨ Noise ⇨
Median, Photoshop produces a Radius option box. For every pixel in a selection, the
filter averages the colors of the neighboring pixels that fall inside the specified

radius—ignoring any pixels that are so different that they might skew the average—and applies the average color to the central pixel. You can enter any value between 1 and 100. However, even at low settings like 16 significant blurring occurs, as you can see from the bottom-right example in Figure 10-43 (in the preceding section). At the maximum Radius value, you wind up with a sort of soft, blurry gradient, with all image detail obliterated.

As with Gaussian Blur, you can achieve some very interesting and useful effects by backing off the Median filter with the Fade command. But rather than creating a *Star Trek* glow, Median clumps up details, giving an image a plastic, molded quality, as demonstrated by the examples in Figure 10-44. To create every one of these images, I applied the Median filter with a Radius of 5 pixels. For the second example, I pressed Ctrl+Shift+F (⌘-Shift-F on the Mac) to display the Fade dialog box and lowered the Opacity value to 65 percent. For the bottom-left image, I raised the Opacity back up to 100 percent in the Fade dialog box and applied the Darken blend mode. And for the final example, I took the Opacity back down to 80 percent and used the Linear Dodge mode.

Median, Radius: 5 pixels   Normal, 65% Opacity

Darken, 100% Opacity   ...plus Linear Dodge, 80% Opacity

Figure 10-44: After applying the Median filter to our Klingon cutie, I reversed the effect slightly using Edit ➪ Fade Median. I varied the blend modes and Opacity values, as labeled beneath the images.

Another difference between Gaussian Blur and Median is that Gaussian Blur destroys edges and Median invents new ones. This means you can follow up the Median filter with Unsharp Mask to achieve even more pronounced sculptural effects.

Sharpening a compressed image

Digital cameras are the hottest thing in electronic imaging. You can take as many images as you like, download them to your computer immediately, and place them into a printed document literally minutes after snapping the picture. In the next couple of years, I have little doubt that you — yes, *you* — will purchase a digital camera (if you haven't already).

Unfortunately, the technology is still very young. And if you're using one of the mid- or low-priced cameras — read that, under $400 — even the slightest application of the Unsharp Mask filter sometimes results in jagged edges and unsightly artifacts. These blemishes stem from a stingy supply of pixels, heavy-handed compression schemes (all based on JPEG), or both. The situation is improving; cameras at the high end of the consumer price range can produce 5-megapixel images and often enable you to store uncompressed images in the TIFF format. But as with all good things in life, it will take a while for those options to be available in moderately priced equipment.

In the meantime, firm up the detail and smooth out the color transitions in your digital photos by applying a combination of filters — Median, Gaussian Blur, and Unsharp Mask — to a layered version of the image. The following steps tell all.

STEPS: Adjusting the Focus of Digital Photos

1. **Select the entire image and copy it to a new layer.** That's Ctrl+A, Ctrl+J (⌘-A, ⌘-J on the Mac). Figure 10-45 shows the image that I intend to sharpen, a picture of a friend's child.

2. **Choose Filter ⇨ Noise ⇨ Median.** After processing several thousand of these images, I've found that a Radius value of 2 is almost always the optimal choice. But if the image is particularly bad, 3 may be warranted.

3. **Choose Filter ⇨ Blur ⇨ Gaussian Blur.** Now that you've gummed up the detail a bit and rubbed out most of the compression, use the Gaussian Blur filter with a Radius of 1.0 to blur the gummy detail slightly. This softens the edges that the Median filter creates. (You don't want any fake edges, after all.)

4. **Choose Filter ⇨ Sharpen ⇨ Unsharp Mask.** All this blurring demands some intense sharpening. So apply Unsharp Mask with a maximum Amount value of 500 percent and a Radius of 1.0 (to match the Gaussian Blur Radius). This restores most of the definition to the edges, as shown in Figure 10-46.

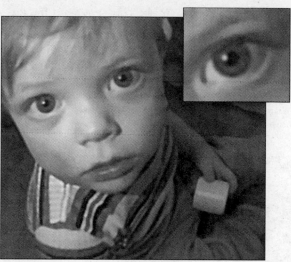

Figure 10-45: I captured this youthful fellow with a low-end digital camera equipped with a removable fish-eye lens. How innocent and happy he looks — obviously not a computer user.

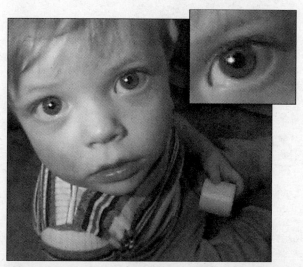

Figure 10-46: Thanks to Median, Gaussian Blur, and Unsharp Mask, Cooper is a much smoother customer. In fact, he's beyond smooth — he's a gummy kid.

5. **Lower the layer's Opacity value.** By itself, the filtered layer is a bit too smooth. So mix the filtered floater with the underlying original with an Opacity value between 30 and 50 percent. I found that I could go pretty high — 45 percent — with Cooper. Kids have clearly defined details that survive filtering quite nicely.

6. **Merge the image.** Press Ctrl+E (Win) or ⌘-E (Mac) to send the layer down.

7. **Continue to correct the image as you normally would.** The examples in Figure 10-47 show the difference between applying the Unsharp Mask filter to the original image (top) and the filtered mixture (bottom). In both cases, I applied an Amount value of 200 percent and a Radius of 1.0. The top photo displays an unfortunate wealth of artifacts — particularly visible in the magnified eye — while the bottom one appears smooth and crisp.

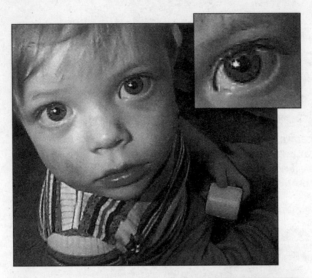

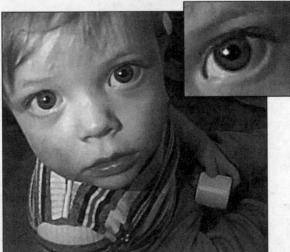

Figure 10-47: Here you can see the difference between sharpening a digital photograph right off the bat (top) and waiting to sharpen until after you've prepared the image with Median, Gaussian Blur, and Unsharp Mask (bottom).

These steps work well for sharpening other kinds of compressed imagery, including old photographs that you over-compressed without creating backups, and images that you've downloaded from the Internet. If applying the Unsharp Mask filter brings out the goobers, try these steps instead.

Cleaning up scanned halftones

Photoshop offers one additional filter in the Filter ⇨ Noise submenu called Dust & Scratches. The purpose of this filter is to remove dust particles, hairs, scratches, and other imperfections that may accompany a scan. The filter offers two options, Radius and Threshold. As long as the offending imperfection is smaller or thinner than the Radius value and different enough from its neighbors to satisfy the Threshold value, the filter deletes the spot or line and interpolates between the pixels around the perimeter.

But like so many of Photoshop's older automated tools — and this one is getting very old — Dust & Scratches works only when conditions are extremely favorable. I'm not saying that you should never use it; in fact, you may always want to give it the first crack at a dusty image. But if it doesn't work (as it probably won't), don't be surprised. Just hunker down and eliminate the imperfections manually using the clone stamp tool or healing brush, as discussed in Chapter 7.

Now, as I say, Dust & Scratches was designed to get rid of gunk on a dirty scanner. But another problem that the filter may be able to eliminate is moiré patterns. These patterns appear when scanning halftoned images from books and magazines. See, any time you scan a printed image, you're actually scanning a collection of halftone dots rather than a continuous-tone photograph. In most cases, the halftone pattern clashes with the resolution of the scanned image to produce rhythmic and distracting moirés.

When scanning published photographs or artwork, take a moment to find out if what you're doing is legal. It's up to you to make sure that the image you scan is no longer protected by copyright — most, but not all, works over 75 years old are considered free game — or that your noncommercial application of the image falls under the fair-use umbrella of commentary, criticism, or parody. I'm not a lawyer; so I can't advise you. But I generally find that it's better to be extremely safe than even slightly sorry.

The Dust & Scratches filter can be pretty useful for eliminating moirés, particularly if you reduce the Threshold value below 40. But this also goes a long way toward eliminating the actual image detail, as Color Plate 10-3 demonstrates. This figure features the first image I ever created for *Macworld* magazine using a photo that I shot during a traveling Tutankhamen exhibit. More than a decade later, I scanned this art from the February, 1991 issue of *Macworld* magazine. Because I own the image, *Macworld* can't reasonably sue me. But even scanning your own stuff can be tricky, particularly if you no longer own the rights.

The first image in Color Plate 10-3 shows the image as it appeared when scanned and then opened inside Photoshop. Figure 10-48 shows each of the individual color channels. In both examples, you can clearly see the halftone dots. These halftone dots interact with the halftone dots required to print this book to create periodic inconsistencies known as moiré patterns. And bless their hearts, they're mighty ugly.

Scanned halftone

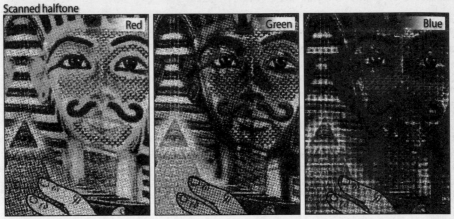

Figure 10-48: Each of the color channels from the scanned halftone, the color version of which appears at the top of Color Plate 10-3. Growing increasingly worse from one channel to the next, these represent some of the worst moiré patterns I've ever seen.

The middle example in Color Plate 10-3, as well as the individual channels in Figure 10-49, show the same image subject to the Dust & Scratches filter with a Radius of 2 and a Threshold value of 20. The moirés are for the most part gone, but the edges have all but disappeared as well. I'm tempted to describe this artwork using adjectives such as "soft" and "doughy," and them are fightin' words in the world of image editing.

But what about that bottom example in Color Plate 10-3? How did I manage to eliminate the moirés *and* preserve the detail that we see here? Why, by painstakingly applying the Gaussian Blur, Median, and Unsharp Mask filters to the individual color channels.

The first step is to examine the channels independently by pressing Ctrl+1, Ctrl+2, and Ctrl+3 (⌘-1, ⌘-2, and ⌘-3 on the Mac). You'll likely find that each one is affected by the moiré pattern to a different extent. As we saw in Figure 10-48, all three channels need work, but the blue channel — the usual culprit — is the worst. The trick, therefore, is to eliminate the patterns in the blue channel and draw detail from the red and green channels.

Dust & Scratches, Radius: 2 pixels, Threshold: 20

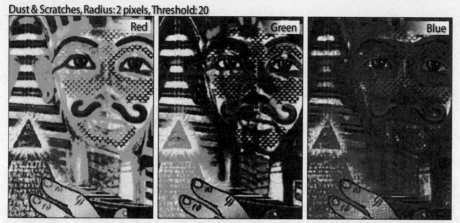

Figure 10-49: The Dust & Scratches filter quickly eliminates the patterns, but results in gummy details and garish color transitions.

To fix the blue channel, I applied both the Gaussian Blur and Median commands in fairly hefty doses. I chose Filter ⇨ Blur ⇨ Gaussian Blur and specified a Radius value of 3 pixels, rather high considering that the image measures only about 900 pixels tall. Then I chose Filter ⇨ Noise ⇨ Median and once again specified a Radius of 3.

The result was a thickly modeled image with no moirés but little detail. To firm things up a bit, I chose Filter ⇨ Sharpen ⇨ Unsharp Mask and entered 200 percent for the Amount option and 3 for the Radius. I opted for this Radius value because it matched the Radius that I used to blur the image. When correcting moirés, a Threshold value of 0 is almost always the best choice. A higher Threshold value not only prevents the sharpening of moiré pattern edges but also ignores real edges, which are already fragile enough as it is.

The green and red channels required incrementally less attention. After switching to the green channel, I applied the Gaussian Blur filter with a Radius of 1.5 and Median with a Radius of 1. Then I sharpened the image with the Unsharp Mask filter set to 200 percent and a Radius value of 1.5 (again matching the blur). In the red channel (Ctrl+1 or ⌘-1), I applied Gaussian Blur and Median, each with a Radius value of 1 pixel. I also sharpened the image with an Amount of 200 percent and a Radius of 1. The results of these channel-by-channel operations appear in Figure 10-50.

Gaussian Blur, Median, & Unsharp Mask applied independently to each channel

Figure 10-50: By attacking the image one channel at a time, I'm able to downplay the considerable problems in the blue channel and draw out the strengths of the red and green channels.

When you're finished, switch back to the RGB view by pressing Ctrl+tilde (⌘-tilde on the Mac) to see the combined result of your labors. Or keep an RGB view of the image up on screen by choosing Window ➪ Documents ➪ New Window. The focus of the image will undoubtedly be softer than it was when you started. You can cure this to a limited extent by applying very discreet passes of the Unsharp Mask filter, say, with an Amount value of 50 percent and a Radius of 1 pixel. Keep in mind that oversharpening may bring the patterns back to life or even uncover new ones.

One last tip: Always scan halftoned images at the highest resolution available to your scanner. Then resample the scan down to the desired resolution using Image ➪ Image Size, as covered in Chapter 3. This step by itself goes a long way toward eliminating moirés.

✦   ✦   ✦

Distortions and Effects

CHAPTER 11

Destructive Filters

Corrective filters enable you to eliminate image flaws and apply special effects. *Destructive filters*, on the other hand, are devoted solely to special effects. Even though Photoshop offers nearly twice as many destructive filters as corrective counterparts, destructive filters are less frequently used and ultimately less useful.

Don't get me wrong — these filters are a superb bunch. But because of their more limited appeal, I don't explain each and every one of them. Rather, I concentrate on the ones that I think you'll use most often, breeze over a handful of others, and let you discover on your own the ones that I ignore.

A million wacky effects

Oh heck, I guess I can't just go and ignore half of the commands on the Filter menu — they're not completely useless, after all. It's just that you aren't likely to use them more than once every lunar eclipse. So here are the briefest of all possible descriptions of these filters:

✦ **Fragment:** Ooh, it's an earthquake! This lame filter repeats an image four times in a square formation and lowers the opacity of each to create a sort of jiggly effect. You don't even have any options to control it. It's quite possible I'm missing the genius behind Filter ➪ Pixelate ➪ Fragment. Then again, maybe not.

✦ **Lens Flare:** Found in the Render submenu, this filter adds sparkles and halos to an image to suggest light bouncing off the camera lens. Even though photographers work their behinds off trying to make sure that these sorts of reflections don't occur, you can add them after the fact. You can select from one of three Lens Type options, adjust the Brightness slider between 10 and 300 percent (though somewhere between 100 and 150 is bound to deliver the best results), and move the center of the reflection by dragging a point around inside the Flare Center box. In addition, you can Alt-click (Win) or Option-click (Mac) inside the preview to position the center point numerically. By way of example, Figure 11-1 shows the effects of the three different Lens Type settings; in each case the Brightness value was set to 140 percent.

Here's another thing the Alt or Option key can do for you in this and many other filter dialog boxes: If you hold down Alt or Option as you drag the slider, you can see the preview update on the fly. This was the default behavior in Photoshop 6, but Adobe has obviously caved in to aggressive lobbying from Alt and Option key special interest groups, and now you have to use these keys to get the same result.

However, behold the larger and more accurate previews in many filter dialog boxes! Why, it's almost like seeing the preview inside the image itself, isn't it? Well, no, not really, but at least it's an improvement. My prediction: In Photoshop 8, the size of the filter previews will revert to being small, and will only grow larger if you hold down the Ctrl or ⌘ key.

Now, which filter was I talking about? Oh yeah, Lens Flare. If you want to add a flare to a grayscale image, first convert it to the RGB mode. Then apply the filter and convert the image back to grayscale. The Lens Flare filter is applicable to RGB images only.

Here's another great tip for using Lens Flare. Before choosing the filter, create a new layer, fill it with black, and apply the Screen blend mode by pressing Shift+Alt+S (Shift-Option-S on the Mac) with a non-painting tool selected. Now apply Lens Flare. You get the same effect as you would otherwise, but the effect floats above the background image, protecting your original image from harm. You can even move the lens flare around and vary the Opacity value, giving you more control over the final effect. Frankly, I've grown more and more fond of Lens Flare over time — it's also a very flexible tool for making specular highlights.

✦ **Diffuse:** Located in the Stylize submenu — as are the three filters that follow — Diffuse dithers the edges of color, much like the Dissolve brush mode dithers the edges of a soft brush. Even with the new Anisotropic mode, which tends to create the least change in an image's colors, Diffuse is not likely to gain a place among your most treasured filters.

✦ **Solarize:** This single-shot command is easily Photoshop's worst filter. It's really just a color-correction effect that changes all medium grays in the image to 50 percent gray, all blacks and whites to black, and remaps the other colors to shades in between. (If you're familiar with the Curves command, the map for Solarize looks like a pyramid.) It really belongs in the Image ⇨ Adjustments submenu or, better yet, on the cutting room floor.

Original digital photograph

Lens Flare, 50-300mm Zoom

Lens Flare, 35mm Prime

Lens Flare, 105mm Prime

Figure 11-1: Starting with a very dark image, I applied the different Lens Type settings available in the Lens Flare filter.

✦ **Tiles:** This filter does its best to break an image up into a bunch of square, randomly spaced rectangular tiles. You specify how many tiles fit across the smaller of the image's width or height — a value of 10, for example, creates 100 tiles in a perfectly square image — and the maximum distance each tile can shift. You can fill the gaps between tiles with foreground color, background color, or an inverted or normal version of the original image. A highly intrusive and not particularly stimulating effect.

✦ **Extrude:** The more capable cousin of the Tiles filter, Extrude breaks an image into tiles and forces them toward the viewer in three-dimensional space. The Pyramid option is a lot of fun, devolving an image into a collection of spikes. When using the Blocks option, you can select a Solid Front Faces option that renders the image as a true 3D mosaic. The Mask Incomplete Blocks option simply leaves the image untouched around the perimeter of the selection where the filter can't draw complete tiles.

Actually, I kind of like Extrude. For the sheer heck of it, Figure 11-2 shows two examples of Extrude applied to what was once a statue. In the middle image, I set the Type to Blocks, the Size to 6, the Depth to 30 and Random, with the Solid Front Faces radio button selected. The example on the right shows the Pyramid option, with Size at 10 and Depth at 20. Pretty great, huh? I only wish that the filter would generate a selection outline around the masked areas of the image so that I could get rid of anything that hadn't been extruded. It's a wonderful effect, but it's not one that lends itself to many occasions.

✦ **Diffuse Glow:** The first of the Gallery Effects that I mostly ignore, Filter ⇨ Distort ⇨ Diffuse Glow sprays a coat of dithered, background-colored pixels onto your image. Yowsa, let me at it.

✦ **Custom:** The first of two custom effects filters included in Photoshop, Filter ⇨ Other ⇨ Custom enables you to design your own *convolution kernel*, which is a variety of filter in which neighboring pixels get mixed together. The kernel can be a variation on sharpening, blurring, embossing, or a half-dozen other effects. You create your filter by entering numerical values into a matrix of options.

✦ **Displace:** Located in the Distort submenu, Displace is Photoshop's second custom effects filter. It permits you to distort and add texture to an image by moving the colors of certain pixels in a selection. You specify the direction and distance that the Displace filter moves colors by creating a second image called a *displacement map*, or *dmap* (pronounced *dee-map*) for short. The brightness values in the displacement map tell Photoshop which pixels to affect and how far to move the colors of those pixels.

✦ **The Artistic filters:** As a rule, the effects under the Filter ⇨ Artistic submenu add a painterly quality to your image. Colored Pencil, Rough Pastels, and Watercolor are examples of filters that successfully emulate traditional mediums. Other filters — Fresco, Palette Knife, and Smudge Stick — couldn't pass for their intended mediums in a dim room filled with dry ice.

Original digital photo   Blocks, Size: 6, Depth: 30   Pyramids, Size: 10, Depth: 20

Figure 11-2: Two examples of the fun Extrude filter, which can turn the most dignified image into one of those toys with hundreds of thin metal rods which you can press your face into to create an impression. (What the heck are those things called, anyway?)

✦ **The Brush Strokes filters:** I could argue that the Brush Strokes submenu contains filters that create strokes of color. This is true of some of the filters — including Angled Strokes, Crosshatch, and Sprayed Strokes. Others — Dark Strokes and Ink Outlines — generally smear colors, while still others — Accented Edges and Sumi-e — belong in the Artistic submenu. Whatever.

✦ **The Sketch filters:** In Gallery Effects parlance, Sketch means color sucker. Beware, most of these filters replace the colors in your image with the current foreground and background colors. If the foreground and background colors are black and white, the Sketch filter results in a grayscale image. Charcoal and Conté Crayon create artistic effects, Bas Relief and Note Paper add texture, and Photocopy and Stamp are stupid effects that you can produce better and with more flexibility using High Pass.

Tip

To retrieve some of the original colors from your image after applying a Sketch filter, press Ctrl+Shift+F (⌘-Shift-F on the Mac) to display the Fade dialog box and try out a few different Mode settings. Overlay and Luminosity are particularly good choices. In Color Plate 11-1, I applied the Halftone Pattern filter with the foreground and background colors set to dark green and light blue. Then I used the Fade command to select first the Overlay blend mode, and then Luminosity.

✦ **The Texture filters:** As a group, the commands in the Filter ➪ Texture submenu are my favorite effects filters. Craquelure, Mosaic Tiles, and Patchwork apply interesting depth textures to an image. Texturizer provides access to several scalable textures and permits you to load your own (as long as the pattern is saved in the Photoshop format), as demonstrated in Figure 11-3. The one semi-dud Texture filter is Stained Glass, which creates polygon tiles like Photoshop's own Crystallize filter, only with black lines around the tiles.

Certainly, there is room for disagreement about which filters are good and which are awful. After I wrote a two-star *Macworld* review about the first Gallery Effects collection back in 1992 — I must admit, I've never been a big fan — a gentleman showed me page after page of excellent artwork he created with the filters. More recently, a woman showed me her collection of amazing Lens Flare imagery. I mean, here's a filter that basically just creates a bunch of bright spots, and yet this talented person was able to go absolutely nuts with it.

The moral is that just because I consider a filter or other piece of software to be a squalid pile of unspeakably bad code doesn't mean that a creative artist can't come along and put it to remarkable use. But that's because *you* are good, not the filter. So if you're feeling particularly creative today, give the preceding filters a try. Otherwise, skip them with a clear conscience.

What about the others?

Some filters don't really belong in either the corrective or destructive camp. Take Filter ➪ Video ➪ NTSC Colors, for example, and Filter ➪ Other ➪ Offset. Both are examples of commands that have no business being under the Filter menu, and both could have been handled much better.

The NTSC Colors filter modifies the colors in your RGB or Lab image for transfer to videotape. Vivid reds and blues that might otherwise prove very unstable and bleed into their neighbors are curtailed. The problem with this function is that it's not an independent color space; it's a single-shot filter that changes your colors and is done with them. If you edit the colors after choosing the command, you may very well reintroduce colors that are incompatible with NTSC devices and therefore warrant a second application of the filter. Conversion to NTSC — another light-based system — isn't as fraught with potential disaster as conversion to CMYK pigments, but it still deserves better treatment than this.

The Offset command moves an image a specified number of pixels. Why didn't I cover it in Chapter 8 with the other movement options? Because the command actually moves the image inside the selection outline while keeping the selection outline itself stationary. It's as if you had pasted the entire image into the selection outline and were now moving it around. The command is a favorite among fans of channel operations, a topic I cover in Chapter 4. You can duplicate an image, offset the entire duplicate by a few pixels, and then mix the duplicate and original to create highlight or shadow effects. But I much prefer the more interactive control of layering and nudging with the arrow keys.

Burlap, Scaling: 100%, Relief: 6, Light Dir: Top Right   Canvas, Scaling: 150%, Relief: 8

Sandstone, Scaling: 200%, Relief: 12   Load Texture: Water.psd, Scaling: 200%, Relief: 25

Figure 11-3: Filter ⇨ Texture ⇨ Texturizer lets you select from four built-in patterns — including the first three shown here — and load your own. In the last example, I loaded the Water.psd pattern located at Photoshop 7/Presets/Patterns/ Adobe ImageReady Only.

Among the filters I've omitted from this chapter is Filter ➪ Stylize ➪ Wind, which is technically a destructive filter but is covered along with the blur and noise filters in Chapter 10. I discussed Filter ➪ Render ➪ Texture Fill in Chapter 7.

As for the other filters in the Filter ➪ Distort, Pixelate, Render, and Stylize submenus, stay tuned to this chapter to discover all the latest and greatest details.

One final note about RAM

Memory—that is, real RAM—is a precious commodity when applying destructive filters. As I mentioned in Chapter 2, the scratch disk space typically enables you to edit larger images than your computer's RAM might permit. But all the filters in the Distort submenu and most of the commands in the Render submenu operate exclusively in memory. If they run out of physical RAM, they choke.

Fortunately, there is one potential workaround: When editing a color image, try applying the filter to each of the color channels independently. One color channel requires just a third to a fourth as much RAM as the full-color composite. Sadly, this technique does not help Lens Flare, Lighting Effects, or NTSC Colors. These delicate flowers of the filter world are compatible only with full-color images; when editing a single channel, they appear dimmed.

The Pixelate Filters

The Filter ➪ Pixelate submenu features a handful of commands that rearrange your image into clumps of color:

✦ **Color Halftone:** This highly practical filter allows you to suggest the effect of a halftone pattern. When applied to a CMYK image, Photoshop simulates a commercially reproduced color separation. Otherwise, the filter merely affects those channels that it can. For example, when working inside an RGB image, the Channel 4 value goes ignored, because there is no fourth channel. When working on a grayscale image or mask, the Screen Angles value for Channel 1 is the only angle that matters.

✦ **Crystallize:** This filter organizes an image into irregularly shaped nuggets. You specify the size of the nuggets by entering a value from 3 to 300 pixels in the Cell Size option.

✦ **Facet:** Facet fuses areas of similarly colored pixels to create a sort of hand-painted effect.

✦ **Fragment:** I already harped on this filter, so here's a quick summary: It jumbles, it bumbles, but more than anything, it dumbles.

✦ **Mezzotint:** This filter renders an image as a pattern of dots, lines, or strokes. See the upcoming "Creating a mezzotint" section for more information.

✦ **Mosaic:** The Mosaic filter blends pixels together into larger squares. You specify the height and width of the squares by entering a value in the Cell Size option box.

✦ **Pointillize:** This filter is similar to Crystallize, except it separates an image into disconnected nuggets set against the background color. As usual, you specify the size of the nuggets by changing the Cell Size value.

The Crystal Halo effect

By applying one of the Pixelate filters to a feathered selection, you can create what I call a Crystal Halo effect, named for the Crystallize filter, which tends to deliver the most successful results. The following steps explain how to create a Crystal Halo, using the worlds in Figures 11-4 and 11-5 as examples.

STEPS: Creating a Crystal Halo Effect

1. **Select the foreground element around which you want to create the halo.** In my case, I select the world.

2. **Choose Select ⇨ Inverse.** Or press Ctrl+Shift+I (⌘-Shift-I on the Mac). The halo appears outside the foreground element, so you have to deselect the foreground and select the background.

3. **Press Q to switch to the quick mask mode.** Now you can edit your selection and see the results of your changes.

4. **Copy the mask.** Press Ctrl+A and Ctrl+C to select the entire mask and copy it to the Clipboard. (That's ⌘-A, ⌘-C on the Mac.) We'll need this image later to complete the effect.

5. **Choose Filter ⇨ Other ⇨ Minimum.** As I explained in the previous chapter, this filter enables you to increase the size of the deselected area. The size of the Radius value depends on the size of the halo you want to create. I entered 50 because I wanted a generous 50-pixel halo.

6. **Choose Filter ⇨ Blur ⇨ Gaussian Blur.** Then enter a Radius value equal to the amount you entered into the Minimize dialog box, in my case, 50 pixels. The result appears on the left side of Figure 11-4.

7. **Choose Filter ⇨ Pixelate ⇨ Crystallize.** Enter a moderate value in the Cell Size option box. I opted for the value 20 to convert the blurred edges to a series of chunky nuggets. The filter refracts the edges, almost as if you were viewing them through textured glass.

8. **Invert the mask.** Press Ctrl+I (⌘-I on the Mac) to swap the blacks and whites. This deselects the area outside the halo.

9. **Paste the copied selection outline.** Press Ctrl+V (⌘-V on the Mac) to paste the version of the mask you copied in Step 4.

Quick mask, Minimum: 50, GBlur: 50

Crystallize: 20, Invert, Paste, Fade: Multiply

Figure 11-4: Create a heavily feathered selection outline (left) and then apply the Crystallize filter, invert the mask, and paste the original selection (right).

10. **Choose Edit ➪ Fade, and then Multiply.** To blend the original mask with the crystallized version, press Ctrl+Shift+F (⌘-Shift-F on the Mac) and choose Multiply from the Mode pop-up menu. This burns one mask into the other, leaving only the halo selected, as in the right example in Figure 11-4.

11. **Press Q to return to the marching ants mode.** Then use the selection as desired. I merely pressed Ctrl+Backspace (⌘-Delete on the Mac) to fill the selection with white, as shown in the top-left image in Figure 11-5.

Figure 11-5 shows several variations on the Crystal Halo effect. To create the upper-right image, I substituted Filter ➪ Pixelate ➪ Color Halftone for the Crystallize filter in Step 7. To create the lower-left image, I applied the Mosaic filter in place of Crystallize, using a Cell Size value of 14 pixels. Finally, to create the lower-right image, I applied Pointillize with a Cell Size of 5 pixels.

Creating a mezzotint

A *mezzotint* is a special halftone pattern that replaces dots with a random pattern of swirling lines and wormholes. Photoshop's Mezzotint filter is an attempt to emulate this effect. Although not entirely successful — true mezzotinting options can be properly implemented only as PostScript printing functions, not as filtering functions — they do lend themselves to some pretty interesting interpretations.

The filter itself is straightforward. You choose Filter ➪ Pixelate ➪ Mezzotint, select an effect from the Type submenu, and press Enter or Return. A preview box enables you to see what each of the ten Type options looks like. Figure 11-6 shows off four of the effects at 300 ppi.

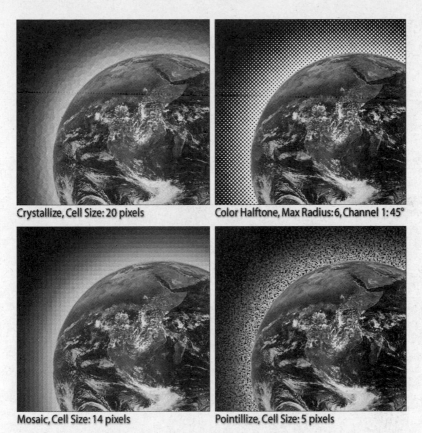

Crystallize, Cell Size: 20 pixels   Color Halftone, Max Radius: 6, Channel 1: 45°

Mosaic, Cell Size: 14 pixels   Pointillize, Cell Size: 5 pixels

Figure 11-5: These images illustrate the effects of applying each of four filters to a heavily feathered selection in the quick mask mode, and then filling the resulting selection outlines with white.

When applied to grayscale artwork, the Mezzotint filter always results in a black-and-white image. When applied to a color image, the filter automatically applies the selected effect independently to each of the color channels. Although all pixels in each channel are changed to either black or white, you can see a total of eight colors — black, red, green, blue, yellow, cyan, magenta, and white — in the RGB composite view. The upper-left example of Color Plate 11-2 shows an image subject to the Mezzotint filter in the RGB mode.

If the Mezzotint filter affects each channel independently, it follows that the color mode in which you work dramatically affects the performance of the filter. For example, if you apply Mezzotint in the Lab mode, you again whittle the colors down to eight, but a very different eight — black, cyan, magenta, green, red, two muddy blues, and a muddy rose — as shown in the middle-left example of Color Plate 11-2. If you're looking for bright happy colors, don't apply Mezzotint in the Lab mode.

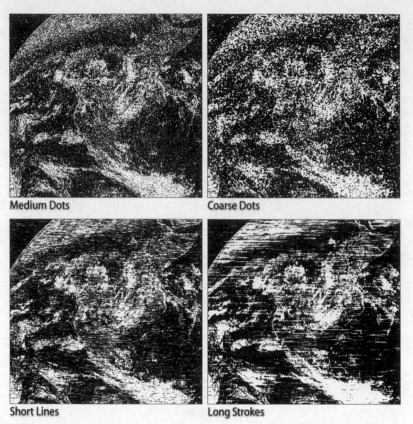

Medium Dots   Coarse Dots

Short Lines   Long Strokes

Figure 11-6: The results of applying the Mezzotint filter set to each of four representative effects. These line patterns are on par with the halftoning options offered when you select Mode ➪ Bitmap, as discussed back in Chapter 4.

In CMYK, the filter produces roughly the same eight colors that you get in RGB — white, cyan, magenta, yellow, violet-blue, red, deep green, and black. However, as shown in the bottom-left example of the color plate, the distribution of the colors is much different. The image appears lighter and more colorful than its RGB counterpart. This happens because the filter has a lot of black to work with in the RGB mode but very little — just that in the black channel — in the CMYK mode.

The right column of Color Plate 11-2 shows the effects of the Mezzotint filter after using the Fade command to mix it with the original image. I chose Overlay from the Mode pop-up menu and set the Opacity value to 40 percent. These three pairs of very different images were all created using the same filter set to the same effect. The only difference is color mode.

Edge-Enhancement Filters

The Filter ⇨ Stylize submenu offers access to a triad of filters that enhance the edges in an image. The most popular of these is undoubtedly Emboss, which adds dimension to an image by making it look as if it were carved in relief. The other two, Find Edges and Trace Contour, are less commonly applied but every bit as capable and deserving of your attention.

Embossing an image

The Emboss filter works by searching for high-contrast edges (just like the Sharpen Edges and High Pass filters), highlighting the edges with black or white pixels, and then coloring the low-contrast portions with medium gray. When you choose Filter ⇨ Stylize ⇨ Emboss, Photoshop displays the Emboss dialog box shown in Figure 11-7. The dialog box offers three options:

✦ **Angle:** The value in this option box determines the angle at which Photoshop lights the image in relief. For example, if you enter a value of 90 degrees, you light the relief from the bottom straight upward. The white pixels therefore appear on the bottom sides of the edges, and the black pixels appear on the top sides. Figure 11-8 shows four reliefs lit from different angles and with different Height settings.

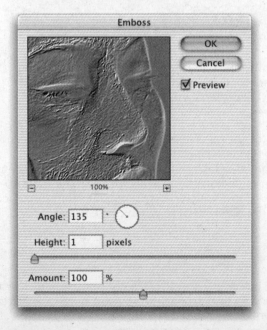

Figure 11-7: The Emboss dialog box lets you control the depth of the filtered image and the angle from which it is lit.

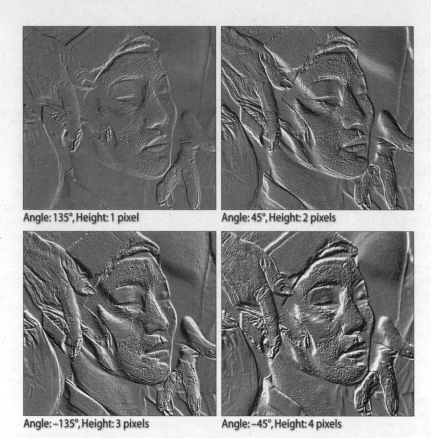

Angle: 135°, Height: 1 pixel   Angle: 45°, Height: 2 pixels

Angle: –135°, Height: 3 pixels   Angle: –45°, Height: 4 pixels

Figure 11-8: Reliefs lit with four different Height settings and from four different angles, in increments that are multiples of 45 degrees. You can imagine a light source in the center of the grouping of four images.

✦ **Height:** The Emboss filter accomplishes its highlighting effect by displacing one copy of an image relative to another. Using the Height option, you specify the distance between the copies, which can vary from 1 to 100 pixels. Lower values produce crisper effects, as demonstrated in Figure 11-8. Values above 4 goop up things pretty well unless you also enter a high Amount value. Together, the Height and Amount values determine the depth of the image in relief.

Tip

The Height value is analogous to the Radius value in the Unsharp Mask dialog box. You should therefore set the value according to the resolution of your image—1 for 150 ppi, 2 for 300 ppi, and so on.

✦ **Amount:** Enter a value between 1 and 500 percent to determine the amount of black and white assigned to pixels along the edges. Values of 50 percent and lower produce almost entirely gray images. Higher values produce sharper edges, as if the relief were carved more deeply.

As a stand-alone effect, Emboss is only so-so. It's one of those filters that makes you gasp with delight the first time you see it but never quite lends itself to any practical application after you become acquainted with Photoshop. But if you think of Emboss as an extension of the High Pass filter, it takes on new meaning. You can use it to edit selection outlines in the quick mask mode, just as you might use the High Pass filter. You also can use it to draw out detail in an image.

Figure 11-9 shows the result of using the Fade command immediately after applying the Emboss filter. First, I applied the Emboss filter at an Angle of 135 degrees, a Height of 2 pixels, and an Amount of 500 percent. Then I pressed Ctrl+Shift+F (⌘-Shift-F on the Mac) to display the Fade dialog box. To create the top-right example, I selected Darken from the Mode pop-up menu and lowered the Opacity to 65 percent. This added shadows to the edges of the image, thus boosting the texture without unduly upsetting the original brightness values. I selected the Overlay blend mode and raised the Opacity back to 100 percent to create the bottom-left example, and then switched to Pin Light at 80 percent Opacity for the bottom-right image.

Emboss, Angle: 135°, Height: 2, 500%   Darken, 65% Opacity

Overlay, 100% Opacity   Pin Light, 80% Opacity

Figure 11-9: After applying the Emboss filter, I used my old friend the Fade command to experiment with blend modes and Opacity levels.

Tip

To create a color relief effect, apply the Emboss filter and then select the Luminosity option in the Fade dialog box. This retains the colors from the original image while applying the lightness and darkness of the pixels from the filtered selection. The effect looks something like an inked lithographic plate, with steel grays and vivid colors mixing together. An example of this effect appears in the next-to-the-last example of Color Plate 11-3.

While this color plate chiefly demonstrates various effects you can achieve by fading the Emboss filter, the final example uses a different technique to improve upon the example directly above it. Rather than let the gray choke out the colors below, I adjusted the Underlying Layer settings in the Layer Style dialog box, permitting the blacks and whites to show through. For a full explanation of this feature, turn to the "Color exclusion sliders" section of Chapter 13.

Tracing around edges

Photoshop provides three filters that trace around pixels in your image and accentuate the edges. All three filters live on the Filter ⇨ Stylize submenu:

✦ **Find Edges:** This filter detects edges similarly to High Pass. Low-contrast areas become white, medium-contrast edges become gray, and high-contrast edges become black, as in the first example in Figure 11-10. Hard edges become thin lines; soft edges become fat ones. The result is a thick, organic outline that you can overlay onto an image to give it a waxy appearance. To achieve the bottom-left effect in the figure, I chose Edit ⇨ Fade Find Edges and applied the Overlay mode.

✦ **Glowing Edges:** This Gallery Effects filter is a variation on Find Edges, with two important differences: Glowing Edges produces an inverted effect, changing low-contrast areas to black and edges to white, as in the top-middle image in Figure 11-10. This filter also enables you to adjust the width, brightness, and smoothness of the traced edges. For example, the top-middle image in Figure 11-10 uses an Edge Width of 2, an Edge Brightness of 10, and a Smoothness of 5. Glowing Edges is a great backup command. If you aren't satisfied with the effect produced by the Find Edges filter, choose Glowing Edges instead and adjust the options as desired. If you want black lines against a white background, press Ctrl+I (Win) or ⌘-I (Mac) to invert the effect.

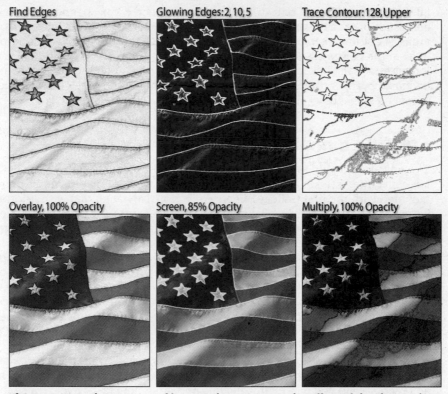

Figure 11-10: The top row of images demonstrates the effect of the three edge-tracing commands available from the Filter ⇨ Stylize submenu. After applying each command, I used the Fade command to apply the blend modes and Opacity values demonstrated in the bottom row.

✦ **Trace Contour:** Illustrated on the right side of Figure 11-10, Trace Contour is a little more involved than the others and slightly less interesting. The filter traces a series of single-pixel lines along the border between light and dark pixels. Choosing the filter displays a dialog box containing three options: Level, Upper, and Lower. The Level value indicates the lightness value above which pixels are considered to be light and below which they are dark. For example, if you enter 128—medium gray, the default setting used in Figure 11-10—Trace Contour draws a line at every spot where an area of color lighter than medium gray meets an area of color darker than medium gray. The Upper and Lower options tell the filter where to position the line—inside the lighter color's territory (Upper) or inside the space occupied by the darker color (Lower).

Like Mezzotint, Trace Contour applies itself to each color channel independently and renders each channel as a 1-bit image. A collection of black lines surrounds the areas of color in each channel; the RGB, Lab, or CMYK composite view shows these lines in the colors associated with the channels. When you work in RGB, a cyan line indicates a black line in the red channel (no red plus full-intensity green and blue becomes cyan). A yellow line indicates a black line in the blue channel, and so on. You get a single black line when working in the grayscale mode.

Creating a metallic coating

The edge-tracing filters are especially fun to use in combination with Edit ⇨ Fade. I became interested in playing with these filters after trying out the Chrome filter included with the first Gallery Effects collection. Now included with Photoshop as Filter ⇨ Sketch ⇨ Chrome, this filter turns an image into a melted pile of metallic goo. No matter how you apply Chrome, it completely wipes out your image and leaves a ton of jagged color transitions in its wake. It's really only useful with color images, and then only if you follow up with the Fade command and a blend mode. Even then, I've never been particularly satisfied with the results.

But all that experimenting got me thinking: How can you create a metallic coating, with gleaming highlights and crisp shadows, without depending on Chrome? Find Edges offers a way. First, copy your image to a separate layer by pressing Ctrl+J (⌘-J on the Mac). Then apply the Gaussian Blur filter. A Radius value between 1.0 and 4.0 produces the best results, depending on how gooey you want the edges to be. Next, apply the Find Edges filter. Because the edges are blurry, the resulting image is light, so I recommend you darken it using Image ⇨ Adjustments ⇨ Levels (raise the first Input Levels value to 100 or so, as explained in Chapter 17). The blurry edges appear in the top-left example in Figure 11-11.

To produce the bottom-left image, I mixed the layer with the underlying original using the Overlay blend mode. The result is a shiny effect that produces a metallic finish without altogether destroying the detail in the image.

If you decide you like this effect, there's more where it came from. The second and third columns of Figure 11-11 show the results of applying Filter ⇨ Sketch ⇨ Bas Relief and (for comparison's sake) Filter ⇨ Sketch ⇨ Chrome, respectively. After applying each filter, I chose Edit ⇨ Fade and selected the Overlay mode, repeating the effect I applied to the Gaussian Blur and Find Edges layer. In this case, the Overlay mode actually makes the Chrome filter look quite respectable.

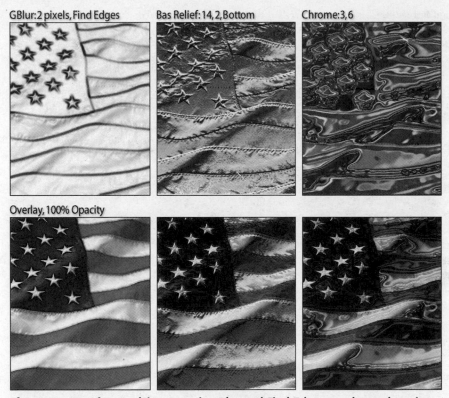

GBlur: 2 pixels, Find Edges   Bas Relief: 14, 2, Bottom   Chrome: 3, 6

Overlay, 100% Opacity

Figure 11-11: After applying Gaussian Blur and Find Edges to a layered version of the image (top left), I composited the filtered image with the original using the Overlay mode (bottom left). The second and third columns show similar effects achieved using the effects filters Bas Relief and Chrome.

Distortion Filters

For the most part, commands in the Distort submenu are related by the fact that they move colors in an image to achieve unusual stretching, swirling, and vibrating effects. They're rather like the transformation commands from the Edit menu in that they perform their magic by relocating and interpolating colors rather than by altering brightness and color values.

The distinction, of course, is that whereas the transformation commands let you scale and distort images by manipulating four control points, the Distort filters provide the equivalent of hundreds of control points, all of which you can use to affect different portions of an image. In some cases, you're projecting an image into a fun-house mirror; other times, it's a reflective pool. You can fan images, wiggle them, and change them in ways that have no correlation to real life, as illustrated in Figure 11-12.

A kind and decent man   What'd you have to go and do that for?

Figure 11-12: This is your image (left); this is your image on distortion filters (right). Six filters, in fact: Spherize, Twirl, Polar Coordinates, Shear, Wave, and Ripple. I also used Liquify for some of the effects toward the top of the image, including those Gollum-like eyes.

Distortion filters are powerful tools. Although they are easy to apply, they are extremely difficult to use well. Here are some rules to keep in mind:

✦ **Practice makes practical:** Distortion filters are like complex vocabulary words. You don't want to use them without practicing a little first. Experiment with a distortion filter several times before trying to use it in a real project. You may even want to write down the steps you take so that you can remember how you created an effect.

✦ **Use caution during tight deadlines:** Distortion filters are enormous time-wasters. Unless you know exactly how you want to proceed, you may want to avoid using them when time is short. The last thing you need when you're working under the gun is to get trapped trying to pull off a weird effect.

✦ **Apply selectively:** The effects of distortion filters are too severe to inflict all at once. You can achieve marvelous, subtle effects, however, by distorting feathered and layered selections. Although I would hardly call the image in Figure 11-12 subtle, no single effect was applied to the entire image. For instance, the black edges were created with the Ripple filter. I also skipped ahead of myself a bit and used the Liquify command to create the distortion in the topmost face and in the main pair of eyes. The section, "Distorting with the Liquify command," explains how to use this tool.

✦ **Combine creatively:** Don't expect a single distortion to achieve the desired effect. If one application isn't enough, apply the filter again. Experiment with combining different distortions.

Distortion filters interpolate between pixels to create their fantastic effects. This means the quality of your filtered images depends on the setting of the Interpolation option in the General Preferences dialog box. If a filter produces jagged effects, the Nearest Neighbor option is probably selected. Try selecting the Bicubic or Bilinear option instead.

Reflecting an image in a spoon

Most folks take their first venture into distortion filters by using Pinch and Spherize. Pinch maps an image on the inside of a sphere or similarly curved surface; Spherize maps it on the outside of a sphere. It's sort of like looking at your reflection on the inside and outside of a spoon.

You can apply Pinch to a scanned face to squish the features toward the center or apply Spherize to accentuate the girth of the nose. Figure 11-13 illustrates both effects. It's a laugh, and you pretty much feel as though you're onto something that no one else ever thought of before. (At least that's how I felt—but I'm easily amazed.)

You can pinch or spherize an image using either the Pinch or Spherize command. Note that a positive Amount value in the Pinch dialog box produces a similar effect to a negative value in the Spherize dialog box. There is a slight difference between the spatial curvature of the 3D calculations: Pinch pokes the image inward or outward using a rounded cone—we're talking bell-shaped, much like a Gaussian model. Spherize wraps the image on the outside or inside of a true sphere. As a result, the two filters yield subtly different results. Pinch produces a soft transition around the perimeter of a selection; Spherize produces an abrupt transition. If this doesn't quite make sense to you, just play with one, try out the same effect with the other, and see which you like better.

Another difference between the two filters is that Spherize provides the additional options of enabling you to wrap an image on the inside or outside of a horizontal or vertical cylinder, as shown in Figure 11-14. To try out these effects, select the Horizontal Only or Vertical Only options from the Mode pop-up menu at the bottom of the Spherize dialog box.

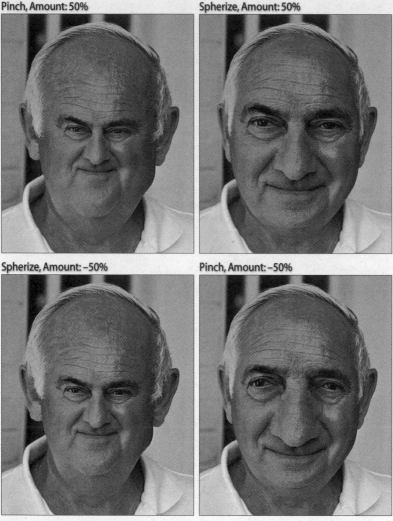

Figure 11-13: My kind and decent subject endures more humiliating abuse—thanks to the Pinch and Spherize filters. Notice how negative values make Pinch spherize, and Spherize pinch.

Both filters can affect elliptical regions only. If a selection outline is not elliptical, Photoshop applies the filter to the largest ellipse that fits inside the selection. As a result, the filter may leave behind a noticeable elliptical boundary between the affected and unaffected portions of the selection. To avoid this effect, select the region you want to edit with the elliptical marquee tool and then feather the selection before filtering it. This softens the effect of the filter and provides a more gradual transition (even more so than Pinch already affords).

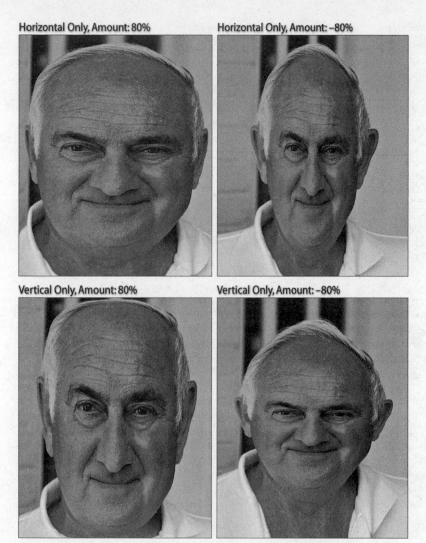

Horizontal Only, Amount: 80%

Horizontal Only, Amount: –80%

Vertical Only, Amount: 80%

Vertical Only, Amount: –80%

Figure 11-14: Spherize also lets you wrap your image around a horizontally (top row) or vertically (bottom row) oriented cylinder.

One of the more remarkable properties of the Pinch filter is that it lets you turn any image into a conical gradation. Figure 11-15 illustrates how the process works. First, you may wish to blur the image to eliminate any harsh edges between color transitions. Then apply the Pinch filter at full strength (100 percent). Reapply the filter several more times. Each time you press Ctrl+F (⌘-F on the Mac), the center portion of the image recedes farther and farther into the distance, as shown in Figure 11-15. After 10 repetitions, the face in the example all but disappeared.

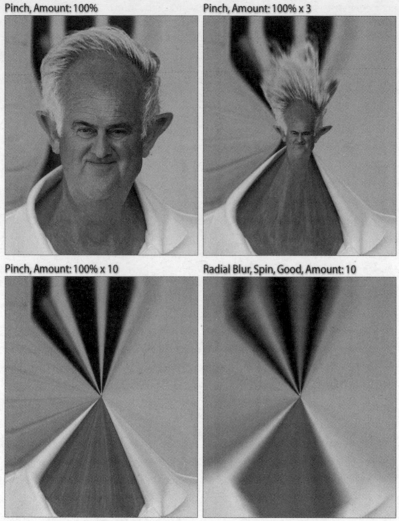

Figure 11-15: I pinched the image 10 times and applied the Radial Blur filter with its default settings to create a conical gradation.

Next, apply the Radial Blur filter set to Spin 10 pixels or so to mix the color boundaries a bit. The result is a type of gradation that you can't create using Photoshop's gradient tool.

Twirling spirals

The Twirl filter rotates the center of a selection while leaving the sides fixed in place. The result is a spiral of colors that looks for all the world as if you poured the image into a blender set to a very slow speed.

When you choose Filter ➪ Distort ➪ Twirl, you can enter a positive value from 1 to 999 degrees to spiral the image in a clockwise direction. Enter a negative value to spiral the image in a counterclockwise direction. Figure 11-16 shows a 30-degree spiral and a 100-degree spiral in both positive and negative directions. As you are probably already aware, 360 degrees make a full circle, so the maximum 999-degree value equates to a spiral that circles around almost three times, as shown in the bottom-right example in Figure 11-17.

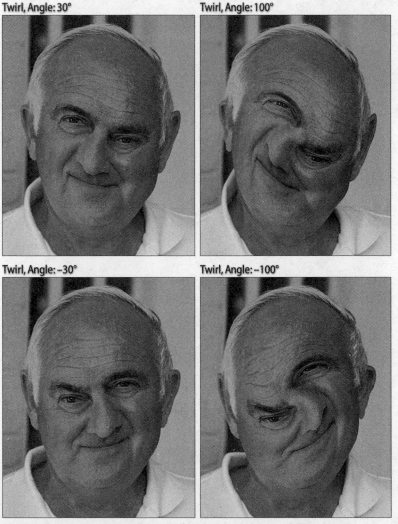

Figure 11-16: You can adjust the direction of the Twirl filter to suit whichever side of the equator you happen to be on.

Tip   The Twirl filter produces smoother effects when you use lower Angle values. Therefore, you're better off applying a 100-degree spiral 10 times rather than applying a 999-degree spiral once, as you can see in Figure 11-17.

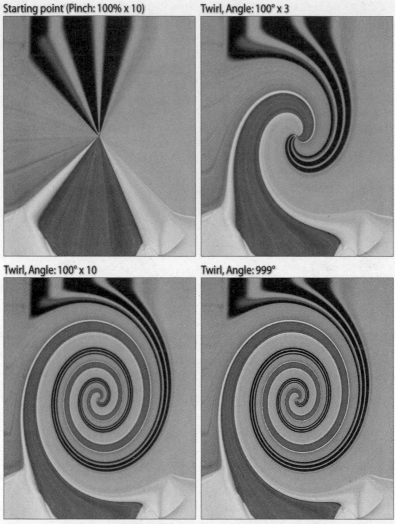

Starting point (Pinch: 100% x 10)   Twirl, Angle: 100° x 3

Twirl, Angle: 100° x 10   Twirl, Angle: 999°

Figure 11-17: Our poor Pinch-headed subject (upper left) gets subjected to the tortures of the Twirl filter (upper right). Repeatedly applying the Twirl filter at a moderate value (bottom left) produces a smoother effect than applying the filter once at a high value (bottom right).

In addition to creating ice-cream swirls like those shown in Figure 11-17, you can use the Twirl filter to create organic images virtually from scratch, as witnessed by Figures 11-18 and 11-19.

To create the images shown in Figure 11-18, I started with Mr. Pinch-head (top left) and used the Spherize filter to flex the image vertically by entering 100 percent in the Amount option box and selecting Vertical Only from the Mode pop-up menu. After repeating this filter several times, I eventually achieved a stalactite-stalagmite effect, as shown in the top-right example of the figure. To increase the contrast in the image, I applied Unsharp Mask and followed that up with a little Gaussian Blur to make things creamier. I then repeatedly applied the Twirl filter to curl the straight spikes like two symmetrical hairs. The result merges the simplicity of pure math with the beauty of bitmapped imagery.

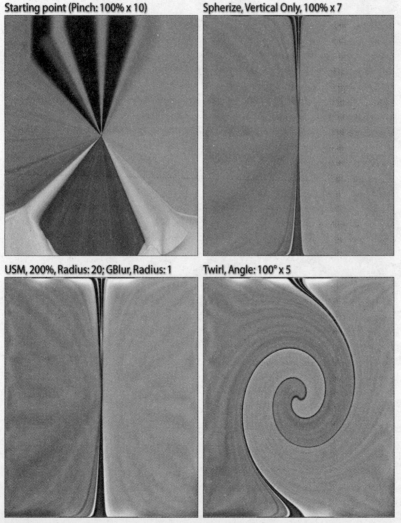

Figure 11-18: You can create surprisingly naturalistic effects using distortion filters exclusively.

Figure 11-19 illustrates a droplet technique designed by Mark Collen. I took the liberty of breaking down the technique into the following steps.

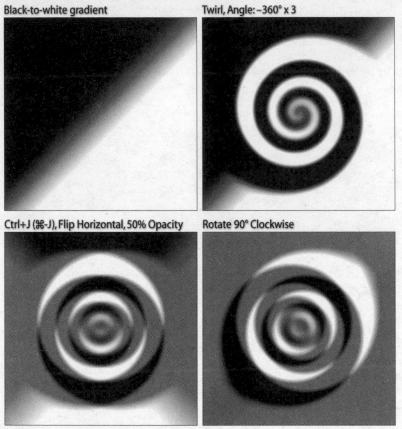

Black-to-white gradient

Twirl, Angle: –360° x 3

Ctrl+J (⌘-J), Flip Horizontal, 50% Opacity

Rotate 90° Clockwise

Figure 11-19: Although they appear as if they might be the result of the ZigZag filter, these images were created entirely by using the gradient tool, the Twirl filter, and a couple of transformations.

STEPS: Creating a Thick-Liquid Droplet

1. **Press D to restore the default foreground and background colors.**

2. **Shift-drag with the rectangular marquee tool to select a square portion of an image.**

3. **Create a linear gradation by dragging inside the selection outline with the gradient tool.** Before you drag, select the linear gradient style in the Options bar and select the foreground to background gradient from the Gradients drop-down palette, also in the Options bar. Drag a short distance near the center of the selection from upper left to lower right, creating the gradation shown in the top-left box in Figure 11-19.

4. **Choose the Twirl filter and apply it at −360 degrees so that the spiral moves counterclockwise.** To create the top-right image in the figure, I applied the Twirl filter three times. Each repetition of the filter adds another ring of ripples.

5. **Press Ctrl+J (Win) or ⌘-J (Mac) to copy the selection to a layer.**

6. **Choose Edit ➪ Transform ➪ Flip Horizontal.**

7. **Lower the Opacity value to 50 percent.** You can do this from the keyboard by selecting the rectangular marquee tool and pressing 5. The result appears in the lower-left example in Figure 11-19.

8. **Choose Edit ➪ Transform ➪ Rotate 90° CW.** This rotates the layer a quarter turn, thus creating the last image in the figure. You can achieve other interesting effects by choosing Lighten, Darken, and others from the brush modes pop-up menu.

Now, if a few twirls and transformations can produce an effect this entertaining in black and white, just imagine what you can do in color. On second thought, don't imagine; check out Color Plate 11-4 instead. Starting with Photoshop's Blue, Red, Yellow gradient, I followed the previous Steps 1 through 4. From there, I made extensive use of floating copies of layers with the Difference blend mode applied. Finishing up with a little Spherize, ZigZag, Lens Flare, and Unsharp Mask to mutate the concentric rings into something a little more interesting, the result was the whirlin', twirlin' work of art at the bottom of the color plate.

If that went a little fast for you, not to worry. More important than the specific effects is this general category of distortion drawings. A filter such as Pinch or Twirl permits you to create wild imagery without ever drawing a brushstroke or scanning a photograph. If you can do this much with a simple three-color gradation, just think of what you can do if you throw in a few more colors. Pixels are little more than fodder for these very powerful functions.

Creating concentric pond ripples

I don't know about you, but when I think of zigzags, I think of cartoon lightning bolts, wriggling snakes, scribbles — anything that alternately changes directions along an axis, like the letter *Z*. The ZigZag filter does arrange colors into zigzag patterns, but it does so in a radial fashion, meaning that the zigzags emanate from the center of the image like spokes in a wheel. The result is a series of concentric ripples. If you want parallel zigzags, check out the Ripple and Wave filters, described in the next section. (The ZigZag filter creates ripples and the Ripple filter creates zigzags. Go figure.)

When you choose Filter ➪ Distort ➪ ZigZag, Photoshop displays a dialog box offering the following options:

✦ **Amount:** Enter an amount between negative 99 and positive 100 in whole-number increments to specify the depth of the ripples. If you enter a negative value, the ripples descend below the surface. If you enter a positive value, the ripples protrude upward.

To illustrate how the Amount value works, I first prepared the sample image pictured in Figure 11-20. Starting with our much-maligned Mr. Pinch as seen in the upper-left example (Oh, you're a lean one, Mr. Pinch), I copied the image to an independent layer, rotated it 180 degrees, and applied the Overlay blend mode (upper right). I floated this layer, used Overlay again, and applied the Twirl filter repeatedly (lower left). Finally, I pasted in the flag image seen earlier, inverted it, used Difference mode on the layer, and flattened the entire image (lower right). Pretty cool, huh? Figure 11-21 shows the final image subject to the ZigZag filter with two different Amount values.

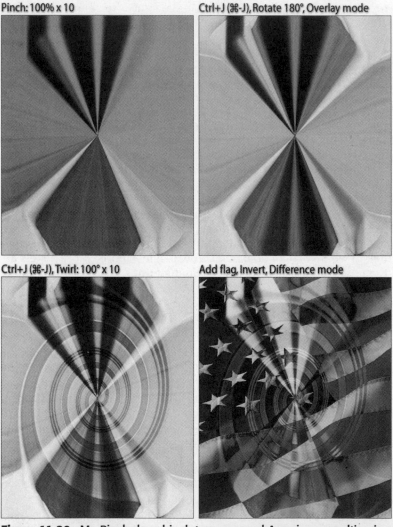

Figure 11-20: Mr. Pinch does his duty as a proud American, resulting in a kaleidoscopic sample image.

Figure 11-21: The results of applying the ZigZag filter using Amount values of 30 percent (top row) and 100 percent (bottom row) and each of the three Style settings. In all cases, the Ridges value was 5.

✦ **Ridges:** This option box controls the number of ripples in the selected area and accepts any value from 0 to 20. Figure 11-22 illustrates the difference between a Ridges value of 5 (top row) and 20 (bottom row).

✦ **Style:** The options in this pop-up menu determine how Photoshop moves pixels with respect to the center of the image or selection.

• **Around Center:** Select this option to rotate pixels in alternating directions around the center without moving them outward, as shown in the left columns of Figures 11-21 and 11-22. This is the only option that produces what I would term a zigzag effect.

• **Out From Center:** When you select this option, Photoshop moves pixels outward in rhythmic bursts according to the value in the Ridges option box. The middle columns of Figure 11-21 and 11-22 show some examples.

• **Pond Ripples:** This option is really a cross between the previous two. It moves pixels outward and rotates them around the center of the selection to create circular patterns. As demonstrated in the right columns of Figures 11-21 and 11-22, this option truly results in a pond ripple effect.

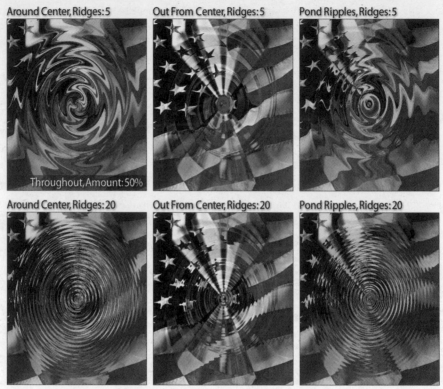

Figure 11-22: The effects of the ZigZag filter using two Ridges values and each of the three Style pop-up menu settings. In all cases, the Amount value was 50.

Creating parallel ripples and waves

Photoshop provides four means to distort an image in parallel waves, as if the image were lying on the bottom of a shimmering or undulating pool. Of the four, the ripple filters — which include Ripple, Ocean Ripple, and Glass — are only moderately sophisticated, but they're also relatively easy to apply. The fourth filter, Wave, affords you greater control, but its options are among the most complex Photoshop has to offer.

The Ripple filter

To use the Ripple filter, choose Filter ➪ Distort ➪ Ripple. Photoshop displays the Ripple dialog box, giving you the following options:

✦ **Amount:** Enter an amount between negative 998 and positive 999 in whole-number increments to specify the width of the ripples from side to side. Negative and positive values change the direction of the ripples, but visually speaking, they produce identical effects. The ripples are measured as a ratio of the Size value and the dimensions of the selection—all of which translates to, "Experiment and see what happens." You can count on getting ragged effects from any value over 300, as illustrated in Figure 11-23.

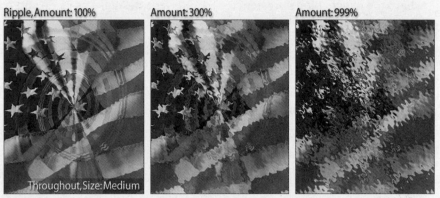

Figure 11-23: The effects of three different Ripple filter Amount values.

✦ **Size:** Select one of the three options in the Size pop-up menu to change the length of the ripples. The Small option results in the shortest ripples and therefore the most ripples. Combining the Small option with a relatively high Amount value results in a textured-glass effect. The Large option results in the longest and fewest ripples. Figure 11-24 shows an example of each Size option.

Figure 11-24: The effects of the three different Ripple filter Size settings.

You can create a blistered effect by overlaying a negative ripple onto a positive ripple. Try this: First, copy the selection. Then apply the Ripple filter with a positive Amount value—say, 300. Next, paste the copied selection and apply the Ripple filter at the exact opposite Amount value, in this case, –300. Press 5 to change the Opacity value to 50 percent. The result is a series of diametrically opposed ripples that cross each other to create teardrop blisters.

Ocean Ripple and Glass

The Ocean Ripple and Glass filters are gifts from Gallery Effects. Both filters emulate the effect of looking at an image through textured glass. These two distorters so closely resemble each other that they would be better merged into one. But where the effects filters are concerned, interface design is as fickle and transitory as the face on the cover of *Tiger Beat Magazine*.

The Ocean Ripple filter's two parameters, Ripple Size and Ripple Magnitude, are illustrated in Figure 11-25. Compare the examples horizontally to observe an increase in Ripple Size values from 3 to the maximum of 15; compare vertically to observe an increase in Ripple Magnitude from 5 to the maximum of 20. As you can see, you can vary the Ripple Size value with impunity. But raise the Ripple Magnitude value, and you're looking through sculpted glass.

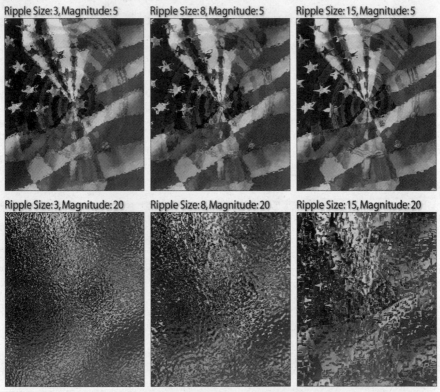

Figure 11-25: Raising the Ripple Size value spreads out the effect; raising the Ripple Magnitude adds more depth and contrast to the ripples.

The principal difference between Glass and Ocean Ripple is that while Ocean Ripple uses one preset distortion texture, Glass gives you four to choose from, plus it lets you load your own (similar to Texturizer). You can invert the texture—high becomes low, low becomes high—and also scale it to change its size relative to the layer you're distorting. Figure 11-26 uses the Tiny Lens texture throughout, and demonstrates how different the effect can be depending on the Distortion and Smoothness settings. Compare the examples in the figure horizontally for proof that Distortion is perhaps the best-named parameter in all of Photoshop. Smoothness, on the other hand, is sort of like an "anti-Ripple Magnitude" setting. High Smoothness settings in Glass are analogous to low Ripple Magnitude settings in Ocean Ripple.

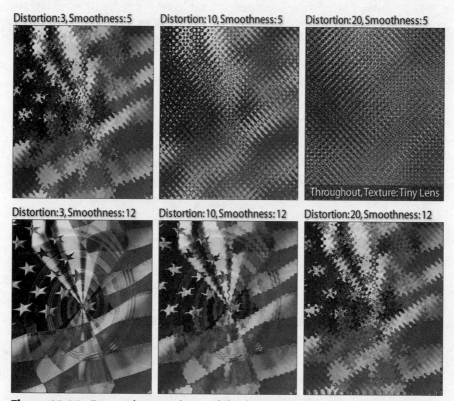

Figure 11-26: For maximum privacy while showering, choose a Glass door with high Distortion and low Smoothness settings (upper right).

The Wave filter

Now that you've met the ripple family, it's time to ride the Wave. I've come to love this filter—I use it all the time—but it's complex enough to warrant its own book. It wouldn't be a very big book and no one would buy it, but you never know what a freelancer like me will do next. Keep an eye out for *Wave Filter Bible* at your local bookstore.

In the meantime, choose Filter ⇨ Distort ⇨ Wave (that's the easy part) to display the Wave dialog box shown in Figure 11-27. Photoshop presents you with the following options, which make applying a distortion every bit as easy as operating an oscilloscope:

✦ **Number of Generators:** Right off the bat, the Wave dialog box boggles the brain. A friend of mine likened this option to the number of rocks you throw in the water to start it rippling. One generator means that you throw in one rock to create one set of waves. You can throw in two rocks to create two sets of waves (see Figure 11-28), three rocks to create three sets of waves, and all the way up to a quarryful of 999 rocks to create, well, you get the idea. If you enter a high value, however, be prepared to wait a few years for the preview to update. If you can't wait, press Escape, which turns off the preview until the next time you enter a value in the dialog box.

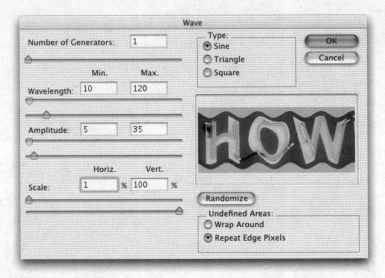

Figure 11-27: The Wave dialog box lets you wreak scientific havoc on an image. Put on your pocket protector, take out your slide rule, and give it a whirl.

✦ **Wavelength and Amplitude:** Beginning to feel like you're playing with a ham radio? The Wave filter produces random results by varying the number and length of waves (Wavelength) as well as the height of the waves (Amplitude) between minimum and maximum values, which can range from 1 to 999. (The Wavelength and Amplitude options, therefore, correspond in theory to the Size and Amount options in the Ripple dialog box.) Figure 11-29 demonstrates the difference between Wavelength and Amplitude.

Number of Generators: 1

Number of Generators: 2

Number of Generators: 5

Number of Generators: 10

Throughout, Type: Sine, Max. Wavelength: 300, Max. Amplitude: 75, Horiz. Scale: 1%, Vert. Scale: 100%

Figure 11-28: The only difference between the examples in this figure is in the Number of Generators. Adding generators increases random action by creating more intersecting waveforms.

Max. Wavelength: 120, Max. Amplitude: 35

Max. Wavelength: 350, Max. Amplitude: 35

Max. Wavelength: 120, Max. Amplitude: 115

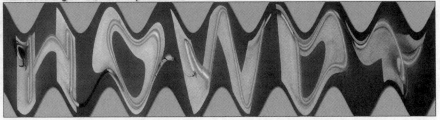

Max. Wavelength: 350, Max. Amplitude: 115

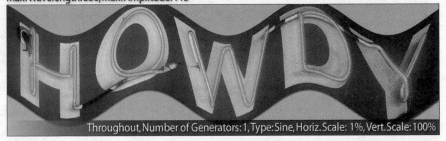

Throughout, Number of Generators: 1, Type: Sine, Horiz. Scale: 1%, Vert. Scale: 100%

Figure 11-29: With all other parameters set according to the specifications at the bottom of the figure, increasing Wavelength creates a larger horizontal distance between the peaks of waves. Increasing Amplitude creates a higher wave peak.

✦ **Scale:** You can scale the effects of the Wave filter between 1 and 100 percent horizontally and vertically. For clarity's sake, all the effects featured in Figures 11-28 and 11-29 use only Vertical Scale, with Horizontal Scale set at the minimum of 1 percent. Increasing Horizontal Scale would make the waves go back and forth as well as up and down.

✦ **Type:** You can select from three kinds of waves. As seen in Figures 11-28 and 11-29, the Sine option produces standard sine waves that rise and fall smoothly in bell-shaped curves, just like real waves. The Triangle option, shown in the first and third examples of Figure 11-30, creates zigzags that rise and fall in straight lines, like the edge of a piece of fabric cut with pinking shears. The Square option, illustrated in the second and last examples of Figure 11-30, has nothing to do with waves at all, but rather organizes an image into a series of rectangular groupings, reminiscent of Cubism. You might think of this option as an extension of the Mosaic filter. All examples in Figure 11-30 utilize a Number of Generators setting of 1; examples of the Triangle and Square types with higher Number of Generator values can be seen in Figure 11-31.

✦ **Randomize:** The Wave filter is random by nature. If you don't like the effect you see in the preview box, click the Randomize button (as illustrated in Figure 11-31) to stir things up a bit. You can keep clicking the button until you get an effect you like.

✦ **Undefined Areas:** The Wave filter distorts a selection to the extent that gaps may appear around the edges. You can fill those gaps either by repeating pixels along the edge of the selection, as in the figures, or by wrapping pixels from the left side of the selection onto the right side and pixels from the top edge of the selection onto the bottom.

Type: Triangle, Max. Wavelength: 120, Max. Amplitude: 35

Type: Square, Max. Wavelength: 120, Max. Amplitude: 35

Type: Triangle, Max. Wavelength: 20, Max. Amplitude: 70

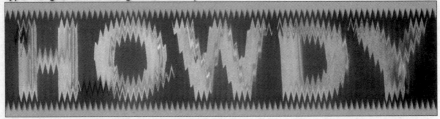

Type: Square, Max. Wavelength: 20, Max. Amplitude: 70

Throughout, Number of Generators: 1, Horiz. Scale: 1%, Vert. Scale: 100%

Figure 11-30: The effects of the unsmooth Triangle and Square types, using relatively high Wavelength and low Amplitude values (top two examples) versus relatively low Wavelength and high Amplitude values (bottom two examples).

Type: Triangle, Number of Generators: 3

Same settings, Randomize

Type: Square, Number of Generators: 2

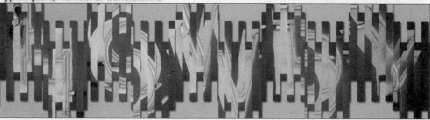

Same settings, Randomize

Throughout, Max. Wavelength: 300, Max. Amplitude: 75, Horiz. Scale: 1%, Vert. Scale: 100%

Figure 11-31: Clicking Randomize "rolls the dice" and gives you another Wave effect based upon the parameters you've set; compare the first example to the second, and the third to the fourth.

Distorting an image along a curve

The Distort command (Edit ⇨ Transform ⇨ Distort), which isn't discussed elsewhere in this book, creates four corner handles around an image. You drag each corner handle to distort the selected image in that direction. Unfortunately, you can't add other points around the edges to create additional distortions, which can be frustrating if you're trying to achieve a specific effect. If you can't achieve a certain kind of distortion using Edit ⇨ Free Transform, the Shear filter may be your answer.

Shear distorts an image or selection along a path. When you choose Filter ⇨ Distort ⇨ Shear, you get the dialog box shown in Figure 11-32. Initially, a single line that has two points at either end appears in the grid at the top of the box. When you drag the points, you slant the image in the preview. This, plus the fact that the filter is named Shear—Adobe's strange term for skewing (it appears in Illustrator as well)—leads many users to dismiss the filter as nothing more than a slanting tool. But in truth, it's more versatile than that.

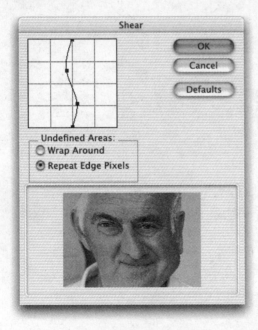

Figure 11-32: Click the grid line in the left corner of the Shear dialog box to add points to the line. Drag these points to distort the image along the curve.

You can add points to the grid line simply by clicking on it. A point springs up every time you click an empty space in the line. Drag the point to change the curvature of the line and distort the image along the new curve. To delete a point, drag it off the left or right side of the grid. To delete all added points and return the line to its original vertical orientation, click the Defaults button.

The Undefined Areas options work just as they do in the Wave dialog box (described in the preceding section). You can either fill the gaps on one side of the image with pixels shoved off the opposite side by selecting Wrap Around or repeat pixels along the edge of the selection by selecting Repeat Edge Pixels.

Tip

While Shear was obviously conceived to create horizontal distortions, you may find you need to create a vertically-based distortion instead. If you can't change the filter, why not change the image? As shown in Figure 11-33, simply rotating the image on its side allowed me to give the desired slant to my subject's face.

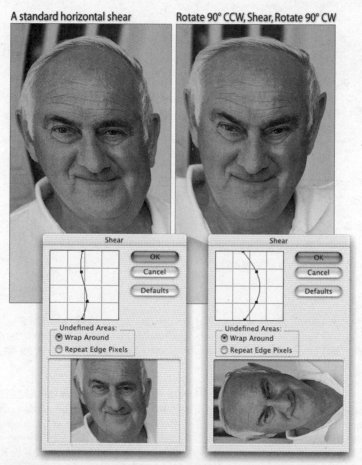

Figure 11-33: Not liking the effect I was able to achieve with a normal application of Shear (left), I chose Image ⇨ Rotate Canvas ⇨ 90° CCW, which allowed me to vertically distort my image with the Shear filter (right). Finally, I chose Image ⇨ Rotate Canvas ⇨ 90° CW to restore the image to its original upright position.

Changing to polar coordinates

The Polar Coordinates filter is another one of those gems that a lot of folks shy away from because it doesn't make much sense at first glance. When you choose Filter ➪ Distort ➪ Polar Coordinates, Photoshop presents a dialog box with two radio buttons, as shown in Figure 11-34. You can either map an image from rectangular to polar coordinates or from polar to rectangular coordinates.

Figure 11-34: In effect, the Polar Coordinates dialog box enables you to map an image onto a globe and view the globe from above.

All right, time for some global theory. The first image in Figure 11-35 shows a stretched detail of a world map. This map falls under the heading of a *Mercator projection*, meaning that Greenland is all stretched out of proportion, looking as big as the United States and Mexico combined.

The reason for this has to do with the way different mapping systems handle longitude and latitude lines. On a spherical globe, lines of latitude converge at the poles. On a Mercator map, they run absolutely parallel. Because the Mercator map exaggerates the distance between longitude lines as you progress away from the equator, it likewise exaggerates the distance between lines of latitude. The result is a map that becomes infinitely enormous at each of the poles.

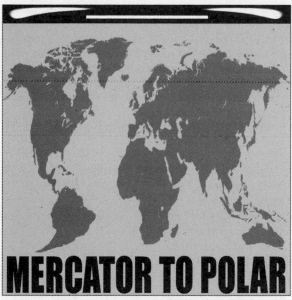

Figure 11-35: The world expressed in rectangular (top) and polar (bottom) coordinates. The decorative ornament atop the first image becomes a happy inhabitant of the North Pole in the second.

When you convert the map to polar coordinates (by selecting the Rectangular to Polar radio button in the Polar Coordinates dialog box), you look down on it from the extreme North or South Pole. This means that the entire length of the top edge of the Mercator map becomes a single dot in the exact center of the polar projection. The length of the bottom edge of the map wraps around the entire perimeter of the circle. The second example in Figure 11-35 shows the result. For this to be completely realistic, I would have to start with a map of just the top half of the globe, with the equator running along the bottom edge, but you get the idea. And as you can see, the Rectangular to Polar option is just the tool for wrapping text around a circle.

If you select the Polar to Rectangular option, the Polar Coordinates filter produces the opposite effect. Imagine for a moment that the image shown in the upper-left corner of Figure 11-36 is a fan spread out into a full circle. Now imagine closing the fan, breaking the hinge at the top, and spreading out the rectangular fabric of the fan. The center of the fan unfolds to form the top edge of the fabric, and what was once the perimeter of the circle is now the bottom edge of the fabric. Figure 11-36 shows two examples of what happens when you convert circular images from polar to rectangular coordinates. Color Plate 11-5 gives the results in full color, with a morphing effect thrown in for good measure.

Tip   The Polar Coordinates filter is a great way to edit gradations. After drawing a linear gradation with the gradient tool (as discussed in Chapter 6), try applying Filter ⇨ Distort ⇨ Polar Coordinates with the Polar to Rectangular option selected. (Rectangular to Polar just turns it into a radial gradation, sometimes with undesirable results.) You get a redrawn gradation with highlights at the bottom of the selection. Press Ctrl+F (⌘-F on the Mac) to reapply the filter to achieve another effect. You can keep repeating this technique until jagged edges start to appear. Then press Ctrl+Z (⌘-Z on the Mac) to go back to the last smooth effect.

Distorting with the Liquify command

The final essential distortion function isn't located under the Filter ⇨ Distort submenu. In fact, in many respects, it's not a filter at all. The Liquify command is more of a separate distortion utility that just happens to run inside Photoshop. It enables you to perform any number of distortions — you can warp, shift, twirl, expand, contract, and even copy pixels. It grants you multiple undos and redos before you apply the final effect. And unlike other distortion filters, which apply a uniform effect across a layer or selection, Liquify lets you modify pixels by pushing them around with a brush.

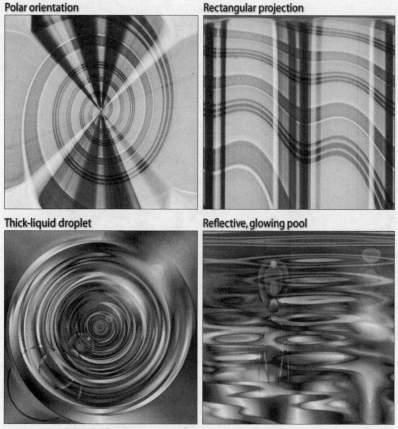

Polar orientation

Rectangular projection

Thick-liquid droplet

Reflective, glowing pool

Figure 11-36: Two familiar circular images (left) converted from polar to rectangular coordinates (right). The top example is simple enough that you might be able to predict the results of the conversion in your head. The lower example looks cool, but you'd need a brain extension to predict the outcome.

The result is a distortion filter that doubles as a powerful retouching tool. Consider the images in Figure 11-37. Raphael's original oil painting on left shows a lad who, in his day, was no doubt regarded as the perfect gentleman. But I worry that if he were to attempt to transport from his century to ours, his ways would be misunderstood. It might be his hair style, all curly on the sides but slicked down on top. Or it could be his languid expression, as if his delicate features had become lost in a torpid sea of big, round face. Then there's his raised pinky, which speaks perhaps too loudly of a young man who very much enjoys the feel of a dainty teacup in his hand. But whatever the culprit, I sense that this boy's presence would not receive warm applause and hearty handshakes were he to step onto a modern metropolitan thoroughfare or playground. In fact, there's the very real possibility that today's spirited teens would greet him with a vigorous beating and help themselves to his lunch money.

But thanks to the Liquify command, I was able to transform Raphael's masterwork into the swaggering, first-person-shooter playing, ill-informed but fiercely opinionated high school graduate that we see on right. Oh sure, he still wears his hair long and likes to dress like his grandmother, but like any good Catholic boy, he's got the chutzpah to pull it off. There's still a bit of action in that pinky, but you know he's only doing that because it seems to irritate people.

Figure 11-37: Using only the Liquify command, I was able to transform Raphael's 16th-century vision of St. Sebastian from a languid, matronly aristocrat (left) into a self-assured senior who managed to snag a part in the high school play (right).

English teachers and ex-spelling bee champions may notice my habitual misspelling of the word "liquefy" throughout this and the following pages. Rather than referring to the strictly accurate "Liquefy command," which would not match your screen, or the condescending "Liquify (sic) command," which gets old fast, I merely bend like the reed and adopt Adobe's spelling. Photoshop's engineers assure me that "liquify" is an acceptable alternative spelling, and that's good enough for me. But here's a head scratcher: If you use the type tool to enter the word "liquify" and then choose Edit ➪ Check Spelling, Photoshop will suggest *liquefy, liquefied, liquefier, liquefies,*

and *liquefying*, but it always wants to replace that second I with an E. So if "liquify" offends, my sincere apologies. The good news is that Photoshop agrees with you.

Liquify basics

To enter the world of Llquify (sic) — oh, sorry, I forgot, I said I wasn't going to do that — choose the Liquify command from the Filter menu or press the keyboard shortcut Ctrl+Shift+X (⌘-Shift-X on the Mac). Photoshop displays the immense Liquify image window shown in Figure 11-38, which tops even the Extract window (see Chapter 9) in its wealth of tools and options.

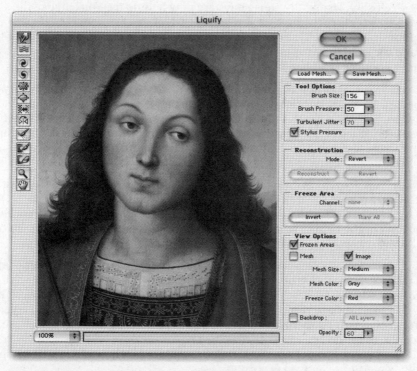

Figure 11-38: Choose Filter ⇨ Liquify to shove pixels around in your image by dragging them with a brush.

The miniature toolbox on the left side of the window contains eight tools for distorting your image. You drag or click with the tools as explained in the next section. (You can even select tools from the keyboard, as indicated by keys in parentheses.) But before you begin, here are a few basic facts:

✦ All tools respond to the Brush Size setting on the right side of the window. Press the right and left bracket keys, [and], to raise and lower the brush size from the keyboard by one pixel. This is a bit of a departure from Photoshop's standard painting tools, where pressing [or] routinely changes the brush size by 10 pixels or more. To change the brush size inside the Liquify window more rapidly, press and hold [or]. Throughout, your cursor reflects the approximate brush size. Note, however, that most distortions affect the pixels at the center of the cursor more quickly than those on the perimeter.

✦ The Brush Pressure option controls the impact of the tools; higher values produce more pronounced effects. If you work with a pressure-sensitive tablet, select the Stylus Pressure check box to make Photoshop adjust the tool pressure based on the amount of pressure you put on the pen stylus.

✦ Before Version 7, Photoshop distorted the image in the dialog box using screen-resolution data. This meant you couldn't zoom in to inspect your image more closely. Thankfully, those days are now behind us. You can use the standard shortcuts Ctrl+plus to zoom in and Ctrl+minus to zoom out (⌘-plus and minus on the Mac). There are no scroll bars, so press the spacebar to get the hand tool and drag the image inside the window. The Liquify window also provides zoom (Z) and hand (H) tools for your navigation pleasure.

✦ If you select a portion of your image prior to choosing Filter ⇨ Liquify, any deselected areas are considered *frozen*, which just means that they're unaffected by the distortion tools. You can freeze and then *thaw* — make available for editing — portions of the image as explained in the upcoming section, "Freezing and thawing pixels." You can even create partially frozen or thawed areas, which further limits the impact of the distortion tools.

✦ By default, frozen regions are covered with a red translucent coating, just like masked areas in the quick mask mode. You can change the appearance of the overlay by selecting a new color from the Freeze Color pop-up menu at the bottom of the Liquify window. If you don't want to see the coating at all, turn off the Frozen Areas check box.

✦ If your image contains layers, then you will see only the current layer against a transparent checkerboard background when you enter the Liquify window. To see other layers, turn on the Backdrop check box in the bottom right corner of the window. You can either view all layers, or select a specific layer from the nearby pop-up menu. The Opacity option controls how well you can see the other layers, but note that they never become fully opaque. Even at 100% Opacity, you get a 50/50 blend. Regardless of what you see, Photoshop lets you edit the active layer only.

✦ Select the Mesh check box to display gridlines on top of the image. You can use the gridlines as a guide if you want to apply very precise distortions. You can even apply your distortions while viewing only the grid by deselecting the Image check box. Set the grid size and color by selecting options from the Mesh Size and Mesh Color pop-up menus.

✦ You can save a distortion for later use by clicking the Save Mesh button. To use the mesh on a Mac or PC, the file name needs to end with the extension *.msh*. Click Load Mesh to load a distortion stored on disk. Note that Photoshop is smart enough to scale the mesh to fit the current image, so a mesh specifically designed for one image may turn out to be useful for another.

Caution

As with other Save buttons found throughout Photoshop's myriad dialog boxes, the Save Mesh button may strike you as the kind of nifty option that may prove useful every once in a while. But I strongly urge you to use it *every time you use the Liquify command.* Did you get that? Last thing you should do, right before you click the OK button, is click Save Mesh. Why? Because Photoshop does not automatically keep track of your previous Liquify settings. So if you spend 15 minutes or so working inside the Liquify window, click OK, and then decide that the distortion doesn't work exactly as well as you had hoped, you're left with two unpleasant options: choose Liquify and try to tweak the image further, which can result in incremental damage to the detail, or undo the previous operation and start over again. But if you saved the mesh, then you always have that last distortion to come back to. And the beauty is, a mesh is purely mathematical until it's applied. So you can use one mesh as a jumping off point for another without doing incremental damage. Pixels only get involved after you click OK. So don't forget, save your mesh, save your mesh, save your mesh.

Oh, and by the way, save your mesh.

The Liquify tools

Okay, so much for the basics. I can see that you're itching to start mucking around in your pixels. So here's how the distortion tools along the left side of the Liquify window work:

Warp tool (W): Drag to shove the pixels under your cursor around the image. At first, it may feel a lot like the smudge tool. But instead of smearing pixels, you're incrementally moving points in the mesh that distorts the image. The first example in Figure 11-39 shows a few large-scale changes made with a large brush and the default Pressure value. That's a lot of fun, of course, but it's only practical if you're trying to produce a caricature of Carrot Top, which, let's face it, no one wants to do. And yet, when used properly, the warp tool is the Liquify command's most practical tool. To create the second image, I used the warp tool set to a smaller brush size. But the biggest difference was in the length of my strokes. Instead of dragging, say, 10 to 20 pixels at a time, I dragged one or two pixels. As you can see, lots of little adjustments — in my case, somewhere in the neighborhood of 30 strokes — produces the best results.

Turbulence (A): New to Photoshop 7, the turbulence tool is a variation on the warp tool that distorts pixels in random directions as you drag. When you select this tool, Photoshop grants you access to a third Tool Options value labeled Turbulent Jitter. If the Brush Size value controls how many pixels are affected at a time and Brush Pressure controls the strength of the stroke, then Turbulent Jitter specifies just how much random variation is permitted. The minimum value of 1 causes the turbulence tool to behave much like the warp tool; a maximum value of 100 mixes pixels in all directions.

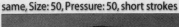
Warp tool, Brush Size: 100, Pressure: 50   same, Size: 50, Pressure: 50, short strokes

Figure 11-39: Making big strokes with the warp tool produces wacky results (left); short, careful drags give you more control (right). But you have to be patient. It took 6 strokes to make the big changes on left and about 30 to make the subtle changes on right—broadening the nose, expanding the lips, raising the chin, and lifting the eyelids and brows.

Figure 11-40 illustrates a few examples. For purposes of demonstration, all four images were created using a very large Brush Size, 400, and the maximum Pressure value, 100. For each image in the top row, I held the brush in place for 15 seconds. The random variations built up from one moment to the next. Not surprisingly, a Turbulent Jitter value of 30 produced a more dramatic effect than one of 10. But things become a bit more complicated when you drag with the tool. For each image in the bottom row, I created two brush-strokes from the bottom of the image to the top, once on the right side of the face and again on the left. This time, the higher Turbulent Jitter value produces more random fluctuation, but both images result in roughly equivalent amounts of distortion, as dictated by the fixed Size and Pressure values.

After all that, what good is the tool? When combined with low Turbulent Jitter values, I find it helpful for introducing small tremors or, if you prefer, turbulence into an image. At higher values, 30 and up, things go haywire very quickly.

 Twirl clockwise (R): Click or drag to spin pixels under your cursor in a clockwise direction, or to the right.

 Twirl counterclockwise (L): This tool spins pixels counterclockwise, or to the left.

Turbulence tool, Jitter: 10 …

Jitter: 30, hold 15 seconds on face

same, Jitter: 10 …

Jitter: 30, drag up both sides of face

Figure 11-40: Four variations created using the turbulence tool, twice holding the mouse in place (top row) and twice dragging with the tool on the left and right sides of the face (bottom row). Throughout, the Size and Pressure were set to 400 and 100, respectively.

Tip

You can toggle between the two twirl tools by pressing the Alt key (or Option on the Mac). When using the twirl clockwise tool, for example, pressing Alt twirls pixels counterclockwise. Best of all, you can press and release Alt in mid-drag to switch the twirl direction on-the-fly.

Figure 11-41 shows how I curled the lad's hair using the twirl tool. Throughout, I used just one tool and pressed Alt (or Option) to change the twirl direction. In the first image, I clicked and held in each of 15 locations to create 15 distinct curls. Then I clicked and dragged between the curls to fill in the hair and achieve a more credible effect.

Twirl tool, Size: 50, Pressure: 100; 15 curls   Second passes over same ground

Figure 11-41: Here I used the twirl tool to curl St. Sebastian's hair. I started by clicking and holding in 15 locations to rough in the basic curls (left). Then I clicked and dragged between those curls to fill in the effect (right).

Pucker (P): Drag with this tool to send pixels scurrying toward the center of the brush cursor. The effect is similar to applying the Pinch filter with a positive Amount value. If you mouse down instead of dragging, Photoshop steadily increases the extent of the distortion until you release the mouse button.

Bloat (B): When you drag or mouse down with this tool, pixels underneath the cursor move outward, like a stomach after too many trips to the buffet line. As is the case with the pucker tool, the longer you hold down the mouse button, the more bloating you get.

Tip

Press the Alt key (or Option on the Mac) to toggle between the pucker and bloat functions on the fly.

The pucker and bloat tools rock. In fact, I use them only slightly less frequently than the warp tool. They are particularly valuable for removing weight or adding bulk. For example, in the first image in Figure 11-42, I used the pucker tool exclusively to slim details in the image. I clicked and dragged around the jaw line. I also clicked and held on the nose and mouth and around the chin. The result is an increasingly feminine version of the one-time man. In the second image, I completed the operation by bloating the eyes, eyelids, and lips. I guess it just goes to show you — there aren't that many planets between men and women after all, just Pucker and Bloat.

Pucker tool, Size: 100, Pressure: 20   Press Alt (Option on Mac) to bloat eyes, lips

Figure 11-42: Armed with the pucker tool, I clicked and dragged along the jaw, chin, nose, and mouth (left) to reduce the masculine elements of what had become a fairly meaty guy. Then I pressed Alt (Option on the Mac) and moused down on the eyes, eyelids, and lips to fill out his feminine attributes.

Shift pixels (S): As you drag with this tool, pixels underneath the cursor move in a direction perpendicular to your drag. For example, if you drag down, pixels flow to the right. Drag straight up, and pixels move to the left. To reverse the direction of the pixels, press the Alt key (Option on the Mac).

At first, the shift pixels tool may seem unwieldy, resulting in dramatic and sometimes unpredictable movements. But you can control it using two techniques. First, reduce the Brush Pressure value to 25 or lower. Figure 11-43 illustrates the difference between drags performed using Pressure settings of 50 and 20. Second, try using it in a straight line by clicking at one point and Shift-clicking at another, as you might with Photoshop's painting and editing tools. The result is a neat line, great for reducing flab along straight elements, such as arms and legs.

Shift pixels tool, Size: 400, Pressure: 50   same, Pressure: 20

Figure 11-43: Here I dragged down on the left side of the face and up on the right to slim the face with the shift pixels tool. The first image used a Brush Pressure value of 50, which produces extreme results. For the second image, I reperformed the edits using a Pressure value of 20. I would still characterize the effect as extreme, but it's better.

 Reflection (M): The M, it appears, stands for mirror. Dragging with this tool creates a reflection, albeit one you might see in a funhouse mirror. As you drag, Photoshop copies pixels from the area perpendicular to the direction you move the cursor. So if you drag up, you clone pixels to the right of the cursor into the area underneath the cursor; drag down to clone pixels from left to right, as shown in Figure 11-44. Press the Alt key (Option on the Mac) to reflect from another direction on-the-fly.

After you drag with any of these tools, you can undo the effect by pressing Ctrl+Z (⌘-Z on the Mac). In Photoshop 7, you also have the option of multiple undos. Press Ctrl+Alt+Z to backstep through your operations (⌘-Option-Z on the Mac). Press Ctrl+Shift+Z (⌘-Shift-Z) to redo undone distortions. To learn how to go back in time nonsequentially and explore additional reversion options, read the section, "Reconstructing and reverting."

Freezing and thawing pixels

As I mentioned a few paragraphs ago, if you make a selection in your image, Photoshop automatically freezes unselected pixels when you enter the Liquify dialog box. This means that any distortions you apply don't affect them. You can't thaw these pixels from inside the Liquify window, but you can freeze and thaw other areas as you see fit.

Reflection tool, Brush Size: 400, drag up on the left, down on the right

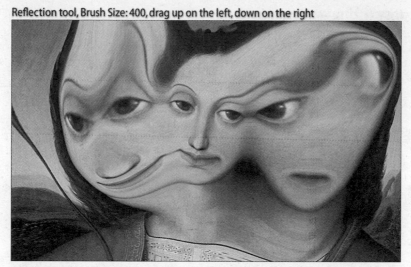

Figure 11-44: Using the reflection tool, I dragged up on the left side of the woman and down on her right side. Pixels are reflected in a clockwise direction.

To freeze a portion of your image from the Liquify window, you have two options:

 Freeze (F): Press F to select the freeze tool and then drag over areas that you want to protect. You can adjust the brush size and pressure as you can when working with the distortion tools. But in this case, the Brush Pressure setting determines how deeply frozen the pixels become. At anything less than 100 percent, the pixels become partially distorted when you drag over them with a distortion tool. If you set the pressure to 50 percent, the distortion is applied with half the pressure as in unfrozen areas.

Tip

If you created a mask channel before choosing the Liquify command, you can freeze the masked area by selecting the channel from the Channel pop-up menu.

Thaw (T): To thaw areas that you have frozen from inside the Liquify window, once again making them slaves to the distortion tools, paint over them with the thaw tool. The Brush Pressure setting affects this tool just as it does the freeze tool. To thaw the entire image, click the Thaw All button.

Tip

Just as you can inverse a selection outline or invert a mask in the quick mask mode, you can click the Invert button to quickly freeze any unfrozen pixels and thaw any frozen ones (except those frozen because they weren't among the selected pixels when Liquify was chosen).

Reconstructing and reverting

In the Reconstruction section of the Liquify window, you see a Mode pop-up menu plus two buttons, Reconstruct and Revert. You can use these options not only to revert an image to the way it looked before you applied a distortion, but also to redo a distortion so that it affects the image differently.

The following list outlines reversion possibilities:

✦ **Undo:** The Liquify window doesn't give you a History palette, but Ctrl+Alt+Z and Ctrl+Shift+Z still let you undo and redo sequences of operations. (That's ⌘-Option-Z and ⌘-Shift-Z on the Mac.)

✦ **Reset:** To return everything back to the way it was the very first time you opened the Liquify window, Alt-click (Win) or Option-click (Mac) the Cancel button, which changes to Reset. Not only do you restore your original image, you restore the Liquify window's default settings.

Believe it or not, Reset and other reversion techniques are undoable. I know, it's too cool. Just press Ctrl+Z (⌘-Z on the Mac) to get your edits back.

✦ **Revert:** To revert the image without resetting all values to their defaults, click the Revert button. This affects frozen and thawed areas alike.

Liquify also offers a handful of reconstruction techniques that are more controlled and more complex than the reversion options. By selecting an option from the Mode menu and then clicking the Reconstruct button or dragging with the reconstruct tool (E), you can reconstruct a distortion so that it extends from a frozen area into neighboring unfrozen pixels. The Reconstruct button affects all unfrozen areas, but dragging with the tool alters only pixels under your cursor, subject to the Brush Size and Pressure values.

All the reconstruction modes calculate the change to the image based on the warp mesh (grid). To get a better feel for how each mode works, deselect the Show Image check box, turn on Show Mesh and then apply a simple distortion across a portion of the grid. Freeze part of the distorted region and then keep an eye on the grid lines at the intersections between frozen and unfrozen regions as you try out each of the modes:

✦ **Revert:** The Revert mode restores unfrozen portions of the image to their original appearance, without regard to the borders between the frozen and unfrozen areas. Compare this to the Revert button, which restores frozen and unfrozen areas alike.

✦ **Rigid:** This mode extends the distortion only as needed to maintain right angles in the mesh where frozen and unfrozen areas meet. The result is unfrozen areas that look very much like they did originally but smoothly blend into the frozen areas.

✦ **Stiff:** Stiff interpolates the distortion so that the effect tapers away as you move farther from the boundary between the frozen and unfrozen areas.

✦ **Smooth, Loose:** These two modes extend the distortion applied to the frozen areas into the unfrozen areas. The Smooth setting tries to create smooth transitions between frozen and unfrozen areas. Loose shares more of the distortion from the frozen area with the unfrozen area. You'll achieve the most dramatic results when frozen and unfrozen areas have been distorted differently.

✦ **Displace, Amplitwist,** and **Affine:** The last three modes work exclusively with the reconstruct tool. Using these modes, you can apply one or more distortions that are in force at a specific reference point in the image. Click to set the reference point and then drag through unfrozen areas to distort them. Use the Displace mode to move pixels to match the displacement of the reference point; select Amplitwist to match the displacement, rotation, and scaling at the reference point; and choose Affine to match all distortions at the reference point.

Although Liquify certainly gives you plenty of ways to reconstruct distortions, predicting the outcome of your drags with the reconstruct tool can be nearly impossible. So be prepared to experiment. And if you don't get the results you want, remember, you can undo a reconstruction just as easily as a distortion.

Wrapping an Image around a 3D Shape

I've long maintained that three-dimensional drawing programs would catch on better if they were sold as plug-in utilities for Photoshop. Imagine being able to import DXF objects, add a line or two of text, move the objects around in 3D space, apply surface textures, and then render the piece directly to independent Photoshop layers. After that, you could change the stacking order of the layers, edit the pixels right there on the spot, or maybe even double-click a layer to edit it in 3D space. Virtually every digital artist working in 3D visits Photoshop somewhere during the process, so why not do the whole process in Photoshop and save everyone a few steps? Experienced artists would love it and novices would take to 3D in droves.

Frankly, my little fantasy isn't likely to take form any time soon. Photoshop would have to modify its plug-in specifications, and some brave programming team would have to spend a lot of time and money producing an aggressive suite of plug-ins. Even so, Adobe seems to share my dream. Filter ⇨ Render ⇨ 3D Transform lets you wrap an image around a three-dimensional shape. Although the drawing tools are rudimentary, the spatial controls are barely adequate, and the filter lacks any kind of lighting controls, 3D Transform is a first tentative step in the right direction.

Figure 11-45 shows exactly what 3D Transform can do. In each case, I started with the brick image shown in the upper-left corner of the figure. Then I wrapped the image around the three basic kinds of *primitives* permitted by the 3D Transform filter — a cube, a sphere, and a cylinder. 3D Transform lets you add points to the side of a cylinder, as I did to get the hourglass shape. You can also mix and match primitives, as the final example in Figure 11-45 illustrates.

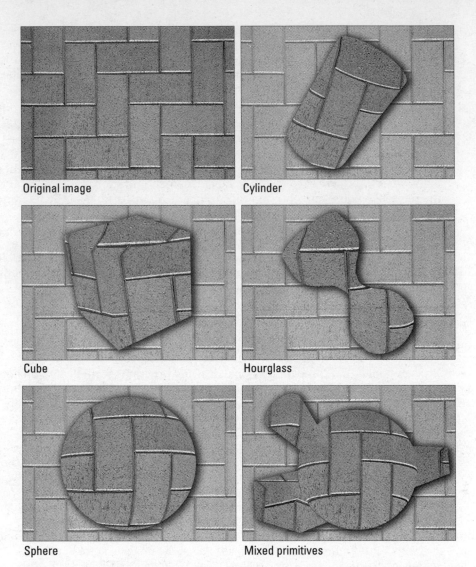

Original image

Cylinder

Cube

Hourglass

Sphere

Mixed primitives

Figure 11-45: The 3D Transform filter lets you wrap an image (upper left) around each of three basic primitives (cube, sphere, and cylinder), a modified cylinder (hourglass), or several shapes mixed together.

Notice that in each case, 3D Transform merely distorts the image. It has no effect on the brightness values of the pixels, nor does it make any attempt to light the shapes (which is why I'd prefer to see it under the Distort submenu as opposed to Render). I added the shadows using Layer ➪ Layer Style ➪ Drop Shadow.

Note

To be perfectly fair, 3D Transform is not the first three-dimensional plug-in for Photoshop. That honor went out years ago to the Series 2 Three-D Filter from Andromeda (*www.andromeda.com*). Series 2 offers features that Photoshop's 3D Transform plug-in lacks, including a wider range of numerical controls and lighting functions — but 3D Transform is easier to use.

Using the 3D Transform filter

Choose Filter ⇨ Render ⇨ 3D Transform to bring up the window shown in Figure 11-46. Less a dialog box than a separate editing environment, the 3D Transform window contains a wealth of tools and a preview area in which you can draw and evaluate the effect. There are a dozen tools in all, but they make a bit more sense if you regard them as members of five basic categories, itemized in the following sections. Like Photoshop's standard tools, you can select the 3D Transform tools from the keyboard (assuming that you have any headroom left to memorize the shortcuts). Shortcut keys are listed in parentheses.

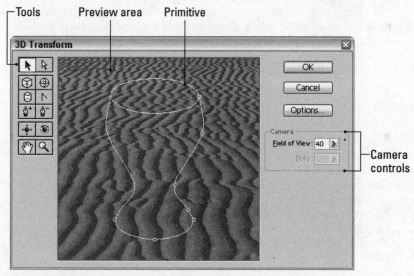

Figure 11-46: The 3D Transform dialog box contains a dozen tools that permit you to draw and edit three-dimensional shapes.

Primitive shape tools

Use one of the primitive shape tools to draw a basic 3D shape in the preview area. This is the shape around which 3D Transform will wrap the selected image.

 Cube (M): Use this tool to draw a six-sided box. Adobe selected *M* as the shortcut to match Illustrator, which uses *M* for its rectangle tool. And that *M* is based in turn on Photoshop's marquee tool.

Sphere (N): This tool creates a perfect sphere. Just remember, *N* follows *M*.

Cylinder (C): This cylinder tool draws your basic, everyday, dowel-like cylinders. But you can edit them to make lots of other shapes, as I explain in the upcoming "Cylinder editors" section. Finally we get a sensible shortcut: *C*.

Basic edit tools

The two arrow tools — the black select tool and the white direct select tool — enable you to change a shape by dragging it around or moving the points. Both tools work just like their counterparts in Illustrator:

 Select (V): Drag a shape with the black arrow tool to move the whole shape. If you know Illustrator, you already know about the weird V-key shortcut. If not, think of Photoshop's own move tool.

Direct select (A): Use the white arrow to move individual points. Dragging a point in a sphere resizes it. Dragging a point in a cube or a cylinder stretches or rotates the shape. Experiment and you'll quickly see how it works. (Unlike paths, dragged points have no control handles. All you have to work with are anchor points.) This tool has the same shortcut — A — as the direct selection tool in Photoshop's main toolbox. Of course, it's also the shortcut for the path selection tool. Oh, never mind.

Cylinder editors

The three path-edit tools are applicable exclusively to cylinders. Why? Because cylinders can be modified to create a whole family of tubular shapes. Throw the cylinder on the lathe and you can make an hourglass, a goblet, a cone — in short, any shape with radial symmetry and a flat top or bottom. To make these shapes, you use the following tools:

 Insert point (+): Click the right side of the cylinder — unless you turn it upside-down, in which case you click the left side — to add a point. Then drag the point with the white arrow tool to move both sides symmetrically. It's a virtual potter's wheel.

Remove point (–): Click a point you've added with the insert point tool to remove it. Don't click any of the square points that Photoshop put in there or the program will whine at you.

Convert point: The insert point tool adds circular smooth points that create continuous arcs in the side of the cylinder. To change the point to a sharp corner, click it with the convert point tool. Click again to change the point back to a smooth point.

Moving in 3D space

The next two tools are the most powerful and the hardest to use. They permit you to move the object in 3D space. When you switch to one of these tools, Photoshop renders the preview so you can see the image wrapped around the shape, as in Figure 11-47.

Pan camera (E): Drag the image to move it up, down, left, or right. How is this different than moving the primitive with the arrow tool? This time, you're moving the image in 3D space across your field of vision. (To be more precise, you're moving the camera—which is your window into the image—while the object remains still.) As you move the image to the left, you see more of its right side. Move it up, and you see its bottom.

Trackball (R): The trackball rotates the image in 3D space. Meanwhile, it's ultimately a 2D control—you can't move your cursor into or out of the screen; just up, down, and side-to-side—making it difficult to predict the outcome of a drag.

Tip

Inevitably, you'll end up exposing the back, empty side of a shape. When this happens, spin the shape by dragging against the grain. To spin the shape head over heels, for example, drag directly up or down. To spin the shape sideways, drag horizontally. Don't fret too much about moving through the 3D world; just watch how the program behaves when you move your mouse from one location to another. In time, you'll see some very simple patterns that you can exploit to your advantage.

Rendered preview

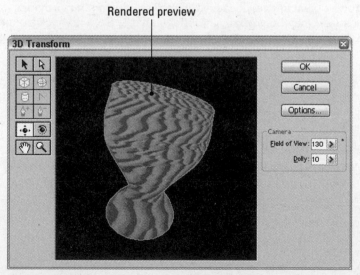

Figure 11-47: When you select either the pan camera or the trackball tool, Photoshop renders the image inside the preview area.

The camera controls

When you select the pan camera or trackball tool, Photoshop offers two Camera options on the right side of the dialog box. At first, the two options seem to do the same thing. A low value moves you in; a high value takes you out. But, in truth, they produce subtly different effects. Think of the Field of View option as a zoom lens and the Dolly option as a moving camera, with both operating at the same time. A low Field of View with a high Dolly results in shallow shapes. A high Field of View with a low Dolly (. . .well, 'ello, Dolly. . .) shrinks you to the size of a bug so that the depth is really coming at you.

Basic navigation

The last two tools in the 3D Transform dialog box are the standard hand and magnifying glass. They work just like their counterparts outside the 3D Transform dialog box:

 Hand (H): Drag the image to move it around inside the preview area. You can press either *H* or the spacebar to get this tool.

Zoom (Z): Click with this tool to zoom in, Alt-click (Win) or Option-click (Mac) to zoom out. When any other tool is selected, Ctrl+spacebar-click and Alt+spacebar-click (⌘-spacebar-click and Option-spacebar-click on the Mac) to zoom in and out.

Layer before you apply

When you press Enter (Win) or Return (Mac), Photoshop merges your new 3D shape with the original image. Because the 3D Transform filter provides no lighting controls, the shape may be virtually indistinguishable from its background, as Figure 11-48 makes abundantly clear. And that, dear friends, is a giant drag.

Figure 11-48: By default, the 3D Transform filter merges the 3D image into the original image, making for an extraordinarily subtle effect.

Tip

Luckily, you can force Photoshop to deliver the 3D shape on a separate layer. Here's what you do. First copy the image to a separate layer by dragging it onto the page icon at the bottom of the Layers palette. Then choose Filter ⇨ Render ⇨ 3D Transform and click the Options button inside the dialog box. Turn off the Display Background check box, spotlighted in Figure 11-49, and press Enter (Win) or Return (Mac).

Figure 11-49: Copy the image to a separate layer and turn off the Display Background check box to make the area outside the 3D shape transparent.

Not only will the 3D Transform filter restrict its efforts to the active layer, it will also make the area outside the 3D shape transparent, as in the first example of Figure 11-50. Then you can apply layer effects or other lighting techniques to distinguish the 3D shape from its background, as in the second example.

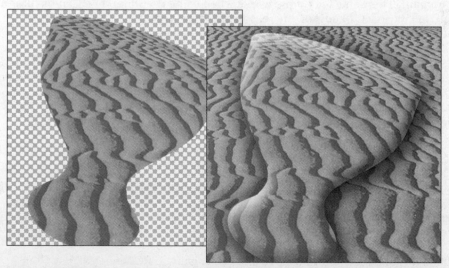

Figure 11-50: After applying the 3D shape to a separate layer (shown by itself at left), I used the Drop Shadow and Inner Bevel effects to add some fake volumetric lighting to my goblet (right).

Adding Clouds and Spotlights

The remaining five filters in the Render submenu produce lighting effects. You can use Clouds and Difference Clouds to create a layer of haze over an image. Lens Flare creates light flashes and reflections (as I mentioned earlier). Lighting Effects lights an image as if it were hanging on a gallery wall. You can even use the unremarkable Texture Fill to add an embossed texture to a piece embellished with the Lighting Effects filter.

Creating clouds

The Clouds filter creates an abstract and random haze between the foreground and background colors. Difference Clouds works exactly like layering the image, applying the Clouds filter, and selecting the Difference blend mode in the Layers palette.

Why on earth should Difference Clouds make special provisions for a single blend mode? Because you can create cumulative effects. Try this: Select a sky blue as the foreground color and then choose Filter ⇨ Render ⇨ Clouds. Ah, just like a real sky, huh? Now choose Filter ⇨ Render ⇨ Difference Clouds. It's like some kind of weird Halloween motif, all blacks and oranges. Press Ctrl+F (Win) or ⌘-F (Mac) to repeat the filter. Back to the blue sky. Keep pressing Ctrl+F (⌘-F on the Mac) over and over and notice the results. A pink cancer starts invading the blue sky; a green cancer invades the orange one. Multiple applications of the Difference Clouds filter generate organic oil-on-water effects. Figure 11-51 shows an example of Clouds and Difference Clouds.

Tip

To strengthen the colors created by the Clouds filter, press Shift when choosing the command. This same technique works when using the Difference Clouds filter as well. In fact, I don't know of any reason *not* to press Shift while choosing one of these commands, unless you have some specific need for washed-out effects.

Also, if you want to make a repeating texture using Clouds and Difference Clouds, make sure your image size is a square with pixel dimensions that are based on a power of two — something like 128 by 128 or 256 by 256 will work well. Your cloudy image will seamlessly tile, making it perfect for creating Web page backgrounds and the like.

Lighting an image

Photoshop ventures further into 3D drawing territory with the Lighting Effects filter. This very complex function enables you to shine lights on an image, color the lights, position them, focus them, specify the reflectivity of the surface, and even create a surface map.

Caution

The Lighting Effects filter is applicable exclusively to RGB images. Also, don't expect to be able to apply 3D lighting to shapes created with the 3D Transform filter. Sadly, the two filters share no common elements that would permit them to work directly with each other.

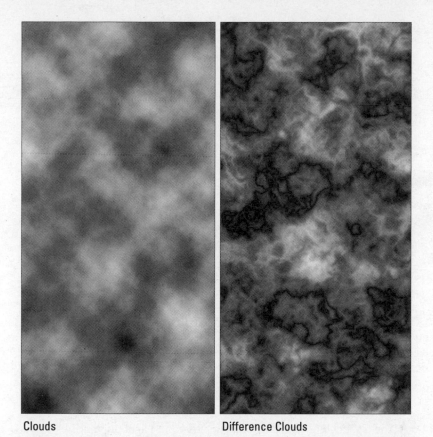

Clouds   Difference Clouds

Figure 11-51: Clouds (left) and Difference Clouds (right) each applied ten times in succession. Repeated applications of the Clouds filter always yield variations on the same theme; repeated applications of Difference Clouds soon result in roiling, plasma-like textures.

When you choose Filter ➪ Render ➪ Lighting Effects, Photoshop displays what is easily its most complex dialog box, as shown in Figure 11-52. The dialog box has two halves: one in which you actually position light with respect to a thumbnail of the selected image, and one that contains about a billion intimidating options.

No bones about it, this dialog box is a bear. The easiest way to apply the filter is to choose one of the predefined lighting effects from the Style pop-up menu at the top of the right side of the dialog box, see how it looks in the preview area, and — if you like it — press Enter or Return to apply the effect.

But if you want to create your own effects, you have to work a little harder. Here are the basic steps involved in creating a custom effect.

Preview area   Footprint   Handle   Color swatches

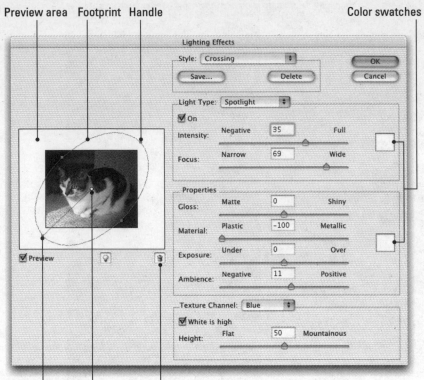

Hotspot   Focus point   Trash icon

Figure 11-52: The Lighting Effects dialog box enables you to light an image as if it were hanging in a gallery, lying on a floor, or perhaps resting too near a hot flame.

STEPS: Lighting an Image

1. **Drag from the light icon at the bottom of the dialog box into the preview area to create a new light source.** I call this area the *stage* because it's as if the image is painted on the floor of a stage and the lights are hanging above it.

2. **Select the kind of light you want from the Light Type pop-up menu.** It's just below the Style pop-up menu. You can select from Directional, Omni, and Spotlight:

   • Directional works like the sun, producing a general, unfocused light that hits a target from an angle.

   • Omni is a bare light bulb hanging in the middle of the room, shining in all directions from a center point.

   • Spotlight is a focused beam that is brightest at the source and tapers off gradually.

3. **Specify the color of the light by clicking the top color swatch.** You can also muck about with the Intensity slider bar to control the brightness of the light. If Spotlight is selected, the Focus slider becomes available. Drag the slider toward Narrow to create a bright laser of light; drag toward Wide to diffuse the light and spread it over a larger area.

4. **Move the light source by dragging at the *focus point* (if you've chosen a color for your light, the focus point appears as a colored circle in the preview area).** When Directional or Spotlight is selected, the focus point represents the spot at which the light is pointing. When Omni is active, the focus point is the actual bulb. (Don't burn yourself.)

5. **If Directional or Spotlight is active, you can change the angle of the light by dragging the hot spot.** The *hot spot* represents the location in the image that's liable to receive the most light. When you use a Directional light, the hot spot appears as a black square at the end of a line joined to the focus point. The same holds true when you edit a Spotlight; the confusing thing is that there are four black squares altogether. The light source is joined to the focus point by a line; the three *handles* are not.

To make the light brighter, drag the hot spot closer to the focus point. Dragging the hot spot away from the focus point dims the light by increasing the distance that it has to travel. It's like having a flashlight in the living room when you're in the garage — the light gets dimmer as you move away from it.

6. **With Omni or Spotlight in force, you can edit the elliptical footprint of the light.** When Omni is in force, a circle surrounds the focus point. When editing a Spotlight, you see an ellipse. Either way, this shape represents the *footprint* of the light, which is the approximate area of the image affected by the light. You can change the size of the light by dragging the handles around the footprint. Enlarging the shape is like raising the light source. When the footprint is small, the light is close to the image so it's concentrated and very bright. When the footprint is large, the light is high above the image, so it's more generalized.

When editing the footprint of a Spotlight, Shift-drag a handle to adjust the width or height of the ellipse without affecting the angle. To change the angle without affecting the size, Ctrl-drag (Win) or ⌘-drag (Mac) a handle.

7. **Introduce more lights as you see fit.**

Duplicate a light in the stage by Alt-dragging (Option-dragging on the Mac) its focus point. To delete the active light, drag the focus point onto the trash can icon below the preview area.

8. **Change the Properties and Texture Channel options as you see fit.** I explain these in detail after the steps.

9. **If you want to save your settings for future use, click the Save button.** Photoshop invites you to name the setup, which then appears as an option in the Style pop-up menu. If you want to get rid of one of the presets, select it from the pop-up menu and click the Delete button.

10. **Press Enter or Return to apply your settings to the image.**

That's almost everything. The only parts I left out are the Properties and Texture Channel options. The Properties slider bars control how light reflects off the surface of your image:

✦ **Gloss:** Is the surface dull or shiny? Drag the slider toward Matte to make the surface flat and nonreflective, like dull enamel paint. Drag the slider toward Shiny to make it glossy, as if you had slapped on a coat of lacquer.

✦ **Material:** This option determines the color of the light that reflects off the image. According to the logic employed by this option, Plastic reflects back the color of the light; Metallic reflects the color of the object itself. If only I had a bright, shiny plastic thing and a bright, shiny metal thing, I could check to see whether this logic holds true in real life (like maybe that matters).

✦ **Exposure:** I'd like this option better if you could vary it between Sun Block 65 and Melanoma. Unfortunately, the more prosaic titles are Under and Over — exposed, that is. This option controls the brightness of all lights like a big dimmer switch. You can control a single selected light using the Intensity slider, but the Exposure slider offers the added control of changing all lights in the stage (preview) area and the ambient light (described next) together.

✦ **Ambience:** The last slider enables you to add *ambient light*, which is a general, diffused light that hits all surfaces evenly. First, select the color of the light by clicking the color swatch to the right. Then drag the slider to cast a subtle hue over the stage. Drag toward Positive to tint the image with the color in the swatch; drag toward Negative to tint the stage with the swatch's opposite. Keep the slider set to 0 — dead in the center — to cast no hue.

The Texture Channel options enable you to treat one channel in the image as a *texture map*, which is a grayscale surface in which white indicates peaks and black indicates valleys. (As long as the White is high check box is selected, that is. If you deselect that option, everything flips, and black becomes the peak.) It's as if one channel has a surface to it. By selecting a channel from the pop-up menu, you create an emboss effect, much like that created with the Emboss filter except much better because you can light the surface from many angles at once and it's in color to boot.

Choose a channel to serve as the embossed surface from the pop-up menu. Then change the Height slider to indicate more or less Flat terrain or huge Mountainous cliffs of surface texture.

Figure 11-53 shows an image lit with a total of five spotlights, two from above and three from below. In the first example, I left the Texture Channel option set to None. In the second example, I selected the green channel as the surface map. And in the third example, I filled a separate mask channel with a bunch of white and black dollops using Filter ➪ Pixelate ➪ Pointillize and then I selected the mask from the Texture Channel pop-up menu in the Lighting Effects dialog box. The result is a wonderfully rough paper texture.

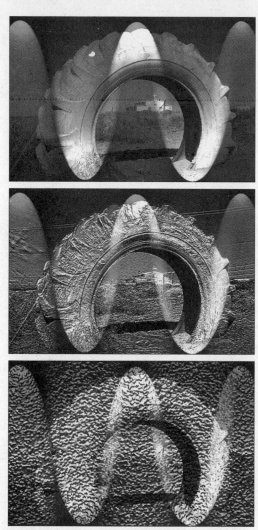

Figure 11-53: Not only can Lighting Effects enhance your images with simulated directional light, it can also be used to create textures.

✦   ✦   ✦

Layers, Objects, and Text

Working with Layers

Layers, Layers Everywhere

Layers started out as little more than their name implies —
sheets of pixels that you could edit and transform independently of each other. But since the feature was introduced
in Version 3, layers have become increasingly more sophisticated and complicated. Photoshop 4 forced you to embrace
the feature by creating a new layer every time you imported
an image; but it also rewarded you with floating *adjustment
layers* that let you correct colors without permanently affecting a single pixel (see Chapter 17). Photoshop 5 witnessed the
birth of layer effects, which included editable drop shadows,
glows, and edge bevels (see Chapter 14). Photoshop 6 permitted you to bundle and color-code layers into logical clusters
(this chapter), blend color channels independently of each
other (Chapter 13), and even add vector-based lines and
shapes (Chapter 14), not to mention object-oriented text
(Chapter 15).

In Photoshop 7, layers have generally maintained the status
quo, witnessing only a few modest enhancements. Mind you,
there's still room for improvement. For example, one day I hope
to see Photoshop integrate parametric effects, in which filters
such as Unsharp Mask and Motion Blur are fully editable,
interactive, and interchangeable, on the order of Adobe's full-
motion editor, After Effects. But in the meantime, Photoshop's
layers still provide us with a rewarding amount of freedom
and flexibility.

For those of you who are wondering what I'm talking about,
permit me to back up for a moment. The first and foremost
benefit of layers is that they add versatility. Because each layer
in a composition is altogether independent of other layers,
you can change your mind at a moment's notice. Consider the

top example in Figure 12-1. Here we see a promotional piece I created for my new video series, *Total Training for Adobe Photoshop 7*, in which I do not actually appear as a lovable robot named roboDeke. I created the top image one morning, utilizing the Layers palette to its fullest extent. Really, just about every element you see in the image is on a separate layer: the background, the motorcycle toy, the chains, each individual bunch of text, and even roboDeke himself. Satisfied with my work, I set it aside and took the rest of the day off.

The next morning, I checked out my multilayered masterpiece with fresh eyes, only to find that I felt it needed some improvement. Luckily, I had worked so extensively in layers, I was able to give my work an extensive overhaul, resulting in the true masterpiece you see at the bottom of Figure 12-1. I made innumerable changes, as reflected in the Layers palette shown in the figure: roboDeke has hair, antennae, and a much more substantial goatee, he's been shrunk and repositioned, the finger and arrow are gone from the image, many of the text elements have been restyled, the background is blurred, and so on. (In fact, there are more than 20 differences between the two images. Can you circle them all?)

Layers make it harder to make mistakes, they make it easier to make changes, and they expand your range of options. More than anything else, they permit you to restructure a composition and examine how it was put together after you assemble it. Layers can be very challenging to use or relatively simple. But whatever you do, don't shy away. If a layer might help, there's no reason not to add one. Layers are a big fact of life inside Photoshop, and it's important to know how to create, modify, organize, and exploit them to their full potential. And that's what this chapter is all about.

Sending a Selection to a Layer

To its credit, Photoshop lets you establish a new layer in roughly a billion ways. If you want to add a selected portion of one image to another image, the easiest method is to Ctrl-drag (Win) or ⌘-drag (Mac) the selection and drop it into its new home, as demonstrated in Figure 12-2. Photoshop makes you a new layer, lickety-split.

Be sure to Ctrl-drag (⌘-drag on the Mac) or use the move tool. If you merely drag the selection with the marquee, lasso, or wand, you drop an empty selection outline into the new image window. Also, be aware that pressing Ctrl (Win) or ⌘ (Mac) delivers the move tool. But if the pen, arrow, or shape tool is active, you get the arrow tool instead, which won't work for you. Press V to get the good old move tool and then try dragging again.

Figure 12-1: Thanks to the flexibility of layers, you can arrange a bunch of elements one way one moment (top) and quite differently the next (bottom). Layers let you modify a composition without sacrificing quality.

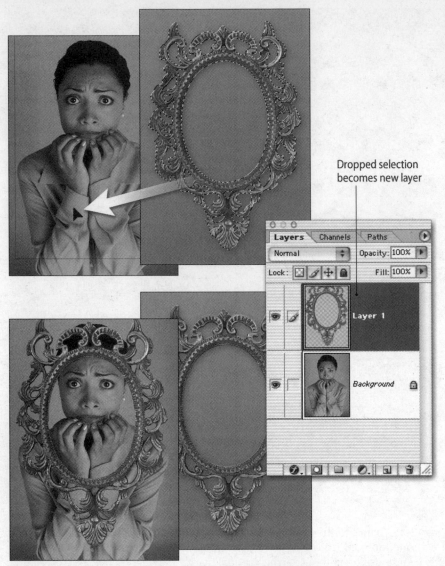

Figure 12-2: Ctrl-drag (Win) or ⌘-drag (Mac) a selected portion of an image and drop it into a different image window to introduce the selection as a new layer. As you can see in the Layers palette, the frame becomes a new layer in front of the frightened woman.

When you drop the selection, your selection outline disappears. Not to worry, though. Now that the image resides on an independent layer, the selection outline is no longer needed. You can move the layer using the move tool, as you would move a selection. You can even paint inside what was once the selection by selecting the first of the Lock buttons in the Layers palette. I explain both the move tool and the Lock buttons in greater detail throughout this chapter.

If you want to clone a selection to a new layer inside the same image window — useful when performing complex filter routines and color corrections — choose Layer ⇨ New ⇨ Layer Via Copy. Or press Ctrl+J (⌘-J on the Mac), as in Jump.

Other ways to make a layer

Those are only two of many ways to create a new layer in Photoshop. Here are a few others:

✦ Copy a selection (Ctrl+C or ⌘-C) and paste it into another image (Ctrl+V or ⌘-V). Photoshop pastes the selection as a new layer.

✦ If you want to relegate a selection exclusively to a new layer, choose Layer ⇨ New ⇨ Layer Via Cut or press Ctrl+Shift+J (⌘-Shift-J on the Mac). Rather than cloning the selection, Layer Via Cut removes the selection from the background image and places it on its own layer.

✦ To convert a floating selection — one which you've moved or cloned — to a new layer, press Ctrl+Shift+J (⌘-Shift-J on the Mac). The Shift key is very important. If you press Ctrl+J (Win) or ⌘-J (Mac) without Shift, Photoshop clones the selection and leaves an imprint of the image on the layer below.

✦ To create an empty layer — as when you want to paint a few brushstrokes without harming the original image — choose Layer ⇨ New ⇨ Layer or press Ctrl+Shift+N (⌘-Shift-N on the Mac). Or click the new layer icon at the bottom of the Layers palette (labeled in Figure 12-3).

✦ When you create a new layer, Photoshop positions it in front of the active layer. To create a new layer behind the active layer, Ctrl-click (Win) or ⌘-click (Mac) the new layer icon.

Incidentally, you can also create a new layer by choosing New Layer from the Layers palette menu. But as you can see in Figure 12-3, nearly all the palette commands are duplicated in the Layer menu. The only unique palette command is Palette Options, which lets you change the size of the thumbnails in front of the layer names. And you can do that more easily by right-clicking (Win) or Control-clicking (Mac) in the empty space below the layer names and choosing an option.

Tip

When you choose the Layer Via Copy or Layer Via Cut command or click the new layer icon, Photoshop automatically names the new layer for you. Unfortunately, the automatic names — Layer 1, Layer 2, and so on — are fairly meaningless and don't help to convey the contents of the layer.

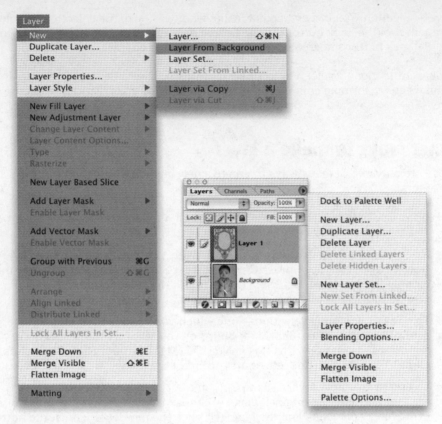

Figure 12-3: All but one of the commands in the Layers palette menu are duplicated in the Layer menu.

If you want to specify a more meaningful name, add the Alt (Win) or Option (Mac) key. Press Ctrl+Alt+J (⌘-Option-J on the Mac) to clone the selection to a layer, press Ctrl+Shift+Alt+J (⌘-Shift-Option-J on the Mac) to cut the selection, or Alt-click (Option-click on the Mac) the new layer icon to create a blank layer. In any case, you see the dialog box shown in Figure 12-4. Enter a name for the layer. If you like, you can also assign a color to a layer, which is helpful for identifying a layer name at a glance. Then press Enter or Return. (For now, you can ignore the other options in this dialog box.)

When creating a new layer from the keyboard, press Ctrl+Shift+Alt+N (⌘-Shift-Option-N on the Mac) to bypass the dialog box. Alt (Option on the Mac) works both ways, forcing the dialog box some times and suppressing it others. The only time it produces no effect is when pasting or dropping an image. Too bad—I for one would get a lot of use out of it.

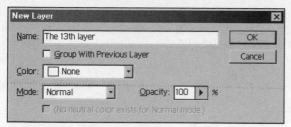

Figure 12-4: Press Alt (Win) or Option (Mac) to force the display of the New Layer dialog box, which lets you name the new layer.

For a long time in Photoshop, renaming a layer used to be as simple as double-clicking on its name in the Layers palette. Then Version 6 made a maddening break with history, bringing up the large and complex Layer Styles dialog box when you double-clicked a layer's name. To rename a layer, you had to Alt- or Option-double-click the layer's name. The huddled masses were not especially pleased with this change. So in Photoshop 7, things are more or less back to the way they were before Version 6. To rename a layer, just double-click on the name and type the new name directly into the Layers palette.

Duplicating a layer

To clone the active layer, you can choose Layer ⇨ Duplicate Layer. But that's the sucker's way. The more convenient way is to drag the layer name you want to clone onto the new layer icon at the bottom of the Layers palette.

To specify a name for the cloned layer or to copy the layer into another image, Alt-drag (Win) or Option-drag (Mac) the layer onto the new layer icon. Always the thoughtful program, Photoshop displays the dialog box shown in Figure 12-5. You can name the cloned layer by entering something in the As option box. To jettison the layer to some other open image, choose the image name from the Document pop-up menu. Or choose New and enter the name for an entirely different image in the Name option box, as the figure shows.

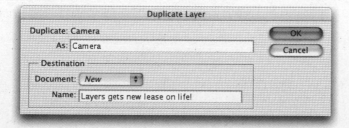

Figure 12-5: You can duplicate the layer into an entirely different image by Alt-dragging (Win) or Option-dragging (Mac) the layer onto the new layer icon in the Layers palette.

You can clone a layer by simply Ctrl-Alt-dragging (Win) or ⌘-Option-dragging (Mac) it inside the image window. This way, you clone the layer and reposition it in one operation. Just be sure not to begin your drag inside a selection outline; if you do, you create a floating selection.

Working with Layers

Regardless of how you create a new layer, Photoshop lists the layer along with a little thumbnail of its contents in the Layers palette. The new layer appears highlighted to show that it's active, and the layer's name appears in bold. The little paintbrush icon in front of the layer name also indicates an active layer.

To the left of the paintbrush icon is a column of eyeballs, which invite you to hide and display layers temporarily. Click an eyeball to hide the layer. Click where the eyeball previously was to bring it back and redisplay the layer. Whether hidden or displayed, all layers remain intact and ready for action.

To view a single layer by itself, Alt-click (Win) or Option-click (Mac) the eyeball icon before the layer name to hide all other layers. Alt-click (Win) or Option-click (Mac) in front of the layer again to bring all the layers back into view.

Switching between layers

You can select a different layer by clicking on its name in the Layers palette. This layer becomes active, enabling you to edit it. Note that only one layer may be active in Photoshop — you can't Shift-click to select and edit multiple layers, I'm sorry to say. So although you *can* link multiple layers and combine them into sets — as I explain in the section "Moving, Linking, and Aligning Layers" — you cannot select, paint, filter, or otherwise change the pixels on more than a single layer at a time.

If your image contains several layers — like the one back in Figure 12-1 — it might prove inconvenient, or even confusing, to switch from one layer to another in the Layers palette. Luckily, Photoshop offers a better way. With any tool, Ctrl+Alt-right-click (Win) or ⌘-Option-Control-click (Mac) an element in your composition to go directly to the layer containing the element. For example, Ctrl+Alt-right-clicking on the dangling hooks in Figure 12-1 would take me to the chains layer.

Why Ctrl+Alt-right-clicking (⌘-Option-Control-clicking on the Mac)? Here's how it breaks down:

✦ Ctrl (⌘ on the Mac) gets you the move tool. (If the move tool is already selected, you don't have to press Ctrl or ⌘; Alt-right-clicking or Option-Control-clicking works just fine.)

✦ Right-clicking (Win) or Control-clicking (Mac) alone brings up a shortcut menu. When you right-click or Control-click with the move tool — or Ctrl-right-click (⌘-Control-click on the Mac) with any other tool — Photoshop displays a pop-up menu that lists the layer that the image is on and any other layers in the image, as in Figure 12-6. (If a layer is completely transparent at the spot where you right-click or Control-click, then that layer name doesn't appear in the pop-up menu.) Select the desired layer to go there.

✦ The Alt key (Option key on the Mac) bypasses the pop-up menu and goes straight to the clicked layer.

Add them all together, and you get Ctrl+Alt-right-click (Win) or ⌘-Option-Control-click (Mac). It's a lot to remember, but believe me, it's a great trick once you get the hang of it.

Ctrl-right-click
(⌘-Control-click)

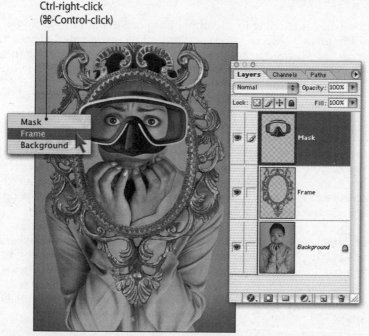

Figure 12-6: Ctrl-right-click (Win) or ⌘-Control-click (Mac) an image to view a pop-up menu. The menu lists all of the layers in the image that contain pixel data on the spot where you clicked.

If you'd prefer Photoshop to *always* go directly to the layer on which you click and avoid all these messy keyboard tricks, press V to select the move tool. The first check box in the Options bar is called Auto Select Layer. Turn it on. Now whenever you click a layer with the move tool — or Ctrl-click (⌘-click on the Mac) with some other tool — Photoshop goes right to that layer.

Switching layers from the keyboard

You can also ascend and descend the layer stack from the keyboard:

✦ **Alt+] (Win) or Option-] (Mac):** Press Alt+right bracket (Win) or Option-right bracket (Mac) to go to the next layer up in the stack. If you're already at the top layer, Photoshop takes you back around to the lowest one.

✦ **Alt+[(Win) or Option-[(Mac):** Press Alt+left bracket (Win) or Option-left bracket (Mac) to go down a layer. If the background layer is active, Alt+[or Option-[takes you to the top layer.

✦ **Shift+Alt+] (Win) or Shift-Option-] (Mac):** This takes you to the top layer in the image.

✦ **Shift+Alt+[(Win) or Shift-Option-[(Mac):** This activates the background layer (or the lowest layer if no background exists).

You have to pardon me for alluding to a feature out of order, but I thought you should note that Photoshop treats a closed folder in the Layers palette (better known as a *layer set*) as if it were a layer. So every one of these tricks skips to or over the set in a single bound. For the complete lowdown on layer sets, see the "Uniting layers into sets" section later in this same chapter.

Understanding transparency

Although the selection outline disappears when you convert a selection to a layer, no information is lost. Photoshop retains every little nuance of the original selection outline — whether it's a jagged border, a little bit of antialiasing, or a feathered edge. Anything that wasn't selected is now transparent. The data that defines the opacity and transparency of a layer is called the *transparency mask*.

To see this transparency in action, click the eyeball icon in front of the Background item in the Layers palette. This hides the background layer and enables you to view the new layer by itself. In Figure 12-7, I hid the background woman from Figure 12-6 to view the mask and frame on their own. The transparent areas are filled with a checkerboard pattern. Opaque areas look like the standard image, and translucent areas — where they exist — appear as a mix of image and checkerboard.

If the checkerboard pattern is hard to distinguish from the image, you can change the appearance of the pattern. Press Ctrl+K and then Ctrl+4 (⌘-K and then ⌘-4 on the Mac) to go to the Transparency & Gamut panel of the Preferences dialog box. Then edit the colors as you see fit (as explained back in Chapter 2).

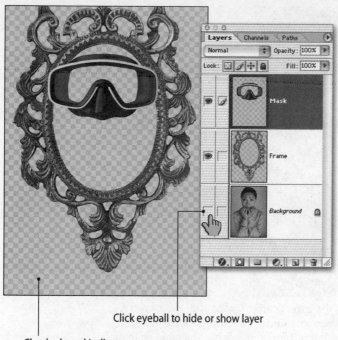

Click eyeball to hide or show layer

Checkerboard indicates transparency

Figure 12-7: When you hide the background layer, you see a checkerboard pattern that represents the transparent portions of the layer.

If you apply an effect to the layer while no portion of the layer is selected, Photoshop changes the opaque and translucent portions of the image but leaves the transparent region intact. For example, if you press Ctrl+I (⌘-I on the Mac) or choose Image ⇨ Adjustments ⇨ Invert, Photoshop inverts the image but doesn't change a single pixel in the checkerboard area. If you click in the left column in front of the Background item to bring back the eyeball icon, you may notice a slight halo around the inverted image, but the edge pixels blend with the background image as well as they ever did. In fact, it's exactly as if you applied the effect to a selection, as demonstrated in Figure 12-8. The only difference is that this selection is independent of its background. You can do anything you want to it without running the risk of harming the underlying background.

Only a few operations affect the transparent areas of a layer, and most of these are limited to tools. You can paint on transparent pixels to make them opaque. You can clone with the clone stamp or smear pixels with the edit tools. To send pixels back to transparency, paint with the eraser. All these operations change both the contents of the layer and the composition of the transparency mask.

Figure 12-8: Applying the Invert command to the mask layer inverts only the mask without affecting any of the transparent pixels. The woman and frame remain every bit as visible as ever.

Tip   You can fill all pixels also by pressing Alt+Backspace (Option-Delete on the Mac) for the foreground color and Ctrl+Backspace (⌘-Delete on the Mac) for the background color. To fill the pixels in a layer without altering the transparency mask, toss in the Shift key. Shift+Alt+Backspace (Shift-Option-Delete on the Mac) fills the opaque pixels with the foreground color; Ctrl+Shift+Backspace (⌘-Shift-Delete on the Mac) fills them with the background color. In both cases, the transparent pixels remain every bit as transparent as they ever were.

When a portion of the layer is selected, pressing plain old Backspace (Win) or Delete (Mac) eliminates the selected pixels and makes them transparent, revealing the layers below.

Note   Transparent pixels take up next to no space in memory, but opaque and translucent pixels do. Thus, a layer containing 25 percent as many pixels as the background layer takes up roughly 25 percent as much space. Mind you, I wouldn't let this influence how you work in Photoshop, but it is something to keep in mind.

Modifying the background layer

At the bottom of the layer stack is the *background layer*, the fully opaque layer that represents the base image. The background image is as low as you go. Nothing can be slipped under the background layer, and pixels in the background layer cannot be made transparent, unless you first convert the background to a floating layer.

To make the conversion, double-click the item labeled Background in the Layers palette. A dialog box appears. Enter a name for the new layer—Photoshop suggests Layer 0—and press Enter or Return. You can now change the order of the layer or erase down to transparency.

Tip

To skip the dialog box and accept Layer 0 as the new layer name, press Alt (Win) or Option (Mac) and double-click the Background item in the Layers palette.

In Figure 12-9, I converted the background woman to a layer. This particular image included a pre-drawn path that encircled the scared subject. I Ctrl-clicked (⌘-clicked on the Mac) on the path to convert it to a selection outline and then I pressed Ctrl+ Shift+I (⌘-Shift-I on the Mac) to reverse the selection. Finally, I pressed Backspace (Delete on the Mac) to erase the pixels outside the woman, as the figure demonstrates. From this point on, I can reorder all of the layers or add layers behind the woman. I can also introduce a new background layer.

Note

While InDesign 2.0 can easily handle layered Photoshop files complete with transparency, QuarkXPress 5.0 can't. As I mentioned in Chapter 8, if you want to export transparency to Quark, you must use a clipping path.

Convert background to independent layer

Ctrl-click (⌘-click) path to make selection

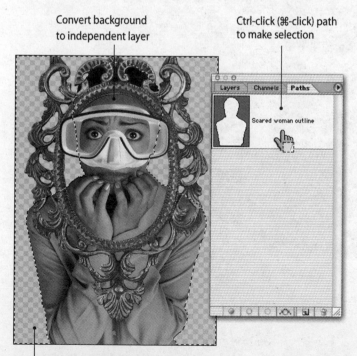

Inverse, delete selected pixels

Figure 12-9: After converting the image of the scared woman to a layer, I Ctrl-clicked (⌘-clicked on the Mac) on the path, inversed the selection, and pressed Backspace (Delete on the Mac) to reveal the transparent void below.

Tip

To convert the active layer to a background layer when there is currently no background layer, choose Layer ➪ New ➪ Background From Layer. It doesn't matter whether the active layer is at the top of the stack, the bottom, or someplace in between — Photoshop takes the layer and makes a new background out of it.

To establish a blank background, create an empty layer by pressing Ctrl+Shift+N (⌘-Shift-N on the Mac) and then choose Layer ➪ New ➪ Background From Layer. In Figure 12-10, I did just that. Next I used the Add Noise and Emboss filters to create a paper texture pattern (as I explain in Chapter 7). Then I selected the Frame layer and chose Layer ➪ Layer Style ➪ Drop Shadow to add a drop shadow that matched the contours of the frame. Finally, I switched back to the Scared Woman layer and gave our frightened friend a drop shadow as well. (I explain all there is to know about layer styles in Chapter 14.)

Create new background layer   Add drop shadows

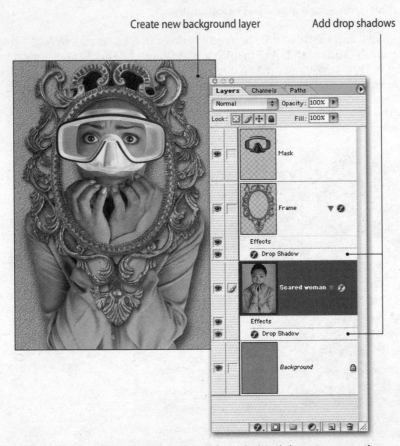

Figure 12-10: I added a background layer behind the woman and applied a paper texture and drop shadows to give my composition a little false depth.

Photoshop permits only one background layer per image. If an image already contains a background layer, the command Layer ⇨ New ⇨ Background From Layer changes to Layer From Background, which converts the background layer to a floating layer, as when you double-click the Background item in the Layers palette.

Reordering layers

What good are layers if you can't periodically change what's on the top and what's on the bottom? You can reorder layers in two ways. First, you can drag a layer name up or down in the scrolling list to move it forward or backward in layering order. The only trick is to make sure that the black bar appears at the point where you want to move the layer before you release the mouse button, as illustrated in Figure 12-11.

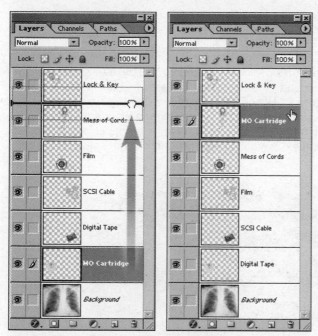

Figure 12-11: Drag a layer between two other layers to make the all-important black bar appear (left). Then release the mouse button to change the hierarchy of the layer (right).

The second way to reorder layers is to choose a command from the Layer ⇨ Arrange submenu. For example, choose Layer ⇨ Arrange ⇨ Bring Forward to move the active layer up one level; choose Layer ⇨ Arrange ⇨ Send to Back to move the layer to above the background layer.

You can move faster if you remember the following keyboard shortcuts:

✦ **Ctrl+Shift+] (Win) or ⌘-Shift-] (Mac):** Press Ctrl+Shift+right bracket (Win) or ⌘-Shift-right bracket (Mac) to move the active layer to the top of the stack.

✦ **Ctrl+Shift+[(Win) or ⌘-Shift-[(Mac):** This shortcut moves the active layer to the bottom of the stack, just above the background layer.

✦ **Ctrl+] (Win) or ⌘-] (Mac):** This nudges the layer up one level.

✦ **Ctrl+[(Win) or ⌘-[(Mac):** This nudges the layer down.

Note   You can neither reorder the background layer nor move any other layer below the background until you first convert the background to a floating layer, as explained in the previous section.

Automated matting techniques

When you convert an antialiased selection to a layer, you sometimes take with you a few pixels from the selection's previous background. These *fringe pixels* can result in an unrealistic outline around your layer that cries out, "This image was edited by a hack." For example, Figure 12-12 shows a magnified detail from one of my original attempts to add a pair of glasses to the frightened woman we met earlier in the chapter. Although the selection outline was accurate, I managed to retain a few white pixels around the edges, as you can see around the outline of the glasses.

Figure 12-12: This enlarged detail of the glasses against the face shows the fringe pixels left over from the white background that was originally behind the glasses.

You can instruct Photoshop to replace the fringe pixels with colors from neighboring pixels by choosing Layer ⇨ Matting ⇨ Defringe. Enter the thickness of the perceived fringe in the Width option box to tell Photoshop which pixels you want to replace.

To create the image shown in Figure 12-13, I entered a Width value of 1. But even at this low value, the effect is pretty significant here, leaving gummy edges in its wake.

Figure 12-13: Here I used the Defringe command set to a Width value of 1 to replace the pixels around the perimeter of the glasses layer with colors borrowed from neighboring pixels.

It's not that Defringe never works; sometimes the results will be satisfactory. But keep in mind that it's not available when a selection is active or when the layer has a layer mask or vector mask.

Photoshop provides two additional commands under the Layer ➪ Matting submenu: Remove Black Matte and Remove White Matte. Frankly, it's unlikely you'll have much call to use them, but here's the scoop:

✦ **Remove Black Matte:** This command removes the residue around the perimeter of a layer that was lifted from a black background.

✦ **Remove White Matte:** This command removes a white ring around a layer.

Adobe tells me that these commands were designed for compositing a scene rendered in a 3D drawing program against a black or white background. But for other purposes, they almost never work. For example, my glasses are a prime candidate for Remove White Matte — they originated from a white background — and yet it leaves behind more white pixels than the Defringe command set to its lowest setting.

Tip

If you encounter unrealistic edge pixels and the automatic matting commands don't solve your problem, you may be able to achieve better results by fixing the edges manually. First, switch to the layer that's giving you fits and Ctrl-click (Win) or ⌘-click (Mac) its name in the Layers palette. This creates a tight selection around the contents of the layer. Then choose Select ➪ Modify ➪ Contract and enter the width of the fringe in the Contract By option box. Next, choose Select ⇨ Feather or press Ctrl+Shift+D (⌘-Shift-D on the Mac) and enter half of the Contract By value in the Feather Radius option box. Finally, press Ctrl+Shift+I (⌘-Shift-I on the Mac) to inverse the selection and press Backspace (Delete on the Mac) to eliminate the edge pixels.

Figure 12-14 shows the results of applying this technique to my glasses. By setting the Contract command to 1 pixel and the Feather command to 0.5 pixels, I managed to remove the edges without harming the layer itself. And the effect looks better than that produced by the Defringe command (as you can compare for yourself with Figure 12-13).

Figure 12-14: Here I removed the edges manually using the Contract, Feather, and Inverse commands. This looks way better than anything Photoshop can do automatically.

Blending layers

Photoshop lets you blend layers like no other program in the business. In fact, Photoshop does such a great job that it takes me an entire chapter — Chapter 13 — to explain these options in detail. I offer this section by way of introduction so that you're at least aware of the basics. If you have bigger questions, Chapter 13 is waiting to tell all.

The Layers palette provides four basic ways to blend pixels between layers (see Figure 12-15). None of these techniques permanently changes as much as a pixel in any layer, so you can always return and reblend the layers at a later date.

✦ **The Opacity value:** Enter a value in the Opacity option box near the top of the Layers palette to change the opacity of the active layer or floating selection. If you reduce the Opacity value to 50 percent, for example, Photoshop makes the pixels on the active layer translucent, so the colors in the active layer mix evenly with the colors in the layers below.

If any tool other than a paint or an edit tool is active — including the selection and navigation tools — you can press a number key to change the Opacity value. Press 1 for 10 percent, 2 for 20 percent, up to 0 for 100 percent. Or you can enter a specific Opacity value by quickly pressing two number keys in a row. For example, press 3 and then 7 for 37 percent.

✦ **The Fill value:** A new arrival to the Layers palette in Version 7, the Fill option lets you adjust the opacity of pixel information in the layer — anything painted, drawn, or typed — without affecting the opacity of any layer effects that might be applied. For instance, if you have a text layer with the Drop Shadow layer effect applied, lowering the Fill slider to 0 fades out the text itself, leaving just the ghostly drop shadow behind. As with all other blending-related options, I explain the Fill option in excruciating detail in Chapter 13.

✦ **The blend mode pop-up menu:** Choose an option from the blend mode pop-up menu — open in Figure 12-15 — to mix every pixel in the active layer with the pixels below it, according to one of several mathematical equations. For example, when you choose Multiply, Photoshop really does multiply the brightness values of the pixels and then divides the result by 255, the maximum brightness value. Blend modes use the same math as the brush modes covered in Chapter 5 (in fact, the two terms are sometimes used interchangeably). But you can accomplish a lot more with blend modes, which is why I spend so much time examining them in Chapter 13.

As with Opacity, you can select a blend mode from the keyboard when a selection or navigation tool is active. Press Shift+plus to advance incrementally down the list; press Shift+minus to inch back up. You can also press Shift+Alt (Win) or Shift-Option (Mac) and a letter key to select a specific mode. For example, Shift+Alt+M (Shift-Option-M on the Mac) selects the Multiply mode. Shift+Alt+N (Shift-Option-N on the Mac) restores the mode to Normal.

✦ **Blending Options:** Choose Layer ⇨ Layer Style ⇨ Blending Options or double-click a layer thumbnail to display the Layer Style dialog box. The General Blending area of this dialog box provides access to a Blend Mode pop-up menu and an Opacity value, but it also offers a world of unique functions. As discussed in Chapter 13, you can hide one or more color channels, specify which colors are visible in the active layer, and force other colors to show through from the layers behind it. Select an item from the left-hand list to apply a layer style, as discussed in Chapter 14.

Although far short of the whole story, that should be enough to prepare you for anything I throw at you throughout the remainder of this chapter.

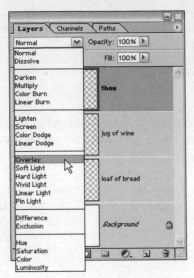

Figure 12-15: The blend mode pop-up menu and the Opacity and Fill option boxes enable you to mix layers without making any permanent changes to the pixels.

Fusing several layers

Although layers are wonderful and marvelous creatures, they have their price. Layers expand the size of an image in RAM and ultimately lead to slower performance. And as I noted in Chapter 3, only three formats — PDF, TIFF, and the native PSD format — permit you to save layered compositions.

In the interest of slimming the size of your image, Photoshop provides the following methods for merging layers together:

✦ **Merge Down (Ctrl+E or ⌘-E):** Choose Layer ⇨ Merge Down to merge a layer with the layer immediately below it. When generating screen shots, I use this command 50 or 60 times a day. I paste the screen shot into the image window, edit the layer as desired, and then press Ctrl+E (Win) or ⌘-E (Mac) to set it down. Then I can save the screen shot to the smallest possible file on disk, essential when e-mailing the screens to my editor.

If the active layer is part of a clipping group or is linked to other layers — two conditions I discuss later in this chapter — the Merge Down command changes to Merge Linked or Merge Group, respectively. Again, these commands use Ctrl+E (⌘-E on the Mac) as a shortcut. Merge Down is forever changing to suit the situation.

✦ **Merge Visible (Ctrl+Shift+E or ⌘-Shift-E):** Choose the Merge Visible command to merge all visible layers into a single layer. If the layer is not visible — that is, if no eyeball icon appears in front of the layer name — Photoshop doesn't eliminate it; the layer simply remains independent.

To create a merged clone, press Alt when applying either Layer ⇨ Merge Down or Layer ⇨ Merge Visible. Pressing Alt (Win) or Option (Mac) and choosing Merge Down — or pressing Ctrl+Alt+E (⌘-Option-E on the Mac) — clones the contents of the active layer into the layer below it. Pressing Alt (Win) or Option (Mac) and choosing Merge Visible — or pressing Ctrl+Shift+Alt+E (⌘-Shift-Option-E on the Mac) — copies the contents of all visible layers to the active layer.

More useful, I think, is the ability to copy the merged contents of a selected area. To do so, choose Edit ⇨ Copy Merged or press Ctrl+Shift+C (⌘-Shift-C on the Mac). You can then paste the selection into a layer or make it part of a different image.

✦ **Flatten Image:** This command merges all visible layers and throws away the invisible ones. The result is a single, opaque background layer. Photoshop does not give this command a keyboard shortcut because it's so dangerous. More often than not, you'll want to flatten an image incrementally using the two Merge commands.

Note that Photoshop suggests that you flatten an image when converting from one color mode to another by choosing a command from the Image ⇨ Mode submenu. You can choose not to flatten the image (by pressing D) but this may come at the expense of some of the brighter colors in your image. As discussed in Chapter 13, many of the blend modes perform differently in RGB than they do in CMYK.

Dumping layers

You can also merely throw a layer away: Drag the layer name onto the trash can icon at the bottom of the Layers palette. Or click the trash can icon to delete the active layer.

When you click the trash can icon, Photoshop displays a message asking whether you really want to toss the layer. To give this message the slip in the future, Alt-click (Win) or Option-click (Mac) the trash can icon.

Here's a much juicier tip for you: If the active layer is linked to one or more other layers (see the upcoming section "Linking layers"), you can delete all linked layers in one fell swoop by Ctrl-clicking (Win) or ⌘-clicking (Mac) the trash can icon.

Saving a flattened version of an image

As I mentioned, only three file formats — PDF, TIFF, and the native Photoshop format — save images with layers. If you want to save a flattened version of your image — that is, with all layers fused into a single image — in some other file format, choose File ⇨ Save As or press Ctrl+Shift+S (⌘-Shift-S on the Mac) and select the desired format from the Format pop-up menu. If you select a format that doesn't support layers — such as JPEG, GIF, or EPS — the program dims the Layers check box.

The Save As command does not affect the image in memory. All layers remain intact. And if you select the As a Copy check box with the Layers option deselected — which I recommend you do — Photoshop doesn't even change the name of the image in the title bar. It merely creates a flattened version of the image on disk. Nevertheless, be sure to save a layered version of the composition as well, just in case you want to edit it in the future.

Selecting the Contents of Layers

A few sections back, I mentioned that every layer (except the background) includes a *transparency mask*. This mask tells Photoshop which pixels are opaque, which are translucent, and which are transparent. Like any mask, Photoshop lets you convert the transparency mask for any layer — active or not — to a selection outline. In fact, you use the same keyboard techniques you use to convert paths to selections (as explained in Chapter 8) and channels to selections (Chapter 9):

✦ Ctrl-click (Win) or ⌘-click (Mac) an item in the Layers palette to convert the transparency mask for that layer to a selection outline.

✦ To add the transparency mask to an existing selection outline, Ctrl+Shift-click (Win) or ⌘-Shift-click (Mac) the layer name. The little selection cursor includes a plus sign to show you that you're about to add.

✦ To subtract the transparency mask, Ctrl+Alt-click (Win) or ⌘-Option-click (Mac) the layer name.

✦ And to find the intersection of the transparency mask and the current selection outline, Ctrl+Shift+Alt-click (Win) or ⌘-Shift-Option-click (Mac) the layer name.

If you're uncertain that you'll remember all these keyboard shortcuts, you can use Select ⇨ Load Selection instead. After choosing the command, select the Transparency item from the Channel pop-up menu. (You can even load a transparency mask from another open image if the image is exactly the same size as the one you're working on.) Then use the Operation radio buttons to merge the mask with an existing selection.

Selection outlines exist independently of layers, so you can use the transparency mask from one layer to select part of another layer. For example, to select the part of the background layer that exactly matches the contents of another layer, press Shift+Alt+[(Shift-Option-[on the Mac) to descend to the background layer and then Ctrl-click (Win) or ⌘-click (Mac) the name of the layer you want to match.

The most common reason to borrow a selection from one layer and apply it to another is to create manual shadow and lighting effects. After Ctrl-clicking (⌘-clicking on the Mac) on a layer, you can use this selection to create a drop shadow that precisely matches the contours of the layer itself. No messing with the brush or the lasso tool — Photoshop does the tough work for you.

Now, you might think with Photoshop's extensive range of layer styles, manual drop shadows and the like would be a thing of the past. After all, you have only to choose Layer ⇨ Layer Style ⇨ Drop Shadow and, bang, the program adds a drop shadow. But the old, manual methods still have their advantages. You don't have to visit a complicated dialog box to edit a manual drop shadow. You can reposition a manual shadow from the keyboard, and you can expand and contract a manual shadow with more precision than you can an automatic one.

On the other hand, the old ways aren't necessarily always better. A shadow created with the Drop Shadow command takes up less room in memory, it moves and rotates with a layer, and you can edit the softness of the shadow long after creating it.

What we have is two equally powerful solutions, each with its own characteristic pros and cons. Therefore, the wise electronic artist develops a working knowledge of both. This way, you're ready and able to apply the technique that makes the most sense for the job at hand.

Cross-Reference

The following sections explore manual drop shadows and highlights. For everything you ever wanted to know about the Layer Styles commands, read Chapter 14.

Drop shadows

In these first steps, I take the lovable, cuddly mutt shown in Figure 12-16 and make him cast a drop shadow on the sign beside him. Hopefully no one will be bitten or eaten as I demonstrate how the effect works.

Figure 12-16: A doggie in dire need of a drop shadow, if not Prozac.

STEPS: Creating a Drop Shadow

1. **Select the subject that you want casting the shadow.** In my case, I selected the pooch by painting a mask inside a separate mask channel. These days, I add a mask to nearly every image I create to distinguish the foreground image from its background. I converted the mask to a selection outline by Ctrl-clicking (⌘-clicking on the Mac) on the mask name in the Channels palette and then pressing Ctrl+tilde (⌘-tilde on the Mac) to switch back to the composite view.

2. **Send the image to a separate layer by pressing Ctrl+J (⌘-J on the Mac).** Now that the selection is elevated, you can slip in the drop shadow beneath it.

3. **Retrieve the selection outline for your new layer and apply it to the background layer.** To do this, Ctrl-click (Win) or ⌘-click (Mac) the new layer name (presumably Layer 1) and then press Shift+Alt+[(Shift-Option-[on the Mac) to switch to the background layer. Because I saved the mask to a separate channel, I could have instead Ctrl-clicked (Win) or ⌘-clicked (Mac) on the Mask item in the Channels palette to retrieve the selection. Or I could have pressed Ctrl+Alt+4 (⌘-Option-4 on the Mac).

4. **To create a softened drop shadow — indicative of a diffused light source — choose Select ➪ Feather or press Ctrl+Alt+D (⌘-Option-D on the Mac).** The Radius value you enter depends on the resolution of your image. As a general rule of thumb, dividing the resolution of your image by 20 can yield pretty good results. My image is 300 ppi, so I entered 15. (Note that this isn't a hard and fast rule; by all means, forget about the math if necessary and do what looks right.) Then press Enter or Return to soften the selection.

5. **Press Ctrl+J (⌘-J on the Mac) to send the feathered selection to a new layer.**

6. **Fill the feathered area with black.** If necessary, press D to make the foreground color black. Then press Shift+Alt+Backspace (Shift-Option-Delete on the Mac) to fill only the area inside the transparency mask. A slight halo of dark pixels forms around the edges of the image.

7. **Press Ctrl (Win) or ⌘ (Mac) with the arrow keys to nudge the shadow to the desired location.** I nudged the shadow 25 pixels to the left. (Press Ctrl+Shift+arrow key or ⌘-Shift-arrow key to nudge the shadow in 10-pixel increments.)

8. **Lower the Opacity setting.** If the shadow is too dark — black lacks a little subtlety — change the Opacity value in the Layers palette to change the opacity of the shadow. Or press M to make sure a selection tool is active and then press a number key to change the opacity. I typically press 7 (for 70 percent), but I'm probably in a rut. Figure 12-17 shows the results so far.

Tip

If you don't like a black drop shadow, you can make a colored one with only slightly more effort. Instead of filling the shadow with black in Step 6, select a different foreground color and press Shift+Alt+Backspace (Shift-Option-Delete on the Mac). For the best result, select a color that is the complementary opposite of your background color. Next, choose Multiply from the blend mode pop-up menu in the Layers palette or press Shift+Alt+M (Shift-Option-M on the Mac). This burns the colors in the shadow into those in the lower layers to create a darkened mix. Finally, press a number key to specify the opacity.

Figure 12-17: A manually created drop shadow behind this canine cutie gives a feeling of depth, yet ironically still a feeling of flatness.

9. **Press Ctrl+T (⌘-T on the Mac) to apply Free Transform, and distort the shadow.** Ctrl-drag (⌘-drag on the Mac) on the corner handles to create a perspective distortion, as seen in Figure 12-18. This is an advantage of creating a drop shadow manually; it can easily be resized, filtered, and transformed to suit your whim.

10. **Press Ctrl+Shift+X (⌘-Shift-X on the Mac) to tweak with the Liquify filter.** The shadow didn't line up perfectly with the dog's legs, so I applied the Liquify filter and nudged the shadow around until things looked perfect, as shown in Figure 12-19.

Figure 12-18: The Free Transform command lets me distort my drop shadow to give a sense of perspective and true depth to the image.

Figure 12-19: A drop-shadowed dog who truly belongs in this image, and knows it.

Halos

Creating a halo is similar to creating a drop shadow. The only differences are that you must expand the selection outline and fill the halo with white (or some other light color) instead of black. Again, doing this manually gives you a good deal of room for creative expression. The following steps tell all.

STEPS: Creating a Less-than-Heavenly Halo

1. **Follow Steps 1 through 3 of the preceding instructions.** You end up with a version of the selected image on an independent layer and a matching selection outline applied to the background image. (See, I told you this was like creating a drop shadow.)

2. **Expand the selection outline.** Unlike a drop shadow, which is offset slightly from an image, a halo fringes the perimeter of an image pretty evenly. You need to expand the selection outline beyond the edges of the image so you can see the halo clearly. To do this, choose Select ➪ Modify ➪ Expand. An Expand By option box greets you; I entered 30. (The maximum permissible value is 100; if you want to expand more than 100 pixels, you must apply the command twice.)

3. **Choose Select ➪ Feather and enter the same value you entered in the Expand By option box.** Again, I entered 30.

4. **Send the selection to a new layer.** Press Ctrl+J (Win) or ⌘-J (Mac).

5. **Fill the halo with white.** Assuming the background color is white, press Ctrl+ Shift+Backspace (⌘-Shift-Delete on the Mac). Figure 12-20 shows the result.

Figure 12-20: I selected, expanded, feathered, and filled our doggie buddy to make a halo.

From there, I applied the ZigZag filter, as shown in Figure 12-21. This created a nice spiraling effect to the glow. I then created another layer, used the brush tool and a Wacom tablet to paint in some lightning bolts shooting out from the glow, and finally dropped some fire from another image into the waiting mouth of Fido. Figure 12-22 shows demon dog in his full glory.

Figure 12-21: The ZigZag filter applies a swirling motion to the pooch's halo.

Tip   Incidentally, you needn't create a white halo any more than you must create a black drop shadow. In Step 5, set the background color to something other than white. Then select the Screen option from the blend mode pop-up menu in the Layers palette, thus mixing the colors and lightening them at the same time. If you don't like the effect, select a different background color and press Ctrl+Shift+Backspace (⌘-Shift-Delete on the Mac) again. With the halo on a separate layer, you can do just about anything to it without running the risk of harming the underlying original.

Figure 12-22: Halos don't always have to be used for an angelic effect.

Moving, Linking, and Aligning Layers

You can move an entire layer or the selected portion of a layer by dragging in the image window with the move tool. If you have a selection going, drag inside the marching-ants outline to move only the selection; drag outside the selection to move the entire layer.

As I mentioned in Chapter 8, you can temporarily access the move tool when some other tool is active by pressing Ctrl (Win) or ⌘ (Mac). To nudge a layer, press Ctrl or ⌘ with an arrow key. Press Ctrl+Shift (⌘-Shift on the Mac) to nudge in 10-pixel increments.

If part of the layer disappears beyond the edge of the window, no problem. Photoshop saves even the hidden pixels in the layer, enabling you to drag the rest of the layer into view later.

Note that this works only when moving all of a layer. If you move a selection beyond the edge of the image window using the move tool, Photoshop clips the selection at the window's edge the moment you deselect it. Also be aware: If you move your cursor outside the image window, Photoshop thinks you are trying to drag-and-drop pixels from one image to another and responds accordingly.

If you Ctrl-drag (Win) or ⌘-drag (Mac) the background image with no portion of it selected, you get an error message telling you that the layer is locked. If some portion of the layer is selected, however, you can drag that selected portion, and Photoshop will fill in the hole with the background color.

Tip   If you regularly work on huge images or your machine is old and kind of slow, Photoshop lets you speed the display of whole layers on the move. Press Ctrl+K and then Ctrl+3 (⌘-K and then ⌘-3 on the Mac) to display the Display & Cursors panel of the Preferences dialog box. Then select the Use Pixel Doubling check box. From now on, Photoshop will show you a low-resolution proxy of a selection or a layer as you drag (or Ctrl-drag) it across the screen.

Linking layers

Photoshop lets you move multiple layers at a time. To do so, you have to establish a *link* between the layers you want to move and the active layer. Begin by selecting the first layer in the Layers palette you want to link. Then click in the second column to the left of the other layer you want to link. A chain-link icon appears in front of each linked layer, as in Figure 12-23. This icon shows that the linked layers move in unison when you Ctrl-drag (Win) or ⌘-drag (Mac) the active layer. To break the link, click a link icon, which hides the icon.

Note   Dragging inside a selection outline moves the selection independently of any linked layers. Dragging outside the selection moves all linked layers at once.

┌─ Link icons
│ ┌─Link column

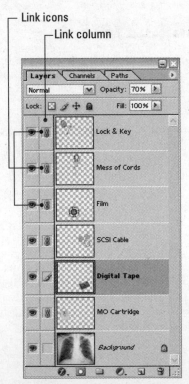

Figure 12-23: Click in the second column in the Layers palette to display or hide link icons. Here I've linked all layers except the background, so I can Ctrl-drag them in unison.

To link many layers at a time, drag up and down the link column. To unlink the active layer from all others, Alt-click (Win) or Option-click (Mac) the paintbrush icon in the link column.

You can also link layers with the shortcut menu. As you may recall from the "Switching between layers" section earlier in this chapter, you can bring up a pop-up menu listing the layers in an image by Ctrl-right-clicking (Win) or ⌘-Control-clicking (Mac) on an image element with any tool. Add Shift while selecting a layer from the pop-up menu to link or unlink the layer rather than switch to it.

But that's not all. If you're plum crazy for shortcuts, you can change the link state without visiting the pop-up menu by — drum roll please — Ctrl+Shift+Alt-right-clicking (Win) or ⌘-Shift-Option-Control-clicking (Mac) on an element in the image window. Okay, I love shortcuts, but even *I* have to admit that this one is gratuitous!

When you drag-and-drop linked layers into another document, all linked layers move together and the layers retain their original order — provided that you Ctrl-drag (⌘-drag on the Mac) the layers from one image window into another. If you want to move just one layer without its linked buddies, drag the layer name from the Layers palette and drop it into another open image window.

If you hold down Shift when dropping, Photoshop centers the layers in the document. If the document is exactly the same size as the one from which you dragged the layers, Shift-dropping lands the image elements in the same position they held in the original document. And finally, if something is selected in the document, the Shift-dropped layers are centered inside that selection.

Uniting layers into sets

Linking isn't the only way to keep layers together. You can toss multiple layers into a folder called a *set*. To create a new set, click the little folder icon along the bottom of the Layers palette. Or better yet, Alt-click (Win) or Option-click (Mac) the icon to display the dialog box shown in Figure 12-24. Here you can name the set, assign a color, and set the blend mode and opacity.

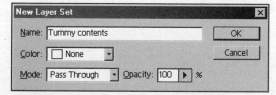

Figure 12-24: Choose the New Layer Set command or Alt-click (Option-click on the Mac) the folder icon at the bottom of the Layers palette to create and name a new set.

Notice in Figure 12-24 that a unique Mode option — Pass Through — appears when working with sets. This tells Photoshop to observe the blend modes assigned to the individual layers inside the set. By contrast, if you apply a different blend mode such as Multiply to the set, Photoshop overrides the blend modes of the layers inside the set and applies Multiply to them all.

The set appears as a folder icon in the Layers palette scrolling list. To add a layer to the set, drag the layer name in the scrolling list and drop it on the folder icon. Layers that are part of a set appear indented, as in Figure 12-25. The triangle to the left of the folder icon permits you to expand and collapse the layers inside the set, a tremendous help when working inside images with a dozen or more layers. Figure 12-26 shows the layers associated with a typical page design I put together for my Web site. When all sets are expanded, the layers don't even begin to fit on screen. But with sets collapsed, you can assess the construction of the image at a glance.

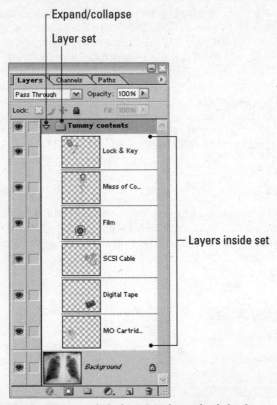

Figure 12-25: Click the triangle to the left of a folder icon to show or hide all layers in a set.

Figure 12-26: Sets are a terrific help when working with complex, multilayer compositions, such as this sketch for a Web page. Witness the difference between all sets expanded (first palette) and all sets collapsed (second).

Here are some other ways to create and modify sets:

✦ Double-click a set name to rename it.

✦ Drag a set name up or down the palette to move it.

✦ When a set is expanded, you can drag a layer within the set, move a layer out of the set, or drop a layer into the set at a specific position.

✦ Drag a set name and drop it onto another set to empty all layers from the former into the latter.

✦ To duplicate a set, drag it onto the folder icon at the bottom of the Layers palette.

✦ Hate dragging all those layers into a set? Wish you could move more than one at a time? Well, you can't, but you can do the next best thing. Link the layers that you want to make part of a set. Then choose New Set From Linked from the Layers palette menu. All linked layers go into the new set.

✦ In case you're wondering, *Can I link layers in different sets?*, yes, you can. If you're wondering, *Can I create sets within sets?*, no, you cannot. But don't be disillusioned, because the moment you ask, *Can I link sets together?*, I'll be happy to tell you that it's possible not only to link sets, but also to link individual layers to whole sets. You have to admit, it's pretty hot stuff.

✦ As you know, Ctrl-right-clicking (Win) or ⌘-Control-clicking (Mac) in the image window displays a shortcut menu of layers under the cursor. If one of the layers belongs to a set, Photoshop lists the set name along with the individual layer names in the shortcut menu. Select the set name to make it active.

Anytime a set name is active in the Layers palette, you can move or transform all layers in the set as a unit, much as if they were linked. To move or transform a single layer inside the set, just select that layer and go about your business as you normally would.

Locking layers

Photoshop lets you protect a layer by locking it. But unlike other programs that lock or unlock layers in their entirety, Photoshop lets you lock some attributes of a layer and leave other attributes unlocked. Figure 12-27 labels the four Lock buttons available in the Layers palette. Here's how they work:

✦ **Lock transparency:** This button protects the transparency of a layer. When selected, you can paint inside a layer without harming the transparent pixels. This option is so useful, I devote an entire section to the topic (see "Preserving transparency" later in this chapter).

✦ **Lock pixels:** Select this button to prohibit the pixels in the active layer from further editing. Paint and edit tools will no longer function, nor will filters or other pixel-level commands. However, you'll still be able to move and transform the layer as you like. Note that selecting this button dims and selects the Lock Transparency button as well. After all, if you can't edit pixels, you can't edit pixels — whether they're opaque or transparent.

✦ **Lock position:** Select this button to prevent the layer from being moved or transformed. You can, however, edit the pixels.

✦ **Lock all:** To lock everything about a layer, select this button. You can't paint, edit, filter, move, transform, delete, or otherwise change a hair on the layer's head. About all you can do is duplicate the layer, move it up and down the stack, add it to a set, and merge it with one or more other layers. This button is applicable to layers and sets alike.

Photoshop shows you which layers are locked by displaying two kinds of lock icons in the Layers palette. As labeled in Figure 12-27, the hollow lock means one attribute or other is locked; the filled lock means all attributes are locked.

Lock transparency
Lock pixels
Lock position
Lock all

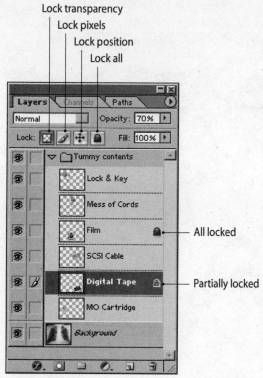

All locked

Partially locked

Figure 12-27: The Lock buttons at the top of the Layers palette let you protect certain layer attributes.

Using guides

Photoshop's grids and guides allow you to move selections and layers into alignment. When combined with the move tool, they also enable you to create rows and columns of image elements and even align layers by their centers.

To create a guide, press Ctrl+R (⌘-R on the Mac) or choose View ➪ Rulers to display the horizontal and vertical rulers. Then drag a guideline from the ruler. At the top of Figure 12-28, you can see me dragging a horizontal guide down from the top ruler. Then Ctrl-drag (Win) or ⌘-drag (Mac) layers and selections in alignment with the guide. In the bottom portion of the figure, I've dragged the MO disk, film reel, and tape — each on different layers — so they snap into alignment at their centers. (The reel has some film hanging from it, which Photoshop considers in calculating the center.) You'll know when the layer snaps into alignment because the move cursor becomes hollow, like the labeled cursor in Figure 12-28.

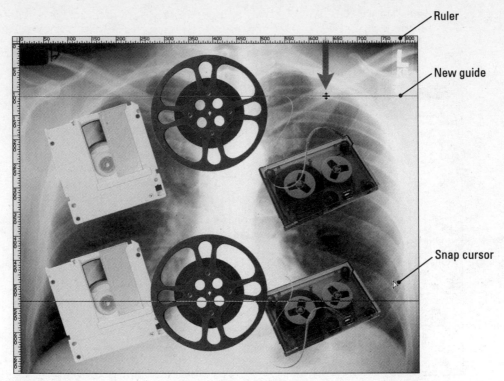

Figure 12-28: Drag from one of the rulers to create a guide (top) and then Ctrl-drag (⌘-drag on the Mac) each layer or selection into alignment (bottom).

Single-line text layers snap to horizontal guides a little differently than other kinds of layers. Rather than snapping by the top or bottom edge of the layer, Photoshop snaps a text guide by its baseline. It's just what you need when aligning type.

Guides are straightforward creatures. I mean, you don't have to study them rigorously for years to understand them — a few minutes are all you need to master them. But there are a few hidden treats:

✦ If you know the exact position where you want to put a guideline, choose View ➪ New Guide. After selecting from a horizontal or vertical guide, enter the location of the guide as measured from the ruler origin, by default in the upper-left corner of the image. For example, enter "1 in" for 1 inch, "2.5 cm" for 2.5 centimeters, or "200 px" for 200 pixels.

✦ You can show and hide all guides by choosing View ➪ Show ➪ Guides. When the guides are hidden, layers and selections do not snap into alignment.

✦ You can also hide or show guides by pressing Ctrl+H (Win) or ⌘-H (Mac). But be aware that this turns on or off the visibility of other elements, including the grid, selection outlines, paths, and notes. To hide and show just the guides, press Ctrl+semicolon (Win) or ⌘-semicolon (Mac).

You can preselect which items are hidden and shown with the Show Extras command by checking and unchecking the items in the View ➪ Show menu.

✦ You can turn a guide's snappiness on and off by choosing View ➪ Snap To ➪ Guides. You can also press Ctrl+Shift+semicolon (⌘-Shift-semicolon on the Mac). Again, this shortcut affects the snappiness of *everything*, including the grid, the perimeter of the image, and Web slices.

✦ To turn off the snappiness in the middle of a brushstroke or layer movement, press Ctrl (Win) or ⌘ (Mac) in mid drag. Release Ctrl or ⌘ to return to snappy land.

✦ As with all image elements in Photoshop, you can move a guide with the move tool. If some other tool is active, Ctrl-dragging (Win) or ⌘-dragging (Mac) also works.

✦ To lock all guides so you can't accidentally move them while you're trying to Ctrl-drag or ⌘-drag something else, press Ctrl+Alt+semicolon (⌘-Option-semicolon on the Mac) or choose View ➪ Lock Guides. Press Ctrl+Alt+semicolon again to unlock all guides.

✦ When moving a guide, press Shift to snap the guide to the nearest ruler tick mark.

✦ To convert a horizontal guide to a vertical guide or vice versa, press Alt (Win) or Option (Mac) while moving the guide.

✦ If you rotate your document in exact multiples of 90 degrees or flip the image horizontally or vertically, your guides also rotate unless they are locked.

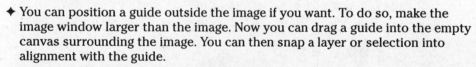

✦ You can position a guide outside the image if you want. To do so, make the image window larger than the image. Now you can drag a guide into the empty canvas surrounding the image. You can then snap a layer or selection into alignment with the guide.

✦ To edit the color of the guides, Ctrl-double-click (Win) or ⌘-double-click (Mac) a guide to display the Guides, Grid & Slices panel of the Preferences dialog box. You can also change the guides from solid lines to dashed. (This is only for screen purposes, by the way. Guides don't print.)

✦ On the Mac, guides are saved with any file format. But on the PC, the only formats that let you save guides are Photoshop (PSD), JPEG, TIFF, PDF, and EPS.

✦ If you don't need your guides anymore, choose View ➪ Clear Guides to delete them all in one housekeeping operation. I wish I had a command like this built into my office—I'd choose Maid ➪ Clear Dust and be done with it.

Automatic alignment and distribution

Photoshop lets you align and distribute layers by choosing commands from the Layer ➪ Align Linked or Distribute Linked submenus. The commands are straightforward—and familiar if you've ever used a drawing or page-layout program—but applying them is a little unusual. The following steps show you how to align two or more layers.

STEPS: Aligning Layers

1. **Select the layer that will serve as the anchor.** Whenever you align layers, one layer remains still and the others align to it. The active layer is the one that remains still.

2. **Link the layers you want to align.** Click in front of the layers you want to align to display the link icon. (And be sure to unlink any layers you *don't* want to align.) You have to link at least two layers — after all, there's no point in aligning a layer to itself.

3. **Choose a command from the Layer ➪ Align Linked submenu.** If you don't like the result, press Ctrl+Z (⌘-Z on the Mac) and try a different command.

You can likewise align linked layers to a selection outline. Just select an area inside any layer, and choose a command from the Layer ➪ Align To Selection submenu. The selection remains stationary, and the layers move into alignment.

The Distribute Linked commands space linked layers evenly. So it doesn't matter which of the linked layers is selected — the command distributes all linked layers with respect to the two horizontal or vertical extremes. Naturally, it's meaningless to space one or two layers, so the Distribute Linked commands require three or more layers to be linked. And there is no such thing as Distribute To Selection.

Photoshop also provides easy access to the align and distribute functions in the Options bar. Just select the move tool (by pressing V) and there they are. You can also align and distribute paths by selecting two or more paths with the black arrow tool and clicking buttons in the Options bar.

Setting up the grid

Photoshop offers a grid, which is a regular series of snapping increments. You view the grid — and turn it on — by choosing View ➪ Show ➪ Grid. Turn the snapping forces of the grid on and off by choosing View ➪ Snap To ➪ Grid.

You edit the grid in the Guides, Grid & Slices panel of the Preferences dialog box, which you can get to by pressing Ctrl+K and then Ctrl+6 (⌘-K and then ⌘-6 on the Mac) or by Ctrl-double-clicking (Win) or ⌘-double-clicking (Mac) on a guide. I explain how to use these options in the "Guides, Grid & Slices" section of Chapter 2. But for the record, you enter the major grid increments in the Gridline Every option box and enter the minor increments in the Subdivisions option box. For example, in Figure 12-29, I set the Gridline Every value to 50 pixels and the Subdivisions value to 5. This means a moved layer will snap in 10-pixel (50 pixels divide by 5) increments. Figure 12-29 also demonstrates each of the three Style settings.

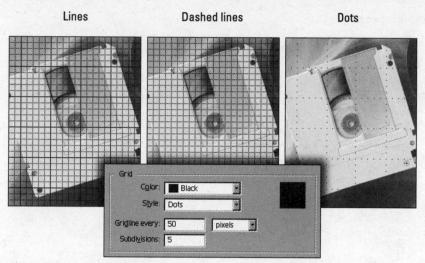

Figure 12-29: Here are the three styles of grid with the Grid Preferences options shown at the bottom.

Using the measure tool

The final method for controlling movements in Photoshop is the measure tool. Alt-click (Win) or Option-click (Mac) the eyedropper tool a couple of times to select the measure tool. Then drag from one point to another point in the image window. Photoshop itemizes the distance and angle between the two points in the Info palette. The measure tool is even smart enough to automatically display the Info palette if it's hidden.

From that point on, any time you select the measure tool, Photoshop displays the original measurement line. This way, you can measure a distance, edit the image, and press I (or Shift+I) to refer back to the measurement.

To measure the distance and angle between two other points, you can draw a new line with the measure tool. Or drag the endpoints of the existing measurement line.

Photoshop accommodates only one measurement line per document. But you can break the line in two using what Adobe calls the "protractor" feature. Alt-drag (Win) or Option-drag (Mac) on one of the endpoints to draw forth a second segment. The Info palette then measures the angle between the two segments. As demonstrated in Figure 12-30, the D1 item in the Info palette lists the length of the first segment, D2 lists the length of the second segment, and A tells the angle between the segments.

Measure cursor

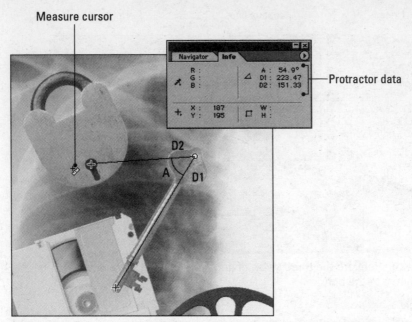

Protractor data

Figure 12-30: Here I measured the angle of the key, and then Alt-dragged (Option-dragged on the Mac) from the top endpoint to measure the angle between the key and lock.

The measure tool is great for straightening crooked layers. After drawing a line with the measure tool, choose Image ➪ Rotate Canvas ➪ Arbitrary. The Angle value automatically conforms to the A (angle) value listed in the Info palette. If you look closely, the two values may not exactly match. That's because Photoshop intelligently translates the value to between –45 and +45 degrees, which happens to be the simplest way to express any rotation. If you're unclear what I'm talking about, just trust in Photoshop. It does the math so you don't have to.

Applying Transformations

Photoshop treats some kinds of edits differently than others. Edits that affect the geometry of a selection or a layer are known collectively as *transformations*. These transformations include scaling, rotating, flipping, slanting, and distorting. (Technically, moving is a transformation as well.) Transformations are a special breed of edits inside Photoshop because they can affect a selection, a layer, multiple layers, or an entire image at a time.

Transforming the entire image

Photoshop has two varieties of transformations. Transformation commands that affect the entire image—including all layers, paths, channels, and so on—are listed in the Image menu. Those that affect layers and selected portions of layers are in the Edit menu, or in the case of selection outlines, in the Select menu.

The following list explains how to apply transformations to every pixel in an image, regardless of whether the image is selected or not:

✦ **Scale:** To resize the image, use Image ➪ Image Size. Because this command is one of the most essential low-level functions in the program, I covered it way back in Chapter 3.

✦ **Rotate:** To rotate the entire image, choose a command from the Image ➪ Rotate Canvas submenu. To rotate an image scanned on its side, choose the 90° CW or 90° CCW command. (That's clockwise and counterclockwise, respectively.) Choose 180° to spin the image on its head. To enter some other specific value, choose Image ➪ Rotate Canvas ➪ Arbitrary.

To fix a crooked scanned image, for example, select the measure tool from the eyedropper flyout in the toolbox (press I or Shift+I, depending on your preference settings, three times). Drag along what should be a vertical or horizontal edge in the image. If you like, note the A value in the Info palette. Then choose Image ➪ Rotate Canvas ➪ Arbitrary. Look, the Angle value is preset to the angle you just measured. That Photoshop, it's one sharp cookie. Press Enter or Return and the job's done.

Whenever you apply the Arbitrary command, Photoshop has to expand the canvas size to avoid clipping any of your image. This results in background-colored wedges at each of the four corners of the image. You need to either clone with the clone stamp tool to fill in the wedges or clip them away with the crop tool.

✦ **Flip:** Choose Image ➪ Rotate Canvas ➪ Flip Horizontal to flip the image so left is right and right is left. To flip the image upside down, choose Image ➪ Rotate Canvas ➪ Flip Vertical.

No command is specifically designed to slant or distort the entire image. In the unlikely event you're keen to do this, you'll have to link all layers and apply one of the commands under the Edit ➪ Transform submenu, as explained in the next section.

Transforming layers and selected pixels

To transform a layer or selection, you can apply one of the commands in the Edit ➪ Transform submenu. Nearly a dozen commands are here, all of which you can explore on your own. I'm not copping out; it's just that it's unlikely you'll use any of these commands on a regular basis. They aren't bad, but one command— Free Transform—is infinitely better.

With Free Transform, you can scale, flip, rotate, slant, distort, and move a selection or layer in one continuous operation. This one command lets you get all your transformations exactly right before pressing Enter or Return to apply the final changes.

To initiate the command, press Ctrl+T (⌘-T on the Mac) or choose Edit ➪ Free Transform. Photoshop surrounds the layer or selection with an eight-handle marquee. You are now in the Free Transform mode, which prevents you from doing anything except transforming the image or canceling the operation.

Note You can reach a slightly less-powerful version of Free Transform by selecting the move tool and turning on the Show Bounding Box check box in the Options bar. You don't have the ability to adjust the transformation origin, but it can be handy nevertheless.

Here's how to work in the Free Transform mode:

✦ **Scale:** Drag one of the eight square handles to scale the image inside the marquee. To scale proportionally, Shift-drag a corner handle. To scale about the central *transformation origin* (labeled in Figure 12-31), Alt-drag (Win) or Option-drag (Mac) a corner handle.

Tip By default, the origin is located in the center of the layer or selection. But you can move it to any place inside the image — even outside of the transformation box — by dragging it. The origin snaps to the grid and guides, as well as to the center or any corner of the layer.

✦ **Flip:** You can flip the image by dragging one handle past its opposite handle. For example, dragging the left side handle past the right side handle flips the image horizontally.

Tip If you want to perform a simple flip, it's generally easier to choose Edit ➪ Transform ➪ Flip Horizontal or Flip Vertical. Better yet, right-click (Win) or Control-click (Mac) in the image window and choose one of the Flip commands from the shortcut menu. Quite surprisingly, you can choose any of the shortcut menu commands while working in the Free Transform mode.

✦ **Rotate:** To rotate the image, drag outside the marquee, as demonstrated in the first example in Figure 12-31. Shift-drag to rotate in 15-degree increments.

✦ **Skew:** Ctrl-drag (Win) or ⌘-drag (Mac) a side handle (including the top or bottom handle) to slant the image. To constrain the slant, which is useful for producing perspective effects, Ctrl+Shift-drag (Win) or ⌘-Shift-drag (Mac) a side handle.

✦ **Distort:** You can distort the image by Ctrl-dragging (Win) or ⌘-dragging (Mac) a corner handle. You can tug the image to stretch it in any of four directions.

Tip To tug two opposite corner handles in symmetrical directions, Ctrl+Alt-drag (Win) or ⌘-Option-drag (Mac) either of the handles. I show this technique in the second example in Figure 12-31.

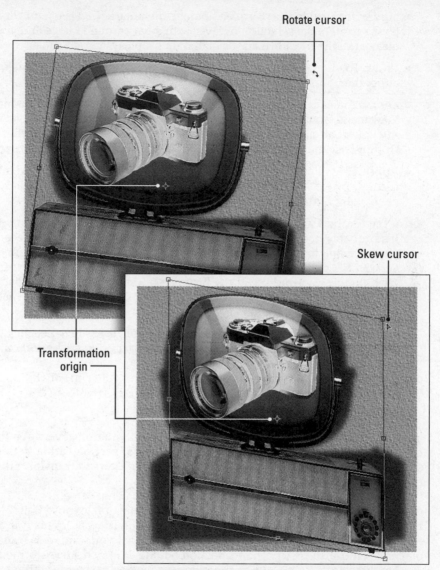

Rotate cursor

Skew cursor

Transformation origin

Figure 12-31: After pressing Ctrl+T (Win) or ⌘-T (Mac) to initiate the Free Transform command, drag outside the marquee to rotate the layer (top). You can also Ctrl+Alt-drag (Win) or ⌘-Option-drag (Mac) a corner handle to move the opposite corner handle symmetrically and skew the layer (bottom).

✦ **Perspective:** For a one-point perspective effect, Ctrl+Shift-drag (Win) or ⌘-Shift-drag (Mac) a corner handle. To move two points in unison, Ctrl+ Shift+Alt-drag (Win) or ⌘-Shift-Option-drag (Mac) a corner handle.

✦ **Move:** Drag inside the marquee to move the image. This is useful when you're trying to align the selection or layer with a background image and you want to make sure the transformations match up properly.

✦ **Undo:** To undo the last modification without leaving the Free Transform mode altogether, press Ctrl+Z (⌘-Z on the Mac).

✦ **Zoom:** You can change the view size by choosing one of the commands in the View menu. You can also use the keyboard zoom shortcuts: Ctrl+spacebar-click, Alt+spacebar-click, Ctrl+plus, or Ctrl+minus on the PC or ⌘-spacebar-click, Option-spacebar-click, ⌘-plus, or ⌘-minus on the Mac.

✦ **Apply:** Press Enter or Return to apply the final transformation and interpolate the new pixels. You can also double-click inside the marquee or click the checkmark button in the Options bar.

If the finished effect looks jagged after you've applied the transformation, it's probably because you selected Nearest Neighbor from the Interpolation pop-up menu in the Preferences dialog box. To correct this problem, press Ctrl+Z (⌘-Z on the Mac) to undo the transformation and then press Ctrl+K (⌘-K on the Mac) and select the Bicubic option from the General panel of the Preferences dialog box. Then press Ctrl+Shift+T (⌘-Shift-T on the Mac) to reapply the transformation.

✦ **Cancel:** To cancel the Free Transform operation, press Escape, click the "no" symbol button in the Options bar, or press Ctrl+period (⌘-period on the Mac).

To transform a clone of a layer or selected area, press Alt (Win) or Option (Mac) when choosing the Free Transform command or press Ctrl+Alt+T (⌘-Option-T on the Mac).

If no part of the image is selected, you can transform multiple layers at a time by first linking them, as described in the "Linking layers" section earlier in this chapter. For example, I could have linked the TV and camera layers to transform the two in unison back in Figure 12-31.

To replay the last transformation on any layer or selection, choose Edit ⇨ Transform ⇨ Again or press Ctrl+Shift+T (⌘-Shift-T on the Mac). This is a great technique to use if you forgot to link all the layers that you wanted to transform. You can even transform a path or selection outline to match a transformed layer. It's a handy feature. In fact, throw the Alt or Option key in there, and the transformation can be repeated on a clone of the selected layer.

Neither Free Transform nor any of the commands in the Edit ⇨ Transform submenu are available when a layer is locked, either with the Lock Position or Lock All button. If a transformation command appears dimmed, therefore, the Lock buttons are very likely your culprits.

Numerical transformations

To track your transformations numerically, display the Info palette (F8) before you apply the Free Transform command. Even after you initiate Free Transform, you can access the Info palette by choosing Window ⇨ Info. You can also track the numerical equivalents of your transformations in the Options bar. Shown in Figure 12-32, the Options bar contains a series of numerical transformation controls anytime you enter the Free Transform mode. These values not only reflect the changes you've made so far, but also permit you to further transform the selection or layer numerically.

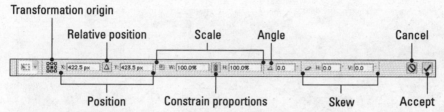

Figure 12-32: Normally, the options in the Options bar change only when you select a different tool, but choosing Free Transform adds a series of controls that permit you to transform a selection or layer numerically.

For the most part, the controls in the Options bar are straightforward. Click in the grid of nine squares to reposition the transformation origin. Use the X and Y values to change the location of the origin numerically. Click the triangular delta symbol to measure the movement relative to the transformation origin. Use the W and H values to scale the selection or layer. Click the link button to constrain the W and H values and resize the selection or layer proportionally. The angle value rotates; the H and V values skew.

I imagine most folks use the Options bar strictly for scaling and rotating. You'd need the spatial awareness of a NASA navigation system to predict a numerical slant.

Masking and Layers

Layers offer special masking options unto themselves. You can paint inside the confines of a layer as if it were a selection mask; you can add a special mask for a single layer; or you can group multiple layers and have the bottom layer in the group serve as the mask. Quite honestly, these are the kinds of thoughtful and useful functions I've come to expect from Photoshop. Although they're fairly complicated to use — you must be on your toes once you start juggling layer masks — these functions provide new realms of opportunities.

Preserving transparency

As you may recall, I mentioned we'd be talking more about the Lock Transparency button, first mentioned in the "Locking layers" section and labeled in Figure 12-33. Well, sure enough, the time has come to do exactly that. When selected, this button prevents you from painting inside the transparent portions of the layer. And although that may sound like a small thing, it is in fact the most useful Lock option of them all.

Lock transparency

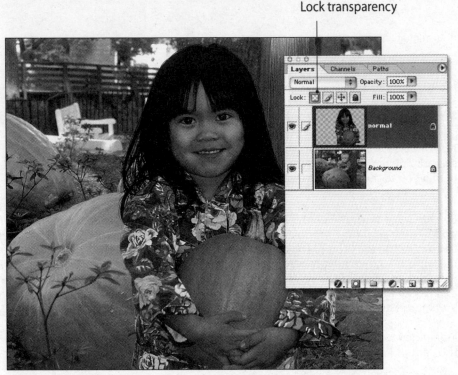

Figure 12-33: The Lock Transparency button enables you to paint inside the layer's transparency mask without harming the transparent pixels.

Suppose I want to paint inside the girl shown in Figure 12-33. If this were a flat, non-layered image, I'd have to draw a selection outline carefully around her. But there's no need to do this when using layers. Because the girl lies on a different layer than her background, a permanent selection outline tells Photoshop which pixels are transparent and which are opaque. This is the *transparency mask*.

The first example in Figure 12-34 shows the girl on her own with the background hidden. The transparent areas outside the mask appear in the checkerboard pattern. When the Lock Transparency button is turned off, you can paint anywhere you want inside the layer. Selecting the Lock Transparency button activates the transparency mask and places the checkerboard area off-limits.

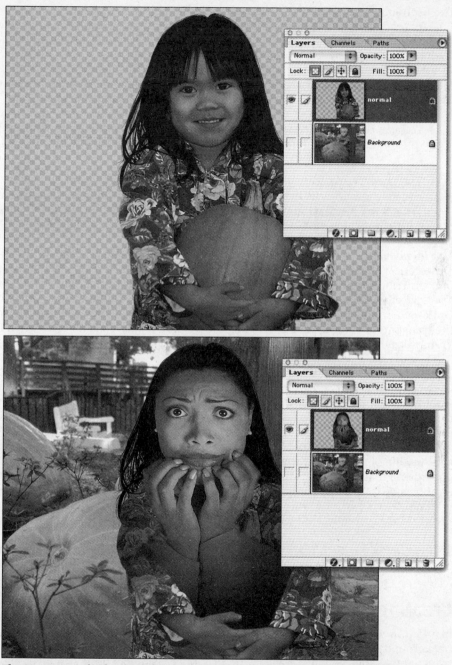

Figure 12-34: The layered girl as she appears on her own (top) and when the scared woman has been clone stamped in with the Lock Transparency button turned on (bottom).

The bottom image in Figure 12-34 shows what happens after I select Lock Transparency and use the clone stamp tool to paint in the scared woman image. I also painted in some black with the brush tool. Notice that no matter how much I painted, it never leaked out onto the background.

Although this enlightening discussion pretty well covers it, I feel compelled to share a few additional words about Lock Transparency:

Tip

✦ You can turn Lock Transparency on and off from the keyboard by pressing the standard slash character, /, right there on the same key with the question mark.

✦ The Lock Transparency option is dimmed when the background layer is active because this layer is entirely opaque. There's no transparency to lock, eh? (That's my impression of a Canadian explaining layer theory. It maybe needs a little polishing, but I think it's just aboot perfect.)

And finally, here's a question for all you folks who think you may have Photoshop mastered. Which of the brush modes (explained in Chapter 5) is the exact opposite of Lock Transparency? The answer is Behind. To see what I mean, turn off Lock Transparency. Then select the brush tool and choose the Behind brush mode in the Options bar. Now paint. Photoshop applies the foreground color exclusively *outside* the transparency mask, thus protecting the opaque pixels. So it follows, when Lock Transparency is turned on, the Behind brush mode is dimmed.

The moral? Behind is not a true brush mode and should not be grouped with the likes of Multiply and Screen in the Options bar. If you ask me, the better solution would be a Lock Opacity button in the Layers palette. Alas, Adobe's engineers seem to have better things to do, such as give us the Clear brush mode. But just because I've been complaining about the Behind "brush mode" for the last, oh gosh, *eight years* doesn't mean that I'm bitter or anything. Heavens no. I *like* to be ignored! It robs my life of meaning, which is precisely what I'm looking for. In fact, I think I'll go and end it all right now. And for what? A button. That's all I want. A small and unobtrusive button, possibly with a picture of my face on it and a little caption reading, "Yes, Deke, you were right. Can you ever forgive us for being such knot-heads?" I mean, really, am I asking too much?

So, in conclusion, Lock Transparency is your friend; Behind is the tool of Satan. Too bad so few things in the world are this black and white.

Creating layer-specific masks

In addition to the transparency mask that accompanies every layer (except the background), you can add a mask to a layer to make certain pixels in the layer transparent. Now, you might ask, "Won't simply erasing portions of a layer make those portions transparent?" The answer, of course, is yes. And, I hasten to add, that was a keen insight on your part. But when you erase, you delete pixels permanently. By creating a layer mask, you instead make pixels temporarily transparent. You can return several months later and bring those pixels back to life again simply by adjusting the mask. So layer masks add yet another level of flexibility to a program that's already a veritable image-editing contortionist.

To create a layer mask, select the layer you want to mask and choose Layer ⇨ Add Layer Mask ⇨ Reveal All. Or more simply, click the layer mask icon at the bottom of the Layers palette, as labeled in Figure 12-35. A second thumbnail preview appears to the left of the layer name, also labeled in the figure. A second outline around the preview shows the layer mask is active.

Tip If the second outline is hard to see, check the icon directly to the right of the layer's eye icon. If the icon is a paintbrush, the layer and not the mask is active. If the icon is a square with a little dotted circle, the mask is active.

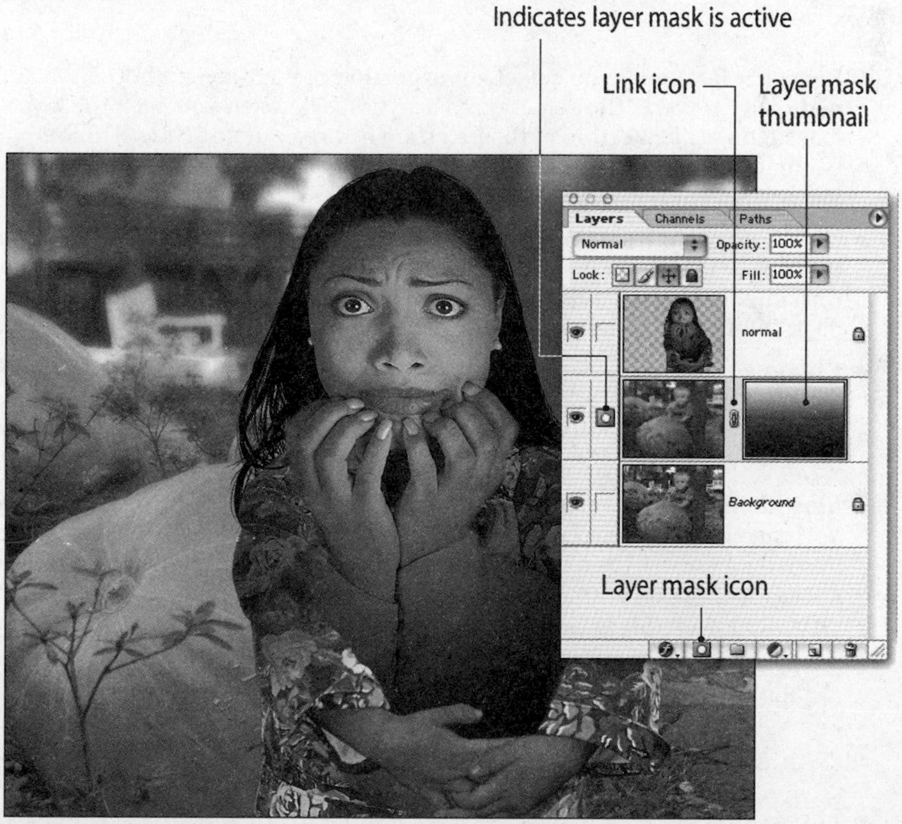

Indicates layer mask is active

Link icon

Layer mask thumbnail

Layer mask icon

Figure 12-35: The black area in the layer mask (which you can see in the thumbnail view in the Layers palette) translates to transparent pixels in the layer.

To edit the mask, simply paint in the image window. Paint with black to make pixels transparent. Because black represents deselected pixels in an image, it makes these pixels transparent in a layer. Paint with white to make pixels opaque.

Thankfully, Photoshop is smart enough to make the default foreground color in a layer mask white and the default background color black. This ensures that painting with the brush makes pixels opaque, whereas painting with the eraser makes them transparent, just as you would expect.

In Figure 12-35, I floated the background to a new layer, applied Gaussian Blur with a Radius of 8 pixels, and drew a simple white to black gradient in the layer mask using the gradient tool. The result was a fading blur, so that the farthest away elements appear the least in focus. If I decide I want the fade to be more abrupt, not to worry. I merely drag a shorter distance in the layer mask with the gradient tool.

Photoshop goes nuts in the layer mask department, adding lots of bells and whistles to make the function both convenient and powerful. Here's everything you need to know:

✦ **Reveal Selection:** If you select some portion of your layer, Photoshop automatically converts the selection to a layer mask when you click the layer mask icon at the bottom of the palette. The area outside the selection becomes transparent. (The corresponding command is Layer ➪ Add Layer Mask ➪ Reveal Selection.)

✦ **Hide Selection:** You can also choose to reverse the prospective mask, making the area inside the selection transparent and the area outside opaque. To do this, choose Layer ➪ Add Layer Mask ➪ Hide Selection. Or better yet, Alt-click (Win) or Option-click (Mac) the layer mask icon in the Layers palette.

✦ **Hide everything:** To begin with a black mask that hides everything, choose Layer ➪ Add Layer Mask ➪ Hide All. Or press Ctrl+D (⌘-D on the Mac) to deselect everything and then Alt-click (Win) or Option-click (Mac) the layer mask icon.

✦ **View the mask:** Photoshop regards a layer mask as a layer-specific channel. You can actually see it listed in italics in the Channels palette. To view the mask on its own — as a black-and-white image — Alt-click (Win) or Option-click (Mac) the layer mask thumbnail in the Layers palette. Alt-click (Win) or Option-click (Mac) again to view the image instead.

✦ **Layer mask rubylith:** To view the mask as a red overlay, Shift+Alt-click (Win) or Shift-Option-click (Mac) the layer mask icon. Or simply press the backslash key, \, which is above the Enter key (Return key on the Mac).

After you have both layer and mask visible at once, you can hide the mask by pressing \, or you can hide the layer and view only the mask by pressing the tilde key (~). So many alternatives!

✦ **Change the overlay color:** Double-click the layer mask thumbnail to access the Layer Mask Display Options dialog box, which enables you to change the color and opacity of the rubylith.

✦ **Turn off the mask:** You can temporarily disable the mask by Shift-clicking on the mask thumbnail. A red *X* covers the thumbnail when it's disabled, and all masked pixels in the layer appear opaque. Click the thumbnail to put the mask back in working order.

✦ **Switch between layer and mask:** As you become more familiar with layer masks, you'll switch back and forth between layer and mask quite frequently, editing the layer one minute and editing the mask the next. You can switch between layer and mask by clicking on their respective thumbnails. As I mentioned, look to the icon to the right of the eye icon to see whether the layer or the mask is active.

Tip

You can also switch between layer and mask from the keyboard. Press Ctrl+tilde (Win) or ⌘-tilde (Mac) to make the layer active. Press Ctrl+\ (Win) or ⌘-\ (Mac) to switch to the mask.

✦ **Link layer and mask:** A little link icon appears between the layer and mask thumbnails in the Layers palette. When the link icon is visible, you can move or transform the mask and layer as one. If you click the link icon to turn it off, the layer and mask move independently. (You can always move a selected region of the mask or layer independently of the other.)

✦ **Convert mask to selection:** As with all masks, you can convert a layer mask to a selection. To do so, Ctrl-click (Win) or ⌘-click (Mac) the layer mask icon. Throw in the Shift and Alt (Win) or Option (Mac) keys if you want to add or subtract the layer mask with an existing selection outline.

✦ **Apply mask to set:** You can also apply a mask to a set of layers. Just select the set and click the layer mask icon. The mask affects all layers in the set. If a layer in the set contains its own mask, no worries; Photoshop's smart enough to figure out how to mix them together. For another method of masking multiple layers, see the section "Masking groups of layers," coming up soon.

When and if you finish using the mask—you can leave it in force as long as you like—you can choose Layer ⇨ Remove Layer Mask. Or just drag the layer mask thumbnail to the trash can icon. Either way, an alert box asks whether you want to discard the mask or permanently apply it to the layer. Click the button that corresponds to your innermost desires.

Pasting inside a selection outline

One command, Edit ⇨ Paste Into (Ctrl+Shift+V or ⌘-Shift-V), creates a layer mask automatically. Choose the Paste Into command to paste the contents of the Clipboard into the current selection, so that the selection acts as a mask. Because Photoshop pastes to a new layer, it converts the selection into a layer mask. But here's the interesting part: By default, Photoshop turns off the link between the layer and the mask. This way, you can Ctrl-drag (Win) or ⌘-drag (Mac) the layer inside a fixed mask to position the pasted image.

Once upon a time in Photoshop, there was a command named Edit ➪ Paste Behind. (Or something like that. It might have been Paste in Back. My memory's a little hazy.) The command (whatever its name) pasted a copied image in back of a selection. Although the command is gone, its spirit still lives. Now you press Alt (Win) or Option (Mac) when choosing Edit ➪ Paste Into. Or just press Ctrl+Shift+Alt+V (⌘-Shift-Option-V on the Mac). Photoshop creates a new layer with an inverted layer mask, masking away the selected area.

Masking groups of layers

About now, you may be growing fatigued with the topic of layer masking. But one more option requires your immediate attention. You can group multiple layers into something called a *clipping group*, in which the lowest layer in the group masks the others. Where the lowest layer is transparent, the other layers are hidden; where the lowest layer is opaque, the contents of the other layers are visible.

Despite the similarities in name, a clipping group bears no relation to a clipping path. That is, a clipping group doesn't allow you to prepare transparent areas for import into QuarkXPress and the like.

There are two ways to create a clipping group:

✦ Alt-click (Win) or Option-click (Mac) the horizontal line between any two layers to group them into a single unit. Your cursor changes to the group cursor labeled in Figure 12-36 when you press Alt (Win) or Option (Mac); the horizontal line becomes dotted after you click. To break the layers apart again, Alt-click (Win) or Option-click (Mac) the dotted line to make it solid.

✦ Select the higher of the two layers you want to combine into a clipping group. Then choose Layer ➪ Group with Previous or press Ctrl+G (⌘-G on the Mac). To make the layers independent again, choose Layer ➪ Ungroup or press Ctrl+Shift+G (⌘-Shift-G on the Mac).

Figures 12-36 and 12-37 demonstrate two steps in a piece of artwork I created for *Macworld* magazine. I had already created some text on an independent layer using the type tool (the subject of Chapter 15), and I wanted to fill the text with water. So I added some photographs I shot of a swimming pool to a layer above the text, as shown in Figure 12-36. Then I combined text and pool images into a clipping group. Because the text was beneath the water, Photoshop masked the pool images according to the transparency mask assigned to the text. The result is a water pattern that exactly fills the type, as in Figure 12-37.

Group cursor

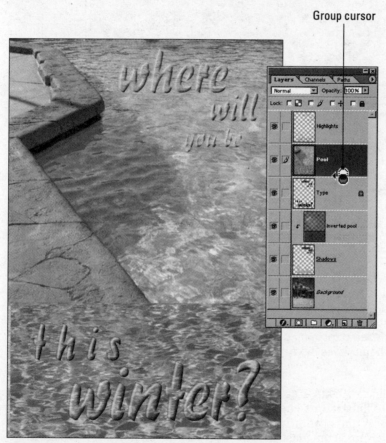

Figure 12-36: Alt-click (Win) or Option-click (Mac) the horizontal line between two layers to group them.

Clipping group

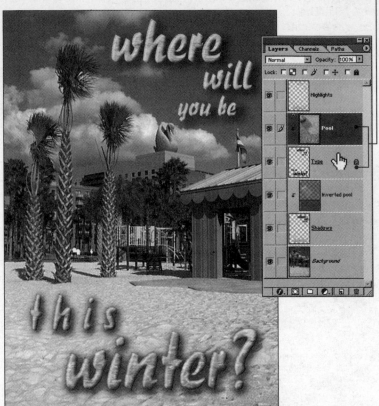

Figure 12-37: After combining pool water and type layers into a single clipping group, Photoshop applies the type layer's transparency mask to the pool layer.

Note   If you're familiar with Illustrator, you may recognize this clipping group metaphor as a relative to Illustrator's clipping mask. One object in the illustration acts as a mask for a collection of additional objects. In Illustrator, however, the topmost object in the group is the mask, not the bottom one. So much for consistency.

✦   ✦   ✦

The Wonders of Blend Modes

It's High Time to Blend, Friend

When recording artist Paul Simon first asserted that there must be 50 ways to leave your lover, I couldn't help but think he was inflating the number a little. I mean, some of the methods he proposed were pretty flimsy. Does it really help Gus to get on a bus? Won't he just have to come back later for a clean shirt and a change of underwear? And when he cautions Roy not to be coy, Simon seems to be more interested in rhyming than providing concrete, helpful suggestions. In the end, the premise simply doesn't hold up. Between Jack, Stan, Roy, Gus, and Lee, Simon gets around to delivering a scant five ways to leave your lover, just 10 percent the number promised. What happened to Just take a pill, Phil; don't be a slob, Bob; and show her the door, Thor? And how about the ladies? Might not Sue, Beth, and Anne benefit from some help in leaving their lovers as well?

Don't get me wrong, I love the song. But I think the songwriter might have had an easier time of it if he had decided to list the many ways you can combine and compare differently colored pixels in Photoshop. Forget 50, there must be 50 thousand! Just give it a nudge, Smudge; flutter and sway, Wave; give layers the purge, Merge — Clone Stamp yourself free. Granted, it would have failed commercially, but assuming Simon managed no more than his trademark 10 percent, the song could have filled seven albums.

Here we are, hundreds of pages into the book, and we've seen how you can smear and blur pixels, trace and sharpen pixels, distort and transform pixels, select pixels using other pixels, layer pixels in front of pixels, compare a pixel to its neighbors, copy pixels from one location to another, and much, much more. Any time that you edit, retouch, mask, composite, or filter an image, you're actually breeding the image with itself or with another image to create a new and unique offspring. Did I say 50 thousand? I meant 50 million!

And yet, despite all that we've seen so far, we're not even close to finished. Consider the subject of this chapter, *blend modes*, one of the most alluring experiments in Photoshop's great genetics laboratory. Alternatively known as *transfer modes* and *calculations*, blend modes permit you to mix the color of a pixel with that of every pixel in a straight line beneath it. A single blend mode can be as powerful as a mask, a filter, and a retouching tool combined. Best of all, it's temporary. As long as one image remains layered in front of another, you can replace one calculation with another as easily as you change a letter of text in a word processor.

To appreciate the most rudimentary power of blend modes, consider Figure 13-1. The first image shows me rendered in robot form on an independent layer with the New Yankee Photoshop set in the background. Aside from the text and accompanying color bars, these are the only layers in the image. For the most part, the robot is as opaque as if I had cut it out with scissors and glued it to the wood behind it. (Admittedly, I'd have to be very skilled with scissors and glue, but you get the idea.) The soft edges of the shadow to the right of the robot mix slightly with the pixels below them. But beyond that, every pixel is a digital hermit, steadfastly avoiding interaction.

The second image in Figure 13-1 paints a different picture. Here I've created several clones of the robot and mixed them with both the background and each other using Photoshop's wide array of calculation capabilities. The robot image itself never changes; each layer contains the same 400 or so thousand pixels that, when combined, scream out, "We are roboDeke!" In all, there are ten layers: three angled robots in the background, one apiece subject to the Hard Light and Linear Light modes on the left, followed by two overlapping layers, one the result of Linear Dodge and the other a function of Multiply and an Opacity value of 50 percent. I created the final photonegative robot using three layers, one subject to Difference, another inverted and subject to Screen, and then again inverted and again subjected to Difference.

Naturally, we'll get into the specifics of every one of these blend modes — including the ever-popular Difference sandwich — later in this chapter. But before we do, a few basics are in order. Photoshop gives you three fundamental ways to mix images:

✦ **The Layers palette:** You can combine the active layer with underlying pixels using the Opacity and Fill values, along with the blend mode pop-up menu, all members of the Layers palette. Figure 13-2 shows these illustrious items in the context of the list of layers for Figure 13-1. To learn everything there is to know about Opacity and Fill options, read the next section. Blend modes are covered in the section after that.

✦ **Blending options:** Right-click a thumbnail in the Layers palette (Control-click on the Mac) and choose Blending Options to display the Blending Options panel of the extensive Layer Style dialog box. Along with the Blend Mode,

Opacity, and Fill Opacity options, you get an assortment of advanced blending options, including the Knockout pop-up menu and Blend If sliders. The Knockout options let you use one layer to cut a floating hole into one or more layers below it. Using the Blend If sliders, you can drop colors out of the active layer and force colors to show through from layers below. For more information about these and other options, read "Advanced Blending Options" later in this chapter.

Figure 13-1: One roboDeke means good training (top), but treat yourself to multiple roboDekes subject to all kinds of blend modes (bottom), and you get the kind of educational overload that leaves you begging for mercy.

Blend mode pop-up menu   Opacity/Fill slider bar

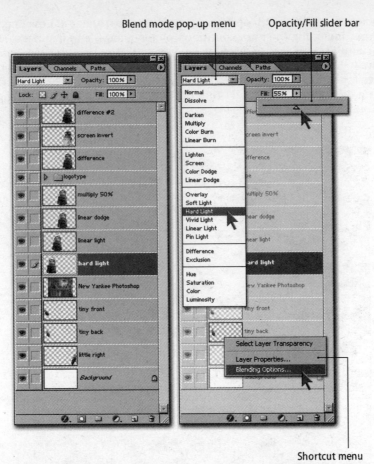

Shortcut menu

Figure 13-2: The list of layers in the "Army of roboDekes" composition, with a few essential layer blending functions labeled on right.

✦ **Channel operations:** The so-called channel operations permit you to combine two open images of identical size, or one image with itself. Photoshop offers two commands for this purpose, Image ➪ Apply Image and Image ➪ Calculations. Largely archaic and completely lacking in sizing and placement functions, these commands are unique in that they provide access to two otherwise hidden blend modes, Add and Subtract. Simply put, unless a technique involves the Add or Subtract mode, or you want to clone two images into a third image window, you can mix images with greater ease, flexibility, and feedback using the Layers palette. For more on this lively topic, see "Whole Image Calculations" in the latter half of this chapter.

Blend modes are not Photoshop's most straightforward feature. There may even come a time when you utter the words, "Blend modes are stupid." They demand a generous supply of experimentation and even then they'll try to fool you. I was a math major in college (with a double-major in art, for what it's worth), so I well understand the elementary arithmetic behind many of Photoshop's calculations. And yet, despite roughly a decade of experience with blend modes in Photoshop and other programs, I am frequently surprised by their outcome.

The key, therefore, is to combine a basic understanding of how blend modes and other compositing features work with your natural willingness to experiment, grow, and bond with pixels. Sometime when you don't have a deadline looming over your head, take some multilayered composition you have lying around and hit it with a few calculations. Even if the result is a disaster that you wouldn't share with your mother, let alone a client, you can consider it time well spent.

Opacity and Fill

The Opacity value permits you to mix the active layer with the layers beneath it in prescribed portions. By way of example, consider Figure 13-3. The first image shows one of my favorite postage stamps, in which patriot and statesman Paul Revere looks for all the world like Betsy Ross. Although quite thoroughly emasculated, he is shown at full opacity, 100 percent. In the second example, I have reduced his Opacity setting to 20 percent, thereby transforming him from Paul Revere in drag to the ghost of Paul Revere in drag.

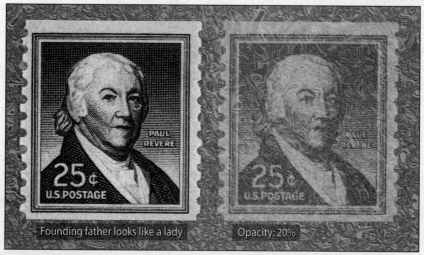

Founding father looks like a lady   Opacity: 20%

Figure 13-3: Paul Revere at 100 percent Opacity (left) and faded into the background (right).

The result is a lot like mixing a drink. Suppose you pour one part vermouth and four parts gin into a martini glass. (Any martini enthusiast knows that's too much vermouth, but bear with me on this one.) The resulting beverage is ⅕ vermouth and ⅘ gin. If the vermouth were a layer, you could achieve the same effect by setting the Opacity to 20 percent, as I did with Paul Revere. So in the case of the right half of Figure 13-3, 20 percent of what you see is Revere and the remaining 80 percent is background.

The option directly below Opacity in the Layers palette is Fill, which controls the *fill opacity* of a layer. Although not technically new to Photoshop 7, its appearance in the Layers palette is, and it's mighty handy. Where Opacity controls the translucency of everything associated with a layer, Fill adjusts the opacity of the filled areas only. Now at first blush, there might not seem to be any difference. In Figure 13-4, for example, changing either the Opacity or Fill setting of the stamp layer to 50 percent produces the same effect: The layer is half visible and half invisible.

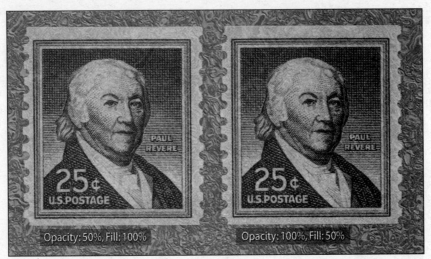

Opacity: 50%, Fill: 100%   Opacity: 100%, Fill: 50%

Figure 13-4: Whether you change the Opacity value to 50 percent (left) or the Fill value to 50 percent (right), Paul Revere looks the same.

Things change, however, if you add one or more layer effects. In Figure 13-5, I added a drop shadow and outer bevel to each of the stamp layers. (You can add a layer effect to a layer by choosing an option from the cursive *f* icon at the bottom of the Layers palette, as discussed in Chapter 14.) Now the difference between Opacity and Fill becomes apparent—Opacity affects pixels and layer effects alike; Fill affects pixels and leaves effects unchanged.

Figure 13-5: But add a layer effect or two, and the difference between Opacity and Fill becomes obvious. Opacity makes layer and effects translucent (left), Fill alters the layer independently of its effects (right).

Fill is also more absolute than Opacity. You can lower the Opacity value to 1 percent, just shy of altogether transparent. But Photoshop lets you take Fill all the way down to 0 percent. Why? Because that allows you to reduce the fill of a layer to nothing while leaving the effects intact. Figure 13-6 shows the results of lowering the Fill value to first 20 and then 0 percent.

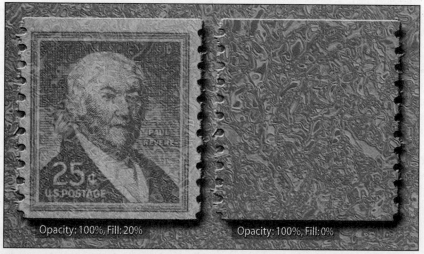

Figure 13-6: Using the Fill value, you can subordinate a layer to its effect (left) or fade the layer away entirely (right).

When a selection or navigation tool is active, you can change the Opacity setting for a layer from the keyboard. Press a single number key to change the Opacity in 10-percent increments. That's 1 for 10 percent, 2 for 20 percent, up to 0 for 100 percent, in order along the top of your keyboard. If you have the urge to be more precise, press two keys in a row quickly to specify an exact two-digit Opacity value.

Hankering to change the Fill just as easily? Then press the Shift key. Shift-1 changes the Fill value to 10 percent, Shift-0 makes it 100 percent. Shift plus two numbers enters a two-digit value.

You also can change the setting by dragging the Opacity or Fill slider in the Layers palette (labeled back in Figure 13-2). Click the arrowhead to the right of the option to display the slider bar and then drag the triangle to change the value. Or press the up and down arrows to nudge the triangle along; press Shift with the arrow key to nudge the value in 10-percent increments. Press Enter or Return to confirm the slider setting, or press Escape to restore the previous setting.

Incidentally, both the Opacity and Fill options are dimmed when working on the background layer or in a single-layer image. There's nothing underneath, so there's nothing to mix. Naturally, this goes double when editing a black-and-white or indexed image, or when editing a single channel or mask, because neither of these circumstances supports layers.

Blend Modes

Photoshop 7 offers a total of 22 blend modes, starting with Normal and ending with Luminosity. If you've been reading the chapters sequentially, you'll notice this isn't the first time I've touched on Normal, Dissolve, Darken, and the like. In fact, given that the blend modes mimic Chapter 5's brush modes both in name and in function, we're covering some familiar territory. But you'll soon find that there's a big difference between laying down a color or pattern with a brush and merging the myriad colors that inhabit a single layer. This difference is the stuff of the following pages.

For you visual learners, I'll be demonstrating the effects of Normal, Luminosity, and the others using the images pictured in Figure 13-7. The default order of the images is that pictured in the figure — that is, the Blistered Paint pattern (one of the predefined patterns included with Photoshop 7) on top and the tranquil background at the bottom. However, I sometimes slide the pattern layer below the gradient layer if it better suits the discussion. In any case, bear in mind how these control images look, because I'll be using two or more of them throughout future figures.

You apply every one of the blend modes to a layer from the keyboard by pressing Shift+Alt (Shift-Option on the Mac) plus a letter, provided that the active tool doesn't offer its own brush mode options. (If the tool supports brush modes — as in the case of the brush tool, pencil, clone stamp, healing brush, and others — the shortcuts set the mode for the tool and not the layer.)

Top

Bottom

Figure 13-7: To demonstrate the effects of Photoshop's blend modes, I'll be compositing these images in more or less the order shown here (with some occasional swapping around). The tranquil background is in fact the background layer, so no blend mode will ever be applied to it. Note that the right half of the face layer is transparent, and the layer includes an automated drop shadow, fading off to the right.

Some of the shortcut letters make perfect sense — Shift+Alt+N for Normal and Shift-Option-S for Screen. Others are a bit of a stretch — such as Shift+Alt+W for Linear Dodge or Shift-Option-Z for Pin Light. That's why I've come up with the following helpful pneumonic. Reading from the top of the blend mode menu to the bottom, it's "Nik mba gsd wof hvjz ex utcy," pronounced "Nick mubba gus-sid woff heev-jizz ex ootsie." Sing that to a song Big Bird might have sung (see Figure 13-8), and you'll have your blend mode shortcuts memorized in no time.

Figure 13-8: Just sing this magical word and you'll be fine. I promise.

Of course, it's always possible a few people won't be able to wrap their brains around my simple poach. Which is why I list the shortcut letter in parentheses with each blend mode description and illustrate the shortcut inside the figures. So whether predictable or not, we got your blend modes covered.

Note

One more note: Every so often, I allude to a little something called a *composite pixel*. By this I mean the pixel color that results from all the mixing that's going on beneath the active layer. For example, your document may contain hordes of layers with all sorts of blend modes in effect, but as long as you're working on, say, Layer 23, Photoshop treats the image formed by Layers 1 through 22 as if it were one flattened image filled with a bunch of static composite pixels.

Cool? Keen. So without any further notes or clarifications, here they are, the 22 blend modes, in order of appearance:

✦ **Normal (N):** In combination with Opacity and Fill settings of 100 percent, this option displays every pixel in the active layer normally, regardless of the colors in the underlying layers. When you use opacity values (whether Opacity or Fill) of less than 100 percent, the color of each pixel in the active layer is averaged with the composite pixel in the layers behind it. Figure 13-9 shows examples applied to the face layer on its own.

Figure 13-9: The face layer subject to the Normal mode when combined with Opacity values of 100 percent (top) and 60 percent (bottom). The superimposed character indicates the keyboard shortcut Shift+Alt+N (Shift-Option-N on the Mac) and 6 for 60 percent opacity.

✦ **Dissolve (I):** This option specifically affects feathered or softened edges. If the active layer is entirely opaque with hard edges, Dissolve has no effect. But when the edges of the layer fade into view, as is the case around the neck and chin in Figure 13-10, Dissolve randomizes, or *dithers*, the pixels. If you look closely, you'll see that Dissolve does not dither pixels in the drop shadow; as discussed in Chapter 14, layer effects are governed by their own, independent blend modes. Things change, however, when you drop the Opacity value below 100 percent, in which case Dissolve dithers all pixels, as demonstrated in the second example of the figure.

Figure 13-10: Here I applied the Dissolve mode to a layer at 100 percent (top) and 60 percent (bottom) Opacity settings. Instead of creating translucent pixels, Dissolve turns pixels on and off to simulate transparency, as shown by the magnified details.

✦ **Darken (K):** The first of the four darkening modes, Darken applies colors in the active layer only if they are darker than the corresponding pixels below. Keep in mind that Photoshop compares the brightness levels of pixels in a full-color image on a channel-by-channel basis. So although the blue component of a pixel in the active layer may be darker than the blue component of the underlying composite pixel, the red and green components may be lighter. In this case, Photoshop would assign the blue component but not the red or green, thereby subtracting blue and shifting the pixel toward yellow. Darken is most useful for covering up light portions of an image while letting dark areas show through.

To illustrate Darken and the other darkening modes, I first established a light background by setting the pattern layer on top of the background and lowering its Opacity to 70 percent. Then I placed the gradient layer on top of that and set it to the Screen mode, which left the white portion of the gradient visible and dropped out the black portion. The result appears in the top example of Figure 13-11. I then added the face layer and set it to the Darken mode, as shown at the bottom of the figure. The result is a face that appears smooth in the midtones and shadows and patterned in the light areas, with relatively sharp transitions between the two.

Figure 13-11: A backdrop composed of the background, pattern, and gradient layers (top) followed by an application of the face in the Darken mode (bottom). Only those pixels in the face that are darker than the pixels in the patterned backdrop remain visible.

✦ **Multiply (M):** Multiply is one of the rare blend modes that emulates a real-world scenario. Imagine that the active layer and the underlying composite are both photos on transparent slides. The Multiply mode produces the same effect as holding these slides up to the light, one slide in front of the other. Because the light has to travel through two slides, the outcome invariably combines the darkest elements from both images. So unlike Darken, Multiply universally darkens, resulting in smooth transitions, ideal for preserving contours and shadows, as in the top image of Figure 13-12.

Tip

If the Multiply mode produces too dark an effect, reduce the Opacity or Fill value. If it isn't dark enough, clone the layer by pressing Ctrl+J (⌘-J on the Mac). In the second example in Figure 13-12, I cloned the face layer and threw away its drop shadow to avoid darkening the shadow. Then I merged the two layers by pressing Ctrl+E (⌘-E). As fortune would have it, the visual effect remained the same, effectively creating a single layer with twice the darkness of the original. This technique holds true throughout Photoshop: provided that two layers share a common blend mode, you can merge the layers and preserve the effect.

Figure 13-12: The Multiply blend mode (top) produces the same effect as holding two overlapping transparencies up to the light. To get an even darker effect, I duplicated the layer, removed its drop shadow, and merged the two face layers into one (bottom).

✦ **Color Burn (B)** and **Linear Burn (A):** If the Multiply mode darkens your image, then the two Burn modes char them. They both use colors in the active layer to reduce brightness values, resulting in radical color transformations. As demonstrated in Figure 13-13, Color Burn results in crisp, often colorful, toasted edges; Linear Burn creates a smoother, less vibrant effect. Both modes have an uncanny ability to draw colors from background layers. For example, even though I lightened the background by applying Screen to the pattern layer in Figure 13-13, we see more contrast in this figure than in the single-pass Multiply example from Figure 13-12. So for high-contrast stamping effects, these are the blend modes to use.

Figure 13-13: After applying Screen to the pattern layer, I applied the Color Burn (top) and Linear Burn (bottom) blend modes to the face layer. Even though the background is lighter, many portions of the face appear darker than they did after a single application of Multiply.

✦ **Lighten (G):** The next four options use the active layer to lighten those below it. If you select Lighten, for example, Photoshop applies colors in the active layer only if they are lighter than the corresponding pixels in the underlying image. As with Darken, Photoshop compares the brightness levels of all channels in a full-color image.

To set the stage for the lightening figures, I modified the background layers, restoring the pattern layer to Normal and switching the gradient layer to Multiply. As a result, Photoshop dropped out the whites in the gradient and kept the blacks, as in the first image in Figure 13-14. In the second image, I assigned the Lighten blend mode to the face. But I also modified the drop shadow — which would have otherwise remained black — by changing its color to white and its blend mode to Screen. The result is a drop glow, which I describe in the section "Inside the Layer Style dialog box" in the next chapter. (If you're having problems finding this discussion, look for the bright and helpful Figure 14-18.)

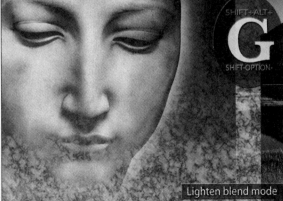

Figure 13-14: Here I prepared a dark background by assigning Multiply to the gradient layer (top). Then I applied Lighten to the face layer and changed its drop shadow to white (bottom).

✦ **Screen (S):** From a creative standpoint, Screen is the opposite of Multiply. In fact, remember those transparent slides from the Multiply analogy? Well this time, place them both in separate projectors and point them at the same screen. The result is the effect you get with Screen. Rather than creating a darker image, as you do with Multiply, you create a lighter image, as demonstrated in Figure 13-15.

You can use the Screen blend mode to emulate film that has been exposed multiple times. Ever seen Thomas Eakin's pioneering *Jumping Figure*, which shows rapid-fire exposures of a naked man jumping from one location to another? Each shot is effectively screened onto the other, lightening the film with each and every exposure. The photographer was smart enough to limit the exposure time so as not to overexpose the film; likewise, you should only apply Screen when working with images that are sufficiently dark so that you avoid overlightening. Screen is likewise useful for creating glows, retaining just the light colors in a gradient, and creating light noise effects such as snow and stars.

✦ **Color Dodge (D)** and **Linear Dodge (W):** When you apply one of the two Dodge modes, each color in the layer becomes a brightness-value multiplier. Light colors such as white produce the greatest effect, and black drops away. As a result, the Dodge modes are Photoshop's most dramatic whitening agents, the equivalent of mounting your image on a gel and projecting it from a spotlight. (This is not an exact equivalent, mind you, but it's close enough to give you an idea of what to expect.) Of the two, Color Dodge produces the sharper, rougher effect; Linear Dodge smoothes out the transitions (see Figure 13-16). Because they send so much of an image to white, the Dodge modes are most useful for simulating hot spots and other intensely bright effects.

✦ **Overlay (O), Soft Light (F),** and **Hard Light (H):** Photoshop's six Light modes darken the darkest colors and lighten the lightest colors, thereby allowing the midtones to intermix, so that foreground and background remain independently identifiable. Of the six, the first three — Overlay, Soft Light, and Hard Light — are the oldest and arguably the most useful, so I'll begin with them.

Each of these three modes alternatively multiplies the blacks and screens the whites, but to different degrees. For example, where Overlay favors the background layers, Hard Light emphasizes the active layer. In fact, the two are direct opposites — Layer A set to Overlay in front of Layer B produces the same effect as Layer B set to Hard Light in front of Layer A. Meanwhile, Soft Light is a modified version of Hard Light that results in a more subtle effect than either Hard Light or Overlay.

When experimenting with these modes, my advice is to always start with Overlay. If Overlay produces too strong an effect, reduce the Opacity or Fill value to favor the composite pixels. Figure 13-17 shows three compositions created using the background, face, and pattern layers. Throughout, the face is set to Normal, fully opaque. To add texture to the image, I set the blend mode for the pattern layer to Overlay. But as we can see in the first example, this overwhelms the image. So I pressed the 5 key to reduce the Opacity to 50 percent, resulting in the second image.

Figure 13-15: The Screen mode produces the same effect as shining two projectors at the same screen. In this case, one projector contains the background layers, and the other contains the face (top). Want a more pronounced ghosting effect? Just duplicate the Screen layer (bottom).

Alternatively, you can switch from Overlay to Soft Light, as I did in the final example of Figure 13-17. On first glance, the second and third examples in the figure—one showing Overlay at 50 percent and the other Soft Light at full opacity—look very close to identical. But on closer inspection, you will

Figure 13-16: After slightly darkening the gradient layer and fading the pattern layer, I applied Color Dodge (top) and Linear Dodge (bottom) to the face. Never subtle, both modes simultaneously bleach the image and draw out some of the dark outlines from the Blistered Paint pattern.

notice that where the balance of lights and darks is roughly equivalent, their distribution is quite different. The Overlay example favors the details in the face; the Soft Light example favors the marbleized edges of the Blistered Paint pattern.

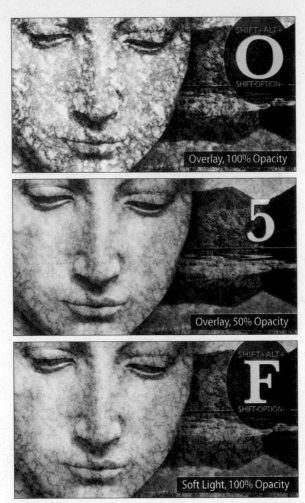

Figure 13-17: With the pattern layer in front, I applied the Overlay mode (top), experimented with reducing its Opacity setting to 50 percent (middle), and finally settled on the Soft Light mode with an Opacity of 100 percent (bottom).

On the other hand, if the Overlay mode at 100 percent seems too subtle, you can try cloning the layer to double the Overlay effect, or switching to the Hard Light mode. Figure 13-18 demonstrates the difference. I start with the gradient layer set to Screen and the face set to Overlay. (For the present, the pattern layer is hidden.) The face is too light, so I clone the face to another layer by pressing Ctrl+J (⌘-J on the Mac) and delete its drop shadow. The final image compares this effect to sticking with a single layer and applying the Hard Light mode instead. In this particular case, Hard Light provides the best marriage of emphasis on the face and balance with the background.

Figure 13-18: Here I have the face layer in front with the gradient set to Screen behind it. Working on the face, I first applied the Overlay mode (top) then duplicated the face to another layer (middle). Deciding I didn't like the contrast, I deleted the cloned layer and changed the original to Hard Light (bottom).

✦ **Vivid Light (V)** and **Linear Light (J):** If Overlay and its ilk combine Multiply and Screen, then the next two Light modes combine Dodge and Burn. More specifically, Vivid Light combines Color Dodge and Color Burn, where Linear Light combines Linear Dodge and Linear Burn. Figure 13-19 shows examples. This time, I've reduced the Opacity setting for the gradient layer to 50 percent and brought back the pattern layer, also at 50 percent Opacity, but set to Soft Light. Sandwiched in between is the face, set to Vivid Light at top and Linear Light at bottom.

Figure 13-19: The effect of setting the face to the Vivid Light (top) and Linear Light (bottom) modes. Because the effects are so hot, I sandwiched them between a Soft Light pattern layer and a Screen gradient layer, each with Opacity settings of 50 percent.

I find both of these modes useful for enhancing contrast, especially when combined with gradients. In Figure 13-20, we have the usual gang: the Blistered Paint pattern at 50 percent Soft Light and the face layer at 100 percent Normal. But this time, I've alternated the gradient layer, fully opaque, between Vivid Light in the first example and Linear Light in the second. In the final example, I cloned the face and set it to Linear Light as well. Both gradient and face set to Linear Light invokes a heightened, haunting effect; cloning the face before applying Linear Light prevents the face and gradient from interacting.

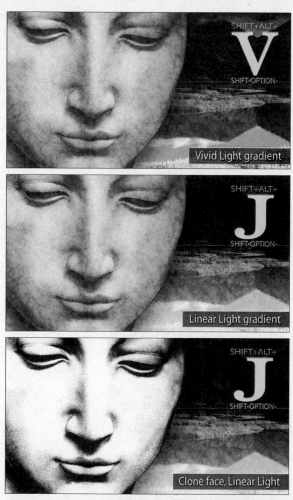

Figure 13-20: The effects of applying Vivid Light (top) and Linear Light (middle) to the gradient layer. In both cases, the Opacity value is 100 percent. I then cloned the face layer and set it to Linear Light as well (bottom).

✦ **Pin Light (Z):** One of the simplest modes in all of Photoshop, Pin Light keeps the darkest blacks and the lightest whites, and then makes everything else invisible. For the sake of comparison, the first example of Figure 13-21 shows the gradient layer set to Pin Light. (The face has been restored to Normal.) As you can see, only the very top and bottom of the gradient is visible; otherwise, the tranquil background lies exposed.

I find Pin Light particularly useful for modifying edge filters. In the second example of Figure 13-21, I cloned the face to a new layer and applied Filter ⇨ Sharpen ⇨ Unsharp Mask with an Amount of 100 percent and a Radius of 20 pixels. By applying the Pin Light mode, I retained just the lightest and darkest edges of the sharpened layer, as the final image shows. The result is a more subtle effect that still manages to exhibit thick, high-contrast outlines.

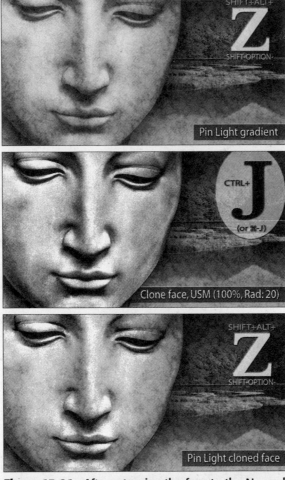

Figure 13-21: After returning the face to the Normal mode, I set the gradient layer to Pin Light (top). Then I cloned the face and sharpened the edges using the Unsharp Mask filter (middle). Finally, I applied the Pin Light mode to keep just the lightest and darkest pixels (bottom).

✦ **Difference (E)** and **Exclusion (X):** Difference inverts lower layers according to the brightness values in the active layer. White inverts the composite pixels absolutely, black inverts them not at all, and the other brightness values invert them to some degree in between. In the first example of Figure 13-22, I applied the Difference mode to the face layer, which is set against the gradient layer set to Screen. The light colors from the background show through the black pixels around the eyebrows, nose, and mouth, while the light areas in the face invert the lake and mountains.

Exclusion works just like Difference except for one, er, difference. Illustrated in the second example of Figure 13-22, Exclusion sends midtones to gray — much as Pin Light sends midtones to transparent — creating a lower contrast, often smoother effect.

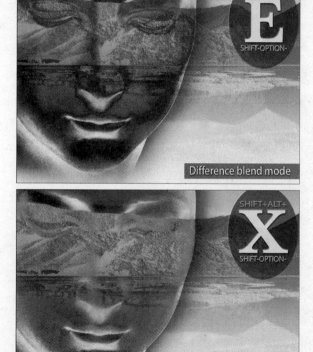

Figure 13-22: When you apply the Difference mode (top), white pixels invert the pixels beneath them; black pixels leave the background untouched. The Exclusion mode (bottom) performs a similar effect, but instead of inverting medium colors, it changes them to gray.

Because these modes invert colors, they can produce interesting effects when combined with inverted layers. Figure 13-23 shows examples in which Difference is applied to the face. In the first example, I inverted the face layer by pressing Ctrl+I (⌘-I on the Mac). In the second example, I restored the face to its previous appearance and then inverted the gradient layer, so it went from white at the top to black at the bottom.

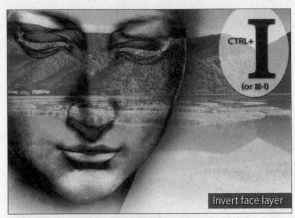

Figure 13-23: Since the Difference mode inverts colors, it only stands to reason that you can invert Difference layers and neighboring layers to achieve still more effects. Here I've alternated between inverting the face layer (top) and the gradient (bottom). In both cases, the face is set to Difference, the gradient is set to Screen.

One of my favorite uses for the Difference and Exclusion modes is to create a "Difference sandwich," in which you slide a filtered version of an image onto a layer between two originals. I explain this and related techniques in the upcoming section "Sandwiching a filtered image."

✦ **Hue (U):** Hue and the remaining three blend modes make use of the HSL color model to mix colors between the active layer and the underlying composite. When you select Hue, Photoshop retains the hue values from the active layer and mixes them with the saturation and luminosity values from the underlying image.

Note

I don't include grayscale figures for the Hue, Saturation, Color, and Luminosity blend modes for the simple reason that these modes affect color images only. In fact, all four options are dimmed when you edit a grayscale document. But in a moment, we'll see how the last of these modes, Luminosity, affects the full color image pictured in Color Plate 13-1.

✦ **Saturation (T):** When you select this option, Photoshop retains the saturation values from the active layer and mixes them with the hue and luminosity values from the underlying image. Saturation produces such subtle effects that you'll typically want to apply it in combination with other blend modes. For example, after applying a random blend mode to a layer, you might duplicate the layer and then apply the Saturation mode to either boost or downplay the colors, much like printing a gloss or matte coating over an image.

✦ **Color (C):** This option combines hue and saturation. Photoshop retains both the hue and saturation values from the active layer and mixes them with the luminosity values from the underlying layers. Because the saturation ingredient of the Color mode produces such a slight effect, Color frequently produces a very similar effect to Hue.

✦ **Luminosity (Y):** The Luminosity blend mode retains the lightness values from the active layer and mixes them with the hue and saturation values from the composite pixels below. So just as the Color mode uses the layer to colorize its background, the Luminosity mode uses the background to colorize the layer.

Color Plate 13-1 gives you a sense of the wonders you can achieve by combining a mere trio of blend modes — one each from the lighten, Light, and HSL categories — in concert. The page begins with the two base layers, the face and tranquil background. The face is fully opaque and set to Normal. In the second image, I introduce three more layers, including the by-now familiar pattern and gradient, as well as an old postage stamp. The gradient and stamp are set to Normal with the stamp lowered to an Opacity value of 70 percent; meanwhile, the pattern enjoys the Overlay blend mode and an Opacity setting of 30 percent. In the final image, I changed the gradient layer to the Screen mode and reduced the Opacity setting to 60 percent. Then I assigned Luminosity to the face and stamp.

Or did I? Clearly if you look at the color plate, you can see the brightness values from the face and stamp interact with the colors from the background. But had I applied Luminosity independently to the layers, they would interact with each other as well, with some of the blend of background and stamp leaking into the face. And yet, there is no such interaction. It's as if the stamp thinks the face is opaque, while the background can see through both.

Tip

And that's exactly what's happening. How? By combining the layers that should not interact into a set and applying a blend mode to the set instead of the layers. In the case of Color Plate 13-1, for example, I added the face and stamp to a set. The modes for both layers were Normal, so the face would cover the stamp. The default mode for a set is Pass Through, which merely means Photoshop will ignore the set and adopt the modes assigned to the independent layers. By changing this set mode to Luminosity, I instructed Photoshop to override the blend modes assigned to the individual layers and adopt Luminosity instead. The result is two layers blending as if they were one.

Blend-mode madness

Remember that scene in *Amadeus* where Mozart is telling the king about some obscure opera that he's writing — "Marriage of Franz Joseph Haydn" or something like that — and he's bragging about how many folks he has singing on stage at the same time? You do remember that scene, don't you? Oh, you're not even trying. Anyway, you can do that same thing with Photoshop. Not with melody or recitative or anything like that, but with imagery. Just as Mozart might have juggled several different melodies and harmonies at once, you can juggle layers upon layers of images, each filtered differently and mixed differently with the images below it.

Predicting the outcome of these monumental compositions takes a brain the magnitude of Mozart's. But experimenting with different settings takes no intelligence at all, which is where I come in.

The hierarchy of blend modes

The most direct method for juggling multiple images is "sandwiching." By this I mean placing a heavily filtered version of an image between two originals. This technique is based on the principal that more than half the blend modes — including Normal, Dissolve, Color Dodge and Burn, the six Light modes, and the four HSL modes — change depending on which of two images is on top.

For example, Figure 13-24 shows two layers, A and B, and what happens when I blend them with the Overlay mode. When the man is on top, as in the third example, the Overlay mode favors the sun; but when the sun is on top, Overlay favors the man. How fair is that?

Fortunately, Overlay is balanced by its opposite, Hard Light, which operates with a keener sense of justice, favoring the layer to which it's applied. For example, I could have achieved the exact effect shown in the third example of Figure 13-24 by placing the man under the sun and setting the sun to Hard Light. Flip-flop the layers and apply Hard Light to the man to get the last example.

Another obvious example of blend mode opposites is Color and Luminosity. If I were to position the man in front of the sun and apply Color, the sun would turn a kind of peachy, fleshy color. The same thing would happen if I placed the sun in front and applied Luminosity.

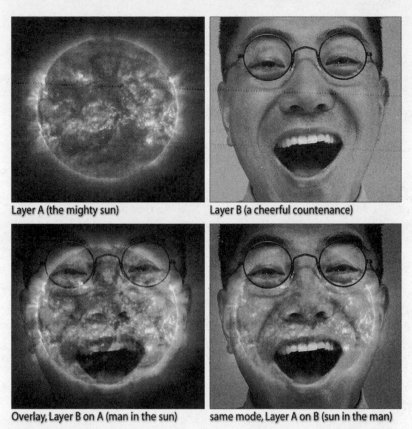

Layer A (the mighty sun)   Layer B (a cheerful countenance)

Overlay, Layer B on A (man in the sun)   same mode, Layer A on B (sun in the man)

Figure 13-24: After establishing two layers, sun and man, I placed the man on top and applied Overlay to get the third image. Then I switched the order of the layers and applied Overlay to the sun to get the last image.

The moral of this minutia is that the order in which you stack your layers is as important as the blend mode you select. Even modes that have no stacking opposites — Color Dodge, Linear Light, and others — produce different effects depending on which layer is on top. For your general edification, Figure 13-25 shows a few examples.

Note

An interesting upshot of Figure 13-25 is that you can see which layer each mode favors. Like Overlay, Color Dodge favors the composite pixels below the active layer. This holds true for Color Burn as well. Meanwhile, Linear Light, Pin Light, and all the other modes with Light in their names favor the active layer. Modes that do not change based on layering order — Multiply, Screen, Difference, and the like — favor neither front nor rear layer.

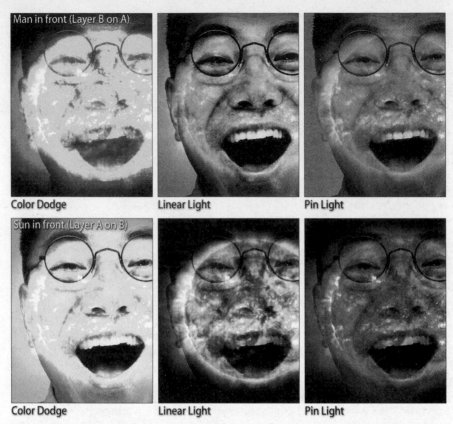

Figure 13-25: A series of blend modes shown with the man in front (top row) and the sun in front (bottom row).

Sandwiching a filtered image

When you sandwich a filtered image between two originals — which, as you may recall, is what all this is leading up to — you can lessen the effect of the filter and achieve different effects than those I discussed in Chapter 11. Layers and blend modes give you the flexibility to experiment as much as you want and for as long as you please.

In Figure 13-26, I copied the happy man's face to a new layer and then applied Filter ⇨ Sketch ⇨ Charcoal with the foreground and background colors set to their defaults, black and white. The right-hand image lists the specific settings.

Like most filters under the Sketch submenu, Charcoal absolutely destroys the detail in the image, replacing all brightness values with the foreground and background colors, in this case, black and white. Fortunately, because I applied Charcoal to a clone of the image, I can use a blend mode to restore some of the detail. Figure 13-27 shows two of the myriad possibilities that exist — one using the Multiply mode, which kept the blacks in the Charcoal effect and threw away the whites, and the other using Pin Light, which allowed colors from the original image to show through the gray areas of the Charcoal rendering.

Control layer (unfiltered image)   Filter ⇨ Sketch ⇨ Charcoal (5, 5, 50)

Figure 13-26: The fixings for our blend mode sandwich include the original happy man layer (left) and a cloned version on an independent layer subject to the Charcoal filter (right). The original will be our bread, the Charcoal is our meat. I mean, come on, who wouldn't want charcoaled meat?

Charcoal on control, Multiply   same, Pin Light

Figure 13-27: Each of two blend modes applied to the Charcoal meat in front of a slice of original image bread. This is what we image editing professionals like to call an open-face blend mode sandwich, great when you only have time for a light snack.

But that's just the beginning. By once again cloning the background layer and moving it above the Charcoal layer, so that the filtered image resides between two originals, I can increase my opportunity for blend mode variations. In this sandwich, the original images serve as the bread and the Charcoal layer is the meat (or the eggplant, for you vegetarians). Figure 13-28 shows the effects of applying a total of four blend modes to the top slice of bread, which in turn interact with the two blend modes applied to the Charcoal meat in the previous figure. For example, in the lower left example, I applied the Multiply mode to the filtered image and the Linear Light mode to the cloned original in front of that. The result is a brightly colored image with charcoal shadows and a bright, white background.

Multiply meat, Color Dodge bread   Pin Light meat, Linear Burn bread

Multiply meat, Linear Light bread   Pin Light meat, Pin Light bread

Figure 13-28: When you've got a hunger, only a full sandwich will do. Here I've thrown on several top slices of bread, each slathered with a different, delicious blend mode.

Creating a Difference sandwich

Check out the last example in Figure 13-28 and you'll see a purist's sandwich, Pin Light on the meat and Pin Light on the bread. In Photoshop 7, that's one of the best, most reliable sandwich combinations you can create. If blend modes were condiments, Pin Light would be mustard — it works for everything.

But every purist has a favorite, and for me, the best sandwich dressing out there is Difference. By applying Difference to both the filtered layer and the cloned original on top, you do a double-invert, first inverting the filter into the original image and then reinverting the original into the composite. The result is a subtler and utterly unique culinary combination.

Figure 13-29 and Color Plate 13-2 show a small sampling of the several thousand possible variations on the Difference sandwich theme. In the top rows of both figures, I've vigorously applied a series of standard filters — so vigorously, in fact, that I've pretty well ruined the image. But no fear. By stacking it on top of the original, cloning the original on top of it, and applying the Difference mode to both layers, you can restore much of the original image detail, as shown in the bottom examples of the two figures.

Note

A few notes about the Difference sandwich:

✦ First, the effect doesn't work nearly so well if you start reducing the Opacity values, so fully opaque is usually the best way to go.

✦ If you want to lighten or darken the effect, try adding a Levels adjustment layer to the top of the stack, as discussed in Chapter 17.

✦ If you want to lower the contrast, try substituting Difference with the Exclusion mode.

✦ Finally, Difference is one of those blend modes that produces the same effect regardless of how you order the layers. This means you can filter either the middle layer or the bottom layer in the sandwich and get the same effect. But the top layer must be the original image. Using the sandwich analogy, you can put the meat between the two slices of bread, or both slices of bread on top of the meat. In either case, set the top two layers to Difference, and life will be a dream, sweetheart.

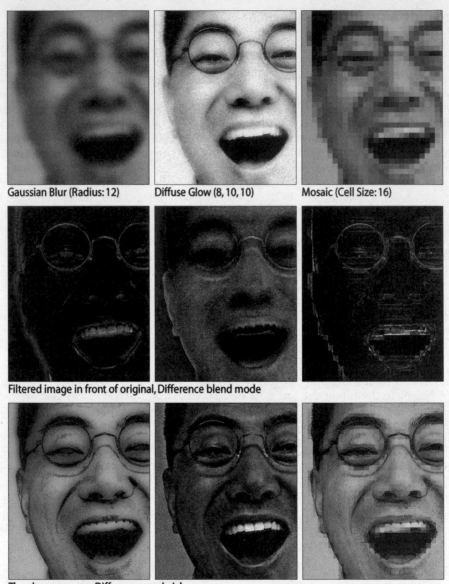

Gaussian Blur (Radius: 12)   Diffuse Glow (8, 10, 10)   Mosaic (Cell Size: 16)

Filtered image in front of original, Difference blend mode

The always yummy Difference sandwich

Figure 13-29: Three different filtering effects as they appear on their own (top row), combined with the original image using the Difference mode (middle row), and when inserted into a Difference sandwich (bottom row).

Advanced Blending Options

Opacity got you down? Blend modes just not enough? Why then, you need the Advanced Blending options, a collection of settings so absolutely terrific you'll be reaching for the phone and calling your mother to thank her for giving birth to you (as well you should anyway—mothers work so very hard).

Getting to the Advanced Blending options is slightly trickier than it used to be. In the old days, you could double-click anywhere on the layer in the Layers palette. Now, double-clicking on a layer name highlights the name so you can enter a new one. To display the Advanced Blending options, you now have three options: First, you can double-click on the layer thumbnail. Second, if you want to modify the Advanced Blending options for a specialty layer—such as type or an adjustment layer—right-click on the layer name or thumbnail (Control-click on the Mac) and choose the Blending Options command. You can also right-click inside the image window with one of the selection tools and access Blending Options that way. Third, you can press Alt (or Option) and double-click the layer name. So you decide.

In any case, you'll see the vast and stately Layer Style dialog box. This one multi-paneled window holds controls for adding layer effects, changing the opacity and blend mode of a layer, and achieving some special blending tricks, which I'll be discussing here. By default, you should see the Blending Options panel, pictured in Figure 13-30. If you're working in some other area of the dialog box, click the Blending Options item at the top of the list on the left side of the dialog box.

You already know how the two General Blending options, Blend Mode and Opacity, work. The same goes for the Fill Opacity slider (though as we'll see, it takes on broader meaning inside this dialog box). These are the same options found in the Layers palette and discussed in the first half of this chapter. The next few sections explain the Advanced Blending options, spotlighted in Figure 13-30. Like so many aspects of blend modes, these options can be perplexing at first. But after you get the hang of them, they enable you to gain a degree of control over your layers unrivaled by any other image editor.

Cross-Reference

Many of the Advanced Blending options affect the performance of layer effects, such as drop shadows, glows, bevels, and so on. These effects fall into the broader category of layer styles, which I discuss at length in the second half of Chapter 14, starting with the section "The Bold and Beautiful Layer Styles."

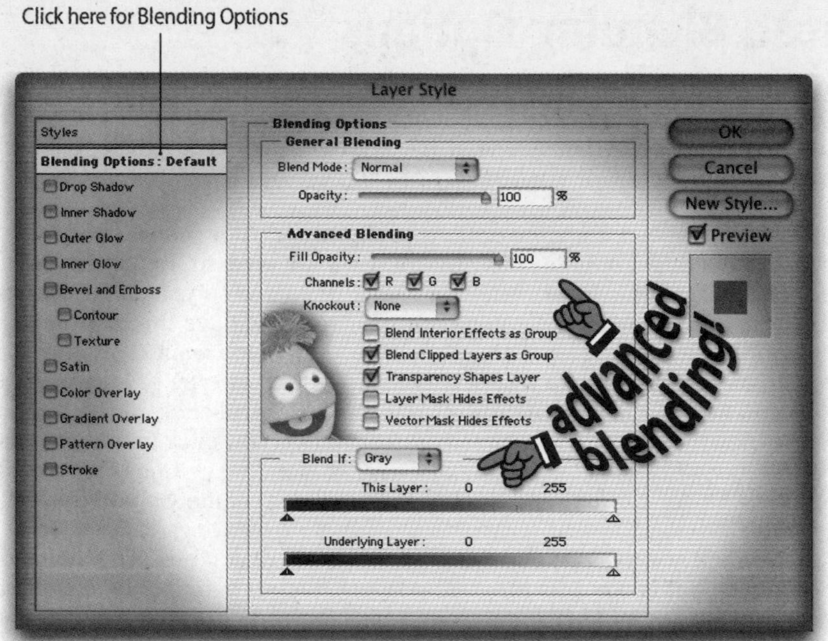

Click here for Blending Options

Figure 13-30: Using the Advanced Blending options, you can turn a layer into a floating hole, make specific color ranges invisible, and more.

Blending interior layer effects

I should say at the outset, the Fill Opacity value behaves exactly like the Fill option in the Layers palette. Enter a number into one option and it appears in the other as well. They are as one. The same goes for the Blend Mode setting inside the dialog box and the selected mode in the Layers palette. However, we are about to discover a few ways to modify the performance of these options that are only possible from the Advanced Blending options.

As you may recall, the Opacity value controls the translucency of all aspects of a layer, including pixels and layer effects alike. This is a fact of life, regardless of any other settings that may be in place. Meanwhile, the Blend Mode and Fill Opacity settings modify the interaction of pixels independently of most or all layer effects. This caveat, "most or all," is where things get interesting.

You see, Photoshop divides layer effects into two groups that you can control independently of each other. *Interior effects* fall inside the boundaries of the filled areas of a layer and include the Inner Shadow, Inner Glow, Satin, and three Overlay effects.

Exterior effects fall either outside or both inside and outside the boundaries of a layer. These include the effects Drop Shadow, Outer Glow, Bevel and Emboss, and Stroke.

Using blend modes and Fill Opacity, Photoshop permits you the option of modifying interior effects independently from exterior effects. The catalyst at the heart of this behavior is the check box labeled Blend Interior Effects as Group. When turned off, as by default, blend modes and Fill Opacity affect the pixels on a layer only. But if you turn the check box on, Photoshop applies the blend mode and Fill Opacity to the interior layer effects as well — only the exterior effects remain unchanged.

Figures 13-31 and 13-32 show examples. In Figure 13-31, we see a layer to which I've assigned three interior effects — Color Overlay, Pattern Overlay featuring the Wrinkles pattern (one of Photoshop's defaults), and a thick white Inner Glow — as well as three exterior effects — Drop Shadow, Stroke, and Bevel and Emboss set to a Stroke Emboss. When I lower the Fill Opacity to 20 percent, the pixels that make up the scanned stamp drop away, but the layer effects do not change. However, if I also turn on Blend Interior Effects as Group, Photoshop reduces the opacity of the three interior effects to 20 percent as well. Figure 13-32 shows the similar relationship that exists between Blend Interior Effects as Group and a couple of blend modes, Multiply and Difference. When the check box is off, the interior effects remain unchanged; when the check box is on, the interior effects are treated as just another part of the layer.

Note however that neither Fill Opacity nor blend mode affects the exterior effects under any circumstance. This is a little odd, since some exterior effects actually fall inside the boundaries of the layer. In particular, the Stroke effect is set to trace the inside of the layer, and the Stroke Emboss covers the stroke. In fact, the only effect that truly exists outside the layer is the drop shadow. However, so far as Photoshop is concerned, an exterior effect is an exterior effect, regardless of where it happens to fall.

Blending clipping groups

Just as you can control whether interior layer effects blend with filled areas of a layer, you can choose to blend the upper layers in a clipping group along with the base layer or leave them unchanged. By default, the Blend Clipped Layers as Group check box is turned on, thus blending all layers in a clipping group as a single unit. So the blend modes inside the group interact, and then the group as a whole inter-acts with other layers in the composition. To adjust the blending of the base layer in a clipping group by its lonesome, deselect the check box. Then, only the Opacity slider will impact the other layers in the group.

Figure 13-31: The results of taking a layer subject to three interior effects and three exterior effects (top), reducing the Fill Opacity value to 20 percent (middle), and then selecting the Blend Interior Effects as Group check box (bottom).

Multiply, ▣ Blend Interior Effects as Group off   Difference, ▣ Blend Interior Effects off

Multiply, ☑ Blend Interior Effects as Group on   Difference, ☑ Blend Interior Effects on

Figure 13-32: Two blend modes, Multiply (left) and Difference (right), when applied to the stamp layer with Blend Interior Effects as Group turned off (top) and on (bottom). The effect is most obvious on the thick Inner Glow, which turns invisible in the Multiply image and inverts colors when set to Difference.

For those of you who are thinking, "Yes, that's all very well and good, but what the heck does that gibberish you just wrote mean?" cast your curious eyes to Figure 13-33. Here, I've pasted the happy man on a separate layer, grouped him with the stamp layer so that the man's face falls entirely inside the stamp's edges, and then set the blend mode for the stamp (which is now the base layer for the group) to Hard Light and the Fill value to 50 percent. Using the Blend Interior Effects as Group and Blend Clipped Layers as Group check boxes, I was able to achieve the following effects:

✦ **Both options off:** By turning off Blend Clipped Layers as Group, I was able to maintain the happy man's face at the Normal blend mode and full opacity. But because Blend Interior Effects as Group was also turned off, the Inner Glow and other effects wrap around the face, just as they do any other layers in the group. The result appears at upper left in the figure.

Hard Light, Fill: 50%, ☑Blend Int. Effects off
☑Blend Clipped Layers as Group off

same, ☑Blend Interior Effects as Group on
☑Blend Clipped Layers as Group off

again, ☑Blend Interior Effects as Group off
☑Blend Clipped Layers as Group on

finally, ☑Blend Interior Effects as Group on
☑Blend Clipped Layers as Group on

Figure 13-33: After adding a face to the composition and grouping it with the stamp, I set the stamp's blend mode to Hard Light and the Fill Opacity to 50 percent. Then I experimented with turning each of the Blend as Group check boxes on and off.

✦ **Interior Effects on, Clipped Layers off:** If I turn Blend Interior Effects as Group on, the interior effects — including the Inner Glow and Pattern Overlay — recede behind the clipped face, as in the upper right image in Figure 13-33. However, exterior effects such as Stroke and Stroke Emboss remain in force.

✦ **Interior Effects off, Clipped Layers on:** Pictured in the lower-left example of Figure 13-33, this is the default condition for a new clipping group. The face adopts the blend mode and fill opacity assigned to the stamp layer. The interior effects, on the other hand, remain as opaque as ever.

✦ **Both options on:** If you want everything to be governed by the base layer of the group — including clipped layers and interior effects — then turn both options on. The result appears in the lower right example of Figure 13-33.

Masking and unmasking effects

The remaining check boxes — Transparency Shapes Layers, Layer Mask Hides Effects, and Vector Mask Hides Effects — permit you to manage the boundaries of interior and exterior effects alike. New to Photoshop 7, these options take us into some weird and rarefied territory. But don't panic. I'm going to briefly explain each one and then walk you through a real-world example.

✦ **Transparency Shapes Layer:** One of the strangest sounding features in all of Photoshop, turning off this check box deactivates the transparency mask that is normally associated with a layer, permitting layer effects and clipped layers to spill outside the boundaries of a layer to fill the entire image window. If the layer includes a layer mask, then effects and clipped layers fill the mask instead. So it serves two purposes: First, you can fill an image or clipping group with a Color Overlay or other interior effect associated with a layer. And second, you can substitute a transparency mask with a layer or vector mask. I'll be showing both of these in the following pages.

✦ **Layer Mask Hides Effects:** When turned on, this check box uses the layer mask to mask both the pixels in the layer and the layer effects. When turned off, as by default, the layer mask defines the boundary of the layer, and the effect traces around this boundary just as it traces around other transparent portions of the layer.

✦ **Vector Mask Hide Effects:** As I discuss in the next chapter, Photoshop's shape tools allow you to draw vector-based shapes, which you can fill with flat colors, gradients, patterns, or even layered images. When working inside a layer inside a shape, you can use the Vector Mask Hides Effects check box to specify whether the shape defines the outline of the layer (check box off) or clips layer effects just as it clips pixels (check box on). For complete information on defining a layer mask, read the "Editing the stuff inside the shape" section of Chapter 14.

Okay, so much for the basics. But why would you ever use these options? The short answer is, because something has gone wrong and you want to correct it. Don't like how your layer effects look? Turn one of these options on or off and see if it makes a difference. Of course, it helps to have a little experience with these options before you start randomly hitting switches, so let's work through an example.

The top image in Figure 13-34 is basically a repeat of the first image in Figure 13-33 — the stamp layer is set to Hard Light with a Fill Opacity of 50 percent. The face layer is grouped with the stamp and both the Blend Interior Effects as Group and Blend Clipped Layers as Group check boxes are turned off. Now let's say I decided to add a layer mask to the stamp layer. Nothing fancy, just a gradient from black at the bottom of the image to white near the middle, as shown in the second example in Figure 13-34. Naturally, this made the layer transparent at the bottom and opaque toward the middle, but it had an unexpected consequence. The mask shaped the boundaries of the layer, giving it a very soft edge that the layer effects didn't quite know how to accommodate. Rather than fading into view, the Inner Glow effect starts abruptly at the point where the layer becomes fully opaque, right under the guy's nose (see the final image in Figure 13-34). As it turns out, it really wasn't the inner glow's fault — it was a function of the Stroke being set to Inside — but who cares? The plain fact of the matter is, it looks absolutely awful.

Figure 13-34: Starting with the face masked inside the stamp (top), I added a layer mask to the stamp layer using the gradient tool (middle). But instead of fading the effects, the mask shoved the edges of the Stroke and Inner Glow so far upward, I worry that our once chipper fellow may soon run out of breath (bottom).

One's natural proclivity in a situation like this is to say, "Gosh, I guess I can't combine a layer mask with Inner Glow and an inside Stroke effect. I think I'll go soak my head now." And in Photoshop 6, that was pretty much your only option. But thanks to Photoshop 7, you can keep your head dry and consult your Advanced Blending options instead. In the first image in Figure 13-35, I fixed the problem by simply turning on the Layer Mask Hides Effects check box. This way, rather than constraining the effects, the layer mask fades them out just like a good gradient mask is supposed to do.

Figure 13-35: After fading out the Inner Glow and Stroke effects by selecting the Layer Mask Hides Effects check box (top), I turned off Transparency Shapes Layer, which permitted the Pattern Overlay effect to fill most of the image (middle). Then I added a vector mask to the stamp layer and left the Vector Mask Hides Effects check box off, as by default (bottom).

The second example of Figure 13-35 shows what happened when I turned off the Transparency Shapes Layer check box (on by default). Suddenly, the layer effects are no longer bound by the boundaries of the stamp layer and grow to fill the entire layer mask. Edge-dependent effects, such as Inner Glow, Drop Shadow, and Stroke disappear. Meanwhile, the Color and Pattern Overlay effects expand to fill the image.

Next, I added a vector mask to the stamp layer. To do this, I pressed the Ctrl key (⌘ on the Mac) and clicked the layer mask icon at the bottom of the Layers palette. After selecting the custom shape tool and selecting the highway sign symbol from the Shape menu in the Options bar, I pressed the plus key (+) to make sure the Add to Path Area button was active and drew my shape. Photoshop automatically traced the Drop Shadow, Inner Glow, and Stroke effects around the shape, as in the final example in Figure 13-35. However, if for some reason this weren't to occur, I had only to visit my handy Advanced Blending options and turn off the Vector Mask Hides Effects check box.

Dumping whole color channels

That takes care of the most complex of the check boxes. All that remain are the Channels options. Located directly below the Fill Opacity slider in the Layer Style dialog box, the Channels check boxes let you hide the layer inside one or more color channels. For example, turning off R makes the layer invisible in the red channel, sending colors careening toward vivid red or turquoise (all red or no red), depending on the colors in the layers underneath.

I have a tendency to make bold pronouncements on the features I like and loathe inside Photoshop, and the Channels check boxes fall into the latter category. They are, for the most part, useless. There are exceptions, of course — in a CMYK image, it can prove helpful to drop a layer inside, say, the Black channel — but for general RGB image editing, they just don't cut the mustard. Which is too bad, because if slightly retooled, they could. For example, I would very much like to control the translucency of a layer on a channel-by-channel basis, but instead we have only on or off controls. One lives in hope for something better.

Making knockouts

Okay, enough grousing. Back to the good stuff. Like the Knockout pop-up menu.

Knockout turns the contents of the active layer into a floating hole that can bore through one or more layers behind it. It's like a layer mask, except that you can use it to mask multiple layers, and their layer effects, at a time. You can also apply layer effects to the knockout, making them extremely flexible.

Creating a knockout is arguably more abstruse than it ought to be, but it ultimately makes a kind of twisted sense. You specify how deep the hole goes using the Knockout pop-up menu. Then use the Fill Opacity or Blend Mode option to define the translucency of the hole. The Knockout pop-up menu provides the following three options:

✦ **None:** This setting is the same as turning the knockout function off. The layer is treated as a standard layer, not a hole.

✦ **Shallow:** Choose this option to cut a hole through a group of layers inside a set and expose the layer immediately below the set. In a clipping group where Blend Clipped Layers as Group is turned off, Shallow burrows down to the layer directly below the base layer of the group. When Blend Clipped Layers as Group is turned on, the knockout layer burrows down to the base layer in the group. If the layer resides neither inside a set nor a clipping group, it typically cuts a hole down to the background layer.

✦ **Deep:** The final setting bores as far down as the background layer, even if the knockout layer resides inside a set. A notable exception occurs when working inside a clipping group. If the Blend Clipped Layers as Group check box is on, Deep burrows down to the base of the clipping group, just like Shallow.

See, I told you it was abstruse. But in truth, making a knockout has less to do with what option you choose from the Knockout pop-up menu and more to do with Fill Opacity, layering order, and sets. Consider my revolutionary idea in motoring shown in Figure 13-36. Here we have a pair of friendly highway markers that tell you where to go. I call out, "Where's the Garden State?" and they yell back, "You're on it, you knucklehead!" Forget global positioning systems—invest in talking highway markers today.

I created my brave new vision using vector masks, as I explained a few pages back in the "Masking and unmasking effects" section. If you look closely, you may notice that I replaced the one-time stamp layer with a pattern, threw out the now unnecessary Pattern Overlay effect, and deleted the gradient layer mask (first featured in Figure 13-34). Finally, I added posts behind the signs and set the background image—a photograph of New Mexico's Ship Rock—on an independent layer, so I could reposition it if need be. Okay, so the signs cast drop shadows onto the Ship Rock image—that's not realistic. But bear in mind, it's all conceptual. The real highway markers will be much cooler.

At this point, I decided that these shouldn't be little signs, like the highway markers we see now. They should be great huge things that emerge from the ground like the ancient moai heads of Easter Island. Otherwise, how will you be able to hear them as you speed on by? To do this, I needed the markers to fade up from the ground. For a single sign, I could use a layer mask, but for multiple signs, I needed a knockout layer.

Figure 13-36: If you're like me, the first thing you do upon arriving in a new city is rent a car and spend a few hours driving around the wrong state, playing the radio too loud and trying to look at an elaborately detailed map while hurtling past one exit after another at 70 miles per hour. Wouldn't it be easier if someone would invent talking highway markers? Here's my sketch, now get on it. Remember, I get 25 percent of net.

In Figure 13-37, I started things off by creating a new layer and filling it with a slightly angled black-to-transparent gradient. Then I double-clicked on the gradient thumbnail in the Layers palette and set the Knockout option to Shallow, which is a good place to start. But nothing happened. That's because you need to follow up by telling Photoshop how transparent to make the knockout. You can do this using a blend mode — for example, setting the gradient to Screen would make the black transparent, thereby cutting a hole. But the most straightforward method is to lower the Fill Opacity value. By reducing the value to 0 percent, I instructed Photoshop to use the filled portions of the gradient layer to burrow through all layers below. (Transparent portions of the knockout layer have no effect.) Note that you have to use the Fill value; the standard Opacity value does not work for this purpose.

So far so good, except for one tiny problem: the knockout went too far, masking all the way down to the white background layer, as illustrated in the second image in Figure 13-37. I set the Knockout to Shallow, which is the least amount of knockout I can apply, but without clipping groups or layer sets to guide it, Photoshop goes ahead and drills down to the bottom of the stack. How do I tell Photoshop to drill down to the Ship Rock layer instead? By combining the knockout and the layers I want to mask into a single set.

Black-to-transparent gradient on independent layer

Knockout: Shallow, Fill Opacity: 0% — reveals white background

Link all layers but Ship Rock, choose New Set From Linked

Figure 13-37: To mask through the many layers that make up the two signs, I made a new layer and filled it with a black-to-transparent gradient (top). Then I set the Knockout option to Shallow and reduced the Fill Opacity to 0 percent, which masked down to the white background (middle). To constrain the knockout, I combined all layers except the Ship Rock image into a set (bottom).

So I link the gradient knockout layer to the many layers that make up the signs and posts (using the link icons on the left side of the Layers palette). Then I choose New Set From Linked from the Layers palette menu. That's all there is to it. The Shallow setting tells the knockout to bore through to the layer immediately below the set, which is the Ship Rock layer. The result appears at the bottom of Figure 13-37.

After all this work to make a so-called shallow knockout even shallower, why would you ever choose Deep? Because your image may contain a network of layer sets and clipping groups, and you want to cut all the way through to the background. For example, let's say I wanted to create a floating crop boundary. In other words, I didn't want to throw away any background details for good, nor did I want to reduce the size of my image window. I merely wanted to add an empty border around my image to indicate how the final composition should be cropped.

To make my crop boundary, I created a new layer and used the rectangular marquee tool to draw the perimeter of my final image. Then I pressed Ctrl+Shift+I to inverse the selection (⌘-Shift-I on the Mac) and filled the area outside the crop with black. (Incidentally, I didn't have to use black; any color will do. It's just important to make the knockout pixels opaque.) The first example in Figure 13-38 shows my progress thus far.

To turn the blackness into knockout, I double-clicked on the layer thumbnail to bring up the Advanced Blending options, set the Fill Opacity to 0 percent, and set the Knockout to Shallow. The knockout works, but it only goes down so far as the Ship Rock layer. This is because I've gone and created the crop layer inside my new set. So I have two choices: move the crop layer in front of the set, in which case it'll burrow through everything inside and outside the set, or just set the Knockout option to Deep. The latter seemed easier, so that's what I did.

Finally, I decided I wanted my cropped image to have some depth. So I added a drop shadow. However, if I were to apply the Drop Shadow effect, the knockout would cast the shadow into the image. I want the shadow to go into the knockout, so I apply the Inner Shadow effect instead. The final image appears at the bottom of Figure 13-38.

At this point, I could move my crop boundary, add to it, change the effects, or otherwise modify it without worrying about harming a single pixel in the composition. Couldn't I do this same thing by simply filling the crop layer with white, as Photoshop artists have been doing for years? Yes, but there are two benefits to using a knockout layer instead: you have more flexibility where layer effects are concerned, and you can later turn around and composite this cropped image against a different background or frame. Simply put, no other cropping technique is this flexible.

Black boundary on independent layer

Knockout: Deep, Fill Opacity: 0%, Inner Shadow (Angle: 130°, Distance: 10, Size: 10)

Figure 13-38: To establish a floating crop boundary, I create a new layer and fill the area outside the desired crop with black (top). Then I set the Knockout to Deep and reduced the Fill Opacity value to 0 percent. I also added an Inner Shadow effect to the knockout layer, which resulted in what appears to be a drop shadow behind the image (bottom).

Dropping Out and Forcing Through

Found at the bottom of the Blending Options panel of the Layer Style dialog box, the Blend If slider bars rank among Photoshop's oldest and most powerful compositing capabilities. Pictured in Figure 13-39, these options enable you to drop out pixels in the active layer and force through pixels from lower layers according to their brightness values. You can even use them in combination with the Knockout option. For example, if you set the Knockout to Deep, you force through pixels from the background layer instead of from the layer immediately below the active layer.

Figure 13-39: Little Puppet Friend ranks the Blend If slider bars among Photoshop's most powerful capabilities, and I'm forced to agree.

Here's how the three Blend If options work:

✦ **Blend If:** Select a color channel from the Blend If pop-up menu to apply the effects of the slider bars according to the contents of a single color channel. If you choose Gray, as by default, Photoshop bases the changes on the grayscale composite. Each time you select a different Blend If option, the slider triangles change to the positions at which you last set them for that color channel. Regardless of how you set the sliders, Photoshop applies your changes evenly to all channels in the image; the selected channel is merely used for the calculation.

✦ **This Layer:** This slider bar lets you exclude ranges of colors according to brightness values in the active layer. You exclude dark colors by dragging the black triangle to the right; you exclude light colors by dragging the white triangle to the left. In either case, the excluded colors disappear from view.

✦ **Underlying Layer:** The second slider forces colors from the underlying layers to poke through the active layer. Any colors outside the range set by the black and white triangles will not be covered and are therefore visible regardless of the colors in the active layer.

✦ **Preview:** Don't forget to select the Preview check box on the right side of the Layer Style dialog box so you can see the effects of your modifications in the image window every time you adjust a setting.

These options are far too complicated to fully explain in a bulleted list. So I invite you to learn more by reading the following sections. You'll be glad you did.

Color-range slider bars

To demonstrate the Blend If options, I've taken the sculpted face and tranquil background composition first introduced in Figure 13-7 and added an oldie but goodie element from *Photoshop Bibles* of yore, The Thinker. (For you longtime readers who might be saying, "Oh no, not The Thinker again! Retire that guy already!" notice that this time, he's facing a different direction. I used to flip him so he was facing right, but this time I kept him facing left, just as photographer Wernher Krutein shot him. No, that's okay, no need to thank me. Putting a smile of genuine satisfaction on a loyal reader's face is reward enough for me.) As shown in Figure 13-40, The Thinker includes a soft drop shadow to distinguish him from the rest of the composition. Like all layers in this composition, he rests contemplatively behind a thin veil of the Blistered Paint pattern set to the Overlay blend mode at 20 percent Opacity.

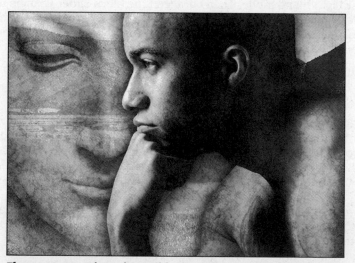

Figure 13-40: *Photoshop Bible* regular and Corbis Royalty Free stock image, The Thinker joins the composition for this very special demonstration of the Blend If slider bars.

The first Blend If slider bar, This Layer, hides pixels in the active layer according to their brightness values. You can abandon dark pixels by dragging the left slider triangle and abandon light pixels by dragging the right triangle. Figure 13-41 shows examples of each.

✦ To create the first example in Figure 13-41, I first set the blend mode to Screen. Then I dragged the black slider triangle until the value immediately to the right of the words This Layer read 130, thereby hiding all dark pixels whose brightness values were 130 or lower.

✦ To create the second example, I changed the blend mode to Multiply. I reset the black slider triangle to 0 and dragged the white slider triangle to 175, which hid those pixels with brightness values of 175 or higher.

✦ The final image in the figure shows the second Thinker layered in front of the first. With the help of the This Layer slider bar, I can combine the Screen and Multiply blend modes to produce an image that is both lighter and darker than its background.

Drag the triangles along the Underlying Layer slider bar to force pixels in the underlying layers to show through, again according to their brightness values. To force dark pixels in the underlying image to show through, drag the black slider triangle; to force light pixels to show through, drag the white slider triangle.

Here's how I achieved the effects in Figure 13-42:

✦ To achieve the effect in the top example in Figure 13-42, I started off by applying the Linear Light blend mode. Then I dragged the black slider triangle until the first Underlying Layer value read 130. This forced the dark colors in the sculpted face and tranquil background with brightness values of 130 or lower to show through.

✦ In the second example, I changed the blend mode to Luminosity. Then I restored the black Underlying Layer triangle to 0 and dragged the white triangle to 175, uncovering pixels at the bright end of the spectrum.

✦ The final image shows the two effects combined, one copy of The Thinker in the Linear Light mode with Underlying Layer values of 130 and 255, and another in front of that set to Luminosity with Underlying Layer values of 0 and 175. The right eye from the sculpted face blends in with The Thinker's face like another one of his tattoos.

Bear in mind, like every other adjustment made inside the Layer Style dialog box, changes made to the Blend If slider bars are temporary. These options hide pixels; they don't delete them. As long as the layer remains intact, you can revisit the Blend If sliders and restore hidden pixels or hide new ones.

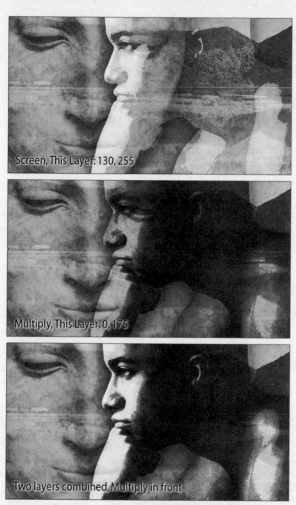

Screen, This Layer: 130, 255

Multiply, This Layer: 0, 175

Two layers combined, Multiply in front

Figure 13-41: Examples of modifying the blend mode and This Layer settings inside the Layer Style dialog box. The final image shows the copy of The Thinker that I set to Multiply layered in front of the copy set to Screen to get a high-contrast effect.

Linear Light, Underlying Layer: 130, 255

Luminosity, Underlying Layer: 0, 175

Two layers combined, Luminosity in front

Figure 13-42: Here I changed the Underlying Layer settings to force through the darkest (top) and lightest (middle) pixels from the sculpted face and tranquil background layers. The third image shows the two effects combined.

Fuzziness

The problem with hiding and forcing colors with the slider bars is that you achieve some pretty harsh color transitions. Although printed at high resolutions, both Figures 13-41 and 13-42 exhibit occasional jagged edges. Luckily, you can soften the color transitions by dropping and forcing pixels gradually over a fuzziness range, which works much like the Fuzziness value in the Color Range dialog box, leaving some pixels opaque and tapering others off into transparency.

To taper the opacity of pixels in either the active layer or the underlying image, press the Alt key (or Option on the Mac) and drag one of the triangles in the appropriate slider bar. The triangle splits into two halves, and the corresponding value above the slider bar splits into two values separated by a slash, as demonstrated in Figure 13-43.

Figure 13-43: Alt-drag (Win) or Option-drag (Mac) a slider triangle to split it in half. You can then specify a range over which brightness values will fade into transparency.

The left triangle half represents the beginning of the fuzziness range—that is, the brightness values at which the pixels begin to fade into or away from view. The right half represents the end of the range—that is, the point at which the pixels are fully visible or invisible. Figure 13-44 shows a bit of fuzziness applied to the This Layer slider. Here are the specifics:

✦ In the top example, I set the blend mode to Screen. After splitting the black slider triangle by Alt-dragging (Option-dragging on the Mac), I set one half of the triangle to 40 and the other to 220. Colors with a brightness value of 40 or darker turn transparent, they fade into view from 41 to 219, and they become opaque from 220 on up.

✦ In the second image, I selected the Multiply blend mode and restored both halves of the black triangle to 0. Then I Alt-dragged (or Option-dragged) the white triangle to split it. I moved the left half of the split triangle to 20 and the right half to 190. The result is an extremely gradual drop off. Those few pixels with brightness values from 0 to 20 are opaque, the pixels become gradually translucent from 21 to 189, and pixels of 190 and brighter are transparent.

✦ Finally, I combined both effects on separate layers, with the Multiply effect on top. As shown in the bottom example in Figure 13-44, the result is a perfect blending of Multiply and Screen, with the background images showing through in the midtones.

Using the Underlying Layer slider is a bit trickier. It typically works best when you're trying to force through very bright or dark details, such as the highlights in the sculpted face or the shadows in the mountains. It also helps to work with a foreground layer that has lots of flat areas of color for the background to show through. Here's what I did to create Figure 13-45:

✦ For starters, I applied Filter ➪ Other ➪ High Pass to The Thinker layer. As shown in the first example of Figure 13-45, this created lots of gray areas that would serve as ample neutral ground for the Blend If slider bars.

✦ I next applied the radical Linear Dodge mode to this layer. I first dropped out most of the dark colors in The Thinker layer by setting the halves of the black This Layer triangle to 80 and 230. Then I split the black triangle for the Underlying Layer slider, leaving the left half at 0 and moving the right half to 190. This forced through virtually all of the darkest pixels from the rear layers, fading them out as they got lighter.

✦ Finally, I duplicated the layer, applied the Multiply mode, and reset the black triangles to 0. I experimented with the white triangles, ultimately setting the This Layer halves to 110 and 180 and the Underlying Layer halves to 90 and 200. The result is a vibrant composition that contrasts elements of the sculpted face with the outline of The Thinker.

Figure 13-44: By Alt-dragging (Win) or Option-dragging (Mac) a This Layer slider triangle, you can create gradual transitions between the opaque and transparent portions of a layer.

High Pass, Radius: 10 pixels

Linear Dodge, This Layer: 80/230, 255
Underlying Layer: 0/190, 255

Multiply, This Layer: 0, 110/180,
Underlying Layer: 0, 90/200

Figure 13-45: After combining a High Pass effect with the Linear Dodge and Multiply blend modes, I used both the This Layer and Underlying Layer slider bars to drop out foreground colors and force through background colors. In the end, I was able to bring out some interesting details from the Michelangelo sculpture and mountain range.

Whole Image Calculations

Image ➪ Apply Image and Image ➪ Calculations provide access to Photoshop's *channel operations*, which composite one or more channels with others according to predefined mathematical calculations. Once hailed as Photoshop's most powerful capabilities, channel operations have been eclipsed by the standard and more accessible functions available from the Layers and Channels palettes. There may come a day when Adobe decides to scrap Apply Image and Calculations altogether. But until that day, I will dutifully document them both.

The Apply Image and Calculations commands allow you to merge one or two identically sized images using 17 of the 22 blend modes discussed earlier plus two additional modes, Add and Subtract. In a nutshell, the commands duplicate the process of dragging and dropping one image onto another (or cloning an image onto a new layer) and then using the blend mode and the Opacity settings in the Layers palette to mix the two images together.

Although Apply Image and Calculations are more similar than different, each command fulfills a specific — if not entirely unique — function:

    ✦ **Apply Image:** This command takes an open image and merges it with the foreground image (or takes the foreground image and composites it onto itself). You can apply the command to either the full-color image or one or more of the individual channels.

    ✦ **Calculations:** The Calculations command works on individual channels only. It takes a channel from one image, mixes it with a channel from another (or the same) image, and puts the result inside an open image or in a new image window.

The primary advantage of these commands over other, more straightforward compositing methods is that they allow you to access and composite the contents of individual color channels without a lot of selecting, copying and pasting, cloning, floating, and layering. You also get two extra blend modes, Add and Subtract, which may prove useful on a rainy day.

The Apply Image and Calculations commands provide previewing options, so you can see how an effect will look in the image window. But thanks to the sheer quantity of unfriendly options offered by the two commands, I suggest that you use them on only an occasional basis. The Calculations command can be a handy way to combine masks and layer transparencies to create precise selection outlines. Apply Image offers the unique ability to composite images in different color models. For example, you could mix a layer or channel from an RGB image with another image in the CMYK mode.

But if your time is limited and you want to concentrate your efforts on learning Photoshop's most essential features, feel free to skip Apply Image and Calculations. I assure you, you won't be missing much.

The Apply Image command

Channel operations work by taking one or more channels from an image, called the *source*, and duplicating them to another image, called the *target*. When you use the Apply Image command, the foreground image is always the target, and you can select only one source image. Photoshop then takes the source and target, mixes them together, and puts the result in the target image. Therefore, the target image is the only image that the command actually changes. The source image remains unaffected.

When you choose Image ➪ Apply Image, Photoshop displays the dialog box shown in Figure 13-46. Notice that you can select from a pop-up menu of images to specify the Source, but the Target item — listed just above the Blending option — is fixed. This is the active layer in the foreground image.

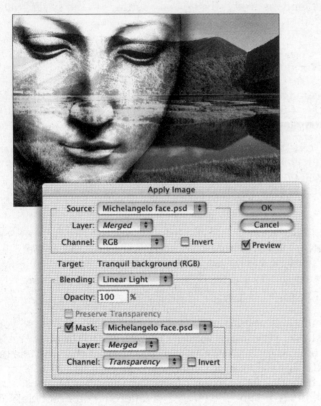

Figure 13-46: The Apply Image dialog box lets you mix one source image with a target image and make the result the new target.

If this sounds a little dense, think of it this way: The source image is the floating selection and the target is the underlying original. Meanwhile, the Blending options are the blend modes pop-up menu and the Opacity value in the Layers palette.

Using the Apply Image command is a five-step process. You can always simply choose the command and hope for the best, but you'll get the most use out of it if you do the following.

STEPS: Applying the Apply Image Command

1. **Open the two images that you want to mix.** If you want to mix the image with itself to create some effect, just open the one image.

2. **Make sure that the two images are exactly the same size, down to the last pixel.** Use the crop tool and Image Size command as necessary. (You don't have to worry about this step when mixing an image with itself.)

3. **Inside the target image, switch to the channel and layer that you want to edit.** If you want to edit all channels, press Ctrl+tilde (⌘-tilde on the Mac) to remain in the composite view.

Tip

If you're thinking of editing a single channel, I recommend you go ahead and display all channels on screen. For example, after pressing Ctrl+1 (⌘-1) to switch to the red channel, click in front of the RGB item in the Channels palette to display the eyeball icon and show all channels. Only one channel is active, but all are visible. This way, you can see how your edits inside the Apply Image dialog box affect the entire image, not just the one channel.

4. **Select the portion of the target image that you want to edit.** If you want to affect the entire image, don't select anything.

5. **Choose Image ⇨ Apply Image and have at it.**

Obviously, that last step is a little more difficult than the text lets on. In fact, it takes an entire section to explain all the stuff you'll need to know. That section is coming up next.

The Apply Image options

The following list explains how to use each and every option in the Apply Image dialog box:

✦ **Source:** The Source pop-up menu contains the name of the foreground image as well as any other images that are both open and exactly the same size as the foreground image. If the image you want to merge is not available, you must not have been paying much attention to Step 2. Press Escape to cancel, resize and crop as needed, choose Image ⇨ Apply Image, and try again.

✦ **Layer:** This pop-up menu lists all layers in the selected source image. If the image doesn't have any layers, Background is your only option. Otherwise, select the layer that contains the prospective source image. Select Merged to mix all visible layers in the source image with the target image.

✦ **Channel:** Select the channels that you want to mix from this pop-up menu. Both composite views and individual color and mask channels are included. Keep in mind that you'll be mixing these channels with the channels that you made available in the target image before choosing the command.

For example, if the target image is an RGB image shown in the full-color composite view, and you choose RGB from the Channel pop-up menu in the Apply

Image dialog box, Photoshop mixes the red, green, and blue channels in the source image with the corresponding red, green, and blue channels in the target image. However, if you switched to the red channel before choosing Apply Image and then selected the RGB option, the program mixes a composite grayscale version of the RGB source image with the red channel in the target and leaves the other target channels unaffected.

✦ **Selection, Transparency, and Layer Mask:** If a portion of the source image is selected, the Channel pop-up menu offers a Selection option, which lets you apply the selection outline as if it were a grayscale image, just like a selection viewed in the quick mask mode. If you selected a specific layer from the Layer pop-up menu, you'll find a Transparency option that represents the transparency mask. If the layer includes its own layer mask, a Layer Mask option also appears.

None of the three options is particularly useful when you work in the composite view of the target image; you'll usually want to apply the Selection, Transparency, or Layer Mask option only to a single channel, as described in "The Calculations command" section toward the end of this chapter.

✦ **Invert:** Select this check box to invert the contents of the source image before compositing it with the target image.

✦ **Target:** You can't change this item. It merely shows which image, which channels, and which layers are being affected by the command.

✦ **Blending:** This pop-up menu offers access to 17 of the blend modes I discussed in the "Blend Modes" section earlier in this chapter. The Dissolve, Hue, Saturation, Color, and Luminosity options are missing. Two additional options, Add and Subtract, are discussed in the "Add and Subtract" section later in this chapter.

✦ **Opacity:** By now, you're well aware of how this one works.

✦ **Preserve Transparency:** When you're editing a layer in the target image — that is, you activated a specific layer before choosing Image ➪ Apply Image — the Preserve Transparency check box becomes available. Select it to protect transparent portions of the layer from any compositing, much as if the transparent portions were not selected and are therefore masked.

✦ **Mask:** Select this option to mask off a portion of the source image. I already mentioned that you can specify the exact portion of the target image you want to edit by selecting that portion before choosing the Apply Image command. But you can also control which portion of the source image is composited on top of the target through the use of a mask. When you select the Mask check box, three new pop-up menus and an Invert check box appear at the bottom of the Apply Image dialog box. For complete information on these options, see the next section.

Compositing with a mask

The Mask option in the Apply Image dialog box provides a method for you to import only a selected portion of the source image into the target image. Select the Mask check box and choose the image that contains the mask from the pop-up menu on the immediate right. As with the Source pop-up menu, the Mask menu lists only those images that are open and happen to be the exact same size as the target image. If necessary, select the layer on which the mask appears from the Layer pop-up menu. Then select the specific mask channel from the final pop-up menu. This doesn't have to be a mask channel; you can use any color channel as a mask.

After you select all the necessary options, the mask works like so: Where the mask is white, the source image shows through and mixes in with the target image, just as if it were a selected portion of the floating image. Where the mask is black, the source image is absent. Gray values in the mask mix the source and target with progressive emphasis on the target as the grays darken.

If you prefer to swap the masked and unmasked areas of the source image, select the Invert check box at the bottom of the dialog box. Now, where the mask is black, you see the source image; where the mask is white, you don't.

Tip

You can even use a selection outline or layer as a mask. If you select some portion of the source image before switching to the target image and choosing Image ⇨ Apply Image, you can access the selection by choosing Selection from the Channel pop-up menu at the very bottom of the dialog box. Those pixels from the source image that fall inside the selection remain visible; those that do not are transparent. Use the Invert check box to create an inverse of the selection. To use the boundaries of a layer selected from the Layer pop-up menu as a mask, choose the Transparency option from the Channel menu. Where the layer is opaque, the source image is opaque (assuming that the Opacity option is set to 100 percent, of course); where the layer is transparent, so too is the source image.

Add and Subtract

The Add and Subtract blend modes found in the Apply Image dialog box (and also in the Calculations dialog box) add and subtract the brightness values of pixels in different channels. The Add option adds the brightness value of each pixel in the source image to that of its corresponding pixel in the target image. The Subtract option takes the brightness value of each pixel in the target image and subtracts the brightness value of its corresponding pixel in the source image. When you select either Add or Subtract, the Apply Image dialog box offers two additional option boxes, Scale and Offset. Photoshop divides the sum or difference of the Add or Subtract mode, respectively, by the Scale value (from 1.000 to 2.000), and then adds the Offset value (from negative to positive 255).

If equations help, here's the equation for the Add blend mode:

Resulting brightness value = (Target + Source) ÷ Scale + Offset

And here's the equation for the Subtract mode:

Resulting brightness value = (Target – Source) ÷ Scale + Offset

If equations only confuse you, just remember this: The Add option results in a destination image that is lighter than either source; the Subtract option results in a destination image that is darker than either source. If you want to darken the image further, raise the Scale value. To darken each pixel in the target image by a constant amount, which is useful when applying the Add option, enter a negative Offset value. If you want to lighten each pixel, as when applying the Subtract option, enter a positive Offset value.

Applying the Add command

The best way to demonstrate how these commands work is to offer an example. To create the effects shown in Figures 13-47 and 13-48, I began with the Michelangelo sculpture and the tranquil background introduced way back in Figure 13-7. The difference is, for purposes of the Apply Image command, both photographs start out in separate image windows.

After switching to the Tranquil Background image and choosing Image ➪ Apply Image, I selected the Michelangelo Face image from the Source pop-up menu. I selected the Add option from the Blending pop-up menu and accepted the default Scale and Offset values of 1 and 0, respectively, to achieve the first example in Figure 13-47. The face went blindingly white, much lighter than it would under any other blend mode, even the Dodge modes. To improve the quality and detail of the image, I changed the Scale value to 1.2 to slightly downplay the brightness values and entered an Offset value of –60 to darken the colors uniformly. The result of this operation is the more satisfactory image shown in the second example of the figure.

For the sake of comparison, the final example in Figure 13-47 shows what happens when I introduce the Tranquil Background image into the Michelangelo Face layer using the Add mode, using a Scale of 1.2 and an Offset of –60. Note that Add automatically respects the transparency mask of the face layer, regardless of whether or not you select the Preserve Transparency check box.

Applying the Subtract command

To create the first example in Figure 13-48, I selected the Subtract option from the Blending pop-up menu, once again accepting the default Scale and Offset values of 1 and 0, respectively. This time, the face turned pitch black because I subtracted the light values of the face from the light values in the background image, leaving no brightness value at all. Meanwhile, shadow details such as the eyes and lips had little effect on the background because shadows range from very dark to black. Subtracting black from a color is like subtracting 0 from a number — it leaves the value unchanged.

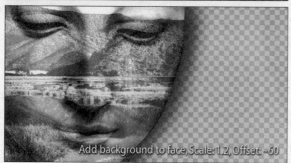

Figure 13-47: Two applications of the Add blend mode from inside the flat Tranquil Background image (top and middle), each subject to different Scale and Offset values. When adding an image into an independent layer, Add always preserves transparency (bottom).

The result struck me as too dark, so I lightened it by raising the Scale and Offset values. To create the second image in Figure 13-48, I upped the Scale value to 1.2, just as in the second Add example, which actually darkened the image slightly. Then I raised the Offset value to 180, thus adding 180 points of brightness value to each pixel. This second image is more likely to survive reproduction with all detail intact.

Subtract face from background, Scale: 1, Offset: 0

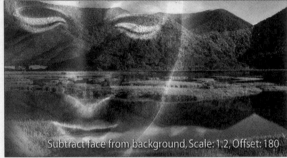

Subtract face from background, Scale: 1.2, Offset: 180

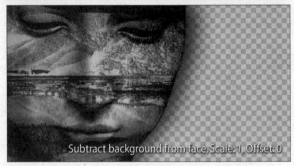

Subtract background from face, Scale: 1, Offset: 0

Figure 13-48: Two applications of the Subtract command on the Tranquil Background image, one subject to Scale and Offset values of 1 and 0 (top) and the other subject to values of 1.2 and 180 (middle). When subtracting into the Michelangelo Face image, subtract not only respects the transparency mask but delivers a very different result.

Subtracting the other direction — that is, applying the Subtract mode inside the Michelangelo Face image — produces a radically different effect, as verified by the final example of Figure 13-48. The mountains are generally quite dark, so they have little effect when subtracted from the face. In fact, by Subtract standards, this is a remarkably successful blend.

The Calculations command

Although its options are nearly identical, the Calculations command performs a different function than Apply Image. Rather than compositing a source image on top of the current target image, Image ➪ Calculations combines two source channels and puts the result in a target channel. You can use a single image for both sources, a source and the target, or all three (both sources and the target). Although Photoshop previews the effect in the foreground image window, the target doesn't have to be the foreground image. The target can even be a new image. But the biggest difference is that instead of affecting an entire full-color image, as is the case with Apply Image, the Calculations command affects individual color channels. Only one channel changes as a result of this command.

Choosing Image ➪ Calculations displays the dialog box shown in Figure 13-49. Rather than explaining this dialog box option by option — I'd just end up wasting 35 pages and repeating myself every other sentence — I'll attack the topic in a less structured but more expedient fashion.

When you arrive inside the dialog box, you select your source images from the Source 1 and Source 2 pop-up menus. As with Apply Image, the images have to be exactly the same size. You can composite individual layers using the Layer menus. Select the channels you want to mix together from the Channel options. In place of the full-color options — RGB, Lab, CMYK — each Channel menu offers a Gray option, which represents the grayscale composite of all channels in an image.

The Blending pop-up menu offers the same 19 blend modes — including Add and Subtract — found in the Apply Image dialog box. However, it's important to keep in mind how the Calculations dialog box organizes the source images when working with blend modes. The Source 1 image is equivalent to the source when using the Apply Image command (or the floating selection when compositing conventionally); the Source 2 image is equivalent to the target (or the underlying original). Therefore, choosing the Normal blend mode displays the Source 1 image. The Subtract command subtracts the Source 1 image from the Source 2 image.

Half of the blend modes perform identically regardless of which of the two images is Source 1 and which is Source 2. The other half — including Normal, Overlay, Soft Light, and Hard Light — produce different results based on the image you assign to each spot. But as long as you keep in mind that Source 1 is the floater — hey, it's at the top of the dialog box, right? — you should be okay.

Tip

The only mode that throws me off is Subtract, because I see Source 1 at the top of the dialog box and naturally assume that Photoshop subtracts Source 2, which is underneath it. But wouldn't you know, this is exactly opposite to the way it really works. If you find yourself similarly confused and set up the equation backwards, you can reverse it by selecting both Invert options. Source 2 minus Source 1 results in the same effect as an inverted Source 1 minus an inverted Source 2. After all, the equation (255 – Source 1) – (255 – Source 2), which represents an inverted Source 1 minus an inverted Source 2, simplifies down to *Source 2 – Source 1*. Then again, if math isn't your strong suit, don't worry. I was just showing my work.

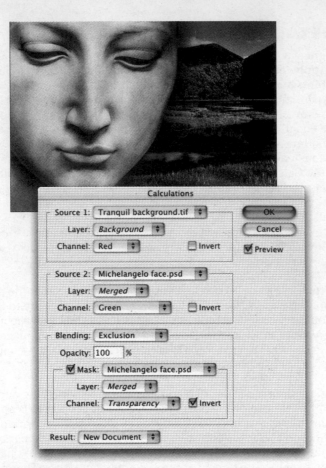

Figure 13-49: Use the Calculations command to mix two source channels and place them inside a new or an existing target channel.

As in the Apply Image dialog box, you can specify a mask using the Mask options in the Calculations dialog box. The difference here is that the mask applies to the first source image and protects the second one. So where the mask is white, the two sources mix together normally. Where the mask is black, you see the second source image only.

The Result option determines the target for the composited channels. If you select New Document from the Result pop-up menu, as in Figure 13-49, Photoshop creates a new single-channel image. Alternatively, you can stick the result of the composited channels in any channel inside any image that is the same size as the source images.

Combining masks

As described for the Apply Image command, the Channel pop-up menus may offer Selection, Transparency, and Layer Mask as options. But here they serve a greater purpose. You can composite layer masks to form selection outlines, selection outlines to form masks, and all sorts of other pragmatic combinations.

Figure 13-50 shows how the Calculations command sees selected areas. The figure starts off with a photograph by Marty Snyderman for the Corbis image library. Next we see two selections, one for the mother manatee and one for wee little Manatee Jr. Whether you're working with masks, selection outlines, transparency masks, or layer masks, the Calculations command sees the area as a grayscale image. So in Figure 13-50, white represents selected or opaque areas, and black represents deselected or transparent areas.

Original manatee image

Figure 13-50: An underwater photograph, followed by two selections expressed as grayscale images (a.k.a. masks). The mommy manatee will serve as our first source, the baby manatee will be the second.

Mommy selection (Source 1)

Baby selection (Source 2)

Screen (same as add)

Figure 13-51: Here I combined the manatee masks using the Calculations command in concert with the Screen and Multiply modes, simulating the effects of adding, subtracting, and finding the intersection of two selection outlines.

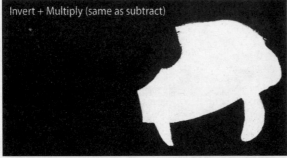

Invert + Multiply (same as subtract)

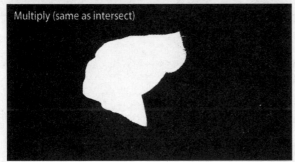

Multiply (same as intersect)

Assuming that I've chosen Image ⇨ Calculations and selected the images using the Source 1 and Source 2 options, the only remaining step is to select the proper blend mode from the Blending pop-up menu. Screen, Multiply, and Difference are the best solutions. Figure 13-51 shows the common methods for combining selection outlines. In the first example, I added the two together using the Screen mode, just as in the preceding steps. In fact, screening masks and adding selection outlines are equivalents. To subtract the Source 1 selection from Source 2, I inverted the former (by selecting the Invert check box in the Source 1 area) and applied the Multiply blend mode. To find the intersection of the two masks, I simply applied Multiply without inverting.

The Calculations command doesn't stop at the standard three — add, subtract, and intersect. Figure 13-52 shows three methods of combining selection outlines that are not possible using single keystroke operations. For example, if I invert the Source 1 mask and combine it with the Screen mode, it's like inversing the mommy manatee selection and adding it to the baby. The Difference mode adds the manatee selections but subtracts the area where they overlap, an operation known as exclusion. And inverting Source 1 and then applying Difference retains the intersection, subtracts the areas that do not intersect, and selects the area outside the manatees — which is equivalent to excluding two selections and then inversing the result. These may not be options you use every day, but they are extremely powerful if you can manage to wrap your brain around them.

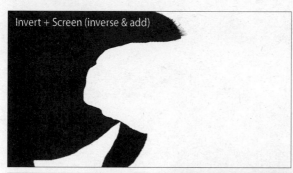

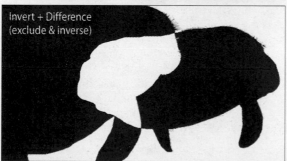

Figure 13-52: Three nontraditional ways to combine selection outlines, all greatly facilitated by the Calculations command.

Shapes and Styles

Adobe Soup

As any longtime user of Adobe products will tell you, things were sure a lot simpler in the old days. You wanted to work in a pixel-based environment, touching up photos and creating artistic images? Photoshop was the only place to be. You wanted to work with vectors, creating object-based art with razor-sharp edges? Illustrator was made just for you. You wanted to create motion graphics for video? Look no further than After Effects, my friend.

But now, things are different. Many people actually use After Effects as an image editor, completely ignoring that program's powerhouse animation capabilities and just taking advantage of its immensely flexible effects palette, arguably a better way to work with filters than Photoshop provides. Illustrator is giving bitmap graphics a full body hug now, signified by the fact that pixels are now one of the built-in units of measurement available to you. And while Photoshop's paths have always been vector-based, the shape tools bring all the advantages of drawing with vectors into Photoshop, ensuring that anything you create with them will stay sharp, whether the final destination is a high-end printer or the World Wide Web.

And it doesn't stop there; Adobe InDesign has extremely capable vector tools as well; Photoshop Elements can create animated GIFs, just like ImageReady; and After Effects outputs to the Flash format, just like LiveMotion, Adobe's dedicated Web animation tool. Sometimes it seems that all these products will eventually converge into one towering Swiss army knife of a graphics application, and when someone admires your work and asks what program you used to create it, you'll simply answer: "I did it in Adobe 1.0."

Until that day arrives, we'll have to take things piecemeal. First up in this chapter are Photoshop's aforementioned shape tools. These permit you to draw object-oriented paths filled with anything from solid colors to gradients to photographic images. Other bitmap image-editing programs may have done it before Photoshop did, but as is so often the case, none has done it better.

Next, we turn our attention to *layer styles*. While the promise of "instant drop shadows and glows" might sound at first like a cheap trick unworthy of inclusion in Photoshop's professional high-end tool set, they've actually proven to be an invaluable addition. Not only do they give you painstaking control over drop shadows, glows, and bevels, but you can coat layers with gradients, patterns, and contoured wave patterns, as well as trace outlines around layers. When combined with the advanced blending options introduced in Chapter 13, layer styles blossom into a powerful special-effects laboratory, one of the most far-reaching and flexible Adobe has ever delivered. Furthermore, you can save the effects and reapply them to future layers.

These features may not be the reason you set out to learn Photoshop in the first place, and there's no question that they'll take time and patience to fully under-stand. But you'll be rewarded with greater proficiency and versatility in the long run—and you'll be that much farther down the road to mastery when the Day of the Grand Adobe Convergence finally arrives.

Drawing Shapes

Photoshop provides six *shape tools* that allow you to draw geometric and prede-fined shapes. By default, the shapes are separated off into independent *shape layers*, which are a mix of objects and pixels. The vector-based outlines of the shapes print at the maximum resolution of your printer, while the interiors may consist of solid colors, gradients, or pixel-based patterns and images.

The pros and cons of shapes

What good are object-oriented shapes inside Photoshop? Well, I'll tell you:

✦ **Shapes are editable.** Unlike pixels, you can change a shape by moving points and control handles. Likewise, you can scale, rotate, skew, or distort shapes, or even transform specific points and segments inside shapes. Nothing is ever set in stone.

✦ **Shapes help to disguise low-resolution images.** Sharply defined edges can add clarity to a printed image. The first example in Figure 14-1 shows a stan-dard image printed at 75 pixels per inch. The second example shows that same 75-ppi image, but this time using an object-oriented shape outline. The low resolution works fine for the blurry fill, but where clarity is needed, the mathematical outline is there to serve.

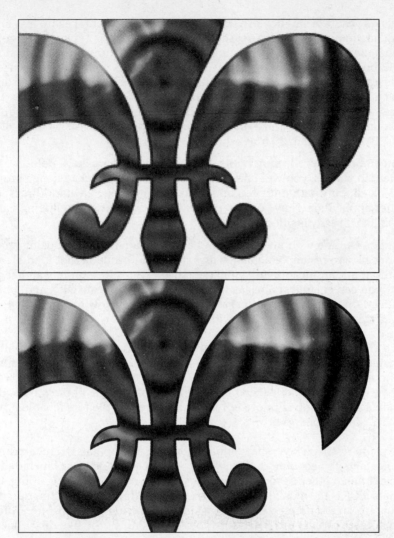

Figure 14-1: The difference between a 75-ppi graphic saved as a
flat image (top) and as an object-oriented path outline (bottom).
Although the blurry interiors appear identical, the shape outline
becomes several times sharper when expressed as a path.

✦ **You can color a shape with a layer style.** As we see later in this same chapter,
layer effects such as drop shadows and beveled edges are equally applicable
to shape layers as they are to standard image layers. And it's amazing what
wild effects you can achieve with a shape, a style, and no talent whatsoever.
To create Figure 14-1, for example, I drew a fleur-de-lis shape and applied the
Striped Cone style from the Styles palette.

✦ **Shapes result in smaller file sizes.** As a rule, an object takes up less space on disk than an image. Expressed in PostScript code, a typical path outline consumes 8 bytes per anchor point, as compared with 3 bytes for a single RGB pixel. But while a shape may contain as few as 4 points in the case of a rectangle or ellipse, an image routinely contains hundreds of thousands of pixels. For example, the illustration pictured in Figure 14-1 consumes 172K on disk when saved as a native PSD file. If I rasterized the image at an equivalent resolution — say, 600 ppi — using exclusively pixels, the file would balloon to 3.5MB, or more than 20 times the size.

✦ **You can preview clipping paths directly inside Photoshop.** Before object-oriented shapes, you were never quite sure if you traced an image properly with a clipping path until you imported it into InDesign, QuarkXPress, or some other application. Now you can preview exactly what your clipping path will look like directly inside Photoshop.

✦ **Shapes expand with an image.** In Chapter 3, I advise against using Image ➪ Image Size to resample an image upward on the grounds that it adds pixels without adding meaningful detail (see the section "Resampling an image"). But you can enlarge shapes as much as you want. Because it's mathematically defined, the shape remains crystal clear no matter how big or small you make it. Layer styles likewise resize without problem.

If vectors are so great, why not forsake pixels and start drawing entirely with shape layers instead? While a shape can clip a continuous-tone photograph, it can't replace one. Although there have been all kinds of experiments using objects and fractals, pixels are still the most viable medium for representing digital photographs. Because Photoshop's primary job is photo editing, pixels are (for the foreseeable future) the program's primary commodity.

One downside to shape layers is compatibility. Photoshop has stretched the TIFF and PDF formats to accommodate any kind of layer — shape layers included — but that doesn't mean other programs have any idea what Photoshop is doing. Of all the formats, PDF is the most likely to work with other programs. Just be sure to proof the document on a laser printer before taking it to a commercial printer. After all, when you create objects in Photoshop, you're working on the bleeding edge, so be prepared for the consequences.

The shape tools

Now that I've painted my rosy picture, let's dig in and look at the tools. Or, if you're not feeling brave enough, take a break and come back later. Either way. Up to you. As you've probably discovered by now, I like to give my readers lots of autonomy. That way, you're responsible for your own actions and you can't sue me if you go and pour this piping hot book all over your lap.

Now as I was saying, click the rectangle tool to display a flyout menu of six shape tools, pictured in Figure 14-2. Or press U to select the rectangle tool. Then press U again (or Shift+U) to switch from one shape tool to the next. Either way — remember, it's totally up to you, I make no recommendations (as my lawyer told me to tell you) — the six shape tools work as follows:

✦ **Rectangle tool:** It used to be a running gag that the hardest thing to do in Photoshop was to draw a simple rectangle. You had to draw a rectangular marquee and then fill it. Not hard, I guess, but what person outside the walls of a sanitarium would think to approach it that way? But the gag is dead — these days drawing a rectangle is easy. Drag to draw a rectangle from one corner to the other, Shift-drag to draw a square, Alt-drag (Win) or Option-drag (Mac) to draw the shape outward from the center.

While drawing a rectangle or any other shape, press the spacebar to reposition the shape. Then release the spacebar and continue dragging to resize the shape as you normally do.

Tip

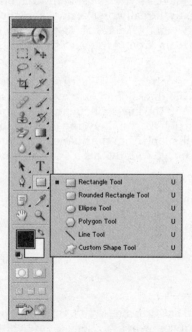

Figure 14-2: Click the rectangle tool to display the shape tools flyout menu. Or press U or Shift+U to switch between tools.

✦ **Rounded rectangle tool:** When you select the rounded rectangle tool, a Radius value becomes available in the Options bar. If you think of each rounded corner as a quarter of a circle, the Radius value is the radius (half the diameter) of that circle. Bigger values result in more roundness.

✦ **Ellipse tool:** The ellipse tool draws ovals. Shift-drag for circles, Alt-drag (Win) or Option-drag (Mac) to draw the oval outward from the center.

✦ **Polygon tool:** This tool draws regular polygons, which are straight-sided shapes with radial symmetry. Examples include isosceles triangles (3 sides), squares (4 sides), pentagons (5 sides), hexagons (6 sides), heptagons (7 sides), octagons (8 sides), decagons (10 sides), dodecagons (12 sides), and a bunch of other shapes with so many sides that they're virtually indistinguishable from circles. Enter a Sides value in the Options bar to set the number of sides in the next polygon you draw. Or better yet, press the bracket keys, [and], to decrease or increase the Sides value from keyboard. You can also draw stars and rounded shapes, as I explain in the next section.

✦ **Line tool:** Some of you are probably thinking to yourselves, "Deke, you blithering nincompoop, how can you call these 'shape tools' when one of them draws lines?" Well, despite your name-calling, I'll tell you. The truth is, even the line tool draws shapes. Enter a Weight value into the Options bar to define the thickness of the so-called "line," and then drag in the image window. The result is an extremely long and skinny rectangle. As you see shortly, this makes editing a line exceedingly difficult. Honestly, it really breaks my heart that The Squirt Gun that Shoots Jelly has to live on the Island of Misfit Toys while The Line Tool that Draws Shapes gets to roam around free as a bird (one that doesn't swim).

✦ **Custom shape tool:** It saddens me to say this, but so far, the shape tools are a bunch of drips. You can't edit the roundness of an existing rectangle or add sides to a polygon while drawing it. And the line tool offends even the otherwise open-minded Cowboy on an Ostrich. Fortunately, the custom shape tool makes up for them all. Select a preset shape from the Shape option in the Options bar, and then draw it in the image window. It's a symbol library of instant clip art.

By grouping the pen tools up in the Options bar along with the rectangle tool and its five cohorts, Photoshop 7 is finally confessing: "Yes! The pen tools are actually shape tools too!" After selecting a pen tool, click the Shape Layers button in the Options bar (see Figure 14-3) to draw your own custom shape layer.

The shape-drawing process

The act of drawing a shape can be as simple as dragging with a tool. How that shape manifests itself, however, depends primarily on which of the first three buttons pictured in Figure 14-3 is depressed. The first option creates a new shape layer when you draw with the shape tool. The second option creates a work path, available for inspection in the Paths palette. And the final option creates a pixel-based shape. Photoshop doesn't add a new layer; it merely recolors the pixels on the active layer. While simple in theory, the program offers you a wealth of additional controls. Just for the record, here's the long way to approach the process of drawing a shape layer.

STEPS: Creating a New Shape Layer

1. **Select the shape tool you want to use.** Remember, U is the keyboard shortcut for the shape tools.

2. **Specify the color.** Select a color for the shape from the Color palette. Alternatively, you can click either the foreground color icon in the toolbox or the Color swatch in the Options bar, and then select a color from the Color Picker. If you want to fill the shape with a gradient, pattern, or image, you can do that after you finish drawing the shape, as I explain in the upcoming section "Editing the stuff inside the shape."

3. **Specify how you want to draw the shape.** Pictured in Figure 14-3, the first three buttons in the Options bar determine what the shape tool draws. Because we're creating a shape layer, you'll want to make sure the first button is selected.

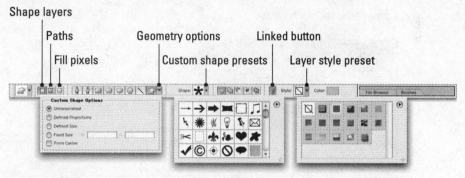

Figure 14-3: Use the options in the Options bar to specify the appearance of a shape before you draw it.

4. **Modify the geometry options.** Click the down-pointing arrowhead to the right of the tool buttons in the Options bar (labeled "Geometry options" in Figure 14-3) to see a pop-up palette of options geared to the selected shape tool. These permit you to constrain rectangles, ellipses, and custom shapes; indent the sides of a polygon to create a star; round off the corners of a polygon or star; and add arrowheads to a line.

   The one unusual option is Snap To Pixels, which is associated with the two rectangle tools. Object-oriented shapes don't have any resolution, so their sides and corners can land in the middle of pixels. To prevent potential antialiasing in rectangles, select the Snap To Pixels check box to precisely align them with the pixels in the image.

5. **Modify other tool-specific settings.** Depending on the tool, you may see options to the right of the geometry options arrowhead. The polygon tool offers a Sides option; the line tool offers a Weight option. When drawing a

custom shape, click the shape button to display a pop-up palette of presets, as shown in Figure 14-3. You can load more shapes by choosing the Load Shapes command or by choosing a predefined presets (.csh) file from the presets palette menu.

6. **Apply a layer style.** When drawing a shape layer, you can assign a layer style to your shape before drawing it. The Layer Style pop-up palette offers all presets available in the Styles palette, as discussed in the "Saving effects as styles" section at the end of this chapter.

7. **Draw the shape.** Because you set the tool to draw a shape layer in Step 3, Photoshop automatically creates a new layer. As shown in Figure 14-4, the Layers palette shows a colored fill (labeled "Layer contents" in the figure) with a clipping path—or *vector mask*, in Photoshop 7 parlance—to the right of it, masking the fill. If you assigned a layer style, a list of one or more effects appears under the layer name.

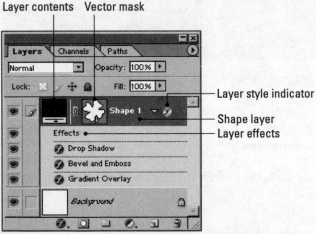

Figure 14-4: A shape layer is actually a vector mask that masks a color or other contents directly inside Photoshop.

8. **Switch tools and draw more shapes.** By default, Photoshop creates a new shape layer for each new shape that you draw. If you prefer to keep adding to the same shape layer so that all shapes will share the same fill, click the Add to Shape Area button in the Options bar (it's labeled in Figure 14-5). Then draw a new shape.

This behavior is contrary to what took place in Photoshop 6. Version 7 adds a new compound path option to the Options bar—the Create New Shape Layer button (labeled in Figure 14-5)—and it's turned on by default. With this option selected, Photoshop creates a new shape layer for every shape that you draw. Photoshop 6 had the Add to Shape Area option selected by default, meaning that every shape you drew was added to the same shape layer.

If you hit the Enter, Return, or Escape key, the current shape layer is deactivated, signifying that you no longer want to add shapes to that layer. This change is visible in the Layers palette; notice that the vector mask thumbnail no longer has a selection border around it. To reactivate the layer, simply click the thumbnail.

That's it. You now have one or more shape layers that you can use as you please. From this point on, it's a matter of editing the shape, as explained in the following sections.

Combining and editing shapes

A few years back, there was an image editor called Live Picture. Its creators heralded it as the first image editor to provide "infinite incremental undos." In fact, the program had a run-of-the-mill single-level Undo/Redo command. The infinite incremental undos were actually a result of an object metaphor that pervaded the program. After drawing an element, you had the option of changing it. It wasn't an automated undo, but rather a manual adjustment.

By this twisted marketing logic, Photoshop's shape layers permit infinite incremental undos. Although I'm being deliberately ironic, there is much to be said for a mask that is perpetually editable. Don't like a segment? Change it. Don't like a point? Move it. Hate the entire shape? Delete it. Here's how:

✦ **Compound path options:** As explained in Step 8 in the previous section, you can draw multiple shapes on a single layer. Because they all share a single fill, Photoshop thinks of the shapes as being bits and pieces of a single, complex path. In drawing parlance, such a path is called a *compound path*. This leads Photoshop to wonder, what do I do when the bits and pieces overlap? Because they share a fill, they could just merge together. Or perhaps you'd rather use one shape to cut a hole in the other. Or maybe you'd like the intersection to be transparent.

You specify your preference by selecting one of the last four compound path buttons, shown in Figure 14-5. (As mentioned previously, the first button, which is on by default, makes Photoshop create every shape on its own shape layer.) Click the second button or press the plus key (+) to add the new shape to the others. Click the third button or press the minus key (–) to subtract the new shape from the others. The fourth button retains the intersection, the fifth makes the intersection transparent. Feel free to experiment with these Boolean operations (if you'll pardon a little techno-speak).

✦ **Selecting shapes:** You have access to all but the first compound path button when selecting shapes with the arrow tool. Press A to get the black arrow tool — if you get the white arrow instead, press A again (or Shift+A if the Use Shift Key for Tool Switch preference setting is turned on) — and then click a shape to select it. Or Ctrl-click (⌘-click on the Mac) a shape when using a shape tool.

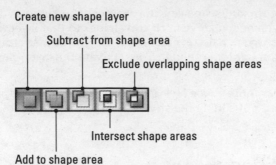

Create new shape layer

Subtract from shape area

Exclude overlapping shape areas

Intersect shape areas

Add to shape area

Figure 14-5: The five compound path buttons; the last four are available when editing or adding to an existing shape layer.

✦ **Moving and transforming:** Drag a selected shape to move it. Select the Show Bounding Box check box in the Options bar to access the transformation controls. Or press Ctrl+T (⌘-T on the Mac) to enter the free transform mode. Then drag a handle to scale, drag outside the bounding box to rotate, and Ctrl-drag (Win) or ⌘-drag (Mac) a handle to skew or distort. If you need a transformation refresher, check out the section "Applying Transformations" in Chapter 12.

✦ **Arranging and combining shapes:** After selecting a shape with the arrow tool, you can apply any of the four available compound path buttons. As you do, bear in mind that the topmost shape takes precedence. So if Shape A is set to Add, Shape B is set to Intersect, and Shape B is in front, then Photoshop fills only the intersection. Meanwhile, the stacking order is entirely dependent on the order in which you draw the shapes, with more recent shapes in front. (The Layer ⇨ Arrange commands affect whole layers; they can't be used to reorder shapes.) Once you get the effect you're looking for, you can fix the relationship by selecting two or more paths and clicking the Combine button in the Options bar. Photoshop fuses the selected paths into one.

Caution

Technically, you can combine multiple shapes that don't overlap. But I advise against it. At first, the shapes behave as if they're grouped together. But try to combine other paths with them, and you may uncover some pretty strange relationships. Something about these paths reminds me of Jeff Goldblum in the last hour of *The Fly*. Some things on this planet just shouldn't be combined.

✦ **Selecting points and segments:** Press A or Shift+A (depending on your preference setting) to get the white arrow tool, which selects individual points and segments. Move individually selected points by dragging them; transform such points by pressing Ctrl+T (Win) or ⌘-T (Mac). To select an entire shape, Alt-click (Win) or Option-click (Mac) on it.

✦ **Adding and deleting points:** The best tool for reshaping a shape is the pen tool. First select part of the shape with one of the arrow tools. Then click a segment to insert a point; drag on a segment to add a smooth point; click a point to remove it. You can likewise use the convert point tool, as well as any other technique that's applicable to paths.

✦ **Disabling a vector mask:** Shift-click the vector mask thumbnail in the Layers palette to turn it off and make visible the entire contents of the layer. Shift-click the thumbnail again to turn the vector mask on.

✦ **Duplicating a vector mask:** So far as Photoshop is concerned, shapes are just another kind of path. So it's not surprising that you can access the paths in an active shape layer from the Paths palette. Drag the *Vector Mask* item onto the tiny page icon at the bottom of the Paths palette to duplicate the shapes so you can use them elsewhere as standard paths (as discussed in Chapter 8).

✦ **Deleting a vector mask:** Click the vector mask thumbnail and then click the trash can icon at the bottom of the Layers palette to delete the shapes from the layer. You can also just drag the thumbnail to the trash can icon. To add a new shape to the layer, first choose Layer ➪ Add Vector Mask ➪ Hide All. Then draw shapes in the layer to expose portions of the layer's contents.

✦ **Defining your own custom shape:** If you create a shape that you think you might want to repeat in the future, select the shape with either arrow tool and choose Edit ➪ Define Custom Shape. Then name the shape and press Enter or Return. Photoshop adds the shape to the presets so you can draw it with the custom shape tool. If you want to keep it around, it's a good idea to save the shape with the Preset Manager, as discussed in Chapter 2.

The moral of the story is, shapes work a lot like paths. If you find yourself strangely drawn to the Dark Art of Shape Editing and you're afraid I've forgotten to mention some amazing technique once known to the Oblique Brotherhood of Vector Druids — as I undoubtedly have — consult the "Reshaping paths" and "Transforming paths" scrolls, which I've sequestered inside the caliginous catacombs of Chapter 8.

Editing the stuff inside the shape

Here are a few ways to modify the color and general appearance of shape layers:

✦ **Changing the color:** To change the color of a shape layer, double-click the layer contents thumbnail in the Layers palette. Then select a new color from the Color Picker dialog box. Or better yet, change the foreground color and then press Alt+Backspace (Option-Delete on the Mac).

✦ **Changing the blending options:** You can change the blend mode and Opacity value for a shape layer using the standard controls in the Layers palette. Or double-click anywhere on the layer except the name or the layer contents thumbnail to display the Blending Options section of the Layer Style dialog box. As discussed in Chapter 13, these options work the same for shape layers as they do for normal layers. You can also apply or modify layer effects, as I explain later in this chapter.

✦ **Changing the layer style:** Another way to apply or switch out layer effects is to apply a predefined style from the Styles palette. Just click a preset in the Styles palette and Photoshop automatically applies it to the active layer. After that, you can edit an effect by double-clicking its name in the Layers palette.

The linked button labeled back in Figure 14-3 comes into play when you make a change to the layer style or color of a shape layer. If the button is selected, changes you make to the style or color are applied, or "linked," to the currently active shape layer; if the button isn't selected, the style or color change applies to the next shape layers you create.

✦ **Renaming the shape layer:** Double-click the name of a shape layer to rename it.

✦ **Fill with a gradient or repeating pattern:** Don't want to fill your shape with a solid color? Don't have to. To fill the active shape layer with a gradient, choose Layer ⇨ Change Layer Content ⇨ Gradient. Or choose Layer ⇨ Change Layer Content ⇨ Pattern to apply a repeating pattern. Figure 14-6 shows the dialog box for each. Most of the options are familiar from the gradient tool (Chapter 6) and pattern stamp tool (Chapter 7) discussions. The only new options are in the Pattern Fill dialog box. Scale lets you resize the pattern inside the shape; Link With Layer makes sure the shape and pattern move together; and Snap To Origin snaps the pattern into alignment with the origin.

You can reposition a gradient or pattern inside its shape just by dragging inside the image window while the dialog box is up on screen.

After applying a gradient or pattern, you can edit it just by double-clicking the layer contents thumbnail in the Layers palette. Photoshop calls these kinds of editable contents *dynamic fills*.

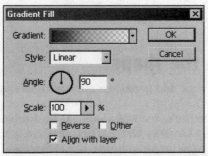

Figure 14-6: Gradients and patterns inside a shape layer are considered dynamic fills, which means you can edit them simply by double-clicking the layer contents thumbnail and editing the options above.

✦ **Making a color adjustment shape:** Where layer content is concerned, shape layers have unlimited potential. You can even fill a shape with a color adjustment. Just choose Levels, Curves, Hue/Saturation, or any of the other color correction classics from the Layer ➪ Change Layer Content submenu. Read the "Adjustment Layers" section of Chapter 17 for complete information.

✦ **Painting inside a shape layer:** Wish you could paint or edit the contents of a shape layer? Well, thanks to subtle genetic alterations to Photoshop's core subroutines, you can. Assuming the shape is filled with a solid color, gradient, or pattern (this technique is not applicable to adjustment layers), choose Layer ➪ Rasterize ➪ Fill Content. From this point on, the fill is no longer dynamic. This means you can't double-click its thumbnail to edit it. However, you can edit it like any other layer full of pixels. Paint inside it, clone from another layer with the stamp tool, apply a filter, go nuts.

✦ **Filling a vector mask with an image:** Applying a vector mask to an image is a more delicate operation. Fortunately, there are several ways to do it, so you can select your favorite. Method number one: Draw a shape not as a new shape layer, but rather as a working path (see "The shape drawing process" earlier in this chapter). Then select the layer that you want to mask (it must be a floating layer, not the background) and choose Layer ➪ Add Vector Mask ➪ Current Path.

Want to avoid that command? After establishing a work path, Ctrl-click (Win) or ⌘-click (Mac) the Add Layer Mask icon at the bottom of the Layers palette to make the path clip the active image layer.

✦ **From clipping group to vector mask:** Okay, so that's one way. But what if you've already gone and made a shape layer, and you want to fill that shape with an image? Again, there are a few approaches, but the easiest is to paste the image onto a layer in front of the shape layer. Then press Ctrl+G (Win) or ⌘-G (Mac) to group it with the shape layer.

✦ **Fusing image and shape layer:** That's enough to create the same visual effect as a shape masking an image, but it involves two layers instead of one. If you want for any reason to fuse the two layers together, you have to take a special approach once again. First, select the shape layer and choose Layer ➪ Rasterize ➪ Fill Content to convert the dynamic fill to pixels. Then select the image layer and press Ctrl+E (Win) or ⌘-E (Mac) to merge it with the shape layer below.

If all this isn't enough, there is one more way to push the boundaries of shape layers and wring the last vestiges of cogent reasoning out of your by-now fragile mind. How? By adding a layer mask to a shape layer. That's right, Photoshop lets you combine pixel masking and vector masking on one layer, as shown in Figure 14-7. Why do it? Well, of course, there's always the chance it appeals to a latent strain of masochism on your part. But also, the combination permits you to have soft and razor sharp edges all in the same layer. For example, in the figure, I Ctrl-clicked (⌘-clicked on the Mac) on the vector mask and then loaded that as a layer mask by clicking the add layer mask icon at the bottom of the Layers palette. In other words, the layer mask is identical to the vector mask. Why in the world would I want to do that? Because in Figure 14-8, I applied Gaussian Blur to the layer mask and then applied the Crystallize filter. The result is soft filtered edges along the inside of the vector shape, but then a hard edge after that. The layer mask masks the layer, and then the vector mask masks that. Pretty spiffy, huh?

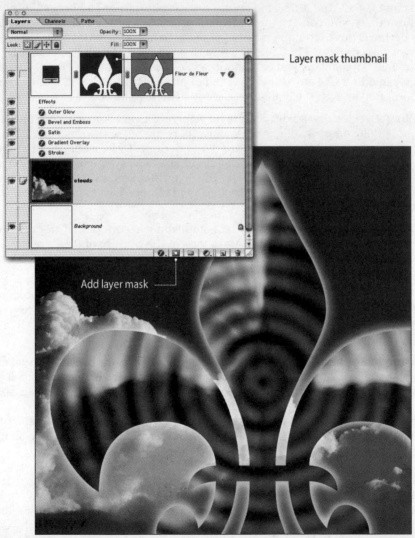

Figure 14-7: Add a layer mask to a shape layer to add pixel-based softening to the razor-sharp vector mask.

Gaussian Blur, Radius: 24 pixels

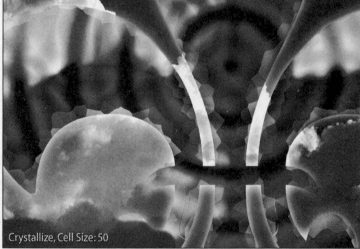

Crystallize, Cell Size: 50

Figure 14-8: Applying the Gaussian Blur (top) and Crystallize filters to the layer mask mixes a soft pixelated effect with the hard edges provided by the vector mask (bottom).

The Bold-and-Beautiful Layer Styles

Photoshop 5 introduced a series of *layer effects* that automate the application of shadows, glows, and beveled edges. Version 6 took that metaphor several steps further, dramatically improving the quality of the existing effects and adding effects that overlay colors, stroke outlines, and create textures and contours. It also let you define exactly how effects are blended with background layers and permitted you to save them as preset *layer styles* for later use. Photoshop 6 elevated layer effects from nifty tools to some of the most powerful functions inside the program, and in Photoshop 7 we can continue to bask in their effulgent glory.

To apply a layer effect, start with an image on an independent layer. In Figure 14-9, I painted the numeral 7 on an independent layer, but you can use any kind of layer, including text (see Chapter 15) or a shape layer. Then click the add layer style icon at the bottom of the Layers palette — the one that looks like a florin (cursive *f*) — and choose any of the commands following Blending Options. Or double-click anywhere on the layer other than the layer name to display the Layer Style dialog box and then select an effect from the left-hand list. Use the check box to turn the effect on and off; highlight the effect name to edit its settings. You can select from one of the following ten effects:

✦ **Drop Shadow:** The Drop Shadow command applies a common, everyday drop shadow, as seen in the first example of Figure 14-10. You specify the color, opacity, blend mode, position, size, and contour of the shadow; Photoshop makes it pretty.

✦ **Inner Shadow:** This command applies a drop shadow inside the layer, as demonstrated in the second example in Figure 14-10. The command simulates the kind of shadow you'd get if the layer were punched out of the background — that is, the background looks like it's in front, casting a shadow onto the layer. Figure 14-10 should give you an inkling of the fact that Inner Shadow is especially effective with type.

✦ **Outer Glow:** The Outer Glow command creates a traditional halo, as seen in the first example in Figure 14-11. However, you have lots of additional controls in case you want to get fancy.

✦ **Inner Glow:** This command applies the effect inside the layer rather than outside, as demonstrated in the second example in Figure 14-11.

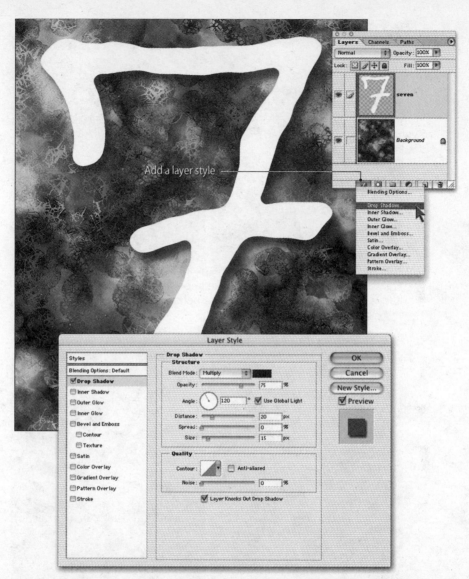

Figure 14-9: Starting with an independent layer, click the add layer style icon at the bottom of the Layers palette and choose an effect (top). Then adjust the settings inside the sprawling Layer Style dialog box (bottom).

Drop shadow, Distance: 25, Size: 30 Inner shadow, Distance: 20, Size: 10

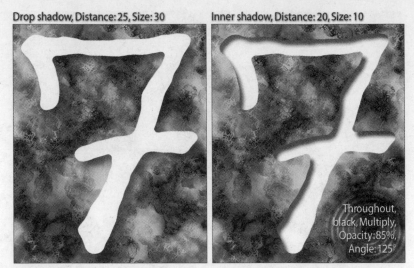

Throughout, black, Multiply, Opacity: 85%, Angle: 125°

Figure 14-10: Layer styles can make it look like the affected layer is above (left) or below (right) the layer behind it.

Outer glow, Size: 30 Inner glow, Size: 20

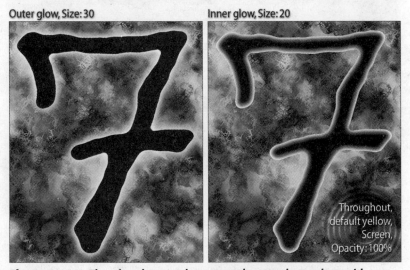

Throughout, default yellow, Screen, Opacity: 100%

Figure 14-11: The glow layer styles can make your layer glow with outer (left) or inner (right) beauty. I filled my numeral 7 with black instead of white to help show off the glows.

Tip

To create a neon strip around the perimeter of a layer, apply both the Outer Glow and Inner Glow commands. Figure 14-12 shows an example of a neon edge (top-right), as well as other effects you can obtain by mixing and matching shadows and glows.

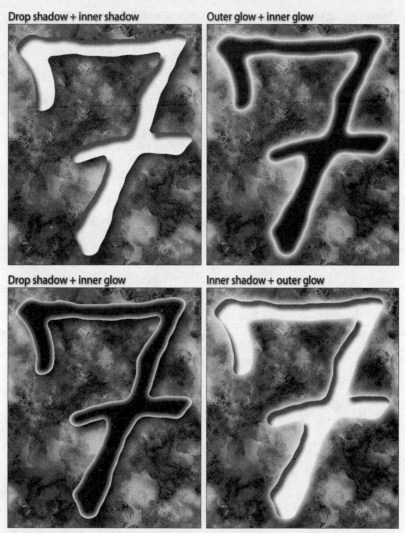

Figure 14-12: Simply sticking with the shadow and glow layer styles, you can come up with some effective combinations.

✦ **Bevel and Emboss:** The Bevel and Emboss option produces one of five distinct edge effects, as defined using the Style pop-up menu. The first four appear in Figure 14-13; the fifth one is exclusively applicable to stroked layers and requires the Stroke effect to be turned on. You can add a three-dimensional beveled edge around the outside of the layer, as in the first example in the figure. The Inner Bevel effect (top-right) produces a beveled edge inside the layer. The Emboss effect (bottom-left) combines inner and outer bevels. And the Pillow Emboss effect (bottom-right) reverses the inner bevel so the image appears to sink in and then rise back up along the edge of the layer.

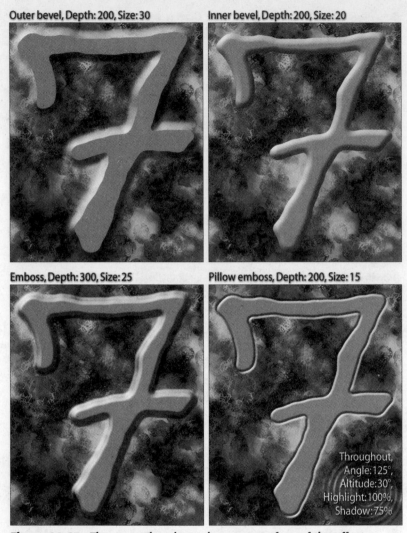

Figure 14-13: The examples above demonstrate four of the effects available when you choose Layer ⇨ Layer Style ⇨ Bevel and Emboss. I filled my numeral 7 with medium gray to better show off the highlights and shadows that Bevel and Emboss creates.

✦ **Contour and Texture:** The Contour and Texture options aren't actual effects, but rather modify the Bevel and Emboss effect. The Contour settings create waves in the surface of the layer that result in rippling lighting effects. Texture stamps a pattern into the surface of the layer, which creates a texture effect. Figure 14-14 illustrates these two options.

Inner bevel, Contour: Ring, Range: 20%   same, Texture, Pattern: Molecular

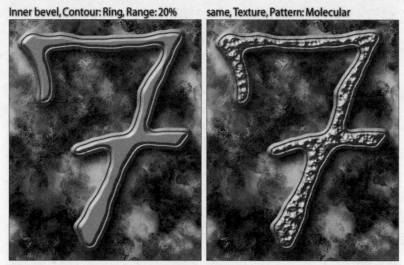

Figure 14-14: The Contour (left) and Texture (right) options available with the Inner Bevel effect let you break up the surface of your layer in interesting ways.

✦ **Satin:** This option creates waves of color, as in Figure 14-15. You define the behavior of the waves using the Contour options. One of the stranger effects, Satin can be difficult to predict. But so long as you keep the Preview check box turned on, you can experiment with a fair amount of success.

Satin, Angle: 125°, Distance: 50, Size: 30   same, with contoured inner bevel

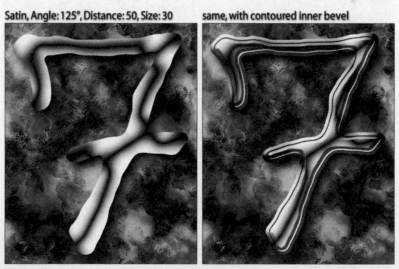

Figure 14-15: After making my numeral 7 white, I applied the Satin option (left) and then added a contoured inner bevel to produce a dramatic, metallic effect (right).

✦ **Color, Gradient, and Pattern Overlay:** These three options fill the layer with a coating of solid color, gradient, or repeating pattern, respectively. They work almost identically to the three dynamic fills available to shape layers, as discussed in the section "Editing the stuff inside the shape" earlier in this chapter. All three can be quite useful when defining your own style presets. Figure 14-16 shows off the Gradient and Pattern Overlay effects.

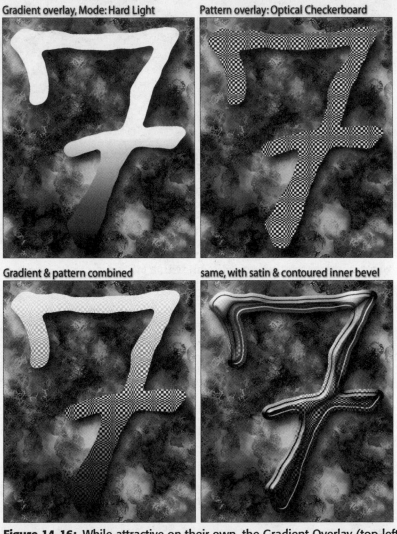

Figure 14-16: While attractive on their own, the Gradient Overlay (top-left) and Pattern Overlay (top-right) options can be combined to create the entrancing effect shown in the bottom-left example. Add in my Satin and Inner Bevel settings from Figure 14-15, and the bottom-right example is the ravishing result.

✦ **Stroke:** Use this option to trace a colored outline around a layer, as shown in Figure 14-17. The Stroke effect is often preferable to Edit ⇨ Stroke because you can edit it long after creating it. By comparison, Edit ⇨ Stroke is a permanent effect.

Stroke, black, 7 pixels, with stroke emboss   same, with satin, gradient, & pattern

 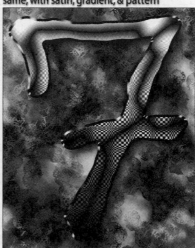

Figure 14-17: The Stroke effect (left) is an editable alternative to the Edit ⇨ Stroke command and can be used in combination with other layer effects (right). Don't worry, I'll make this look better in just a second.

The Layer Style dialog box is a vast labyrinth of options. So it's handy to know a few additional ways to get around. To switch between effects without turning them on or off, press Ctrl (Win) or ⌘ (Mac) plus a number key. Ctrl+1 (⌘-1 on the Mac) highlights Drop Shadow, Ctrl+2 (⌘-2) highlights Inner Shadow, Ctrl+3 (⌘-3) highlights Outer Glow, and so on, all the way to Ctrl+0 (⌘-0) for Stroke. You cannot get to Blending Options, Contour, or Texture from the keyboard.

The advantages of layer effects

The layer effects available in the Layer Style dialog box are a godsend to beginners and intermediate folks, but experienced users might be tempted to turn their noses up at them. After all, you can create many of these effects manually using layers, selection outlines, and blend modes. But there is much to like about automated layer effects:

✦ First, they stick to the layer. Move or transform the layer and the effect tags along with it.

✦ Second, the effect is temporary. So long as you save the image in one of the three layered formats — native Photoshop (PSD), TIFF, or PDF — you can edit the shadows, glows, bevels, overlays, and strokes long into the future.

✦ Third, layer effects are equally applicable to standard layers, shape layers, and editable text. This is unusual because both shape layers and editable text prohibit many kinds of changes.

✦ Fourth, thanks to the Contour presets, layer effects enable you to create effects that would prove otherwise exceedingly difficult or even impossible.

✦ Fifth, you can combine multiple effects on a single layer.

✦ Sixth, you can copy an effect from one layer and paste it onto another.

✦ Seventh, you can save groups of effects for later use in the Styles palette.

✦ Eighth, the effects show up as items in the Layers palette. You can expand and collapse a list of effects, as well as temporarily disable and enable effects by clicking the familiar eyeball icons.

✦ Ninth — why the heck do you need a ninth advantage? Didn't television teach us that *Eight Is Enough*? But what the heck. Ninth, layer effect strokes print as vector output, so they're guaranteed to be smooth. There, satisfied?

Now that you're champing at the bit to get your mitts on these effects, the following sections tell you how, why, and what for.

Inside the Layer Style dialog box

The Layer Style dialog box offers 13 panels containing more than 100 options. I discussed the first panel, Blending Options, in Chapter 13. The remaining 12 panels are devoted to layer effects. Select the desired effect from the list on the left; use the check box to turn the effect on and off.

Although there are gobs of options, many of them are self-explanatory. You select a blend mode from the Blend Mode pop-up menu. (For explanations of these, look to "The blend modes" section of Chapter 13.) You make the effect translucent by entering a value in the Opacity option box.

Other options appear multiple times throughout the course of the dialog box. All the options that appear in the Inner Shadow panel also appear in the Drop Shadow panel; the options from the Outer Glow panel appear in the Inner Glow panel; and so on. The modified dialog box in Figure 14-18 shows four representative effects panels — Inner Shadow, Inner Glow, Bevel and Emboss, and Texture — which together contain most of the options you'll encounter.

The following items explain the options in the order that they appear throughout the panels. I explain each option only once, so if an option appears multiple times (as so many do), look for its first appearance in a panel to locate the corresponding discussion in the following list:

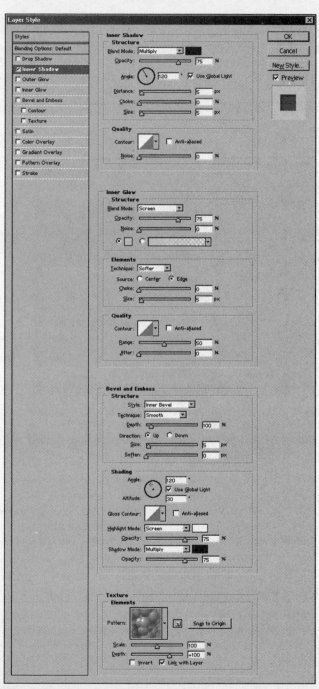

Figure 14-18: A modified picture of the Layer Style dialog box, featuring the Inner Shadow, Inner Glow, Bevel and Emboss, and Texture panels.

✦ **Blend Mode:** This pop-up menu controls the blend mode. So much for the obvious. But did you know that you can use the Blend Mode menu to turn an effect upside-down? Select a light color and apply the Screen mode to change a drop shadow into a directional halo. Or use a dark color with Multiply to change an outer glow into a shadow that evenly traces the edge of the layer. Don't be constrained by pedestrian notions of shadows and glows. Layer effects can be anything. Figure 14-19 offers proof.

Inner shadow, white, Screen   Outer glow, black, Multiply

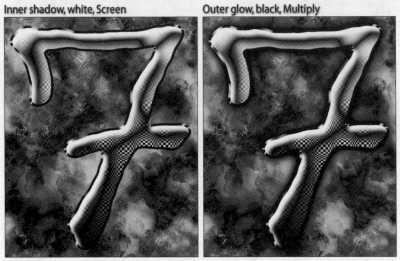

Figure 14-19: Starting with the last example in Figure 14-17 (an image of questionable attractiveness), I add a white inner shadow (left) to create a soft beveling effect, and then surround the whole thing with a black outer glow (right) to make my numeral really stand out from the background.

✦ **Color Swatch:** To change the color of the shadow, glow, or beveled edge, click the color swatch. When the Color Picker is open, click in the image window to eyedrop a color from the layered composition. When editing a glow, you can apply a gradient in place of a solid color. Click the gradient preview to create a custom gradation or select a preset from the pop-up palette.

✦ **Opacity:** Use this option to make the effect translucent. Remember, a little bit of effect goes a long way. When in doubt, reduce the Opacity value.

✦ **Angle:** Associated with shadows, bevels, the Satin effect, and gradients, this value controls the direction of the effect. In the case of shadows and bevels, the option controls the angle of the light source. With Satin, it controls the angle at which contour patterns overlap. And with a gradient, the Angle value represents the direction of the gradient.

Tip

You can avoid the numerical Angle option and simply drag an effect inside the image window. When the Drop Shadow or Inner Shadow panel is visible, drag inside the image window to move the shadow with respect to the layer. You can also drag the contour effect when working in the Satin panel. Other draggable effects include Gradient Overlay and Pattern Overlay, although dragging affects positioning, not angle.

✦ **Use Global Light:** In the real world, the sun casts all shadows in the same direction. Oh, sure, the shadows change minutely from one object to the next, but what with the sun being 90 million miles away and all, the changes are astronomically subtle. I doubt if a single-celled organism, upon admiring its shadow compared with that of its neighbor, could perceive the slightest difference. The fact that single-celled organisms lack eyes, brains, and other perceptual organs does not in any way lessen the truth of this powerful argument.

As I was saying, one sun means one lightness and one darkness. By turning on the Use Global Light check box, you tell Photoshop to cast *all* direction-dependent effects — drop shadows, inner shadows, and the five kinds of bevels — in the same direction. If you change the angle of a drop shadow applied to Layer 1, Photoshop rotates the sun in its heaven and so changes the angle of the pillow emboss applied to Layer 9, thus proving that even a computer program may subscribe to the immutable laws of nature.

Conversely, if you turn the check box off, you tell nature to take a hike. You can change an Angle value in any which way you like and none of the other layers will care.

Tip

If you have established a consistent universe, you can edit the angle of the sun by choosing Layer ⇨ Layer Style ⇨ Global Light. Change the Angle value and all shadows and bevels created with Use Global Light turned on will move in unison. You can also set the Altitude for bevels. "Sunrise, sunset," as the Yiddish fiddlers say. That doesn't shed any light on the topic, but when in doubt, I like to quote a great musical to class up the joint.

✦ **Distance:** The Drop Shadow, Inner Shadow, and Satin panels feature a Distance value that determines the distance between the farthest edge of the effect and the corresponding edge of the layer. Like Angle, this value is affected when you drag in the image window.

✦ **Spread/Choke:** Associated with the Drop Shadow and Outer Glow panels, the Spread option expands the point at which the effect begins outward from the perimeter of the layer. If you were creating the effect manually (as discussed in the section "Selecting the Contents of Layers" in Chapter 12), this would be similar to applying Select ⇨ Modify ⇨ Expand. Spread changes to Choke in the Inner Shadow and Inner Glow panels, in which case it contracts the point at which the effect begins. Note that both Spread and Choke are measured as percentages of the Size value, explained next.

✦ **Size:** One of the most ubiquitous settings, the Size value determines how far an effect expands or contracts from the perimeter of the layer. In the case of shadows and glows, the portion of the Size that is not devoted to Spread or Choke is given over to blurring. For example, if you set the Spread for Drop Shadow to 0 percent and the Size to 30 pixels, as in the top-left example of Figure 14-20, Photoshop blurs the shadow across 100 percent of the 30-pixel size. If you set the Spread to 100 percent as in the bottom-right example, then

0 percent is left for blurring. The shadow expands 30 pixels out from the perimeter of the layer and has a sharp edge. This makes the effect seem larger, but in fact, only the opaque portion of the effect has grown.

Size and Depth observe a similar relationship in the Bevel and Emboss panel, with Depth taking the place of Spread or Choke. When adjusting a Satin effect, Size affects the length of the contoured wave pattern. And in Stroke, Size controls the thickness of the outline.

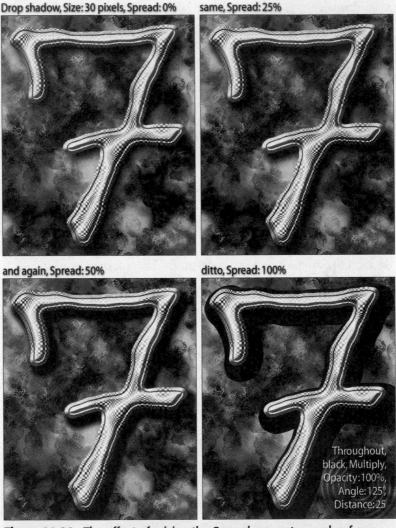

Figure 14-20: The effect of raising the Spread percentage value from 0 (top-left) to 100 (bottom-right) on my now-familiar numeral 7. Note that I changed the color setting of Satin to white (insert your own Moody Blues joke here).

✦ **Contour:** Photoshop creates most effects — namely shadows, glows, bevel, and the Satin effect — by fading a color from a specified Opacity value to transparent. The rate at which the fade occurs is determined by the Contour option. Click the down-pointing arrowhead to select from a palette of preset contours; click the contour preview to design your own. If you think of the Contour preview as a graph, the top of the graph represents opacity and the bottom represents transparency. So a straight line from top to bottom shows a consistent fade. A spike in the graph shows the color hitting opacity and then fading away again. Figure 14-21 shows a few examples applied to — hooray! — a new layer. In case you're curious, I painted this S shape with a scatter brush, and then filled it with the Molecular Pattern Overlay effect, topping it all off with an Inner Bevel garnish.

The most challenging contours are associated with Bevel and Emboss. The Gloss Contour option controls how colors fade in and out inside the beveled edge, as if the edge were reflecting other colors around it. (Figure 14-27 offers a glimpse.) The indented Contour effect — below Bevel and Emboss in the Layer Style list — wrinkles the edge of the layer so that it casts different highlights and shadows.

✦ **Anti-aliased:** If a Contour setting consists of sharp corners, you can soften them by turning this check box on. Most presets have rounded corners, making antialiasing unnecessary.

✦ **Noise:** Associated strictly with shadows and glows, the Noise value randomizes the transparency of pixels. It's like using the Dissolve blend mode, except that you have control over how much randomization to apply. The Noise value does not change the color of pixels; that is the job of an option called Jitter.

✦ **Layer Knocks Out Drop Shadow:** In the real world, if an object was translucent, you could see through it to its own shadow. However, this turns out to be an unpopular law of nature with most image editors. So when creating a drop shadow, Photoshop gives us the Layer Knocks Out Drop Shadow check box, which when selected makes the drop shadow invisible directly behind the layer. Turn the option off for a more natural effect.

✦ **Technique:** Moving out of the Shadow panels and into Outer Glow, the first unique option is the Technique pop-up menu. Also available when creating bevel effects (see Figure 14-26), Technique controls how the contours of the effect are calculated. When a glow is set to Softer, as in all of the examples in Figure 14-21, Photoshop applies a modified Gaussian Blur to ensure optimal transitions between the glow and background elements. Your other option (shown in Figure 14-22) is Precise, which calculates the effect without the Gaussian adjustment. Mind you, the effect may remain blurry, but strictly as a function of the Spread and Contour settings. Precise may work better in tight corners, common around type and shape layers. Otherwise, stick with Softer.

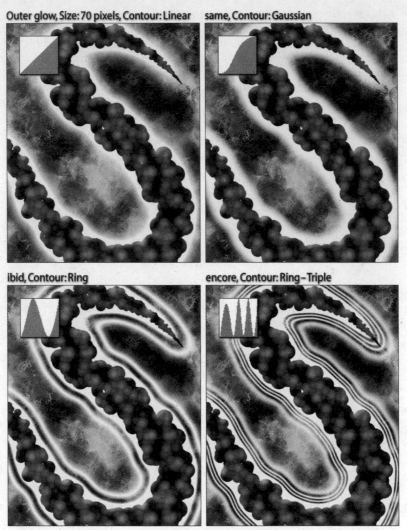

Figure 14-21: Four Contour presets combined with an Outer Glow effect. The Contour setting controls how the halo drops from opacity to transparency, and sometimes back again. These settings were used throughout: Screen mode, 100 percent Opacity, 15 percent Spread, and Softer Technique.

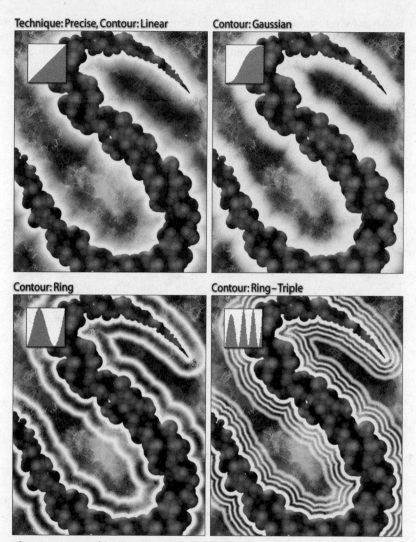

Figure 14-22: This figure is identical to Figure 14-21 in every way, save one: Here the Technique option is set to Precise.

The Bevel and Emboss panel doesn't provide the same kind of blurring functions that you get with shadow and glow effects, so the Technique option works a bit differently. The default setting, Smooth, averages and blurs pixels to achieve soft, rounded edges. The two Chisel settings remove the averaging to create saw-tooth abrasions into the sides of the layer. Chisel Hard results in thick cut marks; Chisel Soft averages the perimeter of the layer to create finer cuts. Up the Soften value (described shortly) to blur the abrasions.

✦ **Source:** When working in the Inner Glow panel, Photoshop wants to know where the glow starts. Should it glow inward from the perimeter of the layer (Edge, as seen in the left example in Figure 14-23) or outward from the middle (Center, as seen on the right in Figure 14-23)?

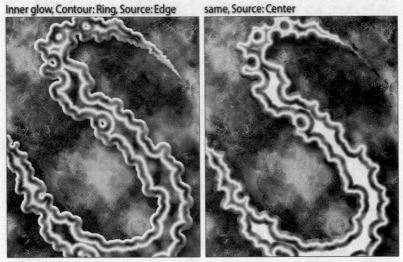

Inner glow, Contour: Ring, Source: Edge   same, Source: Center

Figure 14-23: The two options for the Source setting in the Inner Glow panel. The other settings used in both examples are Blend Mode: Screen, Opacity: 100 percent, Technique: Precise, Choke: 15 percent, and Size: 40 pixels.

✦ **Range:** The two Glow panels and the Contour panel (subordinate to Bevel and Emboss) use Range values to modify the Contour settings. This value sets the midpoint of the contour with respect to the middle of the size. As seen in the left example in Figure 14-24, values less than 50 percent move the midpoint away from the source, extending the effect. Values greater than 50 percent shrink the effect, as shown in the right example in the figure.

✦ **Jitter:** Where the Noise value randomizes the transparency of pixels, Jitter randomizes the colors. This option is operable only when creating gradient glows in which the gradation contains two or more colors (not a color and transparency).

✦ **Depth:** The first unique Bevel and Emboss setting is Depth, which makes the sides of a bevel steeper or shallower. In most cases, this translates to increased contrast between highlights and shadows as you raise the Depth value. Figure 14-25 shows an example.

Outer & inner glows, Range: 20%   same, Range: 80%

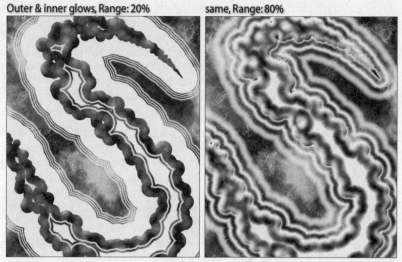

Figure 14-24: The Range setting at 20 percent (left) and 80 percent (right). The outer glow in both examples uses the Ring-Triple Contour preset; the inner glow uses the Ring Contour with a Source setting of Center.

Inner bevel, Depth: 150%   same, Depth: 950%

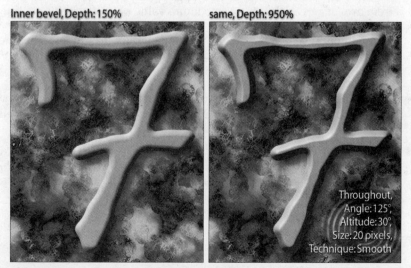

Throughout,
Angle: 125°,
Altitude: 30°,
Size: 20 pixels,
Technique: Smooth

Figure 14-25: The return of the 7 with an inner bevel depth of 150 percent (left) and 950 percent (right).

The Texture panel includes its own Depth setting. Here, Photoshop renders the pattern as a texture map, lighting the white areas of the pattern as high and the black areas as low. The Depth value determines the depth of the texture. The difference is you can enter a negative value, which inverts the texture. Meanwhile, you also have an additional Invert check box, which you can use to reverse the lights and darks in the pattern. So a positive Depth value with Invert turned on produces the same effect as a negative Depth value with Invert turned off.

✦ **Direction:** When working in the Bevel and Emboss panel, you see two radio buttons: Up and Down. If the Angle value indicates the direction of the sun, then Up positions the highlight along the edge near the sun and the shadow along the opposite edge. Down reverses things, so the shadow is near the light source. Presumably, this means the layer sinks into its background rather than protrudes out from it. But, in practice, the layer usually appears merely as though it's lit differently.

✦ **Soften:** This value sets the amount of blur applied to the beveled highlights and shadows. Small changes make a big difference when Technique is set to one of the Chisel options. Figure 14-26 provides a hardcore look at this option.

✦ **Altitude:** The Bevel and Emboss panel includes two lighting controls, Angle and Altitude. The Angle value is just that: the angle of the sun with respect to the layer. The Altitude, demonstrated in Figure 14-27, is measured on a half circle drawn across the sky. A maximum value of 90 degrees puts the sun directly overhead (noon); 0 degrees puts it on the horizon (sunrise). Values in the medium range — 30 to 60 degrees — generally produce the best results. If you find the effect to be too sharp, you can temper it with the Soften setting, as shown in Figure 14-28.

✦ **Scale:** The Texture and Pattern Overlay panels include Scale values, which scale the pattern tiles inside the layer. Values greater than 100 percent swell the pattern; values lower than 100 percent shrink it.

✦ **Link/Align with Layer:** When turned on, this check box centers a gradient inside a layer. If you want to draw a gradient across many layers, turn the option off to center the gradient inside the canvas. When editing a pattern, this option links the pattern to the layer so the two move together.

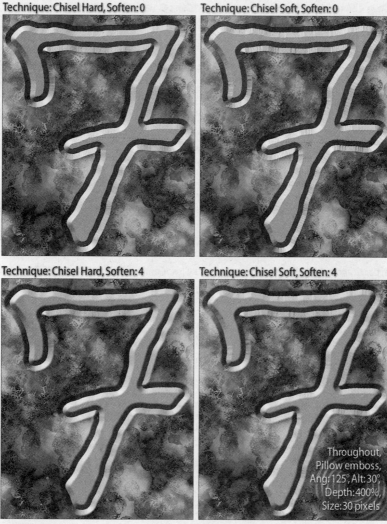

Technique: Chisel Hard, Soften: 0   Technique: Chisel Soft, Soften: 0

Technique: Chisel Hard, Soften: 4   Technique: Chisel Soft, Soften: 4

Throughout,
Pillow emboss,
Ang: 125°, Alt: 30°,
Depth: 400%,
Size: 30 pixels

Figure 14-26: Two Soften values compared with two different Technique settings in the Pillow Emboss effect. Note that higher Soften values (bottom two examples) smooth out the otherwise jagged Technique settings without altogether getting rid of the edge.

✦ **Position:** The final Layer Style option appears inside the Stroke panel. The Position pop-up menu defines how the width of the stroke aligns with the perimeter of the layer. Photoshop can draw the stroke outside the edge of the layer, inside the edge, or center the stroke exactly on the edge. It's up to you.

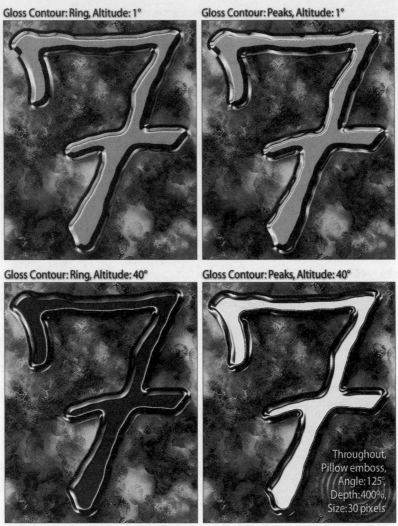

Gloss Contour: Ring, Altitude: 1°

Gloss Contour: Peaks, Altitude: 1°

Gloss Contour: Ring, Altitude: 40°

Gloss Contour: Peaks, Altitude: 40°

Throughout,
Pillow emboss,
Angle: 125°,
Depth: 400%,
Size: 30 pixels

Figure 14-27: A couple of Gloss Contour presets with an Altitude setting of 1 degree (top) and 40 degrees (bottom). Note that the higher setting brings out the difference between the two Gloss Contour presets.

Gloss Contour: Ring, Altitude: 1°, Soften: 4   Gloss Contour: Peaks, Altitude: 40°, Soften: 2

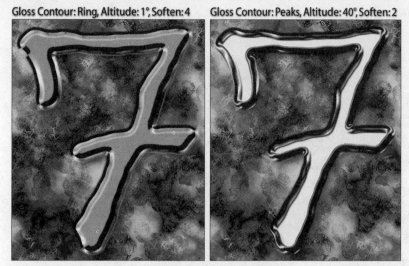

Figure 14-28: The first and last examples from Figure 14-27 with a touch of the Soften option.

Modifying and Saving Effects

After you apply a layer effect, Photoshop stamps the layer with a florin symbol (*f*), as shown in Figure 14-29. A triangular toggle switch lets you collapse the effects to permit more room for layers inside the palette. From that point on, you can edit an effect by double-clicking its name in the Layers palette. Or double-click the florin symbol to display the Blending Options panel of the Layer Style dialog box.

Disabling effects

To temporarily disable all effects applied to a layer, choose Layer ⇨ Layer Style ⇨ Hide All Effects. Or better yet, just click the eyeball in front of the word "Effects" in the Layers palette. Click the eyeball spot again to show the effects. You can likewise hide and show individual effects — without permanently disabling them — by clicking eyeballs. Photoshop even goes so far as to save hidden effects. This makes it easy to bring an effect back to life later without re-entering settings.

To permanently delete an effect, drag it and drop it onto the trash icon at the bottom of the Layers palette. To delete all effects, drag the word "Effects" to the trash.

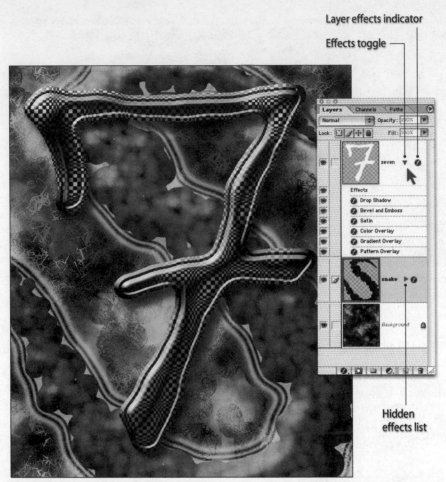

Layer effects indicator

Effects toggle

Hidden
effects list

Figure 14-29: The florin symbol indicates that one or more layer effects have been applied to the layer. Use the toggle to hide and show the list of effects.

Duplicating effects

After you apply an effect to a layer, the effect becomes an element that you can copy and apply to other layers. Select the layer with the effects you want to duplicate and choose Layer ➪ Layer Style ➪ Copy Layer Style. Or right-click (Control-click on the Mac) the layer name in the Layers palette and choose Copy Layer Style from the shortcut menu. Then select another layer, right-click (Win) or Control-click (Mac) it, and choose Paste Layer Style. To paste a copied effect onto multiple layers at a time, link them together (as explained in the section "Linking layers" in Chapter 12) and choose the Paste Layer Style to Linked command.

The Copy and Paste Layer Style commands bypass the Clipboard. This means you can copy an image and then copy an effect without displacing the image.

Paste Layer Style duplicates all effects associated with one layer onto another. But what if you want to duplicate a single effect only? Just drag the effect name from one layer and drop it below another in the Layers palette. Be sure you see a bar below the layer name when dropping the effect — otherwise, it won't take.

Scattering effects to the four winds

When you apply an effect, Photoshop is actually doing all the manual layer work for you in the background. This means if Photoshop doesn't seem to be generating the precise effect you want, you can take over and edit the layers to your satisfaction. Choose Layer ⇨ Layer Style ⇨ Create Layers to resolve the automated effect into a series of layers and clipping groups. In some cases, a warning appears telling you that one or more attributes of an effect cannot be represented with layers. Go ahead and give it a try; you can always undo. If you like what you see, inspect it and edit at will.

After choosing Create Layers, you're on your own. From that point on, you lose the ability to edit the effects from the Layer Style dialog box (unless, of course, you decide to go back in time via the History palette).

Effects and blending options

If you like layer effects as much as I do — and by the way, I really, *really* like layer effects — there's no doubt you'll eventually find yourself experiencing a curious phenomenon. After you've gone and heaped on a bunch of different effects, particularly Color, Gradient, and Pattern Overlays, your layer may no longer respond to blend modes. For example, Figure 14-30 shows two very familiar layers together: the 7 and the S. I applied the Overlay blend mode to the 7 layer (much as I would apply hot sauce to a 7-layer burrito). Then I applied the Hard Light blend mode to the S layer and reduced the Fill Opacity value to 50 percent. (For more on blend modes and fill opacity, see the previous chapter.)

Two layers, two blend modes . . . and yet nothing happens, as the left-hand image in Figure 14-30 illustrates. It looks like both layers are still set to Normal mode, with 100 percent Opacity. Why? Well, both layers contain opaque interior effects, Pattern Overlay being the primary culprit. But there's an easy workaround here: I just double-clicked on each layer and turned on the Blend Interior Effects as Group check box in the Blending Options panel. As shown in the right-hand image in Figure 14-30, I'm now getting the interaction between layers that I was looking for. And by the way, such blending options can happily be saved along with styles, as I explain in the next section.

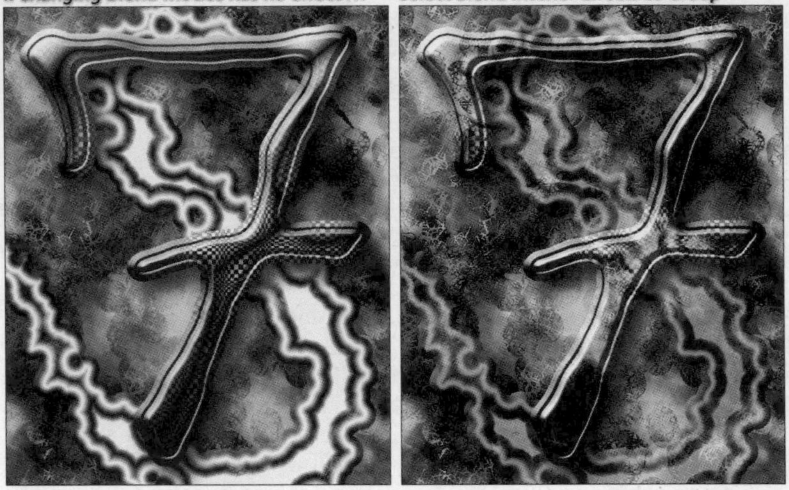

If changing blend modes has no effect ...   select Blend Interior Effects as Group

Figure 14-30: Here I applied the Overlay and Hard Light blend modes to the 7 and S layers, respectively, with the Blend Interior Effects as Group option turned off (left) and on (right).

Color Plate 14-1 shows a very similar scenario, with the added benefit of full color. Note that after piling on the layer effects in the first four examples, I threw in some blend modes and activated Blend Interior Effects as Group to arrive at the pixel-melding masterpiece shown at the bottom of the color plate. It's pretty amazing, I think, that you can start with a couple of plain old black and white layers and completely transform them into richly colored and sculpted objects using layer effects. Oh, yeah—just for the record—I really, really, *really* like layer effects.

Saving effects as styles

Photoshop lets you save layer effects and blending options for later use by creating layer styles, which show up as items in the Styles palette. There are three ways to create a style:

✦ **Click the New Style icon.** When working in the Layer Style dialog box, click the New Style icon to display the options shown at the bottom of Figure 14-31. Name your style and then use the check boxes to decide which settings in the Layer Style dialog box are preserved. The first check box saves the effects covered in this chapter, the second saves the blending options discussed in the previous chapter.

✦ **Click in the Styles palette.** Choose Window ⇨ Styles to view the Styles palette. Then move your cursor inside the palette and click with the paint bucket, as in the top example in Figure 14-31. Photoshop shows you the New Style dialog box. Set the options as described previously.

✦ **Drag and drop a layer.** Start with both the Layers and Styles palettes open. Now drag any layer, active or not, and drop it in the Styles palette. Again, Photoshop shows you the New Style dialog box.

Figure 14-31: Click in the Styles palette (top) to display the New Style dialog box (bottom).

After you press Enter or Return, Photoshop saves the style as a new preset. As with any preset, you can apply it to future images during future Photoshop sessions. Just click a style to apply it to the active layer, or drag the style and drop it on any layer name (active or not) in the Layers palette. And don't forget, Photoshop ships with scads of preset styles that you can explore at your leisure. Load a set of styles from the Styles palette menu, apply one to your favorite layer, and take a look at how it's put together in the Layer Style dialog box. It's a great way to get a feel for the amazing variety of effects that are possible in Photoshop.

Tip

A style may include blending options, layer effects, or both. Applying a new style to a layer replaces all blending options and/or effects associated with that style. If you would rather add the blending options and effects from a style to the existing blending options and effects associated with a layer, Shift-click an item in the Styles palette.

Note

Sadly, there is no way to update a style. And even if you could, the style and layer are not linked, so updating the style would have no effect on the layer. Photoshop lets you create new styles, rename existing styles, and delete old ones — that's about it.

✦   ✦   ✦

Fully Editable Text

The State of Type in Photoshop 7

If you wanted to put text into your image back in the early days of Photoshop, you might as well be carving your words into a big hunk of marble. Spelling definitely counted back then, because you were more or less permanently embedding your words into the image. The introduction of layers in Version 3 loosened things up a bit, but until fairly recently creating type in Photoshop has been a restrictive process.

Then Photoshop 5 came along and gave us something very new and welcome — editable bitmapped type. Long after you created a line of text, you had the option of changing the words, typeface, size, leading, kerning, and so on. In only one upgrade cycle, Photoshop made a quantum leap from grim Stone Age letter wrangling to something that might actually pass for contemporary typesetting. Photoshop 5.5 expanded the type possibilities further, but with Version 6 type finally evolved from a single-celled organism to something resembling *homo sapiens*. At last you could:

- ◆ Scale text as large as you wanted without any repercussions, just as you could with any vector object. That's because the type tool actually created vector text.

- ◆ Create and edit text by typing directly on the image canvas — no more side trips to the Type Tool dialog box required.

- ◆ Create text inside a frame and then apply paragraph formatting to control hyphenation, justification, indents, alignment, and paragraph spacing. You could even create lists that use hanging punctuation and control word and character spacing in justified text, as you can in Adobe PageMaker and InDesign.

✦ Make per-character adjustments to color, width, height, spacing, and baseline shift.

✦ Bend, twist, and otherwise distort text using a simple Warp Text dialog box instead of wrestling with the Wave filter or other distortion filters.

✦ Convert characters to shapes that you could then edit, fill, and stroke just as you do objects you create with the shape tools (explored in Chapter 14). Alternatively, you could convert text to a work path.

✦ Rasterize text so that you could apply any filters or tools applicable to ordinary image layers.

The additions to the world of type found in Photoshop 7 aren't nearly as groundbreaking as those in Version 6; think of them more as gentle refinements. In fact, the reappearance of the vertical and mask type tools in the toolbox could even be viewed as a regression back to the days of Photoshop 5. But the addition of the Check Spelling and Find and Replace Text commands are indeed welcome and bring Photoshop's type features even more in line with those found in page-layout, illustration, and even advanced word-processing programs. You should be able to make them a regular part of your text routine in no time.

I don't cover the options for formatting Chinese, Korean, and Japanese text, which become available when you select the Show Asian Text Options check box on the General panel of the Preference dialog box. Like the rest of Photoshop's type controls, these options should be familiar to you if you work regularly with type in these languages. But if you're not sure what each control does, check the Photoshop online help system for details.

The five flavors of text

As I mentioned a few paragraphs ago, the type tool produces vector type. But you also can create a text-based selection outline or work path, convert each character to a separate vector object, or create a bitmap version of your text. Here's a rundown of your type choices:

✦ To create regular text, select the type tool (also known as the horizontal type tool), click in the image window, and type away. Or, to create paragraph text, drag to create a text frame and then type your text in the frame. You then can choose from a smorgasbord of type formatting options, apply layer effects, and more. There are a few things you can't do, such as apply the commands in the Filter menu or use the standard selection tools. But as for that last one, there's no need to use the selection tools anyway — you can select characters simply by dragging over them, as you do in a word processor.

✦ To produce a text-based selection outline, select either the horizontal or vertical type mask tool from the type tool flyout menu (see the upcoming Figure 15-5) and create your text. Photoshop covers your image with a translucent overlay, as when you work in quick mask mode, and your text appears transparent. You can apply all the same formatting options that are available when you work with ordinary text. When you commit the text, the overlay disappears and your selection outline appears.

Tip

You can also create type masks using the regular old type tool. Simply enter and format your text as usual. Then Ctrl-click (⌘-click on the Mac) on the type layer in the Layers palette to generate the selection outlines. What's the advantage of this approach? Simple — type on a layer is forever editable; a type mask is not. So if you ask me, there's really no reason to ever use the type mask tools.

✦ After creating text, choose Layer ⇨ Type ⇨ Convert to Shape to turn each character into an individual vector shape that works just like those you create with the shape tools (covered in Chapter 14). You then can edit the shape of individual characters, an option explored in "Editing text as shapes," later in this chapter.

✦ Choose Layer ⇨ Type ⇨ Create Work Path to generate a work path from text. One reason to use this option is to create a clipping path based on your text.

✦ Finally, you can convert text to bitmapped type by choosing Layer ⇨ Rasterize ⇨ Type. After rasterizing the text, you can apply Photoshop's filters and other pixel-based features to it.

Caution

After you rasterize text or convert it to a shape or work path, you can't go back and run the spelling checker or change the text formatting as you can while working with vector text or type masks. So be sure that you're happy with those aspects of your text before you convert it. You may even want to save a copy of the vector text in a new layer so that you can get it back if needed.

Caution

Also note that when you save images in the PSD, PDF, or TIFF format, you must select the Include Vector Data option to retain the vector properties of your text. If you turn off the check box or save in a format that doesn't support vectors, Photoshop rasterizes your text. Again, saving a backup copy of the image in the native Photoshop format is a good idea.

Text as art

Before I get into the nitty-gritty of creating text, I want to share a few ideas to inspire you to see text for the creative playground that it can be. Combine the powers of the type tool with the program's effects, filters, paint and edit tools, and layering features, and you can create an almost unlimited array of text effects to enhance your images — even produce text that stands alone as a powerful image in its own right.

With that flowery speech out of the way, allow me to provide some examples of the kind of things you can do with your text:

✦ **Create translucent type.** Because Photoshop automatically creates type on a new layer, you can change the translucency of type simply by adjusting the Opacity value for the type layer in the Layers palette. Using this technique, you can merge type and images to create subtle overlay effects, as illustrated in Figure 15-1.

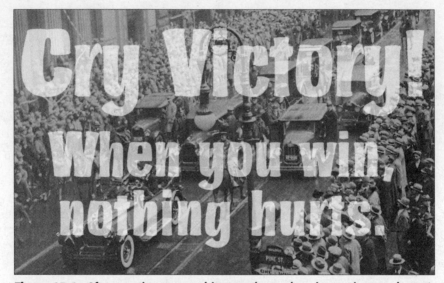

Figure 15-1: After creating some white type layered against a vintage photo, I lowered the type opacity to 70 percent. Though child's play in Photoshop, this effect is difficult to create in many other programs.

✦ **Use type as a selection.** By creating a type mask, you can use type to select a portion of an image, and then move, copy, or transform it. To create Figure 15-2, for example, I used my text to select the vintage photo. Then I dragged it into a different stock photo background and applied the Multiply blend mode from the Layers palette. You'd be hard-pressed to tell that there's a parade inside those letters, but it serves as an interesting texture.

✦ **Apply layer effects.** Photoshop's layer effects are fully applicable to type. In Figure 15-3, I replaced the industrial background from Figure 15-2 with a background texture created with the Clouds and Emboss filters (see Chapter 11). Then I applied a pillow emboss effect to the text layer using Layer ⇨ Layer Style ⇨ Bevel and Emboss.

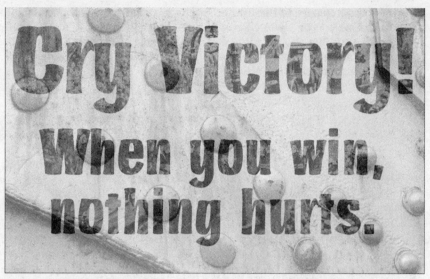

Figure 15-2: Photoshop is virtually unique in permitting you to select an image using type. Here I selected the image from Figure 15-1 and dragged the selection into a different background.

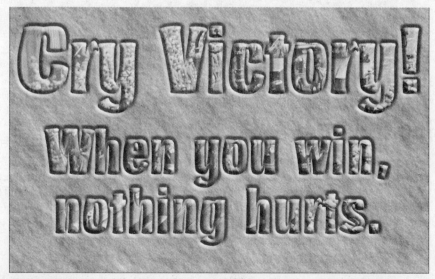

Figure 15-3: I used the Bevel and Emboss layer effect to apply a pillow emboss effect.

✦ **Edit type as part of the image.** After rasterizing text (by choosing Layer ⇨ Rasterize ⇨ Type), you can paint type, erase it, smear it, apply a filter or two, or do anything else that you can do to pixels. In Figure 15-4, I embossed the type, flattened it against its background, applied a few effects filters, and made it sway with the Wave filter.

Figure 15-4: This image is the result of going nuts for 15 minutes or so using the commands in the Filter menu. I used Emboss, Radial Blur, Colored Pencil, Craquelure, and Wave.

Using the Type Tool

In a drawing or desktop publishing program, the type tool typically serves two purposes: You can create text with the tool or you can edit existing text by highlighting characters and either replacing them or applying formatting commands. The following steps assume that you're creating text for the first time in your image (more about adding to existing text later).

STEPS: Creating Text in Photoshop

1. **Select the type tool by clicking its icon in the toolbox or pressing T.** Photoshop activates the type tool, displays the I-beam cursor in the image window, and displays type controls in the Options bar. You can access additional formatting options by displaying the Character and Paragraph palettes, shown in Figure 15-5.

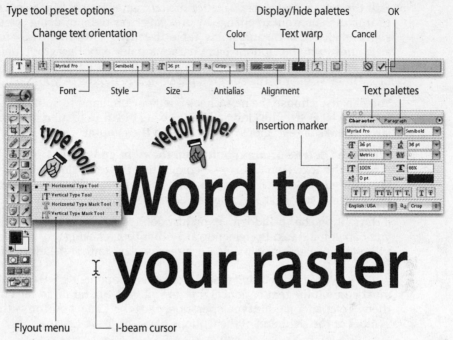

Figure 15-5: Photoshop provides a full complement of text creation and formatting options, which you access from the Options bar, Character palette, and Paragraph palette.

2. **Select the font, type size, and other formatting attributes from the Options bar and palettes.** The upcoming sections explain your options.

3. **Click or drag in the image window.** If you click, Photoshop places the first character you type at the location of the blinking insertion marker, just as when you type in a word-processing program. Adobe calls this creating *point text*. Each line of type operates as an independent entity. Press Enter (Win) or Return (Mac) to begin a new line of text.

Alternatively, you can create paragraph text by dragging with the type tool to draw a frame—called a *bounding box*—to hold the text. Now your text flows within the frame, wrapping to the next line automatically when you reach the edge of the bounding box. If you create your text this way, you can apply standard paragraph formatting attributes, such as justification, paragraph spacing, and so on. In other words, everything works pretty much like it does in every other program in which you create text in a frame. Pressing Enter (Win) or Return (Mac) starts a new paragraph within the bounding box.

4. **Type your text.** If you mess up, press Backspace (Win) or Delete (Mac) to delete the character to the left of the insertion marker. On the PC, pressing Delete wipes out the character to the right of the insertion marker.

5. **Edit the text, if necessary.** To alter the character formatting, select the characters you want to change by dragging over them or using the selection shortcuts listed in the upcoming Table 15-1. Then choose the new formatting attributes from the Options bar, Character palette, or Paragraph palette. If you don't select any text, paragraph formatting affects all text in the bounding box. Otherwise, only the selected paragraph responds to your commands.

You can also choose the new Check Spelling command to spell-check your text, as well as use the Find and Replace Text feature to hunt for words in large chunks of text; more on that later in the chapter.

6. **Click the OK (check mark) button on the right end of the Options bar to commit the text.** Don't worry—"committing the text" simply takes you out of text-editing mode. As long as you don't convert the text to a regular image layer, work path, or shape, you can edit it at any time.

If the Options bar is hidden or you just don't like reaching to click the button, you can commit text by selecting any other tool, clicking any palette but the Character or Paragraph palette, or pressing Ctrl+Enter (⌘-Return on the Mac).

While you're in text editing mode, most menu commands are unavailable. You must commit the text or cancel the current type operation to regain access to them. To abandon your type operation, click the Cancel button—the "no" symbol at the right end of the Options bar—or press Escape.

When you create the first bit of type in an image, Photoshop creates a new layer to hold the text. After you commit the type, clicking or dragging with the type tool has one of two outcomes. If Photoshop finds any text near the spot where you click or drag, it assumes that you want to edit that text and, therefore, selects the text layer and puts the type tool into edit mode. For paragraph text, the paragraph is selected as well. If no text is in the vicinity of the spot you click, the program decides that you must want to create a brand new text layer, and responds accordingly. You can force Photoshop to take this second route by Shift-clicking or Shift-dragging with the type tool, which comes in handy if you want to create one block of text on top of another.

Photoshop automatically uses the first characters you type as the layer name. You can change the layer name by double-clicking on it in the Layers palette.

Creating vertical type

Just as in the bygone days of Photoshop 5, Version 7 provides a type tool entirely dedicated to creating vertically-oriented text. To get this tool, press T or Shift+T (depending on your Use Shift Key for Tool Switch setting in the Preferences dialog box) when the regular type tool is active. In truth, the vertical type tool is nothing more than the standard type tool lifted from the Japanese version of Photoshop. As shown in the first example of Figure 15-6, it creates vertical columns of type that read right to left, as in Japan. If you want to make columns of type that read left to right, you have to create each column as an independent text block.

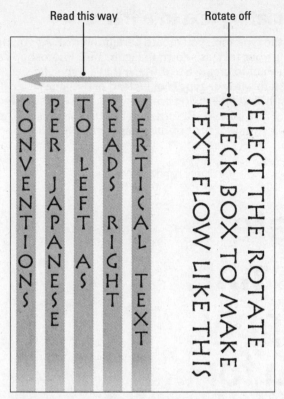

Figure 15-6: By default, vertical type reads right to left, as shown in the first example. If you deselect the Rotate Character option in the Character palette menu, your characters appear like those on the right.

After you click in the image, you have access to the Rotate Character command in the Character palette menu. (If the palette isn't open, click the display/hide palettes button at the right end of the Options bar. It's labeled in Figure 15-5.) By default, the option is turned on, which gives you upright characters such as those on the left side of Figure 15-6. Choose the command again to rotate 90 degrees clockwise and flip characters on their side, as shown in the right side of the figure.

If you want to rotate the type to some other degree, wait until after you commit the text to the layer (by clicking the check mark button in the Options bar) and then use the Edit ⇨ Free Transform command, which I describe in Chapter 12, to rotate the text layer.

You also can choose Layer ⇨ Type ⇨ Horizontal and Layer ⇨ Type ⇨ Vertical to change vertically oriented type to horizontally oriented type, and vice versa. But why bother with those commands when you can just click the text orientation button on the far left side of the Options bar (labeled in Figure 15-5)?

Creating and manipulating text in a frame

By dragging in your image with the type tool, you create paragraph text. As you drag, Photoshop draws a frame to hold your text, as shown in Figure 15-7. Photoshop calls this frame a *bounding box*. If you want to create a text frame that's a specific size, Alt-click (Win) or Option-click (Mac) with the type tool instead of dragging. Photoshop displays the Paragraph Text Size dialog box, in which you can specify the width and height of the box. Press Enter or Return, and Photoshop creates the bounding box, placing the top-left corner of the box at the spot you clicked.

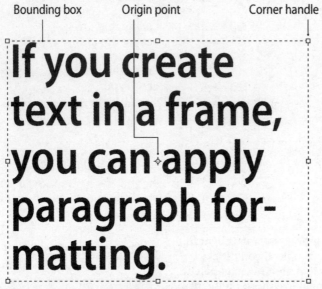

Bounding box   Origin point   Corner handle

If you create text in a frame, you can apply paragraph for-matting.

Figure 15-7: Drag the box handles to transform the frame alone or frame and text together.

The bounding box looks just like the one that appears when you choose Edit ➪ Free Transform, and some of its functions are the same:

✦ Drag a corner handle to resize the box. Shift-drag to retain the original proportions of the box. The text reflows to fit the new dimensions of the box.

✦ Ctrl-drag (Win) or ⌘-drag (Mac) a corner handle to scale the text and box together. Ctrl+Shift-drag (⌘-Shift-drag on the Mac) to scale proportionally. To scale text alone, use the character formatting controls in the Options bar or in the Character palette (explained next). Either way, you can scale up or down as much as you want without degrading the text quality, thanks to the vector-orientation of the type tool.

✦ To rotate both box and text, move the cursor outside the box and drag, just as you do when transforming selections, crop boundaries, and layers. Shift-drag to rotate in 15-degree increments. The rotation occurs respective to the origin point, which you can relocate by dragging, as usual.

Using the bounding-box approach to type has more benefits than being able to use the transformation techniques I just described, however. You also can apply all sorts of paragraph formatting options to control how the text flows within the bounding box, as described in the upcoming section "Applying paragraph formatting."

Note Keep in mind that you also can scale, skew, rotate, and otherwise transform the text layer after you commit the text to the layer. In addition, you can size, distort, and rotate text using the options in the Character palette, as I explain shortly.

If you ever decide that you'd like to work with your text as regular text instead of paragraph text, cancel out of text editing mode by clicking the OK or Cancel buttons in the Options bar. Then select the text layer and choose Layer ⇨ Type ⇨ Convert to Point Text. Photoshop splits the paragraph text into individual lines. To go back to paragraph text, select the text layer and choose Layer ⇨ Type ⇨ Convert to Paragraph Text.

Selecting and editing text

Before you can modify a single character of type, you have to select it. You can select all text on a text layer by simply double-clicking the layer thumbnail in the Layers palette. (This automatically switches you to the type tool as well.) You can select individual characters by dragging over them with the type tool, as in any word-processing program. You also have access to a range of keyboard tricks, listed in Table 15-1.

Table 15-1
Selecting Text from the Keyboard

Text Selection	*Keystrokes*
Select character to left or right	Shift+left or right arrow
Select whole word	Double-click on word
Select entire line	Triple-click the line
Move left or right one word	Ctrl+left or right arrow (⌘-left or right arrow)
Select word to left or right	Ctrl+Shift+left or right arrow (⌘-Shift-left or right arrow)
Select to end of line	Shift+End
Select to beginning of line	Shift+Home
Select one line up or down	Shift+up or down arrow
Select range of characters	Click at one point, Shift-click at another
Select all text	Ctrl+A (⌘-A)

After selecting type, you can replace it by entering new text from the keyboard. You can likewise cut, copy, or paste text by pressing the standard keyboard shortcuts (Ctrl/⌘+X, C, and V) or by choosing commands from the Edit menu. You can undo a text modification by pressing Ctrl+Z (⌘-Z on the Mac) or choosing Edit ➪ Undo. However, if you type a few characters and then choose Undo, you wipe out all the new characters, not just the most recently typed one. If things go terribly wrong, press Escape or click the Cancel button in the Options bar (the "no" symbol) to cancel out of the current type operation.

Tip

Selected text appears highlighted on screen, as is the convention. If the highlight gets in your way, press Ctrl+H (Win) or ⌘-H (Mac) to hide it. This shortcut hides all on-screen helpers, including guides.

Applying character formatting

The Options bar gives you ready access to the collection of formatting controls shown in Figure 15-8. The Character palette and its palette menu, also shown in the figure, offer some of these same controls plus a few additional options. If you use Adobe InDesign, the palette should look familiar to you — with a few exceptions, it's a virtual twin of the InDesign Character palette.

To open the palette and its partner, the Paragraph palette, click the display/hide palettes button in the Options bar. Alternatively, you can choose Window ➪ Character or press Ctrl+T (⌘-T on the Mac) when in text-editing mode.

Note

You can apply formatting on a per-character basis. For example, you can type one letter, change the font color, and then type the next letter in the new color. You can even change fonts from letter to letter.

The next several sections explain the character formatting options. All apply to both paragraph and regular text. You can specify formatting before you type or reformat existing type by selecting it first.

Tip

If you ever want to return the settings in the Character palette to the defaults, make sure that no type is selected. Then choose Reset Character from the bottom of the palette menu.

Font

Select the typeface and type style you want to use from the Font and Style pop-up menus. Rather than offering lowest-common-denominator Bold and Italic check boxes (as was the case back in Photoshop 4), Photoshop is smart enough to present a full list of designer style options. For example, while Times is limited to Bold and Italic, the Helvetica family may yield such stylistic variations as Oblique, Light, Black, Condensed, Inserat, and Ultra Compressed.

Tip

If you're working with multiple linked text layers, you can quickly change the typeface or type style on all linked layers in one fell swoop by pressing the Shift key while choosing an option from the Font or Style pop-up menu.

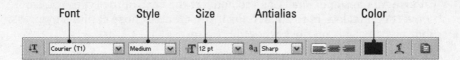

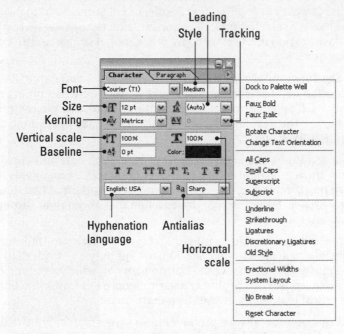

Figure 15-8: Photoshop provides many character-formatting controls in the Options bar and the Character palette.

The Character palette menu contains a bunch of additional style options, which you can see in Figure 15-8. Click these options in the menu to toggle them on and off. A check mark next to the style name means that it's active.

Many of the items relegated to the Character palette menu in Version 6 have come out of hiding and now appear on the Character palette. These lucky menu items can be found in the row of buttons near the bottom of the palette. They include the following (in order from left to right on the palette itself and top to bottom in the palette menu):

✦ Faux Bold and Faux Italic enable you to apply bold and italic effects to the letters when the font designer doesn't include them as a type style. Use these options *only* if the Style pop-up menu doesn't offer bold and italic settings; you get better looking type by applying the font designer's own bold and italic versions of the characters.

✦ Choose All Caps and Small Caps to convert the case of the type. You can't convert capital letters to Small Caps if you created those capitals by pressing Shift or Caps Lock on the keyboard.

Pressing Ctrl+Shift+K (Win) or ⌘-Shift-K (Mac) toggles selected text from uppercase to lowercase, as it does in InDesign and QuarkXPress. Remember that this shortcut works only when text is selected. If you're working with the type tool and haven't selected text, the shortcut affects any new text you create after the insertion marker; with any other tool, it brings up the Color Settings dialog box.

✦ Superscript and Subscript shrink the selected characters and move them above or below the text baseline, as you might want to do when typing mathematical equations. If Superscript and Subscript don't position characters as you want them, use the Baseline option to control them, as I explain in the upcoming section "Baseline."

✦ Underline Left and Underline Right apply to vertical type only and enable you to add a line to the left or right of the selected characters, respectively. When you work with horizontal type, the option changes to Underline and does just what its name implies. Strikethrough draws a line that slices right through the middle of your letters.

✦ It's a bit confusing when working with vertical type to have two Underline options available in the menu — left and right — but only one Underline button on the palette itself. Activating the button turns on whichever type of underlining you used last; it's probably safer to ignore the Underline button when using vertical text, and just use the palette menu.

Keep in mind that you can always produce these styles manually by using the pencil or brush tool — a choice that I prefer because it enables me to control the thickness, color, and opacity of the line and even play with blend modes. Just click to set a starting point and then Shift-click to draw a straight line with these tools.

✦ The Ligatures and Old Style options are available only in the palette menu, and even then they become available only if you select an OpenType font and only if the font designer included the required type variations. A ligature is a special character that produces a stylized version of a pair of characters, such as *a* and *e*, tying the two characters together with no space between, like so: æ. Old Style creates numbers at a reduced size, which may extend below the baseline.

Size

You can measure type in Photoshop in points, pixels, or millimeters. To make your selection, press Ctrl+K and then Ctrl+5 (⌘-K and then ⌘-5 on the Mac) to open the Units and Rulers panel of the Preferences dialog box. (You must exit text mode to do so.) Select the unit you want to use from the Type pop-up menu.

Tip

You can enter values in any of the acceptable units of measurement, and Photoshop automatically converts the value to the unit you select in the Preferences dialog box. Just type the number followed by the unit's abbreviation ("in" for inches, for example). After you press Enter or Return, Photoshop makes the conversion for you. See Chapter 2 for more information about measurement units in Photoshop.

If the resolution of your image is 72 ppi, points and pixels are equal. There are 72 points in an inch, so 72 ppi means only 1 pixel per point. If the resolution is higher, however, a single point may include many pixels. The moral is to select the point option when you want to scale text according to image resolution; select pixels when you want to map text to an exact number of pixels in an image. (If you prefer, you can use millimeters instead of points; 1 millimeter equals 0.039 inch, which means 25.64 mm equals 72 points.)

Note

Whatever unit you choose, type is measured from the top of its *ascenders* — letters such as *b*, *d*, and *h* that rise above the level of most lowercase characters — to the bottom of its *descenders* — letters such as *g*, *p*, and *q* that sink below the baseline. That's the way it's supposed to work, anyway. But throughout history, designers have played pretty loose and free with type size. To illustrate, Figure 15-9 shows the two standards, Times and Helvetica, along with a typical display font and a typical script. Each line is set to a type size of 180 pixels and then placed inside a 180-pixel box. The dotted horizontal lines indicate the baselines. As you can see, the only font that comes close to measuring the full 180 pixels is Tekton. The Brush Script sample is relatively minuscule (and Brush Script is husky compared with most scripts). So if you're looking to fill a specific space, be prepared to experiment. The only thing you can be sure of is that the type *won't* measure the precise dimensions you enter into the Size option box.

Tip

You can change type size by selecting a size from the Size pop-up menu or double-clicking the Size value, typing a new size, and pressing Enter or Return. But the quickest option is to use the following keyboard shortcuts: To increase the type size in 2-point (or pixel) increments, press Ctrl+Shift+> (Win) or ⌘-Shift-> (Mac). To similarly decrease the size, press Ctrl+Shift+< (Win) or ⌘-Shift-< (Mac). Add Alt (Win) or Option (Mac) to raise or lower the type size in 10-point (or pixel) increments. If you select millimeters as your unit of measurement, Photoshop raises or lowers the type size by 0.71 mm, which is the equivalent of 2 points.

Leading

Also called line spacing, *leading* is the vertical distance between the baseline of one line of type and the baseline of the next line of type, as illustrated in Figure 15-10. You set leading via the Leading pop-up menu in the Character palette, labeled in Figure 15-8. Again, either select one of the menu options or double-click the current value, type a new value, and press Enter or Return. Leading is measured in the unit you select from the Type pop-up menu in the Preferences dialog box.

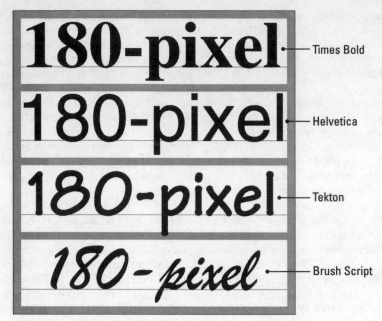

Figure 15-9: Four samples of 180-pixel type set inside 180-pixel boxes. As you can see, type size is an art, not a science.

If you choose the Auto setting, Photoshop automatically applies a leading equal to 120 percent of the type size. The 120 percent value isn't set in stone, however. To change the value, open the Paragraph palette menu and choose Justification to display the Justification dialog box. Enter the value you want to use in the Auto Leading option box and press Enter or Return.

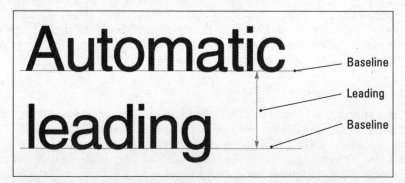

Figure 15-10: Leading is the distance between any two baselines in a single paragraph of text. Here, the type size is 120 pixels and the leading is 150 pixels.

Tip

The easiest way to change the distance between one line and another is like so: First, when adjusting the space between a pair of lines, select the bottom of the two. Then press Alt+up arrow (Option-up arrow on the Mac) to decrease the leading in 2-point (pixel) increments and move the lines closer together. Press Alt+down arrow (Option-down arrow on the Mac) to increase the leading and spread the lines apart. To work in 10-point (pixel) increments, press Ctrl+Alt+up or down arrow (⌘-Option-up or down arrow on the Mac). Again, if you work in millimeters, the leading value changes by 0.71 mm and 3.53 mm — the equivalent of 2 points and 10 points, respectively.

Kerning

Technically, *kern* is the predetermined amount of space that surrounds each character of type and separates it from its immediate neighbors. (Some type-heads also call it *side bearing*.) But as is so frequently the case with our molten magma of a language, kern has found new popularity in recent years as a verb. So if a friend says, "Let's kern!" don't reach for your rowing oars. Get psyched to adjust the amount of room between characters of type. (Yes, there are people who love to kern and, yes, it is sad.) You establish kerning via the Kerning pop-up menu in the Character palette, labeled earlier, in Figure 15-8. Select 0 to use the amount of side bearing indicated by the specifications in the font file on your hard drive.

Some character combinations, however, don't look right when subjected to the default bearing. The spacing that separates a *T* and an *h* doesn't look so good when you scrap the *h* and insert an *r*. Therefore, the character combination *T* and *r* is a special-needs pair, a typographic marriage that requires kern counseling. If you select Metrics from the Kerning pop-up menu, Photoshop digs farther into the font specifications and pulls out a list of special-needs letter pairs. Then it applies a prescribed amount of spacing compensation, as illustrated by the second line in Figure 15-11.

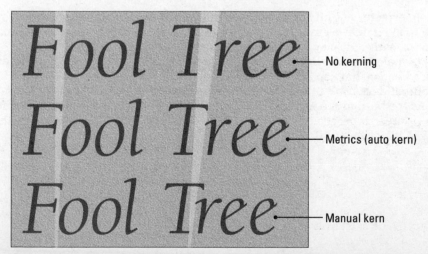

No kerning

Metrics (auto kern)

Manual kern

Figure 15-11: Three examples of the kerning options in Photoshop. I've added wedges to track the ever-decreasing space between the difficult pairs *Fo* and *Tr*.

In most cases, you'll want to select Metrics and trust in the designers' pair-kerning expertise. But there may be times when the prescribed kerning isn't to your liking. To establish your own kerning, click between two badly spaced characters of type. Then select any value other than 0 from the Kerning pop-up menu. Or double-click the current kerning value, type a value (in whole numbers from –1000 to 1000), and press Enter or Return. Enter a negative value to shift the letters closer together. Enter a positive value to kern them farther apart. The last line in Figure 15-11 shows examples of my tighter manual kerns.

To decrease the Kerning value (and thereby tighten the spacing) in increments of 20, press Alt+left arrow (Option-left arrow on the Mac). To increase the Kerning value by 20, press Alt+right arrow (Option-right arrow on the Mac). You can also modify the kerning in increments of 100 by pressing Ctrl+Alt+left or right arrow (⌘-Option-left or right arrow on the Mac).

Incidentally, the Kerning and Tracking values (explained shortly) are measured in ¹⁄₁₀₀₀ em, where an *em* (or *em space*) is the width of the letter *m* in the current font at the current size. This may sound weird, but it's actually very helpful. Working in ems ensures that your character spacing automatically updates to accommodate changes in font and type size.

Fractional Widths and System Layout

If kerning gives you fits, try turning off Fractional Widths, found in the Character palette menu. (Click the option name to toggle the feature on and off.) When type gets very small, the spacing between letters may vary by fractions of a single pixel. Photoshop has to split the difference in favor of one pixel or the other, and 50 percent of the time the visual effect is wrong. Better to turn the feature off and avoid the problem entirely. The top two text blocks in Figure 15-12 show the effects of Fractional Widths both on screen and in printed form.

However, even turning off Fractional Widths isn't always a complete solution, as seen in the middle two examples of Figure 15-12. A better choice when using small type for on-screen display is to turn on the new System Layout option in the Character palette menu. Doing so turns off antialiasing — in fact, choosing System Layout when you have an active text layer makes Photoshop automatically perform three operations visible in the History palette, the first of them being Anti Alias None. As the bottom two examples in Figure 15-12 show, this is the best option for small on-screen type, and a particularly good choice when you need to match the type used in on-screen interface elements.

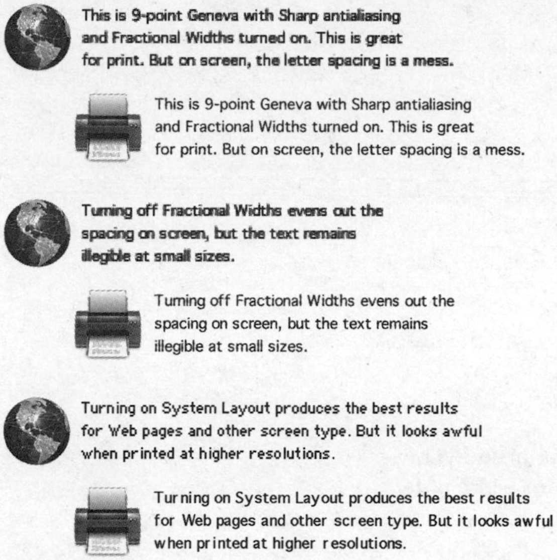

This is 9-point Geneva with Sharp antialiasing and Fractional Widths turned on. This is great for print. But on screen, the letter spacing is a mess.

This is 9-point Geneva with Sharp antialiasing and Fractional Widths turned on. This is great for print. But on screen, the letter spacing is a mess.

Turning off Fractional Widths evens out the spacing on screen, but the text remains illegible at small sizes.

Turning off Fractional Widths evens out the spacing on screen, but the text remains illegible at small sizes.

Turning on System Layout produces the best results for Web pages and other screen type. But it looks awful when printed at higher resolutions.

Turning on System Layout produces the best results for Web pages and other screen type. But it looks awful when printed at higher resolutions.

Figure 15-12: Examples of the Fractional Widths and System Layout options as they appear on screen (signified by the World Wide Web icon) and in printed form (signified by the printer icon).

Tracking

The Tracking value, which you set using the pop-up menu to the right of the Kerning pop-up (see Figure 15-8), is virtually identical to Kerning. It affects character spacing, as measured in em spaces. It even reacts to the same keyboard shortcuts. The only differences are that you can apply Tracking to multiple characters at a time, and Photoshop permits you to apply a Tracking value on top of either automatic or manual kerning. (For folks experienced with Photoshop 4 and earlier, Tracking is more or less the equivalent of the old Spacing option, but measured in ems.) Tracking is usually applied to body text, such as paragraphs, whereas kerning would typically be used in single lines of text, such as headlines.

Horizontal and vertical scaling

The Size pop-up menu scales text proportionally. But using the two scaling options labeled in Figure 15-13, you can scale the width and height of letters individually. A value of 100 percent equals no change to the width and height. Enter a value larger than 100 percent to enlarge the character or lower than 100 percent to shrink it.

Vertical scale

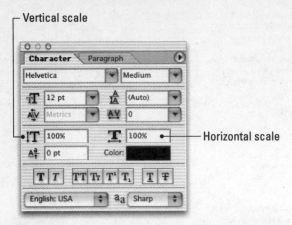

Horizontal scale

Figure 15-13: Change the Horizontal and Vertical scale values to change the height or width of text.

Photoshop applies horizontal and vertical scaling with respect to the baseline. If you're creating vertical type, then the Vertical value affects the width of the column of letters and the Horizontal value changes the height of each character.

 You also can distort text after you create it by applying the Edit ➪ Free Transform command to the text layer. If you go that route and then decide you want the letters back at their original proportions, just open the Character palette and enter scaling values of 100 percent.

 By converting text to shapes, as explained a little later in this chapter, you can reshape characters with even more flexibility, dragging points and line segments as you do when reshaping paths and objects created with the shape tools.

Baseline

The Baseline value, which you set using the bottom-left option box in the Character palette, raises or lowers selected text with respect to the baseline. In type parlance, this is called *baseline shift*. Raising type results in a superscript. Lowering type results in a subscript. An example of each appears in Figure 15-14.

You can also raise type to create a built fraction. Select the number before the slash (the *numerator*) and enter a positive value into the Baseline option box. Reduce the type size of the number after the slash (the *denominator*) but leave the Baseline value set to 0. That's all I did to get the fraction at the bottom of Figure 15-14.

 Press Shift+Alt+up arrow (Shift-Option-up arrow on the Mac) to raise the Baseline value by 2 or Shift+Alt+down arrow (Shift-Option-down arrow on the Mac) to lower the value by 2. To change the value in increments of 10, add in the Ctrl key (or ⌘ key on the Mac).

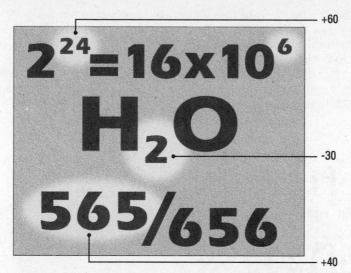

$$2^{24} = 16 \times 10^{6}$$

$$H_2O$$

$$565/656$$

+60

-30

+40

Figure 15-14: Baseline shift frequently finds its way into the worlds of math and science. The labels show the Baseline values.

Of course, since Photoshop offers both a superscript and subscript type style, which you toggle on and off from the Character palette menu, you can use those options to create your fractions, too. But using the Baseline option gives you more control over how much your characters move up or down from the baseline.

Color

Click the Color swatch in the Options bar or in the Character palette to display the Color Picker dialog box. You can apply color on a per-character basis. The color you select affects the next character you type and selected text.

When applying color to selected text, you can't preview the new color accurately because the selection highlight interferes with the display. Press Ctrl+H (⌘-H on the Mac) to toggle the selection highlight (as well as all other on-screen guides) on and off so that you can better judge your color choice.

Antialiasing

So the names of the three antialiasing options in Photoshop 6 — Crisp, Strong, and Smooth — weren't vague enough for you? Let's have a nice warm round of applause for Photoshop 7's new vague antialiasing name: Sharp. Details to follow.

The Antialias pop-up menu, found both in the Character palette and in the Options bar (refer back to Figure 15-8), now offers five choices. Whichever option you choose, the entire layer gets the effect. You can't apply antialiasing to individual characters on a layer, as you can other character formatting options.

Choose None from the pop-up menu to turn off antialiasing (softening) and give characters hard, choppy edges, which is good for very small type. Sharp applies a slight amount of antialiasing, creating sharp contrast. Crisp is similar to Sharp, but a little bit softer. If you notice jagged edges, try applying the Smooth setting. If antialiasing seems to rob the text of its weight, you can thicken it up a bit with the Strong setting. Sharp, Crisp, Strong, and Smooth produce more dramatic effects at small type sizes, as shown in Figure 15-15.

None
ABCdef123#$&
Jagged letters

Sharp
ABCdef123#$&
Slight softening

Crisp
ABCdef123#$&
Just a little more

Strong
ABCdef123#$&
Softens out for thicker letters

Smooth
ABCdef123#$&
Maximum softness

Figure 15-15: The results of the five antialias settings, available from the pop-up menu in the Character palette and in the Options bar.

Applying paragraph formatting

Photoshop offers a full complement of paragraph formatting options, including justification, alignment, hyphenation, line spacing, indent, and even first-line indent. With the exception of the alignment options, all these controls appear only in the Paragraph palette and affect text that you create inside a bounding box. (See the section "Creating and manipulating text in a frame," earlier in this chapter, for information about this method of adding text.)

Figure 15-16 provides a field guide to the Paragraph palette and also shows the palette menu, which offers additional choices related to paragraph formatting.

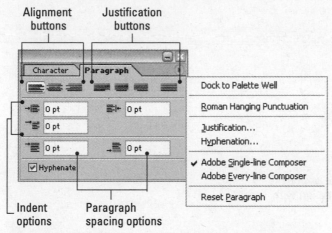

Figure 15-16: You can control the flow of text created in a bounding box by using the options in the Paragraph palette.

Photoshop can apply formatting to each paragraph in a bounding box independently of the others. Click with the type tool inside a paragraph to alter the formatting of that paragraph only. To format multiple paragraphs, drag over them. If you want to format all paragraphs in the bounding box, double-click the type layer thumbnail in the Layers palette, which selects the whole shebang. You also can click the type and then press Ctrl+A (Win) or ⌘-A (Mac).

When no text is selected, you can restore the palette's default paragraph settings by choosing Reset Paragraph from the Paragraph palette menu.

Alignment

The alignment options, found both in the Paragraph palette and in the Options bar, let you control how lines of type align with each other. Assuming that you're using the horizontal type tool, Photoshop lets you align text left, center, or right. Figure 15-17 labels the alignment options. The lines on the alignment buttons indicate what each option does, and they change depending on whether you're formatting vertical or horizontal type.

If you create bounding-box text, Photoshop aligns text with respect to the boundaries of the box. For example, if you draw a bounding box with the right alignment option selected, the text cursor appears at the right edge of the box and moves to the left as you type. For vertical type, the right-align and left-align options align text to the bottom and top of the bounding box, respectively. You must choose a different alignment option to relocate the cursor; you can't simply click at another spot in the bounding box.

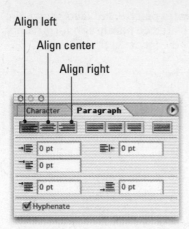

Align left

Align center

Align right

Figure 15-17: Use these options to specify how lines of text align with each other.

When you create point text — that is, by simply clicking in the image window instead of drawing a bounding box — the alignment occurs with respect to the first spot you click and affects all lines on the current text layer.

Tip

You can change the alignment using standard keyboard tricks. Press Ctrl+Shift+L (⌘-Shift-L on the Mac) to align selected lines to the left. Ctrl+Shift+C (⌘-Shift-C on the Mac) centers text, and Ctrl+Shift+R (⌘-Shift-R on the Mac) aligns it to the right.

Roman Hanging Punctuation

One additional alignment option controls the alignment of punctuation marks. You can choose to have punctuation marks fall outside the bounding box so that the first and last characters in all lines of type are letters or numbers. This setup can create a cleaner-looking block of text. Choose Roman Hanging Punctuation from the Paragraph palette menu to toggle the option on and off.

Justification

The justification options adjust text so that it stretches from one edge of the bounding box to another. The different options, labeled in Figure 15-18, affect the way Photoshop deals with the last line in a paragraph.

Assuming that you're using the horizontal type tool, choose left justify to align the line to the left edge of the box; right justify to align to the right edge; and center to put the line smack dab between the left and right edges. With force justify, Photoshop adjusts the spacing of the last line of text so that it, too, fills the entire width of the bounding box. This option typically produces ugly results, especially with very short lines, because you wind up with huge gullies between words. However, if you want to space a word evenly across an area of your image, you can use force justify to your advantage. Drag the bounding box to match the size of the area you want to cover, type the word, and then choose the force justify option. If you later change the size of the bounding box, the text shifts accordingly.

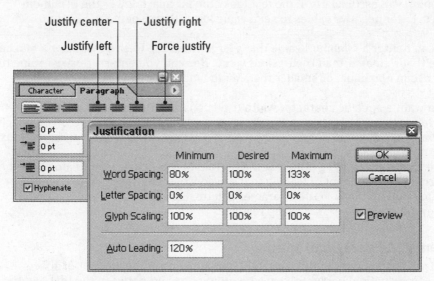

Figure 15-18: The justification options let you control how Photoshop adjusts your text when justifying it.

Photoshop lets you apply a couple of the justification options from the keyboard: Press Ctrl+Shift+J (⌘-Shift-J on the Mac) to left-align the last line; press Ctrl+Shift+F (⌘-Shift-F on the Mac) to force-justify the last line.

You can further control how Photoshop justifies text by using the spacing options in the Justification dialog box, also shown in Figure 15-18. To open the dialog box, choose Justification from the Paragraph palette menu. You can adjust the amount of space allowed between words and characters, and you can specify whether you want to alter the width of *glyphs* — a fancy word meaning the individual characters in a font. Here's what you need to know:

✦ The values reflect a percentage of default spacing. The default word spacing is 100 percent, which gives you a normal space character between words. You can increase word spacing to 1000 percent of the norm or reduce it to 0 percent.

✦ The default letter spacing is 0 percent, which means no space between characters. The maximum letter spacing value is 500 percent; the minimum is –100 percent.

✦ For glyphs, the default value is 100 percent, which leaves the characters at their original width. You can stretch the characters to 200 percent of their original width or squeeze them to 50 percent.

Enter your ideal value for each option into the Desired box. Whenever possible, Photoshop uses these values. The Minimum and Maximum options tell Photoshop how much it can alter the spacing or character width when justifying text. If you wind up with text that's crammed too tightly into the bounding box, raise the Minimum values. Similarly, if the text looks too far apart, lower the Maximum values. Enter negative values to set a value lower than 0 percent.

You can't enter a Minimum value that's larger than the Desired value or a Maximum value that's smaller than the Desired value. Nor can you enter a Desired value that's larger than Maximum or smaller than Minimum.

If you want a specific character width used consistently throughout your text, use the Horizontal scale option in the Character palette rather than the Glyph spacing option. You can apply Horizontal scaling to regular text as well as paragraph text.

As for that Auto Leading option at the bottom of the Justification dialog box, it determines the amount of leading that's used when you select Auto from the Leading pop-up menu in the Character palette. For information on additional paragraph spacing controls, keep reading.

Indents and paragraph spacing

The five option boxes in the Paragraph palette control the amount of space between individual paragraphs in a bounding box and between the text and the edges of the bounding box. Figure 15-19 labels each option.

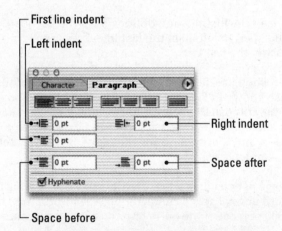

Figure 15-19: Enter values into the top three option boxes to adjust the paragraph indent; use the bottom options to change spacing before and after a paragraph.

Photoshop's indent options work the same as their counterparts in just about every program on the planet. But just to cover all bases, here's the drill:

✦ Enter values in the top two option boxes to indent the entire paragraph from the left edge or right edge of the box.

✦ To indent the first line of the paragraph only, enter a value into the first-line indent option box, which sits all alone on the second row of option boxes. Enter a positive value to shove the first line to the right; enter a negative value to push it leftward, so that it extends beyond the left edge of the other lines in the paragraph.

✦ Use the bottom option boxes to increase the space before a paragraph (left box) and after a paragraph (right box).

Note   In all cases, you must press Enter or Return to apply the change. To set the unit of measurement for these options, use the Type pop-up menu in the Units & Rulers panel of the Preferences dialog box; you can choose from pixels, points, and millimeters. As is the case with options in the Character palette, however, you can enter the value using some other unit of measurement by typing the value followed by the unit's abbreviation ("in" for inches, for example). When you press Enter or Return, Photoshop converts the value to the unit you selected in the Preferences dialog box. (Chapter 2 explains other pertinent facts about units preferences in Photoshop.)

Hyphenation

In most cases, you probably won't be entering text that requires hyphenation to an image. I mean, if you're entering that much text, you're better off doing it in your page-layout program and then importing the image into the layout.

But nevertheless, Photoshop offers the Hyphenate check box in the Paragraph palette. When you select this option, the program automatically hyphenates your text using the limits set in the Hyphenation dialog box, shown in Figure 15-20. Choose Hyphenation from the Paragraph palette menu to open the dialog box.

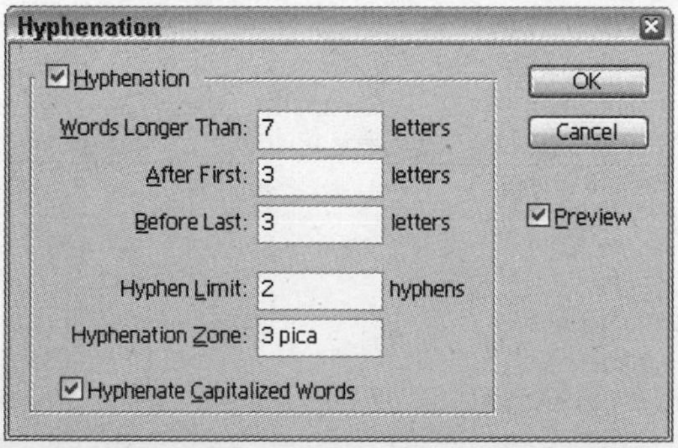

Hyphenation	
☑ Hyphenation	OK
Words Longer Than: 7 letters	Cancel
After First: 3 letters	
Before Last: 3 letters	☑ Preview
Hyphen Limit: 2 hyphens	
Hyphenation Zone: 3 pica	
☑ Hyphenate Capitalized Words	

Figure 15-20: If you ever want to hyphenate text, set the hyphenation controls here.

This dialog box, like several others related to text formatting, comes straight from Adobe InDesign and Illustrator. In case you're not familiar with the controls, they work as follows:

✦ Enter a value into the Words Longer Than option box to specify the number of characters required before Photoshop can hyphenate a word.

✦ Use the After First and Before Last options to control the minimum number of characters before a hyphen and after a hyphen, respectively.

✦ Enter a number into the Hyphen Limit option box to tell Photoshop how many consecutive lines can contain hyphens.

✦ Finally, specify how far from the edge of the bounding box Photoshop can place a hyphen by entering a value into the Hyphenation Zone box.

✦ Turn off the Hyphenate Capitalized Words check box if you want Photoshop to keep its mitts off words that start with an uppercase letter. Hope I didn't insult your intelligence on this one.

Line breaks and composition methods

When you create paragraph text that includes several lines, you may not like the way that Photoshop breaks text from line to line. You may be able to improve the situation by changing the equation that Photoshop uses to determine where lines break.

If you choose Adobe Every-line Composer from the Paragraph palette, the program evaluates the lines of text as a group and figures out the best place to break lines. In doing so, Photoshop takes into account the Hyphenation and Justification settings. Typically, this option results in more evenly spaced text and fewer hyphens.

Adobe Single-line Composer takes a line-by-line approach to your text, using a few basic rules to determine the best spot to break a line. The program first attempts to fit all words on the line by adjusting word spacing, opting for reduced spacing over expanded spacing where possible. If the spacing adjustments don't do the trick, Photoshop hyphenates the last word on the line and breaks the line after the hyphen.

As I've mentioned before, these options may not come into play very often because most people don't create long blocks of text in Photoshop. If you want to control line breaks for a few lines of text, you can just create your text using the regular, text-at-a-point method instead of putting the text in a bounding box. Then you can just press Enter (Win) or Return (Mac) at the spot where you want the line to break, adding a hyphen to the end of the line if needed.

Checking your spelling

As I mentioned near the beginning of the chapter, Photoshop 7 introduces a built-in spelling checker. Located under the Edit menu, the Check Spelling command compares the words in your document with the words in Photoshop's built-in dictionary. If you've typed a word not found in the dictionary, Photoshop brings this to your attention by displaying the Check Spelling dialog box, shown in Figure 15-21.

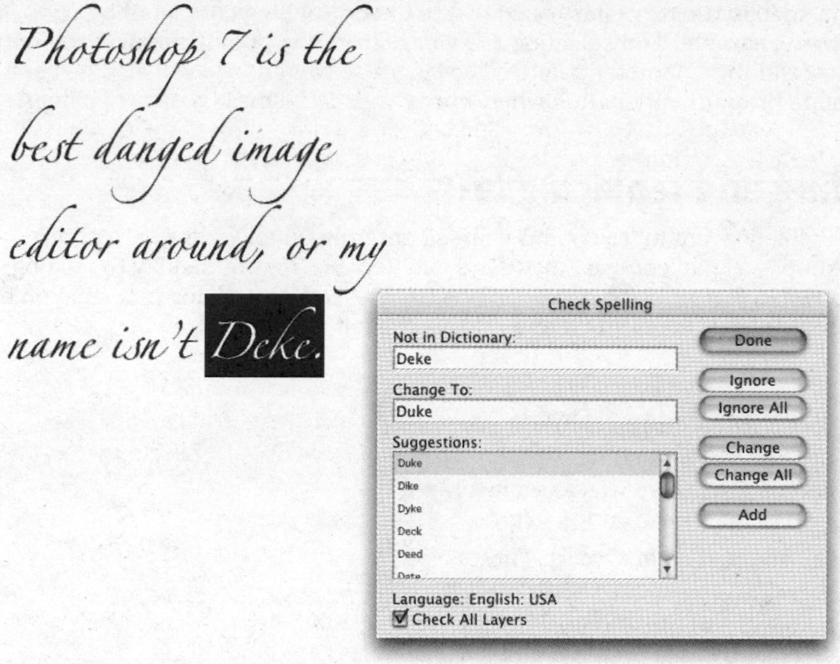

Photoshop 7 is the

best danged image

editor around, or my

name isn't Deke*.*

Figure 15-21: The Check Spelling dialog box offers helpful suggestions for replacing words it doesn't recognize.

The questionable word appears in the Not in Dictionary option box, and Photoshop offers you its favorite replacement word in the Change To option box. Other choices can be found in the Suggestions list. If you have indeed made an error but none of Photoshop's suggested words are correct, you can type the correct word yourself in the Change To option box. Once you have the appropriate replacement word in the Change To option box, click Change. To also change all future instances of the misspelled word, click Change All. If the highlighted word is correct but simply isn't in Photoshop's vocabulary, you can click Ignore to tell it to ignore the word, click Ignore All to tell it to ignore that and all other instances of the word, or click Add to add the word to the dictionary. After you finish making corrections, click Done to exit the dialog box.

If you're in text-editing mode — there's an insertion marker in your text — Photoshop will perform the spell check only on the currently active layer, and only on the text that follows the placement of the insertion marker. In other words, if you want to check the entire text layer, make sure the insertion marker is at the beginning of the text block. Better yet, you can check spelling on all text layers at once. Just make sure there is no active insertion marker in any text layer when you choose Edit ➪ Check Spelling, and make sure the Check All Layers check box is activated in the Check Spelling dialog box.

Note   You can specify the dictionary used by the Check Spelling command by choosing Window ⇨ Character and selecting a language from the pop-up menu in the bottom-left corner of the Character palette. The language you choose will also be used to determine proper hyphenation when words need to be broken over two lines.

Finding and replacing text

In the unlikely event that you find yourself entering huge chunks of text into Photoshop, you can choose Edit ⇨ Find and Replace Text to display the dialog box shown in Figure 15-22. As you may have guessed, this dialog box lets you hunt for specific words in your text and replace them if you so desire.

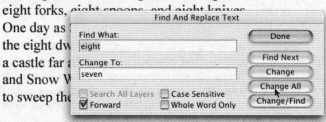

Snow White and the Eight Dwarfs

Once upon a time there was a beautiful
young girl named Snow White who
ran away and met eight dwarfs. These
eight dwarfs were named Sleazy, Thrashy,
Itchy, Frumpy, Drooly, Phlegmatic, and
Blitzen. The eight dwarfs lived in a cottage
with eight little beds, eight chairs, eight bowls,
eight forks, eight spoons, and eight knives.
One day as
the eight dw
a castle far
and Snow W
to sweep the

Find And Replace Text

Find What:
eight

Change To:
seven

☐ Search All Layers   ☐ Case Sensitive
☑ Forward   ☐ Whole Word Only

Done
Find Next
Change
Change All
Change/Find

Figure 15-22: With the Find and Replace Text dialog box, making global changes in your text is easy.

If you've ever used a similar command in a word-processing program, there are no big surprises here. Enter the word you're looking for in the Find What option box. If you want to replace that word with another, type the new word in the Change To option box. The Find Next button locates the next instance of your word relative to the placement of the insertion marker; Change replaces the word; Change All replaces all instances of the word, and Change/Find replaces the current instance and highlights the next. The remaining options are quite common in Find/Replace commands found in word processors. The one quirky thing about Photoshop's version of the command is that should you start your search in the middle of a text block, Photoshop doesn't wrap around when it reaches the end of the text and start looking at the beginning. That's the main use for the Forward option; leave it on and Photoshop searches forward from the text insertion marker; turn it off and Photoshop looks backwards.

Warping Text

For all its glories, text in Photoshop has always lacked an option widely used by designers creating type in drawing programs: the ability to fit text to a path. Prior to Version 6, you were limited to creating straight lines of text only — no wrapping type around a circle or otherwise bending your words.

You still can't fit text to a path in Photoshop 7, but you may be able to get close to the effect you want by using the Warp Text feature. Similar to the text art features that have been available in word-processing programs for some time, Warp Text bends and distorts text to simulate the effect of fitting text to a path. You can choose from 15 different path shapes and choose to curve type, distort it, or both.

Tip

You can warp paragraph text or regular text, but the warp always affects all existing text on the layer. So if you want to reshape just a part of a line of text — for example, to make the last few letters in a word bend upward — put that bit of text on its own layer.

Note

In addition, note that you can't warp type to which you've applied the faux bold style that resides on the Character palette menu. Nor can you warp bitmap fonts or fonts for which the designer hasn't provided the paths, or outlines, that make up the font characters.

After selecting a text layer, click the text warp button in the Options bar, labeled in Figure 15-23, or choose Layer ➪ Type ➪ Warp Text. Photoshop displays the Warp Text dialog box, shown in the figure.

After choosing a warp design from the Style pop-up menu, set the orientation of the warp by clicking the Horizontal or Vertical radio button. Then adjust the Bend, Horizontal Distortion, and Vertical Distortion sliders until you get an effect that fits your needs. You can preview your changes in the image window.

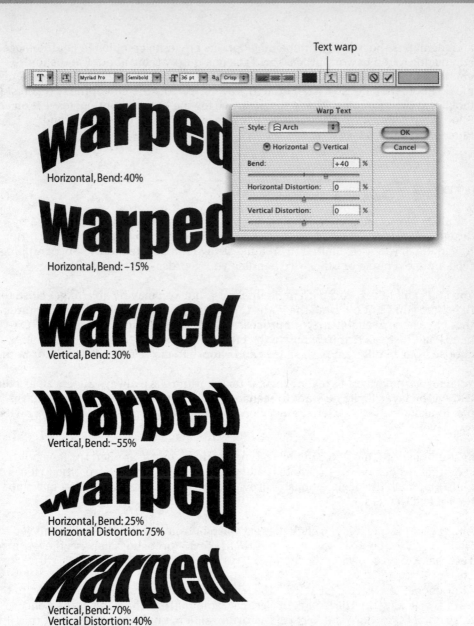

Figure 15-23: Use the controls in the Warp Text dialog box to bend, stretch, and curve type.

I'm sure you can easily figure out how this dialog box works, but a few hints may speed you on your way:

✦ When you select the Horizontal radio button, the warp occurs as the shape in the Style pop-up menu suggests. If you choose Vertical, the warp is applied as if you turned the shape on its side.

✦ Use the Bend value to change the direction of the curve. For the warp style selected in Figure 15-23, for example, a positive Bend value curves the text upward, as shown in the top example in Figure 15-23, and a negative value curves the text in the opposite direction, as shown in the second example.

✦ You can use the Horizontal and Vertical Distortion options to create perspective effects. Horizontal Distortion puts the origin point of the perspective to the left if you enter a positive value and to the right if you enter a negative value. I used a positive value to create the fifth example in Figure 15-23.

Vertical Distortion, as you can probably guess, places the origin point above the text if you enter a positive value and below the text if you enter a negative value. I created the bottom example in Figure 15-23 by entering a positive Vertical Distortion value.

✦ If you edit warped text, Photoshop reapplies the original warp to the layer.

Tip After warping text, you can often improve the effect by tweaking the tracking, kerning, and other character spacing and scaling formatting. If you have trouble achieving the distortion or perspective effect you're after, try choosing Edit ⇨ Free Transform to manipulate the text layer. (You must get out of text-editing mode to access the command.) The steps in the next section offer an example of this technique.

Editing Text as Shapes

Way back near the beginning of this chapter, I mentioned that you can convert each letter in a text layer to individual shapes by choosing Layer ⇨ Type ⇨ Convert to Shape. The command converts all text on a layer; you can't convert part of the text on a layer and leave the rest alone. If the command is grayed out, you're in text-editing mode; click the OK (check mark) or Cancel ("no" symbol) button in the Options bar to exit editing mode.

After you make the conversion, each character works just like a shape that you create with the shape tools. Photoshop creates points and line segments as it sees fit for each letter, as shown in Figure 15-24. This enables you to fool with the shape of each letter by dragging points and segments, as I'm doing in the middle example in the figure. And you can apply all the same effects to your new text shapes as you can to any shape. (Chapter 14 provides a complete rundown of your options.)

Caution Before you convert text to shapes, however, make sure that you don't need to make further changes to character or paragraph formatting or add or delete letters. Photoshop sees your text purely as shapes after the conversion so you can't edit the text using the type tool anymore. For safety's sake, save the text to a new layer or image before choosing Convert to Shape.

Figure 15-24: Starting with some layer effect-laden text (top), I converted the text to shapes and dragged the resulting points and line segments (middle) to reshape the individual characters. A couple of background elements complete my logo for Mississippi's Yazoo River (bottom).

Tip

As do regular shapes, type shapes appear jagged around the edges because of the tiny outline that Photoshop displays around the shape. To hide the outline and smooth out the on-screen appearance of the text, press Ctrl+H (⌘-H on the Mac). Of course, this command also hides the marching ants, guides, and other on-screen aids. The View ⇨ Show ⇨ Target Path command enables you to toggle just the shape outlines.

✦   ✦   ✦

Color and Output

Essential Color Management

Plunging Headlong into Color

Most artists react very warmly to the word *color* and a bit more coolly to the word *management*, especially those of us who have made the mistake of taking on managerial chores ourselves. Put the two words together, however, and you can clear a room. The term *color management* has been known to cause the sturdiest of characters to shriek and sweat like a herd of elephants locked in a sauna.

It's no exaggeration to say that color management is the least understood topic in all of computer imaging. From my experience talking to Photoshop users, most folks expect to calibrate their monitors and achieve reliable if not perfect color. But in point of fact, there's no such thing. So-called *device-dependent color* — that is, synthetic color produced by a piece of hardware — is a moving target. The best Photoshop or any other piece of software can do is to convert from one target to the next.

For what it's worth, most consumer monitors (and video boards, for that matter) are beyond calibration, in the strict sense of the word. You can try your hand at using a hardware calibrator — one of those devices where you plop a little suction cup onto your screen. But calibrators often have less to do with changing screen colors than identifying them. Even if your monitor permits prepress-quality calibration — as in the case of $3,000 devices sold by different vendors over the years, including Radius, Mitsubishi, and LaCie — it's not enough to simply correct the colors on screen; you also have to tell Photoshop what you've done.

Therefore, color management is first and foremost about identifying your monitor. You have to explain your screen's foibles to Photoshop so that it can make every attempt to account for them. In the old days, Photoshop used the screen data to calculate CMYK conversions and that was it. Nowadays, Photoshop embeds a *profile* that identifies the source of the image and uses this information to translate colors from one monitor to another. Photoshop also permits you to work in multiple profile-specific color spaces at the same time — great for artists who alternatively create images for print and the Web — and to specify exactly what to do with images that lack profiles.

The Color Settings command is both wonderful and bewildering. It can just as easily mess up colors as fix them. But if you read this chapter, you and your colors should be able to ride the currents safely from one digital destination to the next. And best of all, color management in Photoshop is consistent with color management found in recent versions of Illustrator and other Adobe applications. Learn one and the others make a heck of a lot more sense.

A Typical Color-Matching Scenario

On the PC, Photoshop 7 devotes three features to color management; Mac users now only have two. Formerly a standard component of Photoshop on both platforms, the Adobe Gamma control panel, which characterizes your monitor, is now a PC-only utility accessible in the Control Panel. Mac users can use the built-in display calibrator, available from the Color section of the Displays system preferences in OS X or of the Monitors control panel in OS 9.

The second color management feature, common to both platforms, is the Color Settings command, found under the Edit menu on the PC and in Mac OS 9 and under the Photoshop menu in Mac OS X. Choose the command or press Ctrl+Shift+K (⌘-Shift-K on the Mac) to display the Color Settings dialog box, which lets you edit device-dependent color spaces and decide what to do with profile mismatches. Finally, use File ⇨ Save As to decide whether to embed a profile into a saved image or include no profile at all.

I could explain each of these features independently and leave it up to you to put them together. But peering into every tree is not always the best way to understand the forest. So rather than explaining so much as a single option, I begin our tour of color management by showing the various control panels, commands, and options in action. In this introductory scenario, I take an RGB image I've created on the Mac and open it up on my PC. The Mac is equipped with a high-end prepress monitor and the PC is hooked up to a generic Sony Trinitron screen, so I've got both extremes pretty well covered. Yet despite the change of platforms and the even more dramatic change in monitors, Photoshop maintains a high degree of consistency so the image looks the same on both sides of the divide. While the specifics of setting up your system will obviously vary, this walk-through should give you an idea of how color management in Photoshop works.

If you already have a rough idea of how profile-based color management works, skip ahead to the section "Color Conversion Central." There I explain the intricacies of the Color Settings dialog box, which is where the vast majority of the color management process occurs.

Setting up the source monitor

If you own a monitor with calibration capabilities, I recommend that you start off by calibrating it. In order to share some common ground here, I'm going to calibrate mine using OS X's built in Display Calibrator. As I mentioned a few paragraphs ago, you can access this by clicking the Calibrate button in the Color tab of the Displays system preferences, as shown in Figure 16-1; it's also located in the Utilities folder of the Applications folder. The Display Calibrator utilizes ColorSync, which is Apple's system-wide color management system.

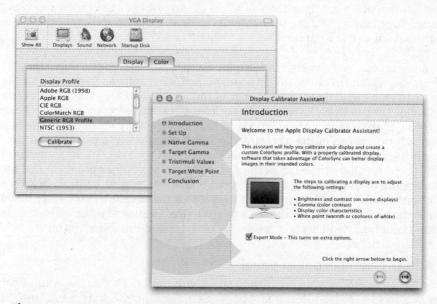

Figure 16-1: In Mac OS X, clicking the Calibrate button on the Color panel of the Displays system preferences launches the Display Calibrator.

The Macintosh Display Calibrator

Once I've fired it up, I'll go ahead and flatter myself by turning on the Expert Mode check box. That gives me access to a few more options. If you're following along at home, you may find that you can't access every step in the Display Calibrator, or for that matter of the Adobe Gamma control panel on the PC. Some monitors, particularly LCD displays, don't allow for every adjustment. You navigate through the Display Calibrator by clicking the buttons in the lower-right corner of the window.

The first step is adjusting the contrast and brightness settings on my monitor. The next step is the most important one of all; I'm presented with sliders I can use to adjust the colors of red, green, and blue apples until they blend in with their respective backgrounds. This allows me to balance the red, green, and blue display functions of my monitor. Next is the gamma control. While you'll probably want to keep this on the Mac Standard default, it can be very enlightening to slide the control down to the PC Standard to see just how much darker PC screens generally are. This is an important thing to remember when designing graphics for the Web.

Incidentally, the term *gamma* refers to the amount of correction required to convert the color signal generated inside the monitor (let's call it x) to the color display that you see on screen (y). Imagine a simple graph with the input signal x along the bottom and the output y along the side. A gamma of 1.0 would result in a diagonal line from bottom-left to upper-right corner. A higher gamma value tugs at the center of that line and curves it upward. As you tug, more and more of the curve is taken up by darker values, resulting in a darker display. So a typical Mac screen with default gamma of 1.8 is lighter than a typical PC screen with a default gamma of 2.2. For a real-time display of gamma in action, check out the discussion of the Curves dialog box included in Chapter 17.

Continuing on our way through the Display Calibrator, next up is the Tristimuli Values pane, which isn't available even on some CRT displays. Tristimuli is a big fancy word signifying the three extremes of red, green, and blue that your monitor can display. On the Mac, ColorSync draws lines between extreme colors to generate a 3D graph of achievable colors. I'm asked here to select my monitor (or the nearest equivalent) from a list. In the next step I'm asked to set a white point for my display; unfortunately there's no way to measure this as with the Adobe Gamma utility, but the three settings at the top of the slider represent popular points in the spectrum. Pick the one that makes on-screen fields of white appear whitest, or select the check box to turn off white point correction if that looks best to you. After being asked to name the profile, I'm done. I can see in the Displays system preferences that the ColorSync display I just created is now assigned to the monitor.

The Adobe Gamma control panel

For the PC users among you, Photoshop ships with the Adobe Gamma control panel. Under Windows systems prior to XP, choose Settings from the Start menu, and then choose Control Panel. After the Control Panel window comes up, double-click the Adobe Gamma icon. (Make sure you're viewing all Control Panel options.) Under Windows XP, the Control Panel is available immediately under the Start menu. If you don't see the Adobe Gamma icon, click the Appearance and Themes option, then double-click the Adobe Gamma icon. (If the control panel displays a warning that your video card doesn't support system-wide color management, don't sweat it. Most video cards don't.) Select the Step By Step (Wizard) option and click the Next button to walk through the setup process one step at a time. If you see a control panel like the one on the right side of Figure 16-2, click the Wizard button to continue.

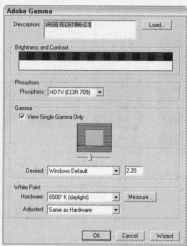

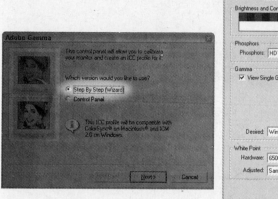

Figure 16-2: Select the Step By Step option (left) to advance one step at a time through the otherwise imposing Adobe Gamma options (right).

When using the Adobe Gamma Wizard, all you have to do is answer questions and click the Next button to advance from one screen to another. For example, after adjusting the contrast and brightness settings, Gamma asks you to specify the nature of your screen's red, green, and blue phosphors. If you own a Trinitron or Diamondtron monitor — which you'll know because you paid more for it — select the Trinitron settings. Or select Custom and enter values according to your monitor's documentation. If the documentation does not suggest settings, ignore this screen and click Next to move on. So you don't know your phosphors — that's life. You've got bigger fish to fry.

As with the Native Gamma section of the Mac Display Calibrator, the next screen, pictured in Figure 16-3, is the most important. It asks you to balance the red, green, and blue display functions of your monitor. But to do so, you need to turn off the View Single Gamma Only check box; this presents you with separate controls over each of the three monitor channels. Then use the sliders to make the inner squares match the outer borders. You are in essence calibrating the monitor according to your unique perceptions of it, making this particular brand of characterization a highly personal one.

The next screen asks you to set the white point, which defines the general color cast of your screen from 5,000 degrees Kelvin for slightly red to 9,300 degrees for slightly blue. A medium value of 6,500 degrees is a happy "daylight" medium. To find the best setting for your monitor, click the Measure button. Then click the gray box that appears the most neutral — neither too warm nor too cool — until you get dumped back into the Gamma Wizard. Then click Next.

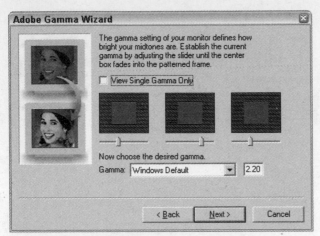

Figure 16-3: Turn off the View Single Gamma Only check box to modify each of the three color channels independently.

After you click the Finish button, the Gamma utility asks you to name your new monitor profile and save it to disk. Name it whatever you want, but don't change the location — to be made available to Photoshop and other applications it has to stay in the default location.

Adobe Gamma generates a custom monitor profile and automatically alerts Photoshop to the change. Your screen may not look any different than it did before you opened Gamma, but you can rest assured that Photoshop is now officially aware of its capabilities and limitations.

Selecting the ideal working space

Now that I've identified my monitor, I need to select an RGB *working environment*, which is a color space other than the one identified for the monitor. This is the strangest step, but it's one of the most important as well. Fortunately, all it requires is a bit of imagination to understand fully.

On my Mac equipped with OS X, I switch to Photoshop and choose Photoshop ➪ Color Settings. (In OS 9, the Color Settings command is found under the Edit menu.) Photoshop displays the dialog box shown in Figure 16-4. I'm immediately faced with a dizzying array of options — no gradual immersion into the world of color management here — but Photoshop does make a small attempt to simplify the process. The program offers several collections of predefined settings via the Settings pop-up menu. Among the settings are Color Management Off, which deactivates Photoshop's color management entirely; ColorSync Workflow, which is useful in all-Macintosh environments; and Emulate Photoshop 4, which both turns color management off and mimics Version 4's screen display.

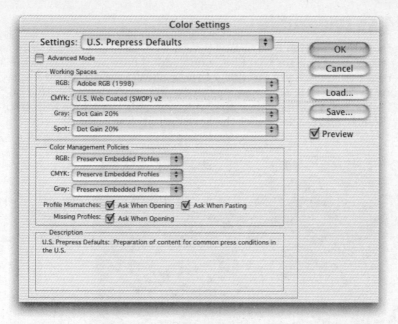

Figure 16-4: I choose U.S. Prepress Defaults to access the Adobe RGB (1998) color space, which affords me a large theoretical RGB spectrum.

Each of these options has its relative advantages in certain settings, but most folks will want to gravitate toward two other options. If you create most of your images for the Web, select the Web Graphics Defaults option. This directs Photoshop's color functions so that they're most amenable to screen display. On the other hand, if most of your artwork finds its way into print, and if you live in the United States or some country that supports U.S. printing standards, select U.S. Prepress Defaults.

For my part, I select U.S. Prepress Defaults, as shown in Figure 16-4. If you have any doubts about whether to favor Web or print graphics, I recommend you do the same. Why? Among its other attractions, the U.S. Prepress option sets the working RGB color space to Adobe RGB (1998), arguably the best environment for viewing 24-bit images on screen.

Adobe RGB includes a wide range of theoretical RGB colors, whether they can truly be displayed on a monitor or not. You may see some *clipping* on screen—where two or more color spaces appear as one—but Photoshop has greater latitude when interpolating and calculating colors.

After selecting U.S. Prepress Defaults, I click the OK button. The source environment is fully prepared. Now to save an image and send it on its way.

Embedding the profile

The final step on the Mac side is to embed the Adobe RGB profile into a test image. (The word *embed* simply means that Photoshop adds a little bit of code to the file stating where it was last edited.) For this, I choose File ➪ Save As, which displays the dialog box in Figure 16-5. After naming the file and specifying a location on disk, I select the Embed Color Profile check box, which embeds the Adobe RGB color profile into the test image. Then I click the Save button to save the file.

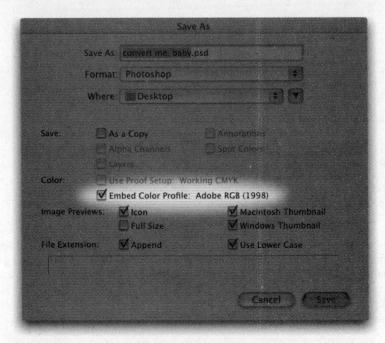

Figure 16-5: I select the Embed Color Profile check box to append the Adobe RGB profile to the image saved on the Mac.

In order to save a profile with an image, you have to select a file format that supports profiles. This includes the native Photoshop (PSD) format, TIFF, JPEG, EPS, and PICT. The two DCS formats also save profiles, but because DCS supports CMYK images only, it converts the RGB image to CMYK and saves a CMYK profile. If you select another format — GIF, PNG, BMP, or the like — the Embed Color Profile check box becomes dimmed.

Note that the Embed Color Profile check box always embeds the device-independent profile defined in the Color Settings dialog box. This is very important — it does *not* embed the monitor profile. Photoshop handles the conversion from monitor space to RGB space internally, without the help of either the Color Settings or Save As commands. This permits Photoshop to accommodate a world of different monitors from a single RGB working space.

Setting up the destination space

After saving the test image with the embedded Adobe RGB profile, I e-mail it from my Mac to my PC. No translation occurs here; this is a simple file copy from one computer to another. Now before I can open this image and display it properly on my PC, I have to set up my RGB colors. I start by characterizing my monitor. This time I'm on the PC, so I perform the calibration using the Adobe Gamma Wizard, as discussed previously in the section "The Adobe Gamma control panel."

After I finish with Adobe Gamma, I go into Photoshop and choose Edit ⇨ Color Settings or press Ctrl+Shift+K. Now if I were really trying to calibrate my systems to match up, I would select U.S. Prepress Defaults from the Settings pop-up menu, just as I did on the Mac. But for purposes of this demonstration, I want to force Photoshop to perform a conversion, and a good conversion requires a little dissension. So this time around, I put on my Web artist cap and choose Web Graphics Defaults from the Settings option, as shown in Figure 16-6. This sets the RGB Working Spaces pop-up menu to the utterly indecipherable sRGB IEC61966-2.1.

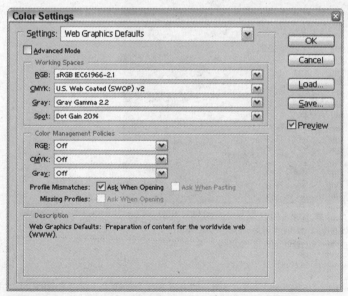

Figure 16-6: On the Windows side, I select Web Graphics Defaults to set my working environment to sRGB. This forces Photoshop to make a conversion.

The truncated name for this working space is *sRGB*, short for *standard RGB*, the ubiquitous monitor space touted by Hewlett-Packard, Microsoft, and a host of others. Although much smaller and drabber than Adobe RGB, the sRGB space is perfect for Web graphics because it represents the colors projected by a run-of-the-mill PC monitor. It also happens to be Photoshop's default setting. Given that many users will never visit this dialog box, sRGB is fast becoming a cross-platform standard.

Defining color-management policies

The Color Settings command determines not only how Photoshop projects images on screen, but also how it reads embedded profiles. The three Color Management Policies pop-up menus determine how Photoshop reacts when it tries to open an image whose embedded profiles don't match the active color settings. When Web Graphics Defaults is active, the RGB pop-up menu is set to Off, which tells Photoshop to resist managing colors when it opens an RGB image. Personally, I'm not a big fan of disabling color management entirely, especially when it threatens to ruin my color conversion scenario. So I set the option to Convert to Working RGB, as shown in Figure 16-7.

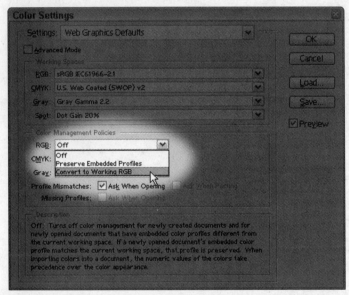

Figure 16-7: Set the first of the Color Management Policies to Convert to Working RGB to convert the image from the Adobe RGB working space to the sRGB space.

Finally, Photoshop wants to know how it should behave when it encounters an image garnishing a profile other than sRGB. Should it convert all colors in the image to the sRGB environment? Or should it ask permission before proceeding? Personally, I like my software to be subservient, so I select Ask When Opening from the Profile Mismatches options, as in Figure 16-7.

Converting the color space

Now I'm ready to open the test image. I choose File ⇨ Open just as I normally would. As Photoshop for Windows opens the test image, it detects the embedded Adobe RGB profile and determines that it does not match the active sRGB profile. Justly troubled by this development, Photoshop displays the alert box shown in Figure 16-8. You can select from three conversion options:

✦ **Use the embedded profile:** Photoshop is perfectly capable of displaying multiple images at a time, each in a different color space. Select this option to tell Photoshop to use the Adobe RGB space instead of sRGB to display the image it's about to open. No colors are converted in the process.

✦ **Convert document's colors to the working space:** This option converts the colors from the Adobe RGB space to sRGB. Because I selected Convert to Working RGB in the previous step, this option is selected by default. Had I not selected the Ask When Opening check box, Photoshop would have performed the conversion without asking me.

✦ **Discard the embedded profile:** Select this option to ignore the embedded profile and to display the image in the sRGB space without any color manipulations. Thanks to the low saturation inherent in sRGB, the result would be a significantly grayer, gloomier image.

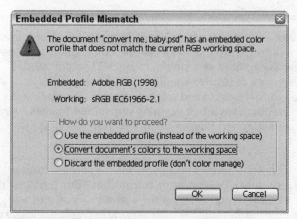

Figure 16-8: The alert box gives you the option of converting the colors from the foreign image or opening the image as is.

I select the Convert Document's Colors radio button and click OK. Photoshop spends a few seconds converting all pixels in the image from Adobe RGB to the smaller sRGB and then displays the converted image on screen. The result is an almost perfect match — much better than the sort of results you could achieve without profile-based color management.

Color Conversion Central

As I mentioned near the outset of this chapter, Color Settings is the command that puts Photoshop's color conversion functions in play. It at once defines the color space parameters and makes the color conversions happen. The following sections explain the specific options as they're grouped inside the Color Settings dialog box. I also make suggestions for what I consider to be the optimal settings, in case you're interested in a little advice.

Description

This portion of the dialog box comes last, but it's also the most important. It tells you what every one of the Color Settings options does. Just hover the cursor over an option to see a detailed description. To see how an option in a pop-up menu works, select the option and then hover your cursor over it. With help like this, what do you need me for?

No seriously, what *do* you need me for? I think I'll take the rest of the chapter off. Well, I guess I could mention that if you save your own color settings, you can enter a description that shows up here in the Description section when you load your settings. There, I suddenly feel important again.

Working spaces

Because every color model except Lab varies according to a piece of hardware—either screen or printer—Photoshop has to tweak the color space to meet your specific needs. There's no such thing as a single, true CMYK color model, for example; instead, there are lots of printer-specific CMYK color models. These color models inside color models are called *working spaces*. You define the default working spaces that Photoshop uses when opening unprofiled images, creating new ones, or converting mismatched images using the four Working Spaces pop-up menus:

✦ **RGB:** The RGB environment defines what you see on screen. Rather than limiting yourself to the circumscribed range of colors that your particular brand of monitor can display—known as the monitor's *gamut*—you can work in a larger, richer color environment, filled with theoretical color options that will serve your image well when projected on other monitors and output from commercial presses. Unless you work strictly on the Web and never create artwork for print, I suggest you select Adobe RGB (1998). Notice that your monitor space also appears in the pop-up menu—this shows that your monitor was correctly tagged with Adobe Gamma or the Display Calibrator.

Tip

If you're a Web artist and you want to preview how an image will look on a different kind of monitor, choose the color space from the View ➪ Proof Setup menu after closing the Color Settings dialog box. For example, choose View ➪ Proof Setup ➪ Windows RGB to see how the image looks on a typical

PC monitor. Choose Macintosh RGB for a typical Mac monitor or Monitor RGB to turn off the RGB working space and see the image as it appears without conversion. Then use Ctrl+Y (Win) or ⌘-Y (Mac) to turn the preview on and off. All these commands work identically regardless of which working space you select, so you might as well use Adobe RGB, the choice most likely to put you in sync with other professionals.

✦ **CMYK:** Use this option to specify the kind of printer you intend to use to print your final CMYK document. This option defines how Photoshop converts an image to the CMYK color space when you choose Image ⇨ Mode ⇨ CMYK Color. It also governs the performance of the CMYK preview (View ⇨ Proof Setup ⇨ Working CMYK). Finally, it decides how the colors in a CMYK image are converted for display on your RGB monitor. So any time you open a CMYK image, the RGB working space becomes dormant and this option kicks into gear. For more information about characterizing a CMYK device, see "Custom CMYK Setup" later in this chapter.

✦ **Grayscale:** This command defines how Photoshop displays a grayscale image (created using Image ⇨ Mode ⇨ Grayscale). You can adjust the gray values in the image to account for a typical Macintosh or PC display (Gray Gamma 1.8 or Gray Gamma 2.2, respectively). Or preview the image according to how it will print, complete with any of several Dot Gain values. (*Dot gain* is the factor by which halftone dots grow when absorbed into paper, as I discuss in the upcoming "Custom CMYK Setup" section.) My preferred setting is Gray Gamma 2.2. It's dark enough to account for dot gains of more than 25 percent, so it accurately reflects the printing conditions typical of grayscale work. Plus it predicts how grays display on a typical PC monitor. Everybody wins.

✦ **Spot:** From a printing perspective, a spot color separation behaves like an extra grayscale print. Specify the dot gain value that correlates to your commercial printer. If you don't know, Dot Gain 20% is a safe bet.

Note

An open profiled image remains in its working space regardless of how you change the settings in the Color Settings dialog box. Suppose that you open an image in sRGB and then change the working space to Adobe RGB. The open image remains unchanged on screen, safe in its sRGB space. If you'd prefer the image to change to the new space, choose Image ⇨ Mode ⇨ Assign Profile. Then select the Working RGB radio button, as shown in Figure 16-9. Because Assign Profile leaves the color values of all pixels unchanged, Photoshop merely displays the old pixels in the new space, which permits the colors to shift on screen. So perhaps perversely, not converting pixels results in a visible color shift, whereas converting pixels does not.

Tip

To permit the image to change on the fly according to the active working space, choose Image ⇨ Mode ⇨ Assign Profile and select the Don't Color Manage This Document option. A pound or number symbol (#) appears in the title bar to show that the image is no longer tagged with a color profile, as in Figure 16-10. Now whenever you change the image's working space in the Color Settings dialog box, the image updates in kind. Select the Preview check box to view changes without exiting the dialog box.

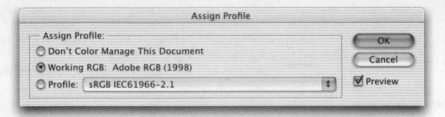

Figure 16-9: Use the Assign Profile command to switch an open image to a different color space without converting pixels. As a result, the image will look different on screen.

Figure 16-10: A pound or number symbol (#) in the title bar shows that the image has not been assigned a color profile. If an asterisk (*) appears, the image uses a profiled space other than the default working space, as when opening an sRGB image in an Adobe RGB environment.

If the Assign Profile command leaves pixels unchanged so they appear to change on screen, there must be a command that converts pixels so they appear consistent on screen. Sure enough, that command is Image ➪ Mode ➪ Convert to Profile, which displays the dialog box pictured in Figure 16-11. The options in the lower half of the dialog box—Engine, Intent, and so on—also appear in the Color Settings dialog box when you enter the advanced mode, so you'll be hearing more about them later. For now, just select the color space that you want to convert the image to from the Destination Space pop-up menu and press Enter or Return.

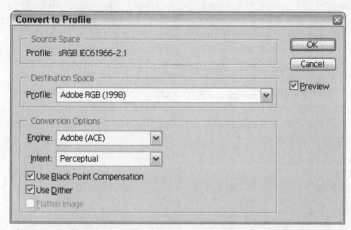

Figure 16-11: Convert to Profile is the complement to Assign Profile. Choose it to both switch an open image to a different color space and convert the pixels. The result is an image that looks the same on screen as it did before.

On first glance, the Destination Space pop-up menu may seem wildly complicated, offering RGB, CMYK, and grayscale working spaces, and even going so far as to permit you to create your own. But in fact, this dizzying array of options may in some situations lead to less work for you. The Destination Space option is unusual in that it permits you to switch color modes. For example, if you open an RGB image, choose the Convert to Profile command and select a CMYK space such as U.S. Web Coated (SWOP), Photoshop not only remaps the colors, it converts the RGB channels to CMYK. In this way, Convert to Profile has an edge over Image ⇨ Mode ⇨ CMYK Color—you can switch color modes and nail a specific working space in one operation.

Color-management policies

Highlighted in Figure 16-12, the next set of options control how Photoshop reacts when opening an image that either lacks a profile or contains a profile that doesn't match the specified Working Spaces options previously listed. These are the options that are most likely to cause confusion because they're responsible for the error messages Photoshop delivers when opening images. The trick is to keep the error messages to a minimum while keeping control to a maximum. Here are my suggestions for each option with what I hope is enough explanation for you to make your own educated decisions:

✦ **RGB:** The first three pop-up menus establish default policies that Photoshop suggests or implements according to the check boxes that follow. For example, when opening an untagged RGB image, I reckon I might as well tag it with the working RGB profile, which in my case is Adobe RGB. So I select Convert to Working RGB and turn the Missing Profiles check box off. This way, when no profile is evident, Photoshop assigns the Adobe RGB profile without bothering me. However, if the image contains a profile, I might go either way. An image tagged with an sRGB profile is probably a Web image, so I might go ahead and open it in the sRGB space without conversion. However, if I encountered an image tagged with the Apple RGB profile—intended to match a typical Apple Macintosh screen—I'd want to convert it to Adobe RGB. Therefore, I set Profile Mismatches to Ask When Opening. This way, Photoshop will ask me what I want to do every time I open an image with a nonmatching RGB profile. It'll suggest I convert the image to Adobe RGB, but permit me to override if I like.

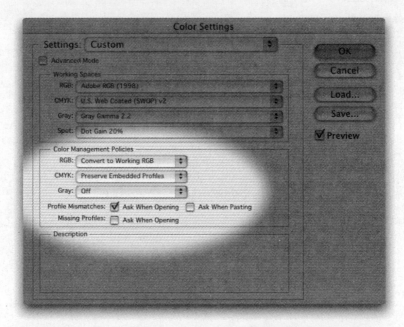

Figure 16-12: Here are my recommended settings for the five Color Management Policies options. They tell Photoshop to ask you when opening images with mismatches, but otherwise proceed automatically.

✦ **CMYK:** Whereas RGB color is a function of your monitor and the RGB working space, accurate CMYK is all about matching colors to a specific output device. Therefore, if you're accepting CMYK images from clients and colleagues, you probably want to be very careful about making arbitrary conversions. By setting CMYK to Preserve Embedded Profiles, I tell Photoshop to open a tagged CMYK image in its own color space and override the default CMYK space specified in the Working Spaces option mentioned previously. Again, setting Profile Mismatches to Ask When Opening gives me the option to change my mind and convert the image to my working CMYK space if I deem it appropriate. If the image has no profile, Photoshop leaves it untagged, giving me the option of testing out multiple CMYK working spaces and assigning the one that fits best.

✦ **Gray:** Making automatic color manipulations to color images is all very well and good. Clipping is bound to occur, but with millions of theoretical colors at your disposal, the clipping is unlikely to do any visible harm. However, grayscale images are another story. Blessed with just 256 brightness values, they are significantly more fragile than color images. Furthermore, few grayscale images are tagged properly, making Photoshop's automatic adjustments highly suspect. The upshot is that I prefer to correct grayscale images manually (as explained in Chapter 17) and keep Photoshop the heck out of it. Therefore, I set the Gray option to Off.

✦ **Profile Mismatches:** These two check boxes tell Photoshop how to behave when opening an image whose profile does not match the working color space. If you select the Ask When Opening check box, Photoshop asks your permission to perform the conversion suggested in the previous pop-up menus. As the top message in Figure 16-13 shows, you also have the option of opening the image in its native color space or leaving the image untagged. Back in the Color Settings dialog box, select Ask When Pasting to tell Photoshop to warn you when you copy an image from one working space and paste it into another. Shown at the bottom of Figure 16-13, this warning is a bit much, in my opinion. In all likelihood, you want Photoshop to convert the colors; so turn off Ask When Pasting and let Photoshop do its work unhindered.

✦ **Missing Profiles:** When Photoshop 5.0 first shipped, it had the regrettable habit of converting images that lacked embedded profiles, even though there was no clearly defined space to serve as the source for the conversion. Photoshop 6 successfully shook that nasty habit, and it's still holding strong in Version 7. However, Photoshop does like to ask you whether you want to manage the colors or not. I say turn Ask When Opening off — enough alert messages already! — and let Photoshop take its cues from the RGB, CMYK, and Gray pop-up menus. According to Figure 16-12, this means Photoshop will tag most unprofiled RGB images with an Adobe RGB profile and leave unprofiled CMYK and grayscale images alone. An exception occurs when opening newer unprofiled images. If you saved an image without a profile using Version 5 or later, Photoshop inserted a tag that explicitly states, "I have no profile." In this case, the file will open untagged and Photoshop will resist color managing the image until you tell it to do otherwise.

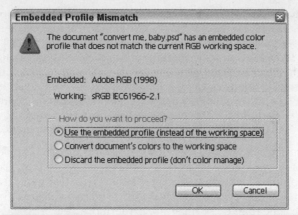

Figure 16-13: The alert message that appears when opening an image with a mismatched profile (top) and then copying part of that image and pasting it into an image that subscribes to the default working space (bottom).

The Color Management Policies options are particularly dense, so I don't blame you if you find yourself reading and rereading my text trying to make sense of it. If you can't for the life of you make heads or tails of what I'm talking about — if it's any consolation, I'm honestly not trying to confuse you — try this instead: Set your options to match the ones I've suggested in Figure 16-12. Then work in Photoshop for a few days or weeks and see how it feels. The good news about my suggestions is that they won't hurt your images, even if you don't know what you're doing. With a little time and practice, you'll get a feel for how the settings work. Then come back, read my text again, and see if it doesn't make more sense. I wouldn't be surprised if it suddenly seems crystal clear.

Advanced mode

Right about now, I picture you scratching your head and thinking, "Wow, this Deke guy really gets off on color management. I mean, dude, give it a rest already!" I have to admit, I do find color management profoundly interesting. It inspires the same twisted feelings I have when watching a highway expansion project. On the one hand, I have to admire all that planning and organization. I mean, gee whiz, what a lot of work, all so I can get to the grocery store faster. But on the other hand, I think surely there has got to be a better way. If these guys would only put this kind of effort into flying cars, I'd be home by now.

Up to this point, my admiration for Photoshop's color management has outweighed my frustration. But the moment I select the Advanced Mode check box, my patience evaporates. Suddenly, this really is too much. But a book called the *Bible* has a responsibility to cover everything, so I guess I'm stuck with it.

Think of the Advanced Mode check box as the key to the color management underworld. When you select it, you unleash two categories of demonic preference settings: Conversion Options and Advanced Controls. Spotlighted in Figure 16-14, each set of options possesses its own special brand of loathsome and horrible power. For the love of God, dear reader, run away now while you still can.

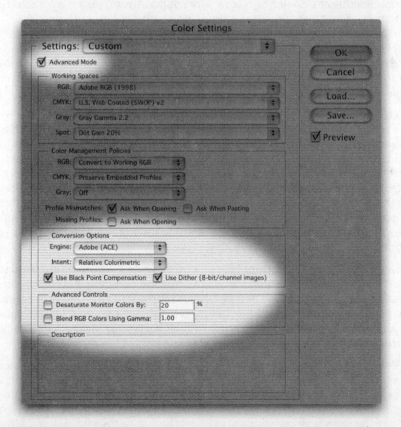

Figure 16-14: Turn on the Advanced Mode check box to display the Conversion Options and Advanced Controls, as well as define your own CMYK working space.

Okay, perhaps that's a bit of an exaggeration. After all, there is one reason to turn on the Advanced Mode check box, and that's because it permits you to change an ill-advised Intent setting. So what the heck, let's give it a whirl. Perhaps even hell can be fun if we give it a chance:

✦ **Engine:** The first of the Advanced Mode options is Engine, and it does just what it sounds like it does. The force behind the color management process is the *engine*. If you don't like one engine, you can trade it for another. If you work in a Macintosh-centric environment, for example, you might want to select Apple ColorSync. But I recommend you stick with the Adobe Color Engine, or ACE. Not only is ACE a great engine, it ensures compatibility with Illustrator, InDesign, and other Adobe applications.

✦ **Intent:** Whenever you remap colors, a little something gets lost in the translation. The trick is to lose as little as possible, and that's the point of Intent. By default, the option is set to Relative Colorimetric, which converts every color in the source profile to its closest equivalent in the destination profile. But while such a direct transfer of colors may sound attractive, it can create rifts in the image. The closest equivalent for two similar colors in the source profile might be a single color in the destination, or they might be two very different colors. As a result, gradual transitions may become flat or choppy. The better setting is Perceptual, which sacrifices specific colors in favor of retaining the gradual transitions between colors, so important to the success of continuous-tone photographs.

Tip

Why should you take my word that Perceptual is better? You shouldn't. To get a second opinion, hover your cursor over the word Perceptual and read the Description text, which tells you that Perceptual "requests a visually pleasing rendering, preserving visual relationships between source colors." The truth is, most folks inside Adobe believe Perceptual to be the better choice. So why is the default setting Relative Colorimetric? Because a direct color translation is the best way to convert object-oriented artwork, like that in Illustrator and InDesign. Because cross-application harmony is very important to the powers that be, Photoshop is stuck towing the line. But don't you get roped in — select Perceptual today.

✦ **Use Black Point Compensation:** Like any other colors, Photoshop wants to convert black and white to new values. Whites are compensated naturally by the Intent setting, which may in many cases map white to a different color in the name of smoother transitions. But if you let black map to a lighter color, you can end up with wimpy gray shadows. To keep your blacks their blackest, turn this check box on.

✦ **Use Dither (8-bit/channel images):** Just so we're all on the same page, a 24-bit image contains 8 bits per channel. So don't think we're talking about 8-bit GIF images here; this option uses *dithering* (random patterns of pixels) to smooth out what might otherwise be harsh color transitions. Ostensibly, it can result in higher file sizes when saving an image in the native PSD format or TIFF with LZW compression. But the effect is usually minimal. Leave this check box turned on.

✦ **Desaturate Monitor Colors By:** The Adobe RGB space in particular has a habit of rendering such vivid colors that the brightest areas in the image flatten out on screen. Because they may or may not have a direct outcome on the appearance of the final image, whether in print or on the Web, such flat areas can be a bit misleading. To better see details in bright areas of color, turn on the Desaturate Monitor Colors check box. Note that this option affects the screen view only; the colors will continue to print as vividly as ever. I recommend you use this option only for running previews from inside the Color Settings dialog box. Leaving this option on for extended periods of time can be more deceiving than turning it off.

✦ **Blend RGB Colors Using Gamma:** When this option is off, as by default, Photoshop blends layers according to the gamma of the working color space. For example, the gamma of Adobe RGB is 2.2, the same as a typical PC screen and a few shades darker than a typical Macintosh screen. On occasion, however, this may result in incongruous highlights around the edges of layers. If you encounter this, try turning on this check box. Photoshop recalculates all blends using a theoretically more desirable gamma value.

To recap, I suggest you turn on the Advanced Mode check box and select Perceptual from the Intent pop-up menu. Then turn off Advanced Mode, click OK, and never set foot inside this dark corner of Photoshop again.

Custom CMYK Setup

To prepare an image for reproduction on a commercial offset or web press, you first need to specify how you want Photoshop to convert the image from the RGB to CMYK color space. This step also affects the conversion from CMYK to RGB, which in turn defines how CMYK images appear on screen.

You specify the CMYK space by choosing Edit ➪ Color Settings. Then select the color profile you want to use from the CMYK pop-up menu in the Working Spaces section of the dialog box. You can select a predefined color profile. Or define a custom CMYK conversion setup by choosing Custom CMYK from the CMYK pop-up menu. When you choose Custom, Photoshop displays the Custom CMYK dialog box, shown in Figure 16-15.

The following list explains each and every option in the Custom CMYK dialog box. If you're not a print professional, some of these descriptions may seem a little abstruse. After reading this section, you may want to talk with your commercial printer and find out what options, if any, he or she recommends.

✦ **Name:** Okay, so this one's not so abstruse after all. Enter a name for your custom CMYK settings here.

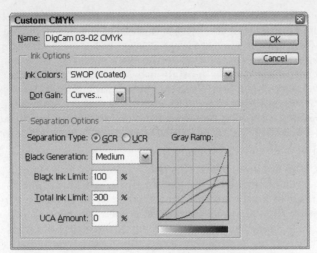

Figure 16-15: Use the options in the Custom CMYK dialog box to prepare an image for printing on a commercial offset or web press.

✦ **Ink Colors:** This pop-up menu offers access to a handful of common press inks and paper stocks. Select the option that most closely matches your printing environment. (Your commercial printer can easily help you with this one.) The default setting, SWOP (Coated), represents the most common press type and paper stock used in the United States for magazine and high-end display work. Regardless of which setting you choose, Photoshop automatically changes the Dot Gain value to the most suitable setting.

✦ **Dot Gain:** Enter any value from –10 to 40 percent to specify the amount by which you can expect halftone cells to shrink or expand during the printing process, a variable known as *dot gain*. When printing to uncoated stock, for example, you can expect halftone cells to bleed into the page and expand by about 25 to 30 percent. For newsprint, it varies from 30 to 40 percent. In any case, Photoshop automatically adjusts the brightness of CMYK colors to compensate, lightening the image for high values and darkening it for low values.

Tip

For more control, select Curves from the Dot Gain pop-up menu. As shown in Figure 16-16, this brings up the Dot Gain Curves dialog box, which permits you to specify how much the halftone dots expand on a separation-by-separation basis. If the All Same option is checked, turn it off. Then use the Cyan, Magenta, Yellow, and Black radio buttons in the lower-right corner of the dialog box to switch between the four separations and modify their output independently. To do this, locate the lone point in the center of the curved line in the graph on the left side of the dialog box. Drag this point up to add dot gain, which in turn darkens the display of CMYK colors on screen; drag the point down to lighten the display. If you need more control, you can add points to the graph by clicking on the curved line. Points added to the left side of the curve affect the display of light colors; points added to the right side of the curve affect dark colors.

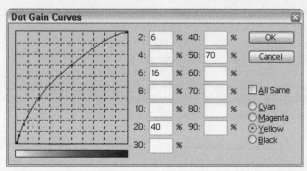

Figure 16-16: Select Curves from the Dot Gain pop-up menu to modify the dot gain values on a separation-by-separation basis. Here, I'm editing the yellow separation.

✦ **Separation Type:** When the densities of cyan, magenta, and yellow inks reach a certain level, they mix to form a muddy brown. The GCR (*gray component replacement*) option avoids this unpleasant effect by overprinting these colors with black to the extent specified with the Black Generation option. If you select the UCR (*under color removal*) option, Photoshop removes cyan, magenta, and yellow inks where they overlap black ink. GCR is almost always the setting of choice except when printing on newsprint.

✦ **Black Generation:** Available only when the GCR option is active, the Black Generation pop-up menu determines how dark the cyan, magenta, and yellow concentrations must be before Photoshop adds black ink. Select Light to use black ink sparingly; select Heavy to apply it liberally. The None option prints no black ink whatsoever, while the Maximum option prints black ink over everything. You may want to use the UCA Amount option to restore cyan, magenta, and yellow ink if you select the Heavy or Maximum option.

✦ **Black Ink Limit:** Enter the maximum amount of black ink that can be applied to the page. By default, this value is 100 percent, which is solid ink coverage. If you raise the UCA Amount value, you'll probably want to lower this value by a similar percentage to prevent the image from overdarkening.

✦ **Total Ink Limit:** This value represents the maximum amount of all four inks permitted on the page. For example, assuming you use the default Black Ink Limit and Total Ink Limit values of 100 and 300 percent, respectively, the darkest printable color contains 100 percent black ink. The sum total of cyan, magenta, and yellow inks, therefore, is the difference between these values: 200 percent. A typical *saturated black* — a mix of inks that results in an absolute pitch-black pigment — is 70 percent cyan, 63 percent magenta, 67 percent yellow, and 100 percent black. And 70 + 63 + 67 + 100 =, you guessed it, 300.

✦ **UCA Amount:** The opposite of UCR, UCA stands for *under color addition*, which enables you to add cyan, magenta, and yellow inks to areas where the concentration of black ink is highest. For example, a value of 20 percent raises the amount of cyan, magenta, and yellow inks applied with black concentrations between 80 and 100 percent. This option is dimmed when the UCR radio button is active.

✦ **Gray Ramp:** The Gray Ramp graph on the right side of the Custom CMYK dialog box shows the effects of your changes. Four lines — one in each color — represent the four inks. Although you can't edit the colored lines in this graph by clicking and dragging them, you can observe the lines to gauge the results of your settings. If you have an urge to grab a curve and yank on it, choose Custom from the Black Generation pop-up menu. The ensuing dialog box lets you edit the black curve directly while you preview its effect on the C, M, and Y curves in the background.

To see how your changes affect an open CMYK image in Photoshop, do this: Prior to choosing the Color Settings command, choose Image ⇨ Mode ⇨ Assign Profile and select Don't Color Manage This Document. Then choose Edit ⇨ Color Settings and turn on the Preview check box. From then on, the image updates every time you press Enter or Return to accept changes from the Custom CMYK dialog box.

Saving and loading color settings

As we've seen, it can be a painstaking process of trial-and-error to arrive at the perfect color settings. Furthermore, the perfect settings for one job might be highly imperfect for another. Clearly, there's a pressing need for a way to save and load color settings — and just as clearly, Photoshop is the sort of obliging application to provide a way to do it.

You might logically surmise that the Load and Save buttons on the right side of the Color Settings box will come into play here — and you'd be correct. Once you have your settings just the way you want them, click the Save button. You'll be prompted by default to save your settings in a Settings folder located deep within the bowels of your computer. (Should you ever need to find it again, here's the path: Under Windows, it's Program Files\Common Files\Adobe\Color\Settings. In Mac OS X, it's located in your Home folder at Library\Application Support\Adobe\Color\Settings. And in Mac OS 9, it's System Folder\Application Support\Adobe\Color\Settings.) Clicking the Load button takes you to the same folder, where you can choose the saved settings you want to load.

And that's not all. Not only can you save and load individual CMYK Working Spaces settings, but with the dreaded Advanced Mode activated, you can also save Working Spaces files for RGB, Grayscale, and Spot color settings as well. You'll find the load and save commands under the individual pop-up menus for each space.

But what if you work with multiple commercial prepress houses? Wouldn't it be nice to be able to select different custom working spaces from the CMYK pop-up menu without having to constantly open setup files using the Load CMYK option? Yes, it would, and here's how you do it:

Steps: Create a Profile That Appears in the CMYK Pop-up Menu

1. **Create an ICM file.** Inside the Color Settings dialog box, choose Save CMYK from the CMYK pop-up menu, and give the file a name ending in the extension *.icm*. Other than the extension, the name you give it here isn't really that important; the original name you assigned when you first created the settings with the Custom CMYK command is the name you'll see when you actually load the settings. Wait to click Save until the next step.

2. **Save the ICM file to the Recommended folder.** For Photoshop to see the CMYK profile, you have to save it to a specific folder. On the PC, the path for that folder is C:\Program Files\Common Files\Adobe\Color\Profiles\ Recommended. On the Mac in OS 9, it's System Folder\Application Support\ Adobe\Color\Profiles\Recommended. In OS X, start with the Library folder on the root level of your hard drive, and then go to Application Support\ Adobe\Color\Profiles\Recommended. When you finally arrive inside the Recommended folder, save the ICM file.

3. **Quit Photoshop.** Regardless of which version of Photoshop you're using, quit it by choosing File ⇨ Exit (File ⇨ Quit on the Mac).

4. **Launch Photoshop.** By starting (or restarting) Photoshop, you force the program to load the ICM profile.

5. **Confirm the profile has loaded.** Press Ctrl+Shift+K (⌘-Shift-K on the Mac) to bring up the Color Settings dialog box and click the CMYK pop-up menu in the Working Spaces area. You should see the profile you saved in the menu.

Tip

Because the ICM file created in the previous steps resides in the Recommended folder, it appears in the CMYK pop-up menu even when the Advanced Mode check box is turned off. Any ICM files saved in the Profiles folder but outside the Recommended folder appear only when Advanced Mode is turned on.

✦   ✦   ✦

Mapping and Adjusting Colors

What Is Color Mapping?

Color mapping is just a fancy name for shuffling colors around.
For example, to map Color A to Color B simply means to take
all the A-colored pixels and convert them to B-colored pixels.
Photoshop provides several commands that enable you to
map entire ranges of colors based on their hues, saturation
levels, and most frequently, brightness values.

Color effects and adjustments

Why would you want to change colors around? For one thing,
to achieve special effects. You know those psychedelic horror
movies that show some guy's hair turning blue while his face
turns violet and the palms of his hands glow a sort of orange-
yellow? No? Funny, me neither. But a grayscale version of this
sort of effect appears in the second example of Figure 17-1.
Although not the most attractive effect by modern standards—
you may be able to harvest more tasteful results if you put
your shoulder to the color wheel—what we think of as a
"psychedelic" color effect qualifies as color mapping for the
simple reason that each color shifts incrementally to a new
color.

But the more common reason to map colors is to enhance
the appearance of a scanned image or digital photograph, as
demonstrated in the third example in Figure 17-1. In this case,
you're not creating special effects; you're just making straightforward repairs, alternatively known as *color adjustments* and
corrections. Scans are never perfect, no matter how much
money you spend on a scanning device or a service bureau.
They can always benefit from tweaking and subtle adjustments, if not outright overhauls, in the color department.

Uncorrected image

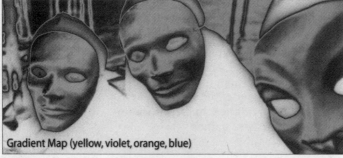

Gradient Map (yellow, violet, orange, blue)

Levels, Curves, & Unsharp Mask

Figure 17-1: Nobody's perfect, and neither is the best of scanned photos (top). You can modify colors in an image to achieve special effects (middle) or simply fix the image with a few well-targeted corrections (bottom).

Keep in mind, however, that Photoshop can't make something from nothing. In creating the illusion of more and better colors, most of the color-adjustment operations that you perform actually take some small amount of color *away* from the image. Somewhere in your image, two pixels that were two different colors before you started the correction change to the same color. The image may look 10 times better, but it will in fact be less colorful than when you started.

Remembering this principle is important because it demonstrates that color mapping is a balancing act. The first nine operations you perform may make an image look progressively better, but the tenth may send it into decline. There's no magic formula; the amount of color mapping you need to apply varies from image to image. But if you follow my usual recommendations — use the commands in moderation, know when to stop, and save your image to disk before doing anything drastic — you should be fine.

Many of the commands I talk about in the following sections can also be applied as *adjustment layers*. Adjustment layers are an extremely flexible tool, giving you all the advantages of the color correction commands without the drawback of having your original image permanently altered. I discuss adjustment layers in full at the end of this chapter, but I wanted to alert you to their welcome presence from the outset. So now you know.

The good, the bad, and the wacky

Photoshop stores all of its color mapping commands under the Image ⇨ Adjustments submenu. Basically, these commands fall into three categories:

✦ **Color mappers:** Commands such as Invert and Threshold are quick-and-dirty color mappers. They don't correct images, but they can be useful for creating special effects and adjusting masks.

✦ **Easy color correctors:** Brightness/Contrast and Color Balance are true color correction commands, but they sacrifice functionality for ease of use. If I had my way, these two commands would be removed from the Image ⇨ Adjustments submenu and thrown in the dust heap.

✦ **Expert color correctors:** The third, more complicated variety of color correction commands provides better control, but they take a fair amount of effort to learn. Levels, Curves, and Hue/Saturation are examples of color correcting at its best and most complicated.

This chapter contains little information about the second category of commands for the simple reason that some of them are inadequate and ultimately a big waste of time. There are exceptions, of course, most notably the new Auto Color command, which usually does a passable job of adjusting an image's midtones and removing color casts. Auto Levels and Auto Contrast are decent quick fixers, and Variations offers deceptively straightforward sophistication. But Brightness/Contrast and Color Balance sacrifice accuracy in their attempt to be straightforward. They are as liable to damage your image as to correct it, making them dangerous in a dull, pedestrian sort of way. I know because I spent my first year with Photoshop relying exclusively on Brightness/Contrast and Color Balance, all the while wondering why I couldn't achieve the effects I wanted. Then, one happy day, I spent about half an hour learning Levels and Curves, and the quality of my images skyrocketed. So wouldn't you just rather learn it correctly in the first place? I hope so, because that's what we're all about to do.

Quick Color Effects

Before we get into all the high-end gunk, however, I take a moment to explain the first category of commands, all of which happen to occupy one of the lower sections in the Image ⇨ Adjustments submenu. These commands — Invert, Equalize, Threshold, and Posterize — produce immediate effects that are either difficult or require too much effort to duplicate with the more full-featured commands.

Invert

When you choose Image ⇨ Adjustments ⇨ Invert or press Ctrl+I (⌘-I on the Mac), Photoshop converts every color in your image to its exact opposite, as in a photographic negative. As demonstrated in Figure 17-2, black becomes white, white becomes black, fire becomes water, good becomes evil, dogs romance cats, and the brightness value of every primary color component changes to 255 minus the original brightness value.

Original digital photo   Image ⇨ Adjustments ⇨ Invert

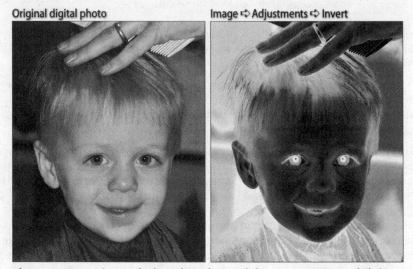

Figure 17-2: An image before the advent of the Invert command (left) and after (right).

Note

By itself, the Invert command is not sufficient to convert a scanned color photographic negative to a positive. Negative film produces an orange cast that the Invert command does not address. After inverting, you can use the Variations command to remove the color cast. Or avoid Invert altogether and use the Levels command to invert the image. Both Variations and Levels are explained later in this chapter.

Image ⇨ Adjustments ⇨ Invert is just about the only color mapping command that retains the rich diversity of color in an image. (The Hue/Saturation command also retains color diversity under specific conditions.) For example, if you apply the Invert command twice in a row, you arrive at your original image without any loss in quality.

When you're working on a full-color image, the Invert command simply inverts the contents of each color channel. This means the command produces very different results when applied to RGB, Lab, and especially CMYK images. Typically, the Invert command changes most pixels in a CMYK image to black. Except in rare instances — such as in night scenes — the black channel contains lots of light shades and few dark shades. So when you invert the channel, it becomes extremely dark.

Just so you know, when I refer to applying color corrections in the CMYK mode, I mean applying them after choosing Mode ➪ CMYK Color. Applying corrections in the RGB mode when View ➪ Preview ➪ CMYK is active produces the same effect as when CMYK Preview is not selected; the only difference is that the on-screen colors are curtailed slightly to fit inside the CMYK color space. You're still editing inside the same old red, green, and blue color channels, so the effects are the same.

As I mentioned back in Chapter 12, inverting the contents of the mask channel is the same as applying Select ➪ Inverse to a selection outline in the marching ants mode. In fact, this is one of the most useful applications of the filter.

Equalize

Equalize is the smartest and at the same time least useful of the Image ➪ Adjustments pack. When you invoke this command, Photoshop searches for the lightest and darkest color values in a selection. Then it maps the lightest color in all the color channels to white, maps the darkest color in the channels to black, and distributes the remaining colors to other brightness levels in an effort to evenly distribute pixels over the entire brightness spectrum. This doesn't mean that any one pixel will actually appear white or black after you apply Equalize; rather, one pixel in at least one channel will be white and another pixel in at least one channel will be black. In an RGB image, for example, the red, green, or blue component of one pixel would be white, but the other two components of that same pixel might be black. The result is a higher contrast image with white and black pixels scattered throughout the color channels.

If no portion of the image is selected when you choose Image ➪ Adjustments ➪ Equalize, Photoshop automatically maps the entire image across the brightness spectrum, as shown in the upper-right example of Figure 17-3. If you select a portion of the image before choosing the Equalize command, however, Photoshop displays a dialog box containing the following two radio buttons:

✦ **Equalize Selected Area Only:** Select this option to apply the Equalize command strictly within the confines of the selection. The lightest pixel in the selection becomes white, the darkest pixel becomes black, and the others remap to shades in between.

✦ **Equalize Entire Image Based on Selected Area:** If you select the second radio button, which is the default setting, Photoshop applies the Equalize command to the entire image based on the lightest and darkest colors in the selection. All colors in the image that are lighter than the lightest color in the selection become white and all colors darker than the darkest color in the selection become black.

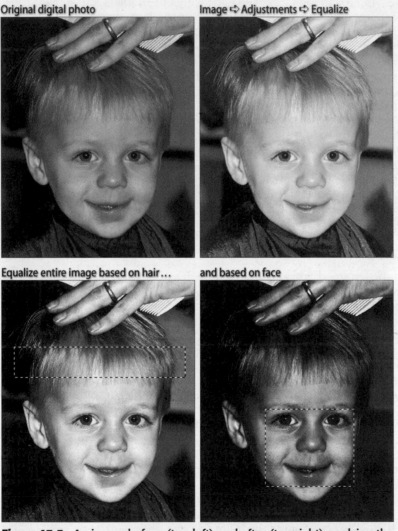

Original digital photo

Image ➪ Adjustments ➪ Equalize

Equalize entire image based on hair...

and based on face

Figure 17-3: An image before (top left) and after (top right) applying the Equalize command when no portion of the image is selected. You can also use the brightness values in a selected region as the basis for equalizing an entire image (bottom left and right).

The bottom two examples in Figure 17-3 show the effects of selecting different parts of the image when the Equalize Entire Image Based on Selected Area option is in force. In the left example, I selected a portion of the image with both light and dark values, which boosted the amount of contrast between highlights and shadows in the image. In many ways, the result is better than the overall adjustment in the upper-right example. In the bottom-right example, I selected a predominantly lighter area, which resulted in an over-darkening of the entire image.

The problem with the Equalize command is that it relies too heavily on some bizarre automation to be of much use as a color correction tool. Certainly, you can create some interesting special effects. But if you'd prefer to automatically adjust the colors in an image from black to white regardless of the color mode and composition of the individual channels, choose Image ⇨ Adjustments ⇨ Auto Levels or press Ctrl+Shift+L (⌘-Shift-L on the Mac). If you want to adjust the tonal balance manually and therefore with a higher degree of accuracy, the Levels and Curves commands are tops. I explain all these commands at length later in this chapter.

Threshold

I touched on the Threshold command a couple of times in previous chapters. As you may recall, Threshold converts all colors to either black or white, based on their brightness values. When you choose Image ⇨ Adjustments ⇨ Threshold, Photoshop displays the Threshold dialog box shown in Figure 17-4. The dialog box offers a single option box and a slider bar, either of which you can use to specify the medium brightness value in the image. Photoshop changes any color lighter than the value in the Threshold option box to white and changes any color darker than the value to black.

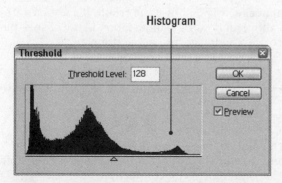

Figure 17-4: The histogram in the Threshold dialog box shows the distribution of brightness values in the selection.

The dialog box also includes a graph of all the colors in the image — even if only a portion of the image is selected. This graph is called a *histogram*. The width of the histogram represents all 256 possible brightness values, starting at black on the left and progressing through white on the right. The height of each vertical line in the graph demonstrates the number of pixels currently associated with that brightness value. Therefore, you can use the histogram to gauge the distribution of lights and darks in your image. It may seem weird at first, but with enough experience, the histogram becomes an invaluable tool, permitting you to greatly improve the colors that you see on screen.

Tip

Generally speaking, you achieve the best effects if you change an equal number of pixels to black as you change to white (and vice versa). So rather than moving the slider bar to 128, which is the medium brightness value, move it to the point at which the area of the vertical lines to the left of the slider triangle looks roughly equivalent to the area of the vertical lines to the right of the slider triangle.

The upper-left example in Figure 17-5 shows the result of applying the Threshold command with a Threshold Level value of 122. Although this value provides a fairly even distribution of black and white pixels, I lost a lot of detail in the dark areas.

As you may recall from my "Using the High Pass filter" discussion in Chapter 10, you can use Filter ➪ Other ➪ High Pass before you use the Threshold command to retain areas of contrast. In the upper-right image in Figure 17-5, I applied the High Pass filter with a Radius of 5.0 pixels, followed by the Threshold command with a value of 122. To get thicker edges in the bottom-left image, I first applied Median and then followed that up with High Pass and Threshold. Next I took all three of these images, put them on separate layers in the same image, used the Multiply blend mode to mix them together, and alternately erased portions of the layers. When I had a satisfactory rough blend, I merged the three layers and used the pencil tool for cleanup. The final image in 17-5 shows the result. It's not an automatic process, by any means — about an hour of manual labor, in my case — but it's the most expedient way to convert an image into a line drawing.

Figure 17-6 shows combinations of various filters on the same image, always topped off with an application of Threshold. While it's not much as a standalone effect, Threshold definitely plays well with others.

If you want to achieve a colorful Threshold effect, try applying the Threshold command independently to each color channel. In an RGB image, for example, press Ctrl+1 (⌘-1 on the Mac) and then apply Image ➪ Adjustments ➪ Threshold. Then press Ctrl+2 (⌘-2 on the Mac) and repeat the command, and press Ctrl+3 (⌘-3 on the Mac) and do it again. Don't forget that you can also apply the same effect to two channels at once by selecting one channel and Shift-clicking the second. Color Plate 17-1 shows examples of what happens when I apply Threshold along with a handful of filters to independent color channels in the RGB, Lab, and CMYK modes. From the end results on the right of each row, I think it's clear that Andy Warhol would have loved the Threshold command.

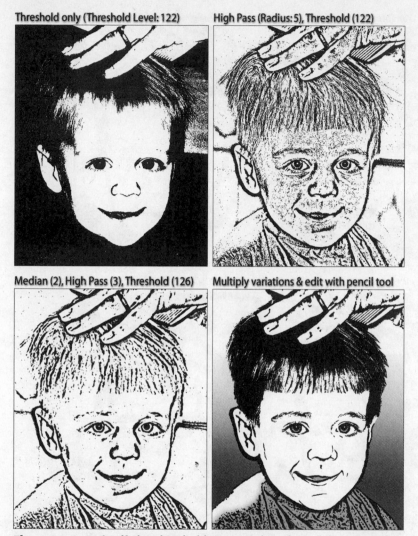

Threshold only (Threshold Level: 122)   High Pass (Radius: 5), Threshold (122)

Median (2), High Pass (3), Threshold (126)   Multiply variations & edit with pencil tool

Figure 17-5: By itself, the Threshold command tends to deliver flat results (top left). But with judicious application of filters, and a fair amount of manual labor, Threshold can ultimately be the cornerstone in turning a photograph into a line drawing (bottom right).

Posterize

The Posterize command is Threshold's rich cousin. Whereas Threshold boils down an image into two colors only, Posterize can retain as many colors as you like. However, you can't control how colors are mapped, as you can when you use Threshold. The Posterize dialog box does not provide a histogram or slider bar. Instead, Posterize automatically divides the full range of 256 brightness values into a specified number of equal increments.

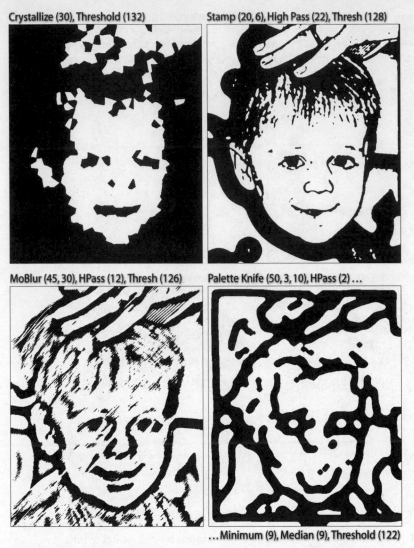

Crystallize (30), Threshold (132)   Stamp (20, 6), High Pass (22), Thresh (128)

MoBlur (45, 30), HPass (12), Thresh (126)   Palette Knife (50, 3, 10), HPass (2) . . .

. . . Minimum (9), Median (9), Threshold (122)

Figure 17-6: You can create some fun and interesting effects by combining Threshold with other filters.

To use this command, choose Image ➪ Adjustments ➪ Posterize and enter a value in the Levels option box. The Levels value represents the number of brightness values that the Posterize command retains. Higher values result in subtle color adjustments; lower values produce more dramatic effects. The first example in Figure 17-7 shows an image subject to a Levels value of 4.

By now, you may be thinking, "By golly, if Posterize is so similar to Threshold, I wonder how it works when applied as a capper with other filters?" Well, you're in luck, because this is exactly what I did in the other examples of Figure 17-7. First I applied Add Noise and then Posterize. Interesting how Median increases the impact of Posterize by melding pixels together, and Add Noise diminishes the impact by dithering the pixels, huh? This Add Noise/Posterize technique is actually great for creating images with very small color palettes, ideal for the Web.

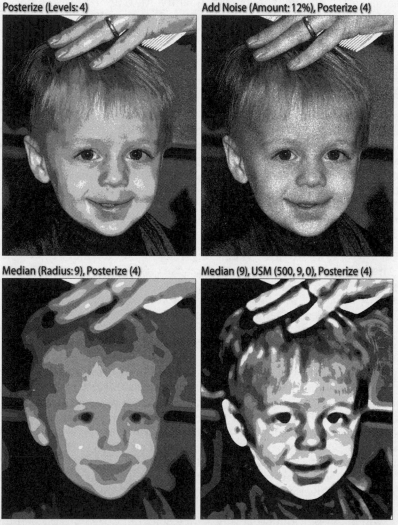

Figure 17-7: Posterize on its own (upper left) and as a follow up to Add Noise (upper right), Median (lower left), and a combination of Median and Unsharp Mask (lower right).

Quick Corrections

Photoshop now offers four quick-correctors under the Image ⇨ Adjustments submenu. The new kid on the block is the Auto Color command, and while it's no substitute for using the advanced tools, it's the most useful of the quick-correctors. Desaturate sucks the saturation out of a selection and leaves it looking like a grayscale image. Auto Levels and Auto Contrast automatically increase the contrast of an image according to what Photoshop deems to be ideal brightness values. Auto Levels examines each color channel independently; Auto Contrast examines the image as a whole. And Auto Color, which works only with RGB images, looks at the whole image as it attempts to automatically correct the image's midtones and remove color casts.

Sucking saturation

The Desaturate command is mostly useful for robbing color from selected areas or from independent layers. There's really very little reason to apply Desaturate to an entire image; you can just as easily choose Image ⇨ Mode ⇨ Grayscale to accomplish the same thing and dispose of the extra channels that would otherwise consume room in memory and on disk. I know of only two reasons to sacrifice all colors in the RGB mode:

✦ You want to retain the option of applying RGB-only filters, such as Lens Flare and Lighting Effects.

✦ You intend to downsize the colors using Image ⇨ Mode ⇨ Indexed Colors and save the final image in the GIF format for use on the Web.

Tip

You can use Edit ⇨ Fade (Ctrl+Shift+F or ⌘-Shift-F) to back off the effects of Desaturate or any other command under the Image ⇨ Adjustments submenu. As always, the Fade command is available immediately after you apply the color correction; if you so much as alter a selection outline, Fade goes dim.

Desaturate isn't the only way to suck colors out of an image. You can also invert the colors and mix them with their original counterparts to achieve a slightly different effect. Just press Ctrl+I (⌘-I on the Mac) to invert the area you want to desaturate. Then press Ctrl+Shift+F (⌘-Shift-F on the Mac), change the Opacity setting to 50 percent, and—here's the important part—select Color from the Mode pop-up menu. You can get a very close approximation of converting an image to the Grayscale mode simply by creating a new layer, filling it with black, and switching the blend mode to Color. And last but certainly not least, the Channel Mixer gives you the most exacting control over converting to grayscale; see Chapter 4 for details.

Note

By the way, you might be wondering why Adobe selected Ctrl+Shift+U (⌘-Shift-U on the Mac) as the keyboard shortcut for Desaturate. Well, Desaturate is actually a renegade element from the Hue/Saturation command, which lets you raise and lower saturation levels to any degree you like. The shortcut for Hue/Saturation is Ctrl+U (⌘-U on the Mac)—for hUe, don't you know—so Desaturate is Ctrl+Shift+U (⌘-Shift-U on the Mac).

The Auto Levels command

Image ➪ Adjustments ➪ Auto Levels (Ctrl+Shift+L or ⌘-Shift-L) goes through each color channel and changes the lightest pixel to white, changes the darkest pixel to black, and stretches all the shades of gray to fill out the spectrum. In Figure 17-8, I started with a drab and murky image. But when I applied Auto Levels, Photoshop pumped up the lights and darks, bolstering the contrast. You could probably get better results by applying Levels and tweaking by hand, but it's not half bad for an automated, no-brainer command that you just choose and let rip.

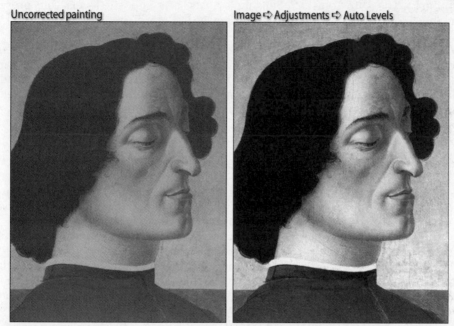

Uncorrected painting
Image ➪ Adjustments ➪ Auto Levels

Figure 17-8: A grayscale image before (left) and after (right) applying the Auto Levels command.

Unlike the Equalize command, which considers all color channels as a whole, Auto Levels looks at each channel independently. Therefore, the active color mode has a profound effect on Auto Levels. Like Invert, Equalize, and other automatic color mappers, Auto Levels is designed for use in the RGB mode. If you use it in CMYK, you're more likely to achieve special effects than color correction.

Cross-Reference

By default the Auto Levels command produces the same effect as the Auto button in the Levels dialog box, as discussed fully in "The Levels command" section later in this chapter.

The Auto Contrast command

The problem with Image ➪ Adjustments ➪ Auto Levels is that it modifies values on a channel-by-channel basis, which means it has a habit of upsetting the balance of colors in an image. Consider Color Plate 17-2, for example. The first image is severely washed out. As shown in the second image, choosing the Auto Levels command results in a bolder and more vibrant image, but it also changes the background from green to blue.

The solution is Image ➪ Adjustments ➪ Auto Contrast (Ctrl+Shift+Alt+L or ⌘-Shift-Option-L). The Auto Contrast command adjusts the composite levels, thus preserving the colors, as in the case of the third image in Color Plate 17-2.

Which should you use when? If a low-contrast image suffers from a color cast that you want to correct, try Auto Levels. If the image is washed out but the colors are okay, try Auto Contrast. (When working on a grayscale image, the two commands work the same, so choose whichever is more convenient.) Bear in mind that neither command is perfect, so you'll very likely want to make additional Levels and Variations adjustments — or try the next command on our roster.

The Auto Color command

New to Photoshop 7, the Auto Color command is indeed a welcome addition, and even manages to erode my faint disdain for any command that starts with the word "Auto." It's true that, depending on the image you're attempting to correct, you might not see any difference between an application of Auto Levels and Auto Color. But on some images, like the one pictured in Color Plate 17-2, Auto Color is definitely worth a shot. Auto Levels helps the skin tones and adds a pleasing blue tint to the background, while Auto Contrast fixes the brightness but leaves the skin jaundiced. Auto Color does the best job on the skin tones, which after all represent the most important colors inside a portrait of this sort.

Choose Image ➪ Adjustments ➪ Auto Color or press Ctrl+Shift+B (⌘-Shift-B on the Mac) to apply the Auto Color command. To get a sense of how the command works, and how it compares with Auto Levels in particular, take a look at Figure 17-9, which shows how each command affects an image on a channel-by-channel basis. (Note that Auto Color works only when applied to images in the RGB mode.)

So what's going on? Like Auto Levels, Auto Color corrects an image one channel at a time. The difference is, rather than set the darks to black and the lights to white, Auto Color neutralizes an image's highlights, midtones, and shadows, thereby restoring balance to other colors in the image. Or, at least, that's the idea. Like any automated command, it fails to achieve the desired results as often as it succeeds. But that's okay. Because while Auto Color might occasionally fix colors when left to its default settings, the real power comes when you customize it using the Levels and Curves commands — a process I discuss in "The Levels command" section later in this chapter.

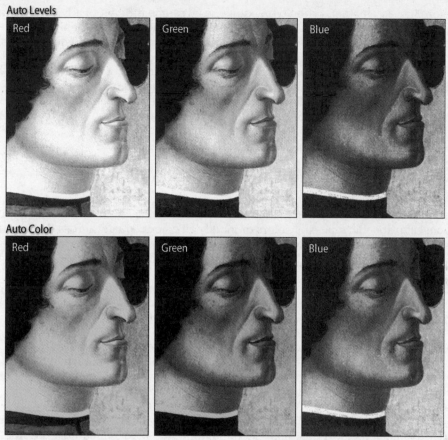

Figure 17-9: The effects of Auto Levels (top row) and Auto Color (bottom row) on the individual channels of an RGB image. Notice that Auto Color turned the red and green channels slightly darker than did Auto Levels, but the blue channel is slightly lighter.

Hue Shifting and Colorizing

The following sections cover commands designed to change the distribution of colors in an image. You can rotate the hues around the color spectrum, change the saturation of colors, adjust highlights and shadows, and even tint an image. Two of these commands — Hue/Saturation and Selective Color — are applicable exclusively to color images. The other two — Replace Color and Variations — can be applied to grayscale images but are far better suited to color images. If you're more interested in editing grayscale photographs, refer to the Levels and Curves commands, both of which I discuss toward the end of the chapter. For those of you who want to correct colors, however, read on.

Before I go any further, I should mention one awesome little bit of advice. Remember how Ctrl+Alt+F (⌘-Option-F on the Mac) redisplays the last filter dialog box so that you can tweak the effect? Well, a similar shortcut is available when you apply color corrections. Press Alt (Win) or Option (Mac) when choosing any of the commands described throughout the rest of this chapter to display that command's dialog box with the settings last applied to the image. If the command has a keyboard equivalent, just add Alt (Win) or Option (Mac) to restore the last settings. Pressing Ctrl+Alt+U (Win) or ⌘-Option-U (Mac), for example, brings up the Hue/Saturation dialog box with the settings you last used.

Using the Hue/Saturation command

The Hue/Saturation command provides two functions. First, it enables you to adjust colors in an image according to their hues and saturation levels. You can apply the changes to specific ranges of colors or modify all colors equally across the spectrum. And second, the command lets you colorize images by applying new hue and saturation values while retaining the core brightness information from the original image.

This command is perfect for colorizing grayscale images. I know, I know, Woody Allen wouldn't approve, but with some effort, you can make Ted Turner green with envy. Just scan him and change the Hue value to 140 degrees.

When you choose Image ⇨ Adjustments ⇨ Hue/Saturation or press Ctrl+U (⌘-U on the Mac), Photoshop displays the Hue/Saturation dialog box, shown in Figure 17-10. Before I explain how to use this dialog box to produce specific effects, let me briefly introduce the options, starting with the three option boxes:

✦ **Hue:** The Hue slider bar measures colors on the 360-degree color circle, as explained back in the "HSB" section of Chapter 4. You can adjust the Hue value from negative to positive 180 degrees. As you do, Photoshop rotates the colors around the Hue wheel. Consider the example of flesh tones. A Hue value of +30 moves the flesh into the orange range; a value of +100 makes it green. Going in the other direction, a Hue of –30 makes the flesh red and –100 makes it purple.

When the Colorize check box is selected, Hue becomes an absolute value measured from 0 to 360 degrees. A Hue value of 0 is red, 30 is orange, and so on, as described in Chapter 4.

✦ **Saturation:** The Saturation value changes the intensity of the colors. Normally, the Saturation value varies from –100 for gray to +100 for incredibly vivid hues. The only exception occurs when the Colorize check box is active, in which case saturation becomes an absolute value, measured from 0 for gray to 100 for maximum saturation.

✦ **Lightness:** You can darken or lighten an image by varying the Lightness value from negative to positive 100.

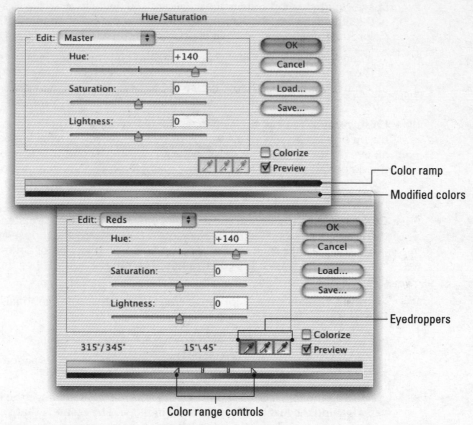

Figure 17-10: The Hue/Saturation dialog box as it appears when editing all colors in a layer (top) or just a specific range of colors (bottom).

Because this value invariably changes *all* brightness levels in an image to an equal extent — whether or not Colorize is selected — it permanently dulls highlights and shadows. I advise that you avoid this option like the plague and rely instead on the Levels or Curves command to edit brightness and contrast.

✦ **Edit:** The Edit pop-up menu controls which colors in the active selection or layer are affected by the Hue/Saturation command. If you select the Master option, as by default, Hue/Saturation adjusts all colors equally. If you prefer to adjust some colors in the layer differently than others, choose one of the other Edit options or press the keyboard equivalent — Ctrl+1 (Win) or ⌘-1 (Mac) for Reds, Ctrl+2 (Win) or ⌘-2 (Mac) for Yellows, and so on.

Each of the Edit options isolates a predefined range of colors inside the image. For example, the Reds option selects the range measured from 345 to 15 degrees on the Hue wheel. Naturally, if you were to modify just the red pixels and left all non-red pixels unchanged, you'd end up with some jagged transitions in your image. So Photoshop softens the edges with 30 degrees of fuzziness at either end of the red spectrum (the same kind of fuzziness described in the "Using the Color Range command" section of Chapter 9).

You can apply different Hue, Saturation, and Lightness settings for every one of the color ranges. For example, to change all reds in an image to green and all cyans to gray, do like so: Choose the Reds option and change the Hue value to +50 and then choose Cyans and change the Saturation value to –100.

✦ **Color ramps:** You can track changes made to colors in the Hue/Saturation dialog box in two ways. One way is to select the Preview check box and keep an eye on the changes in the image window. The second way is to observe the color ramps at the bottom of the dialog box. The first ramp shows the 360-degree color spectrum; the second ramp shows what the color ramp looks like after your edits.

✦ **Color range controls:** You can use the color ramps also to broaden or narrow the range of colors affected by Hue/Saturation. When you choose any option other than Master from the Edit pop-up menu, a collection of color range controls appears between the color ramps. The range bar identifies the selected colors and also permits you to edit them.

Figure 17-11 shows the color range controls up close and personal. Here's how they work:

- Drag the central range bar to move the entire color range.

- Drag one of the two lighter-colored fuzziness bars to broaden or narrow the color range without affecting the fuzziness.

- Drag the range control (labeled in Figure 17-11) to change the range while leaving the fuzziness points fixed in place. The result is that you expand the range and condense the fuzziness, or vice versa.

- Drag the triangular fuzziness control to lengthen or contract the fuzziness independently of the color range.

By default, red is the central color in the color ramps, with blue at either side. This is great when the range is red or some other warm color. But if you're working with a blue range, the controls get split between the two ends. To move a different color to the central position, Ctrl-drag (Win) or ⌘-drag (Mac) in the color ramp. The spectrum revolves around the ramp as you drag.

✦ **Eyedroppers:** To lift a color range from the image window, click inside the image window with the eyedropper cursor. (The cursor automatically changes to an eyedropper when you move it outside the Hue/Saturation dialog box.) Photoshop centers the range on the exact color you clicked.

To expand the range to include more colors, Shift-click or drag in the image window. To remove colors from the range, Alt-click (Option-click on the Mac) or drag in the image. You can also use the alternative plus and minus eyedropper tools, but why bother? Shift and Alt (Shift and Option on the Mac) do the job just fine.

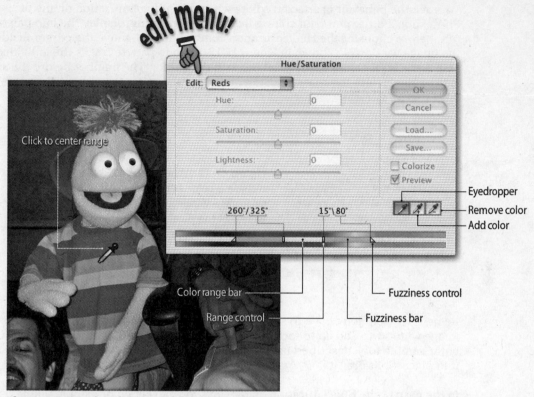

Figure 17-11: After defining a basic range using the Edit pop-up menu, use the color range controls to modify the range or the fuzziness.

✦ **Load/Save:** As in all the best color correction dialog boxes, you can load and save settings to disk in case you want to reapply the options to other images. These options are especially useful if you find a magic combination of color-correction settings that accounts for most of the color mistakes produced by your scanner.

✦ **Colorize:** Select this check box to apply a single hue and a single saturation level to the entire selection or layer, regardless of how it was previously colored. All brightness levels remain intact, although you can adjust them incrementally using the Lightness slider bar (a practice that I strongly advise against, as I mentioned earlier).

Color ranges are not permitted when colorizing. The moment you select the Colorize check box, Photoshop dims the Edit pop-up menu and sets it to Master.

✦ **Restore:** You can restore the options in the Hue/Saturation, Levels, and Curves dialog boxes to their original settings by Alt-clicking (Win) or Option-clicking (Mac) on the Reset button (the Cancel button changes to Reset when you press Alt or Option). Or, you can simply press Option-Escape on the Mac.

Tip

To track the behavior of specific colors when using Hue/Saturation or any of Photoshop's other powerful color adjustment commands, display the Info palette (F8) before choosing the Hue/Saturation command. Then move the cursor inside the image window. As shown in Figure 17-12, the Info palette tracks the individual RGB and CMYK values of the pixel beneath the cursor. The number before the slash is the value before the color adjustment; the number after the slash is the value after the adjustment.

Before   After

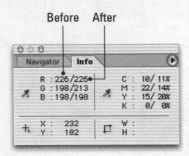

Figure 17-12: When you move the eyedropper outside a color adjustment dialog box and into the image window, the Info palette lists the color values of the pixel beneath the cursor before and after the adjustment.

Remember, you don't have to settle for just one color readout. Shift-click in the image window to add up to four fixed color samples, just like those created with the color sample tool, described in Chapter 4. To move a color sample after you've set it in place, Shift-drag it.

In the case of the Hue/Saturation dialog box, you can set color sample points only when the Edit pop-up menu is set to Master. After you set the samples, select some other options from the pop-up menu to modify a specific range.

Adjusting hue and saturation

All right, now that you know how the copious Hue/Saturation options work, it's time to give them a whirl. Go ahead and turn to Color Plate 17-3, and maybe keep a finger wedged in there as you read on here; we'll be making frequent references to that color plate. The subjects in our sample photo are yours truly (right) and my Little Puppet Friend (left), whose encyclopedic knowledge of digital imaging and dashing good looks have enlivened several of my video training series.

Changing hues

When the Colorize check box is inactive, the Hue slider bar shifts colors in an image around the color wheel. It's as if the pixels were playing a colorful game of musical chairs, except that none of the chairs disappear. If you select the Master option and enter a value of +120 degrees, for example, all pixels stand up, march one third of the way around the color wheel, and sit down, assuming the colors of their new chairs. A pixel that was red becomes green, a pixel that was green becomes blue, and so on. Figure 17-13 shows the result of this color rotation on a channel-by-channel basis. The top right example of Color Plate 17-3 shows the results of my +120 degree Hue shift in full color.

Original digital photo

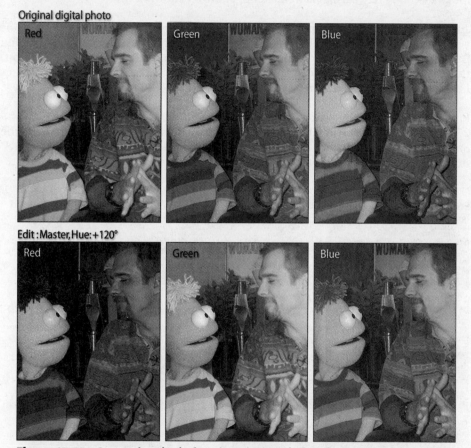

Figure 17-13: Comparing the before (top row) and after (bottom row) of a +120 degree Hue shift, you'll see that the red and green channels are identical, as are the green and blue channels and the blue and red channels.

As long as you select only the Master option and edit only the Hue value, Photoshop retains all colors in an image. In other words, after shifting the hues in an image +60 degrees, you can later choose Hue/Saturation and shift the hues –60 degrees to restore the original colors.

Changing saturation levels

When I was a little kid, I loved watching my grandmother's television because she kept the Color knob cranked at all times. The images leapt off the screen, like they were radioactive or something. *Way* cool. Well, the Saturation option works just like that Color knob. I don't recommend that you follow my grandmother's example and send the saturation for every image through the roof, but it can prove helpful for enhancing or downplaying the colors in an image. If the image looks washed out, try adding saturation; if colors leap off the screen so that everybody in the image looks like they're wearing neon makeup, subtract saturation.

Note

Just as the Saturation option works like the Color knob on a TV set, the Hue value serves the same purpose as the Tint knob, and the Lightness value works like the Brightness knob. So you see, your mother was quite mistaken when she told you that sitting on your butt and staring at the TV wasn't going to teach you anything. Little did she know, you were getting a head start on electronic art.

Figure 17-14 shows the same +120 degree Hue shift with Saturation values of 20 percent (top row) and 60 percent (bottom row). As you can see, increasing the Saturation has the effect of heightening the contrast of the color channels. The middle left example of Color Plate 17-3 shows a Saturation value of 40 percent.

Figure 17-14: The difference between a Saturation increase of 20 percent (top row) and 60 percent (bottom row) on a channel-by-channel basis.

Now that we have some idea how the Hue and Saturation parameters work, let's try applying them to the practical goal of trying to give my Little Puppet Friend a slightly rosier glow. The first thing you need to know is that if you adjust the Hues of an image with any Edit option other than Master, the musical chairs metaphor mentioned earlier breaks down a little. All pixels that correspond to the selected color range move while pixels outside the color range remain seated. The pixels that move must sit on the non-moving pixels' laps, meaning that you sacrifice colors in the image.

For example, in the middle right image of Color Plate 17-3 I switched the Edit menu from Master to Cyans and then performed my Hue shift and Saturation increase, and then repeated this with Edit set to Blues. All pixels that fell inside the cyan and blue ranges shifted to new hues; all non-cyan and non-blue pixels remained unchanged. Though the effect is subtle, my Little Puppet Friend does appear a little rosier than in the upper-left image. Then again, so do the blues in my shirt.

The Saturation option is especially useful for toning down images captured with low-end scanners and digital cameras, which have a tendency to exaggerate certain colors. Back in the early years, I used to work with an Epson scanner that would digitize flesh tones in varieties of vivid oranges and red. I couldn't, for the life of me, figure out how to peel the colors off the ceiling until I tried the Saturation option in the Hue/Saturation dialog box. By selecting the Red color range and dragging the slider down to about −50, I was usually able to eliminate the problem, and so can you.

Correcting out-of-gamut colors

Another common use for the Saturation option is to prepare RGB images for process-color printing. As I explained in Chapter 4, many colors in the RGB spectrum are considered out-of-gamut, meaning that they fall outside the smaller CMYK color space. Photoshop provides a means for recognizing such colors while remaining inside the RGB color space. Choose View ⇨ Gamut Warning or press Ctrl+Shift+Y (⌘-Shift-Y on the Mac) to color all out-of-gamut colors with gray (or some other color that you specify using the Preferences command). The pixels don't actually change to gray; they just appear gray on-screen as long as the command is active. To turn View ⇨ Gamut Warning off, choose the command again.

How do you eliminate such problem colors? Well, you have three options:

✦ Let Photoshop take care of the problem automatically when you convert the image by choosing Image ⇨ Mode ⇨ CMYK Color. This tactic is risky because Photoshop simply cuts off colors outside the gamut and converts them to their nearest CMYK equivalents. What was once an abundant range of differently saturated hues becomes abruptly flattened, like some kind of cruel buzz haircut. Choosing View ⇨ Proof Setup ⇨ Working CMYK gives you an idea of how dramatic the buzz can be while permitting you to continue working in the RGB color space. Sometimes the effect is hardly noticeable, in which case no additional attention may be warranted. Other times, the results can be disastrous.

✦ Another method is to scrub away with the sponge tool. In Chapter 5, I discussed how much I dislike this alternative, and despite the passage of a dozen chapters, I haven't changed my mind. Although it theoretically offers selective control—you just scrub at areas that need attention until the gray pixels created by the Gamut Warning command disappear—the process leaves too much to chance and frequently does more damage than simply choosing Image ➪ Mode ➪ CMYK Color.

✦ The third and best solution involves the Saturation option in the Hue/Saturation dialog box.

No doubt that last item comes as a huge surprise, given that I decided to broach the out-of-gamut topic in the middle of examining the Saturation option. But try to scoop your jaw up off the floor long enough to peruse the following steps, which outline the proper procedure for bringing out-of-gamut colors back into the CMYK color space.

STEPS: Eliminating Out-of-Gamut Colors

1. **Create a duplicate of your image to serve as a CMYK preview.** Choose Image ➪ Duplicate to create a copy of your image. Then choose View ➪ Proof Setup ➪ Working CMYK. Alternatively, you can press Ctrl+Y (Win) or ⌘-Y (Mac) to invoke color proofing. By default, Photoshop selects the working CMYK space. This image represents what Photoshop does with your image if you don't make any corrections. It's good to have around for comparison.

2. **Return to your original image and choose Select ➪ Color Range.** Then select the Out Of Gamut option from the Select pop-up menu and press Enter (Win) or Return (Mac). You have now selected all nonconformist anti-gamut pixels throughout your image. These radicals must be expunged.

3. **To monitor your progress, choose View ➪ Gamut Warning to display the gray pixels.** Oh, and don't forget to press Ctrl+H (⌘-H on the Mac) to get rid of those pesky ants.

4. **Press Ctrl+U (Win) or ⌘-U (Mac) to display the Hue/Saturation dialog box.**

5. **Lower the saturation of individual color ranges.** Don't change any settings while Master is selected; it's not exacting enough. Rather, experiment with specifying your own color ranges and lowering the Saturation value. Every time you see one of the pixels change from gray to color, it means that another happy pixel has joined the CMYK collective. You may want to state, in your best monotone, "Resistance is futile," if only to make your work more entertaining.

6. **When only a few hundred sporadic gray spots remain on screen, click the OK button to return to the image window.** Bellow imperiously, "You may think you have won, you little gray pixels, but I have a secret weapon!" Then choose Image ➪ Mode ➪ CMYK Color and watch as Photoshop forcibly thrusts them into the gamut.

Mind you, the differences between your duplicate image and the one you manually turned away from the evils of RGB excess are subtle, but they may prove enough to produce a better looking image with a more dynamic range of colors.

Avoiding gamut-correction edges

The one problem with the preceding steps is that the Color Range command selects only out-of-gamut pixels without even partially selecting their neighbors. As a result, you desaturate out-of-gamut colors while leaving similar colors fully saturated, an effect that may result in jagged and unnatural edges.

One solution is to insert a step between Steps 2 and 3 in which you do the following: Select the magic wand tool and change the Tolerance value in the Options bar to, say, 12. Next, choose Select ⇨ Similar, which expands the selected area to incorporate all pixels that fall within the Tolerance range. Finally, choose Select ⇨ Feather and enter a Feather Radius value that's about half the Tolerance — in this case, 6.

This solution isn't perfect — ideally, the Color Range option box wouldn't dim the Fuzziness slider when you choose Out Of Gamut — but it does succeed in partially selecting a few neighboring pixels without sacrificing too many of the out-of-gamut bunch.

Colorizing images

When you select the Colorize check box in the Hue/Saturation dialog box, the options perform differently. Returning to that wonderful musical chairs analogy, the pixels no longer walk around a circle of chairs; instead, they all get up and go sit in the same chair. Every pixel in the selection receives the same hue and the same level of saturation. Only the brightness values remain intact to ensure that the image remains recognizable. The bottom left example of Color Plate 17-3 shows the results of shifting the hues in an image using the Colorize option.

In most cases, you'll only want to colorize grayscale images or bad color scans. After all, colorizing ruins the original color composition of an image. For the best results, you'll want to set the Saturation values to somewhere in the neighborhood of 25 to 75.

The final image in Color Plate 17-3 shows my last valiant attempt to give my Little Puppet Friend a rosy glow. This time I started by making a selection using the Color Range command. Then I applied Hue/Saturation with Colorize turned on, and with the same settings as in the bottom left image. It's a stronger effect than I got with just shifting the Hue in the cyan and blue ranges, as in the middle right image. It also played havoc with the blues in my shirt, but I could have tidied up my Color Range selection in quick mask mode to isolate L.P.F.'s skin tones. (Or perhaps that should be "fleece tones.")

To touch up the edges of a colorized selection, change the foreground color to match the Hue and Saturation values you used in the Hue/Saturation dialog box. You can do this by choosing the HSB Sliders command from the Color palette menu and entering the values in the H and S option boxes. Set the B (Brightness) value to 100 percent. Next, select the brush tool and change the brush mode to Color by pressing Shift+Alt+C (Shift-Option-C on the Mac). Then paint away.

Shifting selected colors

The Replace Color command allows you to select an area of related colors and adjust the hue and saturation of that area. When you select Image ⇨ Adjustments ⇨ Replace Color, you get a dialog box much like the Color Range dialog box. The Replace Color dialog box, shown in Figure 17-15, varies in only a few respects: It's missing the Select and Selection Preview pop-up menus and it offers three slider bars, taken right out of the Hue/Saturation dialog box.

In fact, this dialog box works exactly as if you were to select a portion of an image using Select ⇨ Color Range and edit it with the Hue/Saturation command, as I did previously. You don't have as many options to work with, but the outcome is the same. The Replace Color and Color Range dialog boxes even share the same default settings. If you change the Fuzziness value in one, the default Fuzziness value of the other changes as well. It's as if they're identical twins or something.

So why does the Replace Color command even exist? Because it allows you to change the selection outline and apply different colors without affecting the image. Just select the Preview check box to see the results of your changes on screen, and you're in business.

If you're not clear on how to use all the options in the Replace Color dialog box, read the "Using the Color Range command" section in Chapter 9. It tells you all about the eyedropper tools and the Fuzziness option.

Shifting predefined colors

The Selective Color command permits you to adjust the colors in CMYK images. Although you can use Selective Color also when working on RGB or Lab images, it makes more sense in the CMYK color space because it permits you to adjust the levels of cyan, magenta, yellow, and black inks.

Frankly, I'm not very keen on this command. For general image editing, the Variations command provides better control and more intuitive options. Adobe created the Selective Color command to accommodate traditional press managers who prefer to have direct control over ink levels rather than monkeying around with hue, satura-tion, and other observational color controls. If Selective Color works for you, great. But don't get hung up on it if it never quite gels. You can accomplish all this and more with the Variations command, described in the next section.

Figure 17-15: The Replace Color dialog box works like the Color Range dialog box described back in Chapter 9, with a few Hue/Saturation options thrown in.

Choosing Image ⇨ Adjustments ⇨ Selective Color brings up the dialog box shown in Figure 17-16. To use the dialog box, choose the predefined color that you want to edit from the Colors pop-up menu and then adjust the four process-color slider bars to change the predefined color. When you select the Relative radio button, you add or subtract color, much as if you were moving the color around the musical chairs using the Hue slider bar. When you select Absolute, you change the predefined color to the exact value entered in the Cyan, Magenta, Yellow, and Black option boxes. The Absolute option is therefore very much like the Colorize check box in the Hue/Saturation dialog box.

If you examine the Selective Color dialog box closely, you'll notice that it is very much like the Hue/Saturation dialog box. You have access to predefined colors in the form of a pop-up menu instead of radio buttons, and you can adjust slider bars to alter the color. The two key differences are that the pop-up menu lets you adjust whites, medium grays (Neutrals), and blacks — options missing from Hue/Saturation — and that the slider bars are always measured in the CMYK color space.

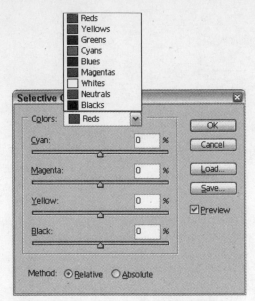

Figure 17-16: Select a predefined color from the Colors pop-up menu and adjust the slider bars to change that color.

Tip

As I mentioned at the outset, the Selective Color command produces the most predictable results when you're working on a CMYK image. When you drag the Cyan slider triangle to the right, for example, you're actually transferring brightness values to the cyan channel. However, you have to keep an eye out for a few anomalies, particularly when editing Black. In the CMYK mode, areas of your image that appear black include not only black but also shades of cyan, magenta, and yellow, resulting in what printers call a *rich black* (or *saturated black*). Therefore, to change black to white, you have to set the Black slider to –100 percent and also set the Cyan, Magenta, and Yellow sliders to the same value.

Using the Variations command

The Variations command is Photoshop's most essential color correction function *and* its funkiest.

On one hand, you can adjust hues and luminosity levels based on the brightness values of the pixels, something Hue/Saturation cannot do. You can also see what you're doing by clicking on little thumbnail previews (see Figure 17-17), which takes much of the guesswork out of the correction process.

On the other hand, the Variations dialog box takes over your screen and prevents you from previewing corrections in the image window. Furthermore, you can't see the area outside a selection, which proves disconcerting when making relative color adjustments.

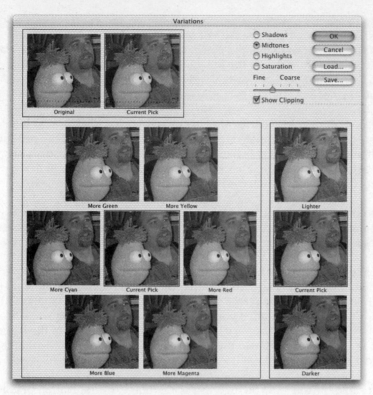

Figure 17-17: Click the thumbnails to shift the colors in an image; adjust the slider bar in the upper-right corner to change the sensitivity of the thumbnails; and use the radio buttons to determine which part of an image is selected.

The Variations command is therefore best suited to correcting an image in its entirety. Here's how it works: To infuse color into the image, click one of the thumbnails in the central portion of the dialog box. The thumbnail labeled More Cyan, for example, shifts the colors toward cyan. The thumbnail even shows how the additional cyan will look when added to the image. In case you're interested in seeing how these thumbnails affect a final printed image in the CMYK color space, check out Color Plate 17-4.

Now notice that each thumbnail is positioned directly opposite its complementary color, with the Current Pick between them. More Cyan is across from More Red, More Blue is across from More Yellow, and so on. In fact, clicking on a thumbnail shifts colors not only toward the named color but also away from the opposite color. For example, if you click More Cyan and then click its opposite, More Red, you arrive at the original image.

Although this isn't exactly how the colors in the additive and subtractive worlds work — cyan is not the empirical opposite of red — the colors are theoretical opposites, and the Variations command makes the theory a practicality. After all, you haven't yet applied the color to the image, so the dialog box can calculate its adjustments in a pure and perfect world. Cyan and red ought to be opposites, so for the moment, they are.

To control the amount of color shifting that occurs when you click a thumbnail, move the slider triangle in the upper-right corner of the dialog box. Fine produces very minute changes; Coarse creates massive changes. Just to give you an idea of the difference between the two, you have to click a thumbnail about 40 times when the slider is set to Fine to equal one click when it's set to Coarse.

The radio buttons at the top control which colors in the image are affected. Select Shadows to change the darkest colors, Highlights to change the lightest colors, and Midtones to change everything in between.

In fact, if you're familiar with the Levels dialog box — as you will be when you read "The Levels command" section later in this chapter — you might have noticed that the first three radio buttons have direct counterparts in the slider triangles in the Levels dialog box. For example, when you click the Lighter thumbnail while the Highlights option is selected in the Variations dialog box, you perform the same action as moving the white triangle in the Levels dialog box to the left — that is, you make the lightest colors in the image even lighter.

The Saturation radio button lets you increase or decrease the saturation of colors in an image. Only one thumbnail appears on each side of the Current Pick image: One that decreases the saturation and another that increases it. The Variations command modifies saturation differently than Hue/Saturation. Hue/Saturation pushes the saturation of a color as far as it will go, but Variations attempts to modify the saturation without changing overall brightness values. As a result, an image saturated with Hue/Saturation looks lighter than one saturated with Variations.

As you click the options — particularly when modifying saturation — you may notice that weird colors spring up inside the thumbnails. These brightly colored pixels are gamut warnings, highlighting colors that exceed the boundaries of the current color space. For example, if you're working in the RGB mode, these colors extend beyond the RGB gamut. Although the colors won't actually appear inverted as they do in the dialog box, it's not a good idea to exceed the color space because it results in areas of flat color, just as when you convert between the RGB and CMYK spaces. To view the thumbnails without the weirdly colored pixels, turn off the Show Clipping check box. (Incidentally, this use of the word *clipping* has nothing to do with paths.)

Enhancing colors in a compressed image

Now that you know every possible way to adjust hues and saturation levels in Photoshop, it's time to discuss some of the possible stumbling blocks. The danger of rotating colors or increasing the saturation of an image is that you can bring out some very unstable colors. Adjusting the hues can switch ratty pixels from colors that your eyes aren't very sensitive to—particularly blue—into colors your eyes see very well—reds and greens. Drab color can also hide poor detail, which becomes painfully obvious when you make the colors bright and vivid.

Consider the digital photograph featured in Color Plate 17-5. Snapped several years back in Boston's Copley Square using a Kodak DC50 digital camera, the original image at the top of the color plate is drab and lifeless. If I use the Hue/Saturation command to pump up the saturation levels, a world of ugly detail rises out of the muck, as shown in the second example. (Obviously, I've taken the saturation a little too high, but only to demonstrate a point.) The detail would have fared no better if I had used the Variations command to boost the saturation.

Unstable colors may be the result of JPEG compression, as in the case of the digital photo. Or you may have bad scanning or poor lighting to thank. In any case, you can correct the problem using our friends the Median and Gaussian Blur commands, as I explain in the following steps.

STEPS: Boosting the Saturation of Digital Photos

1. **Select the entire image and copy it to a new layer.** It seems like half of all Photoshop techniques begin with Ctrl+A and Ctrl+J (⌘-A and ⌘-J on the Mac).

2. **Press Ctrl+U (Win) or ⌘-U (Mac) to display the Hue/Saturation dialog box.** Then raise the Saturation value to whatever setting you desire. Don't worry if your image starts to fall apart—that's the whole point of these steps. Pay attention to the color and don't worry about the rest. In the second example in Color Plate 17-5, I raised the Saturation to +80.

3. **Choose Filter ➪ Noise ➪ Median.** As you may recall, Median is the preeminent JPEG image fixer. A Radius value of 4 or 5 pixels works well for most images. You can take it even higher when working with resolutions of 200 ppi or more. I used 6. This destroys the detail, but that's not important. The color is all that matters.

4. **Choose Filter ➪ Blur ➪ Gaussian Blur.** As always, the Median filter introduces its own edges. And this is one case where you don't want to add any edges, so blur the heck out of the layer. I used a Radius of 4.0, just 2 pixels less than my Median Radius value, to produce the third example in Color Plate 17-5.

5. **Select Color from the blend mode pop-up menu in the Layers palette.** Photoshop mixes the gummy, blurry color with the crisp detail underneath.

My image was still a little soft, so I flattened the image and sharpened to taste. The finished result appears at the bottom of Color Plate 17-5. Although a tad too colorful—Boston's a lovely city, but it's not quite this resplendent—the edges look every bit as good as they did in the original photograph, and in many ways better.

Making Custom Brightness Adjustments

The Lighter and Darker options in the Variations dialog box are preferable to the Lightness slider bar in the Hue/Saturation dialog box because you can specify whether to edit the darkest, lightest, or medium colors in an image. But neither command is adequate for making precise adjustments to the brightness and contrast of an image. Photoshop provides two expert-level commands for adjusting the brightness levels in both grayscale and color images:

✦ **The Levels command is great for most color corrections.** It lets you adjust the darkest values, lightest values, and midrange colors with a minimum of fuss and a generous amount of control.

✦ **The Curves command is great for creating special effects and correcting images beyond the help of the Levels command.** Using the Curves command, you can map every brightness value in every color channel to an entirely different brightness value.

In the back rooms of some print houses and art shops, a controversy is brewing over which command is better, Levels or Curves. Based on a few letters I've received over the years, it seems that some folks consider Curves to be the command for real men and Levels suitable only for color-correcting wimps.

Naturally, this is a big wad of hooey. Levels provides a histogram, which is absolutely essential for gauging the proper setting for black and white points. Meanwhile, Curves lets you map out a virtually infinite number of significant points on a graph. The point is, both commands have their advantages, and both offer practical benefits for intermediate and advanced users alike.

There's no substitute for a good histogram, so I prefer to use Levels for my day-to-day color correcting. If you can't quite get the effect you want with Levels, or you know that you need to map specific brightness values in an image to other values, use Curves. The Curves command is the more powerful function, but it is likewise more cumbersome.

The Levels command

When you choose Image ➪ Adjustments ➪ Levels or press Ctrl+L (⌘-L on the Mac), Photoshop displays the Levels dialog box shown in Figure 17-18. The dialog box offers a histogram, as explained in the "Threshold" section earlier in this chapter, as well as two sets of slider bars with corresponding option boxes and a few automated eyedropper options in the lower-right corner. You can compress and expand the range of brightness values in an image by manipulating the Input Levels options. Then you can map those brightness values to new brightness values by adjusting the Output Levels options.

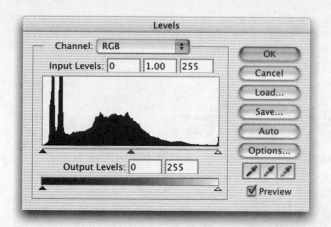

Figure 17-18: Use the Levels dialog box to map brightness values in the image (Input Levels) to new brightness values (Output Levels).

The options in the Levels dialog box work as follows:

✦ **Channel:** Select the color channel that you want to edit from this pop-up menu. You can apply different Input Levels and Output Levels values to each color channel. However, the options along the right side of the dialog box affect all colors in the selected portion of an image regardless of which Channel option is active.

✦ **Input Levels:** Use these options to modify the contrast of the image by darkening the darkest colors and lightening the lightest ones. The Input Levels option boxes correspond to the slider bar immediately below the histogram. You map pixels to black (or the darkest Output Levels value) by entering a number from 0 to 255 in the first option box or by dragging the black slider triangle. For example, if you raise the value to 50, all colors with brightness values of 50 or less in the original image become black, darkening the image as shown in the first example of Figure 17-19.

You can map pixels at the opposite end of the brightness scale to white (or the lightest Output Levels value) by entering a number from 0 to 255 in the last option box or by dragging the white slider triangle. If you lower the value to 200, all colors with brightness values of 200 or greater become white, lightening the image, as shown in the second example of Figure 17-19. In the last example of the figure, I raised the first value and lowered the last value, thereby increasing the amount of contrast in the image.

Tip

One of my favorite ways to edit the Input Levels values is to select the numeric field and then press the up and down arrow keys. Each press of an arrow key raises or lowers the value by 1. Press Shift with an arrow key to change the value in increments of 10.

Tip

Here's another juicy tip for you: If you press and hold the Alt key (or Option key on the Mac) while dragging the black and white Input Levels slider triangles, you can watch where the first shadows appear and where the first highlight detail begins.

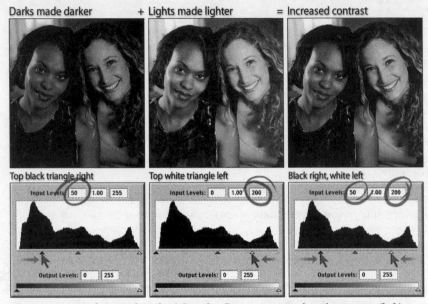

Figure 17-19: The results of raising the first Input Levels value to 50 (left), lowering the last value to 200 (middle), and combining the two (right)

✦ **Gamma:** The middle Input Levels option box and the corresponding gray triangle in the slider bar (shown highlighted in Figure 17-20) represent the midtone, or *gamma value*, which is the brightness level of the medium gray value in the image. The gamma value can range from 0.10 to 9.99, with 1.00 being dead-on medium gray. Increase the gamma value or drag the gray slider triangle to the left to lighten the medium grays (also called *midtones*), as in the first and second examples of Figure 17-21. Lower the gamma value or drag the gray triangle to the right to darken the medium grays, as in the last example in the figure.

You can edit the gamma value also by pressing the up and down arrow keys. Pressing an arrow key changes the value by 0.01; pressing Shift+arrow changes the value by 0.10. I can't stress enough how useful this technique is. I rarely do anything except press arrow keys inside the Levels dialog box anymore.

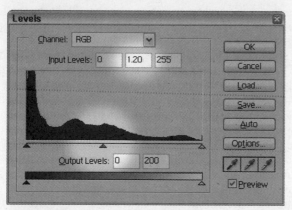

Figure 17-20: To create the spotlighting effects you see here, I selected the circular areas, inversed the selection, and applied the values shown in this very dialog box.

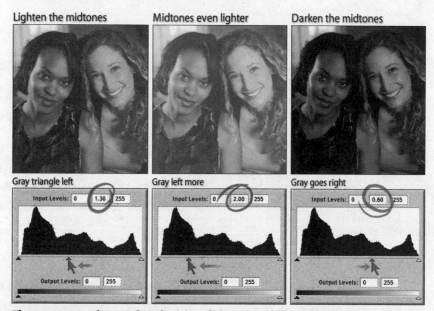

Figure 17-21: The results of raising (left and middle) and lowering (right) the gamma value to lighten and darken the midtones in an image.

✦ **Output Levels:** Use these options to curtail the range of brightness levels in an image by lightening the darkest pixels and darkening the lightest pixels. You adjust the brightness of the darkest pixels — those that correspond to the black Input Levels slider triangle — by entering a number from 0 to 255 in the first option box or by dragging the black slider triangle. For example, if you raise the value to 100, no color can be darker than that brightness level (roughly 60 percent black), which lightens the image as shown in the first example of Figure 17-22. You adjust the brightness of the lightest pixels — those that correspond to the white Input Levels slider triangle — by entering a number from 0 to 255 in the second option box or by dragging the white slider triangle. If you lower the value to 175, no color can be lighter than that brightness level (roughly 30 percent black), darkening the image as shown in the second example of Figure 17-22. In the last example of the figure, I raised the first value and lowered the second value, thereby dramatically decreasing the amount of contrast in the image. Note that any change to the Output Levels values will decrease the contrast of the image.

You can fully or partially invert an image using the Output Levels slider triangles. Just drag the black triangle to the right and drag the white triangle to the left past the black triangle. The colors flip, whites mapping to dark colors and blacks mapping to light colors.

Figure 17-22: The result of raising the first Output Levels value to 100 (left), lowering the second value to 175 (middle), and combining the two (right).

✦ **Load/Save:** You can load and save settings to disk using these buttons.

✦ **Auto:** In previous versions of Photoshop, the Auto button might as well have been labeled Auto Levels, because clicking the button was analogous to choosing the Auto Levels command. This feature has been expanded in Photoshop 7, and the "secret" Options button that you used to obtain by Alt- or Option-clicking the Auto button has now metamorphosed into a permanent Options button in the dialog box. The effect of clicking Auto in the Levels dialog box (as well as in the Curves dialog box) now entirely depends on the settings in the Auto Color Correction Options dialog box, described next.

✦ **Options:** Clicking the Options button in the Levels (or Curves) dialog box brings up the new Auto Color Correction Options dialog box, shown in Figure 17-23. The top section, Algorithms, determines the type of correction you want to apply. Despite the long, somewhat confusing names, these three choices could really be labeled Auto Contrast, Auto Levels, and Auto Color, as that's what the choices are equivalent to. In fact, you can rest your cursor over each name to see an informative tool tip telling you just this. Turn on the Snap Neutral Midtones check box and you'll apply Auto Color's automatic gamma correction as well. If you select the Save as Defaults check box, your settings will be remembered the next time you use the Auto button inside the Levels and Curves dialog boxes.

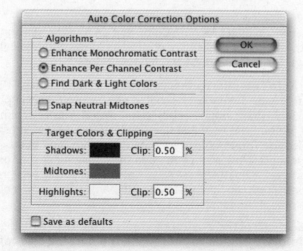

Figure 17-23: Customizing the settings in Auto Color Correction Options dialog box lets you take the "auto" out of Photoshop's auto correction commands.

The Target Colors & Clipping settings come into play not only when you click the Auto button inside the Levels and Curves dialog boxes, but also when you choose the Auto Levels and Auto Contrast commands in the Adjustments sub- menu. (This is assuming that Save as Defaults is selected.) Here you can pick colors to assign to the target values for the highlights, midtones, and shadows in your image. You also have access to the Clip values for the highlights and shadows. Enter higher values to increase the number of pixels mapped to black and white; decrease the values to lessen the effect. Figure 17-24 compares the effect of the default 0.50 percent values to higher values of 3.50 and 9.99 percent. As you can see, raising the Clip value produces higher contrast effects.

Auto Levels: Clip: 0.50%   Clip: 3.50%   Clip: 9.99%

Figure 17-24: The effect of the default Clip values in the Auto Color Correction Options dialog box (left) and the effect after raising the values (middle and right).

The Clip settings have no effect on Auto Color, just on Auto Levels and Contrast. The reason is that Auto Color seeks to neutralize shadows and highlights, as opposed to clipping away the darkest and lightest colors.

Here's where the Auto Color Correction Options can combine with the Auto Color command to create a truly useful tool. If you have a batch of photos you need to correct which share similar problems — maybe you've scanned in an overexposed roll of film from your last family vacation — make adjustments to the first photo with the Target Colors & Clipping settings, and make sure you turn on Save as Defaults. Now when you open the subsequent photos, you can simply choose Image ⇨ Adjustments ⇨ Auto Color — or better yet, press Ctrl+Shift+B (⌘-Shift-B on the Mac) — to instantly apply the same color correction to the rest of the images.

✦ **Eyedroppers:** Select one of the eyedropper tools in the Levels dialog box and click a pixel in the image window to automatically adjust the color of that pixel. If you click a pixel with the black eyedropper tool (the first of the three), Photoshop maps the color of the pixel and all darker colors to black. If you click a pixel with the white eyedropper tool (the last of the three), Photoshop maps it and all lighter colors to white. Use the gray eyedropper tool (middle) to change the color you clicked to medium gray and adjust all other colors in accordance. For example, if you click a light pixel, all light pixels change to medium gray and all other pixels change to even darker colors.

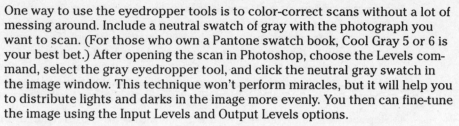

One way to use the eyedropper tools is to color-correct scans without a lot of messing around. Include a neutral swatch of gray with the photograph you want to scan. (For those who own a Pantone swatch book, Cool Gray 5 or 6 is your best bet.) After opening the scan in Photoshop, choose the Levels command, select the gray eyedropper tool, and click the neutral gray swatch in the image window. This technique won't perform miracles, but it will help you to distribute lights and darks in the image more evenly. You then can fine-tune the image using the Input Levels and Output Levels options.

By default, the eyedroppers map to white, gray, and black. But you can change that. Double-click any one of the three eyedroppers to display the Color Picker dialog box. For example, suppose you double-click the white eyedropper, set the color values to C:2, M:3, Y:5, K:0, and then click a pixel in the image window. Instead of making the pixel white, Photoshop changes the clicked color — and all colors lighter than it — to C:2, M:3, Y:5, K:0, which is great for avoiding hot highlights and ragged edges.

To give you a sense of how the Levels command works, the following steps describe how to improve the appearance of a low-contrast, shadow-heavy image, such as the first example in Color Plate 17-6. Luckily, you can bring out the highlights using Levels.

STEPS: Correcting Brightness and Contrast with the Levels Command

1. **Press Ctrl+L (Win) or ⌘-L (Mac) to display the Levels dialog box.** As illustrated in the first example in Color Plate 17-6, most of the colors for this image are clustered on the left side of the histogram, showing that there are far more dark colors than light.

2. **Press Ctrl+1 (Win) or ⌘-1 (Mac) to examine the red channel.** Assuming that you're editing an RGB image, Ctrl+1 (⌘-1 on the Mac) displays a histogram for the red channel. The channel-specific histograms appear inset into the images in Color Plate 17-6.

3. **Edit the black Input Levels value as needed.** Drag the black slider triangle to below the point at which the histogram begins. In my case, there's not much going on in the histogram until the point that's below the "I" in the word "Input." I dragged the black triangle to the beginning of the spike, changing the first Input Levels value to 16, as you can see in the red histogram in the second example of Color Plate 17-6.

4. **Edit the white Input Levels value.** Drag the white slider triangle to below the point at which the histogram ends. I have a lot farther to drag on the right side of the histogram than I did on the left. As seen in the second example of the color plate, I dragged the white slider triangle to the endpoint of the last peak of the histogram.

5. **Edit the gamma value.** Drag the gray triangle to the gravitational center of the histogram. Imagine that the histogram is a big mass, and you're trying to balance the mass evenly on top of the gray triangle. If the histogram is weighted too heavily to the left, drag the gray triangle to the left. In the case of the red channel, I thought the histogram was pretty well balanced, so I left the gamma alone. Looking below to the green channel, however, you can see that I dragged toward the left a little bit, changing the gamma value to 1.10.

6. **Repeat Steps 2 through 5 for the green and blue channels.** Ctrl+2 (Win) or ⌘-2 (Mac) takes you to the green channel; Ctrl+3 (Win) or ⌘-3 (Mac) takes you to blue. At this point, your image probably has a significant preponderance of red about it. To correct this, you need to edit the green and blue channels in kind. The graphs in the third and fourth examples of Color Plate 17-6 show how I edited my histograms. Feel free to switch back and forth between channels as much as you like to get everything just right.

7. **Press Ctrl+tilde (Win) or ⌘-tilde (Mac) to return to the composite RGB histogram.** After you get the color balance right, you can switch back to the composite mode and further edit the Input Levels. I sometimes bump up the gamma a few notches to account for dot gain.

   You may notice that your RGB histogram has changed. Although the histograms in the individual color channels remain fixed, the composite histogram updates to reflect the red, green, and blue modifications. The final RGB histogram for my image is inset into the bottom example of Color Plate 17-6. As you can see, the colors are well distributed across the brightness range.

8. **Press Enter (Win) or Return (Mac) to apply your changes.** Just for fun, press Ctrl+Z (Win) or ⌘-Z (Mac) a few times to see the before and after shots. Quite the transformation, eh?

Tip

If you decide after looking at the before and after views that you could do a better job, undo the color correction and press Ctrl+Alt+L (⌘-Option-L on the Mac) to bring up the Levels dialog box with the previous settings intact. Now you can take up where you left off. Or better yet, use a Levels adjustment layer from the outset, rather than applying the Levels command directly to your image. Skip ahead to the "Adjustment Layers" section later in this chapter to find out about this powerful, flexible feature.

The Curves command

If you want to be able to map any brightness value in an image to absolutely any other brightness value — no holds barred, as they say — you want the Curves command. When you choose Image ⇨ Adjustments ⇨ Curves or press Ctrl+M (⌘-M on the Mac), Photoshop displays the Curves dialog box, shown in Figure 17-25, which offers access to the most complex and powerful color correction options on the planet.

Brightness graph   Brightness curve

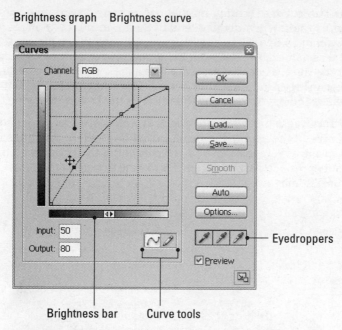

Eyedroppers

Brightness bar   Curve tools

Figure 17-25: The Curves dialog box lets you distribute brightness values by adjusting the curves on a graph.

Quickly, here's how the options work:

✦ **Channel:** Surely you know how this option works by now. You select the color channel that you want to edit from this pop-up menu. You can apply different mapping functions to different channels by drawing in the graph below the pop-up menu. But, as is always the case, the options along the right side of the dialog box affect all colors in the selected portion of an image regardless of which Channel option is active.

✦ **Brightness graph:** The brightness graph is where you map brightness values in the original image to new brightness values. The horizontal axis of the graph represents input levels; the vertical axis represents output levels. The *brightness curve* charts the relationship between input and output levels. The lower-left corner is the origin of the graph (the point at which both input and output values are 0). Move right in the graph for higher input values and up for higher output values. Because the brightness graph is the core of this dialog box, upcoming sections explain it in more detail.

Tip

By default, a trio of horizontal and vertical dotted lines crisscross the brightness graph, subdividing it into quarters. For added precision, you can divide the graph into horizontal and vertical tenths. Just Alt-click (Win) or Option-click (Mac) inside the graph to toggle between tenths and quarters.

✦ **Brightness bar:** The horizontal brightness bar shows the direction of light and dark values in the graph. When the dark end of the brightness bar appears on the left — as by default when editing an RGB image — colors are measured in terms of brightness values. The colors in the graph proceed from black on the left to white on the right, as demonstrated in the left example of Figure 17-26. Therefore, higher values produce lighter colors. This is my preferred setting because it measures colors in the same direction as the Levels dialog box.

If you click the brightness bar, white and black switch places, as shown in the second example of the figure. The result is that Photoshop measures the colors in terms of ink coverage, from 0 to 100 percent of the primary color. Higher values now produce darker colors. This is the default setting for grayscale and CMYK images.

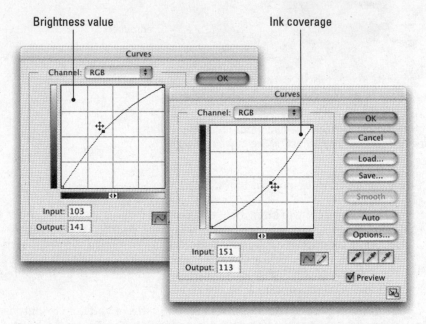

Figure 17-26: Click the brightness bar to change the way in which the graph measures color: by brightness values (left) or by ink coverage (right).

✦ **Curve tools:** Use the curve tools to draw the curve inside the brightness graph. The point tool (labeled in Figure 17-27) is selected by default. Click in the graph with this tool to add a point to the curve. Drag a point to move it. To delete a point, Ctrl-click (Win) or ⌘-click (Mac) it.

The pencil tool lets you draw free-form curves simply by dragging inside the graph, as illustrated in Figure 17-27. This pencil works much like Photoshop's standard pencil tool. This means you can draw straight lines by clicking one location in the graph and Shift-clicking a different point.

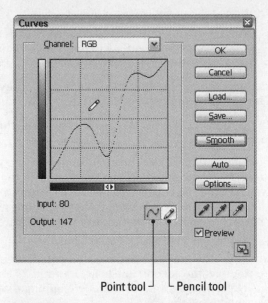

Point tool ⌐   ⌐ Pencil tool

Figure 17-27: Use the pencil tool to draw free-form lines in the brightness graph. If the lines appear rough, you can soften them by clicking on the Smooth button.

✦ **Input and Output values:** The Input and Output values monitor the location of your cursor in the graph according to brightness values or ink coverage, depending on the setting of the brightness bar. You can modify the Input and Output values when working with the point tool. Just click the point on the graph that you want to adjust and then enter new values. The Input number represents the brightness or ink value of the point before you entered the Curves dialog box; the Output number represents the new brightness or ink value.

Tip

You can change the Output value also by using the up and down arrow keys. Click the point you want to modify. Then press the up or down arrow key to raise or lower the Output value by 1. Press Shift+up or down arrow to change the Output value in increments of 10. Note that these techniques — and ones that follow — work only when the point tool is active. (You can't change points with the pencil tool.)

When editing multiple graph points from the keyboard, it's helpful to be able to activate the points from the keyboard as well. To advance from one point to the next, press Ctrl+Tab (Control-Tab on the Mac). To select the previous point, press Ctrl+Shift+Tab (Control-Shift-Tab on the Mac). To deselect all points, press Ctrl+D (Win) or ⌘-D (Mac).

✦ **Load/Save:** Use these buttons to load and save settings to disk.

✦ **Smooth:** Click the Smooth button to smooth out curves drawn with the pencil tool. Doing so leads to smoother color transitions in the image window. This button is dimmed except when you use the pencil tool.

✦ **Auto:** This button is identical to the Auto button available in the Levels dialog box; for details, see "The Levels command" section earlier in this chapter.

✦ **Options:** Identical to the Options button in the Levels dialog box, this is also covered in "The Levels command" section.

✦ **Eyedroppers:** If you move the cursor out of the dialog box and into the image window, you get the standard eyedropper cursor. Click a pixel in the image to locate the brightness value of that pixel in the graph. A circle appears in the graph, and the Input and Output numbers list the value for as long as you hold down the mouse button, as shown in the first example in Figure 17-28.

The other eyedroppers work as they do in the Levels dialog box, mapping pixels to black, medium gray, or white (or other colors if you double-click the eyedropper icons). For example, the second image in Figure 17-28 shows the white eyedropper tool clicking on a light pixel, thereby mapping that value to white, as shown in the graph below the image.

Bear in mind that Photoshop maps the value to each color channel independently. So when editing a full-color image inside the Curves dialog box, you have to switch channels to see the results of clicking with the eyedropper. You can further adjust the brightness value of that pixel by dragging the corresponding point in the graph, as demonstrated in the last example of the figure.

The eyedropper tools aren't the only way to add points to a curve from the image window. Photoshop offers two more keyboard tricks that greatly simplify the process of pinpointing and adjusting colors inside the Curves dialog box. Bear in mind, both of these techniques work only when the point tool is active:

✦ To add a color as a point along the Curves graph, Ctrl-click (Win) or ⌘-click (Mac) a pixel in the image window. Photoshop adds the point to the channel displayed in the dialog box. For example, if the RGB composite channel is visible, the point is added to the RGB composite curve. If the Red channel is visible, Photoshop adds the point to the red graph and leaves the green and blue graphs unchanged.

✦ To add a color to all graphs, regardless of which channel is visible in the Curves dialog box, Ctrl+Shift-click (Win) or ⌘-Shift-click (Mac) a pixel in the image window. In the case of an RGB image, Photoshop maps the red, green, and blue brightness values for that pixel to each of the red, green, and blue graphs in the Curves dialog box. The RGB composite graph shows no change — switch to the individual channels to see the new point.

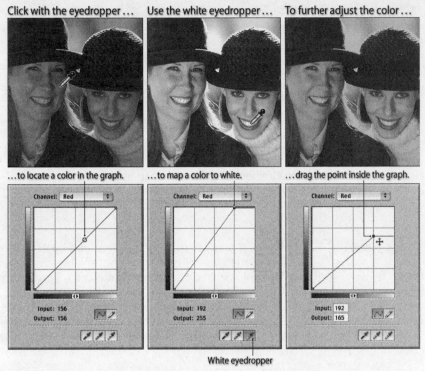

Figure 17-28: Use the standard eyedropper cursor to locate a color in the brightness graph (left). Click with one of the eyedropper tools from the Curves dialog box to map the color of that pixel in the graph (middle). You then can edit the location of the point in the graph by dragging it (right).

Gradient maps

This command permits you to apply a gradation as a Curves map. Just choose Image ➪ Adjustments ➪ Gradient Map to display the dialog box pictured in Figure 17-29. Make sure the Preview check box is turned on. Then click the down-pointing arrowhead to the right of the gradient preview to display the familiar gradient drop-down palette. Select a gradient other than Foreground To Background and watch the fireworks.

In the first row of Color Plate 17-7, I applied a couple of gradient maps to the original image on the left. The Chrome map had jagged edges, which inspired me to apply Gaussian Blur to it and a couple other Gradient Map variations in the middle row. In the bottom row, I mixed these fantastic images with their underlying originals using the Color blend mode.

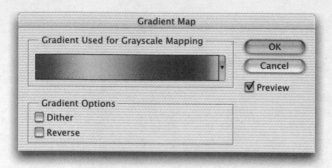

Figure 17-29: Choose the Gradient Map command to apply a preset gradient as a Curves map. Color Plate 17-7 shows examples.

What's going on? As foreign as it may sound, any gradient can be expressed as a Curves graph, progressing through a variety of brightness values in each of the three (RGB) or four (CMYK) color channels. When applied as a gradient map, the beginning of the gradient maps black; the end of the gradient maps white. If you apply the Violet, Orange preset, for example, the dark colors in the image map to violet and the light colors map to orange. Noise-type gradients (introduced in the "Applying Gradient Fills" section of Chapter 6) produce especially interesting effects.

Practical applications: Continuous curves

Note

Due to the complex nature and general usefulness of the Curves dialog box, I spend this section and the next exploring practical applications of its many options, concentrating first on the point tool and then on the pencil tool. These discussions assume that the brightness bar is set to edit brightness values, so that the gradation in the bar lightens from left to right. If you set the bar to edit ink coverage — where the bar darkens from left to right — you can still achieve the effects I describe, but you must drag in the opposite direction. For example, if I tell you to lighten colors by dragging upward, you would drag downward.

When you first enter the Curves dialog box, the brightness curve appears as a straight line strung between two points, as shown in the first example of Figure 17-30, mapping every input level from black (the lower-left point) to white (the upper-right point) to an identical output level. If you want to perform seamless color corrections, the point tool is your best bet because it enables you to edit the levels in the brightness graph while maintaining a continuous curve.

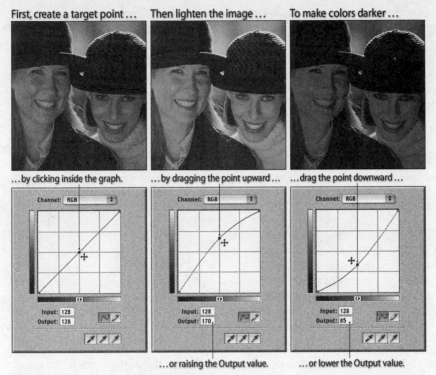

Figure 17-30: Create a single point in the curve with the point tool (left) and then drag it upward (middle) or downward (right) to lighten or darken the image evenly.

To lighten the colors, click near the middle of the curve with the point tool to create a new point and then drag the point upward, as demonstrated in the second example of Figure 17-30. To darken the image, drag the point downward, as in the third example.

Create two points in the curve to boost or lessen the contrast between colors in the image. In the first example of Figure 17-31, I created one point very near the white point in the curve and another point very close to the black point. I then dragged down on the left point and up on the right point to make the dark pixels darker and the light pixels lighter, which translates to higher contrast.

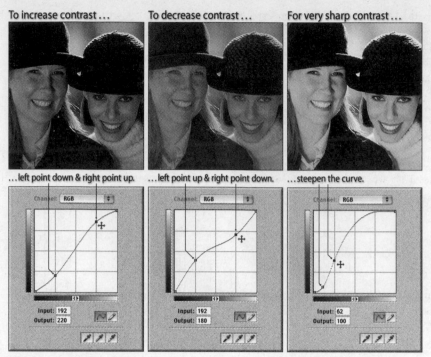

Figure 17-31: Create two points in the curve to change the appearance of contrast in an image, whether by increasing it mildly (left), decreasing it (middle), or boosting it dramatically (right).

In the second example of the figure, I did just the opposite, dragging up on the left point to lighten the dark pixels and down on the right point to darken the light pixels. As you can see in the second image, this lessens the contrast between colors, making the image more gray.

In the final example of Figure 17-31, I bolstered the contrast with a vengeance by dragging the right point down and to the left. This has the effect of springing the right half of the curve farther upward, thus increasing the brightness of the light pixels in the image.

Practical applications: Arbitrary curves

You can create some mind-numbing color variations by adjusting the brightness curve arbitrarily, mapping light pixels to dark, dark pixels to light, and in-between pixels all over the place. In the first example of Figure 17-32, I used the point tool to achieve an arbitrary curve. By dragging the left point severely upward and the right point severely downward, I caused dark and light pixels alike to soar across the spectrum.

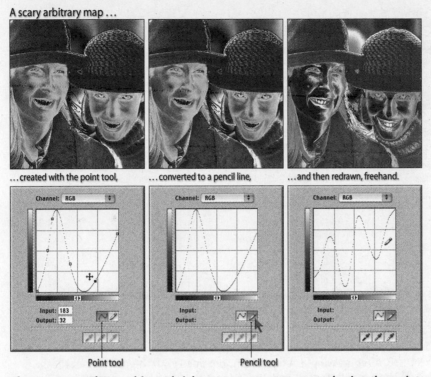

A scary arbitrary map . . .

. . . created with the point tool,   . . . converted to a pencil line,   . . . and then redrawn, freehand.

Point tool   Pencil tool

Figure 17-32: These arbitrary brightness curves were created using the point tool (left) and the pencil tool (right).

If you're interested in something a little more subtle, try applying an arbitrary curve to a single channel in a color image. Color Plate 17-8, for example, shows an image subject to relatively basic color manipulations in the green and blue channels, followed by an arbitrary adjustment to the red channel.

Although you can certainly achieve arbitrary effects using the point tool, the pencil tool is more versatile and less inhibiting. As shown in the last example of Figure 17-32, I created an effect that would alarm Carlos Castaneda just by zigzagging my way across the graph and clicking on the Smooth button.

In fact, the Smooth button is an integral part of using the pencil tool. Try this little experiment: Draw a bunch of random lines and squiggles with the pencil tool in the brightness graph. As shown in the first example of Figure 17-33, your efforts will most likely yield an unspeakably hideous and utterly unrecognizable effect.

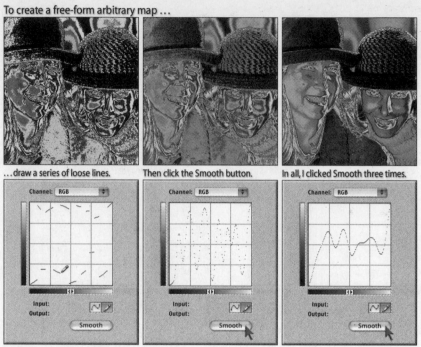

Figure 17-33: After drawing a series of random lines with the pencil tool (left), I clicked on the Smooth button once to connect the lines into a frenetic curve (middle) and then twice more to even out the curve, thus preserving more of the original image (right).

Next, click the Smooth button. Photoshop automatically connects all portions of the curve, miraculously smoothing out the color-mapping effect and rescuing some semblance of your image, as shown in the second example of the figure. If the effect is still too radical, you can continue to smooth it by clicking the Smooth button additional times. I clicked on the button twice more to create the right image in Figure 17-33. Eventually, the Smooth button restores the curve to a straight line.

Adjustment Layers

Every one of the commands I've discussed in this chapter is applicable to a single layer at a time. If you want to correct the colors in multiple layers, you have to create a special kind of layer called an *adjustment layer*. Adjustment layers are layers that contain mathematical color correction information. The layer applies its corrections to all layers beneath it, without affecting any layers above.

You can create an adjustment layer in one of two ways:

✦ Choose Layer ➪ New Adjustment Layer. This displays a submenu of color adjustment commands, ranging from Levels and Curves to Invert, Threshold, and Posterize.

✦ Click the half black/half white circle at the bottom of the Layers palette, as shown in Figure 17-34. The first three options — Solid Color, Gradient, and Pattern — are dynamic fill layers, as discussed in Chapter 14. Choose any one of the remaining 11 options to make a new adjustment layer.

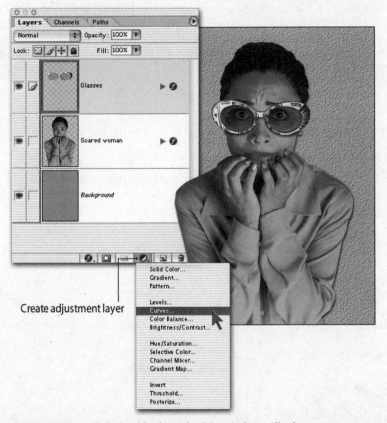

Create adjustment layer

Figure 17-34: Click the black-and-white circle to display a pop-up menu of dynamic fill and adjustment layers.

If you choose a command from the Layer ➪ New Adjustment Layer submenu, Photoshop displays the New Layer dialog box, which permits you to name the layer, assign a color, and set the blend mode. You can also group the adjustment layer with the currently selected layer, which means that the adjustment layer will affect that layer only. If you choose an option from the black-and-white circle in the Layers palette (labeled in Figure 17-34), Photoshop bypasses the New Layer dialog box and heads straight to the selected correction. Choosing Curves, for example, displays the Curves dialog box. (Invert is the only option that produces no dialog box whatsoever.) Change the settings as desired and press Enter or Return as you normally would. If you hold down Alt or Option while clicking the adjustment layer icon in the Layers palette, you'll get the New Layer dialog box just as if you'd chosen from the menu commands.

Regardless of the color adjustment you select, it appears as a new layer in the Layers palette. In Figure 17-35, for example, I've added a total of three adjustment layers. Photoshop marks adjustment layers with special icons that look like miniature versions of their respective dialog boxes. This way, you can readily tell them apart from image layers. As you can also see in Figure 17-35, adjustment layers automatically come with accompanying layer masks. You can take advantage of this fact, as in the top adjustment layer, ignore the mask, as in the bottom adjustment layer, or delete the mask by dragging it to the trash can icon, as I've done with the middle adjustment layer. More on those layer masks in a minute.

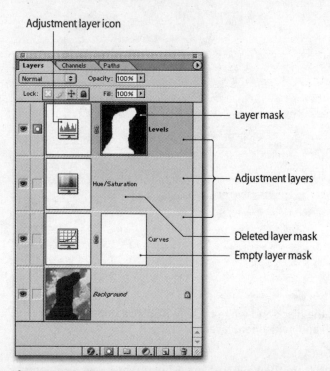

Figure 17-35: Here I've created three layers of color correction in front of a single background image.

The advantages of layer-based corrections

At this point, you might think, "Big whoop. You can apply corrections to multiple layers. That doesn't seem like such a great feature." But lest you judge too hastily, here are a few reasons adjustment layers are so great:

✦ **Forever editable:** As long as the adjustment layer remains intact stored in one of the three formats that support layers (native Photoshop PSD, TIFF, or PDF), you can edit the color correction over and over again without damaging the underlying pixels. Unlike standard color corrections, which alter selected pixels directly, adjustment layers have no permanent effect on the pixels. On the slightest whim, double-click the adjustment layer icon to bring up the color correction dialog box, complete with the settings currently in force. Tweak the settings as the mood hits you and press Enter or Return to make changes on the fly. Toggle the visibility of the adjustment layer by clicking the eyeball icon for the layer. You can't get any more flexible than this.

When editing the settings for an adjustment layer, be sure to double-click the first icon that precedes the layer name (labeled "Adjustment layer icon" in Figure 17-35). Double-clicking elsewhere displays either the Layer Mask Display Options, the Layer Style dialog box, or it allows you to rename the layer.

✦ **Versatile layer masking:** You can likewise adjust the affected area to your heart's content. Unless it's grouped with another layer, an adjustment layer covers the entire image like an adjustable wall-to-wall carpet. You modify the affected area by painting inside the layer. An adjustment layer doesn't contain pixels, so painting inside the layer changes its layer mask. Paint with black to remove the correction from an area; use white to paint the correction back in.

In fact, if a selection is active when you create a new adjustment layer, Photoshop automatically creates a layer mask according to the selection outline. For example, in Figure 17-36, I selected the topiary dinosaur before creating the Levels layer. Photoshop thoughtfully converted my selection into a layer mask, as labeled in Figure 17-35. And like any layer mask, I can edit it well into the future without any adverse side effects.

✦ **Reorder your corrections:** As with any layers, you can shuffle adjustment layers up and down in stacking order. For example, if you decide you don't want the correction to affect a specific layer, just drag the adjustment layer to a level in the Layers palette below the layer you want to exclude. If you're juggling multiple adjustment layers, as in Figure 17-36, you can shuffle the adjustment layers to change the order in which they're applied. This includes the standard reordering keyboard shortcuts, Ctrl+[and Ctrl+] (⌘-[and ⌘-] on the Mac).

✦ **Fade corrections:** You can fade a standard color correction right after you apply it using Edit ⇨ Fade. But you can fade a correction applied with an adjustment layer any old time. Just change the blend mode and Opacity settings in the Layers palette.

✦ **Correct using blend modes without ballooning file sizes:** Some folks prefer to correct overly light or dark images using blend modes. Take an image, copy it to a new layer, and apply the Multiply mode to darken the layer or Screen to lighten it. The problem with this trick is that it increases the size of the image in memory. Duplicating the image to a new layer requires Photoshop to double the size of the image in RAM.

Adjustment layers permit you to apply this same technique without adding pixels to RAM. Create a new adjustment layer with the Levels option selected. After the Levels dialog box appears, press Enter or Return to ignore it. Now select Multiply or Screen from the blend mode pop-up menu in the Layers palette. The adjustment layer serves as a surrogate duplicate of the layers below it, mocking every merged pixel. And it doesn't add so much as a K to the file size. It's an image-editing miracle — layers without the pain.

✦ **Change one adjustment to another:** After applying one kind of adjustment layer, you can convert it to another kind of adjustment layer. For example, you could swap an existing Levels adjustment for a Curves adjustment. To do so, choose the desired color adjustment from the Layer ➪ Change Layer Content submenu. Photoshop doesn't try to preserve the prior color adjustment when making the conversion — in other words, it can't convert the Levels information into Curves data — but it does preserve the layer mask, blend mode, and other layer attributes.

Correcting a flat image using layers

Although many artists use adjustment layers to edit multilayer compositions, they are equally applicable to flat photos. Originally printed in the February, 1996 issue of *Macworld* magazine, Figure 17-36 shows how I corrected an image shot with a Polaroid PDC-2000 using a total of three color corrections, layered one on top of the other. (Much of the following text also comes from that same article.) At first glance, the original photo on the left side of the figure is a textbook example of what happens if you ignore backlighting. But as you have probably figured out by now, an image that appears black may actually contain several thousand colors just itching to get out. Adjustment layers make it easier than ever to free these colors and make them fully visible to the world.

Because my image was in such rotten shape, I decided to start with the Curves command. I clicked on the black-and-white circle button and selected Curves from the pop-up menu. Then I used the pencil tool in the Curves dialog box to draw a radical upswing on the left side of the graph, dramatically lightening the blacks right out of the gate. I clicked on the Smooth button a few times to even out the color transitions, as demonstrated in the second example in Figure 17-36.

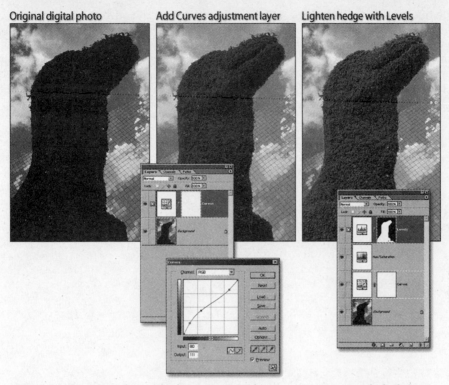

Figure 17-36: After observing that my original image was way too dark (left), I created a new adjustment layer and used the Curves command to lighten the image (middle). I then added two additional layers to increase the saturation levels with Hue/Saturation and correct the brightness levels of the topiary animal with Levels (right).

All this lightening resulted in some very washed-out colors (a typical side effect), so I created a second adjustment layer using the Hue/Saturation command. By raising the Saturation value, I quickly breathed a little enthusiasm into these tired old hues — a sufficient amount, in fact, to make it clear how soft the focus was. So I went back to the original image layer and applied the Unsharp Mask filter. Had it not been for the advent of adjustment layers, I would have had to sharpen the image either before color correcting it, making it impossible to accurately gauge the results, or after correcting, which might bring out compression artifacts and other undesirable anomalies. With adjustment layers, however, I can sharpen and correct at the same time, giving no operation precedent over the other.

The hedge monster remained a little dark, so I selected it with the Color Range command and then created a third adjustment layer for the Levels command. Using Levels, I quickly enhanced the brightness and contrast of the green beast, bringing him out into the full light of day. As I mentioned earlier, Photoshop automatically generated a layer mask for my selection, which appears as a tiny white silhouette in the Layers palette.

✦   ✦   ✦

Printing from Photoshop

Welcome to Printing

On one hand, printing can be a straightforward topic. You choose the Print command, press Enter or Return, wait for something to come out of your printer, and admire yet another piece of forestry that you've destroyed. On the other hand, printing can be a ridiculously complicated subject, involving dot-gain compensation, hardware calibration, under color removal, toxic processor chemicals, separation table generation, and so many infinitesimal color parameters, you're liable to spend half your life trying to figure out what's happening.

This chapter is about finding a middle ground. Although it is in no way intended to cover every possible facet of printing digitized images, this chapter walks you through the process of preparing and printing the three major categories of output: composites, color separations, and duotones. By the end of the chapter, you'll be familiar with all of Photoshop's printing options. You'll also be prepared to communicate with professionals at your service bureau or at a commercial printer, if need be, and to learn from their input and expertise.

 PC users should be aware that although most printer manufacturers now offer Windows drivers, those drivers aren't always perfected. Sometimes you must get seriously down and dirty by using an older printer DLL (*dynamic link library*, a basic component of Windows) with a later printer driver.

If you encounter a Windows-related printing problem, your first cry for help should be to your printer manufacturer's Web site or tech support line. If those sources don't have the answer, check online forums and newsgroups. Your service bureau can also be an excellent source for technical advice. Chances are, you're not the first person to experience the problem and someone, somewhere should have a fix for you.

Understanding Printing Terminology

I'm not a big believer in glossaries. Generally, they contain glib, jargony, out-of-context definitions—about as helpful in gaining understanding of a concept as a seminar in which all the presenters speak pig latin. But before I delve into the inner recesses of printing, I want to introduce, in a semilogical, sort of random order, a smattering of the printing terms you'll encounter. Ood-gay uck-lay.

✦ **Service bureau:** A *service bureau* is a shop filled with earnest, young graphic artists (at least they were young and earnest when *I* worked at one), printer operators, and about a billion dollars' worth of hardware. A small service bureau is usually outfitted with a few laser printers, photocopiers, and self-service computers. Big service bureaus offer scanners, imagesetters, film recorders, and other varieties of professional-quality input and output equipment.

Service bureaus once relied exclusively on the Macintosh. This has changed, but a substantial number of Mac-based service bureaus remain. Most service bureaus are equally ready to help Photoshoppers on both PC and Mac platforms, but many will take your Windows Photoshop file and run it through a Mac. Nothing is wrong with this—Photoshop is nearly identical on the two platforms—but cross-platform problems may crop up. If you're a PC user, try to be sure your service bureau knows how to address cross-platform incompatibilities and has a general working knowledge of Windows.

✦ **Commercial printer:** Generally speaking, a *commercial printer* takes up where the service bureau leaves off. Commercial printers reproduce black-and-white and color pages using offset presses, web presses, and a whole bunch of other age-old technology I don't cover in this miniglossary (or anywhere else in this book, for that matter). The process is less expensive than photocopying when you're dealing with large quantities, say, more than 100 copies, and it delivers professional-quality reproductions.

✦ **Output device:** This is just another way to say *printer*. Rather than writing *Print your image from the printer*, which sounds repetitive and a trifle obvious, I write *Print your image from the output device*. *Output devices* also include laser printers, imagesetters, film recorders, and a whole bunch of other machines.

✦ **Laser printer:** A *laser printer* works much like a photocopier. First, it applies an electric charge to a cylinder, called a *drum*, inside the printer. The charged areas, which correspond to the black portions of the image being printed, attract fine, petroleum-based dust particles called *toner*. The drum transfers the toner to the page, and a heating mechanism fixes the toner in place. Most laser printers have resolutions of at least 300 dots (or *printer pixels*) per inch. The newer printers offer higher resolutions, such as 600 and 1,200 dots per inch (*dpi*).

✦ **Color printers:** *Color printers* fall into three categories. Generally speaking, inkjet and thermal-wax printers are at the low end, and dye-sublimation printers occupy the high end. *Inkjet printers* deliver colored dots from disposable ink cartridges. *Thermal-wax* printers apply wax-based pigments to a page in multiple passes. Both kinds of printers mix cyan, magenta, yellow, and, depending on the specific printer, black dots to produce full-color output. Inkjet output quality can be quite good, but if you want truly photographic quality prints, you must migrate up the price ladder to *dye-sublimation printers*. Dye-sub inks permeate the surface of the paper, literally dying it different colors. Furthermore, the cyan, magenta, yellow, and black pigments mix in varying opacities from one dot to the next, resulting in a continuous-tone image that appears nearly as smooth on the page as it does on screen.

✦ **Imagesetter:** A typesetter equipped with a graphics page-description language (most often PostScript) is called an *imagesetter*. Unlike a laser printer, an imagesetter prints photosensitive paper or film by exposing the portions of the paper or film that correspond to the black areas of the image. The process is like exposing film with a camera, but an imagesetter only knows two colors: black and white. The exposed paper or film collects in a lightproof canister. In a separate step, the printer operator develops the film in a processor. Developed paper looks like a typical glossy black-and-white page. Developed film is black where the image is white and transparent where the image is black. Imagesetters typically offer resolutions between 1,200 and 3,600 dpi. But the real beauty of imageset pages is blacks are absolutely black (or transparent), as opposed to the irregular gray you get with laser-printed pages.

✦ **Film recorder:** A *film recorder* transfers images to full-color 35mm and 4×5 slides perfect for professional presentations. Slides also can be useful to provide images to publications and commercial printers. Many publications can scan from slides, and commercial printers can use slides to create color separations. So, if you're nervous a color separation printed from Photoshop won't turn out well, ask your service bureau to output the image to a 35mm slide. Then have your commercial printer reproduce the image from the slide.

✦ **PostScript:** The *PostScript* page-description language was the first product developed by Adobe — the same folks who sell Photoshop — and is now a staple of hundreds of brands of laser printers, imagesetters, and film recorders. A *page-description language* is a programming language for defining text and graphics on a page. PostScript specifies the locations of points, draws line segments between them, and fills in areas with solid blacks or *halftone cells* (dot patterns that simulate grays). Some newer printers instead use *stochastic screens* that simulate grays and colors using almost-random patterns.

✦ **Spooling:** Printer *spooling* allows you to work on an image while another image prints. Rather than communicating directly with the output device, Photoshop describes the image to the system software. Under Mac OS 9, you can set spooling options when you send the image to the printer. Mac OS X, multitasking master that it is, has spooling turned on at all times. Under

Windows 98, Me, NT, and 2000, set spooling options via the Printer control panel. Choose Settings ➾ Printers, right-click the icon for your specific printer, and choose Properties from the pop-up menu. Inside the printer's Properties dialog box, switch to the Details panel and click the Spool Settings button. Under Windows XP, the spooling settings are located in the Advanced panel of the Properties. When Photoshop finishes describing the image — a relatively quick process — you are free to resume working while the system software prints the image in the background.

✦ **Calibration:** Traditionally, *calibrating* a system means synchronizing the machinery. In the context of Photoshop, however, calibrating means to adjust or compensate for the color displays of the scanner, monitor, and printer so what you scan is what you see on screen, which in turn is what you get from the printer. Colors match from one device to the next. Empirically speaking, this is impossible; a yellow image in a photograph won't look exactly like the on-screen yellow or the yellow printed from a set of color separations. But calibrating is designed to make the images look as much alike as possible, taking into account the fundamental differences in hardware technology. Expensive hardware calibration solutions seek to change the configuration of scanner, monitor, and printer. Less expensive software solutions, including those provided by Photoshop, manipulate the image to account for the differences between devices.

✦ **Brightness values/shades:** As described in Chapter 4, there's a fundamental difference between the way your screen and printer create gray values and colors. Your monitor shows colors by lightening an otherwise black screen; the printed page shows colors by darkening an otherwise white piece of paper. On-screen colors, therefore, are measured in terms of *brightness values*. High values equate to light colors; low values equate to dark colors. On the printed page, colors are measured in percentage values called *shades* or, if you prefer, *tints*. High-percentage values result in dark colors, and low-percentage values result in light colors.

✦ **Composite:** A *composite* is a page that shows an image in its entirety. A black-and-white composite printed from a standard laser printer or imagesetter translates all colors in an image to gray values. A color composite printed from a color printer or film recorder shows the colors as they actually appear. Composites are useful any time you want to proof an image or print a final grayscale image from an imagesetter, an overhead projection from a color printer, or a full-color image from a film recorder.

✦ **Proofing:** To *proof* an image is to see how it looks on paper before the final printing. Consumer proofing devices include laser printers and color inkjet printers, which provide quality and resolution sufficient only to vaguely predict the appearance of your final output. Professional-level proofing devices include the Rainbow dye-sublimation printer and Matchprint laser proofer, both developed by Imation, as well as DuPont's toner-based Cromalin and Creo's Iris, the latter of which uses a special variety of inkjet technology.

✦ **Bleeds:** Simply put, a *bleed* is an area that can be printed outside the perimeter of a page. You use a bleed to reproduce an image all the way to the edge of a page, as in a slick magazine ad. For example, this book includes bleeds. Most of the pages — such as the page you're reading — are encircled by a uniform 2-pica margin of white space. This margin keeps the text and figures from spilling off into oblivion. A few pages, however — including the parts pages and the color plates in the middle of the book — print all the way to the edges. In fact, the original artwork goes 2 picas beyond the edges of the paper. This ensures that if the paper shifts when printing — as it invariably does — you won't see any thin white edges around the artwork. This 2 picas of extra artwork is the bleed. In Photoshop, you create a bleed by clicking on the Bleed button in the Print with Preview dialog box.

✦ **Color separations:** To output color reproductions, commercial printers require *color separations* (or slides, which they can convert to color separations for a fee). A color-separated image comprises four printouts, one each for the cyan, magenta, yellow, and black primary printing colors. The commercial printer transfers each printout to a *plate*, which is used in the actual reproduction process.

✦ **Duotone:** A grayscale image in Photoshop can contain as many as 256 brightness values, from white on up to black. A printer can convey significantly fewer shades. A laser printer, for example, provides anywhere from 26 to 65 shades. An imagesetter provides from 150 to 200 shades, depending on resolution and screen frequency. And this assumes perfect printing conditions. You can count on at least 30 percent of those shades to get lost in the reproduction process. A *duotone* helps to retain the depth and clarity of detail in a grayscale image by printing with two inks. The number of shades available to you suddenly jumps from 150 to a few thousand. Photoshop also lets you create *tritones* (three inks) and *quadtones* (four inks). Note, using more inks translates to higher printing costs.

✦ **Spot color:** Most color images are printed as a combination of four *process color* inks — cyan, magenta, yellow, and black. But Photoshop also lets you add premixed inks called *spot colors*. As I mentioned in Chapter 4, the most popular purveyor of spot-colors in the United States is Pantone, which provides a library with hundreds of mixings. But many large corporations use custom spot colors for logos and other proprietary emblems. Most spot colors fall outside the CMYK gamut and thus increase the number of colors available to you. In addition to using spot colors in duotones, Photoshop lets you add a spot color channel to any image.

Printing Composites

Now that you've picked up some printer's jargon, you're ready to learn how to put it all together. This section explores the labyrinth of options available for printing composite images. Later in this chapter, I cover color separations and duotones.

Like any Windows or Macintosh application, Photoshop can print composite images to nearly any output device you can hook up to your computer. Assuming your printer is turned on, properly attached, and in working order, printing a composite image from Photoshop is a five-step process, as outlined in the following steps. The sections that follow describe each of these steps in detail.

STEPS: Printing a Composite Image

1. **Choose your printer.** Use the Printers control panel on your PC, the Chooser in Mac OS 9, or the Print Center utility in Mac OS X to select the output device to which you want to print. If your computer is not part of a network, you probably rely on a single output device, in which case you can skip this step.

2. **Choose File ⇨ Print with Preview or press Ctrl+P (⌘-P on the Mac).** This command opens the Print with Preview dialog box, where you can position the image on the page, scale the print size of the image, and select a few other options, as discussed later in this chapter. Note that depending on your settings in the General panel of the Preferences dialog box, you may need to add the Alt or Option key to the keyboard shortcut.

   Before you select those settings, however, click the Page Setup button to specify the page size and orientation of the image on the page. Then return to the Print with Preview dialog box and click the Show More Options check box to display and select still more output options.

3. **Adjust the halftone screens, if needed.** Click the Screens button to change the size, angle, and shape of the halftone screen dots. This step is purely optional, useful mostly for creating special effects.

4. **Adjust the transfer function again, if needed.** Click the Transfer button to map brightness values in an image to different shades when printed. This step is also optional, though frequently useful.

5. **Click the Print button to open the Print dialog box.** Depending on your printer, you may also be able to access specialized output functions here. After you've tweaked all relevant print settings, click the Print button to send the image to the printer.

If you already have your printer set up to your satisfaction, you can simply choose the File ⇨ Print command or press Ctrl+Alt+P (⌘-Option-P on the Mac) to skip Steps 2 through 4 and go directly to the Print dialog box. (Again, you might need to drop the Alt or Option key, depending on your Preference settings.) Or, press Ctrl+Alt+Shift+P (⌘-Option-Shift-P on the Mac) to access the Print One Copy command located under the File menu.

At this point, you may be wondering about drag-and-drop printing, where you can drag a file and drop it onto a printer icon at the desktop. Although this approach may seem more convenient, Photoshop still has to launch and access the same functions as when you use the manual process. And in the worst-case scenario, the operating system may print your image from the wrong application. Drag-and-drop printing is great for making quick copies of text files, but when printing photographs and other artwork, don't look for shortcuts.

Choosing a printer on a PC

To select a printer in most Windows systems, choose Start ➪ Settings ➪ Printers. Right-click your printer of choice and select Set As Default Printer on the resulting pop-up menu. If you want to add a printer, double-click the Add Printer icon, and be sure to have either your Windows CD-ROM or a drivers disk from your printer manufacturer.

Under Windows XP, choose Start ➪ Control Panel, select Printers and Other Hardware, and then select Printers and Faxes. Double-click the desired printer, and in the resulting window, choose Set As Default Printer from the Printer menu, as shown in Figure 18-1. To add a printer, choose the Add a Printer option from the Printer Tasks menu and follow the steps in the Add Printer Wizard.

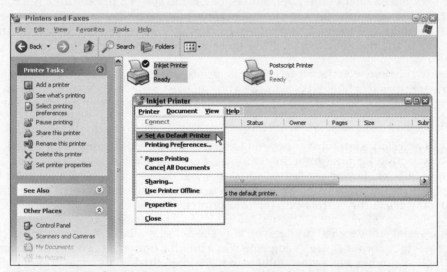

Figure 18-1: Under Windows XP, specify your default printer from inside the Printers and Faxes window.

Printer drivers help the PC hardware, Windows, and Photoshop translate the contents of an image to the printer hardware and the page-description language it uses. You generally want to select the driver for your specific model of printer. But you can, if necessary, prepare an image for output to a printer that isn't currently hooked up to your computer. For example, you can use this technique prior to submitting a document to be output on an imagesetter at a service bureau.

Most high-end graphics applications can take advantage of *PostScript printer description (PPD)* files. A single driver can't account for the myriad differences between different models of PostScript printers, so each PPD serves as a little guidance file, customizing the driver to accommodate a specific printer model. Windows lets you attach a PPD file globally to your PostScript printer, for which you need both the PPD file and the INF file to tell Windows what to install. (Adobe offers its own printer driver called AdobePS — available via *www.adobe.com* — which doesn't require INF files. The setup program works only for Adobe-licensed PostScript printers, however.)

Tip

Windows also lets you switch printers from inside an application. Just choose File ➪ Page Setup (Ctrl+Shift+P) inside Photoshop and select the printer you want to use from the Name pop-up menu. Under Windows XP, click the Printer button inside the Page Setup dialog box.

Choosing a printer on a Mac

If your printer is on a network, you may first need to ensure that you are properly connected to the network. After that, in OS X open the Print Center utility, located in the Utilities folder of the Applications folder, and select a printer from the Printer List. In OS 9 select the Chooser from the Apple menu. The dialog box is split in two, with the left half devoted to a scrolling list of printer driver icons and/or network zones and the right half to specific printer options.

Most of the time, you'll want to select the printer driver for your specific model of printer. But as I mentioned previously, you can use this technique to prepare an image for output on an imagesetter or another device that isn't currently hooked up to your computer.

Any PostScript printer driver beyond LaserWriter 8 includes support for PPD files. After selecting a printer from the right-hand scrolling list, you can access the proper PPD by clicking the Setup button. (Or just double-click the printer name in the list.) Then click the Auto Setup button to instruct the system software to automatically select the correct PPD for your printer.

If you select a networked printer, you may see a Background Printing option in the bottom-right corner of the dialog box. When on, this option lets you print an image in the background while you continue to work in Photoshop or some other application. This enables you to take advantage of spooling, as defined earlier in this chapter. Normally, spooling works fine. But if you encounter printing problems, this is the first option you want to turn off.

Tip

If you use the Macintosh control strip in OS 9, you may be able to bypass the Chooser when switching printers. Just click the printer icon in the control strip and select the desired printer from the pop-up menu. Not all printers support this function, however, so you may have to visit the Chooser whether you like it or not.

Setting up the page

The next step is to define the relationship between the current image and the page on which it prints. You handle most aspects of this part of the printing process in the Print with Preview dialog box, shown in Figure 18-2. To open the dialog box, choose File ➪ Print with Preview or press Ctrl+P (⌘-P on the Mac). When you first open the dialog box, the options shown at the bottom half of the figure aren't visible; select the Show More Options check box to display them.

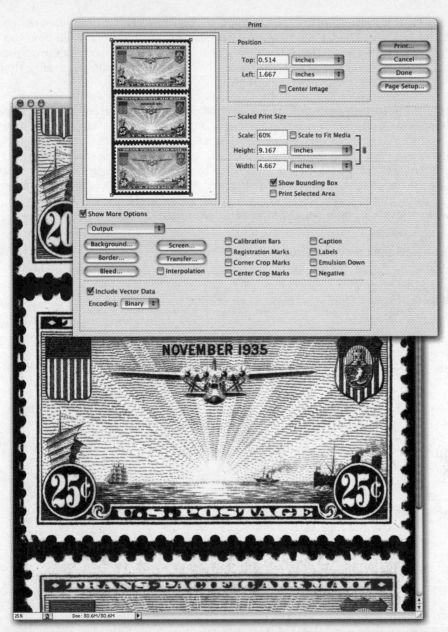

Figure 18-2: The Print with Preview dialog box enables you to precisely position the image, scale the image, and handle almost all other print setup chores.

The settings in the Print with Preview dialog box, however, relate to the printer, paper size, and page orientation you select in the Page Setup dialog box. So unless you want to use Page Setup options that you already established, click the Page

Setup button to transport to that dialog box. Alternatively, you can open the dialog box by choosing File ➪ Page Setup or by pressing Ctrl+Shift+P (⌘-Shift-P on the Mac) when the Print with Preview dialog box isn't open. The next section explains the important choices you need to make in the Page Setup dialog box; after that, I discuss a myriad of other print settings.

Note   Some of Photoshop's print options may appear in several different dialog boxes. For example, you may find image scaling controls in the Page Setup dialog box, as well as in the Print with Preview dialog box. For most print attributes, Photoshop doesn't care where you specify your print options. But if you want to scale the image for output, use the Scaled Print Size controls in the Print with Preview dialog box. If you scale the image in the Page Setup dialog box, the Scale, Height, and Width values in the Print with Preview dialog box may not reflect accurate values. Or better yet, specify these settings using the Image Size command, as discussed in Chapter 3.

The Page Setup dialog box

The Page Setup dialog box varies depending on what kind of printer you use. Figure 18-3 shows the Mac OS X and Windows 2000 Page Setup options for a Tektronix Phaser 750N, a professional-level PostScript printer.

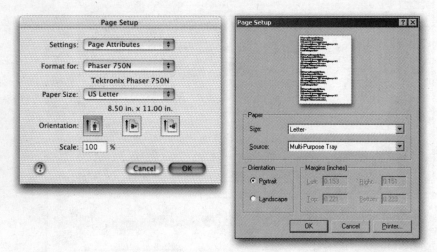

Figure 18-3: Use this dialog box to choose the page size and image orientation.

Even though the Page Setup dialog box offers different options for different printers, you should always have access to the following (or their equivalents):

✦ **Paper size:** Select the size of the paper loaded into your printer's paper tray. The paper size you select determines the *imageable area* of a page — that is, the amount of the page that Photoshop can use to print the current image. For example, the Letter option calls for a page that measures 8.5×11 inches, but only about 7.5×10 inches is imageable.

✦ **Source (Windows only):** Virtually all printers include paper cartridges, but some permit you to manually feed pages or switch between cartridges. Use this option to decide where your paper is coming from.

✦ **Orientation:** You can specify whether an image prints upright on a page (Portrait) or on its side (Landscape) by selecting the corresponding Orientation icon. Use the Landscape setting when an image is wider than it is tall.

Position and scaling options

All of the options I've described so far are constant regardless of what application you're using. However, the settings inside the Print with Preview dialog box (shown earlier, in Figure 18-2) are unique to Photoshop. These settings enable you to position the image on the page and perform a few other handy printing adjustments:

✦ **Position:** If you want the image to print smack dab in the middle of the page, leave the Center Image check box selected. Otherwise, deselect the Center Image check box and enter values into the Top and Left option boxes to position the image with respect to the top-left corner of the page. You can select from five different measurement units for these options. And if you're not overly concerned about placing the image exactly at a certain spot, deselect the Center Image check box and then just drag the image in the preview on the left side of the dialog box.

The preview updates to show you the current image position.

✦ **Scaling:** If you want to adjust the image size for the current print job only, use these controls. They have no effect on the actual image file—they merely scale the image for printing. You can enter a scale percentage; anything over 100 percent enlarges the image, and values under 100 percent reduce the image. Or enter a specific size in the Height and Width option boxes. If you want Photoshop to adjust the image automatically to fit the page size, select the Scale to Fit Media check box.

The Show Bounding Box option, when selected, displays handles at the corners of the preview image. For quick and dirty scaling, you can drag the handles until the image is the approximate print size you want.

✦ **Print selection:** If you selected a rectangular area before opening the dialog box, you can print just the selection by turning on the Print Selected Area check box. Any scaling and position settings still apply to the printed output.

Photoshop prints only visible layers and channels, so you can print select layers or channels in an image by hiding all the other layers or channels. (To hide and display layers and channels, click the eyeball icon next to the layer or channel name in the Layers or Channels palette, respectively.) To print a single layer or channel, Alt-click (Win) or Option-click (Mac) the eyeball.

Output options

To display the special print options shown at the bottom of Figure 18-2, earlier in this chapter, select the Show More Options check box and then select Output from the pop-up menu immediately below. (If any options are dimmed, your printer doesn't support them.)

The five Output buttons work as follows:

✦ **Background:** To assign a color to the area around the printed image, click this button and select a color from the Color Picker dialog box, described in Chapter 4. This button and the one that follows (Border) are designed specifically to accommodate slides printed from a film recorder. If you select either of these options, Photoshop updates the preview to show them.

✦ **Border:** To print a border around the current image, click this button and enter the thickness of the border into the Width option box. The border automatically appears in black.

✦ **Bleed:** This button lets you print outside the imageable area of the page when outputting to an imagesetter. (Imagesetters print to huge rolls of paper or film, so you can print far outside the confines of standard page sizes. Most other printers use regular old sheets of paper; any bleed — were the printer to acknowledge it — would print off the edge of the page.) Click the Bleed button and enter the thickness of the bleed into the Width option box. Two picas (24 points) is generally a good bet. (Bleeds are defined in the "Understanding Printing Terminology" glossary at the beginning of this chapter.)

✦ **Screen:** Click this button to enter a dialog box that enables you to change the size, angle, and shape of the printed halftone cells, as described in the upcoming "Changing the halftone screen" section.

✦ **Transfer:** The dialog box that appears when you click this button enables you to redistribute shades in the printed image, as explained in the upcoming section, "Specifying a transfer function."

Most of the Output check boxes — all except Negative, Emulsion Down, Interpolation, and Include Vector Data — append special labels and printer marks to the printed version of the image. Figure 18-4 illustrates how they look when printed. For all options except Interpolation and Include Vector Data, Photoshop shows the result of selecting the check box in the image preview.

✦ **Interpolation:** If you own an output device equipped with PostScript Level 2 or later, you can instruct Photoshop to antialias the printed appearance of a low-resolution image by selecting this option. The output device resamples the image up to 200 percent and then reduces the image to its original size using bicubic interpolation (as described in the "General preferences" section of Chapter 2), thereby creating a less-jagged image. This option has no effect on older-model PostScript devices.

✦ **Calibration Bars:** A calibration bar is a 10-step grayscale gradation beginning at 10 percent black and ending at 100 percent black. The function of the calibration bar is to ensure all shades are distinct and on target. If not, the output device isn't properly calibrated, which is a fancy way of saying the printer's colors are out of whack and need realignment by a trained professional armed with a hammer and hacksaw. When you print color separations, the Calibration Bars check box instructs Photoshop to print a gradient tint bar and progressive color bar, also useful to printing professionals.

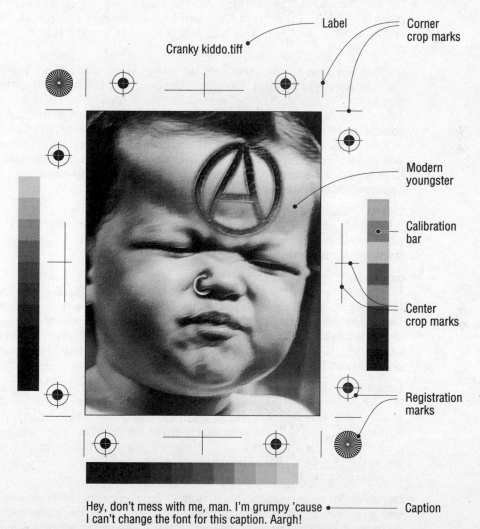

Figure 18-4: An image printed with nearly all the Output check boxes turned on.

✦ **Registration Marks:** Select this option to print eight crosshairs and two star targets near the four corners of the image. Registration marks are imperative when you print color separations; they provide the only reliable means to ensure exact registration of the cyan, magenta, yellow, and black printing plates. When printing a composite image, however, you can ignore this option.

✦ **Corner Crop Marks:** Select this option to print eight hairline crop marks — two in each of the image's four corners — which indicate how to trim the image in case you anticipate engaging in a little traditional paste-up work.

✦ **Center Crop Marks:** Select this option to print four pairs of hairlines that mark the center of the image. Each pair forms a cross. Two pairs are located on the sides of the image, the third pair is above it, and the fourth pair is below the image.

✦ **Caption:** To print a caption beneath the image, select this option. Then press Enter or Return to exit this dialog box, choose File ➪ File Info, and enter a caption in the Caption field of the General section of the File Info dialog box. The caption prints in 9-point Helvetica. This is strictly an image-annotation feature, something to help you 17 years down the road, when your brain starts to deteriorate and you can't remember why you printed the darn thing. (You might also use the caption to keep images straight in a busy office where hundreds of folks have access to the same images, but I don't like this alternative as much because I can't make fun of it.)

✦ **Labels:** When you select this check box, Photoshop prints the name of the image and the name of the printed color channel in 9-point Helvetica. If you process many images, you'll find this option extremely useful for associating printouts with documents on disk.

Incidentally, Figure 18-4 shows the actual labels and marks exactly as they print. I started by printing the Photoshop image to disk as an EPS (Encapsulated PostScript) file (as I describe later in the "Printing pages" section). Then I used Illustrator to open the EPS file and assign the callouts. This may not sound like much, but in the old days this would have been impossible. Figure 18-4 represents a practical benefit to Illustrator's (and Photoshop's) ability to open just about any EPS file on the planet.

✦ **Emulsion Down:** The emulsion is the side of a piece of film on which an image is printed. When the Emulsion Down check box is turned off, film prints from an imagesetter emulsion side up; when the check box is turned on, Photoshop flips the image so the emulsion side is down. Like the Negative option, discussed next, this option is useful only when you print film from an imagesetter, and this option should be set in accordance with the preferences of your commercial printer.

✦ **Negative:** When you select this option, Photoshop prints all blacks as white and all whites as black. In-between colors switch accordingly. For example, 20 percent black becomes 80 percent black. Imagesetter operators use this option to print composites and color separations to film negatives.

✦ **Include Vector Data:** If your image contains any vector objects or type for which outline data is available (not outline or protected fonts), select this check box to send the actual vector data to a PostScript printer. Your vector objects then can be scaled to any size without degrading in quality. Including the vector data increases the image file size, which can slow printing and cause other printing problems. But if you turn off the check box, everything in the image is sent to the printer as raster data. This reduces the file size, but you no longer can scale the vector objects or type with impunity. They're subject to the same quality loss that occurs when you enlarge any pixel-based image.

✦ **Encoding:** Select an option from this pop-up menu to control the encoding method used to send the image file to the printer. In normal printing situations, leave the option set to the default, Binary. If your network doesn't support binary encoding (highly unlikely in this day and age) or your printer is attached through the local parallel printer port, instead of the network, select the ASCII option to transfer PostScript data in the text-only format. The printing process takes much longer to complete, but at least it's possible. If your printer supports PostScript Level 2 or later, you can also choose to use JPEG compression to reduce the amount of data sent to the printer. (This option is applicable to PostScript printers only.)

Color management options

After you select the Show More Options check box in the Print with Preview dialog box, you can display color-management settings by selecting Color Management from the pop-up menu, as shown in Figure 18-5. These options enable you to convert the image color space for printing only. You may want to do this to print a proof of the image on a printer other than the printer you'll use for final output. To convert the color space of the actual image file, you need to use the techniques discussed in Chapter 16.

You can select from two Source Space options, Document and Proof. These options tell Photoshop whether you want to print the image according to the color profile officially assigned to the image file or according to the Proof Setup profile (the so-called "soft proofing" profile). Document uses the actual color profile; Proof uses the profile currently selected in the View ⇨ Proof Setup submenu.

The Profile options control whether Photoshop converts the image to a different profile during the print process. If you select Same As Source from the Profile pop-up menu, no conversion occurs. To convert to a different profile, select the profile from the pop-up menu. You can then specify the rendering method by selecting it from the Intent pop-up menu.

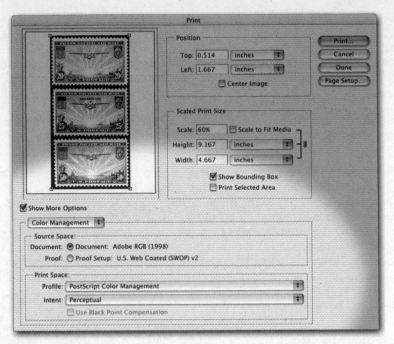

Figure 18-5: Use these options to dictate which color-management settings you want Photoshop to use when printing.

You can convert to any color space offered by Photoshop, Kodak's ICC CMS (Win), or Apple's ColorSync (Mac). Ideally, you want to select the specific profile for your brand of printer. If you can't find such a profile, you'll probably want to stick with the RGB Color space (specified in the Color Settings dialog box). Another option is to choose Working CMYK, which prints the image just as if you had converted it to the CMYK color space. Unfortunately, most consumer printers are designed to accommodate RGB images and fare pretty badly when printing artwork converted to CMYK. (This is precisely the reason I frequently select RGB Color even when printing a CMYK image — it flat out produces better results.)

Tip

If you own a color printer, I encourage you to take an hour out of your day and conduct a few tests with the other Print Space options. For example, if you select Apple RGB, your printed image will darken several shades. This might throw you. Because the Apple RGB profile features the lightest of the monitor gammas — 1.8 — you might expect the image to print lighter. But what Photoshop is really doing is converting the colors as if the printer were as naturally light as an Apple RGB monitor. In order to maintain consistent color, the conversion therefore darkens the image to account for this unusually light device. Select the Wide Gamut setting and the colors appear lighter and washed out, again accounting for this hyper-saturated Space setting. So think opposite.

Yet another alternative is to convert an RGB image to the grayscale color space during printing. But it's generally a bad alternative. Asking Photoshop to perform this conversion on the fly dramatically increases the output time, as well as the likelihood of printing errors. It's better and much faster to simply convert the image to the grayscale mode (Image ⇨ Mode ⇨ Grayscale) and then print it.

Again, if you're unfamiliar with any of these terms or just don't know which options are best for your printing situation, review Chapter 16, where I discuss color management in detail.

Changing the halftone screen

Before I explain this option, available when you select Output from the pop-up menu in the Print with Preview dialog box, I need to explain a bit more about how printing works. To keep costs down, commercial printers use as few inks as possible to create the appearance of a wide variety of colors. Suppose you want to print an image of a pink flamingo wearing a red bow tie. Your commercial printer could print the flamingo in one pass using pink ink, let that color dry, and then load the red ink and print the bow tie. But why go to all this trouble? After all, pink is only a lighter shade of red. Why not imitate the pink by lightening the red ink?

Unfortunately, with the exception of dye-sublimation printers, high-end inkjets, and film recorders, output devices can't print lighter shades of colors. They recognize only solid ink and the absence of ink. So how do you print the lighter shade of red necessary to represent pink?

The answer is *halftoning*. The output device organizes printer pixels into spots called *halftone cells*. Because the cells are so small, your eyes cannot quite focus on them. Instead, the cells appear to blend with the white background of the page to create a lighter shade of an ink. Figure 18-6 shows a detail of an image enlarged to display the individual halftone cells.

The cells grow and shrink to emulate different shades of color. Large cells result in dark shades; small cells result in light shades. Cell size is measured in printer pixels. The maximum size of any cell is a function of the number of cells in an inch, called the screen frequency.

For example, suppose the default frequency of your printer is 60 halftone cells per linear inch and the resolution is 300 printer pixels per linear inch. Each halftone cell must, therefore, measure 5 pixels wide by 5 pixels tall ($300 \div 60 = 5$), for a total of 25 pixels per cell (5^2). When all pixels in a cell are turned off, the cell appears white; when all pixels are turned on, you get solid ink. By turning on different numbers of pixels — from 0 up to 25 — the printer can create a total of 26 shades, as demonstrated in Figure 18-7.

Figure 18-6: A detail from an image (top) is enlarged so that you can see the individual halftone cells (bottom).

Photoshop enables you to change the size, angle, and shape of the individual halftone cells used to represent an image on the printed page. To do so, click the Screen button in the Print with Preview dialog box (after clicking Show More Options and choosing Output from the pop-up menu). The Halftone Screens dialog box shown in Figure 18-8 appears.

Figure 18-7: 5×5-pixel halftone cells with different numbers of pixels activated, ranging from 25 (top left) to 0 (bottom right). Each cell represents a unique shade from 100 to 0 percent black.

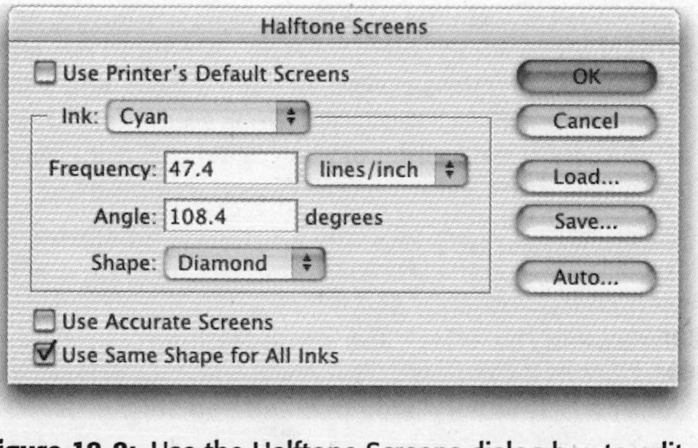

Halftone Screens

☐ Use Printer's Default Screens

Ink: Cyan

Frequency: 47.4 lines/inch

Angle: 108.4 degrees

Shape: Diamond

OK
Cancel
Load...
Save...
Auto...

☐ Use Accurate Screens
☑ Use Same Shape for All Inks

Figure 18-8: Use the Halftone Screens dialog box to edit the size, angle, and shape of the halftone cells for any one ink.

In the dialog box, you can manipulate the following options:

✦ **Use Printer's Default Screens:** Select this check box to accept the default size, angle, and shape settings built into your printer's ROM. All other options in the Halftone Screens dialog box automatically become dimmed to show they are no longer in force.

✦ **Ink:** If the current image is in color, you can select the specific ink you want to adjust from the Ink pop-up menu. When you work with a grayscale image, no pop-up menu is available.

✦ **Frequency:** Enter a new value into this option box to change the number of halftone cells that print per linear inch. A higher value translates to a larger quantity of smaller cells; a smaller value creates fewer, larger cells. Frequency is traditionally measured in *lines-per-inch*, or *lpi* (as in lines of halftone cells), but you can change the measurement to lines per centimeter by selecting Lines/cm from the pop-up menu to the right of the option box.

Higher screen frequencies result in smoother-looking printouts. Raising the Frequency value, however, also decreases the number of shades an output device can print because it decreases the size of each halftone cell and, likewise, decreases the number of printer pixels per cell. Fewer printer pixels mean fewer shades. You can calculate the precise number of printable shades using the following formula:

Number of shades = (printer resolution ÷ frequency)^2 + 1

✦ **Angle:** To change the orientation of the lines of halftone cells, enter a new value into the Angle option box. In the name of accuracy, Photoshop accepts any value between negative and positive 180 degrees.

When printing color composites to inkjet and thermal-wax printers, and when printing color separations, Photoshop calculates the optimum Frequency and Angle values required to print seamless colors. In such a case, you should change these values only if you know exactly what you're doing. Otherwise, your printout may exhibit weird patterning effects. When printing grayscale images, though, you can edit these values to your heart's content.

✦ **Shape:** By default, most PostScript printers rely on roundish halftone cells. You can change the appearance of all cells for an ink by selecting one of six alternate shapes from the Shape pop-up menu. For a demonstration of four of these shapes, see Figure 4-8 in the "Black and white (bitmap)" section of Chapter 4. If you know how to write PostScript code, you can select the Custom option to display a text-entry dialog box and code away.

✦ **Use Accurate Screens:** If your output device is equipped with PostScript Level 2 or later, select this option to subscribe to the updated screen angles for full-color output. Otherwise, don't worry about this option.

✦ **Use Same Shape for All Inks:** Select this option if you want to apply a single set of size, angle, and shape options to the halftone cells for all inks used to represent the current image. Unless you want to create some sort of special effect, leave this check box deselected. The option is unavailable when you are printing a grayscale image.

✦ **Auto:** Click this button to display the Auto Screens dialog box, which auto-mates the halftone editing process. Enter the resolution of your output device in the Printer option box. Then enter the screen frequency you want to use in the Screen option box. After you press Enter or Return to confirm your change, Photoshop automatically calculates the optimum screen frequencies for all inks. This technique is most useful when you print full-color images — because Photoshop does the work for you, you can't make a mess of things.

✦ **Load/Save:** You can load and save settings to disk in case you want to reapply the options to other images. These buttons are useful if you find a magic combination of halftone settings that results in a really spectacular printout.

Tip

You can change the default size, angle, and shape settings Photoshop applies to all future images by Alt-clicking (Win) or Option-clicking (Mac) on the Save button. When you press Alt (Win) or Option (Mac), the Save button changes to read ->Default. To restore the default screen settings at any time, Alt-click (Win) or Option-click (Mac) the Load button (<-Default).

Cross-Reference

The Halftone Screens dialog box settings don't apply only to printing images directly from Photoshop. You can export these settings along with the image for placement in QuarkXPress or some other application by saving the image in the Photoshop EPS format. Make sure you turn on the Include Halftone Screen check box in the EPS Format dialog box, as discussed in the "Saving an EPS image" section of Chapter 3. This also applies to transfer function settings, explained in the following section, "Specifying a transfer function."

Caution

If you decide to include the halftone screen information with your EPS file, be sure the settings are compatible with your intended output device. You don't want to specify a low Frequency value such as 60 lpi when printing to a state-of-the-art 3,600-dpi imagesetter, for example. If you have any questions, make certain to call your service bureau or commercial printer before saving the image. You don't want both a last-minute surprise and a hefty bill, to boot.

Specifying a transfer function

A *transfer function* enables you to change the way on-screen brightness values translate — or *map* — to printed shades. By default, brightness values print to their nearest shade percentages. A 30 percent gray pixel on screen (which equates to a brightness value of roughly 180) prints as a 30 percent gray value.

Problems arise, however, when your output device prints lighter or darker than it should. For example, in the course of using a LaserWriter NTX over the past several years — I know it's going to die one day but, until then, it keeps chugging along — I've discovered all gray values print overly dark. Dark values fill in and become black; light values appear a dismal gray, muddying up any highlights. The problem increases if I try to reproduce the image on a photocopier.

To compensate for this overdarkening effect, I click the Transfer button in the Print with Preview dialog box after clicking Show More Options and choosing Output from the pop-up menu, and then I enter the values shown in Figure 18-9. Notice I lighten 20 percent on screen grays to 10 percent printer grays. I also lighten 90 percent screen grays to 80 percent printer grays. The result is a smooth, continuous curve that maps each gray value in an image to a lighter value on paper.

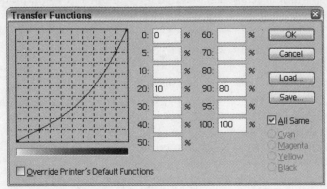

Figure 18-9: The transfer function curve enables you to map on-screen brightness values to specific shades on paper.

The options in the Transfer Functions dialog box work as follows:

✦ **Transfer graph:** The *transfer graph* is where you map on-screen brightness values to their printed equivalents. The horizontal axis of the graph represents on-screen brightness values; the vertical axis represents printed shades. The *transfer curve* charts the relationship between on-screen and printed colors. The lower-left corner is the origin of the graph—the point at which both on-screen brightness value and printed shade are white. Move to the right in the graph for darker on-screen values; move up for darker printed shades. Click in the graph to add points to the line. Drag up on a point to darken the output; drag down to lighten the output.

Cross-Reference

For a more comprehensive explanation of how to graph colors on a curve, read about the incredibly powerful Curves command, covered in Chapter 17.

✦ **Percentage option boxes:** The option boxes are labeled according to the on-screen brightness values. To lighten or darken the printed brightness values, enter higher or lower percentage values in the option boxes. There is a direct correlation between changes made to the transfer graph and the option boxes. For example, if you enter a value in the 50 percent option box, a new point appears along the middle line of the graph.

✦ **Override Printer's Default Functions:** As an effect of printer calibration, some printers have custom transfer functions built into their read-only memory (ROM). If you have problems making your settings take effect, select this check box to instruct Photoshop to apply the transfer function you specify, regardless of the output device's built-in transfer function.

✦ **Load/Save:** Use these buttons to load and save settings to disk. Alt-click (Win) or Option-click (Mac) the buttons to retrieve and save default settings.

✦ **Ink controls:** When you print a full-color image, five options appear in the lower-right corner of the Transfer Functions dialog box. These options enable you to apply different transfer functions to different inks. Select the All Same check box to apply a single transfer function to all inks. To apply a different function to each ink, deselect the check box, and then select one of the radio buttons and edit the points in the transfer graph as desired.

Printing pages

When you finish slogging your way through the Page Setup and Print with Preview dialog boxes, you can initiate the printing process by clicking the Print button in the Print with Preview dialog box or choosing File ⇨ Print. The Print dialog box appears, shown in its Mac OS X and Windows 2000 forms in Figure 18-10.

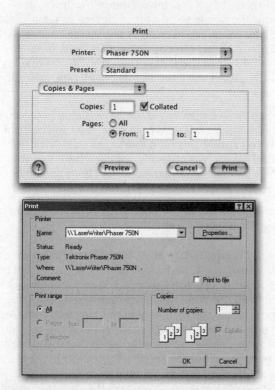

Figure 18-10: The Print dialog box as it appears in Mac OS X (top) and Windows 2000 (bottom).

Several options in this dialog box also appear in the Print with Preview dialog box or the Page Setup dialog box, both discussed earlier in this chapter. The few remaining options you need to understand work as follows:

✦ **Copies:** Enter the number of copies you want to print in this option box. You can print up to 999 copies of a single image if you want to, but I'll just bet you don't.

✦ **Print Range (or Pages on the Mac):** No such thing as a multipage document exists in Photoshop, so you can ignore these options for the most part. If you selected an image area with the rectangular marquee tool, you can print just the selected area by choosing the Selection radio button (Win) or the Print Selected Area check box (Mac). Alternatively, you can turn on the Print Selected Area check box in the Print with Preview dialog box. You may want to use this option to divide an image into pieces when it's too large to fit on a single page.

✦ **Print to File (or Destination on the Mac):** Exclusively applicable to PostScript printing, this option lets you save a PostScript-language version of the file on disk rather than printing it directly to your printer. Under Windows, deselect the Print to File option to print the image to an output device as usual. Select Print to File to write a PostScript-language version of the image to disk. To save a PostScript file to disk on the Mac, choose Output Options from the unnamed pop-up menu in the middle of the dialog box (it's the one displaying Copies & Pages in Figure 18-10), select the Save as File check box, and choose PostScript from the Format menu.

Because Photoshop offers its own EPS option via the Save dialog box, you'll probably want to ignore this option. In fact, the only reason to select Print to File (or File on the Mac) is to capture printer's marks, as I did back in Figure 18-4. If you do, a second dialog box appears, asking where you want to save the PostScript file. You can navigate just as in the Open and Save dialog boxes. For the best results, select the Binary radio button.

Mac OS X offers a handy Preview button at the bottom of the Print dialog box; clicking it will generate a PDF file of your image.

Press Enter or Return inside the Print dialog box to start the printing process on its merry way. To cancel a print in progress, click the Cancel button. If you neglect to cancel before Photoshop spools the print job, don't worry, you can still cancel. On the PC, choose Settings ➪ Printers from the Windows Start menu to display the Printers dialog box. Right-click the icon for the printer you're using and then select Open. Or you can double-click that tiny printer icon that appears on the far-right side of the taskbar. Either way, Windows shows you a window listing the current print jobs in progress. You can pause or cancel the selected print job by choosing a command from the Document menu. Here's what you do if you're using a Mac: If you're using OS 9 and your printer driver installed an icon on the desktop, double-click it. Then select the print job and click the pause button to interrupt it or click the trash can to cancel. If there is no desktop icon, check the Extensions folder in the System Folder to see if there's a Monitor utility for your printer. It may even be running as it spools, in which case you can locate it in the Applications menu on the far-right side of the screen. In OS X, you can cancel the print job from the Print Center utility, which appears in the Dock automatically when you start printing.

Printer-specific options

In addition to the options in the Page Setup and Print dialog boxes, you may be able to control certain print attributes specific to the selected printer. To explore these options from inside the Print dialog box, click the Properties button on the PC or choose the appropriate command from the middle pop-up menu on the Mac. In the case of the Phaser 750N, for example, I chose the Printer Features command on the Mac to get the dialog box shown at top in Figure 18-11; under Windows, I clicked the Properties button to display the bottom dialog box in Figure 18-11. Here I have access to additional options, such as color correction and print quality.

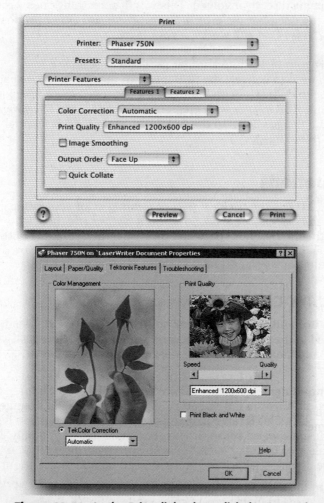

Figure 18-11: In the Print dialog box, click the Properties button (Win) or choose Printer Features from the pop-up menu (Mac) to access still more settings that are specific to the kind of printer you're using.

Creating Color Separations

Unless you're a printing professional, it's rare that you'll ever have to print color separations directly from Photoshop. You'll more likely import the image into QuarkXPress, PageMaker, InDesign, or a similar application before printing separations. It's even more likely that you'll take the image or page-layout file to a commercial printer and have a qualified technician take care of it.

So why discuss this process? Two reasons. First, it's always a good idea to at least peripherally understand all phases of the computer imaging process, even if you have no intention of becoming directly involved. This way, if something goes wrong on the printer's end, you can decipher the crux of the problem and either propose a solution or strike a compromise that still works in your favor.

Second, before you import your image into another program or submit it to a commercial printer, you'll want to convert the RGB image to the CMYK color space. (You don't absolutely *have* to do this — with Photoshop's improved color matching functions, you can exchange RGB images with greater confidence — but it's always a good idea to prepare your images down to the last detail, and CMYK is invariably the final destination for printed imagery.)

Outputting separations

Accurately converting to CMYK is the trickiest part of printing color separations; the other steps require barely any effort at all. So without further ado, here's how you convert an image to the CMYK color space and print separations. Many of the steps are the same as when printing a grayscale or color composite, others are new and different.

STEPS: Printing CMYK Color Separations

1. **Calibrate your monitor and specify the desired RGB environment.** Use the techniques discussed in the "The Gamma control panel," "The Macintosh Display Calibrator," and "Selecting the ideal working space" sections of Chapter 16.

2. **Identify the final output device.** Again, follow the advice I give in Chapter 16, this time, in the section "Custom CMYK Setup." If you're lucky, your commercial printer may provide a CMYK table that you can load. Otherwise, you'll have to grapple with some weird settings. The good news is that you only need to complete this step once for each time you switch hardware. If you always use the same commercial printer, you can set it up and forget about it.

3. **Convert the image to the CMYK color space.** Choose Image ⇨ Mode ⇨ CMYK Color to convert the image from its present color mode to CMYK.

4. **Adjust the individual color channels.** Switching color modes can dramatically affect the colors in an image. To compensate for color and focus loss, you can edit the individual color channels as described in the "Color Channel Effects" section of Chapter 4.

5. **Trap your image, if necessary.** If your image features many high-contrast elements and you're concerned your printer might not do the best job of registering the cyan, magenta, yellow, and black color plates, you can apply Image ➪ Trap to prevent your final printout from looking like the color funnies on a bad Sunday. (When working with typical "continuous-tone" photographs, you can skip this step.)

6. **Choose your printer.** Select the printer you want to use, as described earlier in this chapter.

7. **Turn on a few essential printer marks.** Choose File ➪ Page Setup or press Ctrl+Shift+P (⌘-Shift-P on the Mac) to specify the size of the pages and the size and orientation of the image on the pages, as described in "The Page Setup dialog box" section earlier in this chapter. And in the Print with Preview dialog box, also introduced earlier, be sure to select the Calibration Bars, Registration Marks, and Labels check boxes, at the very least. (You need to select the Show More Options check box and then select Output from the pop-up menu to display these options.)

8. **Adjust the halftone and transfer functions as needed.** Click the Screen and Transfer buttons in the Print with Preview dialog box to modify the halftone screen dots and map brightness values for each of the CMYK color channels, as described earlier in the "Changing the halftone screen" and "Specifying a transfer function" sections. This step is entirely optional.

9. **Send the job to the printer.** Inside the Print with Preview dialog box, make sure the Show More Options check box is turned on and choose Color Management from the pop-up menu. Then choose Separations from the Profile pop-up menu in the Print Space section of the dialog box. This tells Photoshop to print each color channel to a separate piece of paper or film. Finally, click the Print button to bring up the Print dialog box and initiate the print job.

Note

You also can create color separations by importing an image into a page-layout or drawing program. Instead of choosing your printer in Step 6, save the image in the DCS format, as described in the "QuarkXPress DCS" section of Chapter 3.

Steps 6 through 9 are repeats of concepts explained in previous sections of this chapter. Steps 1 through 4 were covered at length in Chapters 4 and 16. This leaves Step 5 — trapping — which I explain in the following section.

Color trapping

If color separations misalign slightly during the reproduction process (a problem called *misregistration*), the final image can exhibit slight gaps between colors. Suppose an image features a 100 percent cyan chicken against a 100 percent magenta background. (Pretty attractive image idea, huh? Go ahead, you can use it if you like.) If the cyan and magenta plates don't line up exactly, you're left with a chicken with a white halo partially around it. Yuck.

A *trap* is a little extra bit of color that fills in the gap. For example, if you choose Image ⇨ Trap and enter 4 into the Width option box, Photoshop outlines the chicken with an extra 4 pixels of cyan and the background with an extra 4 pixels of magenta. Now the registration can be off a full 8 pixels without any halo occurring.

Continuous-tone images, such as photographs and natural-media painting, don't need trapping because no harsh color transitions occur. In fact, trapping actually harms such images by thickening up the borders and edges, smudging detail, and generally dulling the focus.

One of the primary reasons to use the Trap command, therefore, is to trap raster-ized drawings from Illustrator or FreeHand. Some state-of-the-art prepress systems trap documents by first rasterizing them to pixels and then modifying the pixels. Together, Photoshop and Illustrator (or FreeHand) constitute a more rudimentary but, nonetheless, functional trapping system. When you open an illustration in Photoshop, the program converts it into an image according to your size and resolution specifications, as described in the "Rasterizing an Illustrator or FreeHand file" section of Chapter 3. Once the illustration is rasterized, you can apply Image ⇨ Trap to the image as a whole. Despite the command's simplicity, it handles nearly all trapping scenarios, even going so far as to reduce the width of the trap incrementally as the colors of neighboring areas grow more similar.

If you plan on having a service bureau trap your files for you, do not apply Photoshop's Trap command. You don't want to see what happens when someone traps an image that's already been trapped. If you're paying the extra bucks for professional trapping, leave it to the pros.

Printing Duotones

It's been a few pages since the "Understanding Printing Terminology" section, so here's a quick recap: A *duotone* is a grayscale image printed with two inks. This technique expands the depth of the image by allowing additional shades for high-lights, shadows, and midtones. If you've seen a glossy magazine ad for perfume, designer clothing, a car, or just about any other overpriced commodity, you've seen a duotone. Words like *rich*, *luxurious*, and *palpable* come to mind.

Photoshop also enables you to add a third ink to create a tritone and a fourth ink to create a quadtone. Color Plate 18-1 shows an example of each of these. Figure 18-12 shows a detail from the image printed in its original grayscale form. See the difference?

Figure 18-12: A sheet of imperforate souvenir stamps from 1936, scanned in grayscale on a Umax PowerLook 3000 desktop scanner.

Creating a duotone

To convert a grayscale image to a duotone, tritone, or quadtone, choose Image ➪ Mode ➪ Duotone. Photoshop displays the Duotone Options dialog box shown in Figure 18-13. By default, Monotone is the active Type option, and the Ink 2, Ink 3, and Ink 4 options are dimmed. To access the Ink 2, 3, and 4 options, select Duotone, Tritone, and Quadtone, respectively, from the Type pop-up menu.

Specify the color of each ink you want to use by clicking the color swatch associated with the desired ink option. You can define colors with the Color Picker or with the Custom Colors dialog box; it's easy to switch back and forth between the two by clicking the Custom or the Picker button, depending on which dialog box you currently are using.

Photoshop takes the guesswork out of creating a duotone by previewing your settings in the image window when the Preview check box is turned on. Keep in mind that the preview may not exactly match your output when using certain Pantone inks. (This is a common problem when previewing Pantone inks in any program, but it's always a good idea to keep in mind, particularly because Photoshop mixes inks to create its duotone effects.) The next time you create a duotone, Photoshop displays the same colors you defined in your last visit to the Duotone Options dialog box.

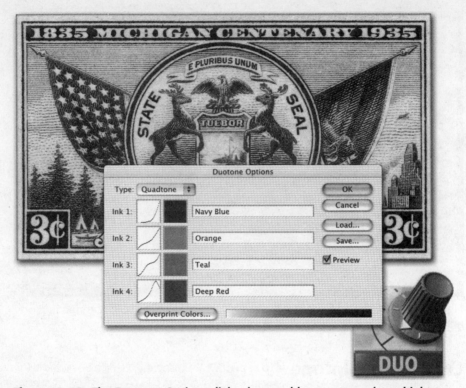

Figure 18-13: The Duotone Options dialog box enables you to apply multiple inks to a grayscale image.

When creating duotones, tritones, and quadtones, prioritize your inks in order — from darkest at the top to lightest at the bottom — when you specify them in the Duotone Options dialog box. Because Photoshop prints inks in the order they appear in the dialog box, the inks print from darkest to lightest. This ensures rich highlights and shadows and a uniform color range.

After selecting a color, you can use either of two methods to specify how the differently colored inks blend. The first and more dependable way is to click the curve box associated with the desired ink option. Photoshop then displays the Duotone Curve dialog box, which works just like the Transfer Functions dialog box described back in the "Specifying a transfer function" section of this chapter. This method permits you to emphasize specific inks in different portions of the image according to brightness values.

For example, Figure 18-13 shows the inks and curve settings assigned to the quadtone in Color Plate 18-1. The Navy Blue color is associated only with the darkest brightness values in the image; Deep Red peaks at about 80 percent gray and then descends; Teal covers the midtones in the image; Orange is strongest in the light values. The four colors mix to form an image whose brightness values progress from light orange to olive green to brick red to black.

The second method for controlling the blending of colors is to click the Overprint Colors button. An Overprint Colors dialog box appears, showing how each pair of colors will mix when printed. Other color swatches show how three and four colors mix, if applicable. To change the color swatch, click it to display the Color Picker dialog box.

The problem with this second method is it complicates the editing process. Photoshop doesn't actually change the ink colors or curve settings in keeping with your new specifications; it just applies the new overprint colors without any logical basis. And you lose all changes made with the Overprint Colors dialog box when you adjust any of the ink colors or any of the curves.

To return and change the colors or curves, choose Image ⇨ Mode ⇨ Duotone again. Instead of reconverting the image, the command now lets you edit the existing duotone, tritone, or quadtone.

Reproducing a duotone

If you want a commercial printer to reproduce a duotone, tritone, or quadtone, you must print the image to color separations, just like a CMYK image. Because you already specified which inks to use and how much of each ink to apply, however, you needn't mess around with all those commands in the Color Settings dialog box. Just take the following familiar steps:

STEPS: Printing a Duotone, Tritone, or Quadtone

1. **Choose the printer you want to use.** Select a printer as described previously in this chapter.

2. **Set the page size, orientation, and printer marks options.** In the Page Setup dialog box (Ctrl+Shift+P or ⌘-Shift-P), specify the size of the pages and the size and orientation of the image on the pages, as described in "The Page Setup dialog box" section earlier in this chapter. Then select the Registration Marks option in the Print with Preview dialog box (Ctrl+P or ⌘-P).

3. **Adjust the halftone screens, if desired.** If you're feeling inventive, click the Screen button to change the size, angle, and shape of the halftone screen dots for the individual color plates, as described previously in the "Changing the halftone screen" section.

4. **Specify output to color separations.** Still inside the Print with Preview dialog box, choose Color Management from the pop-up menu. Then choose the Separations option from the Profile pop-up menu in the Print Space section of the dialog box to print each ink to a separate sheet of paper or film.

To prepare a duotone to be imported into QuarkXPress, Illustrator, or some other application, save the image in the EPS format, as described in the "Saving an EPS image" section of Chapter 3. As listed back in Table 4-1 of Chapter 4, EPS is the only file format other than the native Photoshop format that supports duotones, tritones, and quadtones.

Editing individual duotone plates

If you'll be printing your duotone using CMYK colors and you can't quite get the effect you want inside the Duotone Options dialog box, you can convert the duotone to the CMYK mode by choosing Image ➪ Mode ➪ CMYK Color. Not only will all the duotone shades remain intact, but you'll also have the added advantage of being able to tweak colors and to add color using Photoshop's standard color-correction commands and editing tools. You can even edit individual color channels, as described in Chapter 4.

If your duotone includes Pantone or other spot colors, converting to CMYK is not an option. But you can still access and edit the individual color channels. To separate the duotone inks into channels, choose Image ➪ Mode ➪ Multichannel. Each ink appears as a separate spot color inside the Channels palette, as shown in Figure 18-14. You can experiment with different color combinations by turning eyeball icons on and off. You can even switch out one spot color for another by double-clicking on the channel name and then clicking the color swatch.

To save a duotone converted to the multichannel mode, you have just two options: native Photoshop (as always) and DCS 2.0. For complete information on the latter, read the "QuarkXPress DCS" section in Chapter 3.

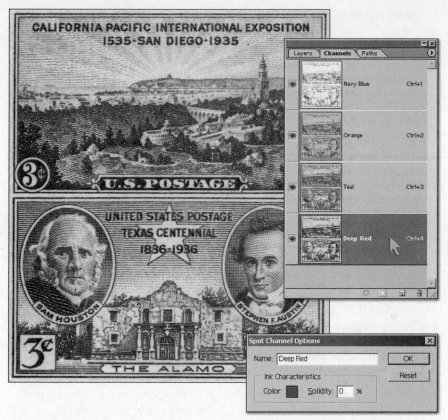

Figure 18-14: Here I chose Image ⇨ Mode ⇨ Multichannel to separate my quadtone into four independent spot-color channels, and then double-clicked the Deep Red channel to access the Spot Channel Options dialog box.

Spot-Color Separations

Photoshop permits you to add spot colors to your images. Although it's unlikely that you'll use spot colors to widen the gamut of your photographs — after all, scanners can't scan spot colors and Photoshop can't automatically lift them out of, say, the RGB color space — you may want to toss in a spot color to highlight a logo, a line of type, and some other special element.

For example, suppose you have a full-color image of a jet ski. The logo along the side of the boat is fully visible, just as the client wants it, but the color is off. Normally, the logo appears in Pantone 265 purple. But the CMYK equivalent for this color looks about three shades darker, four shades redder, and several times muddier. The only solution is to assign the proper spot color — Pantone 265 — to the logo. The following steps tell how:

STEPS: Adding a Spot Color to an Image

1. **Select the logo.** You can use the magic wand tool or a more exacting method, as described in Chapters 8 and 9.

2. **Fill the selection with white.** Press D to get the default foreground and background colors and then press Ctrl+Backspace (⌘-Delete on the Mac). It's important that you erase the old logo so that it appears in pure spot color without any mixing with the CMYK inks. But do *not* deselect your selection! It must remain active for Step 5 to work.

3. **Create a new spot channel.** As explained in Chapter 4, the easiest way to do this is to Ctrl-click (Win) or ⌘-click (Mac) the page icon at the bottom of the Channels palette. But you can also choose New Spot Channel from the Channels palette menu if you prefer.

4. **Set the color to Pantone 265.** Click the Color swatch in the New Spot Channel dialog box. Then select Pantone 265 from the Custom Colors dialog box. (If the Color Picker comes up instead, click the Custom button.)

5. **Press Enter or Return or click OK twice.** Photoshop adds the new spot color to the Channels palette and fills the selection. Your logo automatically appears in the spot color. (Cool, huh?)

6. **Choose Image ⇨ Trap.** It's a good idea to trap the spot color so that it covers up any gaps that may result from misregistration. Enter a value of 1 or 2 pixels and press Enter or Return. Photoshop spreads the logo but leaves the CMYK image alone. Very intelligent program, that Photoshop.

7. **Save the image.** You have two choices of formats, native Photoshop or DCS 2.0. If you want to import the image into a different program, use the latter.

Naturally, you don't want to trust Photoshop's on-screen representation of the spot color any more than you would in Illustrator, QuarkXPress, or any other program. The screen version is an approximation, nothing more. So it's a good idea to have a Pantone swatch book on hand so that you know exactly what the color should look like when printed. (If the printed logo doesn't match the swatch book, it's the printer's fault, not Photoshop's.)

Printing Contact Sheets

In a previous edition of this book, I came down pretty hard on Photoshop's Contact Sheet command, and for good reason. At the time I wrote about the command, it was a big mess. Fortunately, my last sentence — "My guess is that we can expect better things from this command in the future" — turned out to be prescient, for nowadays we have Contact Sheet II.

Choose File ➪ Automate ➪ Contact Sheet II to display the dialog box shown in Figure 18-15. These options permit you to take a folder of images and arrange them as thumbnails on a page, greatly expediting the creation of image catalogs. You specify the location of the folder, the number of columns and rows in the grid, and the color mode, and Photoshop does the rest. Contact Sheet II adds the ability to look into folders inside the specified folder (very useful) and label image thumbnails according to their file names (even more useful). You can even select the typeface and type size for the labels from the Font and Font Size pop-up menus. Figure 18-16 shows the result of applying the settings from Figure 18-15, with a few elements I added later by hand. With a little work after the fact, Contact Sheet II is a great choice for creating full photo album pages and the like.

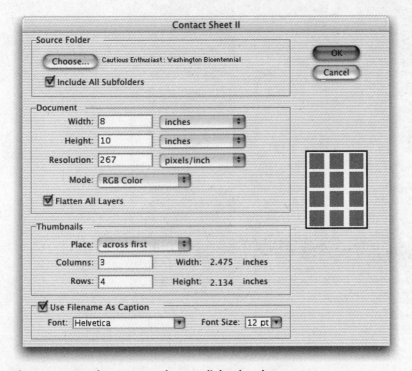

Figure 18-15: The Contact Sheet II dialog box lets you label thumbnails with their corresponding file names.

Contact Sheet II is better than its predecessor, but if you ask me, there's still room for improvement. For example, I'd like control over gutter and spacing, attributes that Contact Sheet II addresses automatically. But until the next sequel, Contact Sheet III comes out, it'll have to do.

Figure 18-16: Because the Contact Sheet II thumbnails are created on a separate layer, it's easy to add custom backgrounds, such as the pattern I used here.

In addition to Contact Sheet II, Photoshop offers two other commands under the File ⇨ Automate submenu that organize multiple images onto a single page:

✦ **Picture Package:** Formerly limited to dealing with a single image, this command can now fill a page with multiple copies of multiple images scaled to common print sizes such as 5×7 inches, 4×5 inches, and wallet snapshots. If you're a photographer, or you simply want to print some pictures of the kids for Grandma, this command does it all. After choosing a layout from the Layout menu, you can replace any image in the layout with a different one by clicking the image thumbnail in the preview to bring up the Select an Image File dialog box.

The new Label section of the Picture Package dialog box, shown in Figure 18-17, lets you add text to your image. The options are pretty self-explanatory, but it's worth pointing out that the Custom Text option box is a welcome addition. It keeps you from having to quit the Picture Package command to jump over to File ⇨ File Info just so you can enter a caption.

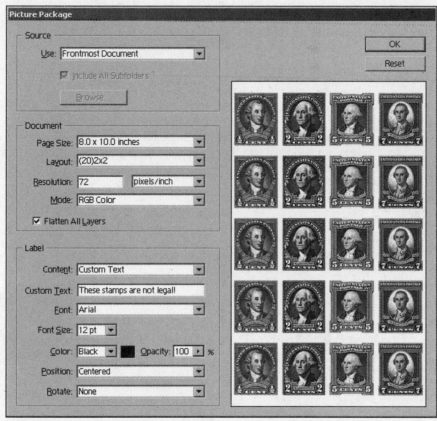

Figure 18-17: Picture Package tiles images for printing on a single sheet of paper. Somewhere a tree is saying "Thank you."

✦ **Web Photo Gallery:** Again geared toward professional and aspiring photographers, this command assembles a folder of images into a Web site, complete with HTML pages and JPEG images. In the Web Photo Gallery dialog box, shown in Figure 18-18, first select a page style from the Styles pop-up menu. The preview on the right side of the dialog box shows a sample page created using that style. You can also enter an e-mail contact and choose between the *.htm* and *.html* extensions. You can make further design choices by selecting the various items in the Options pop-up menu. For each item, you get a different set of accompanying design options:

• **Banner** enables you to name your page and add the photographer's name, contact info, and the date. You also can select the font and type size for these items.

- **Large Images** provides options for adding a border around your images, resizing images, adding titles, and applying JPEG compression.

- **Thumbnails** lets you specify such options as the thumbnail size and the number of columns and rows of thumbnails. You can also add borders around the thumbnails, add captions based either on the image file name or the caption info entered in the File Info dialog box, and specify a font type and size.

- **Custom Colors** enables you to set the colors for the page background, banner, text, and links.

- **Security** lets you create a text message that will be embedded into each image, making people much less likely to steal the images from your Web site for their own nefarious purposes. You can enter custom text, use the File Info caption or the name of the file, choose the placement of the text, and choose whether you want the text to be rotated at an angle on the image.

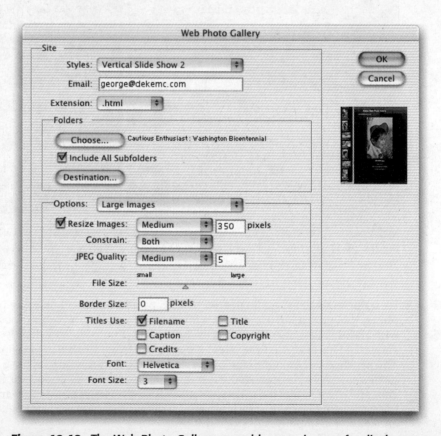

Figure 18-18: The Web Photo Gallery assembles your images for display on a Web page.

The Folders options let you choose a folder of images for use in your Web photo gallery, allow you to determine whether to include folders nestled within that folder, and also pick where the resulting files should finally end up. Figure 18-19 shows a Web page created with the settings from Figure 18-18. In case you're curious, these stamps were created in 1932, to mark the bicentenary of George Washington's birth.

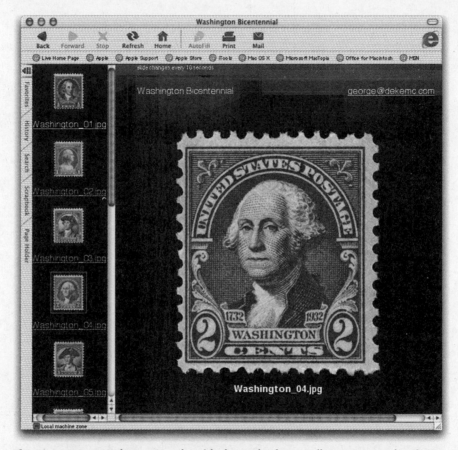

Figure 18-19: A Web page made with the Web Photo Gallery command, using one of the new slide show Styles. The large image changes every ten seconds.

Web pages created via the Web Photo Gallery command aren't going to win any design awards, but the command is easy to navigate and it gets the job done. And if you know a little HTML, you can use the pages as a jumping off point for a more-sophisticated site.

Tip

Photoshop also lets you define custom Web Photo Gallery page styles. Using an HTML editor, you can create a batch of HTML files that contain the instructions for formatting the various elements of the page. To get an idea of how to build your custom style, take a look at the HTML files provided for the Photoshop default styles, found in the Presets\WebContactSheet folder. After creating your custom pages, store them together in a new styles folder in the WebContactSheet folder.

✦   ✦   ✦

Shortcuts and Modifiers

Unlike most graphics programs, Photoshop invests a lot of its capabilities in the keyboard. Literally hundreds of functions are available exclusively at the press of a key. For example, Photoshop provides no menu command that lets you delete multiple layers at a time. There is no command that hides all palettes, nor is there an option that brings up the last-used color-correction settings. Every one of these options is out of your reach if you don't know the right key. The keyboard may seem like an unlikely artistic tool, but it is both a powerful and an essential ally in Photoshop.

There are two basic varieties of keyboard tricks:

+ **Shortcuts:** Some keystroke combinations produce immediate effects. For example, pressing Ctrl and Backspace together (⌘ and Delete on the Mac) fills the selection with the background color.

+ **Modifiers:** Other keys change the behavior of a tool or command. Pressing Shift while dragging with the lasso tool adds the lassoed area to the previous selection. As a result, Shift, Alt, and Ctrl are known collectively as *modifiers*.

Naturally, I discuss both in meticulous detail throughout this chapter. With a keen mind and a little practice, you'll be driving your new Model 7 Photoshop at speeds that would land your butt in jail in the real world.

Hidden Shortcuts and Modifiers

Shortcuts permit you to initiate operations without resorting to the laborious task of choosing commands from menus or clicking a tool icon until your arm falls off. Some shortcuts are fairly obvious. For example, Photoshop lists shortcuts for its commands next to the command in the menu. You can choose File ➪ New by pressing Ctrl+N (⌘-N on the Mac), choose Edit ➪ Undo by pressing Ctrl+Z (or ⌘-Z), choose Select ➪ All by pressing Ctrl+A (⌘-A), and so on. But many of Photoshop's shortcuts are hidden. And, wouldn't you know it, the hidden ones are the most essential.

Alt-key combos

Under Windows (sorry Mac folks) you can perform many operations using so-called hot keys, which are the underlined letters you see in menus and dialog boxes. To access one of these functions, press Alt plus the underlined letter. This can be very useful when choosing commands that lack a Ctrl-key shortcut. For example, to choose Image ➪ Adjustments ➪ Channel Mixer, press Alt+I, then A, and then X. Once inside the Channel Mixer dialog box, you can press Alt+G to select the Green value, Alt+B for Blue, and so on.

You can even access commands that have no underlines. To choose Filter ➪ Sharpen ➪ Unsharp Mask, for example, press Alt+T to bring up the Filter menu, S to highlight Sharpen, Enter to display the Sharpen submenu, and U to choose Unsharp Mask. For Filter ➪ Stylize ➪ Extrude, press Alt+T, S, S, S, Enter, E, E, Enter. I know, it's weird, but try it out a few times and you'll get a feel for how it works. You may love it, you may hate it — it's totally up to you.

You can also waltz through the menus with the arrow keys. After you press Alt plus the underlined letter to display a menu, use the up and down arrows to highlight commands in the menu. Use the left and right arrows to display neighboring menus. To choose a highlighted command, press Enter. To hide the menus and return focus to the image window, press Escape twice.

Under OS X on the Mac, you can arrow through the menus, though for my money, it's hardly intuitive. First press Control-F1. (Or choose System Preferences from the Apple menu, click the Keyboard icon, and turn on Full Keyboard Access.) Then press Control-F2 to highlight the menu bar. Now you're ready to use the arrow keys as described in the previous paragraph.

The shortcut menu

One of the best hidden tricks in Photoshop is right-clicking. If you use a Mac and your mouse doesn't offer a right button, press the Control key and click. When you click the right mouse button (or Control-click) inside the image window, Photoshop displays a shortcut menu of commands tailored to your current activity. For example, if you right-click with the lasso tool while a selection is active, you get the list of commands shown in Figure A-1. Although you can apply other commands to a selection, these are some of the most common.

Deselect
Select Inverse
Feather...

Save Selection...
Make Work Path...

Layer via Copy
Layer via Cut
New Layer...

Free Transform
Transform Selection

Fill...
Stroke...

Unsharp Mask
Fade Unsharp Mask...

Figure A-1: If you grow confused and wonder where you are, right-click to bring up a shortcut menu of helpful commands.

The shortcut menu is *context-sensitive*, which means it changes to suit the active tool and the current state of the image (selected or not). You can also access context-sensitive pop-up menus inside many of the palettes. For example, right-click a layer name in the Layers palette to see a list of actions you can perform on that layer.

Tip

As with the regular menus, you can press the up and down arrow keys to highlight commands in the context-sensitive pop-up menus. To choose a command, press Enter. To hide the menu, press Escape.

Toolbox shortcuts

Usability has always been one of Photoshop's great strengths. One of the ways Photoshop expedites your workflow is to let you select tools from the keyboard. This way, you can use one tool, press a key, and immediately start in with another tool without losing your place in the image. Best of all, the shortcuts work even when the toolbox is hidden. Most of the time, the only reason I even look at the toolbox is to monitor which tool is selected.

Figure A-2 tells the whole, wonderful story. Press the appropriate key, as shown in the figure—no Ctrl, Option, or other modifier required. Many of the shortcuts make sense. M selects the marquee tool, L is for lasso tool. But then there are the weird ones, such as O for dOdge, R for bluR, and my favorite, I for I-dropper.

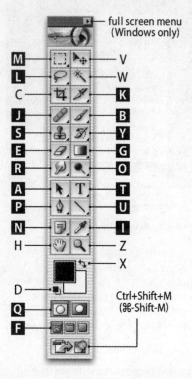

Figure A-2: Press these keys to select tools and activate controls. The white bold letters indicate keys that toggle between alternate tools or settings.

Letters shown in bold reverse switch between one or more tools that share a common slot. By default, you have to press Shift in combination with one of these letters to toggle to an alternative tool. But you can eliminate the need for Shift by choosing Edit ⇨ Preferences ⇨ General (Ctrl+K) and turning off the Use Shift Key for Tool Switch check box, as explained in Chapter 2.

Only one tool shortcut has changed in Photoshop 7, and that's J. Where it used to select the airbrush, it now toggles between the healing brush and the patch tool. Meanwhile, you press Shift+Alt+P (Shift-Option-P) to turn on the airbrush setting when it's available, as when using the brush tool.

Notice that the top of the toolbox in Figure A-2 sports a small pop-up menu arrow. You probably don't see this on your toolbox because it's usually hidden. If you use a PC (alas, it's not available on the Mac), press the F key twice to view the image against a black backdrop. Assuming the menu bar is hidden, click the right-pointing arrow at the top of the toolbox to open a top-secret stash that includes every single one of Photoshop's commands. It is the very essence of coolness.

Palette shortcuts

Photoshop also lets you access palette options from the keyboard. I've documented these options in the following list. As with the tool keys, each of these shortcuts works even when the palette is hidden:

✦ **Palette function keys:** Press F5 to show or hide the Brushes palette. Press F6, F7, F8, or F9 to toggle the display of the Color, Layers, Info, or Actions palette, respectively. If for some weird reason the Options bar is hidden, press the Enter or Return key to bring it back.

✦ **Hide or show all palettes:** Press Tab to hide or show all palettes, including the toolbox, Options bar, and the status bar on the PC. To hide or show the standard palettes only—that is, everything except the toolbox, Options bar, and the status bar—press Shift+Tab.

✦ **Brush size:** Press a bracket key, [or], to decrease or increase the brush size when a paint or edit tool is active.

✦ **Brush hardness:** Press Shift with a bracket key to change the hardness of a brush. Shift+] gives the brush a sharper edge; Shift+[makes it softer. Again, a paint or edit tool must be active.

✦ **Brush preset:** Press the comma (,) and period (.) keys to cycle between preset brushes. If this doesn't work for you, try pressing Shift+comma, which selects the first preset, the single-pixel brush. Then press period to move forward. Shift+period jumps to the last of the preset brushes.

✦ **Gradient style:** Select the gradient tool and press [or] to switch between the five gradient styles.

✦ **Gradient preset:** Press the comma or period key to step backward or forward through the predefined gradients. Press Shift+comma or Shift+period to switch to the first or last gradient in the list.

◆ **Shape layer styles:** Select any of the shape tools and press the comma or period key to step backward or forward through the predefined layer styles. Press Shift+comma or Shift+period to jump to the first or last style in the list.

◆ **Shape attribute:** With the rounded rectangle tool active, press the [or] to decrease and increase the corner radius. Select the polygon tool and press [or] to decrease and increase the number of sides in the next polygon or star you draw. For the line tool, [or] decreases or increases the line weight.

◆ **Custom shape preset:** Select the custom shape tool and press [or] to step backward or forward through the predefined shapes. Press Shift+[and Shift+] to switch to the first or last shape in the list.

◆ **Brush opacity:** When a paint or edit tool is active, press a number key to change the Opacity, Strength, or Exposure value in the Options bar. Press 1 to change the value to 10 percent, 2 for 20 percent, up to 0 for 100 percent. Or enter an exact value by typing two numbers in a row. For example, type 87 for 87 percent or 05 for 5 percent.

◆ **Airbrush:** If a tool offers an airbrush icon in the Options bar, press Shift+Alt+P (Shift-Option-P on the Mac) to turn it on or off.

◆ **Airbrush flow:** If a tool offers the airbrush, it includes both an Opacity value and a Flow value. When the airbrush is turned off, press Shift with a number key to change the Flow value. When the airbrush is on, press a number key to change the Flow value; press Shift with a number key to change the Opacity value.

◆ **Layer opacity:** When any tool other than a paint or an edit tool is selected — that is, any tool in the first, third, or fourth group in the toolbox — pressing a number key changes the Opacity value for the active layer. Again, press one number to modify the Opacity setting in 10-percent increments; press two numbers to specify an exact Opacity setting.

◆ **Fill opacity:** Press Shift with a number key to change the Fill value for the active layer, which modifies the opacity of the pixels in a layer without affecting the layer effects.

◆ **Brush mode:** When a paint or an edit tool is active, you can cycle through brush modes by pressing Shift+plus (+) or Shift+minus (–). Shift+plus takes you down the brush mode pop-up menu and Shift+minus takes you back up.

◆ **Blend mode:** When some other tool is selected, Shift+plus and minus affect the blend mode applied to the active layer. You can also access a particular blend mode by pressing Shift and Alt (or Option) with a letter key. For example, Shift+Alt+M selects the Multiply mode; Shift+Alt+S selects Screen; Shift+Alt+N takes you back to Normal.

✦ **Lock setting:** Press the forward slash (/) to turn on and off the Lock icon that controls transparency inside the Layers palette. If one or more of the Lock icons is already active, press / to turn off all four. Press / again to return the options to their former configuration. Layer locking can be extremely useful for protecting the contents of layers, as I explain in the "Locking layers" section of Chapter 12.

✦ **Switch layer:** Press Alt+] to ascend through the layers. Press Alt+[to descend. Press Shift+Alt+] to activate the top layer in the composition. Press Shift+Alt+[to go all the way down to the bottom of the stack, usually the Background layer.

✦ **Arrange layer:** Press Ctrl+] (or ⌘-] on the Mac) to move the active layer one level forward in the stack; press Ctrl+[to move it back. Press Ctrl+Shift+] to move the layer to the top of the stack. Press Ctrl+Shift+[to move it to the bottom, usually just in front of the Background layer.

The Great-Grandmother of All Shortcut Tables

Since its inception, the *Photoshop Bible* has offered a shortcuts table. But it wasn't until the *Photoshop 4 Bible* that I decided to really pull out the stops and expand the table from a mere four pages to five times that size and growing. That's also when I gave the table its present name. Naturally, I have to tip my hat to Saddam Hussein. Though regarded by most sane people in the universe as an unsavory character — Have you ever noticed all bad men have mustaches? Does it prevent them from breathing properly, I wonder? — you have to give him credit for that "mother of all battles" thing. English isn't even the guy's first language, yet he added a colorful catch phrase to it. Saddam, wicked rodent though he is, has a gift for the turn of phrase.

Even so, that "mother" thing doesn't quite do justice to Table A-1, which lists nearly every keystroke and modifier available to Photoshop 7. This table is so huge and all-encompassing, I am quite convinced it would frighten Saddam Hussein into a power-sharing scenario. In fact, the whole Axis of Evil would probably fall to pieces were this document to fall into the right hands. With 17 categories and more than 300 entries, this table is so grand and filled to the brim with real shortcutty goodness that it skips two whole generations and reaches great-grandmother status.

A few things you should know

Naturally, if you think you might be even a tiny bit evil, you should refrain from reading this table. I wouldn't go so far as to call it righteous; it's just terribly decent. But even those of you with virtuous minds and pure hearts would do well to take heed of a few words of advice.

First, a shortcut won't make much sense if you aren't familiar with the feature it facilitates. I explain both specific features and their shortcuts in context in other chapters. The intent of this table is to serve as a reference you can visit and revisit as your knowledge of Photoshop grows. The more you learn, the more useful the table becomes.

Second, don't press Shift just because a key combination involves a character that normally requires the Shift key. For example, the shortcut for the Zoom In command is Ctrl+plus (⌘-plus on the Mac). Technically, + is the Shifted version of =, so a literal person might think you have to press Ctrl+Shift+=. But the literal person would be wrong, as literal people so often are. The plus sign is used because it implies zooming while the equal sign does not. So when you see Ctrl+plus, just press Ctrl+=.

Third, if you're a Windows user, note that many of Photoshop's keyboard shortcuts involve both the Ctrl and Alt keys. Ctrl+Alt+O invokes the Open As command, Ctrl+Alt+Z undoes an operation from the History palette. Unfortunately, this isn't entirely kosher with Microsoft. Windows likes to reserve Ctrl+Alt combinations to launch applications. For example, let's say you set Ctrl+Alt+Z to launch Nico Mak's popular WinZip. (In case you're unclear how to do this, create a shortcut icon for WinZip. Then right-click the shortcut icon, choose Properties, click the Shortcut tab, and enter Z into the Shortcut Key option box.) From this point on, Windows snags the keystrokes before Photoshop can react to it. So rather than undoing an operation, Ctrl+Alt+Z launches WinZip. The only way to avoid this conflict is to steer clear of the keys Photoshop uses — B, D, E, F, J, K, L, M, N, O, P, S, T, U, W, X, Z, plus, minus, semicolon, and zero through nine — when assigning file-launching shortcuts.

Ready to roll out

So there you have it. You've been briefed, you've been prepped, you've signed all the legal waivers. Now it's time to dive right in and get shortcuts all over you. Throughout the table, operations are listed in the left-hand column. You Windows people will find your shortcuts in the center column. You crazy Macintosh people (crazy like a fox, that is), look to the right-hand column. Incidentally, it's been nice knowing you. This is the last time you'll be hearing from me, so best of luck in there.

Table A-1
Photoshop's Shortcuts and Modifiers

Operation	Windows Shortcut	Macintosh Shortcut
Menu commands		
Actual Pixels	Ctrl+Alt+zero (0)	⌘-Option-zero (0)
Auto Color	Ctrl+ Shift+B	⌘-Shift-B
Auto Contrast	Ctrl+Shift+Alt+L	⌘-Shift-Option-L

Operation	*Windows Shortcut*	*Macintosh Shortcut*
Auto Levels	Ctrl+Shift+L	⌘-Shift-L
Bring Layer Forward	Ctrl+]	⌘-]
Bring Layer to Front	Ctrl+Shift+]	⌘-]
Browse	Ctrl+Shift+O	⌘-Shift-O
Canvas Size	right-click title bar	*none*
Clear	Backspace or Delete	Delete
Close	Ctrl+W or Ctrl+F4	⌘-W
Close All	Ctrl+Shift+W or Ctrl+Shift+F4	⌘-Option-W
Color Balance	Ctrl+B	⌘-B
Color Balance, with last settings	Ctrl+Alt+B	⌘-Option-B
Color Settings	Ctrl+Shift+K	⌘-Shift-K
Copy	Ctrl+C	⌘-C
Copy Merged	Ctrl+Shift+C	⌘-Shift-C
Curves	Ctrl+M	⌘-M
Curves, with last settings	Ctrl+Alt+M	⌘-Option-M
Cut	Ctrl+X	⌘-X
Desaturate	Ctrl+Shift+U	⌘-Shift-U
Deselect	Ctrl+D	⌘-D
Duplicate	click the left-hand icon at bottom of History palette or right-click title bar	click the left-hand icon at bottom of History palette
Exit/Quit	Ctrl+Q or Alt+F4	⌘-Q
Extract	Ctrl+Alt+X	⌘-Option-X
Fade last operation	Ctrl+Shift+F	⌘-Shift-F
Feather selection	Ctrl+Alt+D	⌘-Option-D
File Info	right-click title bar	*none*
Fill	Shift+Backspace	Shift-Delete
Fill from history	Ctrl+Alt+Backspace	⌘-Option-Delete
Filter, repeat last	Ctrl+F	⌘-F

Continued

Table A-1 *(continued)*

Operation	Windows Shortcut	Macintosh Shortcut
Filter, repeat with new settings	Ctrl+Alt+F	⌘-Option-F
Fit on Screen	Ctrl+zero (0)	⌘-zero (0)
Free Transform	Ctrl+T	⌘-T
Free Transform, from clone	Ctrl+Alt+T	⌘-Option-T
Gamut Warning	Ctrl+Shift+Y	⌘-Shift-Y
Group with Previous layer	Ctrl+G	⌘-G
Help Contents	F1	⌘-Shift-?
Hue/Saturation	Ctrl+U	⌘-U
Hue/Saturation, with last settings	Ctrl+Alt+U	⌘-Option-U
Image Size	right-click title bar	*none*
Inverse Selection	Ctrl+Shift+I	⌘-Shift-I
Invert	Ctrl+I	⌘-I
Layer Via Copy	Ctrl+J	⌘-J
Layer Via Cut	Ctrl+Shift+J	⌘-Shift-J
Levels	Ctrl+L	⌘-L
Levels, with last settings	Ctrl+Alt+L	⌘-Option-L
Liquify	Ctrl+Shift+X	⌘-Shift-X
Lock Guides	Ctrl+Alt+semicolon (;)	⌘-Option-semicolon (;)
Merge Down/ Linked/Layer Set	Ctrl+E	⌘-E
Merge copy into layer below	Ctrl+Alt+E	⌘-Option-E
Merge Visible	Ctrl+Shift+E	⌘-Shift-E
Merge Visible, into current layer	Ctrl+Shift+Alt+E	⌘-Shift-Option-E
New	Ctrl+N	⌘-N
New, with default settings	Ctrl+Alt+N	⌘-Option-N
New Layer	Ctrl+Shift+N	⌘-Shift-N

Operation	*Windows Shortcut*	*Macintosh Shortcut*
New Layer, skip options	Ctrl+Shift+Alt+N	⌘-Shift-Option-N
Open	Ctrl+O	⌘-O
Open As	Ctrl+Alt+O	⌘-O
Page Setup	Ctrl+Shift+P	⌘-Shift-P
Paste	Ctrl+V or F4	⌘-V or F4
Paste Into	Ctrl+Shift+V	⌘-Shift-V
Pattern Maker	Ctrl+Shift+Alt+X	⌘-Shift-Option-X
Preferences	Ctrl+K	⌘-K
Preferences, last panel	Ctrl+Alt+K	⌘-Option-K
Print	Ctrl+Alt+P	⌘-Option-P
Print One Copy	Ctrl+Shift+Alt+P	⌘-Shift-Option-P
Print with Preview	Ctrl+P	⌘-P
Proof Colors	Ctrl+Y	⌘-Y
Redo	Ctrl+Z	⌘-Z
Reselect	Ctrl+Shift+D	⌘-Shift-D
Revert	F12	F12
Rulers, show or hide	Ctrl+R	⌘-R
Save	Ctrl+S	⌘-S
Save As	Ctrl+Shift+S	⌘-Shift-S
Save as a copy	Ctrl+Alt+S	⌘-Option-S
Save For Web	Ctrl+Shift+Alt+S	⌘-Shift-Option-S
Select All	Ctrl+A	⌘-A
Send Layer Backward	Ctrl+[	⌘-[
Send Layer to Back	Ctrl+Shift+[	⌘-Shift-[
Show Extras (for example, selection edges, slices, annotation)	Ctrl+H	⌘-H
Show/Hide Grid	Ctrl+Alt+quote (")	⌘-Option-quote (")
Show/Hide Guides	Ctrl+semicolon (;)	⌘-semicolon (;)

Continued

Table A-1 (continued)

Operation	Windows Shortcut	Macintosh Shortcut
Show/Hide Path	Ctrl+Shift+H	⌘-Shift-H
Snap (for example, guides, grid, document bounds)	Ctrl+Shift+semicolon (;)	⌘-Shift-semicolon (;)
Step Backward in History	Ctrl+Alt+Z	⌘-Option-Z
Step Forward in History	Ctrl+Shift+Z	⌘-Shift-Z
Transform Again	Ctrl+Shift+T	⌘-Shift-T
Transform Again, repeat and clone	Ctrl+Shift+Alt+T	⌘-Shift-Option-T
Undo	Ctrl+Z	⌘-Z
Ungroup Layers	Ctrl+Shift+G	⌘-Shift-G
Zoom In	Ctrl+plus (+)	⌘-plus (+)
Zoom Out	Ctrl+minus (–)	⌘-minus (–)
Navigation		
Scroll image with hand tool	spacebar-drag or drag in Navigator palette	spacebar-drag or drag in Navigator palette
Scroll up or down one screen	Page Up or Page Down	Page Up or Page Down
Scroll up or down slightly	Shift+Page Up or Shift+Page Down	Shift-Page Upor Shift-Page Down
Scroll left or right one screen	Ctrl+Page Up or Ctrl+Page Down	⌘-Page Up or ⌘-Page Down
Scroll left or right slightly	Ctrl+Shift+Page Upor Ctrl+Shift+Page Down	⌘-Shift-Page Up or ⌘-Shift-Page Down
Switch to upper-left corner	press Home	press Home
Switch to lower-right corner	press End	press End
Magnify to custom zoom ratio	Ctrl+spacebar-drag or Ctrl-drag in Navigator palette	⌘-spacebar-drag or ⌘-drag in Navigator palette
Zoom in without changing window size	Ctrl+spacebar-click or Ctrl+plus (+)	⌘-spacebar-click or ⌘-Option-plus (+)

Operation	Windows Shortcut	Macintosh Shortcut
Zoom in and change window size to fit (assuming default settings)	Ctrl+Alt+plus (+)	⌘-plus (+)
Zoom out without changing window size	Alt+spacebar-click or Ctrl+minus (–)	Option-spacebar-click or ⌘-Option-minus (–)
Zoom out and change window size to fit (assuming default settings)	Ctrl+Alt+minus (–)	⌘-minus (–)
Zoom to 100%	Ctrl+Alt+zero (0) or double-click zoom tool icon	⌘-Option-zero (0) or double-click zoom tool icon
Fit image on screen	Ctrl+zero (0) or double-click hand tool icon	⌘-zero (0) or double-click hand tool icon
Apply zoom value but keep magnification box active	Shift+Enter	Shift-Return
Cycle through full screen and normal window modes	F	F
Change screen mode for all open windows	Shift-click screen icon in toolbox	Shift-click screen icon in toolbox
Toggle display of menu bar in full screen modes	Shift+F	Shift-F
Bring forward next open image window	Ctrl+Tab	Control-Tab

File browser

Open file browser	Ctrl+Shift+O	⌘-Shift-O
Open selected image	Ctrl+O or Enter	⌘-O or Return
Select continuous range of thumbnails	click one thumbnail, Shift-click another	click one thumbnail, Shift-click another
Select multiple arbitrary thumbnails	click one thumbnail, Ctrl-click others	click one thumbnail, ⌘-click others
Update list of folders	right-click in folder tree or F5	Control-click in folder tree

Continued

Table A-1 *(continued)*

Operation	*Windows Shortcut*	*Macintosh Shortcut*
Move image from one folder to another	drag thumbnail from browser into folder tree	drag thumbnail from browser into folder tree
Copy image from one folder to another	Alt-drag thumbnail from browser into folder tree	Option-drag thumbnail from browser into folder tree
Rotate thumbnail 90° clockwise	click rotate icon at bottom of file browser window	click rotate icon at bottom of file browser window
Rotate thumbnail 90° counterclockwise	Alt-click rotate icon at bottom of file browser window	Option-click rotate icon at bottom of file browser window
Close file browser	Ctrl+W	⌘-W

Painting and editing

Display crosshair cursor	Caps Lock	Caps Lock
Erase to history	Alt-drag with eraser	Option-drag with eraser
Select brush tool or pencil	B or Shift+B	B or Shift-B
Select airbrush	Shift+Alt+P	Shift-Option-P
Cycle between stamp tools	S or Shift+S	S or Shift-S
Select healing brush or patch tool	J or Shift+J	J or Shift-J
Specify an area to clone	Alt-click with clone stamp or healing brush	Option-click with clone stamp or healing brush
Cycle between focus tools	R or Shift+R	R or Shift-R
Sharpen with the blur tool or blur with the sharpen tool	Alt-drag	Option-drag
Dip into the foreground color when smearing	Alt-drag with smudge tool	Option-drag with smudge tool
Cycle between toning tools	O or Shift+O	O or Shift-O
Darken with the dodge tool or lighten with the burn tool	Alt-drag	Option-drag

Operation	Windows Shortcut	Macintosh Shortcut
Paint or edit in a straight line	click and then Shift-click	click and then Shift-click
Change Opacity, Strength, or Exposure in 10% increments	number (1 through 0)	number (1 through 0)
Change Opacity, Strength, or Exposure in 1% increments	two numbers in a row	two numbers in a row
Change Flow in 10% increments	Shift+number (1 through 0)	Shift-number (1 through 0)
Change Flow in 1% increments	Shift+two numbers in a row	Shift-two numbers in a row
Select brush mode	Shift-right-click with paint or edit tool or Shift+Alt+letter	Shift-Control-click with paint or edit tool or Shift-Option-letter
Cycle through brush modes	Shift+plus (+) or Shift+minus (–)	Shift-plus (+) or Shift-minus (–)
Reset to Normal brush mode	Shift+Alt+N	Shift-Option-N
Change brush diameter in increments proportional to brush size	bracket key, [or]	bracket key, [or]
Change brush hardness in 25 percent increments	Shift+bracket, [or]	Shift-bracket, [or]
Cycle between brush presets	comma (,) or period (.)	comma (,) or period (.)
Select first or last brush preset	Shift+comma (,) or Shift+period (.)	Shift-comma (,) or Shift-period (.)
Display Brushes palette	F5 or right-click with paint or edit tool	F5 or Control-click with paint or edit tool
Delete preset brush from Brushes palette	Alt-click preset	Option-click preset
Edit preset name in Brushes palette	double-click preset	double-click preset

Continued

Table A-1 *(continued)*

Operation	Windows Shortcut	Macintosh Shortcut
Applying colors and styles		
Switch foreground and background colors	X	X
Reset foreground and background colors to black and white	D	D
Lift foreground color from image	Alt-click with paint tool or click with eyedropper	Option-click with paint tool or click with eyedropper
Lift background color from image	Alt-click with eyedropper	Option-click with eyedropper
Lift color from different application	click with eyedropper in image window and then drag outside window into other application	click with eyedropper in image window and then drag outside window into other application
Place fixed color sampler in image	click with color sampler tool or Shift-click with eyedropper	click with color sampler tool or Shift-click with eyedropper
Delete fixed color sampler	Alt-click with color sampler tool or Shift+Alt-click with eyedropper	Option-click with color sampler tool or Shift-Option-click with eyedropper
Display or hide Color palette	F6	F6
Lift foreground color from color bar at bottom of Color palette	click color bar	click color bar
Lift background color from color bar	Alt-click color bar	Option-click color bar
Cycle through color bars	Shift-click color bar	Shift-click color bar
Specify new color bar	right-click color bar	Control-click color bar
Lift foreground color from Swatches palette	click swatch	click swatch
Lift background color from Swatches palette	Ctrl-click swatch	⌘-click swatch
Delete swatch or style from palette	Alt-click swatch or style	Option-click swatch or style

Operation	*Windows Shortcut*	*Macintosh Shortcut*
Add new swatch or style to palette	click in empty area of palette	click in empty area of palette
Add new swatch or style without naming	Alt-click in empty area of palette	Option-click in empty area of palette
Apply style to active layer	click icon in Styles palette	click icon in Styles palette
Add effects in style to those applied to active layer	Shift-click icon in Styles palette	Shift-click icon in Styles palette
Fill selection or layer with foreground color	Alt+Backspace	Option-Delete
Fill layer with foreground color, preserve transparency	Shift+Alt+Backspace	Shift-Option-Delete
Fill selection on background layer with background color	Backspace or Delete	Delete
Fill selection on any layer with background color	Ctrl+Backspace	⌘-Delete
Fill layer with background color, preserve transparency	Ctrl+Shift+Backspace	⌘-Shift-Delete
Fill selection with source state in History palette	Ctrl+Alt+Backspace	⌘-Option-Delete
Display Fill dialog box	Shift+Backspace	Shift-Delete
Select gradient tool or paint bucket	G or Shift+G	G or Shift-G
Change gradient style	bracket key, [or]	bracket key, [or]
Cycle between gradient presets	comma (,) or period (.)	comma (,) or period (.)
Select first or last gradient preset	Shift+comma (,) or Shift+period (.)	Shift-comma (,) or Shift-period (.)

Continued

Table A-1 *(continued)*

Operation	Windows Shortcut	Macintosh Shortcut
Type		
Select all text on a text layer	double-click T in Layers palette	double-click T in Layers palette
Select all text when already working inside text layer	Ctrl+A	⌘-A
Select a single word	double-click word with type tool	double-click word with type tool
Select word to left or right	Ctrl+Shift+left or right arrow	⌘-Shift-left or right arrow
Increase type size two pixels (or points)	Ctrl+Shift+greater than (>)	⌘-Shift-greater than (>)
Decrease type size two pixels	Ctrl+Shift+less than (<)	⌘-Shift-less than (<)
Increase type size 10 pixels	Ctrl+Shift+Alt+greater than (>)	⌘-Shift-Option-greater than (>)
Decrease type size 10 pixels	Ctrl+Shift+Alt+less than (<)	⌘-Shift-Option-less than (<)
Kern together 2/100 em	Alt+left arrow	Option-left arrow
Kern apart 2/100 em	Alt+right arrow	Option-right arrow
Kern together 1/10 em	Ctrl+Alt+left arrow	⌘-Option-left arrow
Kern apart 1/10 em	Ctrl+Alt+right arrow	⌘-Option-right arrow
Toggle underlining	Ctrl+Shift+U	⌘-Shift-U
Toggle strikethrough	Ctrl+Shift+slash (/)	⌘-Shift-slash (/)
Toggle all-uppercase text	Ctrl+Shift+K	⌘-Shift-K
Toggle small-caps text	Ctrl+Shift+H	⌘-Shift-H
Toggle superscript text	Ctrl+Shift+plus (+)	⌘-Shift-plus (+)
Toggle subscript text	Ctrl+Shift+Alt+plus (+)	⌘-Shift-Option-plus (+)
Restore 100% horizontal scale	Ctrl+Shift+X	⌘-Shift-X

Operation	Windows Shortcut	Macintosh Shortcut
Restore 100% vertical scale	Ctrl+Shift+Alt+X	⌘-Shift-Option-X
Tighten leading two pixels	Alt+up arrow	Option-up arrow
Expand leading two pixels	Alt+down arrow	Option-down arrow
Tighten leading 10 pixels	Ctrl+Alt+up arrow	⌘-Option-up arrow
Expand leading 10 pixels	Ctrl+Alt+down arrow	⌘-Option-down arrow
Switch to Auto leading	Ctrl+Shift+Alt+A	⌘-Shift-Option-A
Raise baseline shift two pixels	Shift+Alt+up arrow	Shift-Option-up arrow
Lower baseline shift two pixels	Shift+Alt+down arrow	Shift-Option-down arrow
Raise baseline shift 10 pixels	Ctrl+Shift+Alt+up arrow	⌘-Shift-Option-up arrow
Lower baseline shift 10 pixels	Ctrl+Shift+Alt+down arrow	⌘-Shift-Option-down arrow
Left-align text	Ctrl+Shift+L	⌘-Shift-L
Center-align text	Ctrl+Shift+C	⌘-Shift-C
Right-align text	Ctrl+Shift+R	⌘-Shift-R
Justify all text	Ctrl+Shift+F	⌘-Shift-F
Justify all text except last line	Ctrl+Shift+J	⌘-Shift-J
Insert nonbreaking hyphen	Ctrl+Alt+hyphen (-)	none
Insert nonbreaking space	Ctrl+Alt+X	Option-spacebar
Show or hide highlight while editing text	Ctrl+H	⌘-H
Move live text	Ctrl-drag	⌘-drag
Accept changes to text	Enter on keypad or Ctrl+Enter	Enter or ⌘-Return
Cancel changes to text (cannot undo)	Escape	Escape

Continued

Table A-1 *(continued)*

Operation	*Windows Shortcut*	*Macintosh Shortcut*
Highlight font option when type tool active but no type highlighted	Enter	Return
Change formatting for multiple linked text layers	Shift-choose setting from Options bar or enter value and press Shift+Enter	Shift-choose setting from Options bar or enter value and press Shift-Return
Display Character palette	Ctrl+T when text highlighted	⌘-T when text highlighted
Display Paragraph palette	Ctrl+M when text highlighted	⌘-M when text highlighted
Selections		
Select everything	Ctrl+A	⌘-A
Deselect everything	Ctrl+D	⌘-D
Restore last selection outline	Ctrl+Shift+D	⌘-Shift-D
Hide or show marching ants	Ctrl+H	⌘-H
Feather the selection	Ctrl+Alt+D	⌘-Option-D
Reverse the selection	Ctrl+Shift+I	⌘-Shift-I
Toggle between rectangular and elliptical marquee tools	M or Shift+M	M or Shift-M
Draw out from center with marquee tool	Alt	Option
Constrain marquee to square or circle	Shift	Shift
Move marquee as you draw it	spacebar	spacebar
Cycle between lasso tools	L or Shift+L	L or Shift-L
Add corner to straight-sided selection outline	Alt-click with lasso tool or click with polygonal lasso	Option-click with lasso tool or click with polygonal lasso
Add point to magnetic selection	click with magnetic lasso tool	click with magnetic lasso tool

Operation	Windows Shortcut	Macintosh Shortcut
Delete last point added with magnetic lasso tool	Backspace	Delete
Increase or reduce magnetic lasso width	bracket, [or]	bracket, [or]
Close polygon or magnetic selection	double-click with respective lasso tool or press Enter	double-click with respective lasso tool or press Return
Close magnetic selection with straight segment	Alt-double-click or Alt+Enter	Option-double-click or Option-Return
Cancel polygon or magnetic selection	Escape	Escape
Add to selection	Shift-drag (marquee, lasso) or Shift-click (magic wand)	Shift-drag (marquee, lasso) or Shift-click (magic wand)
Subtract from selection	Alt-drag (marquee, lasso) or Alt-click (magic wand)	Option-drag (marquee, lasso) or Option-click (magic wand)
Retain intersected portion of selection	Shift+Alt-drag (marquee, lasso) or Shift+Alt-click (magic wand)	Shift-Option-drag (marquee, lasso) or Shift-Option-click (magic wand)
Select move tool	V or press and hold Ctrl	V or press and hold ⌘
Move selection	drag with move tool or Ctrl-drag with other tool	drag with move tool or ⌘-drag with other tool
Constrain movement vertically or horizontally	press Shift while dragging selection	press Shift while dragging selection
Move selection in 1-pixel increments	Ctrl+arrow key	⌘-arrow key
Move selection in 10-pixel increments	Ctrl+Shift+arrow key	⌘-Shift-arrow key
Clone selection	Alt-drag selection with move tool or Ctrl+Alt-drag with other tool	Option-drag selection with move tool or ⌘-Option-drag with other tool
Clone selection in 1-pixel increments	Ctrl+Alt+arrow key	⌘-Option-arrow key

Continued

Table A-1 *(continued)*

Operation	*Windows Shortcut*	*Macintosh Shortcut*
Clone selection in 10-pixel increments	Ctrl+Shift+Alt+arrow key	⌘-Shift-Option-arrow key
Clone selection to different image	Ctrl-drag selection from one window and drop it into another	⌘-drag selection from one window and drop it into another
Move selection outline independently of its contents	drag with selection tool	drag with selection tool
Move selection outline in 1-pixel increments	arrow key when selection tool is active	arrow key when selection tool is active
Move selection outline in 10-pixel increments	Shift+arrow key when selection tool is active	Shift-arrow key when selection tool is active
Copy empty selection outline to different image	drag selection from one window into another with selection tool	drag selection from one window into another with selection tool
Change opacity or blend mode of floating selection	Ctrl+Shift+F	⌘-Shift-F
Paste image into selection	Ctrl+Shift+V	⌘-Shift-V
Paste image behind selection	Ctrl+Shift+Alt+V	⌘-Shift-Option-V
Layers		
Display or hide Layers palette	F7	F7
View single layer by itself	Alt-click eyeball icon in Layers palette	Option-click eyeball icon in Layers palette
Create new layer above current layer	click page icon at bottom of Layers palette or Ctrl+Shift+Alt+N	click page icon at bottom of Layers palette or ⌘-Shift-Option-N
Create new layer below current layer	Ctrl-click page icon at bottom of Layers palette	⌘-click page icon at bottom of Layers palette
Create new layer above current layer and assign name	Alt-click page icon at bottom of Layers palette or Ctrl+Shift+N	Option-click page icon at bottom of Layers palette or ⌘-Shift-N

Operation	Windows Shortcut	Macintosh Shortcut
Create new layer below current layer and assign name	Ctrl+Alt-click page icon at bottom of Layers palette	⌘-Option-click page icon at bottom of Layers palette
Clone selection or entire layer to new layer	Ctrl+J	⌘-J
Clone selection or entire layer to new layer and assign name	Ctrl+Alt+J	⌘-Option-J
Transfer selection to new layer	Ctrl+Shift+J	⌘-Shift-J
Transfer selection to new layer and assign name	Ctrl+Shift+Alt+J	⌘-Shift-Option-J
Convert floating selection to new layer	Ctrl+Shift+J	⌘-Shift-J
Create adjustment layer	choose from dual-tone icon menu at bottom of Layers palette	choose from dual-tone icon menu at bottom of Layers palette
Create and name adjustment layer	Alt-choose from dual-tone icon menu at bottom of Layers palette	Option-choose from dual-tone icon menu at bottom of Layers palette
Add layer set	click folder icon in Layers palette	click folder icon in Layers palette
Add and name layer set	Alt-click folder icon in Layers palette	Option-click folder icon in Layers palette
Ascend one layer	Alt+]	Option-]
Descend one layer	Alt+[	Option-[
Ascend to top layer	Shift+Alt+]	Shift-Option-]
Descend to background layer	Shift+Alt+[	Shift-Option-[
Go directly to layer that contains a specific image element when using the move tool	Ctrl-click or Alt-right-click layer in image window	⌘-click or Control-Option-click layer in image window

Continued

Table A-1 *(continued)*		
Operation	**Windows Shortcut**	**Macintosh Shortcut**
Go directly to layer that contains a specific image element when using any other tool	Ctrl+Alt-right-click layer in image window	⌘-Control-Option-click layer in image window
Select from layers that overlap when using the move tool	Right-click layer in image window	Control-click layer in image window
Select from layers that overlap when using any other tool	Ctrl-right-click layer in image window	⌘-Control-click layer in image window
Lock the transparency of a layer	slash (/)	slash (/)
Toggle between current lock configuration and no locks in the Layers palette	slash (/)	slash (/)
Convert layer's transparency mask to selection outline	Ctrl-click layer name in Layers palette	⌘-click layer name in Layers palette
Add transparency mask to selection	Ctrl+Shift-click layer name	⌘-Shift-click layer name
Subtract transparency mask from selection	Ctrl+Alt-click layer name	⌘-Option-click layer name
Retain intersection of transparency mask and selection	Ctrl+Shift+Alt-click layer name	⌘-Shift-Option-click layer name
Move layer	drag with move tool or Ctrl-drag with other tool	drag with move tool or ⌘-drag with other tool
Move layer in 1-pixel increments	Ctrl+arrow key	⌘-arrow key
Move layer in 10-pixel increments	Ctrl+Shift+arrow key	⌘-Shift-arrow key
Clone and move layer	Alt-drag with move tool or Ctrl+Alt-drag with other tool	Option-drag with move tool or ⌘-Option-drag with other tool

Operation	Windows Shortcut	Macintosh Shortcut
Clone and move layer in 1-pixel increments	Ctrl+Alt+arrow key	⌘-Option-arrow key
Clone and move layer in 10-pixel increments	Ctrl+Shift+Alt+arrow key	⌘-Shift-Option-arrow key
Clone layer to another open image	Ctrl-drag layer from one window and drop it into another	⌘-drag layer from one window and drop it into another
Clone layer to new image	Alt-drag layer onto page icon at bottom of Layers palette, choose New from Document menu	Option-drag layer onto page icon at bottom of Layers palette, choose New from Document menu
Bring layer forward one level	Ctrl+]	⌘-]
Bring layer to front of file	Ctrl+Shift+]	⌘-Shift-]
Send layer backward one level	Ctrl+[	⌘-[
Send layer to back, just above the background layer	Ctrl+Shift+[	⌘-Shift-[
Link layer that contains a specific image element with active layer	Ctrl+Shift+Alt-right-click layer in image window	⌘-Control-Shift-Option-click layer in image window
Unlink layer that contains a specific image element from active layer	Ctrl+Shift+Alt-right-click layer in image window	⌘-Control-Shift-Option-click layer in image window
Unlink all layers from active layer	Alt-click brush icon in front of layer name in Layers palette or Ctrl+Shift+Alt-right-click active layer in image window	Option-click brush icon in front of layer name in Layers palette or ⌘-Control-Shift-Option-click active layer in image window
Change opacity of active layer in 10% increments	number (1 through 0) when selection tool is active	number (1 through 0) when selection tool is active
Change opacity of active layer in 1% increments	two numbers in a row when selection tool is active	two numbers in a row when selection tool is active

Continued

Table A-1 *(continued)*

Operation	*Windows Shortcut*	*Macintosh Shortcut*
Change opacity of pixels in active layer independently of effects in 10% increments	Shift+number (1 through 0) when selection tool is active	Shift-number (1 through 0) when selection tool is active
Change opacity of pixels in active layer independently of effects in 1% increments	Shift+two numbers in a row when selection tool is active	Shift-two numbers in a row when selection tool is active
Edit layer name	double-click layer name in Layers palette	double-click layer name in Layers palette
Edit blending options for layer	double-click thumbnail in Layers palette or Alt-double-click layer name	double-click thumbnail in Layers palette or Option-double-click layer name
Edit settings for fill or adjustment layer	double-click thumbnail in Layers palette	double-click thumbnail in Layers palette
Change blend mode when selection tool is active	Shift+Alt+letter	Shift-Option-letter
Cycle between blend modes when selection tool is active	Shift+plus (+) or Shift+minus (−)	Shift-plus (+) or Shift-minus (−)
Reset to Normal blend mode when selection tool is active	Shift+Alt+N	Shift-Option-N
Adjust "fuzziness" in Layer Style dialog box	Alt-drag This Layer or Underlying Layer slider triangle	Option-drag This Layer or Underlying Layer slider triangle
Merge layer with next layer down	Ctrl+E	⌘-E
Merge linked layers	Ctrl+E	⌘-E
Merge grouped layers	Ctrl+E	⌘-E
Merge all layers in active set	Ctrl+E	⌘-E
Merge all visible layers	Ctrl+Shift+E	⌘-Shift-E
Copy merged version of selection to Clipboard	Ctrl+Shift+C	⌘-Shift-C

Operation	Windows Shortcut	Macintosh Shortcut
Clone contents of layer into next layer down	Ctrl+Alt+E	⌘-Option-E
Clone contents of linked layers to active layer	Ctrl+Alt+E	⌘-Option-E
Clone contents of all visible layers to active layer	Ctrl+Shift+Alt+E	⌘-Shift-Option-E
Delete active layer	click trash icon in Layers palette	click trash icon in Layers palette
Delete active layer without warning	Alt-click trash icon in Layers palette	Option-click trash icon in Layers palette
Delete multiple linked layers and sets	Ctrl-click trash icon in Layers palette	⌘-click trash icon in Layers palette
Delete multiple linked layers and sets without warning	Ctrl+Alt-click trash icon in Layers palette	⌘-Option-click trash icon in Layers palette
Group neighboring layers	Alt-click horizontal line in Layers palette or Ctrl+G	Option-click horizontal line in Layers palette or ⌘-G
Ungroup neighboring layers	Alt-click dotted line in Layers palette or Ctrl+Shift+G	Option-click dotted line in Layers palette or ⌘-Shift-G
Edit specific layer effect	double-click effect name in Layers palette	double-click effect name in Layers palette
Switch between effects in Layer Styles dialog box	Ctrl+1 through Ctrl+0	⌘-1 through ⌘-0
Save flattened copy of layered image	Ctrl+Alt+S	⌘-Option-S

Brush and blend modes

Normal	Shift+Alt+N or Shift+Alt+L	Shift-Option-N or Shift-Option-L
Dissolve	Shift+Alt+I	Shift-Option-I
Behind	Shift+Alt+Q	Shift-Option-Q
Clear	Shift+Alt+R	Shift-Option-R
Darken	Shift+Alt+K	Shift-Option-K
Multiply	Shift+Alt+M	Shift-Option-M
Color Burn	Shift+Alt+B	Shift-Option-B

Continued

Table A-1 *(continued)*

Operation	Windows Shortcut	Macintosh Shortcut
Linear Burn	Shift+Alt+A	Shift-Option-A
Lighten	Shift+Alt+G	Shift-Option-G
Screen	Shift+Alt+S	Shift-Option-S
Color Dodge	Shift+Alt+D	Shift-Option-D
Linear Dodge	Shift+Alt+W	Shift-Option-W
Overlay	Shift+Alt+O	Shift-Option-O
Soft Light	Shift+Alt+F	Shift-Option-F
Hard Light	Shift+Alt+H	Shift-Option-H
Vivid Light	Shift+Alt+V	Shift-Option-V
Linear Light	Shift+Alt+J	Shift-Option-J
Pin Light	Shift+Alt+Z	Shift-Option-Z
Difference	Shift+Alt+E	Shift-Option-E
Exclusion	Shift+Alt+X	Shift-Option-X
Hue	Shift+Alt+U	Shift-Option-U
Saturation	Shift+Alt+T	Shift-Option-T
Color	Shift+Alt+C	Shift-Option-C
Luminosity	Shift+Alt+Y	Shift-Option-Y
Saturate (sponge tool)	Shift+Alt+S	Shift-Option-S
Desaturate (sponge tool)	Shift+Alt+D	Shift-Option-D
Shadows (dodge and burn tools)	Shift+Alt+S	Shift-Option-S
Midtones (dodge and burn tools)	Shift+Alt+M	Shift-Option-M
Highlights (dodge and burn tools)	Shift+Alt+H	Shift-Option-H
Replace (healing brush)	Shift+Alt+Z	Shift-Option-Z
Pass Through (layer set)	Shift+Alt+P	Shift-Option-P
Cycle to next mode	Shift+plus (+)	Shift-plus (+)
Cycle to previous mode	Shift+minus (–)	Shift-minus (–)

Operation	*Windows Shortcut*	*Macintosh Shortcut*
Channels and masks		
Switch between independent color and mask channels	Ctrl+1 through Ctrl+9	⌘-1 through ⌘-9
View the composite RGB, Lab, or CMYK image	Ctrl+tilde (~)	⌘-tilde (~)
Activate or deactivate color channel	Shift-click channel name in Channels palette	Shift-click channel name in Channels palette
Create channel mask filled with black	click page icon at bottom of Channels palette	click page icon at bottom of Channels palette
Create and name channel mask filled with black	Alt-click page icon at bottom of Channels palette	Option-click page icon at bottom of Channels palette
Create channel mask from selection outline	click mask icon at bottom of Channels palette	click mask icon at bottom of Channels palette
Create and name channel mask from selection outline	Alt-click mask icon at bottom of Channels palette	Option-click mask icon at bottom of Channels palette
View active channel mask as Rubylith overlay	tilde (~)	tilde (~)
Convert channel mask to selection outline	Ctrl-click channel name in Channels palette or Ctrl+Alt+number (1 through 0)	⌘-click channel name in Channels palette or ⌘-Option-number (1 through 0)
Add channel mask to selection	Ctrl+Shift-click channel name	⌘-Shift-click channel name
Subtract channel mask from selection	Ctrl+Alt-click channel name	⌘-Option-click channel name
Retain intersection of channel mask and selection	Ctrl+Shift+Alt-click channel name	⌘-Shift-Option-click channel name
Enter or exit quick mask mode	Q	Q
Toggle quick mask color over masked or selected area	Alt-click quick mask icon in toolbox	Option-click quick mask icon in toolbox

Continued

Table A-1 *(continued)*

Operation	Windows Shortcut	Macintosh Shortcut
Change quick mask color overlay	double-click quick mask icon	double-click quick mask icon
View quick mask independently of image	tilde (~)	tilde (~)
Add spot color channel	Ctrl-click page icon at bottom of Channels palette	⌘-click page icon at bottom of Channels palette
Create layer mask filled with white when nothing selected	click mask icon at bottom of Layers palette	click mask icon at bottom of Layers palette
Create layer mask filled with black when nothing selected	Alt-click mask icon	Option-click mask icon
Create layer mask from selection outline	click mask icon	click mask icon
Create layer mask that hides selection	Alt-click mask icon	Option-click mask icon
Switch focus from layer mask to image	Ctrl+tilde (~)	⌘-tilde (~)
Switch focus from image to layer mask	Ctrl+backslash (\)	⌘-backslash (\)
View layer mask as Rubylith overlay	backslash (\) or Shift+Alt-click layer mask thumbnail in Layers palette	backslash (\) or Shift-Option-click layer mask thumbnail in Layers palette
View layer mask independently of image	backslash (\), and then tilde (~) or Alt-click layer mask thumbnail in Layers palette	backslash (\), and then tilde (~) or Option-click layer mask thumbnail in Layers palette
Add vector mask to layer	Ctrl-click mask icon in Layers palette	⌘-click mask icon in Layers palette
Convert current path to vector mask	Ctrl-click mask icon in Layers palette with path active	⌘-click mask icon in Layers palette with path active
Toggle display of vector mask	click vector mask thumbnail or press Enter when shape or arrow tool is active	click vector mask thumbnail or press Return when shape or arrow tool is active
Disable layer mask or vector mask	Shift-click mask thumbnail in Layers palette	Shift-click mask thumbnail in Layers palette

Operation	Windows Shortcut	Macintosh Shortcut
Toggle link between layer and mask	click between layer and mask thumbnails in Layers palette	click between layer and mask thumbnails in Layers palette
Copy layer mask or vector mask from one layer to active layer	drag mask thumbnail onto mask icon at bottom of Layers palette	drag mask thumbnail onto mask icon at bottom of Layers palette
Convert layer mask to selection outline	Ctrl-click layer mask thumbnail or Ctrl+Alt+backslash (\)	⌘-click layer mask thumbnail or ⌘-Option-backslash (\)
Convert vector mask to selection outline	Ctrl-click vector mask thumbnail	⌘-click vector mask thumbnail
Add layer mask or vector mask to selection	Ctrl+Shift-click mask thumbnail	⌘-Shift-click mask thumbnail
Subtract layer mask or vector mask from selection	Ctrl+Alt-click mask thumbnail	⌘-Option-click mask thumbnail
Retain intersection of layer mask or vector mask and selection	Ctrl+Shift+Alt-click mask thumbnail	⌘-Shift-Option-click mask thumbnail
Paths and shapes		
Cycle between standard, freeform, and magnetic pen tools	P or Shift+P	P or Shift-P
Add corner to end of active path	click with pen tool or Alt-click with freeform pen tool	click with pen tool or Option-click with freeform pen tool
Add smooth arc to end of active path	drag with pen tool	drag with pen tool
Add cusp to end of active path	Alt-click and then drag with pen tool	Option-click and then drag with pen tool
Add point to end of active magnetic selection	click with magnetic pen tool	click with magnetic pen tool
Delete last point added with standard or magnetic pen tool	Backspace	Delete

Continued

Table A-1 *(continued)*

Operation	*Windows Shortcut*	*Macintosh Shortcut*
Draw freehand path segment	drag with freeform pen tool or Alt-drag with magnetic pen tool	drag with freeform pen tool or Option-drag with magnetic pen tool
Increase or reduce magnetic pen width	bracket, [or]	bracket, [or]
Close magnetic selection	double-click with magnetic pen tool or click first point in path	double-click with magnetic pen tool or click first point in path
Close magnetic selection with straight segment	Alt-double-click or Alt+Enter	Option-double-click or Option-Return
Cancel magnetic or freeform selection	Escape	Escape
Select arrow tool	A or press Ctrl when pen tool is active	A or press ⌘ when pen tool is active
Move selected points	drag point with arrow tool or Ctrl-drag with pen tool	drag point with arrow tool or ⌘-drag with pen tool
Select multiple points in path	Shift-click with arrow or Ctrl+Shift-click with pen	Shift-click with arrow or ⌘-Shift-click with pen
Select entire path	Alt-click path with white arrow or Alt-click path in Paths palette	Option-click path with arrow or Option-click path in Paths palette
Clone path	Alt-drag path with arrow or Ctrl+Alt-drag with pen	Option-drag path with arrow or ⌘-Option-drag with pen
Access convert direction tool when pen tool is active	Alt while hovering cursor over anchor point	Option while hovering cursor over anchor point
Access convert direction tool when arrow tool is active	Ctrl+Alt while hovering cursor over anchor point	⌘-Option while hovering cursor over anchor point
Convert corner or cusp to smooth arc	Alt-drag point with pen	Option-drag point with pen
Convert arc to corner	Alt-click point with pen	Option-click point with pen
Convert arc to cusp	Alt-drag handle with pen	Option-drag handle with pen
Insert point in selected path	click segment with pen tool	click segment with pen tool

Operation	Windows Shortcut	Macintosh Shortcut
Remove point from path	click point with pen tool	click point with pen tool
Convert path to selection outline	Ctrl-click path name in Paths palette or Ctrl+Enter when pen or arrow tool is active	⌘-click path name in Paths palette or ⌘-Return when pen or arrow tool is active
Add path to selection	Ctrl+Shift-click path name in Paths palette	⌘-Shift-click path name in Paths palette
Subtract path from selection	Ctrl+Alt-click path name in Paths palette	⌘-Option-click path name in Paths palette
Retain intersection of path and selection	Ctrl+Shift+Alt-click path name in Paths palette	⌘-Shift-Option-click path name in Paths palette
Apply brushstroke around perimeter of path	Enter on keypad when paint or edit tool is active	Enter when paint or edit tool is active
Revert around perimeter of path	Enter on keypad when history brush is active	Enter when history brush is active
Save and name path for future use	double-click Work Path item in Paths palette	double-click Work Path item in Paths palette
Hide path (it remains active)	Ctrl+Shift+H	⌘-Shift-H
Deactivate path	click in empty portion of Paths palette or Enter when pen or arrow tool is active	click in empty portion of Paths palette or Return when pen or arrow tool is active
Cycle between shape tools	U or Shift+U	U or Shift-U
Move shape as you draw it	spacebar	spacebar
Add next shape you draw to active shape layer	plus (+)	plus (+)
Subtract next shape you draw from active shape layer	minus (–)	minus (–)
Adjust roundness of the next rounded rectangle you draw	bracket key, [or]	bracket key, [or]

Continued

Table A-1 *(continued)*

Operation	*Windows Shortcut*	*Macintosh Shortcut*
Change number of sides on the next regular polygon or star you draw	bracket key, [or]	bracket key, [or]
Change weight of the next straight line you draw	bracket key, [or]	bracket key, [or]
Cycle between custom shapes	bracket key, [or]	bracket key, [or]
Cycle between layer styles	comma (,) or period (.)	comma (,) or period (.)
Change color of foreground or background color	Alt+Backspace or Ctrl+Backspace	Option-Delete or ⌘-Delete active shape layer to
Hide shape outlines (shape layer remains active)	Ctrl+Shift+H	⌘-Shift-H
Deactivate shape outlines	Enter when pen or arrow tool is active	Return when pen or arrow tool is active
Delete shape layer when shape outlines are active	Backspace or Delete	Delete
Crops and transformations		
Select crop tool	C	C
Move crop boundary as you draw it	spacebar	spacebar
Move crop boundary	drag inside boundary	drag inside boundary
Scale crop boundary	drag boundary handle	drag boundary handle
Scale crop boundary proportionally	Shift-drag corner handle	Shift-drag corner handle
Scale crop boundary with respect to origin	Alt-drag boundary handle	Option-drag boundary handle
Scale crop boundary proportionally with respect to origin point	Shift+Alt-drag corner	Shift-Option-drag corner

Operation	Windows Shortcut	Macintosh Shortcut
Rotate crop boundary (always with respect to origin)	drag outside boundary	drag outside boundary
Rotate crop boundary in 15° increments	Shift-drag outside boundary	Shift-drag outside boundary
Distort crop boundary	draw crop boundary, select Perspective check box in Options bar, drag boundary handle	draw crop boundary, select Perspective check box in Options bar, drag boundary handle
Constrain distortion effect in Perspective mode	Shift-drag corner handle	Shift-drag corner handle
Scale crop boundary in Perspective mode	Alt-drag handle	Option-drag handle
Accept crop	Enter	Return
Cancel crop	Escape	Escape
Freely transform selection, layer, or path	Ctrl+T	⌘-T
Duplicate selection, layer, or path and freely transform	Ctrl+Alt+T	⌘-Option-T
Move image in Free Transform mode	drag inside boundary	drag inside boundary
Move transformation origin	drag crosshair target	drag crosshair target
Scale image	drag boundary handle	drag boundary handle
Scale image proportionally	Shift-drag corner handle	Shift-drag corner handle
Scale image with respect to origin	Alt-drag boundary handle	Option-drag boundary handle
Rotate image (always with respect to origin)	drag outside boundary	drag outside boundary
Rotate image in 15° increments	Shift-drag outside boundary	Shift-drag outside boundary
Skew image	Ctrl-drag side handle	⌘-drag side handle

Continued

Table A-1 *(continued)*		
Operation	*Windows Shortcut*	*Macintosh Shortcut*
Skew image along constrained axis	Ctrl+Shift-drag side handle	⌘-Shift-drag side handle
Skew image with respect to origin	Ctrl+Alt-drag side handle	⌘-Option-drag side handle
Skew image along constrained axis with respect to origin	Ctrl+Shift+Alt-drag side handle	⌘-Shift-Option-drag side handle
Distort image	Ctrl-drag corner handle	⌘-drag corner handle
Symmetrically distort opposite corners	Ctrl+Alt-drag corner handle	⌘-Option-drag corner handle
Constrain distortion to achieve perspective effect	Ctrl+Shift-drag corner handle	⌘-Shift-drag corner handle
Constrain distortion to achieve symmetrical perspective effect	Ctrl+Shift+Alt-drag corner handle	⌘-Shift-Option-drag corner handle
Apply specific transformation in Free Transform mode	right-click in image window	Control-click in image window
Apply numerical transformation in Free Transform mode	enter values in Options bar	enter values in Options bar
Accept transformation	Enter	Return
Cancel transformation	Escape	Escape
Replay last transformation	Ctrl+Shift+T	⌘-Shift-T
Duplicate selection, layer, or path and replay last transformation	Ctrl+Shift+Alt+T	⌘-Shift-Option-T
Rulers, measurements, and guides		
Display or hide rulers	Ctrl+R	⌘-R
Display or hide Info palette	F8	F8
Change unit of measure	right-click ruler or drag from X,Y pop-up in Info palette	Control-click ruler or drag from X,Y pop-up in Info palette

Operation	Windows Shortcut	Macintosh Shortcut
Reset ruler origin	double-click ruler origin box	double-click ruler origin box
Select measure tool	I, I, I (or I, Shift+I, Shift+I)	I, I, I (or I, Shift-I, Shift-I)
Measure distance and angle	drag with measure tool	drag with measure tool
Move measure line	drag measure line	drag measure line
Change length and angle of measure line	drag endpoint of measure line	drag endpoint of measure line
Measure angle between two lines (protractor option)	Alt-drag endpoint	Option-drag endpoint
Match rotation of entire image to measure line	choose Image ⇨ Rotate ⇨ Arbitrary	choose Image ⇨ Rotate ⇨ Arbitrary
Match rotation of single layer to measure line	choose Edit ⇨ Transform ⇨ Rotate	choose Edit ⇨ Transform ⇨ Rotate
Create guide	drag from ruler	drag from ruler
Move guide	drag guide with move tool or Ctrl-drag with other tool	drag guide with move tool or ⌘-drag with other tool
Change horizontal guide to vertical or vice versa	press Alt while dragging guide	press Option while dragging guide
Snap guide to ruler tick marks	press Shift while dragging guide	press Shift while dragging guide
Display or hide guides	Ctrl+semicolon (;)	⌘-semicolon (;)
Lock or unlock guides	Ctrl+Alt+semicolon (;)	⌘-Option-semicolon (;)
Display or hide grid	Ctrl+quote (")	⌘-quote (")
Toggle guide and grid snapping	Ctrl+Shift+semicolon (;)	⌘-Shift-semicolon (;)
Edit guide color and grid increments	Ctrl-double-click guide	⌘-double-click guide
Filters		
Repeat filter with last-used settings	Ctrl+F	⌘-F

Continued

Table A-1 *(continued)*

Operation	*Windows Shortcut*	*Macintosh Shortcut*
Repeat filter with different settings	Ctrl+Alt+F	⌘-Option-F
Fade the effect of last filter	Ctrl+Shift+F	⌘-Shift-F
Scroll preview box in corrective filter dialog boxes	drag in preview box or click in image window	drag in preview box or click in image window
Zoom preview box in corrective filter dialog boxes	Ctrl-click and Alt-click	⌘-click and Option-click
Zoom full image preview	Ctrl+plus (+) and Ctrl+minus (–)	⌘-plus (+) and ⌘-minus (–)
Increase selected option-box value by 1 (or 0.1)	up arrow	up arrow
Decrease value by 1 (or 0.1)	down arrow	down arrow
Increase value by 10 (or 1)	Shift+up arrow	Shift-up arrow
Decrease value by 10 (or 1)	Shift+down arrow	Shift-down arrow
Adjust Angle value (where offered) in 15° increments	Shift-drag in Angle wheel	Shift-drag in Angle wheel
Reset options inside corrective filter dialog boxes	Alt-click Cancel button	Option-click Cancel button or Option-Escape
Create high-contrast clouds effect	Alt-choose Filter ⇨ Render ⇨ Clouds	Option-choose Filter ⇨ Render ⇨ Clouds
Specify numerical center in Lens Flare dialog box	Alt-click in preview	Option-click in preview
Clone light in Lighting Effects dialog box	Alt-drag light	Option-drag light
Delete Lighting Effects light	press Delete	press Delete

Operation	Windows Shortcut	Macintosh Shortcut
Adjust size of footprint without affecting angle of light	Shift-drag handle	Shift-drag handle
Adjust angle of light without affecting size of footprint	Ctrl-drag handle	⌘-drag handle
Switch between arrow tools in 3D Transform dialog box	press V or A, or Ctrl+Tab	press V or A, or ⌘-Tab
Select 3D cube, sphere, or cylinder tool	M, N, or C	M, N, or C
Edit shape with pan camera or trackball	E or R	E or R
Delete selected 3D Transform shape	Backspace	Delete
Select warp or shift pixels tool inside Liquify dialog box	W or S	W or S
Select twirl clockwise or twirl counterclockwise tool	R or L	R or L
Select pucker or bloat tool	P or B	P or B
Select reconstruct tool	E	E
Select freeze or thaw tool	F or T	F or T
Change Liquify brush diameter in 1-pixel increments	bracket key, [or]	bracket key, [or]
Change Liquify brush diameter in 10-pixel increments	Shift+bracket, [or]	Shift-bracket, [or]
Undo last brushstroke in Liquify dialog box	Ctrl+Z	⌘-Z
Undo brushstroke prior to last one	Ctrl+Alt+Z	⌘-Option-Z
Redo undone brushstroke	Ctrl+Shift+Z	⌘-Shift-Z

Continued

Table A-1 *(continued)*

Operation	Windows Shortcut	Macintosh Shortcut
Color adjustments		
Choose Levels command	Ctrl+L	⌘-L
Switch between channels in Levels or Curves dialog box	Ctrl+1 through Ctrl+3, or Ctrl-tilde (~) for composite	⌘-1 through ⌘-3, or ⌘-tilde (~) for composite
Preview black and white points in Levels dialog box	Alt-drag black or white Input Levels triangle	Option-drag black or white Input Levels triangle
Specify alternate colors for black point, white point, and midtone	double-click black, white, or gray eyedropper tool	double-click black, white, or gray eyedropper tool
Invert image inside Levels dialog box	swap black and white Output Levels triangles	swap black and white Output Levels triangles
Repeat last Levels correction	Ctrl+Alt+L	⌘-Option-L
Choose Curves command	Ctrl+M	⌘-M
Add point in Curves dialog box	click graph line	click graph line
Add specific color as new point on composite curve in point mode	Ctrl-click in image window	⌘-click in image window
Add color as new point on independent channel curves	Ctrl+Shift-click in image window	⌘-Shift-click in image window
Nudge Input value for selected point	left or right arrow key	left or right arrow key
Nudge Output value for selected point	up or down arrow key	up or down arrow key
Select next curve point	Ctrl+Tab	Control-Tab
Select previous curve point	Ctrl+Shift+Tab	Control-Shift-Tab
Delete curve point	Ctrl-click point	⌘-click point

Operation	*Windows Shortcut*	*Macintosh Shortcut*
Select multiple curve points	Shift-click point	Shift-click point
Deselect all points	Ctrl+D	⌘-D
Repeat last Curves correction	Ctrl+Alt+M	⌘-Option-M
Choose Hue/Saturation command	Ctrl+U	⌘-U
Add colors to Hue/ Saturation range when Edit set to anything but Master	Shift-click or drag in image window	Shift-click or drag in image window
Subtract colors from Hue/Saturation range when Edit set to anything but Master	Alt-click or drag in image window	Option-click or drag in image window
Edit all colors in Hue/Saturation dialog box	Ctrl+tilde (~)	⌘-tilde (~)
Edit predefined color range	Ctrl+1 through Ctrl+6	⌘-1 through ⌘-6
Repeat last Hue/ Saturation correction	Ctrl+Alt+U	⌘-Option-U
Desaturation colors	Ctrl+Shift+U	⌘-Shift-U
Undoing operations		
Undo or redo last operation	Ctrl+Z	⌘-Z
Undo operation prior to last one	Ctrl+Alt+Z	⌘-Option-Z
Redo undone operation	Ctrl+Shift+Z	⌘-Shift-Z
Undo to specific point	click item in History palette	click item in History palette
Duplicate previously performed operation	Alt-click item in History palette	Option-click item in History palette
Select state to revert to with history brush	click in front of item in History palette	click in front of item in History palette
Create snapshot from active state	click camera icon at bottom of History palette	click camera icon at bottom of History palette

Continued

Table A-1 *(continued)*

Operation	Windows Shortcut	Macintosh Shortcut
Create duplicate image from active state	click leftmost icon at bottom of History palette	click leftmost icon at bottom of History palette
Revert selection to active History state	Ctrl+Alt+Backspace	⌘-Option-Delete
Revert entire image to saved state	F12	F12
Miscellaneous		
Display or hide all palettes, toolbox, and status bar	Tab	Tab
Display or hide palettes except toolbox, Options bar, and status bar	Shift+Tab	Shift-Tab
Hide toolbox, Options bar, and status bar	Tab, and then Shift+Tab	Tab, and then Shift-Tab
Display Options bar	Enter	Return
Move a panel out of a palette	drag panel tab	drag panel tab
Dock a palette	drag panel tab into docking well	drag panel tab into docking well
Snap palette to edge of screen	Shift-click palette title bar	Shift-click palette title bar
Fully collapse palette	Alt-click collapse box or double-click panel tab	Option-click collapse box or double-click panel tab
Delete item without warning from any palette that includes a trash can	Alt-click trash can	Option-click trash can
Preview how image sits on printed page	click Doc box in the status bar	click Doc box at bottom of image window
View size and resolution of image	Alt-click Doc box in the status bar	Option-click Doc box at bottom of image window
View image tile information	Ctrl-click Doc box in the status bar	⌘-click Doc box at bottom of image window
Change the preference settings	Ctrl+K	⌘-K

Operation	Windows Shortcut	Macintosh Shortcut
Display last used Preferences dialog box panel	Ctrl+Alt+K	⌘-Option-K
Bring up dialog box with last-used settings	Alt+choose command from Image ⇨ Adjustments submenu	Option-choose command from Image ⇨ Adjustments submenu
Duplicate image and bypass dialog box	Alt+choose Image ⇨ Duplicate	Option-choose Image ⇨ Duplicate
Cancel an operation	Escape	⌘-period or Escape
Activate No or Don't Save button when closing image	N	D
Activate Don't Flatten button when changing color modes	D	D
Activate Flatten button when changing color modes	F	F

✦   ✦   ✦

Index

Continued